Social Psychology

Social Psychology

7th Edition

DAVID O. SEARS

University of California, Los Angeles

LETITIA ANNE PEPLAU

University of California, Los Angeles

SHELLEY E. TAYLOR

University of California, Los Angeles

PRENTICE HALL

Englewood Cliffs, New Jersey 07632

Library of Congress Cataloging-in-Publication Data

Sears, David O.
   Social psychology.—7th ed. / David O. Sears, Letitia Anne
Peplau, Shelley E. Taylor.
     p.   cm.
   Rev. ed. of: Social psychology / David O. Sears . . . [et al.]. 6th
ed. © 1988.
   Includes bibliographical references and index.
   ISBN 0-13-817081-9
   1. Social psychology I. Peplau, Letitia Anne. II. Taylor,
Shelley E. III. Social psychology. IV. Title.
HM251.F68 1991
302—dc20
                       90-7761
                       CIP

EDITORIAL/PRODUCTION SUPERVISION: Marina Harrison
INTERIOR AND COVER DESIGN: Lee Goldstein
COVER ART: Stanton Macdonald-Wright, *Synchrony in Green and Orange,*
          1916. Oil on canvas, $34\frac{1}{8} \times 30\frac{1}{8}''$ actual; $40\frac{1}{4} \times 36\frac{1}{4}''$ framed.
          Collection Walker Art Center, Minneapolis. Gift of the T. B.
          Walker Foundation, Hudson D. Walker Collection, 1953.
MANUFACTURING BUYER: Mary Ann Gloriande
PREPRESS BUYER: Debbie Kesar
PHOTO EDITOR: Lorinda Morris-Nantz
PHOTO RESEARCH: Rhoda Sidney

© 1991, 1988, 1985, 1981, 1978, 1974, 1970 by Prentice-Hall, Inc.
A Division of Simon & Schuster
Englewood Cliffs, New Jersey 07632

Printed in the United States of America
10 9 8 7 6 5 4 3 2 1

ISBN   0-13-817081-9   (Student text)

ISBN   0-13-817099-1   (Instructor's edition)

Prentice-Hall International (UK) Limited, *London*
Prentice-Hall of Australia Pty. Limited, *Sydney*
Prentice-Hall Canada Inc., *Toronto*
Prentice-Hall Hispanoamericana, S.A., *Mexico*
Prentice-Hall of India Private Limited, *New Delhi*
Prentice-Hall of Japan, Inc., *Tokyo*
Simon & Schuster Asia Pte. Ltd., *Singapore*
Editora Prentice-Hall do Brasil, Ltda., *Rio de Janeiro*

B R I E F   C O N T E N T S

C O N T E N T S

When we wrote the first edition of this book over twenty years ago, our task was a much simpler one. The field of social psychology then was relatively new and relatively small. In the intervening decades it has changed dramatically.

There has been an explosion of research and theory and a corresponding proliferation of journals meeting the specialized needs of social psychologists. There has been a renewed interest in the practical applications of social psychology for understanding urgent social issues. Women and ethnic minorities have been attracted to the field and have enriched it with new perspectives and new research questions. The students who take social psychology courses today are also a more diverse group: Minority students are better represented than ever before; women are now over half the students in American colleges; and more and more older students are taking our courses.

This book has grown and changed with the times. This seventh edition incorporates the major new topics of research, the outstanding new studies, and the most contemporary examples. But all is not focused on newness; certain basic principles and goals have guided us in the development of this edition.

We believe that social psychology, like any science, is cumulative. As researchers push toward exciting new frontiers, they build on the accumulated knowledge of the field. The new findings of today are best understood as adding to this body of knowledge. Our primary goal in this edition as in each prior edition has been to present the ''basics'' of the field—the core theories and findings that form the shared heri-tage of our discipline. We believe this has been one of the distinctive merits of the book through its several editions.

We have also been sensitive to the important changes taking place in contemporary social psychology. Over time, the core of the field has gradually shifted. There is less emphasis today on group dynamics and more on intimate relationships, less on attitude change and more on social cognition, and so on. This changing core is reflected in this new edition. We have made every effort to include the most recent research and the most advanced theories in social psychology.

Another goal has been to offer an integrated presentation of the field. As we discuss different topics, we try to keep the main theoretical ideas and traditions of social psychology firmly in view, so that students can see the underlying conceptual continuities in the field. For example, we introduce social cognition and attribution theory early in the book and then show how they have been used to understand such topics as attitude change, aggression, prejudice, and bias against women.

The application of research methods and theories to understanding social issues has been a major theme in social psychology. Throughout the text, we highlight ways in which social psychology sheds light on everyday experiences and social problems. We conclude with a section on social psychology in society that explores the most recent research and theory on prejudice, gender roles, environmental psychology, health psychology, and political psychology.

The success of any text depends ultimately

on its ability to communicate clearly to student readers and to spark interest in the field. Our goal has been to present materials simply, without oversimplifying. The text is comprehensive, but not encyclopedic. We have written a textbook for undergraduate students, not a handbook of social psychology for professionals. We have paid special attention to selecting examples that illustrate basic principles in a lively way and to sharing our own personal enthusiasm for the field.

SPECIAL FEATURES OF THE SEVENTH EDITION

This book has been successful throughout its life. Although our basic philosophy about the text remains the same, much has changed in the seventh edition. We think that the old book was good, but we have not left well enough alone. Here are some of the main features of the seventh edition.

Organization

The book is organized to provide a systematic presentation of the material. A beginning chapter on theory and methods is followed by three major sections that progress from individual level topics to dyads and groups, and then to specific applications of social psychology.

Part One on social cognition and attitudes includes expanded coverage of new work on person perception social cognition and attribution. It also presents work on attitudes and attitude change.

Part Two discusses interaction, social influence, attraction and close relationships, behavior in groups, aggression, and prosocial behavior.

Part Three on social psychology in society has chapters on prejudice, gender, environmental psychology, health psychology, and political psychology. We think that this sequence will fit well with the teaching preferences of many instructors. However, each chapter is self-contained and so the chapters can be used in any order.

Style

We have kept the clarity and interest level of the text high. We have made a particular effort in this edition to write in non-technical language, geared for the beginning student of social psychology. We have scrutinized every line of text, every table and figure, and every photograph. We have added new figures and charts in this edition to present information clearly. To help students learn to "think like social psychologists," we have included detailed discussions of a few key research studies, highlighting the research process and the decisions researchers made.

Classic and Contemporary

This edition, like its predecessors, provides a comprehensive survey of the mainstream of contemporary social psychology. Our conviction that social psychology is a cumulative, evolving science leads us to emphasize both the classic studies that have traditionally formed the foundation of the field, and the best new research of today. This approach provides students with a solid understanding of the long-standing issues and controversies in the field, and also with exposure to the exciting new developments shaping social psychology in the 1990s.

Throughout, we emphasize the continuity in theoretical perspectives and empirical approaches between classic early studies and the research of today. Contemporary research does not merely "reinvent the wheel," but rather represents innovative approaches to longstanding core questions about social life that have aroused the curiosity of social psychologists for decades. This emphasis on the continuity between classic and contemporary research is, we believe, a distinctive and valuable component of our approach to social psychology.

Highlights of New Content

The new additions to this edition reflect two major trends in social psychology today: greater interest in the cognitive side of social psychology and greater attention to the application of social psychology to practical problems. Some of the highlights of new material in the seventh edition are:

☐ A consolidated introductory chapter surveys major theories and methods in social psychology. Special attention is given to ethical issues in psychological research. The themes first introduced in this chapter are then expanded in later chapters of the book.

☐ The three chapters on social perception, social cognition, and attribution theory have been reorganized and rewritten to provide an up-to-date and comprehensive view of these key topics in contemporary social psychology.

☐ Recent developments in the study of attitudes, focusing especially on the elaboration likelihood model of persuasion and on systematic processing, have been incorporated into updated chapters on attitudes and attitude change.

☐ To enhance coverage of interpersonal processes, a new chapter on social interaction has been written that examines such topics as self-presentation, social comparison, and social exchange.

☐ A new chapter on social influence provides an integrated presentation of conformity, compliance, and obedience to authority.

☐ The most current research on sexual violence is analyzed in the chapter on aggression.

☐ The chapter on prejudice has been completely updated, giving major emphasis to the cognitive bases of prejudice and to evolving forms and dynamics of intergroup conflict.

☐ The gender chapter includes the latest meta-analyses of sex differences in social behavior, as well as research on the changing social roles of women and men.

☐ The health psychology chapter presents new work on AIDS and psychoneuro-immunology.

☐ The chapter on political psychology includes expanded analysis of international conflict focusing on the rationality of foreign decision-makers and on strategies for increasing international cooperation.

Learning Aids

Various teaching aids further increase the effectiveness of the text. Each chapter begins with an outline. At the end of each chapter is a comprehensive summary of major concepts and findings. Key terms, which are shown in bold-face in the text, are listed at the end of each chapter and are defined in the glossary. Each chapter includes suggestions for further reading. The bibliography at the end of the book is extensive and up-to-date.

Instructor's Manual

Prentice Hall has provided a special Instructor's Manual of our text, which was prepared by Alan Swinkels. This will prove to be an invaluable time-saver for class preparation. In it you will find, in addition to the student text, a wealth of activities and demonstrations, video and film suggestions, lecture ideas, and abstracts of recent important journal articles, discussion questions, and more.

Readings in Social Psychology

For instructors who want to provide students with well-chosen primary source materials, the text may be accompanied by a coordinated paperbound book of readings prepared by the authors. *Readings in Social Psychology: Classic and Contemporary Contributions* introduces students to landmark research in the history of social psychology, including papers by Solomon Asch, Leon Festinger, Harold Kelley, Stanley Milgram, Muzafer Sherif, and others. The reader also includes recent studies, illustrating the latest approaches in social psychology.

All studies are reprinted in original form, with only occasional deletions of peripheral sections or technical footnotes. To facilitate the student's understanding of these research studies, we have selected only those articles that are accessible to the beginning student; articles typically have only simple statistical tests and are written in the most straightforward manner possible. In addition, each selection is prefaced by our own analysis of the most important

themes in the paper and possible limitations of the work. The reader begins with an essay on how to read a social psychology article.

Student Study Guide

An important new feature of this edition is a student *Study Guide* prepared by Tom and Sandra Dunn. For each chapter, the guide includes a detailed outline, a set of learning objectives to highlight the most important material, and a section on key terms and concepts. Multiple choice questions permit students to test their own mastery of each chapter and aid in effective studying. Suggestions for student activities are included to enhance the learning of materials in the text.

Test Item File

An extensive selection of multiple-choice questions test your students' recall of material as well as their ability to comprehend and apply the concepts presented in the text. Essay questions are also provided.

Prentice Hall Datamanager

This electronic classroom management system contains a test generating system (*Test Manager*), an interactive study guide that has computer network features (*Study Manager*), and a grading program that includes scanning features (*Grade Manager*). It is user friendly, offers a wide variety of functions, and is available for IBM and Apple II series computers.

Telephone Test Preparation Service

With one call to 1-800-842-2958, Prentice Hall will provide personalized test preparation on bond paper or ditto master. Within 48 hours of the request, your exam and a separate answer key will be mailed to you at your college or university.

Handout and Transparency Masters

A series of questionnaires, survey materials, and other items to promote class discussion are provided, along with masters for transparencies to accompany your lectures.

Video Offer

Selected videos to augment your course are available. Free to adopters of 100 or more new texts. Contact your local representative for details.

A C K N O W L E D G M E N T S

We wish to express special thanks to Jonathan L. Freedman of the University of Toronto. He, along with the late J. Merrill Carlsmith and David O. Sears, conceived the first edition of this book, and published it in 1970. Jon took the lead in writing the first edition. The book shows the imprint of his approach to the field, in a rigorous attention to methodology and a concern for simple, straightforward, and compelling description. His other activities have over time increasingly crowded out the time required for continued participation in this venture, and so he has not participated in this edition. However, the remaining authors, the book, and generations of social psychology students owe him a great debt of gratitude for what he has contributed in the past.

Special thanks go to Carolyn Drago, Garrett Songhawke, Michelle Nieto, Susan Campbell, Amanda Munoz, and Lisa Silver for their invaluable help in researching and preparing this manuscript. We are grateful to Prentice Hall for continuing support, and especially to our Psychology Editor, Susan Finnemore, and to Marina Harrison, production editor. We also appreciate the useful feedback we have received from students who have used this book. Finally, this text has benefited greatly from the thoughtful reviews of the manuscript by Valerie Scott, Upsala College; Barbara Brown, University of Utah; Edward Sadalla, Arizona State University; Charles A. Alexander, Rock Valley College; John Dovidio, Colgate University; and Brett Pelham, UCLA.

DAVID O. SEARS

LETITIA ANNE PEPLAU

SHELLEY E. TAYLOR

DAVID O. SEARS is Professor of Psychology and Political Science and Dean of Social Sciences at the University of California, Los Angeles. David received his B.A. in History from Stanford University, and his Ph.D. in Psychology from Yale University in 1962, and has taught at UCLA since then. He has been a visiting professor at Harvard University and the University of California, Berkeley, a Guest Scholar at the Brookings Institution, a Fellow at the Center for Advanced Study in the Behavioral Sciences, and a Guggenheim Fellow. He has served on the review panel on social psychology for the National Science Foundation, on the Council of Representatives for the American Psychological Association, and on the Board of Overseers of the National Election Studies. His duties at UCLA have included service as Chair of the So-

cial Psychology Program and of the Human Subject Protection Committee. His other books include *Public Opinion* (with Robert E. Lane), *The Politics of Violence: The New Urban Blacks and the Watts Riot* (with John B. McConahay), *Tax Revolt: Something for Nothing in California* (with Jack Citrin), and *Political Cognition: The 19th Annual Carnegie Symposium on Cognition* (edited with Richard R. Lau). He has published articles and book chapters on a wide variety of topics in social and political psychology, including attitude change, mass communications, ghetto riots, political socialization, voting behavior, and racism.

LETITIA ANNE PEPLAU is Professor of Psychology and acting Co-Director of the Center for the Study of Women at the University of California, Los Angeles. Anne received her B.A. in Psychology from Brown University and her Ph.D. in Social Psychology from Harvard University. Since 1973, she has taught at UCLA, where she helped to found the campus Women's Studies Program and has developed popular undergraduate courses in the psychology of gender and close relationships. She has served on the editorial boards of several journals including the *Journal of Personality and Social Psychology*, the *Journal of Personal and Social Relationships*, and *Psychology of Women Quarterly*. Her other books include *Loneliness: A Sourcebook of Current Theory, Research and Therapy* (with Daniel Perlman), and *Close Relationships* (with Harold H. Kelley, et al.). She has published numerous articles and book chapters in social psychology on such topics as loneliness and social support, friendship, heterosexual dating, homosexual relationships, and social power.

SHELLEY E. TAYLOR is Professor of Psychology and Chair of the Health Psychology Program at the University of California, Los Angeles. Shelley received her A.B. in Psychology from Connecticut College and her Ph.D. in Social Psychology from Yale University. She taught at Harvard University until 1979 when she joined the faculty at UCLA. She has won a number of awards for her work, including the American Psychological Association's Distinguished Scientist Award for an Early Career Contribution, and a Research Scientist Development Award from the National Institute of Mental Health. She is currently a consulting editor for the *Journal of Personality and Social Psychology* and has served on the editorial boards of many other journals. Her other books include *Social Cognition* (with Susan T. Fiske), *Health Psychology*, and *Positive Illusions*. She has published numerous articles and book chapters in social cognition and health psychology.

ONE

Theories and Methods in Social Psychology

WHAT DO SOCIAL PSYCHOLOGISTS STUDY?

THEORIES IN SOCIAL PSYCHOLOGY

THE GOALS OF SOCIAL PSYCHOLOGICAL RESEARCH

RESEARCH QUESTIONS: DESCRIPTIVE AND THEORETICAL

CORRELATIONAL VERSUS EXPERIMENTAL DESIGNS

FIELD VERSUS LABORATORY SETTINGS

METHODS OF DATA COLLECTION

BIAS IN RESEARCH   RESEARCH ETHICS

WHAT DO SOCIAL PSYCHOLOGISTS STUDY?

Social psychology is the scientific study of social behavior. It considers how we perceive other people and social situations, how we respond to others and they to us, and in general how we are affected by social situations. To begin, consider a few examples of the many topics studied by social psychologists.

First Impressions and Lasting Relationships

While driving to school and listening to music on the car radio, Jason was suddenly jolted

Despite the high rate of divorce, some couples remain happily married for many years.

out of his dreamlike state by a young woman driver who cut in front of him on the road. She was driving a bright red sports car considerably faster than the speed limit. She sped around a corner and disappeared. Jason was a little startled, but then reflected on the experience. He was interested to find how quickly he developed strongly negative feelings toward the young woman from such a brief encounter. He quickly categorized her as a spoiled rich kid, probably from the wealthy neighborhood near campus. He also came to a quick judgment about the causes of her behavior—she cut in front of him because she is a reckless driver, not because she was avoiding a hole in the road or because she was getting ready to turn. Jason's experience is typical. We often form clear impressions of a person based on only the briefest contact.

Consider another example of impression formation. Over breakfast at the student union, Karen's mind drifts back to the party she went to this weekend. She is still trying to sort out her reactions to Mark, a new student she talked to for about an hour. He was very handsome and had a great sense of humor. Her roommate's brother had gone to high school with Mark and said he was a good student and people liked him. But Karen has misgivings. She noticed that Mark was wearing a religious medallion, and it was not her religion. He talked about going to church services regularly, and seemed to be quite religious. Karen hasn't been to church in years. Karen learned that Mark comes from a big family and that his mother loves to cook and garden. Mark seemed surprised that Karen's mother has her own successful business, and he wanted to know what Karen's father thought of the situation. Mark wasn't sure, he said, that married women should have jobs. Karen thought about going out with Mark, but wondered if they would be a compatible couple.

How important is physical attractiveness for a good relationship? What about differences in values? Social relationships always involve elements such as these. What is important in a successful relationship? How do relationships change over time? The study of interpersonal relations is central to social psychology.

Helping Others in Distress

At about 9 P.M. on Sunday, March 6, 1983, a 21-year-old woman walked into a bar in a blue-collar neighborhood of New Bedford, Massachusetts, and stopped to have a drink. She later stated that when she tried to leave, a man blocked the door, tackled her, stripped off her clothes except for a sweater, and attacked her. Two other men held her down and tried to force her to perform oral sex. As she struggled, screaming and pleading for help from the other customers at the bar, she was lifted onto the pool table and raped. In the words of the police, "She cried for help, she asked for help, she begged for help—but no one helped her." The bartender told police he gave a customer a dime to call the police, but the customer dialed the wrong number. No one went to the woman's aid, the bartender said, because one of the attackers brandished a butter knife.

The woman finally broke free and ran out of the tavern, naked from the waist down. She flagged down a car, and the driver took her to a telephone. She was treated at a hospital and released. Police later arrested six men between the ages of 23 and 26, though the other men who witnessed the incident did not come forward. Under public pressure, the bar owner handed in his liquor license two days later, and the bar was closed permanently. Ultimately, four men were convicted of aggravated rape and sentenced to long prison sentences.

There have been other highly publicized cases of refusal to help, notably that of another young woman, Kitty Genovese. In 1964, as she was coming home from work late at night, Kitty was attacked and repeatedly stabbed in front of her apartment building in Kew Gardens, New York. During her half-hour struggle with the attacker, she repeatedly screamed that she was being stabbed and begged for help. Thirty-eight people living in adjacent houses and apartments later said they had heard her screams. But no one came to her aid or even called the police. The police were not called until 20 minutes after she died; then they arrived in 2 minutes. Even then, none of her neighbors came

out onto the street until an ambulance arrived to take her body away.

Why didn't either of these victims receive help? How did the bystanders perceive these two victims? How did the bystanders understand their own responsibility and the morality of what they and others were doing? Furthermore, how can we explain the fact that in other situations, bystanders often do volunteer assistance? We know of instances where volunteers work tirelessly for hours to save the lives of people trapped by earthquakes or floods. Or cases in which passersby risk their own lives to help someone being mugged on the street. At times, people act helpfully, even heroically, toward total strangers. Under what conditions do people step forward to help others, and when do they just passively permit suffering to continue? Social psychologists are concerned with uncovering the answers to these questions.

As these examples suggest, the scope of social psychology is quite broad. In reading this book, you will learn that some social psychologists study perceptions and attitudes: how people view each other, how they interpret other people's behavior, and how their attitudes form and change. Other social psychologists focus on various types of interactions between people, including friendship and love, aggression, altruism, conformity, and power. Social psychologists also study how people act in groups, and how groups affect their members. The ideas and methods of social psychology have been applied to a variety of important social issues and everyday experiences, including prejudice, political behavior, sex roles, the effects of the environment, and social factors in physical health. The discipline of social psychology tries to answer questions about how people affect one another and how they behave in social situations. Not all these questions have been answered fully. The job of social psychologists is to ask important questions and then to look for answers.

The Social Psychological Approach

Of course, many other fields also study social behavior. What is unique about social psychology is the distinctive approach taken. The social psychological approach differs, on the one hand, from disciplines that study large-scale social processes, and, on the other hand, from disciplines that focus on the individual.

The *societal level* of analysis is used by sociologists, anthropologists, economists, political scientists, urban geographers, and other social scientists. Scholars in these fields use broad historical, economic, societal, or cultural factors to explain social behavior. According to this viewpoint, people's behavior can be explained by such forces as class conflicts, clashes between competing ethnic groups, a regional crop failure, governmental policies, or technological changes in the economy.

The *individual level* of analysis is typically used by clinical and personality psychologists who explain behavior in terms of the person's unique individual characteristics. According to this viewpoint, personality traits and motives can explain why individuals behave as they do, and why two people may react quite differently to the same situation. Emphasis is given to individual differences in childhood experiences, in ability and motivation, and in personality.

Social psychologists adopt a level of analysis that is in between—the *interpersonal* level. Social psychologists typically focus on a person's current social situation. That social situation includes the other people in the environment, their attitudes and their behaviors, the context within which they are interacting, and so on. For example, what aspects of another person and a particular situation make us more likely to obey the person's orders? Must the person have an official role? act in an authoritative way? issue commands from an official place, such as a laboratory or office? threaten us with punishment if we disobey? In broad terms, what aspects of the immediate social situation determine human behavior?

Let us compare these three levels of explanation in terms of a specific example—the origins

These marchers are protesting the South African government's policy of racial apartheid. What individual, interpersonal, and societal factors might explain this march and the growing opposition to apartheid?

of violent crime in big cities. Figure 1–1 shows how the three levels of analysis might approach this topic. The societal approach would look for broad social explanations. Social scientists might point out that high rates of violent crime tend to be associated with poverty, rapid urbanization, and the industrialization of a society. To provide evidence for such a conclusion, they might point to certain facts: poor people commit more violent crimes than wealthy people do; violent crime is much more common in slum areas than in wealthy neighborhoods; crime rates go up in economic recessions and drop when the economy recovers. Such explanations relate the large social forces on the left of Figure 1–1 to the outcomes shown at the right. They do not consider individual persons at all, nor the immediate social situations in which crime occurs.

The individual approach would tend to explain violent crime in terms of the unique histories and characteristics of the criminal individual. Personality or clinical psychologists might consider individual differences that lead some people to commit crimes when others in seemingly identical situations do not. Of all the bank tellers in Chicago, why does one individual go berserk and shoot five of his co-workers? To understand such behavior, the individual approach would consider the personality and background of the person. Was the bank teller depressed or suffering from paranoid delusions or using drugs? What kind of a life had the bank teller led? For example, was he physically abused as a child? Perhaps abusive parents tend to produce children who are angry at the world, or who do not learn the usual cultural values and morals. The bottom of Figure 1–1 shows that people in the same situation may behave differently because of their unique past experiences.

In contrast, the special focus of social psychology is to understand how people respond to immediate social situations. What feelings and thoughts are produced in a particular social situation, and how do these reactions in turn affect overt behavior? What kinds of interpersonal situations lead to feelings of anger and increase aggressive or criminal behavior? One important answer from social psychology has been that frustrating situations make people angry and so increase the tendency to act aggressively. This has been called the **frustration-aggression hypothesis.** It predicts that when we are blocked from achieving a desired goal, we feel frustrated and angry, and are more likely to strike out. This effect of frustration is one explanation for violent crime.

The frustration-aggression hypothesis can also explain how large-scale economic and soci-

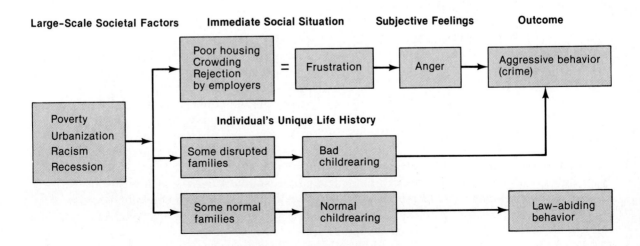

Figure 1–1. How three different approaches might explain aggressive crime.

6   **CHAPTER ONE**

etal factors create situations that lead to violence and crime. For instance, people who are poor and crowded into urban slums are frustrated: they cannot get good jobs, cannot find affordable housing, cannot provide a safe environment for their children, and so on. This frustration may produce anger which can be the direct cause of violent crime. The frustration-aggression hypothesis focuses on the immediate social situation, the feelings and thoughts such situations produce in people of many different backgrounds, and the effects of those subjective reactions on behavior.

Each of these three approaches is worthwhile and indeed essential if we are to understand complex social behavior fully. And there is, of course, considerable overlap among disciplines in the kinds of studies that are done. A single question—What causes violent crime?—can be answered in many different ways. This book will introduce you to the social psychological perspective on human behavior.

THEORIES IN SOCIAL PSYCHOLOGY

In attempting to explain behavior, social psychologists draw on a variety of different theories. Before discussing current theories in social psychology, it is useful to consider some of the historical roots of the field. In the early 1900s, three major theoretical perspectives were developed by pioneering psychologists. These have all left their mark on contemporary social psychology.

Historical Roots of Modern Social Psychology

Sigmund Freud, the founder of **psychoanalytic theory,** was fascinated by the rich mental life of the human animal. Freud proposed that behavior is motivated from within by powerful internal drives and impulses such as sexuality and aggression. He also believed that adult be-

havior is shaped by unresolved psychological conflicts that can be traced to childhood experiences in the family. Psychoanalytic theorists seek to understand the inner forces, both conscious and unconscious, that energize and direct behavior.

Behaviorism offered a very different perspective on human experience. As developed by Ivan Pavlov, John B. Watson, B. F. Skinner, and others, behaviorism focused on the observable behavior of humans and other animals. Behaviorists were not particularly interested in subjective thoughts and feelings; they preferred to study what they could directly observe and measure, which meant overt behavior. Behaviorists examined ways that the environment shapes the behavior of animals and proposed that current behavior is the result of past learning. Behaviorists identified a series of principles to explain the specific processes through which this all-important learning occurs.

The third perspective of **gestalt** psychology was developed by Wolfgang Kohler, Kurt Koffka, Kurt Lewin, and other European psychologists who emigrated to the United States in the 1930s. Their focus was on the way individuals perceive and understand objects, events, and people. In their view, people do not perceive situations or events as made up of many discrete elements, but rather as "dynamic wholes." Think about your best friend. When you last saw her, did you perceive her as a collection of arms, legs, fingers, and other features? Probably not. More likely, you perceived her as a total unit integrating the relationships among her various body parts into the familiar "whole" or person you know and like. This emphasis on perceiving the environment as a whole that is more than the sum of its parts is known as gestalt psychology, from the German word for shape or form.

Each of these three important theories arose from the work of a few charismatic individuals who inspired a fierce sense of loyalty to their own ideas and, often, an equally fierce rejection of other viewpoints. These pioneers modeled their theories on those of the physical sciences. Their goal was to explain and predict all human

John B. Watson (1878–1958)   Kurt Lewin (1890–1947)   B.F. Skinner (1904–1990)

behavior, and they wanted theories as detailed, universal, and complete as, for example, atomic theory in physics. Many of these theories were applied to the analysis of social behavior and to research in social psychology. The idea of developing general theories is important—but in the long run, the problems studied by social psychologists have turned out to be too complex to fit any one of these general theories.

Even so, social psychological approaches to a wide variety of different problems have been guided by a few basic ideas easily traced back to the general theories of yesteryear. In contemporary social psychology, the legacy of psychoanalytic theory can be seen most clearly in the analysis of motivation and emotion in social life. Social psychologists recognize that behavior is influenced by personal motives and by the emotional reactions we have to situations and people. The legacy of behaviorism is a continuing concern with how learning shapes social behavior. Social psychologists are interested, for example, in how people learn to be helpful or to obey authority or to endorse conservative political views. In broad terms, how does experience shape our attitudes and behavior? Finally, the legacy of gestalt psychology is found in the current emphasis on social cognition, the study of how we perceive and understand our social

Sigmund Freud (1856–1939)

world. Basic gestalt principles have been greatly expanded in recent years, as we will see in the next chapters of this book.

In the following sections, we introduce some of the major contemporary theories in social psychology. At this point, our intention is not to be comprehensive or detailed. Rather, we want to convey their essence and particularly the contrasts among them, so that we can refer to these theories in later chapters. To permit a clear comparison of the theories, we will apply each approach to the specific problem of understanding crime.

Consider this situation: At 3 A.M. one morning, a police officer catches a high school dropout, Larry, coming out of the rear door of a liquor store with a bag full of money. The store, like everything else in the neighborhood, has long been closed for the night. The officer shouts at Larry to stop and put his hands up. Larry turns, pulls a pistol from his pocket, and shoots the officer, wounding him in the leg. Larry is later apprehended and ultimately sent to jail. The statistics predict that Larry's stay in jail will not be productive or happy; it will be costly for society, and the chances of his committing further crimes are fairly high. We will refer to Larry in describing major contemporary theories in social psychology.

Learning Theories

For many years, **learning theory** was the dominant approach in psychology. The central idea is that a person's behavior is determined by prior learning. Current behavior is shaped by past experience. In any given situation, a person learns certain behaviors which, over time, may become habits. When presented with the same situation, the person tends to behave in the same habitual way. When a hand is extended to us, we shake it, because that is how we learned to respond to an extended hand. When someone says something nasty to us, we may be nasty back, or we may try to make the other person like us, depending on what we have learned to do in the past. As applied to social behavior by Albert Bandura (1977) and others, this approach has been called **social learning theory.**

There are three general mechanisms by which learning occurs. One is **association** or classical conditioning. Pavlov's dogs learned to salivate at the sound of a bell because they were presented with food every time the bell was rung. After a while they would salivate to the sound of the bell even in the absence of the meat because they associated the bell with meat. We can also learn attitudes by association. For example, the word "Nazi" is generally associated with horrible crimes. We believe that Nazis are bad because we have learned to associate them with atrocities.

A second learning mechanism is **reinforcement,** a principle explored by Clark Hull, B. F. Skinner, and others. People learn to perform a

One of the most powerful mechanisms of learning is imitation. Children often imitate adults, especially their parents and others they like and respect.

particular behavior because it is followed by something pleasurable and need-satisfying (or they learn to avoid behavior that is followed by unpleasant consequences). A child may learn to help other people because her parents praise her for sharing her toys and smile approvingly when she offers to help with chores. Or a student may learn not to contradict the professor in class because each time he does, the professor frowns, looks angry, and snaps back at him.

A third mechanism is **observational learning.** People often learn social attitudes and behaviors simply by observing the attitudes and behaviors of other people, known technically as *models.* Children learn regional and ethnic speech patterns by listening to the speakers around them. Adolescents may acquire their political attitudes simply by listening to their parents' conversations during election campaigns. In observational learning, other people are an important source of information. **Imitation** or **modeling** occurs when a person not only observes but actually copies the behavior of a model. Observational learning can occur without any external reinforcement. However, whether or not a person actually performs a behavior learned through observation will be influenced by the consequences the action has for them. A little boy may learn a lot about baby dolls from watching his sisters, but be discouraged from playing with them himself because his traditional parents say "dolls aren't for boys."

The learning approach has three distinctive features. First, the causes of behavior are believed to lie mainly in the past learning history of the individual. To return to our example of Larry shooting the police officer, we might find that in his previous encounters with the police, they had been rough, rude, antagonistic, suspicious, and unsympathetic. Perhaps Larry had been reinforced in the past for responding violently to situations involving conflict with authority, and nonviolent responses had not worked as well. Or perhaps his father often acted in violent ways so that Larry learned to imitate a violent model. The learning theorist is especially concerned with past experience and somewhat less with the details of the current situation.

Second, the learning approach tends to locate the causes of behavior mainly in the external environment and not in the individual's subjective interpretation of what is happening. It emphasizes the ways others respond to a person's actions and the models to which a person has been exposed. All these are external to the individual.

Third, the learning approach usually aims to explain overt behavior instead of psychological or subjective states. It would try to explain Larry's overt act—shooting the police officer—not such subjective states as perceptions of the situation (whether or not Larry expected the police officer to attack him) or emotions (whether Larry was fearful or angry).

Cognitive Theories

The main idea in the cognitive approach is that a person's behavior depends on the way he or she perceives the social situation. People spontaneously organize their perceptions, thoughts, and beliefs about a situation in simple, meaningful ways. No matter how chaotic or arbitrary the situation, people will impose some order on it. And this organization, this perception and interpretation of the world, significantly affects how we behave in social situations.

The cognitive perspective in social psychology derives from the early work of gestalt psychologists. Kurt Lewin applied gestalt ideas to social psychology, emphasizing the importance of the social environment as perceived by the individual—what Lewin called the person's "psychological field." In Lewin's view, a person's behavior is affected both by the individual's characteristics (such as ability, personality, genetic dispositions) and by the social environment as he or she perceives it.

A core idea in the cognitive perspective is that people tend spontaneously to *group* and *categorize* objects. Put this book down and look around you. Instead of seeing objects individually, you see them as parts of larger groupings. You see a row of books on a shelf as a unit, not as so many individual books. You probably perceive other people in the library in groups—perhaps as students and librarians, or as the line of people at the check-out desk, or as a couple in love. At home, you experience the pile of dirty dishes by the kitchen sink as an oppressive heap, not as individual dishes. We tend to group objects according to some very simple principles, such as similarity (dishes look more like each other than the stove and refrigerator do, so we group the dishes together), proximity (books stacked in a pile go together, the isolated books strewn all over the library table do not), or past experience (tables and chairs go together, so do David and Goliath or Dick and Jane, but a stove and chair do not, nor do Woody Allen and a Stealth bomber).

Second, people readily perceive some things as standing out (*figure*) and some things as just being in the background (*ground*). Usually colorful, moving, noisy, unique, nearby stimuli stand out as figure, whereas bland, drab, stationary, quiet, common, far-away stimuli comprise the background. Our attention is drawn to cheerleaders at a football game, not because they are so numerous—there may be only a dozen in a crowd of nearly 100,000 people—but because cheerleaders move a lot, yell, wave their arms, and wear colorful uniforms. In contrast, we experience the crowd as just that—a crowd—not as a collection of thousands of distinctive, fascinating individuals.

These two principles—that we spontaneously group or categorize the things we perceive and that we focus attention particularly on the most prominent (figural) stimuli—are central to our perception of physical objects and of the social world. As social thinkers, we try to arrive at meaningful interpretations of how people feel, what they want, what kinds of people they are, and so forth.

One important direction for research on cognition has been the study of causal **attributions,** the ways in which people use information to determine the causes of social behavior. For example, how do we decide that a salesperson's ingratiating behavior is caused by a genuine liking for us as opposed to the desire to butter us

up for a big sale? Why do we think someone turned us down for a date? Why did the audience at our music recital give such a loud and enthusiastic response to our performance? The answers to these questions about causes can have a strong influence on our feelings and behavior. Deciding that the recital audience applauded because we gave a flawless performance may lead us to feel proud and to redouble our efforts to become a professional musician. In contrast, deciding that they applauded because they were friends and family who always overlook our faults may not enhance our self-esteem or professional aspirations.

More recently, the cognitive perspective in social psychology has been stimulated by new developments in cognitive psychology—the study of how people process information. As applied to social psychology, research on **social cognition** focuses on how we put together social information about people, social situations, and groups to make inferences about them. Social cognition researchers examine the flow of information from the environment to the person. Three types of social cognition research are important.

First, research on social perception examines the ways people perceive and encode social information. It considers such questions as why we pay attention to some actions that people perform and ignore others. For example, why do we overlook a person scratching his head, but pay attention if he shouts?

Second, research on social inference examines the ways people integrate or put information together to arrive at impressions and conclusions about the social world. For example, when students visit colleges to decide which one to attend, how do they sort the information they have gathered and put it together to arrive at the conclusion that one school is a warm and friendly place and that another school is much too impersonal?

Third, research on social memory examines how individuals store and retrieve information about people and social events. For example, how does an eyewitness to a murder store infor-

What's going on here? Our perception and interpretation of a situation determines how we will respond.

mation about the crime? How can the prosecutor best help this witness to remember specific details of the event?

Cognitive approaches differ from learning approaches in two major ways. First, cognitive approaches focus on current perceptions rather than on past learning. Second, they emphasize the importance of the individual's perception or interpretation of a situation, not the "reality" of the situation as it might be viewed by a neutral observer. To return to Larry's run-in with the law, cognitive approaches would emphasize the importance of the way that Larry interpreted the present situation. How did Larry perceive his actions in taking the money? When the police officer shouted at Larry to stop, how did Larry interpret the situation? He probably perceived this person as a police officer whose job is to arrest criminals and perhaps as someone who is prejudiced against people like Larry. He may have seen the officer as threatening, biased, or perhaps even cruel. Ultimately, it was Larry's interpretation of the situation that led him to shoot the police officer.

Motivational Theories

A third general approach focuses on the individual's own needs or motives. Both everyday experience and social psychological research provide many examples of the ways in which our needs influence our perceptions, attitudes, and behavior. For example, to enhance our self-esteem and satisfy a need to feel good about ourselves, we may blame others for our failures and take personal credit only for successes. The fear aroused by a major earthquake may lead people to seek out the company of others as a way to reduce personal discomfort and feel less frightened. Television commercials often attempt deliberately to arouse insecurity to sell products, promising, for example, to allay our fears that bad breath will wreck our social life if we purchase the brand of mouthwash in the ad.

The Freudian or psychoanalytic view of human motivation emphasized the importance of a few powerful in-born impulses or drives, especially those associated with sexuality and aggression. In contrast, social psychologists consider a much more diverse range of human needs and desires. Social psychologists also emphasize ways in which specific situations and social relationships can create and arouse needs and motives. For example, the experience of moving away from home to go to college often creates feelings of loneliness among young adults. Geographical moves disrupt a person's established social network and sources of companionship, and arouse unmet needs for intimacy and a sense of "belonging." The desire to create a new group of friends at college may lead new students to join clubs, go to social events, and talk to strangers in the cafeteria. Unmet needs for companionship can also lead some students to seek distractions from this discomfort by throwing themselves into their studies or by using alcohol or drugs. The core idea is that situations can create or arouse needs which, in turn, lead people to engage in behaviors to reduce the need.

To understand Larry's behavior in robbing the liquor store, a needs perspective would try to uncover Larry's motives. Was the robbery based on a need for money, perhaps to buy food or to support a drug habit? Or was the robbery a way to gain status in Larry's peer group? Did Larry shoot the police officer out of fear or anger? A social psychological analysis might go further, to try to identify in detail ways in which Larry's social environment fostered the particular needs and motives that led to the robbery and shooting.

Decision-Making Theories

According to **decision-making theories,** people calculate the costs and benefits of various actions and pick the best alternatives in a fairly logical, reasoned way. They choose the alternative that gives them the greatest benefit at the least cost. To return to Larry's situation, let's suppose that he has the choices of fleeing, surrendering, or shooting. He thinks that if he flees, he may be shot, which adds up to a considerable cost. If he surrenders, he will go to jail, another major cost. However, he may think that by shooting the police officer, he can get away—and with the money, too. Numerous decision-making theories have been developed, each using slightly different terms and concepts. For example, **incentive theory** views decision making as a process of weighing the pros and cons of various possible alternatives and then adopting the best one. The pros are positive incentives, and the cons are negative incentives. The relative strengths of the pros and cons determine the final decision.

In this simple form, decision-making theories consider the costs and benefits of each alternative, but not the relative likelihood of each alternative. Larry may try to flee despite the fact that he might get shot and killed, a major con indeed. But he may estimate that the officer is not very likely to hit him with a bullet in the dark and in a backyard with many obstacles. So the probability of being shot is low. Going to jail is not as bad as being shot, but surrendering means he is almost certain to go to jail. The probability of surrender leading to prison is very high. **Expectancy-value theory** extends the simple notion of considering costs and benefits by adding an assessment of the likelihood of each alternative (Edwards, 1954). This theory holds that decisions are based on the product or combination of two factors: (1) the value of each possible outcome or alternative and (2) the probability or "expectancy" that each outcome will actually result from the decision.

To understand how expectancy-value theory works, suppose that you are trying to decide between two new cars, a racy sports car and a solid family-type car. In comparing the two

THEORIES AND METHODS IN SOCIAL PSYCHOLOGY

cars, you are almost certain (high expectancy) that the sports car will give you more fun (high positive value). There is also some possibility (low expectancy) that the sports car will cost you more in repair bills, but since your brother-in-law owns a repair shop, you know that repair bills will not be too expensive (low negative value). A definite high positive value outstrips an uncertain low negative value, so you buy the sports car. Such rational models generate clear predictions about how decisions *ought* to be made.

Sometimes the decisions we make actually do follow fairly well the rational procedures suggested by decision-making theories. In deciding which of two colleges to attend, for example, a student might list the pros and cons associated with each, assess the importance of each factor listed, and come up with some kind of score indicating which college is better. However, social psychologists also recognize that in real life, judgments and decisions do not always follow strict rationality.

As we will see in Chapter 3, people often use shortcuts that enable them to make decisions, form judgments, or solve problems quickly and efficiently, but not always thoroughly and according to strictly rational standards. In addition, many judgments and decisions are swayed by motivational factors, such as emotional reactions or personal goals. The high school senior trying to decide between two colleges may come up with a formal "decision" based on the pros and cons of each school, but if the answer doesn't "feel right," that is, doesn't fit with his or her emotional leanings, the senior may ignore the score sheet in favor of emotional preferences. In short, rational decision-making models sometimes apply to everyday decision making, problem solving, and making judgments. But there are clear limits on the degree to which people actually use rational principles in their daily lives.

Social Exchange Theories

Social exchange theories shift the focus of analysis from the behavior of one individual to the behavior of two or more individuals who interact with each other. The principles of social exchange build on the work of both learning theorists and decision-making theorists. The core idea in social exchange theory is that as two people interact with each other, they exchange benefits and costs. In some instances, they may do this very deliberately. You may agree to help your roommate learn Spanish in return for help with your advanced calculus course. In the heat of an argument, you and a friend may "trade" insults. But even when we are not aware of it, the process of interaction creates rewards or benefits (information, smiles of approval, money, feelings of being loved, etc.) and costs (boredom, disapproval, feelings of being misunderstood, etc.) for the people involved. **Social exchange theory** analyzes interpersonal interaction on the basis of the costs and benefits to each person of possible ways they can interact.

For example, the interactions between Larry and the police officer might be analyzed as turning hostile because of their conflicting interests. Larry would benefit from escaping, while the police officer would benefit from arresting him. In contrast, an exchange theory analysis of the interaction between a nurse and a patient might focus on the benefits to the patient from cooperating with the nurse (the patient gets the right medication and is helped toward recovery) and the benefits to the nurse of being friendly (the patient cooperates, and the nurse gets a reputation for doing a good job). In this case, the interests of both parties converge on sharing a cooperative and friendly interaction. Social exchange theory is particularly useful for analyzing bargaining situations in which two parties must come to a common agreement despite their separate interests. It has also been elaborated by Harold Kelley and others to apply to personal relationships among friends and family. We will discuss social exchange theory in more detail in Chapter 7.

Role Theories

Social psychology is rooted not only in psychology, but also in sociology. The most distinctive legacy from sociology is the analysis of social norms and roles. The term "role" is frequently used in everyday speech to describe the different parts that we play in social interaction. You have probably been in the role of student, or employee, or friend, or customer. In attempting to analyze social roles systematically, sociologists have taken two approaches, one that emphasizes social structure and a second that focuses on interaction processes.

The social structural approach to roles uses imagery borrowed from the theater. The individual acting in society is like an actor in a play. In the theater, the script sets the stage, defines the role that each actor will enact, and dictates what actors say and do. Similarly, sociologists argue, society existed long before we as individuals arrived on the scene, and presents us with many pre-established social rules of behavior.

In technical terms, these rules and expectations are called **social norms.** A few norms apply to everyone in a social situation. On campus, everyone is expected to obey traffic signs and to put litter in wastebaskets. But frequently, the norms that apply depend on your position, for instance whether you are a professor or a student. Professors are supposed to come to class on time, prepare lectures and lead class discussions, write and grade tests, serve on college committees, and so on. In return, professors are entitled to a regular paycheck, to the services of support staff, and to other benefits of their position. Rather different norms apply to students, who are expected to take notes in class, study for tests, write term papers, pay tuition, and so on. The term **social role** refers to the set of norms that apply to people in a particular position, such as teacher or student.

The social structural perspective emphasizes that individuals, like actors, play out pre-existing scripts. This perspective is especially useful in understanding behavior in formal settings such as a college classroom, military unit, or religious organization—where role definitions are fairly clear and detailed. In the case of Larry, a role analysis might consider whether Larry belongs to a gang, and what the gang's expectations are about criminal behavior.

Whereas the social structural approach views people as actors reading fixed social scripts, the contrasting interactionist perspective views people as characters improvising and constructing their own social scripts. This perspective emphasizes the processes of *role making* through which individuals create, modify, and redefine roles during the course of social interaction. For

As these students work together to learn a new computer program, they exchange advice and encouragement.

example, although most people learn general expectations for roles in marriage, newlyweds usually find that they need to negotiate with each other about the specific details of their relationship to arrive at their own understandings of who will do what, when, and how. During the lifetime of a marriage, roles may be reshaped as circumstances change—for instance, when children are born, when one partner becomes ill, or when a spouse decides to return to school or retires. Another idea is that when we learn roles, we learn not only our own part, but also many aspects of the complementary role. Being a wife requires considerable knowledge of the role of husband, since the norms for both roles are closely interrelated.

Whereas the structural view tends to depict people as relatively passive actors playing out their assigned roles on the stage of life, the role-making view depicts people as active creators who, in large measure, write or at least revise their own scripts and define their own characters. From the interactionist approach, a criminal act, like any social act, involves a sequence of choices and behaviors. For example, Larry had to decide which store to rob, how to break in, what time of day is best for the burglary, what to take from the store, whether to carry a weapon, and so on. His choices were guided to some degree by his knowledge of what burglars typically do—that they work at night, try to pick unguarded stores, and so on. But Larry had considerable freedom to shape the course of his own actions and to create his own personal script for burglary.

Social Psychological Theories Today

Over the years, social psychologists have found that the complex topics we study cannot be fully understood by any one of the "grand" theories of yesteryear. Instead, social psychologists have developed more specific **middle-range theories.** These theories attempt to account for a certain limited range of phenomena, such as attitude change, aggression, or interpersonal attraction. In this book, you will be introduced to many of these more focused theories.

But as you will see, these specific theories and models continue to reflect the influence of our basic theoretical traditions.

Another trend in recent years has been for social psychologists to try to combine and integrate ideas from different theoretical traditions. Instead of focusing primarily on overt behavior or primarily on thinking, or primarily on emotions, newer theorists seek to understand the interrelationships among behavior, thoughts, and feelings. As you read about research on specific topics in social psychology such as helping behavior or conformity, consider how current social psychological analyses try to encompass all facets of human experience including behavior, cognition, and motivation. And, as you learn more about social psychology from reading this book, look for ways in which the "grand" theoretical traditions of the past continue to influence social psychology today.

THE GOALS OF SOCIAL PSYCHOLOGICAL RESEARCH

One of the exciting aspects of social psychology is that it explores topics we already know about from everyday experiences. Social psychology strives to help us understand love and altruism as well as conflict and prejudice. Personal experience is often very important in leading psychologists to study particular topics and in generating initial hypotheses about social life. For example, social psychological research on prejudice was sparked by intense concerns about discrimination against Jews, blacks, and other ethnic minorities in our society. It is important to understand, however, that although social psychological research often begins with personal experiences and social concerns, it does not stop at armchair speculation. A hallmark of social psychology is its commitment to scientific methodology.

Social psychology is an empirical science. This means that social psychologists use systematic methods of gathering information to learn about social life and to test the usefulness of our theories. Sometimes research confirms our commonsense views about social life, and sometimes it does not. Consider these statements and decide if you think each one is true or false:

☐ In choosing friends and lovers, a fundamental principle is that opposites attract.

☐ When people are anxious, they prefer to be with other people.

☐ TV ads that try to frighten people usually backfire and are less effective than ads that do not arouse fear.

☐ If you pay someone to give a speech that goes against their own beliefs, they will usually change their minds to agree with the speech. The more money you pay them for the speech, the greater the change in their personal attitudes.

☐ The idea that women are better than men at interpreting other people's "body language" and facial expressions is a myth.

You may not agree with all of these statements, but it is fair to stay that they all sound plausible. Yet research, to be described in later chapters in this book, shows that *all* these statements are oversimplifications and several are false.

Why do our casual observations sometimes lead us to wrong conclusions? Sometimes our own experiences are rather unusual. More often, our own experiences are simply not representative of most people or most social situations. Sometimes we are biased and misinterpret what happens; we see things as we want them to be, not as they really are. Sometimes we see correctly but remember wrong. In contrast, scientific research collects data in ways that reduce bias. Psychologists strive to observe representative groups of people, and to keep track of the "numbers" so we do not rely on memory or general impressions. Psychologists are not always entirely successful in avoiding limitations and bias in their work. For example, psychology has been criticized for relying too often on white, middle-class college students as research subjects—a group that is hardly representative of society at large. What is unusual about scientific research, however, is the conscious effort to

identify and overcome bias—an issue we will discuss more fully later in this chapter.

The main activity of social psychology is to conduct scientific research on social behavior. Our research has several broad goals.

Description. A major goal is to provide careful and systematic descriptions of social behavior that permit us to make reliable generalizations about how people act in various social settings. Are men more aggressive than women? Do children generally grow up to have the same political attitudes as their parents? Are there typical reactions when a love affair ends? In thinking up solutions to problems, do people work better alone or in a group? A thorough knowledge of how people actually behave is crucial to developing theories to explain the causes of behavior.

Causal Analysis. Much research in psychology seeks to establish causal relationships that link cause and effect. Do expensive ad campaigns actually influence how people vote in elections? Does frustration typically lead to anger and aggression? Does a college education cause students to become more liberal in their social attitudes? Fundamental to all scientific inquiry is the search to identify cause-and-effect relations.

Theory Building. Another goal is to develop theories about social behavior that help us to understand why people behave the way they do. As we learn more about general principles and the specifics of particular types of behavior, we gain a better understanding of social life. Theories help us to organize what we know about social behavior and can lead to new predictions that can be tested in further research. As we saw earlier in this chapter, social psychology has been influenced both by very general theories such as behaviorism and by more specific middle-range theories that seek to explain more limited aspects of social behavior.

Application. Social psychological knowledge can be helpful in solving everyday social problems. For example, the application of social psychology may help people to learn to control their own aggressive impulses or develop more satisfying personal relationships. It may also assist social planners to design interventions that can help many people—by reducing smoking, by creating more cooperation in the workplace, and so on. Today, researchers are using social psychological principles to find ways to encourage sexually-active adults to engage in safer sex practices and to understand prejudice against people with AIDS. The possibilities for applying social psychological research are numerous—but to be successful, they must be based on a firm research foundation.

RESEARCH QUESTIONS: DESCRIPTIVE AND THEORETICAL

All research begins with a question. There are two basic kinds of questions in social psychology: those that are directly related to a theory and those that are primarily descriptive.

A *theoretical question* starts with a theory we want to test. A theory can be any abstract generalization that tells us what to expect in more specific, concrete cases. A good example is Darley and Latané's middle-range theory of the diffusion of responsibility in helping situations. Earlier in this chapter, we described two cases in which women were attacked in front of a number of witnesses, yet no one helped stop the attack or even called the police. One woman was repeatedly raped, and the other was ultimately killed. Why didn't people help the women in these situations? Darley and Latané (1968) hypothesized that people are *least* likely to help when they think there are other witnesses to the emergency, so that they do not feel directly and personally responsible. For details on this fascinating research, see Box 1–1 on p. 18.

This hypothesis follows from their more general theory of the **diffusion of responsibility:** anything that diminishes an individual's sense of responsibility for solving a problem makes that person less likely to take action. This general theory leads to many specific hypotheses:

☐ People will be less likely to help in an emergency when there are other witnesses (as in the experiment described).

☐ People will work harder on a task or problem if they are alone than if they are in a large group.

☐ People will pay less attention to instructions when co-workers are also listening.

From one theoretical statement about the diffusion of responsibility, we can deduce what to expect in numerous more specific situations. Theories can usually generate hypotheses or predictions about how people will behave in a variety of situations.

Diffusion of responsibility is a good example of a middle-range theory. It deals with a moderate range of phenomena—situations in which individuals are trying to solve problems and their responsibility for the solution varies. It does not attempt to deal with all social behavior.

In summary, a theoretical research question begins with a specific prediction derived from a theory. The major goal of theoretical research is to evaluate the theory. If the hypothesis is confirmed, the theory is supported. If the hypothesis is disconfirmed, it suggests two possibilities: either we've conducted a poor test of the theory, or the theory is at least partially wrong. We can then go back and discard the theory or alter it to make it consistent with the new finding.

Often, however, research is not concerned with theory. Researchers are simply interested in discovering more about a particular behavior or experience. Research motivated by *descriptive questions* is designed to gather information about the specific phenomenon in question. For example, researchers might be interested in how divorced couples differ from those who remain married for many years. The researchers might compare married and divorced couples on many dimensions, such as how similar the husband and wife are in age, social class background, and political and religious values. The researchers might also investigate how divorced versus married couples handle disagreements and conflicts, whether they have children or not, whether both members of the couple have paid jobs, and so on. Many different factors might be explored systematically in an effort to describe differences that may exist between couples who stay together and those who break up.

The ultimate goal of psychology, indeed of any science, is to have simplifying theories that explain known facts in a particular realm. Theories help us understand, appreciate, and cope with the world. Without a theory, data are often difficult to understand and to fit into the rest of our knowledge. On the other hand, sometimes we need to begin by collecting descriptive data because we do not yet have an adequate theory. A solid understanding of how people actually behave provides the foundation for developing good theories. So there is great value in both kinds of research—research that focuses on testing particular hypotheses that have been generated from theories and research that describes basic facts about important aspects of social life.

BOX 1–1

The Diffusion of Responsibility in an Emergency

To test their theory of the "diffusion of responsibility," Darley and Latané (1968) conducted a laboratory experiment in which every subject overheard an apparent emergency. Some subjects thought they were the only witness. Some subjects believed that other people could also hear the emergency. The hypothesis was that subjects would be more likely to try to help where they thought they were the only witness to the emergency because they would feel more personal responsibility for the victim's fate.

When the college students who participated in this experiment arrived at the laboratory, they were told that they would be participating in a discussion of personal problems associated with college life. The experimenter explained that to avoid embarrassment, students would communicate using an intercom system so that their identity would remain anonymous. The experimenter would not be present for the discussion. All subjects were placed in separate rooms.

To manipulate the diffusion of responsibility, the researchers varied the size of the discussion group. Some subjects were told that there was just one other subject, some were told that there were two other subjects, and some were told that there were five other subjects. A confederate of the experimenters, who acted as if he were one of the real subjects, was always the second subject. Early in the session, the confederate always mentioned that he was prone to seizures. As the discussion proceeded, he said, "I think I need a little help . . . I've got one of these things coming on and I could really use some help . . . (choking sounds) . . . I'm going to die . . . (chokes, then he was quiet)." In reality, his seizure was staged and recorded on a tape recorder so that all subjects would hear the same apparent emergency.

Consistent with the diffusion of responsibility hypothesis, helping was substantially reduced with more witnesses. When the subjects thought no one else had heard the cries for help, 85 percent reported the incident to the experimenters with an average response time of 52 seconds. When the real subject thought there was another subject who could intervene, 62 percent responded, and the response time was 93 seconds. When the subject believed that several others could hear the emergency, only 31 percent responded and the average time to respond was 166 seconds. Bystanders were indeed less likely to intervene to help a stranger in distress when they thought other bystanders were present.

CORRELATIONAL VERSUS EXPERIMENTAL DESIGNS

After an investigator has decided what research question to ask, another difficult decision still remains: how to conduct the study. There are two basic research designs: correlational and experimental. In correlational studies, the researcher carefully observes and records the relationship between two factors. For example, a researcher might ask whether physical attractiveness is related to a student's popularity with other students. In a correlational design, the researcher would not influence the students' behavior in any way, but would merely record information about the attractiveness of each student and how much he or she is liked by other students.

In contrast, the hallmark of an experimental design is intervention: the researcher puts people in a controlled situation to watch how they react. To study the link between physical attractiveness and popularity, a researcher using an experimental design might enlist the assistance of a paid confederate who is sometimes dressed to look very attractive and sometimes dressed to look very unappealing. The researcher might then bring subjects into the laboratory for a brief interaction with another student (really the paid confederate). After a short meeting, the student's liking for the confederate would be measured. In this experimental design, the researcher controls the student's exposure to an attractive versus unattractive peer, the setting in which they interact, and the way in which liking for the peer is measured. We will take a close look at both correlational and experimental research designs, and highlight the advantages and disadvantages of each.

Correlational Research

A correlational research design consists of passively observing the relationship between two or more factors, known technically as "variables." **Correlational research** asks if there is an association between the variables. More specifically, when variable *A* is high, is variable *B* also high (a positive correlation) or low (a negative correlation), or is *B*'s value unrelated (no correlation)? Height and weight are positively correlated because tall people tend to weigh more than short people. In contrast, the amount of clothing worn and the temperature on a given day tend to be negatively correlated—people usually wear less clothing on hot days. However, height and amount of clothing are probably uncorrelated; in general, tall people and short people probably wear about the same number of pieces of clothing.

A good example of correlational research comes from studies of whether or not watching violence on television is related to aggressive behavior. Correlational studies have examined the association between how much time a child spends watching violent programs on television and the amount of aggressive behavior in which the child engages. Are the children who watch the most violence on television also the most aggressive in their daily behavior? Huesmann (1982) found that elementary school children who watched violent programs the most were also described by their peers as the most aggressive. In this study, viewing violent programs on television was positively correlated with aggressive behavior among those children.

Advantages. There are several advantages to correlational designs. Correlational techniques enable us to study problems where intervention is impossible. Many real-world issues of great importance are of this type. For example, we cannot randomly assign people to experience passionate love, earthquakes, or cancer, nor can we randomly assign people to live in big cities or to grow up in small families. Such factors are clearly beyond the control of even the most ingenious and dedicated researchers. Both ethical and practical considerations limit the opportunities that researchers have to intervene in the lives of others. In such situations, correlational designs offer the best method for understanding the connections among various facets of people's lives.

A second advantage of correlational research is efficiency. Correlational studies allow us to collect more information and test more relationships than we can in most experiments. If we use a correlational approach to explore what causes some children to be more aggressive than others, we could collect information on a great many factors, including television viewing, family history, intelligence, personality, relationships with other children, and so on. Moreover, we could measure aggressive behavior in a number of different ways—in terms of teacher's impressions, our own observations of children in school, their reputations for aggressiveness among other children, parents' reports, and so on. We could then use statistical procedures to uncover associations among this large set of variables. The experimental method is relatively inefficient for collecting large amounts of data on many variables.

Disadvantages. Although correlational research is helpful in describing the interrelationships among variables, it does not provide clear-cut evidence of cause-and-effect relationships. In correlational studies, the cause-and-effect relationship can be ambiguous in two ways. The **reverse-causality problem** occurs whenever two variables are correlated with each other, and each one can just as plausibly be the cause as the effect. In this case, we know that variables *A* and *B* are related, but we cannot tell whether *A* causes *B* or whether the reverse is true and so *B* causes *A*. Studies showing a correlation between viewing violent television and levels of aggressive behavior illustrate this problem. Such results could indicate that TV violence causes aggression in everyday life. But the opposite might also be true: perhaps children who are very aggressive in their daily lives are especially interested in watching people fight and so spend more time watching violent TV programs. In other words, perhaps children's aggressive behavior is the cause of their TV viewing. In short, a correlation between two variables does not, by itself, tell you which variable is the cause and which is the effect.

The other serious ambiguity in correlational research is the possibility that neither variable *A* nor variable *B* directly affects the other. Rather,

some other unspecified factor may influence both of them. This is called the **third-variable problem.** For example, aggression is much more common in the homes of disadvantaged people, where there tend to be higher levels of unemployment and divorce, not much money, and a great deal of frustration and anger. In such households, family members may prefer violent television shows because they seem more realistic and familiar. And children in those households may grow up being unusually aggressive themselves because of the high levels of anger and frustration surrounding them. In contrast, children who grow up in more comfortable and affluent homes may find violent programs less appealing and may also be much less aggressive themselves. If all this were true, watching television violence would be correlated with aggressive behavior, but the correlation would be due to a third variable that caused both of them: the level of frustration and anger in the child's family. The correlation between viewing televised violence and aggressive behavior would be called "spurious" because it was artificially created by a third variable that was not considered. Television would have no causal role itself.

These two ambiguities are often, but not always, a problem in correlational studies. Sometimes we can rule out the reverse causality problem. For example, many studies have found a correlation between gender and aggressive behavior, with boys being more aggressive than girls. In this case, we can be confident that aggressive behavior is *not* the cause of the child's gender: children do not begin sexually neutral and then become physiologically male or female depending on whether or not they fight on the playground. So we can be confident in the direction of causality: something about being a boy versus being a girl affects a child's aggressiveness.

Nor is the "third-variable" problem always a fatal difficulty, since we can check to see whether or not the most plausible third variable is really responsible for the correlation we have observed. For example, we could add measures of frustration and anger in the child's family to

Huesmann's (1982) correlational study of elementary school children. Then we could check to see whether or not the correlation of TV viewing with aggressive behavior was in fact due to home life. Does it hold both in angry, aggressive families and in happy, peaceful families? If so, we can conclude that the third variable (home life) was not responsible for the original correlation.

Of course, this procedure does not completely eliminate the third-variable problem. There could be some other "third variable" (now actually a fourth) that we still had not measured, such as verbal skills. Perhaps, children with poor verbal skills prefer watching shows with a great deal of physical activity rather than slower-paced shows with more talking. Again, to test this possibility, the solution would be to measure this new "third variable," verbal skill, and then see if the original correlation held up for both highly verbal children and those below average in verbal skills.

This sounds as if it could go on and on. But at some point the process ends, because we can no longer think of any more plausible "third variables." That does not mean there are none, but that for the moment, we will accept the correlation as reflecting a cause-and-effect relationship until someone else thinks of another possible variable to be examined.

Experimental Research

In an **experiment,** the researcher creates two (or more) conditions that differ in exactly specified ways. People are then randomly assigned to experience these different conditions, and then their reactions are measured. In experiments on media violence, for example, one group of children might be shown a violent film, while another group is shown a nonviolent film. All the children might then be placed in a test situation in which their aggressive behavior can be measured. If those shown the violent film behave more aggressively, filmed violence is demonstrated to be a cause of aggressive behavior in this setting.

A good example of this experimental approach to the study of media violence is a study by Hartmann (1969). He had one group of teenage boys watch a 2-minute film showing two boys shooting baskets and then getting into an argument and finally a fistfight. A second group was shown another 2-minute film depicting an active but cooperative basketball game. After watching the film, each boy was asked to help out in what was described as a study of the effects of performance feedback on learning. The subject was supposed to be a "teacher" and to administer a shock to a "learner" every time that "learner" made a mistake in the learning task. The "teacher" could deliver as strong a shock as he wanted, within certain limits. (In reality, the shocks were fake, and the "learner" was a confederate of the experimenter.) It turned out that the boys who had seen the violent film delivered stronger shocks than those who had seen the nonviolent one. In this situation, at least, observing filmed violence caused an increase in aggressive behavior.

The great strength of the experimental method is that it avoids the ambiguities about causality that afflict correlational studies. In social psychology, experiments consist of randomly assigning people to different conditions and seeing if there is any difference in their responses. If the experiment has been done properly, any difference in responses between the two conditions must be due to the difference in the conditions. In more formal terms, the factor controlled by the researcher (the "cause") is called the **independent variable,** because it is free to take on any value determined by the researcher. In the Hartmann study, the independent variable was the type of film the boys watched. The outcome (or "effect") being studied is called the **dependent variable,** because its value is dependent on the independent variable. In the Hartmann study, the dependent variable was the amount of electric shock the subject administered to another person. Experiments provide clear evidence that differences in the dependent variable are caused by differences in the independent variable.

In experimental research, much attention is

given to creating the independent and dependent variables. The psychologist will usually start with an abstract or conceptual definition of the variable in question. For example, the variable "observing violence" might be defined as watching acts that hurt or are intended to hurt another person. The researcher must then go from this fairly general conceptual definition to an operational definition. An **operational definition** is the specific procedure or operation that is used to manipulate the variable in the experiment. For example, the experimenter might create two versions of a film, one violent and another nonviolent. If the experimenter is attempting to manipulate only the amount of violence in a film, then the two films should not differ in other ways, such as length, being in color versus being in black and white, or being a cartoon versus being realistic. The experimenter's control over the independent variable is crucial because it allows us to pinpoint the cause of any differences that emerge between the two groups of people.

The second essential feature of an experiment is that subjects must be randomly assigned to conditions. This can be done by flipping a coin, cutting a deck of cards, or more commonly and more precisely, by using a set of random numbers. **Random assignment** of subjects to conditions is crucial because we must assume that the groups of subjects did not differ before they experienced the experimental conditions. If they differ in some way beforehand, we cannot interpret any later differences in behavior as being due solely to the experimental conditions. The differences in behavior could be due to those pre-existing factors and not to the independent variable.

In summary, correlational and experimental research complement each other. There are many cases in which both methods are useful. Still, each has its relative advantages and disadvantages. These are summarized in Table 1–1. Correlational studies are particularly effective in the collection of large amounts of data; they provide ideas and hypotheses that can be studied in more detail experimentally. Correlational studies have the disadvantage of causal ambiguity, so it is often helpful for experimental research to supplement correlational studies.

FIELD VERSUS LABORATORY SETTINGS

Another decision in designing research concerns where the study should be conducted: in a field setting or in a laboratory. Research done in the field examines behavior in its "natural habitat." We might study factory workers' productivity right in the factory, or people's television viewing in their own living rooms, or commuters' responses to an emergency on the subway train they normally ride to work, or third-graders' aggressive behavior toward schoolmates on the school playground, or college students' relationships with their roommates in a college dormitory.

Laboratory research, in contrast, is done in an artificial situation, one the person normally does not inhabit. Usually laboratory research is conducted in some specially outfitted room in a psychology building at a university or research institute. The lab room may have all kinds of special equipment, such as video monitors to show films to subjects, audio equipment to record conversations between subjects, one-way mirrors to permit observation of group interactions, physiological recording equipment, or computers. Or it may simply be a room or lecture hall where people can fill out questionnaires. The point is that the subject comes to a setting selected and controlled by the researcher.

Although much research in social psychology during the last 30 years has been conducted in the laboratory, some has always been conducted in the field. Both experimental and correlational research can be done in either the laboratory or the field, and each setting has advantages and disadvantages.

Advantages of the Laboratory

The major advantage of laboratory research is the control it permits over the situation. Re-

T A B L E   1 – 1

CHARACTERISTICS OF CORRELATIONAL AND EXPERIMENTAL RESEARCH

	Correlational	Experimental
Advantages of Experiments		
Independent variable	Varies naturally	Controlled by researcher
Random assignment	No	Yes
Unambiguous causality	No	Yes
Theory testing	Often	Usually
Advantages of Correlational Studies		
Exploratory	Often	Usually not
Real world problems	Often	Usually not
Tests many relationships	Usually	Usually not

searchers can be quite certain about what is happening to each subject. If they are doing experimental work, they can randomly assign the subjects to conditions, expose them to specific experiences, minimize extraneous factors, and go a long way toward eliminating unwanted variations in the procedure. Laboratory researchers have great control over the dependent variable and can measure more precisely than is often possible in the field. Therefore, the laboratory is the ideal place to study the exact effects of one variable on another. All these advantages fall under the heading of **internal validity.** Internal validity is high when we can be confident that the effects we observe in the dependent variable are actually caused by the factors we manipulated in the independent variable (and are not caused by other uncontrolled factors).

In contrast, in field settings, it is generally extremely difficult to assign subjects to conditions randomly, to be certain they are all experiencing the same thing, to get precise measures of the dependent variable, and so on. In particular, it is difficult to find pure manipulations of the independent variable and pure measures of the dependent variable. The researcher must find or arrange circumstances that produce specific differences—and no others—between conditions.

In an ambitious field study of the effects of TV violence, Feshbach and Singer (1971) stud-

ied adolescent boys who lived in seven different boarding schools in California and New York. With the help of the school staff, the researchers were able to assign boys randomly to two different "TV diets." All boys watched selected prime-time TV shows for at least 6 hours a week for 6 weeks. In the violent TV condition, the boys watched shows with aggressive content, including Westerns and crime stories. In the nonviolent condition, boys watched situation comedies and other nonaggressive programs. Staff ratings of the boys' behavior constituted the measure of aggression. Contrary to what you might expect, the researchers found that the boys shown the violent programs were actually somewhat *lower* in aggressiveness than boys shown the nonviolent programs. Observed violence seemed to reduce aggressive behavior. Why might this result have occurred?

The researchers discovered that most of the boys *preferred* the more violent programs. Boys assigned to the nonviolent television condition may have been more frustrated than the other group because they were prevented from watching their favorite programs. Consequently, it is not clear whether the results are due to the content of the shows the boys watched, or to differences in the level of frustration among boys in the violent versus nonviolent TV conditions. This would not be such a problem in a laboratory study, because the re-

Do violent TV shows affect the behavior of children? Correlational studies find that children who watch violent programs are more aggressive. But correlational studies cannot determine clearly the underlying cause and effect relationship.

searchers would not have had to interfere with the boys' normal television viewing practices and, therefore, would not have induced frustration in one group and not in the other.

Another advantage of the laboratory is convenience and cost. It is usually much easier and cheaper for researchers to set up a study in a room down the hall from their office than to go where people are living their daily lives. The advantages of lab and field research are compared in Table 1–2.

Advantages of the Field

The most obvious advantage of field settings is that they are more realistic and, therefore, allow results to be generalized more readily to real-life situations. This is called **external validity** to reflect the fact that the results are more likely to be valid in situations outside of (external to) the specific research situation itself (Campbell & Stanley, 1963). External validity is high when the results of a study can be generalized to other settings and populations. Consider the differences between two studies described

in this chapter: the Hartmann (1969) laboratory experiment on TV violence and the Feshbach and Singer (1971) field experiment on the same topic.

In Hartmann's laboratory study, the independent variable, filmed violence, was artificial. The researcher created a brief film, especially prepared for the study. In Feshbach and Singer's field study, the independent variable was the violence actually shown on prime-time television all over the country. In Hartmann's laboratory study, the dependent variable, aggressive behavior, was artificial—the amount of shock delivered in the "teacher-learner" situation constructed especially for the study. In the Feshbach and Singer field study, the dependent variable was naturalistic and consisted of observers' ratings of how much physical and verbal aggression the boys engaged in during their normal interactions with peers and teachers.

Suppose we want to generalize from these two studies to the effects of prime-time television on teenage boys' aggression in their everyday lives. In the field study, we are already dealing with exactly the kinds of TV violence,

T A B L E 1 – 2 CHARACTERISTICS OF FIELD AND LABORATORY RESEARCH	Field	Laboratory
Advantages of Laboratory		
Control over variables	Low	High
Random assignment	Rarely	Almost always
Convenience and economy	Low	High
Advantages of Field		
Realism	High	Low
Impact of independent variables	Tends to be higher	Tends to be lower
Minimizes suspicion and bias	Yes	No
External validity	High	Low

everyday aggressive behavior, and real-life situations of interest. So it would be more appropriate to generalize from the field study. The field study therefore has greater external validity.

Another advantage of work in the field is that we are sometimes able to deal with extremely powerful variables and situations that could not be studied in the laboratory. We can observe people in extreme situations—when they are waiting for open-heart surgery in a hospital or huddled together under artillery bombardment. Sometimes ingenious researchers are able to take advantage of "natural experiments"—cases in which the independent variable is manipulated by nature rather than by the experimenter. For example, researchers wanting to investigate the effects of heat on violence could take advantage of the fact that the hottest days occur at random through the summer. If more crimes occur on the hottest days of the summer, then heat must be one causal factor.

Because research in the field deals with everyday life, it tends to minimize suspicion by the subjects. Their responses are more spontaneous and less susceptible to the kinds of bias suspicion produces. Whenever college students know they are subjects in an experiment, there is always the possibility that they are not behaving naturally. They may try to please or displease the experimenter, may behave in the way they think they should, may not accept the ex-perimental manipulation because they are distrustful, and so on. Any of these effects could produce bias in the results or obscure actual relationships.

METHODS OF DATA COLLECTION

The next step is to decide on a technique of data collection. Basically, we have three options. (1) We can ask research participants to report on their own behaviors, perceptions, or attitudes. (2) We can observe behavior directly. (3) We can go to an archive and use data originally collected for other purposes.

Self-report. Perhaps the most common technique of data collection in social psychology uses people's self-reports. A person can be asked for her preference between two presidential candidates, as in national polls done before each election. Children can be asked to report on their perception of their classmates' aggressiveness, or on their own actual television viewing behavior, as in Huesmann's study. People can be asked to fill out detailed questionnaires about their romantic relationships. In all these cases, the basic data are the individuals' own reports about their thoughts, feelings, and actions.

The big advantage of self-report questionnaires or interviews is that they allow the investigator to measure subjective states such as perceptions, attitudes, or emotions. These can only be inferred indirectly from observational studies. For example, it would be very difficult for observers to tell how lonely another person feels without getting that person's self-report. The principal disadvantage of self-report is that we must rely on people to give honest descriptions of their own internal feelings. People are often willing to give honest and full answers, especially when their privacy is carefully protected. But researchers also know that people sometimes disguise socially unacceptable feelings (such as racial prejudices) and that people are sometimes not fully aware of their own feelings.

Observational Research. Direct observation is a widely used research technique. In experimental studies, researchers interested in helping behavior have staged fake emergencies in public places to see how many people are willing to come to the aid of a stranger in distress. In studies of group behavior, researchers might make video recordings of a group discussion and systematically count such things as the number of times each person speaks, the number of times each person is interrupted by someone else, the amount of smiling and joking, how frequently group members look at the leader, and so on. Marital researchers have obtained permission to place microphones in homes and to record family interactions so that they can learn about the frequency of conflict, fighting, praising, and other types of interaction.

Archival Research. In **archival research,** the investigator uses data that were previously collected for another purpose. For example, researchers who wanted to examine whether violence against blacks was associated with frustration based on economic difficulties used historical records to correlate cotton prices and lynching of blacks in the U.S. South (Hovland & Sears, 1940). They found that the most lynchings occurred during the years with the lowest cotton prices. Perhaps the best known archival

data come from the U.S. Census that has been collected every 10 years for 2 centuries. But many specialized data banks also exist with the records of polls, surveys, and large-scale studies.

There are many advantages to using archival data. Most obvious is that it is very cheap to use data that may have been enormously expensive to collect. The U.S. Census costs millions of dollars to collect, but the data can be used for next to nothing. Archival data also allow us to test hypotheses at various time points, or even trends over time, rather than being limited to

Every ten years, the U.S. Census Bureau sends trained interviewers to collect vital statistics about the general population. This information then becomes part of a vast data archive, spanning two centuries, that is available for use by social scientists.

one historical moment. We might want to know how many people say they would vote for a woman for president, and the availability of archival data on that question over many years can provide a rich historical context for our findings.

On the other hand, archival data almost always were collected with some research question in mind other than the one we wish now to study. As a result, the questions are usually not exactly the ones we would ask, or they may be worded the wrong way for our purposes, or the participants in the study may not be exactly the group we would prefer. Therefore, the uses of data archives are limited in some ways. Nevertheless, as data archives continue to expand in the years ahead, they will prove of increasing importance to social psychology.

BIAS IN RESEARCH

All scientists are concerned about possible bias in their research, and social psychologists are no exceptions. Three kinds of bias are particularly troublesome in social psychology: the selection of a population to study, the experimenter's behavior, and bias associated with a subject's feelings about being in a study.

Subject Selection

How do we decide which people to study? One obvious starting point is that we should study the people about whom we later want to generalize. If we want to generalize about women who work full time, we should study employed women. But clearly we will never be able to afford to study all working women. So instead we study some smaller number of them, but chosen in such a way that they are representative of the larger group. This is known as a representative sample.

The best way to ensure this general representativeness is to study a random sample of the larger population to which we want to generalize. In formal terms, a **random sample** means

that each person in the larger population has an equal chance of being included in the study. If we selected a sample of telephone numbers from the phone directory at random (using a table of random numbers, for example), we could be assured that ours was a random sample of all listed phone numbers in the area covered by that telephone book. The laws of probability assure us that a large and truly random sample will almost always be representative of the population within a certain margin of error. It will include approximately the same proportion of women, ethnic minorities, unemployed people, older adults, and so forth as the population from which we have sampled.

Most of the time, social psychologists want their research results to apply to people in general, not just to college students in Boston or elementary school children in Austin, Texas, or people who use laundromats in Nashville, Tennessee. Yet it is extremely expensive to study random samples of people in general, as you can readily imagine. So social psychologists try to make realistic compromises between the goal of collecting valid data that can be generalized beyond the few people studied, on the one hand, and practicality on the other.

One very common compromise is to use college students as subjects. It has often been said that American social psychology is based on college sophomores, because they are the ones who are most available for experiments in laboratories. About 75 percent of all published articles in social psychology use undergraduate subjects and about two-thirds use undergraduates in the laboratory (Sears, 1986). Another common compromise is to use volunteer subjects, such as those who might leave their names and phone numbers in response to a plea for subjects left on a church bulletin board or senior citizen center. Clearly, neither college students nor volunteers are representative samples of the general population, and social psychologists usually do not make any pretense that they are. How dissatisfied should we be with such unrepresentative samples?

Our need for a representative sample depends on the question we are asking. For descriptive research in which we are trying to describe the characteristics of a given population, a representative sample is very important. Suppose we are commissioned to study how best to introduce computers into business offices where the employees have worked together for years, are almost all women, and never went past high school. It would be entirely unreasonable to study this question with a sample of college students who had never met each other before the study and who had no experience with any kind of office work. On the other hand, in some basic, theory-testing research the representativeness of the sample is less crucial. For example, according to Darley and Latané's diffusion of responsibility theory, people should be less responsive to a person in need when other people are present than if they are alone. This should be equally true of Ivy League college students, shoppers at a suburban mall, or passengers on an urban subway. The assumption is that all people react in about the same way.

Moreover, for some research topics, college students may be especially appropriate. Suppose we were studying loneliness. National samples indicate that loneliness is greatest among young adults and that the transition to college induces even more loneliness. So it may be that first-year college students are an optimal subject population for loneliness research.

However, there are other areas in which college students may actually be inappropriate as a source of data (Sears, 1986). College students are much younger, higher in social class, and better at test taking than is the general population. For problems in which these are central factors, college students may be misleading. For example, studies of personality should take into account the fact that most college sophomores are still rather young and their personalities have not developed as fully as have those of older adults. The same is likely to be true of their political and social attitudes.

Experimenter Bias

One problem that is particularly troublesome in social psychology is **experimenter bias.** Research participants are extremely susceptible to influence by the experimenter. If the experimenter implies, consciously or otherwise, that he or she would like subjects to respond in a certain way, there is a tendency for participants to respond in that way. Subtle cues tend to be picked up by subjects and to influence their behavior. For example, consider the studies of media violence in which subjects give electric shocks to another person after watching either a violent or a nonviolent movie. A well-intentioned but perhaps overly eager experimenter, knowing that the subjects in the violent movie condition are supposed to be the most aggressive, might subtly encourage these subjects to give more shocks. The researcher might smile, nod, make eye contact, or act encouraging in a variety of subtle ways. For the subjects who had seen the nonviolent movie, the researcher might frown or act cold when they give the shock, because they are violating the hypothesis.

There are two solutions to the problem of experimenter bias. One is to keep the people who actually conduct the research—often research assistants—uninformed about the hypotheses or the experimental conditions to which a particular subject was assigned. For example, in research on TV violence, we could have one experimenter show the movies and a second researcher administer the shock task, and arrange it so that the second experimenter did not know which movie the subject has seen. The second experimenter is said to be "blind" to the condition the subject is in.

A second solution is to standardize the situation in every way possible. If everything is standardized and there are no differences between conditions other than those that are deliberate, there can be no bias. In the extreme case, the subjects might appear for an experiment, find a written instruction on the door telling them to enter and turn on a tape recorder, have all instructions presented on tape, and complete the experiment before they meet a live researcher. In this way, every factor in the situation would be absolutely standardized, and experimenter bias would be eliminated.

In actual practice, the solution to the problem

of bias is usually a combination of the two procedures we have described. As much as possible, the researcher is kept "blind" to the subjects' experimental conditions; also as much as possible, instructions are standardized by the use of tapes or written materials.

Subject Bias and Demand Characteristics

Another source of bias in social psychology research stems from the subject's motives and goals when serving in the role of a research subject. **Demand characteristics** refer to "features introduced into a research setting by virtue of the fact that it *is* a research study and that the subjects know that they are part of it" (Aronson, Brewer, & Carlsmith, 1985, p. 454). The basic idea is that the mere fact of knowing that you are being studied may alter your behavior. In addition, subjects may try to "figure out" the true purpose of the experiment and alter their responses on the basis of their guesses about the study. They may try to give the "correct" or socially desirable response—to portray themselves as smart or politically liberal or religious or sexually responsible, depending on their interpretation of the situation. If subjects' responses are biased in these ways, it becomes difficult for researchers to draw accurate conclusions.

Weber and Cook (1972) have carefully analyzed the roles subjects adopt in laboratory experiments. They distinguish several different roles: "good subjects," who try to help the researchers by confirming the hypothesis; "negativistic subjects," who try to sabotage the experiment; "faithful subjects," who scrupulously follow the instructions and try to avoid acting on the basis of any suspicions about the nature of the study (either to help, or to hurt, the research); and "apprehensive subjects," who are mainly anxious about their own performance.

These biases are almost impossible to eliminate entirely, but they can be minimized in a variety of ways. The goal is to produce a situation in which subjects respond spontaneously without worrying about the correctness of their response or trying to figure out what the situation "demands." Several approaches are commonly used. When possible, researchers may use unobtrusive measures, in which the subjects do not know that they are being studied. For instance, pedestrians who encounter a handicapped person who has fallen on a city street may never know that the person is actually a researcher conducting a study of helping behavior. Another approach is to guarantee participants that their responses are anonymous; no one, including the researcher, will know how any individual reacted.

Perhaps the most common tactic is to try to keep subjects unaware of the goals and hypotheses of the study. For instance, a researcher interested in sex differences in initiating conversations with strangers might ask subjects to volunteer for a study of political attitudes or taste preferences. While the subjects are waiting for the alleged study to begin, their behavior in the waiting room might be observed, perhaps with the help of a confederate who behaves in a standardized way in the waiting room. In this situation, subjects would expect to participate in one type of study and might not suspect that the time they spend in the waiting room is of any interest to the researcher. All these techniques reduce the possibility that participants' reactions will be distorted or changed by their concerns with social desirability.

Replication

We've reviewed a variety of research issues, including the choice of correlational versus experimental designs, the use of lab versus field settings, and the choice of research participants. We have emphasized that each type of research has its own advantages and disadvantages. We also discussed various kinds of bias that can affect social research.

It is important to emphasize that no one study, however beautifully crafted, is ever perfect. Each procedure has its own defects. And we can virtually never test the entire population of interest to us, so there is always some margin of error in our ability to generalize our results. Because any single study is flawed, a hallmark of good research in social psychology is **replication.** In its simplest form, replication means that we are able to reproduce the findings of other researchers if we recreate their methods. So, for example, researchers should be able to recreate the experimental procedures used by Darley and Latané to study the effects of diffusion of responsibility on helping behavior—and should find comparable results. This is a fundamental requirement for all science, that different researchers working in different settings can all produce the same effects. Of course, in social research, it is seldom possible to recreate precisely every aspect of a study, because the subject population may be somewhat different, the social and political climate may have changed over time, and so on. Consequently, when we are able to replicate results, we have much greater confidence in their accuracy.

In addition to conducting exact replications, it is also important to conduct conceptual replications. In a *conceptual replication,* different research procedures are used to explore the same conceptual relationship (Aronson, Brewer, & Carlsmith, 1985). For example, we have seen that research on the effects of TV violence on aggressive behavior has been conducted in both lab and field settings, using both correlational and experimental designs, and using diverse measures of aggressive behavior and a wide variety of violent films. To the extent that all these different techniques yield the same results, we become increasingly confident that we understand the phenomenon in question.

However, as the number of studies on a particular topic increases, researchers are confronted with a new problem—how to read and synthesize research to arrive at general conclusions. Consider work on sex differences in helping behavior. Eagly and Crowley (1986) identified no fewer then 172 separate studies that investigated male-female differences in helping behavior! The number of studies on the effects of TV violence is probably even larger. How are researchers to handle this ever-increasing quantity of empirical research?

In recent years, new statistical techniques

called **meta-analysis** have been developed to help researchers review and synthesize empirical findings systematically (Eagly, 1987; Hyde & Linn, 1986). The first step is for a researcher to find as many studies as possible on the same topic. Then, meta-analysis uses statistical methods to pool information from all available studies. The goal is to arrive at an overall estimate of the size of the finding, for instance, the size of a particular sex difference. We might find, for instance, that the average sex difference on skill X is less than one-tenth of a standard deviation—quite a small effect that may not be of much practical importance.

In meta-analysis, statistics are also used to test for the consistency (homogeneity) of findings across studies. When results from different studies are found to be highly consistent, we can have much confidence in the finding. When results of studies differ, meta-analysis techniques direct the researcher to look for other factors that may be important. For example, if we find 40 studies showing that men are better at skill X and 40 studies showing that women are better at skill X, we might suspect that some factor other than gender makes a difference. Perhaps men are better at skill X only when tested by a male experimenter, or only in group testing situations, or only if they come from working-class backgrounds. Instead of merely commenting that findings are inconsistent, the goal is to try to identify the reasons for the inconsistency. So additional analyses would be conducted, taking these new factors into account.

The basic point is that we should be cautious about taking too seriously the results of a single study on a topic. Rather, we should ask whether any particular finding has been confirmed in other studies. And we should also ask how large and important the finding is in practical terms. For example, of all the possible variation in human aggression, how much can be attributed to TV violence? And are the sex differences we hear about so often really big enough to make a difference in everyday life? As you read magazines and newspapers or watch the nightly news on TV, you will often hear about research on such diverse topics as the health dangers of cholesterol, the latest word on teen sex, the virtue of seatbelts, and the causes of child abuse. Use your knowledge of research methods and the importance of replication to be a sensible and cautious consumer of research reports.

RESEARCH ETHICS

During the late 1950s and early 1960s, many people became concerned about the ethics of research on human subjects. Some of the concern stemmed from the discoveries of Nazi atrocities during World War II, such as the dangerous and often fatal medical experiments carried out by doctors in concentration camps on unwilling camp inmates. Ethical issues were also raised by the discovery of medical experimentation of dubious ethicality in the United States, such as the notorious Tuskegee case. In 1932, the U.S. Public Health Service began a 40-year experiment on 399 poor and semiliterate black men in Tuskegee, Alabama, who had syphilis. The goal was to trace the effects of syphilis on untreated males over many years. The men were told they were being treated, but in fact they never were, despite the fact that penicillin became available in the 1940s and was highly effective against the disease. Even by 1972, treatment was still withheld from the survivors as the study continued.

In social psychology, concern was raised about the use of deception. Consider some of the lab studies of the effects of TV violence on aggression. Is it ethical for a researcher to tell a subject that he or she is administering painful electric shocks to another person when, in fact, the shock machine is fake and the other person is a confederate of the researcher? Might the experiment cause the subject to feel guilty for hurting another person? If at the end of the study the researcher explains that the shock machine was not real, will the subjects feel foolish that they were duped by the experimenter?

Such studies raise a number of issues. When are researchers justified in deceiving subjects about the research they are participating in?

When is it legitimate to do harmful things to subjects? Is it justifiable to expose subjects to risks if the potential scientific value of a study is great? These questions led to efforts within many professional associations to define ethical behavior. In the late 1960s, the U.S. federal government established procedures for the review of all research funded by federal monies. The government required that each university and research institution that received federal funds establish a committee of researchers to review all proposed research using human subjects. This institutional review board would be responsible for ensuring that all research was conducted according to a set of general principles laid down by the federal government. Two important principles are informed consent and minimal risk.

Informed Consent and Debriefing

Federal regulations state that all researchers must obtain the subject's informed consent to participate in the research. **Informed consent** means that the subject must voluntarily agree to participate, without any coercion. And the subject must understand what the participation involves. The researcher has an obligation to tell potential subjects as much as possible about the study before asking them to participate. Subjects should be informed about the research procedures, any risks and/or benefits of the research, and their right to refuse to participate or withdraw during the research without penalty. Any exception to this general guideline must be approved by the institutional review board after careful examination of the planned research.

The requirement of informed consent sounds quite reasonable, but can sometimes create problems for social psychologists. As we have just seen, it may be important not to tell subjects the true purpose of the study, to avoid biasing their responses. Even in the simplest research, subjects are rarely told the specific hypotheses that are being tested. Several of the studies we discussed in this chapter did not provide fully informed consent, and it is hard to see how they could have. In their study of the diffusion of responsibility and helping behavior, Darley and Latané did not tell their subjects that the person in distress was actually a confederate pretending to need help. It is hard to imagine this research being valid if the subjects had really given full "informed consent." Imagine what would have happened if Darley and Latané had first told their subjects the study concerned bystander intervention and that they would be tested to see if they would help in an emergency!

Some people believe that deception of any kind is unethical in psychological research. They think it demeans the subjects and should never be used. A more moderate position endorsed by most research psychologists is that deception should not be used if at all possible, or used only after considering its possible harmful effects. Subjects, however, should always be volunteers. Perhaps they need not be told everything that will happen, but they should know that they are in an experiment and should have freely given their permission. In other words, only someone who has given informed consent or consent based on trust should be exposed to potentially distressing conditions.

At the end of their participation in a study, research subjects should always be debriefed. By **debriefing** we mean that the purposes and procedures of the research are explained in some detail. Participants should be given an opportunity to ask questions and express their feelings. A friendly discussion between the researcher and participants can help subjects to recover from any upset the research may have caused and to learn from their research experience. When research deals with very sensitive topics, it may be important for the researcher to suggest ways in which participants can learn more about the topic by reading or consulting with experts. Sometimes researchers offer to send participants written information about the results of the research, once research findings have been fully analyzed.

Minimal Risk

A second ethical guideline for research is to minimize potential risks to the subjects. The term **minimal risk** means that the risks antici-

pated in the research are no greater "than those ordinarily encountered in daily life." What are the kinds of risk social psychological research can pose?

One of the most important is the invasion of privacy. An individual's right to privacy must be respected and cherished. Researchers studying especially sensitive topics, such as illegal behavior, sex, drug or alcohol use, or religious beliefs must protect the subjects' right to withhold such information and/or to have their responses kept in strict confidence. On the other hand, public behavior and events on the public record do not have to be protected as carefully. Anyone can go to the local courthouse and look up information on births, marriages, and deaths. Threats to privacy, like all risks involved in social psychological research, can change over time as the society itself changes. For example, people are much more willing to discuss details of their sexual relationships now than they were a generation ago. Today, there is widespread concern about keeping the results of AIDS testing confidential, because disclosure that a person has been infected can jeopardize his or her health insurance, employment, and standing in the community. Responsible researchers protect subjects' privacy by guaranteeing confidentiality and often by having the person participate in the study anonymously.

The other main category of risk in social psychology research comes from stresses of various kinds. Subjects in some studies may become bored, anxious, or fearful. Some studies may threaten the individual's self-respect. As we will see in Chapter 4, many studies in recent years have been focused on the causal explanations that people make for their own successes and failures. To do such studies frequently requires that subjects be exposed to success or failure on an experimental task. A gratuitous failure experience in a psychology experiment is no fun. Being deceived is itself an unpleasant experience for some people. Smith and Richardson (1983) surveyed students who had participated in psychology experiments at the University of Georgia. Twenty percent reported experiencing some harmful consequence, such as being deceived, feeling humiliated, experiencing physical discomfort, or being angered. Such reports were almost twice as common among students who had participated in deception experiments as among those who had not. Most students reported no harm, of course, but a substantial minority did.

How much risk should a subject be exposed to? The first and most important principle is once again informed consent. If at all possible, the subjects must be allowed to make that decision for themselves, based on adequate information. The situation is like the decision people face about what surgical procedure to undergo: ultimately, the decision must be in the hands of the patient, but it must be as informed a decision as possible.

It is not always possible to inform a subject fully about the exact nature of a study. In such cases, the researcher and the institutional review board must make a decision about how much risk is allowable. The rule of thumb is this: the risks faced in the research should be no more severe than those the person is likely to encounter in normal life. Being threatened with an injection may be frightening, but it is a usual occurrence—we all get injections. In contrast, being threatened with isolation for 5 hours is also frightening, but it is not a usual occurrence—most people never face this threat. So we would be more hesitant about deceiving a person about isolation than about a harmless injection.

Finally, another general rule many researchers and review boards use in evaluating risk is that the subjects should leave the study in essentially the same state of mind and body in which they entered. That is, participation in the study should have no substantial effect that carries over once the subject has finished. Another way of stating this is that the study may be pleasant, interesting, and enjoyable, or mildly unpleasant, boring, or tedious—but the subjects' state of mind, knowledge of themselves, and general attitudes should not be altered by the experiences. This guideline, if followed closely, would ensure that subjects would not have been exposed to excessive risk.

At its best, social psychological research offers the joy of new discoveries about human experience. The thoughtful use of scientific methods can do much to advance our understanding of social life and social problems. But psychological research also carries with it great responsibility—to treat research participants with sensitivity and high ethical standards and to repay their valuable assistance by sharing our research results with the public. In the chapters that follow, we offer a guided tour of the major findings and theories in social psychology.

Key Terms

archival research

association

attribution

behaviorism

correlational research

debriefing

decision-making theories

demand characteristics

dependent variable

diffusion-of-responsi-
  bility

expectancy-value theory

experiment

experimenter bias

external validity

frustration-aggression
  hypothesis

gestalt

imitation

incentive theory

independent variable

informed consent

internal validity

learning theory

meta-analysis

middle-range theories

minimal risk

modeling

observational learning

operational definition

psychoanalytic theory

random assignment

random sample

reinforcement

replication

reverse-causality
  problem

social cognition

social exchange theory

social learning theory

social norm

social role

third-variable problem

Summary

1. Social psychology has a unique vantage point on social behavior. It emphasizes factors in immediate social situations that induce the same general response from most people. It is less concerned with large social forces than are the other social sciences. And it is less concerned with unique individual responses and individual differences than are personality or clinical psychology.

2. Major theoretical approaches in social psychology include learning theories, cognitive theories, motivational theories, decision-making theories, social exchange theory, and role theories. These are not necessarily contradictory. Rather, each emphasizes one aspect of the causes of behavior without necessarily claiming that the others are unimportant or irrelevant.

3. Today, most social psychologists are working to develop middle-range theories or models to explain specific aspects of human behavior, such as attitude change, aggression, or interpersonal attraction. Another recent trend is for social psychological theories to try to combine and integrate ideas from the "grand" theoretical traditions of the past.

4. We all know a great deal about social behavior from our daily observations and experience. Systematic research is necessary to test which of our intuitions are right and which are wrong. Social psychological research has four goals: description, causal analysis, theory building, and application.

5. Descriptive research starts with a general question about human behavior and tries to describe behavior accurately and discover new relationships. Theoretical research is designed to test a theory, to compare two theories, or to assess the limits and exceptions to a theory.

6. Correlational research asks whether two or more variables are related, without trying to manipulate either. Correlational research can deal with a great many variables at once and can investigate phenomena that cannot usually be manipulated in the laboratory, such as panic, poverty, or divorce. But correlational research usually does not allow strong causal conclusions to be drawn.

7. In an experiment, subjects are randomly assigned to conditions that differ only in specific deliberately varied ways (independent variable). If there is any difference in the resulting behavior (dependent variable), it is due to the independent variable controlled by the researcher. Experiments permit unambiguous causal statements.

8. Research in the laboratory provides more control, but research in field settings is closer to the real world and often has greater external validity. The most common sources of data in social psychology are systematic observations of behavior, self-report, and data archives.

9. Great care must be taken to avoid the effects of bias. Unless the experimenter is "blind" to experimental conditions and hypotheses, he or she can unintentionally bias the results. Responding to demand characteristics of the research situation, subjects may try to give "correct" or socially desirable responses, thus biasing results. Because any one study is inevitably flawed, replication is an essential feature of good research.

10. Social psychologists face many ethical issues in doing research. They must be careful to guard the safety of subjects, to respect their privacy, and to ensure that the research does not cause harm. Current guidelines emphasize obtaining informed consent to whatever extent possible and exposing subjects to no more than minimal risk.

Suggested Readings

Aron, A., & Aron, E. (1989). *The heart of social psychology*, 2nd ed. Lexington, MA: D. C. Heath. A delightful insider's view of the field, filled with fascinating stories about important people and research in social psychology.

Bandura, A. (1977). *Social learning theory*. Englewood Cliffs, NJ: Prentice-Hall. An excellent review of social learning theory, illustrating some of its adjustments to a more cognitive approach.

Cook, T. D., & Campbell, D. T. (1979). *Quasi-experimentation: Design and analysis issues for field settings*. Chicago: Rand McNally. The use of nonexperimental techniques in field studies is becoming increasingly important. This useful book discusses how to design and interpret such studies.

Deutsch, M., & Krauss, R. M. (1965). *Theories in social psychology*. New York: Basic Books. Still the best coverage of the classic theories.

Feshbach, S., & Singer, R. D. (1971). *Television and aggression*. San Francisco: Jossey-Bass. An interesting field experiment on the effects of TV violence.

Lindzey, G., & Aronson, E. (Eds.). (1985). *The handbook of social psychology*, 3rd ed., 2 vols. New York: Random House. A comprehensive survey of the major topics, theories, and methods in social psychology, written by leading experts.

Sears, D. O. (1986). College sophomores in the laboratory: Influences of a narrow database on social psychology's view of human nature. *Journal of Personality and Social Psychology, 51*, 515–520. An analysis of the possible dangers of relying too heavily on college sophomores in laboratory experiments.

Webb, E. J., Campbell, D. T., Schwartz, R. D., & Sechrest, L. (1966). *Unobtrusive measures: Nonreactive research in the social sciences*. Chicago: Rand McNally. An engaging description of many clever techniques for collecting data without letting people know you are doing it.

TWO

Person Perception

*T*wo freshmen destined to be roommates arrive at college and meet for the first time. Each one's personality—how easily each one is to get along with, how nice each is—will have an important effect on the other's life. In the first few minutes of their meeting, each tries to form an impression of the other, because they know they will be spending a great deal of time together during the year. How late does each one stay up studying at night? What kind of music does the other like? How does each feel about parties in the room? They try to find out as much about each other as they can.

People use whatever information is available to form these impressions of others—to make judgments about their personalities or hypotheses about the kinds of persons they are. In this chapter we deal with this process, which is called **person perception:** how we make impressions, what biases affect them, what kinds of information we use in arriving at them, and how accurate our impressions are.

WHAT INFORMATION DO YOU USE?

Our knowledge and expectations about others are determined by the impressions we form of them. A glance at someone's picture or at an individual passing on the street gives us ideas about the kind of person he or she is. Even hearing a name tends to conjure up images of what its owner is like. When two people meet, if only for an instant, they form impressions of each other. With more contact, they form fuller and richer impressions that determine how they behave toward each other, how much they like each other, whether they will associate often, and so on.

As this discussion implies, generally we draw on other people's appearance and behavior to infer qualities about them. Such factors as a person's sex, race, and physical appearance can lead us to form remarkably detailed impressions. The observation that a person is female,

for example, may lead to the imputation of a variety of other characteristics, such as being nice or motherly. The observation that someone is black may call up a stereotype held about black people in general (Devine, 1989). We also use people's behaviors to draw inferences about them. We observe a fellow student helping an elderly person across the street and infer that she is kind.

The central point is that very quickly we move from observable information, such as appearance and behavior, to personality trait inferences about what the person is like (e.g., Albright, Kenny, & Malloy, 1988). Traits are a more economical and general way of describing a person than is referring to behaviors (Allen & Ebbeson, 1981). If someone asked you what your roommate is like and you had to recount each behavior you could remember, it would take you a long time and the person to whom you were describing your roommate might be little better informed by the process. Instead, you would use traits to summarize aspects of your roommate ("He is a good-natured, sloppy, night person with a penchant for loud rock music."). From this, the audience could infer that your roommate is generally easy to get along with, although he stays up late at night, plays his music loud, and doesn't pick up after himself. People use traits to describe others from the moment they first observe them, although the more we know someone, the more likely we are to use traits to describe the person (Park, 1986). In fact, the tendency to infer personality traits from people's appearance and behavior appears to occur rapidly, spontaneously, and automatically, so much so that people may not even be aware that they are doing it (Trope, 1986; Gilbert, Pelham, & Krull, 1988).

The trait inferences that we make about other people fall out along two important dimensions. We tend to evaluate others in terms of their task-related or intellectual qualities, and their interpersonal or social qualities (Rosenberg, Nelson, & Vivekananthan, 1968; Kim & Rosenberg, 1980). But, of course, within these general dimensions, we also make more detailed impressions such as judgments about a person, such as how nice he is to his parents versus his friends or how good he is at physics versus music.

Once we have made personality trait inferences about the meaning of another person's behavior, those inferences take on a life of their own. For example, you may recall your impression of your friend as kind and helpful long after you have forgotten the specific instance when she helped the elderly person across the street (Wyer, Srull, & Gordon, 1984). Asked if your friend is kind and helpful, you are more likely to refer back to your prior trait judgment than to a specific event, such as helping the elderly person across the street (Fiske, Neuberg, Beattie, & Milberg, 1987). Trait inferences, then, are made quickly, virtually spontaneously, on the basis of minimal information about a person, and then often persist long after the information on which they were originally based has dropped from the mind.

Thus, people tend to form extensive impressions of others on the basis of very limited information. Having talked with a person for only a few minutes, people will tell us how much they like him and how much they think they will like the person if they can get to know him better. They will also make judgments about a large number of that person's specific characteristics. They are generally willing to estimate another's intelligence, age, background, race, religion, educational level, honesty, warmth, and so on. Although ordinarily individuals are not overly confident of opinions formed in this way, they generally are willing to make such judgments.

INTEGRATING IMPRESSIONS

As we have seen, people move quite quickly from observations of another's appearance and behavior to inferences about their personality.

People form impressions of others quickly and with confidence from minimal information, such as sex, appearance, or a brief meeting. What impressions of each other are these two college roommates likely to be forming of each other?

But how are these separate inferences put together into an overall impression? What are the most important aspects of impressions, and how do we put together information that may seemingly be inconsistent, such as the observation that our roommate is nice but self-centered?

Evaluation

The most important and powerful aspect of first impressions is **evaluation.** Do we like or dislike this person? How much do we like or dislike him? Our immediate impression may be composed of other dimensions; he may seem friendly, talkative, and helpful. But all these specific traits are fundamentally tied to the question of whether we like or don't like him (Park & Fink, 1989).

Put more formally, the evaluative dimension is the most important of a small number of basic dimensions that organize these unified impressions of people. This point was shown in a classic study by Osgood, Suci, and Tannenbaum (1957) using a measurement procedure called the semantic differential. In this method, subjects were given a list of trait pairs and asked to indicate which trait particular persons and objects fell closest to. The list consisted of such trait pairs as happy-sad, good-bad, strong-weak, and warm-cold, and the items the subjects had to rate ranged from mothers to boulders. For example, the subject had to rate whether "mothers" were "happy" or "sad," and so on. Osgood and his associates then analyzed the responses for any basic dimensions on which all things had been described.

Three underlying dimensions accounted for most of the ratings: *evaluation* (good-bad), *potency* (strong-weak), and *activity* (active-passive). Once a particular person or object was placed on these three dimensions, little additional information could be gotten from getting additional ratings of it. In other words, once we know that someone rates "mother" as very good, moderately strong, and somewhat passive, we learn little more about these perceptions of "mother" by asking for additional ratings.

Of the three, evaluation was the main dimension underlying perceptions, with potency and activity playing lesser roles. Once we place someone on this dimension, many other perceptions of him or her fall into place. Our evaluation of a person pervades our memories of what he or she is like (see Zajonc, Pietromonaco, & Bargh, 1982; Zajonc & Markus, 1984). A favorable or unfavorable impression in one context extends to most other situations and to other seemingly unrelated characteristics.

The Averaging Principle

Suppose you've just met someone, and you notice that she is neat, tall, dark haired, attractive, flirtatious, and "preppy" in dress. Or you meet someone else who is a pre-med, deeply religious, a tennis expert, an extrovert, and engaged to be married. How do we put such separate pieces of information together into simple overall impressions?

Psychologists have two main views on this matter, one emphasizing learning and the other cognitive factors. The learning approach, in its simplest form, suggests that people combine information in a rather mechanical, simpleminded fashion, without thinking about it much. Just as a pigeon or a rat develops a habit rather mechanically, without seeming to interpret or give the experience meaning, so a person forms an impression without reinterpreting or analyzing available information very much. If we receive mainly favorable ideas about a person, we develop a favorable impression of that person. If we hear mainly unfavorable or lukewarm things, we develop that kind of impression instead.

Mixed impressions of others seem to follow an **averaging principle** (Anderson, 1965). Suppose Susan has just met her blind date, John. She quickly perceives that he is witty, intelligent, and courteous—but very short and poorly dressed. She processes this information in terms of how positive or negative she thinks those traits are. Suppose that she were asked to indicate her degree of favorable or unfavorable evaluation of those traits on a scale from +10 (very positive) to −10 (very negative). She might feel that being witty or intelligent are extremely favorable qualities and assign them the maximum value each (+10), that being courteous is quite favorable (+4), that being very short is somewhat unfavorable (−5), and that being poorly dressed is very unfavorable (−9). The averaging model suggests the person would receive an overall evaluation that was approximately an average of the five traits—that is, he would be considered moderately positive (+2). This is shown in Table 2–1.

Others have suggested that inferences are formed on the basis of an **additive principle.** It holds that people integrate separate pieces of information by adding scale values rather than averaging them. The major difference occurs when the person is confronted with two pieces of information on the same side of zero, one more extreme than the other. Suppose Susan had liked John very much (+6) but then she learned something new about him that was only mildly favorable, such as that he is "cautious" (+1). According to the averaging principle, she should like him a little *less* as a result, because the average (+3.5) is lower than the original evaluation (+6). According to the additive principle, however, she should like him more, because adding any additional positive information to an already positive impression should make it even more favorable.

Norman Anderson, in a series of careful experiments (1959, 1965), produced strong evidence in favor of an averaging rather than an additive principle. He found that when a piece of information that is only moderately favorable was combined with a previous very favorable impression, the overall evaluation did not increase and could even decrease. Similarly, two strongly negative traits produced a more negative evaluation than two strongly negative plus two moderately negative traits.

As a result of further research, Anderson proposed a refinement that predicts impression formation even more accurately—the weighted averaging model (1968a). According to this model, people form an overall impression by averaging all traits but giving more weight to those they feel are most important. For example, an administrator interviewing scientists as candidates for a laboratory job would probably weigh "intelligent" more heavily than "attractive," but someone hiring an actor for a television commercial might reverse that priority. An administrator interviewing candidates for a job as a counselor in a rape crisis center might give "warmth" more weight than either intelligence or attractiveness. This research indicates quite convincingly that the best way to account for impression formation is the weighted averaging principle, though it is probably not the only principle at work.

Consistency

Evaluation also introduces distortions and inaccuracies into the person perception process in several different ways. One is that people tend to form evaluatively consistent characterizations of others, even when they have only a few pieces of information. We have a tendency to view others in a way that is internally consistent. Since evaluation is the most important dimension in person perception, it is not surprising that we tend to categorize people as good or bad, not as both.

Following from this basic evaluation, we may go on to perceive other traits as consistent with it. If a person is likable, she should also be attractive, intelligent, generous, and so on. If she is bad, she should be sneaky, ugly, and inept. Another person is not generally seen as both honest and dishonest, warm and frightening, considerate and sadistic. Even when there is

T A B L E 2 – 1	
SUSAN SIZES UP HER BLIND DATE, JOHN	
Individual Traits	Susan's Evaluation
Witty	+10
Intelligent	+10
Courteous	+4
Very short	−5
Poorly dressed	−9
Overall impression	+10/5 = +2.00

contradictory information about someone, he or she usually will be perceived as consistently good or bad, likable or dislikable. The perceiver distorts or rearranges the information to minimize or eliminate the inconsistency. This may also happen when people perceive objects, but it is particularly strong in person perception.

This tendency toward evaluative consistency is called the **halo effect.** A person is seen as likable or not very likable, and all other qualities are perceived as consistent with this judgment. It is called the halo effect because one who is labeled "good" is surrounded with a positive aura, and other good qualities are attributed to him or her. The converse (what might be called a "negative halo" or a "forked tail" effect) is that someone labeled "bad" is seen as having all bad qualities.

Positivity Bias

Another general evaluative bias in person perception is toward positive evaluations of other persons. They are much more common than negative ones. This tendency for positive evaluations of other people to outnumber negative evaluations has been called the **positivity bias** (Sears, 1983).

For example, in one study students rated 97 percent of their professors in college favorably (that is, above "average" on a rating scale), despite all the mixed experiences students have in their college classes (Sears, 1983). Similarly, public opinion polls show that individual political leaders are consistently approved of more often than they are disapproved of (Sears, 1982). In Gallup polls done in the United States since the mid-1930s, about three-fourths of the specific persons asked about were liked by more people than disliked them. As you might expect, then, when an impression changes, it generally tends to become more favorable rather than more unfavorable, everything else being equal (Sears & Whitney, 1973).

There are some plausible hypotheses about why people are evaluated so leniently. One stems from what Boucher and Osgood (1969) have called the "Pollyanna principle" (see also

Matlin and Stang, 1978). They have suggested that people feel better if they are surrounded by good things, pleasant experiences, nice people, good weather, and so on. Even when their houses are falling down, they are sick, neighbors are terrible to them, and the weather is dismal, they will evaluate their situation favorably. The result: most events are evaluated "above average" most of the time; pleasant events are thought more common than are unpleasant ones; good news is communicated more frequently than is bad news; and pleasant words are recalled more accurately and recognized more quickly than are unpleasant ones. As a result, positive words are more common than negative words, in a wide variety of cultures and contexts.

Sears (1983), on the other hand, contends there is a special positivity bias in our evaluations of other human beings which he describes as the *person-positivity bias.* People feel more similarity to any other person they evaluate than they do to more impersonal objects, and therefore extend them a more generous evaluation. In fact, the person-positivity bias operates most in evaluations of individual people, and it does not show up as strongly when impersonal objects are being evaluated.

THE COGNITIVE APPROACH

Up to this point, we have described person perception as dominated by two assumptions: (1) the process of impression formation rather mechanically reflects the nature of the stimulus person, and (2) it is dominated by evaluation rather than cognition. Although there is much value in these two assumptions, they do oversimplify the process. We do not just take in a literal copy of the environment. We are active, organizing perceivers. The focus on evaluation, though central to impression formation, is also incomplete. It ignores cognitive processing mechanisms.

The cognitive approach to impression formation emphasizes somewhat different features of the process. First, although human beings clearly have a greater capacity for processing information than other animals, it is not infinite. We can absorb only a limited amount of the stimulation we are bombarded with every minute, and when we need to retrieve it from our memory, we cannot get it all back in a flash. So any analysis of person perception must start out by acknowledging our limited processing abilities. We might be described as lazy perceivers (McGuire, 1969) or somewhat more charitably as **cognitive misers** (Taylor, 1981a). When we perceive other people and events, we try to cut corners and save effort.

Second, while we take in information selectively, we then organize it into a meaningful **gestalt** that makes sense out of the full input. Each piece of information is taken as an aspect of a coherent whole, rather than as simply another isolated trait to be averaged into the overall impression. The major implication for impression formation is that processing is not mechanical, but involves an attempt to perceive some coherent *meaning* in the stimulus object.

The cognitive approach, therefore, views people as trying to develop meaningful impressions out of the information they have about another person (or event, or whatever), rather than just averaging in each separate element separately. This is what lies behind the old saying that "the whole is greater than the sum of its parts." The perceiver does not just consider each separate piece of information in isolation, but tries to come to an impression about the person as a whole.

This emphasis on cognitive process is one of the main approaches to social psychology (Fiske & Taylor, 1991). At its core is the view that person perception is a cognitive process: people are actively organizing perceivers, not passive receptacles; they are motivated by the need to develop coherent and meaningful impressions, not just likes and dislikes. And our limited processing capacities lead to the use of a series of cognitive shortcuts. These can produce efficiencies in processing, but they can also produce biases and errors. The cognitive approach is a supplement to the simpler, more mechanical processes described earlier. It asks what else is

going on besides the simple judgment of liking or disliking.

Four general ideas that have been developed from the cognitive approach are as follows:

1. Processing information about people involves perceiving some coherent *meaning* in the stimulus object. We try to understand the context for a person's behavior rather than interpret behavior in isolation.

2. Perceivers tend to pay special attention to the most *salient* features of the perceptual field rather than giving equal attention to everything. That is, figural people, or figural aspects of a particular person, get more attention than does the background. On a rainy day, our attention is drawn to the police officer in the middle of a crowded intersection, because he or she is wearing a bright orange raincoat and all the other colors in the intersection are drab.

3. We organize the perceptual field by *categorizing* or grouping stimuli. Of course, everything we see, hear, smell, or feel is a little different from everything else, but we do not perceive them that way. Rather, we tend to see each separate stimulus as part of a category or group— a Porsche as a car and a person wearing a white lab coat as a doctor—even though each of these may have features that make them quite different from other cars or doctors.

4. We perceive stimuli as part of some kind of *structure*. Each separate stimulus tends to be related to others in time, space, and a causal flow. We see a downhill skier as part of a broader context: she is in a ski race, so she begins skiing when the starter gives the order, she skis between the flags down the hill, and she stops when she crosses the finish line. All we literally see is a young woman in motion, but that is part of a much more complex cognitive structure which includes our

Are these people isolated individuals running around on a field or are they a team? We organize our perceptions by categorizing and grouping similar people together, and we see them as part of a structured whole.

knowledge of the rules of slalom racing and our impression of her grace, agility, and power. In other words, we spontaneously embed the individual in a broader structure of knowledge.

Seeking Meaning

Context. The cognitive approach assumes that perceivers are trying to arrive at a meaningful impression of whole persons, rather than just to absorb each new piece of information separately. Their understanding of any new piece of information will depend in part on the context. The meaning of "intelligent" in the context of knowing that a person is a "warm, caring therapist" will probably be quite positive.

But the meaning of "intelligent" when the person is otherwise a "cold, ruthless Russian spy" will probably be more negative; it makes the person seem even more dangerous. To predict the impact of new information, we need to know the context, because that influences its meaning.

Considerable research has shown that context does indeed influence the impact new information has on an existing impression. But the effects of context are a matter of some debate. Anderson (1966), consistent with his averaging approach, suggests that the influence of the context on the value of the new attribute can be predicted by just averaging in its value along with the value of the new information. In this example, suppose "intelligent" is a +2 when it is considered all by itself. And suppose the value of the "cold, ruthless, Russian spy" context is −4. In this case, the contribution of "intelligent" to the overall impression would be influenced by its context, and so would be an average of its own value and that of its context, or −1. On the other hand, if the value of "warm, caring" context is +4, including "intelligent" would produce an overall impression of +3 in that context. Anderson describes this effect of context as a *generalized halo effect*. As you can see, he does not assume much deliberate thought; the new attribute merely mechanically absorbs some of the good or bad feelings associated with the context.

For Asch (1946), on the other hand, working mainly out of the cognitive approach, the whole is more than an average of its parts. Perceivers create a meaningful whole out of the information given, and the whole will change with different information. So any given attribute will have different meaning if it is placed in a different context. Wearing only a bikini has quite a different meaning in a symphony concert hall than it does on a summer beach and would be evaluated quite differently.

Asch says a new attribute undergoes a **shift of meaning** when placed in a new context. "Intelligence" in a cold, ruthless person could be threatening, potentially hostile, and destructive. In a warm, caring person, "intelligence" might be expected to contribute to empathy, to insight, and to the ability to give to another person.

Considerable research has been done on these two explanations for context effects. One way to approach the controversy is to determine whether in fact a given trait has a different meaning in different contexts. Hamilton and Zanna (1974) and Zanna and Hamilton (1977) found that the connotations of a particular trait changed when placed in different contexts. For example, in a positive context the word "proud" bore the connotation of "confident." In a negative context, it connoted "conceited." Further, Wyer (1974) found that the evaluations of these connotations also reflected the context. To use this example, the connotation ("conceited") of the original trait ("proud") implied by a negative context itself bore a negative eval-

uation. Such studies show that contextual effects are partly determined by a shift-of-meaning phenomenon.

Central Traits. A second point at which the evaluative and cognitive approaches potentially differ concerns whether or not certain traits imply more about an individual than others. The averaging approach simply assumes that all traits enter into the impression at whatever value they have; for example, "cold" is always a −5, "warm" is always a +7. The cognitive approach, instead, assumes that some traits are inherently more meaningful than others. For example, the pair of traits "warm-cold" appears to be associated with a great number of other characteristics, whereas the pair "polite-blunt" is associated with fewer. Traits that are highly associated with many other characteristics have been called **central traits** (Asch, 1946).

In a classic demonstration of their importance, Kelley (1950) gave students in psychology courses personality trait descriptions of a guest lecturer before he spoke. Half the students received a description containing the word "warm," and the other half were told the speaker was "cold"; in all other respects the lists were identical. The lecturer then came into the class and led a discussion for about 20 minutes,

T A B L E 2 – 2		
EFFECT OF "WARM" AND "COLD" DESCRIPTIONS ON RATINGS OF OTHER QUALITIES		
	Instructions[a]	
Quality	Warm	Cold
Self-centered	6.3	9.6
Unsociable	5.6	10.4
Unpopular	4.0	7.4
Formal	6.3	9.6
Irritable	9.4	12.0
Humorless	8.3	11.7
Ruthless	8.6	11.0

Source: Adapted from Kelley (1950).

[a] The higher the rating, the more the person was perceived as having the quality.

after which the students were asked to give their impressions of him. The results are shown in Table 2–2. There were great differences between the impressions formed by students who were told he was warm and those who were told he was cold. In addition, those students who expected the speaker to be warm tended to interact with him more freely and to initiate more conversations with him. The different descriptions affected not only the students' impressions of the other person, but also their behavior toward him.

The averaging model has been adapted to handle such phenomena. Its weighted averaged version assumes that some traits are more important than others, and therefore are weighted more heavily. Presumably warmth is one of these. Most of the time, it is very important to us whether someone is warm or cold, and perhaps not very important whether they are good jumpers or not. So we weigh very heavily any information about warmth or coldness in coming to an overall impression and give little weight to information about jumping ability. But this example also illustrates Asch's point about how context influences meaning. In the context of a party, "warm-cold" is probably quite a central trait, because it is so important to whether we enjoy the person or not. In the context of a basketball game or Olympic tryouts, "warm-cold" may not be very central, and jumping ability may be weighted much more heavily.

Salience

People are sensitive to many cues in others, and use these cues to form impressions. But clearly people do not use all the cues available to them. A major relevant principle of perception is the **figure-ground principle.** According to this, people direct their attention to those aspects of the perceptual field that stand out—the figure—rather than to the background of setting—the ground. In the case of impression formation, the main implication is that the most salient cues will be utilized most heavily. If a student appears in a wheelchair the first day of class, everyone else in the room is likely to form an impression that is most heavily influenced by the fact of the person's physical handicap. Clothing, hair style, and perhaps even age, race, and sex will all be secondary.

What determines the **salience** of one cue as opposed to another? A number of clearly specifiable objective conditions make cues stand out. *Brightness, noisiness, motion,* or *novelty* are the most powerful conditions, according to gestalt principles of object perception (McArthur & Post, 1977). A man in a bright red sweater stands out in a crowded classroom, and the sweater is his most salient feature. The student who gets up shouting in the middle of a lecture and leaves the room draws our attention because she is noisy and moving, and almost everything else in the classroom is quiet and stationary. So, anything that makes a cue objectively *unusual* in its context makes it subjectively more salient and more likely to be attended to.

Effects of Salience. Salience has a number of consequences for person perception. Salient behaviors draw more attention than do subtler, less obvious ones (McArthur, 1981). Second, salience influences perceptions of causality in that more salient people are seen as having more influence over their social context. The student who sits in front of the class and asks an occasional question is more likely to be perceived as dominating the discussion than the student who sits at the back and talks just as much.

Third, evaluations of salient people are more extreme than evaluations of less salient people. Taylor, Fiske, Close, Anderson, and Ruderman (1977) ran a series of experiments in which they varied the "solo" status of black group members; some groups had an even mixture of white and black members, other groups had only one black member. The "solo" black was clearly more salient than were the blacks in the evenly divided groups. A pleasant black group member was evaluated more favorably when "solo" than when in an evenly divided group, and an unpleasant one was evaluated more negatively.

Last, salience increases the coherence of an impression (Taylor, 1981b). If the salient person is a member of a stereotyped group, such as

Which person is most salient in this picture? Does the solo woman stand out? Salient people attract attention. We remember more about them and often interpret their behavior in stereotyped terms.

"drug addict," he or she will be seen as possessing other stereotyped attributes of that group, such as having criminal tendencies, weak moral character, slovenly manner and dress, a lack of honesty, and so forth.

Salient stimuli draw the most attention; they are seen as the most causally powerful, they produce the most extreme evaluative judgments, and they produce more consistency of judgment. These effects of salience have been described as "top of the head" by Taylor and Fiske (1978) because they seem to occur at the relatively superficial level of simply directing our attention. That is, they occur because they focus the perceiver's attention one way or an-

other, not because they involve very deep changes in thinking. As might be expected, therefore, they seem to be strongest when the stimuli are sufficiently interesting and exciting to attract the perceiver's real attention. The salience of different stimuli matters more when the perceiver is responding to exciting conversations, such as humorous debates, than when he or she is responding to stiffer, more formal and boring situations (McArthur, 1981). But salience effects appear to be rather general, occurring on important issues as well as unimportant ones (Taylor et al., 1979; Borgida & Howard-Pitney, 1983). Box 2–1 describes some of the consequences when the self becomes salient.

BOX 2–1

Self-awareness: When the Self Is Salient

Usually our attention is focused outward toward the environment, but sometimes our attention is focused inward on ourselves. Certain experiences in the world automatically focus attention inward, such as catching sight of ourselves in the mirror, having our picture taken, or more subtly, being evaluated by others, or even just being in a minor-

ity in a group situation. We begin to think of ourselves not as a moving actor in the environment, but as the object of our own and others' attention. This state is called **self-awareness** (Duval & Wicklund, 1972; Wicklund & Frey, 1980).

In general, self-focus leads people to evaluate

Continued

their behavior against a standard and to set an adjustment process in motion for meeting the standard. Suppose, for example, that you go out to an elegant restaurant and you are seated facing your date but also, to your irritation, you are looking directly into a mirror on the wall behind him. Try as you might, each time you look up, you catch sight of your own face. You notice your windblown hair, the awkward way you smile, and the unattractive way you chew. Feeling utterly foolish by the time the main course arrives, you flee to the bathroom to comb your hair, vowing that if you still look as bad when you return, you will change tables. Self-attention causes people to compare themselves to standards, such as physical appearance, intellectual performance, athletic prowess, or moral integrity. We attempt to conform to the standard, evaluate our behavior against that standard, decide that it either matches the standard or does not, and continue adjusting and comparing until we meet the standard or give up. This process is called feedback, and the theory is called the **cybernetic theory of self-regulation.**

People also differ in whether they attend primarily to public aspects of themselves or to private aspects of themselves. This distinction has been called public versus private self-consciousness (Fenigstein, Scheier, & Buss, 1975). People high in **public self-consciousness** are concerned with what other people think about them, the way they look, and how they appear to others. Those high in **private self-consciousness** try to figure themselves out, think about themselves a lot, and are more attentive to their inner feelings. When the publicly self-conscious person becomes self-aware, he or she may try hard to adjust behavior to conform to external standards, such as others' values or attitudes. In contrast, when the privately self-conscious person becomes self-aware, he or she may be more attentive to internal goals and beliefs, and thus try harder to meet personal standards (Froming & Carver, 1981; Scheier & Carver, 1980). Which are you? Or are you high on both? Answer the questions in Table 2–3.

T A B L E   2 – 3

SELF-CONSCIOUSNESS SCALE

Indicate whether you generally agree (A) or disagree (D) with each of the following items.

_____ 1. I'm always trying to figure myself out.

_____ 2. I'm concerned about my style of doing things.

_____ 3. Generally, I'm not very aware of myself.

_____ 4. I reflect about myself a lot.

_____ 5. I'm concerned about the way I present myself.

_____ 6. I'm self-conscious about the way I look.

_____ 7. I never scrutinize myself.

_____ 8. I'm generally attentive to my inner feelings.

_____ 9. I usually worry about making a good impression.

If you answered "agree" on items 1, 4, and 8 and "disagree" on items 3 and 7, you would be scoring high on the private self-consciousness scale. If you answered "agree" to items 2, 5, 6, and 9, your score would be high on the public self-consciousness scale. Note that the entire scale is considerably longer than the excerpt above.

Source: Adapted from Fenigstein, Scheier, and Buss (1975).

Negativity. People weigh negative information more heavily than positive information in arriving at a complete impression. That is, a negative trait affects an impression more than a positive trait, everything else being equal (Fiske, 1980). This has been called the **negativity**

effect. It follows that a positive impression is easier to change than a negative one (Hodges, 1974). People are more confident of evaluations based on negative traits than those based on positive traits (Hamilton & Zanna, 1972). The averaging principle does not hold for negative traits quite as well as it does for positive traits. The difference is particularly noticeable with more extreme negative traits. They seem to have a "blackball" effect: one extremely negative trait produces an extremely negative impression, no matter what other traits the person possesses (Anderson, 1965). For example, Lau (1982) found that voters' evaluations of presidential and congressional candidates in the period from 1968 to 1980 were more strongly shaped by negative information about the candidate than by positive information. When we are told that a prominent public leader is a "crook," our evaluation of him becomes quite negative, regardless of what else we know about him (e.g., Coovert & Reeder, 1990). If we are told he is "patient," we will just average that mildly positive quality in with whatever else we know about him.

The main explanation for this negativity effect is based on the figure-ground principle. As we noted in the discussion of the person-positivity bias, positive evaluations of other people are much more common than negative evaluations. Negative traits, being more unusual, are therefore more distinctive. In a simple perceptual sense, then, a negative trait is *figural*; it stands out the way an unusual deformity or bright clothing or something of great size stands out (Fiske, 1980). People may simply pay more attention to those negative qualities and give them more weight. For example, Lau (1985) found that negative information had more impact upon evaluations of presidential candidates among those voters who were most trusting of government. That is, the negativity effect was strongest among those who generally respect political leaders, for whom negative information would be most figural.

The negativity effect is probably due mainly to the positivity bias we discussed earlier. The positivity bias suggests that positive evaluations outnumber negative evaluations. The negativity effect suggests that because negative evaluations are therefore more unusual, they then have more impact on impressions when they are present.

Categorization

Perceivers do not respond to salient stimuli in isolation; they immediately and spontaneously perceive them as part of some group or category. We do not see that unshaven, dirty, disheveled man in the park with worn-out shoes and a couple of old shopping bags as just another human being; we immediately categorize him as a derelict. When we go to a basketball game, we usually categorize people right away into members of one or another of five social groups: players on one team or the other, referees, cheerleaders, and spectators. The **categorization** or grouping process is immediate and spontaneous, and does not take any time or thought, any more than you need to think about what category of objects your pencil belongs to.

Categorizing People. At the crudest level, we categorize on the basis of natural similarities in appearance. We tend to assign people to the category of "men" or "women" on the basis of their physical characteristics, usually sex and culturally defined differences in appearance (hair length, makeup, type of clothing). The same is true of assigning people to other social groupings such as racial categories, as illustrated by the story of Lize Venter (see Box 2–2).

How do we go about putting people and objects into categories? Generally speaking, we compare a person or object with the **prototype** of the category. The prototype is an abstract ideal of the category. In our category for football player, for example, we probably have an abstract idea of what the person's body type is like, what he does in his free time, and perhaps even what fraternity he belongs to. Categorizing a new person as a football player, one may compare his attributes with those of the prototype for the category.

For some categories, people pay attention to **exemplars** of the category rather than proto-

---

BOX 2–2

Where Does Lize Fit?

The Union of South Africa categorizes all people into one of three groups: white, colored, or black. All persons of mixed blood are included in the colored category. This categorization determines much of the pattern of the person's life due to the practice of apartheid. Blacks are forbidden to vote; they must go to all-black schools; they generally must leave their families in the countryside if they go to the cities to work; they cannot marry or have romantic or sexual relationships with persons in the other categories; and so on.

Lize Venter was a 2-week-old infant found in a field, and her parents were unknown. The authorities were unable to decide which category to place her in, since she was light-skinned and her face showed no definable racial characteristics: "She's cute, that's all I can say," one nurse was quoted as

saying. The problem arose because the hospital wished to put her out for adoption. But what kind of a family should she go to? If she were colored, she could not be adopted by a white family, would have to live in a nonwhite area, and would be forbidden to marry or have sexual relations with a white. If she were determined to be white, the same prohibitions would hold in reverse. As an orphan, she was entitled to public assistance from the government. But since the public assistance services were also segregated by category, no agency would handle her case until a decision had been made about her category. Ultimately a decision would be made by the Department of Internal Affairs, and that decision would determine much of Lize's future life.

Source: Los Angeles *Times*, July 27, 1983.

---

types (Rothbart & Lewis, 1988). Whereas a prototype is an abstract set of attributes of a category, an exemplar is a real example of the category. Thus, for example, in meeting a new person and trying to figure out if he is a football player, one may compare him to one's friend, Brian, whom one considers to be the exemplar of the category, football player, rather than comparing him to the more abstract prototype for the category, football player. When we learn the abstract attributes of categories, we also learn particular instances of the category that we have actually encountered. In many cases, then, we categorize objects and people by seeing if they resemble the exemplars that we store in that category. For example, if one is sizing up a new partner as a possible long-term boyfriend or girlfriend, usually the person is compared not only with a prototype for the ideal boyfriend or girlfriend, but also with "old flames," particular past boyfriends or girlfriends that made one's heart beat faster for a time (Fiske, 1982; Fiske, Neuberg, Beattie, & Milberg, 1987).

Overall, it is clear that people rely on a complex mix of ways for recognizing and classifying people and their behavior. We use prototypes for categories, groups, and situations about which we have little information, and we use both exemplars and prototypes for categories about which we have more information (Judd & Park, 1988; Linville, Fisher and Salovey, 1989).

What are the consequences of categorization? It speeds information processing time, as the "cognitive miser" idea suggests. For example, Brewer, Dull, and Lui (1981) presented subjects with photos of people in three different categories, "grandmother," "young woman," and "senior citizen," along with verbal labels clearly identifying their category. Then they presented the subjects with additional information about each target person, and measured how long the subjects took to incorporate the information into their impressions. Information consistent with the prototype of the category ("kindly" for "grandmother") was processed faster than information inconsistent with it (such as "aggressive" for grandmother).

Dwight Gooden is an exemplar of the category, athlete.

Schemas

A more complex organization of cognition is called a **schema.** This refers to an organized, structured set of cognitions, including some knowledge about the object, some relationships among the various cognitions about it, and some specific examples (Taylor & Crocker, 1981). We might, for example, have a schema of a "preppie," a WASP college student who wears alligator shirts and khaki pants, buys clothes from L. L. Bean, is partial to pink and kelly green, sports Oxford cloth button-down shirts with madras ties, and likes to sail and jog and play tennis. This "preppie" schema would probably not include going bowling, wearing Caterpillar tractor caps, driving a 1979 Chrysler Imperial, or having a beer belly.

What all schemas have in common is not their content, but their structural characteristics and the effects these have on processing. Schemas help us to process complex bodies of information by simplifying and organizing them. They can help us to remember and organize details, speed up processing time, fill in gaps in

our knowledge, and interpret and evaluate new information. As we will see, such preexisting cognitive structures organize the processing of new information. Our perceptions of new information are biased to make them consistent with what we already know. If we think someone is "warm," for example, we are more likely to talk to him and interpret his behavior as reflecting that warmth.

Some schemas are very abstract and involve the relations among particular traits. This is called an **implicit personality theory** (Schneider, 1973). It is a theory about what traits seem to go together with what other traits and which traits do not go together. An implicit personality theory is not based on a particular person, but may apply to lots of people. On overhearing someone say that Susie is spirited, a person might infer that she was probably also outgoing and self-confident, even in the absence of other information about her. An implicit personality theory, then, is a web of presumed relationships among traits.

Other schemas are more specific. *Person schemas* are structures about people. They can focus

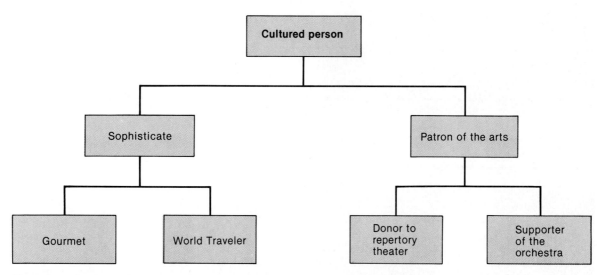

Figure 2–1. A schema for "cultured person." (Adapted from Cantor & Mischel, 1979.)

on particular people, such as Abraham Lincoln. The schema might include such elements as his being deliberate, honest, serious about his duties, and concerned for oppressed people. This would be a schema if in your view these qualities were all related to one another in President Lincoln, in the sense that you perceive them all as aspects of his basically decent and conscientious personality, not unrelated traits he just happened to display from time to time. Person schemas can also focus on particular types of people. For example, our schema of an "extrovert" might include such elements as "spirited," "outgoing," "enthusiastic," and "self-assured." Fig. 2–1 presents a diagrammable representation of a schema for a cultured person.

We also have *role schemas*. These represent the organized, abstract concepts we have of people in a particular role, such as cowboy, professor, receptionist, or devoted lover. Sometimes these schemas are unrealistic. If our schema for "devoted lover" includes elements such as always understanding, always supportive, never angry, never childish, and always concerned first with the other person's happiness, we could be in trouble. Not too many people will live up to that schema.

Other schemas focus on groups. The most familiar is the group *stereotype*, which attributes specific traits to a particular group of people. An early study by Katz and Braly (1933) found white college students checking "superstitious," "lazy," and "happy-go-lucky" as the most common traits of blacks, and "scientifically minded," "industrious," and "stolid" as most common for Germans. Such stereotypes would be schematic if each perceived trait was part of a coherent underlying structure about the group. You might expect a student who is in the Beta fraternity to act like other Betas, or a black football player to act like other black football players, or people from Boston or Texas or Iran to resemble one another. All these involve having a particular schema for the personality and behavior of members of a group. We will take up stereotypes in some detail in Chapter 14.

People also have schemas for events, or standard series of events. Sometimes such schemas are called *scripts* (Abelson, 1976). A script is a standard sequence of behavior over a period of time. One script might be called "ordering for a group in a Chinese restaurant." Everyone sits down, and the waiter brings the menus. Several people talk at once, giving their favorite dishes,

All of us have scripts for common events. In this case, both the customer and the waiter know the standard script for how to order, consume, and pay for food in a restaurant.

while others say they never know what to have and would someone else just please decide. Then people go through the menu section by section, haggling over which soup to have, bargaining away their favorite beef dish (which no one else wants) for sweet and sour pork (which at least one ally does) and finally appointing the most self-confident and brash person to communicate the whole negotiated package to the waiter.

We could generate similar scripts for other ritualized series of events, such as having a baby, taking a shower, taking a final exam, or playing a basketball game. The essence of a

script is in its boundedness in time, its causal flow (early events cause later ones), and in its being a simple, coherent, perceptual unit.

The Self

People not only hold schemas about what other people and events are like, they also hold schemas about themselves. Self-schemas describe the dimensions along which you think about yourself. For example, Markus (1977) investigated the extent to which people thought of themselves as independent or dependent by determining whether or not they would apply to themselves such adjectives as individualistic, unconventional, assertive, cooperative, timid, or moderate.

You may, for example, be very concerned about maintaining and displaying your independence. You might refuse to take money from your parents for college, do your own laundry, not ask your roommate for help with your math, and the like. Or you might consider yourself more dependent, and think a lot about ensuring security for yourself by surrounding yourself with people you can depend on, like your brother, girlfriend, doctor, minister, and so on. In either case, you would have a strong self-schema concerning the independence-dependence dimension. On the other hand, you may not think of yourself very much in connection with that dimension, in which case you would not be thinking schematically in those terms. You would be described as aschematic on the dimension of independence-dependence.

People are schematic on dimensions that are important to them, on which they think of themselves as extreme, and on which they are certain that the opposite is not true. If independence is important to you and you think of yourself as extremely independent and not at all dependent, it implies that you have accumulated considerable knowledge about yourself on that domain. For example, you should be certain that you would never ask anyone for help setting up your stereo, even at the potential cost of damage to it or yourself. When you hold a schema for yourself on a particular dimension, it helps you to identify situations as relevant to that dimension. For example, if you think of yourself as independent, you would be quick to see that the purchase of a new stereo system with complex instructions for installation requires independent behavior. Moreover, the recognition that situations are schema relevant sets guidelines for your own behavior. Thus, you would recognize not only that the situation called for independent behavior, but that you will be the one to wade through the instructions and set it up.

Not all self-schemas are positive. People also hold well-articulated beliefs about themselves on negative qualities. For example, someone who thinks of herself as overweight will quickly decide that eating situations are relevant to her and will plan in advance what she will eat and may count the calories that she consumes. Being weight schematic also means that she is likely to notice weight-relevant behaviors in others (Carpenter, 1988; Dodge & Tomlin, 1987; Hill, Smith, & Hoffman, 1988; Park & Hahn, 1988). Thus, for example, she may more quickly notice and infer that someone who has only cottage cheese and peaches for lunch is on a diet than would someone who is not so concerned with weight (Wurf & Markus, 1983).

People not only hold self-conceptions about their current qualities, they also hold conceptions of themselves that may become self-descriptive at some time in the future (Markus & Nurius, 1986). These are called **possible selves.** Some of these involve goals or roles to which people aspire, such as the 5-year-old's desire to be a firefighter or the student's expectation of becoming a doctor. Most possible selves seem to be positive. That is, people think of themselves in the future primarily in good terms (Markus & Nurius, 1986). However, some possible selves represent fears concerning what one may become in the future, such as the suspicion that one's enthusiastic consumption of alcohol on certain occasions may eventually lead to full-blown alcoholism.

Possible selves function in much the same way as self-schemas. They help people to articulate their goals and develop behaviors that will enable them to get there. In one study, Ruvolo and Markus (cited in Markus & Ruvolo, 1989) asked subjects to imagine themselves either being successful at work, lucky at work, failing at work despite clear effort, or failing because of bad luck. Subsequently, subjects worked on a task that measured persistence. Those subjects asked to envision themselves as successful worked longer on the task than did subjects who envisioned themselves as failing, presumably because they had a vision of the successful possible self firmly in mind. Thus, possible selves provide focus and organization for the pursuit of goals. They enable people to recruit appropriate self-knowledge and develop plans that enable them to rehearse the actions they need to undertake in pursuit of their goals (Markus & Ruvolo, 1989).

Self-referencing

As we have seen, our perceptions of other people are strongly influenced by our perceptions of ourselves. If we perceive ourself as shy, we tend to notice whether another person is shy or not. If we perceive ourselves as smart, we notice whether others are smart or not.

Memory for other people's characteristics is also improved when they are linked to the self. For example, a shy person is more likely to remember her roommate saying that Jeff "has overcome his terrible shyness" than that he is an excellent auto mechanic. A number of experiments have tested for this **self-referencing effect,** that is, improved memory for others' characteristics when they are linked to the self. For example, Kuiper and Rogers (1979) presented trait adjectives such as "shy" or "outgoing" to subjects in several different conditions. In the "self-reference" condition, the subjects were asked "whether the word describes you." In the "other-reference" condition, the subjects were asked "whether the word describes the experimenter." The other conditions asked subjects to rate the word in simple mechanical terms, such as whether it was short or long or whether it was specific or general. Later the subjects were asked to recall all the adjectives with which they had been presented. Those words presented in the self-reference context were much better recalled than were those placed in more neutral contexts, and the person found the task less difficult and had more confidence in his or her ratings. These findings are shown in Table 2–4.

Later experiments obtained similar findings (Lord, 1980; Brown, Keenan, & Potts, 1986; Reeder, McCormick, & Esselman, 1987). Usually, when people think about a trait or utterance in connection with themselves, it is more likely to be remembered than if it is thought about in connection with another person or something impersonal. However, it should be noted that self-reference does not always improve memory relative to the other-person context. When the other people are personally well known to the subject, such as a lab instructor who has been teaching the person all term, the self-reference effect disappears (Kuiper & Rogers, 1979; Bower & Gilligan, 1979).

Why does the self-reference effect occur? The explanation most favored by researchers is that self-referencing produces a "deeper processing" (Craik & Tulving, 1975), because self-refer-encing gets the person to consider a wider and deeper range of associations to the stimulus object (Rogers, Kuiper, & Kirker, 1977). Consistent with this view, the self-reference effect seems to be dependent on getting people to think about traits in connection with their own personal experiences, not just the self. To illustrate this, Bellezza (1984) presented subjects with traits and had them either relate the trait to some real incident from their lives or to some personal body part. For example, the subject might have related the trait "hostile" to an experience of getting into an argument with someone or, alternatively, to the body part "fist." Thinking about the trait in connection with the personal experience made it more memorable than did thinking about it in connection with the body part.

The extra meaningfulness provided by reference to the self seems, therefore, to stem from the rich array of experiences it brings to mind from our past lives. Self-referencing calls up an organized self-schema to which we can relate information about the to-be-recalled stimulus and helps to create an elaborated memory of that stimulus (Klein & Loftus, 1988).

	T A B L E 2 – 4			
SELF-REFERENCE PRODUCES BETTER RECALL, LESS DIFFICULTY, MORE CONFIDENCE				
Experimental Condition	Question	Recall	Mean Difficulty Rating	Mean Confidence Rating
Structural	Rate whether you feel the word is long or short.	.18	3.08	3.83
Semantic	Rate whether you feel the word has a specific meaning or relates to a specific situation.	.15	4.25	3.83
Other-reference	Rate whether you feel the word describes the experimenter.	.18	5.00	2.75
Self-reference	Rate whether you feel the word describes you.	.31	2.00	6.00

Source: Adapted from Kuiper and Rogers (1979).

Note: Recall values can range from 0 to 1.00, where 1.00 indicates that all were recalled. Difficulty and confidence ratings were made on a 7-point scale, with 7 as extremely difficult or extremely confident.

ACCURACY OF JUDGMENTS

How accurately do people usually perceive others? One implication of these various evaluative and cognitive biases is that person perception must not be very accurate. On the other hand, people must be reasonably accurate for society to function as smoothly as it does. After all, we interact with other people a great many times every day, and these interactions usually require fairly accurate judgments of them. Since most interactions proceed without serious difficulties or mistakes, person perception must be fairly accurate.

People perceive external, visible attributes fairly accurately. It is generally no more difficult to judge the height of a person than it is to judge the height of a bookcase. The same is true of weight, skin color, or style of clothing, although as Box 2–3 indicates, sometimes this process, too, can go awry. It is also fairly easy to make judgments about somebody's social role, as long as the appropriate cues are provided. The man in the blue suit with the gun strapped to his side is a police officer, and we treat him accordingly. The woman in the business suit with a briefcase rushing down a platform toward a train is obviously a commuter in a hurry to get to work, and we get out of her way to make it easier for her to catch the train. The contexts in which we see people enable us to make accurate assumptions about their roles.

But person perception becomes more difficult when we try to infer *internal states*—traits, feelings, emotions, and personalities. The bookcase obviously has none of these. However, we do attempt to judge the internal states of human beings. We look at people and perceive them as angry, happy, sad, or frightened. We form an impression of another person and think of her as warm, honest, and sincere. We also make

---

BOX 2–3

Eyewitness Testimony

Criminal charges often rest quite heavily on reports of eyewitness identification. A cashier who has been held up at a 7–11 store must pick the robber out of a lineup and testify to his or her identity in court. A rape victim may have to do the same in more difficult circumstances if the crime happened at night, by surprise, if the victim's life was threatened, if the rapist was partially disguised, and so on. A number of studies have found eyewitness identification not to be very accurate (see Penrod, Loftus, & Winkler, 1982). To be sure, eyewitnesses tend to be highly confident that they are successfully picking out the true perpetrator. But their level of certainty bears almost no relationship to their accuracy level: Highly confident eyewitnesses are no more accurate than those who are uncertain (Wells & Murray, 1984). This is especially distressing because the general public (and thus most jurors, presumably) believes that eyewitness self-confidence is a valid sign of credibility, and it is one

of the standards the U.S. Supreme Court has set for admissibility of eyewitness testimony (Kassin, 1985).

There are techniques for enhancing the accuracy of eyewitness testimony, such as reinstating the original context. Krafka and Penrod (1985) had store clerks identify a previously encountered customer from an array of photographs. When the photograph was accompanied by some physical cues from the original encounter situation, such as a photocopy of identification the customer had shown, and a check like the one the customer had cashed, accuracy was improved. But even so, by 24 hours later, only half the clerks correctly identified the customer (against about one-third in the no-reinstatement condition). Even though the reinstatement manipulation increased accuracy, it had no effect at all on the witness's confidence. Eyewitness confidence continued to bear little relationship to accuracy (see also Shapiro & Penrod, 1986).

judgments about such internal characteristics as the person's attitudes toward various issues. We guess whether she is a Republican or a Democrat, religious or nonreligious, an environmentalist or not.

Judgments of such internal states as emotions, personality traits, and attitudes are often extremely difficult. The person's internal state cannot be observed directly—it must be inferred from whatever cues are available. Therefore, the question of accuracy focuses primarily on the judgments individuals can make of internal states, and on the cues used to make these judgments.

The Eye of the Beholder

One possibility raised by the tendency toward consistency is that perceivers may just impose their own perspectives on the target person, rather than reflecting the real qualities of the target. For example, beauty may truly be in "the eye of the beholder" rather than being in the person being evaluated. This would lead to considerable inaccuracy in person perception, because everyone would have a different perception of the same person.

It does seem to be true that different people organize their perceptions of others along different dimensions. For example, one person might always describe others in terms of their sense of humor, another person in terms of their honesty, and still another in terms of their intelligence. This variety of perspectives was illustrated in a study by Dornbusch, Hastorf, Richardson, Muzzy, and Vreeland (1965). All children at a summer camp were asked to describe, in their own words, every other child. These descriptions were then analyzed in two ways—in terms of the characteristics each child used in making descriptions and in terms of the characteristics used in describing each child. The experimenters could then examine whether the same child was described the same way by most people or whether the same perceiver used the same characteristics to describe all the other children.

Intuitively, we would guess that perceivers would tend to describe a particular child the same way in terms of some outstanding characteristic, such as a sense of humor or aggressiveness. This was not the case. There was no agreement about which dimensions described any given child. Rather, each rater tended to use the same characteristics no matter which child was being described. The children differed among themselves as to which characteristics they used, but they all had their favorites which they used for virtually all their descriptions of others. So perceptions of other children depended more on who was *perceiving* than on who was *being perceived* (see also Beck, McCauley, Segal, & Hershey, 1988). The major implication of this phenomenon is that people do not see the world in the same way; they emphasize different aspects of other people and notice and focus on different qualities. These differences extend to perceptions of physical characteristics too, as Box 2–4 indicates.

Perceivers do arrive at more consensus on the likability of specific target persons than they do on their traits or other attributes, however. When one person talks about another's warmth and sense of humor and someone else talks about his kindness and good-naturedness, the only disagreement may be one of semantics. We generally agree more on how likable other people are than on why they are likable—whether it is their sense of humor, considerateness, intellectual ability, or whatever.

Park (1986) demonstrated this in a study of her seminar students. These seven students, who did not know each other well before the class, agreed to write out impressions of each other each week through the school term. This provided an opportunity to determine whether their impressions were due to the "eye-of-the-beholder" effect—did each perceiver use his or her own favorite dimensions to describe all the various target persons, but different dimensions from those used by the other perceivers? Or were their impressions due to the real qualities of each target person—did the perceivers generally agree on which dimensions applied to each target person?

She found a considerably stronger "eye-of-

BOX 2–4

Is Beauty in the Eye of the Beholder or in the Beauty?

The old saying, "Beauty is in the eye of the beholder," clearly is true to some extent. There are some culturally defined aspects of beauty that not everyone over the globe shares; for example, great body weight is prized in parts of Africa but not on the beach at St. Tropez. But many observers, including Charles Darwin, have been struck by certain constancies in ideas of beauty.

Within our own culture, there is considerable consensus on what characteristics mark beautiful women. Cunningham (1986) had male students rate for beauty pictures of finalists in the Miss Universe beauty contest and pictures of seniors from a women's college. Then he measured the characteristics of those faces along 24 different dimensions. The most beautiful women differed from ordinary women in three general ways. They had (1) the features normally associated with "child cuteness," that is, large and widely spaced eyes, small nose areas, and small chins; (2) two features of more mature faces—wide cheekbones and narrow cheeks; and (3) expressive features of highly set eyebrows, wide pupils, and a large smile. As the "halo effect" would lead you to expect, these features also led perceivers to impute positive characteristics to these attractive people, such as being "bright," "sociable," "assertive," "fertile," and having few medical problems. Interestingly, some of these same child-cuteness features—large round eyes, high eyebrows, and narrow chin—are also considered most attractive in men and are associated with perceptions of warmth and kindness (Berry & McArthur, 1985).

"Baby-faced" people are so associated with positive qualities that in the legal system, they are less often perceived as guilty of charges of intentional criminal behavior. However, perhaps because baby-faced appearance makes people seem childlike, they are sometimes seen as less responsible for their behavior, and in legal settings, may be seen as guilty of negligent criminal behavior. But even when they are judged guilty of negligent criminal acts, they tend to be given lighter sentences (Berry & Zebowitz-McArthur, 1988).

the-beholder" effect on the specific dimensions used to describe other people than on evaluations of those people. That is, two different judges tended to evaluate a given target person in about the same way, but each perceiver tended to use their own particular dimensions to describe the person, such as "yuppie," "the sunny, California beach type," "kind," "aware of her faults," or "loud and boisterous."

Judging Personality

Considerable research has been done judging the accuracy of perceptions of personality traits, such as dominance-submission or need for affiliation. This work is discouraging, for a number of reasons. First, as we have just seen, people's perceptions of others are determined more by their own idiosyncratic preferences for particular personality dimensions than by the objective attributes of the person being evaluated. This, coupled with other biases in person perception described earlier in this chapter leads social psychologists to believe that people are not very accurate in judging other people's personality dispositions. Second, it is very difficult to measure personality traits, so there is a problem in identifying the proper criteria for accuracy.

But a more major problem is that, according to some influential psychologists (such as Mischel, 1979), any given personality trait may only influence behavior consistently in a fairly limited range of situations. That is, we may have unique, idiosyncratic dispositions that make us regularly react in our own distinctive way to any given situation, but these may not be very constant from one set of situations to another. It may, therefore, be more useful to think of personality traits as holding in some fairly limited set of situations, rather than to think of traits as holding in all situations.

For example, we know a man who frequently cheats at pool; or when he is playing golf, he often seems to replay poor shots without giving himself a penalty. But he is scrupulously honest in his dealings with coworkers and subordinates. Should we describe him as generally a "somewhat dishonest person"? Or are we better off saying that he is honest in professional situations and cheats at competitive games?

The problem this raises for the accuracy of person perception is that if personality traits are limited to certain classes of situations, they become more difficult for observers to judge accurately. The observers would need to perceive both the person's tendencies and the situation accurately. But people tend not to do this. As we will see in Chapter 5, observers have a tendency to ascribe general personality traits to people, ignoring the fact that people may behave quite differently in different classes of situations.

Recognition of Emotions

Much of the work on the accuracy of person perception has focused on the recognition of emotions, on whether a person is happy or afraid, horrified or disgusted. The basic procedure is to present a subject with a stimulus representing another person and ask the subject to identify the other's emotion. For some studies, trained actors portrayed a number of different emotions, and pictures were taken of their expressions. One picture was chosen for each emotion. These were then shown to subjects, who were asked to indicate what emotion was depicted. Some of these pictures are shown in Figure 2–2.

Early studies seemed to indicate that people could not judge emotions in facial expressions at better than a chance level. Later studies have shown that people can discriminate among the major groups of emotions, even if they cannot discriminate very well between each individual emotion. Woodworth (1938) suggested that emotions can be arranged on a continuum, with the ease of distinguishing between any two emotions being related to the distance between them on this continuum. The continuum of emotions is

1. Happiness, joy
2. Surprise, amazement
3. Fear
4. Sadness
5. Anger
6. Disgust, contempt
7. Interest, attentiveness

People seem to be quite good at distinguishing emotions in categories that are three, four, or five points apart—they rarely confuse happiness with disgust or surprise with contempt. People have a particularly easy time distinguishing pleasant from unpleasant emotions in others' faces (again indicating the importance of the evaluative dimension in person perception). But they find it almost impossible to discriminate emotions in the same category or only one group away. Happiness and surprise are frequently confused, as are anger and disgust, for example.

More recent studies using the same kind of approach find a simpler structure with two basic underlying dimensions: pleasantness and arousal (Russell & Bullock, 1985). Positive emotions such as excitement and happiness were distinguished from negative ones such as fear, anger, and disgust. Among the positive emotions, arousing ones such as excitement can be distinguished from nonarousing ones such as contentment. Similarly, negative arousing emotions such as fear and anger can be distinguished from nonarousing ones such as sadness.

One artificial aspect of these studies has been that they involve static, posed faces, frequently using just one model. Later studies have used videotaped presentations, such as of ordinary people viewing a variety of emotionally evocative situations (Wagner, MacDonald, & Manstead, 1986). Others have used several different actors portraying different emotions in video-taped scenes (for example, Wallbott & Scherer, 1986). Again, the typical finding has been that expressions can be differentiated fairly well into those that express positive emotions (such as happiness) or negative emotions (disgust, sadness, or anger). To some extent high arousal can be distinguished from low arousal. But beyond that, accuracy is not very great.

The accuracy of recognizing emotions in others also depends upon how intense the emotional experience is. In one study in which a woman watched slides that were slightly pleasant or slightly unpleasant, the emotional expressions she registered in response to the slides were quite modest. Student subjects observing her responses were unable to detect whether she was watching positive or negative slides. However, electrodes attached to her face picked up subtle facial movements, suggesting that nonverbal behaviors that are too subtle to be noticed by an observer may nonetheless indicate a person's affective response (Cacioppo, Petty, Losh, & Kim, 1986; Cacioppo, Martzke, Petty, & Tassinary, 1988).

Universal Emotional Expressions

People are at least crudely accurate in judging others' emotions, then. One reason might be that all people use the same facial expression for expressing a given underlying emotion. Perhaps we all smile when we feel happy, grimace when we feel pain, frown when we are worried, and so on. To illustrate this, Craig and Patrick (1985) induced pain by immersing subjects' hands and wrists into icy water just at freezing temperature. They found such consistent responses as raising cheeks with tight eyelids, raising the upper eyelid, parting the lips, and closing eyes or blinking.

In 1872, on the basis of his evolutionary theory, Charles Darwin proposed that facial expressions convey the same emotional states in all cultures. His argument was that universal expressions have evolved because they have great survival value: they allow animals to com-

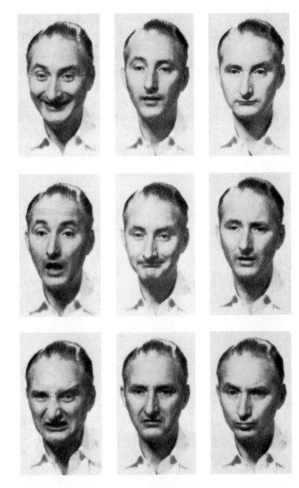

Figure 2–2. Examples of stimuli used in the study of the perception of emotions. The photographs illustrate expressions posed to portray the emotions listed. (You might try to identify them before looking at the following key.) *Top* (left to right): glee, passive adoration, complacency. *Middle:* amazement, optimistic determination, dismay. *Bottom:* rage, mild repugnance, puzzlement.

municate emotions and thereby control others' behavior. For example, if one animal shows an angry or threatening face, others may behave more submissively, which allows the first animal to win the encounter without risking an actual fight.

In fact, virtually all species of Old World monkeys and apes have been found to use facial gestures to signal dominance or submissiveness. Differing eyebrow positions seem to be crucial: typically, the brows are lowered on dominant or threatening individuals and raised on submissive or receptive individuals (Keating et al., 1981). The evolutionary argument is that there may be a link between the facial expressions used by subhuman primates to communicate with and control other species members, and those used by humans for the same purpose. If so, presumably the same link between emotion and facial expression would exist among humans across all (or most) cultures.

Are there such universals in humans? Do we have particular facial expressions or body postures for each emotion? Or is it possible that one person's expression of disgust is another person's expression of contentment? The link between lowered-brow expressions and dominance in nonhuman primates suggests a possible similar link in human beings. To test for this, Keating and others (1981) had people from each of a number of countries in Europe, Africa, North and South America, and Asia pose with brows lowered, and again with brows raised. The researchers also tested for a link between perceptions of smiling and dominance/ submission because a number of studies had suggested that primates' grins may communicate submissiveness. On the other hand, there is also evidence that among humans, smiling is related to happiness. The subjects were presented with pictures of a person from their own country and asked, in their native language, to judge the pose for dominance and happiness. The only differences in poses were brow position and smiling or not. Keating found that nonsmiling and lowered-brow poses were generally associated with dominance, especially among the most Westernized peoples. Smiles were identified with happiness. It is possible that the analog to the human smile is the primate submissive grin. When an ape grins, it means submission. Perhaps there is an evolutionary link to the human tendency to express sociability and submissiveness in the same manner.

These findings parallel those from other studies in the West in which lowered brows are identified with anger, assertive behavior, working on competitive tasks, and dominance. Raised brows are associated with social deference in a number of ways: with children's fleeing during disputes, with perceptions of fear or surprise, and as a signal inviting social contact.

How would you react if asked to imagine finding a dead animal that had been lying in the sun for several days or to imagine that a friend has come to visit? Research shows that the facial expressions of this New Guinea tribesman are remarkably similar to those of American college students given the same instructions. Can you tell which photos show anger, happiness, sadness, or disgust?

Smiles are generally associated with greeting, approval-seeking behavior, and happiness or joy (Keating et al., 1981).

An even tougher test of the universality of particular emotional expressions was a study conducted with people from a remote part of New Guinea who had never lived in any Western settlement or government towns, had seen no movies, understood neither English nor Pidgin, and had never worked for a Caucasian. Presumably these people had had no visual contact with conventional Western facial expression of emotions. Each was given a brief story depicting an emotion, such as for sadness, ''His child has died, and he feels very sad.'' Then the participant was given one photograph Western observers overwhelmingly agreed depicted that emotion and two pictures depicting other emotions. On the average, both children and adults chose the ''correct'' picture more than 80 percent of the time (Ekman & Friesen, 1971). This does not prove there are no cultural differences in the facial expression of emotion, but it does provide evidence of universals that transcend cultural boundaries. In particular, happiness, sadness, anger, and disgust can be detected with high levels of agreement both within and across cultures. Fear and surprise were often confused with each other (Ekman, 1982).

There are some qualifications, however. Cultures do differ substantially in *amount* of emotional expression that is customary. Swedes tend to be relatively impassive; Italians are quite expressive. Sometimes social norms forbid honest expression—we are supposed to conceal disgusted reactions to someone with a terrible deformity, or anger from being belittled by a superior at work. Still, the level of consensus on the meaning of facial expressions is impressive, given the fact that most of these studies have used photographs and hence provide no information about context.

NONVERBAL COMMUNICATION

If you think about it, you will realize that you make judgments about another person's emotional state on the basis of more than facial expression. What other cues do we use? What are the ways in which people communicate their internal states in general, and what cues do observers use in detecting them?

Generally speaking, people communicate information about themselves through three main channels. The most obvious is *verbal communication,* the content of what a person says. The other channels are nonverbal and provide a whole set of much subtler cues. *Nonverbal communication* is the sum of the ways in which we transmit information without using language. The communication comes to us through a visible channel, which includes such expressive behaviors as facial expression, gesture, posture, and appearance. And it comes to us through a paralinguistic channel, namely, what is left in the speech signal when the content has been removed, such as the pitch, amplitude, rate, voice quality, and contour of speech.

The visible and paralinguistic channels have generated a good bit of research and they do prove informative to perceivers. As research has progressed, a wide variety of different nonverbal cues have been identified, and observers seem to get quite different kinds of information from them. However, as helpful as they can be, nonverbal communications provide no magic clues to another person's internal states. Perceivers usually require other information about a person.

The Visible Channel

Some of the main nonverbal cues of the visible channel are expressed through distance, gesture, and eye contact.

Distance. In general, the more friendly and intimate a person feels toward another, the closer he or she will stand. Friends stand closer than strangers (Aiello & Cooper, 1972), people who want to seem friendly choose smaller distances (Patterson & Sechrest, 1970), and people who are sexually attracted to each other stand close (Allgeier & Byrne, 1973). Although most people do not think much about personal space, we are all aware that standing close is usually a sign of friendship or interest. It may be one of the most important and easiest ways of telling someone you have just met that you like him or her. The other person is immediately aware of your interest, and if he or she is not interested, will generally move away to make that clear.

Gestures. In recent years many popular books have been published on the subject of **body language.** These books suggest that you can tell exactly what someone is thinking or perfectly interpret what they say merely by observing their bodily movements and posture. An open palm is an invitation, crossed legs are defensive, and so on. Clearly bodily gestures and posture carry information. There are straightforward, direct gestures and very subtle ones. Many bodily movements are generally accepted and convey specific information or directions—the gestures for "stop" and "come" are examples, as are pointing and gestures for "sit down," "yes," "no," "go away," "goodbye." Various obscene gestures have well-known meanings. In a sense, all these gestures are a sign language.

But gestures have meaning mainly when observers and participants understand the context, and especially when they understand the culture. An open palm is not always an invitation: putting a hand up with palm out means, "stop," not "go"; the reverse gesture, with the palm in and the fingers moving toward the body, means "come" or "enter." No one has constructed a reliable dictionary of gestures. Popular books on body language are usually not based on scientific research and should be read with healthy skepticism. The meaning of gestures depends on the context, on the person doing the action, on the culture, and probably on other factors also.

The importance of nonverbal communications and gestures in particular has now made its way into the popular culture. Media experts who "handle" congressional, senatorial, or presidential candidates often work as much on their candidates' gestures and other nonverbal communication as on the content of their presentation. During the 1988 campaign season, Roger Ailes, George Bush's media consultant, was quoted in *Newsweek* (Warner & Fineman, 1988, p. 19) as telling Bush during a rehearsal

for one of the debates, "There you go with that f---ing hand again. You look like a f---ing pansy!" (cited in DePaulo, 1990).

Eye Contact. Eye contact is an especially interesting form of nonverbal communication. As with other forms, the meaning of eye contact varies greatly and depends on the context. But in nearly all social interactions, eye contact does communicate information.

At the minimum, eye contact indicates interest or lack of it. Hollywood movies often have a couple staring into each other's eyes to portray love, affection, or great concern. Certainly we are all familiar with eye contact held for a long time as a means of demonstrating attraction for someone. An otherwise casual conversation can become an expression of romantic interest if one of the speakers maintains eye contact. Conversely, avoiding or breaking the contact is usually a sign that the person is not interested. Indeed, when someone does not make eye contact during a conversation, we tend to interpret this as an indication that he or she is not really involved in the interaction.

But there are obvious exceptions to this general principle. Someone who is conveying bad news or saying something painful may avoid eye contact. Lack of eye contact can sometimes mean the person is shy or frightened. When people have feelings they are embarrassed about, they do not like to be the focus of a direct gaze. In a study by Ellsworth, Friedman, Perlick, and Hoyt (1978), female college students were told they would have to discuss questions "about rather intimate personal areas of your life, things that college students usually do not like to talk about." Each student then had to wait with a confederate who stared directly at her 75 percent of the time, or just glanced at her once. By far, most subjects preferred the gaze-averting confederate. This was not true of other subjects who were not expecting an embarrassing conversation. The direct gaze apparently threatened the embarrassed women.

Moreover, eye contact can be used more actively, to threaten. In another experiment, someone stared at a subject who was in a position to act aggressively toward the starer. Subjects who were stared at were less aggressive than when there was no staring (Ellsworth & Carlsmith, 1973). Apparently prolonged eye contact can be interpreted as a threat and causes people to escape or act in a conciliatory manner. We can all probably remember teachers who have used this technique very effectively.

It is perhaps not surprising that eye contact can have two seemingly contradictory meanings—friendship or threat. In both cases, eye contact indicates greater involvement and higher emotional content. Whether the emotion is positive or negative depends on the context; the nonverbal cues themselves have no fixed meaning.

Facial Expressions. Facial expressions also can be intended to communicate to others. One interesting case of this is mimicry. It has often been observed that people (and chimpanzees) physically mimic the responses of others. Darwin noted that in particular people mimic distress when others are feeling it. It is possible that this mimicry is an expression of sympathy for the victim; the mimic may want the other person to know that distress about the painful experience is shared.

To test this idea, Bavelas, Black, Lemery, and Mullett (1986) had undergraduate women individually view a person accidentally drop a heavy TV monitor on an already injured finger, one with a heavily taped splint on it. In some cases the victim, a confederate (badly bruised!) then looked directly at the observer; in other cases no eye contact was made. Most of the observers in turn displayed an expression of pain, but it quickly faded in the absence of eye contact. Moreover, the observers were considerably more likely to smile when eye contact was made, probably in an effort to be reassuring. The facial expressions of the observers were in fact rated as more "knowing" and "caring" in the eye contact condition than without, suggesting that they were successfully communicating feelings of empathy and sympathy.

Paralanguage

Variations in speech other than the actual verbal contact, called **paralanguage,** carry a great deal of meaning. Pitch of the voice, loudness, rhythm, inflection, and hesitations convey information. Parents can often tell whether their baby is hungry, angry, or just mildly cranky by how it cries. Dogs bark in different ways, and each means something different to someone familiar with the animal. And, of course, the significance and meaning of adult speech depend in part on these paralinguistic factors.

A simple statement such as "You want to move to Japan" can mean entirely different things depending on emphasis and inflection. Say it aloud as a flat statement with no emphasis, and it sounds like a mere statement of fact. Say it with an inflection (rising voice) at the end, and it questions the wisdom of going to Japan; you are expressing doubt that it is a good place to move to. Say it with added emphasis on the first word, and it turns into a question as to whether or not the person addressed is qualified; you are raising doubts about whether or not the person is capable of getting along in such a foreign country. The short phrase "I like you" may indicate almost anything from mild feelings to intense passion, depending on its paralinguistic characteristics.

These variations are often crucial in conveying emotion. In fact, they are so important that they often must be added to written language. To show that someone thought Japan was an unlikely choice, the sentence might read, " 'You want to move to Japan?' he said with disbelief." To describe the feeling behind a statement of liking, one might write, " 'I like you,' she murmured passionately." Without these paralinguistic clues, the statements are hard to interpret.

One of the difficulties in studying paralanguage (and most other kinds of nonverbal behavior) is that the cues have no fixed meaning. We all agree on the meaning of words. We all know what "Japan" refers to, and with some variations we know that when someone says he "likes" you, he is making a statement of positive feelings. But people differ considerably in the meanings they attach to paralinguistic cues. For some people, a pause may be for emphasis; for others, it may mean uncertainty. Higher pitch may mean excitement or lying; loudness can be anger, emphasis, or excitement. The particular meaning depends on the context. It is hard to interpret what is communicated when a speaker talks louder at you: if the person makes a fist, it is anger; if the person hugs you, it is affection. It also depends on individual habits and characteristics.

Multiple Channels

Which of these three channels of communication—verbal, visible, and paralinguistic—provides the most information about a person's real emotions? Many writers in recent years have speculated that observers weigh nonverbal cues most heavily and tend almost to disregard verbal communication. For example, Birdwhistell (1970) says that no more than 30 to 35 percent of the social meaning of conversation is carried by the words. Mehrabian (1972) estimated that only 7 percent of the communication of emotion was accomplished by the verbal channel, 55 percent was accomplished by the visual channel, and 38 percent by the paralinguistic channel. Other writers have gone even further, arguing that the visible channel dominates over verbal content in the communication of emotion; that is, "video" information is more important than "audio" (DePaulo, Rosenthal, Eisenstat, Rogers, & Finkelstein, 1978).

The question of which channels are taken most seriously becomes particularly important when the observer is receiving conflicting cues from different channels. How do you interpret your girlfriend's feelings when she says she loves you but moves away from you and won't look at you? The verbal and visible channels of her communication seem to conflict. What if your roommate shouts at you at the top of her lungs that she is really *not* mad at you *at all* for breaking her favorite coffee cup? Shakespeare said, "Methinks she doth protest too much." Conflicts across channels ought to be particularly important in interpreting apparently deceptive communications. In such cases, is nonverbal, and especially visible, communication truly relied on most heavily as some of these researchers suggest?

Such claims have now been subjected to rigorous tests. In one of the clearest of such studies, Krauss, Apple, Morency, Wenzel, and Winton (1981) presented subjects with videotapes of the 1976 televised debate between the two candidates for vice president, Walter Mondale and Robert Dole. The debate started pleasantly, but turned rather heated and rancorous. The researchers selected 12 passages for each speaker, half of which seemed to display positive emotions and half negative. Then each subject was presented these passages in one of four conditions: (1) audiovisual—the standard videotaped version; (2) verbal only—a written transcript as published in *The New York Times*; (3) video only—with the audio channel turned off; and (4) paralinguistic—the audio track only, but with content filtered out so that speech was unintelligible, while nonverbal features such as pitch, loudness, rate, and so on were preserved.

The written transcript turned out to be critical for detecting whether positive or negative emotions were being expressed; that is, verbal information was most important, contrary to speculations about the importance of nonverbal communications. The data from this study are shown in Table 2–5.

The visible channel made little contribution to observers' judgments. Paralinguistic information did contribute to judgments of the potency and activity levels of the speakers' presentations. That is, observers who were given only the unintelligible soundtrack gave the same kinds of judgments about energy levels as did those given full audiovisual information. The implication is that paralinguistic information, like eye contact, can be sufficient to detect energy and involvement, even if it is not sufficient to detect the particular kind of emotion expressed.

A follow-up study by Apple and Hecht (1982) found that paralinguistic information could be particularly useful in detecting sadness. They had speakers deliver sentences that varied in the kind of emotion they presented: happiness, sadness, anger, surprise. No visual cues were provided, and the verbal content of the sentence was screened out from the recording. Lis-

T A B L E   2 – 5

IMPORTANCE OF VARIOUS CHANNELS OF INFORMATION IN JUDGMENTS ABOUT VICE-PRESIDENTIAL DEBATERS

	Verbal Only	Video Only	Audio Filtered
Dimension of judgment			
Evaluation	51.8[a]	2.2	8.8
Potency	3.4	29.6	45.1[a]
Activity	0.1	36.8	5.2

[a] $p < .05$.

Source: Adapted from Krauss et al. (1981), pp. 316–317.

Note: The entry is the percentage of variance in judgments of full audiovisual communication that was accounted for by each individual channel. Rows do not sum to 100 percent because factors other than these three channels account for some of the full-channel judgment process.

teners were able to identify the sadness sentences quite readily, but they could identify the others at only slightly better than chance levels. The authors speculate that sadness is expressed through distinctive paralinguistic cues (slow, soft, low-pitched speech), whereas the other emotions are expressed with more energetic cues that easily confuse the listener.

In general, then, nonverbal cues—paralinguistic or visible—are not very precise guides, by themselves, to emotional feelings in others. There is nothing magically or unambiguously communicative about nonverbal cues. Most can communicate a variety of messages depending on the context. A touch on the arm by an attractive acquaintance means something quite different from the same touch made by a homeless person in a subway station. Being tapped on the shoulder by your boss may mean something still different. A smile on the face of a bully as he moves in on a helpless prey means something quite different from the smile on a friend's face when he or she sees you walking across the campus. Nonverbal cues can be informative, but only when they are solidly embedded in a familiar context, when we know the role of the other person, have some notion of his or her general goals, know the norms for the situation, and so on. When we do not have a known or familiar context, as in a first visit to a foreign country, we frequently feel lost and can make little sense of nonverbal cues.

THE PROBLEM OF DECEPTION

A particularly important area of conflict between verbal and nonverbal cues is judging when people are lying or otherwise trying to deceive observers. Police, judges, and jurors are constantly trying to learn the truth from people who try to mislead them.

Nonverbal Leakage

As might be expected from our discussion of nonverbal communication, one important theory is that people will give away deception through nonverbal cues even when they are successful in lying verbally. Ekman and Friesen (1974) argue that people attend more to what they are saying than to what they are doing with their bodies. If they are trying to deceive someone, for example, they may lie verbally in a calm way, but reveal their true emotions through nonverbal cues. In Ekman's terms, there is **nonverbal leakage.** True emotions "leak out" even if the person tries to conceal them. A student may say she is not nervous about a test, but will bite her lower lip and blink more than usual, actions that often indicate nervousness. A young man waiting for a job interview may attempt to appear calm and casual, but will cross and uncross his legs continually, straighten his tie, touch his face, play with his hair. As a result, he will in fact come across as a nervous wreck.

Liars often betray themselves through para-linguistic expressions of anxiety, tension, and nervousness. It sometimes is possible to tell when someone is lying by noting the pitch of the voice. Several studies (Ekman, Friesen, & Scherer, 1976; Krauss, Geller, & Olson, 1976) indicate that the average (or more technically, fundamental) pitch of the voice is higher when someone is lying than when he or she is telling the truth. The difference is small, and one cannot tell just by listening. But electronic vocal analysis reveals lying with considerable accuracy. In addition, shorter answers, longer delays in responding, more speech errors, and more nervous, less serious answers all are characteristic of people perceived as liars or instructed to tell lies (Apple, Streeter, & Krauss, 1979; Kraut, 1978; Zuckerman, DePaulo, & Rosenthal, 1981).

The concept of "leakage" implies that some nonverbal channels "leak" more than others because they are less controllable. The musculature of a smile, for example, changes when people are being truthful as opposed to when they are lying (Ekman, Friesen, & O'Sullivan, 1988). But several studies (Zuckerman, De Paulo, & Rosenthal, 1981) have found that the body is more likely to reveal deception than the face. Paralinguistic cues can also "leak" because, like the body, tone of voice is less controllable than facial expression. Zuckerman, Larrance, Spiegel, and Klorman (1981) have found that liars were better able to modify (suppress and exaggerate) facial expressions than tone of voice. The "leakage" hypothesis proposes, then, that when people are trying to conceal something, they may be able to control their verbal content and facial expressions fairly well, but their deception may "leak" out in bodily gestures and paralinguistic cues.

Nonverbal channels may "leak" more than verbal channels, because when conveying information verbally, a person both produces and hears exactly what he or she said and consequently can correct statements that may not have been said in a way that conveys quite the right impression. However, in the nonverbal channel, we usually do not see our nonverbal behaviors, and consequently may be less able to regulate them (DePaulo, 1990). Thus, while we may try to regulate our nonverbal behavior, we may not always be successful, because we lack the kind of feedback that we get from our own verbal behavior.

Accuracy of Detection

Perceivers do quite consistently perceive deceptive messages as somewhat less truthful than truthful messages (see DePaulo, 1990, for a review). Across dozens of studies, deception accuracy usually exceeds chance, but rarely by an impressive margin (DePaulo et al., 1982). Not surprisingly, people can detect the fact of lying better than they can figure out the nature of the liar's true feelings.

For one thing, people have trouble distinguishing deception from genuine ambivalence. This was illustrated in a study by DePaulo and coworkers (1982). They had people record messages that (1) truthfully described their positive (or negative, as the case may be) feelings about another person, (2) untruthfully described their positive (or negative) feelings, or (3) truthfully described their genuinely mixed feelings about another person. These messages were presented to observers through different channels. They found that observers were not able to distinguish truthful messages about mixed feelings from deceptive messages about positive or negative feelings. Perhaps people are able to distinguish true expressions of positive or negative feelings from everything else, but are not able to isolate deception itself without any further information—all they know is that the person does not sound wholeheartedly positive or negative.

On the other hand, people usually do have other information about the person's motives. They usually know whether or not the person has a reason to want to lie. It may be that we are better at detecting deception when we know the person has such reasons. To test this, DePaulo, Stone, and Lassiter (1985a) had people (hereafter termed "senders") describe their opinions on four issues to their "partners." They manipulated lying by instructing the "senders" to agree or disagree honestly on two issues and to pretend to agree or disagree on two others. Then they varied the incentive for senders to lie in several ways. In the high-incentive conditions, the "partner" was of the opposite sex, the partner was attractive, and the sender was instructed to feign agreement. Presumably all these would give the sender reason to be most ingratiating. In the other conditions, the sender would have less apparent incentive to lie: the "partner" was unattractive, or of the same sex, or the sender was instructed to feign disagreement. These communications were videotaped and later played back to neutral judges, varying which channels were available. The judges rated the communications on a scale of sincerity-insincerity.

The main finding is that lies were easiest to detect when they were apparently motivated by ingratiation, that is, when the sender had the greatest motivation to lie—communicating agreement to an attractive partner of the opposite sex. Deception was harder to detect without any specific information about reasons to lie—that is, when the sender was communicating disagreement to an unattractive member of one's own sex. An interesting example of efforts to detect lying appears in Box 2–5.

Does it help to be warned explicitly that a target person may be lying? One would think so, because perceivers then should attend more closely to "leaky" channels, such as the face and tone of voice. However, it seems not to help very much. In a study by Toris and DePaulo (1984), subjects participated in simulated job interviews. The applicants were told to be honest in some cases and dishonest in others, while the interviewers were told to expect the applicant to try to convey a false impression in some cases and were given no warning in others. However, this warning of deceptiveness just made the interviewers suspicious about everyone, perceiving all applicants as more deceptive; they were no more accurate in singling out the dishonest ones. Not only that, but they were less confident of their own judgments.

Research investigations may actually overestimate the degree to which people can detect deception in everyday life. As social perceivers, most of the time we are very busy trying to form impressions of others, cull what is useful for oneself from the conversation at hand, and manage the impressions that we are conveying to others. Under such circumstances, we tend to take others' self-presentations at face value, rather than questioning whether they are trying to convey a false impression (Gilbert, Krull, & Pelham, 1988; see also Gilbert & Krull, 1988). In fact, when people are deliberately trying to convey an emotion that they may not really be experiencing, their nonverbal behaviors convey that impression even more clearly than when they are actually experiencing the state. Posed expressions of emotion are easier to read than are spontaneous ones (see DePaulo, 1990, for a review). This combination of the deceiver being easy to read and the perceiver being relatively uncritical means that in most social situations, deceptive self-presentations are likely to be taken at face value (DePaulo, 1990).

The Giveaways

When observers are able to discover deception, what cues do they use? Is the leakage hypothesis correct? Is the body less controllable than the face, and do people catch deception primarily through nonverbal bodily cues? Or is the voice an even leakier channel than the body? It may be that the tone of voice—pitch, loudness, speed, and so forth—is even more difficult to control than the body, even when the person can control the content of verbal communication.

Most of the research shows that all these cues help a little to trap a potentially deceptive communicator. But they are really useful only when the observer also has access to the content of the person's speech. A typical study is one done by Zuckerman, Amidon, Bishop, and Pomerantz (1982). They had "senders" describe either a target person they liked (a "liked target") or someone they disliked (a "disliked target"), and they did so in one of three modes: "truth," in which

BOX 2–5

Detecting Smugglers at the Customs Gate

How good are ordinary people at detecting lying? What cues do they use in detecting it? One of the most realistic studies was conducted by Kraut and Poe (1980). They induced airline travelers to try to smuggle some "contraband" past an interview with a real U.S. Customs inspector. The participants were people who happened to be waiting for an airline departure in Syracuse, New York. Some were randomly selected to serve in the "smuggler" condition and were given contraband, such as small pouches of white powder or miniature cameras, and told to hide them on their persons. They were offered a prize of up to $100 for being able to smuggle the contraband successfully past the customs inspector. Others were randomly selected to be in the "innocent" condition and were given no contraband. The whole interaction of passenger and inspector was videotaped. To determine what special nonverbal behaviors were displayed by people actually engaged in deception, each passenger's behavior with the inspector was coded by other judges for many of the visible and paralinguistic variables of nonverbal communication we have been discussing: grooming, postural shifts, relaxed posture, smiling, gaze avoidance, speech errors, response latency, response length, evasiveness, nervousness, and difficulty in answering. Each interaction was also played back to observers who attempted to identify which of the passengers were "smugglers" and which were not.

There were no discernible systematic differences in behavior between the innocent and smuggling passengers. If the "smugglers" were "leaking" their deceptiveness, they were not doing so consistently via the nonverbal behaviors coded. Not surprisingly, then, neither the real customs inspectors nor the observers who later viewed the videotapes were successful in picking out the "smugglers" from the "innocent" passengers. This finding suggests that observers have limited ability to detect deception in a real-life situation, when they only have nonverbal cues to go on.

Despite this lack of accuracy, there was strong consensus among observers on who the actual smugglers were. They also showed considerable consensus on the specific cues associated with "smuggling": the person's apparent nervousness, taking a long time to answer a question, giving short answers, shifting the body more, and avoiding eye contact with the inspector.

In short, neither professional nor untrained observers could accurately determine whether or not a traveler was lying. And in fact the lying and honest travelers did not differ in any way that could be coded in terms of verbal and nonverbal behavior. Yet observers came to a striking level of consensus about who was smuggling, and what cues supposedly revealed it. All this is consistent with the notion that the observers shared a clear but inaccurate schema about how smugglers behave. As in controlled laboratory situations, observers are not terribly accurate detectors of deception on the basis of nonverbal cues, though they are often quite confident about being able to detect it, and have many ready explanations for this "skill."

they conveyed their true feelings; "concealment," in which they tried to conceal their true feelings; and "deception," in which they tried to communicate feelings opposite to those they really had. The "receivers" did not know the senders' true feelings, or which mode the sender was instructed to use.

Some receivers had full audiovisual (face plus verbal content), others heard only the audio channel (verbal content, no face), others had access to visual plus filtered speech (face, no verbal content), and still others, filtered speech only (no verbal content, no face). The question was how access to the face, to verbal content, and to paralinguistic cues affected observers' ability to detect whether the sender really liked or disliked the target.

The results showed that either face or tone of

T A B L E   2 – 6

*ACCURACY OF PERCEPTION OF
COMMUNICATORS' TRUE FEELINGS ABOUT
TARGET PERSON*

	Verbal Content	
	Available	Not Available
Face present	+.85	+.74
Face absent	+.84	+.31

Source: Adapted from Zuckerman et al. (1982), p. 353.

Note: The entry is the perception of communicator's true feeling about the liked target minus the perception of communicator's true feeling about the disliked target, each rated on a nine-point scale.

voice added significantly to ability to detect deception. This can be seen in Table 2–6. The receivers were significantly able to distinguish a liked from a disliked target when given only filtered speech, without being able to see the face or hear any verbal content (as indicated by the fact that they perceived the truly liked target as liked +.31 more, on the average, than the truly disliked target). Second, adding access to the face significantly increased detection of the sender's true feelings, as indicated by the fact that face plus filtered speech is higher (+.74) than filtered speech only (+.31), even when verbal content was not available. Both channels are somewhat "leaky," then, in the sense that both communicated significantly to the receiver about a possibly deceptive sender's true feelings, even when the perceiver could not understand the content of the communications.

The main finding, however, is that accuracy is greatest when verbal content is available. The table shows the highest accuracy in the left-hand column, with verbal content available. Moreover, adding visual nonverbal cues helps the perceiver very little when verbal content is available (+.85 is almost identical to +.84).

A large number of reviews have identified the specific behaviors that reliably distinguish lies from truth. Liars blink more, hesitate more, and make more errors when they are speaking, perhaps because it is arousing to lie. They tend to speak in higher-pitched voices and their pupils are more likely to be dilated. Liars are more

likely to feel guilty or anxious, and this may explain why liars fidget more, speak more hesitatingly and less fluidly, and make more negative and distancing statements than do those telling the truth. The voice tone of liars also often sounds negative. Interchannel discrepancies are more likely to occur. Thus, for example, someone attempting to convey an impression of warmth may smile and make eye contact but lean away from the person with whom he is conversing, rather than leaning forward (DePaulo et al., 1985a; for general reviews, see DePaulo et al., 1985b; Zuckerman, DePaulo, & Rosenthal, 1981; DePaulo, 1990).

Paradoxically, one of the best sources of information regarding deception may be the sender's motivation to lie. Intuitively, it seems that people who are the most highly motivated to deceive others will be most successful. However, considerable research suggests that when people are especially motivated to get away with their lies, they actually become more obvious to observers (e.g., DePaulo, LeMay, & Epstein, in press; DePaulo, Kirkendol, Tang, & O'Brien, 1988). Typically, these lies are not revealed verbally, but nonverbally. Motivated liars seem to work harder to control their nonverbal behavior, sometimes attempting to suppress it altogether in a rigid effort not to give anything away. In other cases, they may deliberately try to control all their verbal and nonverbal behaviors. Both strategies fail because observers can perceive this rigid or controlled behavior through the nonverbal channels and more successfully discern the effort to lie (DePaulo, 1990).

We have discussed a number of studies, then, which have tried to determine what cues help detect lying in another person. For the most part, nonverbal cues do not seem to be sufficient. Rather, people infer lying from other kinds of information they receive about the person: whether the supposed liar seems to have something to gain from lying, or fits the stereotype of a liar, or whether the verbal communication suggests lying. Nonverbal cues add something when this other information is available, but are not sufficient by themselves.

Nonverbal Behavior and Self-presentation

So far, our discussion has implied that nonverbal behavior is either spontaneous and unself-conscious or it is a potential source of leakage about deception. But nonverbal behavior is also subject to a certain amount of self-regulation, although perhaps not as much as verbal behavior (Schlenker, 1986). Think about the last time a friend shared a problem with you. If you listened patiently and sympathetically, as most of us do at least initially, you were probably aware not only of saying the right things, such as "That's too bad" or "That's a terrible way to treat anybody." You may also have been aware of the appropriate nonverbal behaviors, such as making eye contact with your friend while he talked and nodding sympathetically. You knew, for example, not to smile, but to look serious, and not to open your mail and skim it while he was explaining his problem. While not intending to deceive your friend in any way, your nonverbal behaviors were clearly monitored, at least to a degree, so that you conveyed the appropriate sentiments and reactions to your friend's disclosures.

Increasingly, psychologists have been interested in these self-presentational aspects of nonverbal behavior (DePaulo, 1990). Over the lifetime, we learn a great deal about the self-presentation of nonverbal behavior, indeed so much so that it becomes almost automatic in adulthood. For example, by the time we are in college, we may not have to think much about the fact that we should stop fidgeting, make extended eye contact, and look sympathetic when another person is telling us a problem. It may occur virtually spontaneously in response to the friend's distress. But like verbal behavior, nonverbal behavior is learned. Taught to "sit like a lady" in childhood, a behavior that may require uncomfortable amounts of practice, one may do so quite unconsciously in adulthood. Ekman (1972) calls these cultural norms regarding how one conveys emotions to others *display rules.* Display rules govern not only which emotion should be conveyed in a particular situation, but how the emotion should be conveyed.

Generally speaking, people deliberately regulate their nonverbal behavior in ways that enhance the correspondence between their self-presentation and how they truly think about themselves (Swann, 1984; DePaulo, 1990). We wear buttons to convey our political beliefs, choose clothing that represents us as conservative or liberal, and act open and outgoing if we feel we are that way, and more standoffish and shy if we are not.

Nonverbal behavior can also be used to further social goals. Talking with a woman he may wish to date, a man smiles a lot, makes extended eye contact, stands fairly close, and might rest his hand against the wall in back of his intended partner. Caught in a conversation with someone to whom he is not attracted, he stands farther away, glances from time to time around the room, maintains a more serious expression, and keeps his arms folded in front of him.

People's ability to use nonverbal behavior in self-presentational efforts varies considerably and depends upon their knowledge of the appropriate nonverbal behavior for a particular situation, their ability, practice and experience in conveying that impression, and their confidence in conveying the impression. Several factors, however, may paradoxically work against conveying an appropriate self-presentation through nonverbal behavior. As just noted, being highly motivated to convey a particular impression may actually act as an impediment to successful self-presentation when people try too hard to control their verbal and nonverbal behavior (e.g., Baumeister, 1988; Heckhausen & Strang, 1988; DePaulo & Kirkendol, 1989). Similarly, people who are spontaneously expressive, while perhaps more able than those who are not to convey a variety of emotions, may find that their spontaneous expressions interfere with the self-presentation they are attempting to achieve (Friedman & Miller-Herringer, 1990). Spontaneously expressive people probably convey impressions more successfully than people who are not so spontaneous, unless they are trying to convey an impression that is at odds with what they are really feeling.

There are sex differences in the use of nonverbal behavior. Girls and women are more expressive, more involved in their interpersonal interactions, and more open in the expression of emotion (DePaulo, 1990). They use more nonverbal behavior in interacting with others, such as touching, eye contact, expressive body movements, smiling, and gazing. Women are also more accurate interpreters of nonverbal cues than are men (Hall, 1978).

It is easy to interpret such effects in sex-role terms. Generally, women have been regarded as the experts in the social and emotional areas of life, and nonverbal behavior can clearly help in this regard. However, some studies suggest that these sex differences develop very early in life, as early as three months (Malatesta & Havi-land, 1982). Consequently, it is difficult to disentangle the roles of nature and nurture in attempting to understand these robust sex differences (DePaulo, 1990).

In conclusion, it appears that when people are motivated to convey a particular impression of themselves in a social interaction, they will attempt to do so, in part, by controlling their nonverbal behaviors. Although sometimes such behaviors are undertaken to deceive others, more commonly they may be employed to convey an accurate impression of the self and one's feelings in that situation. Moreover, people seem to be fairly successful at it, as long as they are not trying to convey a false impression.

Key Terms

additive principle	**gestalt**	**prototype**
averaging principle	**halo effect**	**public self-consciousness**
body language	**implicit personality**	**salience**
categorization	**theory**	**schema**
central traits	**negativity effect**	**self-awareness**
cognitive miser	**nonverbal leakage**	**self-reference effect**
cybernetic theory of	**paralanguage**	**shift of meaning**
self-regulation	**person perception**	**stereotype**
evaluation	**positivity bias**	
exemplar	**possible selves**	
figure-ground	**private self-consciousness**	
principle		

Summary

1. People decide what other people are like often very quickly and based on minimal information, such as what they look like or what sex they are. They infer enduring qualities in others from brief exposure to behavior in limited situations.

2. The evaluative dimension is the most important organizing principle behind first impressions. People seem to decide first how much they like or dislike another person and then ascribe characteristics to that person that fit this pleasant or unpleasant portrait.

3. People tend to form highly consistent impressions of others, even with very little information.

4. Various identifiable perceptual biases distort our judgments of others, such as the halo effect (we tend to think a person we like is good on every dimension) and the positivity

bias (we tend to like most people, even some who are not so likable).

5. There are two rival points of view about how people process information about other people: the learning approach, which has people essentially averaging information in a quite mechanical manner, and the gestalt approach, which has people forming more coherent and meaningful impressions.

6. Our judgments of other people are not always very accurate. In particular, we have a hard time judging people's emotions from their facial expressions. We can tell fairly easily if the emotion is a positive or a negative one, but we have difficulty telling which positive or negative emotion is being experienced. Nevertheless, there do seem to be some universal connections across cultures between certain emotions and certain facial expressions.

7. We use a wide variety of cues in arriving at impressions of people, including physical appearance, verbal behavior, and nonverbal cues. Nonverbal communication includes cues from both the visible channel (such as facial expressions, gestures, and posture) and the paralinguistic channel (cues in speech when the content has been removed, such as the pitch, rate, and delays of speech).

8. People's verbal communication is probably the single most important source of information about them. However, visible and paralinguistic information make an important additional contribution, particularly when the content helps us to interpret their meaning.

9. Deception "leaks" out in numerous nonverbal ways, such as nervous gestures or high-pitched and rapid speech. Observers can usually detect deception at slightly better than chance levels, but they need all three channels of communication to do so effectively.

Suggested Readings

Anderson, N. H. (1965). Averaging vs. adding as a stimulus-combination rule in impression formation. *Journal of Experimental Social Psychology, 70,* 394–400. This gives the flavor of averaging research, using trait adjectives about hypothetical stimulus persons.

Asch, S. E. (1946). Forming impressions of personality. *Journal of Abnormal and Social Psychology, 41,* 258–290. This is the classic statement of the gestalt approach to impression formation and, indeed, to social perception in general.

Buck, R. (1984). *The communication of emotions.* New York: Guilford. A general resource on emotion and communication with extensive focus on the nonverbal communication of emotion.

Hall, E. T. (1966). *The hidden dimension.* Garden City, NY: Doubleday. An original statement by one of the pioneers in the study of nonverbal communication.

Krauss, R. M., Apple, W., Morency, N., Wenzel, C., & Winston, W. (1981). Verbal, vocal, and visible factors in judgments of another's effect. *Journal of Personality and Social Psychology, 40,* 312–320. An interesting and careful analysis of how people combine cues from different channels to arrive at impressions.

Schneider, D. J., Hastorf, A. H., & Ellsworth, P. C. (1979). *Person perception,* 2nd ed. Reading, MA: Addison-Wesley. Still one of the best resources in the field, this paperback pursues the material in this chapter in more detail.

THREE

Social Cognition

*I*magine that you have completed college and are interviewing at a company for your first job. You have met the personnel director and some prospective coworkers. You also have toured the facilities, seen where your office would be if you were to join the firm, and learned a great deal about the work the company does and your responsibilities to the company. How do you decide if this is indeed the kind of company you want to work for, if you would like the work itself or the people you would work with? Answering these questions involves processes called social cognition.

Social cognition is the study of how people form inferences from social information in the environment (Fiske & Taylor, 1991). It explores how people make social judgments about other individuals or social groups, about social roles, and about their own experiences in social settings. The process of making social judgments is more difficult than we might imagine. Often, the information available to us is incomplete, ambiguous, or downright contradictory. We may be confronted with many complex details. How do we use all this information to arrive at a coherent judgment? This is the core question in research on social cognition.

Much of the early work on social cognition compared the social judgments actually made by people to those we would expect from a **rational model of inference.** By rational model, we mean that there are logical and correct ways to put information together to reach a judgment. Presumably, to make correct decisions and wise judgments, people should try to use social information as logically and carefully as possible (Einhorn & Hogarth, 1981). In the interests of making accurate inferences, people should try hard to avoid logical errors and subjective biases. Consequently, rational models of inference were considered to be appropriate standards against which to evaluate people's everyday processes for forming judgments and making decisions.

Studies comparing actual social judgments to the rational model have taught us much about the processes of social cognition. Contrary to what the rational model predicts, however, people's everyday methods of gathering and combining social information are often illogical. In the next section, we discuss some of the typical errors and biases that affect the social perceiver. Then we turn to newer research that explains some of the good reasons why the social perceiver is not completely rational.

SOCIAL INFERENCE

Any social inference is composed of several steps: gathering information, deciding what information to use to reach a judgment, and integrating the information into a judgment. For example, as you are learning about your possible new employer, you are gathering information about the people, products, and general feel of the organization, and you are gathering information from people around you through the questions you ask and the types of facilities or people that you request to see. When you return home and mull over your visit, you must then decide which of the multitude of information you received will be most relevant to your decision, and then integrate that information into an overall impression or judgment concerning whether or not this company is the right one for you. Each of these steps in the social inference process appears to be subject to particular kinds of errors and biases.

Gathering Information

When people gather information that is relevant to some inference they will ultimately form, they might plan to do so in an even-handed and unbiased manner. However, research suggests that actual information gathering is often colored by people's *prior expectations.* For example, suppose you learn that a college acquaintance of yours, an uptight, serious, humorless fellow, works for the company you are considering and finds it very much to his liking. If he likes the company so much, you might suspect that it is because he has found people there who are like he is. Consequently, you might infer that everyone at the company must be stiff and uptight. Accordingly, as you learn

Are these people prospecting for gold? Searching for a lost contact lens? Interpreting animal tracks? Social inference processes give social interactions structure and meaning.

about the company with this suspicion in mind, you might selectively gather information consistent with this prior expectation. You might note that prospective coworkers seem a little stiff or formal when you meet them and conclude that indeed your classmate is typical of the people at this firm. But in doing so, you might fail to remember that most people are a little stiff or formal when they are meeting someone for the first time. Their formality might simply be due to the fact that you are a stranger to them. They might actually turn out to be very friendly people. But with your prior expectations in mind, you might dismiss them as stiff and formal people without giving them a chance. This is how prior expectations can bias the process of gathering information.

Of course, prior expectations are very helpful in sifting through a lot of information that may otherwise be uninterpretable. They can provide structure and meaning for information that would otherwise be hard to interpret. However, sometimes prior expectations can cause us to draw inaccurate inferences. Three conditions are especially problematic (Nisbett & Ross, 1980). The first is if the expectations are faulty. For example, your belief that the company is

stiff and stodgy merely because it attracted one such individual to its ranks is likely to be incorrect. Therefore, letting this expectation guide your collection of information will probably lead you to incorrect answers. A second condition under which prior expectations can be problematic occurs when the social perceiver fails to recognize how prior expectations bias the collection of information. For example, you may be unaware that your impressions of your stodgy college classmate are actually guiding your judgments of your prospective coworkers. This lack of awareness means that later on you will be unable to correct the biasing effect of your prior impression. Your judgments concerning your prospective coworkers will stray on the stodgy and serious side without your realizing that your own biases contributed to this inference. Third, prior expectations can create problems when they overrule consideration of information altogether. If you decide on the basis of your college classmate's attributes not to meet your potential coworkers at all, you would be guilty of this error.

Once the social perceiver has decided what information is relevant to an inference, information must actually be collected. The individual must determine which bits of information from the wealth that is potentially available should be examined. For example, obviously you cannot meet everybody during your job interview visit, and so the people you do meet will help give you an impression of the qualities of your coworkers. But forming judgments on the basis of limited information can be thrown off when there are *biases in the information*. For example, if you are introduced to a particularly outgoing and friendly coworker, your impression of the attributes of the workers in the company may be falsely influenced toward the outgoing and friendly side.

One study that illustrates this point was conducted by Rothbart, Fulero, Jensen, Howard, and Birrell (1978). Subjects were given information about members of two groups, including the fact that some of the members had committed crimes. For one group, only moderate crimes were listed. In the second group, the same number of crimes were listed, but the list included several particularly severe ones such as rape and murder. Although the actual number of crimes was the same in the two groups, when asked to recall which crimes had been committed by members of which group, subjects misremembered that more individuals had committed crimes in the second group, that is, the group in which a few members had committed highly serious crimes. Presumably, the extreme examples of crimes had led to a strong association between that group and crime in general, leading to the incorrect inference that the second group had actually committed more crimes.

Inferences are also problematic when they are based on very little information. People are sometimes unaware that a *small sample* of information can actually produce a very biased picture. For example, if you are introduced to only two of your prospective coworkers who seem pleasant enough but you will actually be working with 20 individuals, there is the possibility that these two are not typical of the larger group. The other 18 may not be quite as pleasant. But sometimes people forget that they are dealing with very little information and make confident inferences nonetheless (see Nisbett & Kunda, 1986).

Even when people are warned that information may be biased, they sometimes fail to understand the full implications of that bias. For example, in one study (Hamill, Wilson, & Nisbett, 1980), researchers told subjects that they would be viewing a videotape of an interview with a prison guard. Some subjects were told that this prison guard was typical of most prison guards, whereas others were told that he was very different from most prison guards. In the third condition, subjects were not given information about how typical the guard was. Half the subjects then saw a tape in which the prison guard appeared as a highly compassionate, concerned individual. The other half saw a tape portraying him as an inhumane, macho, cruel person. Subjects were later asked a set of questions about the criminal justice system that included questions about what kind of people become prison guards. The results showed that subjects exposed to the interview of the humane guard were more favorable in their attitudes toward prison guards than were subjects who saw the interview with the inhumane prison guard. More important, subjects' inferences about prison guards were unaffected by whether or not they had been told that the interview with the prison guard was typical or not typical.

Consider an analogous situation in your hypothetical job interview. Suppose you wanted to meet some of your coworkers but were told that they were away at a seminar this week and unable to meet with you. But so that you could form some impressions of the workers of the company, you might be introduced to one or two of the company's employees from a neighboring office but with whom you would not be working directly. You might find that your judgments about your prospective coworkers would be influenced by the one or two individuals you do meet. You might fail to correct for the fact that these individuals actually have a different job and would not be in your work group at all. Therefore, your impressions of them might have little if anything to do with the attributes of your actual coworkers.

Another distinction that is important in understanding how people use information is between **statistical information** and **case history information.** Statistical information involves information about a large number of individuals, whereas case history information involves information about only a few specific individuals. It turns out that when people are exposed to both statistical information and a colorful case history, the case history often has more influence on their judgments (Taylor & Thompson, 1982). This occurs even when the statistical information is objectively better. For example, one type of information you might want to gather during your job interview is knowledge about how quickly people advance in the company. Clearly, the most appropriate information to look at is the statistical information about promotion rates for all the employees and for those in your division particularly. However, suppose you are told about Mark Comet, a particularly dynamic fellow who managed to go from clerk to associate vice president in three short years. It is very likely that the case history of Mark Comet's dramatic rise to fame and fortune within the company will bias your impression of how quickly people advance. It may lead you to ignore the more appropriate statistical information that would suggest that most people advance fairly slowly within the company.

Most of us seem to know that we really should use broadly based statistical information in making our judgments. People draw on statistics all the time when they are trying to make a persuasive argument, and a person can often be quite persuasive if he or she has statistical information available. However, generally speaking, when more engaging anecdotal case history evidence is present, people often ignore relevant statistical evidence and are instead overly persuaded by the case histories (Bar-Hillel & Fischoff, 1981; see Schwarz, Strack, Hilton, & Naderer, in press).

Integrating Information

The next task in the inference process involves bringing information together and combining it into a social judgment. When people's integrative capabilities are compared against rational models, it appears that the human judgment process is rather haphazard and does not closely follow the principles of a rational model.

Consider the example of college admissions. When there are many applicants and only a few openings, one must develop criteria for deciding which people to admit and which to reject. Most college admissions departments have a formula for admitting students which dictates how heavily they weight SAT scores, high school grades, letters of recommendation, the personal essay, and other sources of information. With such clear standards available, one would assume that the college admissions decision makers do a good job of using this formula to determine who will be admitted and who will not. However, it turns out that when there are clear standards for combining information into a judgment, a computer typically outperforms a human decision maker (Meehl, 1954; Dawes, Faust, & Meehl, 1989).

Why is this the case? Human decision makers have great faith in their abilities to make decisions. When asked what procedures they use to make decisions, they typically report being more consistent, using more pieces of information, and making more complex judgments than is actually the case. The reason that computers typically outperform human judges is that the computer consistently uses criteria established by people, weights information in a standard way, combines the information according to the formula, and reaches a judgment. The human decision maker, in contrast, may be swayed by pet theories or stereotypes that influence the information selected. Extensive studies have pitted human judges against the computer or other mechanical aids and have yielded the same conclusion (Meehl, 1954; Dawes et al., 1989): When people can specify the rules of inference they want to use to combine information into an overall decision or judgment, computers and other mechanical aids always do a better job of following these rules than human judges do.

Imagine how this process might work after your job interview. A small group of individuals who had met you during your visit would be assigned the task of deciding whether or not to hire you. Each person would have only a modest amount of information about you. One person might point out that you seemed nervous under pressure as evidenced by the fact that you dropped your roll on the floor during

Instead of being a rational, orderly process, decision-making often involves collecting and integrating information in line with a particular theory. People typically believe they are more consistent, use more information, and make more complex judgments than is actually the case.

lunch. Another, however, might argue that you may be a potential Mark Comet, given that you both have competitive tennis in your background. Another might point out that your transcript shows you have high grades in virtually every subject, suggesting great ability. The next person, however, might complain that if you did well in everything, you have not shown any special talents. In short, then, each evaluator may have certain idiosyncratic ways of viewing the information derived from your brief visit which he or she considers relevant to the overall judgment of whether or not you should be hired. It is indeed unnerving to realize one's fate often depends upon this type of decision-making process.

Judgments of Covariation

In addition to putting information together to form coherent impressions of people and events, we are also concerned with figuring out "what goes with what" in social life. Many of our beliefs involve statements about the rela-

tionship between things. For example, the adage "All work and no play makes Jack a dull boy" implies that working too hard and being dull are related and that playing and not being dull go together. Similarly, the statement "Blondes have more fun" implies a relationship between being blonde and having fun and between not being blonde and having less fun. Technically, such ideas about the associations between things are called judgments of **covariation.**

In making judgments about covariation, people are prone to certain errors. Consider the statement, "Blondes have more fun." As Figure 3–1 illustrates, the first step in assessing covariation is deciding what information is relevant. To determine if blondes actually have more fun, one needs to look at both blondes and non-blondes and examine the frequency with which they have fun and do not have fun. However, most people believe that cell A (fun-loving blondes) is the relevant information from which to determine whether blondes have more fun. They fail to recognize that the number of brunettes and redheads who have fun and do not

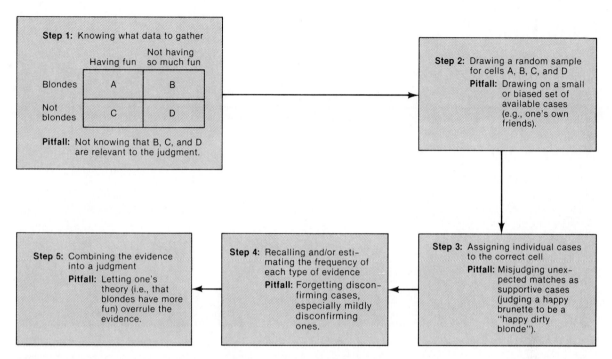

Step 1: Knowing what data to gather

	Having fun	Not having so much fun
Blondes	A	B
Not blondes	C	D

Pitfall: Not knowing that B, C, and D are relevant to the judgment.

Step 2: Drawing a random sample for cells A, B, C, and D
Pitfall: Drawing on a small or biased set of available cases (e.g., one's own friends).

Step 3: Assigning individual cases to the correct cell
Pitfall: Misjudging unexpected matches as supportive cases (judging a happy brunette to be a "happy dirty blonde").

Step 4: Recalling and/or estimating the frequency of each type of evidence
Pitfall: Forgetting disconfirming cases, especially mildly disconfirming ones.

Step 5: Combining the evidence into a judgment
Pitfall: Letting one's theory (i.e., that blondes have more fun) overrule the evidence.

Figure 3–1. The assessment of covariation and its pitfalls. Do blondes have more fun?

have fun are just as relevant as the number of blondes who have fun or do not. After all, to know if blondes have more fun, one needs to know that there are brunettes and redheads who are having less fun.

The second step in assessing covariation is gathering instances of blonde, brunette, and redheaded men and women to see if they are having fun or not. As we already noted, people are very poor at gathering information. They tend to draw on their own acquaintances, which may represent a biased sample. Most people assessing whether or not blondes have more fun would think about a few blonde friends and leave the information-gathering task at that.

The third step in the covariation process is classifying instances as to the type of evidence they represent, and again, the social perceiver's expectations can get in the way. Cases that contradict the proposed relationship may be mislabeled as supportive instances if they are ambiguous, or they may be dismissed as due to error or faulty information gathering if they are not ambiguous. Positive instances are more quickly

or easily identified and incorporated into the inference task (Klayman & Ha, 1987). Thus, for example, happy blondes will quickly be seen as relevant. Happy brunettes may be judged to be happy "dirty blondes" and happy redheads labeled "strawberry blondes." Unhappy blondes might be judged to have dyed their hair blonde—and thus be irrelevant to assessing whether or not blondes have more fun.

Information must next be put together, which requires recalling the frequency of each type of evidence. Unfortunately, the social perceiver remembers confirming cases well but tends to forget cases that contradict the relationship, especially those that are mildly disconfirming (Crocker, Hannah, & Weber, 1983). For example, the ecstatic raven-haired woman might be remembered, but the contented brown-haired individual might be forgotten.

In short, then, when people are making judgments of covariation, they rarely follow the rational model for so doing. Instead, prior expectations lead them to focus primarily on positive instances (such as fun-loving blondes) and to

We often think of decision-making processes as orderly and rational. However, under President Kennedy, the decision to invade Cuba (the Bay of Pigs invasion) was marked by faulty and insufficient information, unrealistically positive assessments of our country's fighting abilities, and gross underassessments of Cuba's resources and willingness to fight. In this case, the result was predictably a disaster.

pay relatively less attention to other evidence (Klayman & Ha, 1987). Thus, when a relationship between two variables is expected (for example, if the perceiver believes that blondes have more fun), a person is likely to overestimate the degree of relationship that exists between the two factors or impose a relationship when none exists. This intriguing phenomenon has been called illusory correlation.

Illusory Correlation. We were introduced briefly to the concept of **illusory correlation** in the preceding chapter. It will be recalled that at least two factors can produce an illusory correlation: *associative meaning,* in which two items are seen as belonging together because they "ought" to be on the basis of prior expectations, and *paired distinctiveness,* in which two items are thought to go together because they share some unusual feature. Thus, as we saw in the previous chapter, members of minority groups are often seen as having attributes stereotypically associated with their group because of their membership when, in fact, any given individual in the group may not exhibit the stereotypic be-

havior or may contradict it altogether (Hamilton & Gifford, 1976; McArthur & Friedman, 1980; Spears, van der Pligt, & Eiser, 1985). Similarly, we noted that individuals who are salient by virtue of an irrelevant factor such as appearance or seating position are thought to have a more potent role in the conversation in which they participate (Taylor & Fiske, 1978). Illusory correlations, then, often substitute for real correlations when people have prior expectations or theories about whether or not two factors go together.

Inference: A Summing Up

Overall, how well does the social perceiver fare on tasks of social inference? The evidence we just considered suggests that, when evaluated against rational models, social inference suffers from predictable errors and biases (Sherman, Judd, & Park, 1989; Taylor & Fiske, 1991). Social inference and its potential pitfalls are shown in Fig. 3–2. This evaluation prompts at least two reactions. The first is concern over disconcerting ways in which social perceivers let their prior expectations override and ignore relevant information. The second reaction is puzzlement. How do people manage in their social lives as well as they seem to if their social judgments are biased?

Some researchers are now coming to the opinion that rational models may often be inappropriate bases for evaluating social inference (e.g., McArthur & Baron, 1983; Funder, 1987; Swann, 1984). One reason is that the conditions of the real world are often such as to make use of a rational model nearly impossible. Much of the time social information is unreliable, biased, and incomplete. Even reliable, unbiased, and complete information may not be presented to the average social perceiver in a clear or usable fashion, and sometimes information that is needed is not available.

Consider, again, the use of the rational model in the judgment, Do blondes have more fun? Is it really worth it to you to get a sample of blondes, observe whether or not they have fun,

get a sample of brunettes and redheads, see whether or not they have fun, and calculate a statistical relationship? How many people would you need to survey? How long should you wait before you decide that any given person is not having fun? The conditions that maximize accuracy seldom occur in real life, and accordingly in many situations, social perceivers could not apply a rational model even if they were so inclined (see Crocker, 1981; Nisbett et al., 1982).

Rational models describe ideal inferential processes under conditions in which time and environment are frozen. Yet people make inferences in environments that are constantly changing and that provide feedback. Inferences are made in a world filled with consequences. Once ventured, an inaccurate inference may be corrected by the environment because other people or new information show it to be wrong. One can then change the inference. For example, if you believe a particular acquaintance is overly serious and say so to a friend, the friend

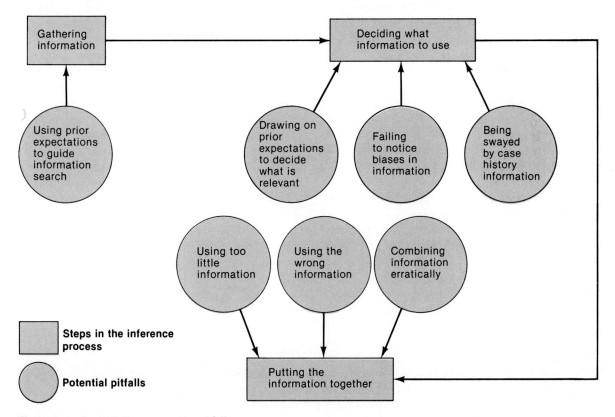

Figure 3–2. Social inference and its pitfalls.

may inform you about the acquaintance's silly side, forcing you to change your belief.

Many of the errors produced by faulty inferential procedures do not truly matter. For example, suppose you pick a particular group of friends on the basis of their flashy fun-filled lives rather than their personal qualities. Suppose you then find out that they are into drugs, fast cars, and hard rock, and these are activities you do not want to participate in. You can gradually withdraw from the circle of friends and make new ones without any long-term repercussions. Spending time with a particular group of people does not force you to spend the rest of your life with them.

Perhaps most important is the fact that the tasks facing the social perceiver may be fundamentally different from the tasks defined by rational models of inference. Rational models of inference place a premium on *accuracy* of inference. For the social perceiver, *efficiency,* that is, processing information quickly, may be at least as important. Consider the sheer volume of information that an individual encounters in a particular day. Even an act as simple as crossing the street requires watching the lights and signs, the flow of the traffic, and the pedestrians on one's own side and the other side of the street. If people truly had to make all their inferences using rational models of inference, they might still be plotting a course to follow across the street when the light changed back to "Don't Walk." In other words, rational models of inference assume that a person has time to do inferential work, and given the blooming, buzzing confusion of the real world, time is a very expensive commodity.

Consequently, people draw on their preexisting conceptions of people and situations and use inferential shortcuts to make social judgments quickly and efficiently. This is not to say that the errors we have just documented in the social inference process are inconsequential. Indeed, they can often have problematic consequences in that people clearly make what are objectively wrong decisions and inferences. Improving the inference process, therefore, is an important priority for social cognition researchers. But it must be done in the context of understanding the processes people typically use,

rather than the rational models of inference developed by statisticians (see Lord, Lepper, & Preston, 1984; Fong, Krantz, & Nisbett, 1986; Nisbett, Fong, Lehman, & Chang, 1987).

To begin to understand how the social perceiver actually forms inferences and why those inferences do not correspond to the assumptions of rational models requires an important observation. The act of bringing information together and solving a problem, as we have noted, can be an extremely time-consuming task involving substantial processing capabilities. When one's attention is absorbed in forming a particular inference, there is relatively little attention that is available to perform other tasks such as monitoring the environment successfully, solving other problems, and the like. However, memory seems to have almost a limitless capacity. Think, for example, of the number of rock songs for which you know all the lyrics. The number may total in the hundreds or even thousands. Or think of all the friends you have and everything that you know about each of them. These simple tasks point out the astonishing amount of information that we are able to carry in our heads and retrieve from memory when we need it. Thus, problem solving is very costly in that it consumes attention and drains resources for other tasks, whereas memory appears to be nearly limitless and does not drain resources for other tasks. For example, knowing a great deal about one friend does not preclude learning a great deal about another friend. This important difference is fundamental to how people actually make inferences. Rather than engaging in elaborate and often time-consuming problem solving for each individual task that the environment presents, instead people often draw on the knowledge that they have stored in memory to interpret the environment that confronts them, namely, their schemas.

SCHEMAS

What we have so far been referring to as prior expectations goes under the general term *schemas.* As we saw in Chapter 2, a schema is an organized, structured set of cognitions about some concept or stimulus which includes knowledge about the concept or stimulus, some relations among the various cognitions about it, and some specific examples (Fiske & Taylor, 1991). As Chapter 2 made clear, schemas can be about particular people, social roles, the self, attitudes about particular objects, stereotypes about groups, or perceptions of common events.

Schemas are important because people draw on them to interpret the environment. That is, each time we are confronted with a new situation, we don't try to understand it afresh. Instead we draw on our knowledge of past similar situations for making interpretations, and this is the way schemas help us to process information. They help us to recognize what aspects of a situation or stimulus are important. They add structure and organization to information. Schemas enable us to remember information better, to organize details, and to process information relevant to the schema very quickly. Schemas can sometimes fill in gaps and knowledge as well as help people interpret and evaluate new information. An example of how schemas and theories can bias information in a self-serving way appears in Box 3–1.

BOX 3–1

Why I Will Never Get Divorced: The Construction of Self-serving Causal Theories

The process of forming social inferences is biased by preexisting theories, as we have seen. Many of these theories are self-serving ones. Ziva Kunda (1987) suggests that people generate and evaluate causal theories in a self-serving manner, constructing theories that are consistent with the belief that good things will happen to them and bad things will not.

For example, upon learning that the divorce rate for first marriages is 50 percent, most people predict that they will not be in that 50 percent, but rather will remain married to their spouse for their lifetime. They convince themselves that this is the case by highlighting their personal attributes that might be associated with a stable marriage and downplaying the significance of or actively refuting information that might suggest a vulnerability to divorce. Thus, for example, one might point to one's parents' 40-year marriage, the close family life that existed in one's early childhood, and the fact that one's high school relationship lasted a full four years as evidence for a likely stable marriage. The fact that one's husband has already been divorced once, a factor that predicts a second divorce, might be interpreted not only as not leading to divorce in one's own case, but as a protective factor ("He does not want this marriage to fail like the last one, so he's working especially hard to keep our relationship strong").

To test this point, Kunda (1987) gave college student subjects a description of a target person and a list of the target's attributes. The list included such facts as the target was extroverted, dependent, religious, and conservative. Other information specified whether or not the target's mother had worked or been in the home while the person was young, and whether or not the target person had had at least one serious relationship before entering college. A third of the subjects read that the target person was divorced, a third that the person was happily married, and a third were given no information about the outcome of the marriage. Subjects then rated each of the target's attributes on a scale ranging from 1 ("made divorce much more likely") to 9 ("made stable marriage much more likely"). After completing this questionnaire, subjects were asked to indicate their own standing on each of the background attributes and the likelihood that they would end up in a divorce.

The results showed that subjects judged attributes on which they matched the target person as better for marriage than attributes on which they did not match the target person. The ability to draw seemingly rational relationships between our own assets and good events and to argue away associations between our own attributes and negative events helps us to maintain the beliefs that we want to hold.

Organization of Schemas

An important feature of schemas is that they often have some hierarchical organization. They have some abstract and general elements, and some more concrete, specific ones. Suppose we had a schema of a "cocktail party." We know that cocktail parties usually are held in the late afternoon or evening, usually in someone's home. They have guests and usually a host and a hostess; they have some food and a lot of alcoholic drinks (all of which are more likely to be prepared and served by the host and hostess rather than by the guests). Normally people interact by standing and talking to each other rather than by watching one common event (like a singer) or sleeping or running in circles. In short, we have a clear, well-developed, somewhat abstract picture in our minds about a "cocktail party." It has a standard sequence, a number of elements, and clear causal interrelationships among them.

At a more specific level, the schema might well have different categories of cocktail parties, all of which would be clearly distinct. For example, a wine-and-cheese party held at the opening of an art gallery would be clearly different from the weekly Saturday night bashes at the country club, where all the local businesspeople and their spouses get together and drink too much, or from a formal diplomatic reception at a foreign embassy. At a still more specific level, our schema might include several specific parties we have attended. All told, we might have a hierarchical schema of a "cocktail party" that would include a general, abstract concept covering all kinds of cocktail parties we have gone to.

So far, our discussion of schemas makes them sound very orderly. However, often the associations contained within a schema more closely resemble a tangled web than a hierarchy (Cantor & Kihlstrom, 1987). For example, a politician, a con man, and a clown are all examples of extroverts. Being socially skilled is associated with being a politician, a con man, or a clown, but being self-confident is associated with being a politician or a con man, but not necessarily with being a clown. Thus, the more specific attributes embedded in a schema (socially skilled, self-confident) may overlap with many or few of the upper-level concepts (politician, clown, con man) (Anderson & Klatsky, 1987). Social categories, then, are related in very flexible and complex ways, not always in neat, tidy, hierarchical fashion.

Individual Differences in Schemas

To some extent, we all share the same schemas. Most of us have schemas about teachers, extroverts, and check cashing. However, many schemas are personal and reflect individual interests and values. For example, a person who loves the out-of-doors may have schemas for hiking, volleyball, and sailing, whereas the stay-at-home television watcher will not. Having a schema for a particular domain will, in turn, greatly modify how one processes information. For example, a veteran baseball coach will have a richer and more detailed set of baseball schemas and will impute more meaning to an outfielder's play than will a foreigner attending his first baseball game (Lurigio & Carroll, 1985; Markus, Smith, & Moreland, 1985). A person to whom honesty is important will be more likely to judge other people according to whether they are dishonest or not than will someone who is not as concerned with the trait of honesty (Cantrambone & Markus, 1987). To summarize, then, some schemas may be widely shared within a given culture, whereas others may be quite idiosyncratic.

SCHEMATIC PROCESSING

Advantages

Schemas are important because they help us process an enormous amount of information swiftly and economically. Indeed, schemas make processing more efficient in several different ways. They help us remember information, interpret new information, draw inferences from it, and evaluate whether or not we agree with it. They help us fill in gaps in our knowledge by suggesting what is likely to be true. And they help us prepare for the future by structuring our expectations about what is likely to happen. These advantages of schematic processing have been demonstrated in a wide variety of studies (see Fiske & Taylor, 1991; Markus & Zajonc, 1986, for reviews).

A schema can aid recall. Memory often works best when we can bring back some schematic representation of past events or people, because the schema will bring many details along with it. For example, Cohen (1981) presented subjects with a videotape of a woman and her husband sitting in their home. Half were told that the woman was a librarian, and half that she was a waitress. Some of the features of the woman fit the schema of a librarian (as measured separately), such as wearing glasses, eating salad, drinking wine, and playing the piano. Others fit the schema of a waitress, such as having a bowling ball in the room and no bookshelves and eating a chocolate birthday cake. Later the subjects were asked to recall the details of the videotape. They remembered the schema-consistent details better, no matter whether recall was assessed immediately or a week later.

But schema-inconsistent material is not always recalled poorly. Both schema-consistent and schema-inconsistent material are remembered much better than things that are simply irrelevant to the schema (Hastie & Kumar, 1979; Brewer, Dull, & Lui, 1981); this may be because it is difficult to learn material that is irrelevant to a schema.

Sometimes information that contradicts a schema is better recalled than information that is consistent with a schema. This is especially likely when a person has a very poorly developed or an extremely well-developed schema. People who are unfamiliar with a schema and attempting to learn it show an initial advantage for remembering schema-inconsistent information (Ruble & Stangor, 1986). Similarly, people who are highly familiar with a domain may more easily recognize inconsistencies. People with moderately well-formed schemas may be most attentive to consistent information (Higgins & Bargh, 1987). Consider, for example, the impressions that might be formed of Harry, a policeman who raises kittens and does needlepoint in his spare time. Those just meeting Harry and those who know him very well may be especially attentive to the schema-inconsistent behaviors, whereas those with a moderately well-developed conception of Harry may attend more to his schema-consistent behavior, such as his concern for abiding by the law or helping people in need (Borgida & DeBono, 1989).

Speed of processing information is affected by schemas. Markus (1977) identified subjects with self-schemas of being independent, self-schemas of being dependent, and neither self-schema. She read them sentences about certain independent or dependent behaviors. People with self-schemas were able to indicate more quickly than those without self-schemas whether or not the behavior was typical of them. Processing time was much longer for schema-inconsistent than consistent information. But not all research finds that schemas speed processing up. In some cases, evoking a schema slows things down by introducing a more complex mass of information that must be processed (Fiske & Taylor, 1991). So, for example, if you are strongly ambivalent about your dependency needs, you might take more time to decide if a dependent behavior is typical of you than would someone who is aschematic with respect to dependency.

Another important attribute of schematic processing is that some schema-related inferences appear to occur almost automatically without any conscious effort on an individual's part. For example, if a particular person you meet seems to be especially friendly, you may automatically attribute other attributes associated with friendliness to him, such as kindness and warmth, and be completely unaware that you have done so. These automatic effects are most likely to occur if the information in the environment strongly suggests a particular schema, or if there is some kind of affective or emotional relationship involved (Bargh, 1984; Smith & Lerner, 1986; Fazio, Sanbonmatsu, Powell, & Kardes, 1986).

A schema can help us fill in missing information when there are gaps in our knowledge. If we read about a policeman but have no information about his clothing, we imagine him to be wearing a blue uniform. We assume a nurse will be warm and caring, and a queen to be rather aloof and haughty. Missing information is filled in by adding schema-consistent details, even when we must invent them.

Schemas also help us interpret new information. For example, when a pediatrician diagnoses a child as having mumps, it enables her to make a whole series of other inferences with confidence: how the child got the disease, what symptoms should be present, what the course of the disease will be, what treatment is best, and so on. To a person with no schema for mumps, none of this would be possible. The problem would just seem mysterious. Schemas allow confident inferences about matters that would otherwise not be clear. This effect seems to occur more for strong schemas than weak ones, however. When people use weakly developed categories, such as day people versus night people, the schema itself seems to be weakened by new and potentially irrelevant information (Fiske & Neuberg, 1990).

Schemas also contain expectations for what should happen. These expectations in turn can determine how pleasant or unpleasant we find a particular situation. When experience matches expectations, the result may be pleasant, whereas violations of expectations are often experienced as unpleasant. Suppose a black student who had worked to educate himself was nonetheless unable to find a job at his level of expertise. This experience might violate his expectations and would be likely to make him quite angry. A sense of deprivation relative to expectation has been cited as one of the causes of ghetto riots and other forms of social rebellion (Sears & McConahay, 1973).

Schemas can also include affect, that is, the feelings we have about the domain. Consequently, use of a particular schema can produce an emotional response, termed *schema-driven affect*. For example, most of us have a fairly well-developed schema for "politician." It may include information about what the politician does in his or her job, and what kinds of people are attracted to being a politician. The schema will also include any affective responses we have to the concept of politician. For example, some of us will feel positively about politicians, thinking of them as helpful statesmen, whereas others may feel negatively about politicians, thinking of them as sly, self-serving, power-hungry individuals. When information in the environment fits a particular schema, then it will trigger the affect attached to that schema (Fiske & Neuberg, 1990). The affect that is triggered by a schema is an efficient affective processing device: One can say "I know that type and I know how I feel about him or her" (Westen, 1988; Pavelchak, 1989; Fiske et al., 1987).

Under some circumstances, bringing a schema to bear on an object or an event can actually change the feelings one has toward that object or event. A series of studies by Tesser (see Tesser & Conlee, 1975; Millar & Tesser, 1986) suggests that simply thinking about something with a schema in mind can intensify the affect one feels for that object. If, for example, you feel that a professor belittled the comments you made in class, the longer you think about it, the more upset you are likely to become. Under other circumstances, however, schemas may make affect simply more complex, not more extreme (Linville & Jones, 1980; Linville, 1982). For example, if a good friend of yours snaps at you one day, this behavior may produce a fairly complex evaluation. You have so much information about your friend and about yourself that coming up with an explanation for this behavior may be difficult (Gilovich, 1987). Your evaluation of the incidence may be complex.

Liabilities of Schemas

All these advantages of schematic processing have their accompanying disadvantages, and many of them are precisely the errors and biases that we discussed at the beginning of this chapter. The tendencies to be overly accepting of information that fits a schema or theory, to fill in gaps in thinking by adding elements that are schema consistent, to apply schemas even when they do not fit very well, and to be unwilling to change schemas can all be *liabilities*. We can easily be misled by oversimplifications.

There are so many familiar examples of the dangers of this kind of stereotyping that it hardly seems necessary to belabor the point. Everyone knows that people frequently behave in ways contrary to the stereotype generally held about their groups. Yet schematic processing can lead the perceiver to some dangerously false inferences about individual members of the group. (We will discuss these issues in somewhat more detail in Chapters 11 and 12). The examples given of "learning from the past" (see Box 3–2) illustrate some of the deficiencies of schematic processing.

Implicit personality theories, a type of schema we discussed in Chapter 2, can also lead to errors, since there is a strong tendency for people to infer from the presence of one trait the presence of others. Knowing someone is intelligent causes most people to expect the person also to be imaginative, clever, active, conscientious, deliberate, and reliable. Knowing someone is inconsiderate leads most people to expect him or her also to be irritable, boastful, cold, hypercritical, and so on. These inferences are not derived logically from the given trait; they are based on assumptions about personality. In-

---

BOX 3–2

Learning from History

A number of writers have observed how political leaders often apply "the lessons of history" when arriving at decisions about foreign policy. The "lessons" they apply frequently turn out to be analogies from events that occurred in their formative years (Jervis, 1976). John F. Kennedy was very impressed during his years in college, in the late 1930s, by the British blunder of appeasing Hitler at Munich.

In 1938, British and French leaders held a highly publicized meeting with Adolf Hitler in Munich, Germany, to discuss his desire to expand the borders of Germany. They arranged a compromise with him that allowed the Germans to take over the Sudetenland, the region of Czechoslovakia closest to Germany. The British prime minister returned to London, triumphantly announcing that they had ensured "peace in our time." In just a few short months, of course, Hitler invaded Poland and Belgium, not in the least bit satisfied by the territory he had been given at Munich.

The "lesson of Munich" was that dictators need to be confronted and stopped or they will continue to make inroads. Kennedy applied this "Munich schema" to the civil wars in Southeast Asia in the early 1960s and came to the conclusion that America needed to stand up militarily to the Communists there, or other "dominos" would fall, just as

they had in Europe after Munich. In contrast, a "Vietnam schema" has become common since the end of that war. It describes the dangers to the United States of becoming involved in faraway civil wars and nationalist, anti-imperialist revolutions in the Third World.

The power of such schemas to dictate preferences about current foreign policy is illustrated in an experiment by Gilovich (1981). He presented two hypothetical case studies of a small democratic country threatened by an aggressive, totalitarian neighbor. They differed only in having salient Munich-like, pre–World War II symbols as opposed to those associated with Vietnam. The first case study mentioned in passing Winston Churchill Hall, *blitzkrieg*, boxcars, and FDR; the second case study mentioned Dean Rusk Hall, chinook helicopters, small boats, and LBJ. Otherwise the two cases were the same, and clearly hypothetical. Subjects given the irrelevant allusions to pre–World War II events were more likely to support intervention than were those given the Vietnam allusions. Exactly the same facts could be interpreted in two quite different ways, with very different implications, depending on whether the irrelevant cues had induced them to apply their Munich or their Vietnam schemas.

telligence does not necessarily denote activity, nor does inconsiderateness denote irritability. The tendency to make these assumptions is sometimes called the **logical error,** because people see certain traits as going together and assume that someone who has one of them also has the others.

So schematic processing has the advantage of speed and efficiency and of making events comprehensible and predictable. It has the disadvantage of leading to wrong interpretations, inaccurate expectations, and inflexible modes of response.

MENTAL SHORTCUTS: USING COGNITIVE HEURISTICS

Because problem-solving activity typically consumes so much time and attention, people often resort to mental shortcuts that reduce seemingly complex problem solving to more simple judgments. These shortcuts help people invoke their schemas to process information in the environment. These shortcuts have been called **heuristics** (Tversky & Kahneman, 1974).

The Representativeness Heuristic

Is John, the new guy in your math class, really the incurable romantic he seems to be, or is he a cad who moves on every woman he meets? Is Linda a dependable person who can be counted on to do her share of a joint project or not? The act of identifying people or events as examples of particular schemas is fundamental to all social inference and behavior. That is, the question, "What is it?" must be answered before any other cognitive task can be performed. A mental shortcut called the *representativeness heuristic* provides a rapid method for accomplishing this task.

Basically, the representativeness heuristic matches information in the environment against schemas to determine the likelihood that the match is appropriate. Consider the following description: "Steve is very shy and withdrawn, invariably helpful, but with little interest in people or the world of reality. A meek and tidy soul, he has a need for order and structure and a passion for detail" (Tversky & Kahneman, 1974). Suppose you are now asked to guess Steve's occupation. Is he a farmer, a circus clown, a librarian, a con artist, or a pediatrician?

With adequate information about the number and characteristics of the people in these different occupations, one could conceivably estimate the likelihood of a meek clown, a shy con artist, and so on. This task, however, would likely take a long time, and good information on which to form these judgments would undoubtedly be lacking. In such cases, the representativeness heuristic provides a quick solution. One decides whether Steve is representative of (or similar to) the average person in each of the occupational categories and makes one's judgment about his occupation accordingly. Students given this task usually guessed that Steve is a librarian because the description of Steve is *representative* of attributes that are stereotypically associated with librarians (Tversky & Kahneman, 1974).

The representativeness heuristic, then, helps one to decide if a particular person or event is an example of a particular schema. However, this quite rapid method of identifying people and events is occasionally fallible because people sometimes fail to take into account other important qualifying information. For example, if Steve lives in a town with lots of farmers and only one librarian, the likelihood that he is a farmer and not a librarian is very high. The representativeness heuristic would not incorporate this qualifying information. As we noted earlier, people often ignore relevant statistical information that they ought to incorporate into their inferences. Under these kinds of circumstances then, use of the representativeness heuristic would probably produce an incorrect answer.

The Availability Heuristic

Sometimes we try to answer such questions as "How often does a person break a leg skiing?" or "How many college students are psychology majors?" These are questions about the frequency of events or the likelihood that a particular event will happen. A common way that people answer such questions is to use examples that come to mind. If you can think of lots of college students who are psychology majors among your friends or acquaintances, you may assume that there are many psychology majors on campus. Or if you can think of several people who broke their legs skiing, you may assume that the chances of breaking your leg skiing are rather high. Using the ease of remembering examples or the amount of information you can quickly remember as a guide to making an inference is called using the *availability heuristic* (Tversky & Kahneman, 1973).

As is the case with the representativeness heuristic, little cognitive work need be performed to accomplish this task. If you have no trouble thinking of psychology majors among your acquaintances, you will probably assume that a great many people in college are psychology majors, whereas if you have trouble bringing to mind examples of psychology majors, you may conclude that relatively few individuals are psychology majors.

Under many circumstances, use of the availability heuristic produces correct answers. After all, when examples of something can be easily brought to mind, it is usually because there are lots of them. Therefore, availability is often a good estimate of frequency. However, there are also biasing factors that can increase or decrease the availability of some kinds of phenomena or events without altering their actual overall frequency. For example, if you are a psychology major, many of your friends and acquaintances are likely to be psychology majors as well, and consequently you will have relatively little difficulty bringing examples of psychology majors to mind. Because of this bias among your friends, you are likely to overestimate the frequency of psychology majors. In contrast, another student who is a chemistry major and who spends most of his time hanging out with chemists or physicists would probably underestimate the number of psychology majors on campus, because he cannot bring examples of many psychology majors to mind (Gabrielcik & Fazio, 1984).

The availability heuristic, then, enables you to answer questions like "how many are there" or "how often does something happen" on the basis of how quickly or easily examples can be retrieved from memory. The ease with which the process can be accomplished, or the volume of information that can be retrieved quickly, determines the answer.

The Simulation Heuristic

Suppose you borrowed your father's car during a college vacation and smashed it up following a party you attended. How would you answer the question, "What is Dad going to think when he finds out I've smashed up the car?" You may think through what you know about your father and his reaction to crises, run through this information in your mind, and generate several possibilities. The ease with which particular endings come to mind is used to judge what is likely to happen. Your father could refuse to pay your college tuition next term, or he could ignore the whole thing, but in your mind it is easiest to imagine that he will strongly suggest that you find a job so that you can help pay for the car. This inferential technique is known as the *simulation heuristic* (Kahneman & Tversky, 1982).

The simulation heuristic may be used for a wide variety of tasks, including prediction ("What will Dad say?"), causality ("Was I driving badly or was the other guy driving badly?") (Wells & Gavanski, 1989; Wells, Taylor, & Turtle, 1987), and affective responses (Kahneman & Miller, 1986; Landman, 1987). On this latter point, consider the situation of a near miss.

Mr. Crane and Mr. Tees were scheduled to leave the airport on different flights, at the same time. They traveled from town in the same limousine, were caught in a traffic jam, and arrived at the airport 30 minutes after the scheduled departure time of their flights.

Mr. Crane is told his flight left on time. Mr. Tees is told that his flight was delayed, and just left 5 minutes ago.

Who is more upset? Mr. Crane or Mr. Tees. (Kahneman & Tversky, 1982, p. 203)

Virtually everyone says, "Mr. Tees." Why? Presumably, one can imagine no way that Mr. Crane could have made his plane, whereas, were it not for that one long light or the slow baggage man or the illegally parked car or the error in the posted departure gate, Mr. Tees would have made it. Thus the simulation heuristic and its ability to generate "if only" conditions can be used to understand the psychology of near misses and the frustration, regret, grief, or indignation they may produce. Abnormal or exceptional events lead people to imagine alternatives that are normal, and consequently dissimilar to the actual outcome (Kahneman & Miller, 1986). The contrast between the exceptional circumstance and the normal situation intensifies the emotional reaction to the unusual situation.

People simulate the future as well as the past, and imagining hypothetic future events makes those events seem more likely (Anderson & Godfrey, 1987). For example, Gregory, Cialdini, and Carpenter (1982) contacted residents of two middle-class neighborhoods on behalf of a local cable television company. Half the residents were given information about the cable company, whereas the other half was instructed to imagine themselves experiencing the benefits and features of the cable service. Those who imagined themselves using the service were more likely to want the cable service, they had more favorable attitudes toward cable, they intended to acquire additional information, and they reported that they would be more likely to subscribe to the cable service in the future. In addition, more subjects in the imagination condition actually accepted a free week of service and subsequently subscribed to the cable service than did those who simply received information about it. Thus, imagining alternatives

via simulation can have a broad impact on expectations, causal attributions, impressions, and the affect experienced in situations (Wells & Gavanski, 1989).

The Anchoring Heuristic

Imagine that someone asks you to guess how many people attended the UCLA-USC football game last night in the Los Angeles Coliseum. You have absolutely no idea, but you do know that last week's game in the Coliseum drew a crowd of 55,000. Assuming that the UCLA-USC contest drew a much bigger crowd, you might guess that 70,000 people attended. In this case, you have no information about the specific event in question, but you use information about a similar event as a reference point or "anchor." You then adjust reference information to reach a final conclusion (Tversky & Kahneman, 1974).

In fact, when people are attempting to form judgments from ambiguous information, they will often reduce ambiguity by starting with the beginning reference point or anchor and then adjusting it. Social judgments are no exception. Information about social situations is often ambiguous, and therefore anchors can be helpful when one is trying to interpret the meaning of ambiguous information and behavior (Plous, 1989; Cervone & Peake, 1986).

A common anchor that is used in social perception is the self. For example, suppose someone asks you whether Ellen, a classmate of yours, is smart. It may be easiest for you to answer this question by trying to decide if Ellen is smarter than you or not. If she seems to be smarter than you are, you may decide that she is very smart. But if she seems to be not as quick as you are, you may decide that she is not very bright. Your judgment about Ellen's intelligence, then, is based not on her absolute standing on an I.Q. test or some other objective information, but rather on whether or not she seems brighter or less bright than yourself (see Markus & Smith, 1981; Markus, Smith, & Moreland, 1985). The anchoring heuristic, then, provides people with a departure point for a judgment

T A B L E   3 – 1

SOME HEURISTIC STRATEGIES FOR MAKING JUDGMENTS UNDER UNCERTAINTY

Representativeness	Probability judgment	Representativeness is a judgment of how relevant A is to B; high relevance yields high estimates that A originates from B	Deciding that George (A) must be an engineer because he looks and acts like your stereotype of engineers (B)
Availability	Frequency of probability judgments	Availability is the estimate of how frequently or likely a given instance or occurrence is, based on how easily or quickly an association or examples come to mind	Estimating the divorce rate on the basis of how quickly one can think of examples of divorced friends
Simulation	Expectations, causal attributions, impressions, and affective experience	Simulation is the ease with which a hypothetical scenario can be constructed	Getting angry because of a frustrating event on the basis of how easily one can imagine the situation occurring otherwise
Adjustment and anchoring	Estimates of position on a dimension	Anchoring and adjustment is the process of estimating some value by starting with some initial value and then adjusting it to the new instance	Judging another person's productivity based on one's own level of productivity

task that might otherwise be ambiguous. In social judgment tasks, the self seems to be a common anchor. For a description of the various heuristic strategies, see Table 3–1.

WHICH SCHEMAS ARE USED?

Suppose you observe two people feverishly searching a room. How do you decide what they are doing? In other words, how do you select which schemas to apply to the situation? Sometimes appropriate schemas are suggested by the nature of the information itself. For example, if you know the two people in question are roommates who keep gerbils and you see an empty cage, you may guess that they are trying to find their missing gerbils. Under other circumstances, information in the environment may not immediately suggest what schemas to invoke. Are the two searchers looking for something that they have lost? Are they burglars? Are they undercover policemen conducting a drug bust? In this section, we consider the factors that influence which schemas people use to interpret information.

Natural Contours

The most obvious and probably also the most powerful determinant of which schema is used is the structure of the information itself. That is, schemas follow the *natural contours* of the information we receive. If you are watching a football game, you will employ your schemas for football games, football players, and cheerleaders for interpreting what is going on in the field. The information in the environment makes it obvious which schemas to use, and you would not invoke your schemas for cocktail parties, tennis games, or final examinations to interpret what is going on.

But people cannot absorb everything in their environment at once. They tend to perceive behavior in coherent, meaningful chunks of action that are marked off by **breakpoints** (Newtson, 1976; Newtson, Hairfield, Bloomingdale, & Cutino, 1987). For example, imagine watching an outfielder break into a run at the sound of the bat hitting the ball; he dashes to the outfield wall, leaps up, catches the ball, lands on his feet, sets for a throw, and then throws the ball to the third baseman to stop the baserunner. Newtson argues that we perceive such a flow of activity as a sequence of separate behaviors, not as one continuous act. Breakpoints occur between the separate actions and mark where one ends and another begins.

Breakpoints are inherent in any stream of behavior; they are not imposed on it by the perceiver. In this sense, they follow the natural contours of the information we receive. To identify these breakpoints, Newtson had subjects watch a film and push a button to indicate when they thought one segment had ended and another had begun. This method is quite reliable: perceivers agree on where certain breakpoints occur in films of someone in action, and they perceive the same breakpoints again when shown the film five weeks later. It also seems quite easy and comfortable for subjects to do. All this argues that the breakpoints occur naturally within the flow of behavior in a given scene.

When do breakpoints occur? Some ingenious research has tied them to changes in behavior, specifically to changes in the movement of different parts of the body (Newtson, Engquist, & Bois, 1977). Breakpoints also occur when the state of objects associated with the person changes. For example, breakpoints would be perceived when a baseball's trajectory is suddenly interrupted by the outfielder's glove, when it disappears from view, or when it suddenly flies through the air back toward the infield. And people use more breakpoints when they encounter unexpected actions or have little prior information, presumably because they need the breakpoints to try to understand the meaning of the action more fully (Wilder, 1986; Graziano, Moore, & Collins, 1988). Breakpoints convey the most information about a sequence of behavior. When the breakpoint moments of a film are shown to subjects as still photos in order, they convey the story almost as well as the full movie itself. People also seem to remember the breakpoints better than any other moments during the sequence.

The more general point, then, is that we do not simply take in environmental information whole when forming an inference. Rather, we absorb meaningful, structured chunks of it. The chunking process is partly imposed on the flow of behavior by the perceiver's own experiences and expectations. And partly the chunks reflect the real changes within the behavioral sequence.

Salience

Environmental salience is also a factor that influences which schemas people use to interpret information. As we saw in Chapter 2, sometimes our interpretation of other people's behavior is influenced by what information about them is made salient by the environment. For example, if Linda is the only woman in a group that is otherwise composed of men, her sex will be particularly salient, and therefore her behavior may be interpreted according to a gender schema for women (Taylor, Fiske, Close, Anderson, & Ruderman, 1978). For example, her request for help from a newcomer to the group might be interpreted as a sign of dependence, a trait sometimes associated with women. However, if Linda is in a group composed of several men and several women, her behavior toward the newcomer might not be interpreted in gender-related terms. Instead, a schema for "newcomers" might be invoked, and her gesture might simply be interpreted as an effort to make the newcomer feel at home. Salience, then, can influence the processing of information in the environment by determining which schemas will be invoked to interpret information that may be subject to multiple interpretations.

The salient physical features that people have, such as their race and sex, appear to be particularly predominant in cueing schemas. Indeed, physical features may take priority over other features, such as social schemas (Deaux & Lewis, 1984). From the earliest moments of perception, people use age, race, sex, attractiveness, and similar qualities to form impressions, and indeed may do so quite automatically. One study, for example (Devine, 1989), found immediate and virtually automatic stereotyped reactions to black-and-white stimulus persons. Surprisingly, both high- and low-prejudice people were equally likely to show these automatic stereotyped reactions. However, when circumstances were provided that allowed for more time to consider the information, low-prejudice people actively rejected the automatic stereotyped responses and replaced them with equality-oriented thoughts. The unnerving conclusion is that schemas, including negatively toned ones, quite automatically guide the processing of information and that tolerance, open-mindedness, and freedom from prejudice come only with enough time to notice that one must adopt such cautions.

Roles

When one seeks ways to organize information about people, role schemas probably take precedence over other kinds of information such as traits. There are many ways to be extraverted (e.g., such as like a comedian, a political leader, or a bully), but there are relatively fewer ways to fulfill a concrete role (such as being a politician). Consequently, role schemas are informative, they are very rich and well articulated, providing greater information across a wide range of dimensions. They are also more distinctive than traits, leading to more unique associations. Knowing that someone is a cheerleader, for example, says a lot about exactly how she is outgoing and in what situations she is outgoing, whereas just being told that she is an extravert does not convey nearly as much information.

Moreover, role schemas are more useful than traits for recall (Bond & Brockett, 1987; Bond & Sedikides, 1988). To see the advantage of role in memory, think of all the people in a particular seminar that you are taking. How easy was that? Now think of all the self-centered people you know. How easy is that? Chances are, the social groupings lead to the generation of more names more quickly than do traits. People seem to think of others first within a role context, and only then according to personality traits.

Primacy

Often, which schema is used to interpret a person or a situation will be determined very early by information present in the situation. For example, when introduced to a friend with the words, "This is George, he's running for student body president," one is inclined to think of George and his subsequent behavior in terms of whether or not he would be a good student body president, and to consider his behavior as determined at least in part by the fact that he is running for office. One reason why **primacy** is so important is that when people have an organizing structure from the very outset, it influences the interpretation of information as that information is taken in. When this occurs, the effects are more powerful than if the schema is applied afterward (e.g., Wyer, Srull, Gordon, & Hartwick, 1982; see Fiske & Taylor, 1990, for a review).

Priming

When a schema has been recently used, it is likely to be used again to interpret new information. Suppose you have just come from a classroom discussion in which the professor castigated the class for its lack of commitment to intellectual pursuits. Walking across campus, you meet Stan who enthusiastically tells you that he has just been appointed to the cheering squad. How do you interpret the enthusiasm? In the context of the prior lecture, you may regard his behavior as shallow and unintellectual. In contrast, if you had just come from a discussion of the importance of being a well-rounded college student, you might interpret the behavior as a sign of extracurricular interests. This tendency for recently used schemas to be employed in unrelated subsequent situations is called the **priming effect.**

A study that demonstrates this point was conducted by Higgins, Rholes, and Jones (1977). Subjects were first exposed to trait words designed to invoke either the positive schema of adventurousness (such as brave) or the negative schema of recklessness (such as foolish, careless). In a second study ostensibly unrelated to the first task, they read about Donald who shot rapids, drove in a demolition derby, and planned to learn skydiving. People who had previously been exposed to the positive schema of "adventurousness" evaluated Donald more positively than did people who had been primed with the negative schema of "recklessness." This priming effect did not occur when the primed schemas were not applicable to the description of Donald (such as neat or shy).

Essentially, then, activating a schema puts it at the top of the mental heap, making it easily accessible for interpreting new information (Srull & Wyer, 1979; Wyer & Srull, 1980, 1981). However, an important qualification is that previously activated schemas are only invoked to explain new information when the schema is relevant to the new information. When new information is irrelevant to the primed schemas, those schemas are not used to interpret it (Higgins & Bargh, 1987; Erdley & D'Agostino, 1988).

Importance

Which schemas are used to interpret information by the environment and how many schemas are called up can also be influenced by the importance of the information being processed. When the circumstances for making inferences are relatively trivial, people may make schematic inferences relatively quickly with little thought. They may, for example, invoke a schema on the basis of which information is most salient. However, in circumstances when the outcome of an inference is important, or a person is accountable for the inference, that person may spend more time studying the situation and invoke more schemas, yielding more complex inferences (Chaiken, 1980; Harkness, DeBono, & Borgida, 1985; Tetlock & Boettger, 1989; Tetlock, Skitka, & Boettger, 1989). For example, if asked your impression of a fellow classmate, you may answer relatively quickly that he or she seems nice, if your judgment of the person has no particular importance to you. However, if you are trying to decide whether or not to ask this classmate out on a date, you would probably spend more time thinking through what you know about the person to decide whether or not he or she is fun, attractive, nice, and attracted to you. Your inferences might consequently be more complex, based on more than one schema.

Individual Differences

Not everyone interprets the same information the same way. One reason is that different people have different schemas. For example, one person might describe other people primarily in terms of their sense of humor or warmth, whereas someone else might consider these characteristics to be relatively unimportant and instead be concerned with another person's diligence and religiousness.

In the last chapter, we noted that people hold self-schemas—organized knowledge structures about themselves that organize important chunks of their self-concept. Self-schemas affect not only how people perceive themselves but how they perceive others. People use their self-schemas to interpret other people's behaviors. For example, a man whose masculinity is very important to him will be more likely to interpret others' behavior in masculine or nonmasculine terms (Markus, Smith, & Moreland, 1985; Cantrambone & Markus, 1987). People also attach more importance to information about another person if it is relevant to their own self-schema, and when they are forming impressions of others, they recall more such material (Carpenter, 1988). So, for example, if being intelligent is important to you as a student, you are particularly likely to notice whether or not another person is intelligent or not and to remember that information when you later think about the person.

Groups of people may differ in their schemas. One interesting case concerns the theories people hold about intelligence. College students have schemas for intelligence that relate it closely to academic performance, whereas nonstudents (people interviewed in supermarkets or at a railway station) viewed intelligence as more closely related to everyday problem solving, social competence, and the like (Sternberg et al., 1981).

Goals

Which schemas are brought to bear on information in the environment is also based on the goals a social perceiver has in a particular situation (Weyer & Srull, 1986; Hastie, Park, & Weber, 1984). As we have seen, schemas are not just passive reflections of the information in the environment. The person must actively organize the information into a more abstract, cognitive structure. One way in which this organizing cognitive activity is triggered is through an individual's goals (e.g., Trzebinski & Richards, 1986). For example, goals have been manipulated experimentally by telling subjects either to form a coherent impression of a person (impression formation goal) or to try to remember the separate bits of information they may be exposed to (remembering goal). Generally speaking, under impression goal conditions people form more organized impressions that reflect the underlying structure of the input information than when their goal is simply remembering the information (Lichtenstein & Srull, 1987; Srull, Lichtenstein, & Rothbart, 1985; Trzebinski, McGlynn, Gray, & Tubbs, 1985).

Anticipating interacting with somebody creates very different social goals than simply trying to learn about them, and research shows that people remember more and organize the information differently when they expect to interact with someone in the future. For example, Devine, Sedikides, and Fuhrman (1989) asked subjects to learn information about five people under various goal conditions. One of the five persons was termed the target, and subjects' goals with respect to the target were manipulated. They anticipated interacting with the target, were told to form an impression of the target, were told to compare themselves with the target, were asked to compare the target with a friend, or were simply asked to recall the target's attributes. As Table 3–2 shows, anticipating interacting with the target in the future produced the greatest recall of the target's behavior. Paradoxically, compared to all the other goal conditions, simply being instructed to remember the target's attributes produced the lowest recall, both compared to other goal conditions and compared to the other four comparison persons.

Do People Always Use Schemas?

Schemas are important because they help people make sense of experience quickly. If we approached every situation as if for the first time, it would be impossible for us to function in our everyday lives. Schemas, then, represent our social learning, the social categories that we use to impute meaning to the people we meet and the situations we encounter.

T A B L E 3 – 2				
THE IMPACT OF GOALS ON RECALLING A PERSON'S ATTRIBUTES: EXPECTING TO INTERACT LED TO GREATER RECALL THAN IN ANY OTHER GOAL CONDITION				
	Anticipated Interaction	Impression	Self-comparison	Friend Comparison	Memory
Recall					
Target	4.38	4.00	3.31	3.38	3.00
Average of four other people	1.80	2.33	2.53	2.22	2.23

Source: Devine, Sedikides, and Fuhrman (1989), p. 686.

But as we also noted earlier in the chapter, there are liabilities to schematic processing. Sometimes we make assumptions about people and situations on the basis of our schemas that turn out not to be true. If we had paid more attention to the information at hand instead of jumping to conclusions on the basis of our schemas, certain mistakes could be avoided. For example, categorizing another person as loud mouthed, opinionated, arrogant, and conservative may not matter much under most circumstances, but if the person happens to be the father of the girl you are hoping to date, you might want to pay closer attention to his qualities and opinions.

The point is that under certain circumstances we pay less attention to our schemas and more attention to the data at hand. What are those circumstances? One condition that leads to less frequent use of schemas and more attention to the information is *outcome dependency*. When your outcomes depend on someone else's actions, you pay more attention to the other person (Bersheid, Graziano, Monson, & Dermer, 1976; Rush & Russell, 1988; Sande, Ellard, & Ross, 1986) and pay more attention to schema-inconsistent information, apparently because it is potentially informative (Erber & Fiske, 1984). When people's outcomes are involved, they probe for more information about others (Darley, Fleming, Hilton, & Swann, 1988). For example, competitors remember more about members of a group with which they are in competition compared with those not in competition with the group (Judd & Park, 1988).

The *need to be accurate* is another condition that leads people to pay more attention to data and less attention to their schemas. Asked if the nerdy guy with glasses and books is smart, you may draw on your schema which tells you that nerds usually are smart. However, if it is up to you to decide whether or not to admit him to your debating team, you will probably want more information than your stereotype about nerds will provide. Consequently, you will pay closer attention to his actual behavior, focusing less on the ways in which he matches your schema for nerds.

When people have to justify their decisions to other people and *accountability* is therefore high, they tend to go beyond the schema to look more closely at the data (Tetlock, 1983, 1985; Tetlock & Boettger, 1989). For example, you will probably pay more attention to information about another person if you must decide whether or not to admit him to your fraternity than if you are simply asked your impression of him.

Conversely, other facts favor schema use over careful consideration of the data. For example, when people are *forming impressions* or *making decisions under time pressure*, they tend to use their schemas more. In one study, male and female subjects were asked to judge the suitability of male and female candidates for particular jobs. When the decisions were made under time pressure conditions, male subjects as well as female subjects with conservative attitudes toward women, tended to discriminate against the female job applicants. In the absence of time pressure, however, discrimination toward the female applicants was less strong. Under time pressure conditions, then, the subjects resorted to their attitudes about men and women in jobs for making the judgments, whereas when they had time to consider the evidence and found that the female applicants were at least as well qualified as the male applicants, their degree of discrimination against the female candidates was considerably less (Bechtold, Naccarato, & Zanna, 1986; see also Devine, 1989).

To summarize, then, when there are pressures in the situation to be accurate, people tend to look at data more closely, sometimes rejecting easy schematically based conclusions. They may attend to more of the information and particularly pay attention to schema-inconsistent information. Conditions that seem to favor this kind of data-driven processing are outcome dependency, accountability, or other situational cues suggesting a need to be accurate. In contrast, other circumstances favor more schematically based processing. In particular, any pressure to form a judgment quickly or in a coherent way that can be communicated easily to others may favor the use of schemas (Fiske & Taylor, 1991).

BOX 3–3

What Are You Doing? Action Identification

If you are engaged in some behavior such as mowing the lawn, and someone asks you what you are doing, you may look at them in surprise. Isn't it obvious what you're doing? But a theory by Vallacher and Wegner (1986) argues that any action can be identified in any of several different ways. Certainly you are cutting the grass, and that would be the most obvious response to the question, "What are you doing?" But you could be just cutting the grass because it needs cutting, or you could be cutting the grass to please your father so that he will loan you the car for the evening. Actions can be identified, then, at relatively low levels of behavior or at higher levels in service of some goal.

Action identification theory maintains that the way one thinks about a particular action has implications for behavior. Actions identified at low levels are subject to context effects that might cue higher levels of action identity. So, for example, if a neighbor passes by and calls to you, "I see you're making your yard beautiful," this would suggest to you a higher goal than just cutting the grass. It might lead you into other behaviors consistent with that goal, such as trimming the hedges and washing the bird droppings off the front steps (Wegner, Vallacher, Kiersted, & Dizadji, 1986). In contrast, if you had identified your action at a higher level to begin with (cutting the grass so your father will loan you the car), your neighbor's comment that you are making the yard beautiful would have less effect on your behavior. You might simply think to yourself, "That's not why I'm doing it."

Actions identified at higher levels are more flexible than actions identified at lower levels. For example, if you have labeled your action as cutting the grass and your lawn mower runs out of gas, the action will come to a stop. However, if you identified the action as doing something to please your father so he would loan you the car, after the lawn mower runs out of gas, you might look for something else you could do that would achieve the same effect, such as washing his car or trimming the bushes.

Actions that are successful tend to be identified and maintained at relatively high levels, whereas actions that are unsuccessful tend to drop down to lower levels of identification (Vallacher, Wegner, & Frederick, 1987; Vallachar, Wegner, & Somoza, 1989). For example, your identification of your action as "cutting the grass" is likely to drop to a lower level if you run into trouble maneuvering around shrubs and stones. You may change the identification of your behavior to "trying to cut around the shrub without mowing it down" or "trying to get the rocks out of the way" rather than the somewhat higher-action identification of cutting the grass.

What are the implications of action identification theory? Sometimes, the level at which we identify an action can keep us from fully experiencing the meaning of the situation. For example, people who have lost a loved one often get through the funeral and burial service not by thinking about the loved one's departure, but by concentrating on very low-level actions, such as wearing the right clothes and making sure that there will be enough food for people after the service. As another example, Vallacher and Wegner (1986) argue that when people are committing crimes, they tend to focus on low levels of identification, such as "getting up to the second-story window," rather than the higher-level action identification of "stealing from somebody." In both these examples, people are able to avoid the full unpleasant implications of their actions by identifying them at lower levels.

SCHEMAS IN ACTION

The use of schemas for processing information is important not only because it helps people to form judgments and make decisions, but because it provides guidelines for interactions with others. Box 3–3 (above) provides one account of the relation between schemas and action. We learn about other people in many ways. Sometimes we hear about them before meeting them, or we may have hints about the kind of people they are like on the basis of their initial behavior. Regardless of how we form an impression of another person, we may relatively quickly develop ideas concerning what the person is like. As we are interacting with the person, how do these ideas (or schemas) influence one's behavior? Considerable research suggests that people behave toward others in ways that tend to confirm the beliefs they hold about those others. Perceivers employ interaction strategies for eliciting information from others that preferentially support these schemas (Snyder & Gangestad, 1981).

How does this process work? Suppose you learned that Susan, an attractive young woman in your psychology class, is with the cheering squad for the school, and you quickly form an image of her as an outgoing, athletic, and enthusiastic person. In talking with her, you might ask her about the various sports she has played, the parties she has been to this year, what she thinks of the games she has attended, and so on. All of this information tends to confirm your view of her as an extroverted, athletic, fun-loving person. However, after seeing her for several weeks, you might discover that she is actually rather shy and introverted, she's fairly klutzy at sports, and she is not a cheerleader at all, but rather coordinates uniform purchases and bus transportation to out-of-town games. You might wonder how you came to be so deceived. Looking back on the situation, however, reveals that Susan may have done nothing at all to deceive you. Rather, you deceived yourself by selectively seeking information that supported your beliefs. There aren't many college students who didn't play some kind of sport in high school or attend at least a couple of parties. Because you asked Susan about these kinds of activities, this is the information she gave you, which augmented your image of her as a fun-loving, athletic party girl (Swann, Giuliano, & Wegner, 1982).

This process has been called **confirmatory hypothesis testing,** and it has been demonstrated under a broad range of circumstances (see Higgins & Bargh, 1987, for a review). For example, M. Snyder and Swann (1978) told college stu-

dent subjects that they would be interviewing another student. Half were told to find out if the other was an extrovert (that is, outgoing and sociable), and half were told to find if the other was an introvert (that is, shy and retiring). All subjects were then given a set of questions assessing introversion and extroversion, and they were told to pick out a set of questions to ask the other student. Students who were told to find out if the person was an extrovert preferentially selected extroversion questions (such as, "What would you do if you wanted to liven things up at a party?"), and those who were told to find out if the person was an introvert picked introversion questions (such as, "What factors make it really hard for you to open up to people?"). These questions, in turn, made the target students appear especially extroverted or introverted, respectively, simply because they answered the questions they were asked (see also Curtis & Miller, 1986).

Although a number of studies have found evidence for confirmatory hypothesis testing, there are conditions under which people are less likely to selectively confirm a hypothesis through leading questions. Holding an opposite hypothesis or having a need for valid information reduces the degree to which people selectively confirm hypotheses (Kruglanski & Mayseless, 1988; Skov & Sherman, 1986; Trope & Mackie, 1987). For example, when people expect to have to work with a target in the future, they ask better questions and are less likely to engage in question-asking techniques that selectively confirm their prior expectations (Darley, Fleming, Hilton, & Swann, 1988).

Sometimes a prior schema you have about an individual will influence not only the kind of information you ask or seek from the person and the subsequent inferences you draw, but will also affect the other person's actual behaviors and self-impressions. When a perceiver's false expectations about another person lead that person to adopt those expected attributes and behavior, this is called a **self-fulfilling prophecy** (see Figure 3–3).

For example, Snyder, Tanke, and Berscheid (1977) gave college student men a folder of information about a woman on campus that in-

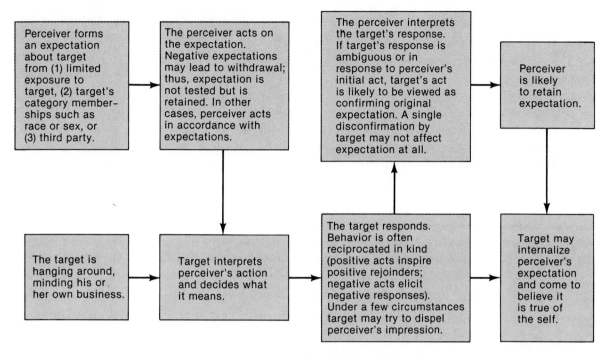

Figure 3–3. The development of a self-fulfilling prophecy. (Adapted from Darley & Fazio, 1980.)

cluded a picture representing the woman as either highly attractive or as unattractive. In actuality, the photos were fake and were randomly assigned to women regardless of their true looks. Each student was then asked to phone the woman whose folder he had read and chat for 10 minutes. Tape recordings were made of the conversations. The men who believed they were talking to attractive women behaved more warmly on the phone than did the men with unattractive women. Even more remarkable, the women who had been miscast as highly attractive were perceived by other students judging the tapes to be more friendly, likable, and sociable in their interactions with the men than those miscast as unattractive. These kinds of self-fulfilling prophecies have been widely demonstrated (see Darley & Fazio, 1980; Jussin, 1989, for reviews).

This implication of the discussion thus far is that schemas are so powerful that they not only influence how information in the environment is interpreted, but also help push the environ-

ment to become consistent with the schema. Obviously, this is not always the case. For example, sometimes people hold beliefs about others that those others feel are untrue about themselves. Consequently, those others may be motivated to disconfirm what they feel is an incorrect belief. For example, if a professor whose opinion you value saw you commit a foolish prank with some of your friends, you might be highly motivated to correct the professor's low opinion of you.

Under these circumstances, whose viewpoint will triumph? The perceiver's misconceptions or the target's beliefs about the self? Research by Swann and Ely (1984) attempted to address this question by considering the certainty of perceiver's expectations and target's self-conceptions. Perceivers first formed relatively certain or uncertain expectations about targets that were inconsistent with the target's self-conceptions. Thus, for example, some perceivers were led to believe that the target was extroverted (when the target perceived herself to be introverted), whereas other perceivers were led to believe the target was introverted (when the target considered herself extroverted). The perceivers then interacted with targets who either possessed relatively certain or uncertain self-conceptions about their introversion or extroversion. The results indicated that the target's self-concept was a stronger determinant than the perceiver's expectancy of the perceiver's ultimate opinion of the target. That is, after they had interacted together, the perceivers' impressions of the targets were more in line with the targets' self-concepts than with the perceivers' initial expectations. Only when targets were uncertain about their introversion or extroversion and perceivers were certain about their expectations did behavioral confirmation occur. That is, when perceivers were certain and targets were

uncertain about their attributes, the perceivers' expectations tended to win out. The general point, then, is that perceivers' expectations may have some effect on a target's behavior. But they do not lead targets to act in ways that are counter to their self-concepts (Miller & Turnbull, 1986; Higgins & Bargh, 1987; Major, Cozzarelli, Testa, & McFarlin, 1988).

Overall, then, schemas and schematic processing are important for several reasons. They help people to organize their past experiences in ways that can be useful in new situations. They help in the processing of new information by determining what is relevant, by filling in gaps, by influencing what is recalled, and by making some inferences automatic. And they can act as effective guidelines for behavior in social interactions.

Key Terms

breakpoints
case history information
confirmatory hypothesis testing
covariation

heuristic
illusory correlation
logical error
primacy
priming effect

rational model of inference
self-fulfilling prophecy
social cognition
statistical information

Summary

1. Social cognition is the branch of social psychology that examines how people form inferences from social information in the environment.

2. When we examine how people make impressions and form inferences and compare those processes against rational methods for accomplishing these tasks, we find that social perceivers are prone to certain errors and biases in their judgments. In particular, prior expectations and theories weigh heavily into the judgment process.

3. These predictable errors and biases appear to stem from the fact that people need to

make judgments relatively quickly and efficiently to process the multitude of information they encounter.

4. Cognitive structures called schemas help us organize information about the world. Schemas make information processing more efficient and speedy, aid recall, fill in missing information, and provide expectations. However, they sometimes lead to erroneous inferences or may lead us to reject good but inconsistent evidence.

5. Heuristics are shortcuts that help relate information in the environment to schemas. Heuristics reduce complex or ambiguous

problems to more simple, judgmental operations.

6. The schemas that are most likely to be used to interpret information are those that match the natural contours of that information. In addition, which schemas a social perceiver uses is influenced by salience, social roles, goals, primacy, priming, the importance of the judgment context, and individual differences.

7. People sometimes attend more to the evidence than to their schemas, especially if they need to be very accurate, they will be held accountable for their judgments, or their future outcomes depend on their judgments.

8. Schemas not only help people form judgments and make decisions but provide guidelines for interactions with others. In some cases, schemas may be so powerful that they bring about self-fulfilling prophecies.

Suggested Readings

Fiske, S. T., & Taylor, S. E. (1991). *Social cognition.* 2nd ed. New York: McGraw-Hill. A readable introduction to the field of social cognition for college students; available in paperback.

Hastorf, A., & Isen, A. M. (1982). *Cognitive social psychology.* New York: Elsevier-North Holland. An edited collection that emphasizes applications of social cognition to such areas as emotion, stereotyping, legal psychology, organizational psychology, and health psychology.

Higgins, E. T., Ruble, D. N., & Hartup, W. W. (1983). *Social cognition and social development.* Cambridge: Cambridge University Press. An edited collection that examines how social cognition research elucidates social development and close relationships in children and adults.

Kahneman, D., Slovic, P., & Tversky, A. (1982). *Judgment under uncertainty: Heuristics and biases.* Cambridge: Cambridge University Press. An edited collection of research on shortcuts, errors, and biases in social inference processes.

Markus, H., & Zajonc, R. B. (1985). The cognitive perspective in social psychology. In G. Lindzey & E. Aronson (Eds.). *Handbook of social psychology.* New York: Random House. A thoughtful analysis of the historical development of social cognition with an emphasis on current work in the field.

FOUR

Attribution

*T*ravelers in the Los Angeles Airport were recently treated to an unusual scene. A well-dressed man with an attache case, obviously waiting for his plane, was approached by two men in gray suits who showed identification and asked to see his. Upon looking over his identification, they put handcuffs on him, confiscated his briefcase, and led him away. Those also waiting for the plane began to talk furiously among themselves, unusual behavior for strangers in a waiting room. Who were the two men in the gray suits? Had the passenger been arrested? Had anyone overheard the conversation? What was in the attache case? Could it have been a bomb? Was it drugs? Who was the man? The waiting passengers shared information and speculated about the causes of the unusual event long after the plane had arrived and they were all airborne.

Often we ask ourselves "why" when we encounter some event. The process of finding a causal explanation reveals the complexity of the task. Usually we do not have direct information about people's internal states. We have access only to limited cues, such as their facial expressions or gestures, what the person says about his or her internal state, what, if anything, we know about the person's past behavior, and so on. So we must make inferences on the basis of the indirect information provided by external cues. Thus, our causal explanation for behavior must be inferred from these cues. The process of so doing is called attribution theory.

When Are Attributions Made?

When do people engage in this process of asking why? Although human beings are supposedly a curious species, they do not go around asking why about everything that happens. They do not ask why the sun comes up in the morning, why a boxer on TV is wearing boxing gloves, or why the bus they are riding has started moving as the red light has changed to green. Most natural events and human actions do not inspire much cognitive effort to search

out correct causal explanations. What, then, are the conditions under which we do undertake the search for a cause?

As the opening example implies, people tend to ask "why" questions when something unexpected or unusual happens (Hastie, 1984; Wong & Weiner, 1981). Unexpected events create a need for greater predictability, both to prevent nasty surprises and because a simple, predictable world permits inferences to be made virtually automatically. As a result, people tend not to ask "why" questions about expected events, such as the sun's rise in the morning or the moon's rise at night. Newspaper readers, government officials, and social scientists want answers when there is a sudden, unexpected outburst of racial violence or student unrest, but not when things are humming along as usual.

Bad, painful, and unpleasant events also inspire a search for causal attributions (Bohner, Bless, Schwarz, & Strack, 1988). To illustrate this point, researchers talked with distressed couples who had come to a clinic for marital therapy. All were asked to list a variety of positive or negative events that happened in their marriage and how frequently those events occurred. They were then asked for their thoughts about these events, which were coded for the presence of causal attributions. The authors found that the most attributional thoughts were made about the most distressing events: their partner's frequent negative behaviors or infrequent positive behaviors (Holtzworth-Munroe & Jacobson, 1985). For example, the frequent event, "he's always late for dinner," might elicit the additional thought, "because he's just not a punctual person," which would attribute his lateness to his personality.

Not surprisingly, the most extremely distressing events in life stimulate the greatest search for causal explanation. Taylor, Lichtman, and Wood (1984) found that 95 percent of a sample of cancer victims made attributions about the cause for their disease. Among family members for whom the disease was presumably less painful, only 70 percent did so. Bulman and Wortman (1977) poignantly document the efforts of paraplegics crippled by spinal cord injuries to analyze why it happened to them. Most

Unexpected or negative events are most likely to lead people to ask why the event happened.

of the injuries were the results of accidents, but still the victims wanted more definitive explanations.

Why Are Attributions Important?

Causal attributions are important for several reasons. First, *attributions help people to predict and control the environment.* The reason unexpected and negative events give rise to more causal explanation than expected or positive events is that people need to be able to avoid, offset, or at least anticipate these kinds of events in the future. Causal attributions, then, fit in with broader needs to predict and control the environment (Kelley, 1972; Pyszczynski & Greenberg, 1981; Bohner et al., 1988).

Causal attributions are also important because they determine our feelings, attitudes, and behavior. According to Weiner (1986), for example, anger usually results when something negative happens to us and we perceive it as being under someone else's control. For example, if you are standing on a curb and a car whips past, splashing dirty water all over you, you might feel angry if you felt the driver could have avoided splashing you. You might feel less angry if there was only one lane and the driver had no choice. Pity arises when a negative event happens to

someone else and no one could have controlled it. You feel sorry for a person with multiple sclerosis; no one could have prevented the disease. Other emotions follow directly from attributions, as we will see.

Our expectations about the future are also influenced by attributions for past events. When we attribute our past successes to ability, we are likely to expect future successes (Weiner, 1986). If we attribute our A's in high school English to a natural talent for literary analysis, we will be more optimistic about similar successes in our college career. But, if we attribute those past A's to teachers who were easy graders, we are not likely to expect such high grades later on.

Attributions not only have a clear impact on expectations and emotions but also on future performance. Dweck (1975), for example, showed that training children to make internal attributions for their behavior—training them, for example, to explain successes and failures as resulting from the amount of effort they put into the task—can make them work harder in the future, increasing the likelihood of success.

In these and numerous other ways, our understanding of the causes of behavior are crucial mediators of our reactions to the social world. Our reactions to other people—liking, aggression, helping, conformity, and so on—frequently depend on how we interpret the world and the causal attributions we make for the events around us.

BASIC PRINCIPLES OF CAUSAL ATTRIBUTION

Although there are different approaches to the attribution process, they rest on a common set of basic principles called **attribution theory.**

Heider's Naive Psychology

Theorizing about attributions began with Fritz Heider (1958). He was interested in how people in everyday life figure out what causes what. Like most in the cognitive tradition in social psychology, he proposed two strong motives in all human beings: the need to form a coherent understanding of the world and the need to control the environment.

One of the essentials for satisfying these motives is the ability to predict how people are going to behave. If we cannot predict how others will behave, we will view the world as random, surprising, and incoherent. We would not know whether to expect reward or punishment for our work performance, a kiss or a punch in the jaw from a friend.

Similarly, to have a satisfactory level of control of our environment, we must be able to predict others' behavior. To avoid an accident, we need to be able to predict that the big truck will not suddenly make a U turn into our front bumper. To control our diet, we need to be able to count on getting a club sandwich when we order it in a restaurant rather than suddenly being presented with an entire roast pig.

To be able to predict how others are going to behave, we need some elementary theory of human behavior. Heider proposed that everyone, not just psychologists, searches for explanations in other people's behavior. He called the result a **naive psychology**—that is, a general theory of human behavior held by each ordinary person.

Dimensions of Causality

Locus of Causality. The central issue in most perceptions of causality is whether to attribute a given act to *internal* states or to *external* forces. That is, what is the "locus of causality"? You have asked the young woman who sits next to you in lecture to go out to a movie this weekend, but she has said she is busy. What is the "real" cause of her refusal? It could be due to some internal state, such as her lack of attraction to you. Or it could be due to some external factor, such as that she really does have some other obligation. **Internal attributions** include all causes internal to the person, such as moods, attitudes, personality traits, abilities, health, preferences, or wishes. **External attributions** would include all causes external to the person, such as pressure from others, money, the na-

ture of the social situation, the weather, and so on. Is this young woman really busy (an external attribution), or has she just decided that she is not interested in dating you (an internal attribution)?

Stability or Instability. A second dimension of causality is whether the cause is *stable* or *unstable*. That is, we need to know whether or not the cause is a relatively permanent feature of that external environment or of the internal dispositions of the person. Some external causes are quite stable, such as rules and laws (the prohibition against running a red light, or against breaking the throwing arm of an overly successful quarterback), or occupational roles (professors are called upon to give lectures year in and year out).

Other external causes are quite unstable: the weather has a lot of influence over whether we spend Saturday out shopping or at home reading, but the weather varies a lot. Sometimes Oral Hershiser gets every pitch where he wants it, and sometimes his control is not so good, and his pitches go where they are easier to hit. So his success is controlled by an unstable, external cause. Certain jobs vary in the external demands they place on the jobholder. Being a general places quite different external forces on a person in wartime than in peacetime.

Internal causes can also be stable or unstable. Woody Allen has a genius for making funny remarks: his talent for humor is quite stable. On the other hand, Hamlet is famous for his lack of stable resolve about what to do with his stepfather. Some baseball players are legendary for going on hot streaks and then becoming mired in terrible slumps; on the average they are quite talented, but the talent seems quite unstable. Similarly, in the achievement domain, a student's success or failure at a particular task could be attributed to ability (which is internal and relatively stable), effort (which is internal and usually fairly unstable), luck (which is external and unstable), or task difficulty (which is external and stable).

Controllability. A third general dimension of attributions is *controllability*, according to Wei-

T A B L E   4 – 1

POSSIBLE CAUSES OF ACHIEVEMENT OUTCOMES ACCORDING TO LOCUS, STABILITY, AND CONTROLLABILITY

	Internal		External	
Controllability	Stable	Unstable	Stable	Unstable
Controllable	Typical effort exerted	Temporary effort exerted (for this particular task)	Some forms of teacher bias	Unusual help from others
Uncontrollable	Ability	Mood	Task difficulty	Luck

Source: Adapted from Rosenbaum (1972), p. 21; Weiner (1979).

ner (1982, 1986). We perceive some causes as within individuals' control and others as beyond their control. Perceived controllability or uncontrollability can coexist with any combination of locus and stability, as Table 4–1 indicates. For example, an internal unstable cause like temporary effort is generally seen as controllable; a student can try to work hard, or can decide not to. A stable internal cause like ability, however, is usually seen as uncontrollable. A "born genius" is someone born with that ability. Similarly, luck, which is an external unstable factor, is also typically seen as uncontrollable, whereas unusual help from others, though external and unstable, is presumably under those others' control.

These three dimensions of causal attribution seem to be the ones people use most frequently in explaining outcomes (Meyer & Koebl, 1982. They help to account for how people understand others' requests for help (Schmidt & Weiner, 1988), how people view others who have stigmas such as having AIDS (Weiner, 1988), and how people interpret the outcomes of sports events (Tenenbaum & Furst, 1986), among other events.

HOW ARE ATTRIBUTIONS MADE?

The Naive Scientist

Harold Kelley has generated the most formal and comprehensive analysis of attribution, which he calls the *covariation model*. The principle of **covariation** means that we tend to look for an association between a particular effect and a particular cause across a number of different conditions. If a given cause is always associated with a particular effect in many different situations, *and* if the effect does not occur in the absence of that cause, we attribute the effect to that cause. The cause always covaries with the effect; whenever the cause is present, so is the effect, and whenever the cause is absent, so is the effect.

Suppose your roommate gets grouchy and complains about everything right before exams, but is quite pleasant the rest of the time. Do you conclude that she is a grouch in general—that is, that she has a generally grouchy personality? Probably not. Instead, you would attribute her complaints to the tensions associated with exams, rather than to her being generally a short-tempered person. Her grouchiness is almost always associated with exams and does not occur in the absence of exams, so you attribute it to exams, not to her personality. This principle of covariation is, of course, exactly the same as the scientific method scientists use. A scientist also arrives at a judgment of causality by seeing that a particular factor is associated with a particular effect across a number of different conditions. This is why Kelley's model is called the naive scientist model. Although most people are not scientists, we are able to use certain scientific principles such as covariation to infer causality. Box 4–1 describes further some of these principles.

BOX 4–1

Perceived Cause and Effect Depends on Proximity in Time and Space

A key factor in arriving at judgments of covariation, and therefore causality, is the proximity of the cause and effect, both in time and in space. If we see one person shoot a gun, and shortly afterward another person close by falls down, we are likely to conclude that the shooting caused the falling down. However, if the second person falls down 5 minutes later and three blocks away, we are less likely to make the causal connection, even though the shooting may again have in fact caused the falling. Johnson and Drobny (1985) demonstrated this importance of both temporal and spatial proximity in producing causal inferences. They varied proximity of cause and effect in simulated jury situations, in which a businessman was being tried for negligence and liability due to a shooting. In the high-proximity case, a maladjusted individual had stolen the businessman's briefcase, which contained handguns and had been left in an airport, and immediately shot a taxi driver. In the comparable low-proximity case, an airport security guard took the same lost briefcase to lost-and-found, from which the maladjusted individual later stole the gun and then shot the taxi driver. The jurors rated the businessman as having more control, negligence, and therefore liability, in the high-proximity case, even though his own actions were identical in both cases. Put another way, they perceived him as more causally responsible in the high-proximity case.

Kelley suggests that people use three specific types of information to arrive at causal attribution. They check to see whether or not the same effect occurs across (1) *stimulus objects,* (2) *actors* (persons), and (3) *contexts.* This is perhaps easiest to grasp with a simple example. Suppose our friend Mary shows up at work one day and tells us that she went to a local nightclub the night before. She tells us the show featured a comedian. She laughed hysterically at his jokes and, in fact, thought he was the funniest comic she had heard in years. We should definitely go see him.

We want a causal attribution for her hysterical laughter. If the cause was that the comedian really is very funny, we should follow her advice. But if it was just something unusual about Mary, or about the situation that night, we would not be so likely to go. That is, we try to decide whether her behavior is caused by something specific to the stimulus object (the comedian), to the actor (Mary), or to the context (the people she was with, the drinks, etc.).

Kelley suggests that we would search for an attribution by checking each dimension in turn. This involves answering three questions for ourselves: (1) Is the behavior specific to a particular stimulus object? Does Mary always laugh at *any* comedian, or did she really laugh unusually hard only at this one? (2) Is the behavior specific to a particular actor? Have we heard the same report from others, or is Mary the only one who laughed at this particular comedian? (3) Is the behavior specific to a particular context or occasion? Did she laugh each night she went to see this comedian, or did she only laugh the night there was a packed house and she was with her best friend and had one more drink than usual?

Kelley's theory suggests that people use all three of these kinds of information in trying to arrive at a causal attribution:

1. *Distinctiveness information.* Does the person act in this manner only in regard to this stimulus object, and not in regard to other objects? Is Mary's reaction distinctive to this particular object?

2. *Consensus information.* Do other people act in the same way in this situation? Did other people like this comedian as well?

3. *Consistency information.* Does this person consistently react the same way at other

times or in other situations? Did Mary react this way to this comedian on only this one occasion?

Kelley hypothesizes this process occurs when we attribute a given effect to a given cause. We quickly review our store of information along these three dimensions. The review may be implicit and rapid rather than deliberate and conscious, but still we review what we know.

For an external attribution to be made—that is, for the comedian's comic ability to be the true cause of Mary's laughter—all three tests have to be passed in the appropriate manner: high distinctiveness, high consensus, and high consistency. Her reaction has to be distinctive to this comedian and not to others, other people have to like the comedian, and she has to like the comedian consistently in this and other situations.

For an internal attribution to be made—that is, for her laughter to be attributed to her general disposition to laugh at anything—low distinctiveness, low consensus, and high consistency must hold. She laughs at all comedians, no one else does, and she laughs in all places and at all times.

In a classic study, McArthur (1972) tested Kelley's predictions. She gave subjects a simple hypothetical event, varied the kind of consensus, distinctiveness, and consistency information available to them, and then measured their attributions. The three main predictions and the results are shown in Table 4–2, using the same

example. The first condition is the same as the example just described and promotes an attribution to the object itself, since it passes all three tests. Everyone else was also laughing, Mary didn't laugh at any of the other performers, but she always laughed at this one. So he must be a funny comedian. Mostly, the subjects saw it that way too; given this pattern of information, 61 percent attributed her reaction to the comedian (the other 39 percent made other attributions).

The second condition leads the observer to make a person attribution: Mary laughs at any comedian and always laughed at this one—but hardly anyone else did. Mary must be a laugher (86 percent). The third condition leads us to think there is something special about the context: she didn't laugh at anyone else, she had almost never laughed at him before, and hardly anyone else had laughed. Something unique must have happened. And 72 percent did attribute her laughter to the particular circumstances.

Does this indicate that people do in fact behave like "naive scientists"? In this study they did tend to arrive at the attributions that we would expect from Kelley's rational decision-making model. At the same time it is obvious that not everyone did so. When the situation genuinely matters, people are even more likely to process information in a systematic manner. Harkness, DeBono, and Borgida (1985) presented a similar task to college women, this time having to do with "Tom's" decisions about dating women with various characteristics. In a

---

T A B L E 4 – 2			
WHY DID MARY LAUGH AT THE COMEDIAN?			
	Available Information		Most Common Attribution
Condition	Distinctiveness	Consensus	Consistency	

Condition	Distinctiveness	Consensus	Consistency	Most Common Attribution
1	High—she didn't laugh at anyone else.	High—everyone else laughed too.	High—she always laughs at him.	Stimulus object: The comedian (61%)
2	Low—she always laughs at comedians.	Low—hardly anyone else laughed.	High—she always laughs at him.	Person: Mary (86%)
3	High—she didn't laugh at anyone else.	Low—hardly anyone else laughed.	Low—she has almost never laughed at him.	Context: (72%)

Source: Adapted from McArthur (1972).

Consensus is one of the sources of information used to make causal attributions. If everyone laughs at the comedian, we infer that he is funny, but if only a few people laugh, we do not.

high-involvement condition, they were told they themselves would date "Tom" later on in the month, while in a low-involvement condition, no mention of dating was made. Their attributions fit the covariation model more accurately when they expected to date him, that is, when the situation had some real stakes for them.

Sometimes there may be several possible causal explanations for a particular behavior, and we need guidelines to determine which attribution is correct. This dilemma raises a second major principle used to make causal attributions, termed the **discounting principle:** "the role of a given cause in producing a given effect is discounted if other plausible causes are also present" (1972, p. 8). That is, we are less likely to attribute the effect to any particular cause, and make less confident attributions, if more than one cause is likely. An insurance salesperson is very nice to us and offers us coffee, but we may not be able to make a confident attribution about why he or she is so friendly. We could attribute the behavior to a real liking for

us. More likely, we may discount that possible cause and attribute the behavior partly to the salesperson's wanting our business. On the other hand, if the person knows we have no money to buy insurance, we may not do any such discounting, because the desire for business is no longer a plausible cause. By and large, research findings do seem to follow the pattern described by the covariation and discounting principles.

ATTRIBUTIONS ABOUT OTHERS

One of the most important and common tasks of causal attribution is understanding why other people do what they do. The most basic question is this: When do we infer that others' actions reflect real dispositions, such as traits, attitudes, or other internal states? When do we assume that others are simply responding to the external situation? Or, using the terms we will use through most of this chapter, when do we make a **dispositional** as opposed to a **situational attribution?**

We know that people do not always say or do what they really believe. A prisoner of war may say things contrary to his real attitudes. Or a boy may try to act cheerful and happy in school the morning after his girlfriend has jilted him. On the other hand, sometimes a POW expresses real, heartfelt criticism of his own nation's war effort. This certainly happened in Vietnam with some American soldiers and airmen. And the boy may have some genuine sense of relief if the relationship had been depressing him for a long time. So how can we tell when a person's actions are a true reflection of his or her internal attitudes or other dispositions?

According to psychologists E. E. Jones and Keith Davis, there are several cues that people can use in situations to determine whether or not a person's behavior reflects an underlying disposition. One is the *social desirability* of the behavior. Socially undesirable behavior leads people to infer underlying dispositions, whereas with socially desirable behavior, the inference is not so clear. For example, suppose a person is applying for the summer job of social director of a summer camp and knows that being extroverted and having people skills are important requirements of the job. If she behaved in an extroverted, socially skilled manner, it might be difficult for the job interviewer to determine if she was really extroverted and socially skilled or if she was simply appearing so for the purpose of creating a positive impression in the job interview. However, if the job called for extroversion and she behaved in an introverted fashion, the job interviewer could infer with some confidence that the candidate was actually introverted. Otherwise, why would she behave in that way when the situation so clearly called for different behavior? (Jones, Davis, & Gergen, 1961; see Jones & McGillis, 1976).

Another basis for inferring dispositions is whether the behavior of an actor is situationally constrained or whether it occurs from the actor's *choice*. Suppose you are asked to take part in a classroom debate and the teacher assigns you a position of arguing in favor of capital pun-

ishment. Knowing that you had been assigned this side of the debate, it would be unwise of your audience to infer that your statements reflected your true beliefs. However, if you had chosen to argue in favor of capital punishment, the audience might appropriately conclude that your statements do reflect your underlying beliefs. Choice enables you to discount the possibility of external pressure.

A number of studies have examined the discounting principle when perceivers are asked to determine another person's true attitude. Jones and Harris (1967) presented subjects with essays written by other students in four conditions: the essays supported Fidel Castro or opposed him and were supposedly written on an assigned topic or with free choice of position. With the free-choice conditions, observers readily inferred that the writer's expressed opinion was the same as his or her underlying attitude. The pro-Castro and the anti-Castro speeches were seen as reflecting underlying pro- and anti-Castro attitudes, respectively. The subjects discounted the possibility of external causality, given the presence of free choice. On the other hand, when the writer was described as having no choice of position (strong external forces), observers still generally felt that the written position reflected the underlying attitude, but they were less sure that this was so. Data from their two very similar experiments are shown in Table 4–3.

A third condition that can help determine whether an action is produced by a person's

T A B L E 4 – 3		
ATTITUDE ATTRIBUTED TO WRITER		
Condition	Pro-Castro	Anti-Castro
Experiment 1		
Choice	59.6[a]	17.4
No choice	44.1	22.9
Experiment 2		
Choice	55.7	22.9
No choice	41.3	23.7

Source: Jones and Harris (1967), pp. 6, 10.

[a] A high score indicates a pro-Castro position attributed to the writer.

dispositional qualities is whether the behavior is part of a *social role*. Behavior that is constrained by a role is not necessarily informative about a persons' underlying beliefs or behaviors. For example, if a firefighter helps to put out a fire, we do not infer that he is helpful; he is simply doing his job. But when people in well-defined social roles display out-of-role behaviors, those actions can be used to infer underlying dispositions, since an explanation related to role is effectively ruled out. For example, if a priest argues in favor of a women's right to an abortion, you may infer confidently that his behavior reflects his true beliefs, since it so clearly contradicts the abortion attitudes one expects in a priest.

Another factor that influences whether or not one will make a dispositional attribution about another's behavior is our *expectancy* about the individual's true dispositions (Jones & McGillis, 1976). Usually we know more about the person than just one behavior. Expectations based on past information can help to rule out certain causal explanations for a particular behavior. We know our friend has long been a supporter of black liberation movements in South Africa. So when we have dinner with her parents and see her nodding agreeably at her parents' conservative statements, we nevertheless infer that she is a strong supporter of the movement and make an external attribution for her nodding. We have past information about her attitudes on this issue that gives us an expectancy about what she really believes. We use that information, along with our perception of her current overt behavior (which seems to be somewhat antimovement) and the external forces (she does not want to get into an argument with her parents), to give us a confident attribution. If people act in a way consistent with our prior expectations about them, we believe the behavior is dispositionally caused. If they behave in a new and different way, we believe it is situationally caused.

To summarize, often we are in the position of wanting to know why a person committed a particular action. The goal of our attributional search is a dispositional attribution, that is, trying to find some stable internal quality of the person that explains the action. To arrive at an explanation for behavior, we use cues about the person and the behavior as well as our past knowledge which includes whether or not the behavior is part of a social role, whether it was undertaken out of choice or not, whether the behavior fits with our past knowledge and expectations about the person, and whether the action is socially desirable or not. As the discounting principle suggests, we use these and other cues to consider whether or not any plausible external forces might have led the person to behave in the particular way, and if so, we should be less likely to make a dispositional attribution for that behavior.

ATTRIBUTIONS ABOUT THE SELF

One of the most interesting hypotheses in attribution theory is that people arrive at perceptions of their own internal states in much the same way as they arrive at perceptions of others' states. We have to infer them from our own overt behavior and from our perceptions of the environmental forces surrounding us. This idea derives from the general assumption that our own emotions, attitudes, traits, and abilities are often unclear and ambiguous to us. We may have quite limited access to our internal processes, being only somewhat aware of the factors that influence our behavior (Nisbett & Wilson, 1977).

Thus, in self-perception, just as in the perception of others, we search for invariant associations of causes and effects and use the discounting principle to divide up responsibility among various plausible causes. If we perceive strong external forces pushing us in the direction of our own behavior, we are more likely to come to a situational attribution. In the absence of clear external forces, we assume that a dispositional attribution is more correct. This approach has generated a good deal of research on the self-perception of attitudes, motivation, and emotion.

Attitudes

Psychologists have long assumed that people figure out their own attitudes by *introspection*, by reviewing the various cognitions and feelings in their consciousness. Bem (1967) argued instead that we receive only minimal and ambiguous internal cues to our attitudes. If so, we must infer our own attitudes by observing our own overt behavior. When we observe our own behavior in a situation with no strong external forces, we assume we are simply expressing our own true attitudes and make an internal attribution. In contrast, when there are strong external pressures on us to do something (such as having been assigned a particular position in a debate), we perceive our statements to be externally caused.

In other words, we learn about our own attitudes by observing how we behave in environments with different external pressures in them, not by introspecting to see how we feel. Bem does not hold that people never use internal evidence, just that, to a surprising degree, people rely on the external evidence of their overt behavior, and the conditions under which it occurs, to infer their own true attitudes (Bem, 1972; Lassiter, 1986).

To test Bem's self-perception theory, we would need to manipulate an individual's perception of his behavior while holding other factors constant (such as the actual behavior and the pressure of the environment). Then we could determine whether the person's perception of his own behavior determined his perception of his own attitudes. To test this, Salancik and Conway (1975) cleverly manipulated subjects' descriptions of their own religious behavior: Some were asked if they "occasionally" read a religious newspaper or magazine, attended a church or synagogue, or consulted a minister about personal problems. Many students had engaged in at least these minimal religious acts, so students in this condition reported lots of religious behavior. Others were asked if they "frequently" did each of these things. Since most college students do not do them "frequently," students in this condition reported very little religious behavior.

Since the two groups were randomly selected, they were presumably in fact almost exactly the same in actual behavior. But because of these differences in the wording of the questions, the first group of subjects described themselves as engaging in quite a variety of religious behaviors, while the second group described few religious acts. And sure enough, when later asked about their own overall religious attitudes in the form of the question "How religious are you?" the first group, which had been subtly induced to describe themselves as engaging in more religious behaviors, said they were more religious in general.

Attributions and Motivation

A similar idea has been applied to the self-perception of motivation. The idea is that performing a task for high rewards will lead to an external attribution—"I did it because I was paid so well for it." Performing the same task for minimal reward will lead to an internal attribution—"I couldn't have done it for that small amount of money, so I must have done it because I really enjoyed it." This leads to the paradoxical prediction that minimal rewards will lead to the greatest intrinsic interest in a task because the person attributes performance to intrinsic interest, not to extrinsic reward. Put another way, **overjustification** (receiving extrinsic rewards for something one would do anyway out of intrinsic interest) undermines intrinsic interest in the activity.

The earliest demonstration of overjustification varied whether or not nursery school children were given awards for engaging in a task (playing with felt-tip pens) which they enjoyed doing anyway (Lepper, Greene, & Nisbett, 1973). Some children were told they would get a "Good Player Award" with a gold star and ribbon if they would draw pictures with a felt-tip pen for a few minutes. Other children were not told about any award. All the children then did the drawing, and the first group was given their awards. A few days later, all the children were observed in a free-play situation with felt-tip pens provided. The children who had been given the awards spent half as much time drawing as the no-award children did. Their intrinsic interest in drawing had been undermined by the extrinsic reward. This finding has been reported in many contexts since then (see Deci & Ryan, 1985).

An interesting consequence of overjustification is that it can even undermine not just the productivity of people's work on a task, but their creativity as well. Amabile, Hennessey, and Grossman (1986) found that the creativity of children's storytelling was significantly reduced when they were offered an explicit reward for telling the story.

If extrinsic rewards for engaging in pleasurable tasks reduce intrinsic interest, then external threats that prevent engaging in specific behaviors ought to increase interest. For example, the stricter the penalty for using an illegal drug, the more attractive the drug should seem to be. Here people attribute their avoidance of the activity to the threat, not the unpleasantness of the activity itself. Wilson and Lassiter (1982) found some evidence for this hypothesis, when they varied threatened punishment for cheating.

The same reasoning would also suggest that the overjustification effect would be increased when external rewards are made more salient (Ross, 1975) and decreased when the initial interest in the activity is made more salient. In an experiment to test this latter point, Fazio (1981) had children play with Magic Markers, and then later varied whether or not they were shown photos of themselves engaged in this highly pleasurable task on the earlier occasion. Otherwise, the experiment closely resembled the Lepper and others (1973) study described earlier. For the children shown those photos of their earlier play, intrinsic interest in playing with the Magic Markers was highly salient, so extrinsic rewards had little undermining effect. They knew they had really enjoyed the Magic Markers, so they attributed their later play to their own pleasure, not to the reward.

 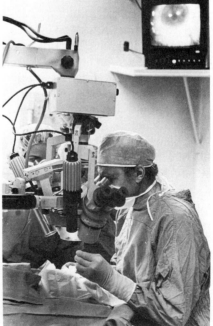

Being overpaid for one's work can undermine intrinsic interest in it. Relative to other professionals, classical musicians are usually paid poorly and even research scientists are usually not paid lavishly. How do you think their payment affects their interest in their work?

The implications of this research are important. Rewards can sometimes backfire: instead of encouraging people, they can turn them away from activities they would otherwise enjoy (Kassin & Lepper, 1984). And punishments may sometimes make a forbidden activity seem all the more attractive.

The Attribution of Emotions

Traditional theories of emotion propose that we recognize what we feel by considering our physiological state, our mental state, and the external stimulus causing these states. But recent evidence indicates that many emotional reactions are biochemically similar. We can distinguish high arousal from low arousal, but not various types of emotion. For example, it is hard to tell the difference between intense jealousy and intense love. We need other information to identify our own emotions.

Stanley Schachter (1964) suggested that perceptions of our emotions depend on (1) the degree of physiological arousal we experience and (2) the cognitive label we apply, such as "angry" or "happy." To arrive at a cognitive label, we review our own behavior and the situation. If we feel physiologically aroused and are laughing at a comedy show on television, we might infer that we are happy. If we are snarling at someone for shoving us on a crowded street, we might infer that we are angry. In each case, our behavior and our interpretation of the situation provide us with the cognitive label that allows us to interpret our internal experience of emotional arousal. Like Bem's theory of self-perception, this point of view emphasizes the ambiguity of internal states and proposes that self-perception is therefore highly dependent on perceptions of overt behavior and of the external environment.

Labeling Arousal. High degrees of physiological arousal give rise to a search for an appropriate attribution. If a plausible attribution exists for the arousal, it will be accepted. If no such attribution exists, the person will search the environment for something that could have caused the arousal. Whatever the environment

provides as an explanation will also provide the label for the emotion.

To illustrate this point, Schachter and Singer (1962) conducted a now classic experiment. One group of undergraduate students was injected with epinephrine: half were told its true side effects (e.g., rapid breathing, flushing, increased heart rate), and half were told to expect effects that are not, in fact, produced by epinephrine (e.g., dizziness, slight headache). A control group of subjects was given no drug. Subjects were then placed in a room with a confederate of the experimenter and were instructed to fill out some papers. After a brief time (during which the epinephrine took effect in those who had received it), the confederate began to act in either a euphoric manner (engaging in silly antics and making paper airplanes) or in an angry manner (ripping up the papers and stomping around the room).

Schachter and Singer reasoned that if physiological experience is indeed subject to various interpretations, then those subjects who had been misinformed about the side effects of epinephrine and who later found themselves in a state of arousal would be searching for an explanation for their state. For these subjects, the behavior of the confederate could act as a salient cue for explaining their arousal, suggesting to those subjects in the euphoric condition that they were also euphoric and to those in the angry condition that they were angry. Subjects who had been informed about the side effects of epinephrine, in contrast, already had an adequate explanation for their arousal state and could remain amused or annoyed by the confederate without acquiring his mood. Subjects in the control condition would have no arousal state to explain and also should not catch the mood of the confederate. Generally speaking, this is what Schachter and Singer found. The procedure and results of this experiment are shown in Table 4–4.

What was important for the experience of emotion was, first, the *arousal* and, second, the *cognitive label* or the attribution made for the arousal. When the experimenter provided a label attributing the arousal to the drug, the subjects acted as if they experienced no particular emotion. When they did not know the drug was

T A B L E   4 – 4

THE SCHACHTER-SINGER EXPERIMENT

Condition	Sequence				
	Step 1	Step 2	Step 3	Step 4	Step 5
	Given Arousing Drug	Told It Would Be Arousing	Confederate's Behavior	Presumed Attribution for Own Arousal (Unmeasured)	Own Behavior (Measured)
No explanation	Yes	No	Euphoric or angry in all cases	Situational	Euphoric or angry
Informed	Yes	Yes		Drug	Calm
No arousal	No	No		None	Calm

Source: Adapted from Schachter and Singer (1962).

responsible for their arousal, they took their cues about the emotions from the external environment.

False Feedback Studies

One implication of Schachter's reasoning is that internal arousal states are so ambiguous that they can be attributed to any plausible stimulus. Which emotion is experienced therefore may depend more on available plausible causes than it does on the nature of the actual internal sensations. Even fake internal sensations should be sufficient, given an external cause that can supply a plausible label.

Valins (1966) tested this idea by giving random false feedback to subjects about their own arousal. He presented heterosexual male sub-

---

BOX 4–2

A Pretty Day Can Make for a Happy Life

People can base self-perceptions about enduring internal states on temporary moods. Schwarz and Clore (1983) showed that people evaluated their lives as a whole as more happy and satisfying on sunny days than on rainy days. Using telephone interviews, they asked people: "What we are interested in is people's moods . . . could you just answer four brief questions? First, on a scale of 1 to 10, with 10 being the happiest, how do you feel about your life as a whole? . . . All things considered, how satisfied or dissatisfied are you with your life as a whole these days? And, how happy do you feel at this moment?" Half the respondents were called on sunny spring days, and half on rainy spring days. The higher the number, the happier they said they were. As the table shows, they were happier at the moment on sunny days and evaluated their "lives as a whole" as happier and more satisfying. Their momentary mood, induced by the chance event of the day's weather, influenced their self-perception of stable internal states.

	Weather	
	Sunny	Rainy
Happiness of mood at moment	7.5	5.4
Happiness of life as a whole	7.4	5.0
Satisfaction with life as a whole	6.6	4.9

Source: Adapted from Schwarz and Clore (1963), pp. 519–520.

jects with slides of nude females. After each slide he provided them with faked feedback through earphones about their heart rates. After some slides, subjects heard increased heartbeats, which they thought were their own; after others, they heard decreased heartbeats; and after still others, they heard what they thought were irrelevant sounds. Valins found that subjects rated the nudes accompanied by the supposedly changed heartbeat as the most attractive.

After the experiment was over, subjects were allowed to take some slides home. Most chose slides that had been associated with the fake feedback about changed heartbeat. Presumably they had searched the environment for a plausible cause for the change in their heartbeats, found the slides of the nude females to be a reasonable cause, and therefore labeled their arousal as sexual. This study suggests that people infer their own emotions from the perception of arousal (in this case, faked changes in heartbeat) and a plausible external cause (in this case, pictures of nudes). Another illustration of misattributing emotion appears in Box 4–2 on p. 115.

Misattribution

Schachter and Singer demonstrated that states of arousal are malleable and can be labeled in any of several ways depending upon the situational cues that make a particular emotional explanation salient. The false-feedback studies conducted by Valins and his associates extended this idea to suggest that when people get false feedback that they are aroused when in fact they are not, they come to attribute affect to those stimuli that they believe aroused them. Nisbett and Schachter (1966) took these ideas a step further and proposed that people may be able to misattribute real arousal to a neutral stimulus. If this is true, they reasoned, it can have major clinical and therapeutic impacts. By leading people to attribute anxiety to neutral external forces, one may cure them of the debilitating effects of anxiety on their own performance.

To demonstrate this point, Nisbett and Schachter (1966) conducted a study to see if peo-

ple could be induced to attribute their arousal to a neutral source. They gave a group of subjects an ordinary sugar pill. Experimental subjects were told the pill would produce physiological symptoms, such as hand tremors and palpitations; control subjects were told it would produce only nonphysiological symptoms. All subjects were then administered painful electric shock. The hypothesis was that the experimental subjects would attribute their physiological reactions after the shock to the pill rather than to the shock itself, and so would perceive the shock as hurting less. The control subjects, having no basis for an attribution to the pill, would blame their reactions on the shock itself. And indeed it was found that these control subjects found the shock more painful than did the experimental subjects. A number of these **misattribution** studies have been done, and they generally share the same basic idea: if people can be persuaded to misattribute their negative emotional states from the real external causes to some other, more neutral cause, the level of emotional distress associated with the real external cause will diminish (Olson, 1988).

Some Limitations. Can it really be the case that we get almost no information about our own attitudes and emotions by introspection? Do outside observers know as much about our own internal feelings as we do? This is surely too extreme.

First, this self-perception process works mainly when there is ambiguity or uncertainty about our internal states. People do have attitudes that endure and are not based entirely on current behavior. They do not decide about whether or not they like steak on the basis of whether or not they have recently eaten steak. They have real feelings toward steak and it is those feelings that determine their responses. Israelis have certain attitudes about Nazis, and bigots have certain attitudes about minorities, which they are quite clear about regardless of their most recent behavior. When we are slapped in the face, we do not have to wait to see if we strike back to know if we are angry. When our boyfriend says he no longer loves us, we know we feel hurt no matter whether tears come or not.

The misattribution of arousal to a neutral source is most likely when the actual source of arousal is unclear or ambiguous (Olson & Ross, 1988). For example, a person is unlikely to attribute arousal caused by the presence of a coiled snake, but might well misattribute residual arousal caused by bumping into a fellow student in the lunch line. Arousal is more likely to be misattributed if the neutral source to which arousal is to be transferred is highly salient and credible (Olson & Ross, 1988). For example, if a male subject is shown a series of beautiful nudes, it may be easy to alter his preferences among them based on false feedback, but it is unlikely that the same subject, shown a nude Miss July and a nude hippopotamus and given false feedback that his heartbeat has accelerated more for the hippo, will seriously think he desires the hippo and want to take the slide home. Another limitation is that the self-perception process seems to work best when people do not care very much about what response they make. When it really matters, people seem to monitor their own attitudes and emotions more carefully and are less influenced by external cues (Taylor, 1975).

When these "misattribution" or "reattribution" studies were first done, they gave some promise of providing a new therapeutic tool for dealing with disruptive anxieties, fears, depressions, low self-esteem, and other seemingly neurotic emotions. A variety of studies have tried to apply reattribution therapies to public speaking anxiety, test anxiety, depression, and other unwanted emotions (Forsterling, 1986). The general technique has been to try to get the person to reattribute anxieties to less threatening sources. However, the effects have been short-lived, unreliable, limited to weak anxieties, or very slight (see Slivken & Buss, 1984; Olson & Ross, 1988; Parkinson, 1985). So the technique is probably not powerful enough for therapeutic purposes.

Attribution and Affect

Some attributions generate specific emotions. Weiner's (1986) theory, shown in Figure 4–1, is that successes produce very general positive feelings (like happiness) and failure produces generally negative feelings (like sadness). Un-

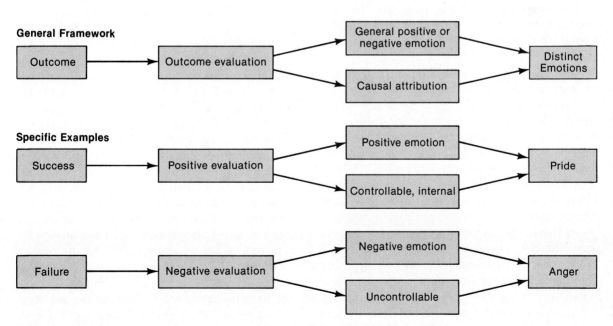

Figure 4–1. Attributional analysis of emotion. (Adapted from B. Weiner, 1986, p. 122.)

der some conditions, such as when the outcome is different from what was expected or when the outcome is extremely important, people try to figure out why they succeeded or failed. The attribution they make stimulates specific kinds of emotions. For example, you may feel bad if you get a "D" on the midterm, but *which* bad emotion you feel will depend on how you explain the low grade. If you think the test was unfair and you blame the teacher, you will feel angry; if you think you did poorly because you are not smart enough to do better, you may feel depressed, but if you feel you didn't study hard enough, you may feel guilty.

Weiner (1982, 1986) has shown that which emotion people experience depends on their attribution. Different attributions produce different emotions. When a person is successful, internal attributions (ability, effort) produce pride, while external attributions (easy test, a helpful roommate) may produce gratitude. Failures explained by internal causes (lack of effort, low ability) breed feelings of shame, while failures explained externally (test harder than expected or unfair) may produce surprise or anger (Weiner, Russell & Lerman, 1979, 1986).

The controllability of perceived causes is also important. Internal attributions for negative outcomes, such as a poor grade on a midterm, can produce quite different emotions, depending on the controllability of the cause. "Guilt" comes from controllable internal causes, such as effort ("I could have studied, and I just wasted the whole evening"), while "depression" comes from causes that cannot be controlled very well, such as lack of ability ("I'm just not smart enough to do this") or personality characteristics ("I'm not self-disciplined enough to be in college") (Weiner et al., 1979; Weiner, 1986). "Anger" is associated with controllable causes. One example Weiner gives is: "My roommate brought her dog into our no-pets apartment without asking me first. When I got home she wasn't there, but the barking dog was . . . . As well, the dog had relieved itself in the entry" (1986, p. 137). The person was angry at the roommate, because she could have controlled whether the dog was there or not. A chronically lying boyfriend or husband, a woman who is on welfare for years but who could be working, a foreign country that deliberately shoots down one of our domestic airliners—all attract anger, because these actions are interpreted as controllable.

"Pity" or "sympathy," on the other hand, is aroused by behavior interpreted as uncontrollable. A handicapped child who accidentally knocks over a vase may elicit sympathy (she couldn't help it); a drunk who does it elicits anger (he should not have been drunk; he could have controlled himself). To show this, Weiner (1980) described to college students either a person who apparently was drunk and fell down in a subway, "He is carrying a liquor bottle wrapped in a brown paper bag and smells of liquor," or a person who was ill and fell down. The college students said that they would have negative affects such as anger toward the drunk, but not toward the ill person. Attributions are important, then, not only because they enable us to make sense of situations and to determine future behavior, but also because they help determine the emotional reactions we experience.

BIASES IN THE ATTRIBUTION PROCESS

Attribution theory, as described up to this point, tends to suggest a rational, logical process. It assumes that people process information in a quite orderly way and that they are fairly objective in assessing the usefulness of information and combining it to produce a conclusion. However, as we saw in the last chapter, people tend to be miserly in their expenditure of cognitive effort. Moreover, we know that people do not spend most of their waking moments diligently trying to ferret out the causes of events. Furthermore, people are far from logical and rational in all their thoughts and behaviors. In that context, we now turn to several biases that have been identified in attributional processes. We begin with a consideration of biases that derive from the tendency to respond more to salient or figural stimuli than to background stimuli and to simplify perception by developing meaningful, structured impressions.

Salience

One way we simplify cognitive processing is by overreacting to salient stimuli. This bias leads us to perceive the most salient stimulus as the most influential. If something is in motion or colorful or loud or novel, we are likely to see it as a cause of whatever else is changing in the environment. The person who is running down the street is seen as having caused the bank alarm to go off. A loud thunderclap is perceived as causing people to scurry for cover.

Sometimes, the most salient stimuli are, in fact, the strongest causes of people's behavior, so such attributions would then be accurate. But biases arise because the most perceptually salient stimuli sometimes dominate causal explanations, even when they are not actually the most powerful causes.

Taylor and Fiske (1975) tested this idea, that whatever is perceptually salient will be seen as the dominant cause. Two confederates served as "actors." They engaged in conversation, facing each other. The subjects were "observers" sitting behind the confederates or next to them. Each actor thus had observers sitting behind him and facing him. Clearly, the actor and his behavior would be more salient for those who faced him than for those who sat behind him. But both actors were equally salient for the observers sitting to the side, equidistant from the two actors.

This arrangement is illustrated in Figure 4–2. The confederates held a standardized 5-minute conversation, chatting as if they had just met. They exchanged information about majors, common job plans, hometowns, family, extracurricular activities, and the like. The conversation was carefully set up to make sure that roughly the same conversation occurred in all experimental groups.

Then the subjects were asked for their causal perceptions: How much had each confederate set the tone of the conversation, determined the kind of information exchanged, and caused the

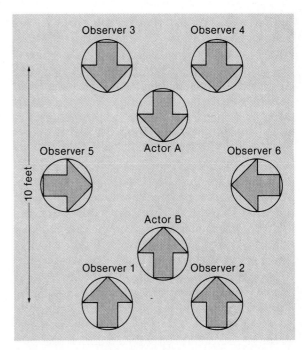

Figure 4–2. Seating arrangements for actors and observers, with arrows indicating visual orientation. (Adapted from Taylor & Fiske, 1975, p. 441.)

other actor to behave as he did? The results are shown in Table 4–5. It shows that the more perceptually salient actor (the confederate the subject faced) was seen as dominant and that the less salient actor (the confederate the subject sat behind) was seen as less influential. Subjects sitting equidistant from both confederates saw

T A B L E 4 – 5		
MEAN RATINGS OF CAUSAL ROLE ATTRIBUTED BY OBSERVERS TO EACH ACTOR AS A FUNCTION OF THE OBSERVER'S SEATING POSITION		
Observer's Position	Actor	
	A	B
Facing actor A (observers 1 and 2)	20.25	15.54
Center (observers 5 and 6)	17.51	16.75
Facing actor B (observers 3 and 4)	12.00	20.75

Source: Taylor and Fiske (1975), p. 441.

both as about equally potent. Thus actor A was seen as most powerful by those facing him (observers 1 and 2), while actor B was seen as most powerful by those facing *him* (observers 3 and 4)—even though all subjects in reality were observing exactly the same interaction (and one in which both actors contributed about equally, according to unbiased observers 5 and 6 in the center).

But what makes people salient? You are salient if you are the only one of your kind in a roomful of other people. For example, if you are the only student in a crowd of professors, the only homosexual in a group of heterosexuals, or the only black in a group of whites, you feel conspicuous. All eyes have a single target. When your solo status is known or obvious, as in the case of salient physical attributes, this is indeed the case. Research on salience supports the idea that it is an uncomfortable experience being the solo and being the center of attention (Taylor, 1981c).

The finding that perceptual salience induces exaggeration of a person's causal role turns out to be quite general (Taylor, Crocker, Fiske, Sprinzen, & Winkler, 1979; Robinson & McArthur, 1982). In fact, people seem to make causal attributions to salient stimuli so readily that some have argued that the causality ascribed to perceptually salient stimuli is a virtually automatic consequence of the perceptual experience and does not involve any deliberate causal inference on the part of the perceiver (McArthur & Baron, 1983).

Overattributing Actions to Dispositions

Another bias in the causal attribution process is that we are too likely to explain others' behavior as resulting from such dispositions as their general personality traits or their attitudes, while we tend to overlook the importance of the situations they are in. When we ask for information from a clerk at a window in the college administration building and he seems impersonal, brusque, and unhelpful, we think he is a

cold, unfriendly person. We tend to ignore the fact that he must have scores of such brief encounters with anonymous complaining students each day. It probably is his particular job situation, rather than his personality, that makes him act brusquely. Overattribution to dispositions, and underestimation to situations, is so common that Ross (1977) has called it the **fundamental attribution error.**

As one example of this fundamental error, recall the Jones and Harris (1967) study of attributions about the attitudes of people writing essays on Fidel Castro. Essay writers who freely chose to take a pro-Castro position were regarded as truly much more pro-Castro than were writers taking an anti-Castro position. But internal attributions were made even when the writer had no choice about which position to take in the essay. Even when the writer had been assigned his essay position, observers overestimated the role of internal dispositions (the writer's true position on Castro) and underestimated the strength of the external situation (that is, the lack of choice about what position to take) in trying to explain the position taken in the essay. This can be seen in Table 4–3.

The finding that observers make internal attributions even when actors have no choice, is an important one. It illustrates the principle that causal attributions for the behavior of others are biased in the direction of overemphasizing dispositions and underemphasizing the environment. Many subsequent studies have found substantially the same thing. The phenomenon seems to hold up even when the subjects have themselves actually and knowingly induced the speaker's behavior (Gilbert & Jones, 1986). And the phenomenon holds up even when observers themselves have been through the same procedure and know that no choice is involved (Miller, Jones, & Hinkle, 1981).

All in all, it appears that the tendency to take speakers' positions as reflective of their true attitudes seems amazingly resilient, even in conditions when it should be easy to make an external attribution: when speakers have no choice, are unenthusiastic, give weak arguments, and are simply reading someone else's speech. Only under the most extreme situational constraints, and with very weak arguments delivered in drab, written form, does the phenomenon disappear and do observers begin to see the full causal role of external forces (see Reeder, Fletcher, & Furman, 1989; Fleming & Darley, 1989; Miller, 1976; Watson, 1982).

Why do we do this? Why do we resist information about external constraints? Salience is one likely explanation for this attributional bias. According to Heider, "Behavior . . . has such salient properties that it tends to engulf the field"; that is, we pay so much attention to the person's behavior that we tend to ignore the situation in which it occurs. The behavior becomes figural and stands out against the surrounding ground of the situation. And as we have seen in the previous section, such salience leads to the perception of causality. Thus the essay writer, rather than the situation, is seen as the primary causal factor. But salience cannot fully explain the fundamental attribution error. It is also strong when paper-and-pencil descriptions of other people's behaviors are used, settings which preclude the dominance of the perceptual field by the actor's behavior (Winter & Uleman, 1984; Winter, Uleman, & Cunniff, 1985).

As we saw in Chapter 3, research now suggests that attributions of dispositional qualities to another person on the basis of their behavior may be made spontaneously without awareness, perhaps even automatically, upon simply learning that another person has committed a particular behavior (Trope, 1986; Gilbert, Pelham, & Krull, 1988). The tendency to make dispositional attributions increases when people are cognitively "busy," that is, thinking about their future activities, trying to make a good impression, or engaging in other tasks that consume attention (e.g., Gilbert, Pelham, & Krull, 1988). Presumably, this is because the "busy" perceiver pays even less attention to nonsalient situational factors than the unbusy perceiver who can take in at least some qualifying contextual information. Most of us are cognitively busy most of the time. Thus, if anything, research may underestimate the strength of the

fundamental attribution error. Another intriguing example of it is described in Box 4–3.

This bias toward interpreting others' behavior as stemming from their dispositions may not be just an irrational blunder. On the contrary, it may be quite functional. As Hoffman, Mischel, and Baer (1984) have pointed out, when we are required to communicate verbally to other people or about them, we need to simplify a rich and detailed store of information about them into brief and meaningful form. Traits (or other dispositions) are very convenient summaries for all that information. It is easier to say, "She's a little immature," than to list all the events that lead us to say that.

Moreover, it appears that most people do not mean what psychologists mean when they use the term "trait." Social perceivers are typically looking for a descriptive shorthand that will enable them to achieve *circumscribed accuracy* in guessing what other people will do (Swann, 1984). That is, in explaining a person's behavior, we are looking for a trait label that summarizes the meaning of the action and enables us to say with confidence, "This person would probably do the same thing, given the same circumstances again." Thus, the trait attributions that people make for others' behavior probably are not intended to explain or predict behavior across a wide range of situations, as is true when psychologists use the term "trait." In serving the goal of circumscribed accuracy, then, dispositional or trait attributions may be perfectly appropriate and not constitute errors at all.

Actors versus Observers

One of the most interesting aspects of the fundamental attribution error is that it holds for observers, but not for actors. Actors instead seem to overemphasize the role of external factors in explaining their own behavior. For example, some parents set fairly restrictive rules for their adolescent children, such as that they can go out on dates during weekends only, they have to be home at a certain hour, they can

BOX 4-3

How to Seem Smart

One ingenious use of this fundamental attribution error made observers considerably overestimate other students' general knowledge. Ross, Amabile, and Steinmetz (1977) set up pairs of Stanford students in a quiz situation. One was a "questioner" and the other a "contestant." In the experimental condition, each questioner was allowed to make up ten "challenging but not impossible" questions on any subject he or she wanted and then pose them to the contestant. Both then rated themselves and their partner for general knowledge.

The questions that were made up were indeed fairly difficult (such as "What is the capital of New Mexico?"), and contestants only got four of ten right, on the average. But the important finding was that contestants vastly overestimated the questioners' knowledge. Contestants rated the questioners as extremely well informed in comparison to themselves, while questioners rated both as about equal, as shown here.

The fundamental attribution error occurs when observers take overt behavior too seriously and ignore the impact of the situation. These contestants apparently thought the questioners were really well informed since they had known the answers to seemingly hard questions. They ignored the fact that the questioners were able to make up any question they liked and were obviously likely to make up questions they knew the answers to. If the contestant had been the questioner instead, he or she would have looked smart instead.

Rating Made by	Rating[a] of:	
	Questioner's Knowledge	Contestant's Knowledge
Questioner	53.5	50.6
Contestant	66.8	41.3

Source: Ross, Amabile, and Steinmetz (1977).
[a] High—more knowledgeable on a 100-point scale.

watch television only during certain hours, and so on. How is this rule making interpreted? The "observers," namely, the adolescents, frequently perceive their rules as dispositionally caused: the parents are mean, authoritarian, arbitrary, and old-fashioned. The "actors" themselves, the parents, are often more likely to explain their behavior in terms of the situation: they are just doing what is best for their children, living up to the role of the parent, or responding to the rebelliousness and irresponsibility of the children themselves.

How do both sides interpret it if the adolescents repeatedly violate the rules? The "observers," this time the parents, interpret it dispositionally: the adolescents are rebellious, irresponsible, and so on. The "actors," this time the adolescents, interpret their own behavior as situationally caused: the party was fun so they didn't want to leave, the parents' rules are un-

reasonably strict, the parents misunderstand them, and so on. In short, observers infer dispositional causes, actors infer situational ones. Both groups are explaining the same behavior, but with quite different attributions.

This **actor-observer bias** (Jones & Nisbett, 1972) has proved to be one of the most widely researched of the various attributional biases. In one of its earliest demonstrations, Nisbett, Caputo, Legant, and Marachek (1973) asked male students to write a paragraph on what they most liked about the woman they dated and why they had chosen their major. Then they were asked to answer the same questions as if they were their best friend. Responses were scored for the extent to which the behavior was attributed to the actor's disposition (such as, "I need someone I can relax with" or "I want to make a lot of money") or externally, to aspects of the woman or major (such as, "she's smart and fun," or "chemistry is a high-paying field"). The subjects gave more situational reasons for their own behavior and more dispositional reasons for a friend's behavior.

A related tendency is that actors not only see their own behavior as less dispositionally based than observers do; they also see their behavior as less stable (Baxter & Goldberg, 1988; Sande, Goethals, & Radloff, 1988). When behavior is thought to result from a disposition, that disposition remains stable across situations, but when behavior is credited to situational factors, it should change as the situation changes. One may regard one's own periods of gloominess as temporary reactions to bad circumstances, but regard another's bouts of gloominess as stable indicators of an inherently gloomy personality.

Jones and Nisbett offered two explanations for this difference in actors' and observers' attributions. One was that the participants have access to *different information* and therefore naturally come to different conclusions. Actors have access to much more historical information about their own behavior in different situations than the usual observer. They know how their own behavior has varied across situations, and therefore attribute it to the characteristics of each particular situation, rather than perceiving themselves as behaving uniformly due to some general predisposition. This explanation comes from the covariation principle described earlier.

The other explanation, and the one pursued by most researchers, is that the difference is due mainly to *different perspectives,* with the key factor again being differences in salience. The observer is naturally focused on the actor. This special salience of the actor leads the observer to overattribute the actor's behavior to dispositions, as we have already seen. This is the "fundamental attribution error." But the actor is not looking at her own behavior. She is looking at the situation—the place, the other people, their expectations, and so on. The actor's own behavior is not as salient to herself as it is to an observer who is watching her. For this reason, the actor will see the situation as more salient and therefore more causally potent. In short, for the observer, the actor's behavior engulfs the field, and so it becomes perceived as the major causal

force. For the actor, the environment rather than behavior is most salient, and *it* engulfs the field and becomes the major causal explanation. There is evidence for both the perceptual explanation (Storms, 1973) and the informational explanation (Eisen, 1979), and it is likely that both types of factors contribute to this effect (see also Van Heck & Dijkstra, 1985).

Differences in actors' and observers' attributions are weakened under certain conditions. People are more likely to attribute positive outcomes to dispositional factors and negatively valenced outcomes to situational factors, regardless of whether they are committed by actors or observers (e.g., Tillman & Carver, 1980; Taylor & Koivumaki, 1976). For example, we are more likely to see a person's friendliness as part of her nature, but her impatience as due to frustrating circumstances. The actor-observer effect can also be reversed when people feel empathy for the person whose behavior they are observing. Regan and Totten (1975) found that if the observer adopted an empathetic attitude and tried to think of and see things the way the actor did, the observer would come to see the world the way the actor does, namely, in terms of situational factors. The surrounding situation became more prominent, presumably as it would for the actor himself or herself. Personal involvement in an actor's plight yields similar effects (Chen, Yates, & McGinnies, 1988). People tend to see the world as the actor does if they believe they will be involved in similar circumstances in the future.

False Consensus

People tend to imagine that everyone responds the way they do. They tend to see their own behavior as typical. This tendency to exaggerate how common one's own opinions or behavior are is called the **false consensus** effect. In an early demonstration of this effect, students were asked if they would walk around their college campus for 30 minutes wearing a large sandwich board with the message "Eat at Joe's." Some students agreed; others refused. But both groups estimated that about two-thirds of the other students on the campus would make the same choice they did. Both groups clearly could not be right (Ross, Greene, & House, 1977).

This false consensus effect has been shown to occur in a broad array of different situations (Mullen et al., 1985; Mullen & Hu, 1988). For example, smokers in junior high and high school are likely to estimate much higher levels of smoking, both among youths in school and in the general population, than are nonsmokers (Sherman, Presson, Chassin, Corty, & Olshavsky, 1983). It begins early: even school-age children demonstrate the effect (Wetzel & Walton, 1985). There are several possible explanations for the false consensus effect. One possibility stems from the fact that people seek out the company of others who are similar to them and who behave as they do (selective exposure). Consequently, estimates of others' beliefs about behavior may simply reflect the biased sample of people one has available for social inference. If our friends think as we do, this provides a certain degree of consensus. Another possibility is that our own opinions are especially salient and that when one focuses on a particular opinion, consensus is increased because the position is the only one in consciousness (Marks & Miller, 1987). Were one to consider the validity of other positions, the estimate of consensus might not be so high.

A third possibility is that in trying to predict how we might respond in a situation, we resolve ambiguous details in our mind in a way that favors a preferred course of action. For example, the person who imagines that others will point and laugh if she appears in a sandwich board will probably decline to wear one and assume that others, anticipating the same harassment, would do the same. A fourth possibility is that people have a need to see their own beliefs and behaviors as good, appropriate, and typical, and so they attribute them to others to maintain high self-esteem. Research investigations suggest that all these explanations have some value in explaining the false consensus effect (Marks & Miller, 1987).

On certain person attributes, people show a *false uniqueness effect* (Marks, 1984; Snyder & Fromkin, 1980; Tesser & Paulhus, 1983). For example, when people are asked to list their best abilities and estimate how others stand on these abilities, they underestimate their peers' abilities. In order to value an ability and consider it special, people seem to need to feel distinctive and uniquely good at the ability (Tesser, 1988). On attitude issues, in contrast, people overestimate the frequency with which others agree with them, providing false consensus. Attitudes and opinions, then, show false consensus effects, whereas one's own highly valued skills and abilities tend to show false uniqueness effects (Kernis, 1984).

The false consensus effect has important implications for how people interpret social reality. It may be one vehicle by which people maintain that their beliefs and opinions are right. It may, for example, lead people to assume that there are lots of others out there who agree with them, when that may not be the case (Granberg, 1987; Judd & Johnson, 1981). Consequently, under certain conditions, the false consensus effect may function as a justification for the imposition of political or religious beliefs on others.

The Self-serving Attributional Bias

After your football team has soundly beaten an opponent, how often do you hear from them a gratifying, "Gee, you're better than we are, aren't you?" Usually you hear that it was luck, the field conditions were poor, and they'll beat you next year. On the other hand, when you have just been badly beaten, the smug look and condescending "Bad luck" from the opponent are particularly grating, because you know that they do not believe it was bad luck for a moment; they simply think they are better. This tendency to take credit for success and deny responsibility for failure is known as the **self-serving attributional bias** (D. T. Miller & Ross, 1975; Mullen & Riordan, 1988; Fletcher & Ward, 1988).

Overall, there is more evidence that people take credit for success than that they deny responsibility for failure. People are sometimes willing to accept responsibility for failure if they

can attribute it to some factor over which they have future control, such as effort. For example, if your team loses the game and blames it on the condition of the field, that will not do much to help them improve next time. But, if they realize that they failed to complete almost every pass, they have something to work on for next week's game.

Much work on self-serving biases has assumed that the biases stem from a need to protect the ego from assault. Presumably, one feels better when one causes good things to happen and not bad things. But cognitive factors appear to be involved, too (Taylor & Riess, 1989). People expect to succeed and may accept responsibility for success because it fits their expectations. People try to succeed, and when they do, their apparent self-enhancing explanation for success may reflect little more than the perceived covariation between their effort and the outcome. When people estimate the amount of control they have in a situation, they utilize instances in which they have been successful more than instances in which they have been unsuccessful, and hence overestimate the amount of control they have. All these factors can contribute to the self-enhancing bias (Miller & Ross, 1975). Indeed, efforts to try to determine if the self-serving bias is cognitively or motivationally based have generally failed, and researchers have assumed that both kinds of factors are involved (Bradley, 1978).

As the football example implies, self-serving biases include not only explanations for one's own behavior, but explanations for one's intimates, close friends, and other groups with which one is allied (e.g., Lau & Russell, 1980; Winkler & Taylor, 1979). At the group level, this bias has been termed the ethnocentric or group-serving bias, and it refers to the tendency of ingroup members to attribute internal causes to positive ingroup behavior and negative outgroup behavior and to attribute negative ingroup behavior and positive outgroup behavior to external causes (Hewstone & Jaspars, 1982; Mullen & Riordan, 1988).

Self-serving attributional biases may actually be quite adaptive, despite their apparent tendency to play fast and loose with the facts. Attributing success to one's own effort, particularly one's enduring characteristics, creates expectations that may make people more likely to attempt related tasks in the future (see Taylor & Brown, 1988). In one study, unemployed workers who attributed their firings to external factors, made greater efforts to become reemployed and actually were more likely to find jobs (Schaufeli, 1988).

Self-centered Bias

People consistently exaggerate their own contributions to shared activities, a bias called the **self-centered bias.** How does this bias differ from the self-serving bias just described? Whereas the self-serving bias involves taking credit for success but not failure, the self-centered bias consists of taking more than one's share of responsibility for a jointly produced outcome, regardless of whether the outcome is successful or unsuccessful. Ross and Sicoly (1979) did several studies of married couples' estimates of relative contributions to joint activities, college basketball players' estimates of their own roles in recent games, and recent college graduates' estimates of their own contribution to their bachelors' theses. In each case, people exaggerated their own contributions.

Thompson and Kelley (1981) found the same thing: each member of a couple consistently claimed that he or she took more than half the responsibility for such joint activities as carrying the conversation when the two of them were alone, waiting for the other person, resolving conflicts, or being sensitive to the other's needs.

What accounts for the self-centered bias? First, it is easier to notice one's own contributions than those of another person. One may be distracted from another's contributions or not even be physically present when the other person is doing his or her share of the joint task. It may also be easier to recall one's own contributions than those of another person, since they are more personally salient. There may be motivational factors involved as well. Thinking about how much I have contributed may increase my self-esteem, particularly for positive tasks. Which of these explanations is correct? As in the previous biases discussed, there appears to be no one factor that accounts for the bias, but several contributing factors.

Self-handicapping

A related but more desperate strategy for dealing with failure has been called **self-handicapping** (Berglas & Jones, 1978; Baumeister & Scher, 1988). People sometimes engage in actions that produce insurmountable obstacles to success so that later, when they experience the resulting inevitable failure, they can attribute it to the obstacle, not to their own lack of ability. The student who stays up all night before the calculus exam can attribute her low grade to fatigue, not to her complete lack of ability to comprehend math; the golfer who rarely practices can attribute his afternoon in the woods and sandtraps to lack of practice, not lack of ability; the alcoholic can attribute the loss of his job to his drinking, not to poor performance. In Kelley's language used earlier, the ability attribution is discounted because another plausible cause is present: the handicap.

In an experiment testing the self-handicapping phenomenon, Shepperd and Arkin (1989) informed college student subjects that they would be taking a test described as either a valid or invalid predictor of academic success. In addition, half the subjects were led to believe that during the course of the test they would hear a high-pitched ringing that might interfere with their test performance, whereas others were not led to believe that there was a distractor in their environment. Subjects were then asked if they wished to listen to music while they performed the test and were given a choice between music that might facilitate their performance on the task or music that might worsen it. The results indicated that subjects "self-handicapped," that is, chose music that was expected to interfere with their task performance, when they anticipated an important task (the test measuring academic success). However, this occurred only when there was no preexisting handicap in the environment. Subjects taking the test but expecting to do so in the presence of the adverse

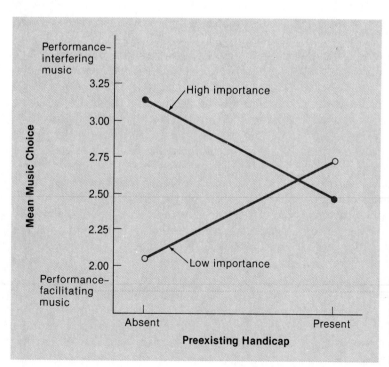

Figure 4–3. Subjects who expected to take an important test chose distracting music, apparently to have an advance explanation for their failure on the test. However, this effect only occurred when there was no preexisting handicap in the environment. (Adapted from Shepperd, J. A., & Arkin, R. M. Determinants of self-handicapping: Task importance and the effects of preexisting handicaps on self-generated handicaps. *Personality and Social Psychology Bulletin, 15,* 101–112, copyright 1989, by Sage Publications, Inc. Reprinted by permission of Sage Publications, Inc.)

ringing sound apparently had no need for additional self-handicapping, and thus were less likely to choose music that interfered with their performance. The results of this experiment are presented in Figure 4–3.

People also protect their images of their own competence by *claiming* to have handicaps that prevent success, even when those handicaps do not necessarily exist. Snyder and others have shown that in evaluative situations threatening failure, people may claim such symptoms as test anxiety, social anxiety, shyness, depression, or a history of traumatic incidents (Snyder & Higgins, 1988). Reporting such symptoms also can protect people from having to make ability attributions for their own failures: the cool response you get from that beautiful girl that just moved onto your dorm floor is just because you are shy, not because you are ugly. As you might expect, when people claim such excuses, it does tend to reduce their negative affect about failure, at least as long as no one else knows the real truth about the situation (Mehlman & Snyder, 1985).

There are two versions of the self-handicapping strategy, then: *behavioral* self-handicapping, in which people actively construct genuine handicaps, such as fatigue, alcohol, drugs, lack of punctuality, inattention, and so on, and *self-reported* handicaps, in which people simply claim to be ill, anxious, shy, or the victim of traumatic incidents, when such states might excuse poor performance (Leary & Shepperd, 1986; Arkin & Baumgardner, 1985). In both cases, as with self-serving attributional biases in general, the key motive is the self-protective or ego-defensive one of avoiding a stable, uncontrollable, internal attribution for failure, such as inherent lack of ability.

Biases: Where Do They Come From?

We have now considered several biases that enter into the process of making causal attributions. Why do they occur? Some represent cognitive shortcuts, ways of cutting through masses of available information efficiently to reach a good explanation. As we saw in the last chapter, people tend to be stingy with their cognitive resources, and were they to spend most of their waking moments diligently trying to ferret out the causes of events, there would be little time and cognitive energy left over for other tasks. Consequently, certain of the biases in causal attributions, such as the tendency to attend to salient stimuli, may simply make the process of forming causal attributions more rapid and efficient. Biases due to cognitive factors, then, represent the need to have a coherent, clear understanding of the environment, and to produce such an understanding with as much efficiency as possible.

Other biases arise from people's efforts to satisfy their own needs and motives. In addition to the need for a coherent understanding of the world, people have other needs—for love, revenge, self-esteem, prestige, material goods, and so on. These factors, too, play a substantial role in biasing causal attributions. Many of these motivational factors fall into two categories: self-serving biases that enhance self-esteem and biases that enhance the sense that people can control their lives.

Finally, biases also stem from the desire to impress others. People typically want to create a favorable impression in the minds of other people and therefore adopt certain of their behaviors as strategic means of enhancing their self-presentation. Most biases seem to stem from a combination of factors: cognitive factors, motivational needs, and self-presentational concerns.

THE ILLUSION OF CONTROL

We have seen how people tend to distort the social world perceptually into a more orderly, organized, predictable, and sensible thing than it really is. They do it in many ingenious ways, using first impressions, schemas, scripts, attributional biases, and a wide variety of other cognitive mechanisms. But people do not only perceive the world as more orderly than it really is. They distort it in more *controllable* directions as well. They systematically overestimate their own control over events and underestimate the role of chance or uncontrollable factors (Taylor & Brown, 1988). Langer (1975) has called this the **illusion of control.**

The typical experiment of illusion of control has led subjects to exaggerate their control over chance outcomes. For example, Wortman (1975) put two different marbles in a can and told subjects that each marble stood for a different prize. Some subjects were told which marble stood for the prize they wanted, and some were not. Then subjects either chose a marble or were given one, without being allowed to see which marble was which. There was no conceivable way they could actually control the outcome. Nevertheless, when they knew in advance which marble stood for the prize they wanted and were allowed to choose a marble, they thought they were more responsible for the outcome than when they were just given a marble. They had the illusion of control.

A Just World

The illusion of control implies that people have more control over their fates than they in fact do. One consequence of this illusion is the tendency to blame victims of misfortune for their adverse circumstances. A person who is involved in a traffic accident must have been driving carelessly. Victims of theft are perceived as having brought it on themselves by not taking adequate security precautions (Tyler & Devinitz, 1981). A woman who is raped must have been acting in a provocative manner and brought it on herself. Even victims blame themselves. For example, many rape victims see themselves as having behaved in the wrong way, such as hitchhiking or leaving their apartment window unlocked (Janoff-Bulman, 1979). Other people also tend to blame the victims of attacks. Women's characters seem particularly to be blamed for such attacks as robbery or rape: they are too passive, or careless, or trusting (Howard, 1984). Minorities who are discriminated against are often seen as being too pushy, unmotivated, or passive and are believed to alienate people with their demands; they therefore are seen as deserving their fates.

To explain such observations, Lerner (1965) has offered the notion that we believe in a **just world:** Good people get good outcomes, and

There is increasing controversy about the homeless. Much of it revolves around disagreements about the causes of their situation. Some attribute it to personal characteristics such as laziness or lack of jobs or mental illness, whereas others blame the failure of government economic programs.

bad things happen to bad people. The key idea is that observers attribute chance events to the victims' moral dispositions. That is, instead of making the seemingly obvious attribution to luck, fate, or some other aspect of the situation, people make an attribution to the victim's moral character. Thus, I blame you for being a lousy driver because someone ran a red light and hit you at an intersection on the way to campus. To test this notion, Lerner ran several laboratory experiments in which victims were picked at random to be given electric shock (Lerner, 1970). Even so, the subjects tended to denigrate them, as if the victims were responsible for their chance misfortunes.

Lerner interprets these indications of a belief in a just world as reflecting a need to believe we can control events, much like the illusion of control. To protect this sense of control, we blame people for the bad things that happen to them. If people in general are responsible for any disaster that befalls them, presumably we ourselves can avoid personal disaster by acting properly. One unfortunate consequence of the tendency to see the world as a just place, as Lerner (1980), Ryan (1971), and others have pointed out, is that it provides a justification for the oppression of society's victims. If people themselves are responsible for the fact that they are sick, poor, or disabled, there is no need for the rest of us to help them.

Control: An Adaptive Illusion?

What happens when this sense of control is threatened? Suppose a woman student is followed by a strange man one night on the way home back to her dormitory from the library. She has always felt safe in this well-lighted part of campus, but suddenly she feels alone and very vulnerable. He finally comes close to her and grabs her arm and tries to pull her off the path. She breaks away and runs to the dormitory, panic-stricken. She arrives there safely. But after this episode, she no longer feels safe walking at night alone on that path. She has lost her sense of control; something bad can happen to her at any moment, no matter what she does. How do people who have lost the illusion of control respond?

Reactions vary all the way from seeking information (Swann & Stephenson, 1981), to experiencing pain and stress more intensely, to declines in performance (Glass & Singer, 1972), and to emotional reactions such as anger or hostility (Brehm & Brehm, 1981) or hopelessness and apathy (Abramson, Seligman, & Teasdale, 1978). But a major response is the attempt to restore control. Even when people get cancer, a disease that is among the most difficult to control and whose causes are very poorly understood, they try to regain a sense of mastery in a variety of ways. Taylor (1983, p. 1164) reports these efforts to restore control among women afflicted with breast cancer.

[Where the cancer came from] was an important question to me at first. The doctor's answer was that it was a multifaceted illness. I looked over the known causes of cancer, like viruses, radiation, genetic mutation, environmental carcinogens, and the one I focused on very strongly was diet. I know now why I focused on it. It was the only one that was simple enough for me to understand and change. You eat something that's bad for you, you get sick.

And one spouse described his wife,

She got books, she got pamphlets, she studied, she talked to cancer patients, she found out everything that was happening to her, and she fought it. She went to war with it. She calls it taking in her covered wagons and surrounding it.

Indeed, a number of psychologists feel that a strong sense of control over oneself and one's life is extremely adaptive—even if it is based in part on illusion: "Far from impeding adjustment, illusion may be essential for adequate coping" (Taylor, 1983, p. 29; see also Taylor & Brown, 1988).

INDIVIDUAL DIFFERENCES IN ATTRIBUTIONS

Locus of Control

Some people's sense of personal control is so great that they almost seem to believe that they make the sun come up in the morning and set at night, whereas other people seem never to see a connection between their behavior and what happens to them. The propensity to explain events in terms of oneself versus the environment is termed **locus of control.** Developed by Rotter (1966), the theory argues that people differ in the expectations they hold about the sources of good and bad things that happen to them. Internals credit themselves with the ability to control the occurrence of reinforcing events, both positive and negative. Other people, termed externals, perceive reinforcing events as under the control of luck, chance, or powerful other individuals—factors external to themselves.

T A B L E   4 – 6
THE ASSESSMENT OF LOCUS OF CONTROL

(Choose one option for each question.)

1. a. Promotions are earned through hard work and persistence.
   b. Making a lot of money is largely a matter of getting the right breaks.
2. a. In my experience, I have noticed that there is usually a direct connection between how hard I study and the grades I get.
   b. Many times the reactions of teachers seem haphazard to me.
3. a. When I am right I can convince others.
   b. It is silly to think that one can really change another person's basic attitudes.
4. a. In our society, a man's future earning power is dependent upon his ability.
   b. Getting promoted is really a matter of being a little luckier than the next guy.
5. a. If one knows how to deal with people, they are really quite easily led.
   b. I have little influence over the way other people behave.

Source: Reprinted with permission from Psychology Today Magazine Copyright © 1971 (PT Partners, L.P.).

Locus of control influences both how people perceive the events that befall themselves and how they interpret the experiences of others. For example, in one study (Phares, Wilson, & Klyver, 1971), college student subjects were made to fail on an intellectual task that they had performed under either distracting or nondistracting conditions. Under the distracting conditions, both internals and externals blamed the distraction for their failure. However, when there was no distraction and accordingly no obvious existing attribution for failure, internals blamed themselves for the poor performance, whereas externals were more likely to blame external factors. Thus, locus of control represents a chronic way of explaining one's own successes, failures, or other experiences when environmental conditions do not provide an obvious explanation.

Locus of control is assessed through a scale that includes items like those in Table 4–6. If you answer option A for all or most of the items, then you would be a high internal locus of control person, whereas more option B answers would push you toward the external extreme.

Attributional Style

Recently, research has examined the pessimistic attributional style, characterized by a tendency to regard negative events as caused by internal, stable, and pervasive factors (Abramson et al., 1978). When a person expects that desirable outcomes are unlikely, when he or she expects undesirable outcomes to occur, and when the person sees no way to change this situation, helplessness, depression, and adverse health consequences can occur, according to the theory. How severe these consequences are and how much of the toll they take on a person's self-esteem depends upon attributions. Global, stable, and internal attributions for negative events produce the most far-reaching, adverse consequences.

Suppose Denise is a college student who wants to go to medical school but does poorly on the MCATs (medical entrance exams). Depression may occur if she believes no amount of effort on her part can change the outcome. If Denise blames the failure on herself, her self-esteem will also decline, and if she blames it on a global factor such as her own incompetence, these adverse responses will generalize, perhaps preventing her from applying to law school, psychology graduate school, or any other training program. If her attribution is stable, such as blaming her lack of ability, it will persist. Taking a year off from school, for example, would not make the situation better. To the extent that Denise is convinced that nothing can change the situation, her ability or motivation to do anything will be worse, and if the outcome is important—she has wanted to be a doctor all

her life like her mother before and her grandmother before that—her depression and low self-esteem will worsen. In addition to its association with depression, explanatory style has now been related to poor health outcomes as well, as Box 4–4 shows. Although whether the so-called **pessimistic explanatory style** actually causes depression remains a debate, it is clearly associated with and may help maintain depression and keep people from being able to shake off the negative effects of their self-destructive attributions (e.g., Barnett & Gotlib, 1988; Cochran & Hammen, 1985; Anderson, Jennings, & Arnoult, 1988; Sweeney et al., 1986).

BOX 4–4

Can the Pessimistic Attributional Style Cause Disease?

Can the way you explain events in your life actually affect your physical and mental health? Recent research on the pessimistic explanatory style suggests that it can. The pessimistic explanatory style is the tendency to perceive negative events as caused by internal, stable, and pervasive factors. People who explain events in their life via the pessimistic attributional style typically credit life's unpleasant events to their own internal, stable, pervasive failings. For some time, psychologists have suspected that this attributional style is implicated in depression (e.g., Peterson & Seligman, 1984). More recently, researchers have investigated whether pessimistic attributional style is also a risk factor for disease.

In a study by Peterson, Seligman, and Valliant (1988), interviews completed by graduates of the Harvard University classes of 1942 to 1944 when they were 25 years old, were analyzed to see how they habitually interpreted the negative events in their lives. The men were asked about difficult experiences they had encountered in World War II, such as combat or relations with superiors, and they were asked whether they had dealt successfully or unsuccessfully with those situations. Their

answers were coded as reflecting either an optimistic or pessimistic attributional style.

An example of explaining a negative event in terms of pessimistic explanatory style was provided by one man who died before the age of 55: "I cannot seem to decide firmly on a career. . . . This may be my unwillingness to face reality." In contrast, one of the healthy men referred to his army career: "My career in the army has been checkered, but on the whole, characteristic of the army." The difference between these responses is that the first man referred to negative events in terms of his own stable qualities, with no apparent hope for escape. In contrast, the second man also described negative experiences, but with reference to external factors ("That's the army").

The authors found that those men who explained negative events by referring to their own internal, stable, pervasive negative qualities had significantly poorer health between ages 45 through 60, some 25 to 30 years later. This was true even when physical and mental health at age 25 were taken into account. Thus, the pessimistic explanatory style in early adulthood seems to be a risk factor for poor health in middle and late adulthood.

Valuing Internal Control

A number of phenomena described in this chapter have been seen to reveal a pervasive bias toward perceiving internal or dispositional control of behavior. The fundamental attribution error overestimates internal control. Work on the illusion of control, the just world, and the pessimistic explanatory style all document how people prefer to believe in internal control, and in fact are often disrupted psychologically when they are forced to face their own helplessness and the randomness of much that affects their lives. Why does this pervasive sense of control exist?

One possibility has been considered in the preceding discussions. Perhaps, at a simple perceptual level, actors and observers alike tend to see an act as so thoroughly connected to the actor (in what Heider called a "unit relation") that they cannot easily attribute it to some external cause (Jones, 1979).

Another possibility is that all human beings share a strong emotional commitment to the feeling of free will, and to feeling that they are free to act any way they choose. The illusion of choice or control may be crucial to our motivational systems and feelings of well-being, for some adaptive reasons deriving from natural selection (Brehm, 1966; Monson & Snyder, 1977). Perhaps it is only the belief in internal control that keeps us actively trying to manipulate our environment, which in turn is crucial for survival (Taylor & Brown, 1988).

There seems little question about the fact that we value a strong sense of internal control. We like other people who believe in internal control more than we like those who believe in external control. When we try to make a positive impression on others, we are more likely to indicate a belief in internal control than a belief in external control, and when other people fail, they are liked better if they make an internal attribution for the failure than if they make an external attribution for it (Jellison & Green, 1981; Carlston & Shovar, 1982; Weary, Jordan, & Hill, 1985). In short, there seems to be a general tendency to

emphasize internal causative factors, and people who display that tendency most are the most liked and approved of. Belief in internal control seems therefore to be a strong and persuasive cultural norm.

But a third possibility is that this bias toward internal attribution is a cultural norm particularly characteristic of Americans. Many observers have noted how dedicated Americans are to individualistic values, to the beliefs that individual people can control their own destinies, are responsible for their outcomes, and so on. The Horatio Alger myth is one of our hardiest: poverty is due to the laziness and stupidity of the poor, while wealth is due to the genius and hard work of the successful. Inkeles (1983), for example, reports that when Americans were asked to explain why one person has succeeded and another failed, despite having the same skill and training, 1 percent invoke fate or God's will. But in six developing countries he found luck or fate was the explanation of about 30 percent. Another example of the same finding is shown in Box 4–5.

This individualism has been traced back to America's Protestant heritage (see, for example, McClelland, 1976; Sears & McConahay, 1973; Sniderman & Brody, 1977). More interdependent cultures emphasize the collective and interpersonal causes of events, and not so much the free acts of individuals (Sampson, 1977). The tradition in the United States, on the other hand, is that individuals stand on their own two feet. Most Americans do not think of themselves as part of a larger social whole, such as an extended family or church or community. For example, in the United States, the decision to marry is supposed to be the free choice of the persons involved and is based on romantic love. In many other cultures, such decisions are made collectively by family or kinship groups because marriages are thought to affect the whole community. Nevertheless, it remains for further research in other cultures to determine how much this emphasis on dispositions, free will and choice, and personal control is limited to our culture, with its strong tradition of individualism, and how much it is a more general human characteristic.

BOX 4–5

Americans Are More Internal

An interesting recent study tested directly for such cultural differences in internal attributions. Miller (1984) asked Americans and Hindus from India of different ages to explain some common events. She found that American adults were more likely to use internal, dispositional attributions, while Hindu adults were more likely to invoke the external context. For example, an American who was asked to explain her neighbor's cheating on taxes said, "That's just the type of person she is. She's very competitive." Or a colleague who stole someone else's idea and presented it as his own was described by an American as "just a very self-absorbed person. He was interested only in himself." In both cases, dispositions were invoked to explain the behavior. What about someone who was cheated of 1,500 rupees by a man who was supposed to do some construction work and didn't, and kept the advance? A Hindu said "The man is unemployed. He is not in a position to give that money [back]." Another, explaining why someone put his name as first author on a paper from his student's thesis, said "She was his student. She would not have the power to . . . publish it by herself" (pp. 967–968). The situation explains behavior, according to these Hindu respondents. Further evidence for the cultural explanation of these findings is that the difference is not present among young children; it only shows up with age, as would be the case if it needed to be learned over time.

	Dispositions		Situation	
	United States	India	United States	India
Adult	40%	18%	18%	40%
15 years	20	12	30	31
11 years	14	11	20	28
8 years	10	10	24	23

Source: Miller (1984), p. 967

Key Terms

actor-observer bias
attribution
attribution theory
covariation
discounting principle
dispositional attribution
external attributions

false consensus
false uniqueness
fundamental attribution error
illusion of control
internal attributions
just world
locus of control
misattribution

naive psychology
overjustification
pessimistic explanatory style
self-centered bias
self-handicapping
self-serving attributional bias
situational attribution

Summary

1. Attribution theory is concerned with how people infer the causes of social events. Although causal attributions can be made by most people for most events, people are most likely to ask "why" questions when something unexpected, unusual, or unpleasant happens.

2. People make causal attributions to help them predict and control the environment. Attributions also influence feelings, attitudes, and behavior.

3. People explain behavior as internal or external to the person, stable or unstable, and controllable or uncontrollable.

4. To infer the causes of behavior, people employ a covariation principle, meaning that they look for an association between a particular effect and a particular cause across a number of different conditions. A second important principle is that people discount the role of one cause in producing a given effect if other plausible causes are also present.

5. Kelley's theory suggests that people base their attributions on three kinds of covariation information: distinctiveness (Is this the only situation in which the person does this?), consensus (Would other people do the same thing in that situation?), and consistency (Does the person always do this in this situation?).

6. Other people's personality traits and attitudes are normally inferred from their overt behaviors by considering the external forces operating on them at the time. If these forces are strong, attributions are shared between external and internal causes. If these forces are weak, internal attributions are made.

7. Attribution theory can be applied to self-perception as well as to the perception of others. That is, the same principles may account for how we infer the causes for our own acts and how we infer the causes of others' acts.

8. To some extent, we infer our own attitudes from our own behavior, particularly when we are not especially involved in our attitudes and when they have little consequence for our future lives.

9. The internal cues we receive from our own emotional arousal state are more ambiguous and undifferentiated than has commonly been assumed in the past. Consequently, we infer both the nature and degree of our own emotional arousal by an attributional process that relies on evidence about our own behavior, indications of our arousal states, and environmental conditions that provide labels for what might have produced the arousal.

10. In its purest form, attribution theory describes a logical, rationalistic mechanism for arriving at causal explanations. But several systematic biases have been discovered.

11. In general, people ascribe more causality to salient stimuli. When inferring the causes of other people's behavior, their explanations rely overly on internal dispositions and less on external forces. This has been called the fundamental attribution error. It is particularly true for observations of other people's behavior. Self-perceptions tend in the opposite direction. We overattribute causality for our own behavior to external forces. Together, these form the actor-observer bias.

12. People are quite heavily influenced by the need to give explanations that support or protect their own self-esteem. This leads to self-serving biases, self-centered biases, self-handicapping, egocentric biases, and false consensus.

13. People seem to need an illusion of control over their environments. Their perceptions exaggerate their own level of control, and they become emotionally distressed when they feel they have no control. They believe in a just world in which people get what they deserve, seemingly based on the assumption that people can control their own outcomes.

14. People differ reliably in their perceived locus of control for events. Some people are more likely to explain outcomes in terms of internal (personal) causes, whereas others are more likely to explain outcomes in terms of external (situational) causes.

Suggested Readings

Kelley, H. H. (1967). Attribution theory in social psychology. In David Levine Ed., *Nebraska symposium on motivation*. Lincoln: University of Nebraska Press. Still the best and most coherent basic statement of attribution theory.

Jones, E. E., Kanouse, D. E., Kelley, H. H., Nisbett, R. E., Valins, S., & Weiner, B. (1972). *Attribution: Perceiving the causes of behavior*. Morristown, NJ: General Learning Press. An influential early collection of theoretical statements on attribution theory. Includes excellent chapters on the actor-observer effect, self-perception, and negativity, among others.

Hewstone, M. *Causal attribution*. Cambridge, MA: Basil Blackwell, Inc. A good contemporary collection of work on attribution.

Ross, M., & Fletcher, G. J. O. (1985). Attribution and social perception. In G. Lindzey & E. Aronson (Eds.), *Handbook of social psychology*. New York: Random House. A thorough presentation of attribution research and its relationships to research on social perception.

Weiner, B. (1986). *An attributional theory of motivation and emotion*. New York: Springer-Verlag. A comprehensive account of Weiner's attributional theory, emphasizing achievement and affect.

FIVE

Attitudes

DEFINING ATTITUDES

THEORIES OF ATTITUDES

ATTITUDES AND BEHAVIOR

COGNITIVE DISSONANCE THEORY

W hat makes someone a Republican or a Democrat, a conservative or a liberal? Why are some people fundamentalist Protestants, others devout Catholics, and others not religious at all? What makes some people racially prejudiced or dedicated environmentalists, and others not? Why do people decide that cigarette smoking is dangerous? What determines whether or not someone will change her mind about toothpastes or cigarettes? How can we convince Republicans to vote for a Democrat? How can we prepare our own supporters to resist the propaganda put out by the other party's candidates? If our friend decides smoking is bad, what will make her actually quit doing it? These questions form the basis for the extensive work on attitude formation and change, which has been a central core of social psychology in the United States for many years.

DEFINING ATTITUDES

Each of the traditional definitions of **attitudes** has grown out of the distinctive theoretical perspectives of the learning and cognitive approaches. Therefore they each contain a slightly different conception of what an attitude is or emphasizes a somewhat different aspect of it. G. W. Allport (1935) proposed that "an attitude is a mental and neural state of readiness, organized through experience, exerting a directive or dynamic influence upon the individual's response to all objects and situations with which it is related" (p. 810). Because this definition was much influenced by the learning tradition, it also emphasized how past experience forms attitudes. For the same reason, it viewed an attitude primarily as a set to respond in a particular way, and thus emphasized its behavioral implications.

In contrast, Krech and Crutchfield (1948, p. 152), who were strongly committed to a cognitive perspective, defined an attitude as "an enduring organization of motivational, emotional, perceptual, and cognitive processes with re-

spect to some aspect of the individual's world." Notice that they omit any reference to the origins of the attitude and instead are concerned with current subjective experience. Note also that they emphasize organization; they view the person as a thoughtful and actively structuring organism. And finally, note there is no mention of overt behavior. The cognitive tradition emphasizes the person's subjective experience.

The Three Components

Today, the most common definition combines elements from both approaches. An attitude toward any given object, idea, or person is an enduring orientation with cognitive, affective, and behavioral components. The **cognitive component** consists of all the thoughts the person has about that particular attitude object—the facts, knowledge, and beliefs concerning the object. The **affective** (or **evaluative**) **component** consists of all the person's affects or emotions toward the object, especially positive or negative evaluations. The **behavioral component** consists of the person's readiness to respond or tendency to act regarding the object.

Consider our friend Susanna's attitude toward smoking cigarettes shown diagrammatically in Figure 5–1. The focus of the whole attitude is on the attitude object, in this case smoking cigarettes. Surrounding the object are the various elements perceived as relevant. Some of these are impersonal entities, such as nonsmoking regulations. Some are people, such as parents or roommates; others are personal states, such as one's own smell; and still others are simple attributes of the object itself, such as its price or taste. This whole cluster of cognitions and their link to the main attitude object constitute the cognitive component of an attitude.

Next there is the affective component. Each separate cognitive element has positive or negative feelings connected to it, and the central attitude object does too. In Figure 5–1 positive and negative evaluations of the elements and central object are indicated by plus and minus signs, respectively. The evaluations of the related ele-

Figure 5–1. Susanna's attitude toward smoking cigarettes. The core object is related to several other cognitions. The signs refer to the affective component of her overall attitude toward smoking and her affects toward the separate cognitions she associates with smoking. A positive sign (+) refers to a favorable affect and a negative (−) to an unfavorable affect.

ments are shown in the boxes. Susanna's negative feelings about smoking come from the dislike her roommate and parents have for smoking, the many places where smokers are unwelcome, its bad smell, and her feelings that smoking is dangerous and too expensive. To be sure, she likes studying to go easier, and to be

relieved of some social discomfort. Still, the affective component of her attitude toward the central object, smoking, combines evaluations of all these separate cognitions. And she plainly has a strong negative evaluation of cigarettes. She dislikes and is afraid of them. This is shown in the diagram by the minus sign in the central circle. The affective component of the attitude, then, can be thought of as consisting of all the feelings toward the central object and toward the separate cognitions linked to the attitude object in question.

Finally there is the behavioral component. An attitude also contains some tendency to behave in connection with the attitude object. The behavioral component of an attitude can manifest itself in a number of ways. In this example, Susanna has a tendency to avoid cigarettes behaviorally. She does not buy them, she does not smoke one when offered it, she tends to avoid places where people are smoking, and indeed she stopped dating a smoker partly because she found his nicotine tasted distasteful when she kissed him.

This three-component definition of attitudes is the one that most social psychologists share today and the one we will use here. The thing to remember is that any attitude toward a particular attitude object has these three different components or aspects. The components are distin-

---

BOX 5–1

Three Components of Attitudes Toward Snakes

Attitudes toward snakes present a good example of this three-component model of attitudes. The cognitive component consists of beliefs in such factual matters as "snakes are soft and smooth" or "snakes control the rodent population." The affective component consists of the person's feelings toward snakes (e.g., "I feel anxious" or "tense" or "affectionate"). The behavioral component consists of relevant behavioral tendencies, describing past behavior (e.g., "I like to handle snakes") or current behavior (e.g., refusing an experimenter's request to handle a live snake). An analysis of items measuring these three components of attitudes toward snakes revealed, as most such analyses do, that they are distinctive but related dimensions (Breckler, 1984). That is, it is sensible to describe these three as separate components of an attitude, but there is a good deal of consistency among them as well. In this study, the correlations among the three components ranged from +.38 to +.70. This consistency will be one of the main themes of the rest of the chapter.

guished for analytic convenience because they follow somewhat different principles. They are not always consistent with each other; indeed, questions about that consistency have led to some of the most interesting research in the area, as will be seen.

Cognitive Complexity

One feature of many attitudes is their cognitive complexity. This can be seen in several respects. First, we often have a great many thoughts and beliefs about the attitude object. They may not all be factually correct, but the cognitions are numerous. In Figure 5–1 we have shown only a few of the cognitions an individual could have regarding cigarettes. Second, the attitude can include a great many cognitions that vary in the nature of their relationship to the core and in their evaluative component. The thought that cigarettes help studying is meaningful only when an attitude toward studying is considered. And then attitudes toward studying can bring in attitudes toward parents, teachers, a future career, and so on. The full cluster would contain all the person's thoughts in connection with cigarettes. And, third, a number of other factors are not included in the structure. For example, each cognition can vary in importance (e.g., the fact that cigarettes are expensive is probably less important than the fact that they are linked to lung cancer). So this figure is an oversimplification of many attitudes in real life.

Evaluative Simplicity

Most attitudes tend to be as evaluatively simple as they are cognitively complex. Even though Susanna has many cognitions about smoking, her evaluation of it is relatively simple: her overall negative evaluation of it dominates and organizes almost all her feelings about it. Smoking alienates her roommate and parents, tastes bad, smells bad, is expensive, runs the risk of lung cancer—even though it would help her study late at night. Her overall attitude is negative, and so are almost all the

attributes or consequences of smoking that she perceives. This pattern is quite common: a multitude of cognitions may exist in people's minds, but by and large, the evaluative components of their attitudes are much simpler. She may even experience a variety of specific negative affects toward smoking, such as fear or disgust, each of which has its own special features, but her overall evaluation of smoking tends to be consistent with these separate affects as well (Breckler & Wiggins, 1989).

Even at the more remote level of attitudes about public affairs, where people often do not have much information, their attitudes are quite consistent, on many important issues such as the performance of the president of our country, race relations, abortion, use of drugs, and so on (Kinder & Sears, 1985). For example, white Americans tend to have evaluatively consistent attitudes on racial issues. Whites who most support civil rights in general tend also to be most supportive of affirmative action for blacks, busing of school children for racial integration, and so on (Sears, 1988).

We might note that the evaluative simplicity of most attitudes closely resembles the evaluative simplicity of our impressions of other people. As noted in Chapter 2, our impressions of other people quickly tend to become evaluatively consistent. No matter how much we know about them, we tend generally either to like them or to dislike them.

Cognition versus Affect

As seen in earlier chapters, much sociopsychological research contrasts affect and cognition. The bases for contextual effects in impression formation or for attributional biases are good examples. These are manifestations of fundamental theoretical differences in perspective, between those who view affect as a primitive, spontaneous, immediate response (Zajonc, 1980) and those who view it as controlled by perceptions and cognitions (Lazarus, 1984; Weiner, 1986). So too, much attitude research concerns itself with the different implications of the cognitive and affective components of attitudes.

One general difference on which most would probably agree is that the affective component of an attitude is more difficult to change than the cognitive component, everything else being equal. This is perhaps easiest to illustrate if we think of the commonsense distinction between ''attitudes''—which include an affective component along with a cognitive component—and beliefs in ''facts''—which have only a cognitive component.

A scientist believes that it is 252,710 miles to the moon or that human beings have 46 chromosomes. She also has a complex collection of other beliefs about the moon and chromosomes. But under most circumstances, she does not have any emotional feelings toward either—she does not think the moon is good or bad. She does not like or dislike chromosomes. In contrast, she has a collection of ''facts'' about Adolf Hitler or toxic wastes, but she also *does* have emotional feelings about these.

As a result, facts and attitudes function differently. Attitudes, once established, are much more resistant to change than beliefs in ''facts.'' Not so many years ago, astronomers were convinced that Neptune had two moons. Then the *Voyager* spacecraft sent back reliable information indicating that Neptune had eight moons. Those who originally believed it had two moons probably changed their belief quite readily when they saw the evidence. Certainly high school and college science students, who were in no way involved in the controversy, changed their ''knowledge'' almost instantaneously.

This is different from the way people react when their attitudes are concerned. Attitudes are more complicated in this respect than facts. People do not change their attitudes without putting up a fight and being exposed to a considerable amount of pressure. The presence of the affective component seems to change the dynamics considerably; it makes the attitude-change process much more difficult.

One reason why the affective component is so resistant to change is that the evaluation of an attitude object can persist long after the content that produced it is forgotten, as Anderson and Hubert (1963), among others, have shown. The affective component is more durable and central than the cognitive component.

This leads to a second general difference between the affective and cognitive components. The affective component tends to have more influence over attitudes and behavior than does the cognitive component. We have already seen one example of this in the ''halo effect.'' Positive or negative evaluations control impressions of a person regardless of the details of that person's characteristics.

Adolf Hitler, the dictator of Germany from 1933–1945, is still reviled all over the world, even though he died nearly a half century ago.

Attitudes and Behavior

The third component of an attitude concerns behavioral tendencies. Our friend was persuaded some time ago that smoking contributes to lung cancer and heart disease, so the cognitive component is in place. She feels that smoking is bad, so the affective component is in place. But it was still hard for her to stop smoking. That is, her behavior did not immediately fall into line.

Much research in social psychology has been devoted to the hypothesis that the affective and cognitive components of an attitude control the behavioral component, or, to put it in the shorthand that most researchers use, that attitudes control behavior. This research suggests that actual behavior is sometimes controlled by attitudes, and sometimes it is not. Everything else being equal, people usually date the person they like best, go to the church of their own preference, and vote for the candidate they think is best qualified. But sometimes overt behavior is inconsistent with attitudes, and people appear to live quite comfortably with the inconsistency. Many smokers do believe smoking is bad for your health, and many do not like the taste of nicotine. But often they keep on smoking nonetheless. Their smoking behavior is not controlled only by their negative evaluations and cognitions about smoking.

And the causal link between attitudes and behavior may run in the opposite direction on occasion. Overt behavior can control the evaluative and cognitive components of attitudes. People can behave in a certain way, and the other components of their attitudes may fall into line. Our friend Jessica got pregnant and gave up smoking because her doctor said it would be bad for the unborn baby, her husband was worried about the baby, and her friends criticized her for jeopardizing the baby's health. For nine months, she stopped smoking. Jessica gradually became convinced that smoking was bad not just for baby but for her, she learned to dislike the smell and taste of nicotine, and she learned new facts about the dangers of smoking. By the time her baby was born, she had a broad reper-toire of antismoking cognitions and negative evaluations of smoking.

So the causal relationships between the cognitive and affective components of an attitude, on the one hand, and overt behavior, on the other, can go in either direction. In the last half of this chapter we will discuss both: ways in which attitudes control behavior, and ways in which behavior controls attitudes.

THEORIES OF ATTITUDES

Now that we have a general view of an attitude, we can consider the theoretical frameworks within which attitudes have been studied. The main theoretical approaches outlined in Chapter 1 have been applied in one form or another to research on attitudes just as with other areas of social psychology. The **learning** approach sees attitudes as habits, like anything else that is learned; principles that apply to other forms of learning also determine the formation of attitudes. The **cognitive consistency** approach asserts that people seek harmony in their attitudes, and between attitudes and behavior. It particularly emphasizes acceptance of attitudes that fit into the person's overall cognitive structure. Motivational approaches, of which the relevant version is **incentive theory,** holds that a person adopts the attitude that maximizes his or her gains. Each side of an issue has its costs and benefits, and the individual will adopt the side on which the net gains are greater. These approaches are not necessarily contradictory or inconsistent. They represent different theoretical orientations and differ primarily in the factors they emphasize when explaining attitudes.

Learning

The learning approach is most closely associated with Carl Hovland and others at Yale University (1953). The basic assumption behind this approach is that attitudes are learned in much the same way as other habits. People acquire information and facts; they also learn the feelings and values associated with these facts. Children learn that a certain animal is a dog, that dogs are friends, that they are good; finally, they learn to like dogs. They learn both the cognitions and affects of an attitude. And they learn them through the same processes and mechanisms that control other kinds of learning. This means that basic learning processes should apply to the formation of attitudes. The individual can acquire information and feelings by the process of association. Associations are formed when stimuli appear at the same time and in the same place. If a history teacher, a parent, or a television reporter shows us a mean-looking military man in a storm-trooper uniform and says the word *Nazi* in a hostile tone, we form an association between negative feelings and the word Nazi. Conversely, we may be exposed to positive things that can become associated with the concept of *democracy*. All our lives we are exposed to people who say that democratic countries are good and totalitarian governments are bad. As a result we have a strongly positive affective association to the term.

This process of association leads to attitudes toward things as well as toward people. Individuals learn the characteristics of a house, a country, an idea, a bill pending in Congress, or anything else. An attitude consists of that knowledge plus the associated evaluative component.

Learning can also occur through *reinforcement*. If you take a class in psychology, and get an "A" in it and enjoy it, the act of taking psychology classes is reinforced and you will be likely to take more in the future. Similarly, if you say that psychology is really interesting and your friends all agree with you and support you, positive attitudes toward psychology are reinforced.

Finally, attitudes can be learned through *imitation*. People imitate others, particularly if those others are strong, important people. So a major source of basic political and social attitudes in early life is the family. Children are likely to imitate their parents' attitudes. In ado-

lescence, they are more likely to imitate peers' attitudes on many matters.

The learning approach to attitudes is relatively simple. It views people as primarily passive. They are exposed to stimuli, they learn by means of one learning process or another, and this learning determines the person's attitude. The final attitude contains all the associations, values, and other bits of information the individual has accumulated. A person's ultimate evaluation of a person, object, or idea depends on the number and strength of the positive and negative elements learned. But the central idea is that the person learns to link a particular affect to the attitude object.

Attitudes vary considerably in the strength of these learned links. The negative affects associated with Adolf Hitler or toxic wastes may be very strong, whereas those associated with other attitude objects such as Jimmy Carter or littering may be rather weak. The strength of this association is known as the *accessibility* of the attitude, to describe how readily the attitude object activates (or *primes*, to use the language introduced in the social cognition chapter) the associated affects (see Higgins, King, & Mavin, 1982; Tourangeau & Rasinski, 1988). Strongly learned evaluative associations (that is, highly accessible attitudes) can be evoked quickly and automatically when the person both has a very well learned response and is presented with a strong stimulus or "prime." Weak associations cannot be (Fazio & colleagues, 1986). For example, people are able to respond with their attitude more quickly if the issue is an important one to them (Krosnick, 1989). And the attitude may be evoked more quickly if we are given a strong stimulus; e.g., a vivid movie of a toxic waste dump should quickly evoke the affects associated with toxic wastes, such as fear, disgust, and anger. This idea of automatic processing portrays the person as responding emotionally, quickly, and without reflective thought.

Association, reinforcement, and imitation are the major mechanisms in the learning of attitudes. Learning theories have dominated the research on the formation of attitudes. But association is also an important mechanism in attitude change. When a neutral attitude object is associated with one that has a strong affective component, a **transfer of affect** takes place such that the first object takes on the affect of the second. When we are told that a Southern white congressman once belonged to the Ku Klux Klan, and only resigned when he ran for Congress, we immediately feel much more negatively toward him.

Cognitive Consistency

Another major framework for studying attitudes emphasizes cognitive consistency. The cognitive consistency approach grows out of the cognitive tradition; it depicts people as striving for coherence and meaning in their cognitive structures. This approach includes a number of somewhat similar theories. They differ in some important respects, but the basic notion behind them is the same: they all assume that people seek consistency among their cognitions.

People who have several beliefs or values that are inconsistent with one another strive to make them more consistent. Similarly, if their cognitions are consistent and they are faced with a new cognition that would produce inconsistency, they strive to minimize the inconsistency. Trying to maintain or restore cognitive consistency is the primary motive.

Balance Theory. There are three main variants on the cognitive consistency idea. The first is **balance theory,** which involves consistency pressures among the affects within a simple cognitive system held by a particular person (Heider, 1958). Such a system typically consists of the person, another person, and an attitude object. There are three evaluations: (1) the first person's evaluations of the other person, (2) the first person's evaluation of the attitude object, and (3) the other person's evaluation of the object. For example, consider Michelle's attitudes toward her teacher and toward legalized abortion. If we consider only simple positive-negative feelings, there is a limited number of combinations of these elements. They are diagrammed in Figure 5–2 with the symbol *P* standing for Michelle (person), *O* for the teacher (other person), and *X* for legalized abortion (attitude object). The arrows indicate the targets of the feelings. A plus sign means a positive affect,

---

BOX 5–2

Things Go Better with Coke (Or Maybe It's Pepsi . . .)

In one study supporting the transfer-of-affect process in attitude change, college students were given peanuts and Pepsi-Cola while they read a series of four persuasive communications on different topics; others read the same communications but were given nothing to eat or drink (Janis et al., 1965). The students who had received food and drink while reading were more positively influenced on all four topics than were those who had not received them, as shown in the accompanying table. The positive associations to the peanuts and Pepsi-Cola apparently transferred to the persuasive communications being read.

Topic	Experimental Condition	
	With Food and Drink	Without Food or Drink
Cure for cancer	81%	62%
Size of armed forces	67	43
Moon shot	55	30
3-D movies	67	60

Source: Adapted from Janis et al. (1965), p. 184. Entry is percentage of subjects changing attitudes in advocated direction minus percent changing in opposite direction.

Balanced Situations   Imbalanced Situations

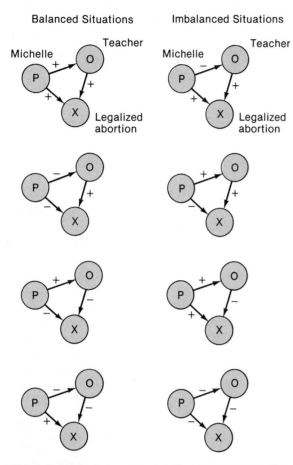

Figure 5–2. The balance model. There are eight possible configurations of two people and one object. According to the model, the imbalanced structures tend to become balanced by a change in one or more elements.

and a minus sign means a negative one. The upper left-hand triad shows that Michelle likes her teacher and that they both support legalized abortion.

The first assumption of balance theory is that some of these simple cognitive systems are cognitively balanced and others are not. The notion of balance comes originally from Gestalt theories of perceptual organization. As we have noted, people try to achieve "good form" in their perceptions of others, just as they try to achieve "good form" or "good figures" in their perceptions of inanimate objects. Balanced relations between people "fit"; they "go together"; they make a sensible, coherent, meaningful picture. The main motive pushing people toward balance is trying to achieve a harmonious, simple, coherent, and meaningful view of social relationships. So a balanced system is one in which you agree with a liked person or disagree with a disliked person. Imbalance exists when you disagree with a liked person or agree with a disliked person.

On the left side of Figure 5–2 are the four balanced situations—situations in which the relations among the elements are consistent with each other. When Michelle likes her teacher and both support abortion, the system is balanced. It is certainly consistent when two people who like each other like the same things; their relationship is harmonious because they both agree. If Michelle likes her teacher and both oppose abortion, balance also exists. Neither supports abortion, and they are united in opposition to it. Finally, if Michelle and her teacher disagree about abortion, but Michelle dislikes the teacher anyway, there is no conflict.

The imbalanced systems occur when Michelle and her teacher like each other but disagree about abortion, or dislike each other and agree about it. The inconsistency lies in the fact that we expect those we like to have similar attitudes to ours, and we expect those we dislike to have different attitudes. In general, imbalance is present when the system has an odd number of negative relations.

The second assumption of the balance model is that imbalanced configurations tend to change toward balanced ones. This assumption gives the model its importance. Imbalanced systems produce pressures toward attitude change and continue this pressure until they are balanced. That is, the systems on the right side of the figure will change toward becoming like those on the left.

The change can occur in many ways. Balance theory uses a *least effort principle* to predict the direction of change. People will change as few affective relations as they can and still produce a balanced system. Any of the relations may be altered to produce balance. For example, if Michelle supports abortion but the teacher does not, and the student likes the teacher, balance could be produced in several ways. Michelle could decide that she really does dislike the teacher or that she actually opposes abortion. Alternatively, she might distort reality by mis-perceiving that the teacher really supports abortion. Which mechanism is chosen depends on the ease of using it and on the individual doing the changing. The important point is that various possibilities exist.

Research on balance theory has generally supported these predictions: people do adjust imbalanced systems toward balance, and in ways that minimize the number of changes that must be made (Abelson et al., 1968). But balance pressures seem to be weaker when you dislike the other person than when you like him or her. Newcomb (1968) calls such situations "nonbalanced" rather than "imbalanced." His idea is that we simply do not care very much whether we agree or disagree with someone we dislike; we just cut off the relationship and forget about the whole thing.

Aside from this, balance theory describes the notion of cognitive consistency in extremely simple terms and provides a convenient way of conceptualizing attitudes. It makes it clear that in a given situation there are various ways to resolve an inconsistency. It focuses our attention on one of the most important aspects of attitude change—the factors that determine which of those various modes of resolution is adopted.

Cognitive-affective Consistency. A second version of the consistency approach is that people also try to make their cognitions consistent with their affects. That is, our beliefs, our "knowledge," our convictions about the facts of the matter are determined in part by our affective preferences, and vice versa.

The idea that information determines our feelings is pretty obvious. If we know that a dictator has imprisoned and murdered most of his opponents, we don't like him. The more interesting version of cognitive-affective consistency is that our evaluations influence our beliefs. Suppose a voter doesn't really know anything about the new governor but develops a strong negative affect toward him because all his friends at work voted against the governor. Consistency theory suggests he will then ac-

quire the cognitions necessary to support that negative evaluation. He will begin to believe the governor is incompetent, has misguided policies, and is surrounded by dishonest cronies. In other words, people will alter their beliefs and sense of the facts to fit their evaluative preferences, even if they do not have any good, new information that would justify doing so.

Rosenberg (1960) provided a striking demonstration of the cognitive changes created by a change in affect toward an attitude object. He obtained from white subjects a comprehensive description of their attitudes toward blacks, racial integration, and the whole question of relations between blacks and whites. He then hypnotized the subjects and told them that their attitude toward blacks moving into their community was the opposite of what it had previously been. If the subject had previously been strongly against integrated housing, he was told he now favored it (or vice versa). That is, Rosenberg reversed the subject's affect toward integrated housing. The subjects were then awakened from their hypnotic trance and questioned about their current attitudes about blacks and integration.

Rosenberg found that the change in this one affect he had produced under hypnosis was followed by many dramatic reversals in the subjects' cognitions relevant to integration. For example, the subjects who had originally been opposed to integrated housing came to believe integration was necessary to remove racial inequality, that it was necessary to maintain racial harmony, that it was the only fair thing to do, and so on. These ramifying changes tended to reduce the inconsistency that had resulted from the induced affective change. The important point is that he changed their affects without supplying any new cognitions or changing any old ones, since he did it by hypnotic induction. As the theories of cognitive consistency would predict, the pressures toward reducing inconsistency resulted in a variety of cognitive changes once affect had been changed.

This process is important because many attitudes are acquired as strong affects without many supporting cognitions. Children who grow up as Democrats because their parents vote Democratic need to rationalize that favorable affect later on by acquiring pro-Democratic cognitions. Children usually grow up loving and patriotically supporting their own country, even though they love it mainly by virtue of having been born in it. They must come up with most of the supporting cognitions later on, such as that it has a noble history, a superior set of political institutions, the finest cuisine and most beautiful countryside, the most interesting sporting contests, the nicest and bravest people, and so on.

Dissonance Theory. A third variant of the cognitive consistency approach is that attitudes will change in order to maintain consistency with overt behavior. **Cognitive dissonance theory** was first proposed by Leon Festinger (1957). Dissonance theory focuses on two principal sources of attitude-behavior inconsistency: the effects of making decisions and the effects of engaging in behavior that goes against one's attitudes.

A decision usually creates some inconsistency, because the behavior of deciding means you have to give up something desirable (all the things you decided not to do) and accept something partially undesirable (even the best choice usually has some flaws). When you engage in counterattitudinal behavior, such as working at a boring job because you need the money or taking an uninteresting class because it is required, inconsistency is produced between your attitudes and your behavior. Such inconsistencies produce an unpleasant psychological state known as cognitive dissonance, which may be reduced in a number of different ways. The most interesting way is to change the attitudes so they are no longer inconsistent with the behavior. We will discuss this theory in a later section of this chapter, spelling out its predictions and describing some of the ingenious research it has led to.

These young Moslem boys are participating proudly in Algeria's independence day parade. What is their likely understanding of this patriotic event?

Incentives

In Chapter 1 we described motivational theories as those that view people as responding in terms of the costs and benefits associated with each possible choice, or in terms of the needs that a particular response might satisfy. Basically, the question is, what has the person got to gain or lose with each response? Thus the third major theoretical perspective on attitudes emphasizes the importance of incentives. Basically, the perspective asks what costs and benefits a person receives from holding particular attitudes. According to this theory, attitude formation is a process of weighing the pros and cons of various possible attitudes on a topic, and then adopting the best alternative.

A student might feel partying is fun, and exciting, and her friends like to do it. These considerations give her a positive attitude. But she knows her parents don't want her just to party while she's in college, and it interferes with her studying, and she wants to go to law school. These considerations give her a negative attitude toward partying. According to the simplest version of incentive theory, the relative strengths of these incentives determine her attitude.

There are two versions of the incentive approach to attitudes in wide use today, each of which modifies this basic theory in one crucial respect. One is **cognitive response theory** (Greenwald, 1968; Petty, Ostrom, & Brock, 1981). This theory assumes that people respond to the various aspects of a particular position with positive or negative thoughts (or "cognitive responses"). These thoughts in turn determine whether or not the individual will support that position. It resembles the simple version of incentive theory in that the person's attitude reflects the pros and cons of the position in question. It differs in that these cognitive responses represent the person's subjective assessments rather than necessarily reflecting the objective pros and cons of the position.

Suppose you listen to a televised speech by a senator in which she advocates cutting government medicare payments to the elderly. You might say to yourself, "But what about retired people on small pensions, or people who can't support themselves, like the handicapped, or the poor? Somebody has to support those people, and government programs are about the only way to do it." These negative cognitive responses would mean you are unlikely to take the senator's position. But if you said to yourself, "That's right! Taxes are too high and those programs are probably just paying for extravagant hospital costs for people who could be paying their own medical bills anyway!" you are likely to come to the speaker's support.

The key assumption of the cognitive response viewpoint is that people are active processors of information who generate cognitive responses to messages, rather than being mere passive recipients of whatever messages they happen to be exposed to.

A second version of the incentive approach is **expectancy-value theory** (Edwards, 1954). This too assumes that people adopt a position based on their thoughtful assessment of its pros and cons, that is, on the basis of the values of its possible effects. But it adds the notion that they take the likelihood, as well as the value, of its possible effects into consideration. People adopt positions that would lead to the most probable good effects, and reject positions that are most likely to lead to bad effects. Put more formally, it assumes that in adopting attitudes, people try to maximize the subjective utility of the various expected outcomes, which is the product of (1) the *value* of a particular outcome and (2) the *expectancy* that this position will produce that outcome.

Suppose you are trying to decide whether to go to your friend's party tonight. The expectancy-value analysis is presented in Figure 5.3. You would try to think of the various possible outcomes of going to the party (dance, drink beer, not study for your midterm tomorrow, meet someone interesting), the values of those outcomes (enjoy the dancing and drinking beer and meeting someone interesting, might be somewhat hungover, and will get a very bad grade on the midterm), and the expectancy of those outcomes (certain to dance and to get a terrible grade, but unlikely to meet anyone new at a small party). Taking both expectancy and

GO TO THE PARTY OR STUDY? AN EXPECTANCY-VALUE ANALYSIS	Value	×	Expectancy	=	Subjective Utility
Choice 1—Go to party					
Dance	+2	×	3	=	+6
Meet someone new	+3	×	1	=	+3
Drink beer	+1	×	3	=	+3
Get hangover	−3	×	2	=	−6
Do poorly on midterm	−3	×	3	=	−9
Total attitude					−3
Choice 2—Study					
Improve midterm grade	+3	×	3	=	+9
Be bored	−1	×	1	=	−1
No hangover	+2	×	3	=	+6
Total attitude					+14

Note: Value is on a +3 (very good) to −3 (very bad) scale; expectancy, on a 3 (certain to happen) to 0 (certain not to happen) scale; subjective utility is the product of value and expectancy.

Figure 5–3. Go to the party or study?

value into consideration, it's time to start studying: an inevitable terrible grade is not balanced by a little fun dancing and drinking beer.

The incentive approach is similar to the learning approach in that the attitude is determined more or less by a sum of the positive and negative elements. One difference is that incentive theories ignore the individual's past history and consider only the current balance of incentives. Another difference is that the incentive theories emphasize what people have to gain or lose by taking a particular position. Whether or not their friends would like them, how enjoyable the experience is, and so forth are the critical considerations. When there are conflicting goals, people adopt the position that maximizes their gains. A third difference is that the incentive approach treats people as more calculating, active, rational decision makers. In contrast, the learning approach treats people as more emotional and possibly controlled by the environment.

A final theory suggests that people can respond either in the thoughtful, deliberate way the incentive theories suggest *or* in the more automatic, emotional way the learning theories suggest, depending on the circumstances. Petty

and Cacioppo's (1986) **elaboration-likelihood model** proposes that, under some conditions, people are motivated and able to engage in thoughtful consideration of the pros and cons of an argument; under others, they are not. When conditions are right, people are likely to attend to the appeal, access relevant memories, scrutinize the arguments, and draw inferences and evaluations on the basis of this scrutiny. Under other conditions, people are likely to draw their conclusions from more peripheral cues irrelevant to the merits of the arguments, such as the attractiveness and prestige of the source, the pleasantness of the context (e.g., a beautiful woman or handsome man smoking the advertised brand of cigarette), and so on. This theory is perhaps more realistic than the others, in that it recognizes that people are capable of processing information in very different ways, depending on the circumstances. The challenge is to identify those conditions that produce one response rather than another. We will return to this question in the next chapter.

Having reviewed the major theories of attitudes, we now turn to research on attitudes. This has focused on two general areas. One is the link between attitudes and behavior. As we have seen, the causal flow between attitude and behavior may well go in both directions, which has given rise to much provocative research. The remainder of this chapter is concerned with such issues. The other area of psychologists' research is what changes attitudes; the next chapter is concerned with that topic.

ATTITUDES AND BEHAVIOR

Originally it was simply assumed that people's attitudes determined their behavior. Devout Christians should be likely to behave honestly, frugally, and compassionately, and people who are prejudiced against Hispanics should be unlikely to send their child to a school with mostly Hispanic students. Much of the interest in attitudes comes from the assumption that they do affect behavior.

And yet we know of many instances in which behavior does not follow from attitudes. How many times have you seen people smile and say how pleased they are to meet someone when, indeed, you know they are bored stiff or hate them? Jim and Tammy Bakker, and other television evangelists involved in public scandals, seem not to have behaved in accordance with conventional religious beliefs. So to what extent do attitudes in fact control behavior?

The degree of influence of attitudes over behavior has become one of the important controversies in attitude research. In a classic study, LaPiere (1934), a white professor, toured the United States with a young Chinese student and his wife. They stopped at 66 hotels and motels and at 184 restaurants. Although at the time there was rather strong prejudice against Asians in the United States, all but one of the hotels and motels gave them space, and they were never refused service at a restaurant. Sometime later, a letter was sent to the same establishments asking whether they would accept Chinese as guests. Of the 128 replying, 92 percent said they would not. That is, the Chinese couple received nearly perfect service in person, but nearly universal discrimination in the subsequent letters.

LaPiere, and many after him, interpreted these findings as reflecting a major inconsistency between behavior and attitudes. Almost all the proprietors behaved in a tolerant fashion, but they expressed an intolerant attitude when questioned by letter. A similar inconsistency between tolerant overt behaviors and intolerant verbal attitudes was found by Kutner, Wilkins, and Yarrow (1952). A group of two white women and one black woman were seated in all 11 restaurants they entered. But later they telephoned for reservations for a group that included blacks and were refused by six of the restaurants.

Part of the controversy centers on how typical these early studies were. Wicker (1969) conducted one widely cited review. He looked at studies testing for consistency between attitudes and behavior in the areas of race relations, job satisfaction, and classroom cheating. Summarizing 31 separate investigations, Wicker concluded: "It is considerably more likely that attitudes will be unrelated or only slightly related to overt behavior than that attitudes will be closely related to actions."

Yet this conclusion has been widely criticized as underestimating attitude-behavior consistency. Indeed, later studies show much higher degrees of consistency than Wicker reported. In one study, a large sample of Taiwanese married women was asked, "Do you want any more children?" In the subsequent three years, 64 percent who had said "Yes" gave birth, whereas only 19 percent who had said "No" had a child.

Another example is voting behavior. Kelley and Mirer (1974) analyzed large-scale surveys conducted during four presidential election campaigns. Voters' partisan attitudes, as revealed in preelection interviews, were highly related to actual voting behavior: 85 percent of the respondents showed a correspondence between attitude and behavior, despite the fact that the interviews took place one month before election day, on the average. Moreover, almost all the inconsistent voters had only weak attitudes.

Such studies led a later careful review to the following conclusion: "Most attitude-behavior studies yield positive results. The correlations that do occur are large enough to indicate that important causal forces are involved, whatever one's model of the underlying causal process may be'' (Schuman & Johnson, 1976, p. 199). But everyone acknowledges there is substantial variation across different situations in just how consistent attitudes and behavior are. In recent years, the major research effort has gone into trying to determine the conditions that yield greater or lesser degrees of consistency.

Strength of the Attitude

One important condition for high attitude-behavior consistency is that the attitude be a strong and clear one. Inconsistencies most often involve weak or ambivalent attitudes. As mentioned, Kelley and Mirer (1974) found that most attitude-vote inconsistencies came from voters with conflicted or weak attitudinal preferences to start with. Similarly, consistent behavior may not follow when the affective and cognitive components of the attitude conflict (Norman, 1975; Millar & Tesser, 1989).

Anything that contributes to a strong attitude should increase attitude-behavior consistency. One factor is the amount of information the person has about the attitude object. For example, Kallgren and Wood (1986) found that students' environmental behaviors (agreeing to a home visit to hear about a recycling project, agreeing to participate in the project, or signing petitions to protect the environment) and attitudes were most consistent among those who knew the most about preservation of the environment.

Another factor that strengthens attitudes is being forced to rehearse and practice them. Fazio and his colleagues (1982) showed that attitude-behavior consistency is greater when people have to think about and express their attitudes, presumably because this helped to strengthen the attitude.

Having direct personal experience with an issue gets us to think and talk more about it than if it is remote to us. So one hypothesis has been that attitude-behavior consistency will be greater when we have direct experience with the attitude object than when we only hear about it from someone else, or read about it, because we will have firmer attitudes about it (Fazio & Zanna, 1981). Regan and Fazio (1977) showed this with students at Cornell University during a severe housing shortage. Many freshmen had to spend the first few weeks of the fall semester in temporary housing, usually a cot in a dormitory lounge. Unlike students assigned immediately to permanent housing, they had direct personal experience with the shortage. While all this was going on, the researchers measured both sets of students' attitudes to-

Abortion is an issue that brings out some of the strongest attitudes in our time. Frequently powerful affects are paired with elaborate cognitive structures.

ward the crisis and their interest in possible behavioral actions, such as signing and distributing petitions, or joining committees to study the crisis. These attitudes and behavior were much more closely related for the students with direct personal experience with the crisis ($r = .42$). In contrast, behavior was not at all related to attitudes among students with only secondhand experience, such as those who only talked to friends or read about it in the student paper ($r = .04$).

There are numerous other examples of the strong relationship of behavior with attitudes based on direct, current experiences. Nonsmoking junior high and high school students with direct experience with smoking (in terms of being around adults or other students who smoke) showed closer correspondence between attitudes about smoking and behavioral intentions (would they start smoking in the near future) than did those with no such direct experience with smoking (Sherman et al., 1982). And Manstead and others (1983) studied predictors of whether mothers would breast-feed or bottle-feed their babies. They found mothers' own attitudes were a better predictor of their feeding choices if they had already had children and so had personal experience with feeding an infant. In contrast, the behavior of first mothers depends less on their own attitudes and relatively more on other people's judgments.

Another source of attitude strength presumably comes from having some vested or selfish interest in the issue. Sivacek and Crano (1982) found support for this notion using the issue of the minimum drinking age. A ballot proposition in Michigan in 1978 would have raised the legal age from 18 to 21. Presumably students under age 21 had more of a selfish interest in the issue than did older students. Indeed, attitudes toward the proposal were considerably more tightly correlated with behavior (volunteering to call voters) among those with a vested interest than among the disinterested.

There are of course other reasons why attitudes are strong. But these examples illustrate the general point: any substantial attitude-behavior relationship depends in part on the attitude itself being a strong one.

Stability of the Attitude

Another critical point is that attitudes may change over time. The attitude held by a person some months or years ago will certainly not affect behavior as much as the person's current attitude. One would not expect to find a close relationship between a college girl's attraction to a boy and her dating behavior with him if her attraction is measured when she is a freshman, and her behavior when she is a senior. Therefore, consistency between attitudes and behavior ought to be maximum when they are measured at about the same time. Kelley and Mirer (1974) found that errors in predicting the vote declined quite rapidly as the preelection interviews got closer to election day.

Partly these longer time intervals diminish the attitude-behavior correlation because attitudes change. But the person and the situation change in other ways as well. We might find that a woman's attitude about having children at age 25 does not predict her behavior at age 30. The woman might continue not to want to have a child, and her husband may have threatened her with divorce if she did not agree to have children.

The longer the interval between measuring the attitude and measuring the behavior, the more such unforeseen contingencies might have arisen. So, when assessing whether or not people "do what they say," make sure you don't try to hold them to something they said two years ago. Things may have changed!

Relevance of Attitudes to Behavior

Another obvious, but often ignored, point is that the more relevant attitudes are to behavior, the more they will be correlated. Attitudes vary quite a bit in how relevant they are to the act in question. LaPiere's asking proprietors about their feelings about Chinese people in general is plainly not as relevant as asking about their attitudes toward this particular couple. In general, behavior tends to be more consistent with attitudes specifically relevant to it than with very general attitudes that apply to a much larger class of potential behaviors.

BOX 5–3

Does the Individual Fit the Stereotype?

The question of inconsistency between attitudes and behavior began with the problem of prejudice and discrimination against minority groups. Is people's behavior toward an individual member of a group consistent with their attitudes toward the group as a whole? But the individual member may or may not be perceived as representative of the group as a whole, and thus may draw behavior inconsistent with general attitudes toward the group; a female Nobel Prize–winning biological scientist may not be perceived as fitting the **stereotype** of women in general, whereas a warmly humanitarian person such as Sister Theresa may be.

Attitude-behavior consistency should be greatest when the individual fits (that is, is most relevant to) the stereotype of the group as a whole. Lord and others (1984) tested this hypothesis using male Princeton students' orientations toward homosexuals. First they measured the students' stereotypes of homosexuals, in terms of their typical traits. Then they were presented with a description of a specific individual, "John B.," who was thinking of transferring to Princeton, and who either fit that stereotype closely or was somewhat uncharacteristic of it. Then they tested for consistency of attitudes toward homosexuals in general with behavioral orientations toward this individual (would they be willing to show him around campus, introduce him to their friends, host a weekend visit). Other students' willingness to interact with him was quite consistent with their attitudes toward homosexuals in general when he fit their stereotype of homosexuals ($r = .38$) but not at all correlated with them when he did not ($r = .02$). Again, attitude-behavior consistency depends on relevance of the behavior to the attitude; here, a close cognitive fit between the individual and stereotype.

Several studies have asked people whether they believe in God or consider themselves religious, and then noted whether they in fact attended church. Typically there was only a weak relationship between those two attitudes and church attendance (e.g., Wicker, 1971). But attending church is not necessarily perfectly relevant to a belief in God or even to being religious. Many people who believe in God, yet consider themselves religious do not attend church. They may not like organized religions or just wish to practice their religious beliefs privately. Other people may only be moderately religious and attend church for a variety of other reasons as well as religion. That may be their one social outing of the week, or their spouses may insist on being accompanied to church. Thus, it is not surprising that these two attitudes do not relate directly to church attendance.

On the other hand, if people were asked whether they thought attending church was a good idea, presumably the relationship to actual church attendance would be much stronger because that attitude would be more directly related to the behavior.

This point is clear in a study of the predictors of oral contraceptive use (Davidson & Jaccard, 1979). Attitudes toward using "the pill" in the next two years correlated .57 with actual behavior, but attitudes toward birth control *in general* correlated only .08 with the use of oral contraceptives in the next two years. This is shown in Table 5–1. Schwartz (1978) found the same to be true with regard to the behavior of volunteering to tutor blind children: attitudes toward that specific behavior predicted it very well, even over several months' or years' time, but attitudes toward altruistic acts in general did not. Similarly, Weigel, Vernon, and Tognacci (1974) found that attitudes specifically toward the Sierra Club were closely related to willingness to engage in various actions on behalf of the Sierra Club, but very general environmental attitudes were not.

T A B L E   5 – 1

THE EFFECTS OF ATTITUDE RELEVANCE ON THE CORRELATION BETWEEN ATTITUDE AND BEHAVIOR (USE OF BIRTH CONTROL PILLS DURING THE FOLLOWING 2 YEARS)

Attitude Measure	Correlation with Behavior
Least relevant	
Attitude toward birth control in general	.08
Attitude toward birth control pills	.32
Attitude toward using birth control pills	.52
Most relevant	
Attitude toward using birth control pills during the next 2 years	.57

Source: Davidson and Jaccard (1979).

Salience of Attitude

In most situations, several different attitudes may be relevant to behavior. Cheating on college examinations might be determined by lax attitudes about honesty or by a strong desire to get into law school. "White flight" behavior, putting one's child in a private school to avoid integrated schools, might be determined by prejudice against Hispanics or by the belief that integration lowers the educational quality of the public schools. A school superintendent's decision to prevent a gay rights sympathizer from addressing a high school assembly might be dictated by his dislike for controversy within the school or by his distaste for gays.

So one important determinant of the consistency of behavior with a particular attitude should be the salience of the attitude in question. The consistency between intolerant attitudes and discriminatory behavior will probably be fairly low if people have other attitudes in mind at the time. Perhaps the restaurant has so little business the proprietor cannot afford to turn anyone away. Serving a Chinese couple may be consistent with the attitude most salient at the moment, which is making some money, even though it is inconsistent with the attitude the proprietor is not even thinking about, such as ethnic prejudice.

As a general matter, when a specifically relevant attitude is made particularly salient, it is more likely to be related to behavior. To show this, Snyder and Swann (1976) assigned subjects to a mock jury situation and gave them a sex discrimination case. In the "salient" condition, subjects' attitudes about affirmative action were made salient by instructing them to take a few minutes before the case to organize their thoughts on affirmative action. In the "not salient" condition, subjects were not given any warning that affirmative action was involved. When attitudes were made salient, they were highly related to jurors' verdicts in the case. But attitudes about affirmative action were not closely related to verdicts when they had not been made salient.

As you might expect, salience is particularly crucial when the attitude is not a very strong one. When the attitude is very strong, presumably it does not have to be brought very forcefully to the person's attention to be strongly related to behavior. Borgida and Campbell (1982) studied students during a campus parking shortage at the University of Minnesota. Students who usually drove to campus were more directly affected by the shortage than were others, because they either spent a long time looking for a parking place or got a lot of parking tickets. Presumably the daily drivers had stronger attitudes, since they had direct experience with the shortages. The researchers exposed some students in each group to a conversation that included complaints about the parking situation, to make attitudes about parking more salient. Others heard a conversation on summer job plans and the merits of racquetball. It turned out that the conversation making the parking issue salient enhanced the consistency of attitude and behavior (willingness to sign a full-page ad in the campus newspaper) only for the students with little experience with the issue, who presumably had the weakest attitudes.

To take this point one step farther, making the affective component of the attitude more salient increases its power over behavior, whereas making the cognitive component more salient makes *it* more powerful (Millar & Tesser, 1986).

However, when the two components are consistent with each other, it does not matter which is made more salient: both will be highly correlated with the behavior when either is made salient (Millar & Tesser, 1989).

Situational Pressures

Whenever people engage in overt behavior, they can be influenced both by their attitudes and by the situation. When situational pressures are very strong, attitudes are not generally likely to determine behavior as strongly as when such pressures are relatively weak. This is easy to see in the LaPiere study. Well-dressed, respectable-looking people asking for rooms are hard to refuse, despite feelings of prejudice against their ethnic group. The external pressures are even stronger when the law requires giving a room to anyone who wants one and can pay for it.

A similar dramatic impact of situational pressures on behavior can be seen in a study of teenage marijuana smoking (Andrews & Kandel, 1979). Attitudes toward marijuana (whether or not it should be legalized, whether use causes physical harm) correlated fairly strongly with actual marijuana use. But situational forces, in this case peer pressure (as indexed by the number of friends using marijuana), had an effect several times greater.

The relative effects of attitudes and situational pressures change from one setting to another. In another study, teenagers' attitudes toward drinking beer, hard liquor, and wine were the best predictors of frequency of actual drinking of them, but only at parties. At home, actual drinking behavior was better predicted by perceptions of their parents' approval or disapproval toward drinking, a situational pressure (Schlegel et al., 1977).

These findings suggest that the theory that attitudes determine behavior is too simple. Sometimes they do and sometimes they do not. We have described some factors that are important, and they are shown in Table 5–2.

T A B L E   5 – 2
CONDITIONS THAT CONTRIBUTE TO HIGH ATTITUDE-BEHAVIOR CONSISTENCY

Attitude is strong
  Unconflicted attitude
  Affective and cognitive components are consistent
  Information about attitude object
  Direct personal experience with attitude object
Attitude is stable over time
Attitude is relevant to the behavior
Attitude is salient
No conflicting situational pressures

The Reasoned Action Model

Perhaps the most influential effort to generate and test a general theory of attitude-behavior links is Fishbein and Azjen's **reasoned action model** (1975; Azjen & Fishbein, 1980). It is an attempt to specify the factors that determine attitude-behavior consistency. It begins with the assumption that people behave fairly rationally. Specifically, the model suggests that people behave in accord with their conscious intentions, which are based in turn on their rational calculations about the potential effects of their behavior and about how other people will feel about it. The model is diagrammed in Figure 5–4.

The reasoned action model has three steps:

1. It predicts that a person's behavior can be predicted from **behavioral intentions.** If a woman says she intends to use the pill to avoid getting pregnant, she is more likely to do so than is someone who does not intend to.

2. Behavioral intentions can be predicted from two main variables: the person's attitude toward the behavior (does she think taking the pill is a good step for her?) and subjective **social norms** (her perception of what others think she should do; does her husband want her to? what about her church, and her mother?).

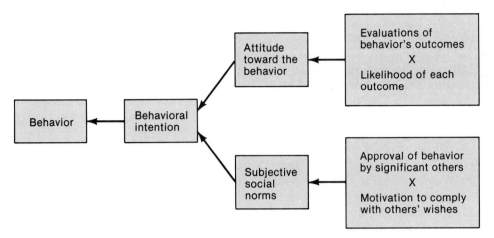

Figure 5–4. The reasoned action model of factors determining a person's behavior.

3a. Attitude toward the behavior is predicted using the expectancy-value framework: the desirability of each possible outcome is weighted by the likelihood of that outcome (avoiding pregnancy is extremely important to this woman, and the pill is almost certain to prevent pregnancy; the pill has mildly unpleasant side effects, but they do not affect everyone who takes it).

3b. Subjective social norms are predicted from the perceived expectations of significant others weighted by motivation to conform to those expectations (her husband strongly wants her to take the pill, and she wants to please him; her church strongly opposes it, but she thinks its views are outdated and no longer cares about them).

The model appeals to many social psychologists both because it makes people seem reasonable and because it places attitudes in a central place in determining behavior. It also has the value of great simplicity: it purports to explain any behavior on the basis of a small number of variables. As a result, the model has been widely used. A simple example is the study mentioned earlier by Manstead and colleagues (1983) predicting whether pregnant women would wind up breast-feeding or bottle-feeding their babies. From prenatal questionnaires the researchers measured behavioral intentions (did the woman intend to breast-feed?), attitude toward the behavior (for example, did she believe that breast-feeding establishes a closer mother-baby bond, and how important is that bond?), and subjective social norms (what did the woman's husband, mother, closest female friend, and doctor prefer, and how motivated was the woman to follow their wishes?). The researchers found the model was very successful in predicting later behavior. The correlation of these various attitudes with actual postbirth breast-feeding was .77, which is quite high.

The model has also been used successfully to predict a variety of other behaviors. It has been shown to apply well to college women's behavioral intentions about the use of contraceptive techniques (Pagel & Davidson, 1984). In another study, college students' exercise, dating, and studying behavior over a two-week period were quite successfully predicted (Bentler & Speckart, 1981), as have a wide variety of other behaviors, such as weight loss, consumer choices, voting behavior, and women's occupational choices (Ajzen & Fishbein, 1980).

Of course no model is perfect. What are some of the difficulties with this one? The notion that our intentions determine our behavior gives the model much of its appeal and distinctiveness. But the role of behavioral intention is a principal source of problems as well. For one thing, as everyone knows, good intentions are not always enough. Sometimes we do not have the ability or resources to do something we intend to do. As a result, it has been suggested that an additional variable—perceived control over outcomes—be added to the model (Ajzen & Madden, 1986). As in the case of the attributional analyses of perceived control discussed in the previous chapter, both internal and external control are relevant. Illustrating the role of a sense of internal control, Schifter & Ajzen (1985) found that female students' intentions to lose weight were more likely to result in genuine weight loss among those who felt they could control their weight and could successfully lose weight if they tried. Attitudes about the desirability of weight loss had little effect on behavior for those who felt helpless about the whole thing.

External constraints and opportunities are also important. Ritter (1988) analyzed interviews with a large national sample of young men about their use of marijuana and cocaine. He found that the intention to use such drugs, as measured ten years earlier, had a significant effect on current use. But so did the current availability of the drug, especially for cocaine. One can intend to use illegal drugs, yet not be able to find a seller. Or one can intend not to, yet wind up using them if they are readily available and everyone else is using them.

And, as we have seen earlier in this chapter, attitudes about the desirability of a behavior do not always control our actions. Prior behavior influences future behavior above and beyond attitudes. To some extent people are simply creatures of habit. How a woman fed her first child influences how she will in fact feed her second, no matter what she or all her friends and family members think is right (Manstead et al., 1983). And, in a study many readers may be able to relate to, Ajzen and Madden (1986) found previous class attendance to be the single strongest predictor of college students' future class attendance, irrespective of any of their attitudes about attending class.

Finally, it is sometimes difficult to get measures of behavioral intention that are truly independent of attitudes toward the behavior, on the one hand, and actual behavior, on the other. Sometimes "behavioral intention" is not, as measured, very different from "attitude toward the behavior." Asking a pregnant woman whether or not she intends to breast-feed her baby may be almost the same thing as asking her whether she thinks it is a good idea or not. Under such circumstances attitudes are a good bit more successful in predicting behavioral intentions than they are actual behavior, as you might expect (e.g., Ajzen & Madden, 1986). But it may not add very much to our understanding to bring behavioral intention in as a separate factor.

This is a particular danger when researchers use self-reported behavior rather than observing it directly. Then it may be artificially correlated with attitudes toward the behavior, especially if the behavior has strong moral implications. Hessing, Elffers, and Weigel (1988), for example, interviewed individuals who had been identified by Dutch tax officials as having knowingly evaded taxes in two separate tax years (and who had paid the resulting bills without protest) as well as individuals identified as having submitted honest tax returns. They found that self-reported tax evasion was scarcely related at all to objective tax evasion: 69 percent of the actual evaders reported that they were not (and 25 percent of the actual nonevaders reported that they *had* evaded taxes!). Not surprisingly, both attitudes toward tax evasion and subjective social norms predicted self-reported behavior much better than they did actual behavior. Apparently people reported their behavior more in terms of what they thought they *should* have done than in terms of what they actually *had* done.

With these reservations, this theory clearly has value in helping to understand the role attitudes play in determining behavior. In general we believe a great deal of evidence now supports the idea that attitudes affect behavior. But clearly there are numerous other factors that play a major role in determining the degree of attitude-behavior consistency.

COGNITIVE DISSONANCE THEORY

We have been discussing attitude-behavior consistency in terms of the conditions under which attitudes determine behavior. But our behavior also can influence our attitudes. Put another way, our attitudes are often rationalizations for the things we have already done. The person who has given up smoking through a long and agonized process becomes the most obnoxious critic of anyone else who smokes. The newlywed couple expecting the birth of an unplanned baby abandon their ambivalence about having children and broadcast their great delight at the prospect. The military commander who commits his troops to a chancy mission that turns out to be a disaster, costing thousands of casualties, now resolutely declares he was certain he was right all along, and would not change his tactics in any way if he had it to do all over again.

All these examples depict a process in which a person's behavior is followed by substantial attitude change. It also assumes pressure toward consistency between attitudes and behavior, but in a far less flattering manner than the theory of reasoned action. It says that people's behavior controls their attitudes no matter how unthinking the behavior was, rather than that people deliberately and reasonably act on the basis of their thinking.

Most of the research on this problem was originally inspired by cognitive dissonance theory (Festinger, 1957). Like several other theories we have discussed, cognitive dissonance theory assumes there is a pressure toward consistency. Although it can be applied to inconsistencies between any cognitions, dissonance theory has dealt most creatively with inconsistencies between behavior and attitudes.

Dissonance is created when some behavior we have engaged in is inconsistent with our attitudes. This dissonance creates psychological tension, and people feel pressured to reduce or remove it. Dissonance operates much like any other drive: if we are hungry, we do something to reduce our hunger; if we are afraid, we do something to reduce our fear; and if we feel dissonance, we do something to reduce it also. Reducing it means restoring consistency, or *consonance*. The main way of reducing dissonance, if the behavior cannot be revoked or changed in some way, is to change one's attitude.

Postdecision Dissonance

One behavior that almost always arouses dissonance is making a decision. Whenever we must decide between two or more alternatives, the final choice is to some extent inconsistent with some of our beliefs. After we decide, all the good aspects of the unchosen alternative and all the bad aspects of the chosen alternative are dissonant with the decision.

This dissonance can be reduced by improving our evaluation of the chosen alternative, because everything positive about it is consonant with the decision. Dissonance can also be reduced by lowering the evaluation of the unchosen alternative. The less attractive it is, the less dissonance is aroused by rejecting it. Therefore, after people make decisions, there is a tendency for them to increase their liking for what they chose and to decrease their liking for what they did not choose.

Suppose that Susan has two rival suitors, Dan the fraternity man and George the honors student. Dan wants her to go to Europe with him after her junior year, while George wants her to go to summer school with him. As shown in Figure 5–5, she likes them both, in different ways. Finally Dan's sense of humor and love for a good time (and his good looks) win out over George's good qualities. After she makes the decision and buys her airline tickets, she reduces dissonance by upgrading Dan's positive attributes and downplaying his shortcomings. Now he becomes a hilarious storyteller, rather than just having a good sense of humor, and she begins to think he will become interested in a long-term relationship with her once they spend more time together. Similarly, she begins to have doubts about George's good qualities

DAN INVITES SUSAN TO SPEND A MONTH IN EUROPE, WHILE GEORGE WANTS HER TO GO
TO SUMMER SCHOOL WITH HIM. SHE DECIDES TO GO WITH DAN. WHAT HAPPENS TO HER
ATTITUDES TOWARD THEM?

	Predecision	Postdecision
Attitudes toward Dan		
Good attributes (consonant)	Good sense of humor (++)	Hilarious storyteller (+++)
	Likes to party (++)	Will be fun to travel with (++)
	Good-looking (++)	Unusually good-looking (+++)
Bad attributes (dissonant)	Drinks too much (−)	Probably won't drink much while traveling (0)
	Doesn't want serious relationships (−)	He'll change when he gets to know me (+)
Overall attitude	+4	+9
Attitudes toward George		
Good attributes (dissonant)	Considerate & thoughtful (++)	Too serious (−)
	Good student (+)	No fun (−−)
	Has a nice family (++)	I won't see his family (0)
Bad attributes (consonant)	Likes to study on weekends (−)	Wouldn't party (−−)
	Not much sense of humor (−−)	Can't take a joke (−−−)
Overall attitude	+2	−8

Figure 5–5. Susan's summer dilemma and the consequences of her decision.

and emphasize his bad ones. Now instead of being a thoughtful good student, she sees him as too serious, with no sense of humor at all, and probably as not much fun in general. These attitude changes should help reduce her dissonance.

A study by Brehm (1956) demonstrated this empirically. College women were shown eight products, such as a toaster, a stopwatch, and a radio, and were asked to indicate how much they would like to have each of them. They were then shown two of the eight products and told they would be given whichever they chose. After the objects were chosen and the subjects received the one they selected, they were asked to rate all the objects again. As shown in Table 5–3, on the second rating there was a strong tendency for the women in the high-dissonance condition to increase their evaluation of the item they had picked and to decrease their evaluation of the rejected item.

A no-dissonance control group (shown on the bottom line in the table) shows that the effect was due primarily to dissonance reduction. These women made the first rating, but, instead of next choosing between two items and receiving their preference, they were simply given one of the products they had rated favorably. When they rerated all the products, they showed no tendency to improve the evaluation of the object they owned. This demonstrated that the reevaluation in the high-dissonance condition was not simply due to pride of ownership—making the decision was the critical factor.

The tendency toward reevaluation is particularly strong when the two alternatives are initially rated close in attractiveness. Then the excellent qualities of the rejected object, and the flaws of the chosen object, create real dissonance. Susan would not have had to change her attitudes nearly as much if Dan were more perfect or if George were a complete nerd. It is

T A B L E   5 – 3

DISSONANCE REDUCTION FOLLOWING A DECISION

Condition	Rating of Chosen Object	Rating of Unchosen Object	Total Dissonance Reduction
High dissonance (objects initially rated close)	+.32	−.53	+.85
Low dissonance (objects initially rated far apart)	+.25	−.12	+.37
No dissonance (gift with no choice)	.00	none	.00

Source: Brehm (1956).

Note: The entries in the first two columns are the mean changes in evaluation of the chosen and unchosen objects from before to after the decision. The difference between the two is the total amount of dissonance reduction, shown in the third column.

Dan's flaws, and George's strengths, that made them almost equally attractive to Susan before she decided to go to Europe, and that created so much dissonance for her. What if Dan turns out to be a selfish pig who takes up with the first French girl he meets on the beach? George would not do that in summer school.

Brehm tested this notion also. In the high-dissonance condition he gave the women a choice between a product they had ranked high and one they had ranked next best. In the low-dissonance condition the women were given a choice between a high-ranked product and one they ranked as much inferior. As shown in Table 5–3, the high-dissonance condition generated considerably more dissonance reduction. As the theory predicts, when two alternatives are close in attractiveness, a great deal of dissonance is aroused. After the decision is made, there should be greater reevaluation of the two alternatives.

In these cases, dissonance was created by choosing between two alternatives. But postdecisional dissonance can also be produced when we commit ourselves to a single course of action. This happened to a group who predicted that the world was going to end on a particular day, and that they would be saved by a spaceship from outer space (Festinger, Riecken, & Schachter, 1956). In the days and weeks after making this prediction, the group members sold many of their belongings and in general prepared for the end of the world. At the same time, the group mainly kept to itself, avoided publicity, and was rather quiet about its beliefs.

When the fateful day arrived and passed without the world being destroyed, they were initially greatly shaken. Their response, however, was not to give up their beliefs and return to normal life. This would not have reduced the dissonance caused by knowing that nothing had come of all the effort they had put into their plans. Instead, they decided that the day was put off but that the end of the world was still coming soon. In addition, they changed their style considerably. Instead of being quiet and avoiding publicity, they argued that their efforts had postponed the end of the world. And they became much more active in trying to get new supporters. Presumably, this helped reduce their dissonance by justifying their original behavior: more and more people were in agreement with them.

Part of the appeal of cognitive dissonance theory is that it often makes counterintuitive predictions. In this case, common sense might have suggested that the group would give up after its prediction failed so miserably. But dissonance theory predicts that this disproof would lead them not to abandon the theory, but to argue it even more forcefully. And that was just what happened.

BOX 5–4

Postdecision Dissonance at Posttime

According to dissonance theory, making a decision produces dissonance and also produces attitude change that will help justify that decision. Knox and Inkster (1968) reasoned that bettors at a horse track ought to be susceptible to this process. After they have irreversibly put their money down on a horse at the betting window, they ought to be in a state of dissonance. To justify the bet, they should overestimate their horse's chances.

So they interviewed one sample of bettors just before they reached the betting window, before they had made an irrevocable commitment, and another sample just after they had completed their bets, when they should have had the maximum dissonance. Indeed, they found the postbet group was considerably more certain their horse would win than was the prebet group, as dissonance the-

ory would predict. A control group was interviewed before making a bet and then again afterward, to determine whether last-minute switches to the favorite might have explained the difference, but none had changed horses in the short time span between interviews.

The authors conclude with a quote from one of the prebet subjects, who approached the postbet interviewer right after making his bet, and volunteered this: "Are you working with that other fellow there?" (indicating the prebet experimenter who was by then engaged in another interview). "Well, I just told him that my horse had a fair chance of winning. Will you have him change that to a good chance? No, by God, make that an excellent chance."

Attitude-Discrepant Behavior

Cognitive dissonance theory has also been applied to the effects of **attitude-discrepant behavior** (sometimes called counterattitudinal behavior). When an individual holds a belief and performs an act inconsistent with it, dissonance is produced. The person has, in fact, performed the act and would find it difficult to convince himself that he did not. Most of the pressure must be relieved by changing the attitude.

For example, many people go into law school because they believe they can help the poor and needy, and improve society. Yet when they later go into legal practice, most of them find that it involves repetitious and routine work that has more to do with business contracts and tax advantages than with helping the poor and needy. These once idealistic individuals then find themselves justifying and even enjoying what they do. They may come to believe that nothing much can be done to help the poor, and even that they do not deserve much help. Why the change?

Dissonance theory would argue that they began engaging in attitude-discrepant behavior when they first got a job, because that was the condition of the job. To get paid, they had to work long hours on relatively uninspiring drudgery. But this created dissonance: their behavior was inconsistent with their attitudes. So with time, they adjusted their attitudes to become more consistent with their behavior.

But dissonance, and the consequent attitude change, is not always generated by engaging in attitude-discrepant behavior. Many young American men who were drafted to fight in Vietnam (and perhaps many young Russian men drafted to fight in Afghanistan) did not believe in the value of the war. And many of them continued to be quite opposed to it throughout their service, despite engaging in the various attitude-discrepant behaviors required of soldiers on active duty. Thus, much of the research on this topic has tried to distinguish the conditions under which attitude-discrepant behavior produces dissonance-reducing attitude change from conditions in which it does not.

Barely Sufficient Incentives. The most interesting prediction from dissonance theory concerns the level of incentive required to produce attitude change. On the one hand, there has to be enough incentive to make the person commit the counterattitudinal act. People normally do not act in a way contrary to their attitudes unless there is some reason to do so. Something has to get that new law school graduate to pore over those boring legal documents until 11:00 P.M. each night. So imagine the person as being subjected to a certain level of pressure to perform the attitude-discrepant act. The pressure had to be enough to produce the act.

But if there is great pressure on the individual to perform the discrepant act, it is consistent with the decision and does not produce much dissonance. If this was the only job the law school graduate could get, he would experience little dissonance about it. He may even joke about it with his friends to show he does not really believe in it. Many of those Vietnam draftees in fact maintained very high levels of cynicism, and especially cynical humor (not to mention drug use) about the war—but military regulations and discipline are such that they were under great external pressure, and indeed usually had no choice about their behavior.

In short, there has to be enough pressure on the person to produce the counterattitudinal act. Yet if too much pressure is exerted, there will be no dissonance, and thus no attitude change. The optimal level of pressure is thus a *barely sufficient* amount—enough to produce the behavior, but not enough to prevent dissonance arousal.

Positive Incentives. The second point is that beyond the minimum incentive required to get the person to engage in the attitude-discrepant behavior, the *more* original pressure to perform the act (that is, the more consonant cognitions), the less dissonance should be produced by performing it. So paradoxically, after a certain point, the *more* incentive, the *less* he will change his attitude to justify having done it. The reason is that increasing the pressure only provides more cognitions consonant with the behavior, so there is less dissonance to be reduced.

The most obvious incentive for performing attitude-discrepant behavior is money. Suppose you are offered a menial summer job but the pay is extremely good, such as day labor on a construction site. There is no dissonance and so there is no pressure to reevaluate the job; it is a crummy job, but at least you earn good money. But suppose you are working at a volunteer job in the local hospital. Then dissonance is created, which you might reduce by reevaluating the job. Perhaps you start to think that it is an educational experience, or that you meet very interesting people, or that you have plenty of freedom to do other things.

The best early example of this point is found in a study by Festinger and Carlsmith (1959). Volunteers for an experiment worked on an exceedingly dull task. After they had completed it, the experimenter explained that he was studying the effect of preconceptions on people's performance on a task. He was studying several groups of subjects who were told good things about the task ahead of time, bad things, or

Well, the incentive *does* have to be sufficient to produce the attitude-discrepant behavior!

nothing. The experimenter then asked the subject to help him out with something because his usual assistant could not be there that day. The next subject was supposed to receive favorable information about the task before performing it. The experimenter asked the subject whether he would be willing to do this for him. All he would have to do is stop the next subject as he was coming into the room, talk to him briefly about the experiment, and tell him that the task was an exceedingly enjoyable one. In other words, he was supposed to pretend to be a regular subject who was just completing the experiment and to lie to the next subject about the dull task by saying that he had found it enjoyable.

At this point, the key experimental manipulation was introduced. Some subjects were told the experimenter would pay them $1 for helping, and others were told they would be paid $20. Virtually all the subjects agreed to the arrangement and proceeded to describe the task to the next subject as very enjoyable. There was also a control group, the members of which were not asked to lie. Soon afterward, the experimenter had all the subjects indicate how much they had actually enjoyed the task. Dissonance about telling the lie could be reduced by changing attitudes about the task—that is, by deciding that the task was quite enjoyable.

Those who were paid $1 rated the task more positively than did those who were paid $20 (Table 5–4). They found the task more enjoyable and were more willing to participate in other similar experiments, despite being paid less money to do it. This is what dissonance theory would predict. The larger amount of money served as an additional reason for performing the task; therefore it was a consonant element in the situation and reduced the overall amount of dissonance. The less dissonance, the less attitude change.

This was an extremely influential experiment. It supported the surprising prediction that liking for a disagreeable task would actually be greatest when the person was paid least to do it. Many similar experiments have been conducted, obtaining similar results, some using money, and others, such incentives as the amount of justification for performing a boring task (Freedman, 1963; Rosenfeld et al., 1984).

Threats. In principle, negative incentives ought to work exactly the same way as positive incentives. One way to try to get people to perform disliked acts is to threaten them with punishment. If they do not wear a tie to work or pay their income taxes or do their homework, they are penalized. Threats are also used to prevent people from doing things they want to do. If people drive too fast, steal cookies from the cookie jar, play with a forbidden toy, or sell cocaine, they may be punished. The severity of the possible punishments varies enormously. They may get a mild reprimand, miss dessert, be fined $100, spend 5 years in jail, or even face execution.

But greater threat also should produce less dissonance and so less attitude change (assuming the threat of punishment is strong enough to produce the desired behavior). In two experiments to test this idea, children were shown a group of toys and then were forbidden to play with one of them (Aronson & Carlsmith, 1963; Freedman, 1965). They were threatened with either mild or severe punishment if they played with that particular desirable toy. If they obeyed and did not play with the toy, dissonance should be aroused. The attitude "I would like to play with that toy" is dissonant with the behavior of not playing with it. On the other hand, the behavior of not playing with the toy should be consonant with the perceived threat of punishment. Therefore, the *less* severe the threat, the more dissonance it should provide. If the

T A B L E 5 – 4		
POSITIVE ATTITUDES RESULTING FROM ATTITUDE-DISCREPANT BEHAVIOR		
	Dependent Variable	
Condition	Enjoyment of Task	Willingness to Participate in Similar Experiments
$1 reward	+1.35	+1.20
$20 reward	−.05	−.25

Source: Adapted from Festinger and Carlsmith (1959).

Note: A positive number indicates greater enjoyment of the task or greater willingness to participate in similar experiments.

BOX 5–5

Cold Cook, Great Grasshoppers

Another possible incentive for engaging in a discrepant act is liking the person trying to get us to do it. If your best friends ask you to do something—lend them ten dollars, drive them to the airport, help them cheat on an exam—there is a considerable amount of pressure to agree. If someone you dislike asks you, you are under considerably less pressure. Thus, if you do something for someone, there should be more dissonance if you dislike the other person than if you like the person. This, in turn, means that performing a discrepant act for somebody you dislike should produce more attitude change than performing the same act for someone you like.

This effect was demonstrated in a study in which subjects were persuaded by two different kinds of experimenters to eat grasshoppers (Zimbardo et al., 1965). In one condition, the experimenter was pleasant, casual, relaxed, and friendly. He presented his arguments in an offhand manner and did his best to be as attractive as possible. In the other condition, the experimenter was cold, formal, somewhat aggressive, and rather forbidding. In general, he did everything he could to be unpleasant. After the subjects who had chosen to eat the grasshoppers had done so, they indicated how much they liked them.

The analysis in terms of dissonance theory is straightforward. Everyone disliked eating grasshoppers, so choosing to eat them produced dissonance. But there would be less dissonance aroused by eating them for the pleasant experimenter, since helping a pleasant person out was consonant with eating them. Helping a cold and aggressive person out, on the other hand, was more dissonant with eating the ugly creatures. So the more they liked the experimenter, the less the dissonance and the less need they would have to decide that they really liked the grasshoppers.

The results were consistent with this analysis. Subjects who ate the grasshoppers when there was a nasty experimenter liked the grasshoppers more than those who ate the grasshoppers when there was a pleasant experimenter. The pleasant experimenter produced less dissonance and therefore made it less necessary to reevaluate the grasshoppers.

---

children did not play with the toy, we would expect the dissonance to produce some change in their attitude toward it, deciding that the toy was not attractive. Little dissonance should be produced by not playing with an unappealing toy. And because the less the threat, the greater the dissonance, there should be more attitude change with lower threats.

In these experiments, none of the children played with the toy, regardless of whether they were threatened with mild or severe punishment, because both threats were strong enough to induce compliance. In one study, the children rerated the toys at this point, and in the other, they were given another opportunity to play with the toy several weeks later. The results of the two experiments are shown in Figure 5–6. It can be seen that the children reduced their evaluation of the forbidden toy more and

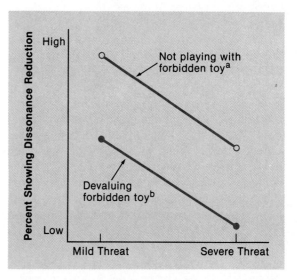

Figure 5–6. Effects of Severity of Threat for Playing with Forbidden Toy on Dissonance Reduction (Aronson & Carlsmith, 1963; Freedman, 1965).

were less likely to play with it later on under mild threat than under severe threat. The greater dissonance in the mild threat condition was reduced by devaluing the toy or deciding it was wrong to play with it.

Other Conditions for Dissonance

We have identified two general situations in which our behavior may change our attitudes: making decisions and engaging in attitude-discrepant behavior. Attitude change depends on the magnitude of dissonance, and minimal positive incentives or minimal threats create more dissonance. What are some of the other factors necessary for dissonance-reducing attitude change to occur?

Choice. Another major contributor to dissonance is the feeling of *choice* about the behavior. If Susan feels she freely and of sound mind chose Dan and Europe, she will have dissonance to reduce afterward. But often we do not feel much sense of choice about what we do. Maybe Dan pressured her into going to Europe by threatening never to see her again if she didn't go. Or maybe her parents would give her the money to go this particular summer but said they might not be able to in later summers. Without the feeling of choice, there is no dissonance.

Similarly, attitude-discrepant behavior creates dissonance only when the behavior is freely chosen (or at least the person feels it is freely chosen). This is shown quite clearly in a study by Linder, Cooper, and Jones (1967). Students wrote an essay that disagreed with their opinions. Some subjects were made to feel they had a choice about whether or not they wrote the essay; others were given no choice. Half the subjects in each condition were paid $2.50, and half were paid $0.50. The amount of attitude change in the four conditions is shown in Figure 5–7.

With free choice, the typical dissonance effect appeared. There was more change with less incentive. With no choice, the dissonance effect did not obtain. There was more change with

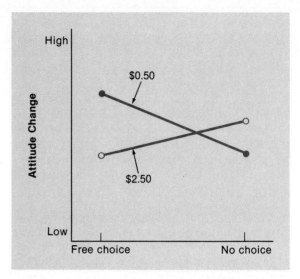

Figure 5–7. The Effects of Incentive and Choice on Attitude Change (Linder, Cooper, & Jones, 1967).

greater incentive. So the feeling of choice about one's behavior is a critical precondition for the occurrence of attitude change produced by one's behavior.

Irrevocable Commitment. An interesting aspect of the effect of decisions is that the reevaluation appears only when the result of the decision is certain. If Susan had bought nonrefundable airline tickets, her decision would create more dissonance than if she knew she could always get a refund if she changed her mind. One key, therefore, to attitude change as a dissonance-reducing mechanism is maintaining the person's **commitment** to the decision or behavior. As long as the person feels irreversibly committed to that course of action, dissonance promotes attitude change. But if the person feels she can get out of the decision if it works out badly, or she can do it half-heartedly, or she may not have to go through with it at all, dissonance will not be present, and no attitude change may occur.

Foreseeable Consequences. In all these cases, the subjects could reasonably foresee the negative consequences of their actions, and expecting those known bad effects creates dissonance. But it turns out that they seem only to need to think they *could* have foreseen the negative consequences, not that they actually *did* foresee them. Dissonance will be avoided only if there was no way for the individual to foresee this negative outcome.

If someone decides to walk to class on the left side of the street rather than the right side, and as she walks along a brick suddenly falls off a roof and hits her on the head, this is a terrible misfortune. But (if she lives) she should not experience dissonance. "I chose to walk on the left side of the street" is not dissonant with "a brick hit me on the head." For all intents and purposes, the two cognitions are not relevant to each other. On the other hand, if she knew that there was some chance that she would get hit on the head, perhaps because in the last week three other people had been hit on the head by bricks, dissonance probably would be aroused.

Following that reasoning, Goethals, Cooper, and Naficy (1979) predicted that either *foreseen* negative consequences, or *foreseeable* consequences even if unforeseen, would produce dissonance and attitude change; only unforeseeable consequences would not. They had students at Princeton record speeches favoring the doubling of the size of the freshman class. That was a disagreeable possibility to the subjects, given Princeton's reputation as a relatively small, elite college. And indeed the speech might help bring about that undesirable change. Some (foreseen consequences) were told the speech might be given to the board of admissions, which was considering such an increase; others (foreseeable consequences) that it would be given to some other groups, but they were not named. Still others (unforeseeable consequences) were not told of any further use of the speech. After the speech was recorded, all were told of the negative consequences: their counterattitudinal speech would be given to the board of admissions.

Under what circumstances did the subjects change their attitudes in the dissonance-reducing direction of their speech? It turned out that either foreseen or foreseeable consequences promoted attitude change, in line with the notion that either can produce dissonance. Only unforeseeable consequences did not.

Responsibility for Consequences. The importance of perceived choice is that it brings with it perceived responsibility for all consequences, whether or not it is "logical" to feel responsible for them. As we saw in the last chapter, people tend to make internal attributions whenever behavior is committed under free choice and assign moral responsibility for behavior that is internally caused. A series of studies has shown the crucial role of this feeling of responsibility for dissonance arousal.

If decision makers feel responsible for the consequences, then dissonance occurs whether the consequence could reasonably have been foreseen or not. If they feel no responsibility for the outcome, there is no dissonance regardless of how disastrous the result. Pallak and his colleagues designed a series of studies to illustrate this point. In the first one (Pallak, Sogin, & Van Zante, 1974) a boring task was reevaluated in a more favorable direction, consistent with dissonance reduction, even when the negative consequences (learning that the task was just wasted time) were not known until after the task was completed—as long as the subject completed it under high perceived choice. In later work (Sogin & Pallak, 1976), they pinpointed the dissonance effect as depending on an internal attribution. If the negative consequences came about because of something the subject felt responsible for, a dissonance-reducing reevaluation would take place whether the effects were foreseen or unforeseen.

So the critical question regarding unforeseen negative consequences is whether or not people *feel* their own prior behavior was responsible for them. That is why perceived choice is so important. When people choose something that works out badly, they feel responsible for the outcome, and it creates dissonance. Indeed some now argue that perceived personal responsibility for aversive consequences is so important in producing attitude change that it does not even matter whether the behavior is counterattitudinal or not. Even acts that are consistent with our attitudes should produce attitude change (strengthening our prior attitudes) if they produce bad outcomes and we feel responsible for the acts (Scher & Cooper, 1989).

Effort. The more effort one takes in executing behavioral acts that have aversive consequences, the more dissonance should be aroused. If you volunteer for the Marine Corps, and basic training is completely exhausting as well as painful and stressful, and you can barely drag yourself out of bed in the morning, more dissonance should be created and the more you should think you made the right choice and love the Marine Corps. The attitude change helps to justify the effort you have expended (or even expect to expend; see Wicklund et al., 1967).

This notion has been applied to the effects of psychotherapy. Therapy usually involves effort and sacrifice, and it can be embarrassing, emotionally painful, and expensive. If the client enters it voluntarily, all of that needs to be justified, and that can lead the person to improve as a result. Axsom (1989) set up a situation in which people were tested for snake phobias, and then told that they would undergo a therapeutic relaxation procedure to reduce phobias. Some were told it would take extreme exertion, and others that it would be very easy. Perceived choice was also manipulated. Subjects actually approached snakes most closely when they had high choice and expected the treatment would take the most effort.

These, then, are the main preconditions for cognitive dissonance, and for the attitude change that results from taking decisive action: minimum incentives, perceived choice, irrevocable commitment, foreseeable consequences, personal responsibility for those consequences, and great effort. This is a somewhat narrower set of conditions than originally proposed by dissonance theorists. Both postdecisional dissonance and dissonance produced by attitude-discrepant behavior are not as common as had been suggested by the earliest versions of dissonance theory. But they do occur fairly reliably, given this restricted set of circumstances.

Self-Perception Theory

Cognitive dissonance theory originally inspired this research on the effects of behavior on attitude change, and for a number of years pro-

These Vietnam veterans did not support the war in which they fought. What prevented military service from producing dissonance-reducing pro-war attitude change?

vided the only theoretical interpretation of these findings. However, Bem (1967) then offered another interpretation, in terms of **self-perception theory.** As we saw in the last chapter, he argued that we often do not really know what our attitudes are and simply infer them from our own behavior and the circumstances in which this behavior occurs. If we choose to eat oranges from a basket with seven kinds of fruit and somebody asks us how we feel about oranges, we say to ourselves, "I just chose oranges; nobody forced me to; therefore I must really like oranges." Accordingly, we tell the person we like oranges. Similarly, if we go to church, we assume that we are religious, and so on.

It is easy to see how this might apply to attitude-discrepant behavior. A subject is paid $1 to tell someone that a particular task was very enjoyable. When the subject is subsequently asked how enjoyable he himself thought the task was, he says to himself, "I said that the task was enjoyable and I was paid only one dollar. One dollar is not enough to make me lie, so I must really think that the task is enjoyable." On the other hand $20 perhaps is a sufficient amount to tell a lie. So the subject then might say to himself, "The reason I said it was enjoyable was just to get the twenty dollars; I didn't really believe it." Thus this self-perception explanation makes the same predictions as dissonance theory: the more people are paid to make a discrepant statement, the less they will believe it.

The major difference is not in the prediction, but in the interpretation. The two theories offer radically different views of attitudes and of the way in which behavior influences attitudes. The more traditional view of attitudes reflected in dissonance theory is that they are strong, enduring predispositions. When people engage in counterattitudinal behavior, they suffer from unpleasant tensions that can be relieved only by giving up these cherished attitudes. Dissonance theory describes people as stubbornly resisting change. They have to be lured and cajoled into a very particular set of circumstances in which they finally feel so involved and committed to the behavior they must change their attitudes. Bem's self-perception theory suggests that people's expressions of attitude are, instead, rather casual verbal statements. People have no great stake in their attitudes; rather, they seem simply to be trying to cooperate with a curious questioner by giving a plausible answer, without strong conviction or feelings. So they readily change these superficial answers.

Dissonance theorists at first reacted with horror to Bem's reinterpretation. The very original, painstakingly created, and ingenious experiments they had done were now being seriously misinterpreted as reflecting some alien process. Their initial response was to try to design experiments that would disprove Bem's interpretations. This proved to be surprisingly difficult. Today, social psychologists assume that both

processes occur on some occasions. The question is, when is one more likely to occur than the other?

The self-perception process should be most likely to occur when people's own attitudes are vague and ambiguous. It would not be surprising if we should arrive at an attitude about a new and unfamiliar laboratory task on the basis of our perceptions of our behavior in the experimental situation. It would be more surprising if we were to use self-perception to figure out our attitude about our favorite foods, like broiled lobster, sushi, or pizza with anchovies. We do not need to feel ourselves salivate or watch ourselves devour every last morsel to know that we love those things; we know that when we think about them.

The hypothesis, then, is that self-perception theory works only when people do not possess well-defined prior attitudes. To test this, Chaiken and Baldwin (1981) separated subjects with strong, consistent attitudes toward the environment (concerning nuclear power, solar energy, outlawing nonreturnable soft drink bottles, aerosol cans, and so on) from those with weak, inconsistent attitudes. Then they varied whether the subjects perceived their own usual behavior as pro- or anti-environment, using the procedures described in the last chapter (Salancik & Conway, 1975). This involves manipulating their perceptions of their own behavior by asking about either easy or hard behaviors. For example, a person asked "Have you ever recycled a soft drink can?" is likely to say, "Yes," and perceive herself as pro-environmental. Someone asked "Do you always recycle your soft drink cans?" is likely to answer, "No," and is likely to feel that she must generally not be very supportive of the environment.

This hypothesis, that the self-perception process would work only for those without strong and well-defined prior attitudes, was quite strongly supported. Among the subjects whose prior attitudes were strong and highly consistent, the manipulation of self-reported environmentalist behaviors had no significant effect on attitudes, as shown in Figure 5–8. However, among those with initially weak and inconsistent attitudes, the manipulation had the large

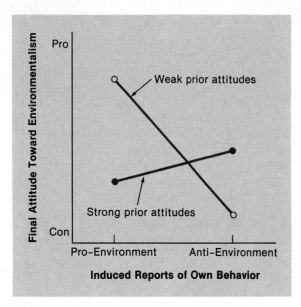

Figure 5-8. Attitudes toward Environmentalism as a Function of Induced Reports of Own Behavior and Prior Attitude Strength

effect predicted by Bem's self-perception theory: People who had been induced to describe their behavior as pro-environment perceived themselves as being more pro-environmental in their attitudes than did those induced to describe their behavior as more anti-environment.

The conclusion was that "the self-perception account of attitude expression holds primarily for individuals who do not possess well-defined prior attitudes toward the target attitude object. . . ." (Chaiken & Baldwin, 1981, p. 8). Later research has elaborated on this conclusion. Well-defined prior attitudes might not be available because the individual has had relatively few prior experiences with regard to the issue (Wood, 1982). Or it might be because the person has no immediate sensory data relevant to the issue—as, for example, never having tasted the food products one is trying to decide between (Tybout & Scott, 1983). On the other hand, when people do have well-defined prior attitudes, we might expect the dissonance process rather than the self-perception process to operate.

Is Dissonance a Drive?

Another approach to this controversy between these theoretical positions involves the contention that dissonance is uncomfortable, that it acts as a drive much like hunger, and that people do what they can to reduce this discomfort. Bem's analysis would not expect attitude-discrepant behavior to arouse discomfort or drive. Fortunately, this difference between the theories is directly testable.

One implication is that dissonance should result in physiological arousal. Elkin and Leippe (1986) had students write counterattitudinal essays, varying choice and effort. The high-choice, high-effort condition should have produced the most dissonance. These authors did find both choice and effort produced greater physiological arousal, in terms of galvanic skin response.

A second implication comes from the misattribution studies discussed in the last chapter. Subjective arousal states can be reduced to the extent that the person attributes them to other stimuli, such as a pill. If dissonance is a subjective arousal state, it could be reduced in this manner.

The dissonance-as-drive idea holds that no attitude change should occur if arousal can be attributed to some cause other than inconsistency. To test this, Zanna and Cooper (1974) gave subjects a pill; in one condition they were told the pill would make them feel tense, in the other, that it would make them feel relaxed. Subjects were then induced to write counterattitudinal essays under either high- or low-choice conditions.

Subjects who were told they would feel tense because of the pill showed no dissonance effect—that is, high choice produced no more attitude change than low choice. Presumably when the subject could attribute arousal to the pill, there was no dissonance, and therefore no dissonance-produced difference in attitude change. However, when they were told the pill would just make them feel relaxed, the high-choice condition produced more attitude change in the direction of the essay than did the low-choice condition, in line with the usual dissonance effect. Presumably the subject could not attribute arousal to the pill, because it was supposedly a relaxation pill. This gives additional evidence for supposing that dissonance effects do depend on some kind of physiological arousal mechanism, which can be eliminated or reduced if the subject can attribute arousal to some extraneous stimulus.

In short, situations involving commitments or counterattitudinal acts create tension under the conditions we have described: choice, fore-seeable negative consequences, minimal external pressure, and so on. Attitude change as a response depends on not being able to reduce the tension in some other way, such as blaming it on external pressure, a drug-induced state (especially if unpleasant; see Higgins et al., 1979), or revoking the behavior. And the two processes probably work best in different arenas: dissonance theory, with more controversial, involving issues, and self-perception theory, with more vague, uninvolving, minor, novel issues.

Key Terms

affective (evaluative) component
attitude-discrepant behavior
attitudes
balance theory
behavioral component
behavioral intention
cognitive component

cognitive consistency
cognitive dissonance
cognitive response theory
commitment
elaboration-likelihood model
expectancy-value approach

incentive theory
learning
reasoned action model
self-perception theory
social norms
stereotype
transfer of affect

Summary

1. Attitudes have a cognitive (thought) component, an affective (feeling) component, and a behavioral component.

2. People often have cognitively complex attitudes. However, like personality impressions, attitudes tend to be organized around the affective (or evaluative) dimension and to be evaluatively simple.

3. The learning approach views attitudes as learned by association, reinforcement, and imitation. Cognitive consistency theories view people as attempting to maintain consistency among their various attitudes, and among the affective, cognitive, and behavioral components of a particular attitude.

The incentive approach views attitudes as reasonable cost-benefit calculations by the individual based on the real pros and cons of the arguments.

4. It is usually assumed that behavior arises from attitudes, but considerable research questions how consistent the two are with each other. Now it appears that attitudes influence behavior most when attitudes are strong, stable, salient, and clearly relevant to the behavior, and when there are few conflicting situational pressures.

5. The reasoned action model holds that behavior is controlled by behavioral intentions, which in turn are determined by

attitudes toward the behavior and by subjective social norms.

6. Dissonance theory focuses on how behavior affects attitudes. Dissonance arises following decisions and following behavioral acts contrary to the individual's attitudes.

7. Dissonance can be reduced in a variety of ways. If the behavior itself cannot be revoked, the most important alternative is attitude change to reduce attitude-behavior discrepancies.

8. Postdecisional dissonance is greatest when people have free choice, remain committed to their decisions, and feel responsible for foreseeable consequences.

9. Dissonance following attitude-discrepant behavior depends upon barely sufficient incentives to commit the behavior, such as threats or promised rewards. The maximum dissonance occurs with minimum incentive and clear personal responsibility for negative consequences of the act.

10. Alternative explanations for these dissonance effects have been generated by self-perception theory. When people have rather vague, undefined attitudes, behavioral acts may lead to new perceptions of one's own attitudes, thus leading to attitude-behavior consistency through self-perception rather than dissonance reduction.

Suggested Readings

Abelson, R. P., Aronson, E., McGuire, W. J., Newcomb, T. M., Rosenberg, M. J., & Tannenbaum, P. E. (1968). *Theories of cognitive consistency: A sourcebook.* Chicago: Rand McNally. An extensive compilation of papers on almost every version of consistency theory, by almost everyone who ever wrote about it. Its nickname is TOCCAS.

Ajzen, I., & Fishbein, M. (1980). *Understanding attitudes and predicting social behavior.* Englewood Cliffs, NJ: Prentice-Hall. A succinct treatment of the "theory of reasoned action," applying it to such social problems as obesity and weight loss, family planning, career choices, and voting behavior.

Chaiken, S., & Stangor, C. (1987). Attitudes and attitude change. In M. R. Rosenzweig & L. W. Porter (Eds.), *Annual Review of Psychology, 38,* 575–630. A thoughtful review of recent research on attitudes.

Cooper, J., & Fazio, R. H. (1984). A new look at dissonance theory. In L. Berkowitz (Ed.), *Advances in experimental social psychology,* Vol. 17. New York: Academic Press. An update of research on cognitive dissonance theory.

Fazio, R. H. (1987). Self-perception theory: A current perspective. In M. P. Zanna, J. M. Olson, & C. P. Herman (Eds.), *Social influence: The Ontario Symposium,* Vol. 5. Hillsdale, NJ: Erlbaum. A recent review of the self-perception approach to attitudes.

Festinger, L. (1957). *A theory of cognitive dissonance.* Stanford, CA: Stanford University Press. The original statement of cognitive dissonance theory. It is elegant in its simplicity and offers plausible speculations about a broad range of psychological phenomena.

Zanna, M. P., & Fazio, R. H. (1982). The attitude-behavior relation: Moving toward a third generation of research. In M. P. Zanna, E. T. Higgins, & C. P. Herman (Eds.), *Consistency in social behavior: The Ontario Symposium,* Vol. 2. Hillsdale, NJ: Erlbaum. A review of research on attitudes and behavior that is sensitive to the complexities of their relationship.

SIX

Attitude Change

W hat makes a person vote for a Democratic candidate in one election and switch to his Republican opponent in the next election? Most Americans were strongly anti-German and anti-Japanese during World War II. Why did so many support these new allies a few years later? Why do people change their attitudes toward long hair, or crew cuts, or pink hair, or miniskirts, or neckties, in such short periods of time?

A major answer is that our attitudes are influenced by other people. Corporations pour millions of dollars into advertising aimed at convincing us that the lithest young women and the most athletic young men on the beach drink Coke (or Pepsi), the men who have the most fun in bars after work drink Bud (or Miller), and the fastest and smoothest cars, with the most beautiful drivers, are Pontiacs (or BMWs).

Political candidates spend sizable fractions of their campaign budgets to buy TV time and put much energy into figuring out how to get additional free exposure. Although it may not seem the same as advertising, the government, schools, and other social institutions also seek to shape and change attitudes. Public debates over the content of school textbooks and school prayer suggest that many people are concerned about the messages being presented by our public institutions.

Our family and friends and coworkers are constantly trying to change our attitudes, about getting good grades, about our new boyfriend, and about our work habits. This chapter analyzes the attitude change that results from such persuasive communication. However, in this chapter we will focus for the most part on mass communications, delivered by a single communicator to a large group of people, whether in a classroom or a newspaper or on television. We will take up face-to-face influence between individuals or in small groups in a later chapter, though as will be seen, the basic principles of attitude change outlined here also apply quite well to that situation.

A MODEL OF PERSUASION

Much of the research on communication and attitude change began with a program organized by Carl Hovland at Yale University after World War II. Figure 6–1 presents a model based largely on Hovland's work but simplified and changed to bring it more in line with recent work in this area. The story begins with the independent variables that affect persuasion.

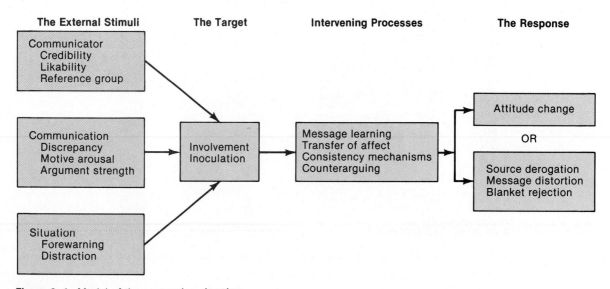

Figure 6–1. Model of the persuasion situation.

The External Stimuli

The *communicator* (or "source") is one of the first things we notice in communication situations. Some communicators are authoritative, like our strict high school geometry teacher or a scientist being interviewed on public television about her research on African apes. Others may be more humorous, like the weekend touch football players who urge us to buy a particular beer from their sweat-stained vantage points in a crowded bar. Others may not seem like communicators at all, like the friend we ask for advice about where to buy a formal skirt and sweater for an upcoming job interview. Still others may seem more like a group than an individual, such as our sorority sisters who would disapprove of us if we fall below a "B" average, or our family back home who expect us to graduate from college in four years. Whatever the nature of those delivering the message, they are crucial ingredients in its persuasive success.

In the typical attitude change situation, individuals are confronted with a *communication* in favor of a position different from the one they hold. They may have a positive attitude toward capital punishment, but someone tells them that it really does not deter crime; they may be

"The Great Communicator," President Ronald Reagan, was extraordinarily successful in generating public support for his proposals through his appearances on television.

Democrats listening to a Republican campaign speech; they may be gays hearing the Surgeon General link AIDS to unsafe sex practices. The discrepancy between the individual's attitude and the attitude expressed in the communication places some pressure on the person to resolve the discrepancy.

But communications always reach the individual in a context. Part of that context involves the external *situation* around the person, such as whether it has provided distraction or forewarning of what the communicator will say. Someone watching a football game briefly interrupted by a beer commercial may be dazzled by a horde of joking retired professional athletes, some flirting with attractive women. Or the person may have deliberately tuned in to watch a hated political candidate argue for some disagreeable position and is ready and waiting.

The Target

Target individuals vary in a number of respects that affect persuasion. They may have a predisposition to agree with the message or a predisposition to disagree with it altogether. A strong liberal Democrat who watches a news conference by a conservative Republican president is predisposed to find flaws and disagree with most of what he says. Sometimes the target person is already familiar with most of the arguments that will be used against his position and knows the rebuttals already; that person may be partially inoculated against persuasion. So the target individual is a major factor in the outcome of the persuasion attempt.

The Response

Usually the communicator intends to produce attitude change in the members of the audience. This means that affects, cognitions, and behaviors regarding the attitude object would all change. The used-car salesman on late-night television wants us to feel that his cars are the best and to believe that they are the cheapest and most reliable used cars in town, and he wants us to come out and buy one the next day. All three components of an attitude would change, if attitude changes were complete.

Yet, as the cognitive consistency theories discussed in the last chapter suggest, other responses are possible. The viewer may wind up thinking the communicator is a fool rather than believing the message. The viewer may misunderstand the message and think that the beer commercial is touting a special kind of dog food for white dogs with black spots. We need to consider those other outcomes as well. The emphasis on alternative responses to communication is one of the important contributions of Carl Hovland's model of attitude change and of the cognitive consistency models.

PROCESSES OF ATTITUDE CHANGE

It would be impossible to keep track of all the factors that can affect attitude change if they were not organized in some way. The theories described in the last chapter are the most commonly cited efforts to account for processes that concern attitudes. But they have not all been equally useful in explaining research results. Here we will emphasize four somewhat more specific versions of those theories that have proved helpful in understanding the results of studies on attitude change.

Message Learning

Perhaps the most obvious idea is that **message learning** is crucial in attitude change. If the person learns the message, change will follow. If this were true, the key question would be what increases or decreases learning. For example, expert communicators might be very effective because people want to remember what they have said, and complex messages might be ineffective because they are difficult to learn.

Surprisingly, however, actually learning the message is much less important than we might expect. Most studies have shown only weak relationships between the learning of the content

of a persuasive communication, or later memory for the information in it, on the one hand, and attitude change on the other (Greenwald, 1968; McGuire, 1985; Chaiken & Stangor, 1987). Similarly, recall of television commercials is usually not closely related to change in brands purchased (Beattie & Mitchell, 1985).

To be sure, it is vital that the listener know what position is being advocated. If the president is advocating military aid to a Central American nation, the listener must learn that and not think the president wants to send toys to Norway. But beyond this learning of the communicator's basic position, remembering the details of the message seems not to be related to the amount of attitude change very much one way or the other. In other words, beyond some necessary minimum, memory for the message has turned out to be relatively unimportant in determining the success of persuasion. It seems to be enough for people to get the general conclusion of the message.

But learning theories also consider motivation. And it may not be sufficient to learn the message; the specific content of the message may need to match the needs of the listener. Motives such as fear or aggression frequently are aroused in the effort to persuade someone to do something. Fanatical religious leaders frighten their followers with threats of eternal damnation and suffering. They also stir hatred of other religious groups in order to get the enthusiastic support of their followers. Political candidates warn that if their opponents are elected, the economy will be ruined, people will starve, or war will break out. Environmentalists warn of chemicals in our vital organs, dying fish in polluted lakes and streams, and mass deaths from cancer. Opponents of environmental improvement warn of rising unemployment.

Another version of the learning approach argues that such motive arousals produce attitude change if accepting the communicator's position satisfies the motive. A fear-arousing message should be accepted if it is accompanied by a fear-reducing recommendation the listener can carry out. If fear is aroused by seeing gruesome pictures of lung cancer victims and we accept the communicator's position and stop smoking, our fear should be reduced. Attitude change depends on reducing arousal. Arousal of aggression should also lead to attitude change if the listeners can reduce their aggression by accepting the recommended new attitude. Political leaders would be able to produce attitude change by stirring up their followers' aggression—but only if they provide their followers with something to hate, like a convenient enemy or scapegoat, so the listeners can express their aggression. In the early 1930s, many Germans were angry about a declining economy and social disorder. Hitler fomented virulent anti-Semitism to get the rest of the Germans to support his costly program of invasion and conquest. Presumably if they accepted his message, it would satisfy some of their anger.

Transfer of Affect

People may simply transfer an affect from one object to another that is associated with it. Imagine a television commercial for an automobile. To persuade you to have a positive attitude toward it, the automobile is associated with many other positive objects. We are not simply shown a sleek car and told how powerful, quiet, and comfortable it is. While the message is being delivered, we are shown beautiful women, handsome men, and lovely children, with perhaps some graceful horses or cute dogs in the background. Or the car may be endorsed by a famous athlete or movie star. Presumably, all this beauty, fame, and popularity becomes associated with the car, thus increasing our positive feelings toward the car and the likelihood that we will buy it. In other words, people simply transfer their feelings about one object (beautiful people) to another (the car). As indicated in the last chapter, this idea of **transfer of affect** comes from the association version of learning theory.

To test for transfer of affect, Lorge (1936) presented American students with the following message: "I hold that a little rebellion, now and then, is a good thing, and as necessary in the political world as storms are in the physical." He found that students agreed with the message when it was attributed to Thomas Jefferson, but disagreed with it when it was attrib-

uted to Lenin. Lorge argued that the positive affect associated with Jefferson transferred to the message, and made it more positive when it was attributed to Jefferson, while the negative affect associated with Lenin—when he was described as the author—transferred to the message with opposite effect. Later research has supported this transfer-of-affect idea in a wide variety of contexts.

A classic case of transfer of affect.

BOX 6-1

Symbolic Attitudes and Transfer of Affect

One application of the transfer-of-affect principle has been to political attitudes. Political symbols are often affect laden, and these affects can get transferred to concrete events, issues, and candidates when they are cognitively linked to them. For example, some of George Bush's attacks on Michael Dukakis in the 1988 presidential campaign revolved around videotapes of a polluted Boston Harbor, and of a "revolving-door" policy of letting convicted criminals out of prison on temporary furloughs, such as the black rapist-murderer Willie Horton. These transferred the very negative affects many people had toward such symbols to Dukakis.

Much research has shown that certain "symbolic attitudes" contain such strong affects that they powerfully influence people's attitudes. Among the most important concern race. The negative affects many whites feel toward blacks are readily transferred to black political candidates (such as Jesse Jackson) and to race-related policy issues such as busing or affirmative action (Kinder & Sears, 1981; Sears, Citrin, & Kosterman, 1987).

The political parties also evoke important symbolic attitudes. When a previously neutral political candidate is associated with one of these symbolic attitudes, evaluations of the candidate quickly change to become consistent with the affect held toward the symbol. For example, Generals Dwight D. Eisenhower and Charles de Gaulle were World War II heroes in the United States and France, respectively. Neither had a clear partisan political affiliation. Because they were so popular, both were eagerly sought after as presidential candidates by the major political parties. When they finally declared as candidates for a specific party, the general positive esteem accorded to them quickly was replaced by a polarization along partisan lines. For example, Eisenhower became even more popular among Republicans, for whom he had declared, and less popular among Democrats. The positive affects Republicans associated with the partisan symbols of the Republican party, and negative ones Democrats did, had transferred to Eisenhower (Converse & DuPeux, 1966).

Consistency Mechanisms

A third approach derives from consistency theories and emphasizes that inconsistency produces psychological tension. Suppose you have always admired the president of your college, but she comes out in favor of some changes you really do not like, such as increased tuition and reduced student aid. You are faced with an inconsistency between your support for her and her endorsement of positions you oppose. According to the consistency theories, this inconsistency should be uncomfortable for you and lead you to change. You may change your attitudes about tuition and student aid, or you may change your attitude about the president, but some change is required if consistency is to be restored.

In general, a communication causes some pressure toward change when it is discrepant from the recipient's original position. Consistency theories suggest the pressure can be reduced in a variety of ways. If the recipients change their attitudes, reducing the discrepancy, then this pressure ought to be reduced. Most research on attitudes has concentrated on this mechanism for restoring consistency.

But the particular insight of the consistency theory approach, and of Hovland's model of attitude change, is that attitude change is only one of several ways of reducing this pressure to change (see Abelson, 1959; Hovland & Janis, 1959). That is, there are other **modes of resolution** of the tension produced by a discrepant communication. The major problem for the communicator is to maximize the likelihood that attitude change will be chosen as the mode of resolution and to minimize or eliminate the use of other modes. Therefore, before discussing attitude change in detail, we will describe briefly the most important alternative responses the individual can make.

Derogating the Source. Someone who is faced with a discrepant communication can reduce the inconsistency by deciding that the source of the communication is unreliable or negative in some other way. This is called **source derogation.** The balance model described in the last chapter suggests that there is nothing inconsistent about disagreeing with a negative source. In fact, people expect to disagree with a negative source.

Such an attack on the source of a communication is common in politics, informal debates, courtroom trials, and practically every kind of disagreement. The defense attorney in a trial tries to discredit the witness whose testimony is damaging. The politician calls his opponent a communist or a liar or some other name when he finds it difficult to argue on the issues themselves.

Attacking the source of the communication is an effective way of reducing the pressure produced by a discrepant communication. It has the additional benefit of making all future arguments from the opponent much less powerful. When an opponent has been discredited, anything he or she later says carries less weight.

Distorting the Message. Another type of resolution is distorting or misperceiving the communication to reduce the discrepancy between it and one's own position. The Surgeon General says that sexually active heterosexuals should use safer sex practices because they are at risk for AIDS. Heterosexuals who do not want to change to using safer sex practices can read this message and decide that the Surgeon General says not to worry too much about AIDS because the evidence about heterosexual transmission is not yet conclusive. Heterosexuals can do this by misperceiving the article when reading it, by distorting the article in memory, or perhaps by reading only part of the article and reconstruct-

ing the rest of it mentally. However, it is accomplished, the result is the same—the message becomes considerably less discrepant. Sadly, in the case of AIDS, the price of distorting a health warning can be high indeed.

An alternative distortion is to exaggerate the communication to make it ridiculous. Many environmentalists want to slow down the development of undeveloped lands and restrict the building of pollution-causing plants and buildings. Developers and many other businesspeople often oppose these restrictions. It is fairly common for them to distort the positions taken by environmentalists to make those positions appear so unreasonable that no thinking person would ever support them. They might argue that environmentalists want such extreme restrictions that no factories could operate in the area at all and so many jobs would be lost.

Blanket Rejection. A discrepant communication is inconsistent with one's prior attitude, so the most primitive (and perhaps most common) mode of resolution is simply to reject the communication altogether. Rather than refuting the arguments on logical grounds or weakening them by attacking their source, individuals simply reject arguments for no apparent reason.

A typical response by a smoker to a well-reasoned, logical attack on cigarette smoking is to say that the arguments are not good enough to make her stop. She does not answer them; she just does not accept them. When someone who believes in capital punishment is shown overwhelming evidence that it does not deter homicide, he tends to be unconvinced. He shrugs off the evidence, says he does not believe it, and continues to maintain his position. So it often takes more than a good argument to convince people of something.

Counterarguing

You read a story in the student newspaper about a proposal to ban all students from driving their cars to campus because of severe parking and traffic problems surrounding the campus. You think this is a bad idea. Right off the

This man quite plainly has not accepted the communication. Which one or more responses has he probably had instead of attitude change?

bat you can think of some serious problems the proposal would create. You know students who live in town 30 miles from campus; how could they get to school? The local bus service goes to some neighborhoods where students live but not to others, and it is too far for those students to walk or bike. Some women students have labs or work in the library until very late at night, and it might be risky for them to walk or hitchhike home at that hour. You have friends who work off campus, and you cannot see how they could make their classes and get to their jobs on time if they used the bus. All in all, you see a lot of arguments against the ban.

Sometimes the recipients can resist by **counterarguing**—by considering and actively attempting to refute the arguments. They can engage in a debate and attempt to demonstrate to themselves that their own position has more merit than the other one. This debate can be implicit or explicit, verbal or nonverbal, perhaps even conscious or unconscious. They can argue against the discrepant communication, produce evidence to support their own positions, or show how the other side is illogical or inconsistent, all to weaken the impact of the communication. To the extent that they are able to do this, the pressure to change should be reduced. Note that this counterarguing mechanism could

well take the merits of the arguments into account, unlike the consistency mechanisms.

Cognitive response theory is one statement of this counterarguing view (Petty, Ostrom, & Brock, 1981). As described in the last chapter, it depicts the recipient as responding to the communication with a series of thoughts about it. These cognitive responses determine the person's overall response to the message. But attitude change will depend on how much and what kind of counterarguing the message triggers. If it stimulates strong and effective counterarguing, resistance to change will follow. Conversely, persuasion can be produced by interfering with the counterarguing process. If the person cannot think of any good counterarguments, or can be distracted from thinking of them while listening to the message, the communicator has a better chance.

This process describes the recipients as actively rehearsing their own attitudes and considering the details of the communication. The problems with this mode of resolution are twofold.

First, recipients are usually rather lazy; most people, most of the time, are not very motivated to analyze the pros and cons of complex arguments. They are cognitive misers, trying to minimize cognitive effort, as we saw in Chapter 3.

Moreover, communicators are usually quite motivated and have designed persuasive messages to be difficult to reject on purely logical grounds. The authors of the communication naturally present as strong a case as they can and are generally better informed on the topic than the recipients. Therefore, although arguing against the discrepant communication is a rational mode of resolution, it is often difficult to employ.

Systematic Processing

These, then, are four simple ideas to keep in mind about why attitude change or resistance to change occurs: message learning, transfer of affect, the consistency mechanisms, and counterarguing. In some cases people are described as learning the arguments, sifting through them for the points that meet their own needs, and counterarguing if they disagree with them. In other cases they are described as acting in a more lazy manner, simply judging a communication on the basis of such superficial cues as who the source is or whether the product is surrounded by attractive men and women.

To take account of this contrast, Petty and Cacioppo (1986) developed their **elaboration-likelihood model** of persuasion, which we discussed in Chapter 5. They characterize detailed information processing, scanning and evaluating the real arguments, as the central route to persuasion and the use of more superficial, **peripheral cues** without thoughtful consideration of the real arguments as the peripheral route to persuasion. Similarly, Chaiken (1980, 1987) has distinguished **systematic processing,** which also involves scanning and considering the arguments, from heuristic processing, which involves using such simple decision rules (heuristics) as that longer arguments are stronger or that consensus implies correctness. Using either terminology, the distinction contrasts an active information processor with a cognitive miser who cuts corners and does not pay close attention to the merits of the actual arguments.

This has become a central distinction in research on attitude change. It is a distinction of major importance because it bears directly on the question of how rationally people respond to persuasion attempts. Does the consumer care about the real quality and price of the product or just about the "hype" that advertising specialists surround it with? Does the voter respond to the real issues and the real qualities of the candidates, or just to some of the superficial images or symbols associated with them by political image makers?

We will refer to this distinction in a number of contexts in the discussion that follows as we consider the determinants of attitude change, and then return to it in a summary manner at the end of the chapter. While there are some differences between the Petty-Cacioppo and Chaiken approaches, those need not concern us here, and we will use a distinction between systematic processing and peripheral cues.

With this in mind, we turn to a consideration of the independent variables that increase or decrease the amount of attitude change produced by a persuasive communication, following the model in Figure 6–1.

THE COMMUNICATOR

One of the most straightforward and reliable findings in attitude change is that the more favorably people evaluate the communicator, the more they are apt to change their attitudes. This follows from any of the cognitive consistency models. It also follows from the transfer-of-affect idea: evaluations of communicators, whether positive or negative, transfer to the positions they advocate. If the teacher says abortion is immoral but the student thinks it is a basic women's right, the system is unbalanced. The student can reduce the imbalance by changing her attitude toward abortion and agreeing with her teacher. In contrast, if she dislikes the teacher anyway because he is a sexist conservative, his discrepant position creates no imbalance and no pressure to change.

Thus, the more favorably people evaluate the source of a discrepant communication, the more likely they will be to change their attitude. But there are several ways in which a communicator can be evaluated favorably, and not all of them yield exactly the same results.

Credibility

Research on this phenomenon began with "the prestige effect." This was illustrated in the work of Lorge on transfer of affect. It simply compared the effectiveness of favorably evaluated authorities like Jefferson with that of unfavorably evaluated authorities like Lenin without attempting to specify the exact characteristics making up "prestige."

Later work narrowed this concept to **credibility,** whose effects were demonstrated in a classic study by Hovland and Weiss (1952). Subjects heard communications concerned with four issues: the advisability of selling antihistamines without a prescription, whether the steel industry was to blame for the steel shortage, the future of the movie industry in the context of the growing popularity of television, and the practicality of building an atomic-powered submarine.

Each communication came from either a high- or low-credibility source. For example, the communication on antihistamines was supposedly from the *New England Journal of Medicine,* or from a monthly mass-circulation pictorial magazine. The results indicated that communications attributed to high-credibility sources produced more change than those from low-credibility sources.

Subsequent research distinguished two separate components of credibility: expertness and trustworthiness (Hovland & Weiss, 1952). However, the mechanisms by which these two factors influenced attitude change turn out to be somewhat different, so it is important to distinguish them.

In a typical study of expertness, subjects were told they were in an experiment on esthetics and were asked to evaluate nine stanzas from obscure modern poems. They then read someone else's evaluation of one of the stanzas they had not liked very much. The communication argued that the poem was better than the subject had indicated. The crucial variable was

that the communication was supposedly from T. S. Eliot, the poet, or Agnes Stearns, who was described as a student at Mississippi State Teachers College. After reading the communication, the subjects reevaluated the poems. There was more change with the high-credibility communicator than with the low-credibility one (Aronson, Turner, & Carlsmith, 1963).

In a more recent study, Wood and Kallgren (1988) had a graduate student give a tape-recorded speech arguing against environmental preservation to undergraduate students. Expertness was manipulated by presenting the graduate student either as specializing in environmental geology, with substantial relevant practical experience, or in modern languages with no relevant experience. Overall, as might be expected, the expert source generated more attitude change.

This effect is fairly straightforward and reasonably noncontroversial. It does raise two additional interesting questions, not yet fully answered. First, how far can experts in one field transfer the influence of their expertise to other fields? Are great scientists or athletes or rock musicians especially persuasive on issues such as international politics that do not directly involve their expertise? The transfer of affect or consistency ideas would suggest they would be, but theories describing more active processing, such as cognitive response theory, suggest they would not. The question of the transferability of prestige is an open one and should be more fully investigated in the future.

The other question concerns the process by which expertness works. Does it motivate the listener to attend more closely to the arguments, and thus be more persuaded by their real merits? Or is the expertness just a simple peripheral cue that allows the cognitive miser to change her attitude without expending any energy actually processing the details of the arguments? We will return to this question presently.

Trustworthiness

Regardless of the expertise of the communicator, it is extremely important for the listener to believe the communicator is unbiased. The graduate student may be a real expert on the effects of environmental controls, but we might not be so influenced by his views if we knew that he was employed by a firm that was trying to develop some farmland nearby and was fighting local environmental regulations tooth and nail. We would be concerned about his objectivity and therefore his trustworthiness. If he is perceived as having something to gain from the position he is advocating or if he is taking that position for personal reasons, he should be less persuasive than someone perceived as advocating the position for entirely objective reasons.

One way for communicators to appear trustworthy is to argue for positions contrary to their self-interest. Consider a situation in which a district attorney and a criminal are each making statements about whether or not law enforcement agencies should be strengthened. Normally the district attorney should be seen as better informed and more prestigious, and therefore be more persuasive. And in a study by Walster, Aronson, and Abrahams (1966), that is exactly what happened—as long as the speaker was advocating less power for law enforcement agencies. With that position, the district attorney was much more persuasive than the convicted criminal, as shown in Figure 6–2. But

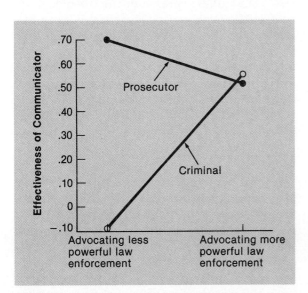

Figure 6–2. Effectiveness of communicators when advocating positions for and against their own self-interest (Walster, Aronson, & Abrahams, 1966, p. 333).

what if the criminal takes a position against his own self-interest and argues in favor of strengthened law enforcement? As shown, the criminal becomes quite persuasive and indeed even matches the persuasive power of the district attorney.

So one way to become more trustworthy, and therefore have more influence, is to argue against your own interest. The head of the state taxpayers' association may really believe that taxes need to be raised, or else the schools will deteriorate so badly that people in the state will be worse off. A union leader may feel that an immediate wage increase is a bad idea because it would damage the financial standing of the company. People do argue against their own self-interest, for a variety of reasons, and it usually makes them more persuasive when they do.

Attributions. How does a recipient decide whether or not the communicator is trustworthy? The audience's judgments must be based on the attributions about the causes of the speaker's statements, as would be suggested by **attribution theory**. Does the listener attribute the communicator's statement to the facts of the matter? Or is it attributed to the communicator's own prejudices and biases? Or to an attempt to please the audience?

Three major types of attributions are possible. The communicator's statement may be attributed to the actual realities of the situation—the criminal arguing for strictness may indeed be reflecting his firsthand knowledge of criminals' behavior. This would be an *entity* attribution, in the language used in Chapter 4. Or the listener may make a *dispositional* attribution. The communicator's statement may be biased because he may not have enough information to know the real facts, or his own prejudices may have blinded him to the truth. The criminal arguing for leniency may be seen as just defending his own past behavior or as reflecting a general disrespect for law and order. Third, a *context* attribution might be made. The communicator may be perceived as simply trying to please the audience. This could happen for any number of reasons, since people frequently have strong incentives to take a public position they do not really hold. A politician running for reelection, an applicant at a job interview, or a person on a first date all have strong incentives to engage in such bias. If either of these last two attributions is made, the communicator's statement should be judged less trustworthy, and thus the audience should be less willing to agree with his position. So a key factor in trustworthiness is making attributions to reality rather than to the communicator's dispositions or to the context.

When do we make attributions to dispositions rather than to reality? As we saw in Chapter 4, observers are especially likely to make dispositional attributions when the actor's statement is consistent with expectations based on his or her past behavior. So we are more likely to attribute a conservative president's statements about Central America to his dispositions when his statements fit those biases than when they do not. If he claims the Russians are behind some guerrilla action, that is consistent with our expectations about him, so we tend to attribute it partially to his dispositions. On the other hand, if he says the rebellion is a genuine nationalistic movement with no Soviet involvement, we are likely to attribute it to some evidence he has.

When communicators say something contrary to expectations, then, they should be perceived as more trustworthy and should produce more attitude change. This sequence has been examined by Wood and Eagly (1981). To set up expectations about the communicator's general political philosophy, subjects were given a short autobiographical statement that described his general attitudes about freedom of speech, abortion, and religion. Then he gave a communication supporting or opposing pornography. This communication could be seen as consistent or inconsistent with his general political views. As Table 6–1 shows, when his message confirmed expectations about him, it was more likely to be attributed to his background rather than to factual evidence, he was perceived as more biased, and he produced less opinion change. Note that expectancy confirmation had little effect on message comprehension: the mechanism responsible for the effects of his background on attitude change is the attribution of trustworthiness, not message learning.

T A B L E 6 – 1
EFFECTS THAT FOLLOW WHEN A COMMUNICATOR'S POSITION CONFIRMS OR DISCONFIRMS EXPECTATIONS BASED ON HIS BACKGROUND

	Expectations	
Effects	Confirmed	Disconfirmed
Attributions about position		
To communicator's background	11.81	6.40
To factual evidence	10.39	11.84
Communicator bias	9.35	7.43
Message comprehension	2.36	2.08
Opinion change	1.56	2.51

Source: Adapted from Wood and Eagly (1981), p. 254.
Note: A high score indicates more of the effect; for example, more attribution to the communicator's background.

When is the communicator's position likely to be attributed to the context rather than to the facts of the matter? As we saw in Chapter 4, perceptions of choice are crucial. Positions that are perceived as freely chosen are usually also perceived as genuine positions. A lack of perceived choice can arise when the communicator has been instructed to present a particular position, as in the experiments by Jones and Harris (1967) and others presented in Chapter 4. A paid public relations spokesperson is often not trusted for that reason. More generally, any strong external incentives for presenting a particular position (whether rewards or threats) might produce attributions to the context. Politicians are often accused of tailoring their messages to the particular audience they are addressing, and their statements are mistrusted for that reason.

Multiple Sources. Another factor that seems to encourage an attribution to reality, rather than to dispositions or context, is having multiple sources saying the same thing—"high consensus information"—in the terms of Kelley's (1967) attribution theory (see Chapter 4). If several people independently take the same position, we regard their views as more credible than if a single person makes the same arguments, presumably because they are less subject to some personal, idiosyncratic bias. Harkins and Petty (1981) initially demonstrated this phenomenon by showing that several communicators produced more attitude change than did a single communicator presenting exactly the same arguments.

But multiple sources have this advantage only if their judgments are regarded as really independent of each other. Harkins and Petty (1987) later demonstrated this in two clever ways. First, they compared three independent sources with a committee of three people and showed that the independent sources produced more attitude change. Indeed the committee was no more effective than a single communicator. Then they created two different kinds of committees, one supposedly chosen to embody a wide diversity of perspectives and the other, to reflect quite similar views (to provide a congenial atmosphere). The diverse committee produced as much attitude change as multiple independent communicators, but the harmonious committee did not. In short, multiple sources produce more attitude changes only when they clearly are putting forward independent judgments; presumably then they are trusted more to reflect the realities of the situation.

It is perhaps for this reason that people tend to discount agreement of leaders from a single partisan group, whether it is Democrats, Republicans, or a pre-*perestroika* Kremlin. They regard the consensus as artificial, resulting from similarity of backgrounds or a desire to present a unified front, rather than as reflecting a series of independent trustworthy judgments about reality.

Liking

Consistency theories suggest that people should change their attitudes to agree with those of the people they like. Anything that increases liking ought also to increase attitude change. As will be seen in Chapter 8, a wide variety of conditions have reliable effects on liking for another person, among them physical attractiveness, similarity, and reciprocal liking. All these have also been shown to increase persuasion. For example, Chaiken (1979) has

shown that students rated by other students as physically attractive were also more persuasive communicators. Similarly, people tend to be influenced more by those who are similar to them than by those who are different. For example, Brock (1965) had salesmen in the paint department of a retail store vary how similar they said their own paint use was to that of a customer. The more similar salesman was more effective than the dissimilar salesman in getting buyers to change their minds about the brand of the paint they wanted to purchase.

Reciprocity is another factor that increases liking: we like those who like us. Wood and Kallgren (1988), in the study cited earlier, also manipulated the likability of the graduate student communicator: he was described as having recently transferred to the subjects' university, and then he either praised their faculty and student body by comparison to those at his old university, or said his previous school was better and its students more responsible and mature. Not surprisingly, in the former guise he was liked better and produced more attitude change in response to his speech against environmental preservation.

Reference Groups

If we are especially likely to be persuaded by communicators who are liked and similar to us, we might expect that we will also be persuaded by a position taken by a majority of our peers. Mackie (1987) demonstrated this quite clearly. She told some subjects that a huge majority (82 percent) of the students at their university had supported the proposition that "the United States should act to ensure a military balance in the Western hemisphere." Others were told that a similarly overwhelming majority opposed it. Then she presented all subjects with speeches of equal strength on both sides, so they all received exactly the same arguments. She found in four such experiments that subjects moved toward the side they had been told the majority supported, whichever side it was.

This influence of a majority of one's peers is a pervasive and important phenomenon. But it is a special case of a more general principle. One of the strongest sources of persuasive pressure is a group with which an individual identifies. The group can be as large and inclusive as all American citizens, all undergraduates at your university, women in general, all members of your ethnic group, the middle class, or a labor union. It can also be a much smaller, more specialized group, such as a college sorority, a ski club, an extended family, or even just a group of high school friends who continue to see each other on vacation.

Note that when we are considering a group's influence, we must consider both its ability to change its members' attitudes to a new position and its ability to help them defend their attitudes against counterpropaganda. If all our friends tell us they like the latest Sylvester Stallone movie, we probably are convinced by them. If most of the members of a fraternity think initiations are a good idea, the others will probably agree with them. But the fraternity member may occasionally be exposed to an attack on initiations from someone outside the fraternity. If this happens, knowing that his group agrees with him makes it easier for him to resist persuasion.

When does a group have such persuasive effects over its members? The same consistency mechanisms operate when a group is the source of the communication as when an individual is. One factor is the clarity of the group's position on the issue, that is, clear **group norms.** The group's position on the issue must be a clear one for it to influence its followers. In the balance theory terms introduced in the last chapter, this refers to the O-X leg of the simple social triad (refer to Figure 5–2). In the case of Mackie's (1987) study of majority influence, the group's norm was very clear: 82 percent of the subjects' fellow students were on a particular side.

Changes in the group's norms can pull people away from their own old positions. Kelley and Woodruff (1956) played subjects a tape recording of a speech arguing against their group's norm—they were education students, and the speech argued against "progressive education." This counternorm speech was interrupted periodically by applause which the experimenters attributed to faculty members and recent graduates of the college in one experimental condition ("members' applause"), or to an audience of college-trained people in a neighboring city, interested in community problems related to education ("outsiders' applause"). Attitude change toward the speech was much greater in the "members' applause" condition. Subjects confronted with an apparent change in their group's norm were likely to change their own attitudes to fit the group's new position.

The consistency approach would suggest that a second critical factor in producing group influence is evaluation of the group, or **group identification.** This is the P-O leg of the balance triad discussed in Chapter 5 (and illustrated in Figure 5–2). The more people want to be a member of the group and the more highly they value it, the more they will be influenced by its beliefs. For example, Converse and Campbell (1960) showed that labor unions influenced voters only when the union made a clear endorsement *and* the voter was strongly identified with the union.

Resistance to persuasion from outside the group also depends to some extent on how strong the individual's ties are to the group. Kelley and Volkart (1952) demonstrated the effect of group identification on members' resistance to outside influence. A communicator attempted to change some Boy Scouts' opinions on various issues away from their troop's norms. The more the Scouts valued their membership in the troop, the less effect the communicator had on their opinions.

This central role of emotional attachment to the group, or group identification, leads us to the distinction between a **reference group** and a membership group. The key factor in the group's influence is that people feel identified with the group, and refer to it for guidance, regardless whether they are actually members of it or not. A person does not have to be a dues-paying member of the Democratic party to regularly prefer its candidates for state assembly and state treasurer. Similarly, a person can be quite influenced by middle-class norms of behavior, dress, and morality even though living, objectively, in poverty; that is, actually being a member of the lower class.

The reasons why reference groups are so effective in producing attitude change are those we have just discussed: liking and similarity (Holtz & Miller, 1985). If people like the group, they want to be similar to the other members. When the other members express a particular opinion, each member thinks his or her own opinion is wrong if it is different from theirs. Only when the opinion is the same as the group's is it correct or "normal." Therefore, they tend to change their opinion to make it agree.

Communicator as Peripheral Cue

What is the process by which these communicator characteristics produce attitude change? Consistency mechanisms are critical to communicator effects, no matter whether the communicator is a group or an individual. In general, any characteristic of communicators which implies they are experts, are trustworthy, or are likable increases the effectiveness of the communication. Any disliking of the communicator or lack of trust in his or her competence or honesty makes it relatively easy to reject the message by attacking the source. In this way, targets free themselves from the pressure of worrying about the complex details of the message itself.

But it is not enough to leave it at that. Sometimes a source's conclusion will be accepted simply because an expert or otherwise favorably evaluated source stated it, regardless of the arguments. On other occasions the arguments themselves are important. What is the difference between these situations?

To start with, the prediction from the elaboration-likelihood point of view would be that communicator characteristics would be used as a simple peripheral cue when people cannot, or are not motivated to, process the arguments carefully themselves. Like good cognitive misers, they engage in the least cognitive effort they can get away with, and knowing that a trusted friend believes something means that they can avoid the effort of thinking it through themselves. On the other hand, being able to access substantial amounts of information should make such simplifying cues as commu-

nicator characteristics less important. The study by Wood and Kallgren (1988) cited earlier, featuring a graduate student arguing for environmental preservation, makes this point. The likability of the source mattered only among subjects who could not recall much information about the issue. Those who could recall many arguments presumably did not need the help of the source as a cue, and so source likability had no effect among them, as shown in Figure 6–3.

Having direct experience with the attitude object also diminishes the need for relying on an

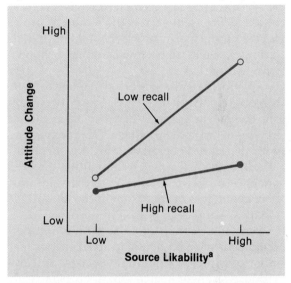

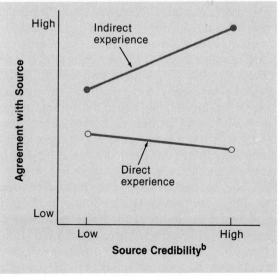

Figure 6–3. Effects of Communicator Characteristics are Greater with Less Prior Information (Wood & Kallgren, 1988; Wu & Shaffer, 1987).

expert, as shown in an impressive study by Wu and Shaffer (1987). They labeled ostensibly different brands of peanut butter products X and Y and presented them as different, but in fact they were identical. Some subjects then tasted them ("direct experience") while other subjects simply looked at the two jars and were given some information about others' reactions ("indirect experience"). Both then rated them on a series of attributes. In both cases the experimenter then mysteriously computed a summary score which told each subject that he or she preferred product X. The subjects then were given a typed message from either a high-credibility professional product evaluator who had tasted the products or one from a low-credibility evaluator who had not.

As shown at the bottom of Figure 6–3, the high-credibility source was more persuasive only when the subjects had had mere indirect experience with the products. Direct experience with the attitude object nullified the advantage of source credibility (even though the direct experience in fact provided no decisive information about the relative superiority of the two identical samples of peanut butter!).

More information about the communicator's characteristics also ought to make people rely more on simple communicator cues, and thus produce stronger source effects on persuasion. For example, an audiovisual communication provides much more information about the source than do most written messages. So Chaiken and Eagly (1983) suggested that communicator likability should be most important in visual or audio communications, where such nonverbal information about the communicator is available. In written communication, however, where nonverbal cues about the communicator are more difficult to access, the message content should be relatively more important.

They varied likability by having the communicator praise or derogate the students, faculty, and overall institutional quality of the university the students were attending (the University of Toronto). Then he delivered a persuasive communication supporting a change to the trimester system on videotape, audiotape, or via a written transcript. As shown in Table 6–2, the commu-

T A B L E 6 – 2		
OPINION CHANGE AS A FUNCTION OF SOURCE AND MEDIUM		
	Communicator	
	Likable	Unlikable
Videotape	4.87	.48
Audiotape	4.82	1.47
Written	3.66	3.43

Source: Adapted from Chaiken and Eagly (1983), p. 246.
Note: The entry is the mean amount of attitude change on a 15-point scale.

nicator's likability contributed to opinion change only in the video or audio versions, where nonverbal cues about him were available.

Additional evidence pointed to the conclusion that communicator attributes were central in video and audio, and message factors relatively more important in written communications. The students' cognitive responses were also measured after the communication. In the video and audio conditions, opinion change was related to the favorability of communicator-oriented thoughts. In the written condition, opinion change was related to the favorability of message-oriented thoughts. In other research, these investigators have shown that written communications have a greater advantage over video or audio communication as the arguments get more complex, presumably because the written medium does induce a message-oriented mentality (Chaiken & Eagly, 1976).

The general principle, then, is that source characteristics have their clearest effects (for better or worse, as far as the source is concerned) when people cannot or will not closely scrutinize the real arguments, and when the source's characteristics themselves are especially easy to figure out, as in audiovisual messages. So the source's characteristics can serve as peripheral cues, and therefore affect attitude change through consistency mechanisms or transfer of affect rather than through enhanced processing of the arguments.

What should be the exceptions to this principle? One should be when the source cues themselves motivate attention to the arguments. One such case occurs when we suddenly realize that a majority of our peers oppose us. Mackie (1987) found systematic processing to be greater among those disagreeing with the vast majority of their peers than among those agreeing with the majority.

THE COMMUNICATION

But what about the actual content of the message? Advertisers try to sell a particular product; is it any good or not? Politicians try to get elected; are they actually qualified for the job or not? Your friend tries to get you to go to a particular party with her; will it actually be a good party or not?

Of course, it is easier to sell something good. Crest became the best-selling toothpaste in part because it really did offer protection against cavities, the automobile became popular because it was a useful product, and some political candidates are more qualified than others. Given a particular product or opinion to sell, however, a number of variables in the communication itself have important effects on the amount of attitude change produced.

Discrepancy

As noted earlier, a major source of pressure for attitude change comes from the **discrepancy** between the target's initial position and the position advocated by the communication. The greater the discrepancy, the greater potential pressure to change. If the typical person needing 8 hours of sleep per night hears a distinguished health scientist say that only 6 hours are necessary, the individual's attitude is under some pressure; if the communication argues that only 4 hours are really necessary, there is much more pressure. As might be expected, therefore, within a wide range, there is more attitude change with greater discrepancy (Hovland & Pritzker, 1957).

However, the effect of discrepancy on pressure and amount of change is not always this simple. There is more pressure with greater discrepancy, but it does not always produce more change. There are two complicating factors. First, as discrepancy becomes quite great, the members of the audience find it increasingly difficult to change their attitudes enough to eliminate the discrepancy. Moreover, an extremely discrepant statement tends to make individuals doubt the credibility of the source. So at high levels of discrepancy, the pressure tends to be reduced more by source derogation than by attitude change. In other words, source derogation rather than attitude change is chosen as the mechanism for restoring consistency.

Suppose a person hears the scientist say that 8 hours of sleep are not really required and that 6 hours are adequate. The scientist's message is at low discrepancy, and the person is likely to be somewhat influenced. In this situation, it is difficult to reject the credible communicator but easy to change one's opinion the little bit required to reduce the discrepancy.

As the discrepancy becomes greater, however, it becomes much harder for individuals to reduce the pressure by changing their opinion. It is more difficult for the person who thinks 8 hours are required to decide that only 4 hours will do. The person then starts to doubt the communicator's credibility. She begins to think that the scientist does not know much about real human beings. The result is that attitude change generally increases with greater discrepancy up to a point and then declines if discrepancy increases still further (e.g., Freedman, 1964; Eagly & Telaak, 1972). At high discrepancy, source derogation starts to occur instead.

Greater credibility should allow communicators to advocate more discrepant positions with success, because they will not be rejected as easily. In contrast, a lower-credibility source makes rejection relatively easy, and the maximum amount of attitude change should occur at lower levels of discrepancy.

These effects of discrepancy and credibility are nicely illustrated in a study by Bochner and Insko (1966), as shown in Figure 6–4. They had a Nobel Prize winner (high credibility) and a YMCA instructor (low credibility) give messages regarding the number of hours of sleep

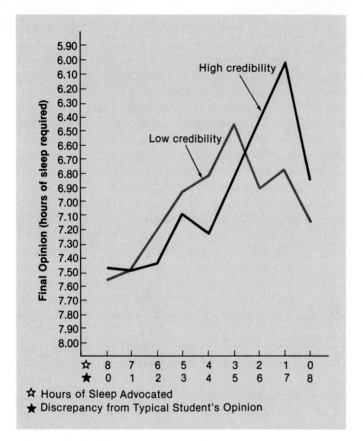

Figure 6–4. Opinion change produced by high- and low-credibility communicators at various levels of discrepancy (Bochner & Insko, 1966).

the average person requires per night. Each subject received one message from one source. Some subjects received a message saying 8 hours were required, others a message saying 7 hours were required, and so on. Since the great majority of subjects initially thought 8 hours was correct, these messages varied in discrepancy accordingly; zero discrepancy for the 8-hour message, 1-hour discrepancy for the 7-hour message, and so on.

As you can see, there was more change at moderate levels of discrepancy than at higher levels. In addition, as expected, the optimal level of discrepancy was greater for the high-credibility source. The YMCA instructor did best by advocating 3 hours of sleep, but the high-credibility source got the maximum attitude change by arguing that only 1 hour was really necessary. Thus, the level of credibility does not change the basic inverted-U relationship between discrepancy and attitude change, but it does change the point at which maximum

change occurs. The more difficult it is to reject the communicator, the greater the discrepancy at which maximum change occurs.

Another example of alternative modes of resolution concerns how discrepancy affects misperception of the message. When a discrepant position is quite close to that of the audience, they perceive it as closer than it actually is. This is called *assimilation.* Exaggerating the closeness of a discrepant position makes it easy to change enough to reduce the small discrepancy, or it may eliminate the need for change by making the two positions essentially identical. The same misperception occurs when people estimate the attitudes of social groups. They tend to overestimate the extent to which members of their own group agree with them; that is, they tend to assimilate fellow group members' attitudes. For example, whites think that other whites agree more with them about racial integration and segregation than is in fact the case (Granberg, 1984).

tion might have two separate effects: it increases the opportunity to consider the content of a persuasive communication (enhanced processing), and it also increases the chances of tedium and therefore a negative reaction. For example, in the just-mentioned example of the children viewing ice cream commercials, the children commonly said, ''Oh, not again'' or ''Not another one'' in the high-exposure condition.

The implication of enhanced processing is that repetition will help strong arguments, because it allows them to be processed better, but will hurt weak ones, because it exposes their flaws. Cacioppo and Petty (1985) found that three exposures to strong arguments for senior comprehensive exams increased their impact, but three exposures decreased the impact of weak arguments.

How can tedium be dealt with? Presumably by varying the content a little. Hence the same authors report evidence that repetition of commercials for a particular product achieves increased effectiveness if the commercials are varied somewhat, but not if exactly the same commercial is used each time.

Peripheral Cues. When a person is poorly motivated to think about the arguments (e.g., when the issue has little importance to the person) or when the person is unable to process them well (e.g., when uninformed or distracted), then more peripheral cues become more important in determining attitude change.

The number of arguments in a message and the length of the arguments are two such peripheral cues. Petty and Cacioppo (1984) have shown that simply presenting more arguments in a message increases attitude change when the issue is not very relevant to the person and therefore provides little motivation to think about it. Presenting more arguments increases attitude change for strong and weak arguments alike, indicating little processing is going on. Similarly, longer messages are more influential than short messages—but only among the uninformed, who presumably give them little thought. Among the better informed, strength of arguments is the more important factor (Wood et al., 1985).

A variety of factors increase attentive pro-cessing of the communication, therefore giving an advantage to strong arguments, such as rhetorical questions and repetition. In their absence, peripheral cues such as source characteristics or the sheer volume of argument have greater impact.

THE TARGET

Even after a message from a particular source has reached the target, the problems of attitude change are not over. Hearing a speech on environmental protection may have quite different effects on the owner of a strip coal mine than it does on a suburban university professor. Characteristics of the target and the target's experience also affect reactions to the message.

Ego Involvement

The earliest work on this topic began with the concept of **ego involvement.** According to Sherif and Cantril (1947), attitudes that become tightly entwined with the ego are highly resistant to change. They believed that ego involvement was most likely to result from anchoring attitudes in important reference groups, especially nationality, religion, ethnicity, and social class groups. Later work has distinguished between several different kinds of involvement, however, each with somewhat different dynamics. It has also treated the link with reference groups as only one possible basis for involvement.

Commitment. One aspect of involvement is the targets' **commitment** to their own initial attitudes on the issue. This is also sometimes called ''position involvement'' because the involvement is specific to the person's position on the issue (Chaiken & Stangor, 1987). Resistance to a persuasive message depends in great part on the strength of this commitment. Commitment to a position can arise from several sources. One is *behavior* engaged in on the basis of the atti-

Such public religious commitments are among the most binding. What are the crucial ingredients in this one that will help keep the young man committed in the years to come?

tude, as we saw in Chapter 5. Someone who has just bought a car is more committed to the belief that it is a fine car than before buying it. And new car owners are generally not very open to hearing that the car they have selected is not a very good one.

Second, *public commitment* to a prior attitude produces more resistance to change, compared with only private commitment or none at all (Hovland, Campbell, & Brock, 1957). Someone who has just told all his friends that he thinks smoking is bad for health and is an evil, dirty habit is more committed to this attitude than if he had kept his thoughts to himself. Changing his attitude is harder if he expressed it publicly because then the change would involve admitting to his friends he was wrong.

Third, free *choice* of a position produces a greater feeling of commitment than being forced. In one study (Freedman & Steinbruner, 1964), subjects were given information about a candidate for graduate school and asked to rate him, under circumstances of either high or low choice. The subjects were either made to feel that they had made up their own minds and freely selected the particular rating, or that they had virtually nothing to do with the decision and had been forced to select the rating. The subjects were then exposed to information that strongly contradicted their initial rating and were allowed to change the rating if they desired. Those who had made the first rating with a feeling of free choice changed less than those in the low-choice condition.

A fourth source of commitment is *direct experience* with the attitude object. For example, Wu and Shaffer (1987) showed that subjects directly exposed to brands of peanut butter were less vulnerable to countercommunications than were those who were indirectly exposed, as indicated earlier (see Figure 6–3). Note that direct experience also promotes greater attitude-behavior consistency, as seen in the last chapter.

In general, then, strong commitment reduces the amount of attitude change produced by a discrepant persuasive communication. Whenever changing an attitude would cause the individual to give up more, suffer more, or change more of his other attitudes or behaviors, his commitment to his initial attitude increases and makes it more difficult for him to change it. Greater commitment makes it harder for people to change an attitude and means that they are more likely to use other modes of resolution instead.

The joint effects of commitment and discrepancy on attitude change are similar to those of credibility and discrepancy. Commitment to an initial position also shifts the amount of discrepancy at which maximum attitude change occurs, but in the opposite direction. The greater the commitment to one's initial attitude, the lower the discrepancy at which rejection of the source starts to substitute for attitude change. Therefore, the greater the commitment, the lower the discrepancy at which maximum attitude change occurs (Freedman, 1964; Rhine & Severance, 1970).

Issue Involvement. A second type of ego involvement occurs when the issue has important consequences for the individual. This has been called *issue involvement* (or sometimes "personal relevance") because the person is involved in the issue rather than in his or her specific position on it. Issue involvement is a key variable in the elaboration-likelihood theory (Petty & Cacioppo, 1986). The main prediction is that issue involvement enhances the role of argument strength in persuasion, since it motivates close scrutiny of the issue and the relevant arguments. For example, proposed tuition increases or comprehensive exams would produce issue involvement for college students if they might be personally affected by them. If you were told your tuition might double next year, you would probably pay close attention to the validity of the reasons for the increase! In contrast, an issue that is not personally relevant tends not to produce as much motivation to process the information. If you heard that tuition was increasing at colleges in Bulgaria, you might not scrutinize the arguments very carefully. Under such conditions people should give more weight to such peripheral cues as communicator expertness or the length of arguments given.

Petty and colleagues (1981) demonstrated this contrast in a marketing study. In the high-

relevance groups, subjects were asked to review magazine ads for a new razor and were told that they would get a free razor in return. In the low-relevance groups they were provided no razor (they got toothpaste instead). As Figure 6–6 shows, with high relevance, the strength of arguments was the key factor; with low relevance, source expertise was. In a later study (Petty et al., 1983) they repeated the same finding about source characteristics, this time comparing famous sports celebrities endorsing the product with endorsements by ordinary citizens.

In short, when the outcome mattered to the subject, the arguments were carefully proc-

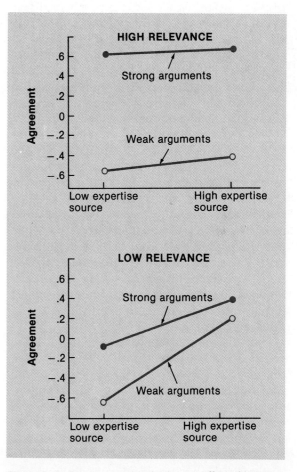

Figure 6–6. Post message attitudes are affected by argument quality, source expertise, and personal relevance of the issue. The top panel shows that any argument quality matters with high issue relevance, but only source expertise matters with low issue relevance (Adapted from Petty & Cacioppo, 1986, p. 144, based on research by Petty et al., 1981).

essed. When it did not, the subject was content to rely on the superficial attributes of the communicator. Most other studies have replicated this finding, and further have found greater counterarguing with higher levels of issue involvement (see Leippe & Elkin, 1987, though in fairness, not all have found that issue involvement does inspire great attention to argument strength; see Axsom et al., 1987).

Response Involvement. Even when the individual is not very committed to her prior attitude and the issue is not very personally relevant, her attitudinal response may be very important to her because it will receive public scrutiny and bring her social approval or disapproval. This kind of involvement is called *response involvement* (Zimbardo, 1960). The response-involved person, then, is mainly concerned with what others will approve, while the issue-involved person is more concerned with the intrinsic quality of the arguments, because the outcome of the issue is what matters.

These contrasting effects of issue and response involvement were compared by Leippe and Elkin (1987). They manipulated issue involvement by telling subjects that their university was considering comprehensive examinations; some were told they would be put into effect the next year and affect current students, and others, that they would not be put into effect until some years hence. Response involvement was manipulated by telling some they would discuss the issue with another subject and a professor, while others were not told of any such discussions.

Only the subjects who were both highly issue involved and weakly response involved—those who expected to be personally affected by the issue but did not have to worry about what image they would present to others—gave real scrutiny to the arguments, as reflected in greater attitude change in response to strong than to weak arguments. With high response involvement—when subjects were preoccupied with their self-presentation—the strength of arguments was ignored, as it was when the issue had no personal relevance.

In short, the original concept of ego involvement has been broken down into three separate types, each with somewhat different psychological dynamics. Commitment (or position involvement) represents involvement in the individual's specific position and produces pressure to defend that position. So exposure to discrepant communications often produces responses other than attitude change, such as source derogation, misperception, or blanket rejection. Issue involvement refers to perceptions that the issue is personally relevant and tends to promote more open and diligent information processing, spurred by an effort to get at the best possible position. And response involvement refers to a concern about how one's overt statement of attitude will be received by others. It breeds concern about self-presentation and the social acceptability of one's attitude rather than about the quality of arguments or merits of the case.

Inoculation

In the aftermath of the Korean war, William McGuire and others became very interested in reports of "brainwashing" of American prisoners of war by Chinese Communists. A number of POWs had given public speeches denouncing the American government, and several said publicly that they wished to remain in China when the war was over, rather than return to the United States. McGuire speculated that some soldiers might have been vulnerable to influence because they were being attacked on matters they were quite inexperienced and ignorant about—many soldiers, especially the less educated ones, had never been forced to defend the United States against the sophisticated Marxist arguments used against them by the Chinese.

McGuire hypothesized that an important source of resistance to change in the target comes from past experience with the issue. He pictured the individual faced with a discrepant communication as being like somebody attacked by a virus or a disease. The stronger the persuasive message (virus), the more damage it would do; but the stronger the person's defenses, the better able he or she would be to resist persuasion (disease).

There are two different ways of strengthening people's defenses against a disease. We can strengthen their bodies generally, by giving them vitamins, exercise, and so on. Or we can strengthen their defenses against that particular disease by building up antibodies. If people are given mild cases of smallpox that they are able to fight off, their bodies produce antibodies which in the future provide an effective and strong defense against more powerful attacks. McGuire argued that these two approaches are also applicable to the influence situation.

The first procedure, to strengthen resistance by building up the person's opinion directly, provides additional arguments supporting the original position. McGuire called this a **supportive defense.** The second approach is the **inoculation defense.** McGuire argued that a more effective way of increasing resistance is to build up defenses. Someone whose opinion has been attacked, and successfully defended, should be able to resist later attacks because a relatively strong defensive system will have been built up. The inoculation defense involves two things. It begins with a weak attack. The attack must be weak, or it would change the attitude and the battle would be lost. Then the target is helped to defend against the mild attack by being given an argument directed specifically at the attack or by being told that the attack is not very good and should be easy to refute.

The key study by McGuire and Papageorgis (1961) used both the supportive and inoculation methods to build up defenses. There were three groups of subjects: one group received support for their position, one group had their position attacked weakly and the attack refuted (the inoculation condition), and the third group received neither procedure. Afterward, all groups were subjected to a strong attack on their initial position. The supportive method helped subjects resist persuasion a little—the group receiving support changed a little less than the group that had no preparation. But the inoculation method helped a great deal; subjects receiving this preparation changed much less than did the other subjects.

One implication would be that supportive defenses are best when the target simply needs to be taught specific arguments. The inoculation defense would be better when the targets must be stimulated to think up their own defensive arguments. Consistent with this view, later research has shown that supportive defenses tend to be particularly effective when the subsequent attack contains arguments similar to the content of the supporting arguments, but it is relatively ineffective when new arguments are used. In contrast, inoculation is effective even when the attack includes new arguments (McGuire, 1964).

Cognitive response theory is most often used to explain these results. It suggests that in refuting the mild attack, people exercise all their defenses. They prepare arguments supporting their own positions, construct counterarguments against the opposing position, derogate the possible sources of opposing views, and so on. This would provide the individual with a stronger, better defended position.

THE SITUATION

The factors described thus far have concerned the communicator, the message, and the target. Yet mass communications usually are delivered within a broader context in which other things are happening, and these also often prove to have decisive effects on the success of persuasion attempts.

When we watch a political candidate's television commercial in an election campaign, we know that she is running for election; her statement is not a dispassionate, academic one. Most people watch television news in the midst of all the hubbub of family members returning home from work, talking to each other, making dinner, children shouting and screaming, and so forth. We watch commercials for new cars during the halftime of football games, in the midst of getting up to get another beer, going to the bathroom, and making sarcastic comments about the commercials with our friends. These situations all are likely to influence the success of attempts at persuasion. Let us now consider some of the most important situational variables in attitude change.

Forewarning of Position

If someone who is highly committed to her position is told ahead of time that she is going to be exposed to a discrepant communication she is better able to resist persuasion by that message. In a study by Freedman and Sears (1965), teenagers were told 10 minutes beforehand that they were going to hear a talk titled "Why Teenagers Should Not Be Allowed to Drive." Other teenagers were not told about the talk until just before the speaker began. Under these circumstances, those who had the warning were less influenced by the talk than were the others. This **forewarning** enabled them to resist this very unpalatable message.

This is certainly a plausible finding, and it seems to be believed by many people in the business of persuasion. For example, we often hear an advertisement on radio or television with no warning that this is going to be an advertisement. Instead, the station sneaks in the ad before we are fully aware of what it is. A similar although more altruistic example is the dentist who warns us that something is going to hurt. He seems to feel that we will be better able to withstand the pain if we are warned. In fact, there is some experimental evidence that sub-

jects who are warned ahead of time that they are going to receive an electric shock report it hurts less than do subjects who are not warned.

All this sounds plausible and reasonable, but why does it occur? Why does a 10-minute warning help people resist persuasion? It is important to keep in mind that all the subjects know the speaker disagrees with them—the only difference is that some people know it 10 minutes ahead of time and others know it only just before the speech. The greater resistance shown by those with the longer warning is due to some mechanism that operates during those minutes between the warning and the speech.

Most likely, as with the inoculation procedure, the individual's defenses are in some way exercised and therefore strengthened. The individual who is warned (or who has just experienced a mild attack) is like a fighter who has prepared for a match. He has been through training, so when the fight comes, he is in better shape and able to meet his opponent. He also spends time convincing himself that his opponent is not very good and that he, himself, is great. This makes him more confident and better able to do his best.

All this work has been done on situations in which the recipient was strongly committed to a

Forewarned is forearmed (except when you like fast cars anyway): She surely was forewarned of the position he would advocate. Does that help her resist persuasion? Or was her position not very discrepant from his to begin with?

position discrepant from the communicator's. When the listener is not very committed to a position, though, warning turns out to have the opposite effect—it actually facilitates attitude change. The warning seems to operate as a cue to propel the listener along the road she was destined for sooner or later anyhow.

For example, Apsler and Sears (1968) hypothesized that forewarning of a discrepant message would actually facilitate attitude change among subjects who were not personally involved in the topic, whereas it would have the usual effect of blocking change among highly involved subjects. They gave subjects a persuasive communication advocating replacement of professors by teaching assistants in many upper-division courses, a change opposed by almost all subjects. Some subjects were told the change would come quickly, in time to affect their own education (high issue involvement); others were told it was several years off and would not affect them (low issue involvement).

Forewarning helped block change among the highly involved subjects, just as it had among the teenagers who were highly involved in the issue of teenage driving in the Freedman and Sears experiment. However, it facilitated change in the low-involvement condition. This is shown in Figure 6–7.

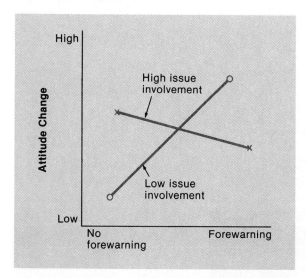

Figure 6–7. Effects of forewarning and issue involvement on persuasiveness of a discrepant message (Adapted from Apsler & Sears, 1968, p. 164).

There are still some other controversies surrounding the exact nature of these responses to warning. The elaboration-likelihood and cognitive response theories contend that forewarning highly committed persons produces more thought, and therefore counterarguing. Indeed Petty and Cacioppo (1977) have shown the delay period between warning and exposure to the communication allows subjects to generate more counterarguments. Listeners also probably use derogation of the discrepant source. The forewarned person has 10 minutes to convince herself that the communicator is unreliable, prejudiced, and misinformed. But it is also possible that the increased resistance is just a by-product of a blanket rejection of the communication, a stubborn refusal to give in.

Forewarning of Intent

Another kind of forewarning is that which signals the intent to persuade. Sometimes we know in advance that a communicator intends to try to change our attitude. Almost all commercials and political speeches take that form. At other times we may be exposed to a persuasive message without realizing persuasion is intended. For example, sometimes a teacher or a friend seems simply to be trying to inform us about something, but in reality is trying to persuade us of a particular position.

Forewarning of intent to persuade generally motivates more thinking about the arguments, if the issue is one of relevance and importance to the recipient. And, as with forewarning of position, if the position is quite discrepant, this additional thinking is likely to produce counterarguments and heightened resistance to change. To show this, Petty and Cacioppo (1979) told subjects either that the message was "designed specifically to try to persuade you and other college students" or that it was prepared as part of a class project. Then the message argued for comprehensive exams for all seniors. In the high-relevance condition, the exam would be instituted at that college the coming year. In the low-relevance condition, it would be far in the future or at another university. They found that the most counterarguing against this unpopular proposal, and the least attitudinal change, occurred with forewarning and high personal relevance.

Distraction

In parts of our discussion, we have described the individual as actively fighting the persuasive message. People whose opinions are attacked usually try to resist changing, especially when they are committed to their attitudes. They counterargue, derogate the communicator, and generally marshal all their forces to defend their own positions. One important implication of this is that the ability to resist persuasion is weakened by anything that makes it harder to fight the discrepant communication. In particular, distracting attention from the battle may enable the persuasive message to get through.

A study by Festinger and Maccoby (1964) demonstrated this effect of **distraction.** Subjects listened to a speech against fraternities while watching a film. For some of the subjects, the film showed the person making the speech. For others, the film was ''The Day of the Painter,'' a funny, somewhat zany satire on modern art. Presumably, those watching the irrelevant film were more distracted from the antifraternity speech than those watching the person speak. Subjects who initially disagreed with the speech (who were in favor of fraternities) were more influenced in the distraction than the nondistraction condition. Taking the subjects' minds off the speech increased its effectiveness.

Mild amounts of distraction do seem generally to enhance persuasion (Petty & Brock, 1981). Much of the relevant research has been guided by a cognitive response approach, which suggests that distraction should increase persuasion only when it interferes with an otherwise effective counterarguing process. So distraction should help persuasion much better on a familiar issue on which we know our own arguments, such as concerning fraternities, than on an issue we do not have ready arguments about. It seems to work best when the communications are highly discrepant and on very involving topics, presumably because these inspire the most vigorous counterarguing (Petty & Brock, 1981). These results are consistent with the elaboration-likelihood hypothesis

Is this salesperson likely to attract more attention to the car or to herself?

that distraction works by interfering with processing the arguments of a communication.

In any case, the effect must depend on the right amount of distraction. Obviously, too much distraction prevents the persuasive message from being heard at all and reduces its effectiveness to zero. Advertisers may want to distract television viewers from the main point of commercials by irrelevant pictures and action. They do not, however, want to have the irrelevancies so fascinating that the message is lost. Having a beautiful woman in the background during a soap commercial may help sell soap, but having her in the foreground dressed in skimpy revealing clothes and acting provocatively may reduce the effectiveness of the ad. Distraction may work under some conditions, but it is important that the distraction not be too great, or the effect will be reversed.

ATTITUDE CHANGE OVER TIME

So far we have focused on immediate responses to one-shot communications—that is, under what conditions does a televised speech, radio ad, or conversation with a friend *immediately* produce attitude change? In many cases, however, we want to know how attitudes change over time. We especially want to know the effects of repeated exposure to a message and what effects are likely to last when the exposure ends.

Spontaneous Attitude Change

Attitudes apparently get stronger the longer people hold them. Tesser (1978) has done a series of studies that find thinking about an attitude object tends to make the attitude more extreme. According to Tesser, people review and rehearse their cognitions, and consistency pressures move them toward more evaluatively consistent clusters. So if you spend more than the usual amount of time thinking about your best friend, you will probably like her better. You might remember additional good qualities or

enjoyable experiences you shared. And you might reinterpret some of your less pleasant memories to excuse your friend's behavior. However, if you think about your enemy more often, you will probably dislike her even more. You would lengthen her list of offenses and find seamy motives for her apparently good and generous acts.

Basically, Tesser's hypothesis is that thinking about an issue produces more polarized attitudes because thinking allows people to generate more consistent attitudes. But all this cognitive activity requires that the individual already have a knowledge structure, or schema, about the issue. Without some schematic understanding of the issue, it would be difficult to generate new beliefs, or know how to reinterpret old ones, and so on.

The implication is that thought will polarize attitudes only if the person already has a schema about the issue, and if the thought is specifically focused on that issue rather than on some other, irrelevant question. To test this, Chaiken and Yates (1985) tested two groups of people, some who already had a highly consistent knowledge structure about the issue (capital punishment), and others who did not. Then every person wrote an essay either about this issue or about a different, irrelevant issue (censorship). Indeed only the highly consistent subjects who wrote an essay on capital punishment developed more extreme attitudes on that topic. No significant polarization occurred in any of the other conditions. To polarize attitudes, then, the thought must be relevant to the issue, and the person must have sufficient cognitive resources.

Persistence of Attitude Change

A last question concerns the persistence of attitude change over time, once it has been induced by a communication. It seems clear that, in general, memory for the details of an argument decays with time in a way resembling an Ebbinghaus forgetting curve—that is, decreases are rapid at first, then diminish later on. In general, though, the persistence of attitude changes is not necessarily dependent on retention of the details of arguments. As indicated earlier, a good bit of research finds memory for arguments of only secondary importance. Other events that occur after the communication are of much greater significance.

One important factor may be whether or not the recipient is later reminded of important cues other than the arguments themselves, such as the credibility of the source. Kelman and Hovland (1953), for example, manipulated source credibility and found the usual difference on an immediate posttest: the high-credibility source had produced more attitude change. Three weeks afterward, the credibility difference was gone. The low-credibility source's message was, by then, just as effective. This rebound in the persuasiveness of the low-credibility source's message was called the **sleeper effect**. The original credibility difference could be reinstated, however, if the subject was reminded of the original source of the message.

A *dissociation* interpretation was offered for the increased effectiveness of the low-credibility source (Hovland, Janis, & Kelley, 1953). The recipient was originally presented with two pieces of information, the message and its endorsement by the low-credibility source. Immediately afterward, the recipient remembers both. But the low-credibility source acts as a discounting cue that enables the recipient to discount or ignore the message. So there was little immediate attitude change. As time goes on, the credibility of the source becomes increasingly dissociated from the message; that is, the recipient remembers the message but forgets who said it. The message therefore becomes more persuasive with time, as it is increasingly relieved of the stigma of being associated with a low credibility source.

An alternative interpretation is the *differential decay* hypothesis (Pratkanis et al., 1988), which assumes that the impact of a discounting cue (such as a low-credibility source) on persuasion dissipates more quickly than does the impact of the message itself. The reason is that it is more difficult to remember the combination of message and source than it is simply to remember your own new position on the issue. Immedi-

ately after hearing the message, both the discounting cue and the message are accessible in memory, so there is little immediate apparent attitude change. But a few days later, the impact of the discounting cue may be lost, while that of the message is retained, producing the surge in attitude change described as the "sleeper effect." This process is shown in Figure 6–8.

The implication is that such sleeper effects should occur primarily when the discounting cue originally followed the message. If you only find out that the source has low credibility *after* you have heard the message, you will have already listened to the arguments and taken them seriously. But if you learn that the source has low credibility before you even hear the message, you probably will not even pay attention to the message, so there will be no original persuasive impact of the arguments to shine through once the suppressing impact of the low-credibility source has dissipated.

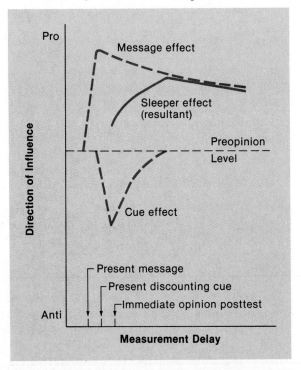

Figure 6–8. The differential decay explanation of the sleeper effect. (At short delays, message and discounting cue are hypothesized [dotted lines] to have near equal impact. However, the impact of the cue dissipates rapidly to yield an observable [solid line] sleeper effect.) (Pratkanis et al., 1988).

Pratkanis and colleagues (1988) report a study demonstrating this effect. When the discounting cue was given before the message, it prevented substantial message impact right off the bat, so little attitude change occurred, either immediate or delayed. But when the cue was given immediately afterward, the sleeper effect occurred. The discounting cue substantially reduced the initial impact of the message, but attitude change surged forward when measured again 6 weeks later. Presumably by that time the discounting cue no longer had any effect, whereas the impact of the message persisted.

Low credibility is not the only discounting cue. Attitude change may also be artificially suppressed by warning the recipient about the communicator's intent. People tend to become stubborn when they feel the source is trying to persuade them. But over time, such people seem to show increased attitude change, presumably as the discounting cue (persuasive intent) is forgotten (Watts & Holt, 1979).

If there is a lesson in all this, it may be that there is no such thing as a free lunch in the day of a persuader. A low-credibility source may get a message through, but the message is always vulnerable to its weak auspices becoming salient again. Or, one may momentarily trick a person into changing by failing to warn her, but with time the persuasive impact will be lost.

PROCESSES OF ATTITUDE CHANGE REVISITED

One theme that has run throughout this chapter is the contrast between systematic processing on the one hand, and the use of peripheral cues on the other. The contrast, as we noted earlier, takes us directly to the most basic questions about attitude change—do people pay attention to the real arguments in persuasive communication, and how thoroughly do they consider the merits of the position?

The factors that induce one or the other style of processing have appeared throughout this chapter. It may therefore be useful to bring them together in one place, so a summary is shown in Table 6–4. This tabulation probably gives a somewhat false sense of the definitiveness of these findings. In many cases it is based

T A B L E   6 – 4

WHEN DOES SYSTEMATIC PROCESSING TAKE PLACE AND WHEN ARE PERIPHERAL CUES USED?

	Conditions Promoting	
	Systematic Processing	Use of Peripheral Cues
Category of Independent Variable		
Source	Number of independent sources	Likability
		Physical attractiveness
		Expertness
Message	Repetition	Length of message
	Rhetorical questions/arguments	Number of arguments
	Written message	Video message
	High discrepancy	
Target	Issue involvement	Response involvement
	Need for cognition	
	Prior information	
Situation	Forewarning	Audience response
	Distraction	Pleasant mood music
	Intent to persuade	Attractive models/actors

on a single study or on partial results or even on contradictory results from different studies. The best evidence in most cases is on attitude change itself; direct evidence on the underlying processes, such as on greater scrutiny of arguments, is usually not as compelling. Still, the general theoretical orientation is a clear one; some evidence for all the findings listed has been presented; and this is the most active line of research on attitude change today. So it well merits *our* systematic processing!

Many factors affect attitude change. Some act by appealing to a person's reason, by increasing the trust in the communication, strengthening the persuasive message, and, in general, determining how much the individual believes what is being said. An attempt to influence someone's opinion need not, however, be done in an entirely logical, unemotional, cognitive situation. The situation may, and often does, involve strong motivations, appeals to deep-seated needs, and a great many factors extraneous to the logical arguments contained in the message itself.

As research on attitude change has developed, there has been some change in theoretical emphasis along these lines. Much of the early research was guided by some version of a transfer-of-affect or rote-learning approach, which treated people as rather emotional and reflexive. More popular now are cognitive theories that place relatively less emphasis on affect and emotion, such as cognitive response theory, the theory of reasoned action, and the elaboration-likelihood model.

Of course, the study of attitude change will always produce a variety of views of human beings, because people are quite various and no one simplified theory will always be correct. But the trend in studying attitude change, like the trend in the study of social perception, has been away from models based on emotion and rote learning and toward models stressing cognitive processes and rational thinking.

Key Terms

attribution theory
cognitive response theory
commitment
counterarguing
credibility
discrepancy
distraction

ego involvement
elaboration-likelihood model
forewarning
group identification
group norms
inoculation defense
message learning

modes of resolution
peripheral cues
reference group
sleeper effect
source derogation
supportive defense
systematic processing
transfer of affect

Summary

1. A useful model of the attitude change situation classifies possible influences on the target in terms of communicator, communication, and situational and target variables.

2. The major mechanisms by which people resist persuasion include derogating the communicator, distorting the message, and counterarguing.

3. Two quite different processes are common in the persuasion situation: systematic processing, which involves close scrutiny of the arguments, and the use of peripheral cues irrelevant to message content.

4. The source of the communication is a critical factor in persuasion. More credible, trustworthy, and liked sources are most po-

tent, as are reference groups with which the target identifies. Source characteristics are often processed as peripheral cues.

5. The most important aspect of the communication is its discrepancy from the target's initial attitude. Attitude change tends to increase with more discrepancy up to a point, when it starts to fall off again. With high source credibility and/or low commitment, this fall-off point occurs at higher levels of discrepancy.

6. Communications can arouse emotional needs such as anger or fear and tend to be accepted if the position advocated reduces the need it has aroused. Very high levels of fear seem to arouse defensive reactions, however, and reduce the likelihood of attitude change.

7. The degree of commitment to an attitude (position involvement) is a critical determinant of persuasion. With higher commitment, there is less persuasion.

8. Strong arguments are more effective than weak ones when the target can be induced to think more about them, such as when the issue is personally relevant (high issue involvement).

9. Repetition of a message is important if attitude change is to be maintained. But too much repetition leads to boredom and lessened support for it.

10. A person can become inoculated against persuasion by being exposed to weak versions of the forthcoming persuasive arguments, and learning to combat them.

11. Forewarning of the position to be advocated tends to increase resistance to change when the listener is highly committed to a very discrepant position.

12. Distraction can help create persuasion by reducing the listener's defenses against very discrepant messages.

Suggested Readings

Alwitt, L. F., & Mitchell, A. A. (Eds.). (1985). *Psychological processes and advertising effects: Theory, research, and application*. Hillsdale, NJ: Erlbaum. A useful and current collection of applications of research on attitude change to advertising.

Chaiken, S., & Stangor, C. (1987). Attitudes and attitude change. In M. R. Rosenzweig & L. W. Porter (Eds.), *Annual Review of Psychology, 38*, 575–630. The best recent statement of social psychologists' thinking about attitudes. It is especially detailed on the question of systematic versus heuristic processing.

Hovland, C. I., Janis, I. L., & Kelley, H. H. (1953). *Communication and persuasion*. New Haven, CT: Yale University Press. The original presentation of the pioneering program in experimental studies of attitude change. Much of the rest of the work described in this chapter springs from work originally presented here.

McGuire, W. J. (1985). The nature of attitudes and attitude change. In G. Lindzey & E. Aronson (Eds.), *Handbook of social psychology*, 3rd ed., Vol. 2. Reading, MA: Addison-Wesley. The most complete review of attitude research and theory.

Petty, R. E., & Cacioppo, J. T. (1986). *Communication and persuasion: Central and peripheral routes to attitude change*. New York: Springer-Verlag. A complete presentation of the elaboration-likelihood model of attitude change.

Petty, R. E., Ostrom, T. M., & Brock, T. C. (Eds.). (1981). *Cognitive responses in persuasion*. Hillsdale, NJ: Erlbaum. Application of the cognitive response approach to many of the problems in attitude change presented in this chapter.

SEVEN

Social Interaction

SOCIAL INTERACTIONS: FROM CASUAL TO CLOSE

SELF-PRESENTATION

SOCIAL COMPARISON

SELF-DISCLOSURE AND INTIMACY

A SOCIAL EXCHANGE PERSPECTIVE

*H*umans are basically social animals who spend most of their time in the presence of other people. In a carefully controlled study, Larson and his colleagues (1982) found that individuals spend almost three quarters of their waking hours with other people. The researchers asked a sample of adults and a sample of teenagers to carry electronic pagers for a week. At random times from early morning to late evening, the researchers activated the pager, sounding a beep that signaled participants to fill out a short questionnaire describing what they were doing and whether they were alone or with others. As shown in Table 7–1, teenagers spent 74 percent of their waking hours with someone else; adults spent 71 percent of their time with others. People were most likely to be with others when they were at school or work. In contrast, they were most likely to be alone when they were doing household tasks, taking a bath, listening to music, or studying at home.

Social interaction occurs when two or more people influence each other—verbally, physically, or emotionally. Talking to a therapist, debating an idea in class, angrily arguing with a friend, and bumping into a person in a crowded elevator are all examples of social interaction. In this chapter, we examine some of the most important features of social interaction. We begin

T A B L E 7 – 1
HOW PEOPLE SPEND THEIR TIME

Activity	Adolescents		Adults	
	Alone	With Others	Alone	With Others
At Home				
Housework	6.7%	5.6%	5.4%	8.6%
Self-care (bathing, etc.)	2.1	0.5	2.2	1.2
Studying (adolescents only)	3.5	1.4	—	—
Eating	0.6	3.1	0.7	2.4
Socializing (includes by phone)	2.6	5.4	—	3.8
Watching television	2.0	3.9	2.2	5.1
Personal reading	2.0	1.4	1.5	1.4
Doing hobbies and art	0.7	0.5	0.3	0.2
Idling, listening to music	1.8	2.5	2.4	3.3
All at home activities	20.0	24.3	14.7	26.0
At Work or School				
Working at work	1.6	2.2	5.9	20.9
In class (adolescents only)	—	15.6	—	—
Other activities at work or school	1.2	13.5	3.6	11.5
All at work or school activities	2.8	31.3	9.5	32.4
In Public				
In transit (on bus, etc.)	1.3	3.3	2.9	3.6
Other practical activities	1.2	6.2	0.8	1.1
Leisure	0.6	9.0	1.2	7.9
All public activities	3.1	18.6	4.9	12.6
TOTAL TIME (Alone + With Others = 100 percent)	25.9	74.1	29.1	70.9

Source: Adapted from R. Larson, M. Csikszentmihalyi, & R. Graef, Time alone in daily experience: Loneliness or renewal? In L. A. Peplau & D. Perlman (Eds.), *Loneliness,* p. 43. Copyright 1982 by John Wiley & Sons.

Note: The table shows what percentage of the time people reported that they were alone or with others doing each specific type of activity. For instance, adolescents reported spending 6.7 percent of their time doing housework alone.

From childhood to old age, close relationships with loved ones, friends, and colleagues are at the core of human experience.

with a general model of how the interaction between two people can develop from a casual acquaintance into a close relationship. Next, we consider the process of self-presentation, in which individuals try to manage the impressions they make on others, and the process of social comparison, in which individuals evaluate their own abilities and opinions by comparison with others. Then we discuss the dynamics of self-disclosure, and how the revelation of personal information can create intimacy in a relationship. We conclude with an exploration of social exchange theory, which offers a systematic analysis of the workings of social interaction.

SOCIAL INTERACTIONS: FROM CASUAL TO CLOSE

When two people interact, they influence each other: what each one does affects the other person. The specific ways people can influence each other are very diverse. Another person can make us feel happy or sad, tell us the latest gossip or criticize our opinions, help us to get something done or get in our way, make us laugh or keep us awake at night worrying, give us advice or tell us off, bring us presents, or make us spend money. As these examples illustrate, influence in social interaction involves feelings, beliefs, and behavior. The basic theme is that two people have mutual influence on each other or, in more technical terms, that they are interdependent (Kelley et al., 1983).

Some interactions are very brief. On an airplane, you may strike up a friendly conversation with your seatmate, knowing that you will probably never see this person again. At the other extreme are relationships that endure for years and that involve countless interactions. A useful way to think about the progress from casual interactions to close relationships is in terms of the increasing **interdependence** of the partners. A model of pair interdependence developed by Levinger and Snoek (1972) is presented in Figure 7–1. The model shows two

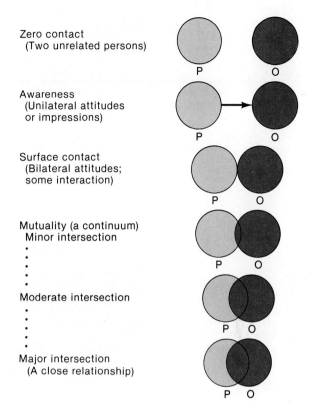

Zero contact
(Two unrelated persons)

Awareness
(Unilateral attitudes
or impressions)

Surface contact
(Bilateral attitudes;
some interaction)

Mutuality (a continuum)
Minor intersection

Moderate intersection

Major intersection
(A close relationship)

Figure 7–1. A model of pair interdependence. (Adapted from Levinger & Snoek, 1972, p. 5.)

people, P and O, at increasing stages of interdependence.

Initially, the two people are completely unaware of each other and are unrelated in any way. They are at a point of *zero contact* when no interaction has occurred. The stage of *awareness* exists when one person notices or learns something about the other, but no direct contact has taken place. For example, we may take an instant dislike to a student who seems to "know it all" in class, even without ever speaking to her directly. Sometimes we learn about another person from a third party; for example, a friend may encourage us to take a particular class because she thought the professor was unusually good.

Awareness can be unilateral (as shown in Figure 7–1 by the one-way arrow from P to O). Or it can be bilateral, as when two strangers glance at each other across a room. The awareness stage can be quite important. If we form a favorable impression of another person, we may take

A high level of interdependence is the hallmark of a close relationship.

the initiative to interact with that person. Indeed, people sometimes have very intense experiences in the awareness stage, as when fans develop passionate feelings for rock singers and movie stars they have never met.

The next level, *surface contact*, begins when two people first interact, perhaps by talking or exchanging letters. Surface contact is the beginning of interdependence. When we exchange small talk with a friendly supermarket checker, we are engaging in surface contact. These interactions are usually brief, the topics of conversation are superficial, the impact people have on each other is limited, and the contact is often defined by specific social roles. Many interactions end at this stage of minimal interdependence.

When interaction continues over time, a relationship begins to develop. As the degree of interdependence increases, the pair moves to the stage of *mutuality*. Levinger and Snoek conceptualize mutuality as a continuum ranging from lesser interdependence (shown by little overlap in the circles in Figure 7–1) to extensive interdependence (shown by much overlap). For example, over the course of their first year at college, the interdependence of roommates may grow from a rather limited and emotionally distant mutuality into a close relationship in which their lives are significantly intertwined.

Social psychologists use the term **close relationship** to refer to relationships that involve much interdependence (Berscheid, Snyder & Omoto, 1989; Kelley et al., 1983). These can be relationships with a parent, a best friend, a teacher, a spouse, a co-worker, or even an important rival or competitor. All close relationships share several basic characteristics. First, they usually involve frequent interaction that continues over a relatively long period of time. Second, close relationships include many different kinds of activities or events. In a friendship, for example, people discuss many different topics, and generally share a wide range of activities and interests. This contrasts with superficial relationships focused around a single activity or topic.

Third, in close relationships, the influence between people is strong. We may quickly forget a snide remark from a salesclerk, but agonize for weeks about a comment made by our best friend. We may be momentarily grateful for the help offered by a bus driver, but benefit daily from the cooperativeness of our roommate. Further, when two people are highly interdependent, they have the potential for arousing strong emotions in each other. We like to think of our close relationships as a source of positive feelings of love, caring, and concern. But it is also true that our strongest emotions of anger, jealousy, and despair are likely to occur in our closest relationships.

SELF-PRESENTATION

John is carefully preparing for an important job interview. He rehearses what he'll say about his past work experience. He gets his hair trimmed and ponders which suit to wear and whether a vest would look too formal. He buys a new briefcase to carry his papers and makes a point of arriving early for his appointment. When he meets the interviewer, John remembers to give a strong handshake, and smiles pleasantly. During the interview, John tries to look attentive and to answer questions thoughtfully. In short, he makes every effort to present himself as an energetic, competent person who would be successful in the job.

A pervasive aspect of social interaction is the desire to manage the impression we make on others. The term **self-presentation** refers to our efforts to control the impression we convey. The fundamental goal of self-presentation is to structure our interaction so that we obtain a desired outcome. In John's case, the goal is to obtain a job offer. We often want people to view us positively—as an interesting, friendly, intelligent, and caring person. But sometimes we strive to convey other images instead (Baumeister & Hutton, 1987). For example, the school yard bully may want to present himself as tough and intimidating. At other times, our goal may be to minimize a bad impression, for instance, by finding a plausible excuse for showing up late for an exam.

Self-presentation is often a deliberate activity. In his job interview, John is quite conscious of his desire to present himself as hard working and talented. However, in familiar situations, self-presentational activities can become automatic (Baumeister, Hutton, & Tice, 1989). With his friends, John may habitually present himself as a fun-loving guy who doesn't take work too seriously. When self-presentation in a particular setting becomes routine, people don't have to think about impression management much and so can focus their attention on other aspects of the situation.

Sociologist Erving Goffman has compared self-presentation to acting in a play (1959). Like dramatic actors, we often pay special attention to appearances—to the way we look and dress and also to our mannerisms and habits. When we "dress up" for a date, or remember not to chew gum on the job, we are controlling appearances in order to convey a desired image. We sometimes rely on props to assist in our self-presentation. Serving the right wine, driving a classy car, and flashing a new engagement ring

are ways people use physical objects to convey a particular impression. Setting the stage can also be important. This might involve turning down the lights and playing soft music as a prelude to romance, or taking a friend on a wilderness hike to convey our interest in nature. Another feature of self-presentation is rehearsal. Before a social event, we may think about what we'll say and do, mentally trying out various approaches.

Goffman observed that people often distinguish between front-stage and back-stage regions in their social interactions. Back regions are where people prepare for a performance; front regions are where the action takes place. When preparing for a dinner party, the nervous amateur chef may spend the entire day in the

Before each performance, a clown puts on special make-up and clothes. In everyday life, people also try to appeal to their audience, and often tailor their appearance and self-presentation to "look good."

kitchen, frantically trying to follow complicated recipes and using every pot in the house. However, the chef's front stage behavior may be quite different. When the guests are seated at the dining table and praise the delectable meal, the chef may appear calm and experienced, saying, "Oh, it's just a little something I whipped up this afternoon."

An important aspect of self-presentation is knowing one's audience. For a fashion-conscious teenager, the trendy clothes and hairstyles that are popular among peers may be considered tasteless and outlandish by older relatives. The ability to "take the role of the other," to anticipate how others will perceive and react to our actions, is essential for successful impression management. Thus, one of the challenges of social interaction is being able to change our behavior from situation to situation, depending on our self-presentational goals and on the nature of the audience.

Making a Good Impression

Perhaps the most common motive in self-presentation is to make a good impression (Schlenker, 1980). How do people accomplish this objective? Several tactics of successful impression management have been identified (Fiske & Taylor, in press).

One strategy is to conform to the norms of the social situation. To look good at a party, a person might tell interesting stories and jokes. In contrast, at a funeral, expressions of sadness and sympathy for the family would be more appropriate. Another strategy is to match the behavior of the other person. If your new acquaintance boasts about her tennis prowess, you might do well to boast about your own accomplishments. But if she behaves modestly and downplays her expertise, a similar degree of modesty might create the most positive impression.

A useful distinction can be made between two additional strategies for creating a positive impression—self-promotion and ingratiation. *Self-promotion* refers to conveying positive infor-

mation about the self, either through one's actions or by saying positive things about the self. In contrast, ingratiation or flattery refers to saying positive things about the listener. Jones and Pittman (1982) have suggested that these two tactics reflect different goals—whereas the self-promoter wants to be seen as competent, the flatterer wants to be liked. In some situations such as a job interview, the person may try to accomplish both goals simultaneously, coming across as both likable and talented.

Self-promotion can be tricky. Telling about one's accomplishments can enhance self-presentation, but it can also backfire and create the impression of being conceited or insecure (Cialdini & De Nicholas, 1989; Jones & Pittman, 1982). This happens because observers often evaluate a person on more than one dimension at the same time. The blatant self-promoter may indeed convince others that he or she is competent, but may also display conspicuous egotism.

An important factor in self-promotion is the context in which people talk about themselves. A recent study compared impressions of people who made positive statements about their intellectual ability under several different conditions (Holtgraves & Srull, 1989). People who mentioned their excellent intellectual accomplishments were seen most favorably if these statements were made in response to specific questions. For instance, if a person was asked how he had done on his midterm, his answer that he got 93 percent correct made a favorable impression. Similarly, positive statements about the self enhanced one's image if they were made in a context of mutual disclosures by both partners. So Andy's statement that he did very well in the chess club tournament was seen positively if it was part of a conversation in which Bob also indicated that he had done very well in bridge. In contrast, if people seemed to go out of their way to say good things about their own ability without being asked and without others providing similar information, they were perceived as less likable, less considerate, and more egotistical. In short, the context of the conversation makes an important difference in how observers interpret self-promoting statements.

Another tactic of positive impression management is the careful use of modesty (Cialdini & De Nicholas, 1989). For example, the female basketball star whose brilliant plays have just saved her team from losing the championship might describe her performance as "pretty good" but emphasize that she couldn't have done it without the work of the entire team. By understating her accomplishments, she will probably be seen as both likable and competent. The trick, of course, is to know when modesty will be effective. There are two rules of thumb. First, modesty boosts a person's public image only when their performance has actually been successful. Modesty about a poor performance is not image-enhancing. Second, modesty works to boost one's public image only when the audience already knows the full extent of the person's success. The champion athlete can afford to be modest because her fame precedes her.

Self-presentation involves both verbal and nonverbal behavior. In Chapter 2, we described ways in which nonverbal behavior contributes to self-presentation. In general, self-presentations are most convincing when verbal and nonverbal messages are the same. A person who says he's "very happy" but uses a glum and depressed tone of voice will not be very credible. In contrast, a person who says she would like to get to know us better, smiles, makes frequent eye contact, and sits close by is much more believable.

We engage in impression management not only by the things we ourselves do, but also by associating ourselves with people who are successful, powerful, or famous. Robert Cialdini and his co-workers have used the term BIRGing to refer to the tendency to *bask in the reflected glory* of others (Cialdini et al., 1976; Cialdini & Nicholas, 1989). Cialdini believes that people enhance their individual self-presentation by highlighting their associations with successful others, even when these connections are quite trivial. If a person tells us that he comes from the same hometown as President Bush, or that he once met Barbra Streisand, or that his friend won a million dollars in the lottery, he is trying to impress us by his mere association with the rich and famous.

Ineffective Self-Presentation

Self-presentation is not always effective. Sometimes our actions do not show us in a positive light. We may forget our mother's birthday or spill a bowl of soup in our lap at a restaurant. In such cases, the best we can do is to minimize our losses.

Embarrassment is a common and unpleasant emotion experienced when there is a disruption in our self-presentation (Parrott, Sabini, & Silver, 1988; Schlenker, 1980). These can be minor lapses in impression management, for instance, when a waiter drops a tray of food or when a person inadvertently calls someone by the wrong name. Flaws in self-presentation can also involve more serious failures in performance — when a professional actor forgets his lines or a famous scientist is shown to have misinterpreted her data. The embarrassed person usually responds with efforts to resume the interrupted pattern of interaction. The person may apologize or give an excuse, and then attempt to pick up where he or she left off. An embarrassing situation is uncomfortable for everyone present, and so others are also motivated to help the embarrassed person "save face."

Excuses can play an important role in impression management. A poor performance on a test or in a sports competition calls into question one's self-presentation. One way to handle a less than stellar performance is to give excuses (Snyder & Higgins, 1988). Consistent with attribution theory (Chapter 4), people often try to excuse their failures as due to external and uncontrollable causes. It is more gratifying to say you failed the test because it was unfair and all the other students also flunked (external, uncontrollable cause) than to admit that the test was easy and you were not able to master the material (low ability).

The importance of excuses is not limited to achievement settings. Failure to meet a social obligation, such as being late for an appointment, can also create impression management problems. Again, you will probably make a better impression—and avoid arousing anger in the other person—if you blame your late arrival on a flat tire, rather than saying you forgot to set the alarm clock (Weiner, Amirkhan, Folkes, & Verette, 1987). In addition to offering excuses after the fact, another strategy for handling a poor performance is **self-handicapping,** a phenomenon we discussed in detail in Chapter 4.

An unfortunate implication of this analysis is that self-presentational pressures may sometimes cause people to lie—to others and to themselves—about the true reasons for their actions. At times, the desire to impress others favorably may conflict with a desire to be honest.

Self-Monitoring

All of us are social actors who consider the impression we make on others. But for some people, a concern with self-presentation is ever-present. **Self-monitoring** is the tendency to emphasize impression management to a great extent. Mark Snyder and his colleagues have developed a paper-and-pencil test to assess this personality disposition (Briggs & Cheek, 1988; Snyder, 1987; Snyder & Gangestad, 1986). Individuals high in self-monitoring are especially sensitive to situational cues about appropriate behavior. On the Self-Monitoring Scale, they would agree with such statements as

"I would probably make a good actor."

"I may deceive people by being friendly when I really dislike them."

"In different situations and with different people, I often act like very different persons."

In contrast, individuals low in self-monitoring are less attuned to situational demands; their self-presentation is controlled to a larger extent by their inner attitudes and values. They would agree with such statements as

"I can only argue for ideas which I already believe."

"I have trouble changing my behavior to suit different people and different situations."

"I have never been good at games like charades or improvisational acting."

High- and low-self-monitoring individuals differ in several ways (Snyder, 1987). In comparison to low self-monitors, high self-monitors make a greater effort to learn about other people and to size up social situations. They pay more attention to information about people they are going to meet and interact with. And they are also more likely to tailor their behavior to fit the demands of the situation. For instance, high self-monitors are more skilled at using their faces and voices to pose particular emotions. Self-monitoring may affect interaction in a wide variety of settings. In dating situations, for example, high self-monitors seem to place greater importance on the physical attractiveness of a partner, whereas low self-monitors seem to give greater weight to personality (Glick et al., 1988; Snyder, Berscheid, & Glick, 1985). Because high self-monitors are attuned to situational demands, their behavior may vary more from one situation to another.

In reading about self-monitoring, you may have tried to figure out where you or your friends fall on this continuum. You may also have wondered which orientation is best or most useful. In fact, there are pros and cons to both high and low self-monitoring. High self-monitors may think of themselves as practical-minded people who try to make the best of social situations. Their perceptiveness and social sensitivity enable them to interact effectively in diverse settings. But carried to an extreme, high self-monitors can be criticized as self-interested opportunists who change themselves and their opinions to suit the situation. A similar dilemma exists for low self-monitors. On the one hand, they may think of themselves as principled people who stick up for what they believe in and remain firm in their goals despite social influences. But carried to an extreme, low self-monitors can be criticized as insensitive, inflexible, and uncompromising. Perhaps fortunately, most people fall in between these two extremes.

SOCIAL COMPARISON

All of us want to know how good we are at the things we care about. Am I a good tennis player, a talented writer, a graceful dancer, a loyal friend? Sometimes we can evaluate ourselves on objective criteria. If we get a perfect score on an exam, we know we did very well. But most of the time there is no convenient objective standard, so we turn to other people to help evaluate ourselves. We assess our personal experiences by comparing them to those of other people. This is especially true when feelings and emotions are involved. Should I enjoy eating chocolate-covered grasshoppers, or laugh at the comedian's dirty jokes, or be afraid of the huge but harmless snake, or like the new movie everyone is talking about? Knowing how others react helps to clarify and evaluate our own thoughts and feelings.

In 1954, Leon Festinger, a pioneer in modern social psychology, formalized these observations in **social comparison theory.** Festinger believed that people are motivated to make accurate assessments of their level of ability and the correctness of their attitudes. To do this, they assess their own standing in comparison to others like themselves. As an illustration of the choice of similar others for comparison, Festinger suggested that beginning chess players would prefer to compare themselves to other beginners rather than to master players. Festinger's theory of social comparison can be summarized in three statements:

1. People have a drive to evaluate their opinions and abilities accurately.

2. In the absence of direct physical standards, people evaluate themselves by comparison with other people.

3. In general, people prefer to compare themselves to similar others.

Young baseball fans often strive to emulate a successful player. Upward comparisons to a "star" can motivate us to improve our own performance.

Today, our understanding of social comparison processes is considerably more complex than Festinger's original model (Goethals & Darley, 1987; Taylor & Lobel, 1989; Wood, 1989). The scope of social comparison theory has been broadened. We now know that people make comparative judgments not only about their abilities and opinions, but also about their emotions, their personality, and their outcomes on such dimensions as salary or prestige. As we will see in later chapters, the process of social comparison affects many aspects of social life. For example, the belief that our current dating partner is more wonderful than anyone we have ever dated before or could be dating now has important implications for our satisfaction and commitment in the relationship. The belief that our social or ethnic group is economically or socially disadvantaged compared to other groups in society can increase discontent and inter-group conflict (see Chapter 13).

The Goals of Social Comparison

Festinger's assertion that accuracy is the only goal of social comparison has been challenged. It now appears that social comparisons can be made in the service of a variety of personal goals and motives, including:

Accurate self-evaluation. As Festinger suggested, sometimes people do desire truthful knowledge about themselves, even if the outcome is not favorable (Trope, 1986). Learning that we are the worst player on the volleyball team may spur us to greater effort or encourage us to change sports.

Self-enhancement. As we first saw in Chapter 4, people often strive to maintain and enhance a positive view of themselves. This can lead them to bias information in self-serving ways (Taylor & Brown, 1988). Rather than seeking truthful self-evaluation, people may seek comparisons that show them in a favorable light. A student who is struggling to learn calculus may prefer to emphasize that he's doing better than other students who are flunking the course. A desire for self-enhancement can lead people to make "downward comparisons" with others who are less fortunate, less successful, or less happy than they are (Wills, 1981).

Self-improvement. Sometimes people compare themselves with others who can serve as models of success. Contrary to what Festinger assumed, an aspiring chess player may deliberately compare his opening strategies to those of great masters, in order to assess his stage of learning accurately, to learn from the insights of the masters, or to be inspired by their model (Wood, 1989). A desire for self-improvement can lead to "upward comparisons" with people who are more successful. The danger, of course, is that comparisons with much better performers can be discouraging and lead to feelings of incompetence.

The Comparison Process

Festinger focused on situations in which a person deliberately chooses to make a social comparison. Illustrations of such situations are easy to find. For example, after surviving a frightening earthquake, a person may actively seek to compare his reactions with others' and spend hours talking with neighbors and friends about their experiences. At other times, however, social comparisons are not intentionally sought, but are rather forced upon us by the situation (Wood, 1989). For example, when elementary school children choose sides for a game of baseball, the best players are usually picked first and the worst players are picked last. Children may not want to undergo this social comparison experience, but find it an unavoidable part of their life at school.

Unsolicited comparisons can have important effects on the individual. This point was demonstrated in a classic experiment by Stanley Morse and Kenneth Gergen (1970). Subjects in their study were undergraduate men who responded to an ad in the school newspaper offering two part-time jobs in "personality research." When the student arrived for his job interview, he was asked to fill out some questionnaires which included a measure of self-esteem. He was then exposed to another job applicant, who was brought into the same room to fill out the application materials. The experimental manipulation was to vary the appearance of the other job candidate (actually a confederate of the researchers).

Half the subjects were confronted with "Mr. Dirty," a young man wearing ripped trousers, a smelly sweatshirt, and no socks. He seemed very disorganized and glanced around the room frequently while filling out the forms. In contrast, half the subjects were randomly assigned to encounter "Mr. Clean," a well-groomed and confident young man who wore a dark suit and carried an attaché case. Later in the study, the subject's self-esteem was reassessed to see what impact exposure to Mr. Clean or Mr. Dirty might have had. As predicted, subjects who had an opportunity for downward comparison with Mr. Dirty increased their self-esteem—

based on the comparison, they felt better about themselves. Subjects who had an opportunity for upward comparison with Mr. Clean suffered a drop in self-esteem—based on the comparison, they felt less good about themselves. The point is that unsolicited opportunities for social comparison can have important effects on our self-evaluation.

Festinger emphasized that people prefer to compare themselves to similar others. But just what dimensions of similarity are most important? Consider the case of a college student enrolled in a large history course who wants to evaluate how well she is doing. She might decide to compare herself with all the other students in the class; she could do this by finding out where she ranks in the class based on her grades. However, she might decide that this is not the best comparison because students in the course differ widely in how many history courses they had in high school.

Instead, she might decide to compare herself only to other nonhistory majors who, like herself, have a limited background in the subject. In technical terms, this would be a comparison based on *related-attributes similarity*. The basis of similarity is not her performance itself, but rather her background or preparation for the course—an attribute that should be related to performance (Goethals & Darley, 1987).

On the other hand, the student might want to know how she compares to other women in the class. In this case, she is selecting comparison targets who are similar on gender, a dimension of similarity that is presumably *unrelated* to performance in the course. There is evidence that people often make comparisons based on similarity in gender, race, or ethnicity—even when it is not directly relevant to task performance. Finally, the student might want information about the range of performance in the course, and so be interested in comparing herself to the best and to the worst students in the group. Here, comparisons with others who are different from the self in performance might prove instructive. In summary, each type of comparison provides different information (Wood, 1989). All may be useful, depending on the individual's goals.

Tesser's Self-Evaluation Maintenance Model

John's best friend Mark recently won a prestigious prize for writing a fictional short story. How will John react? Will he be overjoyed and eager to tell others about his friend's success so he can bask in Mark's reflected glory? Or might he instead feel envious of Mark's success and unhappy to be reminded that he is a less talented writer? More generally, when does the performance of another individual enhance our personal self-evaluation, and when does it threaten our sense of self-worth? Abe Tesser (1988) has spent nearly a decade developing a **Self-Evaluation Maintenance Model** designed to answer this question.

Tesser's model focuses on the motive for self-enhancement—the desire to maintain a positive self-evaluation. The performance of other people in our social environment can affect our self-evaluation, especially when we are psychologically close to them. In the model, perceived closeness can be based on having a relationship with another person, such as being a friend or relative. But closeness can also be based on shared characteristics, such as race, gender, religion or physical proximity. In general, the behavior of people who are close has greater potential impact on us than the behavior of people who are psychologically distant. In addition, Tesser focuses on situations in which the other person performs relatively better than we do. The performance of others is less important to our self-evaluation when it is mediocre. According to Tesser, the critical situation arises when a person whom we are close to performs well.

In such situations, what determines whether our reaction is to bask in their success (a reflection process) or to suffer by comparison? A key factor is whether or not the performance is relevant to our self-definition. If John aspires to be an award-winning creative writer, then knowledge that a close friend has outperformed him is likely to threaten his self-evaluation and lead to feelings of envy and discomfort. On the other hand, if John has no pretensions about his writing ability and sees creative writing as irrelevant to his sense of self, then he should take pleasure in the success of a close friend since it poses no threat to his personal self-evaluation. In more technical terms, the main ideas of the Self-Evaluation Maintenance Model can be summarized as follows:

1. *The comparison effect.* When another person outperforms us on a behavior that is *relevant* to our self-definition, the better their performance and the closer our relationship, the greater the threat to our self-evaluation. A process of upward comparison leads us to feel envious, frustrated, or even angry.

2. *The reflection effect.* When another person outperforms us on a behavior that is *irrelevant* to our self-definition, the better their performance and the closer our relationship, the more we can gain in self-evaluation. A process of reflection leads us to feel positively and to take pride in their success.

It is important to note the crucial role of the personal relevance of the behavior in question. The very same factors—closeness and high performance—can lead to opposite effects depending on whether the behavior is relevant or irrelevant to our self-definition.

The Self-Evaluation Maintenance Model leads to many testable predictions about social interaction, and, in general, research findings have been supportive (Tesser, 1988; Tesser & Collins, 1988). For example, an individual whose self-evaluation has been diminished by the high performance of a close friend can try to repair the situation in several ways. One approach is to reduce the degree of closeness with the high-performing friend. John, for instance, might spend less time with Mark or come to value his friendship less. Another approach is to change one's self-definition. John might decide that creative writing is not really his ambition after all and that he should focus on literary criticism or art history. A third approach is to change the performance difference. John might put greater effort into improving his own writing skills, or try to convince himself that Mark's prize was based on luck rather than high ability.

In short, the successes of people close to us

can be a mixed blessing. They sometimes bring us pleasure, but sometimes cause us to suffer by comparison.

SELF-DISCLOSURE AND INTIMACY

Conversation is an important form of human interaction. People can talk about virtually anything. **Self-disclosure** is a special type of conversation in which we share intimate information and feelings with another person. When a friend reveals that his childhood fear of lawn sprinklers forced him to walk blocks out of his way to get to elementary school, we feel closer to him emotionally. When a co-worker takes us aside to explain that her absence from work was not due to the flu as most believed, but rather to a miscarriage, we sense a bond of trust and

---

T A B L E   7 - 2

FIVE MAIN REASONS FOR SELF-DISCLOSURE

1. *Expression:* Sometimes we talk about our feelings to "get them off our chest." After a hard day at work, we may eagerly tell a friend just how angry we are at our boss and how underappreciated we feel. Simply being able to express our feelings is one reason for disclosure.

2. *Self-clarification:* In the process of sharing our feelings or experiences with others, we may gain greater understanding and self-awareness. Talking to a friend about a problem can help us to clarify our thoughts about the situation.

3. *Social validation:* By seeing how a listener reacts to our self-disclosures, we get information about the correctness and appropriateness of our views. Other people may reassure us that our reactions "seem perfectly normal"—or that we're "blowing things out of proportion." In either case, listeners provide useful information about social reality.

4. *Social control:* We may reveal—or conceal—information about ourselves as a means of social control. For instance, we may deliberately refrain from telling things about ourselves to protect our privacy. We may emphasize things we think will make a favorable impression on our listener. In extreme cases, people may deliberately lie to exploit others, as when an imposter claims to be a lawyer but has actually had no legal training.

5. *Relationship development:* Sharing personal information and confidences is an important way to begin a relationship and to move toward increasing levels of intimacy.

Self-disclosure ranges from a casual chat with strangers to the shared intimacies of long-time friends.

openness. For many people, self-disclosure is a key aspect of intimacy in relationships.

Sometimes we reveal facts about ourselves that might otherwise be unavailable to a listener—the kind of work we do, where we live, how we voted in the recent election. This is known as *descriptive disclosure*, because our revelations describe things about ourselves (Morton, 1978). A different type of self-disclosure occurs when we reveal our personal opinions and feelings—that we like the listener, that we feel guilty about being overweight, that we hate getting up early in the morning. This is called *evaluative disclosure*, because emphasis is given to our personal assessment of people and situations.

There are many reasons why we disclose information to another person (Derlega & Grzelak, 1979). For example, we might tell someone a secret as a way to create greater intimacy in a relationship. Five of the main reasons for self-disclosure are described in Table 7–2.

There is a strong reciprocity effect for self-disclosure (Ludwig, Franco, & Malloy, 1986; Miller & Kenny, 1986). If we share intimate information with another person, they are likely to respond with equally personal information. If we talk in superficialities, so will the other person. One explanation for this effect is the existence of a generalized **norm of reciprocity** (Gouldner, 1960). If someone does us a favor,

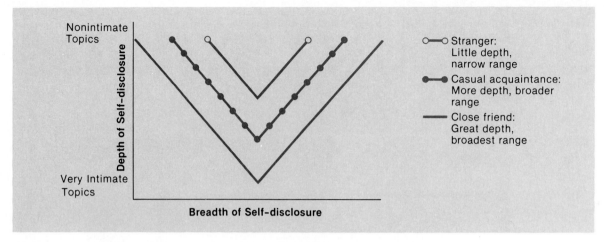

Figure 7–2. The breadth and depth of self-disclosure are represented as "wedges" into the personality and experience of the person. For strangers, the wedge is narrow and superficial. For a close friend, the wedge is deeper (more intimate) and broader in the range of topics disclosed. (Adapted from Altman & Haythorn, 1965, p. 422.)

we feel obligated to do them a favor in return. As applied to self-disclosure, the reciprocity norm implies that if someone tells us something personal, we should respond with a comparable revelation.

Self-disclosure is a major way to get to know another person and to develop a closer relationship. Altman and Taylor (1973) proposed a model to describe how self-disclosure affects the development of a relationship. In their view, the process of forming an intimate relationship involves "penetrating" beyond the surface of another person to gain greater and greater knowledge about their inner self. Altman and Taylor use the term **social penetration** to describe this process. As shown in Figure 7–2, social penetration occurs along two major dimensions of depth and breadth.

As relationships develop from superficial to intimate, people disclose increasingly more personal things about themselves. This is the depth dimension of social penetration. We might willingly talk with a stranger about our preferences in food and music, talk with a casual acquaintance about our attitudes on politics and world events, but reserve for close friends discussions of anxieties and personal ambitions. Only after many years of friendship did one woman reveal to her childhood friend the pain she had suffered in school because her wealthy mother

forced her to wear torn underwear beneath her fashionable clothes since "no one would see."

Relationships also develop from narrow to broad, as over time people discuss a wider range of topics and share more diverse activities. These phases of relationship development are shown in Figure 7–2 as "wedges" that one person makes into the personality and life experiences of another.

Reciprocity and Liking

Liking is an important cause of self-disclosure. People reveal much more to best friends and romantic partners than to co-workers and casual friends. The more interesting question is how the act of self-disclosing affects liking. One view might be that self-disclosure is inherently rewarding, and "the more the better." Research generally supports a different view, however, that we like people most whose self-disclosure is carefully paced and reciprocal (Altman & Taylor, 1973).

For self-disclosure to enhance liking, it must be appropriate to the situation (Derlega & Chaikin, 1975). The disclosure must be slow enough that it does not become threatening to either person. If it races ahead prematurely into areas of great personal intimacy, it will arouse anxiety and defensiveness. Someone who "comes on too strong, too fast" will be disliked (Kaplan et al., 1974). A gradual process of mutual self-disclosure, paced over time, spurs the growth of a relationship.

Altman and Taylor proposed that we like best people who disclose at about the same level of intimacy as we do. Someone who discloses more personal details than we do threatens us with a premature rush into intimate territory, and we may want to put on the brakes. If we are disclosing at a more intimate level than the other person, we may feel vulnerable or foolish. For other potential hazards of sharing personal information, see Box 7–1 on p. 222.

There is much evidence that disclosure reciprocity is a key factor in liking. In an early study, Chaikin and Derlega (1974) used a procedure that enabled them to manipulate experimentally the intimacy level of self-disclosures in a pair. Their method was to videotape two actresses improvising a first-acquaintance encounter in a school cafeteria. Each actress did this in two ways: at a high and a low level of self-disclosure. Then the experimenters presented the videotaped conversations to subjects in each of the four combinations of self-disclosure: both women high in self-disclosure, both low, high-low, or low-high.

In the high-self-disclosure case, one woman told immediately about her relationship with her boyfriend, who was her first sexual partner, and about her parents' reactions. The other woman's high-intimacy disclosures concerned her mother's nervous breakdown and hospitalization, her fighting with her mother, and the possible divorce of her parents. In the low-self-disclosure cases, the women talked about the problems of commuting to school, where they went to high school, and the courses they were taking. After watching one of the videotapes, subjects indicated how much they liked each of the women. The main finding was that liking for both women was higher when they disclosed at the *same* level of intimacy than when they were at different levels. Breaking the reciprocity norm led to less liking, but for different reasons. The woman who disclosed very little (relative to the other) was thought cold, whereas the more intimate norm breaker was seen as maladjusted.

The demands for reciprocal disclosure early in a relationship are different from those later on. Early in a relationship, we expect reciprocity for nonintimate disclosures, but not for highly personal disclosures. If you tell the stranger next to you in the lecture hall that you like this course, she is supposed to reciprocate with her reactions to the course. But if she suddenly changes the subject and tells you about her father's alcoholism, you do not feel obligated at all to tell her anything personal about your life. Indeed, her revelation may seem inappropriately intimate, since she is a complete stranger.

Later in the development of a relationship, reciprocity about intimate details becomes important. Suppose you sit next to a classmate for several weeks, and then go to the campus coffeehouse after the first midterm. If you start telling her your worries about your academic ability, and your concern that maybe you should have gone to an easier college, you are putting yourself out on a limb. It is important that she make some reciprocal gesture to show that she, too, is interested in having a closer relationship. If, in the midst of your disclosures, she suddenly starts talking about the weather, you may feel hurt and want to pull back to a less intimate level. Reciprocity is important for supporting tentative moves toward a closer relationship.

Sex Differences in Self-Disclosure

Stereotypes depict men as "silent types" who keep their feelings to themselves and women as "talkers" who freely share confidences. As one wife complained about her husband, "He doesn't ever think there's anything to talk about. I'm the one who has to nag him to talk" (cited in L. Rubin, 1976, p. 124). How accurate is this stereotype about gender differences in self-disclosure?

In same-sex relationships, women do indeed disclose more than men, on average (Dosser, Balswick, & Halverson, 1986; Reis, Senchak, & Solomon, 1985). Throughout adult life, women are more likely than men to have an intimate, same-sex confidant, and to emphasize the sharing of personal information. In a study of college students, for example, women were more

BOX 7–1

Privacy and the Hazards of Self-Disclosure

Self-disclosure is an important type of interaction that can enhance liking and the development of a relationship. We often want to share our feelings and experiences with others. But it is also true that we sometimes want to conceal our feelings, to keep our thoughts to ourselves, and to protect our private inner life from scrutiny. In short, our goal is often to control the information others have about us—sharing what we want when we want. The term *informational privacy* refers to our ability to control who knows what about us and under what circumstances (Burgoon et al., 1989).

The desire to limit and control the sharing of information highlights the point that self-disclosure can be risky. Revealing personal information can make us vulnerable. A leading expert on self-disclosure, Valerian Derlega (1984), has suggested some of the many possible risks individuals may incur when they self-disclose:

1. *Indifference.* We may share information with another person in a bid to begin a new relationship. Sometimes, our disclosure is reciprocated by the other person, and a relationship develops. At other times, however, we may find that the other person is indiffer-

ent to our disclosures and not at all interested in getting to know us.

2. *Rejection.* Information we reveal about ourselves may lead to social rejection. For example, a college student may not tell her roommate that she has epilepsy, out of a concern that misinformation and fear will lead the roommate to reject her.

3. *Loss of Control.* There is some truth to the old adage that "knowledge is power." Sometimes, others use information we share to hurt us or to control our behavior. Derlega suggests, for instance, that a teenage boy may tell a friend some little-known but potentially embarrassing information about his fear of women. In an angry moment, the friend may remind the young man of his weaknesses to try to establish dominance in the relationship.

4. *Betrayal.* When we reveal personal information to someone we often assume —or even explicitly request—that the knowledge be treated confidentially. Unfortunately, such confidences are sometimes betrayed.

likely than men to say that they enjoy "just talking" to their best female friend and to indicate that talking helped form the basis of their relationship. In contrast, college men emphasized sharing activities with their best male friend (Caldwell & Peplau, 1982).

In opposite-sex relationships, however, gender differences are much less clear cut. In general, people disclose more to their romantic partner or spouse than to anyone else. The most common pattern is for both partners to reveal at equal levels, with some couples sharing a lot and others disclosing relatively little (Komarovsky, 1967). The norm of reciprocity encourages partners to disclose at comparable levels. Today, young people expect more self-disclosure in their intimate relationships than

did earlier generations. Rands and Levinger (1979) asked college students and senior citizens to describe relationships characteristic of 22-year-olds of their own generations. They found that today's young people expect intimate pairs to be more expressive, to do more things together, and to disclose both positive and negative feelings more openly than the young people of two generations ago. Studies also find that college dating couples usually do disclose at quite high and equal levels (see Rubin, Hill, Peplau, & Dunkel-Schetter, 1980). It should be noted, however, that when exceptions to this equal-disclosure pattern occur in male-female couples, it is usually the man who discloses less.

The fact that men and women often disclose

at equal levels does not mean that they necessarily reveal the same kinds of personal information. One study of college students found that in male-female relationships, women were more likely to reveal their weaknesses and to conceal their strengths; men showed a reverse pattern of disclosing their strengths and concealing their weaknesses (Hacker, 1981). Another study found that men disclosed more on "masculine" topics such as when they had been aggressive or had taken risks. Women disclosed more on "feminine" topics such as when they felt childlike or were sensitive about their appearance (Derlega, Durham, Gockel, & Sholis, 1981).

Rosenfeld (1979) investigated why people sometimes avoid disclosure. Consistent with our earlier discussion of impression management, both sexes expressed concern about "projecting an image I do not want to project." In addition, men also worried about losing control over another person; women worried about providing information that might be used against them and about hurting the relationship.

In general, research does not support the stereotype that all men are inexpressive all the time. In heterosexual dating and marriage, men and women often disclose at similar levels. Sex differences are most pronounced in same-sex relationships, with women friends showing a strong preference for talking, and men friends showing a greater interest in shared activities.

Intimacy as an Interpersonal Process

Self-disclosure is one component of intimacy in a relationship. But the mere revelation of personal information is not sufficient to create the psychological experience of closeness. In a recent analysis, Harry Reis and Phillip Shaver proposed a model of the way intimacy is created in the interaction of two people. Their model is illustrated in Figure 7–3, which provides an example of an interaction between Anne and Betty. The model involves three major steps.

Step 1. Anne is upset about a problem she's

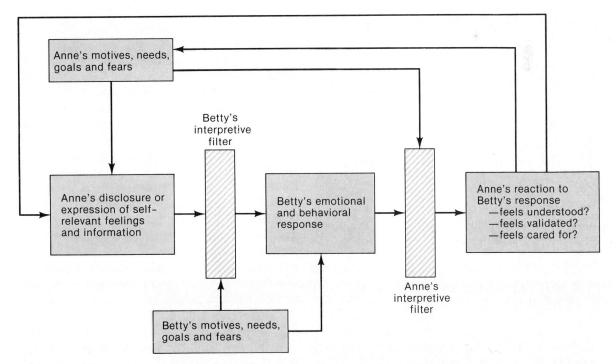

Figure 7–3. Intimacy as an interpersonal process. (Adapted from H. T. Reis and P. Shaver, Intimacy as an interpersonal process. In S. W. Duck (Ed.), *Handbook of Personal Relationships,* p. 375. Copyright 1988 by John Wiley & Sons.)

having at work and decides to share her feelings with her friend Betty. Anne's revelation is triggered by her private mental state—her motives, needs, goals, or fears. The intimacy process begins when one individual reveals personal feelings or information to another. This sharing of information can be done verbally through self-disclosure, or nonverbally by "body language."

Step 2. As the interaction continues, Betty responds to Anne's disclosure with sympathy and warmth. She moves her chair closer to Anne and asks relevant questions. Betty's behavior reflects her own motives (for example, to be a good friend) and her personal interpretation of Anne's story (technically called her "interpretive filter"). Betty believes that her friend has been treated unfairly at work and tells her so.

Step 3. Anne appreciates Betty's concern. She interprets Betty's questions as a sign of interest and a desire to be helpful (this is shown as Anne's interpretive filter). As a result, Anne feels that Betty has understood her and agreed with her views. She feels that Betty cares for her well-being.

According to Reis and Shaver, intimacy results from interactions of this sort, in which one person's actions evoke a response from another that makes the person feel understood, validated, and cared for. Self-disclosure by itself does not create intimacy. Rather, the discloser must feel that the listener accepts and understands the discloser's views. Reis and Shaver believe that intimate interactions of this sort promote feelings of trust and emotional closeness that are fundamental to the development of personal relationships.

A SOCIAL EXCHANGE PERSPECTIVE

The most influential perspective on social interaction is social exchange theory (Blau, 1964; Burgess & Huston, 1979; Kelley & Thibaut, 1978). This perspective analyzes the rewards and costs partners give and receive. The theory proposes that we are attracted to those partners we think are best able to reward us, a point we will explore more fully in Chapter 9. The theory also states that we try to arrange our interactions to maximize our own rewards.

To receive rewards, however, we must also give them. As children we learn a general rule or norm of reciprocity: we are expected to reward those who reward us. If people help us, we feel obligated to help them (Gouldner, 1960). If we invite someone to dinner, we expect that person to return the invitation in the future. Social interaction can thus be viewed as a process of exchange between partners.

Rewards and Costs

A reward is anything a person gains from an interaction, such as feeling loved or getting financial assistance. What is rewarding for one person may be of little value for someone else. A useful analysis of the rewards of social interaction was proposed by Foa and Foa (1974), and is shown in Figure 7–4.

They identify six basic types of rewards: love, money, status, information, goods, and services. These can be classified along two dimensions. The dimension of particularism concerns how much the value of a reward depends upon who provides it. The value of love, or more specifically of such things as hugs and tender words, depends very much on whom they come from. Thus love is a particularistic reward. In contrast, money is useful regardless of whom it comes from; money is a nonparticularistic or universal reward. When we say that a relationship is very special to us, we often mean that it provides us with unique or particularistic rewards that we cannot get elsewhere. The second dimension, concreteness, captures the distinction between tangible rewards—things you can see, smell, and touch—and nonconcrete or symbolic rewards, such as advice or social approval.

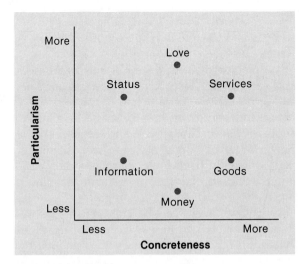

Figure 7–4. Rewards people exchange. (Adapted from U. G. Foa, Interpersonal and economic resources, *Science,* 171, 1971, p. 347. Copyright 1971 by the American Association for the Advancement of Science.)

Costs are the negative consequences that occur in an interaction or relationship. An interaction might be costly because it requires a great deal of time and energy, because it entails much conflict, because other people disapprove of the relationship and criticize us for it, and so on. A further cost of an interaction is that it may deprive us of the opportunity to do other rewarding activities: if you spend the weekend skiing with a friend, you do not have the time to study for an exam or to visit your parents.

Evaluating Outcomes

Social exchange theory assumes that people keep track of the rewards and costs of a particular interaction or relationship. People seldom do this very explicitly; we do not usually make lists of the good and bad things about a relationship. Nonetheless, we are aware of the costs and rewards involved. In particular, we focus on the overall outcome we get in a relationship—that is, whether on balance the relationship is profitable for us (rewards outweigh costs) or whether we are experiencing an overall loss (costs outweigh rewards). People do not necessarily evaluate relationship outcomes very consciously or systematically, but the basic process is reflected

in such statements as "I'm really getting a lot out of this relationship" or "I don't think our relationship is worth it anymore."

At a party, we may avoid talking to John, whom we find totally obnoxious. Instead, we gravitate to Mike, a rather friendly sort who tells good stories. We continue to chat with Mike until we notice that our best friend Seth has just arrived. At this point, we excuse ourself and go talk to Seth. As this example highlights, we evaluate individuals differently as interaction partners—finding John unacceptable, Mike reasonably positive, and Seth best of all.

People use several standards for evaluating relationship outcomes. The simplest standard is whether the relationship is profitable or costly. A conversation with John is a negative, unpleasant experience, whereas conversing with both Mike and Seth is worthwhile. Also important are comparisons we make between relationships, assessing how one relationship compares to others we have been in or that we know about. Thibaut and Kelley (1959) have emphasized two main comparison standards.

The **comparison level** reflects the quality of outcomes a person believes he or she deserves. This baseline standard differs from one type of interaction to another: we have different standards for interacting with a salesclerk and a romantic partner. Our comparison level reflects our past experiences in relationships. For example, we may consider whether a current dating relationship is as good as those we have had in the past. Or we may compare our new boss at work to our past experiences with other supervisors. We may also compare a current relationship to those we have seen in movies, heard about from friends, or read about in pop psychology books. The comparison level is our personal belief about what constitutes an acceptable relationship. Our comparison level may change as we have new experiences.

A second major standard is the **comparison level for alternatives.** This involves assessing how one relationship stacks up against other relationships that are currently available to us. Is our current dating partner better or worse than the other people we could be going out with right now? Is our current boss better or worse than other people we might realistically work for at this point in our lives? Even if a relationship is profitable in absolute terms, we may leave it if a more profitable alternative becomes available. In contrast, if our relationship is the best we think possible, we may stay in it, even if the gains are small. Our dependence on a relationship is based on our perceptions of the relationship as a source of rewards not available elsewhere.

Coordination of Outcomes

A key fact about interaction is that one person's outcomes are interlinked with the outcomes of the partner. Consider some of the coordination problems that might be encountered by two strangers who sit next to each other on a long airplane trip. Carl arrives first, completely fills the overhead compartment with his carry-on luggage, and claims the middle armrest for his use. A rather gregarious type, Carl hopes to spend the trip talking to his seatmate. Kathy, on the other hand, has brought along work to do and plans to spend the trip reading. She's somewhat annoyed to find the overhead compartment full, but manages to find another place for her belongings. After a few pleasantries, Kathy makes it clear that she does not want to begin a long conversation, and Carl thumbs idly through a magazine. Some time later, Carl pulls down the window shade and tries to take a nap. This further annoys Kathy, who was hoping for a glimpse of the Grand Canyon as the plane passed overhead. As Carl nods off, he begins snoring. Finally, in frustration, Kathy gets up to see if there is another vacant seat. In this example, a failure to coordinate their interaction prompts one person to try to end the interchange by leaving.

How easy or difficult it is for two people to coordinate their outcomes depends on how much they share the same interests and goals. When partners like to do many of the same things and value the same activities, they will have relatively few coordination problems. In such cases, they are said to have *correspondent outcomes*, because their outcomes correspond— what is good for one is good for the other, and

what is bad for one is bad for both (Thibaut & Kelley, 1959).

When partners have different preferences and values, they have *noncorrespondent outcomes* and are therefore more prone to conflicts of interest and coordination problems. In general, similarity in backgrounds and attitudes is a powerful factor in relationships because similar people usually have fewer problems of coordination, and so may find it easier to develop a mutually rewarding relationship.

Of course, even well-matched partners experience conflicts of interest from time to time. When this occurs, the partners must negotiate a settlement. Consider a young married couple deciding how to spend the income tax refund they just received. The wife would like to buy a new sofa; the husband would like to buy a video recorder. Since the couple has a limited amount of money available and cannot afford both the sofa and the VCR, they must coordinate their use of the funds and resolve their conflicting interests.

One common solution is to select a less preferred alternative that is acceptable to both partners. The young couple might decide to spend the money on a trip—neither person's first choice, but an alternative that is attractive to both. Another possibility is to take turns—buying the sofa this year and the VCR the next year. Coordinating outcomes is a basic issue in relationships (Thibaut & Kelley, 1959).

Settling conflicts of interest by negotiation is at best a time-consuming activity and at worst, a source of arguments and bad feelings. Over time, partners often develop rules or **social norms** about coordinating their behavior. Neither spouse may like to take out the garbage or pay the bills, but they may agree that he will do one if she will do the other. Shared norms reduce the need for continual negotiation to arrive at coordinated behavior patterns.

In many types of relationships, cultural rules prescribe certain coordinated patterns. At work, there are usually fairly clear understandings about what the employer and employee will do and how they will interact. Lawyers and their secretaries seldom need to negotiate to decide who will draft legal briefs and who will type them, or who will answer the phone and who will make court appearances. Traditional marriage provides another example of a relationship in which roles are predetermined. The traditional pattern is clearly for wives to do the housekeeping tasks and for husbands to have paying jobs.

In Chapter 1, we defined **social roles** as clusters of rules about how people should behave in a particular type of interaction or relationship. Roles provide solutions for some of the problems of coordination that participants are likely to encounter. In some relationships, such as traditional marriage or lawyer-secretary interactions, social roles offer fairly specific guidelines for action. In other relationships, such as between same-sex friends, cultural rules are much less explicit.

When social guidelines are vague or in the process of change, individuals have greater freedom of action, but must put more effort into coordinating interaction successfully. Today, traditional sex roles are being questioned. As a result, dating and married couples may be un-

Learning to share with friends is an important step in understanding principles of fairness in social relations.

certain about who should do what. A couple out on a first date may hesitate as they approach a doorway, trying to decide if the man should open the door for the woman or not. They may pause uncomfortably after a dinner out, waiting to decide whether to split the bill or have the man pay for both.

We can contrast the process of role taking, in which people act out conventional cultural roles, with the process of role making, in which people develop their own shared norms for social interaction (Turner, 1962). In personal relationships, both processes operate. People adopt conventional guidelines about how to behave with classmates, co-workers, friends, and family, but they also improvise and create their own solutions to problems of interdependence.

Fair Exchange

People are most content when their social relations are fair. We don't like to feel exploited by others, nor do we usually like to take advantage of others. Equity theory, an offshoot of social exchange theory, focuses on fairness in relationships (Greenberg & Cohen, 1982; Walster, Walster, & Berscheid, 1978).

People use various rules for determining whether or not a relationship is fair. Consider the case of two teenage boys trying to decide how to divide a chocolate cake. They might decide to "share and share alike," using the equality rule that everyone should receive equal outcomes. Research suggests that people are more likely to use the *equality* principle when they are friends rather than strangers (Austin, 1980). Children are more likely than adults to use the equality rule, perhaps because it is the simplest principle (Hook & Cook, 1979).

The boys might instead use the principle of "to each according to need," the idea that the *relative needs* of the people should be taken into account. By this rule, one boy might get a larger piece of cake if he was especially hungry, or if he hadn't had cake in a long time. This principle is illustrated by a family that spends most of its income to care for a seriously ill child who needs expensive medical treatment.

A third fairness rule is equity or distributive

justice. The key idea is that a person's profits should be proportional to their contributions (Deutsch, 1985). Here, the boy who contributed more to the cost of buying the cake, or who had exerted greater effort by baking the cake himself, should be entitled to a larger portion. In this view, equity exists when:

$$\frac{\text{outcomes of person P}}{\text{contributions of person P}} = \frac{\text{outcomes of person O}}{\text{contributions of person O}}$$

Both people receive the same ratio of outcomes to contributions. This is the fairness rule that has been the focus of equity research.

Equity theory has three basic assumptions:

1. People in relationships try to maximize their outcomes.

2. Dyads and groups can maximize their collective rewards by evolving rules or norms about how to apportion rewards fairly to everyone concerned.

3. When individuals perceive that a relationship is inequitable, they feel distressed and take steps to restore equity.

Research has supported several specific predictions from equity theory (Greenberg & Cohen, 1982). It has been shown, for example, that when relationships are not equitable, both partners feel distressed. It makes sense that the underbenefited (exploited) person feels distress. But research shows that the overbenefited person also feels distress, perhaps because they feel guilty or uncomfortable about the imbalance.

There is also evidence that people will try to restore equity when they perceive a relationship to be unfair. A person can do this in two major ways. First, he or she can restore actual equity: for example, a roommate might agree that he hasn't been doing his share of the housework and do extra work to compensate. Second, individuals sometimes use cognitive strategies to alter their perception of the relationship, thus restoring psychological equity. The roommate might distort reality and argue that he really has

done a fair share of the work, thus avoiding the need to change his behavior. Whether people restore actual or psychological equity depends on the costs and benefits associated with each particular alternative.

Much of the research on equity has come from laboratory studies of strangers interacting for short periods of time. More recently, however, studies have begun to show that equity considerations can also influence close relationships (Kidder, Fagan, & Cohn, 1981; Sprecher, 1988; Walster, Walster, & Traupmann, 1978). A concern with fairness may be especially important early on in a relationship. Over time, individuals may develop trust in their partner's good intentions and may monitor exchange patterns less closely. Recent longitudinal research finds that equity is a stronger factor in satisfaction early in premarital relationships than a few months later (Cate, Lloyd, & Long, 1988).

The Balance of Power

In any interaction, people often have different preferences for their activities and try to influence each other in order to accomplish their own goals. **Social power** refers to a person's ability to influence deliberately the behavior, thoughts, or feelings of another person (Huston, 1983; Molm, 1988). Social exchange theorists have been interested in the balance of power between people. In some relationships, both individuals are equally influential. In other relationships, there is an imbalance of power with one person making more of the decisions, controlling more of the joint activities, winning more of the disagreements, and generally being in a position of dominance. What factors determine whether or not a relationship is equal in power? Three important factors are social norms, relative resources, and the principle of least interest.

Social Norms. Patterns of influence in relationships are often dictated by social norms. When teenagers take a part-time job at a fast-food restaurant, they expect to take orders from the boss and to follow company regulations. It is generally understood that subordinates follow instructions from their superiors—at least in job-related matters. In heterosexual dating and marriage, social convention has traditionally conferred greater authority on men. Until recently, for example, state laws gave husbands legal control over all family property and permitted husbands, as the "head of the household," to decide where the family should live.

Relative Resources. Norms are not the only determinant of the balance of power. Social exchange theory (Blau, 1964) proposes that the relative resources of the two partners also affect their relative power. A resource is anything that "can be used to satisfy or frustrate needs or move persons further from or closer to their goals" (Huston, 1983, p. 206). The prediction from exchange theory is that when partners are imbalanced in their resources, the person who has more resources will have more power. When two students work together on a biology lab assignment, the person who is more knowledgeable or who owns a better microscope is likely to be more influential. In dating or marriage, the partner who earns more money, has more education, has a more prestigious job, is more physically attractive and so on has a power advantage (Scanzoni & Scanzoni, 1981).

The Principle of Least Interest. Exchange theory proposes that another determinant of power is the relative dependency of the two partners on the relationship, based on their comparison level for alternatives. In some relationships, both partners are equally attracted and committed, and this tends to build power equality. In other relationships, one partner is more dependent on the relationship (Molm, 1985) or cares more about continuing the relationship. This sets the stage for an imbalance of power.

Sociologist Willard Waller (1938) called this the **principle of least interest:** the less interested partner in a relationship has greater power. An implicit bargain is struck in which the more interested and dependent person defers to the other's wishes in order to ensure that the relationship will continue. An illustration of this principle is provided by Margaret, an unpopular young woman who had an affair with an older man:

> I accepted his structuring of our relationship. When he chose to deal in wit rather than in real information, I followed suit. When he acted casual about sex, so did I. I wanted something real from him. . . . Even when I knew this was impossible on my terms, I went ahead with it in his way. . . . I didn't back off, because I thought the potential was there, and a dateless summer had taught me that opportunities didn't come up all that often. (Cited in Goethals & Klos, 1970, p. 283)

Ultimately, relationships based on lopsided dependencies usually prove unsatisfactory to both partners. Over time, we would expect these relationships to change toward more equal involvement or to end.

We will continue our discussion of social power in Chapter 8, where we examine processes of social influence.

Conflict

Conflict is the process that occurs when the actions of one person interfere with the actions of another (Peterson, 1983). The potential for conflict increases as two people become more interdependent. As interactions become more frequent and cover a more diverse range of activities and issues, there are more opportunities for disagreement.

Much of the research on interpersonal conflict has involved heterosexual couples. Conflict is usually quite low during casual dating, but increases significantly in serious dating relationships (Braiker & Kelley, 1979). Conflict is common among married couples. In a national survey, 45 percent of married people said they had "problems getting along with each other" (Gurin, Veroff, & Feld, 1960). Couples can apparently fight about almost anything, from politics and religion to work and money, from how to spend their time to how to divide household chores. John Gottman (1979) found 85 different kinds of conflict among young married couples! Of course, conflict is not limited to married couples. It also occurs in relationships with co-

Conflict and arguments are common in many close relationships.

workers and supervisors, family and neighbors, friends and roommates.

Conflict problems can be grouped into three general categories (Braiker & Kelley, 1979):

☐ *Specific behaviors.* Some conflicts focus on specific behaviors of a partner, such as getting drunk at a party or forgetting to pick up milk at the grocery store. A partner's actions may be costly, such as one roommate playing loud music that interferes with another's studying. Or a partner may fail to provide desired rewards, perhaps by refusing to do something that the other wants.

☐ *Norms and roles.* Some conflicts focus on more general issues about the rights and responsibilities of partners in a relationship. Conflicts of this sort might concern a failure to live up to promises, a lack of reciprocity, or the neglect of some agreed-upon task. Thus one roommate might complain that the partner is not doing a fair share of the

cleaning. Or a worker and supervisor might disagree about the worker's job responsibilities.

☐ *Personal dispositions.* People frequently go beyond specific behaviors to make attributions about the intentions and attitudes of a partner. One person might complain that the partner is lazy, inconsiderate, or lacks self-discipline.

These three types of conflict reflect the fact that people are interdependent at three levels (Braiker & Kelley, 1979). At the behavioral level, partners have problems of coordinating specific activities. At the normative level, they have problems negotiating rules and roles for their relationship. At the dispositional level, they may disagree about each other's personality and intentions. This last type of interdependence arises because partners are important sources of validation for our self-image. For example, conflicts could easily arise if a person thinks of herself as kind and considerate, but has a partner who insists she is really selfish and insensitive.

Conflicts can escalate as partners use specific problem behaviors to make more general attributions about each other's character. For example, a person may initially complain that his roommate left the sink full of dirty dishes. As the discussion continues, he may add that the roommate seldom lives up to their agreements about housekeeping. He may finally conclude that the roommate is hopelessly sloppy and self-centered.

Another source of conflict in social interaction is the fact that events are often open to different interpretations (Kelley, 1979). Consider a husband who does not give his wife a present on their wedding anniversary. The wife may interpret this an insult and complain about it to her husband. The husband may see his actions differently and try to justify them to his wife. In such situations, people tend to explain their own and their partner's behaviors differently, consistent with the actor-observer attributional bias discussed in Chapter 4 (Kelley, 1979; Orvis, Kelley, & Butler, 1976).

The complaining person tends to attribute

the event to the partner's negative characteristics. The wife might insist, "You forgot our anniversary because you don't really love me anymore." Her motivation may be to punish the husband's misconduct or to challenge him to show he really does care. In contrast, the person who performed the act tends to excuse the behavior ("I meant to buy you something, but I was preoccupied with a big deadline at work") or to justify the action ("I thought we agreed not to spend money on each other"). The husband's explanations are an attempt to avoid blame and to keep the event from disrupting the relationship.

Conflict can help or harm the development of a relationship, depending on how it is resolved. Conflict can provide an opportunity for clarifying disagreements and changing expectations about the relationship. Lovers' quarrels allow lovers to test their own and their partners' dependence on the relationship, to discover the depth of their feelings for each other, and to renew their efforts to create a satisfying relationship. On the other hand, because conflicts arouse strong emotions, they may not provide the best setting for constructive problem solving. The escalation of conflict and the trading of personal insults are unlikely to benefit a relationship. Conflict may be especially harmful when it leads to defensiveness, stubbornness, and withdrawal from interaction (Gottman & Krokoff, 1989). For recent research on how people react to dissatisfaction in relationships, see Box 7–2 on p. 232.

Satisfaction and Commitment

Employers are often concerned about how to keep workers "happy" and how to increase workers' sense of loyalty to the company. For their part, employees are usually concerned with pleasing their boss and keeping their jobs. When a couple falls in love, the partners often wonder how to make their relationship "good" and how to make sure it will "last." In more technical terms, two important aspects of relationships are personal satisfaction and commitment to continuing the relationship.

There are important differences between satisfaction and commitment (Berscheid & Walster, 1978; Kelley, 1983). In business, for example, a worker may continue in an unhappy job because there are no better alternatives. Or a worker may leave a very satisfying job if a better opportunity comes along. In an "empty-shell marriage," spouses feel little love for each other but stay together because of religious principles, concern for the welfare of their children, or fear of loneliness. They are committed, despite low satisfaction. Or consider the case of a woman who loves a man intensely, but recognizes that he does not return her passion. Despite her current satisfaction, she may realize that continuing her commitment is not in her own best interest, and so she may end the relationship to seek a more compatible mate. Satisfaction and commitment are not the same.

Satisfaction refers to an individual's subjective evaluation of the quality of a relationship. Satisfaction depends on two factors: the outcomes we receive from the relationship and our general comparison level. We are satisfied if a relationship is profitable (rewards exceed costs) and if it compares favorably to our hopes and expectations. Perceptions of fairness also affect satisfaction: even if a relationship provides many benefits, we will not be fully satisfied if we believe that we are being treated unfairly. In business, partners are usually dissatisfied if they perceive the relationship to be inequitable. Similarly, in friendship and love, lopsided relationships in which one person gives much more—or gets much more—than the other are usually not as satisfying as balanced exchanges (Sprecher, 1988).

Commitment refers to all the forces, positive and negative, acting to keep an individual in a relationship. People who are strongly committed to a relationship are likely to stay together "through thick and thin," "for better or for worse." Positive forces of attraction are one determinant of commitment. If we like another person, enjoy that person's company, and find it easy to get along, we will be positively motivated to continue the relationship. Social exchange theory emphasizes, however, that com-

BOX 7–2

Reactions to Dissatisfaction: Voice, Loyalty, Neglect, and Exit

Caryl Rusbult (1987) and her colleagues have investigated the diverse ways people react when they are dissatisfied with a relationship. Rusbult's model is quite general and has been applied to job dissatisfaction (Rusbult et al., 1988) as well as to dissatisfaction with romantic relationships. Rusbult has identified four common reactions to dissatisfaction:

Voice

This occurs when a person voices the problems; tries to compromise; seeks help; tries to change the self, the partner, or the situation; or more generally works to improve the relationship. Fundamentally, voice is an effort to rescue a relationship in trouble. In a job situation, a worker might give voice to his or her dissatisfactions by discussing problems with a supervisor, suggesting solutions, consulting with a union official, or blowing the whistle on corporate wrongdoing. In a romantic relationship, voice might take the form of trying to talk with the partner, suggesting improvements in the relationship, offering to enter counseling, and so on. Voice is most often used when the person has previously been satisfied with the relationship and has invested fairly heavily in it. In romantic relationships, women are somewhat more likely than men to show this response.

Loyalty

This means passively but optimistically waiting for things to improve. Loyalty is a conservative response that attempts to maintain the status quo. In a job situation, a worker might publicly support the organization and perform his or her job well, while hoping that conditions will change. In a personal relationship, a dissatisfied but loyal partner would respond by waiting, hoping, or praying that things will improve with time. This reaction is most likely when the person views the relationship problems as relatively minor, has poor alternatives, has invested a good deal in the relationship, or is not seriously dissatisfied overall.

Neglect

In a job situation, this refers to allowing the situation to deteriorate passively by lack of effort, frequent lateness or absences, or using company time for personal business. In a personal relationship, neglect might be displayed by spending less time with the partner, ignoring the partner, refusing to discuss problems, treating the partner badly, or "just letting things fall apart." This response is most common when the person has not been very satisfied in the past and has made low investments in the relationship.

Exit

In a job situation, exit occurs when a person searches for a different job, transfers, or quits. In a romantic relationship, exit might take the form of moving out of a joint residence, physically abusing the partner, or ending the relationship by leaving or getting a divorce. In personal relationships, people are most likely to leave a relationship when they believe they have little to lose. This occurs when the relationship is unhappy, the person has invested relatively little, or the person has reasonable alternatives.

Rusbult has shown that social exchange factors influence the type of problem solving used in personal relationships. For example, in one study, college students were more likely to use relationship-promoting responses of voice and loyalty when they had been satisfied with the relationship before problems arose, when they had made substantial investments in the relationship, and when they had poor alternatives (Rusbult, Zembrodt, & Gunn, 1982). In contrast, students were more likely to use exit strategies when their preproblem satisfaction was relatively low, their investments were low, and they had good alternatives.

From the perspective of continuing the relationship, loyalty and voice are constructive, relationship-promoting responses; neglect and exit are destructive to the relationship. Of course, for the individuals involved, ending a relationship or quitting a job may be a personally helpful and appropriate action.

mitment is also based on negative forces or constraints that make it costly for a person to leave a relationship.

One barrier to leaving a relationship is a lack of alternatives. We may dislike our boss and regret having to interact daily, but continue the relationship because we need the salary and can't find another job. We may date someone who falls below our comparison level because he or she is the only eligible person we know. If we are dependent on a relationship to provide things we value and cannot obtain elsewhere, we are unlikely to leave.

In more technical terms, commitment is closely related to our comparison level for alternatives. In a recent demonstration of this effect, Jemmott, Ashby, and Lindenfeld (1989) studied college students' perceptions of the availability of opposite-sex dating partners at their college. (They also looked at the actual sex ratios on campus and found that students' perceptions were often inaccurate.) In addition, they asked students who were dating to indicate the strength of their commitment to their current partner. Results showed that students who thought there were relatively few members of the other sex on their campus were more committed to their current romantic relationship, considered the relationship more attractive, and invested more in it compared to other students. Other research suggests that the link between availability of alternatives and commitment can work both ways. Johnson and Rusbult (1989) suggest that people who are highly committed to a romantic relationship may actually reject and devalue alternative partners, as a way of resisting temptation. Convincing ourselves that our current partner is more wonderful than all others makes it easier to sustain commitment.

The investments we have made in a relationship are another factor influencing commitment (Rusbult, 1980, 1983). Investments can include time, energy, money, emotional involvement, shared experiences, sacrifices for a partner, and so on. To invest much in a relationship and then find it unrewarding can arouse cognitive dissonance, and so we may feel psychological pressures to see the relationship in a positive light

and to downplay its drawbacks (Rubin, 1973). The more we have put into a relationship, the more costly it would be for us to leave. Empirical research has demonstrated the importance of exchange considerations for satisfaction and commitment in a variety of types of relationships (Sprecher, 1988). For example, in a study of dating relationships, Caryl Rusbult (1980) explicitly tested an exchange model. College students completed detailed questionnaires assessing the rewards they got from their dating relationship (such as the partner's attractiveness and intelligence, the couple's ability to coordinate activities) and the costs (such as conflict or the partner's embarrassing behaviors). Participants also indicated how much they had invested or "put things into" the relationship and described the quality of the best available alternative to their current partner.

Finally, they completed several measures of satisfaction and commitment. Consistent with exchange theory, the strongest predictors of satisfaction were rewards and costs; investments and alternatives did not affect satisfaction. The most satisfied people reported many rewards and few costs. In contrast, commitment was affected by satisfaction, investments, and alternatives. People felt most committed when they were satisfied with the relationship, had invested a lot, and had relatively less desirable alternatives.

In many relationships, satisfaction and commitment go hand in hand. As a new couple discovers the special rewards of their developing relationship, they take steps to build commitment. They may stop dating other people, exchange presents, and forgo other activities to be with each other. As their affection blossoms into love, they may take public actions to demonstrate their feelings and to build a future together.

A wedding ceremony, buying a home together, having children—these investments in the relationship are usually based on love, and further serve to build commitment. If the couple encounters difficult times of conflict and disagreement, their commitment may provide the motivation to "work to improve the relationship" and to rekindle their love. But satisfaction and commitment are not inseparable. We sometimes find ourselves stuck in unsatisfying relationships, and we sometimes avoid commitment despite strong attraction.

Beyond Exchange

Social exchange principles help us understand many different kinds of relationships. Most people recognize that exchange influences casual relationship, but may resist the idea that exchange factors also govern our most intimate relationships. It is certainly unromantic to suggest, as did sociologist Erving Goffman, that "A proposal of marriage in our society tends to be a way in which a man sums up his social attributes and suggests that hers are not so much better as to preclude a merger or a partnership in these matters" (1952, p. 456).

Social psychologist Zick Rubin voiced the common concern about exchange theory:

> The notions that people are "commodities" and social relationships are "transactions" will surely make many readers squirm. Exchange theory postulates that human relationships are based first and foremost on self-interest. As such, it often seems to portray friendship as motivated only by what one person can get from another and to redefine love as a devious power game. . . . But although we might prefer to believe otherwise, we must face up to the fact that our attitudes toward other people are determined to a large extent by our assessments of the rewards they hold for us. (1973, p. 82)

It may be helpful to remember that although exchange theory borrows terminology from economics, the rewards and costs involved are often very personal and unique: an adorable smile and shared secrets are as much a part of exchange theory as fancy cars and expensive presents.

You may have noticed that in some of your relationships, exchange issues seem to be much more important than in others. For example, you may be willing to trade work shifts with a co-worker this week, but clearly expect that he'll do the same for you next week. In contrast, you and your best friend may do many favors for each other and help each other in times of need without consciously keeping mental records of what you give and receive.

Clark and Mills (1979) have distinguished between what they call *exchange relationships* and *communal relationships*. In both types of relationships, exchange processes operate, but the rules governing the giving and receiving of benefits differ significantly. They believe that in exchange relationships, people give benefits with the expectation of receiving comparable benefits in return soon afterward. Exchange relationships occur most often with strangers or casual acquaintances and in business relations. In exchange relationships, people feel no special responsibility for the welfare of the other person. In contrast, in communal relationships, people feel a special responsibility for the needs of the other. Communal relationships usually occur with family, friends, and romantic partners. In these relationships, people provide benefits to the partner to show concern and to respond to the other's needs, with no expectation of receiving similar benefits in the near future.

Clark and Mills have conducted a program of research to identify the differences between these two relationship orientations (Clark, Mills, & Corcoran, 1989). For example, one study found that people pay more attention to the needs of a partner in a communal relationship than in an exchange relationship (Clark, Mills, & Powell, 1986).

In long-term relationships, patterns of reciprocity and rules of exchange become complex. In our most intimate relationships, we may develop a sense of unity or "we-ness" so that we perceive benefiting a loved one as a way of benefiting ourselves. Exchange principles may not tell the whole story of personal relationships, but they do play an important part.

Key Terms

close relationship

commitment

comparison level

comparison level for
  alternatives

equity theory

interdependence

norm of reciprocity

principle of least interest

self-disclosure

self-evaluation mainte-
  nance model

self-handicapping

self-monitoring

self-presentation

social comparison theory

social interaction

social norm

social penetration

social power

social roles

Summary

1. When two people interact, they influence each other. Interdependence refers to mutual influence between two or more people. As interaction continues over time, a relationship begins to develop. We call a relationship close if there is frequent interaction involving many different kinds of activities and strong mutual influence.

2. Self-presentation refers to our efforts to control the impression we convey to others. A common motive in social interaction is to make a good impression on one's audience. Self-promotion is one strategy for "looking good;" others include ingratiation, the use of modesty, and basking in the reflected glory of successful others.

3. Individuals differ in self-monitoring—the tendency to emphasize impression management. High self-monitors make more effort to learn about other people and to size up social situations than do low self-monitors. There are pros and cons to both orientations.

4. As initially developed by Leon Festinger, social comparison theory proposed that people desire accurate information about their abilities and opinions. In the absence of objective physical standards, people evaluate themselves in comparison to others, especially similar others.

5. Today, we know that the goals of social comparison are quite diverse and can include accurate self-evaluation, self-enhancement, and self-improvement. Social comparison is not always freely chosen; sometimes comparisons are unavoidable.

6. Tesser's Self-Evaluation Maintenance Model addresses the question of when the successful performance of another person enhances as opposed to threatens our sense of self. Successful performance by a close other on a dimension that is relevant to our self-definition can threaten our self-evaluation; if the dimension is irrelevant, a reflection effect may occur in which we bask in the success of a person who is close to us.

7. Self-disclosure is the sharing of personal feelings and information with another individual. There is a norm of reciprocity for self-disclosure, so partners tend to disclose at similar levels. Social penetration describes how self-disclosure contributes to the development of intimate relationships. According to Reis and Shaver, intimacy is created when a person's self-disclosure evokes a response in the listener that leads the person to feel cared for and understood.

8. The most influential analysis of social interaction comes from social exchange theory. In this view, people are concerned with the outcomes (rewards minus costs) they receive in a relationship. People use several standards to evaluate their relationship outcomes including a general "comparison level" and a "comparison level for alternatives." When two people are interdependent, they try to coordinate their activities to maximize their joint profits.

9. People care whether their relationships are fair. Three major rules of fairness are equality, relative needs, and equity. Equity exists when each person's outcomes are proportional to their contributions to the relationship. According to equity theory, when individuals perceive inequity in a relationship, they feel distress and take steps to restore equity.

10. Social power refers to a person's ability to influence deliberately the behavior, thoughts, or feelings of another person.

The balance of power describes whether partners have equal power or whether one person is dominant. Three determinants of the balance of power are social norms, the relative resources of the partners, and the "principle of least interest."

11. Conflict occurs when the actions of one person interfere with the actions of another. Conflicts can be about specific behaviors, norms and roles, or personal dispositions. Rusbult has identified four common reactions to dissatisfaction in relationships; these are called voice, loyalty, neglect, and exit.

12. Commitment refers to all the forces, positive and negative, that keep a person in a relationship. Positive factors include satisfaction, liking, and love. Negative factors are barriers that make it costly to leave a relationship. Two important barriers are the lack of alternatives and the investments a person has already made in a relationship.

Suggested Readings

Altman, I., & Taylor, D. A. (1973). *Social penetration: The development of interpersonal relationships*. New York: Holt, Rinehart and Winston. A thoughtful analysis of the development of intimate relationships, with emphasis on self-disclosure.

Burgess, R. L. & Huston, T. L. (Eds.) (1979). *Social exchange in developing relationships*. New York: Academic Press. Leading experts use exchange theory to discuss such topics as the initiation of relationships, conflict, and breakups.

Derlega, V., & Berg, J. H. (Eds.). (1987). *Self-disclosure: Theory, research, and therapy*. New York: Plenum. An up-to-date review of work on self-disclosure, written by professionals.

Goffman, E. (1959). *The presentation of self in everyday life*. Garden City, NY: Doubleday. A classic analysis of impression management.

Kelley, H. H. et al. (1983). *Close relationships*. New York: W. H. Freeman. A team of psychologists provide a professional-level analysis of interdependence in personal relationships, including topics as interaction, development, emotion, power, roles, conflict, and commitment.

Noller, P., & Fitzpatrick, M. A. (Eds.) (1988). *Perspectives on marital interaction*. Philadelphia, PA: Multilingual Matters Ltd. An excellent set of papers on conflict, power, communication and other facets of interaction in marriage.

Snyder, M. (1987). *Public appearances/private realities: The psychology of self-monitoring*. New York: W. H. Freeman. A well-written review of theory and research about self-monitoring.

Walster, E., Walster, G. W., & Berscheid, E. (1978). *Equity: Theory and research*. Boston: Allyn and Bacon. A clear presentation of equity theory and how it applies to various types of relationships.

EIGHT

Social Influence

CONFORMITY

COMPLIANCE

OBEDIENCE TO AUTHORITY

Consider these illustrations of social influence:

In the 1950s, American college men were virtually all clean shaven, with short hair; only farmers wore blue jeans as everyday clothing; and college women almost invariably had short hair and dressed in blouses and skirts, with hemlines well below the knee. By the late 1960s, college students of both sexes grew their hair long and wore blue jeans regularly. How would you describe fashion trends at your college today? Why do so many students tend to dress so similarly?

As you hurry into the local supermarket, a young woman stops you and asks you to sign a petition urging the city to build a new shelter for homeless families. You somewhat reluctantly read and sign the petition. Next the woman asks you to donate $5 to a campaign to help the homeless. You give her a dollar and duck into the market. Why did you comply, at least partially, with her requests?

In Nazi Germany during World War II, Adolf Hitler commanded his troops into battle—a common practice for heads of state during war-

Many teenagers conform to the norms of their peer group in hairstyles, dress, interests, and values.

time. But he also ordered the construction of concentration camps where millions of civilians were put to death. Why did so many people obey Hitler's extraordinary orders to kill children and unarmed civilians?

Social psychologists have long been interested in how our behavior is influenced by other people and groups. Indeed, Elliot Aronson (1984, p. 6) has defined the core topic of social psychology as "the influences that people have upon the beliefs or behaviors of others." We have already explored some aspects of social influence in our analysis of the processes of attitude change (Chapter 6). This chapter examines three types of social influence: conformity, compliance, and obedience to authority.

When someone voluntarily performs an act because others are doing it, we call it **conformity.** College students are presumably free to pick their own clothes and hairstyles. But students often prefer to dress like others in their social group, thus conforming to current standards of fashion on campus. What factors affect conformity to group pressures?

When people do what they are asked to do, even though they might prefer not to, we call it **compliance.** The distinguishing feature of compliance is that we are responding to a request from another individual or group. Compliance can occur in many settings—when a friend asks us for a ride to the airport, or a group of Halloween trick-or-treaters ask for candy, or a Red Cross volunteer asks for donations.

In some social situations, we perceive one person or group as having the **legitimate authority** to influence our behavior. The government has a right to ask us to pay taxes, parents have a right to ask their children to wash the dinner dishes, and medical personnel have the right to ask us to take off our clothes for a physical exam. In these cases, social norms permit those in authority to make requests. Although authorities often make reasonable and appropriate requests, their power can be abused. During World War II, Nazi military leaders ordered the mass murder of millions of civilians. After the war, when individuals such as Adolf Eichmann were put on trial for carrying out these orders, they often attempted to excuse their behavior by saying they were "just following orders" from those in command.

CONFORMITY

Because conformity is such a powerful phenomenon, it has proved relatively easy to study in the laboratory. We'll begin our discussion with two classic studies that illustrate how conformity works.

A Guess in the Dark: The Sherif Study

The task in this classic study by Muzafer Sherif (1935) seemed straightforward: a college student sat in a darkened room and was shown a single point of light. He was told that the light was moving and that his job was to estimate how far it moved. Most subjects found it extremely difficult to estimate how far the light moved, since it often appeared to move at varying speeds and in different directions. Actually, the study used a perceptual illusion known as the *autokinetic effect;* a single point of light seen in the dark appears to move, even though it is really stationary.

Given the ambiguity of this situation, subjects could not be sure of their own judgments, and their initial estimates varied enormously. Several people thought the light moved only 1 or 2 inches, whereas one person thought it moved as much as 800 feet. Apparently, this person thought he was in a gymnasium, although actually he was in a small room.

After each subject had made several estimates, a second person was brought into the room, also supposedly a subject but in fact a confederate of the researcher. The confederate had been trained to make his estimates consistently lower or higher than those of the real subject. The judgment procedure was repeated for a number of trials.

Under these conditions, the subject soon began to make his estimates more and more similar to those of the confederate. For instance, if the subject began by estimating that the light moved between 10 and 14 inches and the confederate said it moved only 2 inches, on the next trial the subject tended to lower his estimate, and on the following trial he would lower it even more. By the end of the series, the subject's estimates were very similar to those of the confederate.

As Plain as Day: The Asch Study

Solomon Asch wondered if conformity occurs only in ambiguous situations such as the Sherif study where people are quite uncertain about the correct answer. If the stimulus situation were clear, would people conform? Asch reasoned that when people consider an unambiguous situation, they will trust their own perceptions and remain independent even when every member of a group disagrees with them. Asch designed an experiment to test this expectation (Asch, 1955).

Five students arrived to take part in a study on perception. They sat around a table and were told they would be judging the lengths of lines. They were shown a card on which three black lines of varying lengths had been drawn and a second card containing only one line. Their task was to choose the line on the first card that was most similar in length to the line on the second card. As shown in Figure 8–1 on page 240, it was an easy task. One of the lines was exactly the same length as the standard, whereas the other two were quite different from it.

When the lines were shown, the five subjects answered aloud in the order in which they were seated. The first subject gave his choice and then each of the others responded in turn. Since the judgment was so easy, there were no disagreements. When all had responded, a second set of lines was shown, responses were given, and a third set was produced.

At this point, the experiment seems dull and pointless. On the third trial, however, the first subject looked carefully at the lines as before

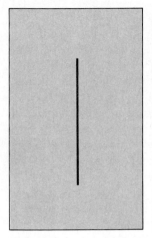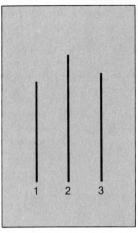

Figure 8–1. A representative stimulus in the Asch conformity study. Subjects were shown two cards. One contained the "standard." The second contained three comparison lines, one of which was the same length as the standard. Subjects were asked which comparison line was the same as the standard. (Adapted from "Opinions and Social Pressure," by Solomon Asch. Copyright © 1955 by Scientific American, Inc. All rights reserved.)

and then gave what was obviously the wrong answer. In the example in Figure 8–1, he might have said 1 rather than 2. The next subject gave the same wrong answer, as did the third and fourth subjects. When it was time for the fifth subject to respond, he was quite disturbed. It was clear to him that the others were giving wrong answers. He knew that 2 was the line

most similar to the standard. Yet everyone else said it was 1.

Under these circumstances many people sitting in the fifth position gave the wrong answer—they agreed with the others even though they knew it was incorrect. In fact, among these college students with good eyesight and presumably sharp minds, the wrong answer was given about 35 percent of the time. Some subjects never gave the wrong answer, some did all the time, but overall they averaged about one wrong response in three. Of course, in this classic study by Solomon Asch, the situation was staged. The first four "subjects" were confederates of the experimenter and were responding according to a prearranged script. But the real subject did not know this and gave the wrong answer rather than disagree with the others.

It is important to keep the clarity of this judgment task in mind if we are to understand the phenomenon. There is a tendency to think that the conforming subjects were uncertain of the correct choice and therefore were swayed by the majority. This is not the case. The subjects were quite sure of the correct choice and, in control conditions with no group pressure, chose correctly 100 percent of the time. When subjects conformed, they conformed despite the fact that they knew the correct answer.

Later studies have demonstrated similar con-

"Well heck! If all you smart cookies agree, who am I to dissent?"

formity effects using other physical stimuli, opinion statements, statements of fact, and logical syllogisms. Subjects have agreed that there is no population problem in the United States because 6,000 miles of continent separates San Francisco from New York; that men are 8 to 9 inches taller than women on the average; and that male babies have a life expectancy of only 25 years. In other words, regardless of the type of stimulus and of how clear the correct choice is, when individuals are faced with a unanimous group opinion, the pressure exerted by the majority is often strong enough to produce conformity.

People often conform—even when doing so means contradicting their own perceptions of the world. In many cases, individuals continue to believe that their private judgments are correct and that the group is wrong. Nevertheless, when asked to respond publicly, they give the same incorrect responses that the others give. This is what we mean by conformity.

Why Do People Conform?

Basically, people conform for two major reasons—to be right and to be liked (Campbell & Fairey, 1989). This is consistent with the analysis of attitude change presented earlier in Chapter 6. There, we saw that people are more likely to be influenced by a persuasive communication from a person (communicator) who is knowledgeable, trustworthy and likable. Similarly, people are more likely to conform to group behaviors when they think the group members are right and when they want to be liked by the group. For an illustration of how conformity pressure may contribute to eating problems in college women, see Box 8–1 on p. 242.

Informational Influence: The Desire to be Right. One reason for conformity is that the behavior of other people often provides useful information. A thirsty traveler at an oasis in the Sahara Desert who sees Arabs drinking from one well and avoiding another well would be smart to copy their behavior. By drinking from the popular well, the traveler may avoid drinking contaminated water. The tendency to conform based on informational influence depends on two aspects of the situation: how well-informed we believe the group is and how confident we are in our own independent judgment.

The more we trust the group's information and value their opinions in a situation, the more likely we are to go along with the group. If our thirsty traveler in the desert sees that the Arabs drinking at the oasis are city dwellers on their first tourist trip to the desert, he or she might be inclined to wonder how much they know about wells and so may not conform to their example. If the Arabs are clearly desert nomads traveling on their usual route, the person would be far more likely to trust them and follow their example. Anything that increases confidence in the correctness of the group should increase conformity. Conversely, anything that leads us to doubt the group's knowledge or trustworthiness should decrease conformity.

Balanced against the individual's confidence in the group is the individual's confidence in his or her own views. Early studies found that the more ambiguous or difficult the task, the more likely people were to conform (Coleman, Blake, & Mouton, 1958), presumably because they were less certain of their own judgment. For example, the Sherif task was more difficult than the Asch task, and so produced more conformity. Other research has found that the more competent and knowledgeable we feel about a topic, the less likely we are to conform (Wiesenthal et al., 1976). Campbell, Tesser, and Fairey (1986) experimentally manipulated subjects' level of self-confidence versus doubt in their ability to solve a hidden figures test. They found that high self-doubt individuals conformed significantly more than those with low self-doubt.

Normative Influence: The Desire to be Liked. A second major reason for conformity is to gain the approval, or avoid the disapproval, of other people. We often want others to accept us, like us, and treat us well. In growing up, people often learn that one way to get along with a

BOX 8–1

Binge Eating in College Sororities

Bulimia is an eating pattern in which individuals first engage in uncontrolled binge eating and then fast or induce vomiting to prevent weight gain. Bulimia is sometimes called the "binge-purge syndrome." Bulimia is almost exclusively a problem of women, and it is estimated that between 4 and 15 percent of college women have serious problems with bulimia. Medical experts agree that bulimia poses a serious threat to the women's health and psychological well-being.

Several explanations have been offered for the fairly recent and sudden increase in bulimia in America. It has been argued that our national obsession with thinness, especially for women, has created a cult of dieting. Support for the importance of cultural factors comes from studies showing that the body size of the women depicted in *Playboy* centerfolds and of the winners of the Miss America Pagent decreased significantly from 1960 to 1980 (Garner, Garfinkel, Schwartz, & Thompson, 1980). Other explanations have emphasized personality and family factors that may predispose women to bulimia.

Recently, Christian Crandall (1988) offered a fascinating social psychological analysis of bulimia. Crandall raises the question of how women learn about binge eating behaviors and suggests that conformity may play an important role. Drawing on research on conformity to group norms, Crandall argues that "social pressures in friendship groups are important mechanisms by which binge eating is acquired and spread. Social groups such as athletic teams, cheerleading squads, dormitories, and sororities develop social norms about appropriate behavior for their members. If eating, dieting, and losing weight are important to the members, then norms will arise in the group defining how much, when and with whom" one should eat or diet (p. 590). Further, Crandall suggests that the stresses associated with college life may make students especially vulnerable to pressures to conform to the norms of their friendship group.

To test these ideas, Crandall studied college sororities. He measured several symptoms associated with bulimia including binge eating, vomiting and restrictive dieting, and so on. Very few of the women Crandall studied showed severe symptoms of bulimia, but many of them reported mild symptoms of the binge eating syndrome.

Crandall found that in one sorority, the more binge eating symptoms a woman reported, the more popular she was. In a second sorority, popularity was greatest for women who binged in moderation; popularity was lower for women who binged too much or too little. By following the women for one academic year, Crandall was able to show that as friendship groups became more

Continued

cohesive, a woman's eating pattern became more similar to that of her friends. The fact that women became more like their friends over time offers clear evidence that social influence processes were at work.

The desire to feel a part of social groups and to be liked by friends is understandable. But participation in social groups also raises the possibility of strong pressures to conform to group norms. Cran-dall's research illustrates how social groups may heighten women's concerns with thinness and physical appearance and, perhaps unknowingly, encourage behaviors that are potentially very harmful. From your own experiences, how might conformity pressures in social groups affect a person's use of drugs and alcohol, their devotion to academic studies, or their involvement in political and social activities?

group is to go along with group standards. In deciding how to dress for the senior prom, we may try to wear the "right" clothes so that we will fit in, give a good impression, and avoid disapproval. We may not really like wearing formal clothes, but do it anyway because it's socially appropriate for the occasion. When we're with our weight-conscious friends, we may eat salads and "health foods" even though we don't especially like them; when we're alone, we're more likely to follow our personal preferences by eating hamburgers and fries. In such situations, conformity leads to an outward change in public behavior, but not necessarily to a change in the individual's private opinions.

This fear of being deviant is justified by the group's response to deviance. When someone does not go along with a group, that person becomes the target of efforts to bring them in line and may ultimately risk rejection. This was shown in an early study by Stanley Schachter (1951), in which three confederates were included in a larger discussion group. One confederate (the deviant) consistently took a position different from that of the group. A second confederate (the "slider") started as a deviant and then changed toward the group. The third confederate took the same position as the group. The rest of the group spent a great deal of time trying to change the position of the two confederates who held deviant positions. They argued with them, presented reasons to support the group position, cajoled, and did whatever they could to change the deviates' stand to agree with the group's. Being the object of such an intense campaign is not pleasant. In this situation, the "slider" who changed toward con-formity was ultimately accepted and treated like any other member of the group. But the confederate who maintained a deviant position was eventually ignored and overlooked for leadership positions.

A group can also apply punishment directly, as shown in a study done at the Hawthorne plant of the Western Electric Company (Homans, 1965). Observations were made of the behavior of a number of workers whose wages depended on their productivity. By working harder and accomplishing more, each worker could receive higher pay. However, the employees had developed their own standards as to the right amount of work to do in a day. Every day, after they did this amount of work, they slacked off. By working just this much, they earned a reasonable sum of money and didn't have to work too hard. Anyone who worked harder would make the others look bad and might cause management to increase its expectation of work output.

The group exerted intense pressure on its members to conform to the group standard for productivity. People who worked too much risked being called "rate busters," and those who worked too little were called "chiselers." In addition, the group devised a novel way to enforce the productivity rule. Anyone who worked too fast or too slow could be "binged." Binging (not to be confused with the binge eating pattern discussed in Box 8-1) consisted of giving the deviate a sharp blow on the upper arm. Not only did this hurt, but it was a symbolic punishment for going against the group. Any group member could deliver the punishment, and the person who was binged could

A classic study of the Hawthorne plant of the Western Electric Company investigated how workers enforce conformity to group standards for productivity and how "rate busters" and "chiselers" were punished for working too much or too little.

not fight back. The punishment had to be accepted and with it, the disapproval it indicated. Binging is a dramatic example of the kinds of pressure present in all groups that cause members to conform to accepted opinions, values, and behavior. In many cases, just being aware of the potential costs of nonconformity and the benefits of conformity leads people to follow group standards. When this fails, groups use persuasion, threats of ostracism, direct punishment, and offers of rewards to pressure individuals to conform.

In summary, the motivation to conform stems from a desire to be right and a desire to be liked by the group. The strength of these two motives varies considerably depending on the situation.

When Do People Conform?

Several important features of the group situation that can affect conformity are commitment, group size, and unanimity. Research also shows that there are individual differences in the desire for individuation or uniqueness.

Commitment to the Group. Conformity is affected by the strength of the bonds between in-

dividuals and the group (Forsyth, 1983). **Commitment** refers to all the forces, positive and negative, that act to keep an individual in a relationship or group. Positive forces attracting an individual to a group might include liking other group members, believing the group accomplishes important goals, feeling that the group works well together, expecting to gain from belonging to the group, and identifying with group values. Another important factor is the individual's sense of identification with the group (Hogg & Turner, 1987).

Negative forces keeping an individual from leaving a group also increase commitment. These include such barriers as having few alternatives or having made large investments in the group that would be costly to give up. Regardless of the sources of commitment, the more committed a person is to a group, the greater the pressures for conformity.

We use the term **cohesiveness** to describe the extent to which group members as a whole are strongly or weakly committed to the group. In general, the more highly cohesive a group, the greater the potential pressures toward conformity. Groups with high morale, where members enjoy working together and believe they function well as a team, are more vulnerable to conformity pressures than are less cohesive groups.

We'll examine this issue further in Chapter 10 when we discuss the dangers of "groupthink."

Group Size. Suppose there were two people in a room and one of them said it was very warm. If the room was in fact quite cold, the second person would be unlikely to agree with the first. She would feel cold and would assume that the other person was mistaken or feverish. If forced to make a public statement on the temperature of the room, she would probably say she thought it was rather cold.

If the room contained five people and four of them said it was warm, the situation would change. Even if one person felt cold, she would be likely to doubt her own perceptions. After all, it is unlikely that all four of the others were feverish or mistaken. If the person were asked how she felt, she might be uncertain enough to agree with the rest. She might say the room was warm and then wonder what was wrong with her. When one person disagrees with you, he or she is feverish; when four others do, you must be sick yourself. Four people tend to be more trustworthy than one, in terms of both honesty and the reliability of their opinions; it is harder to mistrust a group than one person (Insko et al., 1985).

Many experiments have demonstrated that conformity usually increases as the size of the unanimous majority increases, at least up to a point (Tanford & Penrod, 1984). In some of his early experiments, Asch (1955) varied the size of the majority from 2 to 15. As shown in Figure 8–2, he found that 2 people produced more pressure than 1, 3 a lot more than 2, and 4 about the same as 3. Somewhat surprisingly, he found that increasing the size of the group past 4 did not increase the amount of conformity, at least up to 15. He concluded that to produce the most conformity, the optimal group size was 3 or 4.

Using quite a different procedure and a different measure of conformity, Stanley Milgram and associates (1969) produced quite different results. The situation was very simple. On a crowded street in New York City, a number of people played the old game of looking up to see whether anyone else would look up also. This time it was done as a deliberate experiment, and careful observations were made of passersby.

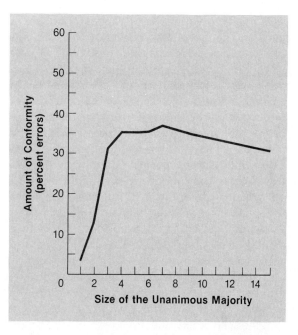

Figure 8–2. Group size and conformity. With one other group member, subjects made few errors (less than 4 percent). As the size of the group increased, the percentage of errors increased, peaking at 37 percent wrong responses with a 7-person unanimous majority. (Adapted from "Opinions and Social Pressure," by Solomon Asch. Copyright © 1955 by Scientific American, Inc. All rights reserved.)

The confederates stood and looked up at the sixth-floor window of an office building across the street. One, 2, 3, 5, 10, or 15 confederates stood around looking up at the window. The chief measure was the percentage of passersby who actually stopped and looked up at the window. When 1 confederate was looking up, only 4 percent of the passersby also looked up; with 5 confederates, it went up to 16 percent; with 10, it was 22 percent; and with 15, it increased to 40 percent.

A similar increase in conformity as group size increased was found in a study of getting in line for the bus in Jerusalem (Mann, 1977). When two or four people lined up, there was little tendency for others to join the line. But when six or more were in line, newcomers usually also joined the line. The more people there were on line, the more likely it was that newcomers would join it.

However, research by Wilder (1977) makes it clear that it is not simply the number of people that makes the difference. In this study, subjects heard the opinions of varying numbers of people. The important difference between this and previous work was that these other people were sometimes expressing their opinions independently and sometimes as members of groups. Some subjects heard the opinions of four people who belonged to one group, some heard the opinions of four people who were members of two different groups, and others heard the opinions of four independent people.

Wilder found that group size had little effect on amount of conformity. But the number of independent opinions, from separate groups or from individuals, had a major effect. This may explain why increasing the size of a group above three or four adds little to conformity. Once the group is seen to be acting as a unit, the number of additional individuals within the group does not matter. But adding independent judgments from people outside the group might increase conformity.

Group Unanimity. An extremely important factor in producing conformity is the unanimity of the group opinion. A person faced with a unanimous group decision is under great pressure to conform. If, however, a group is not united, there is a striking decrease in the amount of conformity. When even one other person does not go along with the rest of the group, conformity drops to about one-fourth the usual level. This is true when the group is small, and it also appears to hold with up to 15 people. One of the most impressive things about this phenomenon is that it does not seem to matter who the nonconforming person is. Regardless of whether this dissenter is a high-prestige, expert figure or someone of low prestige who is not at all expert, conformity tends to drop to low levels (Asch, 1955; Morris & Miller, 1975).

Furthermore, a sole dissenter can reduce conformity even if he or she gives wrong answers. If the correct answer is A, the majority says B, and another person says C, the real subject is less likely to conform than if everyone agreed on one incorrect answer. Simply having some disagreement within the group makes it easier for an individual to remain independent. (Allen & Levine, 1971).

Research has shown that the timing of dissent made a difference (Morris & Miller, 1975). When one person dissented *after* the majority had expressed its opinon, conformity decreased. But when the dissenter answered *before* the majority, conformity decreased even more. Apparently, when the subject heard the correct response at the beginning, the majority's incorrect position carried less weight.

The dramatic decrease in conformity when unanimity is broken seems to be due to several of the factors we have already discussed. First, the amount of trust or confidence in the correctness of the majority decreases whenever there is disagreement, even if the dissenter is less expert or less reliable than those who make up the majority. The mere fact that someone else also disagrees with the group indicates that there is room for doubt, that the issue is not perfectly clear, and that the majority might be wrong. This reduces the individual's reliance on the majority opinion as a source of information and accordingly reduces conformity.

Second, if another group member endorses the position the individual favors, it serves to strengthen self-confidence about that judgment. As we have seen, greater confidence reduces conformity. A third consideration involves reluctance to appear deviant. When one person disagrees with everyone else, that person stands out. The lone dissenter appears deviant, both to himself or herself and to other group members. When someone else also disagrees, neither is as deviant as he or she would be alone.

This last result should probably be taken as encouragement to speak one's mind. In the story of "The Emperor's New Clothes," for example, the whole crowd watched the naked emperor in his supposedly beautiful new clothes. However, when only one child had the courage to say that the emperor was naked, everyone else found strength to defy the majority.

Certainly, this is a strong argument for freedom of speech, because it suggests that even one deviant voice can have an important effect as long as there are other people who inwardly disagree with the majority but are afraid to speak up. It may also explain why totalitarian governments allow no dissent. Even one small voice disagreeing could encourage others to do likewise. After a while, the regime itself might be endangered. The finding that any dissent substantially reduces conformity stands out as one of the most striking aspects of conformity.

The Desire for Individuation. People differ in their willingness to do things that publicly differentiate them from others. Whereas some people are more comfortable blending in with a group and going along with group opinions, others prefer to stand out. Christina Maslach and her colleagues have developed a paper-and-pencil test to measure people's willingness to engage in public behavior that sets them apart from others (Maslach et al., 1985, 1987). A person would score high on individuation by indicating that they would be willing to do such things as "give a lecture to a large audience," "present a personal opinion, on a controversial topic, to a group of strangers," or "speak up about your own ideas even if you are uncertain of whether you are correct." In contrast, a person scoring low on individuation would hesitate to do such behaviors. Research indicates that high-individuation people are more likely to say that they have distinctive ways of dressing, use a distinctive nickname, and own unique possessions. In a laboratory study of conformity, high-individuation subjects were less likely to go along with the majority view and more likely to engage in what the researchers called "creative dissent."

In a related line of research, Burger (1987) has shown that people who are high in the "desire for control" are less susceptible to persuasive messages and less likely to conform in an Asch-type group conformity situation. These studies emphasize the importance of individual differences in susceptibility to group influence.

Minority Influence: Innovation in Groups

Conformity to majority patterns is a basic aspect of social life. But our emphasis on the power of the majority should not blind us to the importance of **minority influence.** Sometimes a forceful minority with a new idea or unique perspective can effectively change the position of the majority.

Early studies showing that dissent reduces conformity began to raise questions about the existence of an "all-powerful" majority. In the past 20 years, the major new developments in conformity research have been attempts to understand the influence of minorities (Maass & Clark, 1984). Pioneering work by the French psychologist Serge Moscovici (1985) has been especially important.

In an early experiment, Moscovici, Lage, and Naffrechoux (1969) used an Asch-type conformity paradigm but with a majority of naive subjects and a minority of confederates. Subjects were shown an unambiguous physical stimulus, namely, slides of colors. In this study, members of six-person groups were asked to rate the color of the slides. In actuality, all slides were blue but varied in their luminance (brightness). In control groups of six naive subjects, virtually all slides were described as blue. In the experimental group, however, two confederates consistently labeled the blue slides as "green." Subjects had previously been told that all group members had normal vision, so these "green" responses could not be attributed to color blindness. With this minority pressure, about a third of the subjects reported seeing at least one "green" slide, and 8 percent of all judgments were that slides were "green." Clearly, the minority view had a noticeable effect on the naive majority.

Moscovici has proposed that the *behavioral style* of a minority is important. To be effective, a minority must be consistent, coherent, and forceful. This behavioral style is interpreted by the majority as a sign of the minority's confidence and certainty in their position (Maass & Clark, 1982). Although members of a consistent minority may be liked less than members of the majority, they tend to be seen as more competent and honest (Bassili & Provencal, 1988). As a minority persists in their position over time, the majority may start to question the correctness of their views. Ultimately, some majority members may "convert" by changing their own position

The first American women who demonstrated for the right to vote were a small minority. Over time, this resourceful and determined minority successfully changed public opinion, obtaining the right to vote for women in 1920.

in the direction of the minority. If enough members change their views, the minority may be transformed into a new majority.

Research has identified other factors that also determine the influence of minorities (Maass & Clark, 1984; Moscovici, Mugny, & van Avermaet, 1985). First, minorities are most effective when their behavioral style is logically consistent but not "rigid," that is, when they are seen as having a well-defined position but a flexible style of presentation. Second, the general social climate also makes a difference. A minority will be more effective if it argues for a position in line with current social trends. For example, in an era of increasing sexual conservatism, a minority arguing for sexual permissiveness will be less effective than will a minority arguing for sexual restraint.

Minorities are also more likely to succeed when they are similar to the majority in most respects except for the behavior or attitude in question. These *single minorities* can be contrasted with *double minorities* who differ not only on the relevant issue, but also in other social characteristics. An example of a double minority

would be a homosexual advocating gay rights to heterosexuals; the gay person differs from the majority of Americans not only in beliefs but also in sexual orientation. A study by Maass and Clark (1984) found that an ostensibly gay minority arguing for gay rights was less influential than was a heterosexual minority arguing for gay rights, in part because the gay minority was seen as having more self-interest in the topic. Another study (Maass et al., 1982) showed that conservative male subjects were more strongly influenced by a man arguing for a liberal position on abortion than by a woman taking the same liberal position. When a minority group can be perceived as having a personal stake in their position, their views can more easily be discounted as reflecting self-interest. More generally, minorities have more influence when their position is taken seriously and seen as reflecting certainty and competence. Minorities are less influential when they can be discounted as bizarre, dogmatic, or self-interested.

A current controversy in this area is whether the processes of majority influence (conformity) and minority influence (innovation) are fundamentally the same or different. There is evidence on both sides of this debate, and it is too soon to decide definitively between the single process versus dual-process perspectives. A brief look at each will highlight the issues in question.

Several theorists (Latané & Wolf, 1981; Tanford & Penrod, 1984) have made the case that the effects of majorities and minorities both reflect a single underlying influence process. Majority and minority influence differ in quantity, not quality; majorities usually have more influence because they have more members. Results from several studies are consistent with this single-process view (e.g., Wolf, 1987).

On the other hand, Moscovici and other researchers (Maass & Clark, 1984; Nemeth, 1986) believe that there may be important qualitative differences between minority and majority influence. For example, they believe that majority influence most often leads to changes in overt behavior (compliance) but not necessarily to changes in private attitudes. In contrast, the influence of minorities is more likely to result in changed attitudes, to a "conversion" in one's opinions.

Charlan Nemeth (1986) has emphasized the potential benefits of dissent in groups. Nemeth has shown that minorities can cause other group members to think more carefully about an issue and to consider a wider variety of possible explanations or novel solutions (Nemeth & Kwan, 1987). In other words, the expression of minority viewpoints can sometimes improve group functioning and can have a beneficial impact out of proportion to the minority's small numbers. Finally, Nemeth and Chiles (1988) have recently demonstrated the potential carryover effects of exposure to a dissenting minority. Subjects first participated in a group color perception task with a confederate who dissented consistently, dissented inconsistently, or never dissented. Later, subjects participated in a new color perception task with a different group. Their experience in the new group was much like that of the Asch subjects: they were exposed to an incorrect and unanimous majority. The results were clear. Subjects who had first been exposed to a dissenting minority were substantially more likely to maintain their independence and provide correct answers than subjects with no prior experience with dissent.

COMPLIANCE

One of the most basic ways we influence other people is to ask them directly to do something. Think of some of the requests you might make of a friend—to water your plants while you are on vacation, to borrow some money for a few days, to refrain from smoking in your car, to tell you what they really think of your new haircut, to join the volunteer group you're organizing, and so on. How might you present these requests to increase the chances that your friend will comply? Research on compliance has attempted to understand some of the processes that lead people to comply (or refuse to comply) with requests.

Sometimes we seem to comply with requests for no reason at all. In one study, researchers approached people using a photocopying machine and asked to go first in line because "I have to make copies" (Langer, Blank, & Chanowitz, 1978). This so-called explanation actually gave no real justification for going out of turn. But many subjects went along with the request, apparently not paying much attention to the content of the explanation. Ellen Langer refers to this behavior as *mindlessness* because people respond without thinking seriously about their behavior. Perhaps out of habit, we have learned that when someone asks for something, especially something trivial, and gives a reason (even a meaningless reason), we should go along. We spare ourselves the mental effort of thinking about the situation and simply comply with the request. Mindlessness may not explain most instances of compliance, but it is a fascinating aspect of human behavior.

Six Bases of Social Power

When David Kipnis (1984, p. 186) asked managers in business organizations how they try to influence their co-workers to do something, they said things like: "I simply order him to do what I ask," "I act very humble while making my request," or "I explain the reasons for my request." In contrast, when he asked dating couples how they influence their partners, they said things like: "I get angry and demand he give in," "I act so nice that she cannot refuse when I ask," or "We talk about why we don't agree." Social psychologists have studied the diverse ways people try to get others to comply with their wishes. For an analysis of how young lovers try to influence each other about sex, see Box 8–2.

BOX 8–2

Come-ons and Put-offs: Power in Sexual Encounters

How do young lovers try to influence each other to have or to avoid sexual intercourse? To find out, Naomi McCormick (1979) asked college students to imagine that they were alone with an attractive dating partner whom they had known for a few weeks. They had "necked," but had not yet had sexual intercourse. Students were asked to describe in their own words how they might influence this partner to have sexual intercourse. In a later question, they were asked to indicate how they would avoid having sex with a "turned on" date. These essays were then coded for the particular power tactics used.

When their goal was to have sex with the partner, both men and women said they were most likely to use indirect strategies of seduction. One student wrote: "First of all, I would put on some soft music and offer some wine, then I would start kissing gently and caressing [the person's] body, then I would give a massage with oil" (p. 199). The use of body language (sitting closer, touching the partner) and of changing the environment (putting on music, dimming the lights) were common. Some students said they would emphasize the nature of their relationship: "I would tell my date that we have a very strong, close relationship and that it is time to express it through sexual intercourse."

Tactics for avoiding sex were usually more direct. The favored approach by both men and women was to emphasize that it was too early to have sex. Others proposed using logic or information—for example, telling the partner that they were concerned about pregnancy or that they weren't in the mood for sex. Some suggested using body language (moving farther away) or manipulating the interaction by changing the conversation. A few would invoke moral principles.

McCormick was interested in whether men and women report using different power tactics in sexual encounters (McCormick & Jesser, 1983). In the study just described, where students were asked to imagine how they might hypothetically try to seduce or reject a partner, few gender differences were found. Both men and women approached seduction similarly, and both proposed similar ways to reject a sexual advance. In other words, the choice of a particular power strategy such as seduction or logic depended on the person's goal, not his or her gender.

In actual dating, however, men and women often have different sexual goals. It is more often men who are the sexual initiators trying to seduce their partner, and women who are the limit setters trying to avoid sex. Despite changing sexual attitudes and the women's movement, this traditional role-playing persists in the early stages of dating.

Thus when people are asked what strategies they have actually used in sexual encounters, women usually report tactics for avoiding sex, and men report tactics for having sex. Similarly, when people are asked how others have typically tried to influence them, women report being the targets of attempted seductions, and men report having been turned down. Because men and women often have differing goals in sexual encounters, they tend to use different influence tactics.

A useful way to classify influence strategies is provided in a model developed by Bertram Raven and his colleagues (French & Raven, 1959; Raven, 1988). They identify six major bases of power, each reflecting a different type of resource a person might use to influence someone.

Rewards. One basis for power is the ability to provide positive outcomes for another person—to help that person accomplish a desired goal or to offer a valued reward. Some rewards are highly personal, such as a smile of approval from a special friend. Other rewards, such as money, are impersonal. Sometimes people use reward power by making explicit bargains: a father might promise to take his daughter to the zoo if she cleans up her room. Sometimes there is no explicit contract, but rather a general awareness that rewards are often reciprocated in the relationship: if I do what you want now, you'll be more likely to do what I want later.

Coercion. Coercion can range from actual physical force to threats of punishment or subtle signs of disapproval. For example, after trying futilely to convince a young child to take a nap, a parent may simply place the struggling child in the crib, walk out, and close the door. Or a supervisor may threaten disciplinary action if an employee continues to arrive late for work.

Rewards and coercion are not exact opposites. To obtain rewards, people are motivated to make their "good" behavior known. In contrast, the target of coercion may do what the influencer wants, but only so long as he or she is being watched. Coercion may lead to secrecy rather than actual compliance. This highlights a central difference among bases of power in the extent to which they require surveillance by the influencer: reward power does not require surveillance but coercion does.

Expertise. Special knowledge, training, and skill are sources of power. We defer to experts and follow their advice because we believe their knowledge will help us to achieve our personal goals. If a trusted physician advises us to take three little green pills daily for an allergy, we are likely to comply whether or not we know what the pills contain or understand how the medicine works. A group of mountain climbers will follow the advice of their experienced guide, even though the route suggested for scaling the mountain looks hazardous.

Information. We often try to influence people by giving them information or logical arguments that we think will suggest the right course of action to them. A friend might convince us to go to a concert by informing us that our favorite rock group is performing. In this case, the influencer is not an expert. Rather, it is the content of the message that produces the

A three-year-old copies the gestures of his brother and friends. In Raven's model, social influence based on identification is called referent power.

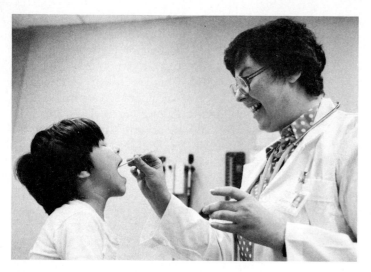

Children can be induced to do quite unusual things in doctors' and dentists' offices, usually without much reward offered or punishment threatened. The power of a simple request from "the doctor" is based on both expertise and legitimate authority.

desired effect. Another name for informational power is persuasion, a process we explored in detail in Chapter 6 on attitude change.

Referent power. A basis of influence with special relevance to personal relationships and groups is referent power. This exists when we admire or identify with a person or group and want to be like them. In such cases, we may voluntarily copy their behavior or do what they ask, because we want to become similar to them. In everyday life we may not think of identification as a type of influence, but it can be very effective. A young child who looks up to an older brother, tries to imitate his mannerisms, and adopts his interests is one illustration. A young man who drinks a particular brand of beer because he identifies with the "macho" image of the sportsmen promoting the product in TV commercials is also being influenced by referent power. Recently, Raven (1988) has discussed the possibility of "negative referent power," which occurs when we want to separate ourself from a disliked or unappealing person or group. To avoid being identified with the unattractive other, we may deliberately avoid copying their behavior.

Legitimate Authority. Sometimes one person has the right or authority to ask another person to act a certain way. The manager who "simply orders" a subordinate to do what she wants or the general who orders his troops into battle are likely to be exercising legitimate authority. Similarly, in most families, parents feel they have the right to tell young children when to go to bed, and children usually feel obligated to comply. Children may try to renegotiate bedtime rules or ask to make an exception for a special occasion, but they usually accept their parents' authority to make rules.

Social roles such as parent-child, teacher-student, or supervisor-employee often dictate the legitimate rights and responsibilities of people in a relationship. Even very young children seem to sense that the requests of physicians and dentists should be obeyed. When someone deviates from agreed-upon rules, we feel we have the right to remind them of their obligations. A prerequisite for effective legitimate authority is that all parties agree about the norms in their relationship.

A recent field experiment by Brad Bushman (1988) illustrates the potential importance of uniforms in indicating that an individual has legitimate authority. In this study, a 52-year-old white female confederate was dressed in one of three ways. In a panhandler (no-authority) condition, she wore an old yellow T-shirt splattered with purple paint and old brown pants. In a second condition, she dressed as a business executive (high status) wearing a professional-looking dress and shoes. In a third "role author-ity" condition, she wore a salient but ambiguous uniform with dark blue pants and shirt and gold insignia. The unknowing participants in this experiment were pedestrians in a major shopping center who encountered a man (also a researcher) standing next to a parked car searching through his pockets for change to put in the meter.

In all conditions, the woman confederate stopped the pedestrian, pointed to the man at the parking meter, and said "This fellow is over-parked at the meter and doesn't have any change. Give him a nickel!" The question of interest was whether the subjects would comply with this request. The majority of subjects went along with this trivial request, but their level of compliance was affected by the influencer's clothing. When the influencer wore a uniform, 72 percent of subjects complied, compared to roughly 50 percent compliance in the other conditions. Apparently the legitimate authority conveyed by the uniform increased the confederate's influence.

A special case of legitimate power is what Raven has called the "power of helplessness." Consider these requests: a small child asks his mother for help in taking off his snow boots; a well-dressed foreign tourist asks in broken English for directions to the bus stop; a partially blind grocery shopper asks for help in reading the price marked on a can of soup. In each case, the person asking for help is in a powerless or helpless condition. And, in each case, others are likely to comply with the request. Our culture has a clear **norm of social responsibility.** We expect people to help those who are less fortunate, and this social obligation makes it legitimate for those in need to ask for help. However, Raven cautions that the legitimate power of helplessness can sometimes be costly for those who use it. People who constantly rely on help-lessness may come to see themselves as incompetent (and so suffer from lowered self-esteem) and may actually perpetuate their powerless situation.

In recent years, Raven has supplemented the six major bases of power with an analysis of other means of influence. For example, "environmental manipulation" occurs when the influencer changes the situation so that the target of influence must comply. An exasperated homeowner, tired of yelling at neighborhood children to stay off her property, may finally

---

T A B L E   8 – 1

THE SIX BASES OF POWER[a]

	Definition	Example
Reward	Power based on providing or promising a positive outcome	If you brush your teeth every night this week, I'll take you to the movies on Saturday.
Coercion	Power based on providing or promising a negative outcome	If you don't brush your teeth, you can't play Nintendo.
Expertise	Power based on special knowledge or ability	The dentist told you to brush twice a day and he knows best.
Information	Power based on the persuasive content of the message	If you don't brush your teeth, you'll get cavities that will hurt. And the dentist will have to drill holes in your teeth to fill the cavities.
Referent power	Power based on identifying with or wanting to be like another person or group	Your big brother Stan always brushes twice a day.
Legitimate authority	Power based on the influencer's right or authority to make a request	I'm your mother and I'm telling you to brush your teeth—now!

Source: Adapted from Raven and Rubin (1983).

[a] According to Bertram Raven and his associates, compliance can be based on six major bases of power. Here we consider how a parent might use each approach to persuade a child to brush her teeth.

erect a sturdy fence to prevent their trespassing. By changing the physical environment, she has changed the children's behavior. Another approach is to invoke the power of third parties. In the heat of an argument, a child may say to his sister, "If you don't stop, I'm going to tell Mommy about what you did." The idea here is to change the sister's behavior by threatening to call on the greater power of a parent.

A summary of the key features of the six major bases of power is provided in Table 8–1 on p. 253.

Specific Compliance Techniques

One line of research has investigated the techniques people use deliberately to gain compliance. Robert Cialdini (1985) has studied car salesmen, con artists, and other professionals who earn a living by getting people to buy their products or go along with their schemes. He and other social psychology researchers have identified several important compliance techniques.

The Foot-in-the-Door Technique. One way of increasing compliance is to induce a person to agree first to a small request. Once someone has agreed to the small action, he or she is more likely to agree to a larger request. This is the so-called **foot-in-the-door technique.** It is used explicitly or implicitly by many advertising campaigns. Advertisers often concentrate on getting consumers to do something connected with the product—even sending back a card saying that they do not want it. The advertisers apparently think that any act connected with the product increases the likelihood that the consumer will buy it in the future.

A classic study by Freedman and Fraser (1966) demonstrated this effect. Experimenters went from door to door and told homemakers they were working for the Committee for Safe Driving. They said they wanted the women's support for this campaign and asked them to sign a petition which was to be sent 'to the state's senators. The petition requested the senators to work for legislation to encourage safe driving. Almost all the women agreed to sign.

Several weeks later, different experimenters contacted the same women and also other women who had not been approached before. At this time, all the women were asked to put in their front yards a large, unattractive sign that read "Drive Carefully."

The results were striking. Over 55 percent of the women who had previously endorsed the petition (a small request) also agreed to post the sign (a relatively large request). In contrast, less than 17 percent of the other women agreed to post the sign. Getting the women to agree to the initial small request more than tripled the amount of compliance to the large request. This effect has been replicated in several studies (e.g., Seligman, Bush, & Kirsch, 1975).

Why this technique works is not entirely clear. One explanation is that people who agree to a small request get involved and committed to the issue itself, to the behavior they perform, or perhaps simply to the idea of taking some kind of action. Any of these factors would probably make someone more likely to comply with future requests.

Another explanation is based on **self-perception theory,** which was introduced in Chapter 5 on attitudes. The idea here is that in some ways the individual's self-image changes as a result of the initial act of compliance. In the safe-driving experiment, for example, a woman may have thought of herself as the kind of person who does not take social action, who does not sign petitions, who does not post signs, or, perhaps, who does not even agree to things that are asked of her by someone at the door. Once she has agreed to the small request—which was actually difficult to refuse—she may have changed her perception of herself slightly. Since she agreed to sign a petition, perhaps she is the kind of person who does this sort of thing. Then, when the second request was made, she was more likely to comply than she would have been otherwise.

The Door-in-the-Face Technique. Sometimes a technique opposite to the foot-in-the-door also works. First asking for a very large request and then making a smaller request can increase compliance to the small request. This is sometimes called the **door-in-the-face technique,** since the first request is typically so outrageously large that people might be tempted to shut the door in the requester's face. In one study, subjects were asked to volunteer time for a good cause (Cialdini et al., 1975). Some were asked first to give a huge amount of time. When they refused, as almost all did, the experimenter immediately said then perhaps they might agree to a much smaller commitment of time. Other subjects were asked only the smaller request, while a third group was given a choice between the two. The results were striking. In the single small-request condition, only 17 percent of subjects agreed. In the choice condition, 25 percent of subjects complied with the smaller request. But in the condition where subjects had first turned down a big request, 50 percent later agreed to the smaller request.

This effect is familiar to anyone who has engaged in bargaining with a used car salesman, a union, or management. The tactic is to ask for the moon and settle for less. The more you ask for at first, the more you expect to end up with eventually. The idea is that when you reduce your demands, the other person thinks you are compromising and the amount seems smaller. In a compliance situation, such as asking for money for charity, the same might apply—five dollars doesn't seem like so much when the organization initially asked for a hundred dollars.

Clearly, both the foot-in-the-door and the reverse tactic work at times, but we do not yet know when each of them will operate (Dillard, Hunter, & Burgoon, 1984). Both seem to work best when the behavior involved is prosocial, that is, when the request is to give money or help a worthwhile cause. One difference seems to be that the door-in-the-face technique works when the smaller request follows the larger request immediately and is obviously connected. The foot-in-the-door technique works even when the two requests are seemingly unconnected and may work best when there is no obvious incentive such as money to perform the small request.

The Low-Ball Technique. Consider how likely you would be to agree to the following requests. In one case, a researcher calls you on the phone and asks you to participate in an experiment scheduled for 7:00 in the morning. In a second case, a researcher calls and asks you to participate in a study. Only after you initially agree to participate does the researcher inform you that the study will be scheduled at 7:00 A.M. When Robert Cialdini and others (1978) actually compared these two procedures, they found that the second approach was much more effective. When students were told from the outset that an experiment would be conducted early in the morning, only 25 percent agreed to participate and showed up on time. In contrast, using the second approach of concealing the time of the study, 55 percent of students agreed to the initial request and almost all of them actually showed up for the early morning appointment. Once having agreed to participate, few people backed out of their agreement when they were informed about the time of day.

This tactic, in which a person is asked to agree to something on the basis of incomplete information and is later told the full story, is called the **low-ball technique.** Essentially, the person is tricked into agreeing to an attractive proposition, only to discover after he or she has agreed that the terms are actually different from those expected. This technique appears to work because once an individual has made an initial commitment to a course of action, he or she is reluctant to withdraw, even when the ground rules are changed. Although this technique can be effective (Burger & Petty, 1981), it is clearly deceptive. To protect consumers from unscrupulous salespersons, laws have been enacted to make low-balling illegal for several industries such as automobile dealers.

Our discussion of the foot-in-the-door, door-in-the-face, and low-ball techniques by no means exhausts the possible tactics people use to gain compliance. Recent research by Jerry Burger (1986) has begun to explore another strategy that he calls the *that's-not-all technique.* Consider this situation. A salesperson describes a new microwave oven to a potential customer and quotes a price. Then, while the customer is mulling over the decision, the salesperson adds, "But that's not all. Today only, we're having a special deal. If you buy the microwave now, we'll give you a five-piece set of microwave dishes at no additional cost." In actuality, the salesclerk intended to include the dishes with the oven all along, but by presenting the dishes as a "special deal" or something "just for you," the salesperson hopes to make the purchase even more attractive. The essence of this technique is to present a product at a high price, allow the customer to think about the price, and then improve the deal either by adding an additional product or by lowering the price.

In a series of seven experiments, Burger (1986) has demonstrated the potential effectiveness of this approach. In one illustrative study, experimenters held a psychology club bake sale on campus. At random, half the people who stopped at the table and asked about the cupcakes were told that they could buy a prepackaged set including one cupcake and two cookies for 75 cents. In this control condition, 40 percent of those who inquired actually purchased a cupcake. In the "that's-not-all condition," people who inquired were first told that the cupcakes were 75 cents each. A moment later, they were told that actually, they would get not only the cupcake but also 2 cookies for the 75 cent price. In this "that's-not-all" condition, 73 percent of people bought a cupcake, a substantially higher proportion than in the control condition.

Limits to External Pressure

We have seen that external pressure can often increase compliance. But we should also be aware of the limits of these approaches. The heroic soldier refuses to divulge the secret information even though cruelly tortured; the long-term smoker refuses to give up cigarettes despite the best efforts of family members, or the letter writer refuses to use zip codes despite a variety of threats from the Postal Service.

Social psychological research has investigated some of the many reasons why efforts to gain compliance fail. In some cases, influencers simply do not control the resources—rewards, punishments, expertise, and so on—that would be needed to induce compliance. In other cases,

psychological processes such as reactance and overjustification may reduce the effectiveness of influence attempts.

Reactance. Sometimes, too much pressure may actually cause a person to do the opposite of what the influencer desires. Brehm (1966) describes this phenomenon as **reactance.** The basic idea is that people attempt to maintain their personal freedom of action. When this freedom is threatened, they do whatever they can to reinstate it. If an individual perceives an influence attempt as a threat to freedom of action, the person protects it by refusing to comply or by doing the opposite of what is requested. We are all familiar with the child who, when asked to do something, says, "I won't." But when her parents say, "All right, then, don't," the child goes ahead and does what was initially requested. This behavior also occurs in adults!

Overjustification. Another limit on external pressure concerns **overjustification,** a concept we introduced in Chapter 4 on attribution. It is not always true that the larger the reward, the more effective it will be in getting someone to do something. Sometimes a large external reward can undermine a person's intrinsic interest in an activity. Larger rewards are often effective, as long as we continue the rewards indefinitely. However, we often use rewards to get someone to comply in the first place, and then withdraw the rewards in hopes that they will continue the behavior. For example, we might give a child an extra cookie for making his bed, or give a third-grade class a prize for mastering a list of spelling words. Advertisers often provide small rewards in the form of prizes or coupons for trying new products. In all these instances, those giving the rewards do not want to continue to offer them forever. Rather, they hope that the behavior will continue after the rewards are discontinued.

The implication of overjustification for compliance is that rewards may sometimes backfire. If an activity is basically uninteresting or even unpleasant, rewards will probably be helpful because they will increase the likelihood of compliance in the first place. And since the task is not enjoyable, there is no basic interest to undermine. But when the activity is inherently enjoyable or satisfying, giving rewards may reduce future compliance. If you think that children can learn to get intrinsic satisfaction from cleaning their rooms or from studying math, offering too many rewards for these activities may be a mistake.

OBEDIENCE TO AUTHORITY

In this final section we take a closer look at one of the six bases of power identified by Raven: obedience to legitimate authority. In any social group, organization, or society, it is important that people obey orders from those who have legitimate authority. In wartime, generals expect soldiers to obey orders and severely punish disobedience. We expect drivers to follow the orders of police directing traffic. Most people believe that public health officials have the right to require vaccinations against polio and other communicable diseases for school chil-

dren. Obedience is based on the belief the authorities have the right to make requests. In many cases, we agree with the policies of those in charge, and obey orders willingly.

But what about situations in which the demands of the authorities conflict with our own beliefs and values? How do parents respond if they believe that a new vaccination required for public schools is potentially hazardous to their children? How do soldiers and citizens react if they believe their government is pursuing a misguided or immoral policy?

Herbert Kelman and Lee Hamilton (1989) have used the term "crimes of obedience" to describe immoral or illegal acts that are committed in response to orders from an authority. Kelman and Hamilton reject the idea that crimes of obedience are things of the past, committed only in Nazi Germany or by fanatical cults. Rather, they suggest that crimes of obedience continue to occur in our society. For example, crimes of obedience occur when employees carry out orders from corporate executives that violate the law or harm public welfare, when political leaders order their subordinates to en-

During World War II, the Nazi regime sent millions to their deaths in concentration camps.

Nazi official Adolph Eichmann testifies from a bullet-proof booth. An Israeli court found him guilty of sending Jews to their death, thus rejecting his claim that he was innocent because he merely obeyed orders.

gage in shady campaign practices, or when soldiers and guerrilla fighters obey orders to torture or kill unarmed civilians.

The Eichmann Defense: Just Obeying Orders

For many people, the mass murder of European Jews by the Nazis has become a tragic and compelling case study in obedience to authority. Before World War II, nearly 9 million Jews lived in Europe. The European Jewish community had a long and brilliant tradition of culture, artistic and intellectual achievement, and religious devotion. Adolf Hitler and the Nazi party came to power in Germany in 1933, contending that the Aryan race was superior to such "mongrel races" as the Jews and Gypsies, and that Europe needed to be racially purified. Within a few years, the Nazi regime had begun to arrest and imprison Jews in Germany. By 1939, when

Germany invaded Poland, hundreds of thousands were already in concentration camps.

Soon thereafter, Nazi officials began secretly exchanging memos on "a final solution to the Jewish problem." Under the effective management of Adolph Eichmann, a dedicated career bureaucrat, Jews from throughout Europe were systematically rounded up and shipped to concentration camps such as Auschwitz and Dachau, mostly by train, where they were starved, gassed, shot, cremated, and buried in mass graves. By 1945, when World War II ended, about 6 million European Jews had died, along with many Gypsies, homosexuals, and political dissidents. Of those Jews who had lived before the war in the 21 countries fully occupied by the Germans, three out of every four were dead. Atomic bombs would have had to have been dropped on 100 cities to have killed as many Japanese.

Eichmann fled to Argentina after the end of the war where he was ultimately captured by Israeli investigators in 1961. He was taken to Israel and tried for murder. His defense was that he was not personally responsible for the deaths of the Jews, because he had simply been following orders. The argument was rejected, and he was held accountable for his crimes and put to death. The "Eichmann defense" has come to stand for the claim that a person is justified in committing terrible actions because he or she is "just following orders."

The virtual annihilation of the European Jewish community could have been carried out only with the conscious cooperation of thousands of ordinary Germans—bureaucrats, soldiers, janitors, doctors, railroad workers, and carpenters. Did these behaviors emerge from pathological characteristics of the German people? Or, more frighteningly, did they arise out of the normal operation of everyday social processes, such as simple obedience to authority? Under what conditions will people commit terrible acts when ordered to? For social psychologists, such events raise fundamental questions about obedience to authority and the conditions under which people will comply with or resist directives that violate their own standards of morality.

The Milgram Experiments

In the 1960s, Stanley Milgram (1963, 1974) designed an important series of laboratory experiments to understand the issues involved in obedience to authority. Milgram began his research by placing newspaper ads asking for men to participate in a psychology study. The volunteers were scheduled in pairs and were told that the purpose of the study was to investigate the effects of punishment on learning. One of them was selected by chance as the "learner" and the other as the "teacher." The teacher's job was to read aloud pairs of words that the learner was supposed to memorize. Each time the learner made a mistake, the teacher was to administer a punishment.

The teacher sat in front of a large, impressive "shock machine" containing a number of levers, each of which was labeled with the amount of shock it would deliver. The range was from 15 volts to 450 volts. Above the numbers representing voltage were labels describing the severity of the shock "Slight," "Extreme Intensity Shock," and "Danger: Severe Shock."

The learner was put in a chair in another room. His arm was strapped down to the chair, and electrodes were taped to his arm. He could not be seen by the teacher or anyone else; they communicated entirely by intercom. Before the testing began, the learner mentioned that he had a slightly weak heart. He was assured by the experimenter that the shocks were not dangerous. Then the experimenter gave the teacher a sample shock, to give him some idea of what the shocks he would be delivering felt like. It was actually fairly severe and hurt considerably, but the teacher was told it was a mild shock.

During the testing, the learner made a number of errors. Each time, the teacher told him he was wrong and delivered a shock. Whenever a shock was given, the learner grunted. As the level of shock increased, the learner's reactions became increasingly dramatic. He yelled, begged the teacher to stop shocking him, pounded the table, and kicked the wall. Toward

The Milgram study of obedience to legitimate authority. (Copyright 1965 by Stanley Milgram. From the film *Obedience,* distributed by the New York University Film Library.)

the end, he simply stopped answering and made no response at all. Through all this, the experimenter urged the teacher to continue. "Please continue." "The experiment must go on." "It is necessary for you to continue." The subject was assured that the responsibility was the experimenter's, and not his.

Under these circumstances, a large number of subjects dutifully delivered supposedly severe electric shocks. All 40 subjects delivered the 300-volt shock, and 65 percent continued to the final 450-volt level. They did this even though the person they were shocking screamed for mercy, had a heart condition, and was apparently experiencing great pain. In reality, of course, the "learner" was a confederate of the experimenter and did not receive any shocks. All responses, including errors, grunts, and groans, were carefully rehearsed and then tape-recorded to make them identical for all subjects. The "teacher," however, had no way of knowing that the situation was staged.

In a series of 18 studies, Milgram (1965, 1974) sought to identify conditions that increased obedience. Situational changes that made individuals feel more responsible for their actions or that emphasized the negative aspect of what they were doing reduced the amount of obedience. Milgram found, for example, that bringing the victim closer to the subject substantially reduced obedience. In the extreme case, when the victim was seated right next to the subject, obedience decreased dramatically. Tilker (1970) supported this finding and demonstrated that reminding subjects of their own total responsibility for their actions made them much less likely to administer shocks.

Subjects in the Milgram studies often experienced considerable stress. Some began to sweat; others broke out into nervous laughter or stuttered. They often pleaded with the experimenter to end the study. The subjects were not callous about the situation, but rather experienced great conflict. On the one hand, they felt enormous pressures from the situation and the experimenter to continue. On the other hand, they were concerned about the welfare of the victim and about their personal responsibility

for inflicting pain. As long as subjects could shift responsibility to the experimenter and minimize in their own minds the pain the victim was enduring, obedience was high. To the extent that they felt personally responsible and were aware of the victim's pain, they were less obedient.

Milgram interpreted his findings as showing that "normal" people can be led to perform destructive acts when exposed to strong situational pressure from a legitimate authority. Miller (1986) calls this the "normality thesis"— the idea that evil acts are not necessarily performed by abnormal or "crazy" people. Rather, average individuals who see themselves as mere agents in an organization, carrying out the orders of those in command, can behave in destructive ways.

Although the pressures to obey legitimate authorities are strong, individuals do not inevitably obey. For example, in Chapter 12 on prosocial behavior, we describe the actions of Christians who risked their lives to shelter Jews from Nazi persecution. What enabled these individuals to resist Nazi policies and, more generally, how can we account for principled resistance to authority?

Several factors seem to make a difference. First, obedience is reduced when the suffering of the victims is highly salient. Second, obedience is reduced when an individual is made to feel personally responsible for his or her actions (Hamilton, 1978). Third, people are more likely to resist authorities when others in the situation model disobedience. Fourth, encouraging individuals to question the motives, expertise, or judgment of authorities can reduce obedience. Finally, sensitizing people to the potential impact of authorities may make a difference.

In this chapter, you have learned a great deal about conformity, compliance, and obedience to authority. Knowledge of influence techniques can sometimes help people to resist social pressures and to follow their individual beliefs. What personal lessons do you draw from the social psychological research on social influence presented in this chapter?

Key Terms

cohesiveness	door-in-the-face technique	minority influence
commitment	foot-in-the-door technique	norm of social responsibility
compliance	legitimate authority	overjustification
conformity	low-ball technique	reactance
		self-perception theory

Summary

1. Three important types of social influence are conformity, compliance, and obedience to authority. Conformity occurs when someone voluntarily performs an act because others are doing it. Compliance occurs when people do what they are asked to do, whether they want to do it or not. Obedience to authority is a particular kind of compliance; it occurs when we believe that the requester has a legitimate right to ask us to do something.

2. Classic studies by Sherif on the autokinetic effect and by Asch on line judgments showed that individuals will often conform to group norms in making both ambiguous and clearcut perceptual judgments. People conform for two main reasons—to be right (informational influence) and to be liked (normative influence).

3. People are most likely to conform when they feel strong commitment to a group, when the group has about three or four members (or subunits), and when the majority view is unanimous.

4. Moscovici and others have shown that a forceful minority can change the position of the majority in a group. Minorities are most effective when they are persistent, and when their behavior is logically consistent but not "rigid." Single minorities (who differ from the group in only one important way) may be more effective than double minorities (who differ in two ways), because single minorities are less likely to be seen as acting out of self-interest.

5. We may comply with a request for many different reasons. Raven and his colleagues have identified six bases of power that can produce compliance: rewards, coercion, expertise, information, referent power, and legitimate authority. A special case of legitimate power is the "power of helplessness"; a strong cultural norm of social responsibility dictates that we should help those who are less fortunate and less powerful than we are.

6. Researchers have identified several specific compliance strategies, including the foot-in-the-door technique, the door-in-the-face technique, the low-ball technique, and the that's-not-all technique.

7. In everyday life, obedience to legitimate authority is adaptive and contributes to smooth social functioning. But sometimes, people obey orders that are harmful to others and that violate their own personal beliefs and values. In one of the most famous research programs in social psychology, Milgram investigated this phenomenon. He found that a majority of "normal" adults would administer severe electric shocks to a helpless victim if ordered to do so by a researcher.

8. Obedience to legitimate authority is lessened when individuals are made aware of the suffering they cause, feel personally responsible for their actions, observe others who disobey the authority, and are encouraged to question the motives and judgment of the authority.

Suggested Readings

Cialdini, R. B. (1988). *Influence: Science and practice.* Glenview, IL: Scott, Foresman/Little, Brown. A very readable discussion of the many ways we try to influence other people. The book is based both on empirical research and on the author's experiences with salespeople, public relations agents, fund raisers, and others whose livelihood depends on successfully influencing people.

Kelman, H. C., & Hamilton, V. L. (1989). *Crimes of obedience: Toward a social psychology of authority and responsibility.* New Haven, CT: Yale University Press. A recent analysis of obedience that gives special attention to the massacre of civilians in My Lai, Vietnam by U.S. soldiers, the Watergate scandal of President Nixon, and the Iran-Contra affair. The book offers suggestions for teaching people to be less accepting of authority.

Milgram, S. (1974). *Obedience to authority: An experimental view.* New York: Harper & Row. A complete description of Milgram's research program and the many variations he conducted plus Milgram's own theoretical analysis of his findings.

Miller, A. G. (1986). *The obedience experiments: A case study of controversy in social science.* New York: Praeger. A thoughtful review of Milgram's original studies and later replication studies by other researchers. The book discusses both ethical and methodological critiques of Milgram's work and considers the applicability of these laboratory studies to understanding the Holocaust and other cases of genocide.

Moscovici, S. (1985). Social Influence and conformity. In G. Lindzey & E. Aronson (Eds.), *Handbook of social psychology,* 3rd ed., Vol. 2. New York: Random House, pp. 347–412. A comprehensive and somewhat technical review of conformity research and theory, with special attention to the influence of minorities.

Staub, E. (1989). *Roots of evil: The psychological and cultural sources of genocide.* New York: Cambridge University Press. A thoughtful analysis of torture and mass murder in such diverse settings as Greece, Cambodia, Argentina, and Russia.

NINE

Interpersonal Attraction

AFFILIATION

BASIC PRINCIPLES OF ATTRACTION

PERSONAL CHARACTERISTICS

SIMILARITY

FAMILIARITY

PROXIMITY

LOVE

LONELINESS

Y ou're sitting in the first meeting of a seminar on American literature, listening to the discussion with one ear and sizing up your new classmates. You've taken an instant dislike to one rather pompous man who seems determined to dominate the conversation. Whenever he opens his mouth, you and the woman sitting across the table exchange knowing glances and smiles. She seems to be friendly, and you decide to talk to her during the coffee break. As your eyes travel around the seminar table, you think about each student, making mental notes about who you like and who you don't like.

In recent decades, social psychologists have probed the mysteries of interpersonal attraction, seeking to understand the basic processes that determine who we like and why we like them. This chapter examines the growing body of scientific research on attraction. We begin with a consideration of affiliation, the basic human tendency to seek the company of other people. Next we review general principles of interpersonal attraction and investigate the importance of such factors as physical attractiveness, attitude similarity, and physical proximity. Then we consider the ultimate form of interpersonal attraction, romantic love. We conclude with an analysis of loneliness, the painful experience we have when our social relationships are inadequate.

AFFILIATION

For most of us, the tendency to affiliate—the desire to be with other people—is quite strong. The earliest roots of human affiliation are to be found in childhood, when infants form strong attachments to one or more adults. This attachment relationship has been described as the child's first love affair. As we grow up, our social needs become more complex and diverse. We affiliate to have fun, to get help, to share sexual intimacies, to feel powerful, to get approval, and so on.

Attachment in Childhood

Infants become attached to the person with whom they interact most often and most lovingly. This is usually the mother, although it could be anyone with whom the infant has regular contact. By **attachment** we mean that an infant responds positively to specific people, feels better when they are close, seeks them out when frightened, and so on. Attachment is typically a two-way process, so parents usually become attached to their children.

Attachment serves two major functions for children (Shaver & Klinnert, 1982). First, children derive a sense of security from being with the attachment person. When children are frightened or confronted with unfamiliar situations, they turn to this person for comfort and reassurance. Infants show less distress when a stranger approaches if they are being held by their mother than if they are several feet away from the mother. A second function of attachment is to provide information about the environment. When children are uncertain about how to respond to a novel situation, they look to their attachment person for guidance.

In one study (Klinnert, 1981), infants aged 12 to 18 months were put in a play room with their mother and presented with such novel stimuli as a large remote-controlled spider, a remote-controlled dinosaur, and a life-size model of the Incredible Hulk's head. When one of these strange objects first appeared, most children looked questioningly at their mothers. If the mother (following instructions from the researcher) showed fear, the child usually moved toward the mother. If the mother showed pleasure and smiled, the child moved toward the new toy. Nonverbal cues from the mother guided the child's response.

All children develop an attachment to their primary caretaker. However, the nature of this attachment between infant and parent may vary. Mary Ainsworth and her associates (1978) have identified three major styles of attachment between infants and parents.

☐ *Secure attachment* occurs when the parent is generally available and responsive to the child's needs.

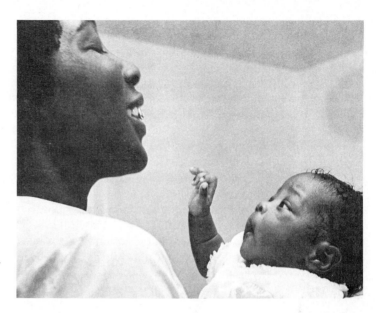

An infant's intense gaze shows her fascination with her mother. At just a few weeks of age, babies begin to form strong attachments to their parents.

☐ *Avoidant attachment* occurs when the parent is generally unresponsive or even rejecting. Infants may initially "protest" this lack of attention, but ultimately become "detached" from the caretaker.

☐ *Anxious/ambivalent attachment* occurs when the primary caretaker is anxious and does not respond consistently to the infant's needs. The caretaker may sometimes be available and responsive, but at other times be unavailable or intrusive.

Children's attachment has been explained both by innate biological factors and by learning. The biological view (see Bowlby, 1969) emphasizes the survival value of attachment for the child. Human infants are helpless creatures who need to be taken care of, protected, fed, and kept warm. When children are old enough to move around, it is important that they not wander too far from their parents because they might get into danger or simply get lost. Attachment was adaptive in human evolution because it ensured that children got the attention they needed to survive. The biological explanation of attachment holds that certain behaviors and responses of the infant and parent are "programmed" genetically, and that these cause the attachment to form.

A second explanation is that attachment is learned. The child becomes attached to the parent because the parent feeds and comforts the child; the parent becomes attached to the child because the child rewards the parent. For example, when the child cries, the parent comes because crying usually means the child needs something. The parent arrives, gives the child food, or changes a diaper. The child stops crying. Both have been reinforced by the interaction: the child feels better because it is no longer hungry or uncomfortable; the parent feels good because the child has stopped crying. Similarly, the parent is reinforced by the child's smile. As we all know, almost nothing is more rewarding than having a baby smile at us, especially if the baby favors us with more smiles than it gives to others. So, the child learns to love its parent if the parent provides the attention and care it needs. And the parent learns to love the child if the child responds to this care with positive reinforcements in the form of smiles, hugs, lack of crying, and so on.

Both the biological and learning approaches probably contain much truth. Clearly, many innate behaviors of the child contribute to the formation of attachment. The child does not have to learn to cry, to smile, or feel good when comforted; all these inborn responses are important for producing an attachment bond between parent and child. On the other hand, there is no question that seeing a child smile or hearing it stop crying in response to your presence is reinforcing and that without this reinforcement you might not develop a strong attachment to a child. So one could say that certain innate behavior patterns help produce attachment and that the mechanism by which they operate is through mutual reinforcement of parent and child.

Work on attachment raises the possibility that the tendency to affiliate is, at least in part, biologically based. As a species, humans may be disposed to form emotional attachments to those with whom they interact regularly and to feel more comfortable and secure in the presence of these people. The capacity for emotional attachment that first appears in infancy continues throughout life, as we form bonds with close friends, lovers, and our own children.

Laboratory Studies of Affiliation

Useful insights about adult affiliative tendencies have come from carefully controlled laboratory studies. In the 1950s, Stanley Schachter began an important series of experiments designed to explore situational factors that increase the desire to be with other people. Schachter (1959) started with the plausible hypothesis that people affiliate to reduce fear. Thus, if we randomly assign adults to a condition where they will experience either high or low fear, we should observe significant differences in their desire for human company.

To test this idea, Schachter recruited women undergraduates. When subjects arrived for the study, they were greeted by an experimenter in a white laboratory coat, surrounded by electrical equipment of various sorts. The experimenter introduced himself as Dr. Gregor Zilstein of the Department of Neurology and Psychiatry, and he explained that the experiment concerned the effects of electric shocks. To make some subjects more afraid than others, the experimenter used two different descriptions of the electric shock.

In the *high-fear condition*, Dr. Zilstein described the shocks in ominous tones. Subjects were told: "These shocks will hurt. . . . In research of this sort, if we're to learn anything at all that will really help humanity, it is necessary that our shocks be intense. . . . These shocks

will be quite painful but, of course, they will do no permanent damage." By continuing at some length in this vein, Dr. Zilstein clearly suggested that the subject was in for a very frightening and painful experience.

In the *low-fear condition,* by contrast, the instructions tried to make subjects feel relaxed and to minimize the severity of the shocks. For example, Dr. Zilstein said, "I assure you that what you will feel [electric shock] will not in any way be painful. It will resemble a tickle or a tingle more than anything unpleasant." Thus, although both groups of subjects were told that the experiment concerned electric shock, one group expected a painful and frightening experience, whereas the other group expected a mild and unthreatening experience. When questioned, women in the high-fear condition were indeed much more afraid.

Following the arousal and measurement of fear, Dr. Zilstein told the subjects there would be a 10-minute delay while he prepared the equipment. He explained that there were a number of rooms in which subjects might wait—comfortable rooms with armchairs and magazines. The experimenter then said it had occurred to him that perhaps some people might prefer to wait alone; others might prefer to wait with other subjects in the experiment. Each subject was asked to indicate whether she preferred to wait alone, with others, or had no preference. She was also asked to indicate the strength of her choice. In this and most subsequent experiments on the topic, the choice and rating of intensity of subjects' desire to affiliate were the basic measure of affiliation.

The results of Schachter's study are shown in Table 9–1. The answer to the question of whether highly fearful subjects want to affiliate more than subjects with low fear is "yes." The greater the fear, the greater the tendency to affiliate. Subsequent studies have confirmed this finding. Research has also shown that fear must be distinguished from other stressful situations that may actually decrease affiliative tendencies. For instance, if we are confronted with a situation that is not only stressful but also embarrassing, we may prefer to avoid other people.

This point was demonstrated by Sarnoff and Zimbardo (1961). Their study included high-fear

T A B L E   9 – 1

EFFECT OF FEAR ON AFFILIATION

Condition	Waiting Preference			Mean Strength of Affiliation Tendency
	Together	Don't Care	Alone	(Scale from −2 to +2)
High fear	62.5%	28.1%	9.4%	.88
Low fear	33.0	60.0	7.0	.35

Source: Adapted from *The Psychology of Affiliation* by Stanley Schachter with the permission of the publishers, Stanford University Press. Copyright 1959 by Stanley Schachter.

and low-fear conditions plus a new condition designed to arouse "oral anxiety." In the high oral anxiety condition, men were asked to perform a series of embarrassing tasks, such as sucking on baby bottles and rubber nipples. The results were that men in the high-fear condition were eager to affiliate, but men in the embarrassing high oral anxiety condition preferred to wait alone.

Given that fearful people usually want company, just what is it that they expect to get from being with others? What is the psychological process involved? Two possibilities have been investigated. The first is the *distraction hypothesis:* Fearful people affiliate to take their minds off their problems. In this case, it should not matter very much who they affiliate with—almost anyone will do. A second hypothesis is suggested by **social comparison theory.** As we discussed in Chapter 7, this theory states that people want to compare their own feelings and reactions with those of others in the same situation. When we are in a new or unusual situation and are uncertain about how to react, we turn to others as a source of information. Thus the social comparison hypothesis is that fearful people should want to affiliate, but *only* with others who are confronted with the same situation.

Several studies have tested these two possibilities, and results generally support the social comparison hypothesis. In one study, for example, some subjects were given a choice of waiting alone or waiting with women taking part in the same study (Schachter, 1959). Other subjects were given a choice of waiting alone or with students who were waiting to see their faculty advisors. As social comparison theory would predict, the fearful subjects preferred to wait with others in the same situation, but not

with others in a different situation. As Schachter concluded, "Misery doesn't love just any company, it loves only miserable company."

You may have noticed that in these laboratory studies, subjects were not given the choice of waiting with someone who had already gone through the experiment and who would therefore know just how painful the electric shocks really were. A recent naturalistic study provided precisely that comparison (Kulik & Mahler, 1989). The subjects were patients about to undergo coronary bypass surgery. The choice they were given was whether to have as their roommate another patient who was awaiting bypass surgery, or a patient who had already had the bypass operation. Given these options, the majority of patients preferred to room with someone who had already had the surgery. Patients explained their choices with such comments as, "You'd rather talk to a guy that's been through it" or "I think talking to someone who's already been through it would give you more confidence" (p. 188).

The results of research on childhood attachment and affiliation among adults lead to similar conclusions: people affiliate to reduce fear and uncertainty. At any age, affiliation is likely to be most beneficial if we can associate with someone who is both knowledgeable and sympathetic.

The Benefits of Social Relations

The reduction of fear and uncertainty are not the only reasons we seek human company. Today, theorists are attempting to classify the major types of benefits people receive in relationships. One illustrative analysis of affiliative needs was proposed by Robert Weiss (1974). He identified what he called six basic "provisions of social relations"—important things relationships provide for individuals:

☐ *Attachment* is the sense of security and comfort provided by our closest relationships. As children we are usually strongly attached to our parents; as adults we may experience this intimacy with dating partners, spouses, or other close friends.

☐ *Social integration* is the sense of having shared interests and attitudes. It is often provided by relationships with friends, co-workers, or teammates. Such relationships offer companionship and give a sense of belonging to a community.

☐ *Reassurance of worth* is provided when people support our sense of being a competent and valued person.

☐ *A sense of reliable alliance* involves knowing that there are people who will assist us in times of need. When emergencies arise, we often turn to our families for help.

☐ *Guidance* is provided by counselors, teachers, doctors, friends, and others to whom we turn for advice and information.

☐ The *opportunity for nurturance* occurs when we are responsible for the well-being of another person. Taking care of someone provides us with a sense of being needed and important.

This analysis of specific social needs highlights several major points about human affiliation. First, the rewards of companionship are numerous and diverse. We could undoubtedly add many other social needs to the list proposed by Weiss. Second, this approach emphasizes that no single relationship can fulfill all our affiliative needs. A love relationship may provide a sense of attachment, but not a sense of belonging to a community. A teacher can provide guidance about academic and career issues, but is not likely to lend us money or drive us to the airport. Third, the importance of specific types of social support varies across time and situations (Cutrona & Russell, 1987). For new moth-

ers adjusting to the demands of caring for an infant, guidance and a sense of belonging appear to be most important. For underpaid nurses working in stressful hospital settings, reassurance of their value as professionals is crucial to warding off burnout. In summary, a rich and healthy social life requires a network of social relations capable of satisfying a variety of needs.

BASIC PRINCIPLES OF ATTRACTION

We saw in Chapter 2 that the major dimension of first impressions is evaluation. Why is it that we like some people and not others? What determines who we will select as friends? Perhaps the most general answer is that we like people who reward us and who help us to satisfy our needs. Learning and social exchange theories explain the specific mechanisms through which rewards influence liking.

Association. A useful principle from classical conditioning is **association.** As applied to interpersonal attraction, the core idea is that we come to like people who are associated with good experiences and dislike people who are associated with bad experiences. More detailed analyses are provided in the newer "reinforcement-affect" model (Clore & Byrne, 1974) and "reinforcement-context" model (Cramer et al., 1985).

A demonstration of the association principle applied to liking comes from a study by May and Hamilton (1980). They were interested in the impact of pleasant versus unpleasant background music on interpersonal attraction. They first determined which type of music college women generally liked most (rock music) and least (avant-garde classical music). They then had other women students rate photographs of male strangers. While the women made their ratings, they heard rock music, avant-garde classical music, or no music. The results were clear-cut. Women rated the men most favorably when they were associated with enjoyable music and least favorably when their photos were associated with disliked music. The idea is that liking for someone can be influenced by a conditioned emotional response to events such as music that are arbitrarily paired with that person.

This association notion is important. Yet, as with so much that occurs with people, its very truth and simplicity should not blind us to other processes that may reverse it on occasion. Someone with whom you spend a very painful or stressful time may wind up a close friend, even though by association the person should make you think of pure misery. For example, in one study subjects were exposed to very noxious, unpredictable bursts of loud noise (Kendrick & Johnson, 1979). Although subjects hated the experience, their liking for each other increased. Sometimes shared misery creates a sense of solidarity that forms the basis for friendship.

Reinforcement. A basic principle from learning theory is **reinforcement.** We like people who reward us in one way or another. One important type of reward is social approval, and many studies have shown that we tend to like people who evaluate us positively. In one experiment, subjects went through a series of brief interactions with another person who was secretly a confederate of the researchers (Aronson & Linder, 1965). After each interaction, the subject overheard an interview between the confederate and the experimenter in which the confederate gave his impressions of the subject.

In one condition, the confederate was quite flattering. He said at the beginning that he liked the subject, and continued to make positive statements about the subject after each interview. In another condition, the confederate was critical. He said he was not sure that he liked the subject much and gave fairly negative descriptions of him. He continued being negative throughout the study. Afterward, the subjects were asked how much they liked the confederate. As expected, subjects liked the confederate significantly more if he said positive things about them than if he was negative in his evaluation.

Social Exchange. This perspective, introduced in Chapter 7, proposes that our liking for another person is based on our assessment of the costs and benefits the person provides us. According to **social exchange theory,** we like people when we perceive our interactions with them to be profitable—that is, when the rewards we get from the relationship outweigh the costs. Thus, we may like Paul because he's interesting and funny, and overlook the fact that he is perpetually late. Social exchange theory also emphasizes that we make comparative judgments, assessing the profits we get from one person against the profits we get from another.

With these general principles in mind, we now turn to research on more specific factors that influence interpersonal attraction. Four powerful determinants of liking are personal qualities of the other individual, similarity, familiarity, and proximity. As we discuss each of these important factors, we will also note occasional exceptions that differ from the general pattern.

PERSONAL CHARACTERISTICS

Just what is it that makes us like one person more than another? There is no single answer to this question. Some people find red hair and freckles irresistible; others dislike them intensely. Some of us prize compassion in our friends; others value intelligence. Individuals vary in the things they find most rewarding in other people. There are also large cultural differences in those personal qualities considered socially desirable. Many Americans equate feminine beauty with being thin, but other societies consider plump women the most attractive. Researchers have sought to identify some of the general characteristics associated with liking in our society.

Some years ago, Norman Anderson (1968b) compiled a list of 555 adjectives that are used to describe people. He then asked college students to indicate how much they would like a person who had each of these characteristics. A sample of these adjectives is given in Table 9–2.

TABLE 9 – 2

LIKABLENESS OF PERSONALITY TRAITS

Highly Likable	Slightly Positive to Slightly Negative	Highly Unlikable
Sincere	Persistent	Ill-mannered
Honest	Conventional	Unfriendly
Understanding	Bold	Hostile
Loyal	Cautious	Loud-mouthed
Truthful	Perfectionistic	Selfish
Trustworthy	Excitable	Narrow-minded
Intelligent	Quiet	Rude
Dependable	Impulsive	Conceited
Thoughtful	Aggressive	Greedy
Considerate	Shy	Insincere
Reliable	Unpredictable	Unkind
Warm	Emotional	Untrustworthy
Kind	Bashful	Malicious
Friendly	Naive	Obnoxious
Happy	Restless	Untruthful
Unselfish	Daydreamer	Dishonest
Humorous	Materialistic	Cruel
Responsible	Rebellious	Mean
Cheerful	Lonely	Phony
Trustful	Dependent	Liar

Source: Adapted from Anderson (1968b), pp. 273–77.

There seemed to be general agreement among the students on which characteristics were desirable and undesirable. One of the most striking results was that for these students, sincerity was the most valued trait. Of the eight top adjectives, six—sincere, honest, loyal, truthful, trustworthy, and dependable—related to sincerity in one way or another. Similarly, the terms rated lowest included liar and phony.

Two other themes that emerged in the list of highly likable traits were personal warmth and competence. Our attraction to others has these same two major components—feelings of affection based on the person's interpersonal warmth and feelings of respect based on the person's competence (Lydon, Jamieson, & Zanna, 1988; Rubin, 1973).

Warmth

What makes one person seem warm and friendly, while another comes across as cold and aloof? We don't yet have a complete answer to this question, but one important ingredient is having a positive outlook (Folkes & Sears, 1977). People appear warm when they like things, praise them, and approve of them—in other words, when they have a positive attitude toward people and things. In contrast, people seem cold when they dislike things, disparage them, say they are awful, and are generally critical.

To test this idea, researchers had subjects read or listen to interviews in which the interviewee was asked to evaluate a long list of things such as political leaders, cities, movies, or college courses (Folkes & Sears, 1977). Sometimes the interviewees expressed predominantly positive attitudes—they liked most of the politicians, cities, movies, or courses. In other cases, the interviewees expressed mainly negative attitudes. As predicted, subjects liked the interviewees more if they were positive rather than negative in their attitudes. Folkes and Sears concluded that the explanation lay in the greater warmth communicated by the positive attitude. Other analyses showed that the liking effect was not due to any greater perceived intelligence, knowledge, or similarity of attitudes on the part of the positive interviewees. Other research shows that in addition to saying positive things, people can also communicate warmth by such nonverbal behaviors as smiling, watching attentively, and expressing emotion (Friedman, Riggio, & Casella, 1988).

Competence

In general, we like people who are socially skilled, intelligent, and competent. The particular type of competence that matters most depends on the nature of our relationship with the person: we are attracted to friends who are good conversationalists, to mechanics who are good at fixing cars, to professors who are interesting lecturers, and so on. Competent people are usually more rewarding to be with than inept people.

Research has investigated one aspect of interpersonal competence—the ability to be an interesting rather than boring conversationalist (Leary, Rogers, Canfield, & Coe, 1986). In a first study, college students reported being bored by speakers who talked too much about themselves or about trivial, banal topics. Students also reported being bored with people who were overly passive, tedious, and serious in their interactions. In a second study, students listened to taped conversations designed so that the target speaker was either boring or interesting. Students evaluated the boring speakers quite negatively. Boring speakers were liked less, and rated as less friendly, enthusiastic,

popular, and more impersonal. In contrast, being a good conversationalist enhanced a person's likability (Leary et al., 1986).

An interesting exception to the competence-leads-to-liking principle is the case of someone who is a little "too perfect" for comfort (Aronson, Willerman, & Floyd, 1966). In one study, participants listened to a tape recording of a student who was trying out for a College Quiz Bowl team. In one condition, the candidate gave an outstanding performance and answered nearly every question correctly. In a second condition, the candidate gave a mediocre performance. As an added twist to the experiment, after the tryout was over, the candidate was sometimes heard to spill coffee on his suit.

The results showed the usual competence-leads-to-liking effect: the outstanding candidate was liked better than the mediocre one. However, the outstanding candidate was liked even better when he made a minor blunder or *pratfall* than when his performance was flawless. Apparently, spilling coffee served to "humanize" the brainy student and so made him more likable. In contrast, the blunder only detracted from the evaluations of the mediocre applicant. He was less liked when he spilled coffee than when he didn't.

Physical Attractiveness

One of the first things we notice about a person is physical appearance. Other things being equal, people considered attractive are liked more than people considered unattractive (Hatfield & Sprecher, 1986). One reason for the strong influence of appearance is the **halo effect** discussed in Chapter 2. This is the tendency to assume that a person who has one good quality will also have other good qualities. For example, people may assume that attractive individuals have better personalities and higher occupational status than less attractive individuals (Dion et al., 1972).

An interesting question is just how far this halo effect for physical attractiveness goes. It is one thing to expect a beautiful woman to be

Beauty is often an advantage in social relations. Other things being equal, attractive people tend to be liked more than people considered less physically attractive.

warm (who wouldn't be, if everyone always reacted as if she were wonderful?), but quite another to expect her to be highly intelligent, innocent of crimes she might be accused of, or especially qualified for high political office. In fact, the halo effect for physical attractiveness has been shown to generalize to a number of areas quite irrelevant to physical beauty.

Here are just a few of the research findings: adults react more leniently to bad behavior by an attractive child than by an unattractive child (Dion, 1972). Teachers evaluate cute children as being smarter and more popular than unattractive kids with identical academic records (Clifford & Walster, 1973). Students rate a lecture by a female teacher as being more interesting and judge the woman to be a better teacher if she is made up to look attractive rather than plain (Chaikin et al., 1978). In mock jury studies, attractive defendants often get lighter sentences than do unattractive defendants for exactly the same crime (Landy & Aronson, 1969).

But, as with all things, the attractiveness effect has its limits. Sigall and Ostrove (1975) hypothesized that jurors would actually be more punitive toward a beautiful defendant if her crime was somehow directly related to her attractiveness. So they gave mock jurors the details of a case, along with a photo of the defendant. The charge was either burglary or swindling. For burglary, the defendant's looks would be irrelevant. But for swindling, which involves using deception to cheat a person out

of money, looks could be an asset. As predicted, a beautiful burglar got a lighter sentence than did an unattractive burglar. But the beautiful swindler was given a somewhat harsher sentence than the unattractive one. The results are shown in Table 9–3.

Further verifying this hunch about connecting the type of crime to attractiveness, a control group, not shown the photographs, did in fact assume that the swindler was probably more attractive than the burglar. Thus, the halo effect for physical attractiveness has important limitations.

A second reason for liking attractive people is the so-called *radiating effect of beauty*. People may find it rewarding to be seen with a particularly attractive person because they think it will enhance their own public image. Michael Kernis and Ladd Wheeler (1981) hypothesized that this radiating effect of beauty occurs if a person is seen with an attractive friend or date, but does not occur if the attractive other is a stranger. To test this idea, they designed a laboratory experiment.

Subjects saw two people, a target person of average attractiveness and a same sex comparison person of either above-average or below-average looks. As a further variation, these people were sometimes presented as being friends and sometimes as strangers. As predicted, the two conditions of friends versus strangers produced opposite results. When the two people were believed to be friends, a radiating effect occurred. The target person was rated as more attractive when seen with a very attractive friend, and less attractive when seen with a very unattractive friend. However, when the two

T A B L E 9 – 3		
EFFECTS OF ATTRACTIVENESS ON LENGTH OF SENTENCE (Numbers are mean years assigned)		
Offense	Attractive Defendant	Unattractive Defendant
Swindle	5.45	4.35
Burglary	2.80	5.20

Source: Adapted from Sigall and Ostrove (1975), p. 412.

BOX 9–1

People Watching: Are Beautiful Friends a Social Asset?

Television presents a world of beautiful people—adorable children, sexy young women, and men with rugged good looks. Even TV news reporters are coached to improve their clothes and physical appearance. Social critics argue that these idealized images create unrealistic standards that few of us can attain. Critics note that even the actors and actresses we see on the screen do not look nearly as attractive in real life, without the help of makeup artists, wardrobe experts, flattering lights, and other props. Do these media beauty standards influence how we react to people in everyday life?

To find out, Douglas Kenrick and Sara Gutierres (1980) designed a clever field study. College men were contacted in their dorm either before or after they had watched "Charlie's Angels," a popular TV show starring three very beautiful young women. To reduce response bias, the men were not told they were in an experiment. Two college students (confederates of the researchers) approached groups of men sitting in a dorm lounge and asked them to help settle a personal debate about how pretty a particular young woman was. The men were shown a photo of the woman and were asked to write their ratings of her beauty secretly, so they wouldn't be influenced by each other. The woman had previously been rated by other college men as being of average attractiveness, about "4" on a seven-point scale.

As predicted, men who had just watched three lovely actresses for an hour rated this typical woman as less attractive than did men who had not seen the TV show. The same researchers replicated this effect in two more laboratory studies. In both, exposure to a photo of a highly attractive woman led to lower attractiveness ratings of an average-looking woman by both male and female subjects. All three studies found a "contrast effect": the average-looking person was seen as less attractive because of the extreme beauty of the recent comparison stimulus.

We need to be cautious in drawing conclusions from this research. These studies involved ratings of strangers. As people learn more about each other, the effects of physical attractiveness may change. Just when contrast and radiating effects occur in interactions with friends and lovers is an important question for future research.

people were thought to be strangers, a contrast effect occurred. The average-looking target person was rated less favorably when paired with a very attractive stranger. Gender did not affect these patterns: the same results were found regardless of whether the subject or the people being evaluated were male or female. Other studies have also shown that both men and women are rated more favorably when they are accompanied by an attractive romantic partner or friend than when they have an unattractive companion (Geiselman, Haight, & Kimata, 1984). For an interesting exception to the radiating effects of beauty, see Box 9–1.

One area in which physical attractiveness is especially important is in heterosexual dating.

In a classic study, Elaine Walster and her colleagues (1966) held a "computer dance" in which college students were randomly assigned to each other as dates for the evening. The researchers secretly made ratings of the physical attractiveness of each participant. At the end of the evening, students were asked to rate how much they liked their assigned partner. Liking was closely related to the person's physical attractiveness. Both men and women who were considered attractive were liked more.

In a more recent study, researchers investigated interpersonal attraction at a commercial dating service (Green, Buchanan, & Heuer, 1984). Clients of this dating service were predominantly white, middle class, and in their thirties. Clients screened prospective partners on the basis of detailed files containing a photograph, background information, and answers to open-ended questions about interests, hobbies, ideals, and relationship goals. As part of the dating service's regular procedures, each client selected five partners he or she would like to date and also indicated five people he or she would definitely not be interested in dating. Physical attractiveness was assessed by having research assistants evaluate the photos. The study found that for both male and female clients, physical attractiveness was a major factor in partner selection: both sexes chose better looking people and rejected less attractive people.

In the dating service study, age was also a factor. Most women selected men who were older than themselves; most men preferred women who were younger. An independent study of a California video-dating service (Woll, 1986) replicated these results, finding that both men and women relied strongly on looks and age in their initial screening of prospective dates. Another facet of physical attractiveness is height, with taller men and shorter women being seen as most attractive (Shepperd & Strathman, 1989).

Why do we consider one face beautiful and another unattractive? Some researchers have investigated the specific physical features that contribute to a person being perceived as attractive in our culture. For example, there is evidence that men give higher attractiveness ratings to women who have certain "cute" features usually associated with children, including large eyes, small noses, small chins, and wide smiles (Cunningham, 1986).

A recent study has investigated an intriguing new possibility—that we are attracted to faces that represent the average of the population. In other words, we prefer faces with noses of average length, foreheads of average height, and so on (Langlois & Roggman, 1990). To test this idea, the researchers obtained photographs of the faces of hundreds of young men and women. They then used computer technology to create composite faces, based on averaging the features of several individuals of the same sex. The composite faces were then rated for attractiveness, as were the original individual faces. The results were clear-cut. Judges found the "average" faces more attractive than the faces of specific individuals. One interpretation of these results comes from social cognition: we prefer faces with features that are prototypical for the population.

Research has also examined individual differences in the importance people give to physical attractiveness as a basis for evaluating others (Snyder, Berscheid, & Glick, 1985). The assumption was that some individuals are more attuned to the "exterior" appearance of prospective partners, while others pay more attention to the "interior" personality characteristics of potential partners. In this research, college men were first classified as high or low on **self-monitoring,** a dimension we described in detail in Chapter 7. Individuals high in self-monitoring seem to monitor the impression they make on others in social situations and try to control the self-image that they convey. It was hypothesized that high self-monitoring men would be particularly concerned about the public image a potential girlfriend conveys, consistent with the folk saying that "a man is judged by the company he keeps." In contrast, men who are low on self-monitoring were hypothesized to pay more attention to "interior" personal qualities of potential partners. The results of two studies supported this hypothesis. In gathering information about prospective partners and in the actual choice of a date, low self-monitoring men gave greater emphasis to personality whereas high self-monitoring men gave greater emphasis to physical attractiveness (Snyder, Berscheid, & Glick, 1985).

SIMILARITY

Another basic factor in interpersonal attraction is similarity. We tend to like people who are similar to us in attitudes, values, interests, background, and personality. This similarity effect applies to friendship, dating, and marriage. There is much truth in the old adage that "birds of a feather flock together."

Research Findings

Theodore Newcomb (1961) provided one of the first demonstrations that similarity leads to friendship. He took over a large house at the University of Michigan and offered male undergraduates free housing in return for taking part in his research. Before the students arrived, they filled out various questionnaires about their attitudes and values. Newcomb controlled the assignment of rooms so that some roommates had very similar attitudes and others had very dissimilar attitudes. By the end of the semester, roommates with similar preacquaintance attitudes generally liked each other and ended up as friends; dissimilar roommates tended to dislike each other and did not become friends.

Attraction through similarity has been the focus of much research. In a series of experiments, Donn Byrne (1971) and his associates carefully examined attitude similarity. To rule out other factors such as appearance or personality that might influence liking, Byrne developed the *phantom-other technique*. In a typical study, participants fill out questionnaires describing their own attitudes. They then read questionnaires allegedly filled out by a stranger. In actuality, there is no other person (hence, the term "phantom other"). Experimenters deliberately write answers to be either very similar, moderately similar, or dissimilar to the person's own answers. Subjects are then asked how much they think they would like the other person. The results of studies using this method have shown that attitude similarity strongly de-

Shared interests are an important factor in interpersonal attraction.

termines liking. The more similar the attitudes, the greater the anticipated liking. This effect has been demonstrated with very diverse groups including children, college students, medical patients, job trainees, and alcoholics.

The importance of similarity extends well beyond attitudes. Similarity in ethnic background, religion, politics, social class, education, and age all influence attraction. A study of the friendships of 2,000 high school students illustrates this point (Kandel, 1978). Each student identified his or her "best friend in school" and completed questionnaires about his or her own background and attitudes. Most best friends were similar in gender, year in school, age, and race. Best friends also tended to be similar in their school grades and their attitudes toward drug use.

A recent study suggests that the specific type of similarity can make a difference (Lydon, Jamieson, & Zanna, 1988). The researchers predicted that similarity in interests would lead to liking, whereas similarity in attitudes would lead to respect. Participants in the study received information about another person who was either similar or different in their interests and attitudes. Similarity of interests was based on the person's ratings of such activities as camping, listening to classical music, going to parties, drinking, and so on. Attitude similarity was based on the person's views about capital punishment, abortion, nuclear weapons, immigration policy, and other issues. In general, similar others were judged more favorably than dissimilar others. But as predicted, attitude similarity was most closely linked to ratings of respect for the person, and interest similarity was most closely linked to ratings of liking.

In dating and marriage, the tendency to choose similar partners is called the **matching principle.** It is unusual for an ardent feminist to date a sex-role traditionalist, or for an orthodox Jew to date a fundamentalist Christian. Dating partners and spouses tend to be relatively matched in their physical and social characteristics (Schoen & Wooldredge, 1989). For example, one study of dating couples found that partners tended to resemble each other in age, intelligence, educational plans, religion, physical at-

tractiveness, and even height (Hill, Rubin, & Peplau, 1976). They were also matched in their attitudes about sexual behavior and sex roles. Furthermore, couples who were most similar in background at the beginning of the study were most likely to be together 1 year and 15 years later.

Explaining the Effects of Similarity

Why should similarity be so important for interpersonal attraction? There are several explanations (Rubin, 1973). First, similarity is usually rewarding. People similar to us will tend to agree with our ideas and bolster our confidence in the rightness of our views. In contrast, it is unpleasant to have someone disagree with us, criticize our beliefs, and challenge our taste and judgment. Similar values and interests provide the basis for sharing activities with another person, whether this be picketing a nuclear power plant or going to a prayer meeting. Conversely, differences in values and interests can lead to dislike and avoidance (Byrne, Clore, & Smeaton, 1986; Rosenbaum, 1986).

A second explanation for the similarity-liking connection comes from the theory of **cognitive dissonance,** described in Chapter 5. According to this theory, people strive to maintain harmony or consistency among their attitudes, to organize their likes and dislikes in a balanced, consistent way. To like someone and at the same time to disagree with that person about fundamental issues is psychologically uncomfortable. We maximize cognitive consistency by liking those who support our views; we minimize cognitive dissonance by disliking those who disagree with us. A desire for cognitive consistency can encourage us to select friends who actually share our views, but it can also lead us to exaggerate the degree to which our friends agree with us. We can maintain cognitive consistency by perceiving that our friends have similar views, even if our perceptions are wrong.

A third explanation of the similarity effect is that people deliberately select partners who are

BOX 9–2

Political Advertising: Does Mere Exposure Work?

One application of the mere exposure principle is to political advertising. Millions of dollars are spent annually on campaigns designed to influence voters. Candidates with more money can clearly buy more ads, but does this increased exposure actually attract more voters?

Grush, McKeough, and Ahlering (1978) proposed that political ads work only under limited conditions:

☐ When there are many candidates (so voters would have difficulty identifying any one candidate without ads),

☐ When there is generally high exposure (all candidates have many ads),

☐ When candidates are previously unknown (so candidates are not overexposed).

Under other conditions, the researchers predicted that voting would be influenced by how well known candidates were before the campaign even began, with the advantage going to office holders who are already familiar to voters.

To test these predictions, they investigated the 1972 primary elections in the U.S. Senate and House of Representatives. All their predictions were confirmed. The amount of money spent by candidates on advertising was the best predictor of success *only* in races with unknown candidates who did not currently hold a major state office and when all candidates spent a good deal on advertising. However, these conditions were unusual, and accounted for only 19% of all races.

In most cases, the best predictor of success was the winner's precampaign visibility, based on being an incumbent, holding a highly visible public office, or having a famous name. The benefits of mere exposure in real-life politics are limited.

Whyte tracked the social activities of residents by reading the social column in the local newspaper. Almost everyone at a baby shower lived within a few blocks of one another, and almost everyone who lived in the area was there. The same was true on the other side of town at a weekend barbecue. In the whole town, there were practically no friends who did not live near one another. Most people who lived close together became friends.

The same proximity effect occurs on a smaller scale in apartment buildings and dormitories. A study by Leon Festinger, Stanley Schachter, and Kurt Back (1950) investigated friendship patterns in Westgate West, a large apartment complex. Westgate West had 17 separate two-story buildings, each containing 10 apartments (5 on a floor). The layout is shown in Figure 9–3.

The apartments were almost identical. More important, residents did not choose where they lived; they were given apartments as the apartments became vacant. In other words, like Park Forest, Westgate came close to being a field experiment with residents randomly assigned to a condition.

All residents were asked, "Which three people in Westgate West do you see socially most often?" Results clearly showed that residents were most friendly with those who lived near them. People on the same floor mentioned their next-door neighbor more often than their neighbor two doors away, and their neighbor two doors away more often than their neighbor at the other end of the hall. Of next-door neighbors, 41 percent were chosen, whereas only 22 percent of those two doors away and 10 percent of those at the end of the hall were chosen. In actuality, the physical distances involved were very small. People who lived next door were 19 feet apart (in the case of the two middle apartments, 32 feet apart), and the maximum distance between two apartments on one floor was only 88 feet. But these distances, only a few extra seconds in walking time, were important factors in determining friendship.

In addition, people who lived on different floors became friends much less often than those on the same floors even when the physical distance between them was roughly the same. This was probably because it takes more effort to go up or down stairs than to walk down a hall. Thus, people on different floors were in a sense farther away psychologically than were those on the same floor. The investigators referred to this as *functional distance,* meaning that the probability people would meet was determined by the design of the apartment house plus actual distance. The closer people lived, as measured by either physical or functional distance, the more likely they were to be friends.

Another demonstration of the proximity effect comes from a study done at the Training Academy of the Maryland State Police (Segal, 1974). Trainees were assigned to dormitory rooms and to seats in classrooms by their last name in alphabetical order. Thus, the closer their last names were alphabetically, the more likely trainees were to spend time in close proximity, both in and out of the classrooms.

After six months, each trainee was asked to name his closest three friends on the force. To an astonishing degree, the trainees' friends

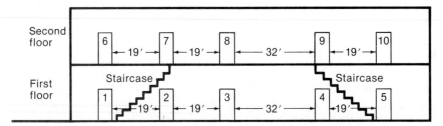

Figure 9–3. Floor plan of Westgate West. All the buildings in the housing development had the same layout. In the study, functional distance was defined as the number of doors apart two people lived. (Adapted from *Social Pressures in Informal Groups* by Leon Festinger, Stanley Schachter, and Kurt Back with the permission of the publishers, Stanford University Press. Copyright 1950 by Leon Festinger, Stanley Schachter, and Kurt Back.)

The social life on these dormitory balconies shows the importance of functional distance. Although the entrances to these rooms are quite far apart, the balconies bring people together and allow the formation of friendships.

turned out to be those with names near theirs in the alphabet. On the average, each person chosen as a friend was only 4.5 letters away from his chooser in the alphabet. So the mere fact of being assigned to a room and sitting close dictated friendship choice, despite an intensive training period in which all trainees became well acquainted.

Explaining the Effects of Proximity

The proximity effect incorporates many of the factors we have already seen are important for interpersonal attraction. First, proximity usually increases familiarity. We see our next-door neighbor more often than the person down the street. This repeated exposure, in and of itself, can enhance liking. Second, proximity is often linked to similarity. Although the citizens of Park Forest did not select their neighbors, people who decided to live in that community tended to start out with things in common. They all had enough money to afford nice homes, they wanted to live in suburbia, and so on. Over time, Park Forest neighbors developed

other points of shared interest, as they gossiped about the noisy teenagers down the block or complained about the pothole in their street. In other words, we often choose to live and work with people who resemble us, and our geographic closeness further enhances our similarities.

A third factor is that people who are physically close are more easily available than those who are distant. Obviously, we cannot like or be friends with someone we have never met. We choose our friends from people we know. The ready availability of people close by also affects the balance of rewards and costs of interacting, a point emphasized by social exchange theory. It takes little effort to chat with a neighbor or to ask her about bus service to the airport. Even if a neighbor's company is only moderately pleasant, we come by it "cheaply"—and so we may find it profitable. In contrast, long-distance relationships require time, planning, and money. When good friends move apart, they often vow to keep in touch regularly. But many find that their contacts dwindle to an occasional birthday card or phone call.

A fourth explanation of the proximity effect is based on cognitive consistency. It is psychologically distressing to live or work side by side with someone we dislike, and so we experience cognitive pressure to like those with whom we must associate. One formulation of this theory was proposed by Fritz Heider (1958). He distinguished between unit relations and sentiment relations. People or objects that "belong together" comprise a unit. Most people would perceive Sam as having a unit relationship with his cat, with his car, with his sister, and with his roommate. Proximity is a common basis for unit relationships. Sentiment relations involve feelings—liking or disliking—between the person and the other. Does Sam like his sister or not? The basic idea of Heider's **balance theory** is that we strive to maintain balance between our sentiment and unit relations. More specifically, we are motivated to like those we are connected to, and to seek proximity with those we like.

When does this desire to balance unit relations with sentiment relations affect liking? The most obvious case is when we are in a unit relation with someone we dislike. Then our positive unit relation is unbalanced by our negative sentiment relation. Suppose you arrive at college to meet your assigned roommate and instantly dislike him or her. To try to balance your unit relation with your sentiment relation, you have two options. You can avoid the roommate as much as possible and try to move to another room. Or you can reevaluate the roommate, trying to see some good qualities, to avoid conflicts, to make the best of the situation.

The issue comes down to which of these relations, unit or sentiment, you are able to change. Often it is nearly impossible to break off the unit relation. Your dorm counselor may insist that you cannot change roommates until the term ends. Therefore, you experience pressure to increase your liking.

This effect has been demonstrated experimentally (Tyler & Sears, 1977). Women participants in this study first met a person who was quite obnoxious. This person (secretly a confederate of the experimenter) forgot the subject's name, snapped gum, blew smoke in her face, claimed the subject was saying silly things, and did not look at the subject when she talked. This was done to establish a negative sentiment relation. Next, the experimenter told the subject either that she would spend another 40 minutes talking to the obnoxious person (creating a unit relation with the unpleasant person) or that she would spend 40 minutes talking to someone else. Finally, the subject was taken into a separate room to fill out a questionnaire which, among other things, asked how much she liked the confederate. As predicted, liking for the obnoxious person increased significantly with the anticipation of continued interaction.

Other studies have also shown that the anticipation of interaction increases liking. In one study, college students agreed to let the experimenters organize their dating life for a period of five weeks (Berscheid et al., 1976). The subjects were shown videotapes of various people, separated at random into those described as future dates and those described as people they would not date. The prospective dates were liked significantly more. In general, if we know we are going to interact with someone in the future, we tend to play up the person's positive traits and to ignore or minimize the negative ones. A desire for cognitive balance motivates us to like our neighbors, roommates, and others in close proximity.

There are, of course, exceptions to the proximity-liking connection. Sometimes no amount of cognitive reevaluation will convince us that the rude secretary in our office is really nice or that our bratty kid sister is really a little angel. Proximity is most likely to foster attraction when the people involved have similar attitudes and goals. Indeed, when there are initial antagonisms or conflicts between people, increased proximity and contact may actually intensify negative feelings.

In summary, research has shown that similarity, familiarity, and proximity are powerful forces in interpersonal attraction. To give a complete account of the processes of interpersonal attraction, we have also noted various exceptions to these patterns. But these minor exceptions should not obscure the importance of the general principles involved.

These factors are not only causes of liking,

but consequences as well. Proximity causes liking, but once we like someone, we often take steps to ensure that we will be close to them in the future. First-year roommates may be thrown together by chance. But if their proximity leads to friendship, they will probably ask to live together the following year. Similarity can work in the same way. Similarity may bring two people together in the first place, but as their friendship continues and they share ideas and experiences, they tend to become even more similar because of their association. Similarity is both a cause and a consequence of liking.

LOVE

Personal relationships are colored by strong emotions—passionate desire for a new lover, anger at an insult from a co-worker, grief at the loss of a grandparent, the joy of playing with a baby. Emotions are basic elements of social life. In recent years, the study of emotion has become a "hot" topic in psychology. New work is underway to develop theories about the nature of emotions, and to understand the social and biological origins of human emotions. Social psychologists have emphasized the importance of the social context of emotional experiences (Gordon, 1981; Schwartz & Shaver, 1987).

In this section, we will focus on love and romance. Long a favored subject for poets and songwriters, love is now a popular topic for scientific research as well. Most Americans consider love to be essential to a successful marriage. In the 1960s, Kephart asked young adults about the love-marriage connection. The question he posed to over 1,000 college students was: "If a boy (girl) had all the qualities you desired, would you marry this person if you were not in love with him (her)?" The results are shown in Table 9–4. Thirty years ago, most men said no, they wouldn't marry a woman they didn't love. However, most women said they were undecided; only one woman in four clearly answered no. In the intervening years, both sexes—but especially women—have become more romantic in their approach to marriage. In 1976 and again in 1984, researchers asked new generations of college students the same question (Simpson, Campbell, & Berscheid, 1986). In 1976, 86 percent of men and 80 percent of women said they would not marry without love; in 1984, the proportion of men who said no was the same, but women had increased to 85 percent. Today, many young people appear to view love as a prerequisite for marriage.

T A B L E 9 – 4					
WOULD YOU MARRY WITHOUT LOVE?					

How college students answered the question "If a man (woman) had all the other qualities you desired, would you marry this person if you were not in love with him (her)? (Numbers are percentages.)

	1967		1976		1984	
	Men	Women	Men	Women	Men	Women
Yes	11.7	4.0	1.7	4.6	1.7	3.6
Undecided	23.7	71.7	12.1	15.4	12.7	11.5
No	64.6	24.3	86.2	80.0	85.6	84.9

In all years, data are questionnaire responses from college men and women. The earliest data were collected by Kephart (1967); his question was worded identically to that above except that he used "boy (girl)" instead of "man (woman)".

Source: Adapted from Simpson, Campbell and Berscheid, *Personality and Social Psychology Bulletin*, Vol. 12, No. 3, September 1986, pp. 364–368. Copyright by The Society for Personality and Social Psychology, Inc. Reprinted by permission of Sage Publications, Inc.

Before turning to other research findings on love, let's set the stage by considering this newspaper story of young love:

On Monday, Cpl. Floyd Johnson, 23, and the then Ellen Skinner, 19, total strangers, boarded a train at San Francisco and sat down across the aisle from each other. Johnson didn't cross the aisle until Wednesday, but his bride said, "I'd already made up my mind to say yes if he asked me to marry him." "We did most of the talking with our eyes," Johnson explained. Thursday the couple got off the train in Omaha with plans to be married. Because they would need to have the consent of the bride's parents if they were married in Nebraska, they crossed the river to Council Bluffs, Iowa, where they were married Friday.

This account may remind you of such starstruck lovers from literature as Romeo and Juliet. But have you personally ever experienced this rather magical love at first sight?

When university students were asked how closely their own most intense love experience corresponded to this romantic model, only 40 percent said that there was a strong resemblance (Averill & Boothroyd, 1977). Another 40 percent said that they had never experienced anything at all like this story. The rest thought their most intense love relationship bore only a partial similarity to this one. This range of answers highlights one of the dilemmas of love researchers—how to capture the essential features of love, and at the same time depict the diverse experiences of people in love.

Love Versus Liking

One of the first researchers to study romantic love scientifically was Zick Rubin (1970, 1973). He was interested in the connection between love and liking. One view is that love is merely a very intense form of liking. According to this unidimensional view, our positive feelings of attraction range along a continuum from mild liking to strong liking to mild love to strong love. A contrasting view, and the one Rubin favored, is that liking and love are qualitatively distinct

and represent two different dimensions. This view seems consistent with folk wisdom that we can like someone a great deal, but not be in love with him or her—and that we can feel passionate love for someone we do not totally like or respect.

To study this issue, Rubin first compiled various statements that people thought reflected liking and other statements that people thought reflected love. These included such things as idealization, trust, sharing emotions, believing someone is intelligent, and tolerating the other's faults. Next Rubin asked several hundred college students to rate how characteristic each of these statements was of their feelings toward their boyfriend or girlfriend and also toward a nonromantic friend of the other sex. Rubin believed that if love and liking are distinct, some statements would characterize a romantic partner but not a friend. The results of this first study supported the idea that love and liking are distinct.

Based on these findings, Rubin constructed two separate paper-and-pencil tests, a Love Scale and a Liking Scale. Each scale consists of nine statements. A sample liking statement is "I have great confidence in _____'s good judgment." Respondents rate each statement on a nine-point scale from strongly disagree to strongly agree.

To collect further evidence that these scales were measuring different attitudes, Rubin recruited 182 dating couples at the University of Michigan. Both members of each couple filled out detailed questionnaires about their relationship and also participated in lab experiments. Rubin's results supported the distinction between love and liking. For example, he found that although students rated their dating partner and best friend equally on the Liking Scale, they rated their boyfriend or girlfriend much higher on the Love Scale.

In an experimental session, Rubin found that couples who scored high on the Love Scale spent more time making eye contact than did low scorers, confirming the idea that lovers often gaze into each other's eyes. Those with high love scores were more likely to say that they and their partner were in love. Strong lovers also

"I suppose I should have let a few minutes elapse between declaring my love for you and announcing that I also loved lobster."

gave a higher estimate of the probability of eventually marrying the partner.

In a follow-up study six months later, Rubin examined whether love scores were related to staying together versus breaking up. Strong lovers were more likely to stay together, but only if they were also high in "romanticism," the belief that true love conquers all. Taken together, these and more recent data suggest that although love and liking are related experiences, there are important qualitative differences between the two.

The Experience of Romantic Love

Research has begun to identify the various thoughts, feelings, and behaviors that are asso-ciated with romantic love (Kelley, 1983). Most of the information we have about love comes from studies of young middle class adults in our society. The experience of love is quite different in other cultures and at other historical times (Hunt, 1959). We need to be cautious about generalizing from current findings to "all lovers."

Thoughts of Love. Rubin's Love Scale conceptualizes love as an attitude toward another person, as a distinctive cluster of thoughts about the loved person. Rubin identified three main themes reflected in his scale items. One theme, which Rubin called attachment, is a sense of needing the partner. A sample statement is: "It would be hard for me to get along without ____." These statements reflect a person's awareness of their dependence on the

1. Saying "I love you" and other verbal statements of affection.
2. Physical expressions of love, such as hugging or kissing.
3. Verbal self-disclosure.
4. Communicating nonverbally such feelings as happiness and relaxation when the other is present.
5. Material signs of love, such as giving presents or doing tasks to help the other person.
6. Nonmaterial signs of love, such as showing interest in the person's activities, respecting his or her opinions, or giving encouragement.
7. Showing a willingness to tolerate the other and to make sacrifices to maintain the relationship.

other to provide valued rewards. A second theme concerns caring for the other person, as illustrated in this item: "I would do almost anything for ____." The desire to promote the other person's welfare and to be responsive to his or her needs is a central idea. The third theme emphasizes trust and self-disclosure.

These ideas of love contrast with the Liking Scale, which concerns beliefs that the other person is likable, intelligent, well-adjusted, and has good judgment. According to Rubin, liking combines feelings of affection and of respect.

Behaviors of Love. In assessing whether someone loves us, we usually depend not only on their words, but also on their actions. If someone professes love but forgets our birthday, goes out with other people, criticizes our appearance, and never confides in us, we may doubt their sincerity. Swensen (1972) asked people of different ages what behaviors they thought were most closely associated with love for a romantic partner or spouse. The answers fell into seven categories or types of love behaviors:

Swensen found that many of these romantic love behaviors were also seen as signs of love for parents, siblings, and same-sex friends.

Researchers have also identified specific events that indicate how far a heterosexual dating couple had progressed toward marriage (King & Christensen, 1983). In most cases, the college couples in this research went through a predictable sequence of events moving toward greater commitment. Events that usually occurred early in the development of a relationship included spending a whole day together and calling the partner by an affectionate name. At a later stage, partners started referring to each other as "boyfriend" and "girlfriend" and received invitations to do things together as a couple. A further development was to say "I love you" and to date each other exclusively. A common next step was to discuss living together or marriage, and to take a vacation together. Events indicating greatest progress included living together or becoming engaged. Although couples varied in how far their relationship had developed and in the speed with which they moved toward permanence, most couples followed a similar sequence of key events.

Feelings of Love: One feature that often distinguishes romantic love from friendship is the experience of physical symptoms. According to popular songs, a lover's heart skips a beat now and then, and a lover loses sleep and has trouble concentrating. To investigate this matter, researchers asked 679 university students to rate the intensity of various feelings they had had during their current or most recent love experience (Kanin, Davidson, & Scheck, 1970).

The most common reactions were a strong feeling of well-being (reported by 79 percent of students) and great difficulty concentrating (37 percent of students). Other reactions included "floating on a cloud" (29 percent), "wanted to run, jump, and scream" (22 percent), feeling "nervous before dates" (22 percent), and feeling "giddy and carefree" (20 percent). Strong physical sensations such as cold hands, butterflies in the stomach, or a tingling spine were reported by 20 percent and insomnia by 12 percent of students.

Researchers also found differences between the love experiences of women and men, with women being more likely to report strong emotional reactions (Dion & Dion, 1973). Whether these results reflect actual sex differences in the experience of love or women's greater willingness to disclose such feelings is not known.

Research has identified some of the thoughts, feelings, and behaviors that Americans commonly associate with love. But studies also find that individuals differ in their specific love experiences. This suggests that there are distinct types of love. In the next section, we examine two major models of love. For a more detailed look at ways people define love, see Box 9–3 on page 290.

Passionate Love and Companionate Love

Passionate love has been described as "a wildly emotional state: tender and sexual feelings, elation and pain, anxiety and relief, altruism and jealousy coexist in a confusion of feelings" (Berscheid & Walster, 1978, p. 177).

Emotions play a central role in passionate love. People are swept off their feet by uncontrollable passions that draw them irresistibly toward the loved person.

The physiological arousal that fuels passionate love can have many sources. Sexual desire, the anxiety of possible rejection, the excitement of getting to know someone, the frustration of outside interference, the anger of a lover's quarrel—all may contribute to the strong emotions experienced in passionate love. The uncontrollable quality of passionate love provides a convenient justification for lovers to engage in behaviors they might otherwise consider unacceptable—such as an extramarital affair (Berscheid, 1983). The lovers' defense is that they "couldn't stop" themselves.

Another element of passionate love is preoccupation with the other person. The lover is obsessed with thoughts of the new love. There is a tendency to idealize the loved person, to see the person as wonderful and perfect in every way. Passionate love is often said to strike suddenly and fade quickly. This type of love is intense, but fragile and often short-lived. In terms of the love styles discussed in Box 9–3, passionate love can be seen as a mix of romantic and possessive love.

Companionate love has been defined as "the affection we feel for those with whom our lives are deeply intertwined" (Berscheid & Walster, 1978, p. 177). This is a more practical type of love that emphasizes trust, caring, and tolerance of the partner's flaws and idiosyncrasies. The emotional tone of companionate love is more moderate; warmth and affection are more common than extreme passions. Companionate love develops slowly as two people build a satisfying relationship (Kelley, 1983). In terms of the six love styles in Box 9–3, companionate love combines being best friends and being pragmatic.

Individuals differ sharply in their beliefs about whether passionate or companionate love is the better or truer form. However, many family researchers believe that companionate love provides the most enduring basis for long-term relationships.

BOX 9-3

Definitions of Love

When people say "I love you," they can mean very different things. How would you personally define love? Researchers have identified six different ways in which people commonly define love (Hendrick & Hendrick, 1989; Lasswell & Lobsenz, 1980; Lee, 1973). These love styles are idealized types; each individual may define love in a way that combines more than one style:

☐ *Romantic love.* Love is an all-consuming emotional experience. Love at first sight is typical. Physical attraction is essential to love. A romantic lover might agree that, "My lover and I have the right physical 'chemistry' between us."

☐ *Possessive love.* The possessive lover is emotionally intense, jealous, obsessed with the beloved. The possessive lover is highly dependent on the beloved, and therefore fears rejection. Preoccupation with the loved one swings quickly from peaks of joy to valleys of despair. The possessive lover might agree, "When my lover doesn't pay attention to me, I feel sick all over."

☐ *Best friends love.* Love is a comfortable intimacy that grows slowly out of companionship, mutual sharing, and gradual self-disclosure. A best friends lover is thoughtful, warm, and companionate. He or she might agree that "My most satisfying love relationships have developed from good friendships."

☐ *Pragmatic love.* This is "the love that goes shopping for a suitable mate, and all it asks is that the relationship work well, that the two partners be compatible and satisfy each other's basic or practical needs" (Lee, 1973, p. 124). The practical lover is logical and thoughtful in selecting a suitable partner, and seeks contentment rather than excitement. The practical lover might agree that "One consideration in choosing a partner is how he/she will reflect on my career."

☐ *Altruistic love.* This style of love is unconditionally caring, giving, and forgiving. Love means a duty to give to the loved one with no strings attached, with no expectations of reciprocity. Altruistic love is expressed through self-sacrifice, patience, and faith in the beloved. An altruistic lover might agree that "I cannot be happy unless I place my lover's happiness before my own."

☐ *Game-playing love.* This person plays at love as others play games: to enjoy the "love game" and to win it. In game-playing love, strategy is important, and commitment is to be avoided. The game player may have several relationships going at once. No relationship lasts for long, usually ending when the love partner becomes boring or too serious. A game player might agree that "I enjoy playing the 'game of love' with a number of different partners."

To study these love styles empirically, John Lee (1973, 1977) and other researchers have developed techniques to assess how individuals rate on each of the six types. The statements quoted above are from a love questionnaire developed by Clyde and Susan Hendrick (1989). Research has found at least preliminary support for the idea of distinct love styles. Individuals are rarely a "pure" type, but instead may score high on two or three styles, or may be moderate in some styles and low in others.

Gender differences in love styles have emerged in several studies (Hatkoff & Lasswell, 1979; Hendrick et al., 1984). In general, men are more likely to be romantics who believe in love at first sight, or game players who enjoy the thrill of the chase. Women are more likely to adopt a best friends or pragmatic approach to love. Intrigued by these finding, researchers have speculated about the possible reasons for sex differences in love styles (Rubin, Peplau, & Hill, 1981). The most common explanation concerns the social and economic context of mate selection. As sociologist Willard Waller (1938) explained, "A man, when he marries, chooses a companion and perhaps a helpmate, but a woman chooses a companion and at the same time a standard of living. It is necessary for a woman to be mercenary" (p. 243). Men, it is argued, can afford to be more frivolous and romantic in love.

The contrast between passionate and companionate love raises interesting questions about the experience of emotions in close relationships. For example, the early stages of a romantic relationship are usually characterized by extreme emotions, whereas the later stages are marked by emotional tranquility and moderation. Why might this be? Ellen Berscheid (1983) has suggested that over time, the novelty and surprise of the relationship wear off. Idealization of the partner confronts the reality of human imperfection. The couple develops routine ways of interacting, and life together becomes more settled.

However, Berscheid also suggests that as a relationship continues over time and interdependence grows, the *potential* for strong emotion actually increases. The greater our dependence on another person, the greater the possible influence of the partner in our lives. But, paradoxically, because long-term couples learn to coordinate their activities smoothly, the actual frequency of strong emotions tends to be fairly low.

The latent potential for strong emotion may emerge occasionally, however. When partners are separated because of travel or illness, they often have intense feelings of loneliness and desire. Another situation that can arouse strong emotions in a long-term relationship is the threat posed by a partner's involvement with another person.

Jealousy occurs when a person perceives a real or potential attraction between the partner and a rival (White, 1981). Jealousy is a reaction to a perceived threat by a rival to the continuity or quality of a valued relationship. A husband's discovery that his wife is having a sexual affair with someone else would be an example. Jealousy involves two types of threats—threats to the relationship from the possible loss of the partner and threats to the person's self-esteem from being rejected by the partner or losing to the rival (Mathes, Adams, & Davies, 1985). Feelings of anger, anxiety, and depression are common.

According to Berscheid (1983), jealousy should be greatest when the person is highly dependent on the partner and when the person perceives that the threat is a serious one. Although empirical research on jealousy is still quite new, there is some evidence linking jealousy with both dependence and insecurity (Buunk & Bringle, 1987; Pines & Aronson, 1983; White, 1976). For example, married people who believed they would have few alternatives if their current spouse left them appeared more vulnerable to jealousy (Hansen, 1985).

Love and Attachment

Cindy Hazan and Phillip Shaver (1987) have recently analyzed romantic love from the perspective of attachment theory. Earlier, we saw that infants develop strong emotional ties to their caretakers—bonds that provide an important sense of security. Although all children become attached to their primary caretaker, this attachment can take three forms: secure attachment, avoidant attachment, and anxious/ambivalent attachment.

Hazan and Shaver propose that adult love relationships are similar to infant attachments in several ways. First, infant attachment and adult romantic love share common features such as intense fascination with the other, distress at separation, and efforts to maintain proximity and to spend time together. Second, adult romantic attachments are similar in form to the three types of infant attachment. That is, adults' styles of romantic involvement can be secure, avoidant, or anxious/ambivalent. Third, like infant attachments, adult romantic bonds are believed to have a biological origin. "Romantic love is a biological process designed by evolution to facilitate attachment between adult sexual partners who, at the time love evolved, were likely to become parents of an infant who would need reliable care" (Hazan & Shaver, 1987, p. 423). Finally, a child's earliest love relationships with parents may influence the way he or she approaches romantic involvements in adulthood.

Hazan and Shaver have found that adults' romantic experiences can be categorized into the same three types described for attachment in infancy. In fact, the proportion of adults classified into each of the three attachment types was remarkably similar to the proportion of infants typically found in each group:

☐ *Secure adults.* Adults were said to have "secure" romantic attachments if they described themselves as finding it relatively easy to get close to others and said they seldom worry about being abandoned. About 56 percent of the adults tested were in the secure group. Secure adults tended to describe their most important actual love relationship as especially happy, friendly, and trusting. Secure adults were also more likely than others to describe their parents in positive terms— as caring, fair, affectionate, and having a good marriage.

☐ *Avoidant adults.* "Avoidant" adults (roughly 24 percent of those tested) reported being somewhat uncomfortable getting close to others or trusting a romantic partner completely. In describing their most important love relationship, avoidant lovers reported emotional highs and lows, jealousy, and fear of intimacy. Compared to secure adults, avoidant adults tended to describe their parents as more demanding, critical, and uncaring.

☐ *Anxious/ambivalent adults.* Finally, those adults (20 percent) who seek intimacy, but worry that others won't reciprocate their love and won't stay with them were called "anxious/ambivalent." The anxious/ambivalent respondents described their most important love relationship as involving obsession, desire for reciprocation and union, emotional highs and lows, and extreme sexual attraction and jealousy. Compared to secure adults, anxious/ambivalent respondents tended to describe their parents as more intrusive and demanding, and their parents' marriage as unhappy.

At present, these findings must be viewed as tentative. But they do raise the fascinating possibility that there are continuities between the emotional bonds we experience in childhood and the attachments we form in adult love relationships (Shaver, Hazan, & Bradshaw, 1988).

LONELINESS

Few people escape the misery of loneliness. As a child, you may have felt lonely when you started in a new school, moved to a new town, or went away to summer camp. As a young adult, you may have suffered the loneliness that follows breaking up with someone you once loved. Life is filled with social transitions that disrupt personal relationships and set the stage for loneliness.

Loneliness Versus Aloneness

Loneliness and aloneness are not the same. **Loneliness** refers to the subjective discomfort we feel when our social relations lack some important feature. This deficit may be quantitative: we may have no friends, or fewer friends than we want. Or the deficit may be qualitative: we may feel that our relationships are superficial, or less satisfying than we would like. Loneliness goes on inside a person and cannot be detected simply by looking at someone.

In contrast to subjective feelings of loneliness, aloneness is the objective state of being apart from other people. Aloneness can be pleasant or unpleasant. If you are stranded on a dark street with a stalled car, being by yourself may be distressing. But solitude can also offer many rewards (Suedfeld, 1982). Religious leaders go off on solitary quests to seek spiritual inspiration. Writers and musicians frequently do their best work alone, away from the distractions of social interaction. In daily life, we may crave time alone to study for an important test, read a good book, or think over a problem. Even living alone can be a positive experience that provides a sense of accomplishment and independence.

There is no inevitable link between aloneness and loneliness: we can be happy alone or lonely in a crowd. Nonetheless, people are somewhat more likely to feel lonely when they are alone. A study of how people spend their time found that people felt lonelier when they were alone than when they were with others (Larson et al., 1982). For teenagers, this pattern resulted primarily from being alone on Friday or Saturday night. Adolescents did not feel particularly lonely if they were alone during the week while shopping or studying. But being alone on a weekend evening when personal preference and social norms suggest you should be out with friends was a major impetus to loneliness.

The Experience of Loneliness

In national surveys, roughly one American in four says he or she has felt "very lonely or remote from other people" in the past two weeks (e.g., Bradburn, 1969). Loneliness can range from fleeting twinges of discomfort to severe and persistent feelings of intense misery (Peplau & Perlman, 1982).

Sometimes loneliness is caused by a life change that takes us away from friends and intimate relationships. *Situational loneliness* occurs when a person has had satisfying relationships until some specific change takes place in his or her life. Situations that commonly cause loneliness include moving to a new town, going away to school, starting a new job, being separated from friends and loved ones while on a trip or in the hospital, or ending an important relationship through death, divorce, or breaking up. People usually recover from situational loneliness and reestablish a satisfying social life, although this is obviously more difficult in some situations than in others. We may make friends at our new job in a few months, but take a year or more to get over the ending of a love relationship.

Some people suffer from loneliness for many years, more or less independent of changes in their lives. They are experiencing *chronic loneliness*. Such individuals might describe themselves as a "lonely person," rather than someone who is in a lonely period of life. Perhaps 10

The misery of time alone is seen in this young man's sense of loneliness and rejection. The pleasures of time alone are seen in this young woman's romp at the beach.

percent of American adults suffer from severe and persistent loneliness.

Robert Weiss (1973) has distinguished two types of loneliness, based on the specific social provisions that a person lacks. *Emotional loneliness* results from the absence of an intimate attachment figure, such as might be provided for children by their parents or for adults by a spouse or intimate friend. *Social loneliness* occurs when a person lacks the sense of social integration or community that might be provided by a network of friends or co-workers.

It is possible to experience one type of loneliness without the other. Young newlyweds who move to Alaska to seek adventure may not feel emotional loneliness—they have each other. But they are likely to experience social loneliness until they make friends and develop a sense of belonging to their new community. A widow may feel intense emotional loneliness after the death of her husband, but continue to have many social ties to family and friends.

Who Is at Risk for Loneliness?

No segment of society is immune to loneliness, but some people are at greater risk than others (Peplau & Perlman, 1982). Certain childhood experiences may predispose individuals to loneliness. Phillip Shaver (1986) has used infant-parent attachment theory to predict that adults will be less vulnerable to loneliness if they were securely attached to their parents during childhood. Two recent studies by Shaver have provided preliminary support for this idea. Other research, presented in Box 9–4, suggests that children of divorce may be at greater risk for loneliness as adults than are children from intact families.

Other factors also affect the risk of loneliness. Married people are less likely to feel lonely than others. It is interesting to note, however, that some married people—18 percent in one study—do feel lonely. Married people might be lonely because their marriage is not personally satisfying or because they lack friends and associates outside the marriage. Loneliness is more common among the poor than the affluent. Good relationships are easier to maintain when people have the time and money for leisure activities.

Loneliness is also related to age. Stereotypes depict old age as a time of great loneliness. But research shows that loneliness is highest among teenagers and young adults, and lowest among older people. In one large survey, 79 percent of people under age 18 said they were sometimes or often lonely, compared to only 53 percent of those 45 to 54, and 37 percent of those 55 and over (Parlee, 1979). Researchers have not yet determined the reason for this age pattern. In part, there may be a "generation gap," with young people being more willing to talk about their feelings and acknowledge loneliness than are older adults. It is also true, however, that young people face a great many social transitions, such as leaving home, living on their own, going to college, or taking a first full-time job—all of which can cause loneliness. As people get older, their social lives may become more stable. Age may also bring greater social skills and more realistic expectations about social relations.

Several personality factors have been linked to loneliness (Peplau & Perlman, 1982). Lonely people tend to be more introverted and shy, more self-conscious, and less assertive (Jones, Briggs, & Smith, 1986). Lonely people often have low self-esteem and, in some cases, poor social skills (Jones, Carpenter, & Quitana, 1985). Loneliness is also associated with anxiety and depression. Several of these personality factors can be both a cause and a consequence of loneliness. For example, people with low self-esteem may be less willing to take risks in social settings. This could make it harder for them to form friendships and thereby increase their chances of loneliness. On the other hand, the experience of being lonely for a long time may lead a person to see himself or herself as a social failure and to suffer a drop in the person's self-esteem.

BOX 9-4

Children of Divorce

Divorce, once an unusual event, is now common, and most divorces today involve families with children. Divorce affected less than 15 percent of children born in 1955. Today, that percentage has doubled. It has been estimated that a third of the children born in the 1980s will experience a parental divorce before they reach age 18. Researchers are only beginning to understand the many ways that divorce can affect children (Guidubaldi, Perry, & Nastasi, 1987). One possibility is that children of divorce may be more vulnerable to loneliness as they become adults.

In a large survey of Americans, Carin Rubenstein and Phillip Shaver (1982) found that adults whose parents had divorced were more likely to feel lonely, especially if the divorce occurred before the person was 6 years old. Perhaps surprisingly, the death of a parent during childhood was not related to adult loneliness. To explain these findings, Shaver and Rubenstein (1980) turned to the work on parent-child attachment discussed in this chapter. They suggested that the loss of a parental attachment relationship through divorce influences children in two major ways.

First, children often blame themselves for the divorce. Although it is an irrational belief, many children think that they have in some way caused their parents' marriage to end. This tendency seems especially strong among preschool children, whose cognitive development is immature and self-focused (Wallerstein & Kelly, 1975). If children are older at the time of the divorce, they are usually better able to understand that the divorce was not their fault. The legacy of this self-blame can be persistent low self-esteem—an enduring belief that one is unlovable and unworthy of affection. Studies of adults show a clear link between low self-esteem and loneliness (Peplau & Perlman, 1982). The person who lacks self-confidence may be less willing to take risks in social situations and may subtly communicate a sense of worthlessness to others. This, in turn, may set the stage for poor social relationships and for loneliness.

Second, Rubenstein and Shaver speculate that children of divorce may come to see other people as rejecting and unreliable. If a child perceives a parent as unresponsive or frustrating, the child may develop a more generalized view of people as untrustworthy and of relationships as undependable. Such a "model" or image of relationships established in childhood may persist into adulthood, making it harder for the individual to form rewarding relationships. Consistent with this idea are data showing that children of divorce have more negative and less trusting views of other people (Shaver & Rubenstein, 1980). This problem may be greater for children of divorce than for children whose parents die. In divorce, children usually continue to see the noncustodial parent and may regard each visit as an opportunity to entice the parent to return. When the parent leaves at the end of the visit, the child may perceive that he or she has been rejected still again.

The possibility that childhood experiences in the family influence loneliness in adulthood is intriguing, and an important topic for additional research. We should be cautious, however, not to overstate the impact of childhood events on later loneliness. Many children of divorce have gone on to create close and satisfying relationships as adults. Greater awareness about the potential effects of divorce may enable divorcing parents to help their children cope more effectively with this major life transition.

Loneliness and the Transition to College

For many people, the social challenges of going to college create feelings of loneliness. The excitement of beginning college is mixed with the temporary loneliness of leaving friends and family, and with anxiety about building a new social life. One student commented:

> Coming to a large university such as this was a big change for me. After being voted in school "Best Personality" and "Most Popular," I had to start over. Seeing nothing but strangers was rather difficult at first, but I find myself getting used to it.

To learn about the social transition of going to college, Carolyn Cutrona, Daniel Russell, and Anne Peplau conducted a study of entering students at UCLA. Participants in the study were contacted during their first few weeks on campus and then seven months later in the spring (Cutrona, 1982).

At the start of the school year, 75 percent of new students had experienced at least occasional loneliness since their arrival on campus. More than 40 percent reported that their loneliness had been moderate to severe in intensity. Fortunately, most students were able to cope successfully with the adjustment to college. By spring, only 25 percent were still lonely.

How did students who overcame their loneliness differ from those who remained lonely throughout their first year of college? The most striking difference was found in their attitudes. Students were more likely to recover from loneliness if they began the school year with positive expectations that they would be successful in making friends and if they felt good about themselves and their personality. In other words, optimism and high self-esteem were significant ingredients in creating a satisfying social life at college.

Successful and unsuccessful students reported about the same frequency of such activities as joining clubs, playing intramural sports, going to parties, or talking to strangers in classes. Both groups were also equally likely to report efforts to improve their appearance and social skills or to find new ways to meet people. Students living at home with parents were no more lonely than students living in a dorm on campus.

But there may be more subtle differences in the behavior of students who do and do not recover from loneliness. One study found that lonely college students interacted in a more self-focused way than did the nonlonely (Jones, 1982). In a conversation with a new acquaintance, lonely students asked fewer questions about the other person, made fewer statements focusing on the other, and responded more slowly to comments by the partner. Lonely people tended to be more negativistic and self-absorbed and were less responsive to others. Other research suggests that lonely college students may also differ in their patterns of self-disclosure, either pouring out their heart to someone they've just met or revealing unusually little about themselves (Solano, Batten, & Parish, 1982). These inappropriate disclosure levels may interfere with the development of close relationships.

Key Terms

association	**halo effect**	**reinforcement**
attachment	**jealousy**	**self-monitoring**
balance theory	**loneliness**	**social comparison theory**
cognitive dissonance	**matching principle**	**social exchange theory**
companionate love	**mere exposure effect**	
expectancy value theory	**passionate love**	

Summary

1. The tendency to affiliate begins in childhood, when infants form strong attachments to the significant adults in their lives. Hazan and Shaver have recently analyzed adult love relationships in terms of attachment theory.

2. Adults have diverse social needs. Laboratory experiments have shown that affiliative tendencies are increased when people are afraid or uncertain. Weiss and others have attempted to classify specific social needs, such as needs for attachment, for social integration, and for guidance.

3. In general, we like people who reward us and who help us to satisfy our needs. Three important principles affecting interpersonal attraction are association, reinforcement, and social exchange.

4. People differ in the qualities they most value in others. In general, we tend to like people who are sincere, warm, competent, and physically attractive. Being seen with a beautiful date or friend may have a "radiating effect," causing others to evaluate us more favorably. Sometimes, however, being associated with a very attractive stranger leads to a "contrast effect": a person of average attractiveness suffers by comparison with a particularly beautiful other.

5. We tend to like people who are similar to us in attitudes, values, interests, background, and personality. In dating and marriage, the tendency to select similar partners is called the "matching principle." The importance of similarity can be explained in terms of rewards, cognitive consistency, and the expectancy-value theory of decision making.

6. Familiarity also enhances liking; this is known as the mere exposure effect. If a person or object is initially evaluated as neutral or mildly positive, repeated exposure usually increases liking.

7. A final factor in attraction is proximity. People who are physically close to us tend to be more familiar and are often, coincidentally, similar to us in background or interests. Social exchange theory suggests that people close by are more easily available for interaction, and so the costs of a relationship are usually less. According to cognitive balance theory, we may experience psychological pressure to like those with whom we must interact.

8. Psychological research on romantic love is relatively new. Rubin has shown that liking and love are qualitatively distinct. Although the two often go together, it is possible to like someone a lot without loving them, and to love a person without fully liking them.

9. Theorists have distinguished between passionate love (the exciting and emotionally charged experience some people have early in a love relationship) and companionate love (the deep affection, trust, and caring a person feels for a long term partner).

10. Loneliness is the subjective discomfort we feel when our social relations are lacking in some important way. Loneliness can range from a temporary state resulting from a change in our social life to a chronic and enduring condition. Emotional loneliness is caused by the lack of an attachment relationship; social loneliness is caused by the lack of social integration.

Suggested Readings

Brehm, S. S. (1985). *Intimate relationships.* New York: Random House. A well-written undergraduate textbook that provides an excellent introduction to the field.

Burns, D. D. (1985). *Intimate connections.* New York: William A. Morrow. A detailed and very readable presentation of a cognitive-behavioral approach to helping lonely individuals.

Hatfield, E. & Sprecher, S. (1986). *Mirror, mirror . . . The importance of looks in everyday life.* Albany: State University of New York Press. A lively paperback that explores the many ways in which physical attractiveness influences us from childhood through old age.

Hendrick, C. (Ed.) (1989). *Close relationships.* Newbury Park, CA: Sage Publications. An excellent up-to-date anthology with articles by professionals on such topics as closeness, communication, trust, jealousy, and friendship.

Peplau, L. A., & Perlman, D. (Eds.). (1982). *Loneliness: A sourcebook of current theory, research, and therapy.* New York: Wiley-Interscience. A survey of research findings and theories.

Rubin, Z. (1980). *Children's friendships.* Cambridge, MA: Harvard University Press. A delightful paperback about how young children learn to be friends.

Sternberg, R. J., & Barnes, M. (Eds.). (1988). *The psychology of love.* New Haven, CT: Yale University Press. Leading experts present the latest research and theories about love.

TEN

Behavior in Groups

BEHAVIOR IN THE PRESENCE OF OTHERS

IDENTITY IN GROUP CONTEXTS

BASIC FEATURES OF GROUPS

TASK PERFORMANCE IN GROUPS

COMPETITION VERSUS COOPERATION

LEADERSHIP

We are all members of groups that have enormous influence on our lives. Most of us are born into a family group and spend much of our childhood interacting with parents and siblings. As we venture into the larger social world, we encounter new groups—perhaps a neighborhood play group, a kindergarten class, Cub Scouts or Brownies, or a group at a church or a synagogue. As we grow up, we begin to join clubs, sports teams, work groups, political parties, and other organizations.

In this chapter, we begin by considering how the mere presence of other people affects our behavior. Then, we examine two ways in which social groups can affect the self, through processes of social identity and deindividuation. Next, we define the nature of groups and explore some of the basic processes of group interaction, including communication, decision making, and competition versus cooperation. We conclude by investigating the topic of leadership in groups.

BEHAVIOR IN THE PRESENCE OF OTHERS

How does the presence of other people influence an individual's performance on a task? Consider two examples. John is an outstanding high school runner who hopes one day to try out for the Olympics. He trains very hard, and notices that he runs better with a training partner than by himself. His best performances have been during actual track meets where he was running against tough competition. Susan is taking her first class in acting. At home in the privacy of her bedroom, she delivers her lines with accuracy and self-confidence. But in front of her classmates, she stumbles over her part. As these examples suggest, the presence of others sometimes enhances and sometimes impairs an individual's performance.

Social Facilitation

People sometimes perform better in the presence of others than when they are alone. This is called **social facilitation.** Social psychologists have long been fascinated by this phenomenon. Indeed, experimentation in social psychology is often traced to an experiment on social facilitation conducted by Triplett in 1898. Triplett observed that cyclists seem to race faster when they are in competition than when they are alone. To test this observation, he devised an experiment to see whether children would work harder pulling in a fishing line in a group setting than alone. As predicted, the children worked harder in the presence of others.

Many studies have demonstrated this effect (see review by Guerin, 1986). In the 1920s, for example, Allport (1920, 1924) had subjects work on such tasks as crossing out all the vowels in a newspaper column, doing easy multiplication problems, or writing refutations of a logical argument. Even though participants always worked individually on the task, they were more productive when there were five other people in the room than when they were alone. Social facilitation has been found when the others who are present are actually performing the same task (are "co-actors") and when the other person is an observer or experimenter. Social facilitation is not limited to humans. It has also been demonstrated in rats, cockroaches, and parakeets. For instance, Chen (1937) found that individual ants dug three times more sand when they were in groups than when they were alone.

On the other hand, the presence of others sometimes inhibits individual performance, as suggested by the example of Susan who could recite her lines flawlessly alone, but stumbled over her words in public. This is called the *social inhibition* of performance. In Allport's early studies (1924), people in a group setting wrote more refutations of a logical argument, but the quality of the work was lower than when they worked alone. Another study found that the presence of a spectator reduced individual performance on a memory task (Pessin, 1933). Why does this happen?

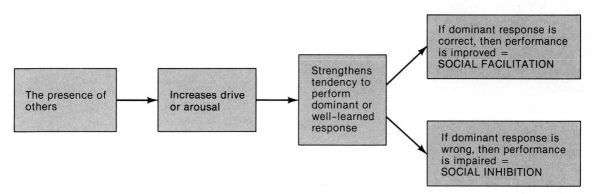

Figure 10–1. How the presence of others affects performance: Social facilitation versus inhibition.

A major answer was offered by Robert Zajonc (1965) and is presented in Figure 10–1. Zajonc suggested that being in the presence of others increases an individual's drive or motivation. Whether this increased drive facilitates or interferes with performance depends on the task. When a task requires a response that is well-learned or innate, called a *dominant response,* increased motivation is helpful. Therefore, the presence of others facilitates performance on relatively simple tasks, such as crossing out vowels or doing easy arithmetic. Similarly, for a highly trained athlete, the presence of others is likely to improve performance. But when a task requires behavior that is complex or poorly-learned, then the increased motivation of having others present impairs performance. Examples would be solving difficult arithmetic problems, memorizing new material, or writing complex logical deductions. For Susan, struggling to remember her lines, an audience may simply increase her stage fright and inhibit a good performance. If she were more experienced and had performed the part every night for months, the audience might improve her performance. In summary, when a dominant or well-learned response is involved, heightened motivation improves performance, and this is more likely to occur for simple rather than complex tasks.

Research has generally supported the basic idea that the effect of the presence of others depends on the kind of task. An interesting illustration comes from an observational study of the behavior of people playing pool in a college

student union building (Michaels et al., 1982). The researchers identified pairs of players who were either above or below average in their play and secretly recorded their scores. Then, teams of four confederates approached the players and watched them closely during several more rounds of play. Zajonc's theory predicts that good players will benefit from an audience, but poor players will not. The results provide clear support for this prediction. When good players were being watched by four others, their accuracy rose from 71 to 80 percent. When poor players were being watched, their accuracy dropped from 36 to 25 percent.

Although there is general agreement that the presence of others increases individual drive or motivation, there is considerable controversy about the nature of the motivation (Geen & Bushman, 1987; Geen, 1989). Zajonc suggested that there is a fairly simple, innate tendency to become aroused by the mere presence of others.

A second view is that others motivate us because we have learned to be concerned about looking good in public—an effect known as **evaluation apprehension.** It is not the mere presence of other people that matters, but rather the belief that others are evaluating the quality of our performance. On simple tasks, an awareness that we are being evaluated can spur us to greater effort. But on complex tasks, the pressure of being evaluated may be detrimental.

A third view is that the presence of others is distracting. On easy tasks that do not require full attention, we may compensate for the distraction by trying harder and may actually perform better. But the distraction created by other people works in reverse on complex tasks. A recent extension of this idea is the *distraction-conflict model* (Baron, 1986), which suggests that the presence of others is arousing because it creates a conflict between two basic tendencies—(1) to pay attention to the audience and (2) to pay attention to the task. This conflict increases arousal, which then either helps or hinders task performance, depending on whether the dominant response is correct. These explanations are not necessarily contradictory: it is possible that all these processes can affect human performance, depending on the situation.

Social Loafing

Social facilitation highlights the point that the presence of others can sometimes motivate individuals and spur them to greater efforts. But the opposite pattern can also be found: sometimes individuals work less hard in the presence of others then they would alone. This effect, known as **social loafing,** was first discussed in the late 1880s by a French agricultural engineer named Max Ringelmann (Kravitz & Martin, 1986).

As part of a study of work efficiency in horses, oxen, and men, Ringelmann asked student volunteers to pull as hard as they could on a rope. He measured their effort in kilograms of pressure using a strain gauge. Sometimes the participants worked alone and sometimes in groups of 7 or 14 people. Common sense and research on social facilitation might predict that the men would work harder when they were part of a team than when they were alone. Just the opposite happened. When pulling alone, individuals averaged about 85 kg per person. In groups of 7, the total group force was only 65 kg per person, and in the largest groups, each individual's contribution fell to 61 kg.

More recent studies by Latané and his colleagues (Latané, Williams, & Harkins, 1979) have provided further evidence about social loafing. In one study, undergraduate men were asked to make as much noise as they could by cheering or by clapping. Each person performed alone, in pairs, in groups of four, and in groups of six. The results, presented in Figure 10–2, clearly show that the noise produced by each

As the number of workers in a group increases, so does the tendency toward loafing on the job.

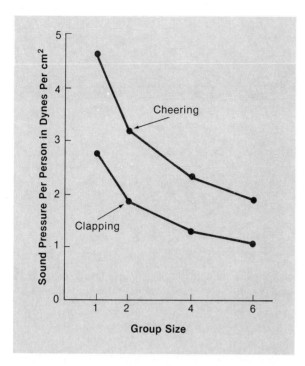

Figure 10–2. A comparison of the intensity of noise an individual makes alone and in groups. (Adapted from Latané, Williams & Harkins, 1979, p. 825.)

individual decreased as the size of the group increased. This is the same pattern Ringelmann found. More recent studies show that social loafing can occur not only on physical tasks, such as clapping or shouting, but also on intellectual tasks (Weldon & Gargano, 1988).

Why does social loafing occur? Social evaluation appears to be a key factor. Working in a group leads to a relaxation of effort when individuals believe that their own work will be "lost in the crowd"—that no one will know how well they performed and that they cannot be held responsible for their individual actions (Harkins & Szymanski, 1987, 1989). Apparently, people tend to slack off when working in a group provides anonymity. The antidote to social loafing is to make each individual's contribution identifiable. If people believe that their contribution can be evaluated by the researcher, or if subjects are given an opportunity to evaluate themselves, social loafing can be eliminated.

Other factors also influence social loafing. For instance, social loafing is less likely to occur on complex tasks than on simple ones. When the task is difficult or challenging, individuals are less likely to slack off (Jackson & Williams, 1985). Providing rewards for high group productivity can also reduce social loafing. In one study, some students were told they could leave an experiment early if their group generated many solutions to a problem; other students were given the same problem-solving task but were not offered the incentive of leaving early (Shepperd & Wright, 1989). In this case, the anticipation of a reward for high effort counteracted the social loafing effect.

In summary, we have seen that the presence of others sometimes leads to social facilitation and sometimes causes social loafing (Harkins, 1987). Working in the presence of others can spur us to greater effort or lull us into complacency about our individual efforts. Which effect occurs depends on the complexity of the task at hand. It also depends on whether the group context increases our concerns about social evaluation (because others are judging our performance) or reduces social evaluation concerns (because our individual effort is hidden by working in a group).

Social Impact Theory

Our discussion so far has concerned the question of when the presence of others has positive or negative effects on individual performance. **Social impact theory** addresses the more general issue of how strong an influence (either positive or negative) these others have. As developed by Latané (1981), this theory suggests that the total impact of other people on an individual depends on the characteristics of the observers or source of influence: their number, strength, and immediacy.

As the number of observers increases, so does their impact. To return to the earlier example of our fledgling actress Susan learning lines for a play, the impact of the audience should increase with the number of people present. Susan should experience more stage fright performing in front of 50 people than 5.

Another factor is the *strength* of the social forces, that is, the importance or power of the observers. Strength is determined by such things as status, age, and the relationship between the individual and those others. Susan might feel significantly worse about performing in front of her teacher or a casting director than in front of her friends.

The third factor is the *immediacy* of the audience, their closeness to the individual in time or space. Susan's reactions should be stronger if she has a live audience than if she is being watched on a video monitor located in another room (Borden, 1980). Latané suggests that social impact can be compared to light falling on a surface: the total amount of light depends on the number of light bulbs, the wattage of the bulbs, and their closeness to the surface. Figure 10–3 illustrates a situation in which a group of people (sources) are influencing a single individual (target).

Latané believes that social impact theory can help explain why the presence of others sometimes leads to social facilitation and sometimes causes social loafing. Latané proposes that these patterns occur in different situations. In facilitation situations, the person is the sole target of

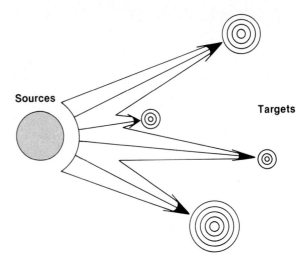

Figure 10–4. When each individual is only one of several targets of social influence, the impact of the audience on the target is lessened. (Adapted from Latané, 1981, p. 349.)

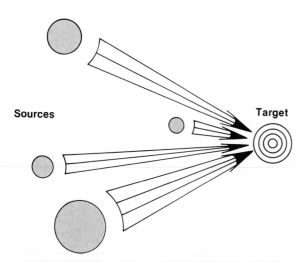

Figure 10–3. The impact of an audience on a target depends on the number of people present (number of circles or "sources"), the immediacy of the people (nearness of the circles to the target), and the strength or importance of the people (size of the circles). (Adapted from Latané, 1981, p. 344.)

influence from an audience or from co-workers (as shown in Figure 10–3). The social impact of the others is all directed at the single individual; as the number of people present increases, their social impact on the individual also increases. In contrast, social loafing situations occur when several group members work together on a task assigned by an outsider. As shown in Figure 10–4, each individual is only one of several targets of forces coming from outside the group. Consequently, the social impact of the outsider is divided among group members. As the size of the group increases, the pressure felt by each individual decreases.

Social impact theory is still relatively new and controversial (Jackson, 1987; Mullen, 1985, 1986). To date, empirical evidence has supported predictions about the impact of group size. The larger the group or audience, the more impact it has on an individual's performance. However, evidence about the importance of strength and immediacy is not clear at this point. Put in broader context, social impact theory illustrates a major goal in theory development—to create theories that can explain diverse social phenomena within a single set of unified principles.

IDENTITY IN GROUP CONTEXTS

Our sense of self is intimately linked to social groups. On the one hand, our identification with social groups defines who we are in important ways. When asked to answer the question "Who am I?" people typically refer to social groups. One person might explain that she is a woman, a Catholic, a Canadian, and a school teacher. Another person might say that he is a conservative Jew, a New Yorker, and a member of the Republican party. Most of the time, groups provide a sense of meaning and identity for our lives. On the other hand, people occasionally seem to lose themselves in a group and find that the anonymity of a group can weaken their sense of individual identity. In this section, we consider the widespread importance of social identity, and the intriguing case of deindividuation.

Social Identity

Today, one of the most active research areas in the social psychology of groups concerns the nature of social identity (Hogg & Abrams, 1988; Turner, 1985). **Social identity theory** recognizes that we humans have a basic tendency to group people into various social categories, a process we introduced in Chapter 2 on person perception. From the wide array of dimensions that could be used to categorize people such as foot size or age of toilet training, some dimensions are perceived as more meaningful in particular social contexts. In Northern Ireland, the categories of Catholic and Protestant are especially salient. On college campuses, the distinction between men who do and don't belong to fraternities may be prominent. In general, categories based on sex, age, ethnicity, occupation, and religion are often salient.

The social identity perspective emphasizes the psychological importance of identification with groups (Tajfel, 1982; Turner, 1985). We first mentioned this idea in our discussion of the importance of **reference groups** in forming and changing a person's attitudes (see Chapter 6). The key idea there was that people's attitudes are strongly influenced by the opinions and behavior patterns of groups with which they identify.

A person's self-concept is also affected by identification with groups. As shown in Figure 10–5, the self-concept is comprised of a set of self-categorizations, some based on unique personal characteristics of the individual and some based on membership in broad social categories and groups. Figure 10–5 shows that the self-concept is a mix of both personal and social identities. In any particular social situation, some identities will be more salient than others.

Another basic idea in social identity theory is that people are motivated to maintain or enhance their self-esteem and self-image. We feel proud when a group we identify with is successful, whether that group is a sports team, a political party, or a nation. This was illustrated in a study of college football fans (Cialdini et al., 1976). The day after their team was victorious,

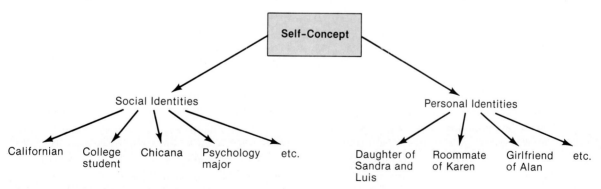

Figure 10–5. The self-concept is made up of social identities based on group affiliations and personal identities based on one's unique individual characteristics.

Belonging to a group can be a meaningful experience that is central to personal identity.

students were more likely to show their pride in the college by wearing school sweaters and scarves than on a day following a defeat.

Social comparison processes are also important. We enhance our self-esteem by evaluating groups to which we belong (ingroups) more favorably than other groups (outgroups). Much research has documented this ingroup favoritism effect (Brewer, 1979). It's comforting to bask in the reflected glory of belonging to a group that is more powerful, important, or successful than other groups. Social identity theory highlights the psychological attachment that people feel toward groups and the ways in which group membership affects one's self-concept. We will explore the social identity perspective in more detail in Chapter 13 on prejudice when we consider its application to such topics as racial discrimination and conflict between groups.

Deindividuation

Sometimes, people in groups seem to lose their sense of personal identity, and to behave in violent and antisocial ways that they would not do individually. In 1931, a young black man, accused of raping a white woman, was being held in a southern jail. There was no evidence against him except that he was in the general vicinity of the crime. A crowd gathered outside the jail and became more and more excited and enraged. Members of the crowd talked of lynching, and before long the crowd had turned into an angry mob. It rushed the jail, broke down the doors, and dragged the prisoner from his cell. He was tortured and killed in a sadistic orgy of violence.

How can we explain such seemingly irrational and destructive group behavior? In 1896 Le Bon suggested that in a mob, the emotions of one person spread through the group. When one person does something, even if it would ordinarily be unacceptable to most of the others, everyone else tends to do it also. Le Bon (1896) called this *social contagion:* mob behavior is infectious, like a cold spreading through members of a school classroom. Le Bon explained social contagion in terms of a breakdown of normal control mechanisms. Our actions are usually controlled by our values and ethics, and the social rules we have learned. In groups, we sometimes lose a sense of responsibility for our own actions; we feel that the group is responsible. Our own control system is weakened and so primitive aggressive and sexual impulses are free to be expressed. This can result in violent, immoral acts.

Social psychologists have translated these ideas into more modern terms (Festinger, Pepitone, & Newcomb, 1952; Zimbardo, 1970). They propose that people in groups sometimes experience **deindividuation.** Personal identity is replaced by an identification with the goals and actions of the group. The individual becomes less aware of his or her own personal values and behavior, and instead focuses on the group and the situation (Diener, 1980). Deindividuation involves a loss of personal responsibility, as well as heightened sensitivity to what the group is doing. In a sense, each person in the group thinks of his or her own actions as being part of the *group's* behavior. This causes people to feel less responsible for their own actions and less concerned about the consequences. And it can set the stage for antisocial acts, if the group favors such actions.

A key factor in deindividuation is anonymity. Anything that makes members of a group less personally identifiable should increase the effect. The more anonymous the group members are, the less they feel they have an identity of their own and the less likely they are to be held accountable for their acts, the more irresponsibly they may behave. In a mob, most of the people do not stand out as individuals. They blend together and, in a sense, do not have an identity of their own. Conversely, to the extent that they know they are identifiable, they retain their feelings of individuality and are less likely to act irresponsibly.

An experiment by Zimbardo (1970) illustrates the deindividuation effect. Groups of four young women were recruited to take part in a study supposedly involving empathic responses to strangers. In one condition, participants were greeted by name, wore name tags, and were easily identifiable. In another condition, subjects wore oversized white lab coats and hoods, were never called by name, and were difficult to identify. All the groups were given an opportunity to deliver electric shocks to a person not in the group. (In fact, the shocks were fake and the "victim" was a confederate.) The subjects who were not identifiable gave almost twice as many shocks as the others. Apparently being less identifiable produced a marked increase in aggression, supporting the idea that loss of individuality is one cause of the violence and antisocial behavior sometimes exhibited by groups.

A naturalistic demonstration of the deindividuation effect involved children who were trick-or-treating on Halloween. In this study (Diener et al., 1976), the researchers stationed themselves in homes in the neighborhood. When children arrived at the door, some were asked their names by the adults in the homes, and others were not. Then the children were all given an opportunity to steal extra candy when the adult was not present. Those children who had been asked their names were less likely to steal, even though the chances of being caught were virtually zero in all cases.

Johnson and Downing (1979) have pointed out that in almost all the research, subjects have worn disguises or masks that have negative implications. Zimbardo used Ku Klux Klan outfits; most Halloween masks are of monsters or ghosts. Perhaps it is not the anonymity that increases the violation of norms, but the kind of disguise. To test this, anonymity was produced by having people wear Ku Klux Klan outfits or nurses' outfits consisting of white hats and coats. Those wearing outfits were compared to others wearing normal clothing. It was found that the Ku Klux Klan outfit had only a slight

A cross-burning ceremony of the Ku Klux Klan. The anonymity of a hooded uniform can lead to deindividuation.

effect on the level of shock subjects gave (thus not replicating Zimbardo's results). Perhaps more important, the nurses' uniforms actually reduced the number of shocks given. Although anonymity sometimes produces increased aggression, these results indicate that people are influenced by the social context—in this case by the type of uniform they wore. If the uniform implies positive, prosocial behavior, the wearer may behave accordingly.

The critical factor in deindividuation is not membership in a group, but rather anonymity and reduced self-awareness (Diener, 1980). There is no evidence that simply being in a group produces deindividuation or increases antisocial behavior. For example, Diener (1976) observed young adults in a situation in which they were free to act aggressively toward someone who would not harm them in any way. In all conditions, the subjects first observed someone else acting aggressively toward the "victim" and thus had a model to imitate. Yet subjects who were alone with the victim were actually more aggressive than those who were in a group. In this case, being in a group *decreased* aggressiveness. Being in a group leads to deindividuation only when the group provides anonymity (which means that a person cannot be held responsible for their actions) and directs the individual's focus away from the self and toward the actions of the group.

BASIC FEATURES OF GROUPS

Defining a Group

We spend time in many different kinds of social units, not all of which qualify as groups. Table 10–1 provides some common examples, including being part of an audience or crowd. In everyday language we often speak of all social units "groups." But social scientists typically use the term group in a narrower, more technical way. In a **group,** people are *interdependent* and have at least the potential for mutual *interaction*. In most groups, members have regular face-to-face contact. This definition of a group is

an extension of the basic definition of an interpersonal relationship given in Chapter 7. The definition emphasizes that the essential feature of a group is that members influence one another in some way.

Based on this definition, a social category such as all professional football players does not comprise a group, since the people in this category do not know one another, have face-to-face contact, or influence one another directly. However, the members of the Dallas Cowboys football team are a group because they interact regularly and their actions affect one another. Similarly, all the children who watch "Sesame Street" on television are part of a common audience, but they are not a group. However, all the children in Mrs. Asawa's second-grade class are part of a group.

T A B L E   1 0 – 1
TYPES OF SOCIAL UNITS

For various purposes, it is useful to group people together into a variety of social units. Not all of these social aggregates meet the criteria for being a "group."

Social categories: We often group people together on the basis of a shared attribute. Examples of social categories are teenage boys, unemployed heads of household, lesbians, Sunday school teachers, and truck drivers. Members of social category all have some common characteristics, although they are not likely to know each other or to interact. As our discussion of social identity indicated, social categories often have considerable psychological importance for individuals.

Audience: All the people watching the 6 o'clock news on Channel 4 in New York City are part of the same audience, even though they are not necessarily aware of each other and do not interact.

Crowd: When people are in physical proximity to a common situation or stimulus, we call them a crowd. Examples are fans gathered outside a rock star's dressing room, people lining up outside a department store waiting for a special sale to begin, or people gathering to watch a street brawl.

Team: A set of people who interact regularly for some particular purpose or activity, such as a work group, sports team, or bridge club, make up a team.

Family: Although there are many types, families usually consist of a set of people who are related by birth or legal arrangements and who may share a common residence.

Formal organization: Larger aggregates of people often work together in some clearly structured way to accomplish a joint goal. Examples are a school system, a church or synagogue, or the National Rifle Association.

In climbing a dangerous ice glacier, the lives of these men are interlinked. Interdependence is a basic feature of all groups.

Groups vary in many ways: size, duration, values, goals, and scope. One of the most important dimensions is size. The smallest group is the dyad or couple. Most group research has focused on small groups ranging from about 3 to 20 people. As social aggregates get much larger, they tend to become formal organizations and may no longer involve knowledge and interaction among all members. To emphasize the distinctions, some researchers prefer the term "small group" for social units in which members have face-to-face interaction.

Groups differ widely in values and goals. Consider for a moment the differences among a chess club, the local Young Republicans group, the Gay and Lesbian Student Association, and a religious education class. Which, if any, of these groups you might consider joining depends a great deal on your own personal values, inter-

ests, and goals. Groups also vary in duration. Families may continue to exist for many generations, with new members joining the group through birth or marriage and others leaving through death or divorce. In contrast, members of a jury might work together for a few days on a particular case, and then be disbanded at the end of the trial.

The breadth or scope of activities performed by a group is another important dimension. Some groups focus on a single issue. For instance, in response to a threatened tuition increase, a group of college students might form a task force to formulate alternatives and present them to the school administration. Here, a group is created for one specific purpose. In contrast, groups such as families engage in a great many different activities.

Research on small groups has sometimes

studied naturally occurring groups such as families, teammates, or work groups. But there is also a long tradition of studying "concocted groups" (McGrath, 1984), groups deliberately created by a researcher. In a typical study, groups of strangers are brought together in a lab to spend a few hours working on a group decision-making task. We'll discuss the results of experimental studies on groups later in this chapter. For the moment, it is useful to note that whereas naturally occurring groups are often relatively enduring and broad in scope, most experimental groups are short-lived and relatively narrow in focus.

Group Structure

When people are brought together in a group, they do not remain entirely undifferentiated. They develop patterns of behavior, divide tasks, and adopt different roles (Brown, 1988). We refer to these patterns as the social structure of the group. For example, Merei (1949) observed that after three or more meetings, groups of young children formed traditions: they decided where each child would sit in the room, who could play with each toy, what sequence of activities would be followed, and so on. In informal groups such as this one, differentiated behavior patterns emerge over time as a result of group interaction.

Often, however, the basic structure of a group is predetermined. The student entering school, the worker taking a new job, and the person joining a bridge club are all confronted with a preexisting social structure. For example, in a small computer software business, there may be four distinct positions: the owner who created the business, the programmers who develop new software packages, a sales representative, and a secretary.

As we saw in our earlier discussion of social roles (Chapter 7), the positions in nearly any social system differ in *social status* (prestige or ranking). In the software company, the owner probably has the highest status and the largest salary; the secretary probably has the lowest status and salary. Associated with each position is a particular set of rules and understandings about what the person in that position is expected to do, what the responsibilities are, and so on. In technical terms, these rules and expectations are called **social norms.**

The cluster of norms that apply to people in a particular position, such as the programmer or secretary, constitutes their **social role.** Roles define the division of labor in the group. In some groups, such as the software company, positions, roles, and status are explicit and may even be described in a formal organizational chart. Individuals must adapt to the requirements of their position in the group, although they may try to redefine or renegotiate existing patterns.

Cohesiveness

In some groups, the bonds among members are strong and enduring. In other groups, members are loosely linked, lack a sense of "groupness," and tend to drift apart over time. **Cohesiveness** refers to the forces, both positive and negative, that cause members to remain in a group (Festinger, 1950). Cohesiveness is a characteristic of a group as a whole, based on the combined commitment of each group member.

A key positive force increasing cohesiveness is the interpersonal attraction that exists among group members (Ridgeway, 1983). When group members like each other and are connected by bonds of friendship, cohesiveness is high. Indeed, researchers have often measured cohesiveness by assessing the amount of liking among group members.

Second, people's motivation to remain in a group is also influenced by the instrumental goals of the group. We often participate in groups as a means to an end—a way to earn a salary, to play a sport we enjoy, to work for a worthy cause. So our attraction to a group depends on the match between our goals and those of the group, and also on how successfully the group accomplishes its objectives. This point was illustrated in a recent study. Synder, Lassgard, and Ford (1986) investigated how individuals react when they belong to a group (even one artificially constructed by researchers) that fails in performing a group task. Compared to people in successful groups, members of unsuccessful groups did more to "distance" themselves from the group, for example, by not wearing their team badge. Individuals apparently wanted to avoid identification with an unsuccessful group, a finding consistent with the social identity perspective.

A third positive factor affecting cohesiveness is the extent to which a group interacts effectively and harmoniously. We would undoubtedly prefer to be on a team that works effectively rather than on one that wastes our time and misuses our skills. More generally, anything that increases group satisfaction and morale should enhance cohesiveness.

Group cohesiveness is also affected by negative forces that discourage members from leaving, even if they are dissatisfied. Sometimes people stay in groups because the costs of leaving are high or because they have no available alternatives. We may despise our co-workers, but stay at the job because there are no other job openings in town. We may dislike our teachers, but stay in their classes because we have no choice in the matter.

Communication

Communication is essential to group activities, be it the endless talking at a committee meeting, or the shared intimacies of a late-night conversation among friends.

A feature of most groups is that some people talk a great deal and others say very little. In a seminar, for example, there usually seem to be one to two people who monopolize the discussion, regardless of the topic. They do most of the talking, and the rest say only an occasional word or two.

Perhaps the most striking aspect of this phenomenon is that it occurs no matter what the size of the group. Regardless of how many members there are, communication follows a fairly regular pattern that can be represented by a logarithmic function. Figure 10–6 illustrates this pattern for groups of four, six, and eight. Note that in all cases, one person does a great deal of talking, the next most talkative person

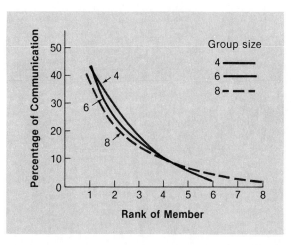

Figure 10–6. The amount of communication by members of a group follows a logarithmic or exponential curve. Regardless of the size of the group, the most talkative person does about 40 percent of the talking, and other group members talk much less. (Adapted from Stephan & Mishler, 1952, p. 603.)

talks considerably less, and so on. In an eight-member group, two people contribute 60 percent of the conversation, one contributes 14 percent, and the other five contribute only 26 percent among them. The exact percentage contributed by each person will vary from group to group. There are even some groups in which all members make equal contributions. But by and large, a pattern roughly similar to the one illustrated appears in most groups.

We have been discussing groups as though every member were free to communicate with every other member. This is true in a discussion group, but there are many groups in which communication is limited. Several studies have investigated the effects of a variety of so-called **communication networks.**

The typical study in this area consists of forming a group to work on some problem and imposing limits on the communication permitted among the members. This is done by putting the subjects in separate rooms or booths and allowing them to communicate only by written messages or an intercom system. The experimenters are then able to control who can talk with whom, and a large number of different communication patterns can be imposed.

Some of these patterns are represented for groups of five people in Figure 10–7. You can

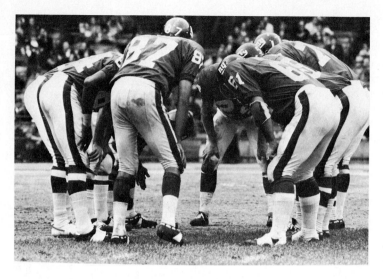

In this football huddle, the quarterback gives teammates instructions for the next play. This illustrates a wheel communication network in which messages are channeled through one person.

see that the structures determine freedom of communication. In the circle, all members are equal—each can talk to two neighbors and to no one else. In the chain, two of the members can each talk to only one person. Obviously, in terms of communication it is worse to be at the end of a chain. The three other members are equal in terms of the number of people they can talk to, but the person in the middle is more central. The two intermediate people are somewhat isolated from the opposite ends. This progression is carried a step further in the Y-shaped structure. With three end members, only one of the others is able to talk to two people, and the fifth member is able to talk to three. In the wheel, one member can talk to everyone else, but all the other members can talk only to the central one.

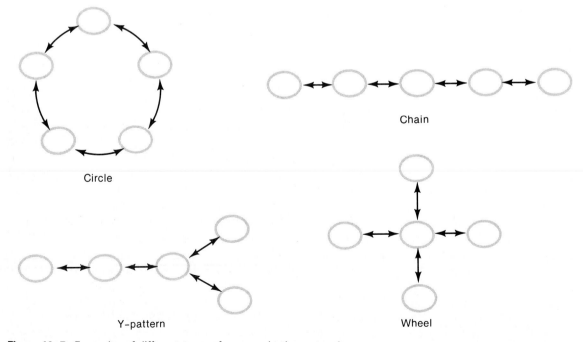

Figure 10–7. Examples of different types of communication networks.

Research shows that communication patterns such as these affect many aspects of group life (Ridgeway, 1983; Shaw, 1981). Communication networks influence group morale. In general, the more freedom group members have to talk, the more satisfied they are. So people are often happier in decentralized groups. Communication networks can also affect the efficiency of group problem solving. In general, centralized groups are more effective when they work on simple problems, and decentralized groups are more effective with complex problems.

Imagine, for example, that each member of a group is given a card with a different symbol on it and that the group task is to make a list of all the symbols. This kind of simple task is ideal for groups with highly centralized communication networks: the leader can easily collect the information from each individual and compile the final list. But complex problems are usually solved more effectively by groups with decentralized communication patterns, where freer interaction among members is possible.

TASK PERFORMANCE IN GROUPS

Are two heads better than one? Are groups usually more successful in getting a task done than individuals alone would be? Social psychologists have studied these issues in depth.

Problem Solving

To understand when a group is better at problem solving than an individual, we first need to consider the variety of tasks that groups can perform (Steiner, 1972).

An *additive task* is one in which group productivity is the sum of effort of a set of individuals. When several friends work together to push a pickup truck with a dead battery out of a busy intersection, the group effort is the sum of how hard each person works. A crucial factor in additive tasks is whether group members are able to coordinate their efforts effectively. In the truck example, it would be important for everyone to push at the same time, and in the same direction. The rope pulling task used by Ringelmann was also an additive task—the total effort exerted was the sum of the effort of each individual. Although social loafing may diminish the contribution of each individual to an additive task, the total contribution still usually exceeds what any one person could do alone. (Try pushing a stalled truck by yourself if you doubt this generalization.) On additive tasks, group productivity is generally superior to the efforts of any one person.

Neighbors struggle together to free a car trapped in a snowdrift. In an additive task such as this, the success of the group depends on the combined efforts of all individuals.

A *conjunctive task* is one in which all group members must succeed for the group to succeed. For a spy team to slip successfully across enemy lines, it is essential that every member remain undetected. A false move by any one person endangers the whole mission. For conjunctive tasks, group productivity is only as good as the *least* competent group member, the "weakest link."

In a *disjunctive task,* only one person needs to solve a problem for the entire group to succeed. If a research group is trying to solve a complex mathematical equation, any one person with the right answer can ensure the group's effectiveness. Group performance on disjunctive tasks depends on the skills of the *most* competent member. In tasks of this sort, groups usually have an advantage over individuals.

An even more complex situation occurs when a group has a task that can be subdivided among group members. In a football game, for example, teammates specialize in particular types of activities. Group productivity depends not only on the effort and skill of the best or worst player, but also on the group's ability to coordinate individual activities, often under time pressure (Kelly & McGrath, 1985) or other situational constraints.

A special type of group problem solving is the technique known as "brainstorming," which is discussed in Box 10–1.

BOX 10–1

Brainstorming: A Classic Method for Problem Solving

If an advertising executive must develop catchy slogans for a campaign to encourage drivers to use seat belts, should he have his staff members work on the problem individually, or should he bring them together as a group to work jointly on the task? Much of the early work on group problem solving involved an activity called brainstorming that was devised by an advertising executive named Osborn (1957).

Brainstorming is a technique for coming up with new or creative solutions to problems. A group is given a specific problem to discuss, such as writing advertising slogans for a new brand of toothpaste. Members are instructed to think of as many different suggestions as they can in a short time period. The rules of brainstorming, as outlined by Osborn, included these:

1. Criticism is ruled out. Negative evaluations of ideas must be withheld until later.
2. Freewheeling suggestions are welcomed. The wilder the idea, the better. It is easier to tame down an idea than to perk it up.
3. Quantity is wanted. The greater the number of ideas, the greater the likelihood of winners.

4. Combinations and improvements are sought. In addition to contributing ideas of your own, you should suggest how the ideas of others can be turned into better ideas or how two or more ideas can be joined into still another one.

In a classic study on brainstorming, participants were assigned at random to five-person groups or to an individual condition (Taylor, Berry & Block, 1958). The people in both conditions were then given five problems and 12 minutes to work on each one. One problem was stated as follows: "Each year a great many American tourists visit Europe, but now suppose that our country wished to get many more European tourists to visit America during their vacations. What steps can you suggest that would get more European tourists to come to this country?" The subjects were told that their task was to consider the problem and to offer as many and as creative solutions as they could. There were obviously no "correct" solutions.

Subjects in the alone condition were divided at random into five-person aggregates. That is, although each person worked alone, for purposes of analysis they were considered a unit, and their total

Continued

production was compared to the production of the actual groups. The researchers compared 5 hours of work done by a five-person interacting group with 5 hours done by five individuals working alone.

The results, presented in Figure 10–A, can be considered in terms of the quantity of ideas produced and also in terms of their originality. Quantity consisted of the number of different ideas produced by the real groups and the aggregates. If two people in an aggregate produced the same idea, it was counted only once. As the table shows, individuals working alone (the aggregates) scored higher than the actual groups. Five individuals working alone produced almost twice as many solutions and unique ideas as five people working together. Why? Someone working alone can concentrate better and also does not worry about competing with others in order to express his or her own ideas. Whatever stimulation a brainstorming group may produce is apparently more than offset by the interfering and distracting effects of other people (Diehl & Stroebe, 1987).

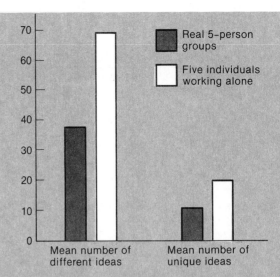

Figure 10–A. Comparing the brainstorming productivity of groups and individuals. (Adapted from Taylor, D. W., Berry, P. C., and Block, C. H. (1958). Does group participation when using brainstorming facilitate or inhibit creative thinking? Published in *Administrative Science Quarterly, 2*, pp. 34–35 by permission of *Administrative Science Quarterly*.)

Group Decision Making

The dean of a major law school has to make an important and controversial decision about the school's policy on the admission of ethnic minority students. Should she make the decision alone, or consult with a group of advisors? Common sense suggests that groups are likely to make better decisions than individuals. After all, a group is likely to have more information than a single individual, a group may be better able to examine all sides of an issue, and group discussion should help to prevent a rash or extreme decision. However, social psychological research indicates that groups do not necessarily make wiser or more moderate decisions. Groups are vulnerable to special social forces that can affect decision making. We will consider two group processes—polarization and groupthink.

Group Polarization. In 1961 James Stoner observed that group decisions are often riskier than the individual views held by the members before discussion. This finding, called the **risky shift,** sparked considerable interest, in part because it seemed to contradict popular belief that groups are relatively conservative and stodgy about decision making.

In a typical risky-shift study, subjects read about a number of complex situations, such as the one described in Table 10–2 on p. 316. In each situation several choices, ranging from very high to very low risk, were available. Subjects were asked to consider each situation carefully and to decide what recommendation they would make or which choice they would prefer. Subjects made their decisions individually and did not know they were going to discuss them later. Then subjects were brought into a group and asked to discuss each problem and to reach a unanimous group decision. Under these conditions, there was a strong tendency for the group decision to involve greater risk than the average of the decisions made by the individuals.

Many studies conducted in the United States, Canada, and Europe replicated this basic find-

T A B L E   1 0 – 2

AN EXAMPLE OF THE SITUATIONS USED TO STUDY GROUP POLARIZATION

Mr. E is president of a light metals corporation in the United States. The corporation is quite prosperous, and has strongly considered the possibilities of expansion by building an additional plant in a new location. The choice is between building another plant in the U. S., where there would be a moderate return on the initial investment, or building a plant in a foreign country. Lower labor costs and easy access to raw materials in that country would mean a much higher return on the initial investment. On the other hand, there is a history of political instability and revolution in the foreign country under consideration. In fact, the leader of a small minority party is committed to nationalizing, that is, taking over, all foreign investments.

Imagine that you are advising Mr. E. Listed below are several probabilities or odds of continued political stability in the foreign country under consideration. Please check the LOWEST probability that you would consider acceptable for Mr. E's corporation to build in that country.

_____ The chances are 1 in 10 that the foreign country will remain politically stable.

_____ The chances are 3 in 10 that the foreign country will remain politically stable.

_____ The chances are 5 in 10 that the foreign country will remain politically stable.

_____ The chances are 7 in 10 that the foreign country will remain politically stable.

_____ The chances are 9 in 10 that the foreign country will remain politically stable.

_____ Place a check here if you think Mr. E's corporation should *not* build a plant in the foreign country, no matter what the probabilities.

Source: Kogan, N. & Wallach, M. A. (1967). Risk taking as a function of the situation, the person, and the group. In *New Directions in Psychology,* Vol. III, pp. 234–235. Copyright 1967 by Holt, Rinehart & Winston.

ing of a group shift toward greater risk, but some began to find exceptions. Some groups actually made more conservative decisions (Fraser, Gouge, & Billig, 1971). Today, research has shown that when the initial opinions of group members are conservative, group discussion results in a shift toward more extreme conservatism. When the initial opinions tend toward risk, group discussion results in a shift toward greater risk. The basic finding is that group discussion leads to more extreme decisions, a phenomenon called **group polarization.** Several explanations for group polarization have been offered (Myers & Lamm, 1976). In a review of

published research, Isenberg (1986) found support for two main explanations.

The *persuasive arguments* perspective emphasizes that people gain new information as a result of listening to pro and con arguments in the group discussion (Burnstein & Vinokur, 1976). The more numerous and persuasive the arguments in favor of a position, the more likely group members are to adopt that decision. However, group discussions do not usually examine all conceivable pro and con arguments, nor do they present all positions with equal conviction (Stasser & Titus, 1985). Often, the majority of arguments tend to support each member's initial position, so that people usually hear more reasons in favor of their own opinion than against it. Group discussion may also encourage members to think about various arguments and to commit themselves more actively to a particular position. The information presented during the discussion may thus convince people of the correctness of their original views, and so lead to more extreme opinions.

A second major explanation emphasizes *social comparison* and self-presentational processes (Goethals & Darley, 1987). The idea is that group members are concerned with how their own opinions compare to those of others in the group. During discussion, individuals may learn that others have similar attitudes and indeed that some people even have stronger (more extreme) views than they do. A desire to be seen positively, as confident or bold, may therefore lead individuals to shift toward even more extreme positions than those of their fellow group members. This is essentially a form of one-upmanship, in which individuals try to be "better" than average. As Brown explained, "To be virtuous . . . is to be different from the mean—in the right direction and to the right degree" (1974, p. 469). Current research provides support for both persuasive arguments and social comparison processes, and suggests that both occur simultaneously.

Other possible explanations have also been proposed (Fraser & Foster, 1984). People may feel freer to make risky decisions in a group because of a diffusion of responsibility for their actions. Another possibility is that social identity processes are at work (Mackie, 1986; Turner,

1985). The idea is that discussion causes individuals to focus on their group membership. This in turn leads to a more stereotyped perception of the group's opinions; members come to perceive the group's position as more extreme than it really is. As a result, individuals feel pressure to shift their own views to conform with this perceived norm.

Groupthink. Sometimes a seemingly reasonable and intelligent group of people comes to a decision that in retrospect is obviously a disaster. Irving Janis (1982) says this may be the result of a process he calls **groupthink.** As outlined in Figure 10–8, the process begins with the group feeling invulnerable and excessively optimistic. The group comes to a decision without allowing any member to express doubts about it. Members shield themselves from any outside information that might undermine this decision. Finally, the group believes its decision is unanimous, even when considerable unexpressed dissent exists. Under these circumstances, the group maintains extremely high morale because of the mutual support for the decision. But since disagreements both inside and outside the group are prevented, the decisions can sometimes be disastrous.

Janis suggests that groupthink occurs most often in highly cohesive groups that are able to seal themselves off from outside opinions and that have very strong, dynamic leaders. These leaders propose a particular solution to a problem and argue strongly for it. Group members do not disagree, partly because they are afraid of being rejected and partly because they do not want to lower morale. According to Janis, skeptical members do not just go along with the group; they may actually convince themselves that their own doubts are trivial and not worth expressing.

Janis claims that groupthink contributed to several disastrous episodes in U.S. foreign policy. He cites the lack of preparation for the Japanese attack on Pearl Harbor in 1941, the Bay of Pigs invasion of Cuba in the 1960s, the escalation of the Vietnam war and Nixon's attempted Watergate cover-up in the early 1970s. In all these cases, a small group of powerful politicians, generally led by the president, made a

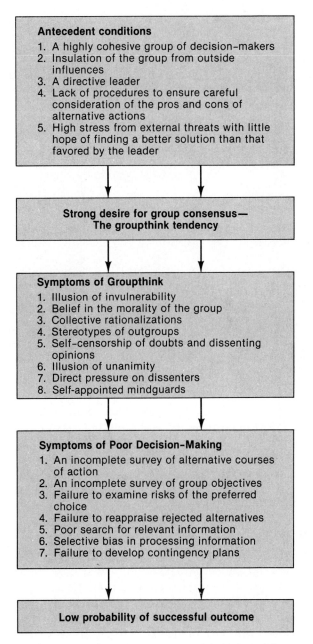

Figure 10–8. An analysis of groupthink. (Adapted from Janis, 1982, p. 244.)

decision in isolation from dissenting voices or from information that would have changed the eventual decision.

Here is how Janis describes the Bay of Pigs fiasco: President John Kennedy and his advisors hatched a plan to land anti-Castro agents, mostly Cubans living in exile in the United

President George Bush meets with his top advisors. How might group processes affect their decision?

States, on Cuban territory. Their ultimate goal was to overthrow the Communist Castro government. The plan called for the invaders to land at the Bay of Pigs. If the initial landing was unsuccessful, the invaders were to retreat into the Escambry Mountains. The planners apparently thought this escape route was a good one, since there were anti-Castro guerrillas in these mountains. Incredibly, no one in the planning group bothered to look at a detailed map of the area. If they had, they would have realized that the mountains were separated from the landing area by 80 miles of swamps and marsh that no army could have gotten through. As it happened, the rest of the plan was also so badly conceived that the invading force was virtually wiped out before it could even consider a retreat.

Janis has offered various suggestions for combatting groupthink and enhancing the effectiveness of group decision making. These include:

1.   The leader should encourage each group member to air objections and doubts about proposed decisions. For this to be effective, the leader must be willing to accept criticism of his or her ideas.

2.   The leader should initially remain impartial in discussions, stating preferences and expectations only *after* group members have expressed their own views.

3.   The group should divide into subcommittees to discuss issues independently and then come together to hammer out differences.

4.   Outside experts should be invited to participate occasionally in group discussions and should be encouraged to challenge the views of the group members.

5.   At each meeting, at least one person should be assigned to play devil's advocate to challenge group ideas.

These suggestions are designed to force the group to consider many alternatives, to avoid a false illusion of consensus, and to consider all relevant information.

Empirical support for the notion of groupthink comes from two sources. First, at least some of Janis's ideas are based on and supported by basic research on group processes (Janis, 1982). Second, there have been a few direct tests of specific predictions from the model (Longley & Pruitt, 1980). In one laboratory study, for example, teams of students met to discuss a hypothetical problem (Flowers, 1977). Some group leaders were trained to use a "closed" style that should increase groupthink; others were trained to use an "open" style. As predicted, groups with open leaders made more use of the information available to them and came up with more possible solutions to the problem. Contrary to prediction, however, there was no difference in the amount of groupthink in high-cohesion groups (made up of acquaintances) and low-cohesion groups (made up of strangers).

The group processes Janis calls groupthink are apparently quite complex (Longley & Pruitt, 1980). Many cohesive groups with strong leaders make excellent decisions. Indeed, the various groups involved in the disasters studied by Janis often made reasonable decisions on other occasions. Both the Roosevelt and Kennedy administrations are thought by many to have been extremely effective in dealing with other crisis situations. More research will be needed to clarify the conditions under which decision makers engage in groupthink. Nonetheless, Janis provides a useful reminder of some of the potential pitfalls of group decision making.

COMPETITION VERSUS COOPERATION

In some groups, people interact cooperatively: they help each other, share information, and work together for mutual benefit. In other groups, people compete: they put their own individual goals first and strive to outperform the rest. What determines whether group behavior is competitive or cooperative?

An important factor is the reward structure of the situation—the way in which rewards and desired outcomes are allocated. A *competitive reward structure* exists when one person's gain is another's loss. If you win a pot in poker, the other players must lose. In an Olympic swimming match, only one person can get the gold medal. If a course is graded on a curve, only a few students can get "A" grades. In these situations, the outcomes of group members are negatively linked; an individual does best when others do poorly.

In other situations, there is a *cooperative reward structure.* For a soccer team to win games, teammates must work together. People's rewards are positively linked, so what happens to one affects all the others. The better each player does, the more likely it is that the entire team will be victorious.

A tug-of-war game can be fiercely competitive. One side wins at the expense of the other.

An *individualistic reward structure* exists when the outcomes of individuals are independent of each other. Here, what happens to one person has no impact on the others. If a teacher gives an "A" to everyone who gets 90 percent correct on a test, it is possible for all students to get "A"s, or for none to get "A"s. Each person's grade is independent of how classmates perform.

Often, however, the reward structure in a situation is mixed or unclear. People have choices about whether to cooperate or to compete. How do people behave when the situation permits either competition or cooperation?

Classic Laboratory Studies

Much of the research on competition and cooperation has used laboratory games that simulate key features of everyday interaction. We will discuss research using two of the most popular games: the trucking game and the prisoner's dilemma. A common finding from these studies is that subjects (usually middle-class, white college students) tend to compete, even when cooperation would be a more rewarding strategy.

The Trucking Game. In a classic experiment on competition, Deutsch and Krauss (1960) used a simple two-person game called the *trucking game.* Subjects were each asked to imagine that they were running a trucking company (either the Acme Company or the Bolt Company) and had to get a truck from one point to another as quickly as possible. The two trucks were not in competition; they had different starting points and different destinations. There was, however, one hitch—the faster route for both converged at one point to a one-lane road, and the two trucks had to go in opposite directions. This is shown in Figure 10–9. The only way both could use the road would be for one of them to wait until the other had passed through. If either truck entered the road, the other could not use it, and if they both entered the road, neither of them could move until one had backed up. In addition, each player had a

gate across the direct route that could be raised by pressing a button. The gate prevented the road from being used.

Each truck was provided with an alternative route that did not conflict with the other's, but was much longer. In fact, the game was set up so that taking the alternative route was guaranteed to lose points, whereas taking the direct route would gain points for both sides, even if they alternated at the one-lane section of the road. The players were told that their goal was to earn as many points as possible for themselves. Nothing was said about earning more points than the other player.

The results of this experiment were striking. It was clear to the participants that the optimal strategy was to cooperate by alternating in using the one-lane road. In this way, they could both use the direct route, and one would be delayed only a few seconds while the other was getting through. Despite this, there was little cooperation between the players. Instead of allowing each other to use the one-lane road, they fought for its use, they raised their gates, and both of them ended up losing points.

In a typical trial, both sides would try to use the road and would meet in the middle, head on. They would stubbornly stay there for a while, each refusing to retreat. The players might laugh nervously or make nasty comments. Finally, one of them would back up, erect the barrier, and use the alternate route. On the next trial, they would do the same thing, and so it went. An occasional cooperative trial might occur, but most trials were competitive.

The Prisoner's Dilemma. The tendency to compete is not due to unique characteristics of the trucking game. It also occurs in many other games, such as the **prisoner's dilemma,** so-called because it is based on a problem faced by two suspects at a police station. The district attorney thinks the suspects have committed a major crime together but has no proof against either one. The prisoners are put into separate rooms, and each is told that he has two alternatives—to confess or not to confess. If neither confesses, they cannot be convicted of a major crime. But the district attorney tells them he can

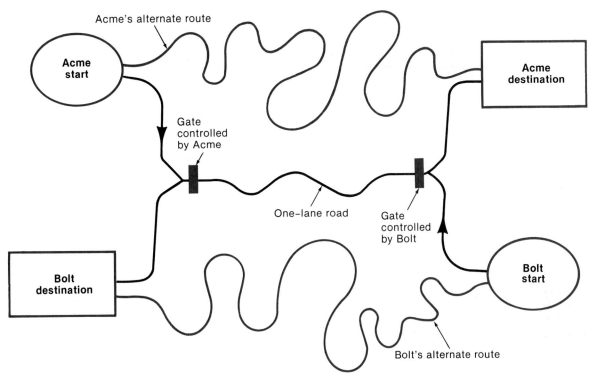

Figure 10–9. Road map of the trucking game. The players must get their truck to its destination as quickly as possible. Although they can do this efficiently only by cooperating and sharing the one-lane road, they often compete, particularly when gates are provided. (Adapted from Deutsch & Krauss, 1960, p. 183.)

get them convicted of minor crimes and that they will both receive minor punishments. If they both confess, they will definitely be convicted of the major crime. But the district attorney says he will ask for leniency. If one of them confesses and the other does not, the confessor will be freed for helping the state, and the other suspect will get the maximum penalty. The situation is shown in Figure 10–10.

Obviously, there is a conflict. If one suspect thinks his partner is going to confess, it is essential for him to confess also; on the other hand, the best joint outcome is for neither to confess and then for both to take the minor sentences. Thus, if the suspects trust each other, they should not confess. However, if one suspect trusts his partner and is convinced his partner will not confess, he would do even better to confess and in that way be freed.

We do not know what real prisoners would do under these circumstances. In research on

the problem, much of the drama is removed, but the game is basically similar. Instead of playing for their freedom, subjects play for points or money. They play in pairs but usually are not allowed to talk to each other. Each player has a choice of two strategies, and each player's payoff depends both on what he does and on what his partner does.

The exact pattern of payoffs varies; a typical one is shown in Figure 10–11 for two players, Pete and Joe. If both choose option X, each gets 10 points. If Pete chooses X and Joe chooses Y, Pete loses 15 and Joe wins 15. If both choose Y, they both lose 5 points. In other words, they can cooperate (choose X) and both win, or they can compete (one or both choosing Y) and try to win a lot but risk losing.

The players are told that the goal is to score as many points as they can. It is clear to virtually all of them that the way to have the highest score is for both to select X (the cooperative

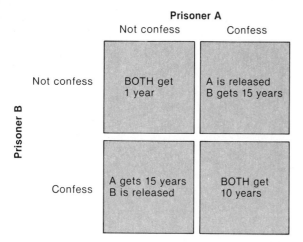

Figure 10-10. Example of the prisoner's dilemma game. Two prisoners have the choice of confessing or not confessing. If they trust and support each other by not confessing, each receives a light sentence; if they both confess they receive relatively heavy sentences; and if one confesses and the other does not, the former is released while the latter gets a very heavy sentence. The dilemma is that if either one has complete trust in the other, he would do best by being untrustworthy himself and confessing.

choice) on every trial. But just as with the trucking game, there is a strong tendency to compete. In a typical game, only about a third of the choices are cooperative. Moreover, as the game progresses (and the players have usually won only a few points), the number of cooperative choices actually goes down. The players choose the competitive strategy more and more, despite the fact that they know they can win more by cooperating.

One factor in this competitive behavior is that for any single play, the competitive choice has a short-run advantage. Let us analyze the game shown in Figure 10-11 more closely. If Pete selects the cooperative strategy, his payoff depends on what Joe does. If Joe chooses the cooperative strategy, Pete wins 10 points; if Joe chooses competitively, Pete loses 15 points. If Pete chooses the competitive strategy, once again his payoff depends on Joe. If Joe chooses the cooperative strategy, Pete wins 15 points; if Joe chooses competitively, Pete loses 5. In either case, Pete would do better by competing (Choice y) than he would by cooperating (Choice x). If Joe picks cooperatively, Pete wins

15 instead of 10; if Joe chooses competitively, Pete loses 5 instead of 15.

The dilemma is that over a long series of trials, Pete would be much better off if both he and Joe agreed to cooperate. They would both win on all trials rather than winning on some and losing on others. This would clearly maximize their individual gains, and so it would be the most rational strategy.

The only advantage of the competitive choice is that one player can score more than the other, even though he always scores less than he would have if both had picked the cooperative choice. When subjects in these studies were questioned about their reasons for behaving as they did, many of them reported that they wanted to "beat" the other player. This occurred despite the fact that the experimenter had told them the aim of the game was to get as high a score as possible.

Determinants of Competition Versus Cooperation

Many factors determine whether people interact cooperatively or competitively. Experimental game studies show that when the re-

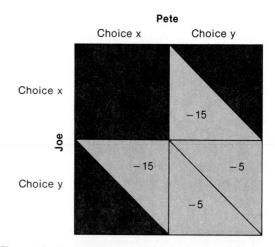

Figure 10-11. Typical prisoner's dilemma game matrix. The top figure in each square cell indicates A's payoff; the bottom indicates B's payoff. X is a cooperative choice, because it allows both members to win. The choice of Y is competitive, because only the one who chooses it has a chance of winning and both may lose. With this matrix there is a great deal of competition.

ward structure of a situation is mixed or ambiguous, college students often adopt a competitive strategy that prevents them from maximizing their rewards. But in situations where the reward structure is more explicit and where the rewards themselves are more important than in simulation games, rewards can enhance cooperation. The same students who strive to "beat" their partner in the trucking game may behave very cooperatively in their families or with their roommates—in settings where cooperation is expected and rewarded. Researchers have identified several factors that influence competition.

Personal values make a difference. It has been suggested that Americans are some of the most competitive people on earth, and cross-cultural studies of children would seem to support this view (Werner, 1979). A program of research by Millard Madsen (1971) and his colleagues investigated the development of competitive behavior in children from around the world. In these studies, children were asked to play games with peers, and the extent to which they selected cooperative versus competitive strategies was assessed. Children from Western technological societies were consistently more competitive than children from developing countries in Latin America, Africa, and the Middle East. In one study (Madsen, 1971), for example, 8-year-old Mexican children cooperated on about seven of ten trials, whereas 8-year-old Americans cooperated on fewer than one trial in ten. In other words, there are cultural differences in the tendency for people to compete or cooperate.

At the same time, there are also individual differences within a particular culture. Children from urban areas are more competitive than are children from rural areas. And children from middle-class homes compete more than do children from lower-class homes. It appears that one of the correlates of industrialization and affluence is greater competitiveness.

Individual differences are also found in the behavior of adults. Research suggests that individuals tend to adopt one of three value orientations or strategies for interacting (Kuhlman & Wimberley, 1976; McClintock & Liebrand, 1988):

☐ *Cooperators* are concerned with maximizing the joint rewards received by both self and the partner.

☐ *Competitors* are oriented toward maximizing their own gains relative to those of the partner—they want to do better than the partner.

☐ *Individualists* are oriented toward maximizing their own gains, with no concern for the gains or losses of the partner.

When people are confronted with a situation such as the trucking game or prisoner's dilemma, their value orientation has a strong impact on their initial behavior. Cooperators usually initiate cooperative interactions; competitors begin in a more competitive mode. Over time, however, individuals will change their own behavior if the partner does not reciprocate. Confronted with a highly competitive partner, even the most dedicated cooperator may begin to behave competitively.

Communication among partners also influences cooperation. In general, more communication leads to more cooperation (Orbell, van de Kragt, & Dawes, 1988). For example, in the Deutsh and Krauss trucking game study, three different communication conditions were included. Some subjects were required to communicate; others were given the opportunity to talk if they wanted to; a third group was not allowed to communicate. Cooperation was greatest when communication was required, and least when communication was impossible.

Similar results have been found using the prisoner's dilemma game. Wichman (1970) showed that competition was greatest when no communication was possible, somewhat less when partners could talk but not see each other, and least when partners could see and talk to each other. Wichman found that when there was no communication, about 40 percent of responses were cooperative; when verbal communication was permitted, cooperation increased to more than 70 percent of trials. Communication enables partners to urge each other to cooperate, to discuss their plans, to make promises, to convince each other that they are trustworthy, to learn about each other, and so on. Assuming that partners have any tendency to cooperate, knowledge about each other should facilitate it.

The size of a group also influences cooperation. In several studies, researchers have adapted the general prisoner's dilemma situation so that groups of three or more people can play. Studies (such as Komorita & Lapworth, 1982) have found that as the size of the group increases, cooperation decreases. The specific reasons for greater competition in larger groups have not been determined. It seems likely that as groups increase in size, there will more often be at least one person who adopts an exploitative, selfish orientation. Further, larger groups may feel less pressure to cooperate because of a general diffusion of responsibility among group members.

A final factor is reciprocity. We have seen throughout this book that there is a general norm of reciprocity: people often feel obligated to return both favors and insults. There is some evidence that in the course of interaction, initial competition provokes more competition and that cooperation sometimes (but not always) encourages further cooperation. One strategy that seems especially successful in fostering cooperation is reciprocal concessions. The players take turns giving up a little. This is the traditional compromise solution to most conflicts: each side starts with an extreme position and then retreats gradually until a common meeting ground is found.

If one player makes a small concession and then waits for the other to do the same, there is indeed greater eventual cooperation (Esser & Komorita, 1975). However, a crucial element of this strategy is timing. A person who gives in too much at once may appear weak and the other will not reciprocate. The concessions must be gradual and sequential. In fact, according to Wall (1977), the most effective technique is to make reciprocal concessions slightly larger than those made by the other person. This reinforces the other's cooperation and results in large concessions and quick agreement. Obviously, this does not work unless both sides are willing to cooperate to some extent. If one is totally competitive, the one who tries cooperating will only

be exploited and end up with a weaker position than before.

Social Dilemmas

As you hike along a beautiful mountain trail, you stop for a snack. You're tempted to throw away your empty water container and granola bar wrappers, knowing that your backpack will be lighter if you don't have to carry your trash to the top of the mountain and back. But you hesitate, knowing that if all hikers litter the trail, it will soon be unpleasant for all who use it. Back at home, there's a heat wave and you consider turning up your air conditioner to its coldest setting. But again, you hesitate, knowing that if everyone turns on their air conditioners full blast, there may be a power failure that will lead everyone to suffer.

Each of these examples represents a **social dilemma**—a situation in which the most rewarding short-term choice for an individual will ultimately lead to negative outcomes for all concerned. As Brewer and Kramer (1986, p. 543) describe it, "Social dilemmas exist whenever the cumulative result of reasonable individual choices is collective disaster."

Social dilemmas pit the short-term interests of the individual against the long-term interests of the group (including the individual). Today, as we are becoming more aware of the dangers of pollution and the wanton use of natural resources, an understanding of social dilemmas is especially timely. Research on social dilemmas extends earlier studies of the trucking game and prisoner's dilemma to more complicated situations. Social dilemma research is currently an active field in social psychology. Much of this research has been done in the laboratory, in game-playing situations that replicate essential features of real-life social dilemmas. Central questions are how to resolve social dilemmas and how to encourage individuals to cooperate, in ways that will have long-range benefits for the group.

One approach to solving social dilemmas is to change the reward structure in the situation.

For example, an effective way to encourage people to use less water is to change the billing system so that customers are charged higher rates if they use more of this valued resource (Messick & Brewer, 1983). We can encourage people to donate to charities by making contributions deductible as an expense on federal income tax. We can take decision making about the use of a valuable resource out of the hands of individuals, and set up an oversight agency or committee. The Environmental Protection Agency is one such effort.

Other factors are also important. Not surprisingly, some of the same factors we identified earlier as affecting competition and cooperation are also relevant to social dilemmas. A person's value orientation—whether cooperative, competitive, or individualist—can make a difference in how they approach a social dilemma (Liebrand & van Run, 1985). Fostering a sense of group identity can also increase the tendency to show restraint and to use resources wisely, especially in small groups (Brewer & Kramer, 1986). Communication among the individuals involved may also be important, because it provides an opportunity for individuals to make public promises to cooperate.

LEADERSHIP

Some form of leadership exists in all groups (Hollander, 1985). The central attribute of leadership is social influence. The leader is the person who has the most impact on group behavior and beliefs. He or she is the one who initiates action, gives orders, makes decisions, settles disputes among group members, offers encouragement, serves as a model, and is in the forefront of group activity.

Leadership Structure

Social scientists refer to a group's unique pattern of leadership as the leadership structure of the group. In some groups, this is relatively simple. The committee responsible for planning a New Year's party at the office may consist of one enthusiastic leader and several followers. In other groups, the pattern of leadership is more complex. Who are the leaders in a professional football team? Possible leaders might include the owners, the general manager, the head coach, the captains of the various team units, the quarterback who calls the plays, or individual team members who serve as informal spokespeople for the team. In this case, various individuals are in charge of different aspects of team functioning. So whereas some groups have only one leader, other groups have two or more. In general, groups have several leaders when they face diverse and complex tasks requiring many types of skills. Then it makes sense to have multiple leaders, each a specialist in some aspect of the group's activities (Ridgeway, 1983).

Formal and Informal Leaders. Groups differ in the extent to which their leadership structure is formal or informal. Large organizations such as a business or school have formal organization charts indicating the official chain of command and giving guidelines about patterns of decision making and supervision. Even in smaller groups, such as clubs and fraternities, there may be elected officers with specified responsibilities. At the other extreme, some groups have no formal leaders at all. Friendship groups are one example.

What is important to recognize, however, is that groups without formal leaders still have patterns of informal leadership. One person may be more articulate and persuasive than others in group discussions, and so have more influence on decisions. Someone else may emerge as the person to whom others turn to smooth over conflicts within the group. All groups have some leadership structure. And even in groups with formal leaders, there is often a pattern of informal leadership that can be very different from the official structure. The president of the student council may be the official head of the group, but unofficially it may be another officer who actually has the greatest influence in decision making.

Paths to Leadership. Individuals can become group leaders in several ways. Some leaders are appointed. An army lieutenant is the official leader of his or her company, and is appointed by people higher up in the military organization. Because of this position, the lieutenant can give orders to everyone else in the company, but none of them can give the lieutenant orders. In other situations, such as clubs or student government, a leader is elected.

In a third process, a group member emerges over time as a leader. When people interact repeatedly, as in a group of friends or classmates, some individuals typically emerge as informal leaders. These leaders do not have official titles, but most group members would generally agree that a particular person or set of people are the leaders. Outside observers can also spot emergent leaders by watching such things as who talks most in group discussions and whose opinions are most likely to prevail in group decision making. A recent review of 25 studies concluded that there is a strong tendency for the person who talks most to be perceived as the leader both by other members of the group and by outside observers (Mullen, Salas, & Driskell, 1989).

Types of Leadership Activities. In general, leaders must perform two types of activities. **Task leadership** concerns accomplishing the goals of the group—getting the work of the group done successfully. The task leader gives suggestions, offers opinions, and provides information for the group. He or she controls, shapes, directs, and organizes the group in carrying out a specific task. **Social leadership** focuses on the emotional and interpersonal aspects of group interaction. The social leader concentrates on keeping the group running smoothly and happily, is concerned about people's feelings, uses humor to relieve tension, and tries to encourage group cohesiveness.

Extensive research has shown that both task and social leadership are important to successful group functioning (Bales, 1970; Burke, 1971). The qualities necessary for the two types of leadership are somewhat different. A social leader must be friendly, agreeable, conciliatory, concerned with feelings, and socially oriented.

A task leader must be efficient, directive, and knowledgeable about the particular task at hand. In some groups, one person is the task leader and a different person is the social leader. But in other situations, one person may combine the functions of both.

It has sometimes been speculated that women usually function as social leaders and men as task leaders. In general, research does not confirm this gender stereotype (Eagly & Johnson, 1990). Studies of managers and other leaders in organizations find little evidence of sex differences. Differences are somewhat more likely to emerge in laboratory studies of college students. But here the overall pattern seems to be a tendency for women to emphasize both types of leadership and for men to give greater emphasis to task leadership.

Who Becomes a Leader?

The search for factors that cause some people and not others to become leaders is an old one. Two contrasting views have emerged: one emphasizes the unique personal characteristics of the leader, and the other emphasizes the situational forces acting on the group.

Characteristics of the Person. The "great person" theory of leadership suggests that some people, because of personality or other unique characteristics, are destined to lead. To test this idea, many empirical studies have compared the characteristics of leaders and followers (Yuki, 1981). Surprisingly few qualities have been found that consistently separate leaders from followers. In a general way, however, three factors are associated with leadership (Ridgeway, 1983).

First, leaders tend to excel in those abilities that help the group to accomplish its goals. In some situations, intelligence correlates with leadership (Fiedler, 1986). In other situations, leadership might be linked to political expertise, physical strength, or skills relevant to the activities and goals of the group. A great quarterback like Joe Montana or the star of a basketball team like Magic Johnson almost automatically becomes a task leader of the team.

What complex paths have led individuals to become world leaders? From top to bottom, left to right: Mikhail Gorbachev, Margaret Thatcher, Nelson Mandela, Benazir Bhutto.

Second, leaders tend to have interpersonal skills that contribute to successful interaction. In general, being cooperative, organized, articulate, and interpersonally sensitive would be an asset. The ability to perceive group needs and to respond to them is also important (Ellis, 1988). Such characteristics enhance a person's functioning as a social leader.

A third factor is motivation. Leaders usually desire recognition and prominence; they are more ambitious, achievement oriented, and willing to assume responsibility. We emphasize, however, that although these qualities enhance a person's leadership potential, none is a sure guarantee of actually becoming a leader.

Characteristics of the Situation. Another approach to leadership emphasizes situational fac-

tors. A striking demonstration of situational forces comes from the research on communication networks described earlier in this chapter (Leavitt, 1951). The basic idea is that communication is essential for leadership, so the person who can communicate most freely tends to become the leader. In situations such as a wheel network, where all communications are channeled through one person, that individual should become the leader.

Today, most researchers believe that becoming a leader depends in large part on the *match* between the characteristics of the person and the needs of the situation confronting the group. It should be obvious that different situations require different qualities in a leader. Take the case of expertise. The particular types of knowledge or ability that are relevant vary dramatically from one situation to another. Being able to pitch well may be a real asset in becoming captain of the fraternity softball team, but it would not contribute much to heading the debate team. Further, expertise is a relative matter. A first-year law student might be the "legal expert" in her family, but would not necessarily become a leader among her law school classmates or professors.

Transactional Approaches. Neither the "great person" approach nor the situational approach considers the role of followers in determining who becomes the leader. The transactional approach serves to remedy this gap (Hollander, 1985). The central point of this approach is that the interaction between the leader and followers works both ways. The perceptions and attitudes of followers partly determine who becomes leader. Leaders, in turn, usually pay close attention to the views of followers and may modify their leadership behavior in response to the actions of their followers. In small groups, the willingness of group members to accept the leader's influence depends on processes of social exchange discussed in Chapter 7. Leaders who fail to provide rewards or to move the group toward its goal, who are perceived as unfair, and who are unresponsive to group needs will be disliked and may jeopardize their leadership position. On a larger scale, voters select candidates they perceive as sharing their values and goals. Elected officials who ignore the wishes of their constituents may not win reelection.

Leadership Style

Think back to your high school teachers and the different ways they led a class. One may have been a dictator who insisted on discipline and obedience. Another may have been a "nice guy" who emphasized student participation and created a relaxed classroom atmosphere. Researchers have tried to classify styles of leadership and to determine how they affect group functioning. Box 10–2 describes a classic study of "democratic" and "authoritarian" leaders.

Fiedler's Contingency Model. Researchers generally agree that group performance is affected by the match between the style of the leader and the circumstances of the group. The consequences of a particular style depend on (are contingent on) various characteristics of the group itself. One prominent version of this approach is Fiedler's **contingency model of leadership effectiveness.**

Fiedler (1978, 1981) identifies two styles of leadership, corresponding roughly to the distinction between task and social leadership that we made earlier. Those leaders who give highest priority to getting the work of the group done successfully and who deemphasize relations among group members are called *task-oriented leaders.* The coach who says that "winning is the only thing" and ignores the feelings of team members is an example. In Fiedler's model, those leaders who reverse these priorities by putting group relations first and task accomplishment second are called *relationship-oriented leaders.* This sort of coach would say that it doesn't matter whether you win or lose, so long as you get along with your teammates.

Fiedler also classifies group situations along a continuum. As one extreme are high-control situations in which a leader has high legitimate power and is well liked and respected by the group, and in which the group's task is structured and clear cut. An example would be a popular Scout leader showing a group of preteens how to set up a tent. At the other extreme are low-control situations in which the leader has little legitimate authority, has poor relations with group members, and is confronted with a task that may require creative or complex solutions. An example would be an inexperienced and unpopular student teacher who is asked to lead a group discussion with high school seniors about ways to improve school spirit.

A main goal of Fiedler's research has been to determine which types of leaders are most effective in which situations. His results, replicated in a number of different studies, are shown in Figure 10–12. Task-oriented leaders are more effective in increasing group productivity in *both* extremely high and extremely low control situa-

BOX 10–2

Democratic and Authoritarian Leaders

At the end of World War II, a classic series of studies on leadership was conducted by Lewin, Lippitt, and White (1939). Kurt Lewin, a refugee from Nazi Germany, and his colleagues investigated the differences between "democratic" and "authoritarian" leaders. They conducted a naturalistic experiment in which they formed several clubs for boys, each with an adult male leader trained to adopt a different style of leadership. In the *authoritarian style*, all decisions were made by the leader. He was very directive and controlling, gave few explanations, and remained rather aloof from the group. In the *democratic style*, boys were encouraged to discuss group policies and to make their own decisions with the assistance of the leader. Members could select their own partners and decide how to divide up the work. All clubs met for several months. To study group reactions, the researchers staged various events, such as the leader coming late to a group meeting or leaving the group for a while. The boys' behavior was observed during club meetings, and follow-up interviews were conducted outside the group.

Clear differences emerged in the behavior of members in democratic and authoritarian groups. First, the groups differed in emotional tone. The democratic groups were friendlier and more relaxed; members were more group-minded and used the word "we" (instead of "I") with greater frequency. The atmosphere in the authoritarian groups was tense. Boys showed more hostility and aggression, sometimes toward the leader and sometimes toward a group member who became the scapegoat. Boys in authoritarian groups also seemed to form weaker ties to the group.

A second major difference was that democratic groups encouraged boys to take more initiative. If an authoritarian leader left the room, the boys stopped working on their assigned project. If a democratic leader left, the boys kept on working. Boys in authoritarian groups seemed more dependent on the leader and less capable of working on their own. Apparently, boys in democratic groups participated more, got to know other boys better, identified more with the group, and consequently were more satisfied with the group activities (Ridgeway, 1983).

It is important to note, however, that these results favoring democratic groups occurred in the context of American society. In cultures where people do not expect or value participatory democracy, the results might be very different. For instance, in a society where elders are supposed to instruct the young, a democratic leader could be perceived as irresponsible, lazy, or inept, and so group morale might be lower in democratic groups.

Lewin, Lippitt, and White also examined the effect of democratic and authoritarian leadership styles on group productivity. They found that authoritarian groups actually spent somewhat more time working on their projects and completed slightly more projects. The researchers argued, however, that democratic groups made products of higher quality and that members took a more personal interest in their projects. Unfortunately for champions of participatory democracy, subsequent research has not supported this finding (Ridgeway, 1983). Although members of democratic groups are generally happier than members of authoritarian groups, they are not necessarily any more productive.

tions. In other words, both the Scout leader and the student teacher would be advised to give priority to the task. Relationship-oriented leaders are most effective in situations where the leader has moderate control: when the leader gets along well with group members but has a complex task or when the leader is disliked but the task is clear.

One conclusion we can draw from Fiedler's model is that the effectiveness of either type of leader will change if there is a change in control. For example, one study of army infantry squads

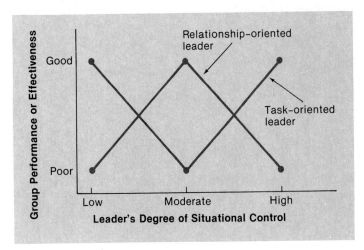

Figure 10–12. Fiedler's model of how group performance is determined by the leader's style and situational control. When control is either very low or very high, task-oriented leaders are more effective in encouraging productivity. When situational control is moderate, relationship-oriented leaders are more effective. (Adapted from Fiedler, *American Behavioral Scientist,* Vol. 24, No. 5, 1981, p. 625. Reprinted by permission of Sage Publications, Inc.)

(Bons & Fiedler, 1976) found that a squad leader's situational control increased from moderate to high as he gained experience and on-the-job training. In accord with Fiedler's theory, task-oriented squad leaders were at first less effective than were relationship-oriented leaders. But as the situation changed, task leaders increased and relationship leaders decreased in effectiveness. The key point is that no one style of leadership is effective in all situations. Ultimately, the most effective leader may be the person who can adapt his or her leadership style to match the situation.

Key Terms

brainstorming
cohesiveness
communication networks
contingency model of leadership effectiveness
deindividuation
evaluation apprehension

group
groupthink
group polarization
prisoner's dilemma
reference group
risky shift
social dilemma
social facilitation

social identity theory
social impact theory
social leadership
social loafing
social norm
social role
task leadership

Summary

1. Working in the presence of others sometimes leads to social facilitation and sometimes causes social loafing. Which effect occurs depends on the complexity of the task. It also depends on whether the group context increases the individual's concerns about social evaluation (because others are judging the person's performance) or reduces social evaluation concerns (because the individual's own effort is hidden by working in a group).

2. Social impact theory proposes that the influence of an audience on an individual depends on the number of observers, the strength (importance) of the audience, and the immediacy of the audience.

3. Our sense of self is intimately linked to social groups. The social identity perspective emphasizes that our self-concept includes social identities based on group affiliations as well as unique personal identities. A desire to enhance our self-esteem leads people to perceive ingroups more favorably than outgroups.

4. People in groups sometimes behave in unusual or antisocial ways that individuals alone would not. This deindividuation occurs because anonymity reduces the individual's feelings of personal responsibility, and because the person's attention is focused on the group rather than on the self.

5. A group is a social unit in which people are interdependent: what happens to one person affects the outcomes for the other group members. Social norms are rules and understandings about how people should behave; social roles define the rights and responsibilities of individuals in particular positions in the group.

6. Cohesiveness refers to the positive forces that cause members to want to stay in a group and also to the negative forces that discourage members from leaving a group.

7. Communication is essential to group activities. In most groups, some people talk more than others. Limits imposed on communication create various communication networks. Centralized networks (one person is allowed to talk to everyone, but the other people can talk only to the central person) are efficient for solving simple problems. Decentralized networks produce higher morale and are probably superior for solving complex problems.

8. There is a tendency for groups to make more extreme decisions than individuals alone. This group polarization effect sometimes leads to riskier decisions, and sometimes to more conservative decisions. Two main explanations for polarization emphasize the importance of persuasive arguments and social comparison processes.

9. Highly cohesive groups with a directive leader may be vulnerable to groupthink. This is a decision-making process that discourages criticism and can lead to poor decisions.

10. Much research on competition and cooperation has used laboratory games such as the trucking game and prisoner's dilemma. More recently, researchers have investigated social dilemmas. In these studies, Americans often tend to compete, even when they would obtain greater external rewards from cooperation. Situational factors affecting competition include the reward structure of the situation, the amount of communication among people, and the size of the group. One strategy for reducing competition is reciprocal concessions.

11. Group leaders are those who have the most impact on group behavior and beliefs. A task leader focuses on accomplishing group goals successfully. A social leader strives to maintain harmony and high morale. People who become leaders tend to be socially skilled, to excel in abilities that help the group achieve its goals, and or to be highly motivated to be a leader. According to Fiedler's contingency model, the success of a leader depends on the match between the leader's style (task oriented versus relationship oriented) and the nature of the situation.

Suggested Readings

Fiedler, F. E., & Garcia, J. E. (1987). *New Approaches to effective leadership: Cognitive resources and organizational performance*. New York: John Wiley. A comprehensive review of Fiedler's theory and research with attention to the impact of intelligence and other "cognitive resources" on leadership.

Forsyth, D. R. (1983). *An introduction to group dynamics*. Monterey, CA: Brooks/Cole. A readable textbook that discusses such group processes as leadership, problem solving, and deindividuation.

Hogg, M. A., & Abrams, D. (1988). *Social identifications: A social psychology of intergroup relations and group processes*. New York: Routledge. A comprehensive presentation of the social identity perspective on groups.

Hollander, E. P. (1985). Leadership and power. In G. Lindzey & E. Aronson (Eds.), *Handbook of social psychology*, 3rd ed., Vol. 2, pp. 485–538. New York: Random House. A professional level review and analysis of research and theory on leadership.

Janis, I. L. (1982). *Groupthink: Psychological studies of policy decisions and fiascoes*, 2nd ed. Boston: Houghton Mifflin. Presents Janis's theory and reviews research testing hypotheses about groupthink.

Janis, I. L. (1989). *Crucial decisions: Leadership in policy making and crisis management*. New York: Free Press. Offers research-based guidelines for effective leadership and decision making.

Paulus, P. B. (Ed.) (1989). *The psychology of group influence*, 2nd ed. Hillsdale, NJ: Erlbaum. An excellent collection of articles on group behavior written by leading experts. Contains detailed discussions of such topics as social facilitation, group polarization, and deindividuation.

McGrath, J. E. (1984). *Groups: Interaction and performance*. Englewood Cliffs, NJ: Prentice-Hall. A comprehensive textbook covering most aspects of group functioning.

Mullen, B., & Goethals, G. R. (Eds.) (1987). *Theories of group behavior*. New York: Springer-Verlag. Presents eight social psychological theories about group behavior.

ELEVEN

Aggression

DEFINING AGGRESSION

SOURCES OF ANGER   **AGGRESSIVE BEHAVIOR**

REDUCING AGGRESSIVE BEHAVIOR

MEDIA VIOLENCE   **SEXUAL VIOLENCE**

When we think of aggression and violence, most of us probably think first of crimes committed by one individual against another. The United States experiences over 20,000 murders per year, over 75,000 rapes, and over 600,000 assaults—in reported crimes alone. The murder rate in the United States far exceeded that in most other civilized countries. New York City had 22 murders per 100,000 population but London had fewer than 2, and New Delhi only 0.1.

We probably also think of war. In recent years, there have been about 50 wars each decade, almost all in Third World countries—those most oppressed by poverty, disease, and all manner of other problems. And the greatest threat of all comes from the threat of nuclear war. By the early 1980s, the United States had over 1,000 intercontinental ballistic missiles (ICBMs), each with the explosive power of 700 Hiroshima bombs.

This is violence and aggression on a global scale, but in fact most violence is committed against people closest to us—against those in our own families, our spouses, children, and lovers. According to a recent national survey (Straus & Gelles, 1986), each year 16 percent of all married persons engage in some act of physical violence against their mate. They estimate that each year about 1.6 million American husbands engage in severe violence (hitting with fist, using gun or knife) against their wives. Similarly, parents commit a surprising number of violent acts against their own children. The same study showed that 10 percent of the parents had hit their child with an object in the previous year, while 55 percent had slapped or spanked their child. Among college students, the phenomenon of "date rape" has drawn increasing attention. One careful national survey found that 15 percent of female college students report they have experienced forced or unwanted sexual intercourse, which the authors note meets the legal standard for rape (Koss, Gidycz, & Wisniewski, 1987).

Not surprisingly, then, aggression has been

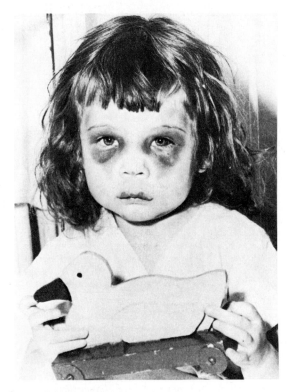

A surprising number of small children are subjected to real brutality, even from their parents and often even in quite affluent, comfortable life circumstances.

an important topic for social psychological research. In this chapter we consider the origins of aggressive behavior and ways to reduce violence. We also take a look at the possible effects of violence shown on TV and in films, and we examine the nature of sexual violence.

DEFINING AGGRESSION

Although it might seem that everybody understands what aggression is, there is considerable disagreement about how to define it precisely. The simplest definition of aggression, and the one favored by those with a learning or behaviorist approach, is that aggression is any behavior that hurts others. The advantage of this definition is that the behavior itself determines whether or not an act is aggressive.

Unfortunately, this definition ignores the *intention* of the person who does the act—and this factor is critical. If we ignored intent, some actions intended to hurt others would not be labeled aggressive because they turned out to be harmless. Suppose an enraged man fires a gun at a business rival, but the gun turns out to be unloaded. The act is harmless because firing an unloaded gun is not dangerous. Despite the fact that the man was enraged and was trying to kill someone, he was not being aggressive because no actual harm was done.

Ignoring intention can also produce the opposite error—calling some acts aggressive that are not, by the usual meaning of the term. If a golfer's ball accidentally hits a spectator, has the golfer committed an aggressive act? She has in fact caused somebody a great deal of pain, but surely no one would believe the golfer was being aggressive. Similarly, criminal law provides exceptions for acts that are painful but intended to help the victim, such as surgery performed by physicians.

Thus we need to distinguish hurtful behavior from hurtful intentions. We will define **aggression** as any action that is *intended* to hurt others. This conception is more difficult to apply, because it does not depend solely on observable behavior. Often it is difficult to know someone's intention. But we will accept this limitation because we can define aggression meaningfully only by including intent.

A second major distinction is also needed, between **antisocial** and **prosocial** aggression.

BOX 11–1

Instinct Theories of Aggression

It has been proposed by Freud, McDougall, Lorenz, and others that humans have an innate drive or instinct to fight. Just as they experience physiologically based feelings of hunger, thirst, or sexual arousal, so too it is argued that they have an innate need to behave aggressively. Although there are no known physiological mechanisms connected with aggressive feelings as there are for the other drives, they argue that aggression is a basic drive.

It is true that many subhuman animals respond aggressively to certain stimuli whenever they appear and that these responses appear to be instinctive. If two male Siamese fighting fish are put in the same tank, they immediately attack and fight until one is badly mauled or dead. The presence of another male is sufficient to produce this aggressive behavior in each one. The aggression seems to be triggered automatically by the other's presence and was obviously not learned.

There are countless other examples of similar reactions. Animals certainly do a great deal of fighting. They fight to obtain food, to protect their territory, to defend their young, and so on.

But our definition of aggression as requiring the intent to harm may not be appropriate to much of this behavior. A lion that chases and kills a buffalo obviously intends to harm the buffalo. On the other hand, as far as we know, the killing is not done in response to anger or with intent to cause suffering. The lion must hunt for food and the buffalo happens to be its natural prey. The lion kills to satisfy hunger, not to satisfy some aggressive drive. Fighting for mates and for territory also seems to be motivated by sexual drives or the need for food.

The work by ethologists on animal behavior is fascinating. It indicates that many species respond instinctively to specific cues and have many instinctive drives. It does not, however, provide evidence concerning humans. Although some ethologists continue to be convinced that all animals have instinctive aggressive drives, most psychologists now dispute this. Among animals relatively low on the phylogenetic scale, instinct plays an important role in producing aggression, but there seems little reason to believe that humans have instinctive impulses toward aggressiveness.

BOX 11–2

Who Are the Worst Aggressors?

Because prosocial aggression obeys the law, and antisocial aggression does not, we usually think antisocial aggression is worse. But which is in fact the most destructive? The most terrible atrocities seem to have been committed as official acts of government. The murder of 6 million European Jews by the Nazis in World War II was by official order of the German government. The murder of more than 3 million Cambodians in the mid-1970s by the Pol Pot regime was by government order. Widespread torture of and violence against dissidents, such as that uncovered by Amnesty International in repressive regimes in Argentina, Chile, El Salvador, Iran, and the USSR, has all been by government order.

The irony is that all these atrocities are examples of *prosocial* aggression. Each was committed by the legitimate leadership of the nation or group, and supposedly for the broader social good. The Nazis claimed the noble goal of "purifying" the German race, leaders in Argentina and other nations wanted to restore "law and order," and so on.

Sanctioned aggression too can open the doors to much cruelty and barbarism. Consider the near extinction of the American bison; although it was not caused by government order, it was certainly legal and was encouraged by the economic system. In contrast, there are, relative to these mass atrocities, few individual murders in any society at any given time. Even the terror campaigns waged by the drug cartels in Colombia kill a comparative handful.

Crime is a major problem in the United States today. Yet the Founding Fathers felt in some respects that unrestrained governments as well as unrestrained private citizens could be extremely dangerous. The Bill of Rights is a partial response to that fear. What do you think? Is the most serious problem of civilized societies prosocial aggression or antisocial aggression?

Normally we think of aggression as bad. After all, if an aggressive act results from an intent to hurt another person, it must be bad. But some aggressive acts are good. We applaud the police officer who shoots a terrorist who has killed innocent victims and is holding others hostage. The question is whether the aggressive act violates commonly accepted social norms, or supports them.

Unprovoked criminal acts that hurt people, such as assault and battery, murder, and gang beatings clearly violate social norms, so they are described as antisocial. But many aggressive acts are actually dictated by social norms, and therefore are described as prosocial. Acts of law enforcement, appropriate parental discipline, or obeying the orders of commanders in wartime are regarded as necessary.

Some aggressive acts fall somewhere between prosocial and antisocial, and we might label them **sanctioned aggression.** This includes aggressive acts that are not required by social norms, but that are well within their bounds. They do not violate accepted moral standards. A coach who disciplines a disobedient player by benching him or her is usually thought to be well within his rights. So is a shopkeeper who in self-defense hits someone who is criminally assaulting him, or a woman who strikes back at a rapist. None of these acts is required of the person, but they fall within the bounds of what is permitted by social norms.

A third distinction is between aggressive behavior and aggressive feelings such as **anger.** Our overt behavior does not always reflect our internal feelings. Someone may be quite angry inside, but make no overt effort to hurt another person. Society discourages and condemns most forms of aggressive behavior, and indeed can exist only if people control their aggressive feelings most of the time. We cannot have people hitting other people, breaking windows, or acting violently whenever they feel like it. Society places strong restraints on such expression, and most people, even those who feel angry much of the time, rarely act aggressively.

We need to consider both the factors that increase anger and the restraints that may prevent it from being translated into aggressive action. We thus have two separate questions—what produces angry feelings and what produces aggressive behavior?

SOURCES OF ANGER

An aggressive feeling is an internal state that cannot be observed directly. We all experience anger, and virtually everyone at one time or another would like to hurt someone else. Indeed, most people report they feel at least mildly or moderately angry anywhere from several times a day to several times a week (Averill, 1983). What causes anger? We will discuss two main factors: attacks by others and frustration. As will be seen, the victim's perceptions of the aggressor's motives also play a major role in generating anger.

Attack

One of the most common sources of anger is being attacked or bothered by another person. Imagine that you are waiting at a red light, and the driver of the car behind you blows the horn just as the light turns green. Or imagine that you are reading a newspaper, and someone unexpectedly pours a glass of water down your neck. Or, finally, imagine a student's reaction when he expresses an opinion in class and someone else disagrees with him and says he is stupid to hold such an opinion. In all these cases, someone has done something unpleasant to someone else. Depending on how the injured person takes it, he or she has been annoyed or attacked. It is extremely likely that the person will become angry and feel aggressive toward the source of the attack. Similarly, aversive stimulation of a wide variety of other kinds pro-

duces aggression. For example, people exposed to foul odors, irritating cigarette smoke, and disgusting scenes show increased aggressive feelings (Berkowitz, 1983).

People often respond to attack with retaliation, in an "eye for an eye" fashion (Baron, 1977). This can produce an escalation of aggression. Gang warfare often starts out with a few insults and ends up in murder, as depicted so clearly in Shakespeare's *Romeo and Juliet* or the musical *West Side Story*. Similarly, domestic violence often breeds more domestic violence. Cases of family violence too often involve not one aggressor and one victim, but a pattern of mutual violence within a married couple or between parents and children (Straus et al., 1981). Attack provokes retaliation, and the violence simply escalates.

Frustration

A second major source of anger is **frustration**. Frustration is the interference with or blocking of the attainment of a goal. If one wants to go somewhere, perform some act, or obtain something and is prevented from doing so we say that person is frustrated.

One of the basic tenets in psychology is that frustration tends to arouse aggressive feelings, as indicated in Chapter 1. Dollard, Doob, and others at Yale began the work on this problem. They asserted that *"aggression is always a consequence of frustration. . . . the occurrence of aggressive behavior always presupposes the existence of frustration and, contrariwise, . . . the existence of frustration always leads to some form of aggression"* (Dollard et al., 1939, p. 1).

The behavioral effects of frustration were demonstrated in a classic study by Barker, Dembo, and Lewin (1941). Children were shown a room filled with attractive toys but were not allowed to enter it. They stood outside looking at the toys, wanting to play with them, but were unable to reach them. After they had waited for some time, they were allowed to play with them. Other children were given the toys without first being prevented from playing with them. The children who had been frustrated

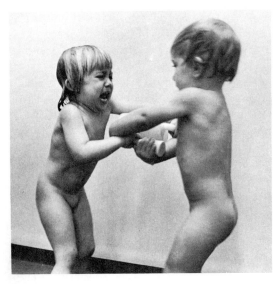

A common source of frustration occurs when someone tries to take something away from you. Sometimes our anger is so intense that we are oblivious to our surroundings.

smashed the toys on the floor, threw them against the wall, and generally behaved very destructively. The children who had not been frustrated were much quieter and less destructive.

Family life is one major source of frustration. Surprisingly, the most commonly reported source of conflict in American families concerns housekeeping. Families argue and fight endlessly about what and how much to clean, about the quality of food served, about taking the trash out, mowing the lawn, and fixing things. One-third of all American couples say that they *always* disagree about housekeeping. Close behind are conflicts about sex, social activities, money, and children, in that order (Straus et al., 1981).

Economic problems produce especially high levels of frustration within families. There is more family conflict and more domestic violence in working-class than in middle-class families, and more in families with unemployed breadwinners or with especially large numbers of children (Straus et al., 1981). Of course, many working-class families with large numbers of children and marginal economic situations are loving, relatively conflict-free, and free of do-

mestic violence. But on the average, these life stresses lead to greater frustration, and ultimately to more violent incidents.

This effect of frustration may also be seen in broader perspective in society at large. Economic depressions produce frustration that affects almost everyone. The consequence is that various forms of aggression become more common. For example, before World War II, the economy in the southern states of the United States was heavily dependent on cotton. Hovland and Sears (1940) found that lower cotton prices were associated with more lynchings of blacks in the South during the years 1882 to 1930. A drop in the price of cotton signified a depressed period economically, producing frustration and in turn heightened aggressive behavior in terms of lynchings (see also Hepwirth & West, 1988).

Job-related problems are also among the greatest sources of frustration and anger. In one study of employed women, such as conflicts between supervisors' and coworkers' expectations, job dissatisfaction, and perceived underutilization of skills were all among the strongest predictors of their general hostility levels (Houston & Kelly, 1989).

These examples illustrate the typical effect of frustration, but the original theory suggested that aggression always stemmed from frustration, and frustration always produced aggression (Dollard et al., 1938). It appears now that neither *always* in these assumptions is correct. Although frustration usually arouses anger, there are circumstances when it does not; increased anger may not always lead to more aggressive behavior. And, as we will see below, factors other than frustration can also produce aggressive behavior.

Attributions

In most cases, for an attack or frustration to produce anger and aggressive behavior, the person must perceive it as intended to harm him or her. Our tendency to aggress often depends more on the apparent motives or intentions behind the other person's actions—

especially when these are potentially provocative—than on the nature of these actions themselves. In terms of **attribution theory** (Weiner, 1982), anger is most likely when the attack or frustration is perceived as intended by the other person, that is, as being under that person's internal control. However, if the victim attributes the frustration to mitigating circumstances—that is, to conditions beyond the frustrator's control—it should not create so much anger. For example, we would expect more anger among unemployed workers if they have been fired by a boss who said she did not like them than if they were laid off because an economic recession forced the entire plant to shut down. Indeed, a survey of occasions on which people felt angry showed that anger was a response to an act perceived as voluntary and unjustified in

59 percent of the episodes, to a potentially avoidable accident or event 28 percent of the time, and to an unavoidable accident or event only 2 percent of the time (Averill, 1983).

The role of perceived internal control in generating anger was shown clearly in an experiment by Greenwell and Dengerink (1973). Male college students were placed in a competitive task with a fictitious opponent. Each was allowed to shock the other. They received information, supposedly from the opponent, indicating either that (1) he was intentionally raising the level of his shock settings over trials or that (2) he was deliberately maintaining those shocks at a constant, moderate level. For half the subjects within each of these groups, the strength of the shocks received actually *did* increase; for the others, it remained constant. The

---

BOX 11–3

Experimenting with Aggression

Aggressive behavior, by its nature, is nasty and hurtful. How then can we do experimental research on it? Measuring one person's impression of another, or their social attitudes and attitude change, or their liking for each other is not generally harmful to anyone, but how can we do an experiment measuring a person's tendency to harm another person without actually hurting anyone?

Two techniques have been widely used and will be referred to quite often throughout this chapter. The **shock-learning technique,** designed by Arnold Buss (1961), involves both a naive subject and a confederate. They are informed that the experiment concerns the effects of punishment on learning. The confederate is to be the learner and the subject, the teacher. When the confederate-learner makes an error, the subject-teacher is to deliver punishment to the learner in the form of electric shock (or sometimes loud noise). Of course no shock or noise is actually delivered to the confederate-learner, but the subject thinks he or she really is hurting the person. The confederate-learner makes errors on a standard, prearranged schedule, and

the subject-teacher can punish for as long and as intensely as he wants. The measure of aggression is the duration and intensity of punishment.

The **shock-competition technique** was developed by Stuart Taylor (1967). It begins by informing two naive subjects they will compete against each other in a reaction-time task. On each trial, they are allowed to set the level of electric shock (or loud noise) their opponent will receive if the opponent loses. In reality the experimenter sets both the outcome of the competition (who wins or loses) and the level of shock either one receives.

Both techniques have been used fairly widely, and to a large extent they both seem to measure the same thing (Bernstein et al., 1987). They both pose ethical problems, of course. They both rely on deceiving the subjects, so fully informed consent is impossible. It also can be argued that either being shocked or shocking another person is harmful. On the other hand, there is plainly great value to society in understanding aggression and how to control it. So if the costs of the research are high, so perhaps are its potential benefits.

results indicated that the opponent's intentions were more important in determining the subjects' own shock settings than was the strength of the actual shocks they received from this person.

But the timing of information about intention or mitigation is also important. If people already understand the mitigating reasons before they are frustrated, they are less likely to get angry and become aggressive. Explaining all the good reasons afterward, while the person is already steaming, is not so likely to reduce the anger!

To show this, Johnson and Rule (1986) had a confederate anger male undergraduates by giving them bursts of loud noise while insultingly evaluating an essay they had written, describing them as uncreative, poor students. Then the subject could administer loud noise in return to the confederate, under the guise of evaluating the confederate's essay. Mitigating information about the confederate that would explain his behavior was provided to the subject: the confederate had just gotten a poor grade in an important midterm, which would prevent him from entering medical school. This mitigating information was only effective in reducing physiological arousal and aggression when it was given prior to the insults.

However, even prior information about mitigating circumstances or the other person's intentions may have little effect if the attack or other provocation to anger is very great (Zillmann, 1988). Family violence often occurs because intense arguing escalates without any consideration for the reasons for the other person's actions. So mitigating information may come too late or just be ineffective in the heat of passion. People really do kill "in the heat of anger," no matter what information they are given.

AGGRESSIVE BEHAVIOR

What is the relationship between anger and aggression? Attack and frustration tend to make people feel angry. But angry people do not always behave aggressively. In the survey mentioned earlier, people reported engaging in overt physical aggression on only 10 percent of the occasions when they felt angry, expressed verbal aggression 49 percent of the time, and engaged in various kinds of nonaggressive calming activities 60 percent of the time (Averill, 1983). Indeed, people typically did *not* behave aggressively when they felt angry, though they usually felt some urge to do so.

It is also possible for people to act aggressively without *feeling* angry. A foot soldier is ordinarily not angry at the anonymous, often unseen, and usually equally frightened enemy soldier he has been ordered to kill. So the factors that control aggressive behavior are as important as those that arouse anger in the first place. The issue is like the attitude-behavior problem discussed in the chapter on attitudes. Feelings—like attitudes—control behavior to some extent, but other factors play a role as well. We will consider the learning of aggressive behavior, social norms that control when and how aggressive behavior occurs, and aggression designed to achieve other goals.

Learning to Be Aggressive

The main mechanism determining human aggressive behavior is *past learning*. A newborn infant expresses aggressive feelings quite impulsively. Whenever it is the least bit frustrated, whenever it is denied anything it wants, it cries in outrage, flails its arms, and strikes out at anything within range. In the earliest days of life, an infant does not realize that other people exist and therefore cannot be deliberately trying to harm it. When the infant does discover the existence of others, it continues to vent its rage and probably directs much of it toward these people.

But by the time the individual is an adult, this little savage has his or her anger under firm control and aggresses only under certain circumstances, if at all. This development is primarily due to learning. We learn habits of behaving aggressively in some situations and suppressing anger in others, to aggress against some kinds of people (like siblings) and not others (like po-

BOX 11–4

Heredity Versus Environment as Influences on Crime

One possible source of individual differences is heredity. But the role of genetic influences in human aggression remains something of an open question. How might one demonstrate a genetic effect? If some form of aggressive behavior were inherited, identical twins should resemble each other behaviorally more than fraternal twins would, because their genes are more similar. And that proves to be true for criminal behavior (Mednick et al., 1988). This difference cannot be unequivocally attributed to genetic endowment, though, because parents and others probably treat identical twins more similarly as well, so environment is more similar as well.

Another strategy is to look at adopted children, to see if they resemble their biological parents (heredity) more than their adoptive parents (environment). In a careful study of all adoptions in Denmark from 1924 to 1947, Mednick and his colleagues (1988) found adoptees' rates of criminal conviction resembled their biological parents' rates more closely than their adopted parents', as the genetic view would suggest. However, further analysis revealed that this held for property offenses and not violent offenses! So, at least in these data, heredity does not seem to explain violent crime.

lice), and in response to some kinds of frustration and not others. These habits are crucial to our control of our own aggressive behavior.

Imitation. **Imitation** is one important mechanism that shapes a child's behavior. All people, and children in particular, have a strong tendency to imitate others. A child watches people eat with a fork and tries to do the same. After a while, the child also uses a fork. This imitation extends to virtually every kind of behavior, including aggression. A child observes other people being aggressive or controlling their aggression and copies them. Thus the child's own aggressive behavior is shaped and determined by what he or she observes others doing.

An experiment by Albert Bandura and his coworkers (Bandura, Ross, & Ross, 1961) illustrated this imitative learning of aggressive behaviors. Children watched an adult play with tinker toys and a Bobo doll (a 5-foot, inflated plastic doll). In one condition, the adult began by assembling the tinker toys for about a minute and then turned his attention to the doll. He approached the doll, punched it, sat on it, hit it with a mallet, tossed it in the air, and kicked it about the room, all the while shouting such

things as "Sock him in the nose," "Hit him down," "Pow." He continued in this way for 9 minutes, with the child watching. In the other

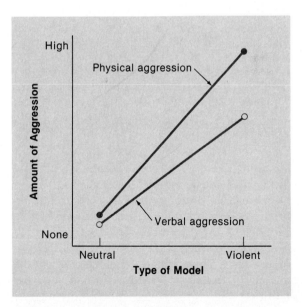

Figure 11–1. Aggression by children witnessing violent or neutral model. Note: The entry is the mean amount of physical or verbal aggression children administered to the Bobo Doll after watching the type of model indicated. (Adapted from Bandura, Ross, & Ross, 1961.)

BOX 11-5

Contagious Violence and Deindividuation

One form of imitative aggression that is important in crime and in crowd behavior is *contagious violence*. The French sociologist Tarde introduced the idea of contagious violence when he noted that news of a spectacular crime in one community produced imitative crimes. He pointed out that lurid news stories about the Jack the Ripper murders inspired a series of female mutilation cases in the English provinces (Tarde, 1903).

Mob behavior is another example of contagious violence. The sociologist LeBon (1896) observed that people in crowds often feel free to gratify "savage, destructive" instincts, feeling both invincible and anonymous. "The individual forming part of a crowd acquires . . . a sentiment of invincible power which allows him to yield to instincts." Moreover, "a crowd being anonymous, and in consequence irresponsible, the sentiment of responsibility which always controls individuals disappears entirely" (p. 30).

More recently, Zimbardo (1970) described this phenomenon as *deindividuation* (as we indicated in the chapter on groups), and suggested a number of factors that would produce it: anonymity, diffused responsibility, size, activity, a novel unstructured situation, arousal due to noise, and fatigue. So, for example, the most extreme violence in warfare by primitive peoples is carried out by those who use such deindividuating devices as masks,

face and body paint, and special garments (Watson, 1973). Similarly, early twentieth-century white lynch mobs in the United States engaged in more atrocities such as burning, lacerating, or dismembering the black victim when the crowds were especially large (Mullen, 1986).

To test experimentally whether these deindividuating factors do in fact lead to more aggressive behavior, Prentice-Dunn and Rogers (1983) used the shock-learning technique. In a "deindividuating cues" condition, subjects were not addressed by name; they were told the experimenter would not know what shock intensities they chose; they were told they would not meet or see the victim. The experimenter took full responsibility for the victim's well-being, and the room was dimly lit. In contrast, in an "individuating cues" condition, the subjects wore name tags, were addressed by their first names, and the experimenter took keen interest in the shock intensities selected. Subjects were told that they would meet the victim after the experiment and that the victim's well-being was the subjects' responsibility. The room was well-lit. As expected, deindividuation led to significantly greater shock being administered as well as to a lack of feeling of inhibition, and a lack of concern for the victim's, experimenter's, and other group members' reactions.

---

condition, the adult worked quietly with the tinker toys and ignored the doll.

Some time later, each child was frustrated mildly and then left alone for 20 minutes with a number of toys, including a 3-foot Bobo doll. The children's behavior was rated as shown in Figure 11–1. They tended to imitate many of the actions of the adult. Those who had seen the adult act aggressively were much more aggressive toward the doll than those who had witnessed the adult working quietly on the tinker toys. The first group punched, kicked, and hammered the doll and uttered aggressive com-

ments similar to those expressed by the aggressive adult.

The key theoretical notion in these experiments is that children learn specific aggressive responses by observing others perform them. It therefore follows that such vicarious learning should be increased when the adult's behavior is reinforced, and when the situation promotes identification with the adult model. So in these Bandura experiments, there was more imitative aggression when (1) the model was rewarded, (2) the model was of the same sex as the child, and (3) the model had had a previous nurturant relationship with the child, such as being a friend or teacher of the child (Bandura et al., 1963).

The children in this situation learned to attack a certain type of doll. They might also attack the same kind of doll in a different situation, and perhaps a different kind of doll, as well. Just how far this would extend—whether or not they would also punch their siblings—is not clear, but it is clear that they would be somewhat more likely to attack some things than they were before. Through the process of imitation, these children showed more aggressive behavior.

Reinforcement. A second mechanism by which aggression is learned is **reinforcement.** When a particular behavior is rewarded, an individual is more likely to repeat that behavior in the future; when it is punished, he or she is less likely to repeat it. A boy may come home in tears after being knocked down by another boy at school. His father chastises him for not hitting the boy back. The next time it happens, he does fight back, and even though he comes home a complete mess from his bloody nose, his father praises him effusively. This is one way that children learn the use of retaliatory aggression.

For example, in one study subjects were verbally reinforced ("that's good," "you're doing fine") for shocking a confederate (Geen & Pigg, 1970). Other subjects in a control group shocked the confederate but were not rewarded. The reinforced subjects gave considerably more intense shocks than did nonreinforced subjects. We could give many other examples making the same point: aggressive acts are, to a major extent, learned responses, and reinforcement is a major facilitator of aggression.

Children do not imitate indiscriminately—they imitate some people more than others. The more important, powerful, successful, and liked the other people are, the more a child will imitate them. Also, the people they see most often are the ones they imitate most. Parents fit all these criteria, and they are the primary models for a child during the early years, Since parents are both the major source of reinforcement and the chief object of imitation, a child's future aggressive behavior depends greatly on how parents treat the child and on how they themselves behave.

This joint dependence on the parents for reinforcement and imitation produces an interesting consequence. Punishing a child for acting aggressively might be considered an effective method of teaching the child not to be aggressive, but it often produces the opposite effect. A child who is punished for fighting does tend to be less aggressive—at home. Home is where the risk of punishment is greatest and therefore where the threat of punishment has the strongest inhibiting effect. Unfortunately, the situation is quite different when this child is out of the home. A child who is punished severely for being aggressive at home tends to be more aggressive outside (Sears, Whiting, Nowlis, & Sears, 1953).

The explanation for this effect is that the child imitates the parents' aggressive behavior. When she is in a situation in which she has the upper hand, she acts the way her parents do toward her. They are aggressive and so is she. The punishment teaches her not to be aggressive at home, but it also teaches her that aggression is acceptable if she can get away with it. Regardless of what parents hope, children will continue to do what their parents do as well as what they say.

Social Norms

Through imitation and reinforcement we learn when and how and against whom it is appropriate to aggress. People learn whether or not to aggress in response to certain cues. Which cues are associated with expressing aggression, and which are associated with suppressing it, is regulated in a very fine-tuned manner by the **social norms** we are all taught for specific situations. It is all right to fight back at a boy who hits you on the playground, but it is usually not okay if it is a girl or a crippled child. It is not all right to yell at a teacher who marks your spelling as incorrect or at your grandmother who serves you boring meatloaf every

BOX 11–6

The Social Heredity of Domestic Violence

This tendency for punishment to make the target even more aggressive—whether it occurs because of modeling or because of increased anger—passes aggressiveness down from one generation to the next, as well. The best data come from the national survey of domestic violence cited earlier (Straus et al., 1981). Men and women who had been physically punished as children were much more likely to be violent themselves toward their families in adulthood. Of the married men who had seen their parents attack each other, 35 percent had hit their own wives in the past year; of those who had not seen any such violence between their parents, only 11 percent had hit their own wives. The same held for wives: 27 and 9 percent, respectively, had hit their own husbands (though presumably much of that is simply retaliation for having been hit by their husbands). This relationship between family violence experienced in growing up, and marital violence engaged in as an adult, is shown quite clearly in the following figure.

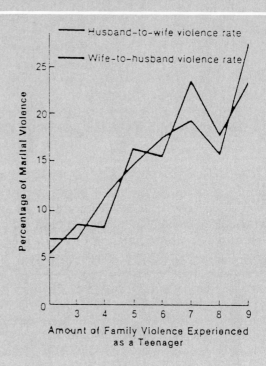

time she sees you. It is all right to honk at someone stopped at a green light but not at a red light. Of course, some aggressive behavior is impulsive, and some is inappropriate to the situation. But the most impressive thing is how much aggressive behavior is controlled by the very complex, and often subtle, social norms developed by every human culture or subculture.

These social norms specify what kind of aggression is antisocial, what kind is sanctioned, and what is actually prosocial. Slapping or spanking a disobedient 12-year-old is generally regarded as prosocial aggression; in one national survey, 70 percent regarded it as "necessary" (Straus et al., 1981). We also share norms about sanctioned aggression; 60 percent

"strongly agreed" that "a man has a right to kill another man in a case of self-defense" (Blumenthal et al., 1972). And most of the time we also agree on what is antisocial aggression. There is broad agreement about what is meant by such terms as "murder" or "assault," reflecting consensus about when violence is antisocial.

Sometimes these norms apply to the whole society; for example, we all generally share the view that it is wrong to kill another person, except under such extreme conditions as self-defense or executions. But occasionally we do not agree. In the 1960s, many blacks felt they were justified in rioting to protest racial discrimination, whereas most whites felt they were not justified in rioting (Sears & McConahay, 1973). Members of youth gangs may feel that retalia-

Complex social norms regulate aggression: The norms that regulate aggression in a civil disobedience protest are very complex indeed, but they have become quite predictable and everyone seems to share them and understand them. The protestors must be passive and nonviolent, while the police are supposed to be firm, make arrests, but not physically harm nor verbally abuse the protestors. When either side breaks these rules, they tend to get into trouble.

tory killings are justified, whereas most other people would disagree.

Sometimes social norms change, and with them, the frequency of certain types of aggressive behavior. The most obvious cases occur when wars begin and end, and the killing of enemy soldiers changes abruptly from being antisocial to being prosocial aggression and back again. Another example comes from comparing national surveys done in 1975 and in 1985 on the frequency of child abuse (Straus & Gelles, 1986). In the interim, the problem of child abuse had received a great deal of new publicity, and considerable resources were put into law enforcement and treatment programs to try to reduce it. The norms about allowable physical punishment of children changed correspondingly. And so the frequency of very severe violence reported by parents against their children (kicked, bit, hit with fist, used gun or knife) dropped by 47 percent in that period.

But such dramatic instances of disagreement and change should not obscure the consensus almost all humans share about the vast majority of aggressive acts. Understanding the differences among antisocial, sanctioned, and prosocial aggression depends on knowing what the relevant social norms are. The distinctions are sometimes quite subtle. But individuals must learn them to function effectively in society. Almost everyone can tell us when aggression is all right and when it is not. The few who cannot make at least the broad distinction are thought insane and are not held responsible for their actions.

Instrumental Aggression

Instrumental aggression occurs when a person uses aggression to attain some practical goal by hurting others, even when they are not angry at them. Boxers are paid to injure their opponents, but may scarcely know them at all. Some people are paid killers or paid assassins; they kill for money, not because of anger. Sometimes young thugs mug people in big cities not because they are angry, but to steal money. Slave-trading Europeans committed many acts of violence against seventeenth- and eighteenth-century Africans not out of anger, but for commercial motives.

One particularly important form of instrumental aggression stems from what LeVine and Campbell (1972) have called **realistic group conflict.** Sometimes two groups are in a situation in which they are competing for the same scarce resources. The two groups may aggress against each other as a way of trying to get those resources. They may or may not be angry at each other. For example, national leaders often take their countries to war with their neighbors not out of anger, but because they want to acquire territory, raw materials, or a better defensive position. In all these cases, aggressive behavior is committed simply as a way to attain other valued goods, and not necessarily because of angry feelings. We will discuss this form of aggression in more detail in the chapter on prejudice.

REDUCING AGGRESSIVE BEHAVIOR

Aggressive behavior is a major problem for human societies. Individual crimes and large-scale social violence are extremely damaging and harmful both to individual well-being and to the general social fabric. All societies expend much energy simply to control this tendency toward violence. So it is vital to understand how to reduce aggressiveness. But every solution proves to have its own risks and unintended consequences. So let us look systematically at the possible techniques for reducing aggressive behavior.

Punishment and Retaliation

It seems obvious that the fear of punishment or retaliation should suppress aggressive behav-

ior. The kind of people described earlier by rational decision-making theories would certainly include such future consequences in their calculations about aggression and would avoid behaving aggressively if punishment seemed likely. Indeed, when ''teachers'' in shock-learning experiments were told that the roles would later be reversed, thereby making them ''learners'' and vulnerable to being shocked themselves, they reduced their own aggression (Wilson & Rogers, 1975). Consistent with these findings, younger children are consistently more likely to be victims of domestic violence than older children because they are weaker and less likely to retaliate (Straus et al., 1981).

But the threat of punishment or retaliation turns out not to be such a simple way of reducing aggression. As suggested earlier, children who are frequently punished for being aggressive turn out themselves to be more aggressive than normal (Sears, Maccoby, & Levin, 1957). As Box 11–5 indicates, they often even go on to be especially likely to abuse their spouses. Perhaps it is because they model themselves on an aggressive parent. Perhaps it is because frequent punishment, like any attack, generates a lot of anger itself. In any case, punishment of children's aggressiveness does not result in a simple reduction of their aggressive behavior.

One of the dangers of aggressing when you are angered by others in traffic is that they will retaliate.

A second problem is that fear of punishment or retaliation seems to spark *counteraggression*. People who are attacked have a tendency to retaliate against their attackers, even when retaliation is sure to provoke more attacks (Dengerink, Schnedler, & Covey, 1978). Many lives have been lost on battlefields (and in presidential and royal palaces) because national leaders have felt that "national honor" demanded counteraggression, even though it almost guaranteed further retaliation and bloodshed.

There is some evidence that this escalation of aggression can be halted by the judicious use of apologies. In one study by Ohbuchi and his colleagues (1989), a confederate made some errors that ensured that the subject would fail at an experimental task. Then the experimenter roundly criticized the subject for doing so poorly. The confederate either then apologized for causing the subject to fail, or did not. The subject then was allowed to rate the confederate in a way that might affect the latter's grade. The apology significantly reduced the subject's hostility in these ratings.

The effects of anticipated punishment or retaliation are not simple, then. Sometimes they simply suppress aggression, as the person quite rationally wants to avoid future pain. But sometimes the threats are simply interpreted as attacks and inspire even more direct or indirect aggression. A rebellious adolescent boy may interpret even the routine and uniform application of rules in a family or a school as a personal attack, and may become belligerent, surly, and uncooperative.

Even if punishment, or threat of retaliation, were usually temporarily effective in suppressing direct aggression, it is too expensive to be a general solution to the problem. There are too many people in too many places for all to be monitored constantly. As it is, many people who commit serious crimes, such as murder, are never caught and punished. It is simply impossible to depend on external controls to minimize violence, and anyway we would not want a society with such repressive control of individual citizens' behavior. So the threat of punishment or retaliation is not a general solution to the problem.

Reducing Frustration and Attack

Since frustration and attack are major sources of anger, a better technique might be to reduce the potential for them. All societies, to one degree or another, try to ensure some minimal access to the necessities of life, such as food, clothing, shelter, and family life. A major reason is to avoid large-scale violent disruptions of daily life from especially frustrated groups. Large-scale hostile political demonstrations resulting from collective frustration are usually met by government attempts to relieve that frustration. Sometimes it is somewhat successful, as in the New Deal's response to the Depression of the 1930s. Sometimes it is not, as in France in 1789 and Russia in 1917.

Some societies, particularly those organized around socialist philosophies, make a particular effort to minimize the frustration of their citizens. Capitalist societies, on the other hand, tend to accept some frustration as part of the price of freedom. The evidence is that socialist societies generally do provide more economic equality, perhaps at the cost of overall productivity, individual freedom, and so on.

Similarly, most societies make some provision for collective police protection so that ordinary people are not continually subject to attack from bandits or otherwise violent persons. This helps to reduce the chances for widespread violence in two ways: people are protected, and they are not themselves goaded into retaliation. In the nineteenth century, life on the frontier in the United States was often lived without benefit of such tight community control over attack. The result was that people were quite vulnerable to attack and sometimes responded with retaliatory vigilantism.

But even the nations most conscientiously dedicated to the public's well-being cannot eliminate all individual frustration, attack, and instrumental aggression. No one ever will have exactly what and as much as he or she wants to eat when he or she wants it. That is the nature of life. So while forward-looking societies are wise to try to minimize as much large-scale frustration as they can, they can never completely eliminate it, or probably even come close. So other techniques for reducing aggression are necessary.

Learned Inhibitions

Another technique is for people to learn to control their own aggressive behavior, whether or not they are in danger of being punished. Just as people learn when aggression is desirable or permissible, so too they must learn when aggressive behavior must be suppressed. That is, they learn inhibitions against expressing aggression. Many factors appear to affect the inhibitions of aggression. We will consider generalized learned inhibitions, cues that bring those inhibitions into play, and substances that cause those inhibitions to be overridden.

Aggression Anxiety. To some extent, people learn to suppress aggressive responses in general. This general learned inhibition is called **aggression anxiety.** This is the anxiety people feel when they are about to commit an aggressive act. They may feel very anxious, or quite calm, depending on the inhibitions they have learned about aggression in general and this aggressive act in particular. Not everyone has equal amounts of aggression anxiety, of course. Women have more than men do. Children reared in middle-class homes tend to have more than children raised in lower-class homes. Parents who use reasoning and withdrawal of affection as disciplinary techniques produce children with more aggression anxiety than do parents who use high degrees of physical punishment (Feshbach, 1970). Presumably reasoning produces more strongly internalized inhibitions about aggression, which is more effective than a simple fear of punishment by others.

We also learn anxiety about expressing aggression in certain very specific situations. All through our lives we are learning and relearning "the ropes," the norms of our social environments. Students learn not to curse their professors to their faces, and professors learn not to throw things at their students. It is legal to kill animals for sport or food, but not to kill each other or someone's pet animal. We all possess a great many finely graded distinctions about what is and what is not permissible aggression. These learned inhibitions represent the most potent controls of human violent behavior we have.

Pain Cues. These learned inhibitions are triggered by cues that tell us what kind of a situation we are in—one that calls for expression, or one that calls for inhibition of it. One particularly important set of cues concerns a potential victim's reactions. What effect does it have if the victim shows signs of real pain? Will the aggressor have empathy for the person's suffering and inhibit further attack? Or will it make the aggressor feel he is successfully hurting the victim, as intended, and strengthen the tendency to aggress?

To test between these possibilities, Baron conducted a number of studies varying whether or not the aggressor got cues about the pain experienced by his victim. First, using the shock-learning technique, he transmitted the supposed physiological reactions of the shock victim to the subject in the form of a "pain meter." Such pain cues reduced further aggression, whether the subject had been angered or not. Even when the victim was quite dissimilar from the subject, and therefore might be difficult to empathize with, pain cues proved to reduce aggression. Indeed, pain cues reduced aggressive behavior in all conditions except when the aggressor was extremely angry to begin with. Then the victim's pain cues did promote more aggression (Baron, 1971a; 1971b; 1974). In general, then, signs of a victim's suffering seem to inhibit further aggression, except in cases of extreme anger, when they are taken as signs of successful hurting.

For such reasons, the phenomenon of *dehumanization* is thought to increase aggression against victims who are far away or anonymous to their attackers. For example, antiwar protestors during the Vietnam war felt that it was easier to bomb North Vietnamese from the great heights of a B-52 or to order troops into battle from the distance of Washington, D.C., than to attack at closer, more personal range. Having the victim distant or anonymous should make aggression easier, because the pain cues are absent. Conversely, making the victim more human, so that the attacker empathizes with the person's suffering, should reduce aggression.

Alcohol and Drugs. Inhibitions can be released as well as implemented, as all of us know. Such **disinhibition** can then result in outbursts of anger and aggression. For example, it is sometimes said that "the conscience is soluble in alcohol." Learned inhibitions against expressing aggression would seem to be among the more common aspects of conscience that are ignored when drinking. Barroom brawls and murders by drunken husbands are legendary, and not just in Hollywood movies. Intoxicated offenders commit as much as 60 percent of the murders in the United States and comparably high proportions of other violent crimes such as rape (including date rape), robbery, assault, domestic violence, and child abuse (Lisak & Roth, 1988; Steele & Southwick, 1985).

Such anecdotes and statistics do not isolate the particular effects of alcohol in these complex situations, however. And they do not prove it reduces inhibitions against aggression. Belligerent men may be attracted to bars and to arguments, or alcohol may stimulate sexual desire, and so on. To test more specifically the effects of alcohol on aggressive behavior, Taylor and Gammon (1975) gave subjects either a high dose of alcohol (about three or four stiff drinks for the average subject) or a low dose (about one drink). Then they were given the opportunity to aggress using the shock competition technique (see Box 11–2). The subject delivered significantly more shock if he had drunk more alcohol. This is a typical finding: most laboratory studies show that consumption of alcohol generally does increase aggression (see the meta-analysis by Hull & Bond, 1986).

Why does alcohol usually produce more violence? When sober people are provoked to aggression, they are responsive to such inhibiting cues as the instigator's intent and potential retaliation, whereas intoxicated subjects tend to plunge ahead with retaliatory aggression, oblivious to the potential consequences of their behavior (Zeichner & Pihl, 1979). In another

shock-competition study, intoxicated subjects who expected their opponent to behave aggressively plunged ahead with retaliatory aggression even if the opponent actually gave the lowest level of shock possible. They seemed to be oblivious to the change in the opponent's behavior. Nonintoxicated subjects noted the change in the opponent and reduced their own aggressive behavior (Leonard, 1989). In short, alcohol would seem to produce a loss of inhibitory control, in part because of a loss of perceptiveness about themselves and others.

But as well as disinhibiting the individual, alcohol may heighten his or her response to any conditions that instigate aggression, again presumably because it interferes with normal cognitive functioning (Taylor & Sears, 1988). In particular, alcohol tends to increase the individual's aggressive responses to such provocations as threat, frustration, or malicious intents. For example, in a shock-competition experiment, intoxicated subjects initiated more attacks than did nonintoxicated subjects only when the opponent was more threatening. They did not differ when competing against a nonaggressive opponent (Taylor et al, 1979; also see Lindman et al., 1987).

A further implication of this theory is that alcohol should increase aggression in response even to instigators that do not involve threat, attack, or frustration. For one thing, it should make people more responsive to simple social pressure to aggress. To test this, Taylor and Sears (1988) repeated the earlier shock-competition experiment but using only an opponent who behaved nonaggressively. So the subject was not threatened or attacked at all. They also varied how strongly two peer observers attempted to persuade the subject to deliver shock to the opponent; on some trials they tried hard, and on others, tried a little or not at all. As can be seen in Figure 11–2, alcohol (relative to a placebo ginger ale drink with just a disguising taste of vodka) increased the aggressive response to peer pressure to aggress—even though the victim was wholly innocent and harmless. So alcohol seems to have both a disinhibiting effect and the effect of heightening response to provocation.

Another disinhibiting drug, marijuana, has been shown in other experimental research actually to reduce aggression (see Taylor et al., 1976). Similarly, a careful review of the extensive clinical and field research on marijuana concludes that marijuana does not precipitate violence in the majority of those people who use it chronically or periodically. It does leave open the possibility that some people might have such weak inhibitions against aggression that marijuana would trigger their aggressiveness, but the research evidence on this point is too skimpy to draw a firm conclusion now (Abel, 1977). In contrast, other drugs such as PCP ("angel dust") or crack cocaine do seem to trigger extremely violent reactions, but systematic behavioral research on their effects is still in its infancy.

Displaced Aggression

What happens to aggressive feelings when, for one reason or another, they cannot be expressed against the cause of the anger? People are often frustrated or annoyed by someone but unable to retaliate against that person—the person may be too powerful, not available, or they may be too anxious and inhibited to do it. In such a situation, they are likely to express aggression in some other way, one of which is called **displaced aggression**—that is, expressing aggression against a substitute target. The child frustrated by her parents may deliberately pour her milk on the dog, or a man whose firm will not promote him may become increasingly angry at ethnic minorities. Either way, the individual expresses anger toward a safer target than the source of the frustration. When people do displace their aggression to an alternate target, what determines who will be selected as the target, and how much aggression will be expressed?

The basic principle of displacement is that the more similar a target is to the original source of frustration, the stronger will be the individual's aggressive impulses toward that target. But anxiety operates in much the same way as anger. Just as the impulse to hurt the source of frustration generalizes to other people, so does the anxiety about attacking the source. The more similar the person is to this source, the stronger the anxiety felt toward him or her. In general, therefore, displaced aggression is most likely to be directed toward targets who are perceived as weaker and less dangerous.

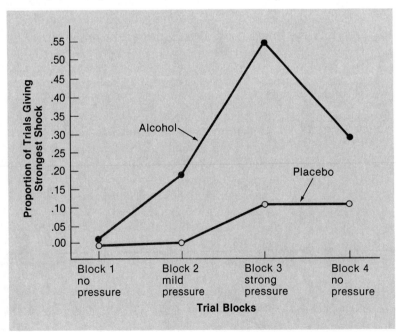

Figure 11–2. Shock administered to non-aggressive opponent as a function of alcohol consumption and social pressure to give shock. Note: Entry is the proportion of trials on which the subject administered the strongest possible shock to his opponent. (Adapted from Taylor & Sears, 1988, p. 241.)

When children are punished by their parents, they sometimes take out their feelings of aggression on dolls or other surrogate objects.

Catharsis

Another idea is that pent-up angry feelings might be reduced by expressing aggression. With less anger, the chance of further aggression would be reduced. Freud called this process **catharsis.** In common sense language, it involves "letting off steam" or "getting it out of your system." If someone annoys us by honking a horn at us, we feel angry. If, at the next traffic light, we find ourselves behind that car and honk at it, this should reduce the anger.

Freud's version of the catharsis theory presupposed that we always have a reservoir of instinctual aggressive energy within us. No matter what the situation is, we have a certain amount of aggressiveness that we need to "get off our chest." The frustration-aggression hypothesis, on the other hand, assumed that an-

ger comes from frustrations and attacks, and so expressing it would reduce aggressiveness only for those people in whom it had been built up through frustration or attack.

Research on catharsis has considered the effects of both *direct* and *indirect aggression*. Direct aggression is retaliation directly against the person who has made you angry by frustrating or attacking you. Catharsis can be successful in reducing aggression when an angry person has expressed that anger directly against his or her frustrator. In one experiment, a confederate insulted some subjects, criticized them for being so slow on an experimental task, and expressed doubts about their intellectual ability. Then some subjects were given the opportunity to aggress against the confederate, while others were not. The results clearly showed that delivering blasts of noise at the confederate reduced a sub-

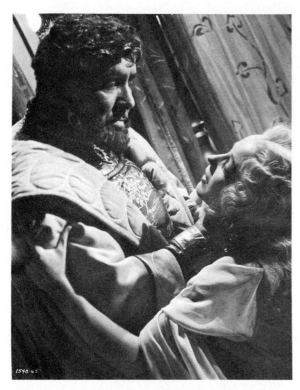

Classical dramas often present interpersonal violence, which the ancient Greeks and Freud thought might induce catharsis. Here Othello is strangling Desdemona in the 1947 film version of Shakespeare's *Othello*.

sequent tendency to do so (Konecni & Ebbesen, 1976). That is, catharsis resulted from delivering loud noise to the confederate.

However, relying on this kind of direct retaliatory catharsis as a way of reducing aggression is risky because it may have a number of undesirable side effects. There is the possibility of disinhibition. We all control our anger fairly tightly most of the time. But if it is once released, we may relax our inhibitions about further hostilities. Geen and Quanty (1977) cite the reaction of a man who killed four people: "He said . . . he had a funny feeling in his stomach but after the first [killing] . . . it was easy" (p. 29). Another risk is that within any given sequence of behavior, aggression seems to escalate rather than to decline. For catharsis to reduce aggression rather than escalate it, the

sequence of behavior needs to be interrupted: there must be a break in the action, or a change in the victim, or a change in the mode of expression of aggression (Goldstein, Davis, & Herman, 1975).

The catharsis hypothesis also predicts that expressing aggression indirectly should provide catharsis, and thus reduce further aggression. Aristotle felt that watching tragic dramas could produce catharsis, because the audience could vicariously experience the actors' emotions. Freud developed the same idea by hypothesizing that people could reduce their aggressive impulses through aggressive fantasy, such as in violent daydreams, cruel jokes, or writing stories. If such indirectly expressed aggression truly did cathart aggressive energy, aggressive behavior might be reduced without all the negative side effects we have enumerated.

By this theory, then, subsequent aggression should be reduced by modes of expressing aggression other than direct physical acts against a frustrator, such as *displaced aggression, vicarious aggression* (that is, aggression against your tormentor actually committed by someone else), or *verbal aggression*. There are some studies that find cathartic effects from indirect aggression (e.g., Feshbach, 1955; Konecni & Doob, 1972) but more that do not (see Geen & Quanty, 1977). In fact, these more indirect kinds of aggression turn out to be relatively highly correlated with direct aggression. For example, 56 percent of the married couples in the highest quarter of the population in verbal aggression had engaged in at least one violent episode within the past year, while only 0.5 percent of the couples in the lowest quarter on verbal aggression had had a violent incident (Straus et al., 1981; also see Carlson et al., 1989). So in married couples, verbally "getting it off your chest" is not associated with peace and harmony, but with later outbreaks of even more serious violence.

At the moment, then, social psychologists are somewhat skeptical that expressing anger often produces cathartic reduction in aggressive behavior. It does seem to reduce the expression of aggression only when the person is angry and is able to express aggression in a fairly direct manner against the person whom he or she perceives as responsible for the anger. But even then, sometimes aggression just escalates. And these are fairly stringent limitations on the catharsis effect.

MEDIA VIOLENCE

It is an understatement to say that in recent years movies have begun to portray a great deal of violence. Content analyses show a long-term trend of increasing violence in films shown in theaters dating from the early 1930s (Comstock, 1982). And more recent movies have escalated the amount of carnage as well as its vividness. People do not just die at a distance or clutch their stomachs and fall slowly to the ground. They bleed and suffer, the bullet wounds gape and blood pumps rhythmically from victims' bodies rather than slowly staining their clothes. Whether it is Rambo taking on the communists, gangs of thugs taking over Manhattan, or slashers materializing out of the night, the violence has become extraordinarily vivid.

Television also uses quite a bit of violence in its programming. Police, gangster, and spy shows, and most television movies include a full complement of fighting, shooting, and killing. Saturday morning cartoons feature more of the same. Although the violence on television is much less explicit and vivid than that in the movies, it is remarkably pervasive.

It is certainly widely assumed that such media violence stimulates people to aggressive behavior. In 1983 the chief of the California state prisons adopted a policy of preventing "any movie that glorifies sick violence" after he discovered that the movie *The Texas Chainsaw Massacre* had been shown at the men's prison in Chino. But as we have seen, aggression is a very complex behavior. Mere exposure to films may or may not have much effect on it one way or the other. This question has become one of the more controversial areas in the application of social psychological research to everyday life.

The Surgeon General's Report

Both the public and politicians are concerned about media violence. The U.S. Congress first held public hearings on TV violence in 1952. Later, the U.S. Surgeon General commissioned a report on the topic which was published in 1972 (Surgeon General's Scientific Advisory

Such horror films have become much more popular in recent years. What effects do you think they have on viewers, especially on young viewers? Do they inspire imitation? Fear? Repulsion?

Committee on Television and Social Behavior). After reviewing available research, the report concluded, rather cautiously, that

> [There is] a preliminary and tentative indication of a causal relation between viewing violence on television and aggressive behavior; an indication that any such causal relation operates only on some children (who are predisposed to be aggressive); and an indication that it operates only in some environmental contexts. (Surgeon General's Scientific Advisory Committee on Television and Social Behavior, 1972, p. 11).

This report immediately came under harsh attack, partly because some of the members of the committee that prepared it had worked for the television networks, and it was felt (quite understandably, but not necessarily accurately) that they therefore could not be disinterested scientific observers (Cater & Strickland, 1975). Most critics argued that the commission had underestimated the effects of media violence.

Ten years later, the National Institute of Mental Health asked a panel of behavioral scientists to evaluate the effects of televised violence once again. This time the reviewing committee concluded that "the consensus among most of the research community is that violence on television does lead to aggressive behavior by children and teenagers who watch the programs. . . . A causal link between televised violence and aggressive behavior now seems obvious" (National Institute of Mental Health, 1982, p. 6). A similar report was issued in seven volumes by the Canadian Royal Commission.

These reports met with much approval from many researchers in the field who had long since become persuaded of this conclusion (e.g., Friedrich-Cofer & Huston, 1986; Huesmann, 1982). However, other social scientists were more skeptical, feeling that the available evidence did not support a firm conclusion one way or the other, and so did not justify efforts to influence public policy (Freedman, 1984).

There are many theories of how and why media violence affects behavior. Most theories suggest that watching violence should increase the likelihood of aggressive behavior among viewers. For example, learning theory would emphasize that observing aggressive models teaches viewers to behave violently through *imitation*. A related idea is that children learn entire *scripts* about aggression from the media. Then events in their later lives prime those memories and generate aggressive behavior (Berkowitz, 1984; Huesmann, 1988). For example, one common television script is that the bad guy provokes the good guy, who retaliates. The child who has learned this script from television might in later life be too quick to retaliate to minor insults. Another theory begins with the observation that much violence in the media is rewarded rather than punished, as in the case of the retaliating good guy. Viewing such rewarded violence *disinhibits* the person: it sends the message that learned inhibitions against aggression should be set aside, freeing the individual to act more aggressively. Only the *catharsis* theory proposes that watching media violence should actually reduce aggression among viewers.

What does research actually find about the effects of media violence? The answer depends in part on the exact method used to study media effects. We will review three types of research: laboratory experiments, correlational surveys, and field experiments. By considering each of these approaches, we can gain a fuller understanding of this important issue.

Laboratory Experiments

An excellent example of a laboratory experiment on media violence is the work done by Albert Bandura and his colleagues discussed earlier in this chapter. Remember that the point of these experiments was to demonstrate that young children can learn aggressive behavior by imitating the aggressive behavior of adults. Preschool-age children were mildly frustrated, and then they observed an adult batting a Bobo doll around. When the children themselves were placed in the room with the doll, they repeated many of the aggressive behaviors performed by the adult.

Leonard Berkowitz and his colleagues subsequently conducted another series of laboratory experiments, typically showing a brief film with violent physical aggression to some college students who had been angered and to some who had not been angered. One of the films often used was a 7-minute clip from a boxing film starring Kirk Douglas called *The Champion*. The dependent variable usually was shock supposedly administered to a confederate in the standard shock-learning situation. Viewing the violent film generally produced more attacks on the confederate.

Most of these studies were tests of the theory that the cue properties of the situation stimulate learned aggressive responses (Berkowitz, 1974). Anything that associated the subject with the film aggressor, or the confederate with the film victim, should tend to increase aggression. In many respects this theory was supported (see Berkowitz, 1984, for a review). For example, subjects displayed more aggression when told to identify with the winner of the boxing match than with the judge; the confederate received more shock when described as a boxer than as a speech major; and a confederate named "Kirk" got more shocks than one named "Bob" after seeing the actor Kirk Douglas play the boxer

Violent scenes such as this from the film "The Champion", starring Kirk Douglas, have been used in many experiments on the effects of media violence.

who got beaten up in the film. When the film presented justified aggression, by presenting the loser of the boxing match in an unfavorable light, more aggression was displayed. Some studies found that subjects had to be frustrated or angered for the violent film to increase their aggression (though other studies did not find that prior angering had any effect; see Freedman, 1986).

Laboratory experiments have also been used to test the catharsis hypothesis. Seymour Feshbach did a pioneering experiment (1961) in which angered and nonangered subjects were shown either a violent boxing film or a neutral film. Measures of aggression taken after the film showed that watching the boxing film lowered the aggressiveness of angered subjects, supporting the catharsis prediction.

However, most laboratory experiments have in fact shown that observing aggression provokes greater aggressive behavior, not less. The catharsis effect rarely occurs. Whether one explains the media effect as resulting from imitation, priming, activating, or disinhibition, the result is the same: In these laboratory experiments, observing aggression usually increases aggressive behavior.

External Validity

As clear as the implications of these findings may be, it is quite a long step from such laboratory studies to the real-life situations to which we might want to generalize. Are these laboratory findings likely to hold up in real life? These laboratory experiments must be judged, therefore, in terms of their **external validity,** as discussed in Chapter 1.

Laboratory situations differ in some important and obvious ways from watching TV at home. First, the laboratory film segments are normally brief and almost entirely composed of a single violent episode, like a few rounds from a boxing match, or an adult beating up a Bobo doll. In contrast, the normal child in real life watches a variety of different television programs. And each program contains quite a mixture of human acts having nothing to do with violence. Even "Miami Vice" has humor, romantic entanglements, loyalty between cops, colorful scenery, and other nonviolent matters. It presents children with a wide variety of possible behaviors to imitate.

Second, in the laboratory the viewing situation is controlled and socially isolated, providing few distractions from the violence. In real life, people usually watch television with other people and simultaneously engage in other activities, ranging from eating, doing homework, conversing, and playing games to dancing (Comstock et al., 1978).

Third, the dependent variable in virtually all laboratory experiments is fully sanctioned, and often even prosocial, aggression. Children know it is perfectly all right to hit the Bobo doll. A 5-year-old playing with what is obviously a

new toy is a far cry from a gang of teenagers holding up a gas station and shooting the manager. Indeed, when the film model was punished for hitting Bobo, imitative aggression was markedly reduced. The shock-learning technique also involves prosocial aggression; the subject is supposedly in a learning experiment and is instructed to punish the victim for errors in order to improve learning. The concern about aggression in real life, in contrast, focuses primarily on such antisocial aggressive acts as unprovoked assaults, armed robbery, assault and battery, rape, and murder.

Fourth, in the laboratory there is usually little possibility of retaliation for being aggressive. And, as we have seen, when the victim can retaliate, the aggressor typically reduces his or her aggression. Finally, in these experiments the aggression measure is usually taken immediately after exposure to the film. Any delay would obviously reduce the effect of the film, and in fact, several studies have shown that the film's effect typically wears off within a matter of minutes. But in real life, the boy does not rush out of his living room with a knife and attack the first person he sees. Most crime is committed quite a long time after the person has watched television. People who are roaming the streets are not home watching television; in fact, we might all be safer if they were.

So the external validity of these experiments is open to some question, particularly since all these special conditions of laboratory experiments have themselves been shown to increase aggression. So they may exaggerate the aggression produced by violent films. They do show that media violence *can* produce increased aggressive behavior, but to learn whether or not it generally *does* so we need to turn to studies done under conditions that more nearly resemble real life.

Correlational Surveys

One solution to the problem of external validity is to conduct **correlational research** to determine whether the children who watch the most violent television are also the ones who are the

Does this little girl perceive her actions as antisocial aggression? Or would she think it was sanctioned, or even prosocial? Looks like the doll did something wrong!

most aggressive. If they were, the causal interpretation might still be open to question as indicated in Chapter 1. But if the correlation between the two was zero, it would be much harder to make a case for the causal role of media violence. So the results from correlational surveys would be valuable, even if not decisive.

Since one interesting question is whether viewing violence in childhood produces more aggression in adulthood, a particularly important type of correlational survey is the *longitudinal study:* children's television viewing is measured at one time, and their aggressive behavior is assessed some years later. Several such studies have been done (Eron et al., 1972; Huesmann et al., 1984; Milavsky et al., 1982). Overall, the correlations between early viewing of violence and later aggressive behavior usually tend to be positive but rather small, and statistically significant in only a minority of cases (Friedrich-Cofer & Huston, 1986; Freedman, 1984). Moreover, if children who view violence the most are the most aggressive, then the effects of their heavier viewing should cumulate over the years, so the correlation between viewing violence and aggressive behavior should increase with age. Yet in longitudinal studies this has generally not been the case: the correlation between viewing violence and aggressive behavior has been about the same at each age level (Freedman, 1984). It is possible to argue that consistently positive, even if very weak, correlations reflect socially significant effects (Rosenthal, 1986). But the fact is that the relationship is simply not a very strong one.

Even if we take these relatively weak correlations as reflecting a real relationship, they lend themselves to other causal interpretations. Both of the standard problems with correlational designs pose dangers here. The "reverse causality" problem is that being especially aggressive may generate interest in watching violence rather than vice versa (Friedrich-Cofer & Huston, 1986). The "third-variable" problem also emerges. The viewing of violent programs is highly correlated with the amount of total television viewing, and when that has been taken into account, the effect of violent viewing often disappears (Friedrich Cofer & Huston, 1986).

This suggests that viewing unusual amounts of television in general, rather than of violence in particular, may be more characteristic of children who are especially aggressive. And there may be important personality characteristics that produce both aggressive behavior and a special interest in watching violent films; these have not yet been taken account in these studies (Freedman, 1986). So the correlational studies do not provide strong evidence for a causal role of media violence in producing aggressive behavior in real life.

Field Experiments

Field experiments would seem to be the answer to these criticisms. A number have been done, which typically present the standard movie and television fare of the day, experimentally varying exposure to violent (as opposed to neutral or nonviolent) films. The subjects have usually been male adolescents living in their normal life situations (though most of these have been in boarding schools, rather than living at home with their parents). They have measured genuine interpersonal aggression in a free, unconstrained atmosphere. By being done in real life situations, they do not present the artificialities and biases present in laboratory studies. And by using experimental designs, they are not vulnerable to alternate causal interpretations.

Only a few major field experiments have been done. In the first, boys in private boarding or state residential schools were randomly assigned to two groups. One group watched largely aggressive television programs such as "Gunsmoke" and "The FBI," while the other group was limited to nonaggressive programs such as the "Ed Sullivan Variety Show" and "Bachelor Father." The boys watched only shows on the designated lists and could watch as much as they wanted as long as they spent at least 6 hours a week watching television. Various measures of aggressiveness were given before and after the six-week viewing period, and both peers and adult supervisors also rated the boys' aggressiveness (Feshbach & Singer, 1971).

The results showed that boys in the state schools who watched aggressive programs actually became less aggressive. They engaged in fewer fights and argued less with their peers. The effect was the same but somewhat weaker for the boys in the private schools. This study thus indicates that, at least under some conditions, observing television violence in real-life situations might actually decrease aggressive behavior.

Three other studies were done in minimum security penal institutions for juvenile offenders in the United States and Belgium (Leyens et al., 1975; Parke et al., 1977). The boys in some living cottages were shown up to five full-length violent movies while boys in other cottages were shown neutral films. The Belgian study found an increase in aggression for one cottage shown the violent films but not the other, and one American study found a similar increase but the other did not. In no case was there any cumulative or lasting effects of exposure. Similarly, Friedrich and Stein (1973) put nursery school children on a diet of 12 violent cartoons ("Batman," "Superman"), or prosocial entertainment ("Mister Rogers") or neutral films (e.g., about nature), but on most of their several measures of aggression, the groups did not differ significantly. Other similar studies show no effects (Wells, 1973; Milgram & Shotland, 1973). So these studies did not find that violent films consistently increased aggresiveness.

Some "natural experiments" have occurred when television has been newly introduced into areas where there had been no television. Hennigan and her colleagues (1982) studied the relationship between the introduction of television to various areas of the U.S. and changes in the crime rate. They found no increase in violent crimes, burglary, or auto theft—the crimes usually portrayed on television. The only change was an increase in larceny—a crime rarely shown on television.

Each of these studies has its flaws. In the Feshbach-Singer study, the adolescent boys in the nonviolent conditions were deprived of their normal favorite programs. This frustration could by itself have increased their aggressiveness, thus eliminating any possible differences between the violent and nonviolent conditions.

The Leyens, Parke and associates studies used group-viewing situations in dormitories where boys in prison had been living together for some time. This was perhaps a little like watching movies in a fraternity (except with juvenile delinquents instead of college boys), and it evidently stimulated a good bit of rowdiness during and right after the movies. But this rowdy-group context is not the usual one for TV viewing in the home.

But all studies in social science are flawed. It is a myth that a perfect study can be devised. The minute we patch up one problem, another emerges (often created by the patch, in fact). The way to come to a conclusion about an important area of research is to look at the pattern of the data. And overall, the results of these violent versus nonviolent TV field experiments are not very dramatic. Rather, observed violence in movies or television seems not to have affected aggressive behavior much in these real-life situations, one way or the other.

Conclusions

The effects of media violence have become one of the most passionate and most political of research topics in social psychology. We have discussed three different methods of researching the effects of media violence. Laboratory studies seem quite generally to show that observed violence increases aggressive behavior. But we do not have much confidence in generalizing from these laboratory studies to crime in the streets. Most correlational surveys find a modest positive association between children's liking for violent television programs and their behavioral aggression. However, these relationships are never very strong, and in some of the best studies are not even statistically significant. And they are vulnerable to alternative interpretations. The field experiments we have described come close to being realistic replicas of real life, with the methodological protection of an experimental design. However, these studies have generally shown that media violence has little or no systematic effect on interpersonal aggression.

From a policy point of view, the question is whether this evidence is strong enough to urge the suppression of certain kinds of entertainment programs. There are social conditions we all know are important in producing violence, such as unemployment, racial prejudice, poor housing, poor medical care (especially for people with mental health problems), the widespread availability of guns and alcohol and illegal drugs, a highly mobile population that does not settle into tight little self-policing communities, parental indifference to the welfare of their children, among many other things. Given the evidence accumulated to date, it seems to us that television and the movies contribute only a small amount to crime and violence beyond these large social factors.

And we must be very careful about censorship of any kind. Today the government might decide that it is illegal to depict a knifing on television, and tomorrow, that it is illegal to depict protest demonstrations, because people might imitate that. Once the principle of censorship is accepted, it becomes harder and harder to draw the line. We should recognize that no matter how passionately we feel about the issue, we must be cautious about taking a stand before we have sufficient evidence. Many psychologists today believe that media violence does generally increase aggressiveness. In our view however, the actual empirical evidence is weak and has not shown a role of media violence in increasing crime.

SEXUAL VIOLENCE

A related question concerns the possible role of sexually explicit films, books, and magazines in promoting sexual violence. According to recent studies about one-quarter of North American women have been or will be raped or sexually assaulted at some point in their lives (Malamuth & Briere, 1986, p. 75). Many women have been threatened with physically coercive sex by male acquaintances. Many argue that such pornography degrades women and encourages sexual coercion and violence. For example a few years ago, a television drama, *Born Innocent*, portrayed an artificial rape scene. A few days later, some adolescent boys carried out a similar artificial rape which some observers blamed on the movie. Does pornography, and perhaps especially violent erotica, generally contribute to such sex crimes?

In the late 1960s, the liberal President Lyndon Johnson appointed a Commission on Obscenity and Pornography. After a careful review of the research evidence, the committee reported (1970) that it could document no antisocial effects of pornography. Laboratory studies of the effects of pornography had not detected harmful effects. Rather, early socialization and peer influence were the key factors in sexual violence. The early background of sex offenders was generally sexually repressive and restrictive, not permissive. Antisocial aggression among young men was more heavily influenced by peers than by the media. This conclusion was attacked by political conservatives, religious groups, and feminists, so the conservative President Ronald Reagan's administration appointed another commission. This concluded that sexually explicit depictions of violence are likely to increase sexual violence and coercion, and recommended stricter antiobscenity legislation and prosecution (Attorney General's Commission on Pornography, 1986).

What can social psychology contribute to this debate? Much research has been done in recent years. Most of it has been guided by the theories we have just discussed, hypothesizing that violent sex in the media increases sexual violence through imitation, association of sexual pleasure with violence, and disinhibition. The best studies have used films and some variant of the shock-learning procedure. Most of these studies have used either full-length feature films or short stag films. They have typically manipulated exposure to erotic and violent material independently. Table 11–1 shows some examples of recent feature films that represent each possible combination of these two dimensions.

Violent Erotica

One basic question is whether or not there is something special about the *mixture* of violence

In this scene from the film, "Modern Girls", the man tries to force himself on the young woman before her friends can come to her aid. Such scenes of sexual violence have become more common in the movies in recent years.

clothes off, slap her around, and rape her (Donnerstein & Berkowitz, 1981A). Other subjects were presented in a similar violent but nonerotic film in which the woman is tied up and slapped around without any nudity or sexual activity. Male subjects angered by a female and then given the violent-erotic film gave more intense shocks to a confederate than in any other condition. Whether this latter finding is replicable or not remains an open question, but at least it does provide some concrete evidence for a harmful effect of violent erotica.

A second important finding is that the female film victim's own emotional reaction to being sexually coerced is crucial in determining the viewer's later aggression. In the Donnerstein and Berkowitz (1981) study, the subjects were either angered or not by a female confederate, against whom they could later retaliate. Then they were shown the film in which the victim was raped by two men. But the ending was varied: in one, she is smiling and not resisting, and even becomes a willing participant. In the other, she seems to find the experience humiliating and disgusting. As shown in Figure 11–3, the male viewers delivered more intense shocks to the female confederate when angered, consistent with earlier research. But when they were not angry, they did so only when the film depicted the woman as enjoying the experience. As will be indicated shortly, men's perception of women's feelings about sexual coercion play an important role in their responses.

Even if violent erotica do not directly contribute to violence, they might contribute to the **de-**

and sexual themes that triggers unusual levels of aggression against women. We have seen that violent films produce more such aggression in laboratory experiments than do nonviolent films. However, what are the effects of witnessing uniquely *sexual* violence? The most relevant comparison, then, is between witnessing a violent erotic film and witnessing a violent nonerotic film.

To test this, Donnesterin (1983) presented some subjects a violent-erotic stag film. This depicted a young woman who comes into view, apparently to study with two men. They have been drinking, and she is forced to sit between them and drink. They then tie her up, strip her

		TABLE 11 – 1	
	TYPOLOGY OF FILMS USED IN RESEARCH ON SEXUAL VIOLENCE		
	Sexual		Nonsexual
Violent	Some R-rated films (*Blue Velvet, Straw Dogs*)		Horror films (*Friday the 13th, Texas Chainsaw Massacre*)
	Some X-rated films (*Story of O*)		War films (*Rambo*)
Nonviolent	Teen sex comedies (*Spring Break*)		Situation comedies (*Rainman, On Golden Pond*)
	Nonviolent R-rated films (*Body Heat*)		Family films (*101 Dalmatians, E.T.*)
	Most X-rated films (*Emmanuelle*)		

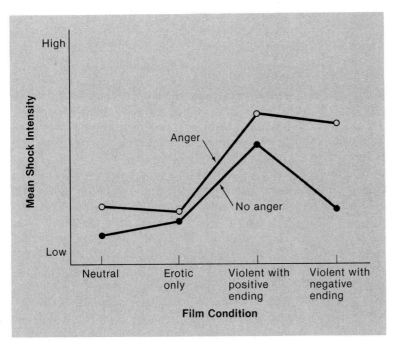

Figure 11-3. Shock intensity as a function of prior angering and type of erotic film. Note: Erotic film had little or no aggression; positive ending depicted coercive sex with a woman who was a willing participant, and the negative ending, with a woman who was not. (Adapted from Donnerstein and Berkowitz, 1981, p. 150.)

sensitization of men to violence against women. They might lead to demeaning or callous attitudes toward women and therefore make violent or coercive sexual behavior more acceptable.

Numerous studies have indeed shown that viewing violent sexuality produces more accepting attitudes about violence against women, and to accepting such myths as that women often enjoy being forced to perform various sexual acts or even being raped.

A typical example of desensitization comes from a study by Malamuth and Check (1981). They compared the effects of viewing the films *Swept Away* and *The Getaway* showing women as victims of both erotic an nonerotic aggression, with those of viewing more neutral film. This study was particulary useful because the films were viewed in regular theaters, while the viewers' attitudes were measured in regular class sessions, so they were not aware of being subjects in an experiment. The more aggressive films increased males', but not females', acceptance of violence against women. Later studies did find that repeated exposure over a period of days or weeks to stag films depicting sexual violence against women did produce desensitization in terms of reducing perceptions that the material was violent and degrading to women, reducing support for sexual equality, and lessening sympathy for victims of rape (e.g., Linz, Donnerstein, & Penrod, 1984; Zillmann & Bryant, 1982; see Malamuth & Briere, 1986, for a review).

As with laboratory experiments on media violence, however, these studies raise problems of external validity. One problem is that most of these studies have tended to present single, brief stag films depicting little other than a wide variety of sexual activities, rather than the full-length films to which most men are usually exposed. Later studies, which presented anywhere from two to six full-length, commercially released films, including a wide variety of other normal daily activities, found no effect on the male subjects' aggressive behavior, attitudes toward women, or sympathy for the victim in a rape trial (Malamuth & Ceniti, 1986; Linz et al, 1988).

A second problem is that such studies may create experimental **demand characteristics** because the purpose of the experiment may seem obvious. The danger is that the subjects will then try to do the expected thing, to try to seem normal, and thus will inadvertently comply with the researcher's hypothesis. Watching a brief clip of women being sexually abused in a film, and then being asked to shock another woman or express attitudes about sexual violence may be so obviously connected to each other that they yield a biased test of the hypothesis. One solution is to collect the dependent variable under different auspices and in a wholly different context from the films, thus disguising the connection between the two. This is called a *separated post-test*. For example, after the film exposure, Linz and colleagues (1988) had another researcher phone subjects at home to ask them to participate in a study in the law school evaluating a trial. When they arrived, they were asked to be jurors in a rape case. As just noted, prior exposure to the films had no effect on evaluations of the rape victim. Similarly, Malamuth and Ceniti (1986) used the shock-learning technique as a separated post-test, and the films had no effect.

In short, the original one-shot laboratory studies, or longer-term studies using short, concentrated clips of sexual violence, did report increased acceptance of violence on attitude measures taken immediately following exposure. But responses to full-length films and/or on separated post-tests yielded only weak effects.

Nonviolent Erotica

The use of force is not a common theme in most men's sexual fantasies or in the erotic materials they most often see. For men it is less common than purely heterosexual or voyeuristic fantasies (Arndt et al, 1985). *Playboy,* which has the largest circulation of the erotic men's magazines, displays violence very rarely; only 0.3 percent of all its pictorials and cartoons have contained violence (and even that is declining; see Scott & Cuvelier, 1987). Similarly, many popular R-rated movies display at least some female nudity and nonexplicit sexual acts, and many depict violence against women as well as men, but relatively few portray sexual violence against women. Indeed, the written stories most sexually arousing to men are those that are sexually explicit and nonaggressive (Malamuth et al., 1986, p. 332).

Nevertheless, some theorists contend that even nonviolent erotica induce sexual coercion and aggression, since they dehumanize women by treating them as sexual objects, portray women as subordinate to men, as existing solely for their sexual satisfaction, as promiscuous and insatiable, and even as desiring coercive sex, thus encouraging men to pursue women even when they do not want sex.

In general, nonviolent erotica seems not to increase aggression below the levels of no-film or neutral-film control groups. For example, nonviolent erotic scenes from the films *Body Heat* and *Crimes of Passion,* displaying couples in mutually consenting but nonexplicit sexual activity, had no more effect on male subjects' attitudes toward sexual violence than did watching a couple have a nonsexual, nonviolent conversation (Sweaton & Byrne, 1987). Similarly, a sexually graphic but nonviolent X-rated film (depicting a young female singer's efforts to establish herself in the music industry), shown to a large audience in a largely residential college, produced no increased violence by male viewers against their female companions as recorded in questionnaires completed by the women several days before and after the film (Smith & Hand, 1987).

Exposure to nonviolent erotica may turn out to increase violent behavior under one set of limited conditions: when subjects are angry to start with; the erotic materials are extremely explicit, ''hard core'' pornography, and the predominant affect experienced by the subject is negative (disgust or distaste). For example, Donnerstein and Barrett (1978) angered male subjects by having confederates shock them, then showed them some hard-core black-and-white stag films depicting oral and anal intercourse and female homosexuality. Such subjects shocked the offending confederate more than did nonangered subjects, or subjects shown no film or a neutral wildlife documentary.

Why did this nonviolent erotica increase aggressive behavior? Probably for two reasons. Angering the subjects beforehand provided aggressive cues. And negative affective experiences contribute to aggression, and most ''hard-core'' material is inherently not very pleasant to most people (White, 1979). So presumably erotic materials that depict sex in an ugly, disgusting way would be more likely to inspire aggression. However, the most common nonviolent erotic materials are considerably more pleasant, depicting nudity and conventional lovemaking. So it would appear that nonviolent erotica does contribute to aggression only under some quite limited conditions, even in laboratory situations.

Other Factors

What else can we say about the origins of sexual violence? The clearest finding is that attitudes condoning sexual violence against women are, among men, associated with men's self-reported likelihood of engaging in violence against women and laboratory aggression against women. For example, attitudes condoning coercive sex were correlated with delivering shock to a woman confederate (Malamuth & Ceniti, 1986) and to unsympathetic responses to

a rape victim (Linz et al., 1988). Rapists also endorse such attitudes more than do ordinary male citizens (Malamuth & Briere, 1986). Anger toward women and need for dominance over them prove to be fairly strong characteristics of convicted rapists and of college men who have engaged in sexual aggression (Lisak & Roth, 1988). Such basic attitudes and personality characteristics may well be more important than erotic films in understanding and ultimately reducing violence against women.

In real life peer influence may also be a most powerful factor in producing sexual aggression. Ageton (1983) and Alder (1985) found that in two separate samples of adolescent boys and adult males, the strongest predictors of sexual aggression were, in the first case, involvement with delinquent peers, and second, having sexually aggressive friends.

In short, it seems likely that most actual acts of sexual violence involve a wide variety of converging factors, of which the media may at best be only one: attitudes, personality, disinhibition due to alcohol, and social influence (Malamuth & Briere, 1986; Lisak & Roth, 1988).

Key Terms

aggression	desensitization	prosocial aggression
aggression anxiety	disinhibition	realistic group conflict
anger	displaced aggression	sanctioned aggression
antisocial aggression	external validity	shock-competition technique
attribution theory	field experiment	shock-learning technique
catharsis	frustration	social norms
correlational research	imitation	
demand characteristics		

Summary

1. Aggression is defined as any action that is intended to hurt another person.

2. Aggressive acts can be antisocial, prosocial, or merely sanctioned, depending on

whether they violate or conform with social norms.

3. Aggressive feelings, or anger, need to be distinguished from aggressive behavior.

4. The major determinants of anger seem to be attack and frustration, particularly if attributed to intent to injure.

5. Major determinants of aggressive behavior are angry feelings and the learning of aggressive responses. This learning can take place through imitation or reinforcement of aggressive responses.

6. Social norms are crucial in determining what aggressive habits are learned.

7. Fear of punishment or retaliation can reduce aggressive behavior. However it may sometimes result instead in covert aggression, or actually increase aggression over the longer run.

8. Learned inhibitions of aggression are the most important control over it. Such inhibitions can also result in the displacement of aggression to other innocent parties.

9. Observed aggression generally increases aggression in laboratory studies, especially when the model is rewarded or when the observed victim is similar to the target of the subject's own aggression. However these results may not generalize to real-life situations.

10. Field experiments of televised or movie violence, on the other hand, have not generally shown that it increases aggressive behavior in real-life settings. The evidence that media violence contributes to violence and crime in our society is still rather indirect.

11. The main determinants of sexual violence seem to lie in inegalitarian and coercive attitudes toward women, peer group norms, and abuse of substances such as alcohol. Written and filmed erotica seem to play a relatively minor role.

Suggested Readings

Bandura, A. (1973). *Aggression: A social learning analysis.* Englewood Cliffs, NJ: Prentice-Hall. The definitive statement by the most influential spokesman for the social learning and imitation approach to aggression.

Baron, R. A. (1977). *Human aggression.* New York: Plenum Press. A thorough, readable, comprehensive treatment of aggression from a social-psychological perspective.

Berkowitz, L. (1984). Some effects of thoughts on anti- and prosocial influences of media events: A cognitive-neoassociation analysis. *Psychological Bulletin, 95,* 410–427. A recent statement from one of the most important researchers in the field on the effects of aggression, reflecting the influence of social cognition.

Dollard, J., Doob, L., Miller, N. E., Mowrer, O. H., & Sears, R. R. (1939). *Frustration and aggression.* New Haven, CT: Yale University Press. The original statement of the theory that frustration breeds aggression. As well as discussing their laboratory experiments, it ranges far into the larger social manifestations of aggression, such as criminality, war, and fascism.

Freedman, J. L. (1984). Effect of television violence on aggressiveness. *Psychological Bulletin, 96,* 227–246. A careful and thorough, deliberately provocative critique of research on the effects of television violence.

Freud, S. (1955). *Civilization and its discontents.* London: Hogarth Press, first published in 1930. The classic exposition of how civilization must deal with aggressive instincts. One of Freud's most brilliant and influential critiques of society.

Malamuth, N. M., & Donnerstein, E. (Eds.). (1984). *Pornography and sexual aggression.* New York: Academic Press. A useful collection of writings on the role of erotica in producing sexual aggression.

National Institute of Mental Health. (1982). *Television and behavior: Ten years of scientific progress and implications for the eighties.* Rockville, MD: NIH. This is the follow-up report on the effects of television, following all the research done in the ten years since the Surgeon General's original report. It is a useful summary, though influenced by the authors' own perspectives.

TWELVE

Prosocial Behavior

On a cold winter night, 11-year-old Timothy Diakis ran to the burning apartment next door to rescue his 83-year-old neighbor. Awakened from sleep and clad only in his underwear, the young boy crawled on his hands and knees through the smoke-filled apartment to reach the bedroom where the woman he called "Grandma" was trapped. He pulled her to the floor where a few pockets of air remained, and then tried desperately to lead her to safety. As they made their way toward the exit, they faced flames creeping down the hallway. Overcome by smoke at last, Sarah Sherman and Timothy lapsed into unconsciousness just as fire engines arrived. Firefighters wearing protective masks and clothing ultimately rescued both and rushed them to a nearby hospi-

The bravery of firefighters risking their lives to save others contrasts vividly with scenes of people ignoring the plight of those in need of help.

tal. Sarah suffered minor injuries, but Timothy spent months in the hospital undergoing skin grafts for severe burns. Firefighters say Sarah would have died if the youngster had not rushed in and dragged her at least part way to safety. When newspaper accounts of the story reported that the family had no medical insurance, readers inspired by the boy's altruism sent more than $50,000 in donations to help pay his medical bills.

Acts of altruism and public generosity such as this stand in stark contrast to stories of public apathy to the plight of victims. In Chapter 1 we recounted the tragic story of Kitty Genovese, a young woman stabbed to death on a city street while at least 38 people watched and did nothing. There are countless stories of this sort. People are beaten, raped, robbed, and killed while those who could give assistance stand by. Why do people sometimes help others? And why, sometimes, do they fail to give badly needed assistance?

DEFINING ALTRUISM AND PROSOCIAL BEHAVIOR

Before trying to answer these questions, we should be clear about the meaning of altruism and prosocial behavior. **Altruism** refers to an act performed voluntarily to help someone else when there is no expectation of receiving a reward in any form (except perhaps a feeling of having done a good deed). By this definition, whether or not an act is altruistic depends on the *intentions* of the helper. The stranger who risks his or her own life to pull a victim from a burning car and then vanishes anonymously into the night has performed an altruistic act.

Prosocial behavior is a much broader category. It includes any act that helps or is designed to help others, regardless of the helper's motives. Many prosocial acts are not altruistic. For example, if you volunteer to work for a charity in order to impress your friends or to build up your resume for future job hunting, you are not acting altruistically in the pure sense. Prosocial behavior ranges over a continuum from the

Throughout life, family and friends help each other in many ways both small and large.

most selfless acts of altruism to helpful acts motivated entirely by self-interest.

Our everyday experiences provide many examples of prosocial behavior. As infants, we all benefit from the help and nurturance of adult caretakers. Throughout the life cycle, families and friends are important sources of help and support. Research shows that people often help each other in a wide variety of ways. Helping activities can be seen even in young children. One study observed children ages 3 to 5 at play in a university preschool (Strayer, Wareing, & Rushton, 1979). On average, each child engaged in 15 helpful acts per hour, ranging from giving a toy to another child to comforting an upset friend or helping a teacher.

Prosocial behavior is affected by the type of relationship between people. Whether because of liking, social obligation, self-interest, or empathy, we are more helpful to those we know and care about than to those we don't know (Schoenrade, et al., 1986). Nonetheless, people often do help total strangers. Research conducted in a midwestern American city found that over half of women shoppers were willing to give money for bus fare to a university student who explained that his wallet had "disappeared" (Berkowitz, 1972). In New York City, most pedestrians responded positively to requests for help from a passerby. Eighty-five percent of New Yorkers gave the time of day, 85 percent gave directions, and 73 percent gave change for a quarter (Latané & Darley, 1970). In another study on the streets of New York, 50 percent of people who found a wallet that had been "lost" (intentionally by researchers) mailed it back to its owner (Hornstein, Fisch, & Holmes, 1968). Prosocial behavior even occurs on city subways. When a passenger (actually a researcher) fell down with an apparent knee injury, 83 percent of those in the subway offered assistance (Latané & Darley, 1970). In another subway study, a researcher pretending to be physically disabled repeatedly fell down and always received help (Piliavin, Rodin, & Piliavin, 1969).

THEORETICAL PERSPECTIVES ON HELPING

Our understanding of prosocial behavior has benefited from several broad theoretical perspectives that were presented in Chapter 1. The decision-making perspective focuses on the processes that influence judgments about when help is needed. It also emphasizes the weighing of costs and benefits in the decision to give help. Second, a learning approach proposes that people learn to be helpful, following basic principles of reinforcement and modeling. Third, sociobiologists have proposed that a predisposition to help is part of our genetic, evolutionary heritage. Finally, others have emphasized the importance of social rules that dictate when we should help people in need. We will discuss each of these four theories of helping.

The Decision-Making Perspective

Helping occurs when an individual decides to offer assistance and then takes action. In any particular situation, the decision to help involves complex processes of social cognition and rational decision making (see Latané & Darley, 1970; Schwartz, 1977). There are several steps in the decision to help, as shown in Figure 12–1. A person must first notice that something is happening and decide whether or not help is required. If help is needed, the person may consider the extent of his or her own personal responsibility to act. Third, the person may evaluate the rewards and costs of helping or not

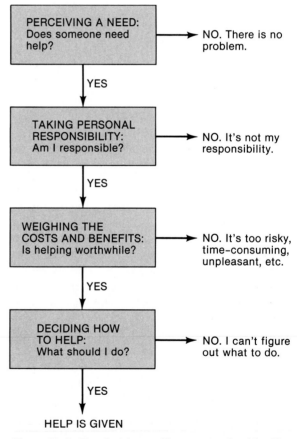

Figure 12–1. The decision-making perspective identifies four crucial steps in the process leading to giving help to a person in distress. At each point, different decisions may lead the person not to offer assistance.

helping. Finally, the person must decide what type of help is needed and just how to provide it. Let's consider each step in detail.

Perceiving a Need. It's 2 A.M. and a piercing scream fills the night air. Some people sleep on, oblivious to all but their private dreams. You wake up with a start. A woman shouts, "Stop it! Leave me alone!" You hear an angry male voice, but you can't quite make out what he's saying. Quickly you ask yourself what is going on—is it merely a noisy lovers' quarrel or a serious physical attack? Is this an emergency requiring outside intervention?

The crucial first step in any prosocial act is noticing that something is happening and deciding that help is required. In some situations, the need is clear: flood waters are rising in the river in your town and all able-bodied people are needed to fill sandbags to hold back the water. Or a child has gashed her head playing soccer and needs medical attention. But in many situations, such as hearing screams in the night, it can be difficult to decide. Uncertainty is a major reason why people sometimes fail to offer assistance. For example, one study found that when students heard an unmistakable emergency—a maintenance man falling off a ladder and crying out in agony—all of them went to the man's aid. In another condition, where students heard an ambiguous emergency—the sounds of an identical fall but without verbal cues that the victim was injured—help was offered only about 30 percent of the time (Clark & Word, 1972).

What cues do people use in deciding whether there is an emergency requiring intervention? Research by Shotland and Huston (1979) identified five important characteristics which lead us to perceive that an event is an emergency:

1. Something happens suddenly and unexpectedly.
2. There is a clear threat of harm to a victim.
3. The harm to the victim is likely to increase over time unless someone intervenes.
4. The victim is helpless and needs outside assistance.
5. Some sort of effective intervention is possible.

For example, most people considered these events to be emergencies: a drug overdose, a heart attack, a rape in progress, and a car accident with the driver motionless on the ground. People were less certain that an emergency existed if there was a power blackout, if a friend said he was miserable and depressed, or if there was a disabled car on the side of a road.

Our interpretation or definition of a situation is a vital factor in whether or not we offer aid. Shotland and Straw (1976) showed that people respond quite differently to an identical fight scene, depending on whether they perceive it as a lovers' quarrel or a fight between strangers. In this study, students came to the psychology department individually in the evening to fill out an attitude questionnaire. While working alone on the task, the student heard a loud fight break out in the corridor (actually staged by drama students). A woman screamed and pleaded with a man to "get away from me." In a "marriage" condition, where the victim yelled "I don't know why I ever married you," only 19 percent of students intervened. But in a "stranger" condition, where the woman yelled, "I don't know you," 65 percent of subjects intervened either directly or by calling the police. Even though the fights were identical in all respects, subjects perceived the situation as more serious and the woman as more eager for help in the stranger condition.

In a real-life fight where the relationship between the participants is unclear, onlookers may assume it to be a lovers' quarrel and so decide not to intrude. Perhaps this is unfortunate, but it means that the lack of help is due to a misunderstanding of the situation, not to unwillingness to help.

Taking Personal Responsibility. The second step in deciding to help is taking personal responsibility. Consider this situation. You're at the beach, lying in the sun. A woman spreads her blanket near yours and turns on her portable radio to a local rock station. After a few minutes she goes for a swim, leaving her radio on the blanket. A bit later a man comes along, notices the radio, snatches it up quickly, and walks off. What do you do? Chances are that you do not try to stop the thief—reminding yourself, perhaps, that it's not your responsibility.

In an experiment recreating the scene just described, only 20 percent of people intervened by going up to the thief and demanding an explanation (Moriarity, 1975). In a second condition, however, the owner of the radio first approached the person next to her on the beach and asked if they would "watch my things." Once such a commitment had been established, 95 percent of people intervened to stop the thief. When individuals feel personal responsibility, they are significantly more likely to act in a prosocial way.

Another demonstration of the importance of taking personal responsibility comes from a clever field study (Maruyama, Fraser, & Miller, 1982). On Halloween, groups of children who came to a certain house while trick-or-treating were asked to donate candies for hospitalized children. There were three experimental conditions, designed to manipulate the children's perceptions of responsibility. In one condition, the woman who greeted the kids made each child personally responsible for donating candies by putting the child's name on a bag for the candies. In another condition, she made one child responsible for the entire group. In the third condition, no one was given responsibility.

The variations in responsibility had clear effects on the number of candies donated by the children, as shown in Figure 12.2. When each child was individually responsible, the average donation was five candies; when one child was responsible for the group, this dropped to three; when no one was responsible, an average of only two candies per child was given.

Another factor influencing perceived responsibility is competence. We feel a greater sense of obligation to intervene if we have the skills to help effectively. In one study, for instance, participants witnessed a person (actually a confederate) pass out from an electrical shock from malfunctioning equipment (Clark & Word, 1974). Of participants who had formal training or experience in working with electrical equip-

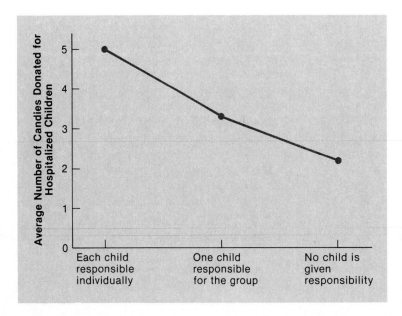

Figure 12–2. Increased personal responsibility increases helping. In this study, researchers varied the instructions given to Halloween trick-or-treaters about their responsibility for giving candy to needy children. (Adapted from Maruyama, Fraser, & Miller, 1982.)

ment, 90 percent intervened to help; among those with no electrical skills, only 58 percent intervened.

Weighing the Costs and Benefits. The decision-making perspective suggests that people consider the potential gains and losses that will result from a particular action, including helping another person (see Lynch & Cohen, 1978; Piliavin et al., 1981). A person will act prosocially if the perceived profits (rewards minus costs) for helping outweigh the profits from not helping.

Sometimes it is relatively easy to help. At other times, helping may involve considerable costs in time, energy, and complications. Telling a passerby the time of day requires little effort; pulling off the freeway to help a stranded motorist would be more time-consuming. In both situations, the cost will depend in part on whether you perceive any inconvenience or possible threat to your own safety. Does the person needing help look respectable, or is there some chance you will be robbed? The greater the perceived costs, the less likely you are to help. This point is illustrated in Box 12–1 on page 372.

There may also be costs to *not* giving assistance. You may feel guilty about not helping. Other people may see that you have not been helpful, and you may feel badly because they have a poor opinion of you. You may have a general moral value that says you should help when you can, and not helping will make you feel that you have not been a good person. Thoughts such as these influence whether or not you offer help.

On the other hand, there are benefits to helping which provide positive incentives. The greater the good you believe you will do, the more likely you are to help. The more the person deserves to be helped, and the more help you are able to give, the better you may feel about offering assistance. For example, Gruder, Romer, and Korth (1978) had a female confederate telephone people and request aid. The woman's story was that her car had broken down and she needed to reach a service station. She had gotten a wrong number and asked the per-

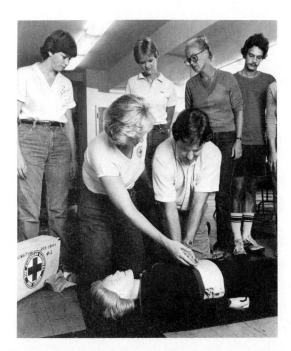

We are more likely to intervene in an emergency if we know how to help effectively. By taking a course in cardio-pulmonary resuscitation (CPR), these people will have the knowledge to help heart attack victims.

son to call the service station for her. In some cases, she was in great need; in others less. In some cases, her problem was largely her own fault because she said she had forgotten to take the car in for servicing even though she knew it needed repairs; in others, it was not her fault because the car had broken down with no warning. People helped more when her need was greater and when she was not at fault (and so presumably more deserving of help).

Several researchers have tested this model of helping and have found generally supportive results (Lynch & Cohen, 1978; Morgan & Leik, 1979). It seems likely that cost-benefit considerations do influence helping, at least in some situations. On the other hand, they do not fully explain all helping decisions. The person who instantly rushes into a burning building to save a child is unlikely to have weighed carefully the expected profits of the action. Rather, such acts may be motivated by basic emotions and values having to do with human life and personal courage.

BOX 12–1

Avoiding Helping

A request for aid often arouses mixed feelings. On the one hand, people would like to help because it is a good thing to do. On the other hand, they realize that costs are involved, costs that they would perhaps rather not assume. Indeed, one study demonstrated that people sometimes actively avoid a situation in which they will be asked for help (Pancer et al., 1979). A table was set up in a passageway. In some conditions, it held a box for donations to charity; in others, it did not. People tended to walk farther away from the table when donations were requested than when no donations

were requested. Similarly, when someone was sitting at the table collecting donations, people avoided it more than when no one was there. And finally, when a handicapped person was sitting at the table, people steered farther away than when the person was not handicapped.

In each case, the stronger the potential request for aid, the more people avoided the situation. Clearly, helping situations can create conflict, and people tend to minimize this conflict by keeping away. Presumably, it is easier not to donate money when you are far away than when you are close.

Deciding How to Help and Taking Action. A final step in the decision-making process is figuring out what type of assistance to offer, and then taking action. Should you intervene directly in the fight outside your door, or act indirectly by calling the police? Should you try to administer CPR to the accident victim, or call the paramedics? Whether a person takes direct action or seeks further assistance from someone else depends on many factors, such as the type of aid needed and the expertise or physical size of the potential helper. In emergencies, decisions are often made under great stress, urgency, and sometimes even personal danger. Well-intentioned helpers are not always able to give assistance or may even mistakenly do the wrong thing.

Our analysis of different steps in the decision to help highlights the many reasons why people fail to give needed assistance. They may not notice that a problem exists, or may perceive the problem as trivial. They may recognize a need, but not feel personally responsible for helping. They may believe the costs of helping are too great. They may want to help, but be unable to do so. Or they may hesitate, caught in a state of indecision.

Foster grandparent Linwood Blunt helps his two "grandsons" practice reading. When adults assist children, they provide an important model of helpfulness. The boys, who are partially hearing impaired, are teaching Linwood sign language.

The Learning Perspective

A second perspective on prosocial behavior emphasizes the importance of learning. In growing up, children are taught to share and to help. You can probably remember times when you were praised for being helpful or chided for forgetting to help when you should have. Two general learning principles discussed in Chapter 1 are again important here. People learn to help through reinforcement, the effects of rewards and punishment for helping. People also learn through modeling, by observing others who help.

Studies show clearly that children will help and share more when they are rewarded for their prosocial behavior. For example, one study found that 4-year-olds were more likely to share marbles with another child when they were rewarded with bubble gum for their generosity (Fischer, 1963). In everyday life, parents and teachers are more likely to reward helpfulness with praise than with bubble gum. Research suggests that some forms of praise may be more effective than others. In a recent study with 8- and 9-year olds, children played a game to win chips that could be traded for toys (Mills & Grusec, 1989). In an initial phase of the study, the researcher urged children to share their chips with poor children who didn't have any toys. With prompting, all children gave away some of their chips. Children were then given one of two types of praise for their helpfulness. In a dispositional praise condition, the experimenter emphasized the child's personality by saying, "I guess you're the kind of person who likes to help others whenever you can. Yes, you're a very nice and helpful person." In a general praise condition, the researcher emphasized the child's actions rather than personality, saying, "It was good that you gave some of your chips to the poor children. Yes, that was a nice and helpful thing to do" (p. 305). The children were then left alone to play the game again and were told that they could share "with the poor children if you want to, but you really don't have to" (p. 312). Children who had received the dispositional praise, emphasizing that they were a helpful person, were significantly more likely to share than children who received the general praise or no praise at all. Dispositional praise appears to be more effective than global praise.

A study of sixth-grade girls showed the impact of seeing a helpful model (Midlarsky, Bryan, & Brickman, 1973). Girls played a special pinball machine to win chips that could be exchanged for candy and toys. Before her own turn came, each girl watched an adult model play the game. In one condition, a selfish model put all the chips she won into a jar labeled "my money." In another condition, a charitable model put some of her chips into a jar labeled "money for poor children." Regardless of the condition, the model then urged the girl to think about the poor children who would "love to receive the prizes these chips can buy." Results showed a clear effect of modeling. Girls who had seen a charitable model donated an average of 19 tokens to the poor compared to only 10 tokens given by the girls who saw the selfish model.

The possibility that childrens' television programs can enhance helpfulness by showing prosocial models is discussed in Box 12–2.

Another study combined both modeling and reinforcement (Rushton & Teachman, 1978). First, a helpful adult model was used to get boys to behave altruistically by giving some of the tokens they won at bowling to an orphan named Bobby. Then the model rewarded the child for his generosity ("Good for you." "That's really nice of you.") or punished him ("That's kind of silly for you to give to Bobby."). There was also a no-reinforcement condition in which the adult said nothing. As Figure 12–3 shows, children who were rewarded gave more to Bobby on later trials than did children who were punished. Two weeks later, when children again played the same game and were reminded about Bobby, the effects of the earlier reward or punishment still influenced how much they gave to Bobby.

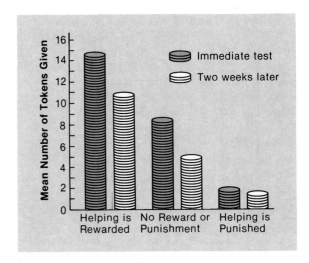

Figure 12–3. Rewards and punishments have clear effects on children's willingness to help. In this study, children were praised, criticized, or given no reinforcement for donating tokens to an orphan named Bobby. Children were then given other opportunities to help Bobby, both immediately and then two weeks later. Children who were rewarded gave the most tokens; children who were punished gave the fewest. (Adapted from Rushton and Teachman, *Personality and Social Psychology Bulletin*, Vol. 4, No. 2, 1978, p. 324. Copyright by the Society for Personality and Social Psychology, Inc. Reprinted by permission of Sage Publications, Inc.)

Adults can also be affected by observing helpful models, as a study of adult blood donors clearly showed. In this clever experiment, female college students first talked to a friendly woman (actually a confederate of the researchers) as part of a study of social interaction (Rushton & Campbell, 1977). The researchers arranged things so that as the two women left the interaction study, they passed a table set up in the corridor, staffed by people asking for blood donations. Half the time, the confederate immediately volunteered, modeling prosocial behavior. In the no-model condition, the confederate stepped aside to talk to someone else and did not volunteer to give blood.

The effects of the model's behavior were striking. A helpful model led 67 percent of subjects to pledge to donate blood, compared to only 25 percent of subjects who saw no model. More impressive were data on whether the women actually followed through on their pledges to give blood. None of the women in

BOX 12–2

Lassie to the Rescue

Can children's television shows influence prosocial behavior? Research suggests that they can. In one study, 3- to 5-year-old children were exposed to one of three television diets for a four-week period (Stein & Friedrich, 1972). In an aggressive condition, children watched "Batman" and "Superman" cartoons. In a prosocial condition, they watched episodes from "Mister Rogers' Neighborhood." In a neutral condition, they watched scenes such as children working on a farm. At the end of the testing, children who had seen prosocial programs showed an increase in helping relative to children in the other two conditions. A problem with this study, however, was that the programs varied in many ways, such as format, interest level, and educational goals.

To correct these problems, a later study exposed children to different episodes from the popular children's TV show "Lassie" (Sprafkin, Liebert, & Poulos, 1975). Half the first-graders in the study watched an episode that focused on Lassie's efforts to keep her puppy from being given away. At the story's climax, the puppy falls into a mining shaft. Unable to rescue the puppy herself, Lassie brings her owner Jeff and his grandfather to the scene. Jeff risks his life by hanging over the edge of the shaft to save the puppy. In the neutral condition, children watched an episode of Lassie that dramatized Jeff's attempt to avoid taking violin lessons. It contained no examples of humans helping a dog, although Lassie was obviously featured in a positive light.

Children watched the TV program individually and then were given an opportunity to help some puppies, but only at the cost of forgoing personal benefits. A female researcher took the child to another room and showed the child how to play a game to earn points. The more points scored, the better the prize the child would receive. The woman also explained that she had to leave the room briefly, and asked the child to do something for her while she was gone. She said that she was using earphones to listen to some dogs who were in a nearby kennel to make sure they were safe. The child was asked to wear the earphones while playing the game.

If the child heard barking, he or she could help the puppies by pressing a button marked "Help." The researcher left the room and shortly turned on a tape recording in which the dogs began to bark frantically. Would the children give up playing their point game in order to help the dogs? During the 3-minute testing period, most children pressed the Help button at least briefly. But children who had watched the prosocial TV show were significantly more helpful: they helped for 93 seconds compared to 52 seconds for children who had watched the neutral show. This and other studies (Ahammer & Murray, 1979) show that watching helpful models on TV can indeed increase children's prosocial behavior.

the no-model condition actually gave blood, but 33 percent of those who saw the altruistic model did. Similar evidence of modeling effects has been found in a variety of situations, such as donating money to a Salvation Army kettle at Christmas or helping a stranded motorist fix a flat tire (Bryan & Test, 1967).

Adult helping is also influenced by reinforcement. In one study, individuals walking along the main street in Dayton, Ohio, were approached by an attractive woman who asked how to get to a local department store (Moss & Page, 1972). After getting instructions, she either rewarded the helper (by saying, "Thank you very much, I really appreciate this.") or punished the helper ("I can't understand what you're saying, never mind, I'll ask someone else."). When the naive subject continued walking down the street, he or she encountered another woman who accidentally dropped a small bag and continued walking as if she didn't know she had lost it. The question of interest was whether the subject would help the woman by returning the bag to her. In the reward condition, 90 percent of people helped; in the punishment condition, only 40 percent helped.

Taken together, these and other studies provide convincing evidence of the power of reinforcement and modeling to shape prosocial behavior. Over time people develop habits of helping and learn rules about who they should help when. For young children, prosocial behavior may depend largely on external rewards and social approval. But as we grow older, helping can become an internalized value, not dependent on external supports. It can be enough to know that you've lived up to your own standards and to feel the warm glow of having done a good deed.

Sociobiology

Scientists have long observed prosocial behavior among animal species. Charles Darwin (1871) noted that rabbits will make noise with their hind feet to warn other rabbits of predators. In termite hives, the soldier termites will defend a nest against an intruder by putting themselves in front of the other termites and exposing themselves to great danger (Wilson, 1971). Many soldier termites die so that others may live and the nest survive. Some varieties of baboon have a characteristic pattern of responding to threats (Hall, 1960). The dominant males take the most exposed positions to protect the group and may even rush at an intruder. As the tribe moves away from the threat, the males risk their own safety by remaining behind to protect the rest of the group.

Dolphins show a fascinating pattern of rescuing injured peers. Since dolphins are mammals, they must breathe air to survive. If an injured animal sinks below the surface, it will die. Several observers have reported that dolphins will aid an injured companion. In one case; a dolphin was stunned by an explosion in the water (Siebenaler & Caldwell, 1956). Two other adults came to its aid by holding the animal afloat until it recovered and was able to care for itself.

Animals other than humans also help each other. Here, one monkey grooms another, perhaps because it expects to be groomed in return.

Among many animals, parents will sacrifice themselves when their young are threatened. An impressive example is the female nighthawk, which responds to a potential attack on her young by flying from the nest as if she had a broken wing, fluttering around at a low level, and finally landing on the ground right in front of the intruder but away from the nest (Armstrong, 1965).

This portrait of animals helping and sacrificing for each other runs counter to the dog-eat-dog, survival-of-the-fittest image that some humans have of the animal kingdom. The existence of altruism has posed a problem for evolutionary theorists: if the most helpful members of an animal species sacrifice themselves for others, they will be less likely to survive and pass along their genes to the next generation by having offspring. How then does a biological predisposition to act altruistically persist among animals or humans (Hoffman, 1981)?

Sociobiology, a theoretical perspective introduced in Chapter 1, has tried to resolve this paradox (Krebs & Miller, 1985; Wilson, 1975). According to sociobiology, any genetically determined trait that has a high survival value (that helps the individual survive) will tend to be passed on to the next generation. In the case of altruism, the tendency to help others may have high survival value for the individual's genes, but not necessarily for the individual. Imagine a bird that has fathered six chicks. Half the genes in each chick come from the father. Together, the six chicks have three times as many of the father's genes as he does himself. If the father sacrifices himself to save the chicks, his particular gene pool is still ahead of the game. Similar analyses can be done for other relatives who have varying percentages of the individual's genes. From the sociobiological viewpoint, helping close relatives contributes to the survival of an individual's genes in future generations, and so can be understood by the basic principles of evolutionary biology.

Sociobiologist Robert Trivers (1971) has argued that only mutual or *reciprocal altruism* is biologically based. In his view, the potential costs of altruism to the individual are offset by the possibility of receiving help from others. But such a system of mutual help giving is threatened by potential "cheaters" who accept help but offer none in return. To minimize cheating, natural selection may have favored a disposition to feel guilt and a tendency to enforce mutual helping through social means such as punishing those who do not follow group rules.

The sociobiological approach leads to several specific predictions. For example, animals should be most altruistic to those who are genetically most closely linked to themselves. They should be more helpful to immediate family than to distant relatives or strangers. The theory also predicts that parents will behave more altruistically to healthy offspring than to unhealthy ones who are less likely to survive. A further prediction is that mothers will usually be more altruistic to their offspring than will fathers. The reasoning here is that males have the biological potential to sire a great many offspring and so can perpetuate their genes without investing much in any one infant. Females can produce only a relatively small number of offspring, and so must help each of these young to thrive to ensure the survival of the mother's genes.

The idea that altruism is a genetically deter-

mined part of "human nature" is quite controversial. Just how well the theory applies to people is still an open question (Rushton et al., 1986). Nonetheless, the theory raises the intriguing possibility that self-preservation is not always the overwhelming motive that we sometimes think. Biological dispositions to aggression may coexist with biological dispositions to altruism.

Social Norms: Responsibility, Reciprocity and Justice

Critics of sociobiology argue that social factors are much more important than biology in determining prosocial behavior among humans. Donald Campbell (1975) suggests that genetic evolution may help explain a few basic prosocial behaviors such as parents' caring for their young, but that it does not apply to more extreme instances of helping a stranger in distress. Such cases are better explained by what Campbell calls "social evolution"—the historical development of human culture or civilization. In this view, human societies have gradually and selectively evolved skills, beliefs, and technologies that promote the welfare of the group. Because prosocial behavior generally benefits society, it has become part of the social rules or, in more technical terms, norms. Three norms in particular may be most important for helping behavior: social responsibility, reciprocity, and social justice.

First, a **norm of social responsibility** prescribes that we should help others who depend on us. Parents are expected to care for their children, and social agencies may intervene if parents fail to live up to this obligation. Teachers are supposed to help their students, coaches to look after team members, and co-workers to assist each other. The religious and moral codes of many societies emphasize the duty to help others. Sometimes this obligation is even written into the law.

The state of Minnesota has enacted a statute requiring that "Any person at the scene of an emergency who knows that another person is exposed to or suffered grave physical harm shall, to the extent that he can do so without danger or peril to himself or others, give reasonable assistance to the exposed person.'' Laws are one way of emphasizing to people that they have a responsibility to help. As we saw earlier in this chapter, an increased sense of personal responsibility does indeed increase the likelihood that a person will provide assistance.

Second, a **norm of reciprocity** says that we should help those who help us. Several studies have shown that people are more likely to help someone from whom they have already received aid. A study by Regan (1968) illustrated this idea that favors are reciprocated. College students were tested in pairs, one partner secretly being a confederate of the experimenter. The study was described as dealing with perceptual and esthetic judgment. The participants were put in separate rooms, and asked individually to rate a series of pictures. They were then given a short break.

In one experimental condition, the confederate did a favor for the subject. During the break, the confederate left the building and returned carrying two bottles of Coca-Cola. He handed one to the subject, saying "I asked him [the experimenter] if I could get myself a Coke and he said it was okay, so I brought one for you, too." All subjects took the Coke. In a second experimental condition, the researcher gave the subject and the confederate drinks, saying "I brought you guys a Coke." In a third condition, no drinks were provided. After the break, the experimenter gave all subjects a second series of pictures to rate.

After the new pictures were rated, there was another short break, during which the confederate asked the experimenter (loud enough for the subject to hear) whether he could send a note to the subject. The experimenter said that he could as long as it did not concern the experiment. The confederate then wrote the following note (Regan, 1968, p. 19):

> Would you do me a favor? I'm selling raffle tickets for my high school back home to build a new gym. The tickets cost 25 cents each and the prize is a new Corvette. The thing is, if I sell the most tickets I get 50 bucks and I could use it. If you'd buy any, would you just write the number on this note and give it back to me right

away so I can make out the tickets? Any would help, the more the better. Thanks.

The measure of helping was how many tickets the subject would agree to buy. The results are shown in Figure 12–4. When the confederate gave the subject a drink and then asked him to do a favor, there was considerably more helping than when the experimenter gave the subject a drink or when no drink was given.

The reciprocity norm seems to be quite strong and has been shown to operate in many cultures (Gergen et al., 1975). The strength of feelings of obligation is influenced by factors in the situation. For example, a larger favor is reciprocated more often than a smaller favor (Greenberg & Frisch, 1972). People's attributions about the motives of the helper also matter. We are more likely to return a favor when the original help is perceived to be given intentionally and voluntarily. Goranson and Berkowitz (1966) found that subjects who had been helped by someone tended to repay that specific person, but were not especially likely to offer aid to someone else.

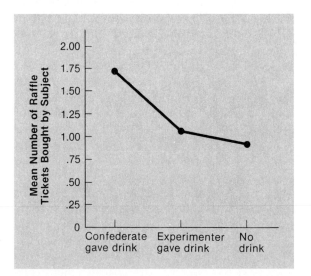

Figure 12–4. According to the norm of reciprocity, we should help someone who has helped us. In this study subjects who had been given a Coke by another subject (actually a confederate) were more likely to help him by purchasing raffle tickets. Subjects who were given a Coke by the experimenter or who received no Coke purchased fewer tickets. In everyday life, favors are often reciprocated. (Adapted from Regan, 1968.)

Third, human groups also develop **norms of social justice,** rules about fairness and the just distribution of resources. One common fairness principle is **equity,** which we introduced in Chapter 7. According to this principle, two people who make equal contributions to a task should receive equal rewards. If one receives more than the other, the people will feel pressure to try to restore equity by redistributing the rewards. The short-changed or underbenefited person obviously feels distressed. The more interesting fact is that even the person who receives more than a fair share (the overbenefited person) may give some to the person who got too little. And a third person, observing the unfair situation, might also be tempted to give to the one who suffered. Everyday acts of "helping the less fortunate" such as donating to a charity seem to be motivated by a desire to promote equity.

Numerous studies have demonstrated that overbenefited people will act to restore equity when they can (Walster, Walster, & Berscheid, 1978). In several experiments, subjects played a game in which one person, through no fault of her own, lost a lot of money or trading stamps while the partner won a good deal (Berscheid & Walster, 1967). At the end of the game, the winner (the real subject) was given an opportunity to give some of her winnings to the partner who lost. There was strong tendency to give some of the money to the loser, even though the winner had won legitimately. In contrast, in a condition where both partners had equal winnings, there was little tendency for the subject to give any winnings to the other player.

In another study, one member of a team was given more money than his partner. This overbenefited person tended to give some of the money to the partner in order to make their rewards more equitable (Schmitt & Marwell, 1972). In addition, the overrewarded partner often chose to play a different game when assured that this would result in a more equal division of the rewards. In other words, not only did he give away some of his own money to produce an equitable division, but he also changed the situation to avoid producing more inequity in the future.

These three norms—social responsibility, reciprocity, and social justice—are common in human societies. They provide a cultural basis for prosocial behavior. Through the process of socialization, individuals learn these rules and come to behave in accord with these guidelines for prosocial behavior.

Having reviewed the major theoretical perspectives on helping, we now take a closer look at three specific factors that influence our willingness to give help: characteristics of the situation, characteristics of the potential helper, and characteristics of the person in need.

SITUATIONAL FACTORS: WHEN DO PEOPLE HELP?

Even the most dedicated altruist is less likely to offer aid in some situations than in others. Research has documented the importance of several situational factors, including the presence of other people, the nature of the physical environment, and the pressures of limited time.

The Presence of Others

One of the shocking things about the Kitty Genovese murder is that so many people heard the young woman's screams and yet did not even call the police. Many social commentators interpreted this as a sign of widespread moral decay and alienation in society. Another hypothesis was offered by social psychologists Bibb Latané and John Darley (1970). They proposed that the very presence of so many onlookers may have caused the lack of helping. Those who witnessed the murder may have assumed that others had already called the police, and so may have felt little personal responsibility to intervene. Darley and Latané called this the **bystander effect.**

To test this idea that the number of witnesses affects helping, Darley and Latané designed a series of experiments, both in the laboratory and in naturalistic settings. In one experiment, college students taking part in a study overheard an "emergency" next door. They were much more likely to respond if they were alone than if they thought others also knew about the situation (Darley & Latané, 1968). The more people present, the less likely it was that any one individual actually offered help, and the longer the average delay before help was given.

Many studies have replicated this finding in different settings. For example, Latané and Darley (1970) conducted a field study in the Nu-Way Beverage Center in Suffern, New York. The researchers staged a series of robberies with the help of the salesclerk and two pretend criminals. The robberies were staged when either one or two customers were in the store. When the salesclerk went to the back of the store to check on something, two husky young men entered, muttering "They'll never miss this," and walked off with a case of beer. As expected, people who witnessed the crime alone were significantly more likely to report the theft to the clerk than were people who were in the store with another customer.

Why does the presence of others inhibit helpfulness? A decision-making analysis of prosocial behavior suggests several explanations. One is the **diffusion of responsibility** created by the presence of other people. If only one person witnesses a victim in distress, then he or she is totally responsible for responding to the situation and will bear all the guilt or blame for nonintervention. But if several people are present, help can come from several people. The obligation to help and the possible costs of failing to help are shared. Further, if a person knows that others are present but cannot actually talk to them or see their behavior, as in the Kitty Genovese case, the person may assume that others have already done something to help, such as calling the police.

Experiments have supported this idea that it is not simply the number of people present that is crucial, but rather the lessened feelings of personal responsibility that result from being in a group (Korte, 1971; Ross, 1971). Recent research has also shown that a group leader—presumably the person most responsible for group activities—is much more likely than other group members to help a victim in distress (Baumeister et al., 1988). It appears that group leaders are less susceptible to the diffusion of responsibility than are other group members.

A second explanation for the bystander effect concerns *ambiguity* in the interpretation of the situation. Potential helpers are sometimes uncertain whether a particular situation is actually an emergency. The behavior of other bystanders can influence how we define a situation and react to it. If others ignore a situation or act as if nothing is happening, we too may assume that no emergency exists. The impact of bystanders on interpreting a situation was demonstrated by Latané and Darley (1970).

In this experiment, college men sat filling out a questionnaire. After a few minutes, smoke began to enter the room through a vent. Soon the smoke was so thick that it was difficult to see and to breathe normally. When subjects were alone, they usually walked around the room to investigate the smoke, and 75 percent reported the smoke to the researcher within four minutes. In a condition where the real subject was in a room with two confederates who deliberately ignored the smoke, only 10 percent of subjects reported the noxious smoke.

A third factor in the bystander effect is **evaluation apprehension.** If we know that other people are watching our behavior, we may get "stage fright." We may worry that we will do something wrong or that others will evaluate our reaction negatively (Baumeister, 1982). Subjects in the smoke-filled room may have feared they would look foolish or cowardly by showing concern about the smoke when others were apparently so calm. The desire to avoid the cost of social disapproval can inhibit action. Of course, there are also situations in which evaluation apprehension can make us more likely to help. If we see someone fall down a flight of stairs or have a heart attack, the socially appropriate response is clearly to offer assistance. In such situations, the knowledge that others are watching us may actually increase our tendency to help (Schwartz & Gottlieb, 1980).

Environmental Conditions

The physical setting also influences helpfulness. Think for a moment about whether you are more likely to stop to help a stranded motorist on a pleasant, sunny day or on a cold, rainy one? on a dark street in a poor section of town, or in a well-lighted affluent area? on a country lane, or in a big city? Much research has documented the impact of environmental conditions such as weather, city size, and noise level on helping.

The effects of weather were investigated in two field studies by Cunningham (1979). In one study, pedestrians were approached outdoors and were asked to help the researcher by completing a questionnaire. People were significantly more likely to help when the day was sunny and when the temperature was comfortable (relatively warm in winter and relatively cool in summer). In a second study conducted in a climate controlled restaurant, Cunningham found that customers left more generous tips when the sun was shining. Other research suggests that people are more likely to help a stranded motorist in sunny rather than rainy weather (Ahmed, 1979) and during the day rather than at night (Skolnick, 1977). In short, weather makes a difference in helping.

A common stereotype is that city dwellers are unfriendly and unhelpful, whereas small-town residents are cooperative and helpful. Research finds that when it comes to helping strangers in distress, city size is important (Steblay, 1987). Strangers are more likely to be assisted in small towns than in large cities. There is apparently something about being in a small town that encourages helping and, conversely, something about the urban context that reduces the tendency to help. Incidentally, studies show that the size of the hometown in which a person grew up is *not* related to helping; it's the current environmental setting in which the need for help occurs that matters.

Amato (1983) investigated helping in 55 Australian communities ranging from small villages to major cities. To ensure a diverse sample of prosocial behaviors, five different types of help-

ing were studied. These included a student asking pedestrians to write down their favorite color as part of a school project, a pedestrian inadvertently dropping an envelope on the sidewalk, a request to donate money to the Multiple Sclerosis Society, overhearing a salesclerk give obviously wrong directions to someone, and witnessing a man with a bandaged leg fall to the ground and cry out in pain.

The results of this study are presented in Figure 12–5 on p. 382. On four of the five helping measures, the percentage of people who helped was significantly greater in small towns than in larger cities. The one exception to this pattern was the lost envelope. It generally brought little helping, and seemed to elicit more help in the largest cities. What also should be kept in mind, of course, is that these studies dealt only with help offered to strangers: there is no reason to believe that city dwellers are any less helpful than small-town people when it comes to aiding friends and relatives.

Many explanations for the lesser helpfulness of city dwellers to strangers have been offered. These include the anonymity of urban life, the overload experienced by city dwellers who are constantly bombarded by stimuli including other people, and possible feelings of helplessness from dealing with unresponsive urban bureaucracies and governments. We don't yet know which explanation is most important.

Another environmental factor that can affect prosocial behavior is noise. Starting with the idea that noise can reduce people's responsiveness to events in the environment, several researchers have investigated whether noisy conditions reduce the likelihood of helping a stranger in distress (Sherrod & Downs, 1974). In one lab study, for example, it was found that noise decreased the likelihood that students would help a person who had dropped some papers on the floor (Mathews & Canon, 1975). When only regular room noise was present, 72 percent of subjects helped, compared to only 37 percent when very loud noise was present. In a field study, the same investigators arranged to have a man wearing a cast on his arm drop some of the books he was carrying. When only

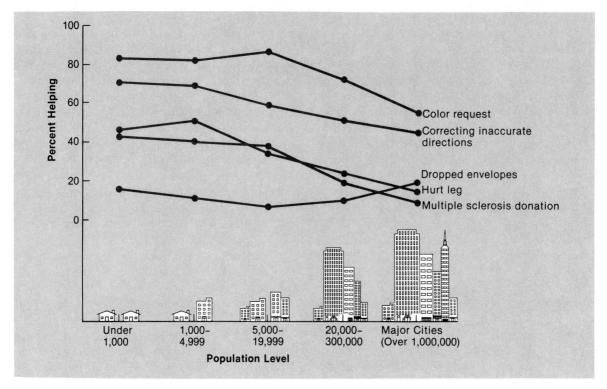

Figure 12–5. Research shows that strangers are more likely to receive help in small towns than in large cities. This figure shows the percentage of times that a stranger received 5 different kinds of help in cities of varying sizes. (Adapted from Amato, 1983, p. 579.)

typical street noises were present, 80 percent of passersby helped; when a noisy lawn mower was going, only 15 percent helped. The researchers suggested that loud noise causes people to ignore others in their environment and motivates them to leave the situation quickly, thus creating less helpful bystanders.

Time Pressures

Sometimes people feel that they are too hurried to help. A clear demonstration of this effect comes from an experiment by Darley and Batson (1973). As part of this study, individual students were asked to walk to another building where they were to give a short talk. Some were told to take their time, that the talk wouldn't begin for several minutes. Others were told to hurry because they were already late and the researcher was waiting. As the subject went from one building to the other building, he encountered a shabbily dressed man slumped in a

doorway, coughing and groaning. The question of interest was whether or not the subject would offer assistance.

A further twist to the study was that all participants were theology students studying religion. For some, the assigned topic for their talk was the Bible story of the Good Samaritan, about a person who came to the aid of a man who lay injured on the roadside, the victim of robbers. Other students were to talk about a topic not relevant to helping, namely, the sorts of jobs theology students might pursue after graduation. The results of the study showed that time pressure had a strong impact on helping. In a postexperiment interview, all students recalled seeing the victim. But only 10 percent of those in a hurry helped, compared to 63 percent of those who were not in a hurry.

Surprisingly, the speech topic made no difference. Students about to talk on the Good Samaritan were no more likely to offer assistance than were those preparing to talk on jobs. The researchers suggested that time pressure caused some students to overlook the needs of the victim. Another factor may have been a conflict about whom to help—the experimenter or the victim.

The possibility that conflict rather than callousness was at work is supported by a second study using a somewhat similar design (Batson et al., 1978). When students arrived for this study, they were sent individually to another building to interact with a computer. Some were told to hurry, and others were not. In addition, some were led to believe that their participation was of vital importance to the researcher, whereas others were told that their data were not essential. As the student walked to the new building, he encountered a male undergraduate slumped on the stairs, coughing and groaning. Would the subject help this victim? Results presented in Figure 12–6 show that students in

a hurry were less likely to help (40 percent) than were those with no pressures (65 percent). But this was primarily true for subjects who thought their research participation was essential. When subjects thought the researcher was not counting on them, those in a hurry were just about as likely to help (70 percent) as were those not in a hurry (80 percent). These results are consistent with the cost-benefit model discussed earlier. Apparently subjects weighed the costs and benefits to both experimenter and victim before arriving at a final course of action.

THE HELPER: WHO IS MOST LIKELY TO HELP?

Some people offer aid even when situational forces discourage helping, and others fail to help even under the most favorable conditions. Individual differences do exist. In an effort to understand why some people help more than others, researchers have investigated both relatively enduring personality characteristics and more fleeting moods and psychological states.

Personality Factors

Efforts to identify a single personality profile of the "helpful person" have not been very successful. Rather, it appears that specific personality traits dispose people to help in some types of situations, but not in others (Romer, Gruder, & Lizzadro, 1986). For instance, one study found that adults with a high need for approval were more likely to donate money to charity than were those low in need for social approval, but only when other people were watching them (Satow, 1975). Presumably, people high in need for approval were motivated by a desire to win praise from others and so acted more prosocially only when their good deeds would be noticed (Deutsch & Lamberti, 1986).

In another study, people high in the need to be nurturant were most likely to volunteer to give advice about personal problems to a same-sex high school student (Gergen, Gergen, & Meter, 1972). But nurturance was not related to willingness to counsel someone of the other sex, or to volunteer to help in a research project, nor

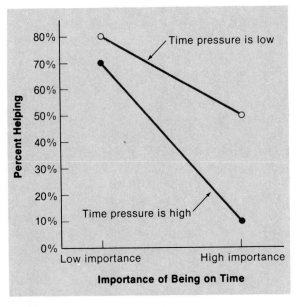

Figure 12–6. Sometimes time pressures create conflicts: should we help a stranger in distress or keep an important appointment? In this study, researchers varied both time pressure, and the importance of being on time. This figure shows the percentage of subjects in each condition who offered to help a person in distress. Students in a hurry were less likely to help, especially when it was important to the experimenter that they be on time. (Adapted from Batson, Cochran, Biederman, Blosser, Ryan and Vogt, *Personality and Social Psychology Bulletin*, Vol. 4, No. 1, 1978, p. 99. Copyright by the Society for Personality and Social Psychology, Inc. Reprinted by permission of Sage Publications, Inc.)

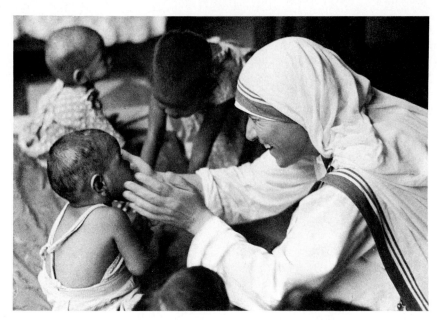

Mother Theresa has devoted her life to helping the homeless children of India.

to assist in preparing course materials. In other words, the link between personality and helping depends on the specific trait in question and on the specific type of assistance needed.

What personal qualities might lead a person to intervene in a potentially dangerous emergency? Consider this true story:

As a young man drove by a dance hall, he noticed a man assaulting a young woman. This is how he described the event and his intervention:

> I went over there and I grabbed the dude and shoved him over and I said lay off the chick. So me and him started going at it. I told him to get out of here, man, look at her, man, the girl's mouth's all bleeding, she got her teeth knocked out, she got a handful of hair pulled out. Everybody was just standing around. (quoted in Huston, Ruggiero, Conner, & Geis, 1981, p. 17)

Before the police arrived, the men exchanged more blows, one of which broke the intervener's jaw. What motivated this man and other "Good Samaritans" to endanger their own welfare to help a stranger?

To find out, Huston, Ruggiero, Conner, and Geis (1981) conducted in-depth interviews with 32 people who had intervened in dangerous crime episodes, such as bank holdups, armed robberies, and street muggings. The responses of these Good Samaritans were compared with a group of noninterveners matched for age, sex, education, and ethnic background. Given the dangerous situations involved, it is perhaps not surprising that the Good Samaritans were significantly taller, heavier, and better trained to cope with emergencies than were the noninterveners. All but one of the interveners were men, the exception being a woman who rescued her 83-year-old neighbor from a knife-wielding attacker. The Good Samaritans were more likely than were the noninterveners to describe themselves as strong, aggressive, and principled. And they had more lifesaving, medical, and police training.

The results suggested that these interveners were not primarily motivated by humanitarian concern for the victim, but rather acted from a sense of their own ability and responsibility, based on their training and physical strength. Of course, the personal qualities that lead someone to stop a crime or mugging may be quite different from those that lead someone to donate money to charity or to help a stranger who collapses from a heart attack. Whether a potential helper intervenes depends on the match between the person's competence, values, and motives, and the requirements of the particular situation.

Further insights about the people most likely to help come from studies of individuals who regularly donate their services. Consider the case of blood donors (Callero, Howard, & Piliavin, 1987; Piliavin, Evans, & Callero, 1984). Many people have never given blood or have done so only rarely. But a helpful minority give blood frequently, perhaps every two or three months. How can we explain their persistent helpfulness? Research suggests that over time, committed blood donors gradually develop an internal motivation to give blood—they donate because they think they should, not because they have been asked to give blood. Repeat blood donors come to view giving blood as a meaningful activity that enhances their self-concept. So, for example, repeat donors are more likely than others to agree that "blood donation

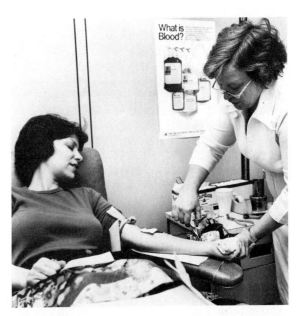

Many adults never donate blood. But a minority of committed donors gives blood regularly.

BOX 12–3

Rescuers of Jews in Nazi Europe

In Europe during World War II, Hitler's government undertook the systematic "extermination" of millions of Jews—a tragedy now known as the Holocaust. For many, the Holocaust symbolizes the very worst aspects of human nature, not only in the brutal acts of murder and genocide committed by the Nazis, but also in the complacency and inaction of the general public. How could so many people look the other way as innocent children and families were sent to specially constructed death camps? The Holocaust raises fundamental questions about the origins of evil. But it also provides examples of great altruism, in the stories of individuals who risked their lives to shelter Jews from death.

In the summer of 1942, 12-year old Samuel Oliner and his family were forced to live in the squalid, walled-in Bobowa Ghetto in Poland. One day, Samuel's entire family was rounded up and shoved into trucks. Samuel's stepmother, hoping that the boy might escape from certain death,

urged him to run and hide. For two days, the boy stayed in the deserted ghetto, hiding from the uniformed officers who searched door to door for Jews. Finally, he cautiously crawled through a hole to escape the ghetto. Once outside, he made his way to the home of a nearby peasant woman named Balwina, a casual acquaintance of his father. Despite grave danger to herself and her family, Balwina sheltered the Jewish boy, taught him ways to pass for Christian, and later arranged for him to work as a hired hand on a farm some miles away. Samuel's family was murdered, but the boy survived because of the brave and altruistic actions of a Christian woman he barely knew.

Samuel ultimately moved to the United States, became a professor of sociology, and undertook a detailed study of "rescuers" who saved the lives of Jews in Nazi Europe. The goal of the research was to identify distinctive characteristics of the rescuers that enabled them to act altruistically. The research

Continued

team conduced in-depth interviews with 406 rescuers and a matched sample of 126 nonrescuers.

Several patterns emerged from the interviews. Rescuers typically reported having a close relationship with their parents during childhood. For many, a parent had served as a model of moral conduct. One rescuer said, "My mother was a model of Christian faith and love of neighbor." Another commented, "I learned to be good to one's neighbor, . . . to be responsible, concerned and considerate. To work—and work hard. But also to help—to the point of leaving one's work to help one's neighbor" (Oliner & Oliner, 1988, p. 164). Many rescuers reported that their parents had emphasized moral reasoning rather than blind obedience to parental authority. Moral lessons learned in childhood laid the foundation for the actions of the rescuers in adulthood.

Another finding was that rescuers tended to apply ethical principles universally to all people, not just to members of their own group. Speaking of his father, one rescuer said: "He taught me to love my neighbor—to consider him my equal whatever his nationality or religion. He taught me especially to be tolerant" (p. 165). In addition, the majority of rescuers emphasized the importance of feelings of compassion and concern as guiding their actions. "I could not stand idly by and observe the daily misery that was occurring."

The experiences of these rescuers illustrate the general concepts discussed in this chapter. Many rescuers emphasized the importance of social norms they had learned from their family, community or religious group such as the responsibility to help those in need and the religious injunction to "love thy neighbor." Others were motivated by empathy and compassion. In describing how she cared for a ragged and starving Jewish man who had escaped from a concentration camp, one woman said: "How could one not have helped such a man? . . . He was shivering, poor soul, and I was shivering too, with emotion. I am very sensitive and emotional" (p. 189). The capacity to respond to the suffering of others and the adherence to moral principles of justice and concern enabled rescuers to overcome fear and to overlook serious risks to their own safety.

Source: Oliner and Oliner (1988).

---

is an important part of who I am" and that "for me, being a blood donor means more than just donating blood." In other words, for repeat donors, the act of giving blood becomes a personal statement about the kind of person they are. In addition, committed donors overcome or "neutralize" the fear of giving blood, a factor that prevents many people from giving in the first place. For many committed donors, giving blood regularly becomes a habit or routine.

Box 12–3 highlights a case of extraordinary helping behavior, the story of Christians who risked their own lives to shelter Jews from Nazi persecution during World War II.

Mood

There is considerable evidence that people are more willing to help when they are in a good mood. For example, people are more likely to help if they have found a dime in a phone booth (Isen & Simmonds, 1978), been given a free cookie at the college library (Isen & Levin, 1972), succeeded on some experimental tasks (Isen, 1970), or listened to soothing music (Fried & Berkowitz, 1979) than if these mood-enhancing events have not occurred. Apparently a warm glow of positive feeling increases the willingness to act prosocially. The specific reasons why feeling good promotes helpfulness are currently under investigation (Carlson, Charlin & Miller, 1988).

There are important limitations to the "feel good" effect, however. First, the effects of positive moods can be quite short-lived—only 20 minutes in one study (Isen, Clark, & Schwartz, 1976). Second, a good mood may actually *decrease* helpfulness when giving assistance would detract from the person's good mood (Isen & Simmonds, 1978). People in a good mood apparently want to maintain their positive feelings.

The effects of bad moods such as sadness or depression are more complicated, and research results have not been entirely consistent (Carlson & Miller, 1987). If a bad mood causes us to focus on ourself and our own needs, it may lessen the likelihood of our helping someone else (Thompson, Cowan, & Rosenhan, 1980). On the other hand, if we think helping someone else might make us feel better and so relieve our bad mood, we may actually be more likely to offer assistance (Cialdini et al., 1987). A further complication is that the link between feeling bad and helping others is clearer in adults than in children (Cialdini et al., 1981). One reason for this may be that children have to learn, as part of growing up, that helping others is a gratifying act that can improve their own feelings.

Does providing assistance actually make helpers feel better? A recent study demonstrates that it can (Williamson & Clark, 1989). College students who were able to provide help reported feeling in a better mood (e.g., more cheerful, less nervous) than did students who were not given an opportunity to provide help. Helpful students also reported feeling better about themselves (e.g., more generous and considerate, and less selfish or unreliable). In short, helping can improve the helper's mood and self evaluations.

Motives for Helping: Empathy and Personal Distress

We noted earlier that true altruism is defined by the person's intentions; we act altruistically only when we help with no expectation of receiving personal benefit. This reasoning has led researchers to study the motives that lead people to help, and to contrast helping based on personal distress versus empathy.

To understand this distinction, picture for a moment the sight of people in serious distress: the mangled bodies of victims in a train crash, a starving child in ragged clothes, an anguished father whose child has disappeared. Witnessing people in need often evokes powerful emotions. **Personal distress** refers to our own personal reactions to the plight of others—our feelings of shock, horror, alarm, concern, or helplessness. Personal distress is prominent when people who witness others in distress are preoccupied with their own emotional reactions to the event. In contrast, **empathy** refers to feelings of sympathy and caring for others, in particular to sharing vicariously or indirectly in the suffering of others. Empathy is prominent when the observer focuses on the needs and emotions of the victim. Personal distress leads us to feel anxious and apprehensive; empathy leads us to feel sympathetic and compassionate. Recent research suggests that the distinctive emotions generated by personal distress and empathy may actually be accompanied by distinctive physiological reactions, including heart rate patterns and facial expressions (e.g., Eisenberg et al., 1989).

Personal distress motivates us to reduce our own discomfort. We might do this by helping a person in need, but we can also feel better by escaping from the situation or ignoring the suffering around us. In contrast, empathic concern typically motivates us to help the person in need. Since the goal of empathic concern is to enhance the welfare of someone else, it would clearly be an altruistic motive for helping. In contrast, helping motivated by a desire to reduce our own personal distress is egoistic and not truly altruistic.

Several studies have shown that empathy increases prosocial behavior (Eisenberg & Miller, 1987). For example, in one study, college students learned of the plight of Carol, another student who had broken both legs in a car accident and was seriously behind in her schoolwork (Toi & Batson, 1982). After listening to a tape-recorded interview with Carol, each subject was asked if she would be willing to help Carol. Empathy was manipulated by varying the instructions given to subjects. In a high-empathy condition, subjects were told: "Try to take the perspective of the person who is being interviewed, imagining how she feels about what has happened and how it has affected her life." In a low-empathy condition, subjects were told: "Try to be as objective as possible, carefully attending to all the information presented. . . .

Try not to concern yourself with how the person being interviewed feels about what happened."

As expected, subjects in the high-empathy condition experienced significantly greater empathy, as reflected in self-ratings of feeling sympathetic, compassionate, and "moved" by Carol's story. Also as predicted, subjects in the high-empathy condition were significantly more likely to volunteer to help Carol than those in the low-empathy condition, even when it would have been easy to avoid helping. Help was offered by 71 percent of subjects in the high-empathy condition compared to only 33 percent in the low empathy condition. Taking the perspective of someone in distress can increase helpfulness.

A controversy currently exists, however, about how to interpret studies showing this empathy-helping link (Fultz et al. 1986). One view is that instructions emphasizing empathy increase altruistic motivation to help (Batson, et al., 1988). In contrast, it has been suggested that when experimenters give instructions designed to enhance empathy, they may actually increase not only the subject's concern for the victim, but also increase the subject's own personal feeling of sadness, depression, or distress (Schaller & Cialdini, 1988). According to the second interpretation, helping based on empathy would not be entirely altruistic because the helper's goal may be to improve his or her own mood.

As this continuing controversy suggests, it is

BOX 12–4

The Heroic Truck Driver

Wilson Ross, 54, was driving his bread delivery van on the Ventura Freeway outside of Los Angeles when he was hit from behind by a truck. The van went out of control and overturned, leaving Ross unconscious. As flames began to appear, Ross dangled helplessly, suspended upside down in the van by his seatbelt. Several passersby saw the accident and stopped, but were deterred from aiding the victim by the flames. But Jackson E. Stallcup, a Vietnam war veteran who drives a hazardous materials truck for a living, stopped his massive 18-wheeler on the freeway to offer help.

Quickly sizing up the situation, Stallcup crawled through the shattered windshield of the truck. He tried unsuccessfully to free Ross by cutting the nylon seat belt with a knife. At this point, Ross regained consciousness and asked Stallcup not to leave him. "I told him I wouldn't leave," Stalllcup remembers. Finally, as flames set Ross's clothes on fire, Stallcup located the belt buckle and released Ross, who fell on top of his rescuer. With difficulty, Stallcup pulled the semiconscious man through the windshield. "I crawled out with him on top. As soon as we got out, I heard an explosion. I was lucky. It was a good day for him, a good day

for me." The explosion engulfed the van in flames. For his act of heroism, Stallcup has been awarded a $2,500 prize and a medal from the Carnegie Hero Fund Commission. Since 1904, the commission has given awards to 7,367 individuals who risked their lives to help others in need.

Stallcup's story hints at the complex factors that affect helping in real-life situations. According to newspaper accounts, the crash scene reminded Stallcup of his earlier experiences in the Vietnam war. "I remembered Vietnam and people crying for help when they were hurt or dying. I knew I couldn't handle it if it would happen again. I wouldn't be able lo live with myself if I left this guy and heard him screaming while the truck burned." Stallcup's desire to help was facilitated by his strength and expertise. He carried a knife, which he used to try to free the injured man. His war experience and current job driving hazardous materials may have increased his confidence in his ability to handle the crisis. Whereas others were deterred by the dangerous situation, Stallcup was willing to risk his life.

Source: Connelly (1989).

often difficult to sort out the motives that lead one person to help another. Our behavior often has multiple causes. These theoretical debates should not diminish our admiration for individuals who risk their own safety in courageous acts of helping. The earthquake victims rescued from a collapsed building care little about the motives of the individual who brings them to safety, and consider the rescuer a hero regardless of whether their help was motivated by empathy or personal distress. Consider the case of Jackson E. Stallcup, described in Box 12–4.

THE PERSON IN NEED: WHO IS MOST LIKELY TO RECEIVE HELP?

As you near the Student Union, someone approaches you and asks for money to make a phone call. Are you more likely to help if the person is clean-cut and neatly dressed, or instead looks rather disheveled? Would it matter if the person explained that his wallet was just stolen or said that he had forgotten to bring any change to school? Although the true altruist may be blind to everything but the needs of a person in distress, everyday prosocial behavior is often influenced by characteristics of the person in need.

For example, people on a college campus were more likely to give money to the March of Dimes if they were asked for a donation by a paraplegic woman in a wheelchair than if asked by a nonhandicapped woman (Slochower et al., 1980). In another study, subway riders in New York saw a man carrying a cane stumble and fall to the floor (Piliavin, Piliavin, & Rodin, 1975). Sometimes the victim had a large red birthmark on his face; sometimes he did not. In this situation, the victim was more likely to receive aid if his face was unblemished (86 percent) than if he had an unattractive birthmark (61 percent). In understanding these and other research findings, two themes seem most important: we are more willing to help people we like and people we think deserve assistance.

Helping Those We Like

In Chapter 9 we saw that our initial liking for another person is affected by such factors as physical attractiveness and similarity. Research on prosocial behavior finds that these same characteristics also influence helping. In at least some situations, those who are physically attractive are more likely to receive aid. For example, in a field study, researchers placed a completed application to graduate school in a telephone booth at the airport (Benson, Karabenick, & Lerner, 1976). The application was stamped and ready to be mailed, but had apparently been "lost." To manipulate appearance, the photo attached to the application was sometimes of a very good-looking person and sometimes of a less attractive person. The measure of helping was whether the individual who found the envelope actually mailed it or not. Results showed that people were much more likely to send in the application if the person in the photo, whether male or female, was physically attractive.

The degree of similarity between the potential helper and the person in need is also important. Some years ago, researchers had confederates dressed as a "hippie" or as a "straight" person approach students and ask to borrow a dime (Emswiller, Deaux, & Willits, 1971). The researchers also used appearance to categorize the potential helpers as "hippie" or "straight." Results clearly showed that people were most likely to help those similar to themselves. For example, hippie men helped a fellow hippie about 77 percent of the time, but helped a straight person only about 32 percent of the time. There is also evidence that helpfulness is greater toward someone who is from the same country rather than a foreigner (Feldman, 1968) and toward someone with similar attitudes (Tucker et al., 1977).

Helping Those Who Deserve Help

Whether a person receives help depends in part on the "merits" of the case. For example, people in a supermarket were more likely to give someone money so they could buy milk rather than cookie dough (Bickman & Kamzan, 1973), presumably because milk is more essential for health than cookies. Passengers on a New York subway were more likely to help a man who fell to the ground if he appeared to be sick rather than drunk (Piliavin, Rodin, & Piliavin, 1969). In both cases, beliefs about the legitimacy or appropriateness of the problem made a difference.

In addition to evaluating the deservingness of the need itself, potential helpers may also make inferences about the causes of the person's need, following the principles of **attribution theory** outlined in Chapter 4. A teacher might spend more time helping a student who missed classes because of a death in the family rather than because of a trip to a beach resort. Several studies indicate that the key causal factor is personal control: we are more likely to help someone if we believe the cause of the problem was outside the person's control. For instance, in one study (Meyer & Mulherin, 1980), college students said they would be more willing to lend rent money to an acquaintance if the need arose due to illness (an uncontrollable cause) rather than laziness (a controllable cause).

In another study, students said they would be more likely to lend their lecture notes to a classmate who needed them because of something uncontrollable, such as the professor's being a poor lecturer, rather than something controllable, such as the classmate's not trying to take good notes (Weiner, 1980). If a person could have prevented the predicament, we are less likely to help. Attributions may also influence how we feel about a person in need. We feel sympathy and concern for those who suffer through no fault of their own; we feel anger and disgust toward those who are responsible for their own problems. In short, attributing a person's need for help to a controllable cause may give rise to anger and avoidance or neglect; attributing the person's plight to uncontrollable

	Perceived Cause of the Person's Need	Emotional Reaction to the Person in Need	Willingness to Offer Help
	Something Outside the Person's Control (e.g., a person is out of work because there are no jobs available)	Sympathy, Pity	High—the person is perceived as deserving help
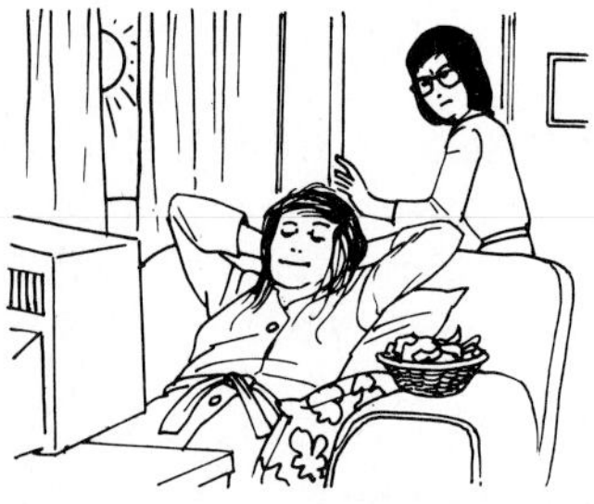	Something the Person Could Control (e.g., a person is out of work because she is lazy and doesn't like to work)	Anger, Irritation	Low—the person is perceived as not deserving help

Figure 12–7. An attribution-theory analysis of help-giving. When we encounter a person in distress, we first try to understand the causes of their need. Attributing need to causes under the person's control leads to reactions of anger and contempt, and diminishes the likelihood of offering help. In contrast, attributing the person's need to uncontrollable causes leads to sympathy and increases the probability of offering assistance. (Adapted from Schmidt and Weiner, *Personality and Social Psychology Bulletin,* Vol. 14, No. 3, September 1988. Copyright by the Society for Personality and Social Psychology, Inc. Reprinted by permission of Sage Publications, Inc.)

causes may elicit sympathy and lead to help giving (Schmidt & Weiner, 1988). Figure 12–7 summarizes the impact of attributions on helping.

THE EXPERIENCE OF RECEIVING HELP

Sometimes we react to getting help with happiness and gratitude. The novice swimmer saved from drowning by an alert lifeguard is thankful to be alive and grateful for the help. The student who gets a ride to the airport from a friend is genuinely thankful for the favor. A soldier may come to like and respect a particularly helpful platoon buddy (Cook & Pelfrey, 1985). But there are also instances when people react negatively to receiving help. When Dad offers to help his 5-year-old get dressed, she may indignantly insist she'd rather do it herself. Welfare recipients may react toward social workers with veiled hostility rather than warmth. Countries receiving millions in U.S. foreign aid complain about American policies and ''exploitation'' of developing nations. What these examples point out is that receiving help can be a mixed blessing. Several social psychological theories help to explain these reactions.

Social Exchange Theory: The Costs of Indebtedness

Providing help involves an exchange of resources from one person to another. When the exchange of help in a relationship is largely one way, it leads to indebtedness and can create an imbalance of power in the relationship (Worchel, 1984). Young adults who receive financial support from their parents may appreciate the assistance, but may also feel that accepting help gives their parents greater rights to influence their lives.

Social exchange theory suggests that help will be most appreciated when it can be reciprocated, hence maintaining a balance of equity and power in the relationship. Research shows that people are less likely to ask for help when they think they will be unable to repay the aid in some form (Fisher, Nadler, & Whitcher-Alagna, 1982). There is also evidence that people like a benefactor more if they are able to give something in return for the aid they receive (Gross & Latané, 1974). In short, lopsided help giving can threaten equity in a relationship, create power imbalances, and increase negative feelings on the part of the recipient.

Reactance Theory: Loss of Freedom

Further insights into the experience of receiving help are provided by reactance theory (Brehm, 1966). According to this theory, people want to maximize their personal freedom of choice. If we perceive that our freedom is threatened, we often react negatively with annoyance and hostility. The prospect of losing freedom may also lead us to take steps to reassert our independence. So when foreign aid recipients criticize U.S. policies, they may be symbolically proving their independence and thereby reducing feelings of psychological **reactance.**

Evidence that those who receive aid perceive a substantial loss of freedom comes from a study of welfare recipients (Briar, 1966). Nearly 70 percent of the welfare families surveyed believed they should not complain if a social worker made a surprise visit in the middle of the night, even though they knew this was probably not legal. Most families (67 percent) also said they would feel obligated to get marriage counseling if asked to do so, whether or not they thought it necessary. Intrusions on privacy and personal freedom can easily lead to feelings of hostility toward those providing aid (Gross, Wallston, & Piliavin, 1979).

Attribution Theory: Threats to Self-esteem

Accepting help can have important implications for our self-esteem. If we perceive that people are helping us because they genuinely care about us and our welfare, we may get an ego boost. If accepting aid implies that we are incompetent, unsuccessful, and dependent, it may threaten our self-esteem (Fisher et al., 1982). For instance, people are sometimes reluctant to seek aid from social agencies because they fear humiliation and embarrassment (Williamson, 1974).

According to attribution theory, people are motivated to understand why they need help and why others are offering to help them. If people can attribute their need to external or uncontrollable forces rather than to personal inadequacies, they will be able to maintain positive self-esteem. Several studies have found that people are more likely to seek help when they can attribute their problem to a difficult situation rather than to a personal deficiency (Fisher et al., 1982; Tessler & Schwartz, 1972). Further, help may be easier to accept when the person in need does not have to ask for it explicitly. A year-long study of welfare recipients found that people used more of the social services available if their caseworker initiated contacts than if the family had to initiate contacts (Gross, Wallston, & Piliavin, 1979). People may avoid asking for help to protect their sense of pride and self-worth.

New Ways to Obtain Help: Self-help Groups and Computers

We have seen that the experience of receiving help is not always positive. There are times when accepting aid can limit our freedom, diminish our power, and lower our self-esteem. An understanding of these processes helps to explain why people sometimes react negatively or ambivalently toward help givers and why people may prefer not to ask for help even when they badly need it.

Social psychological factors may also explain the popularity of two contemporary sources of help: self-help groups and computers. In self-help groups, people with a common problem work together to help one another. Examples would be groups for single parents, or victims of child abuse, or older returning college students. Self-help groups minimize the costs of receiving help because they are run by the people in need, offer opportunities for reciprocal helping, and foster the knowledge that others have the same problem.

Computers offer a unique opportunity to receive help from a machine rather than a human being. Computers are now being used to teach a variety of subjects from spelling to chess; these teaching computer programs offer users help and advice without the embarrassment of acknowledging one's errors to another person. The appeal of computer assistance was dramatically illustrated in a recent study by Karabenick and Knapp (1988). College students performed a complex and difficult task on a computer. Half were told they could receive help from a research assistant and half were told that they could get help from the computer. The results were clear cut. In the personal help condition, students were reluctant to request assistance; only 36 percent of subjects asked the research assistant for help. In contrast, in the computer-help condition, 86 percent of students requested help at least once, and most people asked for help more than once. By offering private assistance with no expectation of reciprocity, computers can reduce the psychological costs of receiving help.

In reading this chapter, you have learned a good deal about helping behavior. You now understand many factors that inhibit people from helping, such as the diffusion of responsibility that comes from being with others. You also know that we can teach people to become more altruistic, for instance by showing children TV models who help others, or by giving adults training in life-saving techniques such as CPR that make it possible for them to help people in need.

Research shows that people who are taught about the factors that influence helping are more likely to overcome these obstacles. In one study, college students either heard a lecture or saw a film about prosocial behavior and how the bystander effect can inhibit helping (Beaman et al., 1978). Two weeks later, in a seemingly unrelated context, students encountered a person in need of help, specifically a student sprawled on the floor in a hallway. Some students were alone when they encountered the victim; others were with an unresponsive confederate who ignored the victim. In all conditions, students who had learned about prosocial behavior were significantly more likely to intervene. What effect do you think learning about prosocial behavior has had on you? Will knowledge increase your willingness to help people in distress?

Key Terms

altruism

attribution theory

bystander effect

diffusion of responsibility

empathy

equity

evaluation apprehension

norm of reciprocity

norm of social responsibility

norm of social justice

personal distress

prosocial behavior

reactance

social exchange theory

sociobiology

Summary

1. Altruism is helping someone with no expectation of reward or personal benefit. Prosocial behavior includes any act that helps or is designed to help, regardless of the helper's motives.

2. A decision-making perspective emphasizes the complex cognitive processes leading to prosocial behavior. The potential helper must perceive that help is needed, take personal responsibility, weigh the costs and benefits, and decide how to intervene.

3. A learning perspective emphasizes that children learn prosocial behaviors and norms by reinforcement and modeling.

4. Sociobiologists believe that a tendency to help is part of our human evolutionary heritage. In contrast, others emphasize that societies create rules about helping which include social norms of responsibility, reciprocity, and justice.

5. Situational factors affect helping. Research shows that people are less likely to intervene when others are present. This so-called bystander effect may result from several causes including: a diffusion of responsibility, other people influencing how an individual interprets the situation, and evaluation apprehension. Other situational factors that influence helping are weather, city size, noise and time pressures.

6. Characteristics of the helper and the recipient of help are also important. People are more likely to help when they are in a good mood and feel empathy for the plight of the victim. People are also more helpful to those they like and to those they believe deserve help.

7. People sometimes react to receiving help with a mixture of gratitude and discomfort. Receiving help may make us feel indebted to others, threaten our sense of freedom, and lower our self-esteem.

8. Knowledge about factors that inhibit helping may enable people to overcome these barriers and to act in more prosocial ways.

Suggested Readings

DePaulo, B. M., Nadler, A., & Fisher, J. D. (1983). *New directions in helping: Help-seeking.* New York: Academic Press. An analysis of factors that lead people to seek help and factors that determine how people respond to receiving help.

Eisenberg, N. (1986). *Altruistic emotion, cognition, and behavior.* Hillsdale, NJ: Erlbaum. A recent discussion of how prosocial behavior is affected by empathy, casual attributions, self-perceptions, and moral reasoning.

Krebs, D. L., & Miller, D. T. (1985). Altruism and aggression. In G. Lindzey & E. Aronson (Eds.), *Handbook of social psychology*, 3rd ed., Vol. 2, pp. 1–71. New York: Random House. A comprehensive overview that links research and theory on prosocial behavior to work on aggression.

Latané, B., & Darley, J. M. (1970). *The unresponsive bystander: Why doesn't he help?* New York: Appleton-Century-Crofts. Reviews the classic studies of bystander intervention conducted by these authors.

Oliner, S. P., & Oliner, P. M. (1988). *The altruistic personality: Rescuers of Jews in Nazi Europe.* New York: Free Press. A well-written account of Christians who risked their lives to help Jews escape from Nazi persecution, based on a large-scale study of several hundred rescuers.

Piliavin, J. A., Dovidio, J. F., Gaertner, S. L., & Clark, R. D. (1981). *Emergency intervention.* New York: Academic Press. Reviews research and theory on bystander intervention with an emphasis on cost-benefit factors.

Staub, E., Bar-Tal, D., Karylowski, J., & Reykowski, J. (Eds.). (1984). *Development and maintenance of prosocial behavior.* New York: Plenum. An excellent collection of theoretical and research reviews written by leading experts.

THIRTEEN

Prejudice

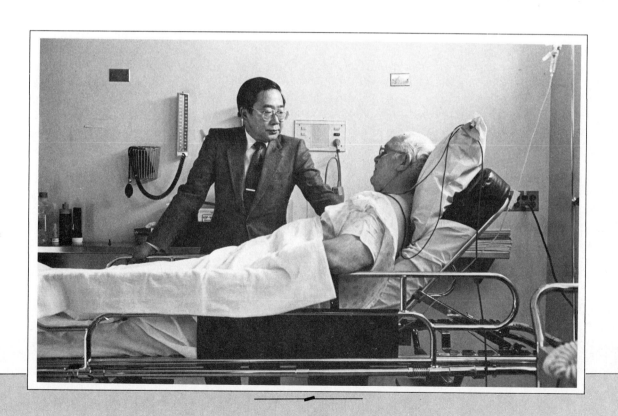

*P*eople's prejudices concern their perceptions of other individuals and groups, and their attitudes and behavior toward them. Prejudice can be one of the most destructive dispositions treated in this book. It has produced chilling acts of violence. Over 6 million European Jews were murdered by the Nazis in the 1940s under the guise of "purifying" the European racial stock. Today only a fraction of that number of Jews remain in Europe. The number of North American Indians dropped from an estimated 3 million in the seventeenth century to 600,000 today. The Spanish genocide of Indians in Latin America is even more appalling.

African-Americans have historically been among the most common victims of prejudice. In the half-century before World War II, thousands of individual blacks were lynched by mobs of whites, usually on some suspicion (often unjustified, or at least uninvestigated) of their involvement in a crime against whites. After World War II, racial lynchings came to a nearly complete halt, but violent incidents continue. In 1989, four young black men went to the predominantly white Bensonhurst section of Brooklyn to look at a used car advertised for sale. They were attacked by a group of about 30 white youths carrying bats and golf clubs and guns, who mistakenly thought a white neighborhood girl had been dating one of the black youths. One of the black men was shot to death. But in analogous fashion a 29-year-old white stockbroker was attacked in 1988 while she was jogging in New York's Central Park and was repeatedly raped and stabbed and beaten nearly to death. The attackers were a group of black and Hispanic youths who had explicitly set out that evening to attack a white woman.

Virtually every social group is the victim of prejudice at one time or another. One indication is the wide variety of derogatory labels that have been applied to every imaginable ethnic group in America, whether Irish (micks), Germans (krauts), French (frogs), Italians (wops, dagos), Poles (polacks), Jews (kikes, hebes, hymies), blacks (niggers, coons, jigaboos, jungle bunnies), Hispanics (spics, greasers, wetbacks, beaners), or Asians (slants, slopes, Chinks, Japs, flips). Even white Anglo-Saxon Protestants are called "WASPS" on occasion, not always fondly. Gay men, lesbians, people with AIDS, and the disabled are among the many other victims of prejudice.

But racial prejudice against blacks by whites has been perhaps the most severe and tenacious social problem faced by the United States. It dates back at least as far as the earliest contact between English travelers and Africans in the sixteenth century. The English were especially struck by the Africans' blackness, a color with overwhelmingly bad connotations for the English of the day. They perceived the Africans as looking like apes, as engaging in savage and uncivilized behavior, and as having "heathen" religions (Jordan, 1968). These earliest white impressions contain most of the antiblack stereotypes still common in the twentieth century.

When Africans were imported into America as slaves, they were treated as property, and often as subhuman beings. Although the slave trade was abolished in 1808, almost 90 percent of all blacks in the United States were still slaves in 1860, just before the outbreak of the Civil War. And emancipation did not noticeably improve their lot. At the beginning of World War II, most blacks lived in the South, where they still were largely segregated by law. Restaurants, movie houses, and buses had separate sections for blacks and whites. This formal, legalized segregation was not outlawed until 1964. The civil rights movement resulted in many improvements for blacks. But in recent years, life has again gotten worse for many blacks. More blacks live below the poverty line, housing and public schools continue to deteriorate in inner-city areas, and the crack epidemic has taken a major toll in increased crime and personal misery.

Prejudice and discrimination toward a wide variety of groups have been common throughout history and all over the world. However, in the United States the "peculiar institution" of slavery, and the legalized system of segregation that followed it, were unique to the black population. As a result, achieving equality has been much more difficult for blacks than for any

Public Sale of Negroes,

By RICHARD CLAGETT.

On Tuesday, March 5th, 1833 at 1:00 P. M. the following Slaves will be sold at Potters Mart, in Charleston, S. C.

Miscellaneous Lots of Negroes, mostly house servants, some for field work.

Conditions: ½ **cash, balance by bond, bearing interest from date of sale. Payable in one to two years to be secured by a mortgage of the Negroes, and appraised personal security.** *Auctioneer will pay for the papers.*

A valuable Negro woman, accustomed to all kinds of house work. Is a good plain cook, and excellent dairy maid, washes and irons. She has four children, one a girl about 13 years of age, another 7, a boy about 5, and an infant 11 months old. 2 of the children will be sold with mother, the others separately, if it best suits the purchaser.

A very valuable Blacksmith, wife and daughters; the Smith is in the prime of life, and a perfect master at his trade. His wife about 27 years old, and his daughters 12 and 10 years old have been brought up as house servants, and as such are very valuable. Also for sale 2 likely young negro wenches, one of whom is 16 the other 15, both of whom have been taught and accustomed to the duties of house servants. The 16 year old wench has one eye.

A likely yellow girl about 17 or 18 years old, has been accustomed to all kinds of house and garden work. She is sold for no fault. Sound as a dollar.

House servants: The owner of a family described herein, would sell them for a good price only, they are offered for no fault whatever, but because they can be done without, and money is needed. He has been offered $1250. They consist of a man 30 to 33 years old, who has been raised in a genteel Virginia family as house servant, Carriage driver etc., in all which he excels. His wife a likely wench of 25 to 30 raised in like manner, as chamber maid, seamstress, nurse etc., their two children, girls of 12 and 4 or 5. They are bright mulattoes, of mild tractable dispositions, unassuming manners, and of genteel appearance and well worthy the notice of a gentleman of fortune needing such.

Also 14 Negro Wenches ranging from 16 to 25 years of age, all sound and capable of doing a good days work in the house or field.

Almost all blacks in the United States are descendents of slaves forcibly imported from Africa, whereas almost all other Americans are descended from people who immigrated by choice. What kinds of behaviors might have been adaptive for people trapped in this "peculiar institution" with almost no hope for escape? What traces of those behaviors might exist today?

other minority group, and racial prejudice has been a central reason. Our discussion will emphasize this problem because it has been so difficult and important in the United States, and because most of the research on prejudice has focused on it.

COMPONENTS OF GROUP ANTAGONISM

Prejudice is exhibited when members of one group (called the **ingroup**) display negative attitudes and behavior toward members of another group (called the **outgroup**). Such group antagonisms have three interrelated but distinguishable elements.

Stereotypes are beliefs about the typical characteristics of group members, such as beliefs that blacks are lazy, not very smart, and good at athletics, or that Jews are shrewd, mercenary, and ambitious. **Prejudice** refers to negative attitudes toward the outgroup, such as that blacks should not live in white neighborhoods. **Discrimination** refers to overt behavior, such as hiring a white rather than an equally qualified black for a job.

Stereotypes

Stereotypes, the cognitive component of group antagonism, are beliefs about the personal attributes shared by people in a particular group or social category. For example, the most common stereotypes of nineteenth-century Native Americans as presented in novels, textbooks, and films, are that they were dirty, cruel, and warring savages, wearing feathers or warbonnets, riding horses, and using nonverbal signals to communicate with each other. Twentieth-century Native Americans are more often depicted as silent, passive, drunken, lazy, and immoral (Trimble, 1988).

Stereotypes often influence perceptions about individual members of the outgroup. For example, Sagar and Schofield (1980) presented

sixth-graders with brief verbal descriptions and artist's drawings of interactions between two children, such as one asking another for cake or one bumping the other in the hallway. The races of the two children were systemically varied in the drawings. Other children were then asked to tell a story about what had happened. Both black and white children described the behavior as more mean and threatening when blacks were involved than when whites were. Presumably this is due to the stereotype that such interactions are likely to be more hostile than friendly if blacks are involved.

Prejudice

Prejudice is the evaluation of a group or of a single individual based mainly on the person's group membership. Usually it is a negative evaluation; we say someone is prejudiced against members of an outgroup. But sometimes people are prejudiced in favor of a group (usually their own!). As a result, prejudice has the same like-dislike quality of the affective or evaluative dimensions discussed earlier regarding impressions (Chapter 2) and attitudes (Chapter 5). But prejudice has the additional quality of prejudgment. The perceiver evaluates other people on the basis of their social or racial category rather than on the basis of information or facts about them as individuals.

Unflattering stereotypes often go together with unfavorable prejudices, but they are not identical. Stereotypes of different groups can differ quite a bit in cognitive content, but yield equally strong negative prejudices. Historically, the majority of Americans have had quite different stereotypes about blacks and Jews, as we have indicated, but until recent years the level of prejudice against the two groups was quite similar.

The effects of prejudice are destructive and wide ranging. For one thing, our judgments about individuals are influenced by our prejudices about their group. For example, white college students at a Midwestern university were asked to participate as jurors in a study of jury behavior. They read a description of an alleged

Until 1964, Southern cities such as Dallas required blacks to sit in the back of the bus, while whites sat in the front.

rape of a 19-year-old woman by a 21-year-old man on the campus. The race of both victim and defendant were varied. The strength of the evidence against the defendant was also varied: in a strong evidence condition, both the victim and an eyewitness could identify the assailant; in a weak evidence condition, neither was sure. A middle or "marginal" condition pitted the victim's identification against the defendant's denials, with ambiguous reports by witnesses and police. Then the subjects were asked how much harm the defendant intended, how responsible he was for the rape, whether or not he was guilty, and what penalty he deserved. The responses were graded to form an index of perceived culpability.

The jurors' racial prejudices influenced their decisions. A black defendant was seen as more culpable than a white, especially when the victim was white and the evidence was marginal, as shown in Table 13–1. This is typical: such prejudices usually do influence perceptions of individual group members most when there is some ambiguity about the real situation.

Prejudice also influences people's political responses to minorities. For example, in elections that pit a black candidate against a white candidate, a white voter's prejudice is often the best predictor of which candidate he or she will support. In 1984, when Jesse Jackson first ran for the presidency, he was most opposed by the most prejudiced whites; less prejudiced whites

TABLE 13–1

PERCEIVED CULPABILITY OF MALE DEFENDANT AS A FUNCTION OF HIS RACE AND STRENGTH OF EVIDENCE

	Strength of Evidence			
	Near Zero	Marginal	Strong	Total
Race of defendant				
Black	7.2	17.1	24.4	15.9
White	6.5	12.9	21.7	13.8

Source: Adapted from Ugwuegbu (1979), p. 140. Entries are ratings of culpability on a 36-point scale where high values indicate greater perceived culpability.

were more supportive of him (Sears, Citrin, & Kosterman, 1987). Similarly, prejudice against blacks increases whites' opposition to affirmative action or busing, prejudice against Hispanic-Americans increases opposition to bilingual education and affirmative action for Hispanics, and prejudice against Asian-Americans increases opposition to similar policies benefiting them (Citrin, Reingold, & Green, 1989; Jessor, 1988; Kluegel & Smith, 1983; Sears & Huddy, 1989). In short, prejudice strongly influences people's political attitudes and behavior, whether it is their preferences about public policy or their voting behavior.

Prejudice refers only to negative attitudes toward the outgroup. **Ethnocentrism** refers to the belief that the ingroup is the center of every-

thing and is superior to all outgroups. Thus the ingroup is perceived as most virtuous, superior, and holding the best values; the outgroup is contemptible, immoral, inferior, weak, distrusted, and criminal (Brewer, 1986).

These positive attitudes toward the ingroup can have some of the same effects as prejudice against the outgroup. Among Anglo adults in California, "traditional Americanism" (based on beliefs about what makes someone a "true American," such as speaking and writing English or defending America when it is criticized) also generated increased opposition to policies that would benefit Hispanics and Asians, such as voting rights for non-English speakers (Citrin et al., 1989).

Prejudice against a group also influences at-

Despite many major changes in race relations since World War II, African Americans remain, on the average, economically and educationally disadvantaged, and racial segregation remains a fact of life even though no longer enforced by segregationist laws.

tributions about the causes of its members' behavior. A good example concerns whites' explanations for racial differences in socioeconomic status. Blacks, on the average, have always been lower in income, employment, educational level, and occupational status than have whites. Years ago the whites' main attribution for this relative lack of success was stable and internal; blacks were innately inferior in a variety of ways. Whites have gradually surrendered this notion, but have replaced it with attributions to such unstable internal causes as lack of effort and low aspirations. For example, in 1981, 59 percent believed blacks' worse jobs, income, and housing were due to their lack of motivation or willpower, while only 39 percent blamed discrimination. Blacks, on the other hand, are more likely to attribute their disadvantage to external causes such as discrimination. In the same survey, only 46 percent blamed lack of motivation, while 72 percent blamed discrimination (Bobo, 1989).

Why do the perceptions held by the two races differ so much? One possibility is that blacks are simply more familiar with the situations they confront than whites are, and therefore are more accurate about them. Another possibility is that a variant of the self-serving attribution (discussed in Chapter 4) is responsible. In this case, whites may make external attributions for blacks' successes and internal attributions for their failures, bolstering the esteem of their ingroup (whites) and derogating the outgroup (blacks). Indeed perceivers do generally make more favorable attributions for ingroup members than they do for outgroup members (Hamilton & Trolier, 1986). And there is substantial evidence that these internal attributions about blacks' disadvantages are made most often by the most prejudiced and politically conservative whites, while less prejudiced whites are more likely to explain them as due to external factors such as discrimination and lack of educational opportunity (Bobo, 1989, Apostle et al., 1983). Thus racial prejudice may lead many whites to make the "ultimate attributional error," of attributing the negative aspects of blacks' lives to their dispositions (Pettigrew, 1985). And blacks' tendency to defend their own group may lead them to blame their lack of success on external factors.

Discrimination

Discrimination is the behavioral component of group antagonism. This consists of negative behaviors toward individuals based on their group membership. For many years, Southern restaurants that served whites refused to seat Asian or black customers. Similarly, there is much documentation of preferential treatment for whites in the criminal justice system. Blacks are more likely to be excluded from juries, especially in cases involving black defendants; if convicted, they get harsher sentences, they serve longer in prison, and they are more likely to be sentenced to death (especially for raping a white woman). These racial differences hold up even when such factors as severity and frequency of offense are held constant (Nickerson, Mayo, & Smith, 1986). Finally, the use of quotas in college admissions has been particularly controversial. Before the 1960s, many private universities had quotas that limited the number of Jewish students admitted (and it is often charged that they now have similar quotas for Asian students). More recently, the use of quotas to aid minorities has been described as "reverse discrimination" because it favors a minority group at the expense of the majority. These are all examples of discriminatory behavior.

Another form of negative behavior motivated by prejudice is the expression of derogatory ethnic labels. Whether meant seriously or in humor, these can have quite harmful effects. In one study, white college students who were members of a mock jury were presented with a black defense attorney and a white defendant charged with transporting a stolen vehicle across state lines. Two of the jurors were confederates, and at one point, one said to the other, "God, Mike, I don't believe this. That nigger defense attorney doesn't know s--t!" In two other conditions either the word "shyster" replaced the word "nigger" or no comment at all was made. As shown in Figure 13–1, the derogatory ethnic label lowered the jurors' eval-

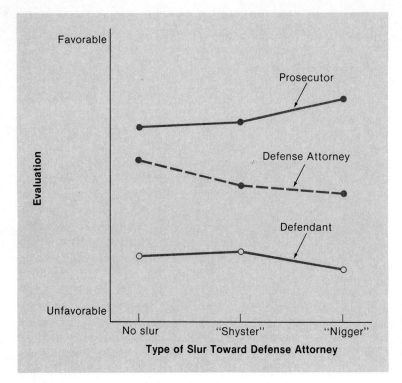

Favorable

Prosecutor

Defense Attorney

Defendant

Evaluation

Unfavorable

No slur   "Shyster"   "Nigger"

Type of Slur Toward Defense Attorney

Figure 13–1. Effects of ethnic slur toward defense attorney on evaluations of participants in trial. (Adapted from Kirkland, Greenberg, & Pyszcynki, 1987, p. 223.)

uations of the defense attorney and the defendant, and increased sentiment for conviction. Even calling the lawyer a "shyster" had a weaker effect than calling him a "nigger" (Kirkland et al., 1987).

Discrimination, as the behavioral component of group antagonism, is not always consistent with prejudiced attitudes. This was illustrated earlier (in Chapter 5) by the study showing that restaurant and hotel owners verbally refused to accept Asian customers, but behaviorally did accept the Chinese couple who appeared on their doorsteps (LaPiere, 1934). Conversely, a great deal of prejudice can exist with very little discrimination, particularly if there are firm legal prohibitions against discriminatory behavior. Today, many people continue to hold racially prejudiced attitudes or are prejudiced against women, but it is illegal to refuse to serve someone based on his or her race or gender, so discriminatory behavior is less common.

LEARNING PREJUDICE

There are a number of theories about the origins of prejudice, most of which derive from the general theories introduced in Chapter 1 and applied to attitudes in Chapter 5. Perhaps the simplest, *social learning theory,* views prejudice as being learned the same way people learn other attitudes and values.

Socialization

Children are not born with stereotypes and prejudiced attitudes. They must learn them, from their family, their peers, the media, and the society around them. *Socialization* refers to the process by which children and adolescents learn those attitudes. This can take place through each of the social learning mechanisms described earlier: for example, children may simply imitate the prejudices of adults and friends, they may be reinforced for using derogatory ethnic humor, or they may simply associate particular minority groups with poverty, crime, dirtiness, and other bad things.

But much of the learning of prejudice occurs outside the home. It is a **social norm** of the group in which the individual lives, or even of the society at large. Such norms are learned as part of the process of socialization. It is easy to

BOX 13–1

Dark Uniforms and Bad Behavior

The color black has historically been closely identified with bad people and bad events. In old Western movies, the bad guys wore black hats and the good guys wore white hats. When we do something seriously wrong, our reputation can become "blackened." Indeed in virtually all cultures, black is seen as the color of evil, death, and badness (Adams & Osgood, 1973). Presumably such norms are transmitted to children as part of their cultural heritage.

In two of the most violent professional sports, football and ice hockey, teams that wear black uniforms (like the Los Angeles Raiders and the Philadelphia Flyers) also receive the most penalties. But why does that happen? It seems not to be because the team management recruits unusually aggressive players and then dresses them to suit their behavior. Teams that have switched to black have done it for other reasons.

Is it because referees share the common stereotype about the color black, that it is associated with evil, and misperceive these teams as misbehaving more than they actually do? Frank and Gilovich (1988) found considerable evidence that they do. They had students who were unfamiliar with both sports rate all the teams' uniforms from pictures (without players in them). The black uniforms were consistently rated as the most bad, aggressive, and mean. Indeed the five black uniforms in football were rated as the most malevolent five in the entire league, and in ice hockey, five of the worst six had black uniforms.

Then these authors staged two brief football scrimmages in which the defensive team wore either black or white uniforms. The players were strictly instructed to behave in the same way in the two segments. The skirmishes were videotaped and then viewed for infractions of the rules by both professional referees and by college students. Both groups were more likely to assign penalties when the uniforms were black. To control for the possibility that the team really did play more illegally when wearing the black uniform, other students viewed the action with color and contrast dials turned down so that the uniform colors were very similar. Then the "black" team received no more penalties than the "white" team.

A self-perception explanation might also explain the excessive penalties: wearing a black uniform may make a player feel especially aggressive. To test this, the authors had students rate 12 competitive games for attractiveness, before and after outfitting them in black or white uniforms. Those wearing the black uniforms chose an increased number of aggressive games, such as dart-gun duels, while those wearing white uniforms did not change their ratings.

The authors conclude that the higher rate of penalties is due both to a stereotype-induced bias that results in black-uniformed players being perceived as more aggressive and to a self-perception process by which they actually come to behave more aggressively.

document the existence of norms of ethnic and racial prejudice all over the world. For example, white North Americans have historically tended to be prejudiced against those who originally came from Africa, Asia, and Latin America and to favor those who came from Western Europe (Lambert & Klineberg, 1967). Russians have historically been prejudiced against Jews, the English against Africans (as in Shakespeare's play, *Othello*), Chinese against Japanese, the Japanese against Koreans, and so on.

And these social norms of prejudice are often acquired very early in life. By the early grade school years, most American children are aware of racial differences in our society and of the prevailing norms about the races, at least in some form. In a careful study of black and white children, Goodman (1952) found that racial awareness was already present in many children at ages 3 and 4 and that 25 percent of the 4-year-olds were already expressing strongly entrenched race-related values. No white child ever expressed a wish to be like a black child, while the black children expressed much more conflict about their color. The experiences children have during these early years are crucial, because by early adolescence racial prejudice has crystallized and is much more difficult to break down.

Parents play a particularly important role in the child's acquisition of prejudice. There are consistent correlations between parents' and children's racial and ethnic attitudes (Ashmore & DelBoca, 1976). Parents often transmit these attitudes without directly instructing their children, since attitudes can be learned by association or by imitation as well as by direct reinforcement. Children observe their parents' attitudes and behavior and pick up many nonverbal cues in their reactions to people of other races.

As children grow older, peer groups become increasingly important. Normally peer groups mostly reinforce parents' views, because of the similarities in social background and values of people sharing a common community environment. But occasionally the parents' attitudes conflict with peers' attitudes, and the older the child gets, the more influential peers will be (Tedin, 1974).

The Media

The media represent another potential source of social learning, especially for children. Minorities have historically been given relatively little attention in the media. For example, before television, magazines such as *Life* and *The Saturday Evening Post* reached very large national audiences. As of 1949–1950, blacks were in only .5 percent of all ads and in 2.5 percent of all non-advertising material, despite the fact that they comprised about 10 percent of the population. Skimpy as this coverage was, it tended to be highly stereotyped; 80 percent of the blacks in ads were maids, cooks, or servants for whites (Greenberg & Mazingo, 1976).

This has changed considerably. On prime-time television, blacks appear much more often than they used to. During the 1977 and 1978 television seasons, blacks appeared in 20 percent of the product commercials and 59 percent of the drama shows (Weigel, Loomis, & Soja, 1980). And for a number of years, "The Cosby Show," featuring a black doctor and his family, was one of the most popular of network television series. Moreover, blacks are no longer shown only in subordinate roles. The same study showed that over 70 percent of the cross-racial interactions "occurred within institutional settings in which at least some black characters appeared to hold positions of authority or positions requiring technical sophistication" (Weigel et al., 1980, p. 889). Blacks and whites were about equally likely to have the higher-status roles in these interactions (see Table 13–2).

But the cross-racial interactions tended to be infrequent, distant, formal, and centered on the workplace. Table 13–2 shows that blacks' ap-

	T A B L E 1 3 – 2			
PRIME TIME COMMERCIALS AND PROGRAMMING ON TELEVISION: RELATIVE FREQUENCIES OF WHITE AND BLACK APPEARANCES, AND CROSS-RACIAL APPEARANCES AND INTERACTIONS				
	Percentage of Human Appearance Time			
Timing Category	Drama	Comedy	Total	Commercials
White appearances	99.5%	86.0%	95.8%	96.6%
Black appearances	3.3	22.0	8.3	8.5
Cross-racial appearances	2.8	7.9	4.1	5.1
Cross-racial interactions	1.5	3.6	2.0	1.7

Source: Weigel et al. (1980), p. 888.

pearances on television tended to be quite brief; some whites were almost always in view, whereas only rarely were one or more blacks in view. Further, blacks' appearances remain quite segregated: blacks and whites were shown as interacting with each other less than 4 percent of the time, even in comedies. Only 10 percent of the cross-racial interactions occurred outside the workplace, whereas 47 percent of the white-white interactions did. So if children were to take their cue from television today, they would assume that relations between the races were somewhat rare, distant, formal, and occur primarily at work. Of course, all this is still a great improvement over the invisibility and the stereotyped behavior presented earlier in this century.

MOTIVES FOR PREJUDICE

Other theories of prejudice focus on the needs of the individual and how prejudice can help satisfy them. Such theories fall into the category of motivational or incentive theories because they focus on individuals' motives and on the incentives offered to individuals for adopting prejudiced attitudes. There are several distinct versions of such theories.

Psychodynamic Approaches

Theories of prejudice that analyze it as an outgrowth of motivational tensions within the individual are sometimes called **psychodynamic theories** because they emphasize the particular dynamics of the specific individual's personality.

One such theory treats prejudice as *displaced aggression.* Displacement occurs when the source of frustration or annoyance cannot be attacked because of fear or simple unavailability. If there is an economic depression and a man loses his job, he feels angry and aggressive, but there is no obvious person at fault. Under these circumstances, people look for a scapegoat—someone whom they can blame for their difficulties and whom they can attack. One example

discussed earlier is the study showing that lynchings of blacks in the South increased as economic conditions deteriorated (Hovland & Sears, 1940). Poor whites could not aggress against the real sources of their frustration—large economic forces—so they aggressed against a more convenient and probably safer target—local blacks.

Another psychodynamic theory treats prejudice as a personality disorder, just like a phobia about snakes or a neurotic need for approval. The best known example of this theory is found in work on the *authoritarian personality* (Adorno et al., 1950). This impressive program of research was sponsored by the American Jewish Committee to try to understand the rise of anti-Semitism in the 1930s and the compliant behavior of Germans toward Hitler. Their conclusion was that anti-Semitism developed from a particular personality syndrome called the authoritarian personality. It is characterized by (1) rigid adherence to (and harsh punishment for deviation from) conventional values and patterns of behavior; (2) an exaggerated need to submit to, and identify with, strong authority; (3) generalized hostility; and (4) a mystical, superstitious cast of mind.

The authoritarian personality was thought to stem from early rearing by a domineering father and punitive mother. As an adult, the individual repeats the experience, but now he or she is in the driver's seat, bullying and punishing those who are different or inferior. People of other races and religions, the handicapped or weak of all kinds, or those with unconventional life-styles all fall under the authoritarian's iron boot. The authoritarian thinks his or her group is wonderful, and all other groups are disreputable and disgusting.

Research on authoritarianism quickly got caught up in technical disputes about the data (see Christie & Jahoda, 1954; Kirscht & Dillehay, 1967). The psychological analysis just presented also became somewhat controversial. A central problem was that researchers failed to distinguish adequately between sociocultural learning and personality factors in its explanation of anti-Semitism. It may not have resulted from a personality disorder, but may have been learned as a normal aspect of socialization.

Many of the most anti-Semitic Americans came from families only a generation or two removed from areas of Europe where extreme anti-Semitism had reigned for centuries. So anti-Semitism could have stemmed from learning a traditional norm, and not from a personality obsessed with authority and domination. As a result of these complexities, the authoritarian personality perspective is not as popular in social psychology as it was some years back.

Realistic Group Conflict

The theory of **realistic group conflict** argues that when two groups are in competition for scarce resources, they threaten each other. This creates hostility between them and thus produces mutually negative evaluations. So prejudice is an inevitable consequence of a reality conflict over resources both groups want. This is a motivational analysis of prejudice: it is created by one group's frustrating the other group's needs. Perhaps prejudice can be minimized if somehow both groups could get more of their needs satisfied, but it cannot be eliminated altogether because it is created by unavoidable realities (Bobo, 1988a; LeVine & Campbell, 1972).

The theory would lead us to expect antagonism between the Palestinians and Israelis: because they claim the same territory, they fight each other. Whites will be angry at blacks if blacks are hired on affirmative action programs and whites are excluded from those jobs. In recent years, increasing numbers of Asian-Americans have been excelling in academic work. If they are to be admitted to prestigious universities, correspondingly fewer students from other groups will be admitted, so it would not be surprising if prejudice against Asian-Americans began to rise.

Indeed, historical analyses suggest that Chinese and Japanese immigrants to the United States were well received as long as they did menial work no one else wanted to do. Only later, when they began to compete with Caucasians for jobs, did prejudice mount. Similarly studies of ethnic conflicts in South Africa, Belgium, and Northern Ireland do trace them to real competition in such areas as labor and housing markets. A breakdown in ethnic segregation is particularly likely to bring ethnic groups into such direct conflicts (Olzak & Nagel, 1986).

If prejudice arises because one group really threatens the other, then the most threatened individuals ought also to be the most preju-

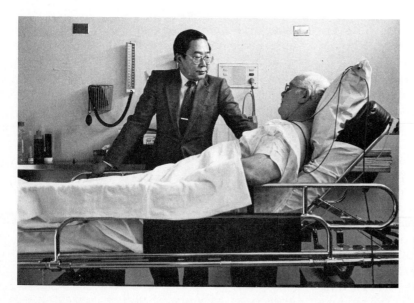

The rapid rise of Asian-Americans into universities, the professions, and business has caused some tensions with other groups. Here a Japanese-American doctor questions an emergency room patient about his chest pains.

diced. The whites who most perceive their neighborhoods as being threatened with racial integration, or with crime by blacks, or with influxes of black children into the schools, ought to be the most prejudiced (Rothbart, 1976).

However, a number of studies have shown that threats posed by blacks to whites' own lives have surprisingly little impact on their levels of prejudice or on their preferences regarding government racial policies (Sears, 1988). For example, parents of white children in school districts with busing (or threatened with busing) show no more opposition to busing than do nonparents or those who live in areas remote from any possibility of busing (McConahay, 1982; Sears & Allen, 1984). Other studies have shown that the past, current, or future impact of affirmative action programs on a white person's own life has little effect on his or her attitudes toward them (Jessor, 1988; Kluegel & Smith, 1983). This is not to say that realistic group conflict is never an important factor. But it seems not to create prejudice because it directly affects the personal lives of ingroup members; it seems to do so through perceptions of threats to the group, not to the individual.

Relative Deprivation

Another motivational theory focuses on the subjective feeling of being deprived as a source of intergroup antagonism. In particular, when people feel deprived relative to others, they may express their resentment in the form of antagonism against some group. This feeling of being deprived relative to other people is described as **relative deprivation** (Bernstein & Crosby, 1980). For example, in a fast-growing economy, most people's economic situations may be improving quite impressively. But they usually improve more slowly for some people, and so will create feelings of relative deprivation among them, as they see others increasingly able to afford things they cannot. This in turn might lead to antagonism against the favored group. This was one explanation for the ghetto riots of the 1960s. Although everyone was doing better, blacks felt that their situations were not

improving as much as those of whites, and the result was antiwhite violence (Sears & McConahay, 1973).

But there are two kinds of relative deprivation, and one is more potent than the other. One is *egoistic deprivation*—the feeling that we ourselves are deprived relative to other people with whom we compare (generally, people we already know, and so members of the ingroup). Other research suggests that the key discontent is instead that our own group is deprived relative to other groups, regardless of whether or not we ourselves are. This is called *fraternal deprivation* (Runciman, 1966). The threat is to "us," not to "me." Even individual whites who are not affected by busing, because they live in towns with no blacks at all or have no children, can be upset about it because it signals a displacement of whites by blacks (Bobo, 1988a; Sears & Kinder, 1985).

Fraternal deprivation proves to have a much stronger effect on group antagonism, nationalism, and voting behavior than does egoistic deprivation. For example, it has been stronger in activating support for social and political protest among unemployed youths in Australia, or among gays and lesbians in Toronto, or among whites who felt that they were not gaining as fast as blacks were (Birt & Dion, 1987; Bobo, 1988b; Vanneman & Pettigrew, 1972; Walker & Mann, 1987).

Part of the reason for the weak impact of egoistic deprivation seems to be that people tend to separate their attitudes about their own situations from their attitudes about society. And prejudice is first and foremost a set of attitudes about how groups should be treated in society, not about how one's own life should be going.

COGNITIVE BASES OF PREJUDICE

Earlier we analyzed extensively the cognitive processes that produce the impressions one person has of another (Chapters 2 and 3). Extending such cognitive theories from impressions of individual persons to impressions of groups and of group members has been one of the most active research areas on prejudice in recent years. The central idea is that certain systematic cognitive biases naturally accompany the perception of other people. These seemingly harmless cognitive biases can, all by themselves, produce stereotyping and prejudice even in the absence of prejudiced socialization, neurotic motives, or real competition between groups for resources.

Categorization

Perceivers naturally categorize other people into groups, the most common being gender, racial, and age groups. We immediately identify a stranger as a man or woman, black or white, child or grownup or old person. Beyond that, we quickly pigeonhole the person into such other social categories as class and nationality. Then we use subtler categories, such as tall ones, pretty ones, jocks, obnoxious ones, or whatever.

This **categorization** process has a number of important consequences. Processing information about individuals is markedly simplified and more efficient if they can readily be placed in categories. In *category-based processing*, the perceiver categorizes the stimulus person, then attends to additional information only to determine if it is consistent with the category. The alternative is to process information about the individual on a piecemeal basis, attribute by attribute, which is called *attribute-based processing* (Fiske et al., 1987). The great advantage of category-based processing is that it allows the perceiver to process a great deal of information quickly and effortlessly. The perceiver does not have to consider all the individual attributes of the other person.

The problem is that it leads to oversimplified stereotypes that frequently simply feed prejudices. Such social categories as "redneck" or "do-gooder" immediately provide rich associations and connotations (Anderson & Klatsky, 1987). But they gloss over the important individual characteristics of those in each category. For example, observers of group discussions including equal numbers of blacks and whites were more likely to confuse the contributions of people within a race than to confuse their contributions across race, as we indicated in Chapter 2 (Taylor et al., 1978). The implication is that information is stored in terms of social category, not in terms of the specific individuals. Observers remember that something was said by a black person or a white person, not which person said it.

Categorization into groups is often based simply on some very prominent, salient cues. Skin color differentiates blacks and whites; body type, hair length, clothing, and voice differentiate men and women; accent differentiates foreigners from natives, and so on.

This kind of *salience* has a number of predictable effects, as we saw in Chapter 2. We pay more attention to salient stimuli, so these differences tend to be on our mind when we encounter members of other groups, especially when they stand out in the environment. A white researcher in a ghetto school stands out; so did Jackie Robinson when he was the first black major league baseball player.

Is categorization into groups, and the ensuing stereotyping, therefore based in reality? If so, it would be less irrational and unfair than it is usually described as being. To some extent it usually is; blacks and whites do look different. But it must be remembered that salience depends to a large degree on where our attention is directed, and that in turn depends to a large degree on the norms we have learned. In the United States, for example, race is extremely salient, primarily because of our history of having placed African-American slaves in a lower caste. By contrast, in Cuba or Brazil, race is not as salient; people's skin colors span the full range, and categorization by race is less common. And in Lebanon, religious preference is the major basis for categorization; people are either Muslim or Christian. In Northern Ireland, the same is true; people are either Catholic or Protestant, not much else matters. In the United States, on the other hand, we tend to categorize on several other dimensions before we even get to religion. Lots of categories are potentially salient, but we tend to rely heavily on only a few, and that selection is based on the conventional norms of our society. So we must not think that categorizing on the basis of salient attributes necessarily means it is rational or accurate.

BOX 13-2

The Perceived Power of the "Solo"

Some of the most salient people in our society are the "solos"—the one black astronaut in a news conference, the only woman engineer in an office, the one white starting in a professional basketball game, and so on. If mere perceptual salience is responsible for biasing observers' perceptions of causal importance, one would think these "solo" individuals would be perceived as having an exaggerated causal role in their social settings. The effects of the salience created by being a solo member of a minority group in a context dominated by majority group members are illustrated in a series of studies conducted by Taylor and her colleagues (1977; see Taylor, 1981b). They varied the distinctiveness of a minority person in a discussion group by setting up discussions by groups that were all white, had one black, or were evenly divided in race. The discussion was presented via tape recording, and exactly the same tape was used in all cases. However, each speaker was identified with a still slide as he spoke, and in this way the race of the speakers was varied. Observers of this mixed-media discussion rated the speakers for amount of contribution to the discussion. The "solo" black stood out as talking more and being more influential than did the same speaker in either of the other contexts, where his race did not make him so salient because he was portrayed as just one black in a group that was racially evenly divided, or as a white in an all-white group. The token's contributions were also remembered better than those of the minorities in the integrated group. Interestingly enough, these tokens may themselves suffer cognitive deficits as a result of their token status; in one study (Lord & Saenz, 1985), tokens remembered less of the discussion in which they had participated (and supposedly dominated!) than did other participants or observers.

Ingroups Versus Outgroups

Numerous studies show that the mere act of categorization can produce discrimination when it involves categorizing people into "us" (an ingroup) and "them" (an outgroup). Members of the ingroup have quite different perceptions about their group than they do about outgroups, and different from those held by outgroup members. Americans are likely to per-

BOX 13-3

How Much Black Does It Take To Make a "Black"?

The arbitrariness of this categorization process is perhaps illustrated most vividly by the famous "separate-but-equal" Supreme Court decision in 1896, *Plessy* v. *Ferguson*. In the racially segregated South during the century following emancipation, the definition of who was black and who was white varied considerably. In some states a single drop of Negro blood classified a person as a Negro. *Plessy* v. *Ferguson* defined a Louisiana pupil with one black great-grandparent and seven white ones as colored and assigned the pupil to an all-Negro segregated school. The Chinese who settled in Mississippi after the Civil War were designated as colored and were subject to the same restrictions as blacks. But this categorization gradually changed, and by World War II Chinese were largely treated as if they were white. The point is that although these classifications were quite arbitrary, they had serious consequences for the people involved, since Negroes could not attend the same schools or restaurants as whites, or usually, even vote.

BOX 13–4

Do "They" Really All Look Alike?

One implication of the outgroup homogeneity effect is that eyewitnesses should be more accurate in distinguishing among members of the ingroup than among members of the outgroup. If "all Asians look alike" to a white American, they should be more readily confused with each other.

Studies testing this hypothesis typically have shown black and white subjects a series of slides with faces of members of both races, then a much larger set of slides from which they are asked to identify the faces they saw earlier. Error rates are computed separately for same-race and other-race identification. A number of such studies have been done, and all have shown that white subjects show the own-race bias, and almost all show it for black subjects as well (Bothwell, Brigham, & Malpass, 1989). Indeed, there is a tendency for all of "them" to look alike, and all of "us" to look quite uniquely different.

ceive Japanese very differently than a Japanese person would. And the Japanese in turn will perceive both groups quite differently. Being in an ingroup places one in a unique perspective. It has three important consequences.

One is that ingroup members perceive other ingroup members as more similar to them than outgroup members are. This is the so-called **assumed similarity effect.** This greater assumed similarity occurs with real groups that do in fact have distinctive opinions. For example, fraternity members perceive themselves as more similar to each other than to commuter students, and vice versa (Holtz & Miller, 1985). But even when group members have been arbitrarily or randomly assigned to the group, observers perceive members of the group as being similar to each other, and dissimilar to members of other groups. Allen and Wilder (1979) assigned students to groups ostensibly on the basis of artistic preferences and found that they assumed other ingroup members were especially similar to them on matters wholly unrelated to art. Making group membership more salient, by discussing possible conflicts with other groups, enhances this assumed similarity still further (Miller & Brewer, 1986).

A second consequence of categorization into ingroup and outgroup is that we tend to see the outgroup as more homogeneous than the ingroup in terms of traits, personality, and even number of subtypes "*They* are all alike, whereas *we* are quite diverse!" The implication is that we tend to perceive a member of an outgroup as just another anonymous group member rather than perceiving them as individuals. We see the person as "an Asian" rather than as Stanley Wong.

This is called the **outgroup homogeneity effect.** For example, members of one sorority or undergraduate club rated the members of their own sorority or club as more dissimilar from each other than they did the members of each of several other sororities or clubs (Jones, Wood, & Quattrone, 1981; Park & Rothbart, 1982). One reason is that we are more likely to perceive the ingroup in terms of subcategories. We can distinguish several different groups of friends within our sorority, and the new pledges seem quite different from the seniors, as well. Similarly, the elderly are more likely than the young to distinguish between such subcategories of old people as grandmothers, elder statesmen, and senior citizens (Brewer, Dull, & Lui, 1981).

In like fashion, people also perceive any individual member of the ingroup as more complex than they do individual members of the outgroup. Their personalities are seen as more multidimensional and as having more variety and richness. For example, white subjects see whites as more complex than blacks, and young subjects see the young as more complex than the elderly (and vice versa!) (see Linville, 1982; Linville & Jones, 1980; Brewer & Lui, 1984). In all these ways, then, we perceive less diversity in the outgroup.

Finally, this categorization of individuals into ingroup and outgroup leads to more favorable attitudes and behavior toward members of the ingroup, and less favorable toward members of the outgroup. This is the so-called **ingroup favoritism effect** (Tajfel et al., 1971). Once people feel they belong to a group, they tend to favor other group members at the expense of members of other groups, in terms of more favorable evaluations or more favorable allocations of rewards.

The simplest demonstrations of such effects use the **minimal intergroup situation** designed by Henri Tajfel (1969). In these studies, students were brought into a laboratory and divided into two groups on the basis of some arbitrary procedure. In one typical study, they were divided into two groups supposedly on the basis of their preferences between the two modern painters Klee and Kandinsky (though in fact they were assigned randomly to the two groups). They had no actual interaction with fellow group members (the ingroup) or members of the other group (the outgroup), but they were asked to evaluate all individuals in the experiment and distribute some rewards to them.

The general finding has been that the participants evaluated ingroup members more positively, and rewarded them more, than they did outgroup members (Brewer, 1979). This ingroup favoritism also has shown up in more favorable descriptions of other ingroup members' traits, expecting more favorable treatment from the ingroup and making more favorable attributions about fellow ingroup members' behavior (Allen & Wilder, 1975; Hamilton & Trolier, 1986; Howard & Rothbart, 1980).

The intriguing thing about these findings is that they occur so consistently despite the fact that the ingroup-outgroup distinction in these experiments is in reality almost completely meaningless. These subjects were not allowed to reward themselves, and they could not be rewarded by other ingroup members. They had no interaction with members from either group. The purely cognitive act of categorization, on whatever basis, seems to trigger ingroup favoritism and discrimination against the outgroup, even when there are no selfish gains to be made or any especially pleasurable interaction with the ingroup, or any especially unpleasant interaction with the outgroup.

Why does the mere act of categorization of individuals into an ingroup and an outgroup exaggerate perceived differences between the groups and lead to more favorable treatment of ingroup members? There are three main explanations. The most obvious is the learning idea that we generally have more direct experience with members of the ingroup, and so are less likely to oversimplify our perceptions of them. While this is no doubt true, it is only part of the explanation, since as we have seen, experimental studies of newly formed groups yield the same results even when they provide no experience with group members at all, as in the minimal intergroup situation, or hold constant real experience with members of both groups (Judd & Park, 1988; Linville et al., 1986). A second possibility is more cognitive: people store information separately about the group as a whole and about particular representatives of it (called *exemplars* or *prototypes*). It may be easier to retrieve memory of individuals from the ingroup because they are more familiar, which would explain the outgroup homogeneity effect (Park & Rothbart, 1982; Judd & Park, 1988). However, that would not explain such effects in groups where experience with individual group members is nonexistent.

Social Identity

Perhaps the most common explanation comes from **social identity theory** as developed by Henri Tajfel (1982). As we indicated in the chapter on groups, it is a blend of the motivational and cognitive approaches and involves three basic assumptions. First, people categorize the social world into ingroups and outgroups, as we have seen. Second is a motivational assumption, that people strive for a positive self-concept and derive a sense of self-esteem from their social identity as a member of the ingroup. Third, their self-concept is partly dependent on how they evaluate their ingroup relative to other groups. Therefore they engage in behavior that both distinguishes their group from other groups, and benefits their group and fellow ingroup members relative to outgroup members (Tajfel & Turner, 1986). This process produces a kind of social competition between groups, in which people try to boost the status of their own group as a way of boosting their own self-esteem.

This theory has two important implications. First, if one's social identity is based on self-categorization into an ingroup, and one's self-esteem is partially based on feeling the ingroup is superior, both self-categorization and ingroup favoritism should bolster the individual's self-esteem. A woman who identifies herself as a member of a particular sorority, and then helps a sorority sister to win a student government election, should have enhanced self-esteem. In one study, people had higher self-esteem if they were both categorized into groups *and* could discriminate against the outgroup than if they were not categorized and could discriminate, or were categorized and could not discriminate (Lemyre & Smith, 1985). People like to be part of a group that is superior.

Second, if ingroup favoritism is motivated by the need to enhance self-esteem, it should be greater when one's self-esteem is low or threatened. Prejudice against outgroups should also be greatest under the same circumstances. So far the evidence on these latter two points is not very clear. People with low self-esteem are usually the most prejudiced, but also are most negative about the ingroup as well (Wills, 1981). They just seem to be the most negative about everything. And mixed results have come from experiments designed to test the assumption that ego-threatened people are the most hostile to outgroups (e.g., Crocker et al., 1987). The value of social identity in enhancing individual self-esteem remains the weakest link in social identity theory, then. But it is an interesting blend of cognitive and motivational approaches, and it will no doubt continue to generate considerable attention.

In the white population in America, hostility toward outgroups such as blacks or Latinos is more common than extreme pro-white identification. But some do engage in advocacy of "white power," like these American Nazis.

Schemas

If stereotypes are cognitive structures regarding a social group, they can be thought of as **schemas,** with the same consequences we have already discussed in the social cognition chapter. New information inconsistent with schemas tends to be rejected, and ambiguous information becomes interpreted as consistent with the group stereotype. This was illustrated in the Sagar and Schofield (1980) study cited earlier, in which children interpreted a black child's behavior in a drawing as more mean and threatening than a white child's. Like any schema, stereotypes distort reality to achieve order. In that sense, they are not necessarily bizarre, deviant, or pathological. They become destructive when they ignore the evidence of reality and are generalized to all group members.

Priming a schema should make it salient and increase its influence over the individual's thinking, as we saw in the social cognition chapter. Indeed imagining stereotypes seems to prime them and increase their believability. Subjects who were asked to imagine a situation involving a stereotype about an occupational group (such as "an aggressive lawyer") subsequently believed those stereotypes more than did subjects not asked to imagine them or asked to imagine a scene with a nonstereotyped trait (Slusher & Anderson, 1987).

But frequently people have more than one schema about a particular object, so it is important to know which schema is being primed. For example, Sears and Huddy (1989) experimentally varied the prime given to a national sample of non-Hispanics regarding bilingual education. Some were presented a version of it that involved the maintenance of Spanish language abilities in children who were native Spanish speakers. This implied that special treatment would be given to immigrant minorities, the "melting pot" idea would be abandoned, and Hispanics would maintain their foreign culture and not assimilate to the mainstream of America. Others were presented a version that simply involved immersion in the English language, and so implied rapid assimilation to American ways. The maintenance version seemed to prime anti-Hispanic and anti-immigrant schemas, since attitudes toward it were more strongly influenced by such racial prejudices.

Priming one's own *self-categorization* as a member of an ingroup has much the same effects as priming any other schema (Turner et al., 1987). Individuals are then more likely to perceive themselves as possessing the stereotyped attributes of the ingroup. For example, Hogg and Turner (1987) made gender salient in small discussion groups. This seems to have primed the subjects' gender self-schemas, because they then saw themselves as more typical of their own gender group and aligned their self-descriptions more closely to their own gender stereotypes. The men perceived themselves as more competitive, assertive, and forceful, while the women perceived themselves as more helpful, compassionate, and sympathetic.

Schemas about an outgroup can, in turn, pro-

duce stereotype-confirming behavior on the part of the outgroup member. That is, our stereotypes influence not only our own thinking, but also the behavior of the *victims* of stereotyping when we interact with them. In this sense, a stereotype can be a **self-fulfilling prophecy.** This further step in the process is in some ways even more damaging. Members of the victimized group begin to live up to the stereotype, to exhibit the very characteristics the stereotype says they have. If we think all Poles are bumblers, we are likely to interact with them as if we expected them to bumble at any opportunity. And, interestingly enough, this will increase the likelihood that they will behave in a stereotype-confirming way and become real bumblers (Word et al., 1974).

The chain of self-fulfilling prophecy involves five steps, as shown at the top of Figure 13–2: (1) the stereotype about how the other person will behave (2) influences the stereotype holder's own behavior, which (3) influences the target person's behavior, and that in turn contributes to (4) the perception of the target person's behavior as confirming the stereotype rather than as a response to the holder's own behavior. This then leads to (5) the target person's coming to accept that stereotype as an accurate self-description.

Snyder and Swann (1978) showed this in an ingenious way, as shown at the bottom of Figure 13–2. They told each subject (the "perceiver") he was going to interact with another subject (the "target") who was described either as hostile, liking contact sports, cruel, and insensitive, or as nonhostile, liking poetry and sailing, kind, and cooperative. This description set up the perceiver's stereotype of the target (step 1). Then the perceiver and target (who was also a naive subject) engaged in a series of reaction time tests that allowed both to behave in a hostile way (by administering loud, painful, distracting noises to each other).

Not surprisingly, it turned out that expecting a hostile partner led perceivers to administer more high-intensity noises (step 2). But the targets, completely ignorant of how they had been described to the other person, also administered more noise if they had been described as hostile

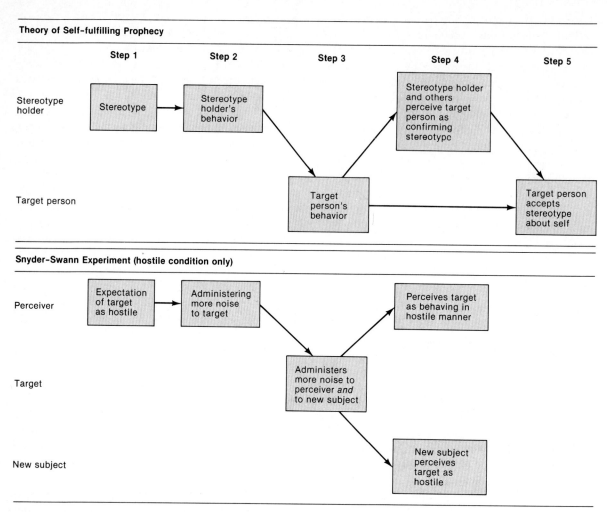

Figure 13-2. Stereotypes as self-fulfilling prophecies: Theory and experiment. (Adapted from Synder & Swann, 1978.)

(step 3). Remember, the targets had been described as hostile or nonhostile at random, so this higher level of hostile behavior had to be caused by the perceiver's expectations. And the perceivers, reasonably enough, saw the "hostile" target as more hostile than the "nonhostile" target, in view of the behavioral confirmation of their expectations (step 4).

The most interesting aspect of this experiment then followed. The target was put through the same task with a new, completely naive subject. Neither knew about the "hostile" or "nonhostile" description randomly assigned earlier to the target. Nevertheless, the target continued to live up to expectations. He gave more noise (step 3, again) and was regarded as more hostile in this new interaction (step 4, again).

So this experiment demonstrates that expectations affect the stereotyper's own behavior toward the person, whose behavior in return confirms the stereotype. Not only that, but the victim later behaves in a stereotype-confirming manner in other situations, even toward people who are completely ignorant of the stereotype. So even in neutral environments, with people who do not share the stereotype, the victim of prejudice still tends to exhibit stereotype-confirming behavior.

Perhaps the most destructive result comes from the fifth step in this process: the target person actually comes to believe that the stereotype accurately applies to him or her. In a similar study by Fazio and his colleagues (1981), the subjects exhibited behavior in the experiment itself that confirmed the expectations of their partners. But they were then placed in a completely different social situation, where they interacted with a new confederate. The subject still lived up to the original expectations in interacting with this new person. And the subject's own self-ratings also lived up to the original partner's expectations. Through the self-perception process described earlier (Chapter 4), the subjects took their own behavior as genuinely reflecting their own personalities, even though it had been induced by the other person's expectations. In short, not only was the stereotype holder's behavior influenced by these arbitrary expectations, but the victims' behavior and self-perceptions also came to reflect the stereotype.

Comparison of Theories

Each of the foregoing broad theoretical approaches points to different factors as causes of prejudice. There is some truth in all of them. For example, normal cognitive processes of categorization and of special attention to salient stimuli can increase stereotypes and discriminatory behavior. It is doubtful that such cognitive processes are sufficient to produce a consistent pattern of bias all by themselves, however. They require learning that produces prejudice against particular groups, and specific stereotypical content. Blacks are stereotypically thought to be lazy and musical, and Asians hardworking, though both are perceptually quite different from whites. But the perceptual distinctiveness of these minority groups may be necessary to get a pattern of group discrimination started, and it certainly helps to maintain it.

In general, social learning plays a major role in defining what is "appropriate" prejudice, what the "correct" stereotypes are, and what is acceptable behavior toward other groups and what is not. The wide variations in the treatment of any given group around the globe and across history testify to that, as do the major differences in the treatment of different groups within a society. In 1850, blacks could be bought and sold like cattle; today elaborate legal machinery protects their right to be treated like other people. Slavery hardly existed for other groups in this country, nor for blacks in many other societies. In most Muslim countries women must wear veils, may not engage in premarital or extramarital sexual relations, and do not compete with men for jobs. American women are not so restricted today, though in the nineteenth century they were much less free. Personality tensions and cognitive biases therefore operate within a cultural framework that determines how much prejudice exists, when it can be expressed, and toward whom. This cultural framework is transmitted through learning.

THE CHANGING FACE OF PREJUDICE

Much has changed since the earliest sociopsychological studies of prejudice in the 1930s. Hitler has come and gone, discrediting anti-Semitism with his slaughter of European Jewry. The women's movement and activism on behalf of people with AIDS and many other disadvantaged groups have filled the news hours and occasionally the streets as well. What has changed, and what has not? Again we will focus primarily on racial prejudice, because it has been most researched, but similar findings hold for prejudice against Hispanics, women, gays and lesbians, the disabled, and other groups.

Declining Old-fashioned Racism

The traditional forms of racism against blacks involved stereotypes of their lack of intelligence, laziness, and so on, along with prejudice against racial integration in a variety of arenas such as housing, schools, jobs, and marriage. This has been called **old-fashioned racism** (Mc-

Conahay, 1986). And it plainly has declined. In years gone by, most whites felt that blacks had less ambition than did whites, that white and black children should go to separate schools, and that whites should get preference for available jobs. Even in 1964, 25 percent of whites favored racial segregation. But in recent years, few or none continue to hold these attitudes (Hochschild & Herk, 1989; Schuman et al., 1985). A number of such examples are shown in Table 13–3.

There is also some evidence that racial prejudice may be a declining factor in whites' responses to black political candidates, at least to some of the longer-established ones. In Tom Bradley's first two campaigns for mayor of Los Angeles, in 1969 and 1973, whites' votes were more strongly influenced by racial prejudice than by any other factor (Kinder & Sears, 1981). But by 1982, when he ran for governor of California, he won as many white votes as did his fellow Democratic candidates (all of them white), and racial prejudice was a factor but no greater than it was for those white running mates (Citrin, Green, & Sears, 1990).

Nevertheless, substantial evidence of continuing racial prejudice exists, in three ways. Large minorities of whites continue to wish to maintain distance from blacks. As of 1983, 60 percent did not approve of interracial marriages, the highest level of disapproval in 13 Western nations (Pettigrew, 1988; Schuman et al., 1985). About one-third do not want black neighbors, and about 20 percent continue not to want integrated schools (Dovidio & Gaertner, 1986). And there is a hard core of real racists; as late as 1978, 15 percent of white adults agreed that "blacks are inferior to white people" (Hochschild & Herk, 1989).

Second, while racism has declined according to most indicators, white support for government policies designed to promote racial equality has not kept pace. Support for affirmative action, open housing laws, busing for integration, or government spending for other programs benefiting blacks has remained weak, and is not visibly increasing (Schuman et al., 1985). Some of those data are shown in Table 13–3.

Third, blacks continue to be much less con-

T A B L E   1 3 – 3

CHANGES OVER TIME IN WHITES' RACIAL ATTITUDES: GENERAL PRINCIPLES OF RACIAL EQUALITY AND IMPLEMENTING POLICIES

	Historical Era		
	Early	Late	Change
General Principles			
Oppose *segregation*	75% (1964)	95% (1978)	+20%
Oppose laws against *intermarriage*	39 (1964)	66 (1982)	+27
White and black students should go to same *schools*	32 (1942)	90 (1982)	+58
Negroes should have as good a chance as whites to get any kind of *job*	45 (1944)	97 (1972)	+52
Vote for well-qualified black for president if nominated by own party	37 (1958)	81 (1983)	+44
Implementing Policies			
Federal government should ensure that white and black children go to same *schools*	42 (1964)	25 (1978)	−17
Favor *busing*	13 (1972)	21 (1983)	+8
Government provide *special aid to minorities*	22 (1970)	18 (1982)	−4
Support increased *government spending on blacks*	27 (1973)	26 (1983)	−1

Source: Adapted from Schuman, Steeh, and Bobo (1985), Tables 3–1 and 3–2. The years involved in the comparison are shown in parentheses.

vinced than are whites that prejudice and discrimination are things of the past. In 1981, over 60 percent of blacks felt that they were discriminated against in getting jobs, while only 25 percent of whites did (Bobo, 1989). In 1988, 69 percent of blacks, as against 37 percent of whites, believed that blacks do not have the same opportunities as whites have (Hochschild & Herk, 1989).

New Forms of Prejudice

A lively set of controversies has arisen about the possible interpretation of this contrast between the seeming disappearance of old-fashioned racism and evidence of continued resistance to change. There are four discernibly different points of view.

Illusory Change. Some have argued that the new liberalism in whites' support for integration merely represents **illusory changes**: whites just mouth the socially desirable responses to such questions, while underneath, their real attitudes contain the same old racism. By this view, old-fashioned racism is on the wane only because it is socially unacceptable to voice it, not because it has really gone away. So, when asked, whites reject old-fashioned racism: they say yes, black children are as intelligent as white children, and yes, they should have the right to go to the same schools. But on questions that pose issues of racial equality more indirectly, where opposition to equality is less likely to be regarded as racist—for example, on support for such efforts to redress the effects of inequality as affirmative action—they allow their true racism to come through, and they resist. Experiments designed to test this view show that whites express less old-fashioned racism to black interviewers than they do to white interviewers, as if they were deliberately holding it back, whereas they express about the same amount of indirect forms of racism to both kinds of interviewers (McConahay et al., 1981).

Ambivalence. In 1944, the great Swedish social scientist Gunnar Myrdal wrote that "the

American dilemma" lay in white Americans' contradictory beliefs in freedom and equality for all, on the one hand, and their racial prejudice and discrimination, with the attendant personal convenience and safety they provided, on the other. Some contemporary social psychologists see the same *ambivalence* operating in white Americans today. Most, it is said, do feel some special sympathy for blacks, out of a recognition that they have been handicapped by special disadvantages. But they also perceive blacks as contributing to their own plight, particularly through lack of ambition, criminal behavior, drug and alcohol abuse, promiscuity, and so on. This leaves the white person with "conflicting sentiments, consisting of friendliness and sympathy on one side and disdain and aversion on the other" (I. Katz et al., 1986, p. 42).

A similar view is that old-fashioned racism has been replaced by **aversive racism** (Kovel, 1970; Gaertner & Dovidio, 1986). This describes whites as conflicted between their genuinely egalitarian value systems and their negative feelings toward blacks. But whites are ashamed of their negative feelings, so they avoid blacks. This allows them to avoid being confronted with their true prejudices, and thus to protect their images of themselves as unprejudiced persons. They feel discomfort, uneasiness, and fear toward blacks, then, rather than hostility or hate, as in old-fashioned racism. To put these theories in the language we have been using, whites have two racial schemas—one that links concern for social justice (egalitarian values) with racial tolerance and the other that links emphasis on self-reliance (individualism) with racial prejudice.

To test this, their order of presentation was varied (Katz & Hass, 1988). When whites answered egalitarian questions first, their prejudice scores went down. When they answered individualism questions first, their prejudice scores went up. This is the result that would be expected if in fact most people genuinely held both schemas, either of which could be primed.

Other evidence for this view comes from studies of whites' nonverbal behavior in interactions with blacks. Whites tend to sit farther away, use less friendly voice tones, make less eye contact and more speech errors, and terminate an interview more quickly when talking to blacks than when talking to other whites (Pettigrew, 1985). In another set of studies, the Donnersteins (1972) found that the potential for retaliation by blacks against a white aggressor markedly reduced the direct aggression performed by whites. Instead it increased whites' covert, disguised, and indirect forms of aggression. They did not find similar effects on blacks resulting from the threat of white retaliation. This too suggests that whites avoid direct expression of whatever real negative feelings they have toward blacks.

Symbolic Racism. Others suggest that old-fashioned racism is simply not very widespread or potent anymore. Instead, it has been replaced by another, more modern, form of prejudice called **symbolic racism** (Kinder & Sears, 1981; McConahay & Hough, 1976; Sears & McConahay, 1973). This view is that the most powerful version of racial prejudice today focuses on racial symbols such as "forced busing," "reverse discrimination," or "welfare." Whites' opposition to racial progress is at an abstract, symbolic level, both because of their unfavorable emotional reaction to blacks and because it violates their other values. More specifically, rather than simply reflecting antagonism toward

blacks, symbolic racism combines antiblack affect with traditional American values that have nothing to do with race, such as self-reliance, the value of hard work, the belief that people should get only the rewards they have worked for, and the belief that no group should get special favors. Symbolic racism therefore is reflected in such attitudes as that blacks are making unfair demands for special treatment and that they therefore are getting undeserved gains in areas such as jobs or college admissions. The symbolic racism model is presented in Figure 13–3.

Research on symbolic racism has focused on three points. First, it is a stronger predictor than old-fashioned racism of whites' attitudes about such racially relevant policies as busing, affirmative action, bilingual education, and welfare. It also predicts opposition to black political leaders such as Mayor Tom Bradley of Los Angeles and Jesse Jackson. Old-fashioned racism is not a strong predictor of these attitudes anymore. Second, attitudes toward these racial policies and leaders are not well predicted by variables central to other theories, such as realistic group conflict theory. Real personal threats that blacks pose to whites' personal lives, such as of criminal violence, busing, or loss of jobs due to affirmative action, do not have the same force. And, third, symbolic racism itself seems to be a

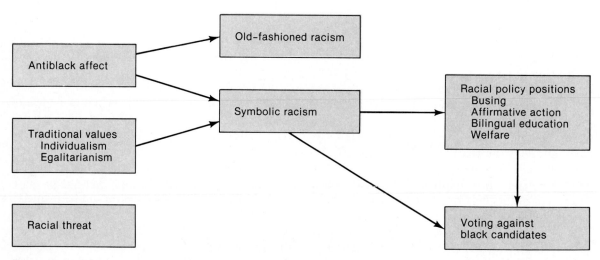

Figure 13–3. The symbolic racism approach. (Adapted from Sears, 1988, p. 58.)

Jesse Jackson denouncing South African apartheid at Harvard University. During the 1980s, Jackson came to symbolize black activism in the eyes of many Americans. As a result he aroused passionate feelings both for and against him.

joint product of antiblack attitudes and of non-racial traditional values (see Jessor, 1988; McConahay, 1982; Sears, 1988).

Realistic Group Conflict. Finally, the *realistic group conflict* interpretation also assumes that the new support for general principles of equality is genuine, but holds that it is superficial. It is easy to support equality in the abstract, but supporting actual implementation has real and costly implications such as busing white children across town, so whites resist that (Jackman, 1978). In other words, such implementing policies produce realistic group conflict, with whites' dominant status being threatened by black activism, so they oppose activists and policies that directly threaten white superiority. Opposition to implementing policies, by this view, represents an ideological defense of the dominant group's interests. In essence whites try to buy off blacks with vague promises of equality, but when push comes to shove, as with affirmative action and busing or electing a black candidate such as Jesse Jackson as president, whites resist any real change (Bobo, 1988a; Jackman & Muha, 1984).

There is some evidence for this view. Over time, data show that whites were most negative toward the black political movement when it was at its strongest, in the 1960s. Second, whites' resistance to policies implementing equality are indeed closely linked to negative attitudes toward black political activism. And, finally, whites' rejection of the black political movement may be influenced by a sense of fra-

Affirmative action has resulted in many unfamiliar situations, such as a white man being interviewed for a job by a black woman. Realistic group conflict theory predicts that whites will often react negatively to such erosions of their traditionally favored position.

ternal deprivation—that blacks are getting too much at the expense of whites (Bobo, 1988a, b).

Much research is currently underway to test among these several theories. They are all somewhat different, but they do share some similar elements. They all assume that whites have some genuine sympathy for general egalitarian principles and that most do reject the old ideas of white superiority and segregation. But they all acknowledge that prejudice has clearly not disappeared; whites have continuing antagonism toward blacks, whether it is based on early socialization or on real conflicts of interest.

REDUCING PREJUDICE

Studies of attitude change, as summarized in Chapter 6, would make it appear that people's attitudes are quite susceptible to change. Similarly, the studies of conformity and obedience presented in Chapter 8 suggest that people's behavior can be influenced rather readily. So it might seem that prejudice and discrimination might be easily controlled as well. But things turn out not to be so easy. As Hovland (1959) pointed out, it is generally easy to change attitudes in the controlled environment of a laboratory. Even a simple written essay can produce changes in attitudes toward foreign aid on brushing teeth. But attempts to change attitudes and behavior in the world outside the laboratory tend to be much less successful, at least of such attitudes as racial and ethnic prejudices.

The main approach to prejudice reduction has been through direct intergroup contact. The pervasiveness of racial segregation in America in housing, schools, jobs, and most areas of life led many social scientists after World War II to conclude that sheer ignorance of blacks and their lives helped to create whites' erroneous and oversimplified racial stereotypes. Greater interracial contact was expected to inform whites, break down their stereotypes, and ultimately reduce their prejudice (Myrdal, 1944).

Does contact really reduce prejudice? The classic early studies took advantage of the fact that America's major institutions gradually be-

came less segregated in the decades following World War II. Changes in the military, schools, professional sports, and many work situations gave social scientists opportunities to test the effects of contact. The first studies examined desegregation of the Army. At the start of World War II, military policy was constructed to avoid racially mixed units. However, as time went by and white infantry replacements came to be in short supply, the Army allowed black volunteers to join previously all-white units. Surveys before this desegregation showed most white soldiers opposed it, but afterward there was much less opposition (Stouffer et al., 1949). The greatest support came from those white soldiers who were most closely associated with the blacks. Unrealistic stereotypes decreased markedly because of the greater knowledge gained by familiarity. And no realistic conflicts arose between the groups because instead of competing, they were fighting a common enemy.

Some other early research focused on desegregation of housing and work situations. Deutsch and Collins (1951) compared two housing projects in which tenants were assigned to apartments without regard to race with two projects in which blacks and whites were kept in different buildings. White homemakers in the integrated projects were less prejudiced and more likely to have a black as a "best friend." Similarly, when blacks were hired to work in department stores in New York City, white clerks became progressively more accepting of them. White customers had similar positive reactions. Comparable results have been found among police officers and government workers.

More generally, whites who have black friends and acquaintances prove to be the least racially prejudiced. A national survey of friendship patterns found evidence of much racial separation: only 9 percent of white adults could name a "good friend" who was black, and only 21 percent, at least one black acquaintance (Jackman & Crane, 1986). But those whites who did have a black friend or acquaintance were the least prejudiced. They were the least likely to say that more whites were intelligent than blacks, and least likely to say they would prefer living in an all-white neighborhood, as shown

The armed services were among the first public institutions to be racially desegregated, but for the most part not until after World War II. The descendents of these troops in an all-black unit could march in racially integrated units in the 1980s.

in Figure 13–4. Interracial contact was particularly successful in reducing prejudice when whites interacted with blacks of higher socioeconomic status than themselves. Indeed, on several indices having lower-status black friends was actually worse than having no black contacts at all. This would suggest that contact is successful in reducing prejudice, at least under some conditions.

On the other hand, school desegregation does not invariably reduce prejudice. The "separate-but-equal" doctrine that permitted Southern states to maintain separate school systems for white and black children was overthrown by the Supreme Court in the *Brown* v. *Board of Education* decision in 1954. But in Northern metropolitan areas, housing segregation had resulted in extensive de facto school segregation. Court-ordered busing plans were adopted over the vehement opposition of many whites, but in many cases they did not have the effects hoped for (see Aronson & Gonzalez, 1988; Gerard, 1988). As a result, most experts have concluded that the specific *type* of interracial contact, rather than mere contact itself, is the crucial factor.

Contact Theory

The original *Brown* v. *Board of Education* Supreme Court decision was advised in part by a brief prepared by several distinguished social psychologists. They testified that segregation lowered black children's self-esteem and school achievement and contributed to perpetuating white children's racial prejudice. They predicted that desegregation would help solve these problems, if it was carried out in a way that ensured four key conditions: interracial contact, an absence of interracial competition for scarce resources, equal status for members of both races, and firm support from the relevant authorities (Cook, 1988). This reflected the consensus within social psychology at the time, best represented in Gordon Allport's (1954) **contact theory.** This held that intergroup contact decreases hostility between the groups only when it meets these four necessary conditions (also see Brewer & Miller, 1984; Cook, 1978).

Sustained close contact is important—it is not enough for people to coexist occasionally in the same geographical space; they must be brought together often in close interaction. Some forms of school or work desegregation do not promote very close contact, such as when white and black students are in different "tracks" in a high school and attend quite different classes, or when the executives of a firm are all white and the clerical workers are black, and they have little close interaction.

Sustained contact is required if prevailing stereotypes about outgroup characteristics are to be disconfirmed. We have earlier seen numerous examples of the difficulties people have in overcoming their own schemas, stereotypes, and expectations. As a result, a great deal of new evidence is often required to produce change, especially when these structures have been in place for many years, and are constantly reinforced by others. And very close contact with individual minority members may be required. We saw in Chapter 9 how important proximity and familiarity are in producing liking. Occasional, superficial contact is not likely

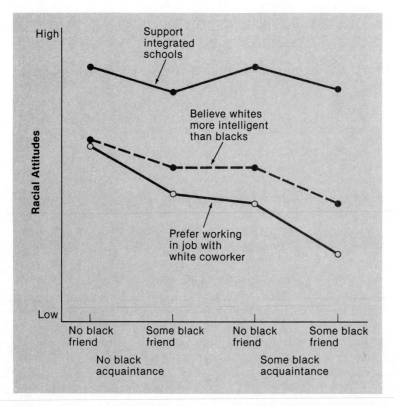

Figure 13–4. Whites' racial prejudice as a function of their friendship with blacks. (Adapted from Jackman & Crane, 1986, p. 469.)

BOX 13–5

Race versus Belief

We have seen how pressures toward cognitive consistency cause changes in attitude or behavior. **Cognitive consistency theories** argue that people mold their attitudes and behavior to their preexisting dispositions. In the context of prejudice, they would suggest that people form prejudiced attitudes or engage in discriminatory behavior to promote consistency with other prior attitudes.

One example of consistency processes is the idea that "similarity breeds liking," as indicated in Chapter 8. We like a new person or group on the basis of consistency of their attitudes or values with our own. One provocative implication is that whites' prejudices against blacks do not arise because of their race per se, but because they assume blacks do not share similar values and attitudes. If that were true, people who had similar values would be liked even if they were black. If so, it would suggest that getting to know someone of another race and discovering that his or her attitudes are similar to one's own would make one like

him or her regardless of the racial difference. The implication would be that a simple program of educating people about other races or of contact with them would reduce racial conflicts.

A series of studies (Byrne & Wong, 1962; Rokeach & Mezei, 1966; Stein et al., 1965) has compared the relative importance of racial and attitudinal similarity. The typical, although not unanimous, finding was that similarity of attitudes was more important in determining liking than belonging to the same racial group. These findings have been interpreted as showing that racial differences are relatively unimportant when compared to differences in attitude. However, these findings held only for relatively nonintimate relationships such as working together. Race was considerably more important than belief when closer relationships, such as dating or marriage, were concerned. So the need for consistency has some impact on the level of prejudice, but it does not always override the fact of real group differences.

to produce the close relationships that break down the distance between groups.

Cooperative interdependence is also necessary. Members of the two groups need to be working together for common goals and to depend upon each others' efforts, as in World War II, rather than competing with each other for scarce resources. The classic study demonstrating the destructive effects of competition on intergroup relations is Sherif and colleagues' (1961) "robbers' cave experiment." They initially encouraged competition between two groups of boys at a summer camp. But this created so much anger and hostility between the groups that it emerged even at such noncompetitive events as watching a movie. The researchers later successfully reduced this hostility by getting the boys to work cooperatively to solve a common problem.

Third, the contact must be of *equal status*—resentments build up if the traditional status im-

balance is maintained, and stereotypes cannot easily be broken down. Contact occurs, for example, when an Hispanic cleaning woman works for a wealthy white woman, but contact of this kind simply perpetuates traditional stereotypes.

Social norms favoring equality must be the consensus among the relevant authorities and the community at large. When intergroup contact is forced upon a situation in which everyone in the ingroup opposes the contact—as for instance in a school district in which a court orders busing and the white school board, superintendent, teachers, and parents all want continued racial segregation—it will be hard for the contact between children to have beneficial effects.

Much research has been done in recent years to test these hypotheses from contact theory. For example, Clore and coworkers (1978) ran an interracial summer camp in which campers, administrative staff, and counselors were all evenly divided between blacks and whites. The researchers tried to maximize (1) close contact, by mixing the living arrangements by race; (2) cooperative interdependence, by creating primitive conditions that demanded cooperation such as fire building, cooking, and planning activities; and (3) equal status, by selecting campers from similar backgrounds. The one-week experience was successful in increasing the percentage of interracial choices campers made for partners in playing games. Similar findings have emerged from Stuart Cook's (1984) program of research involving long-term interaction either in school or in work situations.

Social psychologists have been quite active in trying to introduce such procedures into desegregated schools, with the idea that desegregation can reduce prejudice only if these conditions prevail. Standard educational procedures have been compared with new procedures introducing interdependent "teams" that cooperate to complete classroom assignments.

For example, Eliot Aronson and his colleagues have used what they call a *jigsaw technique*. Children are placed in small learning groups, usually consisting of six participants. They meet in the group for about an hour a day to focus on one particular lesson. Each person is assigned one portion of the day's lesson and is responsible for teaching that material to the rest of the group. For example, in one exercise the students are given the biography of Joseph Pu-

litzer, the newspaper publisher. Paragraph 1 is about his ancestors, paragraph 2 about his preadult life, and so forth. Since no one can put together the whole biography without the information contributed by others, the students are interdependent. Furthermore, since each student is put into the role of being an expert, they all have equal status as well. They should learn to cooperate and learn from each other. Ultimately, each student's learning is evaluated separately, but unless all cooperate in contributing their unique pieces of knowledge, none can do very well.

Aronson and his coworkers report good success with this technique in increasing peer liking across ethnic and racial groups, and in increasing the self-esteem of minority children (Aronson et al., 1978; Aronson & Gonzalez, 1988). The most extensive review found that 63 percent of the cooperative classrooms showed improved academic performance, against 4 percent of the traditional competitive classrooms (Slavin, 1983).

Prospects for Tolerance

Using the principles of appropriate contact laid out above, what are the prospects for prejudice reduction in our society? First, what kinds of situations would be likely to reduce prejudice, and what kinds would not? Being teammates on a professional football team would.

What techniques might this school librarian use to get these children involved in cross-racial cooperative learning?

Being fellow conspirators in a prison break would. Having a black janitor in an office building or Hispanic maid in a middle-class household would not. Having students of different groups in a lecture class probably would not. Pitting a black basketball team against a white team would not. But having interracial teams solve homework problems in a statistics class would.

Are the most helpful kinds of intergroup situations common in our society? Unfortunately, through most of our history they have not been. Prior to the 1950s, American society was organized in a way that afforded almost no opportunities for equal status, cooperative, interdependent contact between blacks and whites. Almost all American institutions were segregated. There were white colleges and there were black colleges. Only whites were permitted to play professional sports in the major leagues. Black athletes had to play on all-black teams in black leagues. Military units were either all black or all white. Most blacks lived in the South, and of course in the South segregation was the law in public accommodations, schools, transportation, politics, and every other social institution. There were such gross differences between blacks and whites in income, education, and occupational status that the chance of widespread equal-status contact was minimal.

Today, contact of this type does occur in the armed forces, where blacks and whites work and fight together with more or less equal rank (at least among enlisted soldiers), and in factories and stores in which members of the two races hold comparable jobs. But in most areas of life, whites and blacks have relatively little contact with each other. For example, in a 1988 survey, only 31 percent of the white adults claimed both to live in a racially mixed neighborhood and to know the name of at least one black neighbor, and only 37 percent said they had entertained a black person in their home in the past year (*Life* Magazine, 1988). Even when interracial contact is intended, as in most urban school systems that have implemented desegregation plans, it often happens less than one might think. The phenomenon of "white flight," whereby white children leave the public schools as soon as they are desegregated, illustrates how hard it is to ensure any interracial contact at all. And even if substantial numbers of children from both races are in the school, there is no guarantee that they will have much meaningful contact. They show a strong tendency to associate more with their own race than any other (Schofield, 1978). And a single integrated experience, or contact with a "token" member of a minority group, is usually not enough to disconfirm stereotypes. One "exception to the rule" does not do the job (Weber & Crocker, 1983).

Cooperative interdependence is important and works—but only if it is successful. If people are cooperating and they fail, it is too easy to blame the minority member. If people work together in wars, or games, or classroom jobs and things go badly, they may resent each other and become even more hostile. For this reason, Cook (1984) reports that the competence of the group member, rather than the person's race, is the critical factor in determining respect and attraction from others. On the other hand, Cook also reports that group success boosts respect for less competent teammates.

Another complication is with equal status (Brewer & Miller, 1984). Integration frequently occurs by bringing minorities in at the bottom of the ladder, whether as students or apprentices, or in the least desirable jobs. Then they have to interact with whites who outrank them. The school or work situation may seem to provide equal status, such as giving two employees the same job title or a teacher treating two children equally. But preexisting differences in group status may carry over into the situation. The new immigrant child who can barely speak English and who has only one dress to wear to school will not be of equal status to a wealthy doctor's daughter whatever the teacher's efforts.

Finally the norms of the surrounding community are also very important. Even if the interracial experience is successful within one limited site, people will go back into their normal lives. If they are then surrounded by prejudiced people, they may quickly revert. This is one of the difficulties in trying to prevent prejudice in the children of prejudiced parents. The children may begin to develop more tolerant attitudes, but if their parents do not support that tolerance at home, it will weaken the effects of the school experience.

As a result, many efforts at school desegregation do not meet these four conditions. Voluntary social contacts, "white flight," and "tracking" within the school limit interracial contact; the traditional competitive classroom has remained the norm; whites have held on to the highest-status positions, whether among administrators, teachers, or students; and many authorities and the white public have opposed busing plans (Gerard, 1988). A relatively few desegregation plans, as implemented, resemble the favorable conditions specified by the social psychologists' contact theory, and they tend to yield positive effects (Cook, 1988; Taylor & Katz, 1988). But they are the exceptions.

These practical difficulties do not mean that the effort to reduce prejudice should be abandoned, because there are important moral and legal reasons for it. And indeed it may be more important than ever, as our nation once again becomes more ethnically diverse and as groups such as gays and the disabled increasingly demand equality. But we must remember that no one approach is going to solve the problem. Intergroup antagonism seems to be a fundamental aspect of the human condition. Every society in the world takes group membership into consideration when determining how it will treat any individual. In a sense, the United States has embarked on a particularly ambitious program of group equality, set up by the idealistic guidelines of the Bill of Rights and the later constitutional amendments (especially the Fourteenth). At the same time, it has tried to accommodate a bewildering variety of groups from all parts of the world, including Africans, Vietnamese, Hungarians, Latinos, Russian Jews, and British Puritans. It is not surprising, therefore, that it should have failed to some degree. We cannot be complacent, because all too much suffering in our society is caused by prejudice. But it is also well to remember the very considerable harmony and group tolerance that has allowed such a Noah's ark of humanity to coexist and cooperate for so many years.

Key Terms

assumed similarity effect	minimal intergroup situation	realistic group conflict
aversive racism		relative deprivation
categorization	old-fashioned racism	schema
contact theory	outgroup	self-fulfilling prophecy
discrimination	outgroup homogeneity effect	social identity theory
ethnocentrism		social norms
ingroup	prejudice	stereotype
ingroup favoritism effect	psychodynamic theories	symbolic racism

Summary

1. Prejudice, stereotypes, and discrimination correspond to the affective, cognitive, and behavioral components of intergroup antagonism.

2. Stereotypes and prejudice strongly influence the individual's attitudes and behavior in a variety of areas.

3. Social learning is probably the strongest determinant of stereotypes and prejudices against minority groups. Prejudices frequently develop in childhood and adolescence and are difficult to change thereafter.

4. Group conflict theories view prejudice as stemming from the realities of intergroup competition; and psychodynamic theories, from the individual's particular personality dynamics.

5. Cognitive approaches view stereotyping and prejudices as arising from such normal cognitive processes as categorization, especially into ingroup and outgroup, and schematic processing, as well as getting self-esteem from one's own social identity.

6. The various theories tend to focus on somewhat different phenomena rather than providing competing explanations for the same events.

7. Although some forms of racial prejudice have diminished in recent years, others have emerged to take their place.

8. Interracial contact is probably the most effective technique for reducing prejudice. But by itself, it is not extremely effective; it is more likely to be successful if it involves sustained close contact, cooperative interdependence, and equal status, and is supported by local norms.

9. Our society is not organized very well to provide the kinds of interracial contact that best break down racial prejudices. For that reason, special efforts need to be made if prejudice is to be reduced substantially.

Suggested Readings

Dovidio, J. F., & Gaertner, S. L. (Eds.). (1986). *Prejudice, discrimination, and racism.* New York: Academic Press. An excellent collection of essays on race relations, summarizing the most interesting recent research.

Katz, P., & Taylor, D. (Eds.). (1988). *Towards the elimination of racism: Profiles in controversy.* New York: Plenum. A stimulating collection of essays on the major controversies in race relations research, presenting one pro and one con on each controversy.

Miller, N., & Brewer, M. B. (Eds.). (1984). *Groups in contact: The psychology of desegregation.* New York: Academic Press. A comprehensive collection of research articles on the contact hypothesis.

Schuman, H., Steeh, C., & Bobo, L. (1985). *Racial attitudes in America: Trends and interpretations.* Cambridge, MA: Har-vard University Press. The best account of postwar changes in Americans' racial attitudes.

Stephan, W. G. (1985). Intergroup relations. In G. Lindzey and E. Aronson (Eds.), *Handbook of social psychology,* 3rd ed., Vol. 2, pp. 599–658. New York: Random House. A thorough review of research, from the cognitive perspective.

Tajfel, H. (1982). *Social identity and intergroup relations.* Cambridge: Cambridge University Press. An authoritative account of social identity theory.

Worchel, S. & Austin, W. G. (Eds.). (1986). *Psychology of intergroup relations,* 2nd ed. Chicago: Nelson-Hall. A collection of essays on the major topics of research in the social psychology of intergroup relations.

FOURTEEN

Gender

*O*n a radio talk show, the host is discussing teenage sexuality with a medical expert. The first caller, Chris, asks a question about the birth control pill. The researcher begins his answer by asking Chris if she herself is considering using the pill. After a pause, Chris blurts out, "I'm a boy." Everyone seems embarrassed, the researcher apologizes, and the host rephrases the question. I, like other listeners, think about Chris's high-pitched voice and gentle manner. Would I have made the same mistake?

A noted psychologist begins a study of the behavior of young children. Concerned that knowledge of a child's gender might influence the way observers interpret the child's activities, the researcher asked parents to bring their children to the study dressed in overalls and T shirts. To the researcher's surprise, her effort to conceal the toddlers' gender backfires. Although all children arrive in denims, many of the little girls wear overalls with ruffles or bows.

You glance casually at the driver of the sports car stopped at a traffic light. Noticing a gray sweatshirt and prominent chin, you assume the person is a man. But something about the face makes you look again. You quickly study the person's physique. The smooth cheeks give no hint of stubble. The shoulders are a bit broad for a woman, but perhaps she's a swimmer. The arm resting on the car door conceals the person's chest, but reveals slender, delicate fingers. Neither rings nor earrings are visible. Then the light changes and the car moves off, leaving you wondering about the driver's sex.

As these examples indicate, gender is one of the basic categories in social life. In meeting new people, we inevitably try to identify them as male or female. There are many reasons for this tendency. One is that the English language has gender-linked pronouns such as "he" and "she," "his" and "hers." (For a discussion of gender and language, see Box 14–1).

The process of categorizing things and people as masculine or feminine is known technically as **gender typing.** This process usually occurs automatically, without our giving it much thought. Most of the time, cues about gender

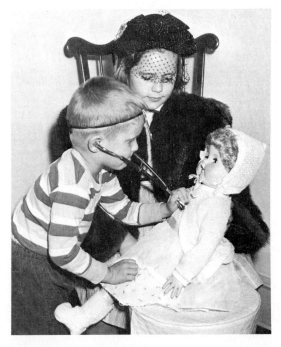

These children practice traditional male-female roles—she as the well-dressed and caring mommy, and he as the expert physician. Childrens' toys and games teach lessons about what males and females can and should do.

are readily available from physical characteristics such as facial hair or breasts and from style of dress. People usually display their gender as a prominent part of their self-presentation.

Parents typically dress their children in ways that readily communicate the child's sex. A study of infants observed in surburban shopping malls found that 90 percent of infants were dressed in clothes that were sex-typed in color or style. For instance, whereas 75 percent of the girls wore or carried something pink, none of the boys did. In contrast, 79 percent of the boys wore or carried something blue, while only 8 percent of girls did (Shakin, Shakin, & Sternglanz, 1985). Situations where we cannot identify a person's gender are unusual. They call attention to the categorization process and typically lead us to seek information to resolve the matter.

The tendency to divide the world into masculine and feminine categories is not limited to person perception; many objects and activities are also defined as masculine and feminine. At

BOX 14–1

Gender Bias in Language

In English, the words "he" and "man" have had to serve two functions. They refer both to specific males and to human beings in general (Martyna, 1980). Many of us learned in high school that it is grammatically correct to say "each person took *his* turn," even when most of the people involved are female. Similarly, we were taught that "mankind" includes both sexes, just as a "chairman" can be a woman. When "he" and "man" are used to refer to both sexes, they are said to be *generic* terms. Grammarians have justified the use of the generic masculine as a convenient shorthand. Recently, however, feminists have criticized this linguistic practice, arguing that it subtly reaffirms male dominance and contributes to the "invisibility" of women in society.

Psychological research shows that the so-called generic masculine is *not* necessarily perceived as including both sexes (Hamilton, 1988). For example, Martyna (1980) asked a large sample of students from kindergarten through college to complete sentence fragments such as "When a police officer leaves the station," "When a secretary first arrives at the office," or "When a teenager finishes high school." Martyna found that when the sentences contained a traditionally masculine role such as "police officer," 96 percent of subjects used "he" in completing the sentence. When the sentences contained a traditionally feminine role such as "secretary," none of the students used "he" and 87 percent used "she." In gender-neutral sentences such as that about a teenager, 65 percent of subjects used "he," 5 percent used "she," and 30 percent used alternatives such as "they." Clearly, students did not always use "he" to refer to both sexes.

Given that people do not always use the generic masculine, do they nonetheless understand it when they encounter it? MacKay and Fulkerson (1979) designed a study to find out. College stu-dents listened to a series of sentences read aloud on a tape recording. Examples included "A lawyer must frequently argue his case out of court," and "A nurse must frequently help his patients get out of bed." These sentences used the word "he" generically and so could logically refer to both sexes. Some students were asked whether each sentence could refer to a man, and 99 percent responded correctly that each sentence could. In contrast, other students were asked if each sentence could refer to a woman. This time, 87 percent of responses were wrong: students said that the sentences could not refer to a woman, when logically they could. This and other studies indicate that the use of pronouns such as "he" can bias interpretations.

We do not always use the generic masculine the way grammarians say we should. When we hear a discussion of the "best man for the job," we often conjure up a mental image of a male. When we read about the "chairman of an important committee," we assume the person is a man. If we were asked to think carefully about these terms, we would most likely acknowledge that "he" can refer to a female, but this is not our first reaction. The use of the so-called generic masculine simplifies communication at the expense of accuracy.

One consequence of these findings is that many organizations, including the American Psychological Association and most textbook publishers, have developed new guidelines for writing that explicitly discourage the use of the generic masculine. Instead, authors are urged to substitute terms that will be understood accurately, such as "chairperson" (for chairman), "human nature" (for "the nature of man"), and "firefighter" (for "fireman"). Alternatives to the use of the generic "he" include using the plural, alternating the use of "he" and "she" throughout the text, or using a phrase such as "he or she."

---

an early age, children learn that dolls and cooking utensils are for girls and that toy trucks and guns are for boys (Robinson & Morris, 1986). Most 4-year-olds believe that doctor, police officer, and construction worker are male jobs and that secretary, teacher, and librarian are female jobs (Gettys & Cann, 1981).

The process of gender typing continues in adulthood. College students identify icepicks, barbells, wrenches, and chest strengtheners as masculine objects, and eggbeaters, thimbles, rolling pins, and laundry baskets as feminine. Some objects, such as headphones, electric outlets, and corkscrews, are seen as gender neutral (Reis & Jackson, 1981). Married couples often distinguish between "men's work," such as mowing the lawn, taking out the garbage, or barbecuing, and "women's work," such as housecleaning or child care. Although a few occupations such as psychologist and personnel officer are seen by adults as gender neutral, most jobs are perceived as gender typed (Shinar, 1975). You should have no trouble guessing how most people categorize the following jobs: receptionist, brain surgeon, day care provider, truck driver, nurse, and judge.

The distinction between male and female is a universal organizing principle in all human societies. As children, boys and girls are expected to learn different skills and to develop different personalities. As adults, men and women typically assume distinctive gender-linked roles as husband or wife, mother or father. Cultures vary in exactly what is defined as masculine or feminine and in the degree to which they accentuate gender differences or similarities. But the use of gender to structure at least some elements of social life has been basic.

GENDER IN THE EYE OF THE BEHOLDER

We begin with a seemingly simple question: How does the gender of other people influence our perception and evaluation of them and their behavior? The emphasis here is on gender as a characteristic of the *target* of impression formation. Research shows that our beliefs about what typical men and women are like can color our perception of individuals and bias our evaluations of their performance.

Gender Stereotypes

How do you think men and women differ? Do you believe that one sex is usually more aggressive or more nurturant than the other? How do the sexes typically compare on such qualities as being courageous, neat, logical, gentle, squeamish, dominant, or gullible? Beliefs about the personal attributes of women and men are **gender stereotypes.** As we saw in Chapter 2, all stereotypes, whether based on gender, race, ethnicity, or other groupings, refer to an image of what the typical member of a particular social category is like. A useful distinction can be made between cultural and personal stereotypes (Ashmore, Del Boca, & Wohlers, 1986).

Cultural stereotypes. We are all exposed to images of the sexes presented by our culture. Movies, pop music, television, and other mass media convey messages about the nature of masculinity and femininity. So do religious teachings, school books, art, and literature. The societal-level images of the sexes conveyed in these places are **cultural stereotypes.** You probably know these stereotypes quite well, although you may not have thought about them very much.

On TV, for example, we can see anxious housewives desperately trying to avoid telltale spots on the family's clothes or pondering the best food for a finicky cat. Young women appear obsessed with staying thin or competing for a man's attention by wearing the right pantyhose or jeans. Off camera, the voices of male experts solemnly offer advice. On screen, men in impressive offices extol the virtues of razor blades or copying machines. Systematic research has found that the most common TV commercial depicts a male expert instructing a female consumer about a particular product. In a study conducted in the 1970s, 70 percent of men were shown as experts, whereas 86 percent of women were product users (McArthur & Resko, 1975). Female experts and male consumers were the exception. In recent years, sex differences in commercials may be lessening (Bretl & Cantor, 1988). A study conducted in 1985 found that increasing numbers of men were shown as parents and as consumers of products. But when commercials had an expert narrator or "voice of authority," this was almost always a man (91 percent of the cases).

A trip to an art museum would also find men and women portrayed in traditional gender-

These women represent quite different images of femininity—beauty queens, a "tomboy" baseball player, and a kindly grandmother. We combine information about gender and other characteristics to form stereotypes about distinct types of males and females. What might you infer about the personality and life aspirations of each of these women?

typed activities. A study of highly acclaimed paintings and sculptures found that men were often shown in professional work or warfare, whereas women were shown doing housework or childcare (O'Kelly, 1980). Significantly more women than men were portrayed as passively "doing nothing": nearly a quarter of women but only 2 percent of men were depicted as "objects" who were not engaged in any identifiable activity.

These studies and other analyses of newspaper articles, award-winning children's books, college textbooks, and other diverse elements of culture have found several general themes in the portrayal of the sexes:

☐ Whereas men are shown in a wide variety of social roles and activities, women are more often restricted to domestic and family roles.

☐ Men are commonly portrayed as experts and leaders, women as subordinates.

☐ Men are usually depicted as more active, assertive, and influential than women.

☐ Although females are slightly more than half the population, they are often underrepresented in the media.

In recent years there have been efforts to change these media images so they portray men and women in less rigidly gender-typed ways. We are slowly beginning to see a few women in the business world and a few men in the kitchen.

Do these cultural portraits of the sexes actually have an effect on people's daily lives? As we have seen elsewhere in this book, it is surprisingly difficult to show that the mass media influence peoples' behavior (Durkin, 1987). Although a few correlational studies have suggested that people with more traditional attitudes about sex roles may watch more television, the direction of causality is not clear. Does TV encourage traditional attitudes in viewers? Or do sex-role traditionalists watch more television because they find media portrayals of women and men consistent with their preexisting personal beliefs?

Experimental studies provide more clear-cut evidence about the potential impact of the media. For example, in Chapter 9, we saw that watching beautiful actresses on TV affected the way college men evaluated a woman's attractiveness. An experimental study of women college students also demonstrated the potential influence of TV (Jennings, Geis, & Brown, 1980). Participants were randomly assigned to one of two conditions. Half the participants saw four commercials depicting the sexes in traditional roles. Men were portrayed as the authorities and were the center of attention; women were shown as sex objects or in domestic roles. The experimental commercials were closely modeled after real ones. In one, for example, a tiny woman serves her large, hungry husband a packaged dinner. The implicit message was that the wife's role is to cater to and please her husband. In another, an attractive man authoritatively extols the virtues of an alcoholic beverage. At the end of the commercial, a seductive woman slithers up and coyly says that she would also choose the same drink. Here the woman is presented as a sex object who follows the man's advice.

In the second experimental condition, participants saw reversed-role versions of the same commercials in which the females were the central figures and the males were shown in the homemaking and seductive roles.

Results indicated that exposure to TV commercials had a significant effect on subsequent behavior. After watching the films, participants engaged in one of two tasks. Some performed a test designed to measure their conformity, while others were rated on self-confidence as they gave a short, extemporaneous speech. Women who had watched traditional commercials conformed more and showed less self-confidence than women who had watched the nontraditional commercials. The researchers concluded that regardless of whether people buy the product advertised in commercials, they may buy the implicit images of femininity and masculinity conveyed. How well the results of laboratory experiments such as this generalize to everyday life has not yet been demonstrated.

Personal stereotypes. As individuals, we may or may not agree with cultural depictions of the sexes. **Personal stereotypes** are our own unique beliefs about the attributes of groups of people such as women and men. Individuals construct personal stereotypes in at least two different ways.

One way individuals think about gender is in terms of general personality traits that characterize each sex. Most of us have beliefs about the global features that distinguish males and females. To get some idea of your own views on this matter, read the list of adjectives in Table 14–1. Decide whether you personally think each trait is more characteristic of men or of women, or equally true of both sexes. You probably found this a fairly easy task. People usually develop broad generalizations about the traits shared by men and women and about the traits that distinguish the sexes.

Research finds that men are commonly rated higher than women on traits associated with competence, such as leadership, objectivity, and independence (Rosenkrantz et al., 1968). In contrast, women are usually rated higher on traits associated with warmth and expressiveness, such as gentleness and awareness of the feelings of others. How do your own personal gender stereotypes compare with these findings?

Some psychologists believe that instead of calling these sets of traits "masculine" and "feminine," we should use terms that are not inherently linked to gender. Thus, traditionally masculine traits are often described as instrumental or "agentic," meaning that they focus on accomplishing tasks and acting independently. Traditionally feminine traits are described as expressive or "communal," because they emphasize the expression of feelings and a sense of caring for others.

A second way in which people think about gender is to develop images of different types of males and females (Ashmore et al., 1986; Brewer & Lui, 1989). Instead of thinking about females "in general," we may think of more specific categories of women, such as mothers, career women, beauty queens, tomboys, or spinsters. Similarly, instead of having a single, uniform image of males, our beliefs about men may distinguish such types as fathers, businessmen, hardhats, sissies, jocks, chauvinists, or nerds (Holland & Skinner, 1987). In other words, we may form **schemas** about specific types of males and females who embody distinctive clusters of traits. Thus one person might believe that mothers are nurturant and self-sacrificing, that beauty queens are gorgeous but emptyheaded, or that tomboys are youthful, athletic, and adventurous. An important point is that these stereotypes often incorporate some attributes typically associated with the other sex: a career woman may be seen as assertive

T A B L E 1 4 – 1	
COMMON GENDER STEREOTYPES	
Typical Man	Typical Woman
Aggressive	Gentle
Unemotional	Cries easily
Likes math and science	Enjoys art and literature
Worldly	Does not use harsh language
Ambitious	Tactful
Objective	Religious
Dominant	Interested in own appearance
Competitive	Aware of feelings of others
Self-confident	Strong need for security
Logical	Talkative
Acts as leader	Neat in habits
Independent	Dependent

and independent (masculine traits) as well as attractive and tactful (feminine traits).

Activating Stereotypes

What determines whether we relate to a person largely on the basis of stereotypes or as a unique individual? In other words, what situations increase or decrease the influence of stereotypes? Social psychologists are just beginning to answer this question. Two important factors are the amount of information we have about the person and the salience of the person's group membership.

Amount of information. The less information available about a person, the more likely we are to perceive and react to him or her on the basis of stereotypes. For example, when adults know nothing about a baby except its gender, they sometimes react to the child in stereotyped ways (Stern & Karraker, 1989). In one study, adults watched a videotape of a baby (Condry & Condry, 1976). Although everyone watched the same videotape, half were told they were watching a boy and half were told they were watching a girl. People who thought the child was a boy rated the child as significantly more active and forceful than people who thought the child was a girl. The child's ambiguous response to a jack-in-the-box toy was rated as showing more "fear" if the child was a girl and more "anger" if the child was a boy.

When we have more information about the unique attributes of a particular person, we rely less on stereotypes (Locksley et al., 1980). For instance, we may believe that most males are highly assertive, and so assume when we meet a new man that he too will be assertive. But we may also have learned from past experience that our friend Leon is shy and unassuming. The effect of gender stereotypes can be eliminated when we have relevant information about a specific person.

Salience of group membership. A second factor that can activate the use of stereotypes is the salience of the person's group membership, in

If you saw this woman in a supermarket, you might assume her to be a suburban homemaker or school teacher. In reality, Sandra Day O'Connor is the first woman to serve on the U.S. Supreme Court. The less information we have about a person, the more we fall back on gender stereotypes.

this case gender. By salient we mean that the person's gender stands out and is a prominent characteristic. For example, a woman's gender is more salient if we can see her than if we talk to her by phone or read an article she has written. Another factor affecting gender salience is the proportion of women to men in a group. A person's gender is more salient when he or she is in a numerical minority, such as being the only woman in an all-male work group. "Token integration" often creates groups with just one minority person. Token or "solo" status calls attention to the person's distinctive social category and makes solos especially vulnerable to stereotyping.

A study by Shelley Taylor (1981) illustrates this point. Students evaluated the members of a six-person tape-recorded discussion group. Some groups had a "solo" man or just a "solo" woman; others were evenly divided between men and women. After listening to the tape recording, subjects rated the group members. In actuality, the solo's contribution to the discussion was *identical* to that of one of the members of the gender-balanced group. But Taylor found that the solos were perceived as talking more and making a stronger impression than members of the more gender-balanced groups. In addition, solos tended to be perceived as playing gender-stereotyped roles. Solo women were seen as "motherly, nurturant types, bitches, or as the group secretary." Solo men were perceived as "father figures, leaders, or macho types." Group composition accentuated the solo's gender and fostered stereotyped perceptions of the solo's behavior.

The Dangers of Stereotypes

As Chapter 3 on social cognition indicated, it is quite natural for us to try to simplify complex life experiences by categorizing and generalizing. Personal stereotypes, like other social schemas, are one way in which we try to make sense of life. But like other mental crutches, stereotypes have certain inherent problems. One is that stereotypes always oversimplify and sometimes are dead wrong, as we'll see later in the chapter. For example, the belief that men are more intelligent than women has been disproved by scientific research. Unfortunately, people seldom examine the accuracy of their stereotypes. If we encounter someone who does not fit a stereotype, we often simply decide the person is "the exception that proves the rule." We do nothing to change our stereotype. Further, as Box 14–2 indicates, we sometimes act in ways that turn stereotypes into self-fulfilling prophecies.

A second problem is that stereotypes exaggerate differences *between* groups and minimize differences *within* groups (Martin, 1987). Gender stereotypes can make it seem that all men are alike, when in fact there are enormous individual differences among men. The same is true

about differences among women. Gender stereotypes can also make it seem that men and women are utterly different, when in fact similarities are usually much greater than differences. For example, there is great variation among men in aggressiveness: individuals range from nonassertive males who wouldn't hurt a fly to mass murderers. In contrast, the average difference between males and females in aggressiveness, while real, is much smaller in magnitude. Gender stereotypes can create a very distorted view of human nature.

A final danger of stereotypes is that they are often used to justify prejudice and discrimination against members of certain groups. Historically, the false belief that women were not as smart as men and that women lacked ambition was used to deny women an education and to keep them at home. Stereotypes that have a basis in fact can also be misused in a discriminating way. For instance, there appear to be sex differences in visual spatial ability—the ability to manipulate objects visually in space. A person who has good visual spatial ability will be able to judge easily whether your newly purchased king size bed will fit through the front door, make the narrow turn in the hall, and fit in the upstairs bedroom. Yet if we were recruiting applicants for a job that requires visual-spatial ability, it would be foolish to exclude all female candidates, since some women will be more talented than some men. Recruitment and hiring practices that categorically reject one sex are not only discriminatory but foolish. A sounder policy is to use a task-relevant selection procedure, such as giving all applicants a skill test and then selecting the high performers regardless of sex.

Evaluating Performance

Do we typically give women and men equal credit for equal work? Or do gender stereotypes distort judgments of performance? In the world of work, stereotypes often depict men as more competent than women. In one national survey, for example, male managers generally perceived women workers as lower than men in

BOX 14–2

Making Stereotypes Come True

A young man goes on a blind date with a woman he has never met before. Based on hearsay, he believes her to be a rather traditional "Southern belle" type. Accordingly, he dresses rather formally, puts on his most gentlemanly manners, and treats her in a somewhat old-fashioned way. Just as he expected, she defers to his suggestion, waits for him to open doors, and acts in what he considers a very "ladylike" way. Only later does he learn that his advance information was wrong; she is, in fact, usually a fairly assertive nonconformist. This story shows how expectations can become self-fulfilling prophecies. The man's beliefs about his date shaped his own behavior toward her. The woman, wanting to spend a pleasant evening, responded by acting in a conventionally "ladylike" way herself. The result was that the man's expectations set in motion an interpersonal process that appeared to confirm his prior beliefs.

Gender stereotypes often become self-fulfilling prophecies. This point was cleverly demonstrated in a study by Berna J. Skrypnek and Mark Snyder (1982). A male college student is led to believe that his partner for an experiment is either a stereotypic man (independent, assertive, ambitious, and masculine) or a stereotypic woman (shy, gullible, soft-spoken, and feminine). In reality, the partner is always a woman, a naive subject who has been randomly assigned the label of "man" or "woman." Since the two partners communicate from separate rooms by a system of lights, the partner's real gender is never revealed. The woman is told nothing about her partner, how she has been described to him, or the goals of the study. In this way the researchers systematically manipulate the gender expectations of the male subject.

In the first phase of the study, the partners must negotiate how to divide work on 12 hypothetical tasks. Some tasks are traditionally masculine (fixing a light switch or baiting a fish hook), some are feminine (icing a birthday cake or ironing a shirt), and some are neutral (coding test results, washing windows). The rules set by the experimenter give the man greater initiative in the bargaining process. As predicted, the man's expectations about his partner shape his own actions significantly. If he thinks his partner is a conventional woman, the male subject is more likely to select masculine tasks for himself and to refuse to switch tasks than if he thinks his partner is a man. As a result, the female subject winds up being assigned more of the feminine tasks if she is arbitrarily labeled a "female" than if she is believed to be a "male."

In the second phase, the researchers investigate whether this initial behavior pattern would continue over time. Accordingly, they change the rules of the interaction so that the woman now has greater control over the bargaining. Nonetheless, a woman who is labeled as "female" continues to select more feminine tasks than does a woman labeled as a "male." The woman actually comes to initiate behavior consistent with the gender to which she has been randomly assigned.

This study provides a powerful demonstration that in dyadic interaction, one person's beliefs and stereotypes about another can channel their interaction so that the other person engages in stereotype-confirming behavior. Our actions are shaped not only by our own interests and preferences, but also by the expectations of those with whom we interact. When others expect us to act in gender-typed ways and communicate these expectations through their behaviors, we may put aside personal preferences and instead act out the other's stereotypes.

skill, motivation, and work habits (Rosen & Jerdee, 1978). Women were believed to be less employable and promotable, and to have less ability to make decisions and to cope with stress.

Research shows that general stereotypes such as these can bias evaluations of the performance of individuals (Nieva & Gutek, 1981). This evaluation bias can cut both ways, however; sometimes it favors men, and occasionally it favors women.

One of the first demonstrations of gender bias in evaluation was provided by Philip Goldberg in 1968. He investigated whether women were biased in evaluations of other women. Goldberg selected six professional articles from such fields as law, elementary education, and art history. The articles were edited to about 1,500 words each and combined into test booklets. The experimental manipulation concerned the gender of the authors. The same article bore a male name (such as John T. McKay) in one booklet and a female name (such as Joan T. McKay) in another. Each booklet contained three articles by "men" and three by "women." College women read the six articles and then rated each on persuasiveness, style, and competence.

Results indicated that the same article was judged more favorably when it had a male author than when it had a female author. Goldberg's results appeared to show that women are indeed prejudiced against women. But before leaping to a hasty conclusion, it is important to know that Goldberg's findings sparked a rash of research. The results of over a hundred studies suggest that evaluation bias is considerably more complex than might first be imagined. The challenge today is to understand when and how gender bias occurs. Many factors seem to be important. For instance, a recent study suggests that gender bias is increased when evaluations are made under time pressure (Jamieson & Zanna, 1989). Let's review some of the most important factors influencing gender bias in evaluation.

First, the gender typing of the task or job makes a difference. In general, men have an advantage in masculine jobs and women have an advantage in feminine jobs (Glick et al., 1988). In one study, professional personnel consultants rated applicants' résumés for traditionally masculine jobs such as automobile salesperson, feminine jobs such as office receptionist, and gender neutral jobs such as motel desk clerk (Cash, Gillen, & Burns, 1977). For masculine jobs, men were perceived as better qualified, were expected to be more successful, and

Women are still a small minority of air force pilots. How might their gender affect evaluations of the job performance of these women?

were given stronger recommendations. For feminine jobs, women were rated more favorably. For gender-neutral jobs, men and women were given similar ratings.

Another study investigated how employers react to male versus female job applicants (Levinson, 1975). College students working on the research team responded by phone to actual job ads that had appeared in the local newspaper (Levinson, 1975). Some of the jobs were traditionally masculine (bus driver, management trainee, security guard) and some were feminine (receptionist, housekeeper, dental assistant). None required advanced training. A male and female applicant with equivalent qualifications called about each job. How would the employers respond to the male and female applicants?

Gender bias was said to occur when the "sex-appropriate" caller was encouraged to apply, but the "sex-inappropriate" caller was not. In one case, for example, a female caller for a restaurant management training program was told that she was disqualified because she had only two years of college and no prior management experience. But a male with the identical background was scheduled for an interview. In all, 28 percent of the women asking about masculine jobs were discouraged, as were 44 percent of the men asking about feminine jobs. This suggests considerable gender bias linked to the gender typing of occupations. In this case, the bias was actually stronger against men than against women.

A second factor influencing evaluation bias is the amount of relevant information available about the person. Gender bias in evaluations is least likely when much information is provided about the individual's ability. One study gave extensive information about a male or female manager, including copies of letters, memos, and other materials allegedly written by the person (Frank & Drucker, 1977). Subjects used this material as a basis for evaluating the manager's sensitivity, organizing and decision making ability, and communication effectiveness. The experimental manipulation was whether the materials were written by "John Griffin" or "Joan Griffin." Given all this information about the specific individuals, John and Joan were rated identically. No evaluation bias occurred.

Third, there is some evidence that stereotype-breaking behavior can occasionally win a person "extra" credit. In particular, when a woman excels in a traditionally masculine job, she may be perceived more favorably than an equally successful man. One study found that a highly successful female attorney was rated more vocationally competent than was an identically successful male attorney (Abramson et al., 1977). Similarly, another study presented students with descriptions of a person whose quick thinking in an armed robbery helped the police capture a criminal (Taynor & Deaux, 1973). When the person was a woman, she received more positive evaluations than a man in the identical situation. The unusualness of a woman's successful performance in masculine situations appears to win her a more favorable evaluation than her male counterpart. Whether something comparable occurs for men who excel in traditionally feminine activities is an interesting but unanswered question.

Finally, it is also important to add that the size of the sex bias in evaluations is often very small. In laboratory studies, it is rare for Joan McKay to be seen as a complete incompetent and John McKay to be rated as a stellar performer. When gender effects are found, they usually reflect small mean differences in ratings—perhaps a difference of one point on a ten-point rating scale. In a recent review of 106 studies, Janet Swim and her associates (1989) found that the size of the bias varied from study to study. Gender typically accounted for less than 1 percent of all the variation in ratings. The authors speculate that sex bias may be greater in the real world than in laboratory experiments where subjects are often on their "best" behavior.

We can conclude that sex bias in evaluation is real but elusive. Gender is only one of many factors that affect how we assess other people.

So far, we have considered evaluations of the quality of women's and men's performance. Another way in which gender bias can occur is in the **attributions** people make to explain success or failure. Research has found that men's success is more often seen as resulting from ability. In contrast, women's success is more often attributed to the ease of the task (Feather & Simon, 1975), to extreme effort (Taynor & Deaux, 1975), or to luck (Deaux & Emswiller, 1974). Ability attributions usually produce more favorable evaluations of successful performance. Differences in attributions for men's and women's performance may create a subtle bias that diminishes recognition of women's skills and instead explains female success as due to situational or chance factors.

Consider two school children who both do well in math. When Tina shows her mom the "A" grade in math on her report card, her mother proudly credits Tina with "really working hard" in that course. In contrast, when Tim shows his "A" to his mom, she proudly credits

Tom with being "a little math genius." The girl's success is attributed to high effort and the boy's to high ability.

A recent study of junior high school students and their parents indicates that gender-based attributional differences such as these may be common (Yee & Eccles, 1988). The researchers investigated how parents perceived their child's math performance. In general, parents were fairly accurate in their assessment of the level of their children's math achievement. But parents gave significantly different explanations for the performance of sons versus daughters. For example, mothers credited a son's success more to talent than a daughter's; mothers attributed a daughter's success more to effort than a son's. The researchers suggest that well-meaning parents may unintentionally discourage their talented daughters from pursuing the study of math by subtly communicating that the girl is hardworking rather than gifted.

In summary, a person's gender can influence the way we evaluate that person and explain his or her performance. Evaluation bias sometimes favors men, especially in masculine situations. However, women may have an advantage in feminine situations and when they excel in masculine activities. When substantial information is available about a person, gender bias in evaluation often disappears. Finally, it appears that female and male evaluators are equally prone to engage in evaluative bias based on the performer's gender. Having seen how the perceptions of other people are affected by whether they are female or male, we turn now to the question of how gender influences our self-perception.

GENDER AND THE SELF

Gender is a basic element in self-concept. Knowing that "I am a woman" or "I am a man" is as core part of our personal identity. Further, many people perceive themselves as having gender-typed interests and personalities.

Gender Identify

Knowledge that we are a male or female, our sense of **gender identity,** is acquired early in life. By age 2 or 3, children are aware of their own gender and can tell us whether they are a girl or a boy. By age 4 or 5, children can correctly label other people by gender. However, this understanding of gender differs from that of adults. Research by Lawrence Kohlberg (1966) and other developmental psychologists has documented the surprising fact that young children think they can change gender if they want to.

In one study, Kohlberg showed children a picture of a girl and asked whether she could be a boy if she wanted to or if she played boys' games or if she wore a boy's haircut and clothes. Most of the 4-year-olds said that she *could*. By age 6 or 7, however, children insisted that such a gender transformation would be impossible. Kohlberg believes this shift in children's conception of gender is part of a more general pattern of cognitive development. The same 4-year-old who says she could change gender might also say the family cat could become a dog by cutting off its whiskers. Adults know that if you pour a pint of water from a tall skinny glass into a short fat one, the volume of water stays the same. But the 4-year-old would probably disagree, perhaps arguing that the short glass had less.

Young children do not see the physical world as constant. As children get older, a combination of experience and maturation enables them to reach a more advanced stage of mental development in which they understand that gender, water volume, and other physical properties remain the same despite changes in external appearance. An important developmental milestone occurs when children understand that gender is fixed and unchanging: once a boy, always a boy, and once a girl, always a girl.

Knowing that we are male or female does not mean we think about our gender identity all the time. In one study, for example, only about 20 percent of sixth-graders spontaneously mentioned their gender when asked to "tell us about yourself" and to "describe what you look like"

As a young man, James Morris led an adventurous life that included serving as a war correspondent and climbing Mt. Everest. Through it all, he secretly believed that he was a woman trapped in a male body. After sex-change surgery, Jan Morris lives more happily as a woman. Jan's fascinating biography, *Conundrum,* details her puzzling life experiences.

(McGuire & Padawer-Singer, 1976). For many children, other characteristics were more salient, as for a girl who answered: "I am twelve years old. I was born in South Carolina. I have two sisters and a dog. I have a babysitting job every day after school. . . . I hate arithmetic but I like our teacher." (pp. 746–747). The salience of gender identity depends on many factors, including the proportion of males and females in our environment. The study found that boys and girls were twice as likely to mention their own gender if their classroom at school had an excess of children of the other sex. We are apparently more aware of our own gender when we are in a numerical minority. This is like the token or solo effect discussed earlier for gender stereotypes, where the gender of a lone man or woman in a group is more salient to observers than it would be in a gender-balanced group.

For most of us, the acquisition of gender identity is a smooth and trouble-free process. We are classified as male or female at birth, treated as a boy or girl by our parents, and easily learn our own gender as we grow up. For a few people, however, developing gender identity is a problem. *Transsexuals* are a case in point. Such individuals are biologically members of one sex, but develop the belief that they are really members of the other sex. In the most common case, a person is to all outward appearances a male, but the person's psychological reality is being a woman trapped in a male body.

The causes of transsexualism are still a mystery. Most often, transsexuals show no signs of biological abnormality. Genetically, hormonally, and physiologically, they are "normal" members of their sex. Yet at a very early age they develop a self-concept at odds with their physical characteristics. This puzzling situation is profoundly disturbing to the individuals involved. Efforts to help transsexuals by psychotherapy have had very little success; it is not easy to change a deeply rooted sense of gender identity. As a result, some have advocated sex-change surgery as one way to reconcile this mind-body problem by altering the body to fit the person's mental identity.

Psychological Masculinity, Femininity, and Androgyny

Gender identity is an either-or matter; people believe they are either a male or a female. However, individuals differ markedly in the degree to which they perceive themselves as having all the different masculine or feminine characteristics that make up conventional gender stereotypes. In terms of their **gender self-concept,** highly "masculine" individuals believe they possess the attributes, interests, preferences, and skills society typically associates with maleness. Highly "feminine" individuals believe they possess the attributes, interests, preferences, and skills associated with femaleness. Psychologists have long been interested in self-perceptions of psychological masculinity and femininity.

A typical masculinity-femininity test might ask such questions as whether a person prefers showers (masculine) or tub baths (feminine), whether the person would rather work as a building contractor (masculine) or librarian (feminine), whether the person is active (masculine) or passive (feminine). An important feature of these tests is that they view masculinity and femininity as mutually exclusive polar opposites. People get a single score on the test: high scores indicate masculinity (many masculine choices), and low scores indicate femininity (few masculine choices).

In more recent times, some psychologists have challenged this one-dimensional view of psychological masculinity and femininity (Spence, 1985; Spence & Helmreich, 1978). Sandra Bem (1974, 1985), for example, proposed that some people might see themselves as having both masculine and feminine characteristics. Such a person might enjoy both carpentry and cooking, might be very assertive (a masculine trait) at work but very nurturant (a feminine trait) at home, and so on. Bem called these people psychologically androgynous, borrowing from the Greek terms for male (*andro*) and female (*gyne*). Bem emphasized that the androgynous person is not a moderate who falls halfway between extreme masculinity and femininity. Rather, the androgynous person views himself or herself as combining strong masculine and strong feminine attributes. This two-dimensional model is shown in Figure 14–1.

To investigate **androgyny,** Bem (1974) constructed a new test with separate dimensions for masculinity and for femininity, making it possible for a person to score high on both. In the Bem Sex-Role Inventory, people rate their personal qualities using 60 adjectives: 20 masculine (assertive, independent), 20 feminine (affectionate, understanding), and 20 gender neutral (sincere, friendly). When Bem administered her test to samples of college students, she found some traditionally gender-typed individuals, both masculine men (who scored high on M and low on F) and feminine women (who scored high on F and low on M). More interesting, however, was the fact that some people rated themselves high on both masculine and feminine characteristics, showing the androgynous pattern Bem predicted.

The exact percentages of gender-typed and androgynous people vary somewhat from study to study. Typical are results from a study of California college students (Bernard, 1980). Roughly 40 percent of students perceived themselves as traditionally gender typed and 25 percent were androgynous. An "undifferentiated" subgroup included 29 percent of men and 21 percent of women who scored low on both masculine and feminine traits. Finally, a few people showed a pattern of reverse gender typing—

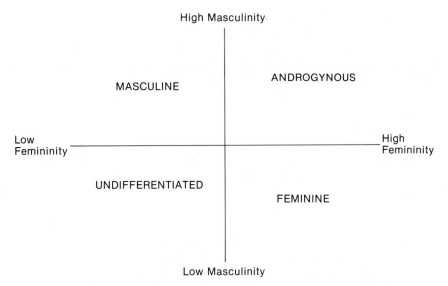

High Masculinity

MASCULINE   ANDROGYNOUS

Low
Femininity   High
                                        Femininity

UNDIFFERENTIATED

                   FEMININE

Low Masculinity

Figure 14–1. A two-dimensional model of psychological masculinity and femininity.

specifically feminine men (5 percent) and masculine women (12 percent). The important point is that although traditional gender typing is the most common pattern, a sizable minority of people perceive themselves as combining both masculine and feminine qualities.

Research on androgyny has raised basic questions about how psychological masculinity and femininity affect well-being. One long-standing view has been that to ensure mental health, boys and men should be masculine in their interests and attributes, whereas girls and women should be feminine. This *congruence model* (Whitley, 1983) proposes that adjustment is enhanced when there is an ''appropriate'' match between gender and self-concept. In contrast, the newer *androgyny model* of well-being argues that it is better for people to have both masculine and feminine traits. In particular, it has been proposed that androgynous individuals surpass traditionally sex-typed individuals in having greater behavioral flexibility and better psychological adjustment.

Behavioral Flexibility. Sandra Bem hypothesized that masculine people will perform well in situations calling for task competence or assertiveness; feminine people will do well in situa-

tions requiring nurturance or emotional expressivity, and androgynous people will do well in *both* types of situations. Some empirical support for this prediction has been found (Jose & McCarthy, 1988).

Some research has focused on situations in which psychological masculinity should affect performance. For example, in a study by Bem (1975), masculine and androgynous individuals did better than feminine individuals on a test of ability to resist group pressure for conformity. In a more recent study of Israeli soldiers, both masculine and androgynous individuals viewed themselves as more likely to succeed in the army and received more positive evaluations from fellow soldiers than did feminine individuals (Dimitrovsky, Singer, & Yinon, 1989).

Other studies demonstrate situations in which femininity and androgyny are advantageous. In one study, feminine and androgynous individuals did better on tasks requiring nurturance, including playing with a baby and responding to a transfer student who was having problems adjusting to a new college (Bem, Martyna, & Watson, 1976). Higher femininity has also been linked to greater marital satisfaction for both husbands and wives (Bradbury & Fincham, 1988).

Self-Esteem. Feeling good about oneself is a key ingredient in mental health. The congruence model predicts that self-esteem and psychological adjustment should be highest for masculine men and feminine women—people with "appropriate" gender self-concepts. In contrast, the androgyny model asserts that androgynous individuals who perceive themselves as having both positive masculine and positive feminine attributes should have higher self-esteem than gender-typed individuals. A large number of studies have investigated this topic (Markstrom-Adams, 1989; Orlofsky & O'Heron, 1987; Whitley, 1983, 1988), and they suggest an unexpected conclusion.

Basically, research once again provides no support for the congruence model. But results offer only weak support for the androgyny model. Instead, the biggest factor influencing self-esteem seems to be how a person scores on the dimension of psychological masculinity. Both masculine and androgynous individuals usually have high self-esteem. The added benefit for androgynous people of being feminine as well as masculine is statistically significant, but very small in size.

Researchers are still puzzling about why masculinity appears to be so central to self-esteem. One possibility is that in this culture, self-esteem is closely linked to traits traditionally labeled as masculine, such as independence, assertiveness, and competence. Another possibility is that self-esteem tests are biased and do not adequately assess elements of self-esteem that are associated with femininity; in other words, the pattern of results may be due to a methodological weakness in the tests being used (Whitley, 1988).

Some Cautions. Research on the behavioral flexibility and self-esteem of gender-typed and androgynous individuals challenges the model that "appropriate" gender typing is essential to mental health. Masculine men and feminine women do not seem to have an advantage over androgynous individuals. Although the concept of androgyny has provided a useful correction to earlier work on masculinity and femininity, we should be cautious about accepting it uncritically.

First, androgyny measures are very limited in scope; they focus on self-perceptions of task competence and emotional expressiveness. In actuality, most people probably view masculinity and femininity much more broadly as including appearance, sexual behavior, and social roles as well as personality (Myers & Gonda, 1982). Further, these different components of masculinity and femininity are probably not part of a single, consistent dimension (Spence & Helmreich, 1980). One woman might, for instance, think of herself as masculine in personality (assertive, ambitious, and independent), feminine in appearance (short and voluptuous), and androgynous in social roles (both a mother and a career woman). Existing androgyny instruments do not capture this complexity.

Second, androgyny is possible only in areas such as personality; a person could perceive himself or herself as warmly nurturant in some situations and coldly competitive in others. But in different domains, masculinity and femininity actually are mutually exclusive. In reproduction, for example, insemination and childbearing are each exclusive to one sex.

Third, current work on androgyny tells us little about how salient masculinity and femininity actually are in people's thinking about themselves. The Bem Sex Role Inventory and other tests ask people to rate themselves on traits society labels as masculine or feminine (Spence & Helmreich, 1980). But responses to these tests do not tell us whether people spontaneously label their own actions this way. If gender typing is really important, a person might think: "Gee, it makes me feel feminine to have prepared such a fine meal for my family," or "I feel more masculine for having stood up to my boss today." But if gender typing is not so vital, people might recognize their own nurturance or assertiveness, but identify these as human traits unrelated to gender. We just do not know how prominent masculine and feminine labels actually are in people's self-concepts.

Finally, discussions of masculinity and femininity often touch on personal values and ideals. For those who endorse more traditional views about the sexes, the preservation of clear-cut distinctions between masculinity and femininity is an important goal. For those who want to expand the options available to both sexes, the blurring of distinctions is seen as desirable. Indeed, some feminists have rejected androgyny as an ideal because it preserves the notion that there are distinct masculine and feminine qualities even as it gives permission to people to have both types of attributes. Instead, some have argued that we should move toward "sex-role transcendence" (Garnets & Pleck, 1979). Personal attributes and preferences should no longer be associated with gender. Psychological research can clarify how gender affects our self-concept and can identify the consequences of various patterns, but it cannot tell people what to adopt for their own lives.

So far, our discussion of gender has focused on perception—impressions of others and of ourselves. Now we turn to the topic of actual differences in the behavior of women and men.

THEORETICAL PERSPECTIVES ON GENDER

Debates about the nature of sex differences raged long before the existence of social psychology. For centuries, personal experience and intuition were the basis for such discussions. Today, scientific theories and research are providing a more balanced and comprehensive understanding of gender differences in behavior.

Early discussions often asked whether gender differences are caused by "'nature or nurture," by biology or learning. We now know that such simple dichotomies are misleading. A full explanation of gender differences must consider *both* the biological capacities of the sexes and the social environment in which males and females live. It has also become clear that there is no single, general explanation for all differences between males and females. Rather, the causes of gender differences in math ability may be quite distinct from the causes of gender differences in self-disclosure, and so on. Four broad perspectives on the causes of gender differences emphasize the influence of biology, childhood socialization, social roles, and social situations.

The Influence of Biology

Gender differences are undoubtedly affected by biology. Physical differences in height, in the ability to bear children and to breast-feed them, and so on, are obvious. The impact of sex hormones, both on the unborn fetus and on adults, is a lively topic of investigation, as are possible sex differences in the brain. Some sociobiologists even suggest that genetic evolution contributes to gender differences in human behavior, a possibility discussed in Box 14–3 on page 446.

The point social psychologists emphasize is that the importance of basic biological differences can be greatly increased or reduced by social forces. For example, sex differences in physical size and strength may once have given males a clear-cut advantage over females in warfare. But with modern aircraft and pushbutton weapons, brute force is less important for soldiers of either sex.

Childbirth provides another illustration of the interplay of biology and society. Women are physically capable of having a dozen or more babies during a lifetime. In colonial days, American women had many children; childbirth was hazardous; and as a result, men usually lived longer than women. Today, women's biological capacity remains the same. But because of contemporary social attitudes and medical technology, the typical American woman has only two or three children and the dangers of childbirth are greatly reduced. Consequently, American women now typically outlive men by several years. The impact of biological gender differences can vary dramatically depending on the social environment.

Childhood Socialization

This perspective emphasizes the ways in which people learn about gender and acquire "sex-appropriate" behavior during childhood. An important idea is that society has different expectations and standards for the behavior of males and females. Imagine a father whose young daughter enters the living room dressed in Mommy's earrings, silk robe, and high heels, and climbs on Daddy's knee. The father is likely

BOX 14–3

The Evolution of Sex Differences

In his book, *The Evolution of Human Sexuality* (1979), Donald Symons outlines a sociobiological analysis of sex differences. Like other sociobiologists, he looks to genetic inheritance and the process of evolution for the causes of many gender differences.

Symons argues that humans have evolved in ways that maximize the likelihood of their individual genes being passed on to offspring and thus "surviving" in future generations. Whereas men produce many sperm, women typically produce only one egg per month and then must invest time and energy in pregnancy and nursing a baby. As a result, the most effective reproductive strategies for the two sexes differ. For men, the survival of one's own genes ("reproductive success") is enhanced by impregnating as many women as possible and investing little time and energy in the rearing of any one child. Hence, Symons believes, men are biologically disposed to have many sexual partners and limited contact with infants. In contrast, for women reproductive success depends on maximizing the chances that the few children a woman can produce will survive to maturity. Women are disposed to be involved in the care of infants and to seek a long-term relationship with a man who can also contribute to the development of their children.

Symons and other sociobiologists believe that males and females have distinctive genetically based dispositions. They recognize, however, that whether such dispositions are translated into gender differences in actual behavior depends a good deal on the environment. The sociobiological perspective is still quite controversial, but it provides a good example of how biological factors might influence gender differences in attitudes and behavior.

---

to smile at his daughter, give her a big hug, and compliment her on being such a pretty little girl. Now imagine a 4-year-old boy doing exactly the same thing. Although a modern Daddy might not punish his son, it is likely he would communicate firmly that feminine clothes are not appropriate for boys.

Through such experiences and the processes of reinforcement and modeling described in Chapter 1, children learn what society expects for boys and girls. The different social experiences of boys and girls lead to relatively enduring sex differences in attitudes, interests, skills, and personality traits that continue into adulthood.

Social Roles

A third perspective emphasizes that a person's behavior is strongly influenced by social roles (Eagly, 1987). The lives of adults are structured by their various roles as family members and workers. A key idea is that many important social roles are defined differently for the two sexes. Within the family, people usually have quite different expectations for mothers and fathers, for husbands and wives, for sons and daughters. In the world of work, occupational roles are often sex typed. Consider your images of nurses versus truck drivers, of kindergarten teachers and business tycoons. Further, women's work roles are often lower in social status, prestige, and power than those of men: he's the "boss" and she's the secretary.

Traditional social roles affect the behavior of women and men in several ways. They perpetuate a division of labor by gender, with women as homemakers and child care providers and men as breadwinners. Roles influence the skills and interests people first develop in childhood and later refine as adults. Little girls often play with cooking sets and dolls in preparation for adult roles as wives and mothers. In addition, the effects of gender-linked roles may "spill over" into new situations. We may learn from experiences in the family and at work that men have higher status and are more authoritative than women. When we meet a new person, we may use their sex as a cue, inferring, for example, that a man is likely to be a confident leader and that a woman is likely to be a supportive follower (Eagly, 1987). As we saw earlier in this chapter (Box 14–2), such expectations can become self-fulfilling prophecies.

Social Situations

Another major influence on behavior is the social setting. A man might talk about football and cars with his male buddies, peppering his speech with four-letter words, but "clean up his act" and change the topic of conversation with a new girlfriend. The basic assumption in situational models is that "men and women are relatively equal in their potentialities for most social behaviors and [their] behaviors may differ widely as a function of personal choice, the behavior of others, and the situational context" (Deaux & Major, 1987, p. 371). Research is beginning to uncover important situational factors that contribute to sex differences in behavior.

Our desire to be liked by other people often leads us to conform to their expectations about how males and females should behave, regardless of personal beliefs. In one experiment, college women participated in a simulated job interview (von Baeyer, Sherk, & Zanna, 1981). By random assignment, half the women were informed that the male interviewer was a traditional person, who believed that the ideal woman should be gentle, sensitive, attractive, and passive, and should be assigned to easier jobs such as making coffee. Other women were informed that the interviewer preferred nontraditional women, who were independent, assertive, and could assume equal job responsibilities with men. Not surprisingly, the women's knowledge about the interviewer influenced how they prepared for the interview. Women expecting a traditional interviewer "dressed up" by wearing more makeup and jewelry than did women expecting to meet a nontraditional interviewer. Women with traditional interviewers also talked less during the interview, and tended to make more traditional statements about themselves. The desire to be liked and accepted by others can lead us to act in more or less gender-typed ways, depending on the situation.

The gender of the person we are with is a

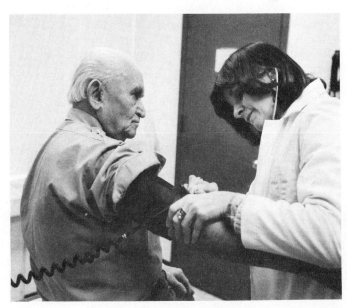

Is the woman taking this man's blood pressure a nurse or a physician? In our society, many jobs have traditionally been segregated by sex. Although many more women are now going to medical school, nurses are still typically women and doctors are usually men.

powerful situational determinant of behavior. An empirical demonstration of this idea comes from a study of who interrupts whom in casual conversations. The researchers unobtrusively tape-recorded the conversations of male-male, female-female, and male-female pairs as they chatted spontaneously in coffee shops, drugstores, and other public places (Zimmerman & West, 1975). Interruptions were ten times more frequent in the male-female conversations than in the same-sex ones. More striking, in same-sex pairs, men and women were equally likely to interrupt, but in mixed sex dyads, men initiated 96 percent of all interruption.

A laboratory study of conversations in mixed-sex groups found similar results (McMillan, Clifton, McGrath, & Gale, 1977). As shown in Table 14–2, men and women were equally likely to interrupt another person of the same sex. But when cross-sex interruptions occurred, it was five times more likely for a man to interrupt a woman as vice versa. For another illustration of the impact of group gender composition, this time in the society as a whole, see Box 14–4.

Situational constraints can prevent people from acting in accord with their own preferences and beliefs about gender. For example, many parents believe that mothers should have greater responsibility for child care than fathers, and mothers usually do spend more time with children, even when the mother has a full-time job. However, an exception occurs when a wife's work schedule literally prevents her from doing all the child care. One study found that when wives worked an evening shift so that

they had to leave home before dinner, fathers wound up, of necessity, giving the kids dinner and putting them to bed (Berk & Berk, 1979). The more general point is that a variety of situational factors, such as the gender composition of a group, the expectations of other people, or the constraints of a work schedule, can have great impact on how men and women behave.

In summary, the causes of sex differences in behavior are complex. The focus of contemporary research is to understand the many interwoven factors that affect specific behaviors.

SEX DIFFERENCES IN BEHAVIOR

In recent years, a great deal of research has compared the abilities and behavior of males and females, especially that of American children and college students. But the results of these studies are often contradictory and sometimes downright confusing. It turns out to be considerably more difficult to pin down gender differences than might be imagined. We begin by considering sex differences in intellectual abilities, and then turn to the social behaviors of aggression, helping, conformity and nonverbal communication. Before beginning our discussion, however, we need to review some basic ideas about meta-analysis, a statistical method first discussed in Chapter 1.

Meta-Analyses of Sex Differences

As the number of studies of sex differences has increased, it has become more difficult for investigators to summarize research findings to arrive at general conclusions. Traditionally, reviews of research literature have relied heavily on the judgment of the reviewers to select a balanced sample of studies and to eliminate methodologically flawed research. A persistent problem for reviewers has been inconsistency across studies. What can we conclude if 20 studies find boys are better at some activity, but 10 studies find women are better, and 10 studies find no differences? Often, researchers have

T A B L E   1 4 – 2

MEAN NUMBER OF INTERRUPTIONS PER HALF-HOUR IN MIXED SEX DISCUSSION GROUPS

Sex of person who is interrupted	Sex of interrupter	
	Male	Female
Male	2.36	0.93
Female	5.24	2.50

Source: Adapted from McMillan, Clifton, McGrath, & Gale (1977), p. 553.

BOX 14–4

Too Many Women: Sex Ratios and Social Life

In their book, *Too Many Women: The Sex Ratio Question* (1982) Marcia Guttentag and Paul Secord investigate the social effects of the ratio of males to females in society. Although approximately equal numbers of males and females are born each year, the ratio of male-to-female adults of marriageable age is quite variable cross-culturally. It is affected by wars, the hazards of childbearing, migration, infanticide of girl children, and so on. On the American frontier, for example, men outnumbered women, often by substantial proportions. By contrast, in 1980, for every 100 women aged 33 to 37 in the United States, there were only 95 men. Ethnic differences in sex ratios have also been noted. Among black Americans, the current sex ratio imbalance is even more extreme, with an average of only 89.6 males per 100 females (Tucker, 1986). What are the social and personal consequences of imbalanced sex ratios?

Guttentag and Secord begin by arguing that in all societies, men have relatively greater structural power than women: men control the economy, religion, government, and so on. However, sex ratios influence patterns of dominance in the personal relations of men and women in courtship and marriage. When there is an undersupply of women, as in America before World War II, young women are highly valued and protected. Men are eager to form a committed relationship through marriage. Women gain status through marriage and are able to achieve economic mobility by "marrying up." Husband and wife roles are highly differentiated

and complementary. Both sexes stress sexual monogamy, although a double standard may permit greater sexual freedom for men.

In contrast, Guttentag and Secord propose, when women are in oversupply, as in the 1970s and 1980s in America, the relations between the sexes are quite different. Specifically, marriage and commitment are deemphasized. A high proportion of women are never-married or divorced, and single-parent families headed by women increase. For example, 1980 census data for Los Angeles county in California showed that 14 percent of all white women were divorced and 24 percent of white women aged 25 to 34 had never been married (Tucker, 1986). For black women, confronted with a more severe shortage of black men, the overall rate of divorce was 23 percent, and the proportion of black women aged 25 to 34 who have never married was 31 percent. Under such conditions, Guttentag and Secord believe, women may feel personally devalued and powerless, and feminist movements are likely to arise.

The basic argument of Guttentag and Secord—that sex ratios in society have a profound impact on heterosexual relationships—is provocative. The researchers support their argument with examples of societies ranging from ancient Greece to medieval Europe to contemporary Africa. Their views have sparked scientific research (South, 1988), and their work provides a fascinating illustration of a way in which societal-level factors may influence the daily lives of women and men.

---

used a "vote-counting" approach to resolving these discrepancies, assuming, for example, that a sex difference "exists" if it occurs in the majority of studies.

In an effort to develop more systematic ways to review and synthesize empirical findings, researchers have begun to use new techniques called **meta-analysis** (Eagly, 1987; Hyde & Linn, 1986). This approach uses statistical methods to pool information from many studies in order to

arrive at an overall estimate of the size of sex differences. We might find, for instance, that the average sex difference on a particular measure is less than one tenth of a standard deviation—quite a small effect. Meta-analyses also encourage reviewers to consider very carefully how they select a sample of studies to review. It has been suggested, for instance, that reviews should include not only published studies, but also unpublished doctoral dissertations. The reasoning here is that studies finding no sex differences may be less likely to be accepted for publication, thus biasing published research toward overestimating sex differences. In the following sections, we present some of the findings of recent analyses of sex differences.

Intellectual Abilities

Psychologists have long been interested in individual differences in ability, and this research has often led to comparisons of the performance of males and females. In 1974, Eleanor Maccoby and Carol Jacklin published a landmark book called *The Psychology of Sex Differences*. They reviewed hundreds of studies of sex differences in many psychological characteristics, such as verbal ability and achievement motivation. Maccoby and Jacklin attempted to evaluate this research carefully, excluding studies with methodological weaknesses and accepting as true only those findings replicated in several studies by different investigators. Maccoby and Jacklin concluded that some stereotypes about sex differences were clearly wrong. The sexes do *not* differ in overall intelligence, or in general level of achievement motivation or striving for excellence. The authors also debunked the idea that girls are better at rote learning and simple repetitive tasks, whereas boys are better at tasks requiring higher-level cognitive processing.

Maccoby and Jacklin concluded that sex differences had been established in only three major areas of intellectual ability: verbal ability (favoring females), math ability (favoring males), and visual-spatial ability (favoring males). In the years since Maccoby and Jacklin's review, research on sex differences has continued to increase, and meta-analysis techniques have provided better ways for researchers to summarize the results of many empirical studies. Currently, Maccoby and Jacklin's conclusions about sex differences in verbal and math ability are controversial (Feingold, 1988b). Let's take a closer look at verbal ability as an illustration.

For years, girls consistently did better than boys on tests of verbal ability such as the Scholastic Aptitude Test (SAT)—a test taken by students applying to college. In recent years, however, the gap between male and female performance on the SAT verbal test has been reversed. In 1985, the mean verbal score was 437 for males and 425 for females (Ramist & Arbeiter, 1986). Today, researchers are divided about whether or not there really are sex differences in verbal ability.

At one extreme, Janet Hyde and Marcia Linn (1988) used techniques of meta-analysis to review the results of many studies of sex differences in verbal abilities on a variety of different tests. They found that the average size of tested sex differences had declined over time. In studies published after 1973, the mean sex difference was roughly one-tenth of a standard deviation (comparable to the 12-point difference found for the 1985 SAT verbal scores)—a difference that they considered so small as to be of no practical significance. Hyde and Linn concluded,

> We are prepared to assert that there are no gender differences in verbal ability, at least at this time, in American culture, in the standard ways that verbal ability has been measured. We feel that we can reach this conclusion with some confidence, having surveyed 165 studies that represent the testing of 1,418,899 subjects. (1988, p. 62)

In contrast, Diane Halpern (1989) recently argued that females do have a clear verbal advantage over males. She suggests that current testing procedures may underestimate the true size of this sex difference.

> The notion that cognitive gender differences are diminishing in size is at odds with virtually hundreds of studies that have found consistent differences [showing] female superiority in verbal ability. (p. 1156)

Similar controversies are currently raging about sex differences in math ability (Feingold, 1988b; Kimball, 1989). How can reasonable researchers arrive at such different conclusions?

First, researchers disagree about how to interpret recent changes in test results such as the

SAT. What does this narrowing of the gender gap mean? One possibility is that the sexes are actually more similar in ability than we once thought. But changes in test scores could also reflect other factors. For example, today more boys than girls drop out of high school. The 1985 SAT was taken by roughly 472,000 males compared to 505,000 females. This may mean that low-ability boys are less likely to be tested than are low-ability girls, which might explain why boys seem to be catching up with girls in verbal ability. Another possibility is that test makers may have changed the items on the tests, perhaps to eliminate items on which boys and girls have average differences or to include more technical vocabulary terms that may favor boys.

Second, researchers may adopt different criteria for determining when sex differences are large enough to warrant attention. For example, Hyde and Linn acknowledge that there is a small average sex difference in verbal ability, which they calculate to be about one-tenth of a standard deviation. But they consider this difference so small that it does not have "any meaningful psychological or educational implications" (p. 62).

Third, some researchers suggest that we should consider not only average group scores on tests, but also the distribution of scores. For example, Halpern (1989) emphasized that boys have long been overrepresented among those with language problems. Males are three to four times more likely than females to be stutterers (Skinner & Shelton, 1985). Dyslexia, a serious reading disability, is 5 to 10 times more common among males than females (Sutaria, 1985). Others have emphasized that boys are overrepresented among the math "geniuses" who score at the very top of the ability curve. The point here is that average scores may not be as informative as a close examination of the entire range of performance.

The general conclusion that we offer is this. At the level of basic intellectual abilities, there are enormous individual differences. People range from those who can barely add a column of numbers to brilliant mathematicians, and from those who can't read to those who write

beautiful poetry. Within this broad arc of human variation, gender is usually of relatively little importance. Global statements about sex differences in general abilities are probably less useful than more focused efforts to describe sex differences in specific abilities, such as reading comprehension, vocabulary, and essay writing or in specific verbal disabilities such as dyslexia. And, given the large size and increasing diversity of our population, efforts to characterize the abilities of "all females" and "all males" are probably less useful than discussions of more specific groups.

At the same time, our everyday experiences repeatedly show that men and women frequently use their basic talents in different ways. Boys who are good in math are more likely than equally talented girls to pursue careers in science and engineering (Kimball, 1989). A man with high achievement strivings may channel his energies into starting his own business; a traditional woman with equally great desire for achievement may take up gourmet cooking or become a "supermom." In other words, traditional definitions of appropriate roles for men and women can dramatically influence how individuals use their intellectual abilities.

Aggression

One of the most consistent sex differences in social behavior is men's greater aggressiveness (Eagly & Steffen, 1986; Hyde, 1986). Around the world, it is men who are the warriors. Violent crime is also largely a male domain. Whether it be the activities of teenage gangs, underworld crime figures, or a lone assassin, it is usually men who use physical force in illegal pursuits. According to FBI statistics, 88 percent of those arrested for murder in 1987 were men. (See Table 14–3 on p. 452 for other statistics.) During childhood, boys are usually rated as more aggressive than girls by teachers, parents, and peers. So whether we consider socially approved aggression in wartime, illegal violence, or children's play, males take the lead in aggressive behavior.

Two recent meta-analyses reviewed more

| T A B L E   1 4 – 3 | | | |
| FBI STATISTICS COMPARING ARRESTS FOR VIOLENT CRIMES BY MEN AND WOMEN | | | |
Type of offense	Total Number	Committed by Men (%)	Committed by Women (%)
Murder and nonnegligent manslaughter	16,714	88	12
Robbery	123,306	92	8
Aggravated assult	301,734	87	13
All violent crime	473,030	89	11

Source: Adapted from Uniform Crime Reports for the United States, 1987 (Federal Bureau of Investigation, U.S. Department of Justice, 1987), p. 181.

than a hundred studies of aggression (Eagly & Steffen, 1986; Hyde, 1986). They found that males are more aggressive than females in both verbal and physical aggression, although the gender gap is bigger for physical aggression. Larger sex differences are found in naturalistic settings (e.g., hitting and kicking on a playground) than in more controlled laboratory settings (e.g., hitting a plastic bobo doll in a research room). Hyde (1986) suggests that males may be more likely than females to engage in spontaneous aggression, but that males and females respond more similarly in controlled laboratory conditions.

In addition, there is evidence that women feel more guilt and anxiety about behaving ag-

Football provides a socially-approved context for male aggression. But theorists disagree about whether aggressive sports provide a wholesome outlet for innate male aggressive drives, or rather teach men to become even more aggressive.

gressively (Eagly & Steffen, 1986). Our society is more tolerant of aggression in males than in females. In childhood, boys are much more likely to be given toy guns and swords, and to be taught about fighting and self-defense. A recent study investigated children's expectations about the consequences of various aggressive acts, such as hitting a child who takes a ball (Perry, Perry, & Weiss, 1989). Compared to boys, girls anticipated more parental disapproval for aggression and expected to feel greater guilt. There is also evidence that females are more concerned about the harm their aggression may cause the victim and about the danger of retaliation (Eagly & Steffen, 1986). As a result, females may feel more guilt, anxiety, and fear about aggressive acts and so inhibit their aggressive impulses.

Helping

Is one sex more helpful than the other? A meta-analytic review of 172 studies of prosocial behavior (Eagly & Crowley, 1986) found a significant sex difference: men were more likely than women to offer assistance. However, the researchers noted several important qualifications to this general conclusion. First and foremost, they emphasized that most social psychological studies of helping have investigated bystander intervention, that is, offering aid to a stranger in distress. Studies have not typically investigated other important kinds of prosocial behavior such as caring for children, comforting a friend, or taking an elderly relative to a clinic.

Using a social roles perspective, Eagly and Crowley (1986) propose that whereas female roles foster helping that is nurturant and caring, male roles foster helping that is heroic and chivalrous. Bystander intervention research documents men's greater chivalry. Men are more likely than women to help strangers in distress, and the average size of the sex difference is about one-third of a standard deviation. Men are especially likely to help when the victim or requester is female, when there is an audience, and in situations that women perceive as dangerous.

Unfortunately, existing research tells us little about helping that occurs in private relations among friends and relatives. Eagly and Crowley identified five studies showing that women were more likely than men to do personal favors for friends and to provide advice about personal problems. Clearly, a more complete understanding of sex differences in helping will require studies that go beyond bystander intervention to investigate helping in a wide variety of settings.

Conformity

Stereotypes portray women as more yielding, gullible, and conformist than men. According to Eagly (1987), traditional social roles dictate that men should be less easily influenced than women. Social psychological studies have typically investigated conformity and compliance in laboratory settings where an individual interacts with strangers.

Careful reviews of the empirical research on social influence lead to two conclusions. First, when modern meta-analytic techniques are used to pool findings from a large number of studies, there is a small but statistically significant tendency for women to be more easily influenced than men (Eagly, 1987). Second and equally important is the finding that results are often very inconsistent from study to study. Alice Eagly (1978, 1983) found 62 studies that had investigated sex differences in persuasion—that is, the extent to which a person is influenced by hearing arguments in favor of or against an issue. Only 16 percent of these studies found that women were significantly more easily persuaded; the vast majority found no differences. Similarly, Eagly found 61 studies of responses to group pressures for conformity, as in the Asch experiment described in Chapter 8. Here again, only 34 percent found that women conformed significantly more; in most cases, the sexes did not differ significantly. Whether sex differences occur or not appears to depend on specific details of the testing situation, such as the nature of the social influence task or the testing materials.

One interesting idea is that sex differences in influenceability may have more to do with the gender typing of the task than with a general disposition for women to conform. People are generally more likely to conform if they lack information about a topic or consider it unimportant. Thus women are more likely to conform on tasks traditionally viewed as masculine, and men are more likely to conform when confronted with feminine tasks.

This point was demonstrated by Sistrunk and McDavid (1971). They asked college women and men to answer a questionnaire about matters of fact and opinion, some concerning masculine topics such as sports cars, politics, and mathematics, and others concerning feminine areas such as cosmetics, sewing, or cooking. To introduce conformity pressure, the questionnaire indicated next to each question how a majority of college students had supposedly responded. Results clearly showed the effect of gender typing. Men conformed more than women on feminine items; women conformed more than men on masculine items. Overall, there were no significant differences between the level of conformity of men and of women. Although this interpretation seems quite plausible, more research will be needed to establish its general applicability (Eagly, 1987).

If empirical studies find that sex differences in influenceability are somewhat elusive and small in magnitude, why does the stereotype persist that women are much more yielding? The answer may be found in the roles that men and women typically play in society (Eagly & Wood, 1985). In real life, an important determinant of social influence is a person's prestige or power relative to others in a group. In a business, for example, subordinates are expected to go along with the boss; a nurse usually follows a physician's order. Since men typically have higher occupational status than women, it is more common to observe a woman yielding to a man than vice versa.

Although this behavior pattern is actually based on job status, people may mistakenly infer that women have a general tendency to go along with others. To test this idea, Eagly and Wood (1982) had students read a description of a man influencing a female co-worker or a woman influencing a male co-worker. Subjects then answered questions about the people described. When subjects had no information about the job titles of these persons, they assumed that women held lower-status jobs and that women were more likely to comply behaviorally with men than vice versa. When explicit job titles were provided, subjects believed that compliance would be based on status rather than gender. Such results support the idea that stereotypes about women's greater influenceability are based in part on knowledge that men often have more prestigious and powerful positions in society.

Nonverbal Communication

Stereotypes about female "intuition" suggest that women may be better than men at decoding or "reading" nonverbal behavior. Thus it might be speculated that mothers are more expert than fathers at telling whether a crying baby is hungry, wet, or suffering gas pains. Similarly, the stereotype would suggest that women may be better able to sense whether another person is feeling depressed or embarrassed or tired. Many studies have addressed this question by comparing men's and women's accuracy at decoding another person's emotions from facial cues, body language, or tone of voice.

In a typical study, subjects watch a videotape of a person expressing a series of emotions, such as happiness, disgust, or fear. After viewing each segment of the film, subjects indicate which of several emotions they think is being expressed. In other studies, subjects listen to recordings of voices that have been "content filtered"—altered so that the words are garbled and only the tone is distinct. Judith Hall (1978) reviewed 75 studies that permitted gender comparisons. In 68 percent, women were better decoders than men; in 13 percent, men were better than women; and in 19 percent, no gender differences occurred.

More recent meta-analyses have confirmed and expanded these results (Hall, 1984). On average, women are more skilled at decoding nonverbal cues. The female advantage is greatest for "reading" facial expressions, next largest for body cues, and smallest for decoding voice tone. Women are also better at recognizing faces. This gender difference has been found in school children, teenagers, and adults. Although the size of the sex difference in decoding nonverbal cues varies from study to study, women's greater skill in this domain has consistently been documented by research.

Several possible explanations have been offered for women's greater nonverbal skill. One is that females have a genetically "programmed" sensitivity to nonverbal cues because of their role in caring for preverbal infants. Another suggestion is that women are trained to be experts in emotional matters, and so learn to be more skillful in nonverbal communication. A third explanation emphasizes men's greater dominance in many social settings. Consistent with this interpretation is work showing that, regardless of sex, subordinates may be more sensitive to the feelings of leaders than leaders are to the feelings of subordinates (Snodgrass, 1985).

Having reviewed a good deal of research on sex differences, we can consider a frequently asked question: aside from the biological facts of life, just how different are males and females? Psychological research offers no simple answer. At the level of basic abilities and personal dispositions, gender differences are often small in magnitude, no more than a few points on a standardized test. Yet sex differences do seem to exist (for whatever complex reasons) in aggressive behavior and in nonverbal communication skills. And the daily activities and roles of men and women are often very different. Whether we conclude that the sexes are "fundamentally different" or "basically the same" is a question of perspective. There is probably some truth and some exaggeration in both positions (Hare-Mustin & Marecek, 1988).

CHANGING ROLES FOR WOMEN AND MEN

Newspapers today are filled with stories about the changing roles of men and women. Whether a writer heralds these changes as a "stride toward equality" or laments the collapse of "traditional values," few would deny that the lives of men and women are not what they used to be. One way to assess these changes is to compare contemporary gender roles with the older, traditional patterns. Traditional gender roles were organized around two basic principles. The first idea was that men and women should perform distinctive activities, that there should be a division of labor by gender. The second idea was that men should be the dominant sex, both at home and in society at large. Let us look at these social roles and how they are changing.

Division of Labor

There is much evidence that rigid distinctions between what men should do and what women should do are breaking down. During this century, women have increasingly come to do things formerly considered "for men only." In particular, women's participation in paid work has increased dramatically, decreasing men's exclusive role as the family breadwinner. In 1940, only 15 percent of married women worked for pay. Today, more than half of all married women have paying jobs, including many mothers with school age children. In 1988, 56 percent of all married women worked for pay, as did 71 percent of married women with children ages 6 to 17 (U.S. Department of Labor, 1989).

Women are also participating more in higher education. In 1978, for the first time in history, more women than men entered college in the United States. Women have also begun to enter occupations such as law and medicine that were once the near exclusive domain of men. In 1986, women received 39 percent of the professional

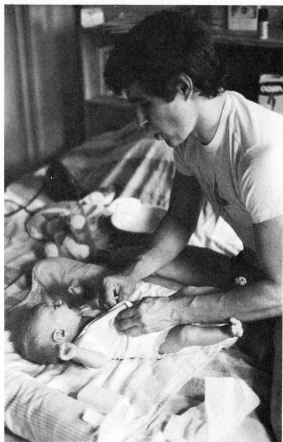

Traditional rules about what males and females should do are breaking down. Here, a high school woman learns carpentry and a new father cares for his infant son.

degrees awarded in law, 31 percent of the degrees in medicine, and 23 percent of degrees in dentistry (Rix, 1988). These are changes of great personal and social significance. These behavioral changes have been accompanied by increasing public acceptance of education and employment for women.

Yet women are far from equal partners in the world of work. Women continue to be concentrated in lower-status "female jobs" such as secretary, nurse, and teacher. Partly as a result, the average woman worker earns only about 65 cents for every dollar earned by a man, with black and Hispanic women faring worse than white women. Even when women make it into high-status jobs, they often experience bias not encountered by their male peers.

Are men today doing more things formerly considered "for women only"? Everyday examples of such changes are easy to find. It is not unusual these days to see a father in the delivery room assisting in the birth of his child or taking his toddler to the supermarket. In public schools, many home economics classes have gone "coed"; more boys are learning to cook and to baby-sit. Research also finds that men are spending more time with their children now than in the past (Douthitt, 1989). However, men's participation in housework and child care—*family work* as some call it—is still relatively small compared to women's. One study found that husbands' total time in child care and housework averaged only 11.2 hours per week (Robinson et al., 1977).

A surprising finding is that the amount of time a husband spends on housework and child care is *not* related to whether or not his wife has a paid job (Douthitt, 1989). On average, a husband whose wife has a 40-hour-a-week job spends no more time on household chores than does a husband whose wife is home full time! Women perform most homemaking and child care activities, regardless of whether they have a paid job or not. The only difference is that employed wives spend less time on family work (about 28 hours per week) than do full-time homemakers (about 53 hours per week). Whether or not men have increased their contributions to family work in recent years is a matter of some debate (Thompson & Walker, 1989). The undisputed fact, however, is that homemaking and child care continue to be largely "women's work."

Male Dominance

The second basic idea in traditional gender roles is that men should be the leaders both at home and in society at large. Changes are clearly occurring in both arenas. In the public section, laws denying women the vote, forbidding women to own property, and in general defining women as second-class citizens are largely a thing of the past. In recent years we've seen the first woman elected governor and the first woman appointed to the U.S. Supreme Court.

Nonetheless, the numbers of women in the power circles of society are still small. In 1988, women comprised only 5 percent of members of the U.S. Congress, and less than 16 percent of members of state legislatures (Rix, 1988). For an example closer to home, consider the college you attend. Chances are that there are many women secretaries and a few women professors, but that the chairperson of most departments, most of the deans and top-level administrators and the president are male. Women are

still very far from being equal partners in public affairs.

In personal relationships, the extent of male dominance is harder to assess. At the level of personal dispositions, men and women do not differ in their interest in power or their power motivation (Winter, 1988). However, social convention has traditionally conferred greater authority on men in dating and marriage. Until recently, for example, state laws gave husbands legal control over all family property and permitted husbands, as the "head of the household," to decide where the family should live. More informally, women were taught to "look up to" the man they married and to defer to his wishes (Bernard, 1972).

Today, people are increasingly rejecting these traditional power norms as outdated and unfair. In 1981, when Lady Diana married Prince Charles, the future king of England, she broke tradition in her wedding vows: she did not promise to obey her husband. A Westminster Abbey spokesperson explained: "Marriage is the kind of relationship where there should be two equal partners, and if there is to be a dominant partner it won't be settled by this oath" (*Los Angeles Times,* July 2, 1981, p. 18). Many other young couples seem to share this view—they believe that dating and marriage relationships should ideally be equal in power. In one study (Peplau, 1984), 87 percent of college men and 95 percent of college women said that ideally both partners in a dating relationship should have "exactly equal" influence in the relationship. It seems likely that male dominance in marriages is less pronounced than it used to be (Scanzoni & Scanzoni, 1981).

Nonetheless, couples sometimes find it hard to achieve their egalitarian ideals. Although individuals reject the abstract principle of male dominance, they often continue to follow social scripts that encourage male leadership. A recent study of dating illustrates this idea (Rose & Frieze, 1989). Researchers asked college students to list separately the actions that a man and a woman would do as each prepared for a first date, met the date, and spent time together. The typical dating script is presented in Table 14–4. Note that it is generally assumed

T A B L E   1 4 – 4

TYPICAL SCRIPT FOR A FIRST DATE

The Woman's Role	The Man's Role
Tell friends and family	*Ask for a date
	*Decide what to do
Groom and dress	Groom and dress
Be nervous	Be nervous
Worry about or change appearance	Worry about or change appearance
Wait for date	Prepare car, apartment
	*Check money
Welcome date to home	Go to date's house
Introduce parents or roommates	Meet parents or roommates
Leave	Leave
	*Open car door for date
Confirm plans	Confirm plans
Get to know date	Get to know date
Compliment date	Compliment date
Joke, laugh, and talk	Joke, laugh, and talk
Try to impress date	Try to impress date
Go to movies, show, or party	Go to movies, show, or party
Eat	Eat
	*Pay
	*Initiate physical contact
	Take date home
Tell date she had a good time	Tell date he had a good time
	*Ask for another date
	*Tell date will be in touch
Kiss goodnight	Kiss goodnight
	Go home

Note: The man's script has more elements than the woman's. The man typically takes the leadership role (see actions with asterisk).

Source: Adapted from Rose and Frieze, *Gender & Society*, Vol. 3 No. 2, June 1989. Copyright 1989 by Sociologists for Women in Society. Reprinted by permission of Sage Publications.

that the man will take the leadership role in the dating context, asking the woman for a date, deciding where they go, paying for the date, initiating physical contact, and being the one to ask for a second date. In other words, contemporary dating rules continue to cast the man as the person "in charge."

In addition, culturally based patterns of dating and marriage may continue to create situations in which women have fewer personal resources than their romantic partners. To the extent that women marry men who are older, have more education, earn more money and so on, women may be at a relative power disadvantage.

Young adults often have somewhat ambivalent attitudes toward power in dating and marriage. On the one hand, they endorse abstract democratic principles of shared decision making for male-female relationships. On the other hand, they follow traditional patterns of male-female interaction that can have the unintended consequence of giving men greater control.

In contemporary society, multiple definitions of gender roles coexist. The options available to people today, both at work and in personal relationships, are much less limited by gender than in the past.

Key Terms

androgyny	**gender self-concept**	**meta-analysis**
attribution	**gender stereotype**	**personal stereotype**
cultural stereotype	**gender typing**	**schema**
gender identity		

Summary

1. Gender is one of the most basic categories in social life. The process of labeling people, things, and activities as "masculine" and "feminine" is called gender typing.

2. Gender stereotypes are beliefs about the typical personal attributes of males and females. Cultural stereotypes are societal-level images of the sexes found in the media, art, and literature. Personal stereotypes are the unique beliefs held by an individual about the typical attributes of men and women.

3. Stereotypes are most likely to influence our perception of other people when we have little information available and when a person's gender is especially salient. One problem with gender stereotypes is that they can bias evaluation of the performance of individual men and women.

4. Gender identity, the knowledge that we are female or male, is acquired early in childhood. An important developmental milestone occurs when children come to understand that gender is constant and unchanging. Transsexuals have a severe gender identity conflict: they believe their true psychological gender is different from their biological gender.

5. Beliefs about masculinity and femininity are important elements in our self-concept. Androgynous people rate themselves high in both masculine (instrumental) and feminine (expressive) qualities. Recent research has challenged the congruence model assertion that psychological well-being is greatest among traditionally "masculine" men and "feminine" women.

6. There are four major theoretical perspectives on the causes of sex differences. A biological approach emphasizes the impact of physical differences, sex hormones, and genetics. A childhood socialization approach emphasizes ways in which we acquire relatively stable gender-typed characteristics through social learning processes. A social roles perspective emphasizes that people tend to conform to the expectations of gender-linked social roles such as husband or nurse. A final approach emphasizes that people's behavior varies from situation to situation, depending on such factors as the sex composition of the group, the nature of the task or activity, and the social expectations of others.

7. Much research has investigated sex differences in abilities and social behaviors. A new technique called meta-analysis provides a quantitative way to integrate findings from many different studies. Research finds that, on average, males are more aggressive and more likely to help a stranger (especially a female) in distress. In some situations, men may be less vulnerable to social influence. Females tend to be better at decoding nonverbal communication.

8. In daily life, women and men often use their basic talents and drives in distinctive, gender-linked ways. Traditional gender roles prescribed a division of labor by sex and conferred great power on men. Despite social change, both these traditional patterns continue. In general, however, people today are less constrained by gender than in the past.

Suggested Readings

Ashmore, R. D., & Del Boca, F. K. (Eds.) (1987). *The social psychology of male-female relations.* New York: Academic Press. An excellent collection of review articles by experts in the field. Topics include gender stereotypes, sex-role attitudes, and the nature of male-female relations at work and in personal life.

Eagly, A. H. (1987). *Sex differences in social behavior: A social-role interpretation.* Hillsdale, NJ: Erlbaum. A social role perspective on gender plus an excellent summary of research using meta-analysis.

Fausto-Sterling, A. (1985). *Myths of gender: Biological theories about women and men.* New York: Basic Books. A feminist critique of biological analyses of sex differences including sociobiology, sex differences in genes, hormones, and the brain. A readable book that assumes little prior scientific knowledge.

Henley, N. M. (1977). *Body politics: Power, sex, and nonverbal communication.* Englewood Cliffs, NJ: Prentice Hall. A classic analysis of gender differences in the use of touch, space, time, and other aspects of nonverbal behavior. Written for students and available in paperback.

Hochschild, A. (1989). *The second shift: Working parents and the revolution at home.* New York: Viking. A fascinating description of the lives of dual-worker families and their struggles to deal with changing sex roles.

Matlin, M. W. (1987). *The psychology of women.* New York: Holt, Rinehart and Winston. A basic college text on the psychology of gender. Available in paperback.

Pleck, J. H. (1981). *The myth of masculinity.* Cambridge, MA: MIT Press. A detailed analysis of research and theories of masculinity; somewhat technical, but well worth the effort.

FIFTEEN

Environmental Psychology

HUMAN SPATIAL BEHAVIOR

CROWDING

ENVIRONMENTAL STRESS NOISE

ARCHITECTURAL DESIGN

LIFE IN THE CITY

*P*eople are becoming more and more concerned about the environment. The environmental movement has focused attention on the quality of the air we breathe and the water we drink. The nightly news raises questions about the possible destruction of the ozone layer, or the impact of the destruction of the South American rain forest on weather around the globe. We are beginning to realize that virtually all aspects of the world around us can have profound and potentially negative effects on our health and well-being.

Social scientists, including psychologists, have also become concerned about how the environment affects us. Just as toxic chemicals in the air and the ground can damage physical health, so other characteristics of the environment can damage mental and social health. Noise, crowding, building design, and community structure all influence the quality of our lives and our day-to-day functioning. **Environmental psychology** is a relatively new branch of psychology that focuses on the relationship between the physical environment and human behavior and well-being (Stokols & Altman, 1987). We will consider some of the main findings of environmental psychologists, beginning with how humans use space.

HUMAN SPATIAL BEHAVIOR

How do people use the space around them to regulate their social interactions? This is one of the questions asked by environmental researchers, who use the term **proxemics** to refer to the study of human spatial behavior (Hall, 1959). A key idea is that individuals try to achieve an optimal degree of involvement and physical closeness with other people, depending on the specific situation. In other words, our use of space is one way of influencing our interaction with other people. We will consider two issues in more detail: personal space and territoriality.

Personal Space

Suppose you are standing by yourself in a physician's waiting room, and the nurse walks up to you. How close does she actually come? 3 inches? 10 inches? 2 feet? Suppose you are sitting on a park bench and a well-dressed man sits down immediately next to you. How does that make you feel? Would you feel differently if he sat 5 feet away? How close to other people do you usually stand? Does it make any difference if they are friends, strangers, or members of your family? Does it make any difference if you are standing at a party, on a bus, or in line at the post office?

As these examples suggest, people have preferred distances for social interaction, depending on who they are with and the activity. People treat the physical space immediately around them as though it were a part of themselves; this zone has been called their **personal space.** According to Sommer (1969),

> Personal space refers to an area with an invisible boundary surrounding the person's body into which intruders may not come. Like [porcupines], people like to be close enough to obtain warmth and comradeship but far enough away to avoid pricking one another. (p. 26)

In social interactions, people try to maintain an acceptable balance between being too close for comfort or awkwardly distant.

Personal space is often measured by the physical distance a person maintains from others. But personal space involves much more than physical distance. At very close distances, we can touch and smell another person, talk in hushed whispers, and see their features very clearly. At far distances, we may need to talk loudly and have quite different possibilities for social contact.

Edward Hall (1966), an anthropologist, suggested four basic zones for interpersonal interaction, shown in Figure 15–1 on p. 464. These range from the very close "intimate distance" of a lovers' embrace to the "public distance" between a speaker and the audience in a large

According to Edward Hall, there are distinct zones for interpersonal interaction. Lovers maintain "intimate distance" of less than 18 inches. A friendly conversation takes place at a "personal distance" of 18 inches to 4 feet. We use "social distance" of 4 to 7 feet for a formal business meeting.

auditorium. According to Hall, the social situation determines which of these zones people prefer. Intimate and personal distances are typically used for informal interactions with friends, family, or close associates. Social and public dis-

tances are used for more formal interactions among casual acquaintances or strangers.

Research has generally supported Hall's basic idea (Aiello, 1987). For instance, friends prefer to stand closer together than do strangers

Intimate distance, from 0 to 18 inches, is illustrated by a couple making love, by a mother nursing an infant, by wrestlers locked in a tight hold.

Personal distance, from 18 inches to 4 feet, is the distance for friendly conversation.

Social distance, from 4 to 7 feet, is the distance for a formal business meeting.

Public distance, from 12 to 25 feet, requires a loud voice and is illustrated by someone giving a lecture.

Figure 15–1. Basic zones of interpersonal interaction. (Adapted from *The Hidden Dimension* by Edward T. Hall, copyright © 1966, 1982 by Edward T. Hall. Used by permission of Doubleday, a division of Bantam Doubleday Dell Publishing Group, Inc.)

(Ashton, Shaw, & Worsham, 1980), and people who want to seem friendly choose smaller distances (Patterson & Sechrest, 1970). People who are sexually attracted to each other also stand close (Allgeier & Byrne, 1973). Although most people do not think much about personal space, we are nonetheless aware of the unwritten rules about space use in our culture. For example, we know that standing close together is usually a sign of friendship or interest. It may be one of the most important and easiest ways to tell someone we have just met that we like him or her. The other person is immediately aware of our interest, and if the person is not interested, he or she will generally move away to make that clear.

Group Differences in Spatial Behavior. Many factors affect our use of space. As an anthropologist, Hall was especially interested in cross-cultural differences. If you have traveled much outside the United States, you have no doubt noticed that people in other countries differ in how close they stand while talking. People in some cultures stand closer together than you are accustomed to, whereas people in other cultures maintain a greater distance. Cultural norms determine typical personal space preferences. White North Americans, the English, and the Swedes stand the farthest apart; Southern Europeans stand closer; and Latin Americans and Arabs stand the closest (Little, 1968; Sommer; 1969). Although much observation remains to be done in Africa, Eastern Europe, and Asia, it is clear that consistent differences exist all over the world.

These cultural differences might be considered a piece of interesting but trivial information if it were not for the fact that preferences in personal distance can sometimes have important consequences. People from cultures with different preferences may misinterpret one another's actions. Consider, for example, the possible miscommunication between a white American businessman and a Pakistani businessman when they stand next to each other to talk. The American likes to stand about 3 or 4 feet away, whereas the Pakistani would ordinarily stand much closer. Obviously, they cannot both have their way. If they are unaware of the cultural difference, they may execute a little dance around the room. The Pakistani feels uncomfortably far away and moves closer. The American feels uncomfortably close and retreats, which in turn causes the Pakistani to move closer again. Moreover, as this is going on, the Pakistani may feel the the American is being cold and unfriendly, while the American thinks the Pakistani is being overly intimate and pushy.

Personal space may also vary within a culture. As you may have guessed, men and women tend to use personal space somewhat differently (Aiello, 1987). Pairs of women stand closer together than do pairs of men, and women often tend to stand closer to whomever they are with.

Territorial Behavior

You arrive at the library to study for your midterm exam in social psychology. To your distress, every seat is taken. Most seats are physically occupied by someone, and the rest are "staked out" with coats, books, briefcases, and other markers. You consider whether or not to move someone's belongings and take the chair, but think better of it, not wanting to face an argument.

People often lay claim to a particular place as "theirs." A **territory** is an area controlled by a specific individual or group. Territorial behavior includes actions designed to stake out or mark a territory and to claim ownership. Whereas personal space is physically connected to a person—a distance from the person's body to that of other people—territories do not necessarily require physical presence. As the library example suggests, people often try to guard their territory from intrusion while they are absent.

Territorial behavior is a way that people regulate social interaction, and it can serve many specific functions (Brown, 1987). Territorial rules can simplify and bring order to daily interactions. For instance, when family members share bedrooms, they usually designate some areas for personal use. Each person has his or her own part of the closet, dresser, or side of the bed (Altman, Nelson, & Lett, 1972). Family members tend to have fixed places at the dinner table, places that are changed only when individuals eat alone or when guests are present.

Territoriality also contributes to the maintenance of privacy—control over the information others have about us and the extent to which social contact occurs. The goal of territorial behavior is not necessarily to be alone, but rather to *control* access to oneself and one's property. Finally, territorial behavior provides a way to communicate information about our self and our interests. The rose-covered white picket fence surrounding a suburban house marks the property line, but it also conveys an image of the owners.

Irwin Altman (1975) has distinguished three main types of human territories: primary, secondary, and public. Territories differ in the degree of control and ownership exerted by particular individuals. As described below in Table 15–1, a primary territory such as one's home or private office is clearly under personal control.

T A B L E 1 5 – 1	
MAJOR TYPES OF HUMAN TERRITORIES	
Type	Characteristics
Primary	A space that is owned and used exclusively by an individual or group who uses it frequently and often on a long-term basis. For example, a house or apartment is clearly owned by a person or family, controlled on a relatively permanent basis, and important in their daily lives. Unwelcome intrusions into a primary territory are a serious matter.
Secondary	A space that is used regularly, but shared with others. For example, you may always take the same seat in your chemistry lab and get annoyed if someone else sits in it before you arrive, but you know that the space is not exclusively yours. Secondary territories are semipublic, and so there is more ambiguity of ownership and control.
Public	Places such as a park or airport waiting lounge where everyone presumably has an equal right of access. For example, we may stake out a spot on the beach with a blanket and umbrella, but we know our claim is temporary; getting a choice spot depends on getting there ahead of the other beachgoers. Public territories provide little if any personal control or privacy.

A secondary territory such as a dormitory lounge, sorority house, or school cafeteria may be used regularly by members of a group. In contrast, a public territory such as a seat in an airport waiting room or on a city bus is available to all interested parties on a first-come basis. For a fascinating example of the importance of the territories, see Box 15–1 on the home field advantage in sports.

BOX 15–1

THE HOME FIELD ADVANTAGE IN SPORTS

In competitive sports, teams usually do better when playing at home than "on the road." A study of professional basketball, baseball, and football teams found that all teams won a greater percentage of their home games than games played elsewhere (Hirt & Kimble, 1982). The home field advantage was most striking for basketball, where professional teams won about 65 percent of home games but only 35 percent of away games. An analysis of the 1976–77 National Basketball Association season found that even teams that finished last in their division won nearly 60 percent of their home games (Watkin, 1978). And even the most powerful division champions performed relatively poorly on the road. Schwartz and Barsky (1977) have concluded that playing at home is as strong a factor in a team's performance as the quality of the players.

Why is it better to play on your home territory? Greater familiarity with the home field and the fatigue of travel may contribute, but they are not the whole answer (Schwartz & Barsky, 1977). Psychological factors are also important. Territorial dominance may be one explanation. Home teams may do better because they are on their own turf. Visitors may feel wary and inhibited because they are not on their home ground. An even more important factor may be the behavior of the spectators. A team usually has more fans on hand for home games. According to Schwartz and Barsky, the social support provided by the home audience is a crucial factor. They also suggested that encouragement from an audience is most effective when it is sustained for some time and when the audience is most compact (high in social density). This may explain why the home team advantage is most pronounced for indoor sports such as basketball, where spectators are in a small enclosed space, rather than for outdoor games such as football, which are played in large arenas.

Audience encouragement may influence sports performance through the process of social facilitation, discussed in Chapter 10. In this view, supportive audiences increase an athlete's arousal or motivation. When someone performs a well-learned task, increased arousal usually improves performance. Thus highly skilled athletes should benefit from heightened arousal.

In an extension of this work, Greer (1983) looked at negative behavior by fans, such as booing and hissing. Researchers observed the behavior of home and visiting men's college basketball teams over a two-year period. The researchers noted every instance of sustained crowd protest that lasted for at least 15 seconds, and then recorded the behavior of both teams during the next five minutes. Performance measures included scoring, violations, and turnovers.

Greer found that very short crowd protests occurred in virtually every game, but sustained outbursts happened only about half the time, for a total of 15 games. All protests were in support of the home team. Ten of these booing incidents were directed at the referees for calls made against the home team. In four cases, the protest expressed displeasure with referees who failed to call violations on visiting players. One protest was directed at the players on the visiting team. Following these episodes, there was a consistent improvement in home team performance and a decline in visitor performance. Greer suggested that protests by home fans may interfere with the concentration of visiting players and reduce their effectiveness.

Recently, an interesting reversal of the home

Continued

field advantage has been documented by Baumeister and Steinhilber (1984). They proposed that when a team is on the brink of winning a championship, playing before a supportive audience may lead to increased self-attention that can impair performance. In a final, decisive game, playing at home may cause players to "choke." To support their claim, the researchers examined records for baseball World Series games and for national basketball championships. Consistent with previous research, they found that playing at home was an advantage for games early in the season. But at the end of the season, teams did worse when they played at home. For example, home baseball teams won 60 percent of the first two games in the World Series, but won only 41 percent of the final games. Although playing at home is often an advantage, it may become a disadvantage when the pressure to win is greatest.

Territorial Markers. How do people mark and personalize their territories? (Brown, 1987). **Territorial markers** often serve a preventive function by letting others know that a particular area is claimed. In a study of behavior in the library, Becker (1973) found that people were least likely to select a table that was physically occupied by another person. Not surprisingly, physical presence is a strong marker. But people were also discouraged by the presence of books and personal belongings on a table; the more markers present, the greater the avoidance.

A study in a game arcade (Werner, Brown, & Damron, 1981) found that body gestures were territorial markers. A confederate stood by an electronic game called Space Invaders. The researchers varied how far the confederate stood from the machine, and whether or not the confederate placed a hand on the edge of the machine. The confederate never touched the actual controls. New players were significantly less likely to approach the machine when the confederate stood close and when he touched the machine. In public settings where it is not possible to use permanent markers, touch and physical proximity may be subtle signs of temporary "ownership."

Territorial markers also serve to display aspects of an individual's personality or interests. In one study (Vinsel, Brown, Altman, & Foss,

We use territorial markers to claim a particular space and prevent unwanted intrusions. This woman has used her sandals, bookbag, and newspaper to indicate her control of the area.

1980), photographs were taken of the wall decoration in dorm rooms of newly entering first-year university students. Virtually all students hung at least one object, such as a poster or photograph, on the wall by the bed. Women were more likely than men to use relationship items, such as personal photos; men were more likely to use impersonal items, such as a sports poster. Differences were also found between the markers of students who later dropped out of the university and those who remained in school. The decorations of continuing students showed more identification with the new school and community, such as school posters and maps of the local area. The displays of dropouts suggested a greater commitment to past life and families.

Defending and Sharing Space. Personal space and territorial behavior are used to control social interaction. On the one hand, we want to defend ourselves and our territory from unwanted "invasions." But equally important, we often want to share ourselves and our space with friends and loved ones. Thus, our reaction to someone who enters our space can vary greatly, depending on the way we define the situation.

Our attributions about the other person's motives—whether we interpret the actions as friendly, rude, or possibly even dangerous—are important. When we perceive a person's presence as an intrusion, we can either leave the situation or defend our turf. A study by Koneci and his associates (1975) illustrates the reaction of flight. They had a confederate stand very close to a person who was waiting on a corner to cross the street. In this situation, people apparently interpreted the stranger's behavior as an unwelcome invasion and crossed the street much faster than usual to escape from the stranger's presence.

At other times, however, people defend their territory and resist encroachments by others. For example, a recent study observed the reactions of people using public telephones (Ruback, Pape, & Doriot, 1989). People talked significantly longer if another person approached and stood waiting to use the phone than if no

"intruder" was present. A similar effect was found for people browsing in the open stacks of a university library. Individuals who were looking at books in a particular aisle stayed longer if another person appeared than if they were alone—a reaction consistent with the idea of defending one's space (Ruback, 1987).

Another experiment investigated the effect of having a stranger ask permission to sit next to a person (Sundstrom & Sundstrom, 1977). Confederates approached a same-sex stranger sitting on a public bench. Before sitting down, half the confederates asked permission—they asked whether it was okay if they sat down on the bench. The other half of the time, the confederates sat down without asking permission. It appears that women and men interpreted this situation quite differently. Women seem to have interpreted the request for permission as the beginning of an unwanted social contact. They left sooner when the confederate asked permission than when the confederate did not. In contrast, men seemed to have interpreted the request for permission as a sign of politeness. Men who were asked permission stayed on the bench longer than men who were not asked. The point is that our reaction to others who enter our space depends on how we interpret the situation and the person's motives.

When physical space is limited and we are forced to share it with others, we may feel crowded. The experience of crowding has been an important research topic in environmental psychology.

CROWDING

Rush-hour commuters crammed into a bus on a hot summer day are likely to feel crowded. So, too, are holiday shoppers swarming down the escalators of a department store and competing for the attention of a sales clerk. Feeling crowded can occur regardless of the amount of space we actually have available. It is more likely to be aroused when we are cramped, but we sometimes feel crowded even when we have plenty of space around us. There are times

When we must share limited space with others, we usually feel unpleasantly crowded.

when three is a crowd, no matter how much space is available. If you like to swim at deserted beaches, the presence of a few other people may make you feel that the beach is overcrowded, whereas you might not feel crowded at a party even if there were 50 other people in a fairly small room. Crowding refers to the psychological state of discomfort and stress associated with wanting more space than is available.

Researchers who study crowding find it essential to distinguish between objective measures of population density and subjective feelings of being crowded. **Social density** refers to the objective number of people in a given space. Density might be measured in terms of the number of people per square foot. **Crowding** refers to the subjective experience of feeling cramped and not having enough space. Density may or may not be unpleasant, but crowding is always unpleasant and negative, by definition. When we say we feel "crowded," we are usually complaining.

Theories of Human Crowding

When do people experience the presence of others as crowding? A number of explanations

have been given that emphasize cognitive processes—the way people perceive, interpret, and react to their social environment.

Sensory Overload. Stanley Milgram (1970) proposed that whenever people are exposed to too much stimulation, they experience sensory overload. Social density is one source of stimulation that can sometimes produce overstimulation and feelings of being crowded. Milgram believed that sensory overload is always unpleasant and interferes with a person's ability to function properly. People deal with overload by screening out some of the stimulation and attending only to what is most important.

Individual differences in reactions to social density may reflect differences in preferred level of stimulation. Some people may like high levels of stimulation—they like the radio blaring all the time, study in busy rooms, and watch television while carrying on a conversation or doing a crossword puzzle. Others like low levels of stimulation. When they work, it has to be quiet; if they watch television, they do not want any distraction. For high-stimulation people, high social density may be the right level of stimulation and so be perceived as pleasant and exciting. In contrast, for low-stimulation people, high social density may be disruptive and so be perceived as crowding. Research provides support for the importance of sensory overload, but suggests that other factors are also important (Baum & Paulus, 1987).

Density-Intensity Theory. A different explanation, offered by Jonathan Freedman (1975), is that high density intensifies usual reactions to a social situation. Just as turning up the volume on a stereo magnifies our reaction to music, so increasing density magnifies our reaction to other people. If we dislike the music, we will dislike it more when it is loud than when it is soft; if we like it, we will like it more when it is loud. Similarly, whatever our response to other people who are near us, increasing density intensifies that response. If we like them, we will like them more; if we dislike them, we will dislike them more. If we are afraid, nervous, angry, friendly, or anything else in low-density situations, we will feel more of it in high-density situations.

Some direct support for this view is provided in a series of studies by Freedman and his colleagues (Freedman, 1975). In this research, situations were deliberately made pleasant or unpleasant. Increasing density should intensify responses, making the pleasant situation more pleasant and the unpleasant more unpleasant. That is what these studies show.

Loss of Control. High density can make people feel they have less control over their actions, and so create feelings of being crowded (Baron & Rodin, 1978). The idea is that with so many people in a small space, each individual is less able to control the situation, to move around freely, or to avoid undesired contact.

This loss of control can have several negative features. Since people often want as much control as possible over their lives, simply feeling powerless or helpless is, in itself, negative. Further, high density may prevent people from maintaining a desired degree of privacy (Altman, 1975). High density may also lead to problems in the coordination of activities. When three people share a small dorm room, they may literally bump into each other, making it difficult for individuals to study or sleep when they want. Under high-density conditions, people are more likely to interfere with each other's activities, leading to feelings of frustration and anger (Schopler & Stockdale, 1977).

Research has begun to provide evidence that a lack of perceived control produces the feeling of being crowded. For example, Sherrod (1974) had students work under high-density conditions and provided some with a button that, if pushed, would signal the experimenter to remove them from the situation. Although no one actually used the button, students who were given this sense of control over their environment were less negatively affected by the high-density environment.

Closely related to control may be the ability to predict what a situation will be like. Klein and Harris (1979) told subjects to anticipate a high- or low-density room, and then confirmed or did not confirm their expectation. The results were that the objective number of people in the room

by itself had no effect. Instead, subjects did better when their expectations were confirmed than when their expectations were not confirmed. In other words, there were no negative effects of being in a high-density room so long as it was anticipated.

Attributions. A final explanation for crowding emphasizes causal attributions, a concept we first discussed in Chapter 4. According to Stephen Worchel and his colleagues, we feel crowded when we experience physiological arousal and attribute it to the excessive closeness of other people (Worchel & Teddie, 1976). In this view, the subjective experience of crowding requires two elements—a physiological state of arousal and a cognitive label attributing the arousal to the presence of too many people.

According to the attribution perspective, if people in a high-density situation can be induced to attribute their arousal to something other than the people present, they should feel less crowded. This point was demonstrated by Worchel and Yohai (1979). In their study, subjects who were falsely told that they were being exposed to stressful "inaudible noise" reported feeling significantly less crowded than did subjects in the identical situation who were given no alternate attribution for the source of their arousal.

In general, Worchel and his colleagues argue, when people can be distracted away from focusing on the people present in a situation, they should feel less crowded (Webb et al., 1986). For example, when subjects in high-density conditions were exposed to arousing (humorous, sexual, or violent) television shows, they experienced significantly less crowding than did people watching a nonarousing program under the same conditions. Indeed, people in cramped quarters rated the humorous movie as funnier and the violent movie as more violent, and tended to enjoy the arousing movies more.

It is likely that sensory overload, density intensification, loss of control, and causal attributions can all play a part in producing the experience of crowding. With these general principles in mind, we now turn to empirical studies of the psychological consequences of crowding.

Researchers have used many approaches to

study the effects of human crowding. An important distinction can be made between "inside density" and "outside density." Inside density refers to the social density in one's primary territories, such as the home, classroom, or workplace. In contrast, outside density refers to the social density of the community, school, or public transportation (Zlutnick & Altman, 1972).

Stokols (1976) has suggested that perceived crowding in primary environments may be more detrimental than crowding in one's larger community. We will consider research that illustrates these two types of crowding. First, we examine the impact of population density in cities on such social ills as crime and suicide. Then, we consider the effects of crowded living conditions in families, schools, and prisons.

Population Density in Cities

Several studies have investigated the effects of population density in the largest metropolitan areas of the United States. The measure of density is the number of people per square mile. In other words, this type of study is concerned simply with how many people live within the boundaries of the city relative to the physical size of the city. How does this measure of density affect the quality of life?

In general, urban density does not seem harmful to psychological well-being. Consider, for example, the relationship between population density and the amount of crime in cities. It has been found (Freedman, Heshka, & Levy, 1973) that there is a small but significant correlation between density and crime when only those two factors are considered. However, density tends to be highly correlated with other factors such as income, and income in turn is also highly correlated with the crime rate. It is therefore impossible to tell from the simple correlation whether density causes crime or whether some other factor, such as income, leads to both higher density and higher crime rates. This is the "third-variable" problem discussed in Chapter 1. When researchers have used statistical procedures to control for the effect of income and other social factors, the rela-

tionship between population density and crime disappears. Across the major U.S. metropolitan areas, once income is controlled, there seems to be little relationship between density and crime rates.

This result may seem surprising, given our stereotype of urban life as crowded and crime-ridden. Yet studies show that most people in major cities function well psychologically (Fischer, 1984). The incidence of mental disturbance is no higher in large cities than in smaller communities (Srole, 1972). People in cities are no more likely to commit suicide than people in smaller communities (Gibbs, 1971). In fact, urban dwellers say they are just as happy as people who live in suburbs, small towns, or rural areas (Shaver & Freedman, 1976). Research does not support the belief that urbanites are more stressed, disordered, alienated, or unhappy than ruralites (Fischer, 1984). Population density in cities is not the generally harmful factor it is often thought to be. Apparently, people can live successfully in fairly crowded public environments. But what about crowding closer to home?

Residential Density

Several studies have examined the effects of social density in households on well-being. Findings on this issue are somewhat mixed. Some studies find that people are able to live successfully in highly crowded conditions. Probably the most impressive research of this type was conducted by Mitchell (1971), who went into a vast number of homes in Hong Kong, one of the most crowded cities in the world. He measured the exact size of each family's living space, computed the density of people in the home, and took measures of anxiety, nervousness, and other symptoms of mental strain. In this study, a typical person shared a space of about 400 square feet with 10 or more people. Yet despite these cramped conditions, Mitchell found no appreciable relationship between density and pathology. Similar results were found in a study in Toronto (Booth, 1976).

Another dramatic demonstration of people's ability to cope successfully with high-density

This large migrant farm worker family shares a single small room. Researchers are investigating the psychological effects of such high residential density.

living comes from a case study of Peace Corps volunteers (MacDonald & Oden, 1973). In this study, five married couples agreed voluntarily to share an unpartitioned 30-by-30-foot room during the 12-week training program. The volunteers agreed to this experience in order to gain some insight into the hardships they might encounter once overseas. They were compared to other Peace Corps couples living in more spacious hotel rooms. Despite their very dense living conditions, the couples living communally showed no adverse effects and saw their experience as a positive challenge. They apparently developed high morale and a spirit of cooperation. Clearly, those who volunteered for the communal living arrangement may have had different personalities than the nonvolunteers, and they knew that the situation was only temporary. The point of the example, however, is that very high density living can be a positive experience under certain circumstances.

On the other hand, studies of crowded conditions in college dormitories and prisons do find evidence of psychological distress. Studies at Rutgers University (Karlin, Epstein, & Aiello, 1978) compared students living two to a room versus three to a room, all in rooms designed to hold two students. Tripled students reported significantly more stress and disappointment than doubled students. These effects were more severe for women, who attempted to make their cramped quarters into a homelike environment, than for men, who spent more time away from their rooms. Tripled students of both sexes got significantly lower grades. However, in later years when students were no longer living in high-density environments, their grades improved. In another study, students in triple rooms reported feeling less control over their environment (Baron, Mandel, Adams, & Griffen, 1976), suggesting that this may be one reason for the negative effects of tripled dorms.

Studies of prison inmates also show that higher density living is associated with more frequent health complaints and lower morale (McCain, Cox, & Paulus, 1980; Ruback & Innes, 1988).

In summary, the effects of crowded living quarters can be quite variable. Crowded living conditions are often stressful and upsetting. These effects are minimized when the crowding lasts for only a short time, and when residents have a cooperative attitude. But when residential crowding persists over time, it can lead to feelings of loss of control, frustration, and discontent (Baum & Paulus, 1987).

ENVIRONMENTAL STRESS: NOISE

The physical environment can be a major source of stress (Evans & Cohen, 1987). Some environmental stressors, such as earthquakes or

Cities are noisy places. Today, the sounds of music blaring from portable stereos often accompanies noise from cars, construction, and people.

floods, are sudden and powerful; they dramatically alter people's lives. Also important, however, are the daily hassles created by environments that expose us to noise, heat, air pollution, and other irritants. Much research on stress in the physical environment has studied the effects of noise, and we will focus our discussion on that topic.

Unless you are in a specially constructed soundproof chamber, you are always exposed to noise. For those with normal hearing, sound is one of the most important means of knowing about and experiencing the world. A silent world is virtually impossible to imagine. Psychologists are especially concerned about the effects of noise because so much of modern industrial life involves the production of noise, and because the amount of noise to which people are exposed in cities is often extremely high. Not only do traffic, construction, machinery of all kinds, and powerful stereo equipment produce noise of great intensity, but millions of people in a relatively small area create high noise levels. Just what effect does noise have on us?

Adaptation to Short-Term Noise

Sometimes we are exposed to short bursts of very loud noise—sounds of a dynamite blast from the construction site next door or the shrill barking of a neighbor's dog. Our initial reaction to a burst of very loud noise is strong. Everyone is familiar with one typical response—the so-called startle reflex. An unexpected loud noise causes us to jump, flex our stomach muscles, blink, and generally react physically. Even if we are expecting the noise, we respond physiologically with increased blood pressure, sweating, and other signs of arousal. In addition, loud noise interferes with our ability to perform tasks. We do less well on both simple and complex tasks. Clearly, loud noise is upsetting, causes physiological arousal, and prevents us from functioning at our usual level.

However, these disruptive effects generally last only a short while. The most important finding from studies of short-term noise is that people adapt very quickly. It takes only a few minutes for physiological reactions to disappear and for performance to return to normal. After 10 minutes or less, people who are subjected to short bursts of extremely loud noise behave very much like people who hear moderate or low noise. This is true even for noise levels over 100 decibels, which is roughly equivalent to a big jet coming in low over your head or a huge truck rumbling by right next to you. As long as the noise is not so loud that it actually produces pain or physical damage, people adapt to it very quickly (Glass & Singer, 1972).

You can see this effect in a study by Glass and Singer in which people were exposed for 23 minutes to one of two conditions: background noise (no noise condition) or a meaningless jumble of noise at 108 decibels in short bursts. As shown in Figure 15–2, the loud noise did cause physiological arousal, but the arousal lasted only a few minutes. Moreover, after 4 minutes, all subjects did equally well on a variety of tasks, including simple arithmetic, matching sets of numbers (deciding whether 68134 and 68243 are identical), scrambled words, and higher-level mathematics. Once they have gotten used to the noise, people perform almost any task as well with loud noise as they do in quieter environments.

There are a few important exceptions to this finding, however. In particular, noise does seem to affect performance on some kinds of tasks, especially complex ones. Donald Broadbent (1957) and others have shown that certain kinds of monitoring tasks are more difficult to do with loud noise. For example, if someone is required to watch three dials to be sure none of them goes over a certain point, high levels of noise interfere with performance. Similarly, it is apparently harder to do two tasks at the same time in a noisy environment. In one study (Finkelman & Glass, 1970), subjects had to repeat digits they heard over headphones while at the same time turning a steering wheel to track a moving line. Noise level did not affect the primary task, which was the tracking, but it made the subjects less accurate at repeating the digits. Presumably, noise is distracting and interferes with the performance of complex tasks that already strain our capacity to concentrate.

Most of the time we are only doing one thing at a time, so the effects of noise are probably quite limited. On the other hand, it is well to remember that some sensitive jobs do involve exactly the kinds of complex monitoring tasks that seem to be affected by loud noise. The pilot of a plane must watch many different dials while operating a variety of instruments, flight controllers have similar problems, and even the typical driver of a car has many things to attend to at once. It is a little frightening to realize that these critical jobs are often performed under conditions of considerable noise.

The Importance of Predictability and Control. We have seen throughout this book that our reactions to situations are influenced by our ability to predict what will happen and to control it. A series of experiments by Glass and Singer (1972) demonstrated that loud noise may have negative aftereffects if the noise is not under the control of the individual. In particular, if the noise is predictable (occurring every 60 seconds or only when there is a warning) or if the person can turn off the noise, no bad effects occur. But if the noise seems to be totally out of the control of the person, certain kinds of performance may suffer once the noise ceases.

The experiments were straightforward but ingenious. Subjects heard bursts of noise for a set period of time while they performed tasks such

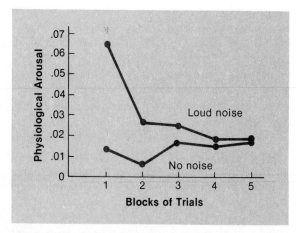

Figure 15–2. Physiological response (GSR) to loud noise. After a strong initial response, subjects adapted quickly. (Adapted from Glass & Singer, 1972, p. 29.)

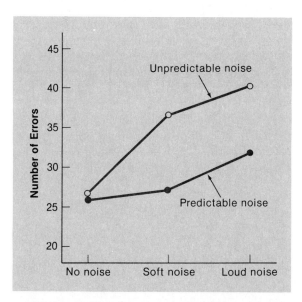

Figure 15–3. Aftereffects of predictable and unpredictable noise on proofreading accuracy. (Adapted from Glass & Singer, 1972, p. 53.)

as proofreading. Then they performed other tasks with no noise. The crucial variation was that the circumstances under which the noise occurred gave the person a sense of control or did not. In one study, people heard short bursts of loud or soft noise. The major variation was that the noise bursts came either exactly 1 minute apart (and were therefore predictable) or at random intervals. Even though subjects heard just as much noise in the two conditions, the effects were entirely different.

During the noise section of the study, all groups performed equally well regardless of how loud the noise was or whether it was predictable. But afterward, as shown in Figure 15–3, those who had heard the predictable noise performed better than those who had heard random noise. In fact, unpredictable soft noise caused more errors than did predictable loud noise. This was true despite the fact that subjects reported finding the predictable and unpredictable noise equally annoying. In other studies, subjects were given a feeling of control by telling them they could stop the noise whenever they wanted to by pressing a button or by signaling their partner, who would then stop the noise. This feeling of control was apparently enough to eliminate the negative effects. There

was no decline in performance either during or after the noise.

A later study (Sherrod, Hage, Halpern, & Moore, 1977) replicated and extended these results. Subjects were allowed to start the noise, stop it, both start or stop it, or allowed no control whatever. As in the earlier work, control reduced the negative effects of the noise. Moreover, the more control they had, the better the people performed. In this study, unlike any previous work, the presence of uncontrollable noise actually caused subjects to do less well on a proofreading task while the noise was present. In line with the earlier work, the main result was that those exposed to controllable noise performed better on problems after the noise ended.

How Noise Affects Social Behavior. In recent years, researchers have begun to investigate the impact of noise on social behaviors (Cohen & Weinstein, 1981). One finding is that noise appears to reduce attention to social cues. In one study (Cohen & Lezak, 1977), students watched slides while learning lists of nonsense syllables in a noisy or a quiet room. The slides showed people in common daily activities and in dangerous situations. For example, one slide showed two men shaking hands in front of a house; another slide showed one man threatening another with a knife in front of a house. After seeing the slides, students were unexpectedly asked questions about them. Those exposed to noise remembered significantly fewer slides than did those in the quiet condition. Similarly, in a field study (Korte & Grant, 1980) pedestrians on noisy streets were less likely to notice unusual objects on the sidewalk (such as a woman holding a large teddy bear) than were pedestrians on a quiet street. In other words, loud noise may cause people to narrow the focus of their attention and so miss social cues in the environment.

In the chapter on prosocial behavior, we reviewed several studies showing that people are less helpful in noisy situations than in quiet ones. There is also some evidence that noise can increase aggressiveness (Geen & O'Neal, 1969). In one study (Donnerstein & Wilson, 1976), students were either angered or treated in a neutral manner, and then were given an opportunity to give electric "shocks" to another person as part of a learning experiment. Angered students in a noisy room gave significantly more shocks than did nonangered students or angered students in a quiet room.

A second experiment (Donnerstein & Wilson, 1976) demonstrated that perceived control can alter the noise-aggression link. In this study, students first worked on math problems in a high-noise or no-noise condition. Later, students were able to give electric "shocks" to another person as part of a learning experiment. Some students had been angered by a confederate of the researcher; some had not. Students who had been exposed to loud noise and angered gave more shocks than did those who had not been angered or who had not been exposed to the noise. However, angered students who had been able to control the loud noise (to turn it off if they wanted to) were no more aggressive than were those not exposed to the noise, even when they did not actually use their control. These and other studies suggest that noise can sometimes increase aggressive behavior, but that this may only occur when people perceive no control over the noise and when they have an independent reason to be angry. In other words, noise may not be a direct cause of aggression, but rather may intensify preexisting aggressive tendencies.

Long-Term Exposure to Noise

Long-term exposure to noise can have detrimental effects. A large apartment house in New York City is built over a highway, and because of the design of the building, the noise levels inside are quite high. Lower floors are almost always noisier than higher ones, and this situation provides an ideal setting for a natural experiment on the effects of long-term noise. Cohen, Glass, and Singer (1973) measured reading achievement and ability to make auditory discriminations of children who had lived in the building for at least four years.

Those who lived on lower floors did worse on both measures. The louder the noise on their floor, the less well they read and the poorer their auditory discriminations. More recent studies (such as Cohen, Evans, Krantz, Stokols, & Kelly, 1981) have also found that noisy environments can impair children's intellectual performance. Studies further suggest that although people are able to adapt to short-term noise, they may not adapt to long-term noise, such as that experienced by those who live near a busy airport (Cohen & Weinstein, 1981).

ARCHITECTURAL DESIGN

One of the most fascinating questions facing environmental psychologists is how the design of buildings, roads, and shopping centers affects us. Certainly the structures we produce, the so-called **built environment,** are an extremely important part of our world. And some of them seem to "work" better than others. Some houses are pleasant to be in and function smoothly, others are drab and inconvenient. Some stores minimize congestion and generally make the shopping experience pleasant; others are cramped and uninviting. And, as we discuss in Box 15–2, some college classrooms may provide a better setting for learning than others.

Architects are concerned with making their designs work well, but by and large they have to rely entirely on their own intuition and experience. Until very recently there was no systematic research on how architectural designs affect people, and even now psychologists and sociologists are only beginning to study the problem seriously. But at least they are beginning to understand some of the ways in which designs influence people. For the moment, most of the research done by psychologists has been on the structure of college dormitories (obviously of interest to many people at universities) and the design of high-rise versus low-rise housing.

Dormitory Design

College dormitories are generally built according to two different designs. One type has single or double rooms located along a long cor-

---

BOX 15–2

Building Better Classrooms

College classrooms are often drab and dreary places. Walls are painted a variation of "institutional gray"; furniture is easy to clean, but uncomfortable and unattractive. Chairs are lined up in straight rows facing the teacher's desk or lectern. In one study, over 80 percent of students at one university rated their classrooms negatively, describing them as ugly, cramped, stuffy, and uncomfortable (Farrenkopf, 1974). Research by environmental psychologists is beginning to show that unattractive classrooms are not only unappealing, but may also affect academic performance.

In a demonstration study by Sommer and Olsen (1980), a typical small classroom was converted into what the researcher called a "soft classroom." Rows of chairs were replaced with cushioned benches around the walls, carpets were added, lighting was made softer, and colorful mobiles were hung. Students reacted enthusiastically with such comments as "It's dynamite!" or "I'm really impressed!" Comparisons of student behavior in the soft classroom and other classrooms on campus suggested that student participation in class discussion was two or three times greater in the more attractive room.

A more carefully controlled study of classroom environments was conducted by Wollin and Montage (1981). They selected two identical classrooms located side by side in the psychology building. The control classroom, which they called the "sterile classroom," had white walls, a gray carpet, and rows of plastic desks. The experimental classroom, which they called the "friendly classroom," was redecorated with the help of a design consultant. Several walls were painted bright colors, art posters were hung on the walls, large plants were added to the room, and colorful Chinese kites were hung from the ceiling. In addition to traditional desks, a part of the room was outfitted with area rugs, color-coordinated cushions, and wooded cubes to provide nontraditional seating.

The researchers investigated how these two different environments affected performance in actual college classes. Two professors teaching introductory psychology agreed to participate in the study although they were not informed of the purpose of the research. When school began, each class was randomly assigned to one of the two rooms. Halfway through the term, the classes switched rooms, so that students in both classes spent half the term in the control room and half in the "friendly" room. Students were not told they were being studied; the switch in rooms was explained as occurring because the original room was needed for videotaping.

The most striking finding from this study was that students performed significantly better on regular course exams when they were in the friendly rather than the sterile classroom. It thus appears that the physical environment can affect the amount of learning that occurs, at least as measured by scores on tests. In addition, students were asked to evaluate their instructor halfway through the term and again at the end of the term. The instructors were rated significantly more positively during the time the class met in the attractive classroom. In the experimental room, instructors were evaluated as more knowledgeable, more interesting, and better organized than they were in the control room. So our evaluations of other people are at least partly influenced by the physical setting in which we interact with them.

---

ridor, with social areas and bathrooms shared by all corridor residents. A second type has suites of room consisting of several bedrooms located around a common living room, usually with the residents of just these bedrooms sharing bathroom facilities. The amount of space available to each resident is approximately the same for both designs. Yet the two designs seem to have different effects on the residents.

A series of studies (Baum & Valins, 1977; Baum et al., 1978) compared corridor and suite arrangements. The research indicates that students who live in suite-type dormitories are more sociable and friendlier. At first glance, this seems obvious. Clearly, if you share a living room with, say, nine other people (five bedrooms with two people each), you will get to know these nine other students. In a sense, you have a "family" living situation. If you share a room with only one person, it takes greater effort to get to know other people on the floor.

As we noted in Chapter 9, proximity is one of the major factors in liking and friendship. The suite arrangement puts more people in close proximity and therefore should lead to more friendships. Thus far, this follows directly from our knowledge of the effects of proximity and certainly would be expected. The striking aspects of the work by Baum and Valin is that these sociability differences seem to carry over into the world outside the dormitory. When the students are observed in the psychology laboratory, the suite residents are friendlier than the corridor residents. For example, in one study a student arrived at the laboratory and was shown into a room in which another student (actually a confederate) was sitting. There were several chairs in the room, and the question was how close to the other student the subject would sit. Suite residents tended to sit closer than corridor residents and to initiate more conversations.

One problem with this research is that students are not always randomly assigned to rooms. Perhaps more sociable people request assignment to suites. Another problem is that suites are sometimes newer than corridor dorms, and the two types of housing are sometimes located on different parts of the campus. To overcome these problems, Baum and Davis (1980) conducted an intervention experiment. They obtained permission to assign first-year women students randomly to living conditions. To control the environment further, the researchers devised the architectural intervention shown in Figure 15–4.

Baum and Davis selected two identical long-corridor floors in the same building, each housing about 40 students. On the intervention floors, they converted several bedrooms in the middle of the corridor into lounges and installed doors to divide the corridor into two smaller units, each housing about 20 students. As a further comparison, they studied a "short" corri-

BR = Bedroom
B = Bathroom
L = Lounge

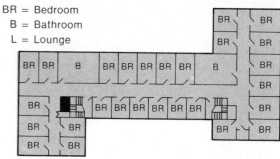

Long-corridor floor

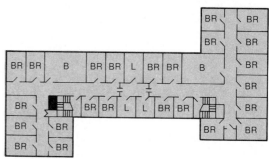

Intervention floor

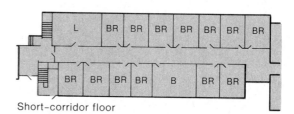

Short-corridor floor

Figure 15–4. Floor plans of the dormitory floors. The intervention floor was originally identical to the long-corridor floor but was remodeled to form two short corridors separated by doors and lounges. The short-corridor floor was in another building. (Adapted from Baum & Davis, 1980, p. 475.)

dor in another building that also housed about 20 students. In all settings, students had about the same amount of physical space, and the density was relatively high. The researchers gave questionnaires to dorm residents at the beginning of the school year and at several times during the year. They made systematic observations of social interaction in the dorm and of behavior in a laboratory situation.

The results of the experiment were very consistent with earlier findings. After living in the dorm for several weeks, residents on the short corridors reported feeling less crowded, having fewer problems regulating social contacts in the dorm, and having a greater sense of control over life in the dorm than did students in the long corridor. Short-corridor residents also reported that they were more successful in forming friends in the dorm, and they were observed to have more social interactions in lounges and corridors. In the laboratory, students who had been randomly assigned to short corridors showed greater friendliness toward a research confederate and expected to have more control over the experiment than did long-corridor residents. These results provide strong evidence that an architectural design feature—in this case the size of the residential living group—can significantly affect feelings and social interactions.

Two main factors appear to be at work in these dormitory settings. First, smaller residential units (suites and short corridors) are more conducive to group formation and friendship than are larger units. Since it is usually more pleasant to interact with friends than with strangers, dorm designs that encourage friendships are experienced as more positive. Second, smaller residential units increase students' sense of personal control over the environment. In long-corridor dorms, students are constantly required to meet and interact with many others on the floor. When they walk to the bathroom or common lounge areas, they necessarily share the corridor and facilities with many others, most of whom are not friends and with whom they might prefer not to interact.

Thus, they are overloaded with social contacts and have difficulty avoiding them. In contrast, those who live in suites or short corridors have a self-contained living unit they share only with people they get to know quite well. They therefore have much more control over their social interactions, which presumably increases satisfaction with their residence and their general sense of control over their lives.

High-Rise and Low-Rise Housing

Although students are naturally quite concerned about dormitory design, a much more serious problem for our society is how high-rise housing affects people. Since the 1950s, vast numbers of high-rise buildings have been constructed for our rapidly expanding population. Some of these buildings are huge—30 or 40 stories, with hundreds or even thousands of individual apartments. Others are smaller. But all contrast sharply with the private homes or 4-story apartment houses characteristic of previous housing. It has become a matter of great social importance to determine whether high-rise housing provides a good living environment.

The Failures: Pruitt Igoe. Some high-rise buildings have been major failures. They have gotten run down, the halls have been defaced, the apartments have been allowed to deteriorate, crime and vandalism have made the buildings unsafe, and people have moved out whenever they could. The most dramatic example of this kind of failure is the Pruitt Igoe project built in the 1950s in St. Louis. Designed by a leading architect, the complex had 33 high-rise buildings with 2,800 modern apartments. Built with public funds for low- and middle-income families, the "showcase" project soon became a disaster.

Located in the midst of an urban slum, the project never attracted middle-income families who could afford to live in better neighborhoods, and so rental revenues were less than anticipated. Teenage gangs invaded the halls and elevators to rob and terrorize residents. Walls were covered with graffiti, and physical conditions deteriorated as needed maintenance and repairs were not made. Tenants who could find other housing moved out. Ultimately, conditions worsened to such a point that the buildings were condemned and torn down. The multi-million-dollar housing project was a total loss.

Psychological Effects. On the one hand, we know that most high-rise buildings, both public and private, have been successful at least to the extent that people continue to live in them and function reasonably well. In cities such as Toronto, San Francisco, and Boston, high-rise apartments and condominiums in fashionable neighborhoods are considered very desirable. The central question addressed by environmental psychologists is whether high-rise and low-

Environmental psychologists study how housing design affects our mental health and social relationships.

rise buildings have different psychological effects on residents, and in particular, whether high-rise housing is typically harmful.

In general, research does not find major differences between the health or general well-being of those who live in high-rise versus low-rise housing. A few studies (Holahan & Wilcox, 1978; McCarthy & Saegert, 1978) have found that high-rise residents are less happy with their social relations, more concerned about safety, and feel more crowded. But other studies (Friedman, 1979; Michelson, 1977) have found the opposite: high-rise residents reported feeling more content with their buildings and more satisfied with their social relations. Overall, few consistent differences have been found.

In understanding these results, it is important to keep in mind that the experience of high-rise living can vary considerably. Living in the penthouse of a beautiful high-security apartment building is quite different from living at the top of a poorly maintained public housing

project in a rundown area. Further, it is likely that high-rise housing (or for that matter any kind of housing) may not be suitable for everyone. Although research has not produced consistent differences between high- and low-rise housing, there is no question that some people prefer one or the other.

Parents with young children often complain that high-rise housing presents great difficulties in supervising the children (Michelson, 1970). Someone who lives on the twentieth floor cannot watch a child in the playground on the street floor. Many parents are reluctant to let their young children ride elevators alone, so that even if they can play on the street, it is inconvenient to get them there. Perhaps because of this, residents of high-rise housing are often less satisfied with their housing than are people who live in their own homes. None of these differences is large or related to any noticeable differences in health or general satisfaction, but the differences do exist. In other words, people complain more about high-rise housing, even though research has not shown any actual negative effects on well-being.

As with the dormitory design studies, research on high-rise housing faces enormous difficulty in equating the residents of the various kinds of buildings. People are not randomly assigned to housing in our society, so that residents of different buildings almost always differ in potentially important ways. In cities like New York, which has many high-rise apartments, upper-, middle- and working-class families all live in high-rise buildings. Many people who can afford to live anywhere choose to live in a high-rise building in the center of New York City. In other words, high-rise buildings are not only for low-income families. But middle-class and upper-class families do generally have a choice, whereas poorer families often are forced to live in a high-rise because it is the only housing available.

This lack of choice may itself cause problems, and it should therefore probably be a matter of public policy to provide choice for all people. That is, if we continue to build high-rise apartments for low-income people, we should also provide the alternative of low-rise buildings for these same people. Although high-rise buildings may not have major harmful effects, being forced to live in one (or to live anywhere with no choice) may be psychologically harmful.

LIFE IN THE CITY

The United States and Canada are largely urban societies, with more than 70 percent of the population living in or around cities. So it is important to ask how living in cities differs from living elsewhere. This question is especially relevant today. In addition to financial problems, our cities are beset by high crime rates, rundown schools, heavy welfare rolls, and high unemployment. In recent years, public opinion about cities has become increasingly negative. In a 1978 Gallup poll asking Americans whether they would prefer to live in a city, a suburb, a small town, or on a farm, only 13 percent chose the city. Of those who actually lived in cities, only 21 percent said they preferred city living.

City dwellers are more likely than others to criticize their community and to complain about schools, housing, taxes, and lack of safety (Fischer, 1984). On the other hand, people continue to move to metropolitan areas, suggesting that cities must also hold positive attractions. In fact, as we will see, research indicates that city life does not typically have negative psychological effects on people. The city may not be to everyone's liking, but it is not inherently harmful to mental health or personal relationships.

The Urban Environment. The experience of living in cities is affected by both the physical and the social environment (Fischer, 1984). Physically, big cities are typically noisier, dirtier, and more polluted than are small towns.

City dwellers often encounter crowds of people, traffic congestion, massive skyscrapers, noise and air pollution. Do the benefits of city living outweigh these potential costs?

Urban population density often necessitates high-rise apartments rather than single-family homes. In the city, trees and grass give way to concrete and asphalt. But although such factors as noise and high-rise buildings may be unpleasant, they do not necessarily have negative psychological consequences. Further, cities offer many advantages that may compensate for the difficulties of urban life. It is in cities that we find major art museums, theaters, and concert halls, the latest medical technology, financial and political centers, and specialized stores and services.

The social context of city living also differs from that of towns and rural areas. High social density is the hallmark of the city, and urbanites are more often exposed to crowds. Cities also have people from many ethnic, racial, and religious backgrounds. The social composition of cities differs from that of small towns. Cities tend to attract people who are younger, less likely to be married, have fewer children, and are higher in socioeconomic status. New immigrants are also likely to gravitate to urban centers. Do these differences in the physical and social environment of cities harm city dwellers?

Physical and Mental Health. In terms of physical and mental health, living in a town versus a city is not an important factor (Fischer, 1984). Whatever advantages people in small communities may have in terms of lower stress and a more healthful environment are apparently offset by the urbanite's greater access to health care services. Rates of mental disturbance and psychosis are about the same for those who live in cities, small towns, and even rural communities (Srole, 1972). Nor do city people feel any more anxious or unhappy than other people.

In a survey of a large number of Americans (Shaver & Freedman, 1976), those who lived in cities said that they were just as happy and calm as did those who lived in small town or rural areas. These findings are all the more striking since city dwellers do report less satisfaction with their living environment than do those who live outside of cities. Apparently dissatis-faction with facets of city living does not affect people's personal feelings of happiness and overall life satisfaction.

A study (Franck, 1980) of people who had recently moved to New York City or to a small town in upstate New York sheds light on this finding. The newcomers in this research were all beginning graduate students who were interviewed during the first year in their new environment. Newcomers to New York City were more likely than those in the small town to report that the move increased their fears about crime and safety, and made them more distrustful of other people. City residents were more likely to report being stressed by exposure to panhandlers, drunks, addicts, and "crazies."

However, the big city people also reported many compensating positive features of the urban experience. They came to enjoy the variety of people they saw in the city and felt that they had become more broadminded. In other words, city life has not only unique problems, but unique pleasures as well.

Social Relations. It has been suggested that one of the most pernicious effects of urban life may be to weaken social relationships. Sociologist George Simmel (1903) thought that city residents would be so overloaded by superficial contacts that they would have fewer intimate friends than those who live in smaller communities. However, despite the common belief that life in the big city leads to alienation and social isolation, empirical research seriously challenges this view.

In a large-scale survey study, Claude Fischer (1982) obtained detailed information about the social relations of more that 1,000 people living in large cities, suburbs, small towns, and semi-rural areas in northern California. Overall, no differences were found between city dwellers and others in the number of their social ties or the quality of their relations. For example, city dwellers were as likely as townspeople to report having someone they could talk to about personal matters; the overall level of social support available to an individual was not related to community size.

Fischer did find, however, that people in cities differed somewhat in the types of relationships they have. Urbanites reported fewer ties to relatives, neighbors, or church groups, and more ties to friends, co-workers, and others with similar interests or hobbies. Fischer explains this pattern in terms of self-selection. For instance, city dwellers are more likely to be young, foreign-born, or unmarried—all factors that would reduce relations with relatives and increase ties to friends and associates. The important point is that those who live in big cities report just as much "social connectedness" as those who live in smaller communities.

The newcomer study adds further to this portrait of city life. Franck (1980) found that newcomers to New York City and to a smaller town were equally successful in making friends, but it took the city dwellers somewhat longer to do so. Shortly after arriving, city dwellers reported having fewer friends than those in the small town, but several months later this difference had disappeared. City dwellers said they found it harder to make friends, but ultimately they had just as many friends as people in the smaller community.

The one aspect of social relations that is affected by community size is interaction with strangers (Korte, 1980). We have already seen that city dwellers are more fearful of crime, more concerned about their personal safety, and more distrustful of others. Perhaps not surprisingly, people in cities are less likely to help a stranger in distress than are people in smaller communities (see Chapter 12). Research has found that in urban environments people are usually less likely to help someone who dials a wrong telephone number, to return a "lost" letter, to do small favors, to help a lost child, or to let a stranger use a phone (Korte, 1980).

Diversity of Lifestyle. Although city dwellers are less helpful to strangers, they are also more accepting of others whose lifestyles differ from their own. The populations of small towns tend to be more homogeneous than do those of cities with respect to race, religion, ethnic background, sexual orientation, political views, and just about anything else you can think of. People who do not fit comfortably in a small town often seek like-minded companions in the big city. Cities tend to attract people who are "different" from the average, and to treat these groups better. It is not surprising, for example, that the largest and most visible homosexual communities are found in major metropolitan areas. It is not that cities produce alternate lifestyles, but rather that city dwellers are more accepting of individual differences.

In fact, one study (Hansson & Slade, 1977) found that city people were actually more helpful toward an extremist group, in this case the Communist party, than were people in small towns. In this study, the experimenters dropped letters that were addressed to an individual, to someone who was apparently performing at the "Pink Panther Lounge," or to the Communist party headquarters. The researchers counted how many of each "lost" letter were returned. The townspeople returned somewhat more letters to the individual and the Pink Panther Lounge, but many fewer to the Communist party. The authors concluded that people in small towns may be somewhat more helpful as long as the person in need belongs to an acceptable category; the city people were much more helpful toward nonconformists.

By this point, it should be clear that reactions to the city depend on the particular individual. Just as some people like high levels of stimulation and others do not, so some people are city lovers and others are not. Individuals have optimal levels of stimulation, which may actually change as they live in one type of environment or another (Geller, 1980). If you like a high level of stimulation, you may enjoy cities, find them exciting and invigorating, and dislike small towns as dull and uninteresting. The key issue is the match between the person's characteristics and the community. Indeed, research indicates that people who do not like their community (whatever it is) tend to be less happy and healthy (Shaver & Freedman, 1976). Although the size of the community does not affect happiness, an individual's satisfaction with the community does.

Key Terms

built environment

crowding

environmental psychology

personal space

proxemics

social density

territorial markers

territory

Summary

1. Environmental psychology considers how the physical environment affects people's behavior and well-being. Major topics in environmental psychology include how humans use space, crowding, noise, the design of buildings, and life in the city.

2. Proxemics is a general term for the study of how people use space. Personal space refers to the physical space immediately around a person that the person treats as an extension of the self. The distance we prefer to stand from other people depends on our ethnic or cultural background, our gender, and our relation to the other people. Hall has distinguished four basic zones for interpersonal interaction: intimate, personal, social, and public distance.

3. A territory is an area controlled by a person or group. Altman has distinguished primary, secondary, and public territories. People use various markers to identify and lay claim to their territory. Our reaction to someone who enters our territory depends on how we interpret the act—as friendly, rude, hostile, and so on.

4. Crowding is the subjective experience of feeling cramped and not having enough space. In contrast, social density refers to the objective number of people in a given area. According to the sensory overload theory of crowding, high social density creates an unpleasantly high level of stimulation. According to the density-intensity theory, high social density intensifies usual reactions to a social situation, making bad situations worse and good ones better. A third view is that high density may cause people to experience a distressing loss of personal control. A final perspective is that we feel crowded when we attribute our physiological arousal to the presence of too many people.

5. Research shows that crowding does not always have harmful consequences. High population density in cities is not necessarily a cause of crime or mental illness. In some situations, however, high density can be harmful. For example, students living in tripled dorm rooms and prisoners sharing cramped cells may show signs of distress. High density is probably most harmful when it interferes with accomplishing specific goals and when it is associated with a perceived loss of control.

6. Noise affects us less than we might think. If noise is not so loud that it causes physical damage, people usually adapt to short exposure to loud noise and perform most tasks at their normal level. Only complex tasks seem to be impaired by short-term loud noise. Prolonged exposure to loud noise can have negative effects on hearing and intellectual performance.

7. Architectural design can influence people's behavior. College students who live in suite-type dormitories and in small living units are more sociable and friendlier than those who live on long corridors. Smaller residential units may make it easier to form friendships and may also increase a sense of personal control. However, high-rise housing is not necessarily worse than low-rise housing.

8. Urban living is not generally less healthy than living in other kinds of communities. People often find that the difficulties of city life are offset by the advantages of living in a cultural and business center. The effect of community size depends on the preferences and characteristics of the individual.

Suggested Readings

Cohen, S., Evans, G. W., Stokols, D. S., & Krantz, D. S. (1986). *Behavior, health and environmental stress.* New York: Plenum. Considers the impact of environmental stress on human behavior and well-being.

Fischer, C. S. (1984). *The urban experience,* 2nd ed. New York: Harcourt Brace Jovanovich. A readable textbook that reviews research and theories about life in cities.

Fisher, J. D., Bell, P. A., & Baum, A. (Eds.). (1984). *Environmental psychology,* 2nd ed. New York: Holt, Rinehart and Winston. A comprehensive survey of the field of environmental psychology.

Jones, D. M., & Chapman, A. J. (Eds.). (1984). *Noise and society.* New York: John Wiley. A detailed look at the effects of noise.

Seligman, C., & Syme, G. J. (1989) Managing the environment. *Journal of Social Issues, 45* (2). This special issue of the journal explores the role of social science in helping to protect and preserve our natural environment.

Sommer, R. (1969). *Personal space: The behavioral basis for design.* Englewood Cliffs, NJ: Prentice-Hall. A classic discussion of the topic.

Stokols, D., & Altman, l. (Eds.). (1987). *Handbook of environmental psychology.* New York: John Wiley. This two-volume collection of chapters by leading experts provides a professional-level overview of current research and theory in the field.

SIXTEEN

Health Psychology

HEALTH BEHAVIORS   **STRESS AND ILLNESS**

COPING WITH STRESSFUL EVENTS

SYMPTOMS, ILLNESS, AND TREATMENT

SOCIAL PSYCHOLOGICAL PERSPECTIVES ON CHRONIC ILLNESS

M ost of us think about our health in physical terms. Either we are sick or we are healthy, and we know which state we are in on the basis of the cues we get from our body. However, as the following anecdotes suggest, health is a psychological issue as well as a physical one.

☐ Bob, a 22-year-old member of the tennis team, has been told to stop smoking because it is sapping his energy during matches. He wants to stop, but so far, he has been unable to do so.

☐ Lisa broke up with her boyfriend last week, and she faces a major test in her chemistry course next week. She has just come down with the flu.

☐ Ellen recently went to see a physician about her headaches. The doctor was cold and aloof, and seemed to dismiss her complaints as trivial. She has decided not to follow her doctor's advice, but instead to go to a relaxation training course to see if it can help her.

☐ Mark, who is currently 19, has suffered from diabetes since he was 12 years old. Although he knows he should inject himself with insulin twice a day, he sometimes "forgets" and has ended up in the hospital as an emergency case four times in the last six months.

The realization that health is a psychological as well as a physical issue has given rise to an exciting new field, health psychology. The psychological study of health considers four main areas: (1) promoting and maintaining health; (2) preventing and treating illness; (3) identifying the causes and correlates of health, illness, or other dysfunctions; and (4) improving the health care system and the formation of health policy (Matarazzo, 1980; Rodin & Salovey, 1989).

An important lesson of health psychology is that health is not a purely physical matter, but rather a **biopsychosocial state.** According to the **biopsychosocial model,** a person's state of health is a complex interaction of several factors: biological factors such as a genetic predisposition to a particular disease or exposure to a flu virus, psychological factors such as the experience of stress, and social factors such as the amount of social support one receives from one's friends and family. Once we recognize that psychological and social factors as well as biological ones are involved in health and illness, it is clear that good health is something that everyone achieves by engaging in a healthy life-style, rather than something merely to be taken for granted.

HEALTH BEHAVIORS

At one time, our major health problems involved infectious diseases such as influenza, pneumonia, and tuberculosis. Now, however, these problems have been largely brought under control. Currently, the major health problems faced by citizens of industrialized nations are "preventable" disorders such as heart disease, cancer, and diabetes. These problems are called preventable because they result at least in part from health behaviors which people can control. For example, annual cancer deaths in the United States could be reduced by 25 to 30 percent if everyone stopped smoking (American Cancer Society, 1989). Deaths due to heart disease would decline substantially if people lowered the cholesterol in their diet, stopped smoking, and reacted more effectively to stress (American Heart Association, 1984). Deaths due to vehicular accidents could be reduced by 50 percent if simultaneous drinking and driving were eliminated (DHHS, 1981). An examination of the nation's health goals for 1990 (see Table 16–1), developed by the Department of Health and Human Services, clearly shows that the majority of these goals are related to life-style factors.

What Is a Health Behavior?

Health behaviors are actions undertaken by people who are healthy to enhance or maintain

T A B L E 1 6 – 1

FIFTEEN SPECIFIC WAYS TO IMPROVE HEALTH FOR AMERICANS BY THE YEAR 1990

In the 1970s the U.S. Department of Health and Human Services, under Patricia Harris, developed a set of goals to improve the health of the American populace. These goals served as targets for intervening in local health services. The important point to note in this list is how many to them involve life-style changes and behavior modification.

A. *Preventive Health Services*
1. Teaching people how to control high blood pressure
2. Implementing programs of effective family planning
3. Establishing programs to improve health care for pregnant women and infants
4. Establishing effective immunization programs for children and at-risk adults
5. Educating adolescents and adults regarding the control of sexually transmitted diseases

B. *Health Protection*
6. Managing toxic chemicals and wastes
7. Developing and implementing effective occupational safety and health standards
8. Developing procedures to reduce accidents (especially vehicular accidents) and injuries
9. Fluoridating water and improving preventive dental helath care
10. Surveillance and control of infectious diseases

C. *Health Promotion*
11. Reducing smoking
12. Reducing the misuse of alcohol and drugs
13. Developing programs for effective nutrition
14. Improving physical fitness and increasing exercise
15. Developing effective techniques for the control of stress and violent behavior

Source: Adapted from Harris (1980); Matarazzo (1983).

their good health. The importance of basic health habits was illustrated in a classic study conducted by Belloc and Breslow (1972). These scientists began by defining seven health habits: sleeping 7 to 8 hours a night, not smoking, eating breakfast each day, having no more than one or two alcoholic drinks each day, getting regular exercise, not eating between meals, and being no more than 10 percent overweight. They then interviewed 6,000 residents of Alameda County, California, and asked them to indicate which of these behaviors they regularly practiced. The residents were also asked to indicate how many illnesses they had had, how much energy they had, and how disabled they had been (for example, how many days of work they had missed) over the previous 6 to 12 months. The more health behaviors people practiced, the fewer illnesses of all kinds they reported having, and the more energy they said they had.

Unfortunately, few people follow all these good health behaviors. Although most of us practice some, such as not smoking or keeping our weight down, most of us violate at least a few others, such as not getting enough sleep or not exercising as much as we should (Steele, Gotmann, Leventhal, & Easterling, 1983). Some of the worst offenders are college students. Why is this the case? Most of the country's major health problems strike older people and are uncommon among college students. Therefore, these diseases often seem very remote to a student. It may seem almost impossible that the health habits developed in adolescence and

Poor health habits such as smoking are responsible for the major causes of death in this country. Unfortunately, they often begin early in life before people realize the damage their actions will produce.

young adulthood could possibly influence health so many years away (Maddux, Roberts, Sleddin, & Wright, 1986). Yet this is clearly the case.

Health Attitudes and Health Behaviors

Since health behaviors are so essential to good health, it is important to understand the attitudes that lead people to practice good health behaviors or to continue to practice faulty ones. The practice of health behaviors centers on five sets of beliefs (Hochbaum, 1958; Rosenstock, 1966; Bandura, 1986; Rogers, 1984).

1. *General health values,* including interest in health and concern about health

2. The perception that the *threat to health* posed by a disorder is severe

3. A belief in *personal vulnerability* to a disorder

4. A belief that one is able to perform the response necessary to reduce the threat (*self-efficacy*)

5. A belief that the response will be effective in overcoming the threat (*response efficacy*)

To understand these points, consider the experience of one of our students a few years ago. This student (call him Bob) was the only person in the class who smoked, and he was the object of some pressure from the instructor and the students to quit. Although he acknowledged that smoking is linked to both lung cancer and heart disease, he believed that the links are fairly weak. Moreover, because he was in good health and played a number of sports, he felt relatively invulnerable to these diseases. However, over Thanksgiving vacation, Bob went home to a large family gathering and discovered to his shock that his favorite uncle, a chain smoker all his adult life, had lung cancer and was not expected to live more than a few months. Suddenly his general health became a

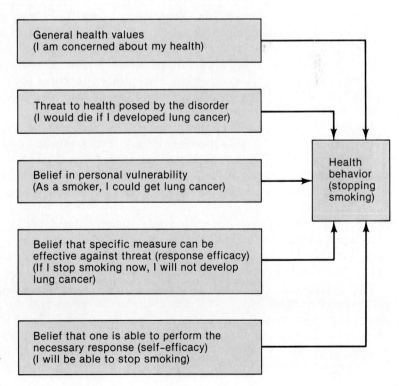

Figure 16–1. The relation of health attitudes to health behaviors.

more salient value for Bob. Bob's feelings of vulnerability to lung cancer changed dramatically because now a member of his own family had been affected Moreover, he came to realize in graphic fashion how severe the outcome of smoking can be. Bob's perceptions of the need to stop smoking changed as well. He concluded that stopping might be sufficient to ward off the threat of disease (response efficacy). Moreover, he developed a belief in his own self-efficacy, that he would be able to stop. When Bob returned from Thanksgiving vacation, he had stopped smoking altogether. These relations are diagrammed in Figure 16.1.

Generally, understanding these *health beliefs* has done a good job of predicting health behaviors as varied as flu immunizations (Cummings, Jette, & Rosenstock, 1978), smoking reduction/cessation (Kaufert, Rabkin, Syrotuik, Boyko, & Shane, 1986), exercise (Wurtele & Maddux, 1987), and genetic screening (Becker et al., 1975), as well as the practice of breast self-examination (Calnan & Moss, 1984), the use of condoms by gay men to avoid exposure to HIV (the virus that causes AIDS) (Coates, Morin, & McKusick, 1987), and dieting to control obesity (Uzark, Becker, Dielman, & Rocchini, 1987).

A final attitudinal component that predicts health behavior has been added by Fishbein and Ajzen's theory of reasoned action that we considered in Chapter 5 (Ajzen, 1985; Ajzen & Fishbein, 1977; 1980; Ajzen & Madden, 1986; Fishbein, 1980). The theory of reasoned action maintains that a behavior is a direct result of a behavioral intention. To take the specific case of dieting to reduce cholesterol, suppose that your father believes cholesterol is a threat to his health and that the outcome (namely, a potential heart attack) is serious. Suppose he also believes he could change his diet in a healthier direction and believes that if he were to do so, it would reduce his risk. He still may not be inclined to undertake the behavior. Knowing if he *intends* to change his diet, then, also adds a certain amount of predictability in trying to understand who will practice health behaviors when (e.g., Gielen, Eriksen, Daltroy, & Rost, 1984; Valois, Desharnis, & Godin, 1988).

Through understanding the determinants of health behaviors, it may be easier to see why so few people actually practice good health behaviors overall. The smoker may decide that it is too hard to change (low self-efficacy). The nonexerciser may believe that exercise alone would not reduce the risk of a particular disease (low-response efficacy). The obese individual may not perceive that being overweight is actually a threat to her health (low perceptions of threat). For a health behavior to occur, all these beliefs must fall into place, and there are any number of beliefs or rationalizations a given person may have for not undertaking a particular health behavior.

Changing Health Attitudes

Research on health attitudes is useful not only because it helps us predict who will practice a particular health behavior. It also explains the conditions under which people might change their health behaviors. In theory, by designing persuasive messages that increase feelings of vulnerability while simultaneously increasing feelings of self-efficacy and response efficacy, one could get people to modify their behavior in a healthy direction. But how would we get this information out to people? One of the goals of preventive health education is to reach as many people as possible, as through the mass media. We have all been exposed to televised or radio messages urging us to increase the fiber in our diet, reduce our cholesterol, or stop smoking. How successful are these messages?

Unfortunately, evaluation of these efforts suggests somewhat limited success (Atkin, 1979; Lau, Kane, Berry, Ware, & Roy, 1980). Mass media communications seem to bring about changes in health attitudes but only modest changes in behavior. A classic study conducted by the Stanford Heart Disease Prevention Program (Meyer, Nash, McAlister, Maccoby, & Farquhar, 1980) illustrates this point. These researchers developed a mass media intervention designed to get people to change their health habits and reduce their risk of heart disease. Three communities of similar size and social composition were identified and evaluated concerning risk factors associated with heart disease both before and after the study. The risk factors examined included smoking, diet, and exercise.

One town served as a control group and received no campaign. The second and third towns were both exposed to a mass media campaign concerning smoking, diet, and exercise over a 2-year period. In the third town, the media campaign was supplemented by face-to-face instruction in the modification of risk factors directed at those people at highest risk for heart disease.

The results indicated modest attitude change and behavior change in the community exposed only to the mass media campaign. The residents

IS THIS WHAT YOUR KISSES TASTE LIKE?

If you smoke cigarettes, you taste like one.
Your clothes and hair can smell stale and unpleasant, too.
You don't notice it, but people close to you do.
Especially if they don't smoke.
And non-smokers are the best people to love.
They live longer.   **AMERICAN CANCER SOCIETY**
This space contributed by the publisher as a public service.

Mass media messages designed to change health behaviors can be effective in inducing the motivation to change, but alone they may produce little behavior change.

were more knowledgeable about risk factors, and they reported that they had reduced their consumption of dietary cholesterol and fats somewhat. There was also some evidence that blood pressure and blood cholesterol levels had been reduced. However, much more dramatic and lasting effects were found when the media campaign was coupled with behavioral instruction for individuals at highest risk (Leventhal, Nerenz, & Strauss, 1980).

This study illustrates two important points. Media may be quite effective in informing people about risks and in gradually changing public opinion about health practices over time (Lau et al., 1980; Leventhal & Cleary, 1980; Mogielnicki et al., 1986). They are not, however, in themselves necessarily effective in modifying behavior. Second, what is often needed to modify health behavior successfully is intensive training directly targeted to those at risk for a particular health problem.

Cognitive Behavioral Approaches to Health Behavior Modification

But how do we modify behavior? Increasingly, those who want to alter stubborn health behaviors have focused on the specifics of each individual's habits, health cognitions, and environment that may promote a faulty health behavior or undermine the practice of a desirable new one. This approach, which comes out of social learning theory (Chapter 1), is called cognitive-behavior therapy (Lazarus, 1971; Thoresen & Mahoney, 1974).

Consider, for example, the case of a woman who is 40 pounds overweight and at risk for heart disease. To get her to reduce her weight, first one needs to understand her eating, the factors that give rise to it, and the stimuli that are associated with it. To address these issues, a psychologist might begin an intervention for weight reduction by having her systematically observe her eating, a procedure termed *self-monitoring* (Abel, Rouleau, & Coyne, 1987; Thoresen & Mahoney, 1974). She would be trained to take notes about her eating and the circumstances under which it occurred. The psychologist might then attempt to alter the stimuli that are associated with eating. For example, if this woman eats while she is watching television, she might be retrained only to eat at the kitchen table with the television off. By removing the association of television with food, one of the enjoyable factors associated with overeating would thereby be removed. Similarly, the presence of desirable and fattening foods like cookies and ice cream might also act as stimuli for eating, and so this woman might be urged to clear her refrigerator and shelves of these foods. Next she might be taught to reward herself for changing her eating patterns. For example, she might be encouraged to set up a schedule of projected weight goals and then be told to reinforce herself with some pleasurable activity such as going to a movie each time she met a particular weight-loss goal. She might also be encouraged to use techniques of self-punishment. For example, if she failed to bring her eating under control and ate forbidden foods, she might punish herself by unplugging her television for a day or two.

The thoughts people have about their health habits also influence the practice of those health habits. In particular, cognitions about one's sense of self-efficacy or self-control are especially important (Abel et al., 1987; Bandura, 1986b; Thoresen & Mahoney, 1974). For example, this woman might inadvertently undermine her diet by thinking, "I'll never be able to do this" or "I've tried to diet many times before and always been unsuccessful." Teaching her to think positively ("I'm going to be successful at this") can help promote health habit change. To increase the sense of personal control, a person may be given behavioral assignments to complete at home that will help further the goals of the health behavior change program. For example, our obese woman might be encouraged to keep a log of her eating each day (Cox, Tisdelle, & Culbert, 1988; Shelton & Levy, 1981).

Psychologists recognize that many health behaviors are related to social factors (Chaney, O'Leary, & Marlatt, 1978). For example, smoking or overeating may occur primarily in social settings to control anxiety. Accordingly, psychologists may encourage smokers or over-

eaters to join social-skills training programs or assertiveness training programs so that they can develop new social skills to substitute for their old faulty health behaviors. Our overweight woman might be taught effective social skills to prevent overeating at parties.

The kind of cognitive behavioral change program described here is called *broad-spectrum cognitive-behavioral therapy* because it draws on a wide variety of behavior change techniques (Lazarus, 1971). Such programs have shown at least modest effectiveness in modifying problems of alcohol abuse (DHHS, 1981), smoking (Leventhal & Cleary, 1980), and obesity (Brownell, 1982; Lovibond, Birrell, & Langeluddecke, 1986). Some of these programs are undertaken individually with private therapists. Others are implemented through self-help groups, such as Overeaters Anonymous or Alcoholics Anonymous. In other cases, the schools may be the target for an intervention, such as programs designed to prevent children from beginning to smoke, and worksite interventions have increasingly been used to help people change their health habits (e.g., Cataldo, Green, Herd, Parkinson, & Goldbeck, 1986). Box 16–1 describes one cognitive-behavioral intervention that has been used with college students to control drinking.

It is very easy to get people to agree to stop smoking, to lose weight, and/or to change their diet for short periods of time. Unfortunately, the problem comes in in long-term maintenance. Most people exposed to most health behavior modification programs return to their unhealthy behavior, a problem termed relapse. Consequently, it is important that relapse prevention techniques be integrated into treatment programs from the outset (Brownell, Marlatt, Lichtenstein, & Wilson, 1986). One useful method of *relapse prevention* is getting people to identify high-risk situations for relapse. For example, an exsmoker might identify being in a bar, having a cup of coffee after dinner, or playing poker with friends as likely trigger situations for resuming smoking. The person would then be encouraged to think of ways to avoid those situations or to substitute better responses that would make relapse less likely. The exsmo-

Box 16–1

The Drinking College Student

Between 70 and 96 percent of U. S. college students drink alcohol, and as many as 15 to 25 percent of them are heavy drinkers (Kivilan, Coppel, Fromme, Williams, & Marlatt, 1989). If anything, these statistics are increasing, as college women begin to drink as heavily as college men. Many colleges have tried to deal with the heavy drinking problem by providing educational materials about the harmful effects of alcohol (Kivilan et al., 1989). However, the information conflicts markedly with the personal experiences of many college students who find drinking in a party situation to be satisfying, even exhilarating behavior. Moreover, most college students do not see drinking as a problem (Baer, Kivlahan, Fromme, & Marlatt, 1988), but rather regard it as a natural outgrowth of their social environment. Consequently, motivating students even to attend alcohol abuse programs, much less to follow their recommendations, is difficult.

Therefore, some of the more successful efforts to modify college students' drinking have encouraged students to gain self-control over drinking, rather than explicitly trying to get them to reduce or eliminate alcohol altogether. These programs typically begin by getting students to monitor their drinking and to understand what blood alcohol levels mean and what their effects are. Often, merely monitoring one's drinking and recording the circumstances in which it occurs actually leads to a reduction in drinking (Alden, 1988, cited in Baer et al., 1988).

The consumption of alcohol among students is heavily under the control of peer influence and the need to relax in social situations (Collins & Marlatt, 1981; Murphy, Pagano, & Marlatt, 1986). Thus, many intervention programs include a skills-training component designed to get students to find alternative ways to relax and have fun in social situations. Since alcohol use is also related to negative emotional states such as anxiety or depression (Marlatt, 1987), training in alternative ways to relax can sometimes improve mood overall.

To gain personal control over drinking, students are first taught to identify the circumstances in which they are most likely to drink and especially to drink to excess. Then students are taught specific coping skills so that they can moderate their alcohol consumption. For example, one technique for controlling alcohol consumption in high-risk situations such as a party is "placebo drinking." This involves either the consumption of nonalcoholic beverages while others are drinking, or the alternation of an alcoholic with a nonalcoholic beverage to reduce the total volume of alcohol consumed.

Finally, students are encouraged to engage in "life-style rebalancing" (Marlatt & George, 1988). This involves developing a healthier diet, engaging in aerobic exercise, and making other positive health changes, such as stopping smoking. As the student comes to think of himself or herself as health oriented, excessive alcohol consumption becomes incompatible with other aspects of the new life-style.

Evaluations of eight-week training programs with college students involving these components have shown a fair degree of success. Students reported significant reductions in their drinking, compared to a group that received only educational materials about the dire effects of excessive drinking. Moreover, these gains persisted over a year-long follow-up period (Baer et al., 1988).

ker, for example, might avoid bars altogether and play poker only with friends who do not smoke.

Another aspect of relapse prevention is called life-style rebalancing (Marlatt & George, 1988; Marlatt & Gordon, 1985). By getting exercise, changing diet in a healthy direction, trying to reduce stress, and drawing on the social support of others, people alter their life-style generally in a healthy direction, and this change may help them to increase adherence to any particular health habit change as well. While there is currently no foolproof method of relapse prevention, researchers have identified relapse prevention as the most important target for additional work, given the high rate of relapse that does occur (Taylor & Aspinwall, 1990).

Health habits alone are not sufficient to ward off the threat of illness, although they help substantially. Stressful life experiences and the ways people cope with those stressful events also have an impact on health and illness. We examine these issues in the next section.

STRESS AND ILLNESS

Most of us have more experience with stress than we care to remember. Stress is discovering that your alarm clock did not go off the morning of a major test or finding out that your car won't start when you need to drive to a job interview. The experience is fundamentally a physiological one. Your body moves into a state of heightened arousal, your mouth goes dry, your heart beats faster, your hands may shake a little, and you may perspire more heavily.

Most of us think of these experiences as unnerving but temporary, not producing any lasting damage. However, researchers now believe that over time, stress can wear down the body, making it more vulnerable to illness. Repeated exposure to stressful events and repeated engagement of the physiological changes that accompany stress (increased blood pressure, blood sugar level, respiration, and the like) exert wear and tear on the physiological system. This, in turn, may lay the groundwork for a variety of disorders, including heart disease, hypertension, and even cancer (e.g., Jemmott & Locke, 1984; Friedman & Rosenman, 1974; Selye, 1956, 1976).

But what is **stress**? Most of us think of stress as intrinsic to particular events such as being stuck in traffic, getting a poor grade on a test, being late for an appointment, or losing a notebook. Yet despite some commonalities in the experience of stress, not everyone perceives the same events as stressful. For example, one person may experience a job interview as threatening, while another may welcome it as a challenge. The fact that stress is, to some degree, in

the eye of the beholder makes it clearly a psychological process. That is, events are stressful when they are regarded as stressful and not otherwise (Lazarus, 1966; Lazarus & Folkman, 1984).

What Makes Events Stressful?

Some types of events are more likely to be appraised as stressful than others. Any event that requires a person to adjust, make changes, or expend resources has the potential to be stressful. For example, although Christmas is usually viewed as a positive event, it may also be highly stressful, since it can involve last-minute shopping, extensive travel, social occasions with relatives, excessive consumption of alcohol and rich food, and little sleep.

Negative or unpleasant events are more likely to be perceived as stressful than positive ones. For example, a $20 parking ticket typically causes a person more distress than does spending $20 to go to a noisy, crowded rock concert, even though the latter experience may actually be more physiologically arousing. Unpleasant events cause people more psychological distress and produce more physical symptoms than do more positive stressful events (e.g., McFarlane, Norman, Streiner, Roy, & Scott, 1980; Myers, Lindenthal, & Pepper, 1972; Sarason, Johnson, & Siegel, 1978).

Uncontrollable or unpredictable events are more stressful than controllable or predictable ones (Bandura, Cioffi, Taylor, & Brouillard, 1988; McFarlane et al., 1980; Suls & Mullen, 1981). This is because an event that is uncontrollable or unpredictable does not enable the person going through the stress to make a plan or develop ways of coping with the problem. For example, the sound of static on your own radio may be less distressing than static from a neighbor's radio, because you can always turn off your own radio whereas you may not have the same degree of control over your neighbor's radio.

Ambiguous events are often perceived as more stressful than clear-cut events. For example, if you have been attracted to a fellow student in a class, and one day this person treats you in a

Even positive events, such as Christmas, can be stressful because they produce change and frenzy in people's lives.

cold, aloof manner, you may ruminate over why this is the case. Did you do something to offend this person? Is he or she simply having a bad day? Presumably if you knew what was wrong you could correct it quickly, but not knowing means you are stuck trying to figure out what has gone wrong. Clear stressors let people get on with finding solutions and do not leave them stuck at the problem-solving stage (Billings & Moos, 1984; Gal & Lazarus, 1975).

How Stress Can Cause Illness

The experience of stress is a problem for people not only because it produces emotional distress and physiological arousal, but because over time it may lay the groundwork for illness.

Major stressful life events. The earliest research to demonstrate this point examined the role of major **stressful life events** in the onset of illness. Newspapers and magazines often high-

light colorful cases in which individuals who have experienced a major stressful event suddenly develop a serious illness or even die.

> A dramatic example is the death of the 27-year-old army captain who had commanded the ceremonial troops at the funeral of President Kennedy. He died 10 days after the president of a "cardiac irregularity and acute congestion," according to the newspaper report of medical findings. (Engel, 1971, p. 774)

Much of the research designed to show the importance of major life events in the onset of illness has used a questionnaire called the Social Readjustment Rating Scale. As can be seen in Table 16–2, the Social Readjustment Rating Scale lists a variety of potentially stressful events that require people to make changes in their lives. Through extensive testing, the events selected for the scale were determined to be the ones that, on the average, force people to make the greatest change. The points reflect the relative amount of change that must be made.

T A B L E 1 6 – 2

Rank	Life Event	Mean Value
1.	Death of spouse	100
2.	Divorce	73
3.	Marital separation from mate	65
4.	Detention in jail or other institution	63
5.	Death of a close family member	63
6.	Major personal injury or illness	53
7.	Marriage	50
8.	Being fired from work	47
9.	Marital reconciliation with mate	45
10.	Retirement from work	45
11.	Major change in the health or behavior of a family member	44
12.	Pregnancy	40
13.	Sexual difficulties	39
14.	Gaining a new family member (e.g., through birth, adoption, oldster moving in)	39
15.	Major business readjustment (e.g., merger, reorganization, bankruptcy)	39
16.	Major change in financial state (e.g., a lot worse off or a lot better off than usual)	38
17.	Death of a close friend	37
18.	Changing to a different line of work	36
19.	Major change in the number of arguments with spouse (e.g., either a lot more or a lot less than usual regarding childrearing, personal habits)	35
20.	Taking out a mortgage or loan for a major purchase (e.g., for a home, business)	31
21.	Foreclosure on a mortgage or loan	30
22.	Major change in responsibilities at work (e.g., promotion, demotion, lateral transfer)	29
23.	Son or daughter leaving home (e.g., marriage, attending college)	29
24.	Trouble with in-laws	29
25.	Outstanding personal achievement	28
26.	Wife beginning or ceasing work outside the home	26
27.	Beginning or ceasing formal schooling	26
28.	Major change in living conditions (e.g., building a new home, remodeling, deterioration of home or neighborhood)	25
29.	Revision of personal habits (dress, manners, associations, etc.)	24
30.	Trouble with the boss	23
31.	Major change in working hours or conditions	20
32.	Change in residence	20
33.	Changing to a new school	20
34.	Major change in usual type and/or amount of recreation	19
35.	Major change in church activities (e.g., a lot more or a lot less than usual)	19
36.	Major change in social activities (e.g., clubs, dancing, movies, visiting)	18
37.	Taking out a mortgage or loan for a lesser purchase (e.g., for a car, TV, freezer)	17
38.	Major change in sleeping habits (a lot more or a lot less sleep, or change in part of day when asleep)	16
39.	Major change in number of family get-togethers (e.g., a lot more or a lot less than usual)	15
40.	Major change in eating habits (a lot more or a lot less food intake, or very different meal hours or surroundings)	15
41.	Vacation	13
42.	Christmas	12
43.	Minor violations of the law (e.g., traffic tickets, jaywalking, disturbing the peace)	11

Source: Holmes and Rahe (1967).

Thus, for example, if one's spouse dies, virtually every aspect of life is disrupted, and so this event has the highest number of "life change units" assigned to it. On the other hand, getting a traffic ticket may be annoying but, in and of itself, it is unlikely to produce much change in one's life.

To obtain a score on the Social Readjustment Rating Scale, one simply checks the events that have occurred within the past year and totals up the point values associated with those events. Although all people will have experienced at least a few stressful events during the year, some will have experienced a lot, and it is this group, according to Holmes and Rahe, that is most vulnerable to illness. In one study, Rahe, Mahan, and Arthur (1970) obtained scores on the SRRS from sailors who were about to depart on a 6-month cruise. They selected this group because during the 6 months that the men would be on board ship, they would be subjected to the same rather dull and unchanging environment. Therefore, if life events have an impact on the likelihood of illness, one should be able to see differences in the rates of illness of the sailors who had highly stressful lives just before departure, relative to those with less stressful lives just before departure. In fact, the predictions were borne out. Sailors who had experienced more major stressful life events were most likely to get sick and to be sick longer than were those who had experienced few stressful life events.

Daily Hassles. More recently, psychologists have begun to suspect that the more minor stressful events or the daily hassles of life may also have a cumulative and negative impact on health. Such hassles include being stuck in a traffic jam, waiting in line, doing household chores, or having difficulty making a small decision. Although research is not yet conclusive, it may emerge that the wear and tear of daily life predicts illness and psychological stress as well or better than the more major but relatively rare stressful events (Kanner, Coyne, Schaeffer, & Lazarus, 1981; Lazarus, DeLongis, Folkman, & Gruen, 1985; Reich, Parrella, & Filstead, 1988). Now you have a really good reason not to let anyone hassle you!

In short, research suggests that both major stressful events and minor stressors are problematic, not only because they produce psychological distress but because they can also increase the likelihood of physical illness.

COPING WITH STRESSFUL EVENTS

Once a person experiences an event as stressful, he or she usually begins to make efforts to cope with that event. **Coping** is the process of attempting to manage demands that are viewed as taxing or exceeding one's resources (Lazarus & Folkman, 1984; Lazarus & Launier, 1978). It is the process of trying to manage and master stressful events.

Coping with a stressful event is a dynamic process. For example, the impending breakup of a romantic relationship can produce a variety of responses, including actions such as efforts at reconciliation or attempts to find activities that will distract one from emotions such as sadness or indignation. Generally, researchers distinguish between two types of coping efforts: problem-solving efforts and efforts at emotional regulation (Lazarus & Folkman, 1984; Leventhal & Nerenz, 1982; Pearlin & Schooler, 1978). *Problem-solving efforts* are attempts to do something constructive to change the stressful circumstances. *Emotion-focused coping* involves efforts to regulate the emotional reactions to the stressful event. Both types of coping can occur simultaneously. For example, when the romantic partners break up, each person may try to cope with the loss by mulling over the past events and taking steps to meet new people. Box 16–2 presents examples of some coping strategies used by men with Aids.

What Is Successful Coping?

What constitutes successful coping? This is not an easy question to answer, and researchers differ in the criteria they use to measure successful coping. Some emphasize the effects of coping on measures of physiological and bio-

BOX 16–2

Coping with AIDS

AIDS has killed many thousands of people, and thousands more live, sometimes for years, with the knowledge that they have the disease. Such a threat requires and elicits many forms of coping, some of which are illustrated in the following excerpts from interviews with gay men living with AIDS. (Reed, 1989).

Social Support or Seeking Information

A key point in my program is that I have a really good support network of people who are willing to take the time, who will go the extra mile for me. I have spent years cultivating these friendships.

—

My family has been extremely supportive, and my lover has been extremely supportive, but it really wasn't quite enough. They weren't helping me in the right ways. That's when I went and got a therapist. Basically, she is the one who has helped me cope with [AIDS] and understand it.

—

I try to find people that have manifested long-term living with AIDS or have been healed. There are a few people out there, and I try to listen to them. There are also a lot of people who are angry and bitter and more than willing to give advice. I have learned a lot from them about what not to do, which is just as important as learning what to do.

—

Direct Action

My main concern is making it through another day without getting any disorder. I would really like to completely beat it.

—

My first concern was that, as promiscuous as I have been, I could not accept giving this to anyone. So I have been changing my life-style completely, putting everything else on the back burner.

—

The main thing I did was to get all my paperwork in order. I was good at it before, but when AIDS hit, I made sure everything was spelled out perfectly, and I figure that makes it easier for my lover left behind. He will go through grief, but he will not have to be sorting through all my junk.

—

Strategies of Distraction, Escape, or Avoidance

I used to depend on drugs a lot to change my mood. Once in a while, I still find that if I can't feel better any other way, I will take a puff of grass or have a glass of wine, or I use music. There are certain recordings that can really change my mood drastically. I play it loud and I dance around and try to clear my head.

—

I do exactly what I want to do, as much as possible, things that amuse me, entertain me, and pamper me.

—

There's an old disco song that says, "Keep out of my mind what's out of my hands." I try to do that, to not fret over things I really don't have control over.

—

It was important to me to focus on something besides AIDS, and my job is the most logical thing. I'm very good at what I do. I have a supervisory position, so I deal with other people's problems, which is good for me, because I take their problems and solve them and I forget about mine. I think that's a real constructive distraction for me.

—

I drive. I feel so much more at peace when I am driving down the road in a car, listening to music, having my dog next to me. It is wonderful.

—

Continued

Emotional Regulation/Ventilation

When you're sad, you cry. That's what I've done a lot lately, over silly, well, not silly things, but over small things, and over reminders of a life that's probably cut short, the expectations of things that you were going to do and planned on doing and don't seem possible now.

⎯

I try to be like Spock on "Star Trek." So this is an emotion. So that's what it makes you feel like. I try to analyze it and look as a third party would, like I am an observer from the fiftieth century.

⎯

Sometimes I will allow myself to have darker feelings, and then I grab myself by the bootstraps and say, okay, that is fine, you are allowed to have these feelings but they are not going to run your life.

⎯

Personal Growth

In the beginning, AIDS made me feel like a poisoned dart, like I was a diseased person and I had no self-esteem and no self-confidence. That's what I have been really working on, is to get the self-confidence and the self-esteem back. I don't know if I will ever be there, but I feel very close to being there, to feeling like my old self.

⎯

I've made sure everybody knows how I feel about them. I have given away some of my precious things, some back to the people who gave them to me. I make sure that everyone has something from my past, everyone who's been important in my life and for the most part I've sent them all letters too. Not that it was always received well. . . .

⎯

When something like this happens to you, you can either melt and disappear or you can come out stronger than you did before. It has made me a much stronger person. I literally feel like I can cope with anything. Nothing scares me, nothing. If I was on a 747 and they said we were going down, I would probably reach for a magazine.

⎯

I really have an advantage in a sense over other people. I know there is a possibility that my life may not go on for as many years as other people's. I have the opportunity to look at my life, to make changes, and to deeply appreciate the time that I have.

⎯

Positive Thinking and Restructuring

Everyone dies sooner or later. I have been appreciating how beautiful the Earth is, flowers, and the things I like. I used to go around ignoring all those things. Now I stop to try and smell the roses more often, and just do pleasurable things.

⎯

I have been spending a lot of time lately on having a more positive attitude. I force myself to become aware every time I say something negative during a day, and I go, "Oops," and I change it and I rephrase it. So I say, "Wonderful," about 42,000 times a day. Sometimes I don't mean it, but I am convincing myself that I do.

⎯

I made a list of all the other diseases I would rather not have than AIDS. Lou Gehrig's disease, being in a wheelchair; rheumatoid arthritis, when you are in knots and in terrible pain. So I said, you've got to get some perspective on this, and where you are on the Great Nasty Disease List.

⎯

The last chapter has not been written. The fat lady has not sung. I'm still here.

---

chemical functioning. Coping efforts are generally considered to be more successful if they reduce physiological arousal and its indicators such as heart rate, pulse, and skin conductivity. A second criterion of successful coping is whether or not and how quickly people can return to their previous life activities. Many stressful events disrupt ongoing daily life activities, interfering with work or leisure. To the extent that coping efforts enable a person to re-

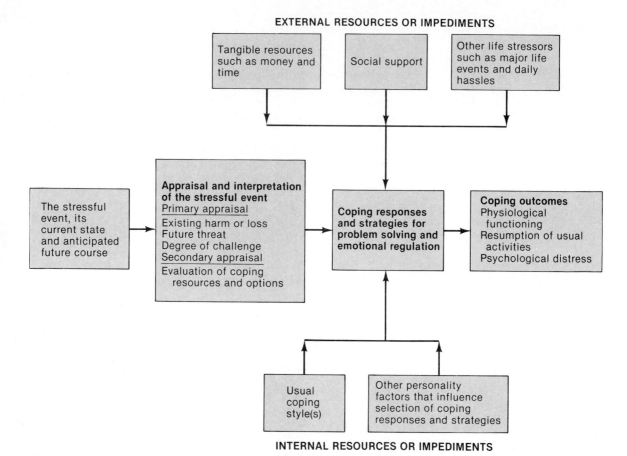

Figure 16–2. The coping process.

sume such activities, coping may be judged to be successful. Finally, and most commonly, researchers judge coping according to its effectiveness in reducing psychological distress. If negative emotions such as anxiety and depression are reduced by a coping effort, the coping effort is judged to be successful (Lazarus & Folkman, 1984).

Successful coping depends upon a variety of coping resources. Internal resources consist of coping styles and personality attributes. External resources include money, time, social support, and other life events that may be occurring at the same time. All these factors interact with each other to determine coping processes (e.g., Wiebe & McCallum, 1986). A model of the coping process is presented in Figure 16–2. In the next section, we consider a few of these coping resources in detail.

Coping Style

Coping style is one internal coping resource. It consists of a general tendency for a person to deal with a stressful event in a particular way.

Avoidance versus Confrontation. Some people meet stressful events head on and seem to tackle problems directly, whereas other people avoid stressful events by minimizing their significance or withdrawing from them through alcohol, drugs, or television.

In fact, neither coping style is necessarily more effective than the other in managing stress. Each seems to have its own advantages and liabilities. People who cope by minimizing or avoiding stress appear to cope effectively with short-term threats. However, if the threat is repeated or persists over time, avoidance may not be so successful. Avoiders may be unable to deal with the possibility of future threat and may not make enough efforts to anticipate and manage subsequent problems (Suls & Fletcher, 1985; Taylor & Clark, 1986).

In contrast, individuals who cope with threatening events through confrontation may deal effectively with long-term threats. But in the short run, they may be more anxious as they deal with the stressor directly (e.g. Miller & Mangan, 1983). For example, the avoider may cope well with a trip to the dentist because he puts the event out of his mind until just before it happens. However, the avoider may cope poorly with constant job stress because this is not an event that can easily be put out of mind; the stress recurs daily despite efforts to avoid it. In contrast, the vigilant coper may fret over a visit to the dentist and create internal distress. However, he or she may make constructive efforts to reduce stress on the job, and thereby ameliorate the situation. An example of coping through catharsis appears in Box 16–3.

Type A Behavior. Some coping styles may succeed in dealing with the psychological discomfort of stressful events but may nonetheless have an adverse effect on health. Perhaps the best example is the "Type A behavior" syndrome that has been associated with heart disease. The Type A person has a behavioral and emotional style marked by an aggressive, unceasing struggle to achieve more and more in less time, often in competition with other individuals or forces. Type A behavior has three components: easily aroused hostility, a sense of

---

BOX 16–3

Is Catharsis Good for Your Health?

For many years, psychologists have suspected that people recover better from traumatic events if they talk about them with others. This is an extension of the general idea of catharsis—that is, it's better to express emotions than to bottle them up inside. Traumatic events such as the death of a family member, a sexual assault, or a public humiliation may fester inside a person, producing obsessive thoughts for years and even decades (Silver, Boon, & Stones, 1983). This perspective suggests that the ability to confide in others or consciously confront their feelings may eliminate obsessive thoughts about the event and reduce physiological activity associated with it.

To test these points, Pennebaker and Beall (1986) had 48 undergraduates write either about the most traumatic and stressful event of their life or about a trivial topic. Each day for several days, they wrote about the topic, and their emotional reactions and blood pressure were measured both immediately after writing and over a six-month period. Pennebaker and Beall also recorded the number of visits the students made to the health service during the following six-month period. Students who had written about the facts and their emotional reactions concerning the traumatic event were more upset immediately following writing the essays and showed elevated blood pressure compared to those who wrote about trivial topics. However, over the following six months, they were less likely to visit the student health service for illness.

Why would talking through a traumatic event improve health? Talking with others allows one to gain information about the event or about how to cope effectively with it. Confiding in others may elicit positive feedback from them as well as emotional support. There may also be reliable cognitive effects associated with talking about or writing about a traumatic event. For example, in the process of talking or writing, one organizes one's thoughts and may also be able to find meaning in the experience. Talking through a traumatic event may even bolster the immune system (Pennebaker, Kiecolt-Glaser, & Glaser, 1988).

time urgency, and competitive achievement striving (Rosenman, 1978). So-called Type Bs, with whom Type As are usually compared, are less driven individuals who do not show these behavior patterns in response to stressful events. There are several measures of Type A behavior; items from one scale/test are given in Table 16–3.

Type A individuals lead fast-paced lives. They work longer hours and put in more overtime than do Type Bs. They are impatient with what they perceive as people's slow behavior and may complete people's sentences for them. They often concentrate on several activities si-

---

T A B L E   1 6 – 3

THE JENKINS ACTIVITY SURVEY: A MEASURE OF TYPE A BEHAVIOR

The Jenkins Activity Survey measures Type A behavior by asking people about their typical responses to frustrating, difficult, and competitive situations. The following are a few examples of items that appear on that survey:

1. When you listen to someone talking and this person takes too long to come to the point, how often do you feel like hurrying the person along?
   Frequently
   Occasionally
   Never

2. Do you ever set deadlines or quotas for yourself at work or at home?
   No
   Yes, but only occasionally
   Yes, once a week or more

3. Would people you know well agree that you tend to get irritated easily?
   Definitely yes
   Probably yes
   Definitely no
   Probably no

4. Would people who know you well agree that you tend to do most things in a hurry?
   Definitely yes
   Probably yes
   Definitely no
   Probably no

Note: If your answered these questions by giving the high-frequency answers, you show at least some characteristics of the Type A individual.

Source: Adapted from Jenkins, Zyzarisku, and Rosenman (1979).

Jenkins Activity Survey. Copyright © 1965, 1966, 1969, and 1979 by The Psychological Corporation. Reproduced by permission. All rights reserved.

multaneously. Despite the fact that Type As often achieve substantial accomplishments, they may evaluate their achievements in terms of quantity instead of quality and be dissatisfied with their output. They are likely to challenge and compete with others, especially in moderately competitive situations (Rosenman, 1978).

Type A behavior is important because it has been reliably related to the development of coronary artery disease (Haynes, Feinlieb, & Kannell, 1980; Matthews, 1988). Type As experience excessive arousal in response to stressful events, followed by dramatic decreases in arousal. This pattern may be the mechanism that produces damage to the arteries, although this issue is still under debate (Glass, 1977). Recently, investigators have found that the hostility aspect of Type A is the most important in the development of heart disease, more so than time urgency or competitiveness (Dembroski & Costa, 1987; Friedman & Booth-Kewley, 1987; Hecker, Chesney, Black, & Frautschi, 1988).

Social Support

In Chapters 7 and 9, we saw how important social relationships are to people for satisfying their social needs. Recent work by health psychologists indicates that socially supportive relationships may also mute the effects of stress, help people cope with stress, and enhance health.

Social support is an interpersonal exchange in which one person gives help to another. Social support may be provided in any of several ways. First, *emotional concern* expressed through liking, love, or empathy can be supportive. For example, if you are going through an awkward breakup with a romantic partner, expressions of caring from friends can be very welcome. Second, *instrumental aid*, such as the provision of goods or services during stressful times, can be an act of social support. For example, if you are having difficulty getting to your classes on time because your car is unreliable, a friend's offer to fix your car or to drive you to class would be very supportive. Third, *providing information* about a stressful situation can be helpful. For example, if you feel poorly prepared for an exam and someone who took the course last year gives you information about types of questions on the midterm and final, this may be very useful in helping you study. Finally, information may be supportive when it is relevant to *self-appraisal*, that is self-evaluation. For example, if you are uncertain whether you have made the right decision in breaking up with your boyfriend or girlfriend, information from your friends telling you that you did the right thing for the right reasons can be very comforting. Social support can come from a spouse or partner, family members, friends, or social and community contacts such as clubs and churches or temples.

Research demonstrates that social support effectively reduces psychological distress during stressful times (Cohen & Wills, 1985; Kessler & McLeod, 1985). For example, a study of residents' reactions following the nuclear reactor accident at Three Mile Island, Pennsylvania, revealed the importance of social support (Fleming, Baum, Gisriel, & Gatchel, 1982). After the event, residents were interviewed by a team of researchers about their reactions to the nuclear accident and about the support they received from family and friends. Those who reported having family and friends they felt close to showed lower levels of psychological distress in response to the accident than those who reported lower levels of social support.

Social support also appears to lower the likelihood of illness and to speed recovery from illness (House, Landis, & Umberson, 1988). Some impressive evidence for the importance of social support in combating the threat of illness comes from a survey of adults in Alameda County, California (Berkman & Syme, 1979). Almost 7,000 people were interviewed regarding their personal, social, and community ties. Then their death rate was tracked over a nine-year period. The results showed that people who had few social and community ties were more likely to die during this period than were people who had more such ties.

Research has tried to identify exactly how social support affects stress, and two possibilities have been extensively explored. One hypothesis, called the *direct effects hypothesis*, maintains that social support is always beneficial, during nonstressful as well as during stressful times.

Socially supportive relationships can help keep people well and help them to recover quickly from illness.

The other hypothesis, termed the *buffering hypothesis*, maintains that the physical and mental health benefits of social support chiefly occur during periods of high stress and not during periods of low stress. Extensive research suggests that social support can have both direct effects and buffering effects (Cohen & Hoberman, 1983; Pilisuk, Boylan, & Acredolo, 1987; Wills, 1984). Unfortunately, effective coping and the practice of good health behaviors do not always prevent the onset of illness.

Stress Management

Some individuals have difficulty coping with stressful events on their own. Stress management programs have developed to help people deal with these events more effectively (e.g. Chesney, Eagleston, & Rosenman, 1981; Ganster, Mayes, Sime, & Tharp, 1982; Roskies, 1980). Such programs train people in stress management techniques that can be used for a wide variety of stressful events or they may focus on coping with a particular stressful event (e.g., Meichenbaum & Jaremko, 1983).

As an example, consider the stress of college. College can be a trying experience for many students. For some, it is the first time they are away from home, and they must cope with the problems of living in a dormitory surrounded by strangers. They may have to share a room with a person of very different background and habits. High noise levels, communal bathrooms, institutional food, and difficult academic schedules may all be very trying. In addition, the fledgling college student may discover that academic life is more rigorous than he or she had expected. Whereas each student may have been a star in high school, there is more competition in college. Consequently, course loads are heavier and grades are typically lower. Coping with the first "C," "D," or "F" can be a deflating and anxiety-arousing experience.

Some colleges and universities have instituted programs to help students cope with these stressful events by learning stress management techniques. Commonly, in the first phase of such programs, the student learns what stress is and how it creates wear and tear on the system. Students learn that stress is in the eye of the beholder, that college life is not inherently stressful but can become stressful depending on how a student perceives it. Through these messages, students begin to see that if they acquire appropriate stress management techniques, they may come to experience currently stressful events as less stressful. In sharing their experiences of stress, many students find reassurance in the fact that other students have experiences similar to their own.

In the next phase, students are trained to observe their own behavior closely and to record the circumstances they find most stressful. They also typically record their physiological, emotional, and behavioral reactions to the stressful events. They may write down any efforts they make to cope with the stressful events such as sleeping, eating, watching television, or taking drugs.

Once they learn to chart stressful responses, students are encouraged to examine what causes those experiences. For example, one student may feel overwhelmed with academic life only when she must deal with speaking out in class, whereas another student may experience stress primarily when he thinks about having to use the computer in a particularly demanding course. By pinpointing precisely the circumstances that initiate a student's feelings of stress, that student can more clearly identify his or her own trouble spots.

Students are next trained to recognize the negative self-talk they may go through when they face stressful events. Thus, for example, the student who fears speaking out in class may come to recognize how her self-statements contribute to the stress she feels ("I hate asking questions" and "I always get tongue-tied"). Such negative self-talk undermines feelings of self-efficacy and will become a target for modification later in the intervention.

Typically, a student will next set specific goals that he or she wants to meet to reduce the experience of college stress. For example, one student's goal may be to learn to speak in class without suffering overwhelming anxiety. For another, the goal may be to go see a particular professor about a problem. Once the goals have been set, the student identifies some behaviors that can help meet those goals. For example, the student who fears speaking out in class may decide that she will begin to raise her hand whenever she knows the answer to factual questions that will require only a one- or two-word response. By beginning with relatively little speaking out in class, she may then be able to train herself to give longer answers that can ultimately enable her to speak more effectively.

Once the student has set some realistic goals and identified some target behaviors, he or she will learn how to engage in positive self-talk. For example, the student desiring to overcome a fear of oral presentations might remind herself of the occasions when she has spoken successfully in public. Once some success in speaking publicly has been achieved, the same student might encourage herself by highlighting the positive aspects of the experience (for example, holding the attention of the audience or making some good points). As she becomes more effective, she might try to create opportunities to speak publicly and reward herself each time she does so by engaging in some desirable activity such as going to a movie.

Typically, students also learn some ways of modifying the physiological reactions associated with stress. Usually, these methods involve relaxation-training techniques and may include deep breathing, muscle relaxation, guided imagery, meditation, and similar techniques (English & Baker, 1983; Benson, Greenwood, & Klemchuck, 1975). Such methods can help reduce heart rate, muscle tension, and blood pressure. Then, if a student finds the stress of college life is becoming overwhelming, he or she can take a 5- or 10-minute break, breathe deeply and relax completely, and then return to tasks freer of previous tensions.

As may be evident, most stress management programs include a wide array of cognitive behavioral techniques that an individual can use to combat stress. Some will work better for some students, and others will work better for

other students. By presenting a broad array of coping techniques, students have a broad set of skills from which to choose ones that work for them individually.

SYMPTOMS, ILLNESS, AND TREATMENT

When and how a person decides that he or she is sick is a heavily social and psychological process.

The Recognition and Interpretation of Symptoms

To label yourself as sick, you first have to notice that you are. Noticing symptoms is, in part, a psychological process that depends on focus of attention. If your focus of attention is directed inward, symptoms are detected more quickly than when your focus of attention is directed externally toward the environment. So, for example, people whose attention is chronically focused on themselves, who are socially isolated or live alone, or who have relatively inactive lives are more likely to notice symptoms in themselves. Conversely, people who are externally focused on their environment and activities, who have active social lives and work outside the home, or who live with others are less likely to notice symptoms (Pennebaker, 1983).

Similarly, situational factors influence whether or not a person will recognize a particular situation by directing attention inward or outward. Boring situations make people more attentive to their symptoms, whereas interesting situations distract them from attending to bodily states. Joggers, for example, are more likely to experience fatigue and to be aware of their running-related symptoms if they are running on a boring course than if they are running on one that is more interesting (Pennebaker & Lightner, 1980; see also Fillingim & Fine, 1986).

People's expectations can guide the interpretation of information, and so it is with symptom information as well (Leventhal et al., 1980). For example, women who believe they are close to their menstrual periods may interpret vague sources of discomfort as premenstrual symptoms, whereas women who believe their periods are several days away may ignore these same bodily sensations.

Prior experience also shapes reactions to symptoms (Safer, Tharps, Jackson, & Leventhal, 1979; Jemmott, Croyle, & Ditto, 1988). If you have a long history of sore throats, you are more likely to ignore any particular one than if it is an unusual symptom for you.

As we saw in Chapter 3, cognitive theories or schemas about events often strongly affect how those events are perceived and interpreted. Beginning research suggests that such beliefs can be important in symptom interpretation and the management of illness as well. Researchers have suggested that patients form organized, cognitive pictures of their symptoms that influence their illness-related activities (e.g., Bishop, 1990; Nerenz & Leventhal, 1983; Lau, Bernard, & Hartman, 1989; Turk, Rudy, & Salovey, 1986). In essence, these are illness schemas. They include such factors as the name of the illness and its symptoms (i.e., its identity), its cause, duration, and consequences.

People have at least three models of illness (Nerenz & Leventhal, 1983). *Acute* illness is short in duration with no long-term consequences and is believed to be caused by specific viral or bacterial agents. An example is flu. *Chronic* illness is caused by many factors, including faulty health habits, and is long in duration with often severe consequences. Cancer is an example. *Cyclic* illness is marked by alternating periods when there may be no symptoms and others when there are many. Recurrent episodes of herpes is an example.

Sometimes patients adopt an inappropriate model for their disorder. For example, patients suffering from hypertension (high blood pressure) may believe the disease is acute, when in fact, it is chronic. Consequently, they may think that if they feel well, their blood pressure must be under control, and therefore they need no longer take their medication (Meyer, Leventhal,

& Gutmann, 1985). In fact, hypertension is called the silent killer precisely because patients often experience no symptoms and conclude erroneously that they no longer need treatment. Consequently, it is important for practitioners and others involved in health care to explore patients' schemas for their illnesses to see if they are using an appropriate illness model in understanding their disorder and its treatment.

Finally, social interaction also affects how people interpret symptoms. Sometimes when we are ill we consult our friends to find out if they have had similar symptoms or to get their opinions on what the symptoms might mean. Warned that a minor sore throat is the first symptom of a serious flu that is going around, you might take better care of yourself than if you learned that others were experiencing a similar symptom and attributing it to pollution in the air. Often, then, people exchange information with family and friends about the interpretation of symptoms well before they seek any treatment (Freidson, 1960).

Patient-Practitioner Interaction

Sometimes symptoms lead us to the medical practitioner's door. Interacting with a physician or nurse regarding medical treatment is a complex social process involving interpersonal communication, person perception, social judgments, and social influence. One of the earliest judgments that most patients make is whether or not they think the practitioner is technically competent. But most of us know little about medicine and standards of practice, and so we evaluate medical care using the only information we have: whether we like the practitioner and whether he or she is warm and friendly or cool and uncommunicative. When people are asked what is important to them in their medical care, they rate the manner in which the care is delivered at least as high as the technical quality of care (Feletti, Firman, & Sanson-Fisher, 1986; Scarpaci, 1988).

One of the problems that arises in interactions with practitioners, even when patients and practitioners have some basic confidence in each other, is faulty communication. Practitioners often use jargon and technical language that patients do not understand, and they may inadvertently depersonalize the patient by referring to the patient's symptoms rather than the patient as a person (Chafetz, 1970; Kaufman, 1970).

> Recently, when I was being given emergency treatment for an eye laceration, the resident surgeon abruptly terminated his conversation with me as soon as I lay down on the operating table. Although I had had no sedative or anesthesia, he acted as if I were no longer conscious, directing all his questions to a friend of mine—questions such as, "What's his name?" "What occupation is he in?" "Is he a real doctor?" etc. As I lay there, these two men were speaking about me as if I were not there at all. The moment I got off the table and was no longer a cut to be stitched, the surgeon resumed his conversation with me, and existence was conferred upon me once again (Zimbardo, 1970, p. 298).

Patients, too, contribute to faulty communication by failing to pay attention to what they are being told, and by responding to the wrong cues in the situation and reading too much into a physician's comment (DiMatteo & DiNicola, 1982; Golden & Johnston, 1970; Greer, 1974). For example, a patient may be so distressed by swollen glands that he fails to listen to a physician's instructions about taking penicillin.

The treatment setting contributes to undermining effective communication (see Taylor, 1979). For example, a physician may have a backlog of patients in the waiting room, and accordingly is under pressure to see each patient for as little time as possible. The patient is asked to describe symptoms efficiently and effectively to a physician when the patient may be in a poor state to do so. It is difficult to be coherent when one is in pain, running a fever, or simply anxious about the meaning of a particular problem. In summary, a variety of factors can inadvertently impede communication.

Faulty communication between patient and practitioner is problematic for several reasons. First, it may undermine the use of health ser-

Communication between patient and practitioner can be improved by training physicians in effective communication techniques.

vices in the future. Patients whose emotional needs are not met in their interactions with physicians are less likely to return to that physician in the future (Ware, Davies-Avery, & Stewart, 1978). Even more important, patients may not adopt the behaviors and treatments recommended by their practitioners.

Adherence to Medical Treatment

The seventeenth-century French playwright, Molière, aptly described the relationship that physicians and patients often have with respect to treatment recommendations:

> The King: You have a physician. What does he do?
> Moliere: Sire, we converse. He gives me advice which I do not follow, and I get better.
> (Treue, 1958, p. 41, cited in Koltun & Stone, 1986)

Depending upon the disorder and recommendation, nonadherence to treatment ranges from a low of 15 percent for such recommendations as tablets or ointments to a staggering high of 93 percent for life-style advice such as to stop smoking or lose weight (Davis, 1968; Turk & Meichenbaum, 1989).

Failure to follow medical advice can be traced to several factors. First, patients who are dissatisfied with the quality of their care may decide deliberately not to follow advice. Second, to follow through on a treatment, a patient must understand it, and often, understanding is not achieved. Adherence is high when a patient receives a clear, jargon-free explanation of the origin, diagnosis, and treatment recommendations associated with the disorder (Hauenstein, Schiller, & Hurley, 1987). Adherence is also increased if the instructions are written down, if the patient has repeated back the instructions, if any unclear sections are clarified, and if the instructions are repeated more than once (DiNicola & DiMatteo, 1984). Unfortunately, these seemingly simple steps are often not followed.

The nature of the treatment also influences the patient's behavior. Complex treatments involving several medications are less likely to be taken as directed than treatments involving one medication (Blumenthal & Emery, 1988; Siegel, Grady, Browner, & Hulley, 1988). Patients are less likely to follow treatments that must be continued over several months than treatments that continue for just a few days; over time, adherence simply falls off. Treatments that interfere with regular life activities produce lower rates of adherence than those that can be implemented relatively easily (Kirscht & Rosenstock, 1979). For example, a patient who has been advised to rest in the middle of a busy working day might find it nearly impossible to do so (Turk & Meichenbaum, 1989).

Adherence is higher with treatments that seem "medical." For example, a patient is more likely to take a foul-tasting pill every three hours for three days than to rest, avoid stressful experiences, stop smoking, or lose weight. The reason is that patients may not see life-style recommendations as truly medical, and therefore may not follow through. They may believe that their social activities, the stressful nature of their work life, and whether or not they smoke are their own business and that the physician's job is restricted to providing "medical" treatments for diagnosable conditions.

Another reason why physicians' recommendations to alter life-style behaviors often show low rates of compliance is because these aspects of life are difficult to modify. As we noted earlier in the chapter, such stubborn health habits as overeating, smoking, or drinking to excess may have become habitual and may be tied to certain cues and stimuli in the social environment. These cues alone can maintain a behavior, even when the motivation to change the behavior is there.

Sometimes people experience *reactance,* a psychological state that results when people feel their freedoms have been arbitrarily restricted (Brehm, 1966; Brehm & Brehm, 1981). The withdrawal of freedom can be very threatening, especially when valued activities are involved. Many illnesses and treatments have precisely these effects. For example, being put on bed rest by a physician may seem like an arbitrary and useless step to you. It may also cause you to miss a midterm and several weekend parties. Under such circumstances, adherence is low, both because the treatment recommendations threaten freedoms and because personal frustration can result when one is unable to do what one wishes (Leigh & Reiser, 1986; Rhodewalt & Strube, 1985; Rhodewalt & Marcroft, 1988).

Improving Patient-Practitioner Communication

How can we improve patient-practitioner communication? Training practitioners to communicate effectively is a good way to begin. For example, in medical school, physicians may be trained how to provide information to patients in a manner that is comprehensible and jargon-free without being simpleminded. Training programs also stress the importance of communicating information clearly and asking the patient to repeat the information to be certain that the patient has understood it. Methods of

communicating warmth and friendliness to a patient through such simple nonverbal behaviors as smiling, leaning forward, or shaking hands can also help improve the communication process (DiMatteo, Friedman, & Taranta, 1979; DiMatteo, Hays, & Prince, 1986).

Training physicians in the effective use of techniques of social influence identified in Chapter 8 can also improve the communication process and ultimately increase adherence to treatment (Rodin & Janis, 1979). Physicians are high-status people and have a high degree of authority by virtue of their medical expertise. This type of power is termed *legitimate* power. But doctors can also draw on their *referent power* by becoming significant individuals in their patients' lives. If the patient feels that the physician's approval and acceptance are rewarding, then the practitioner has an additional mode of influence. When the practitioner is able to use both referent power and legitimate power, adherence is increased (Janis, 1983; Raven, 1988; Rodin & Janis, 1979).

Physicians are also in a unique position to influence a patient's behavior because they interact on a one-to-one basis (Raven, 1988). Health recommendations can be tailored to the individual needs and vulnerabilities of that particular patient. These conditions maximize attitude and behavior change. For example, patients who are told by their physicians that they are particularly vulnerable to lung cancer by virtue of their smoking are more likely to stop than in response to other health communications about smoking such as mass media campaigns (Pederson, 1982). The face-to-face interaction provides an effective setting for holding the patient's attention, repeating and clarifying instructions, extracting commitments from the patient to adhere to the treatment, and assessing any possible sources of resistance to compliance. Thus, for example, the patient for whom bed rest was recommended can explain to the physician about the importance of midterms and not missing social activities, and the patient and physician together may be able to work out a compromise. Finally, because of the face-to-face situation and the likelihood of additional visits, the physician has the patient under surveillance at least to some degree and can monitor progress during subsequent visits.

In summary, then, the processes of diagnosis, treatment recommendations, and following through on treatment are clearly social-psychological ones. Information must be effectively communicated in order for a patient to adhere to treatment, and effective techniques of social influence can help instill the desire to follow through on treatments.

Psychological Control and Adjustment to Treatment

As has already been noted, feelings of control over one's health and treatment regimen appear to be important for health behaviors and adherence to treatment. So important is control that many psychologists have used it to design interventions with medical patients. The idea is that if patients are given a sense of control during an unpleasant medical procedure, it will enable them to adjust to that procedure more successfully than if they do not have such feelings of control (Averill, 1983; Fiske & Taylor, 1984; Miller, 1979; Thompson, 1981).

An example is interventions with patients undergoing cardiac catheterization. Cardiac catheterization is an exploratory diagnostic procedure that is used with people suspected of having irregularities in coronary circulation. A catheter (a hollow tube) is inserted into the base of the aorta next to the heart, and dye is injected, which makes it possible for the practitioner to visualize the entire coronary area to detect abnormalities. Patients are fully conscious during the procedure and receive only a local anesthetic and a tranquilizing agent, such as Valium. As might be expected, although the procedure is not particularly painful, it does arouse a lot of anxiety in many patients.

In a study designed to reduce the stressfulness of this procedure (Kendall et at., 1979), patients who were scheduled for cardiac catheterization were assigned to one of four intervention groups. In the first group (cognitive-control intervention), patients were first taught to recognize the signs of their own anxiety. They were then instructed to use these internal signals to initiate cognitive coping skills of their own. The intervention trainer provided a model by confessing her own fears about a stressful event in her own life and by describing the techniques she used to overcome her fears. Patients were then encouraged to discuss their fears and the coping techniques they typically used to overcome anxiety. The goal of this intervention, then, was to help patients recognize their anxiety and initiate personal coping techniques to achieve relaxation.

In the second group (information-control intervention), patients received individual instruction, using a model of the heart to illustrate points about heart disease and the catheterization procedure. They were also given reading materials about the procedure, and their questions were answered. In the third group (social support), patients were told that a therapist would talk to them before and during the procedure to help them relax and cope. The therapist engaged the patient in general conversation, which lasted as long as the orientation interventions with the first two groups. This condition is a comparison condition because there is no reason to think that merely talking to a patient during a stressful medical procedure will necessarily reduce anxiety. Inclusion of this group enabled the researchers to see if the cognitive- and information-control intervention groups experience benefits over and above the effects that mere talking has. Finally, a fourth group of patients received the hospital's standard preparatory information, which consisted of a brief description of the procedure. All patients then went through the cardiac catheterization procedure.

Patients were asked to report their anxiety before the procedure; to say, in retrospect, how much anxiety they felt during the procedure; and to indicate their level of anxiety after the procedure was over. In addition, physicians and technicians made ratings of patient adjustment. Results clearly showed that the cognitive-control intervention and the information-control intervention had significant roles in reducing anxiety during the procedure. Of the two interventions, the cognitive intervention was the more successful. These effects persisted after the procedure, thus ameliorating post-procedural anxiety as well. Another example of how beliefs in control can improve coping appears on Box 16–4 on page 511.

SOCIAL PSYCHOLOGICAL PERSPECTIVES ON CHRONIC ILLNESS

At any given time, 50 percent of the population has some chronic condition that requires medical management (Cole, 1974), This includes major conditions such as cancer or heart disease, as well as more minor ones such as a partial hearing loss or recurrent episodes of herpes. Perhaps a more startling statistic is that most of us will eventually develop at least one chronic disability or disease that may alter our daily lives for many years and ultimately be the cause of our death. As we noted at the beginning of this chapter, chronic illness now accounts for the major health problems in this country, and these are conditions with which people often live for many years. Precisely because chronic diseases are chronic, they often have a major impact on the social and psychological lives of these patients. The impact of chronic illness is a relatively new area of investigation for social psychologists, and consequently there is much work to be done in understanding exactly what the psychosocial effects of the various chronic diseases are. A beginning effort toward such understanding has been made in several specific areas.

Illness Cognitions

Researchers have noted that most people suffering from chronic illness develop theories about where their illnesses came from (e.g., Meyerowitz, 1980; Schain, 1976). Such theories about the origins of chronic illness include stress, physical injury, disease-causing bacteria,

---

BOX 16–4

Control and Health: The Nursing Home Study

Feelings of psychological control appear to affect not only adjustment to specific unpleasant medical procedures, but also health more generally. This point was dramatically illustrated in a study of nursing home residents by Langer and Rodin (1976). The purpose of their study was to see if the introduction of an element of control into a nursing home environment could improve the morale and health of these institutionalized elderly people.

Patients on one floor were given small plants to care for (behavior control); they were also asked to choose when they wished to participate in some of the nursing home activities (decision control). Patients on a comparison floor were also given plants, but they were told that the staff would care for them. They participated in the same activities as the first group of patients, but they were assigned to times rather than being able to choose those times.

Several weeks later, nurses rated the mood and activity level of the patients, patients reported their own mood, and behavioral measures of patients' activity levels were collected. The results revealed that the patients who had been given some control were more active and had a greater sense of well-being than were those on the comparison floor. A year later, those patients were still psychologically and physically healthier than were the patients who had not received the interventions designed to enhance feelings of control (Rodin & Langer, 1977).

The importance of feelings of control is well illustrated by this study, because the control-enhancing manipulations were actually quite modest. Thus, this study illustrates how powerful and helpful the variable of psychological control can be, and how it can have a long-term effect on major health outcomes.

---

and God's will. Of perhaps greater interest is where patients ultimately place the blame for illness. Do they blame themselves, another person, the environment, or a quirk of fate?

Self-blame for illness is widespread. Patients frequently perceive themselves as having brought on their own illnesses by engaging in bad health practices such as smoking or even just by exposing themselves to stress. What are the consequences of self-blame? Unfortunately, a definitive answer to this question is not yet available. Some researchers have suggested that self-blaming patients may adjust poorly to their illness because they focus on things they could have done or should have done to prevent it (see Krantz & Deckel, 1983). On the other hand, some researchers have suggested that self-blame may sometimes be adaptive, because it leads people to believe they have control over the illness in the future (Bulman & Wortman,

1977). It may be that self-blame is adaptive for some disorders and not others (Taylor, Lichtman, & Wood, 1984).

It does appear, however, that individuals who blame other people for their disorders often adjust more poorly (Taylor et al., 1984; Bulman & Wortman, 1977). Perhaps poorly adjusted people single out others to blame for their illness, or it may be that by blaming other people, these patients adjust less well to their illness because of the unresolved anger and hostility they experience toward those who they believe are responsible for their illness.

Researchers have also examined whether patients who believe they can control their illnesses are better adjusted than are those who do not see their illnesses as under personal control. Patients develop a number of control-related beliefs with respect to chronic illness. They may believe, as do many cancer patients,

A chronic illness affects not only the patient's life, but the lives of family and often friends as well.

that they can prevent a recurrence of the disease through good habits or even sheer force of will (Taylor et al., 1984). Heart patients or patients suffering from multiple sclerosis may believe that by avoiding stressful situations, they will avoid exacerbating their disorder. We have already noted that feelings of personal control appear to be adaptive in the practice of preventive health behavior, illness-related behaviors, and adjustment to medical procedures. Self-generated feelings of control also appear to be adaptive for chronically ill patients. For example, breast cancer patients who believed that they had some control over their illness were better adjusted to their cancer than were patients without such beliefs (Taylor et al., 1984).

Chronic Disease and Patients' Changing Lives

A chronic disease like cancer or diabetes can affect all aspects of a patient's life. Work may be threatened or terminated by the need for extensive treatments or by the debilitating side effects of the disorder. The patient's psychological state is almost certainly affected. The diagnosis of a chronic illness can produce extreme fear and anxiety or depression, as the patient realizes that his or her life activities may be permanently curtailed by the disorder (Burish & Bradley, 1983; Taylor & Aspinwall, 1990). Because of physical changes that occur, loss of income due to job restriction, or the need for help from others, the entire family and even friends are often affected by one individual's experience of chronic illness (Turk & Kerns, 1985). A patient's spouse may suddenly have to take on additional responsibilities that once fell to the partner who is now ill. Young children are sometimes forced into taking on more responsibilities than would normally be expected for their age group. Often, then, it is not just the patient who may experience psychosocial difficulties, but also the spouse, children, and others who must adjust to these changes.

Problems in social communication and social support can also arise. For example, Wortman and Dunkel-Schetter (1979) have suggested that cancer patients are sometimes inadvertently treated badly by their family members and friends. Cancer can create conflicting reactions in family and friends. Feelings of fear and aversion to cancer develop because the disease is so frightening to most people. But most people also believe appropriate behavior toward cancer patients requires a cheerful, optimistic front, so the patient will feel better. The conflict between these reactions may produce ambivalence toward the patient and anxiety about interacting with him or her. Consequently, family and friends may physically avoid the cancer patient or may avoid open communication about the disease (Dakof & Taylor, 1990). These discrepancies in behavior (i.e., positive verbal but negative nonverbal behavior) can create confusion and upset, as we saw in Chapter 2, and can lead the patient to feel rejected or abandoned by loved ones.

So far, we have focused primarily on the problems and stressors created by chronic disease. This focus obscures an important point, namely, that chronic disease can confer positive as well as negative outcomes. In one study (Collins, Taylor, & Skokan, in press), over 90 percent of cancer patients reported at least some beneficial changes in their lives as a result of the cancer. These patients reported an increased ability to appreciate each day and the inspiration to do things now instead of postponing them. In terms of relationships, these patients reported that they were putting more effort into their relationships and deriving more pleasure from them. They believed that they had acquired more awareness of others' feelings and more sympathy and compassion for others.

They reported feeling stronger, more self-assured, and more compassionate toward the unfortunate. Similar results have been reported for patients who have had heart attacks (Laerum, Johnsen, Smith, & Larsen, 1987; Waltz, 1986) and AIDS (Reed, 1989). What seems evident, then, is that sometimes people are able to derive value and benefits from a chronic illness experience while simultaneously accommodating their lives to the adverse changes posed by disease. Thus, while chronic disease can be a trying and unpleasant experience, it can also be an enobling one, allowing people to derive meaning from their lives (Taylor, 1983).

To summarize, because people often live with chronic illnesses for long periods of time, these illnesses may pervade all aspects of their lives. Until relatively recently, the health care community largely ignored the changes in self-concept, personal relationships, and work that can result from chronic disease. However, health psychologists are now beginning to examine the social and psychological factors that not only give rise to these chronic conditions but also those that follow from them. Through such efforts, there is hope that health can be improved by keeping those who are currently healthy in good health and by ameliorating the life circumstances of those who have developed illnesses.

Key Terms

biopsychosocial model	**health belief**	**stress**
broad-spectrum cognitive-behavioral therapy	**psychological control**	**stressful life event**
	relapse prevention	**theory of reasoned action**
coping	**self-monitoring**	**type A behavior**
health behavior	**social support**	

Summary

1. Health psychology examines the role of psychological factors in the promotion and maintenance of health; the prevention and treatment of illness; the identification of causes and correlates of health, illness, or dysfunction; and the improvement of the health care system and health policy formation.

2. The major health problems of our country involve life-style disorders— including cancer, diabetes, heart disease, drug and alcohol abuse, and vehicular accidents. Life-style disorders are preventable and can potentially be influenced by psychological interventions.

3. Attitude-change techniques have been applied to understanding the practice of health behaviors. Whether or not a person practices a health behavior depends on: general health values, the perceived threat of the particular health hazard, the perceived severity of that hazard, the perceived effectiveness of the particular health practice, and a sense of self-efficacy that one can undertake the recommended health practice. Overall, however, attitudinal approaches to the modification of health behaviors have had fairly modest effects.

4. Increasingly, psychologists have drawn upon cognitive-behavioral analyses of health habits to understand the specific stimuli in an environment and the health cognitions that control health habits. By modifying these stimuli and cognitions, one may encourage the development of more healthy behaviors.

5. Stress is a major health issue, because it causes psychological distress and because it can have an adverse effect on health. Stress, however, is not intrinsic to situations but is rather the consequence of a person's appraisal processes. Negative, uncontrollable, and ambiguous events are most likely to be perceived as stressful.

6. Coping consists of problem-solving efforts and efforts at emotional regulation that attempt to reduce the stress of stressful events. Coping resources and liabilities include coping style, social support, time, money, and the presence of other stressful events in one's life. Stress management

programs help people to make more effective use of their coping resources in dealing with stressful events.

7. The recognition and interpretation of symptoms are influenced by social-psychological factors. When attention is directed outward, people are less likely to notice symptoms than when attention is directed inward. The interpretation of symptoms is influenced by prior expectations, experience, and illness schemas. Communications with others are influential in whether or not people seek treatment for symptoms.

8. Adherence to treatment is often very low, in part because of communication difficulties between patient and practitioner. Practitioners often provide jargon-filled and simplistic explanations, whereas patients are guilty of not learning or following through on treatment recommendations. Interventions that draw on principles of social influence can help improve this situation.

9. Interventions that utilize the principle of psychological control with patients awaiting noxious medical procedures have been very successful in helping patients adjust to these procedures.

10. Adjustment to chronic illness depends in part on the cognitions people have about their illness such as its cause and whether or not they feel they can control it.

11. Communication problems between chronically ill patients and their family members often occur. Friends and family members may not understand or may be unable to meet the communication needs of chronically ill patients who have to work through the impact that the illness is having upon their lives.

12. Chronic illness can provide meaning and value to patients even as it also produces adverse changes and poses problems of adjustment.

Suggested Readings

Burish, T. G., & Bradley, L. A. (Eds.) (1983). *Coping with chronic disease: Research and applications.* New York: Academic Press. This edited collection describes the difficulties and issues confronted by patients facing a variety of specific chronic diseases.

Rodin, J., & Salovey, P. (1989). Health psychology. *Annual Review of Psychology, 40,* 533–579. A scholarly review of recent trends in the field of health psychology.

Taylor, S. E. (1991). *Health psychology* 2nd ed. New York: Random House. A readable and comprehensive introduction to the field of health psychology.

SEVENTEEN

Political Psychology

POLITICAL SOCIALIZATION

PUBLIC OPINION AND VOTING

MASS MEDIA

PERSONALITY AND POLITICS

INTERNATIONAL CONFLICT

CONCLUSION

*I*n 1961, in the earliest days of John F. Kennedy's presidency, his administration engineered a disastrous and ill-conceived invasion of Cuba in an effort to overthrow the Communist regime of Fidel Castro. Soon thereafter, the Soviet Union began to place nuclear missiles in Cuba. In 1962, the United States discovered the presence of these missiles, and Kennedy ordered a naval blockade of Cuba, demanding their removal. This confrontation sent the world into a crisis, since neither Kennedy nor the Soviet leader, Khrushchev, seemed willing to back down. American preparations to destroy the missiles accelerated, as did the Soviet and Cuban preparations to make them ready. A week of escalating tension seemed to bring the two superpowers ever closer to an exchange of nuclear arms which would destroy much of human civilization. Finally a private deal was struck which allowed the Soviets to remove the missiles in exchange for American concessions elsewhere in the world.

The world has never come closer to nuclear annihilation. Much depended on the two leaders themselves: on their emotions (was it too humiliating to back down?), on their own goals (how important was victory over the enemy compared to the avoidance of nuclear holocaust?), and on the perceptions they had of each other (did the other want peace or victory at all costs? could he be reasoned with?). Moreover, each leader spent long hours each day deliberating with groups of advisors. What role was played by the dynamics of those groups?

Kennedy and Khrushchev were not the leaders of their nations forever, of course. A critical question, then, is how such leaders come into power, and how they are replaced. In the United States the answer would seem to be fairly simple: presidents are elected by the voters, so we must look at the determinants of voting behavior. President Kennedy was a Democrat, as was his successor, Lyndon B. Johnson. But four of the five presidents since then have been Republicans. Why do such changes occur? Do voters make reasoned and informed decisions based on the issues? Or do they just respond to superficial political commercials on television? We all remember George Bush's televised ads in 1988, attacking Michael Dukakis for his "revolving-door" policy of letting criminals out on furlough programs or depicting pollution in Boston Harbor. Do such ads sway the voter? Or are voters really more concerned with fundamental issues such as national defense, a balanced budget, and the environment?

Such questions are the stuff of political psychology. They have resulted in basic research on political socialization, public opinion and voting behavior, the impact of the media, the personality of political leaders, and international conflict. These are the topics we will discuss in this chapter.

POLITICAL SOCIALIZATION

Our political lives begin in childhood just as do many other aspects of our lives. Fundamental political attitudes, like basic social and moral values, racial attitudes, and other crucial predispositions, seem to be acquired prior to adulthood (Hyman, 1959). Indeed, most theories and research on the political decision making of the general public have concluded that the central variable in the voting decision is **party identification,** a standing preference for one political party or the other, typically developed before adulthood and significantly influenced by one's family (e.g., Campbell et al., 1980). This suggests a close look at preadult political socialization.

Preadult Socialization

As mentioned earlier, attitudes are assumed to be learned in the same way as any other disposition, through the basic processes of association, reinforcement, and imitation. This means that parents may have a great deal of influence. For example, one major national survey of high school seniors showed that they strongly tended to favor the political party of their parents; only about 10 percent favored the opposite party (Jennings & Niemi, 1974). This is shown

T A B L E 17 - 1				
RELATIONSHIP BETWEEN PARTY PREFERENCES OF PARENTS AND THEIR ADOLESCENT OFFSPRING				
	High School Seniors (N = 1,852)			
Parent	Democratic	Independent	Republican	Total
Democratic	66.0%	26.7%	7.3%	= 100.0%
Independent	29.2	53.6	17.2	= 100.1
Republican	12.7	36.3	50.9	= 99.9
Total	43.0	35.7	21.3	= 100.0%

Source: Adapted from Jennings and Niemi (1974).

in Table 17–1. The same survey revealed that in the last election, 83 percent of the high school students favored the same presidential candidate as their parents had.

However, parent-offspring agreement was much less in many other areas. For example, the high school students were asked a series of questions about how much "the people in government" can be trusted. As many students disagreed with their parents on these questions as agreed with them. Why do parents sometimes have a major impact on their children's attitudes, and sometimes not?

Surprisingly, the adolescents' feelings about their parents had relatively little to do with their political agreement or disagreement. Adolescents who were angry at their parents were about as likely to agree with them as those who felt warmly toward Mom and Dad (Jennings & Niemi, 1974). Rather, the most important factor seems to be the clarity and frequency of the communication of parents' attitudes to their offspring. And this varies greatly. Parents communicated clearly and repeatedly their presidential preference in the heat of an election campaign; 92 percent of the students were able to report accurately which candidate their parents favored. But on other issues, they were strikingly inaccurate—indeed it often appeared they were simply guessing about their parents' orientations. For example, they were quite inaccurate in assessing how interested their parents were in politics (Niemi, 1974; also see Tedin, 1974).

So parents' influence tends to be more limited than many early observers originally

thought (Jennings & Niemi, 1974). In general, parents have maximum influence on simple, concrete, recurrent issues like partisan choice, religious denomination, or prejudices against minority groups. They have relatively little influence on more diffuse, subjective, occasional issues, where communication is likely to be sporadic and fuzzy, such as religious philosophy, political cynicism, interpersonal trust, or civil liberties. And peers tend to have more influence than do parents about matters peers tend to discuss with each other, but not with parents, such as drugs and music.

Persistence of Early Socialization

This raises the question of the persistence of such early-socialized predispositions across the life span. Do people in fact maintain the same basic political attitudes throughout their lives? Persistence clearly is quite high for party identification and racial attitudes (Converse & Markus, 1978; Jennings & Markus, 1984). But even they do change on occasion. For example, young adults' party identifications have changed somewhat in response to major political events such as the Vietnam War or racial conflict (Markus, 1979). Similarly, they can change when young adults make major geographical moves into an area with quite a different partisan complexion (Brown, 1987). In general, basic attitudes can change whenever the dominant political complexion of the individual's social environment changes. And such changes are more likely to occur among young adults than among those over age 30, whose attitudes tend to have hardened with time.

One particularly interesting case of such changes occurs when the individual is exposed to new peer group norms through higher education. Students who have spent most of their years living in their parents' home and surrounded by childhood friends can, at college, be introduced to many new and different kinds of people with many new and different beliefs. Not surprisingly, this exposure can have a profound effect on many of them.

A classic demonstration of such change was provided by Newcomb's (1943) study of alumnae of Bennington College. This small, exclusive women's college in Vermont first opened, with a very liberal faculty, in the early 1930s. Most of the students came from affluent, conservative families, yet there were large and marked changes toward liberalism as the women progressed through the school. These attitude changes were most common among students who identified most with Bennigton and who had the closest social relationships with other students and faculty. For these students, Bennington served as an important reference group, and its dominant liberal norms brought about substantial attitude change.

What happened to the students' attitudes after they left school? Did their liberalism persist, or did they regress to their parents' conservatism? In fact, 20 years later their political views had remained remarkably stable. Those who left college as liberals were still liberals, and the conservatives were still conservatives (Newcomb et al., 1967). The critical factor determining this persistence was the social environment the women entered after college, particularly their husbands and their friends. Liberal women had generally married liberal husbands. The occasional regressions could be attributed to the fact that some liberal women had married husbands in occupations such as banking or corporation law, and so had moved into a politically conservative world.

Of course it is a rare college that shows the political homogeneity of the small, exclusive, isolated, and highly liberal Bennington campus. The most important conclusion of the Ben-

Drawing by Saxon; © 1963 The New Yorker Magazine, Inc

"They sent her to Bennington to lose her Southern accent, and then she turned her back on everything."

nington study is that mere exposure to information is not sufficient to change basic political attitudes. Intense, interpersonal contact such as that in the Bennington experience is necessary and, indeed, may be necessary for years afterward if the change is to be maintained. And such contact is most likely to produce change if it occurs relatively early in life.

PUBLIC OPINION AND VOTING

A second major focus in political psychology has been on public opinion and voting behavior. An influential early product was *The People's Choice* (Lazarsfeld, Berelson, & Gaudet, 1948), a careful analysis of voter decision making during the 1940 campaign. It explained individuals' voting behavior as stemming from their membership in social groups with clear political norms. Catholics, the working class, and city dwellers were more likely to vote Democratic, while Protestants, the middle class, and those living in rural areas were more likely to vote Republican. These differences were later explained as resulting from direct interpersonal influence: parents pass their partisan preferences on to children, and husbands and wives and coworkers influenced each other, making sure that each other did not stray from the "right" vote for their social category (Berelson, Lazarsfeld, & McPhee, 1954). The dominant causal factors were groups and social influence.

Party Identification

Later national studies resulted in a theory of voting behavior that focused on individual decision making (rather than social influence), published in the important book, *The American Voter* (Campbell et al., 1960). It had two dominant features. First, it argued that voters are minimally informed and largely nonideological. In the absence of much information about the candidates and issues, and without strong ideological moorings, how do voters decide? Primarily by applying their own party identification, a

"standing decision" to favor one side rather than the other. By a simple process of **cognitive consistency** (as outlined earlier in Chapter 5), party identification determines the voter's attitudes toward the candidates and issues of the current election campaign. A lifelong Republican would tend to evaluate George Bush very favorably and his Democratic opponent unfavorably and approve of Bush's opposition to tax increases and support for "Star Wars" and the B-2 bomber. These attitudes toward the candidates and issues of the campaign, shaped by a stable and powerful party identification, proved to predict quite accurately the individual's vote.

The American Voter has been challenged from a number of other perspectives in the years since it was published. Much of the criticism has contended that the key factors are current political and economic realities rather than such long-standing psychological dispositions as party identification. The underlying question is one that runs through the political psychological approach: Is *homo politicus* uninformed, inconsistent, irrational, operating from anachronistic preferences and prejudices out of touch with current reality—or is he or she informed, consistent, sensible, and rational, operating from a set of stable preferences and values, and responsive to external reality?

Thus, other researchers argue that voters do not just ritualistically vote for the same party year after year, but make sensible judgments about the past performance of the president, and then vote to support or oppose his continuing in office accordingly. Indeed poor performance by one's party when in power can also weaken one's party identification (Fiorina, 1981). Similarly, they suggest that congressional incumbents' service to their constituents is a key factor in their re-election campaign; some members of Congress are quite visible and effective in dealing with their constituents' problems with the federal government, while others are not. The key factor is the reality of whether that constituent service is done effectively or not (Mann & Wolfinger, 1980).

Overall, the emphasis among researchers has probably shifted away from believing that party identification is acquired in permanent form in

These children are being socialized to anti-busing attitudes. What is their cognitive understanding of the issues? What about their affective reactions?

early adolescence, toward believing that early adulthood is a formative period with lasting effects (see Jennings & Markus, 1984). There is greater appreciation for how people adjust their preferences (even if only modestly) later in life to accommodate changed realities. And, of course, times change; party identification has not been socialized as strongly in early life in the late 1970s and 1980s as it was in the 1940s and 1950s; today's young people do not have the strong party loyalties their parents and grandparents did (Wattenberg, 1984). But other attitudes generally persisting through adulthood can replace it to some extent, such as racial attitudes or self-identification as a liberal or conservative (Sears, 1989).

Economic Voting

A major area of contention is the role of current economic realities. Kramer (1971) observed that the outcomes of elections were strongly correlated with the health of the general economy. Hence the president's political party tended to lose congressional seats when the economy was weak, and did well when the economy was strong. This finding would seem on the surface to indicate that voters were voting their pocketbooks: when they were doing

This young girl is witnessing a peace march with her parents. What do you think the lasting impact of such socializing experiences will be on her later in life?

well financially, they supported the party in power; when they were doing poorly, they threw the rascals out. This would be a **self-interest** hypothesis. On the other hand, voters may vote against the president's party when the national economy is doing poorly even if they themselves are not particularly badly hurt. That is, people may vote on the basis of what is good for the society as a whole rather than on the basis of what is good for them selfishly. This is the **sociotropic** hypothesis.

Considerable careful research has been done to test these alternative hypotheses. The clear finding is that voters' ''sociotropic'' judgments of the economy are the deciding factor rather than more egocentric, self-interested judgments about their personal financial situations (Kinder & Kiewiet, 1979; Lewis-Beck, 1988). This mirrors the finding that material self-interest often plays a surprisingly minor role in racial and ethnic prejudices, as discussed in Chapter 13.

Why is self-interested voting comparatively rare? The voters' *attributions* about change in their own personal well-being seems most likely to be responsible. Most people normally attribute such changes to personal factors, such as their own abilities and efforts, and to the particular features of their own situations, rather than to the broader political situation involving the government or the president. If we lose our job, we blame the boss, our own lack of skill or lazy work habits, or perhaps an inept firm that is losing business. We usually do not blame the president. This is consistent with our observation in Chapter 4 that Americans are biased toward internal attributions for their own situation, the so-called ''ethic of self-reliance.''

On the other hand, people are likely to attribute responsibility for the nation's economy as a whole to the president. Herbert Hoover found that out, to his great regret; he was personally blamed for the Great Depression of the 1930s! People might tend, then, to vote on the basis of conditions for which the president is plausibly responsible—the state of the general economy—but not on the basis of conditions for which he is not likely responsible—the voter's own pocketbook (Feldman, 1982).

Consistency and Ideology

Another question that has drawn much attention is the degree of consistency and ideological thinking in public opinion. This again raises the fundamental question of whether the general public thinks politically in an informed, sensible, coherent, and sophisticated manner, or simply uses such superficial cues as party identification without greater thought.

Early research suggested that most members of the general public do not think about politics in terms of a general personal political *ideology* such as liberalism or conservatism (Campbell et al., 1960). Similarly, Converse (1964) found that people did not seem to have strong, consistent views across policy issues; people who were strong environmentalists were not necessarily likely to favor cuts in the defense budget or to favor government aid for child care, and most people oppose higher taxes and want smaller government (in the abstract), but also want to maintain or even expand existing government social programs (Sears & Citrin, 1985). Such inconsistencies also suggested a low level of ideological thinking in the mass public. Moreover, people are often inconsistent on issues of civil liberties and civil rights; most are tolerant in the abstract, but many are also intolerant in more concrete situations. For example, most people believe in free speech for all, but far fewer would grant free speech to such unpopular groups as Communists or the Ku Klux Klan; most support racial integration in the abstract, but oppose busing (Sears & Allen, 1984; Sullivan, Piereson, & Marcus, 1982).

This view of the public as inconsistent and illogical has been extensively challenged by scholars who believe that citizens respond in a rational way to political realities. They argue that the public thinks ideologically only when political elites offer genuinely different ideological alternatives, as they generally do not (Nie et al., 1979); that freedom of speech for groups such as Communists is denied only when they are perceived as being dangerous, as in the early 1950s (Sullivan et al., 1982); that the white public supports integration but not such obvi-

BOX 17–1

Wonderful Winners and Victimized Losers

The self-serving attributional bias discussed in Chapter 4 is one clear example of consistent thinking. Even political candidates are susceptible to it. Interviews were conducted by Kingdon (1967) with the winning and losing candidate in each of 33 races in Wisconsin for the U.S. Senate, House, state senate, state assembly, and five statewide offices. The candidates were asked a series of questions about why they thought they had won or lost. The winners thought the most important factor was the characteristics of the candidates. The losers downplayed that factor and blamed the outcome on party label ("the voters just voted a party line against my side"). Some of the results are shown in the table below. In addition, the losers blamed their loss on the voters' ignorance: 70 percent of the losers said the voters were "not informed," compared to 32 percent of the winners.

For "wins" throughout their careers, 75 percent of the respondents emphasized matters within their control: "their hard work, personal service to constituents, matters of campaign strategy, build-

ing a reputation, and publicizing themselves." For their "defeats," 90 percent of the respondents emphasized matters beyond their control: "the party makeup of the district, the familiar name or other unbeatable characteristics of the opponent, national and state trends, lack of money, or other uncontrollable circumstances" (p. 141).

COMPARISON OF WINNERS AND LOSERS ON PERCEIVED CAUSES OF ELECTION OUTCOMES

Most Important Causes	Winners	Losers
Characteristics of the candidates	62%	35%
Election issues	17	7
Party label	21	59
	100%	101%[a]

[a] Rounding error.
Source: Kingdon (1967).

ously ineffective policies as busing; and that most people support tax cuts to reduce waste in government rather than wanting cuts in essential government services. But no matter whether one interprets these inconsistencies as rational or irrational, there is general agreement that they exist.

Group Conflict

The early voting studies emphasized social and political groups as key determinants of political behavior, as indicated earlier. Today there is renewed interest in groups in politics, but with an emphasis on racial and gender conflict. Racial attitudes clearly play an important role in determining policy preferences on issues such as busing and affirmative action; evaluations of black political candidates; and welfare, tax, and

government spending reductions (Kinder & Sears, 1981; Sears & Citrin, 1985). As we saw in Chapter 13 on prejudice, there is disagreement about whether these racial attitudes are mainly learned in preadult socialization, perhaps therefore not having much to do with today's realities (Sears, 1988), or whether they are a realistic response to the threats posed by blacks to whites' superior position in our society (Bobo, 1988). Whichever is the case, it is generally agreed that threats posed by blacks to whites' *personal* lives have much weaker effects; these are *political*, not personal, judgments (Jessor, 1988).

Another theoretical approach to racial conflict in politics focuses on the attributions people have about the causes of blacks' disadvantages in such areas as jobs, income, housing, and education (Kluegel & Smith, 1986). The "dominant

T A B L E   1 7 – 2

WHAT DO YOU THINK CAUSED THE WATTS RIOTS?

| | Blacks | | Whites |
Perceived Causes	Arrestees	Community Sample	Community Sample
Stable external (grievances about society, pent-up hostility)	85%	64%	34%
Unstable external (weather, accident, chance happening)	8	11	28
Stable internal (Communists, criminals, agitators)	2	9	29
Don't know, no answer	6	17	10
	101%[a]	101%[a]	101%[a]

[a] Rounding error.
Source: Adapted from Sears and McConahay (1973), p. 160.

ideology" held by many whites attributes such disadvantage to blacks' lack of effort (i.e., to controllable internal causes), while blacks attribute them to situational factors such as discrimination and lack of opportunity. This racial difference can be viewed as a special case of the *self-serving attributions* discussed in Chapter 4: people tend to provide explanations that make their own group look good and exonerate it from blame. Another good example concerns blacks' and whites' attributions for the ghetto rioting in the 1960s. As Table 17–2 shows, blacks tended to attribute the rioting to the miserable situation blacks found themselves in, and to the justifiable hostility those conditions produced. Whites, on the other hand, were more likely to blame chance external factors or bad individual rioters.

This difference in attributions for blacks' disadvantage has great political significance. If the real causes lie in bad conditions, as blacks believe, then those conditions should be changed, through governmental housing, health, jobs, education programs, income redistribution, and so on. If the true causes lie in blacks' internal characteristics, such as lack of effort or ability, or criminality, or in the case of the rioting, in unstable external factors such as hot weather, nothing need be done. If criminals were responsible, a harsh "law and order" policy might be appropriate.

The women's movement and the many postwar changes in women's roles in society have also prompted renewed attention to gender conflict in politics. Women today, compared to 30 years ago, are more likely to be working, highly educated, unmarried, and free of caretaking for small children. This new reality has the potential for increasing sensitivity to discrimination against women, and in turn, converting those perceptions into potent motivators of political action.

The major hypothesis linking these changes in women's social roles to political behavior is that they have influenced their **group consciousness.** This raised consciousness is said to have increased women's support for women's issues, such as equal pay, affirmative action, child care, abortion, and the Equal Rights Amendment. And it is said to have contributed to their greater liberalism on other political issues (Klein, 1984; Gurin, 1985).

Indeed, women have increasingly held distinctive political attitudes. They are now consistently more Democratic and liberal than are men, more opposed to Ronald Reagan, and more favorable to social services and unfavorable to military action, differences usually described as the ''gender gap.'' And, consistent with this hypothesis, young, single, well-educated, working women are more liberal in all these respects than are women in more traditional social roles: older, married, less educated homemakers. But whether or not these differences are due to their group consciousness is less clear. Women's sense of group consciousness seems to be too weak to explain the political effects (Gurin, 1985). Women in general, and women in these more modern social roles in particular, tend not to be more favorable to women's issues than do men or more traditional women. Nor do women vote more on the basis of how candidates stand on women's issues than do male voters (Mansbridge, 1985). In general, the circumstances of women's private lives seem to have rather little spillover into their political attitudes (Sapiro, 1983; Sears & Huddy, 1990). Rather, the best evidence is that the ''gender gap'' is mostly due to women's longstanding greater aversion to the use of force, such as war, defense spending, capital punishment, or harsh responses to crime (Smith, 1984).

MASS MEDIA

Another major area of research focuses on the role of the media in politics. Everyone is familiar with seeing the president speak on television, and watching the news at night. We live in a mass media era, in which people are said to spend more time with the media than they do with one another. So sometimes it seems that nothing of any importance occurs in politics that is not due to television. But as we discovered in Chapter 11 on aggression when we examined the effects of media violence on real-life behavior, the media may not dominate people's lives as much as this would imply.

Three Eras

Research on the effects of the media in politics has gone through three phases. The first began in the 1920s and 1930s when radio became widely available throughout the Western world, and talking movies, with accompanying newsreels, became a source of mass entertainment. For the first time, charismatic political leaders such as Hitler, Mussolini, Churchill, and Franklin Roosevelt could reach huge masses of people not merely through the printed word but through radio and movie newsreels. They seemed to have an almost magical power to sway ordinary people. Though social scientists conducted little empirical analysis, they assumed that this propaganda was extremely persuasive. Why? Because, they as-

Adolf Hitler, here addressing the masses at a giant Nazi demonstration in Nuremberg, in 1933, was a hypnotic orator.

BOX 17–2

The Ratings Game versus Real Audiences

How can we reconcile these modest audiences with the network claims of vast audiences? The networks generally rely on Nielsen ratings, which are based mainly on whether a household's television set is on or off, though they also make some use of viewer diaries. The Nielsen ratings showed, for example, that in 1976 the average household had a TV set on 6.82 hours per day (Comstock et al., 1978, p. 89).

This figure overestimates actual viewing in several obvious ways. First, the Nielsen sample probably includes an excessive number of regular television viewers, since the family must contract with Nielsen to be included in the study. Second, it does not tell us if anyone is watching the set. It could be just sitting there in the living room playing to nobody. Movies taken of living rooms indicate that the TV set is on, but no human being is even in the room part of the time (19 percent in one study), and some of the time people are in the room and the set is on, but no one is watching (an additional 21 percent; see Comstock et al., 1978, p. 142). So 40 per-

cent of the time the set is on, but no one is watching. And, finally, even when they are supposed to be watching, the viewers may be doing something else and not paying close attention. Another study videotaped people watching TV and found an amazing variety of other activities going on, including pacing, ironing. playing Monopoly, answering the phone, conversing, wrestling, dancing, and undressing (p. 144). The mother often fills out the viewing diaries for all family members for the whole week on Saturday, when she finally has some spare time, but cannot remember their viewing in great detail, and she is likely to "remember" that they watched their usual programs, whether or not they actually did.

In 1987, Nielsen switched to a new system of electronic monitoring in which each individual in the sample is required to press a button when starting or stopping viewing. The reliability of this system remains to be seen. (For a more detailed analysis of television ratings, see Beville, 1985).

---

sumed, the audience was captive, attentive, and wholly gullible (Institute for Propaganda Analysis, 1939).

These speculations highlighted the need for more systematic tests of media impact. A second phase therefore consisted of systematic empirical research on the impact of the mass media, using the new method of public opinion polling. The most influential early study, of the 1940 election campaign already referred to (Lazarsfeld et al., 1948), reported four main findings. First, relatively few voters changed their preferences throughout the whole campaign. Second, those changes that did occur were not closely linked to mass media exposure, contrary to the fears of the earlier analysts. Rather, people ultimately voted in line with their own social background. True, many voters had been undecided and subsequently made up their minds, but even these people decided ac-

cording to their predispositions. Third, each candidate's campaign communications mainly reached people who had already supported him anyway. That is, voters tended to expose themselves to the side they already preferred, a phenomenon called **selective exposure.** Finally, personal contacts were more important than media propaganda. The authors concluded that the voting decision was "a social experience." The major implication was that the media simply reinforced prior predispositions, rather than creating large numbers of converts. A good deal of other research in the 1940s and 1950s yielded a similar viewpoint called the **minimal effects model** (see Klapper, 1960).

The last two decades have ushered in still a third era, this of renewed respect for the power of the media in politics. The media, and television in particular, were again thought to have powerful persuasive effects, making the pre-television "minimal effects model" outdated. Several kinds of evidence have been given to support this changed perspective. There is the seeming devotion of the American public to television; supposedly, the average adult spends as much time watching television as working. There are important changes in the political uses of television. Presidents have increasingly been able to reach vast audiences through "command performances" on prime-time television. "Media experts" have become increasingly prominent in producing television commercials for political campaigns. Political "spindoctors" are hired by candidates to help put a positive "spin" on events, so that the media interprets their candidate favorably. In this new media world, selective exposure should be no obstacle because brief political commercials are snuck into the middle of entertainment programs, television news covers all sides of a campaign, and televised debates present all candidates to large audiences. And, finally, predispositional factors such as party identification, social class, region, and religion seem to have declining impact on voting behavior, and so should control neither what people watch nor how they feel about it.

Let us then take a closer look at the contemporary role of the media, first assessing the overall impact of the media in politics, and then looking at some areas in which the media play their most substantial role.

Limited Effects

Are the media in fact as effective as the "new look" suggests? In general, the mass media are not as successful in producing massive changes in attitudes as one might think. Many apparent cases of mass persuasion turn out, on close study, to have produced remarkably little real change.

Among the big media events in recent years have been televised debates between the major presidential candidates. For example, the 1980 Carter-Reagan debate, held a week before election day and often regarded as a major influence in Reagan's last-minute victorious surge, brought only 7 percent of Carter's previous sup-

As President, Ronald Reagan was known as "the Great Communicator." Although he had expert media consultants, he had personal qualities that made him especially appealing on television. What do you think they were?

porters to Reagan's side, according to a CBS News poll done immediately after the debate. In a close race such changes were important, but they cannot be said to have been massive.

Research has also examined the effects of regular media programming on political attitudes. Some television series have dealt explicitly with problems of racism and prejudice, and have been enormously popular. The television series "Roots," depicting the history of African-Americans from preslavery life in Africa to the present, played to record-breaking audiences in 1976. However, exposure to the series had no significant effect on whites' perceptions of the hardships of slavery or on racial egalitarianism. Viewers' reactions to the series were most strongly determined by their preexisting racial attitudes (Hur & Robinson, 1978; Ball-Rokeach et al., 1981).

Similarly, reactions to Archie Bunker, the bigoted working-class white man who was the lead character in the series "All in the Family," were

TABLE 17–3

VOTERS' JUDGMENTS OF WHO WON THE CARTER-REAGAN DEBATE, 1980

Predebate Preference	Who Won?			Total (percent)
	Carter	No Choice	Reagan	
Carter	69%	21%	10%	100%
Anderson	31	28	41	100
Undecided	27	43	30	100
Reagan	5	13	82	100

Note: Data from a nationwide CBS News/*New York Times* telephone survey of Americans of voting age.
Source: Adapted from CBS News release, October 29, 1980.

strongly determined by the viewer's prior level of racial prejudice (Brigham & Giesbrech, 1976). In both cases, reinforcement of prior predispositions, rather than attitude change, seemed to be the major effect. Why are the media generally so ineffective in producing major changes of political attitudes? That is, what are the major obstacles they face in political life?

Low Levels of Exposure. People in the business of affecting public attitudes know that their most critical and difficult problem is reaching the people they want to influence. For example, television news is very often thought to be highly influential because so many people watch it. But do they? One typical study found that on an average weeknight, only 23 percent of the adult population watched one of the nightly national network news programs. Most adults (53 percent) never watched even one such program in a two-week span (J. Robinson, 1971). Even these relatively few watchers seem not to have been watching very carefully. In another study, people who had watched an evening network news show could recall, later on in the evening, only an average of 6 percent of the stories it covered (Neuman, 1976).

Major political events, like presidential debates, would seem to be exceptions. For example, during the presidential campaign of 1976, 80 million people were said to have watched at least one debate. But only a minority watched more than one debate, and only about a quarter

of the public watched even one debate all the way through (Sears & Chaffee, 1979). Most viewers consider a situation comedy, football game, or a good movie more interesting than a political speech. Thus, in politics and public affairs, the percentage of the potential audience reached by any message is quite small. With such poor attention among the minority who are reached by it, massive attitude change would seem to be unlikely.

Resistance. Even a communicator who has been successful in getting the message to the target is a long way from changing the target's opinion. For example, both Democrats and Republicans watched the Reagan-Carter TV debate in 1980, but they differed enormously in their evaluations of them. The overwhelming journalistic consensus was that Reagan had "won" the debate. Yet, as you can see in Table 17–3, only 10 percent of pro-Carter viewers thought Reagan had won.

The new information seems to be incorporated into existing attitudes without changing them very much. This seems to be a typical response to most such mass communications. Why is this so? The communications that draw a large audience usually happen also to encounter strong, highly committed attitudes in a great many people. The result is that people use **modes of resolution** other than attitude change to restore cognitive consistency.

All the modes of resolution discussed in

Chapter 6 are relevant here. For one thing, people are likely simply to reject outright arguments that are discrepant from their own previous attitudes. Many of the pro-Carter viewers simply felt that the debate had reaffirmed their initial judgment and did not need to think about it further. Source derogation also takes place. Many of the pro-Carter voters thought that Reagan was poorly informed and too old and that Carter had a better grasp of the complexities of the presidency, so they simply rejected Reagan. Perceptual distortions follow the same pattern. Voters distort the positions on issues taken by candidates to make them more consistent with their own preferences. Many of the pro-Carter voters saw Reagan as a war-hungry hawk, perceiving him as likely to get us into a war, disregarding his desire to achieve "peace through strength." Similarly, they perceived Carter as promoting peace, disregarding his increasingly confrontive stance toward Iran and the USSR. The result of using all these modes of resolutions is that people can expose themselves to discrepant information in the media and not show any real attitude change.

A New Look

It seems to be true that the political media do not create vast changes most of the time. But, as indicated, researchers have increasingly gone beyond such simple demonstrations of modest impact to look closely at media events that do break through these barriers and produce considerable change all by themselves. When do such exceptional events occur?

Massive Exposure. Truly massive public exposure to political events can produce major effects. For example, following the assassination of President John F. Kennedy, at about 12:30 P.M. (CST) Friday, November 22, 1963, the three television networks covered the story virtually nonstop for four days. They covered the confusion at the hospital where the dying president

This famous photo shows Lyndon Johnson being sworn in as president on Air Force 1, alongside his wife and Jacqueline Kennedy, shortly after the death of John F. Kennedy.

was taken; the swearing-in of his successor, Lyndon B. Johnson; the murder of Lee Harvey Oswald, the alleged assassin; the services; the cortege to Arlington Cemetery; the burial there; several processions through the streets of Washington; and countless retrospectives and interviews with prominent people. The networks devoted, on the average, almost 70 hours to these events (Rubin, 1967). The average American adult watched 34 hours of this coverage.

The emotional and attitudinal effects of this massive exposure were extraordinary. According to a survey completed the week after his death (Sheatsley & Feldman, 1965), 53 percent said they cried, 30 percent said they felt *more* upset than *most* people (and only 8 percent, less). Only 19 percent of the public said they had carried on "pretty much as usual" (Sheatsley & Feldman, 1965). The attitudinal effects were no less impressive. Before the assassination, Kennedy had not been thought of as a particularly exceptional president. He had barely won election, was rated by the public as doing no better a job than most presidents, and was judged by historians to be only a little above average among American presidents. Yet in the postassassination survey, half the population called Kennedy one of the best two or three presidents in history, and only 2 percent called him "somewhat below average." It is impossible to separate the effects of the assassination itself from those of its television coverage in producing these changes. But it is widely agreed that the television coverage was instrumental in making the event among the most memorable in American history.

Another dramatic series of events was the Watergate revelations. At the height of his political fortunes, immediately after a smashing re-election victory in 1972, President Richard M. Nixon slowly but surely was revealed as having participated in covering up a burglary of Democratic party headquarters carried out by some of his campaign workers. Most of his top aides were sooner or later implicated in the scandal and were imprisoned, and Nixon himself ultimately became the first American president to resign, in disgrace. The events came to a head when a tape recording of Nixon's private con-versations was made public revealing his complicity in the cover-up. This quickly became common knowledge and produced, in a period of just three days, an increase of 15 percent in those desiring Nixon's forceful removal from office (Laing & Stevenson, 1976). This major change in public attitude forced the president to resign.

These instances of major media impact rank among the relatively few political events that have attracted very high levels of media exposure in the general public. So part of the key to overcoming the obstacles to change is massive exposure.

Long-term Exposure. Most studies of media impact deal with relatively brief or short-term mass communications—single programs or short series on TV or newspaper endorsements in a particular campaign. But many important changes of attitude may occur over extended periods of time—attitudes toward the enemy in wartime or value changes over many years on matters such as religion or sexuality. These more gradual changes may be responsive to equally long-term patterns of media communication.

One example is the effect of American casualties on support for conflicts in Korea and Vietnam. The earliest casualties caused big declines in public support; later casualties made less difference, as if the public had become "hardened" to the fighting (Mueller, 1973). This study provides no direct information on the media's role, but that was surely the main vehicle by which the public as a whole learned about the casualties.

Weak Attitudes. Not all attitudes are emotionally laden and deeply held. The media may have a major persuasive impact when members of the audience are not especially committed to their attitudes. Similarly, attitudes toward relatively new and unfamiliar attitude objects, such as crack cocaine or the 1989 U.S. invasion of Panama or a new toxic waste problem may depend on media coverage. And the media may be more decisive in primary and nonpartisan elections than in general elections, because

---

BOX 17–3

Does Money Talk?

A somewhat more direct test of long-term impact treats campaign expenditures as a determinant of election outcomes. One might think that the more money a candidate spends on a campaign, and the more media expenditure and exposure, the more votes he or she should receive.

But careful research shows that the amount of campaign expenditures is most decisive when little is known about the candidates and the choice is moderately confusing, for example, when (1) three or more candidates are running, (2) they are all relatively unknown, and (3) only moderate levels of expenditure are involved. So Grush and others

(1978) found that in House and Senate primary elections, campaign expenditures were strongly related to the vote when no incumbent or "notorious" candidate (past incumbent, famous person, or past governor or attorney general) was running. Similarly, in presidential primaries campaign expenditures are related to voting success only in the early phase of the primary season, particularly for the less successful candidates (Grush, 1980). Again, the media are primarily important with massive exposure about candidates the public has only weak attitudes about.

---

these elections involve fewer standing predispositions.

Conveying Information. Nevertheless, the media are much more successful in providing information than in changing deeply held attitudes. Presidential debates increase voters' familiarity with the candidates' positions on campaign issues (Sears & Chaffee, 1979). Children learn a great deal from television, ranging from "Sesame Street" to weather forecasts (Comstock et al., 1978).

One of the earliest demonstrations of this information gain from mass communication came from wartime research by Hovland, Lumsdaine, and Sheffield (1949). The Army commissioned them to evaluate the effectiveness of orientation films shown to draftees and volunteers. These films were intended to explain the reasons for World War II, to make new soldiers enthusiastic about the war effort and more eager to fight.

They, too, did not find much evidence of the hoped-for attitude change. Attitudes toward the British and the war—such as whether the British were going all out, whether or not they would have given up with more bombing, or whether they would hold out to the end, along

with attitudes toward the Germans and Japanese—were largely unaffected.

But the researchers did find that viewing the films markedly increased levels of information about the war. For example, the films clearly communicated factual details about the air war over Britain, such as the relative sizes of the German and British air forces, the focusing of German bombings on ports and ships, and the fact that the Germans would have physically invaded England except for the resistance of the British air force.

Nevertheless, it would be a mistake to expect that the media convey a great deal of information. We already mentioned Neuman's (1976) study indicating viewers could recall only 6 percent of the stories they had seen and heard on the national news earlier that evening. People do not usually pay close attention to television news. Also, TV news tends to emphasize the more entertaining features of the day's events. For example, when it comes to elections, TV news emphasizes the "horse race" or "hoopla" aspect of the campaign, not the issues. It focuses on who is ahead, what the campaign strategies are, who made the latest mistake, and pictures of motorcades or people in funny hats, not complex policy positions. So regular viewers of TV news often know little more about candidates' policies than do nonviewers (Patterson & McClure, 1976).

Agenda Setting. In recent years, much attention has been paid to the media's role in **agenda setting.** Issues given a great deal of media coverage tend to become regarded as the most important problems facing the nation. Political leaders then tend to be evaluated in terms of their ability to solve those problems. In this sense the media are said to set the agenda for political debates.

One important early study showed that the public's sense of priorities (as reflected in the Gallup poll question, "What is the most important problem facing the nation?") was determined by the volume of news coverage given various issues. Thus media coverage of the Vietnam war, the ghetto riots, assassinations, and campus unrest of the 1960s, and of Watergate all made them the number one problems of the day. Interestingly enough, the public's priorities bore more relationship to the volume of media coverage than to such indicators of "reality" as the number of troops actually involved in Vietnam, the real crime rate, and so on (Funkhouser, 1973; also see MacKuen, 1981).

Such studies might only reflect a decision by the media to cover the problems already worrying the public; that is, the public's priorities may dictate media coverage, rather than vice versa. But a number of careful experiments have indicated that greater television news coverage induces higher issue salience regardless of the viewer's previous priorities. In one, adults viewed television newscasts in which the amount of coverage given particular issues was varied experimentally. This manipulation significantly influenced the perceived importance of these issues, even on a questionnaire given 24 hours later. In a second, this salience manipulation influenced the basis for the respondents' evaluations of the president. They tended to base their approval of his performance on his handling of the particular issue made salient in the experiment. For example, when energy shortages were most intensely covered, viewers tended to evaluate the president's overall performance primarily in terms of how well they felt he was handling the energy problem (Iyengar & Kinder, 1986). These experiments indicate that television news can, under the right circumstances, have an agenda-setting effect.

The media, therefore, do not often seem to produce major political attitude changes except when exposure is massive or quite long term. They are more likely to have significant effects in providing information or influencing the public agenda. But even in these cases we should not overestimate the magnitude of effects. As with media violence, it is much easier to document effects in the laboratory than in real life.

PERSONALITY AND POLITICS

Another major focus of political psychology has been on the personality of political leaders and followers. Most psychologists would define **personality** as a set of generalized predispositions to behave in a particular way, regardless of the person's situation or role. So to what extent is political behavior determined by individuals' own personal qualities, rather than the situation they are in? In understanding this question, a major influence on political psychology has been psychoanalytic theory, and especially **psychobiography,** the analysis of a specific individual.

The Question of Pathology

One approach centers on political recruitment: What kind of people become political leaders? Lasswell (1930), a major early psychoanalytic theorist, asserted that people went into political life to satisfy their private personality conflicts, but then rationalized their neurotic behavior as being in the public good. For example, a young man might have a strong unconscious antagonism toward authority, and then take up revolutionary causes on behalf of the underprivileged, cloaking his neurotic conflict about authority in the noble rhetoric of democracy and equality. In particular, Lasswell (1948) felt that politics drew people with low self-esteem. The exercise of power should compensate for their feelings of inadequacy by demonstrating how important they are. The "power-hungry" politician is therefore seen as motivated by feelings of inadequacy.

Is this typical? Are political leaders in fact likely to be drawn to politics because of hidden anxieties, conflicts, and neuroses? A number of important psychobiographies have been done of major political decision makers who seemed to evidence signs of real psychopathology. For example, Woodrow Wilson, as the president responsible for U.S. entry into World War I, wanted it to be "the war to end all wars" by instituting a world government to ensure peace. To do so, the United States needed to join the League of Nations (the predecessor of the United Nations). The proposal aroused some opposition in Congress, of course, but Wilson stubbornly refused to compromise, which ultimately resulted in the United States not joining it. The Georges' (1956) excellent biography of Woodrow Wilson depicts his identification with, and repressed hostility toward, a stern and demanding father. When Wilson became frustrated, this conflict could be expressed by rage and rigidity. The Georges suggest that this aspect of Wilson's personality was partly responsible for his fatal stubbornness regarding the League of Nations.

Another example of pathology in high office concerns James Forrestal, the first U.S. Secretary of Defense, who committed suicide at the height of the Cold War. Rogow (1963) argues that Forrestal's suicide was brought on by progressive paranoia, surely a potentially dangerous condition for someone in charge of the armed services of the United States! Similarly, Mazlish's (1972) biography of Richard Nixon describes his need to create crises in order to cope with his fear of death, along with such potentially hazardous traits as suspiciousness, social isolation, difficulty in decision making, and a need for an emotional enemy. Such in-depth case studies of political leaders indeed frequently do turn up pervasive feelings of insecurity, low self-esteem, early deprivation, ungratified social and personal needs, and the like.

In contrast, Lane (1959) argues that a successful democratic politician requires a healthy, well-balanced personality. Success requires that the person work easily with others, be popular, be able to manage complex political campaigns competently, and be able to effectively deal with the complexities of political office. And indeed most data show that political participation is associated with healthy personalities. The most active citizens have high self-esteem and a strong sense of personal efficacy, and their basic physical, safety, and social needs are satisfied (e.g., Renshon, 1974).

The conflict between these two sets of findings is partly due to the fact that analyses of the inner lives of the political leaders focus especially on their failures rather than on their successes, and failure is most likely to be linked to conflicts and anxieties. This has been the case, for example, in studies of such leaders as Lenin, Woodrow Wilson, Eleanor Roosevelt, Lyndon Johnson, and Richard Nixon. But most of the time, compared to most people, these individuals were surely strikingly strong, confident, effective human beings. Current research tends, therefore, to focus more on how particular disabilities produce difficulties in certain specific political tasks or roles, rather than assessing the over-all level of mental health among the politically active.

Personality Types

Such studies of individual leaders have limited capacity for generalizing beyond the person in question. As a result, various more general personality types have been proposed to capture major differences in political orientation. In one such effort, American presidents were classified in terms of two cross-cutting dimensions: (1) whether they were active or passive and (2) whether their dominant affect was positive, such that they enjoyed their work, or negative, so they were always fighting it (Barber, 1985, see Table 17–4). In this scheme, the most dan-

T A B L E 1 7 – 4		
TYPES OF PRESIDENTS		
	Positive	Negative
Active	Franklin D. Roosevelt Harry S Truman John F. Kennedy	Woodrow Wilson Lyndon Johnson Richard M. Nixon
Passive	Warren Harding Ronald Reagan	Calvin Coolidge Dwight D. Eisen- hower

Source: Barber (1985).

gerous are the "active negatives," such as Wilson, Johnson, and Nixon. This type is characterized by unusual self-concern, perfectionism, an all-or-nothing quality in self-perception, denial of self-gratification, and great concern with control of one's aggression. When threatened, the active-negative type has a tendency to rigidify. One consequence is that he may focus anger on a personal enemy; another is that he may cling tightly to a failing policy, stand and fight, and even order others to die for him.

We have already mentioned Harold Lasswell's hypothesis (1930) that the *power motive* is central to political leaders' personalities, particularly because the seeking of power helps to compensate for low self-esteem. In one early study, especially strong power motives were found among elected county officials who had initiated their own political activity, who ran for offices with relatively high-power opportunities, and who aspired to higher office (Browning & Jacob, 1964). A later study analyzed the inaugural addresses of American presidents for their power motivation. The strongest power motives emerged from speeches of the most effective presidents (as evaluated by historians). The highest were Harry S. Truman and John F. Kennedy, with Ronald Reagan and Franklin D. Roosevelt coming in right behind them. Among the lowest in power motivation were such undistinguished presidents as Hoover, Coolidge, Harding, and Ford (Winter, 1987; Winter & Stewart, 1977). But it should be noted that this research has not yet tested the hypothesis that power motives are based on low self-esteem. Indeed most biographical studies of Truman, Kennedy, Reagan, and Roosevelt have contended that they were men with exceptional self-confidence.

Another type is the *authoritarian personality* discussed in the chapter on prejudice. Such individuals tend to use authoritarian aggression against subordinates (or people who are weaker, dependent, or different), to be submissive to authority, to emphasize power and toughness, to be contemptuous of tenderness, and to be especially cynical as well (Adorno et al., 1950). A great deal of research has associated the authoritarian personality with political conservatism, as well as with racial or ethnic prejudice (Kirscht & Dillehay, 1967).

A third personality type is the *machiavellian personality*. Machiavelli wrote his best known book, *The Prince*, in 1513. It was ostensibly a primer on how to attain and make effective use of political power. It tended toward a cynical view of human nature, regarding people as selfish, greedy, vain, and self-protective. Christie and Geis (1970) developed scales by which they could measure the tendency for people who hold this same machiavellian view of human nature, indexed by agreement with items such as "the best way to handle people is to tell them what they want to hear." They expected that people high in machiavellianism would demonstrate a lack of interpersonal affect, ideological commitment, or concern with conventional morality. Indeed, in experimental studies "high machs" used more deception in interpersonal relations than "low machs" did, and used deceit more successfully; they remained cool and collected in interpersonal interaction, and were more successful in bargaining games, especially when emotions were involved. Such individuals may therefore be especially appropriate for foreign minister positions (such as those held with great effect by Bismarck and Henry Kissinger), who can be held in check by heads of state. But they would usually be unsuited for the head of state position itself, which requires behavior more conventionally approved of (Elms, 1976).

Finally, there is the male *machismo* or "male narcissism syndrome." This tends to produce male leaders who like to "play hardball" or threaten force; they perceive international relations in competitive, coercive, combative, adversarial terms (Etheredge, 1979). Such individuals, like Fidel Castro in Cuba, Mussolini in Italy, or the former dictator General Noriega in Panama, run the risk of precipitating conflicts that cost them high office or more.

Personality or Situation?

Another question pits the situation against personality dispositions. Is an action caused by the person's disposition or by the situation? Are "great men" in politics great because of unusual personal qualities or because they just happened to have been in power during good times?

One major study tested whether the greatness of American presidents (as evaluated by historians) was better explained by their situation or by their own personality traits. The more effective presidents shared five helpful situational characteristics: they were more likely to be war heroes (like Washington, Jackson, or Eisenhower), to serve during wars, to be free of scandal, to serve for relatively long periods of time, and/or to be assassinated in office. However, no personality dimensions (such as power or affiliation motives, dominance and extroversion orientations, or dogmatism) explained differences in greatness (Simonton, 1986). These data would suggest it is the president's situation, rather than his personality, that is the most important to his success.

A related study compared elected presidents with vice presidents who assumed the presidency because of the death or resignation of the

Fidel Castro, shown here making an emotional speech on the 30th anniversary of his revolution, is a fine example of a *machismo* leader.

president. These "accidental" presidents did not, on the average, perform as well as the presidents elected in their own right: their terms were marked by such evidence of ineffectiveness as cabinet resignations, Senate rejections of cabinet and Supreme Court nominees, and congressional overrides of presidential vetoes. Again, the question is whether this is due to the situation—they were not elected—or to their personalities.

Elected presidents prove not to differ from "accidental" presidents in such personal characteristics as age, education, and political or electoral experience, so it would seem to be the situation—how accidental presidents take office—that is responsible for the difference in performance (Simonton, 1981, 1985). Presumably, accidental presidents are regarded as less legitimate than presidents elected in their own rights. While such investigations cannot ultimately resolve "the man versus the times" question, they do begin to specify the factors that are important in our judgments of greatness and effective political leadership.

INTERNATIONAL CONFLICT

Another major influence on political psychology has been international conflict. During the 1950s and 1960s, the Cold War inspired much psychological work on international conflict, just as today much work is focused on international tensions in and around the Middle East. Specific crises have also been a focus of attention, such as the Cuban Missile Crisis or the negotiations at Munich in 1938 that led to Hitler's takeover of parts of Czechoslovakia.

Earlier in this book we have discussed a number of theories about the origins of interpersonal or intergroup conflict. The frustration-aggression theory suggests that when one person (or group) frustrates another, the other will respond aggressively. Social identity theory suggests that people get self-esteem by identifying with a group that is superior to its rivals and therefore strive to get better outcomes for their own group than for its rivals. Realistic group conflict theory suggests that antagonisms between groups arise from real conflicts over scarce resources; the same two nations cannot both inhabit the same rich oil fields that lie between their capitals. Presumably all these factors are at work in producing international conflicts. A comprehensive psychological analysis of such conflicts should consider many factors, including mutual perceptions of contending parties, attitudes toward each (such as nationalism and outgroup antagonisms), economics, social roles, organizational behavior and group dynamics within decision-making groups, and bargaining and negotiation (e.g., Stagner, 1967). We can discuss only a small portion of this terrain here.

Images and Misperception

A convenient starting point is the images that contending adversaries hold about themselves and each other. These can focus on nations, political leaders, or populaces. For example, we might be interested in whether or not American decision makers view the Soviet government as fundamentally hostile to the United States. Similarly, we might be interested in the images that officials in the U.S. State Department have of the Soviet government's intentions in Central America, and in the images that the Soviet decision makers have, in turn, of American leaders' intentions.

The Berlin Wall (with East Germany to the left) became the prime symbol of the Cold War, from its building in 1961 until it was broken in 1989.

The first priority for psychologists has been to identify patterns of misperception. Cognitive consistency theories (see Chapter 5) generate numerous examples of decision makers' biases in favor of decisions consistent with their predispositions and images. People seem to delight in having a foreign enemy, and so tend to distort their perceptions to create enemy figures. Enemies are perceived as having bad intentions, poor morals, and indeed, bad traits in general (Finlay, Holsti, & Fagan, 1967). During the Cold War, American decision makers tended to perceive the Soviet Union as expansionist, ruthless, heartless, atheistic, and deceitful. Soviet leaders were thought to support peaceful solutions to conflict only when faced with superior power. Consistency pressures also may be responsible for a number of other common misperceptions, such as "the diabolical enemy," "the moral self," and "the virile self" (White, 1970).

But if Americans perceived the Soviets as the enemy and the United States as moral and honest, it would not be surprising if the Soviets had a very similar black-and-white portrait of the United States in mind. This pattern of distortion that is mutually engaged in by two opposing nations has been described as the **mirror image** (White, 1970). Each side believes *it* has peaceful intentions, and is afraid of the other side; the other side is perceived as aggressive and threatening, so one's own militarism is justified as self-defense.

Belief Systems

A central tenet of social cognition theories in psychology (see Chapter 3) is that information processing tends to be "theory driven" rather than "data driven." We used the term *schema* to describe these theories in that earlier chapter. This leads us to consider the "schemas," or belief systems, that decision makers have about international conflicts.

Two quite different belief systems are the "deterrence" and "spiral" models of international relations (Jervis, 1976). The deterrence model holds that a powerful nation must be firm in its resolve, and not give potential aggressors concessions; indeed it must be willing to go to war to defend its interests. Firmness can check aggression. The idea is that if you give them an inch, they will take a mile. A classic example is British Prime Minister Neville Cham-

Neville Chamberlain and Adolf Hitler shake hands sealing their Munich agreement in 1938, surrendering part of Czechoslovakia to German control. Chamberlain naively said that this meant "peace in our time"; Hitler invaded Poland one year later.

berlain's capitulation to Adolf Hitler at Munich in 1938, an act which is widely believed to have unleashed Hitler's aggressive aspirations. The spiral model, instead, holds that other nations are likely to develop aggressive intentions sooner or later, so to protect one's security it is necessary at all times to be the aggressor. This viewpoint, not surprisingly, tends to bias the perceiver toward seeing danger everywhere.

An especially important notion is that of a leader's **operational code** (Leites, 1951; George, 1969), his beliefs about the nature of politics and political conflict, historical developments, and strategy and tactics. This is similar to the schema notion discussed earlier. Leites suggests that the operational codes of the Bolshevik leaders who led the Russian Revolution, and led the Soviet Union for many years, were quite different from those of contemporary American leaders. The Bolsheviks were willing to engage in high-risk activities as long as subsequent events could be controlled, so that the sequence could be aborted in the event of failure; American leaders, with their sensitivity to public opinion and concern about the next election, abhor the idea of public failure, and thus poorly understood Soviet leadership.

One particularly interesting set of theories held by decision makers involve the "lessons" they have "learned from history" (Jervis, 1976). For example, Franklin Roosevelt, who was secretary of the navy at the end of World War I, was much impressed by Woodrow Wilson's failure to bring the United States into an international peace-keeping organization, and so at the end of World War II was willing to make important concessions to the Soviet Union to ensure that all nations joined the United Nations. On the other hand, John F. Kennedy, whose father was ambassador to Great Britain when the British government was appeasing Hitler at Munich, later in life was resolutely opposed to making concessions to the Soviet Union. Each had "learned from history" during his formative years, but quite different lessons! As in these cases, too often those lessons are learned too early in life and hence are anachronistic when applied later in life, or give too much weight to firsthand or vivid experiences,

or to efforts that were successful even if for accidental reasons.

Belief systems should produce more rational decisions if they are well informed and well integrated. The notion of **integrative complexity** has been used to describe such belief systems. It is composed of two dimensions: differentiation (the number of aspects of the problem perceived by the leader) and integration (perceiving the various parts of the problem as related to each other). A leader is likely to be thought more sensible if he takes into account many factors in thinking about the Russians' military intentions—their economic resources, their real national interests, their fear of invasion, and their ideological desires for world domination. Similarly, his thinking is likely to be regarded as more rational if his perceptions of the Russians' intentions are integrated with his knowledge about what kinds of military forces they have, their economic resources, the relevant geography, and so on.

The integrative complexity of decision makers' belief systems depends in part on the situation. For example, one hypothesis is that revolutionary leadership requires single-minded devotion to the cause, simple messages around which followers can unite, and simple goals that can be the basis of swift and concerted action. As a result, the writings of Washington, Lenin, and Mao Tse-Tung prove to be rather low in integrative complexity during their revolutionary phases. On the other hand, after the revolution has succeeded, the enemy has been defeated, and the revolutionaries take power, they must administer the country in all its complexities. At that point they need to be more aware of complexity, qualify their assertions, and so on. Indeed the integrative complexity of such revolutionaries' rhetoric increased substantially after they took power. And it increased more for those who were successful—like Lenin—than for those who were unsuccessful—like his failed rival Trotsky (Suedfeld & Rank, 1976).

Another hypothesis is that international crises are more likely to be solved without use of force when decision makers are using integratively complex thinking. In such highly com-

BOX 17–4

Rigidity of the Right?

One longstanding hypothesis is that extremely conservative attitudes develop as a means of coping with psychodynamic conflicts. These attitudes are accompanied by oversimplified, black-and-white, rigid cognitive styles, because ambiguity is ego threatening (Adorno et al., 1950; Tetlock et al., 1984). As a result, conservatives are said to be more intolerant of ambiguity, dogmatic, and prone to think in rigid, black-and-white terms. Tetlock and colleagues have tested this hypothesis in several studies from the public statements of public figures by developing measures of integrative complexity. They find, for example, that conservative senators and Supreme Court justices have regularly thought in less complex, more simplified ways than do liberal senators and justices (Tetlock et al., 1985). Even when conservatives were in con-

trol of the Senate, and presumably responsible for dealing with the complexities and trade-offs of practical legislation, they displayed less complex thinking than did liberals—though the difference was much less marked; responsibility for formulating legislation did force more complex thinking (Tetlock et al., 1984). Finally, the most integratively complex members of the British House of Commons were the moderate socialists, with the least complex being both the extreme socialists and extreme conservatives (Tetlock, 1984). In short, these studies provide considerable support for the rigidity-of-the-right hypothesis, with some qualifications: the extreme left is also quite intolerant of ambiguity, and even conservatives become more complex when forced to cope with the practical realities of exercising power.

---

plex situations, integrated thinking is required to discuss and evaluate all possible alternatives. Indeed the integrative complexity of messages exchanged by American and Soviet leaders prior to the outbreak of the Korean conflict, in 1950, was quite low. But during the Cuban Missile Crisis, which was resolved without bloodshed, both sides exhibited much more complex thinking (Suedfeld & Tetlock, 1977).

A central question motivating much of this research is whether foreign policy decision makers are making rational or irrational decisions. A formal definition of rationality would surely not fit most of the cases we have discussed. Many biases and errors intrude, just as we would have expected from our discussions of decision making in earlier chapters. Yet a more modest definition of rationality may come closer. Simon (1985) has offered the notion of **bounded rationality** that suggests practical decision makers are pretty rational within their limits—they do not have all the information, they do not have all the time necessary to evaluate even the information they have, and they

take various cognitive shortcuts. They choose alternatives that are "good enough" rather than "perfect." They are subject to a wide variety of irrational pressures. But still, they are often as rational as can be expected under the circumstances.

Conflict Resolution

At the most general level, conflict arises from **competitive interdependence,** as we saw in the chapter on groups. When two groups are in a relationship in which the outcomes one gets depend in part on what the other gets, they compete for the resources, and conflict is produced (Sherif et al., 1961). Yet when there are realistic conflicts between groups or nations, it is not necessarily the case that competition benefits anyone, even the winner. Rather, there often are cooperative solutions that would benefit both more. To be sure, the United States and the Soviet Union benefited more than Germany or Japan from World War II. But it was at terri-

This 1952 H-bomb test explosion in the South Pacific was photographed from a distance of 50 miles.

ble cost to all concerned, in terms of civilian and military dead and wounded, and devastated cities and economies. Twenty-seven million Russians alone died during that war. There might have been cooperative solutions that would have benefited everyone more. Relationships of competitive interdependence between groups (or individuals)—often have both competitive and cooperative solutions, then. The two parties can fight it out, with one winning and one losing. Or, sometimes they fight it out, and both lose, as in a nuclear exchange. Or, sometimes they cooperate, such that neither gains as much as they might by winning, but both profit in the long run.

Such reward structures that are mixtures of cooperation and competition are often described in terms of the **prisoner's dilemma game** (see Chapter 10). Remember that this is the situation in which one prisoner cannot talk to his pal. The jailer offers a deal: either prisoner can get off if he confesses and implicates the other prisoner. If neither confesses, they both

get short jail terms. But if they both confess, they both get long terms. So the prisoner can cooperate with his partner in crime and keep mum and get a short jail term. Or he can compete, and confess; he may get off altogether, or he may be in jail for the maximum term. International conflicts have much of this same character. By cooperating with other nations with whom we have conflicts, we may at least get something. By going to war, we may win, or everyone may lose big.

How can international conflicts best be resolved? Deutsch (1973) has offered what he describes as a "crude law of social relations": cooperative behavior breeds cooperation in return, and competition inspires competition from others. In an interaction with another group or individual, the person who makes the first move can set the tone of the interaction. In the prisoner's dilemma game, if one person takes a cooperative stance initially, sacrificing the chance for a really big gain for the possibility that both players will win small gains, it is more likely that the other person will also cooperate. If the first person chooses a response that is likely to hurt the other person grievously, that is likely to be reciprocated as well.

Tit for Tat and GRIT. The interesting aspect of the prisoner's dilemma game is that the most effective strategy for earning points for one's own side, over the long term, may be exactly Deutsch's principle. This is called the **"tit-for-tat" strategy.** It starts the interaction with a co-operative response. Thereafter, each time the opponent responds cooperatively, the player cooperates. But if the opponent chooses a competitive response, the player retaliates. Axelrod (1984) held an electronic tournament that came up with exactly this outcome. He invited 14 experts in game theory to program optimal strategies for playing the game. Then he played each of them against the others, and against a computer program that generated random responses, in games of 200 trials each. He found that the tit-for-tat strategy consistently produced the best outcomes for the individual. To win, then, Axelrod concluded the best player should not start a fight (that is, should always initiate cooperation, or respond cooperatively to the opponent's cooperative stance), should not hold grudges (that is, if the opponent switches to cooperation after a period of competition, the player should not vindictively continue to compete), and should not allow himself or herself to be taken advantage of (that is, should retaliate if the opponent switches to a competitive stance).

The implication is that a peaceful gesture is usually helpful unless the opponent has been consistently hostile. This idea has been applied to international relations in the form of a strategy called **GRIT** (graduated reciprocation in tension reduction). This was proposed by Charles Osgood (1962) at a time of extreme tension over nuclear weapons between the United States and the Soviet Union. It proposed that one side make small concessions on its own to reduce tensions between the two superpowers, as a way of seducing the other side into making reciprocal concessions. It assumed that the tit-for-tat strategy would occur, but that it needed to be triggered by some unilateral gesture of tension reduction.

He advocated that we gradually reduce armaments unilaterally, but without jeopardizing our own security either in terms of the potential for nuclear retaliation or in conventional arms. Our own reductions should be graduated depending on the opponent's response: if the Soviet Union makes small cuts, so do we; if they make large cuts, so do we. They need to be clear cut and verifiable, and public, and include an explicit invitation for the opponent to reciprocate. And they should take place over a wide range of geographical regions and dimensions of conflict—diplomatic, military, educational, and whatever.

Several examples of the GRIT strategy seemed to have occurred during the Cold War. Khrushchev appears to have used it in trying to defuse tension around the status of Austria, which was occupied by both Soviet and U.S. forces. A resulting treaty neutralized that country (Larson, 1986). Not long after the world came to the brink of nuclear war in the Cuban Missile Crisis, President Kennedy announced a unilateral initiative, the ending of nuclear tests in the atmosphere. Several minor mutual diplomatic concessions followed, and then an agreement to put in a "hot line" between the two national leaders to help avoid accidental nuclear war, direct air traffic between Moscow and New York, surplus wheat sales to the Russians, and other tension-reducing moves. Shortly before President Kennedy was assassinated later that year, tensions seemed to resume again, perhaps because the president began to look forward to his campaign for reelection and did not wish to appear "soft" toward the Soviet Union. But the episode represents an interesting experiment in international negotiation (Etzioni, 1967).

Third-party Mediation. Another approach to international conflict involves the good works of some third party who serves as a mediator. Perhaps the most successful recent example of this was President Jimmy Carter's success in mediating conflicts between Israel, as represented by Prime Minister Begin, and Egypt, represented by President Sadat. He succeeded in isolating

President Jimmy Carter mediated the quite remarkable 1979 agreement between Egypt's President Anwar Sadat (left) and Israel's Menachim Begin (right) that restored amicable relations between those two warring nations.

the two leaders at the presidential retreat at Camp David, and then engaged in "shuttle diplomacy," personally shuttling back and forth between the two leaders. Finally, he obtained an historic agreement between the two warring nations, one that resulted in mutual diplomatic recognition, a peace treaty, and return of the captured Sinai Peninsula to Egypt.

Later efforts have been made by a wide variety of social scientists to play a similar mediating role to create understanding between hostile parties. One has been the effort by Kelman and Cohen (1986) to reduce tensions between Palestinians and Israelis. The basic idea is that the participants need to analyze not only their own perspectives but those of their adversaries and to recognize the shared nature of the problem. While there have been no extensive evaluations of this approach, it is a promising one and has the value of keeping communication open between groups that frequently seem to prefer to go to war with each other.

Crisis Management

How do political leaders deal with international (or even domestic) crises? When John F. Kennedy and his advisors attempted to deal with the missiles in Cuba, what determined whether they would be successful or not? Clearly they could have triggered a major war, but they did not. On the other hand, they might have defused it without risking war, and they did not. What makes leaders more or less successful in dealing with such crises?

One factor inherent in international crises is psychological stress. Such stress can have a number of negative effects, such as reducing the complexity of information processing, and it can lead to defensive avoidance and wishful thinking. Janis and Mann's (1977) conflict theory of decision making centers on emotion-laden decisional conflicts, the various patterns of coping behavior common in such conflicts, the antecedents of such coping patterns, and their various consequences for decisional rationality. Janis and Mann offer various techniques for coping constructively with stress, primarily relying on vigilance. Decision makers need to inform themselves adequately beforehand about the decision, but particularly about the emotions likely to accompany the decision and its aftermath, and come to grips with them.

Finally, most foreign policy decisions are made with extensive small-group deliberation, so it is perhaps not surprising that one of the most influential efforts by a political psychologist involves **groupthink.** As discussed in Chapter 10, groupthink occurs when a group of people working together form a highly cohesive, tight group of high morale. Subtly they begin to reject people who don't agree with the group, reject differing ideas, and take on an illusion of invulnerability. They then begin to exhibit many symptoms of poor decision making, such as incompletely surveying of alternative possibilities, failure to examine the risks of the preferred choice, and selective biases in evaluating information.

As we indicated earlier, Janis (1982) has applied this theory to numerous cases of foreign policy decision making. He suggests that the American government's lack of response to information suggesting a forthcoming Japanese attack on Pearl Harbor came about through groupthink, an unwillingness to take seriously information that would threaten the foundations of their current policies. He also suggests that groupthink helped to foster all the illusions that led to the disastrous American invasion of Castro's Cuba at the Bay of Pigs in 1961.

On the other hand, there are things that can be done to prevent or at least minimize groupthink. As we indicated earlier, the leader can encourage each member to air objections and be critical of the group's consensus. Outside experts can be called in to challenge the group's

decision. Devils' advocates or subcommittees can be formed within the group to come up with any plausible alternative. Indeed, Janis suggests that the Kennedy administration's handling of the Cuban Missile Crisis exhibited some of these desirable features. The president even arranged to be absent at some key meetings so that the others would not be so concerned with pleasing him by agreeing with whatever he said.

CONCLUSIONS

The psychological approach to politics is a distinctive one in two respects. First, it tends to be a comprehensive one; the psychologist tries to take account of any and all forces on human behavior. A rival point of view, in many areas, is an economic approach, that views the person as more narrowly motivated by the rational pursuit of material interests. Moreover, the political psychologist emphasizes distinctively psychological factors, such as stress, cognitive consistency, cognitive biases, and group influence. These tend to emphasize irrational influences on the individual's behavior. As with many other topics discussed in this book, this contrast of perspectives provides a creative tension that in the long run helps to illuminate the many complex aspects of the human species.

Key Terms

agenda-setting	integrative complexity	prisoner's dilemma game
bounded rationality	minimal effects model	psychobiography
competitive interdependence	mirror image	selective exposure
GRIT	modes of resolution	self-interest
group consciousness	operational code	sociotropic
groupthink	party identification	tit-for-tat strategy
	personality	

Summary

1. Basic political attitudes are often acquired before adulthood and may be quite resistant to change thereafter. Party identification is influenced to some extent by one's parents, although not as exclusively as once thought. Today's young voters have weaker party identifications than did their predecessors.

2. The dominant theory of voting behavior views a longstanding party identification, acquired early in life, as the major influence on the vote. Voters are thought to be generally ill informed and nonideological, and to have rather weak attitudes on issues.

3. This dominant theory has been challenged in recent years by the view that voters do respond in a moderately informed manner to the realities of life, in terms of their economic situations, issue differences between candidates, presidential performance, and constituency service.

4. Racial and gender issues are receiving much current attention, especially the bases of whites' negative political responses to racial issues and black candidates, and of women's political mobilization.

5. In the 1930s the mass media were thought to be awesomely powerful new weapons and in the 1940s and 1950s to have minimal effects. Today there is renewed respect for their role. Nevertheless, far-ranging attitude changes are rarely produced by the media.

6. Major obstacles include lack of exposure to discrepant information and resistance to change of highly committed attitudes.

7. The media can produce major changes in political attitudes, but only when there is a high level of exposure. The media can be effective, however, in agenda setting, providing information, or changing low-commitment attitudes, or in producing change through repeated exposure over long time periods.

8. One major debate in political psychology is whether people recruited to political leadership tend to be fulfilling neurotic needs or are among the most healthy and effective human beings.

9. A number of common misperceptions in international relations have been identified, including the need to identify an enemy, the mirror images that contending powers have of each other, and the tendency to overuse the "lessons of history."

10. Elite decision making in international relations is also subject to bias due to the stress and emotionality inevitably associated with it, and to the group dynamics of decision-making elites.

Suggested Readings

Janis, I. L. (1982). *Victims of groupthink*, 2nd ed. Boston: Houghton Mifflin. A series of case studies analyzing foreign policy "fiascoes" (and some successes) as a result of "groupthink." Includes chapters on Pearl Harbor, the Bay of Pigs, Watergate, among others.

Jervis, R. (1976). *Perception and misperception in international politics*. Princeton, NJ: Princeton University Press. The best application of social cognition theory and research to government decision makers' perceptions of international relations; many fascinating case studies.

Kinder, D. R., & Sears, D. O. (1985). Public opinion and political action. In G. Lindzey and E. Aronson (Eds.), *Handbook of social psychology*, 3rd ed., Vol. 2. New York: Random House. A comprehensive account of research on public opinion concerning politics in the United States. Relates that research to the social psychological principles discussed in this chapter.

Kraus, S., & Perloff, R. M. (Eds.). (1985). *Mass media and political thought: An information-processing approach*. Beverly Hills: Sage. The best of the contemporary sociopsychological approaches to mass media effects, including nonverbal communication, schemas, and agendasetting.

Lau, R. R., & Sears, D. O. (1986). *Political Cognition: The 19th Annual Carnegie Symposium on Cognition*. Hillsdale, NJ: Erlbaum. A recent collection of papers that apply social cognition research and theory to politics. The "schema" concept appears most often.

McGuire, W. J. (1986). The myth of massive media impact: Savagings and salvagings. In G. Comstock (Ed.), *Public Communication and Behavior*, Vol. 1. Orlando, FL: Academic Press. A thorough but surprisingly brief review of the empirical evidence on the 12 principal areas of hypothesized media impact: "The demonstrated impacts are surprisingly slight."

Political Psychology. A quarterly journal that publishes a wide variety of research, ranging from psychobiography and peace research to voting behavior.

White, R. K. (Ed.) (1986). *Psychology and the prevention of nuclear war.* New York: New York University Press. A broad collection of the best of psychologists' thinking about international conflict in the nuclear era.

Actor-observed bias. The tendency for observers to overestimate the importance of the actor's dispositions, and for the actor to overestimate the importance of the situation in explaining the actor's behavior.

Additive principle. In impression formation, the idea that information about a person or attitude is processed in terms of its evaluative implications, and then added together to form an overall impression. Sometimes contrasted with the *averaging principle*.

Affective component. That part of an *attitude* consisting of a person's emotional feelings associated with beliefs about an attitude object; consists mainly of the evaluation of the object (like-dislike, pro-con).

Agenda-setting. Mass communications can focus the public's attention on certain issues, and therefore determine which issues the public is concerned about. If the media focus intensively on inflation, the public becomes concerned with inflation; if they focus on Central America, so will the public.

Aggression. Any action intended to hurt another person.

Aggression anxiety. Anxiety about expressing overt aggression, usually with respect to a particular target.

Aggressive behavior. Any behavior that is intended to hurt another person.

Altruism. An act performed voluntarily to help another person when there is no expectation of receiving a reward in any form. See also *prosocial behavior*.

Androgyny. In psychology, the term used to refer to people who believe they possess both traditionally feminine and masculine characteristics. An androgynous person's self-concept includes both masculine or instrumental qualities (e.g., being independent and strong) and feminine or expressive qualities (e.g., being nurturant and gentle).

Anger. Aggressive feelings.

Antisocial aggression. Aggressive acts such as murder that violate commonly accepted social norms.

Archival research. The analysis of data already collected for another purpose, such as census data or legal records of births, deaths, and marriages.

Association. A link in memory between different stimuli that occur together in time and place. Through pairing, reactions to one stimulus become associated with the other. This is one of the basic processes by which learning occurs.

Assumed similarity effect. The tendency for members of an ingroup to assume that fellow members share their attitudes and values.

Attachment. The emotional bonds that form between people in a close relationship. During infancy, attachment is seen when a child responds positively to one special person, wants to be with that person, seeks the person out when frightened, etc.

Attitude. Enduring response disposition with a *cognitive component*, an *affective component*, and a *behavioral component*. We develop and hold attitudes towards persons, objects, and ideas.

Attitude-discrepant behavior. Acts inconsistent with a person's attitudes. When an individual behaves in a way inconsistent with a belief, *cognitive dissonance* is produced and there is a tendency for the attitude to change.

Attribution. The process by which people use information to make inferences about the causes of behavior or attitudes.

Attribution theory. The principles that determine how attributions are made and what effects these causal attributions have.

Averaging principle. In impression formation, the idea that information about a person or attitude is processed in terms of its evaluative implications, and then averaged together to form an overall attitude. Sometimes contrasted with the *additive principle*.

Aversive racism. Attitudes toward members of a racial group that embody both egalitarian social values and negative affects, resulting in avoidance of that racial group. For example, whites often avoid blacks because of conflicting attitudes: they value equality but have negative feelings toward blacks.

Balance theory. Heider proposed that we strive to maintain consistency among our sentiment and unit relations. We are motivated to like people we are connected to by physical proximity or other links, to like people we agree with, and to dislike those we disagree with.

Behavioral component. That part of an attitude consisting of the person's tendencies to act toward the attitude object. A child's attitude toward a pet cat may include the tendencies to pet and cuddle the animal.

Behavioral intention. The conscious intention to carry out a specific act.

Behaviorism. The influential analysis of learning associated with Watson, Pavlov and Skinner which investigates only overt behavior, not subjective states such as thoughts, feelings, or attitudes. Behaviorism identifies association and reinforcement as the key determinants of learning.

Biopsychosocial model. The view that a person's state of health is jointly determined by biological factors (such as exposure to a virus), psychological factors (such as stress),

and social factors (such as degree of social support).

Body language. Information transmitted about attitudes, emotions, and so on by nonverbal bodily movements and features, such as posture, stance, or touch.

Bounded rationality. A definition of rational decision-making that describes it as rational if it utilizes available information in an efficient and sensible way, even if it is not perfectly rational in formal terms.

Brainstorming. A technique for coming up with new and creative solutions for problems. Members of a group discuss a problem and generate as many different solutions as they can, withholding criticism until all possibilities have been presented.

Breakpoints. The starting or ending points of a behavioral act, as perceived by an observer.

Built environment. Buildings, roads, shopping centers, and other structures built by humans.

Bystander effect. When other people are present, it is less likely that any one person will offer help to a stranger in distress. The diffusion of responsibility created by the presence of other people is one explanation for the bystander effect.

Case history information. Information about a particular person or event. This kind of information often has a more persuasive impact on people's judgments than objectively better but more pallid and dull statistical information.

Categorization. The process by which we perceive stimuli in groups or categories rather than perceiving each individual stimulus in isolation from the others.

Catharsis. Freud's idea that by expressing aggression, a person's aggressive drive can be reduced.

Causal attribution. See *attribution*.

Central traits. A trait is central to the extent that it is associated with many of the stimulus person's other characteristics. Traits such as being warm or cold are considered central because they are important in determining overall impressions.

Close relationship. A personal relationship involving much interdependence. Partners in close relationships usually interact frequently, have relatively strong influence on each other, and engage in a variety of activities together.

Cognitive component. That part of an attitude consisting of the person's beliefs, knowledge, and facts about the attitude object.

Cognitive consistency. Tendency for people to seek consistency among their attitudes; regarded as a major determinant of attitude formation and change.

Cognitive dissonance. Theory developed by Festinger according to which inconsistency (dissonance) between two cognitive elements produces pressure to make these elements consonant. It has been applied to a wide range of phenomena, including decisions and attitude-discrepant behavior.

Cognitive miser. Description of people as having limited information-processing capabilities, and therefore adopting various cognitive shortcuts. For example, we cannot perceive all stimuli in our perceptual field at once, so we focus on the most salient ones.

Cognitive response theory. The theory that attitude change following receipt of communication depends on the cognitive responses it evokes. If it produces negative thoughts, it will be rejected; if it evokes positive thoughts, it will be accepted. Counterarguing is a crucial mechanism for resisting persuasion, according to this theory.

Cohesiveness. In group dynamics, the forces, both positive and negative, that cause members to remain in a group. Cohesiveness is a characteristic of a group as a whole, and results from the degree of *commitment* of each individual to the group.

Commitment to an attitude. The perception that one's decision cannot be revoked; a key determinant of cognitive dissonance.

Commitment to a relationship. All the forces that act to keep a person in a relationship or

group. Positive forces include interpersonal attraction and satisfaction with a relationship; negative forces include such barriers to ending a relationship as the lack of alternatives or having made large investments in the relationship.

Communication networks. In some groups, there are constraints on the channels of communication available to members. Four types of communication networks are the circle, chain, wheel, and Y-pattern.

Companionate love. A somewhat practical type of love that emphasizes trust, caring and tolerance of the partner's flaws. Companionate love may develop slowly in a relationship as partners become more interdependent. Sometimes contrasted with *passionate love*.

Comparison level. One standard we use to evaluate the quality of our social relationships. Our comparison level refers to the level of outcomes (benefits and costs) we expect or believe we deserve based on our past experience in relationships.

Comparison level for alternatives. A second standard we use to evaluate the quality of our social relationships. Our comparison level for alternatives refers to evaluating one particular relationship against other relationships that are currently available to us.

Competitive interdependence. Situation in which the outcomes of two persons or groups depend on each other in such a way that the rewards one gets reduce the rewards the other gets. Wars, athletic contests, or business competition are good examples; each has winners and losers.

Compliance. Performance of an act at another's request.

Confirmatory hypothesis testing. Selectively extracting from others information that preferentially confirms a hypothesis, instead of gathering information evenhandedly that both favors and opposes the hypothesis.

Conformity. Voluntary performance of an act because others also do it. Conformity often results from a person's desire to be right (informational influence) and/or desire to be liked (normative influence).

Contact theory. The theory that prejudice against a social group can be reduced by appropriate kinds of contact with individual members of that group.

Contingency model of leadership effectiveness. Fiedler's model distinguishing between task-oriented and relationship-oriented leaders. When the group situation is either highly favorable or highly unfavorable to control by the leader, task-oriented leaders are more effective. In intermediate situations where the leader has moderate control, relationship-oriented leaders are more successful.

Contrast. In the study of attitude change, the tendency to perceive a communicator's position as being farther away from the individual's own position than it actually is.

Cooperative interdependence. Situation in which the outcomes of two persons or groups depend on each other in such a way that they must cooperate to get rewards both desire.

Coping. The process of managing internal or environmental demands that are appraised as taxing or exceeding one's resources. Coping may involve active problem-solving efforts and/or efforts at emotional control.

Correlational research. Passively measuring two variables and determining whether or not they are associated with each other. Studies relating smoking to lung cancer are correlational: They measure the amount of smoking each person has done and whether or not he or she gets lung cancer in order to determine if the two are related. The major problem with correlational designs is determining whether or not a correlation reflects a cause-and-effect relationship.

Counterarguing. In attitude change, resisting persuasion by considering and actively refuting the arguments in a persuasive communication.

Covariation. Judgments of covariation involve determining how strongly two things are related such as the time of day and frequency of crime, or the ingestion of caffeine and alertness. When social perceivers expect two things to go together, they tend to overestimate the actual degree of covariation.

Credibility. In attitude change, a communicator's credibility depends on his or her perceived expertise about the topic and how much he or she is trusted by the individual receiving the communication.

Crowding. The subjective experience of feeling cramped or not having enough space.

Cultural stereotypes. Societal-level images of members of a social group such as those found in art, literature, religious teachings, and the mass media. See also *personal stereotypes*.

Cybernetic theory of self-regulation. The process by which people compare their behavior to a standard, decide that it either matches the standard or not, and continue adjusting and comparing until the standard is met or abandoned. Self-awareness is argued to be a precondition for this type of self-regulation.

Debriefing. An essential feature of ethical research is debriefing. After their participation is over, subjects should have the purposes and procedures of research explained, their questions answered, and the scientific value of the research discussed.

Decision-making theories. According to decision-making theories, people calculate the costs and benefits of various actions, and pick the best alternatives in a fairly logical way. Two specific examples of this perspective are *expectancy-value theory* and *incentive theory*.

Deindividuation. Loss of a sense of personal identity and responsibility in a group which can lead people to do things they would normally not do when alone. Anonymity is a key factor in deindividuation.

Demand characteristics. Aspects of a study that make subjects more aware of their participation in research and thus bias their behavior. Subjects may try to avoid negative evaluations from the experimenter, try to cooperate with the experimenter to verify the hypothesis, etc.

Dependent variable. In an experiment, the responses to the independent variable being manipulated or measured.

Desensitization. When over-exposure to material that normally evokes strong emotions, such as violence or sexuality, makes the individual insensitive to it.

Diffusion of responsibility. The presence of other people can make each individual feel less responsible for events that occur or for solving problems. This can decrease the likelihood that a person will take action, for instance to help a stranger in distress.

Discounting principle. In making attributions, the tendency to reduce reliance on one particular cause to the extent that other plausible causes exist. If, for example, a judge gives the death penalty to a criminal, we might conclude that she was generally a tough judge, but we would be less likely to do so if we also discovered that the law required the death penalty for this particular crime.

Discrepancy. In the study of attitude change, the distance between the communicator's and the target's position on the issue discussed in the communication. A communicator may argue that tuition should be doubled; that position will be highly discrepant to a student who believes it should not change, but only moderately discrepant to a student who thinks a modest increase is reasonable.

Discrimination. The behavioral component of group antagonism. People discriminate against the disliked group by refusing its members access to desired jobs, educational opportunities, country clubs, restaurants, places of entertainment, and so on.

Disinhibition. General loosening of control over anger when it has once been released under socially approved conditions; that is, once a person has committed a socially approved aggressive act, he or she has fewer inhibitions about aggression under other conditions.

Displaced aggression. The expression of aggression against a target other than the source of attack or frustration, usually a safer target.

Dispositional attribution. Perceiving the cause of a person's action as being in his or her own dispositions, such as personality, ability, or attitudes.

Distraction. Stimulus that draws attention away from a persuasive message. It sometimes increases attitude change by making it harder for people to defend a position against the arguments in the message.

Door-in-the-face technique. A technique for gaining compliance with a request by first asking for a much larger request. After the larger request is refused, the person is more likely to agree to the second, smaller request.

Ego-involvement. The subjective linking of an attitude to strong ego needs, thereby making the attitude more emotionally-laden and more resistant to change.

Elaboration-likelihood model. A theory of persuasion and attitude change in which the key variable is amount of careful thought given to the arguments (elaboration likelihood). With more careful processing, attitude change will depend more on the real strength of the arguments and less on peripheral cues.

Empathy. Feelings of sympathy and caring for others—in particular, sharing vicariously or indirectly in the suffering of other people. Strong feelings of empathy can motivate a person to help someone in need.

Environmental psychology. A branch of psychology that studies the relationships between the physical environment and human behavior and well-being.

Equity theory. An offshoot of *social exchange theory* that focuses on fairness in relationships. A relationship is equitable when the ratio of a person's profits to contributions is the same for everyone. The theory postulates that when individuals perceive inequity, both underbenefited and overbenefited partners feel distress and take steps to restore equity.

Ethnocentrism. The belief that the ingroup is the center of the social world and superior to outgroups.

Evaluation. Most important basic dimension underlying impression formation and attitudes; the goodness or badness of another person, object, or concept. See also *affective component*.

Evaluation apprehension. Concern for how others evaluate oneself and often for looking good in public.

Exchange theory. See *social exchange theory*.

Exemplar. An example of a category that embodies the significant attributes of that category or the ideal of that category. For example, a robin is an exemplar of the category "bird."

Expectancy-value theory. This theory predicts that decisions are based on the combination of two factors: (1) the value of the various possible outcomes of the decision and (2) the likelihood or probability that each outcome will actually occur.

Experiment. Type of research in which the researcher randomly assigns people to two or more conditions, varies in a controlled manner the treatment each condition is given, and then measures the effects on the subjects' responses. Though experiments are often difficult to arrange, they have the advantage of yielding clear information about cause and effect. Any differences between groups in the outcome of the experiment must be due to the variables that were experimentally manipulated.

Experimenter bias. Biases introduced into the results of an experiment, usually in the direction of falsely confirming the hypothesis, through unintentional actions of the experimenter.

External attributions. Attributions of causality for a person's behavior or attitudes to factors external to the individual, such as luck, or other people, or the situation.

External validity. Extent to which the results of a study are generalizable to other populations and settings.

False consensus. Bias in perceptions of others such that one exaggerates how common one's own opinions or behaviors are.

False uniqueness. Bias in perceptions of others such that one exaggerates how uniquely good one's own abilities are.

Fantasy aggression. An imagined act of aggression. It may tend to reduce direct aggression.

Field experiment. Study in which variables are systematically manipulated and measured in real-life, nonlaboratory settings.

Figure-ground principle. In social perception, the basic principle that attention is drawn to stimuli that stand out against a background. Figural stimuli are those that stand out; the background is called the ground. This principle has generated much of the research on salience in the area of social perception.

Foot-in-the-door technique. A technique for gaining compliance with a request by first getting the person to comply with a smaller request. After agreeing to a small request, the person is more likely to comply with the larger request.

Forewarning. In attitude change, informing recipients of the position to be taken in a persuasive communication, or that the communicator is intending to persuade them, prior to the receipt of the communication.

Frustration. The blocking or thwarting of goal-directed behavior. A child is frustrated when a parent refuses to let the child color the bathroom wallpaper with crayons or smear ice cream on the dining room table.

Frustration-aggression hypothesis. In its strongest form, this hypothesis asserts that frustration always creates feelings of aggression, and that aggression is always caused by frustration.

Fundamental attribution error. The tendency for observers to overestimate the causal importance of a person's dispositions and underestimate the importance of the situation when they explain the person's actions.

Gender identity. The knowledge that one is male or female. Gender identity is acquired early in life.

Gender self-concept. The degree to which a person perceives that he or she possesses traditionally masculine or feminine characteristics.

Gender stereotypes. Beliefs about the typical personal attributes of males and females. According to traditional gender stereotypes, women are believed to have expressive or communal qualities, such as being nurturing and gentle. Men are believed to have instrumental or agentic qualities such as being independent, assertive, and competent.

Gender typing. The process of labeling things, activities and people as "masculine" or "feminine." For example, many people consider dolls, ruffles, and housecleaning to be feminine.

Gestalt. The theory that people form coherent and meaningful perceptions based on the entire perceptual field, so that the whole is different from the sum of its parts.

GRIT. Graduated reciprocation in tension reduction; a complex formula for de-escalating conflict between two superpowers, initiated by small unilateral concessions by one side.

Group. A social aggregate in which members are interdependent (have mutual influence on each other) and have at least the potential for mutual interaction.

Group consciousness. Strong identification with the ingroup plus the feeling that the ingroup is being treated unfairly. This is theorized to increase political action to further group aims.

Group identification. The individual's affective attachment to a reference group.

Group norms. See *social norms*.

Groupthink. Term used by Janis to describe an impairment in decision making and sound judgment that can occur in highly cohesive groups with a strong, dynamic leader. Group members isolate themselves from outside information, try to please the group leader, and agree on a decision even if it is irrational.

Group polarization. When a group discusses an issue, people often come to support more extreme positions than they did initially. This sometimes leads to a *risky shift*, and sometimes to a cautious shift, depending on the initial views of group members.

Halo effect. A liked person is assumed to have good qualities of many kinds, whether or not the observer has any information about those qualities.

Health behavior. An action undertaken by a person who is healthy to enhance or maintain good health.

Health belief. An attitude about a particular health practice that influences the willingness to adopt that practice; may include beliefs about personal susceptibility, the efficacy of the health practice, or the severity of the health risk among others.

Heuristic. A shortcut for problem solving that reduces complex or ambiguous information to more simple judgmental operations.

Illusion of control. A bias whereby we perceive ourselves as being able to control our lives and the events around us more than is the case in fact.

Illusory correlation. The belief that two things are related to each other because prior expectations dictate that they ought to go together, when in fact those things bear little or no relationship to each other.

Imitation. See *modeling*.

Implicit personality theory. The ordinary person's theory about which personality traits go with other traits, such as "weak" going with "cowardly," or "calm" going with "decisive."

Incentive theory. An attitude theory that predicts people will adopt whichever attitude position offers the most positive incentives and the fewest negative incentives.

Independent variable. The variable in a study that is interpreted as the cause of changes in the dependent variable. The independent variable may be systematically manipulated by the researcher in an experiment, or passively measured in a correlational study.

Informed consent. The requirement that research subjects must freely choose to participate, after being informed about the study, the procedures that will be used, and the costs and benefits of the study.

Ingroup. The group to which the individual belongs and which forms part of his or her social identity. See also *outgroup*.

Ingroup favoritism effect. The tendency to give more favorable evaluations and greater rewards to members of one's ingroup than to members of outgroups.

Inoculation. McGuire's notion that people become more resistant to the effects of persuasive communications when they have been exposed to weak counterarguments.

Integrative complexity. An index of the complexity of a person's thinking about a particular issue: How many dimensions are taken into consideration and how complex are the connections among these dimensions?

Interdependence. The condition in which two or more people have some degree of mutual influence on each other's feelings, thoughts or behaviors.

Internal attributions. Attributions of causality to factors internal to the individual, such as his or her attitudes, personality, ability, emotions, or effort.

Internal validity. The extent to which cause and effect conclusions can validly be drawn from the research.

Jealousy. Occurs when a person perceives a real or potential attraction between his or her partner and a rival. Jealousy is a reaction to a perceived threat by a rival to the continuity or quality of a valued relationship. Feelings of anger, anxiety, and depression are common.

Just world. The belief that people get what they deserve. If good things happen to people, it is because they have worked hard, been honest, or been foresighted; if bad things happen to them, it is because they were lazy, careless, stupid, or dishonest. One consequence is that victims are blamed for their misfortunes, even if in reality they are not to blame.

Learning theory. The central idea in learning theory is that a person's behavior is determined by prior learning. Current behavior is shaped by past experience. In any given situation, a person learns certain behaviors which, over time, may become habits. When presented with the same situation, the person tends to behave in the same habitual way.

Legitimate authority. In many situations, social norms permit those in authority to make requests. Illustrations of legitimate authority include the government's right to ask citizens to pay taxes; parents' right to ask their children to wash the dinner dishes; and an employer's right to assign duties to an employee.

Locus of control. The tendency to explain events in terms of one's own behavior versus forces in the environment. Those favoring explanations centering on the self are said to have an internal locus of control; those favoring explanations centering on environmental factors are termed external in locus of control.

Logical error. The tendency to impute attributes to people that are consistent with what we already know about them. For example, upon learning that a man is warm, we might also regard him as generous and sociable.

Loneliness. The psychological discomfort we feel when our social relations lack some essential feature. This deficit may be quantitative (too few relationships) or qualitative (unsatisfying relationships).

Low-ball technique. A technique for gaining compliance in which the influencer obtains a commitment from the person before revealing hidden costs of the request.

Matching principle. In dating and marriage, people tend to select partners who are similar to themselves in attitudes, values, ethnic background, religion, social class, education, and many other personal characteristics.

Membership group. A group of which the individual is a member.

Mere exposure effect. Simply being exposed frequently to a person or object tends to increase our liking for that person or object. Repeated exposure most often enhances liking when our initial reactions to the person are neutral or positive, when no conflict of interests exists, and when the repetition is not so great that it causes satiation.

Message learning. The theory that attitude change depends on the individual's learning the content of the communication.

Meta-analysis. A quantitative approach to summarizing and synthesizing the results of many empirical studies on a topic, such as sex differences in aggression. Statistics are used to estimate the overall size of the "effect" or sex difference, and also to test for the consistency (homogeneity) of a finding across studies.

Middle-range theories. Theories that attempt to account for major categories of behavior, but do not attempt to cover all human behavior in general. A middle-range theory might attempt to explain attitude change, or attribution or aggression, but not all three at once.

Minimal effects model. The description of mass communications as mainly reinforcing the recipient's prior attitudes rather than as creating widespread attitude change.

Minimal intergroup situation. The basic research situation used to test social identity theory: People are arbitrarily classified into groups, and then allowed to allocate rewards to each other.

Minimal risk. The idea that the risk anticipated in any research project must be no greater than the risk encountered in daily life.

Minority influence. Influence that members of a minority have over the larger majority in a group.

Mirror image. Images held by members of two conflicting nations, each of which feels their own nation is peace-loving and afraid of the other nation, which is regarded as hostile and threatening.

Misattribution. Assigning the cause of a particular behavior or emotional state to a stimulus other than the actual cause, such as thinking a lecture is exciting when actually you are excited by having drunk ten cups of coffee.

Modeling. In observational learning, people often learn behaviors and social attitudes simply by observing the attitudes and behaviors of other people, known technically as models. Modeling occurs when a person not only observes but actually copies the behavior of a model. Observational learning can occur without any external reinforcement. However, whether or not a person actually performs or models a behavior learned through observation will be influenced by the consequences the action has for them. Modeling is also known as *imitation*.

Modes of resolution. In attitude change, the various alternative ways in which a target of a discrepant communication can reduce inconsistency, such as attitude change, source derogation, or misperception.

Naive psychology. The ordinary person's informal theories about what determines human behavior.

Negativity effect. Tendency for impressions to be influenced more by negative traits than by positive traits. Hence positive impressions are more vulnerable to change than negative impressions.

Nonverbal leakage. The communication of true emotions through nonverbal channels even when the person's verbal communication tries to cover them up.

Norm. See *social norms*.

Norm of reciprocity. The social norm that we are expected to reward those who reward us. For example, if someone helps us, we feel obligated to help them in return.

Norm of social justice. Human groups develop norms about fairness and the just distribution of resources. Norms of social justice may contribute to prosocial behavior.

Norm of social responsibility. A social norm dictating that we should help others who depend on us. This may contribute to prosocial behavior.

Observational learning. Learning by watching what others do and doing the same; also applies to forming attitudes by modeling those of others, such as parents or teachers.

Old-fashioned racism. Old-fashioned stereotypes of white racial superiority, segregationist attitudes and opposition to formal racial equality.

Operational code. In political psychology, a leader's beliefs about the nature of politics, history, and strategy.

Operational definition. The specific procedure or operation that is used to measure or manipulate a variable in a research study.

Outgroup. Any group other than the *ingroup*.

Outgroup homogeneity effect. Perception that members of the outgroup are more similar to each other than members of the ingroup are to each other.

Overjustification. Giving people rewards for performing a task can undermine their intrinsic interest in the task, presumably because they attribute their liking for the task to the reward rather than to their own intrinsic interest in the task.

Paralanguage. Information conveyed by variations in speech other than actual words and syntax, such as pitch, loudness, hesitations, and so on.

Party identification. A person's underlying, stable preference for one political party over its rivals.

Passionate love. The emotionally charged type of love that sometimes characterizes the early stages of romantic relationships. Often contrasted with *companionate love*.

Peripheral cues. Aspects of the communication situation that are irrelevant to the content of the message, but which can influence attitude change when the individual is not engaged in systematic processing (e.g., nice music, long or beautifully written messages).

Person perception. Process of forming impressions of others, making judgments about their personalities, and adopting hypotheses about the kind of persons they are.

Personal distress. An individual's reactions to the suffering of others, including horror, shock, helplessness, or concern. Since personal distress focuses on the self, it can motivate people to ignore or avoid the suffering of others, rather than to offer assistance.

Personal space. The physical space immediately around their bodies that people treat as though it were a part of themselves. Hall has suggested four basic zones for interpersonal interaction: intimate, personal, social, and public.

Personal stereotypes. An individual's own beliefs about the attributes of members of a particular group. Personal stereotypes may be similar to or different from *cultural stereotypes*.

Pessimistic explanatory style. The tendency to explain negative events that befall the self in terms of internal, stable and global qualities of the self.

Positivity bias. General tendency to express positive evaluations of people more often than negative evaluations. Also called the "leniency effect" or "person positivity bias."

Possible selves. Schemas that people hold concerning what they may become in the future.

Power. See *social power*.

Prejudice. The affective component of group antagonisms; disliking a group or members of a group.

Primacy. The tendency to use an initial impression to organize and interpret subsequent information.

Priming effect. The tendency for recently used or thought about material to influence the interpretation of subsequent information.

Principle of least interest. According to social exchange theory, the balance of power in a relationship is affected by the relative dependency of the two partners. According to the principle of least interest, the partner who is less interested (less dependent) will tend to have greater power.

Prisoner's dilemma game. A laboratory game widely used in studies of competition. So-called because it is based on a problem faced by two suspects at a police station.

Private self-consciousness. A chronic tendency to focus on the private self. Privately self-conscious people try to figure themselves out, think about themselves a lot and are attentive to their inner feelings.

Prosocial aggression. Aggressive acts that support commonly accepted social norms, such as a soldier shooting an enemy sniper during combat.

Prosocial behavior. An act that helps or is intended to help others, regardless of the helper's motives. Prosocial behavior is a broader category than *altruism*.

Prototype. A schema defined by the specific features of a particular type of person, such as librarian or effete snob.

Proxemics. The term used by Hall to describe the study of how people use space.

Psychoanalytic theory. Theory of human behavior based originally on Freud's work. It emphasizes instincts, unconscious motivation, and the ego defenses people construct to protect themselves against their own irrational drives.

Psychobiography. Biographies of prominent political leaders, often written from the perspective of psychoanalytic theory.

Psychodynamic theories. Theories that analyze attitudes and behavior as resulting from deep motivational tensions and conflicts. *Psychoanalytic theory* is the best known of these.

Psychological control. The belief that one can exert personal control over events, independent of whether or not that control actually exists or is ever exercised.

Public self-consciousness. A chronic tendency to be concerned with how one appears to others. Publicly self-conscious people are concerned with what others think of them, the way they look, and how they appear to others. Contrasts with *private self-consciousness*.

Random assignment. Placement of subjects into experimental conditions in a manner which guarantees that assignment is made entirely by chance, such as by using a random numbers table. This is an essential characteristic of an experiment.

Random sample. A group of people participating in a study who are selected from the broad population by a random process, and who therefore are representative of that broad population.

Rational model of inference. A model assuming a logical, correct way to put information together to reach a judgment.

Reactance. Brehm's concept that people attempt to maintain their freedom of action. When this freedom is threatened, they do whatever they can to restore it, for instance, by refusing to comply with a request.

Realistic group conflict. The theory that antagonism between groups arises from real conflicts of interest and the frustrations those conflicts produce. Two groups in conflict over the fishing rights in a certain segment of the ocean may start to hold prejudices and act aggressively toward each other as a result of the reality-based intergroup conflict.

Reference group. A group to which a person belongs or uses a basis of comparison. The group serves as a standard for the person's own behavior and attitudes. Group norms can act as a persuasive force leading to attitude change, or can prevent change by supporting the individual's position when it is attacked.

Reinforcement. The process by which a person or animal learns to perform a particular response by being rewarded when it is performed.

Relapse prevention. Procedures incorporated into health behavior change programs that train people to identify situations that may lead them to return to prior faulty health habits; usually involves training in coping skills for use in high-risk-for-relapse situations.

Relative deprivation. The theory that the amount of personal or social discontent depends on the level of deprivation relative to what other people or groups have, or what the deprived person or group had in the past, rather than on the absolute amount of deprivation.

Replication. Because any single study is flawed, a hallmark of good research in social psychology is replication. In its simplest form, replication means that we are able to reproduce the findings of other researchers if we recreate their methods. It is also important to conduct conceptual replications, in which different research procedures are used to explore the same conceptual relationship.

Reverse-causality problem. The problem that arises in correlational research when the presumed cause might in fact be the actual effect. Children who watch a lot of television do less well in school than children who watch little television. But is their television viewing causing their poor grades? Or does their poor school performance cause them to escape from schoolwork by watching TV?

Risky shift. After taking part in a group discussion of an issue, people are sometimes willing to support riskier decisions than they were before the group discussion. This is part of a more general process of *group polarization,* which can lead either to riskier or more cautious decisions, depending on the initial views of group members.

Role. See *social role.*

Salience. The quality that makes a particular stimulus stand out and be noticed. Bright, noisy, colorful, unusual, and novel stimuli are usually the most salient.

Sanctioned aggression. Aggression that is permissible (though not necessarily encouraged) according to the norms of the individual's social groups.

Schema. An organized system or structure of cognitions about some stimulus or type of stimulus, such as a person, personality type, group, role, or event.

Selective exposure. Tendency for persuasive communications not to reach the intended audience because audience members tend to be exposed mostly to sources they agree with. Should be distinguished from "motivated selectivity," a presumed psychological tendency to avoid nonsupportive information.

Self-awareness. The state of experiencing one's self as an object of one's own attention.

Self-centered bias. Taking more than one's share of responsibility for a jointly-produced outcome.

Self-disclosure. A special type of conversation in which we share intimate information or feelings about the self with another person. Self-disclosure can be descriptive (revelations describe things about ourselves) or evaluative (emphasis is given to our personal assessment of people and situations).

Self-evaluation maintenance model. Tesser's analysis of when people react to the success of others with pride (basking in reflected glory) versus discontent (suffering by comparison). A key factor is whether or not the performance of the other is relevant to our self-definition.

Self-fulfilling prophecy. The tendency for an individual's expectations about the future to influence that future. Prejudice can serve as a self-fulfilling prophecy by determining how the prejudiced person acts toward the other, which may in turn influence the target to act in a way that confirms the first person's prejudices.

Self-handicapping. Engaging in actions that produce insurmountable obstacles to success, so the inevitable failure can later be attributed to the obstacle rather than one's own lack of ability.

Self-interest. In political psychology, the hypothesis that the individual's political behavior is motivated by what is best for his or her short-term material well-being.

Self-monitoring. In the study of self-presentation, self-monitoring refers to the tendency to emphasize impression management to a great extent. Snyder et al. have developed a paper-and-pencil test to assess this personality disposition. On the Self-Monitoring Scale, high scorers are especially sensitive to situational cues about appropriate behavior.

In health psychology, self-monitoring refers to observing and recording a target behavior (such as smoking) to highlight its frequency and the factors with which it co-occurs.

Self-perception theory. The idea that people infer their attitudes from their overt behavior and from their perceptions of the external situation, rather than from their own internal states.

Self-presentation. Deliberate efforts to behave and appear in ways that create a particular impression of the self, often a favorable impression.

Self-reference effect. The improved memory for others' characteristics that results from perceivers linking them to their own characteristics.

Self-serving attributional bias. The tendency for people to see their positive behaviors as internally caused and their negative behaviors (such as failure) as caused by external circumstances.

Shift of meaning. Tendency for the connotations of a trait to change when placed in a different context. This is the explanation for context effects given by cognitive theories of impression formation.

Shock-competition technique. Experimental procedure in which subjects compete in a reaction time game, and the winner shocks the loser.

Shock-learning technique. Experimental procedure in which a naive subject is a "teacher" and is supposed to shock the "learner" (who is a confederate) when the learner makes an error.

Situational attribution. Perceiving the cause of a person's action as lying in situational forces acting upon the person, such as social influence or economic incentives.

Sleeper effect. Delayed attitude changes that are not apparent immediately after exposure to the communication.

Social cognition. The study of how people form inferences and make judgments from social information.

Social comparison theory. Festinger proposed that people have a drive to evaluate themselves. In the absence of objective nonsocial criteria, people evaluate themselves by comparison with other people. In an uncertain or ambiguous situation, people may want to affiliate with others in order to make social comparisons.

Social density. The objective number of people in a given space, such as the number of people living per square mile in a major city.

Social dilemma. A situation in which the most rewarding short-term choice for an individual will ultimately lead to negative outcomes for all concerned. Social dilemmas pit the short-term interests of the individual against the long-term interests of the group (including the individual).

Social exchange theory. An analysis of interpersonal interaction in terms of the costs and benefits each person gives and receives. Because people in a relationship or group are interdependent (that is, the outcomes one person receives depend on what others do, and vice versa), individuals must coordinate their behavior to maximize their joint benefits.

Social facilitation. The tendency for people (and other kinds of animals) to perform better on simple, well-learned tasks when others are present than when they are alone.

Social identity theory. A theory that people spontaneously categorize the social world into ingroups and outgroups, and develop higher self-esteem if their ingroups have more status than the outgroups.

Social impact theory. According to Latané, the influence (either positive or negative) of an audience on a target individual depends on three factors: the number of observers, the strength of the audience (e.g., their importance), and the immediacy of the audience in time or space.

Social interaction. Occurs when two or more people influence each other—verbally, physically, or emotionally. Talking to a therapist, debating an idea in class, angrily arguing with a friend, and bumping into a person in an elevator are examples.

Social leadership. Refers to activities designed to promote group harmony and *cohesiveness*. The social leader focuses on the social and emotional aspects of interaction in order to keep a group running smoothly and happily. Sometimes contrasted with *task leadership*.

Social learning theory. A modern derivative of behaviorism that places primary emphasis on how people learn social behaviors from one another, especially through social reinforcement and modeling.

Social loafing. Individuals sometimes work less hard as members of a group than they would if they worked alone. Individuals may feel that their own efforts will be less recognizable in a group, which leads to a diffusion of responsibility and diminished effort by individuals.

Social norms. Rules and expectations about what members of a social group should do or be like. The standards of behavior that determine whether specific actions, attitudes, or beliefs are approved or disapproved by the individual's social group. Also called "group norms."

Social penetration. Altman and Taylor's theory about the process by which people gradually attain closeness and intimacy in a relationship. The theory emphasizes that as relationships develop, self-disclosure increases in both breadth (range of topics) and depth (intimacy).

Social power. This refers to one person's ability to influence deliberately the behavior, thoughts or feelings of another person.

Social role. A set of social norms (rules and understandings) about how a person in a particular social position (such as mother or professor) is expected to behave. Roles define the rights and responsibilities of members of couples, groups, and other social units.

Social support. An interpersonal exchange characterized by emotional concern, instrumental aid, the provision of information to another, or help in self-appraisal. Social support is believed to buffer people against the adverse effects of stress and may promote physical health as well.

Sociobiology. A field in biology that uses evolutionary theory to explain the social behavior of humans and other animals.

Sociotropic. In political psychology, the idea that political behavior is motivated by percep-

tions of what is best for the collectivity (the nation, the society), not best for the self.

Source derogation. In persuasive communication situations, reducing inconsistency by derogating the source of a discrepant communication rather than changing one's attitudes.

Stereotype. Beliefs about the characteristics of members of a group or social category. This is the cognitive component of group antagonism.

Statistical information. In social cognition, this refers to information based on a number of individuals or events, such as averages or totals. Such information tends to be less persuasive and to have less impact on judgments than inferior but more vivid *case history* information.

Stress. A process of appraising environmental events as harmful, threatening, or challenging and of responding to that appraisal with physiological, emotional, cognitive, and behavioral changes. Stress occurs when people perceive that their personal resources may not be sufficient to meet the demands of the environment.

Stressful life event. An event in a person's life that requires him or her to make changes; negative, ambiguous and uncontrollable events as most likely to be perceived as stressful; believed to contribute to the likelihood of illness.

Supportive defense. In attitude change, positive arguments for an individual's own position, provided in advance of a persuasive attack to help protect that attitude.

Symbolic racism. Antagonism toward a social group based on symbols and values rather than self-interest. For example, opposition to the progress of blacks, or to policies promoting that progress, that is based both in antagonism toward blacks and in support for traditional values.

Systematic processing. Careful scrutiny of the arguments in a persuasive communication. Gives argument strength more weight, induces counterarguing, and makes attitude change more enduring. Minimizes the role of peripheral cues.

Task leadership. Activities designed to accomplish the goals of a group and to get the work of the group done successfully. The task leader directs and organizes the group in carrying out a specific task. Sometimes contrasted with *social leadership*.

Territorial markers. Objects and nonverbal gestures that people use to mark and personalize their territories. For example, a person may stake out a seat in the library using a sweater, sunglasses, and notebook.

Territory. An area controlled by a specific individual or group. Altman has distinguished primary, secondary, and public territories.

Theory of reasoned action. A model predicting an individual's overt behavior from conscious behavioral intentions, which in turn are based in calculations about the effects of his or her behavior and others' evaluations of it.

Third-variable problem. A problem with interpreting correlational research. When two variables are correlated with each other, is one the cause of the other? Or is some third variable the cause of both? Couples' satisfaction with their sex life is correlated with how long they remain a couple. But is sexual compatibility the cause of long-lasting relationships? Or are both caused by a more general level of trust and understanding?

Tit-for-tat strategy. In the prisoner's dilemma game, tit-for-tat is the optimal strategy. The player should start by cooperating, and then do whatever the opposing player did the round before.

Transfer of affect. Changing attitude A by transferring to it the affect one already has toward object B.

Type A behavior. A behavioral and emotional style of coping with stress, marked by hostility and an aggressive struggle to achieve more and more in less time, often in competition with others. This method of coping with stress is a risk factor for coronary heart disease.

Abel, E. L. (1977). The relationship between cannabis and violence: A review. *Psychological Bulletin, 84,* 193–211.

Abel, G. G., Rouleau, J.-L., & Coyne, B. J. (1987). Behavioral medicine strategies in medical patients. In A. Stoudemire & B. S. Fogel (Eds.), *Principles of medical psychiatry* (pp. 329–345). Orlando, FL: Grune & Stratton.

Abelson, R. P. (1959). Modes of resolution of belief dilemmas. *Journal of Conflict Resolution, 3,* 343–352.

Abelson, R. P. (1976). Script processing in attitude formation and decision making. In J. S. Carroll & J. W. Payne (Eds.), *Cognition and social behavior* (pp. 33–46). Hillsdale, NJ: Erlbaum.

Abelson, R. P., Aronson, E., McGuire, W. J., Newcomb, T. M., Rosenberg, M. J., & Tannenbaum, P. H. (Eds.). (1968). *Theories of cognitive consistency: A sourcebook.* Chicago: Rand McNally.

Abramson, L. Y., Seligman, M. E. P., & Teasdale, J. D. (1978). Learned helplessness in humans: Critique and reformulation. *Journal of Abnormal Psychology, 87,* 49–74.

Abramson, P. E., Goldberg, P. A., Greenberg, J. H., & Abramson, U. M. (1977). The talking platypus phenomenon: Competency ratings as a function of sex and professional status. *Psychology of Women Quarterly, 2,* 114–124.

Adams, F. M., & Osgood, C. E. (1973). A cross-cultural study of the affective meanings of color. *Journal of Cross-Cultural Psychology, 4,* 135–156.

Adorno, T. W., Frenkel-Brunswik, E., Levinson, D. J., & Sanford, R. N. (1950). *The authoritarian personality.* New York: Harper & Row.

Ageton, S. S. (1983). *Sexual assault among adolescents.* Lexington, MA: Lexington Books.

Ahammer, I. M., & Murray, J. P. (1979). Kindness in the kindergarten: The relative influence of role playing and prosocial television in facilitating altruism. *International Journal of Behavioral Development, 2,* 133–157.

Ahmed, S. M. S. (1979). Helping behavior as predicted by diffusion of responsibility, exchange theory, and traditional sex norms. *Journal of Social Psychology, 109,* 153–154.

Aiello, J. (1987). Human spatial behavior. In D. Stokols & I. Altman (Eds.), *Handbook of environmental psychology.* New York: Wiley.

Aiello, J. R., & Cooper, R. E. (1972). The use of personal space as a function of social affect. *Proceedings of the 80th Annual Convention of the American Psychology Association, 7,* 207–208.

Ainsworth, M. D. S., Blehar, M. C., Waters, E., & Wall, S. (1978). *Patterns of attachment: A psychological study of the strange situation.* Hillsdale, NJ: Erlbaum.

Ajzen, I. (1985). From intentions to actions: A theory of planned action. In J. Kuhl & J. Beckman (Eds.), *Action control: From cognition to behavior* (pp. 11–39). New York: Springer.

Ajzen, I., & Fishbein, M. (1977). Attitude-behavior relations: A theoretical analysis and review of empirical research. *Psychological Bulletin, 84,* 888–918.

Ajzen, I., & Fishbein, M. (1980). *Understanding attitudes and predicting social behavior.* Englewood Cliffs, NJ: Prentice-Hall.

Ajzen, I., & Madden, T. J. (1986). Prediction of goal-directed behavior: Attitudes, intentions, and perceived behavioral control. *Journal of Experimental Social Psychology, 22,* 453–474.

Albright, L., Kenny, D. A., & Malloy, T. E. (1988). Consensus in personality judgments at zero acquaintance. *Journal of Personality and Social Psychology, 55,* 387–395.

Alder, C. (1985). An exploration of self-reported sexually aggressive behavior. *Crime and Delinquency, 31,* 306–331.

Allen, R. B., & Ebbesen, E. B. (1981). Cognitive processes in person perception: Retrieval of personality trait and behavioral information. *Journal of Experimental Social Psychology, 17,* 119–141.

Allen, V. L., & Levine, J. M. (1971). Social support and conformity: The role of independent assessment of reality. *Journal of Experimental Social Psychology, 7,* 48–58.

Allen, V. L., & Wilder, D. A. (1975). Categorization, belief similarity, and intergroup discrimination. *Journal of Personality and Social Psychology, 32,* 971–977.

Allen, V. L., & Wilder, D. A. (1979). Group categorization and attribution of belief similarity. *Small Group Behavior, 10*, 73–80.

Allgeier, E. R., & Byrne, D. (1973). Attraction toward the opposite sex as a determinant of physical proximity. *Journal of Social Psychology, 90*, 213–219.

Allport, F. H. (1920). The influence of the group upon association and thought. *Journal of Experimental Psychology, 3*, 159–182.

Allport, F. H. (1924). *Social psychology*. Boston: Riverside Editions, Houghton Mifflin.

Allport, G. W. (1935). Attitudes. In C. Murchison (Ed.), *A handbook of social psychology*. Worcester, MA: Clark University Press.

Allport, G. W. (1954). *The nature of prejudice*. Garden City, NY: Doubleday.

Altman, I. (1975). *The environment and social behavior*. Monterey, CA: Brooks/Cole.

Altman, I., & Haythorn, W. W. (1965). Interpersonal exchange in isolation. *Sociometry, 23*, 411–426.

Altman, I., & Taylor, D. A. (1973). *Social penetration: The development of interpersonal relationships*. New York: Holt, Rinehart and Winston.

Altman, I., Nelson, P. A., & Lett, E. E. (1972). The ecology of home environments. *Catalog of Selected Documents in Psychology*. Washington, D.C.: American Psychological Association.

Amabile, T. M., Hennessey, B. A., & Grossman, B. S. (1986). Social influences on creativity: The effects of contracted-for reward. *Journal of Personality and Social Psychology, 50*, 14–23.

Amato, P. R. (1983). Helping behavior in urban and rural environments: Field studies based on a taxonomic organization of helping episodes. *Journal of Personality and Social Psychology, 45*(3), 571–586.

American Cancer Society. (1989). *Cancer facts and figures—1989*. Atlanta, GA: American Cancer Society.

American Heart Association (1984). *Heartfacts, 1984*. Dallas, TX: American Heart Association.

Andersen, S. M., & Klatzky, R. L. (1987). Traits and social stereotypes: Levels of categorization in person perception. *Journal of Personality and Social Psychology, 53*, 235–246.

Anderson, C. A., & Godfrey, S. S. (1987). Thoughts about actions: The effects of specificity and availability on imagined behavioral scripts on expectations about oneself and others. *Social Cognition, 5*, 238–258.

Anderson, C. A., Jennings, D. L., & Arnoult, L. H. (1988). The validity and utility of the attributional style construct at a moderate level of specificity. *Journal of Personality and Social Psychology, 55*, 979–990.

Anderson, N. H. (1959). Test of a model for opinion change. *Journal of Abnormal and Social Psychology, 59*, 371–381.

Anderson, N. H. (1965). Averaging vs. adding as a stimulus-combination rule in impression formation. *Journal of Experimental Psychology, 70*, 394–400.

Anderson, N. H. (1966). Component ratings in impression formation. *Psychonomic Science, 6*, 279–280.

Anderson, N. H. (1968a). A simple model for information integration. In R. P. Abelson et al. (Eds.), *Theories of cognitive consistency: A sourcebook* (pp. 731–743). Chicago: Rand McNally.

Anderson, N. H. (1968b). Likableness ratings of 555 personality-trait words. *Journal of Personality and Social Psychology, 9*, 272–279.

Anderson, N. H., & Hubert, S. (1963). Effects of concomitant verbal recall on order effects in personality impression formation. *Journal of Verbal Learning and Verbal Behavior, 2*, 379–391.

Anderson, S. M., & Klatsky, R. L. (1987). Traits and social stereotypes: Levels of categorization in person perception. *Journal of Personality and Social Psychology, 53*, 235–248.

Andrews, K. H., & Kandel, D. B. (1979). Attitude and behavior. *American Sociological Review, 44*, 298–310.

Apple, W., & Hecht, K. (1982). Speaking emotionally: The relation between verbal and vocal communication of affect. *Journal of Personality and Social Psychology, 42*, 864–875.

Apple, W., Streeter, L. A., & Krauss, R. M. (1979). Effects of pitch and speech rate on personal attributions. *Journal of Personality and Social Psychology, 37*, 715–727.

Apostle, R. A., Glock, C. Y., Piazza, T., & Suelzle, M. (1983). *The anatomy of racial attitudes*. Berkeley: University of California Press.

Apsler, R., & Sears, D. O. (1968). Warning, personal involvement, and attitude change. *Journal of Personality and Social Psychology, 9*, 162–166.

Archer, R. L., & Berg, J. H. (1978). Disclosure reciprocity and its limits: A reactance model. *Journal of Experimental Social Psychology, 14*, 527–540.

Arkin, R. M., & Baumgardner, A. H. (1985). Self-handicapping. In J. H. Harvey & G. Weary (Eds.), *Basic issues in attribution theory and research* (pp. 169–202). New York: Academic Press.

Armstrong, E. A. (1965). *Bird display and behavior: An introduction to the study of bird psychology*, 2nd ed. New York: Dover.

Arndt, W. B., Jr., Foehl, J. C., & Good, F. E. (1985). Specific sexual fantasy themes: A multidimensional study. *Journal of Personality and Social Psychology, 48*, 472–480.

Aron, A. (1988). The matching hypothesis reconsidered again: Comment on Kalick and Hamilton. *Journal of Personality and Social Psychology, 54*, 441–446.

Aronson, E. (1984). *The social animal*, 4th ed. New York: W. H. Freeman.

Aronson, E., Stephan, C., Sikes, J., Blaney, N., & Snapp, M. (1978). The Jigsaw Classroom. Beverly Hills, CA: Sage.

Aronson, E., & Carlsmith, J. M. (1963). The effect of the severity of threat on the devaluation of forbidden behavior. *Journal of Abnormal and Social Psychology, 66,* 584–588.

Aronson, E., & Gonzalez, A. (1988). Desegregation, jigsaw, and the Mexican-American experience. In P. A. Katz & D. A. Taylor (Eds.), *Eliminating racism: Profiles in controversy* (pp. 301–314). New York: Plenum.

Aronson, E., & Linder, D. (1965). Gain and loss of esteem as determinants of interpersonal attractiveness. *Journal of Experimental Social Psychology, 1,* 156–171.

Aronson, E., & Osherow, N. (1980). Cooperation, social behavior, and academic performance: Experiments in the desegregated classroom. In L. Bickman (Ed.), *Applied social psychology annual* (Vol. 1). Beverly Hills, CA: Sage Publications.

Aronson, E., Brewer, M., & Carlsmith, J. M. (1985). Experimentation in social psychology. In G. Lindzey & E. Aronson (Eds.). *The handbook of social psychology,* 3rd ed. (Vol. 1, pp. 441–486). New York: Random House.

Aronson, E., Turner, J. A., & Carlsmith, J. M. (1963). Communicator credibility and communication discrepancy as determinants of opinion change. *Journal of Abnormal and Social Psychology, 67,* 31–36.

Aronson, E., Willerman, B., & Floyd, J. (1966). The effect of a pratfall on increasing interpersonal attractiveness. *Psychonomic Science, 4,* 227–228.

Asch, S. E. (1946). Forming impressions of personality. *Journal of Abnormal and Social Psychology, 41,* 258–290.

Asch, S. (1955). Opinions and social pressure. *Scientific American, 19,* 31–35.

Ashmore, R. D., & Del Boca, F. (1976). Psychological approaches to understanding intergroup conflict. In P. A. Katz (Ed.), *Towards the elimination of racism* (pp. 73–124). Elmsford, NY: Pergamon Press.

Ashmore, R. D., Del Boca, F. K., & Wohlers, A. J. (1986). Gender stereotypes. In R. D. Ashmore & F. K. Del Boca (Eds.), *The social psychology of female-male relations* (pp. 69–119). New York: Academic Press.

Ashton, N. L., Shaw, M. E., & Worsham, A. P. (1980). Affective reactions to interpersonal distances by friends and strangers. *Bulletin of the Psychonomic Society, 15,* 306–308.

Atkin, C. (1979). Research evidence on mass mediated health communication campaigns. In D. Nimmo (Ed.), *Communication yearbook 3.* New Brunswick, NJ: Transaction Books.

Attorney General's Commission on Pornography. (1986). *Final Report.* Washington, D.C.: U.S. Department of Justice.

Austin, W. (1980). Friendship and fairness: Effects of type of relationship and task performance on choice distribution rules. *Personality and Social Psychology Bulletin, 6,* 402–408.

Averill, J. R. (1983). Studies on anger and aggression: Implications for theories of emotion. *American Psychologist, 38,* 1145–1160.

Averill, J. R., & Boothroyd, P. (1977). On falling in love in conformance with the romantic ideal. *Motivation and Emotion, 1*(3), 235–247.

Axelrod, R. (1984). *The Evolution of Cooperation.* New York: Basic Books.

Axsom, D. (1989). Cognitive dissonance and behavior change in psychotherapy. *Journal of Experimental Social Psychology, 25,* 234–252.

Axsom, D., Yates, S., & Chaiken, S. (1987). Audience response as a heuristic cue in persuasion. *Journal of Personality and Social Psychology, 53,* 30–40.

Baer, J. D., Kivlahan, D. R., Fromme, K., & Marlatt, G. A. (in press). Secondary prevention of alcohol abuse with college student populations: A skills-training approach. In G. Howard (Ed.), *Issues in alcohol use and misuse by young adults.* Notre Dame, IN: Notre Dame University Press.

Bales, R. F. (1970). *Personality and interpersonal behavior.* New York: Holt, Rinehart and Winston.

Ball-Rokeach, S. J., Grube, J. W., & Rokeach, M. (1981). Roots: The next generation—Who watched and with what effect? *Public Opinion Quarterly, 45,* 58–68.

Bandura, A. (1986a). Self-efficacy mechanism in psychological activation and health-promoting behavior. In J. Madden IV, S. Matthysse, & J. Barchas (Eds.), *Adaptation, learning and affect.* New York: Raven Press.

Bandura, A. (1986b). *Social foundations of thought and action: A social cognitive theory.* Englewood Cliffs, NJ: Prentice-Hall.

Bandura, A. (1977). *Social learning theory.* Englewood Cliffs, NJ: Prentice-Hall.

Bandura, A., Cioffi, D., Taylor, C. B., & Brouillard, M. E. (1988). Perceived self-efficacy in coping with cognitive stressors and opioid activation. *Journal of Personality and Social Psychology, 55,* 479–488.

Bandura, A., Ross, D., & Ross, S. A. (1961). Transmission of aggression through imitation of aggressive models. *Journal of Abnormal and Social Psychology, 63,* 575–582.

Bandura, A., Ross, D., & Ross, S. A. (1963). Imitation of film-mediated aggressive models. *Journal of Abnormal and Social Psychology, 66,* 3–11.

Barber, J. D. (1985). *The presidential character: Predicting performance in the White House,* 3rd ed. Englewood Cliffs, NJ: Prentice-Hall.

Barker, R. G., Dembo, T., & Lewin, K. (1941). Frustration and regression: An experiment with young children. *University of Iowa Studies in Child Welfare, 18*(1).

Baron, R. A. (1971a). Magnitude of victim's pain cues and level of prior anger arousal as determinants of adult aggressive behavior. *Journal of Personality and Social Psychology, 17,* 236–243.

Baron, R. A. (1971b). Aggression as a function of magnitude of victim's pain cues, level of prior anger arousal, and aggressor-victim similarity. *Journal of Personality and Social Psychology, 18,* 48–54.

Baron, R. A. (1974). Aggression as a function of victim's pain cues, level of prior anger arousal, and exposure to an aggressive model. *Journal of Personality and Social Psychology, 29,* 117–124.

Baron, R. A. (1977). *Human aggression.* New York: Plenum Press.

Baron, R. A., & Bell, P. A. (1977). Sexual arousal and aggression by males: Effects of type of erotic stimuli and prior provocation. *Journal of Personality and Social Psychology, 35,* 79–87.

Bargh, J. A. (1984). Automatic and conscious processing of social information. In R. S. Wyer & T. K. Srull (Eds.), *Handbook of social cognition* (Vol. 3, pp. 1–43). Hillsdale, NJ: Erlbaum.

Bar-Hillel, M., & Fischhoff, B. (1981). When do base rates affect predictions? *Journal of Personality and Social Psychology, 41,* 671–680.

Barnett, P. A., & Gotlib, I. H. (1988). Psychosocial functioning and depression: Distinguishing among antecedents, concomitants, and consequences. *Psychological Bulletin, 104,* 97–126.

Baron, R. M., & Rodin, J. (1978). Perceived control and crowding stress: Processes mediating the impact of spatial and social density. In A. Baum & Y. Epstein (Eds.), *Human response to crowding.* Hillsdale, NJ: Erlbaum.

Baron, R. M., Mandel, D. G., Adams, C. A., & Griffen, L. M. (1976). Effects of social density in university residential environments. *Journal of Personality and Social Psychology, 34,* 434–446.

Baron, R. S. (1986). Distraction-conflict theory: Progress and problems. In L. Berkowitz (Ed.), *Advances in experimental social psychology* (Vol. 20). New York: Academic Press.

Bassili, J. N., & Provencal, A. (1988). Perceiving minorities: A factor-analytic approach. *Personality and Social Psychology Bulletin, 14,* 5–15.

Batson, C. D., Cochran, P. J., Biederman, M. F., Blosser, J. L., Ryan, M. J., & Vogt, B. (1978). Failure to help when in a hurry: Callousness or conflict? *Personality and Social Psychology Bulletin, 4*(1), 97–101.

Batson, C. D., Dyck, J. L., Brandt, J. R., Batson, J. G., Powell, A. L., McMaster, M. R., & Griffit, C. (1988). Five studies testing two new egoistic alternatives to the empathy-altruism hypothesis. *Journal of Personality and Social Psychology, 55*(1), 52–77.

Baum, A., & Davis, G. E. (1980). Reducing the stress of high-density living: An architectural intervention. *Journal of Personality and Social Psychology, 38*(3), 471–481.

Baum, A., & Paulus, P. (1987). Crowding. In D. Stokols & I. Altman (Eds.), *Handbook of environmental psychology.* New York: Wiley.

Baum, A., & Valins, S. (1977). *Architecture and social behavior: Psychological studies of social density.* Hillsdale, NJ: Erlbaum.

Baum, A., Aiello, J. R., & Calesnick, L. E. (1978). Crowding and personal control: Social density and the development of learned helplessness. *Journal of Personality and Social Psychology, 36,* 1000–1011.

Baumeister, R. F. (1982). A self-presentational view of social phenomena. *Psychological Bulletin, 91,* 3–26.

Baumeister, R. F. (1988). Anxiety and deconstruction: On escaping the self. In J. M. Olson & M. P. Zanna (Eds.), *Self-inference processes: The Ontario Symposium* (Vol. 6). Hillsdale, NJ: Erlbaum.

Baumeister, R. F., & Hutton, D. G. (1987). Self-presentation theory: Self-construction and audience pleasing. In B. Mullen & G. R. Goethals (eds.) *Theories of group behavior* (pp. 71–88). New York: Springer-Verlag.

Baumeister, R. F., & Scher, S. J. (1988). Self-defeating behavior patterns among normal individuals: Review and analysis of common self-destructive tendencies. *Psychological Bulletin, 104,* 3–22.

Baumeister, R. F., & Steinhilber, A. (1984). Paradoxical effects of supportive audiences on performance under pressure: The home field disadvantage in sports championships. *Journal of Personality and Social Psychology, 47*(1), 85–93.

Baumeister, R. F., Chesner, S. P., Senders, P. S., & Tice, D. M. (1988). Who's in charge here: Group leaders do lend help in emergencies. *Personality and Social Psychology Bulletin, 14*(1), 17–22.

Baumeister, R. F., Hutton, D. G., & Tice, D. M. (1989). Cognitive processes during deliberate self-presentation: How self-presenters alter and misinterpret the behavior of their interaction partners. *Journal of Experimental Social Psychology, 25,* 59–78.

Bavelas, J. B., Black, A., Lemery, C. R., & Mullett, J. (1986). "I show how you feel": Motor mimicry as a communicative act. *Journal of Personality and Social Psychology, 50,* 322–329.

Baxter, T. L., & Goldberg, L. R. (1988). Perceived behavioral consistency underlying trait attributions to oneself and another: An extension of the actor-observer effect. *Personality and Social Psychology Bulletin, 13,* 437–447.

Beaman, A. L., Barnes, P. J., Klentz, B., & McQuirk, B. (1978). Increasing helping rates through information dissemination: Teaching pays. *Personality and Social Psychology Bulletin, 4*(3), 406–411.

Beattie, A. E., & Mitchell, A. A. (1985). The relationship

between advertising recall and persuasion: An experimental investigation. In L. F. Alwitt & A. A. Mitchell (Eds.), *Psychological processes and advertising effects: Theory, research, and applications* (pp. 129–155). Hillsdale, NJ: Erlbaum.

Bechtold, A., Naccarato, M. E., & Zanna, M. P. (1986). *Need for structure and the prejudice-discrimination link.* Paper presented at the annual meetings of the Canadian Psychological Association, Toronto, Ontario.

Beck, L., McCauley, C., Segal, M., & Hershey, L. (1988). Individual differences in prototypicality judgments about trait categories. *Journal of Personality and Social Psychology, 55,* 286–292.

Becker, F. D. (1973). Study of spatial markers. *Journal of Personality and Social Psychology, 26*(3), 439–445.

Becker, L. B., McCombs, M. E., & McLeod, J. M. (1975). The development of political cognitions. In S. H. Chaffee (Ed.), *Political communication: Issues and strategies for research* (pp. 21–63). Beverly Hills, CA: Sage Publications.

Bellezza, F. S. (1984). The self as a mnemonic device: The role of internal cues. *Journal of Personality and Social Psychology, 47,* 506–516.

Belloc, N. D., & Breslow, L. (1972). Relationship of physical health status and family practices. *Preventive Medicine, 1,* 409–421.

Bem, D. J. (1967). Self-perception: An alternative interpretation of cognitive dissonance phenomena. *Psychological Review, 74,* 183–200.

Bem, D. J. (1972). Self-perception theory. In L. Berkowitz (Ed.), *Advances in experimental social psychology* (Vol. 6, pp. 1–62). New York: Academic Press.

Bem, S. L. (1974). The measurement of psychological androgyny. *Journal of Consulting and Clinical Psychology, 42,* 155–162.

Bem, S. L. (1975). Sex role adaptability: One consequence of psychological androgyny. *Journal of Personality and Social Psychology, 31,* 634–643.

Bem, S. L. (1985). Androgyny and gender schema theory: A conceptual and empirical integration. In T. B. Sonderegger (Ed.), *Nebraska Symposium on Motivation: Psychology and gender* (pp. 179–226). Lincoln: University of Nebraska Press.

Bem, S. L., Martyna, W., & Watson, C. (1976). Sex typing and androgyny: Further explorations of the expressive domain. *Journal of Personality and Social Psychology, 43,* 1016–1023.

Benson, H., Greenwood, M. M., & Klemchuck, H. (1975). The relaxation response: Psychophysiological aspects and clinical applications. *International Journal of Psychiatry in Medicine, 6,* 87–98.

Benson, P. L., Karabenick, S. A., & Lerner, R. M. (1976). Pretty pleases: The effects of physical attractiveness, race, and sex on receiving help. *Journal of Experimental Social Psychology, 12,* 409–415.

Bentler, P. M., & Speckart, G. (1981). Attitudes "cause" behaviors: A structural equation analysis. *Journal of Personality and Social Psychology, 40,* 226–238.

Berelson, B. R., Lazarsfeld, P. F., & McPhee, W. N. (1954). *Voting: A study of opinion formation in a presidential campaign.* Chicago: University of Chicago Press.

Berglas, S., & Jones, E. E. (1978). Drug choice as a self-handicapping strategy in response to noncontingent success. *Journal of Personality and Social Psychology, 36,* 405–417.

Berk, R. A., & Berk, S. F. (1979). *Labor and leisure at home: Content and organization of the household day.* Beverly Hills, CA: Sage Publications.

Berkman, L. F., & Syme, S. L. (1979). Social networks, host resistance, and mortality: A nine-year follow-up study of Alameda County residents. *American Journal of Epidemiology, 109,* 186–204.

Berkowitz, L. (1972). Social norms, feelings, and other factors affecting helping and altruism. In L. Berkowitz, (Ed.), *Advances in experimental social psychology* (Vol. 6). New York: Academic Press.

Berkowitz, L. (1974). Some determinants of impulsive aggression: The role of mediated associations with reinforcements for aggression. *Psychological Review, 81,* 165–176.

Berkowitz, L. (1983). Aversively stimulated aggression: Some parallels and differences in research with animals and humans. *American Psychologist, 38,* 1135–1144.

Berkowitz, L. (1984). Some effects of thoughts on anti- and prosocial influences of media events: A cognitive-neoassociation analysis. *Psychological Bulletin, 95,* 410–427.

Berkowitz, L., & Frodi, A. (1979). Reactions to a child's mistakes as affected by her/his looks and speech. *Social Psychology Quarterly, 42,* 420–425.

Bernard, J. (1972). *The future of marriage.* New York: Bantam.

Bernard, L. C. (1980). Multivariate analysis of new sex role formulations and personality. *Journal of Personality and Social Psychology, 38,* 323–336.

Bernstein, M., & Crosby, F. (1980). An experimental examination of relative deprivation theory. *Journal of Experimental Social Psychology, 16,* 442–456.

Bernstein, S., Richardson, D., & Hammock, G. (1987). Convergent and discriminant validity of the Taylor and Buss measures of physical aggression. *Aggressive Behavior, 13,* 15–24.

Berry, D. S., & McArthur, L. Z. (1985). Some components and consequences of a babyface. *Journal of Personality and Social Psychology, 48,* 312–323.

Berry, D. S., & Zeibrowitz-McArthur, L. (1988). What's in a face? Facial maturity and the attribution of legal responsibility. *Personality and Social Psychology Bulletin, 14,* 23–33.

Berscheid, E. (1983). Emotion. In H. H. Kelley et al., *Close relationships* (pp. 110–168). New York: W. H. Freeman.

Berscheid, E., Graziano, W., Monson, T., & Dermer, M. (1976). Outcome dependency: Attention, attribution, and attraction. *Journal of Personality and Social Psychology, 34,* 978–989.

Berscheid, E., & Walster, E. (1967). When does a harm-doer compensate a victim? *Journal of Personality and Social Psychology, 6,* 435–441.

Berscheid, E., & Walster, E. H. (1978). *Interpersonal attraction,* 2nd ed. Reading, MA: Addison-Wesley.

Berscheid, E., Snyder, M., & Omoto, A. M. (1989). Issues in studying close relationships: Conceptualizing and measuring closeness. In C. Hendrick (Ed.), *Close relationships* (pp. 63–91). Newbury Park, CA: Sage Publications.

Berscheid, E., Graziano, W., Monson, T., & Dermer, M. (1976). Outcome dependency: Attention, attribution, and attraction. *Journal of Personality and Social Psychology, 34,* 978–989.

Beville, H. M., Jr. (1985). *Audience ratings: Radio, television, and cable.* Hillsdale, NJ: Erlbaum.

Bickman, L., & Kamzan, M. (1973). The effect of race and need on helping. *Journal of Social Psychology, 89,* 37–77.

Billings, A. C., & Moos, R. H. (1984). Coping, stress, and social resources among adults with unipolar depression. *Journal of Personality and Social Psychology, 46,* 877–891.

Birdwhistell, R. I. (1970). *Kinetics and context: Essays on body motion communication.* Philadelphia: University of Pennsylvania Press.

Birt, C. M., & Dion, K. L. (1987). Relative deprivation theory and responses to discrimination in a gay male and lesbian sample. *British Journal of Social Psychology, 26,* 139–145.

Bishop, G. D. (1990). Understanding the understanding of illness: Lay disease representations. In J. A. Skelton & R. T. Croyle (Eds.), *Mental representation in health and illness.* New York: Springer-Verlag.

Blau, P. M. (1964). *Exchange and power in social life.* New York: Wiley.

Blumenthal, J. A., & Emery, C. F. (1988). Rehabilitation of patients following myocardial infarction. *Journal of Consulting and Clinical Psychology, 56,* 374–381.

Blumenthal, M. D., Kahn, R. L., Andrews, F. M., & Head, K. B. (1972). *Justifying violence: Attitudes of American men.* Ann Arbor, MI: Institute for Social Research.

Bobo, L. (1988a). Group conflict, prejudice, and the paradox of contemporary racial attitudes. In P. A. Katz & D. A. Taylor (Eds.), *Eliminating racism: Profiles in controversy* (pp. 85–114). New York, Plenum.

Bobo, L. (1988b). Attitudes toward the black political movement: Trends, meaning, and effects on racial policy preferences. *Social Psychology Quarterly, 51,* 287–302.

Bobo, L. (1989). Worlds apart: Blacks, whites, and explanations of racial equality. Paper presented at the meetings of the Midwest Political Science Association, Chicago.

Bochner, S., & Insko, C. A. (1966). Communicator discrepancy, source credibility, and opinion change. *Journal of Personality and Social Psychology, 4,* 614–621.

Bohner, G., Bless, H., Schwarz, N., & Strack, F. (1988). What triggers causal attributions? The impact of valence and subjective probability. *European Journal of Social Psychology, 18,* 335–345.

Bond, C. R., Jr., & Brockett, D. R. (1987). A social context-personality index theory of memory acquaintances. *Journal of Personality and Social Psychology, 52,* 1110–1121.

Bond, C. R., Jr., & Sedikides, C. (1988). The recapitulation hypothesis in person retrieval. *Journal of Experimental Social Psychology, 24,* 195–221.

Bons, P. M., & Fiedler, F. E. (1976). Changes in organizational leadership and the behavior of relationship- and task-motivated leaders. *Administrative Science Quarterly, 21,* 433–472.

Booth, A. (1976). *Urban crowding and its consequences.* New York: Praeger.

Borden, R. J. (1980). Audience influence. In P. B. Paulus (Ed.), *Psychology of group influence* (pp. 99–132). Hillsdale, NJ: Erlbaum.

Borgida, E., & Campbell, B. (1982). Belief relevance and attitude-behavior consistency: The moderating role of personal experience. *Journal of Personality and Social Psychology, 42,* 239–247.

Borgida, E., & DeBono, K. G. (1989). Social hypothesis-testing and the role of expertise. *Personality and Social Psychology Bulletin, 15,* 212–221.

Borgida, E., & Howard-Pitney, B. (1983). Personal involvement and the robustness of perceptual salience effects. *Journal of Personality and Social Psychology, 45,* 560–570.

Bothwell, R. K., Brigham, J. C., & Malpass, R. S. (1989). Cross-racial identification. *Personality and Social Psychology Bulletin, 15,* 19–25.

Boucher, J., & Osgood, E. E. (1969). The Pollyanna hypothesis. *Journal of Verbal Learning and Verbal Behavior, 8,* 1–8.

Bower, G. H., & Gilligan, S. G. (1979). Remembering information related to one's self. *Journal of Research in Personality, 13,* 420–432.

Bowlby, J. (1969). *Attachment and loss:* Vol. 1. Attachment. New York: Basic Books.

Bradburn, N. (1969). *The structure of psychological well-being.* Chicago: Aldine, 1969.

Bradbury, T. N., & Fincham, F. D. (1988). Individual difference variables in close relationships: A contextual model of marriage as an integrative framework. *Journal of Personality and Social Psychology, 54,* 713–721.

Bradley, G. W. (1978). Self-serving biases in the attribution process: A reexamination of the fact or fiction question. *Journal of Personality and Social Psychology, 36,* 56–71.

Braiker, H. B., & Kelley, H. H. (1979). Conflict in the development of close relationships. In R. L. Burgess & T. L. Huston (Ed.), *Social exchange in developing relationships.* New York: Academic Press.

Breckler, S. J. (1984). Empirical validation of affect, behavior, and cognition as distinct components of attitude. *Journal of Personality and Social Psychology, 47,* 1191–1205.

Breckler, S. J. (1989). Affect versus evaluation in the structure of attitudes. *Journal of Experimental Social Psychology, 25,* 253–271.

Brehm, J. W. (1956). Post-decision changes in desirability of alternatives. *Journal of Abnormal and Social Psychology, 52,* 384–389.

Brehm, J. W. (1966). *A theory of psychological reactance.* New York: Academic Press.

Brehm, S. S., & Brehm, J. W. (1981). *Psychological reactance: A theory of freedom and control.* New York: Academic Press.

Bretl, D. J., & Cantor, J. (1988). The portrayal of men and women in U.S. television commercials: A recent content analysis and trends over 15 years. *Sex Roles, 18,* 595–609.

Brewer, M. B. (1979). In-group bias in the minimal intergroup situation: A cognitive-motivational analysis. *Psychological Bulletin, 86,* 307–324.

Brewer, M. B. (1986). The role of ethnocentrism in intergroup conflict. In S. Worchel & W. G. Austin (Eds.), *Psychology of intergroup relations* (pp. 88–102). Chicago: Nelson-Hall.

Brewer, M. B., & Kramer, R. M. (1986). Choice behavior in social dilemmas: Effects of social identity, group size, and decision framing. *Journal of Personality and Social Psychology, 50,* 543–549.

Brewer, M. B., Dull, V., & Lui, L. (1981). Perceptions of the elderly: Stereotypes as prototypes. *Journal of Personality and Social Psychology, 41*(4), 656–670.

Brewer, M. B., & Lui, L. (1984). Categorization of the elderly by the elderly: Effects of perceiver's category membership. *Personality and Social Psychology Bulletin, 10,* 585–595.

Brewer, M. B., & Lui, L. N. (1989). The primacy of age and sex in the structure of person categories. *Social Cognition, 7*(3), 262–274.

Brewer, M. B., & Miller, N. (1984). Beyond the contact hypothesis: Theoretical perspectives on desegregation. In N. Miller & M. B. Brewer (Eds.), *Groups in contact: The psychology of desegregation* (pp. 281–302). New York: Academic Press.

Briar, S. (1966). Welfare from below: Recipients' view of the public welfare system. In J. Brock (Ed.), *The law of the poor.* San Francisco: Chandler.

Briggs, S. R., & Cheek, J. M. (1988). On the nature of self-monitoring: Problems with assessment; problems with validity. *Journal of Personality and Social Psychology, 54,* 663–678.

Brigham, J. C., & Giesbrecht, L. W. (1976). All in the family: Racial attitudes. *Journal of Communication, 26,* 75–84.

Broadbent, D. E. (1957). Effects of noise on behavior. In C. M. Harris (Ed.), *Handbook of noise control.* New York: McGraw-Hill.

Brock, T. C. (1965). Communicator-recipient similarity and decision change. *Journal of Personality and Social Psychology, 1,* 650–654.

Brown, B. B. (1987). Territoriality. In D. Stokols & I. Altman, (Eds.), *Handbook of environmental psychology.* New York: Wiley.

Brown, P., Keenan, J. M., & Potts, G. R. (1986). The self-reference effect with imagery encoding. *Journal of Personality and Social Psychology, 51,* 897–906.

Brown, R. (1974). Further comment on the risky shift. *American Psychologist, 29,* 468–470.

Brown, R. (1988). *Group processes: Dynamics within and between groups.* New York: Basil Blackwell.

Brownell, A. (1982). Obesity: Understanding and treating a serious, prevalent and refractory disorder. *Journal of Consulting and Clinical Psychology, 50,* 820–840.

Brownell, K. D., Marlatt, G. A., Lichtenstein, E., & Wilson, G. T. (1986). Understanding and preventing relapse. *American Psychologist, 41,* 765–782.

Browning, R. P., & Jacob, H. (1964). Power motivation and the political personality. *Public Opinion Quarterly, 28,* 75–90.

Bryan, J. H., & Test, N. A. (1967). Models and helping: Naturalistic studies in aiding behavior. *Journal of Personality and Social Psychology, 6,* 400–407.

Bulman, R. J., & Wortman, C. B. (1977). Attributions of blame and coping in the "real world": Severe accident victims react to their lot. *Journal of Personality and Social Psychology, 35,* 351–363.

Burger, J. M. (1986). Increasing compliance by improving the deal: The that's-not-all technique. *Journal of Personality and Social Psychology, 51*(2), 277–283.

Burger, J. M. (1987). Desire for control and conformity to a perceived norm. *Journal of Personality and Social Psychology, 53,* 355–360.

Burger, J. M., & Petty, R. E. (1981). The low-ball compliance technique: Task or person commitment? *Journal of Personality and Social Psychology, 40,* 492–500.

Burgess, R. L., & Huston, T. L. (Eds.). (1979). *Social exchange in developing relationships.* New York: Academic Press.

Burgoon, J. K., Parrott, R., Le Poire, B. A., Kelley, D. L., Walther, J. B., & Perry, D. (1989). Maintaining and restoring privacy through communication in different types of relationships. *Journal of Social and Personal Relationships, 6,* 131–158.

Burish, T. C., & Bradley, L. A. (1983). *Coping with chronic disease: Research and applications.* New York: Academic Press.

Burke, P. J. (1971). Task and social-emotional leadership role performance. *Sociometry, 34*, 22–40.

Burnkrant, R. E., & Howard, D. J. (1984). Effects of the use of introductory rhetorical questions versus statements on information processing. *Journal of Personality and Social Psychology, 47*, 1218–1230.

Burnstein, E., & Vinokur, A. (1975). What a person thinks upon learning he has chosen differently from others: Nice evidence for the persuasive-arguments explanation of choice shifts. *Journal of Experimental Social Psychology, 11*, 412–426.

Bushman, B. J. (1988). The effects of apparel on compliance: A field experiment with a female authority figure. *Personality and Social Psychology Bulletin, 14*, 459–467.

Buunk, B., & Bringle, R. G. (1987). Jealousy in love relationships. In D. Perlman & S. Duck (Eds.), *Intimate relationships: Development, dynamics, and deterioration* (pp. 123–147). Beverly Hills, CA: Sage Publications.

Byrne, D. (1971). *The attraction paradigm*. New York: Academic Press.

Byrne, D., & Wong, T. J. (1962). Racial prejudice, interpersonal attraction and assumed dissimilarity of attitudes. *Journal of Abnormal and Social Psychology, 65*, 246–253.

Byrne, D., Clore, G. L., & Smeaton, G. (1986). The attraction hypothesis: Do similar attitudes affect anything? *Journal of Personality and Social Psychology, 51*(6), 1167–1170.

Cacioppo, J. T., & Petty, R. E. (1979). Effects of message repetition and position on cognitive response, recall, and persuasion. *Journal of Personality and Social Psychology, 37*, 97–109.

Cacioppo, J. T., & Petty, R. E. (1985). Central and peripheral routes to persuasion: The role of message repetition. In L. F. Alwitt & A. A. Mitchell (Eds.), *Psychological processes and advertising effects: Theory, research, and applications* (pp. 91–111). Hillsdale, NJ: Erlbaum.

Cacioppo, J. T., Martzke, J. S., Petty, R. E., & Tassinary, L. G. (1988). Specific forms of facial EMG response index emotions during an interview: From Darwin to the continuous flow hypothesis of affect-laden information processing. *Journal of Personality and Social Psychology, 54*, 592–604.

Cacioppo, J. T., Petty, R. E., Losch, M. E., & Kim, H. S. (1986). Electromyographic activity over facial muscle regions can differentiate the valence and intensity of affective reactions. *Journal of Personality and Social Psychology, 50*, 260–268.

Caldwell, M. A., & Peplau, L. A. (1982). Sex differences in same-sex friendship. *Sex roles, 8*(7), 721–732.

Callero, P. L., Howard, J. A., & Piliavin, J. A. (1987). Helping behavior as role behavior: Disclosing social structure and history in the analysis of prosocial action. *Social Psychology Quarterly, 50*(3), 247–256.

Calnan, M. W., & Moss, S. (1984). The health belief model and compliance with education given at a class in breast self-examination. *Journal of Health and Social Behavior, 25*, 198–210.

Campbell, A., Converse, P. E., Miller, W. E., & Stokes, D. E. (1960). *The American voter*. New York: Wiley.

Campbell, D. T. (1975). On the conflicts between biological and social evolution and between psychology and moral tradition. *American Psychologist, 30*(12), 1103–1126.

Campbell, D. T., & Stanley, J. C. (1963). *Experimental and quasi-experimental designs for research*. Chicago: Rand McNally.

Campbell, J. D., & Fairey, P. J. (1989). Informational and normative routes to conformity: The effect of faction size as a function of norm extremity and attention to the stimulus. *Journal of Personality and Social Psychology, 57*, 457–468.

Campbell, J. D., Tesser, A., & Fairey, P. J. (1986). Conformity and attention to the stimulus: Some temporal and contextual dynamics. *Journal of Personality and Social Psychology, 51*(2), 315–324.

Cantor, N., & Kihlstrom, J. F. (1987). *Personality and social intelligence*. Englewood Cliffs, NJ: Prentice-Hall.

Cantor, N., & Mischel, W. (1979). Prototypes in person perception. In L. Berkowitz (Ed.), *Advances in experimental social psychology* (Vol. 12, pp. 4–52). New York: Academic Press.

Carlson, M., Marcus-Newhall, A., & Miller, N. (1989). Evidence for a general construct of aggression. *Personality and Social Psychology Bulletin, 15*, 377–389.

Carlson, M., & Miller, N. (1987). Explanation of the relation between negative mood and helping. *Psychological Bulletin, 102*(1), 91–108.

Carlson, M., Charlin, V., & Miller, N. (1988). Positive mood and helping behavior: A test of six hypotheses. *Journal of Personality and Social Psychology, 55*(2), 211–229.

Carlston, D. E., & Shovar, N. (1983). Effects of performance attributions on others' perceptions of the attribution. *Journal of Personality and Social Psychology, 44*, 515–525.

Carpenter, S. L. (1988). Self-relevance and goal-directed processing in the recall and weighting of information about others. *Journal of Experimental Social Psychology, 24*, 310–322.

Cash, T. F., Gillen, B., & Burns, D. S. (1977). Sexism and "beautyism" in personnel consultant decision making. *Journal of Applied Psychology, 62*, 301–310.

Cataldo, M. F., Green, L. W., Herd, J. A., Parkinson, R. S., & Goldbeck, W. B. (1986). Preventive medicine and the corporate environment: Challenge to behavioral medicine. In M. F. Cataldo & T. J. Coates (Eds.), *Health and industry: A behavioral medicine perspective* (pp. 399–419). New York: Wiley.

Cate, R. M., Lloyd, S. A., & Long, E. (1988). The role of rewards and fairness in developing premarital relationships. *Journal of Marriage and the Family, 50*, 443–452.

Cater, D., & Strickland, D. (1975). *TV violence and the child*. New York: Russell Sage.

Catrambone, R., & Markus, H. (1987). The role of self-schemas in going beyond the information given. *Social Cognition, 5*, 349–368.

Cervone, D., & Peake, P. K. (1986). Anchoring, efficacy, and action: The influence of judgmental heuristics on self-efficacy judgments and behavior. *Journal of Personality and Social Psychology, 50*, 492–501.

Chafetz, M. E. (1970). No patient deserves to be patronized. *Medical Insight, 2*, 68–75.

Chaikin, A. L., & Derlega, V. J. (1974). Liking for the norm-breaker in self-disclosure. *Journal of Personality, 42*, 117–129.

Chaikin, A. L., Gillen, H. B., Derlega, V., Heinen, J., & Wilson, M. (1978). Students' reactions to teachers' physical attractiveness and nonverbal behavior: Two exploratory studies. *Psychology in the Schools, 15*, 588–595.

Chaiken, S. (1979). Communicator physical attractiveness and persuasion. *Journal of Personality and Social Psychology, 37*, 1387–1397.

Chaiken, S. (1980). Heuristic versus systematic information processing and the use of source versus message cues in persuasion. *Journal of Personality and Social Psychology, 39*, 752–766.

Chaiken, S. (1987). The heuristic model of persuasion. In M. P. Zanna, J. M. Olson, & C. P. Herman (Eds.), *Social influence: The Ontario Symposium* (Vol. 5). Hillsdale, NJ: Erlbaum Associates.

Chaiken, S., & Baldwin, M. W. (1981). Affective-cognitive consistency and the effect of salient behavioral information on the self-perception of attitudes. *Journal of Personality and Social Psychology, 41*, 1–12.

Chaiken, S., & Eagly, A. H. (1976). Communication modality as a determinant of message persuasiveness and message comprehensibility. *Journal of Personality and Social Psychology, 34*, 605–614.

Chaiken, S., & Eagly, A. H. (1983). Communication modality as a determinant of persuasion: The role of communicator salience. *Journal of Personality and Social Psychology, 45*, 241–256.

Chaiken, S., & Stangor, C. (1987). Attitudes and attitude change. In M. R. Rosenzweig & L. W. Porter (Eds.), *Annual review of psychology, 38*, 575–630.

Chaiken, S., & Yates, S. (1985). Affective-cognitive consistency and thought-induced attitude polarization. *Journal of Personality and Social Psychology, 49*, 1470–1481.

Chaney, E. F., O'Leary, M. R., & Marlatt, G. A. (1978). Skill training with alcoholics. *Journal of Consulting and Clinical Psychology, 46*, 1092–1104.

Chen, C. E. (1981). Person categories and social perception: Testing some boundaries of the processing effects of prior knowledge. *Journal of Personality and Social Psychology, 40*, 441–452.

Chen, H., Yates, B. T., & McGinnies, E. (1988). Effects of involvement on observers' estimates of consensus, distinctiveness, and consistency. *Personality and Social Psychology Bulletin, 14*, 468–478.

Chen, S. C. (1937). Social modification of the activity of ants in nest-building. *Physiological Zoology, 10*, 420–436.

Chesney, M. A., Eagleston, J. R., & Rosenman, R. H. (1981). Type A behavior: Assessment and intervention. In C. K. Prokop & L. A. Bradley (Eds.), *Medical psychology: Contributions to behavioral medicine* (pp. 20–34). New York: Academic Press.

Christie, R., & Geis, F. L. (1970). *Studies in Machiavellianism*. New York: Academic Press.

Christie, R., & Jahoda, M. (Eds.). (1954). *Studies in the scope and method of "the authoritarian personality": Continuities in social research*. Glencoe, IL: The Free Press.

Cialdini, R. B. (1985). *Influence: Science and practice*. Glenview, IL: Scott, Foresman.

Cialdini, R. B., Baumann, D. J., & Kenrick, D. T. (1981). Insights from sadness: A three-step model of the development of altruism as hedonism. *Developmental Review, 1*, 207–223.

Cialdini, R. B., Cacioppo, J. T., Bassett, R., & Miller, J. A. (1978). Low-ball procedure for producing compliance: Commitment then cost. *Journal of Personality and Social Psychology, 36*, 463–476.

Cialdini, R. B., Schaller, M., Houlihan, D., Arps, K., Fultz, J., & Beaman, A. (1987). Empathy-based helping: Is it selflessly or selfishly motivated? *Journal of Personality and Social Psychology, 52*(4), 749–758.

Cialdini, R. B., Vincent, J. E., Lewis, S. K., Catalan, J., Wheeler, D., & Darby, B. L. (1975). Reciprocal concessions procedure for inducing compliance: The door-in-the-face technique. *Journal of Personality and Social Psychology, 31*, 206–215.

Cialdini, R. B., & De Nicholas, M. E. (1989). Self-presentation by association. *Journal of Personality and Social Psychology, 57*, 626–631.

Cialdini, R. B., Borden, R. J., Thorne, A., Walker, M. R., Freeman, S., & Sloan, L. R. (1976). Basking in reflected glory: Three (football) field studies. *Journal of Personality and Social Psychology, 34*, 366–375.

Citrin, J., Reingold, B. A., & Green, D. P. (1989). American identity and the politics of ethnic change. Working paper 89-1, Institute of Governmental Studies, University of California, Berkeley.

Citrin, J., Green, D. P., & Sears, D. O. (1990). White reactions to black candidates: When does race matter? *Public Opinion Quarterly, 54*, 74–96.

Clark, M. S., & Mills, J. (1979). Interpersonal attraction in exchange and communal relationships. *Journal of Personality and Social Psychology, 37*, 12–24.

Clark, M. S., Mills, J., & Powell, M. C. (1986). Keeping track of needs in communal and exchange relationships. *Journal of Personality and Social Psychology, 51*(2), 333–338.

Clark, R. D., & Word, L. E. (1972). Why don't bystanders help? Because of ambiguity? *Journal of Personality and Social Psychology, 24,* 392–400.

Clark, R. D., & Word, L. E. (1974). Where is the apathetic bystander? Situational characteristics of the emergency. *Journal of Personality and Social Psychology, 29,* 279–287.

Clark, M. S., Mills, J. R., & Corcoran, D. M. (1989). Keeping track of needs and inputs of friends and strangers. *Personality and Social Psychology Bulletin, 15,* 533–542.

Clifford, M. M., & Walster, E. (1973). Research note: The effects of physical attractiveness on teacher expectations. *Sociology of Education, 46,* 248–258.

Clore, G. L., Bray, R. B., Itkin, S. M., & Murphy, P. (1978). Interracial attitudes and behavior at a summer camp. *Journal of Personality and Social Psychology, 36,* 107–116.

Clore, G. L., & Byrne, D. (1974). A reinforcement-affect model of attraction. In T. L. Huston (Ed.), *Foundations of interpersonal attraction* (pp. 143–165). New York: Academic Press.

Coates, T. J., Morin, S. F., & McKusick, L. (1987). Behavioral consequences of AIDS antibody testing among gay men: The AIDS behavioral research project. *Journal of the American Medical Association, 258,* 199.

Cochran, S. D., & Hammen, C. L. (1985). Perceptions of stressful life events and depression: A test of attributional models. *Journal of Personality and Social Psychology, 48,* 1562–1571.

Cohen, C. E. (1981). Person categories and social perception: Testing some boundaries of the processing effects of prior knowledge. *Journal of Personality and Social Psychology, 40,* 441–452.

Cohen, S., & Hoberman, H. M. (1983). Positive events and social supports as buffers of life change stress. *Journal of Applied Social Psychology, 13,* 99–125.

Cohen, S., & Lezak, A. (1977). Noise and attentiveness to social cues. *Environment and Behavior, 9,* 559–572.

Cohen, S., & Weinstein, N. (1981). Nonauditory effects of noise on behavior and health. *Journal of Social Issues, 37*(1), 36–70.

Cohen, S., & Wills, T. A. (1985). Stress, social support, and the buffering hypothesis. *Psychological Bulletin, 98,* 310–357.

Cohen, S., Evans, G. W., Krantz, D. S., Stokols, D., & Kelly, S. (1981). Aircraft noise and children: Longitudinal and cross-sectional evidence on adaptation to noise and the effectiveness of noise abatement. *Journal of Personality and Social Psychology, 40,* 331–345.

Cohen, S., Glass, D. C., & Singer, J. E. (1973). Apartment noise, auditory discrimination, and reading ability in children. *Journal of Experimental Social Psychology, 9,* 407–422.

Cole, P. (1974). Morbidity in the U.S. In C. L. Erhardt, & J. Berlin (Eds.), *Mortality and morbidity in the U.S.* (pp. 65–104). Cambridge, MA: Harvard University Press.

Coleman, J. F., Blake, R. R., & Mouton, J. S. (1958). Task difficulty and conformity pressures. *Journal of Abnormal and Social Psychology, 57,* 120–122.

Collins, R. L., & Marlatt, G. A. (1981). Social modeling as a determinant of drinking behavior: Implications for prevention and treatment. *Addictive Behaviors, 6,* 233–240.

Collins, R. L., Taylor, S. E., & Skokan, L. A. (in press). A better world or a shattered vision? Changes in perspectives following victimization. *Social Cognition.*

Commission on Obscenity and Pornography. (1970). *Report of the commission on obscenity and pornography.* New York: Bantam.

Comstock, G. (1982). Violence in television content: An overview. In D. Pearl, L. Bouthilet, & J. Lazar (Eds.), *Television and behavior: Ten years of scientific progress and implications for the Eighties.* Vol. II: *Technical reviews.* Rockville, MD: National Institute of Mental Health.

Comstock, G., Chaffee, S., Katzman, N., McCombs, M., & Roberts, D. (1978). *Television and human behavior.* New York: Columbia University Press.

Condry, J., & Condry, S. (1976). Sex differences: A study in the eye of the beholder. *Child Development, 47,* 812–819.

Connelly, M. (1989, Sept. 15). Truck driver honored for heroism in fire. *Los Angeles Times,* Part II, pp. 8, 12.

Converse, P. E. (1964). The nature of belief systems in mass publics. In D. E. Apter (Ed.), *Ideology and discontent* (pp. 206–261). New York: Free Press.

Converse, P. E., & Campbell, A. (1960). Political standards in secondary groups. In D. Cartwright & A. Zander (Eds.), *Group dynamics,* 2nd ed. (pp. 300–318). Evanston, IL: Row, Peterson.

Converse, P. E., & Dupeux, G. (1966). DeGaulle and Eisenhower: The public image of the victorious general. In A. Campbell, P. E. Converse, W. E. Miller, & D. E. Stokes (Eds.), *Elections and the political order* (pp. 292–345). New York: Wiley.

Converse, P. E., & Markus, G. B. (1979). Plus ça change . . .: The new CPS election study panel. *American Political Science Review, 73,* 32–49.

Cook, S. W. (1978). Interpersonal and attitudinal outcomes in cooperating interracial groups. *Journal of Research and Development in Education, 12,* 97–113.

Cook, S. W. (1984). Cooperative interaction in multi-ethnic contexts. In N. Miller & M. Brewer (Eds.), *Groups in contact: The psychology of desegregation* (pp. 156–186). New York: Academic Press.

Cook, S. W. (1988). The 1954 social science statement and school desegregation: A reply to Gerard. In P. A. Katz & D. A. Taylor (Eds.), *Eliminating racism: Profiles in controversy* (pp. 237–256). New York: Plenum.

Cook, S. W., & Pelfrey, M. (1985). Reactions to being helped in cooperating interracial groups: A context effect. *Journal of Personality and Social Psychology, 49*(5), 1231–1245.

Cooper, J., & Fazio, R. H. (1984). A new look at dissonance

theory. In L. Berkowitz (Ed.), *Advances in experimental social psychology* (Vol. 17, pp. 229–265). New York: Academic Press.

Coovert, M. D., & Reeder, G. D. (1990). Negativity effects in impression formation: The role of unit formation and schematic expectations. *Journal of Experimental Social Psychology, 26,* 49–62.

Cox, D. J., Tisdelle, D. A., & Culbert, J. P. (1988). Increasing adherence to behavioral homework assignments. *Journal of Behavioral Medicine, 11,* 519–522.

Craig, K. D., & Patrick, C. J. (1985). Facial expression during induced pain. *Journal of Personality and Social Psychology, 48,* 1080–1091.

Craik, F. I. M., & Tulving, E. (1975). Depth of processing and the retention of words in episodic memory. *Journal of Experimental Psychology: General, 194,* 268–294.

Cramer, R. E., Weiss, R. F., Steigleder, M. K., & Balling, S. S. (1985). Attraction in context: Acquisition and blocking of person-directed action. *Journal of Personality and Social Psychology, 49,* 1221–1230.

Crandall, C. S. (1988). Social contagion of binge eating. *Journal of Personality and Social Psychology, 55,* 588–598.

Crocker, J. (1981). Judgment of covariation by social perceivers. *Psychological Bulletin, 90,* 272–292.

Crocker, J., Hannah, D. B., & Weber, R. (1983). Person memory and causal attributions. *Journal of Personality and Social Psychology, 44,* 55–66.

Crocker, J., Thompson, L. L., McGraw, K. M., & Ingerman, C. (1987). Downward comparison, prejudice, and evaluations of others: Effects of self-esteem and threat. *Journal of Personality and Social Psychology, 52,* 907–916.

Cummings, K. M., Jette, A. M., & Rosenstock, I. M. (1978). Construct validation of the health belief model. *Health Education Monographs, 6,* 394–405.

Cunningham, M. R. (1979). Weather, mood, and helping behavior: Quasi-experiments with the sunshine Samaritan. *Journal of Personality and Social Psychology, 37*(11), 1947–1956.

Cunningham, M. R. (1986). Measuring the physical in physical attractiveness: Quasi-experiments on the sociobiology of female facial beauty. *Journal of Personality and Social Psychology, 50*(5), 925–935.

Curtis, R. C., & Miller, K. (1986). Believing another likes and dislikes you: Behaviors making the beliefs come true. *Journal of Personality and Social Psychology, 51,* 284–290.

Cutrona, C. E. (1982). Transition to college: Loneliness and the process of social adjustment. In L. A. Peplau & D. Perlman (Eds.), *Loneliness: A sourcebook of current theory, research and therapy* (pp. 291–309). New York: Wiley-Interscience.

Cutrona, C. E., & Russell, D. (1987). The provisions of social relationships and adaptation to stress. In W. H. Jones & D. Perlman (Eds.), *Advances in personal relationships* (Vol. 1, pp. 37–67). Greenwich, CT: JAI Press.

Dabbs, J. M., Jr., & Leventhal, H. (1966). Effects of varying the recommendations in a fear-arousing communication. *Journal of Personality and Social Psychology, 4,* 525–531.

Dakof, G. A., & Taylor, S. E. (1990). Victims' perceptions of social support: What is helpful from whom? *Journal of Personality and Social Psychology, 58,* 80–89.

Darley, J. M., & Batson, C. D. (1973). "From Jerusalem to Jericho": A study of situational and dispositional variables in helping behavior. *Journal of Personality and Social Psychology, 27,* 100–108.

Darley, J. M., & Fazio, R. H. (1980). Expectancy confirmation processes arising in the social interaction sequence. *American Psychologist, 35,* 867–881.

Darley, J. M., Fleming, J. H., Hilton, J. L., & Swann, W. B., Jr. (1988). Dispelling negative expectancies: The impact of interaction goals and target characteristics on the expectancy confirmation process. *Journal of Experimental Social Psychology, 24,* 19–36.

Darley, J. M., & Latané, B. (1968). Bystander intervention in emergencies: Diffusion of responsibility. *Journal of Personality and Social Psychology, 8,* 377–383.

Darwin, C. (1871). *The descent of man.* London: Murray.

Davidson, A. R., & Jaccard, J. J. (1979). Variables that moderate the attitude-behavior relation: Results of a longitudinal survey. *Journal of Personality and Social Psychology, 37,* 1364–1376.

Davis, M. S. (1968). Variation in patients' compliance with doctors' advice: An empirical analysis of patterns of communication. *American Journal of Public Health, 58,* 274–288.

Dawes, R., Faust, D., & Meehl, P. E. (1989). Clinical versus actuarial judgment. *Science, 243,* 1668–1674.

Deaux, K., & Emswiller, T. (1974). Explanations of successful performance on sex-linked tasks: What is skill for the male is luck for the female. *Journal of Personality and Social Psychology, 29,* 80–85.

Deaux, K., & Lewis, L. (1984). Structure of gender stereotypes: Interrelationships among components and gender label. *Journal of Personality and Social Psychology, 46,* 991–1004.

Deaux, K., & Major, B. (1987). Putting gender into context: An interactive model of gender-related behavior. *Psychological Review, 94,* 369–389.

Deci, E. L., & Ryan, R. M. (1985). *Intrinsic motivation and self-determination in human behavior.* New York: Plenum.

Dembroski, T. M., & Costa, P. T., Jr. (1987). Coronary prone behavior: Components of the Type A pattern and hostility. *Journal of Personality, 55,* 211–235.

Dengerink, H. A., Schnedler, R. W., & Covey, M. K. (1978). Role of avoidance in aggressive responses to attack and no attack. *Journal of Personality and Social Psychology, 36,* 1044–1053.

Department of Health and Human Services. (1981). *Alcohol and health.* Rockville, MD: Secretary of Health and Human Services, National Institute of Alcohol Abuse and Alcoholism.

DePaulo, B. M. (1990). *Nonverbal behavior and self presentation.* Manuscript submitted for publication.

DePaulo, B. M., & Kirkendol, S. E. (1989). Motivational impairment effect in the communication of deception. In J. C. Yuille (Ed.), *Credibility assessment* (pp. 51–70). Brussels: Kluwer.

DePaulo, B. M., Kirkendol, S. E., Tang, J., & O'Brien, T. (1988). The motivational impairment effect in the communication of deception: Replications and extensions. *Journal of Nonverbal Behavior, 12,* 177–202.

DePaulo, B. M., LeMay, C. S., & Epstein, J. (in press). Effects of importance of success and expectations for success on effectiveness of deceiving. *Personality and Social Psychology Bulletin.*

DePaulo, B. M., Stone, J. I., & Lassiter, G. D. (1985a). Deceiving and detecting deceit. In B. R. Schlenker (Ed.), *The self and social life* (pp. 323–370). New York: McGraw-Hill.

DePaulo, B. M., Stone, J. I., & Lassiter, G. D. (1985b). Telling ingratiating lies: Effects of target sex and target attractiveness on verbal and nonverbal deceptive success. *Journal of Personality and Social Psychology, 48,* 1191–1203.

DePaulo, B. M., Rosenthal, R., Eisenstat, R. A., Rogers, P. L., & Finkelstein, S. (1978). Decoding discrepant nonverbal cues. *Journal of Personality and Social Psychology, 36,* 313–323.

DePaulo, B. M., Rosenthal, R., Green, C. R., & Rosenkrantz, J. (1982). Diagnosing deceptive and mixed messages from verbal and nonverbal cues. *Journal of Personality and Social Psychology, 18,* 433–446.

Derlega, V. J. (1984). Self-disclosure and intimate relationships. In V. J. Derlega (Ed.), *Communication, intimacy, and close relationships* (pp. 1–10). New York: Academic Press.

Derlega, V. J., & Chaikin, A. L. (1975). *Sharing intimacy: What we reveal to others and why.* Englewood Cliffs, NJ: Prentice-Hall.

Derlega, V. J., & Grzelak, A. L. (1979). Appropriate self-disclosure. In G. J. Chelune (Ed.), *Self-disclosure: Origins, patterns, and implications of openness in interpersonal relationships.* San Francisco: Jossey-Bass.

Derlega, V. J., Durham, B., Gockel, B., & Sholis, D. (1981). Sex differences in self-disclosure: Effects of topic content, friendship, and partner's sex. *Sex Roles, 7*(4), 433–447.

Deutsch, F. M., & Lamberti, D. M. (1986). Does social approval increase helping? *Personality and Social Psychology Bulletin, 12*(2), 149–157.

Deutsch, M. (1973). *The Resolution of Conflict: Constructive and Destructive Processes.* New Haven, CT: Yale University Press.

Deutsch, M. (1985). *Distributive justice: A social psychological perspective.* New Haven, CT: Yale University Press.

Deutsch, M., & Collins, M. E. (1951). *Interracial housing: A psychological evaluation of a social experiment.* Minneapolis: University of Minnesota Press.

Deutsch, M., & Krauss, R. M. (1960). The effect of threat on interpersonal bargaining. *Journal of Abnormal and Social Psychology, 61,* 181–189.

Devine, P. G. (1989). Stereotypes and prejudice: Their automatic and controlled components. *Journal of Personality and Social Psychology, 56,* 5–18.

Devine, P. G., Sedikides, C., & Fuhrman, R. W. (1989). Goals in social information processing: The case of anticipated information. *Journal of Personality and Social Psychology, 56,* 680–690.

Diehl, M., & Stroebe, W. (1987). Productivity loss in brainstorming groups: Toward the solution of a riddle. *Journal of Personality and Social Psychology, 53,* 497–509.

Diener, E. (1976). Effects of prior destructive behavior, anonymity, and group presence on deindividuation and aggression. *Journal of Personality and Social Psychology, 33,* 497–507.

Diener, F. (1980). Deindividuation: The absence of self-awareness and self-regulation in group members. In P. B. Paulus (Ed.), *Psychology of group influence.* Hillsdale, NJ: Erlbaum.

Diener, F., Fraser, S. C., Beaman, A. L., & Kelem, Z. R. T. (1976). Effects of deindividuation variables on stealing among Halloween trick-or-treaters. *Journal of Personality and Social Psychology, 33,* 178–183.

Dillard, J. P., Hunter, J. E., & Burgoon, M. (1984). Sequential-request persuasive strategies: Meta-analysis of foot-in-the-door and door-in-the-face. *Human Communication Research, 10,* 461–488.

DiMatteo, M. R., & DiNicola, D. D. (1982). *Achieving patient compliance: The psychology of the medical practitioner's role* (pp. 55–84). New York: Pergamon.

DiMatteo, M. R., Friedman, H. S., & Taranta, A. (1979). Sensitivity to bodily nonverbal communications as a factor in practitioner-patient rapport. *Journal of Nonverbal Behavior, 4,* 18–26.

DiMatteo, M. R., Hays, R. D., & Prince, L. M. (1986). Relationship of physicians' nonverbal communication skill to patient satisfaction, appointment noncompliance, and physician workload. *Health Psychology, 5,* 581–594.

Dimitrovsky, L., Singer, J., & Yinon, Y. (1989). Masculine and feminine traits: Their relation to suitedness for and success in training for traditionally masculine and feminine army functions. *Journal of Personality and Social Psychology, 57,* 839–847.

DiNicola, D. D., & DiMatteo, M. R. (1984). Practitioners, patients, and compliance with medical regimens: A social psychological perspective. In A. Baum, S. E. Taylor, & J. E. Singer (Eds.), *Handbook of psychology and health* (Vol. 4, pp. 55–84). Hillsdale, NJ: Erlbaum.

Dion, K. K. (1972). Physical attractiveness and evaluations of children's transgressions. *Journal of Personality and Social Psychology, 24,* 285–290.

Dion, K. K., Berscheid, E., & Walster, E. (1972). What is beautiful is good. *Journal of Personality and Social Psychology, 24,* 285–290.

Dion, K. L., & Dion, K. K. (1973). Correlates of romantic love. *Journal of Consulting and Clinical Psychology, 41,* 51–56.

Dodge, K. A., & Tomlin, A. M. (1987). Utilization of self-schemas as a mechanism of interpretational bias in aggressive children. *Social Cognition, 5,* 280–300.

Dollard, J., Doob, L., Miller, N. E., Mowrer, O. H., & Sears, R. (1939). *Frustration and aggression.* New Haven, CT: Yale University Press.

Donnerstein, E. (1983). Erotica and human aggression. In R. Geen & E. Donnerstein (Eds.), *Aggression: Theoretical and empirical reviews* (pp. 127–154). New York: Academic Press.

Donnerstein, E., & Barrett, G. (1978). Effects of erotic stimuli on male aggression toward females. *Journal of Personality and Social Psychology, 36,* 180–188.

Donnerstein, E., & Berkowitz, L. (1981). Victim reactions in aggressive erotic films as a factor in violence against women. *Journal of Personality and Social Psychology, 41,* 710–724.

Donnerstein, E., & Donnerstein, M. (1972). White rewarding behavior as a function of potential for black retaliation. *Journal of Personality and Social Psychology, 24,* 327–333.

Donnerstein, E., Donnerstein, M., & Evans, R. (1975). Erotic stimuli and aggression: Facilitation or inhibition. *Journal of Personality and Social Psychology, 32,* 237–244.

Donnerstein, E., & Wilson, D. W. (1976). Effects of noise and perceived control on ongoing and subsequent aggressive behavior. *Journal of Personality and Social Psychology, 34,* 774–781.

Dornbush, S. M., Hastorf, A. H., Richardson, S. A., Muzzy, R. E., & Vreeland, R. S. (1965). The perceiver and the perceived: Their relative influence on the categories of interpersonal cognition. *Journal of Personality and Social Psychology, 1,* 434–440.

Dosser, D. A., Balswick, J. O., & Halverson, C. F. (1986). Male inexpressiveness and relationships. *Journal of Social and Personal Relationships, 3*(2), 241–258.

Douthitt, R. A. (1989). The division of labor within the home: Have gender roles changed? *Sex Roles, 20,* 693–704.

Dovidio, J. F., & Gaertner, S. L. (Eds.). (1986). *Prejudice, Discrimination, and Racism.* New York: Academic Press.

Durkin, K. (1987). Sex roles and the mass media. In D. J. Hargreaves, & A. M. Colley (Eds.), *The psychology of sex roles* (pp. 201–214). New York: Hemisphere.

Duval, S., & Wicklund, R. A. (1972). *A theory of objective self-awareness.* New York: Academic Press.

Dweck, C. S. (1975). The role of expectations and attributions in the alleviation of learned helplessness. *Journal of Personality and Social Psychology, 31,* 674–685.

Dworkin, A. (1985). Against the male flood: Censorship, pornography, and equality. *Harvard Women's Law Journal, 8,* 1–25.

Dyck, R. J., & Rule, B. G. (1978). Effect on retaliation of causal attributions concerning attack. *Journal of Personality and Social Psychology, 36,* 521–529.

Eagly, A. H. (1978). Sex differences in influenceability. *Psychological Bulletin, 85,* 86–116.

Eagly, A. H. (1983). Gender and social influence: A social psychological analysis. *American Psychologist, 38*(9), 971–981.

Eagly, A. H. (1987). *Sex differences in social behavior: A social-role interpretation.* Hillsdale, NJ: Erlbaum.

Eagly, A. H., & Crowley, M. (1986). Gender and helping behavior: A meta-analytic review of the social psychological literature. *Psychological Bulletin, 100*(3), 283–308.

Eagly, A. H., & Johnson, B. T. (1990). Gender and leadership style: A meta-analysis. Unpublished manuscript, Purdue University.

Eagly, A. H., & Steffen, V. J. (1986). Gender and aggressive behavior: A meta-analytic review of the social psychological literature. *Psychological Bulletin, 100*(3), 309–330.

Eagly, A. H., & Telaak, K. (1972). Width of the latitude of acceptance as a determinant of attitude change. *Journal of Personality and Social Psychology, 23,* 388–397.

Eagly, A. H., & Wood, W. (1982). Inferred sex differences in status as a determinant of gender stereotypes about social influence. *Journal of Personality and Social Psychology, 43,* 915–928.

Eagly, A. H., & Wood, W. (1985). Gender and influenceability: Stereotype versus behavior. In V. E. O'Leary, R. K. Unger, & B. S. Wallston (Eds.), *Women, gender, and social psychology.* Hillsdale, NJ: Erlbaum.

Eagly, A. H., Wood, W., & Chaiken, S. (1978). Causal inferences about communicators and their effect on opinion change. *Journal of Personality and Social Psychology, 36,* 424–435.

Edwards, W. (1954). The theory of decision-making. *Psychological Bulletin, 51,* 380–417.

Einhorn, H. J., & Hogarth, R. M. (1981). Behavioral decision theory: Processes of judgment and choice. *Annual Review of Psychology, 32,* 53–88.

Eisen, S. V. (1979). Actor-observer differences in information inference and causal attribution. *Journal of Personality and Social Psychology, 37,* 261–272.

Eisenberg, N., & Miller, P. A. (1987). The relation of empathy to prosocial and related behaviors. *Psychological Bulletin, 10*(1), 91–119.

Eisenberg, N., Fabes, R. A., Miller, P. A., Fultz, J., Shell, R., Mathy, R. M., & Reno, R. R. (1989). Relation of sympathy and personal distress to prosocial behavior: A multimethod study. *Journal of Personality and Social Psychology, 57*(1), 55–66.

Ekman, P. (1972). Universals and cultural differences in facial expressions of emotion. In J. K. Cole (Ed.), *Nebraska symposium on motivation, 1971* (pp. 207–283). Lincoln: University of Nebraska Press.

Ekman, P. (1982). *Emotion in the human face* (2nd ed.) Cambridge: Cambridge University Press.

Ekman, P., & Friesen, W. V. (1971). Constants across cultures in the face and emotion. *Journal of Personality and Social Psychology, 17*, 124–129.

Ekman, P., & Friesen, W. V. (1974). Detecting deception from the body or face. *Journal of Personality and Social Psychology, 29*, 288–298.

Ekman, P., Friesen, W. V., & O'Sullivan, M. (1988). Smiles when lying. *Journal of Personality and Social Psychology, 54*, 414–420.

Ekman, P., Friesen, W. V., & Scherer, K. (1976). Body movements and voice pitch in deceptive interaction. *semiotica, 16*, 23–27.

Elkin, R. A., & Leippe, M. R. (1986). Physiological arousal, dissonance, and attitude change: Evidence for a dissonance-arousal link and a "Don't Remind Me" effect. *Journal of Personality and Social Psychology, 51*, 55–65.

Ellis, R. J. (1988). Self-monitoring and leadership emergence in groups. *Personality and Social Psychology Bulletin, 14*, 681–693.

Ellsworth, P. C., & Carlsmith, J. M. (1973). Eye contact and gaze aversion in an aggressive encounter. *Journal of Personality and Social Psychology, 28*, 280–292.

Ellsworth, P. C., Friedman, H. S., Perlick, D., & Hoyt, M. E. (1978). Some effects of gaze on subjects motivated to seek or to avoid social comparison. *Journal of Personality and Social Psychology, 14*, 69–87.

Elms, A. C. (1976). *Personality in politics.* New York: Harcourt Brace Jovanovich.

Emswiller, T., Deaux, K., & Willits, J. E. (1971). Similarity, sex, and requests for small favors. *Journal of Applied Social Psychology, 1*(3), 284–291.

Engel, G. L. (1971). Sudden and rapid death during psychological stress. *Annals of Internal Medicine, 74*, 771–782.

English, E. H., & Baker, T. B. (1983). Relaxation training and cardiovascular response to experimental stressors. *Health Psychology, 2*, 239–259.

Erber, R., & Fiske, S. T. (1984). Outcome dependency and attention to inconsistent information. *Journal of Personality and Social Psychology, 47*, 709–726.

Erdley, C. A., & D'Agostino, P. R. (1988). Cognitive and affective components of automatic priming effects. *Journal of Personality and Social Psychology, 54*, 741–747.

Eron, L. D., Huesmann, L. R., Lefkowitz, M. M., & Walder, L. O. (1972). Does television violence cause aggression? *American Psychologist, 27*, 253–263.

Esser, J. K., & Komorita, S. S. (1975). Reciprocity and concession making in bargaining. *Journal of Personality and Social Psychology, 31*, 864–872.

Etheredge, L. (1979). Hardball politics: A model. *Political Psychology, 1*, 3–26.

Etzioni, A. (1967). The Kennedy experiment. *Western Political Quarterly, 20*, 361–380.

Evans, G. W., & Cohen, S. (1987). Environmental stress. In D. Stokols & I. Altman (Eds.), *Handbook of environmental psychology.* New York: Wiley.

Farrenkopf, T. (1974). *Man-environment interaction: An academic department moves into a new building.* Unpublished doctoral dissertation, University of Massachusetts.

Fazio, R. H. (1981). On the self-perception explanation of the overjustification effect: The role of the salience of initial attitude. *Journal of Experimental Social Psychology, 17*, 417–426.

Fazio, R. H. (1987). Self-perception theory: A current perspective. In M. P. Zanna, J. M. Olson, & C. P. Herman (Eds.), *Social influence: The Ontario Symposium* (Vol. 5). Hillsdale, NJ: Erlbaum.

Fazio, R. H., Chen, J., McDonel, E. C., & Sherman, S. J. (1982). Attitude accessibility, attitude-behavior consistency, and the strength of the object-evaluation association. *Journal of Experimental Social Psychology, 18*, 339–357.

Fazio, R. H., Effrein, E. A., & Falender, V. J. (1981). Self-perceptions following social interaction. *Journal of Personality and Social Psychology, 41*, 232–242.

Fazio, R. H., Sanbonmatsu, D. M., Powell, M. C., & Kardes, F. R. (1986). On the automatic activation of attitudes. *Journal of Personality and Social Psychology, 50*, 229–238.

Fazio, R. H., & Zanna, M. P. (1981). Direct experience and attitude-behavior consistency. In L. Berkowitz (Ed.), *Advances in experimental social psychology* (Vol. 14, pp. 161–202). New York: Academic Press.

Feather, N. T., & Simon, J. G. (1975). Reactions to male and female success and failure in sex-linked occupations: Impressions of personality, causal attributions, and perceived likelihood of different consequences. *Journal of Personality and Social Psychology, 31*(1), 20–31.

Feingold, A. (1988a). Matching for attractiveness in romantic partners and same-sex friends: A meta-analysis and theoretical critique. *Psychological Bulletin, 104*, 226–235.

Feingold, A. (1988b). Cognitive gender differences are disappearing. *American Psychologist, 43*, 95–103.

Feldman, R. E. (1968). Response to compatriot and foreigner who seek assistance. *Journal of Personality and Social Psychology, 10*(3), 202–214.

Feldman, S. (1982). Economic self-interest and political behavior. *American Journal of Political Science, 26*, 446–466.

Feletti, G., Firman, D., & Sanson-Fisher, R. (1986). Patient satisfaction with primary-care consultations. *Journal of Behavioral Medicine, 9*, 389–399.

Fenigstein, A., Scheier, M. F., & Buss, A. H. (1975). Public and private self-consciousness: Assessment and theory. *Journal of Consulting and Clinical Psychology, 43,* 522–527.

Feshbach, S. (1955). The drive-reducing function of fantasy behavior. *Journal of Abnormal and Social Psychology, 50,* 3–12.

Feshbach, S. (1961). The stimulating versus cathartic effects of a vicarious aggressive activity. *Journal of Abnormal and Social Psychology, 63,* 381–385.

Feshbach, S. (1970). Aggression. In P. Mussen (Ed.), *Carmichael's Manual of Child Psychology* (Vol. 2). New York: Wiley.

Feshbach, S., & Singer, R. D. (1971). *Television and aggression.* San Francisco: Jossey-Bass.

Festinger, L. (1950). Informal social communication. *Psychological Review, 57,* 271–282.

Festinger, L. (1954). A theory of social comparison processes. *Human Relations, 7,* 117–140.

Festinger, L. (1957). *A theory of cognitive dissonance.* Evanston, IL: Row, Peterson.

Festinger, L., & Carlsmith, J. M. (1959). Cognitive consequences of forced compliance. *Journal of Abnormal and Social Psychology, 58,* 203–210.

Festinger, L., & Maccoby, N. (1964). On resistance to persuasive communications. *Journal of Abnormal and Social Psychology, 68,* 359–366.

Festinger, L., Pepitone, A., & Newcomb, T. (1952). Some consequences of deindividuation in a group. *Journal of Abnormal and Social Psychology, 47,* 383–389.

Festinger, L., Riecken, H. W., & Schachter, S. (1956). *When prophecy fails.* Minneapolis: University of Minnesota Press.

Festinger, L., Schachter, S., & Back, K. (1950). *Social pressures in informal groups: A study of human factors in housing.* Stanford University Press.

Fiedler, F. E. (1978). Recent developments in research on the contingency model. In L. Berkowitz (Ed.), *Group processes* (pp. 209–225). New York: Academic Press.

Fiedler, F. E. (1981). Leadership effectiveness. *American Behavioral Scientist, 24*(5), 619–632.

Fiedler, F. E. (1986). The contribution of cognitive resources and behavior to leadership performance. In C. F. Graumann & S. Moscovici (Eds.), *Changing conceptions of leadership* (pp. 101–114). New York: Springer-Verlag.

Fillingim, R. B., & Fine, M. A. (1986). The effects of internal versus external information processing on symptom perception in an exercise setting. *Health Psychology, 5,* 115–123.

Finkelman, J. M., & Glass, D. C. (1970). Reappraisal of the relationship between noise and human performance by means of a subsidiary task measure. *Journal of Applied Psychology, 54,* 211–213.

Finlay, D. J., Holsti, O. R., & Fagen, R. R. (1967). *Enemies in politics.* Chicago: Rand McNally.

Fiorina, M. P. (1981). *Retrospective voting in American national elections.* New Haven, CT: Yale University Press.

Fischer, C. S. (1982). *To dwell among friends: Personal networks in town and city.* Chicago: University of Chicago Press.

Fischer, C. S. (1984). *The urban experience,* 2nd ed. New York: Harcourt Brace Jovanovich.

Fischer, W. F. (1963). Sharing in pre-school children as a function of amount and type of reinforcement. *Genetic Psychology Monographs, 68,* 215–245.

Fishbein, M. (1980). A theory of reasoned action: Some applications and implications. In M. M. Page (Ed.), *1979 Nebraska Symposium on motivation.* Lincoln: University of Nebraska Press.

Fishbein, M., & Ajzen, I. (1975). *Belief, attitude, intention, and behavior: An introduction to theory and research.* Reading, MA: Addison-Wesley.

Fisher, J. D., Nadler, A., & Whitcher-Alagna, S. (1982). Recipient reactions to aid. *Psychological Bulletin, 91,* 33–54.

Fiske, S. T. (1980). Attention and weight in person perception: The impact of negative and extreme behavior. *Journal of Personality and Social Psychology, 38,* 889–906.

Fiske, S. T. (1982). Schema-triggered affect: Applications to social perception. In M. S. Clark & S. T. Fiske (Eds.), *Affect and cognition: The 17th annual Carnegie Symposium on Cognition* (pp. 55–78). Hillsdale, NJ: Erlbaum.

Fiske, S. T., & Neuberg, S. L. (1990). A continuum of impression formation, from category-based to individuating processes: Influences of information and motivation of attention and interpretation. In M. P. Zanna (Eds.), *Advances in experimental social psychology* (Vol. 23, pp. 1–73). New York: Academic Press.

Fiske, S. T., Neuberg, S. L., Beattie, A. E., & Milberg, S. J. (1987). Category-based and attribute-based reactions to others: Some informational conditions of stereotyping and individuating processes. *Journal of Experimental Social Psychology, 23,* 399–427.

Fiske, S. T., & Taylor, S. (1984). *Social cognition.* Reading, MA: Addison-Wesley.

Fiske, S. T., & Taylor, S. E. (in press, 1991). *Social cognition,* 2nd ed. New York: McGraw-Hill.

Fleming, J., & Darley, J. M. (1989). Perceiving choice and constraint: The effects of contextual and behavioral cues on attitude attribution. *Journal of Personality and Social Psychology, 56,* 27–40.

Fleming, R., Baum, A., Gisriel, M. M., & Gatchel, R. J. (1982 September). Mediating influences of social support on stress at Three Mile Island. *Journal of Human Stress,* September, 14–22.

Fletcher, G. J. O., & Ward, C. (1988). Attribution theory and processes: Cross-cultural perspective. In M. H. Bond (Ed.), *The cross-cultural challenge to social psychology* (pp. 230–244). Newbury Park, CA: Sage Publications.

Flowers, M. L. (1977). A laboratory test of some implications of Janis's groupthink hypothesis. *Journal of Personality and Social Psychology, 35,* 888–896.

Foa, U. G. (1971). Interpersonal and economic resources. *Science, 71,* 345–351.

Foa, U. G., & Foa, E. B. (1974). *Societal structures of the mind.* Springfield, IL: Charles C. Thomas.

Folkes, V. S. (1982). Forming relationships and the matching hypothesis. *Personality and Social Psychology Bulletin, 8*(4), 631–636.

Folkes, V. S., & Sears, D. O. (1977). Does everybody like a liker? *Journal of Experimental Social Psychology, 13,* 505–519.

Fong, G. T., Krantz, D. H., & Nisbett, R. E. (1986). The effects of statistical training on thinking about everyday problems. *Cognitive Psychology, 18,* 253–292.

Forsterling, F. (1986). Attributional conceptions in clinical psychology. *American Psychologist, 41,* 275–285.

Forsyth, D. R. (1983). *An introduction to group dynamics.* Monterey, CA: Brooks/Cole.

Franck, K. A. (1980). Friends and strangers: The experience of living in urban and nonurban settings. *Journal of Social Issues, 36*(3), 52–71.

Frank, F. D., & Drucker, J. (1977). The influence of evaluatee's sex on evaluation of a response on a managerial selection instrument. *Sex Roles, 3,* 59–64.

Frank, M. G., & Gilovich, T. (1988). The dark side of self- and social perception: Black uniforms and aggression in professional sports. *Journal of Personality and Social Psychology, 54,* 74–85.

Frankovic, K. A. (1982). Sex and politics—new alignments, old issues. *PS, 15,* 439–448.

Fraser, C., & Foster, D. (1984). Social groups, nonsense groups and group polarization. In H. Tajfel (Ed.), *The social dimension: European developments in social psychology* (Vol. 2, pp. 473–497). London: Cambridge University Press.

Fraser, C., Gouge, C., & Billig, M. (1971). Risky shifts, cautious shifts, and group polarization. *European Journal of Social Psychology, 1,* 7–30.

Freedman, J. L. (1963). Attitudinal effects of inadequate justification. *Journal of Personality, 31,* 371–385.

Freedman, J. L. (1964). Involvement, discrepancy, and change. *Journal of Abnormal and Social Psychology, 69,* 290–295.

Freedman, J. L. (1965). Long-term behavioral effects of cognitive dissonance. *Journal of Experimental Social Psychology, 1,* 145–155.

Freedman, J. L. (1975). *Crowding behavior.* New York: Viking Press.

Freedman, J. L. (1984). Effect of television violence on aggressiveness. *Psychological Bulletin, 96,* 227–246.

Freedman, J. L. (1986). Television violence and aggression: A rejoinder. *Psychological Bulletin, 100,* 372–378.

Freedman, J. L., & Fraser, S. C. (1966). Compliance without pressure: The foot-in-the-door technique. *Journal of Personality and Social Psychology, 4,* 195–202.

Freedman, J. L., & Sears, D. O. (1965). Warning, distraction, and resistance to influence. *Journal of Personality and Social Psychology, 1,* 262–266.

Freedman, J. L., & Steinbruner, J. D. (1964). Perceived choice and resistance to persuasion. *Journal of Abnormal and Social Psychology, 68,* 678–681.

Freedman, J. L., Heshka, S., & Levy, A. (1973). Population density and pathology: Is there a relationship? *Journal of Experimental Social Psychology, 11,* 539–552.

Freidson, E. (1960). Client control and medical practice. *American Journal of Sociology, 65,* 374–382.

French, J., & Raven, B. (1959). The bases of social power. In D. Cartwright (Ed.), *Studies in social power* (pp. 150–167). Ann Arbor, MI: Institute for Social Research.

Fried, R., & Berkowitz, L. (1979). Music hath charms . . . and can influence helplessness. *Journal of Applied Social Psychology, 9,* 199–208.

Friedman, L. (1979). *The relationship of some architectural variables to the social behavior of building residents.* Unpublished doctoral dissertation, Columbia University.

Friedman, H. S., Riggio, R. E., & Casella, D. F. (1988). Nonverbal skill, personal charisma, and initial attraction. *Personality and Social Psychology Bulletin, 14,* 203–211.

Friedman, H. S., & Booth-Kewley, S. (1987). The ''disease-prone'' personality: A meta-analytic view of the construct. *American Psychologist, 42,* 539–555.

Friedman, H. S., & Miller-Herringer, T. (1990). *The nonverbal display of emotion: Effects of expressiveness, self-monitoring, and personality.* Manuscript submitted for publication.

Friedman, M., & Rosenman, R. H. (1974). *Type A behavior and your heart.* New York: Knopf.

Friedrich, L. K., & Stein, A. H. (1973). Aggressive and prosocial television programs and the natural behavior of preschool children. *Monographs of the Society for Research in Child Development, 38*(4, Serial No. 151).

Friedrich-Cofer, L., & Huston, A. C. (1986). Television violence and aggression: The debate continues. *Psychological Bulletin, 100,* 364–371.

Froming, W. J., & Carver, C. S. (1981). Divergent influences of private and public self-consciousness in a compliance paradigm. *Journal of Research in Psychology, 15,* 159–171.

Fultz, J., Batson, C. D., Fortenbach, V. A., McCarthy, P. M., & Varney, L. L. (1986). Social evaluation and the empathy-altruism hypothesis. *Journal of Social and Personality Psychology, 50*(4), 761–769.

Funder, D. C. (1987). Errors and mistakes: Evaluating the accuracy of social judgment. *Psychological Bulletin, 101,* 75–90.

Funkhouser, G. R. (1973). The issues of the sixties: An exploratory study in the dynamics of public opinion. *Public Opinion Quarterly, 37,* 62–75.

Gabrielcik, A., & Fazio, R. H. (1984). Priming and frequency estimation: A strict test of the availability heuristic. *Personality and Social Psychology Bulletin, 10*, 85–89.

Gaertner, S. L., & Dovidio, J. F. (1986). The aversive forms of racism. In J. F. Dovidio & S. L. Gaertner (Eds.), *Prejudice, discrimination, and racism* (pp. 61–89). Orlando, FL: Academic Press.

Gal, R., & Lazarus, R. S. (1975). The role of activity in anticipating and confronting stressful situations. *Journal of Human Stress, 1*, 4–20.

Ganster, D. C., Mayes, B. T., Sime, W. E., & Tharp, G. D. (1982). Managing organizational stress: A field experiment. *Journal of Applied Psychology, 67*, 533–542.

Garner, D. M., Garfinkel, P. E., Schwartz, D., & Thompson, M. (1980). Cultural expectations of thinness in women. *Psychological Reports, 47*, 483–491.

Garnets, L., & Pleck, J. (1979). Sex role identity, androgyny, and sex role transcendence: A sex role strain analysis. *Psychology of Women Quarterly 3*, 270–283.

Geen, R. G. (1976). Observing violence in the mass media: Implications of basic research. In R. G. Geen & E. O'Neal (Eds.), *Perspectives on aggression* (pp. 193–234). New York: Academic Press.

Geen, R. G. (1989). Alternative conceptions of social facilitation. In P. B. Paulus (Ed.), *Psychology of group influence*, 2nd ed. (pp. 15–48). Hillsdale, NJ: Erlbaum.

Geen, R. G., & Bushman, B. J. (1987). Drive theory: Effects of socially engendered arousal. In B. Mullen & G. R. Goethals (Eds.), *Theories of group behavior* (pp. 89–110). New York: Springer Verlag.

Geen, R. G., & O'Neal, E. C. (1969). Activation of cue-eliciting aggression by general arousal. *Journal of Personality and Social Psychology, 11*, 289–292.

Geen, R. G., & Pigg, R. (1970). Acquisition of an aggressive response and its generalization to verbal behavior. *Journal of Personality and Social Psychology, 15*, 165–170.

Geen, R. G., & Quanty, M. B. (1977). The catharsis of aggression: An evaluation of a hypothesis. In L. Berkowitz (Ed.), *Advances in experimental social psychology* (Vol. 10, pp. 2–39). New York: Academic Press.

Geiselman, R. E., Haight, N. A., & Kimata, L. G. (1984). Context effects on the perceived physical attractiveness of faces. *Journal of Experimental Social Psychology, 20*, 409–424.

Geller, D. M. (1980). Responses to urban stimuli: A balanced approach. *Journal of Social Issues, 36*, 86–100.

George, A. L. (1969). The "operational code": A neglected approach to the study of political leaders and decision making. *International Studies Quarterly, 13*, 190–222.

George, A. L., & George, J. L. (1956). *Woodrow Wilson and Colonel House: A personality study*. New York: John Day.

Gerard, H. B. (1988). School desegregation: The social science role. In P. A. Katz & D. A. Taylor (Eds.), *Eliminating racism: Profiles in controversy* (pp. 225–236). New York: Plenum.

Gergen, K. J., Ellsworth, P., Maslach, C., & Seipel, M. (1975). Obligation, donor resources, and reactions to aid in three cultures. *Journal of Personality and Social Psychology, 31*, 390–400.

Gergen, K. J., Gergen, M. M., & Meter, K. (1972). Individual orientations to prosocial behavior. *Journal of Social Issues, 8*, 105–130.

Gettys, L. D., & Cann, A. (1981). Children's perceptions of occupational sex stereotypes. *Sex Roles, 7*, 301–308.

Gibbs, J. P. (1971). Suicide. In R. K. Merton & R. A. Nisbet (Eds.), *Contemporary social problems*, 3rd ed. (pp. 271–312). New York: Harcourt Brace Jovanovich.

Gielen, A. C., Eriksen, M. P., Daltroy, L. H., & Rost, K. (1984). Factors associated with the use of child restraint devices. *Health Education Quarterly, 11*, 195–206.

Gilbert, D. T., & Jones, E. E. (1986). Perceiver-induced constraint: Interpretations of self-generated reality. *Journal of Personality and Social Psychology, 50*, 269–280.

Gilbert, D. T., & Krull, D. S. (1988). Seeing less and knowing more: The benefits of perceptual ignorance. *Journal of Personality and Social Psychology, 54*, 193–202.

Gilbert, D. T., Krull, D. S., & Pelham, B. W. (1988). Of thoughts unspoken: Social inference and the self-regulation of behavior. *Journal of Personality and Social Psychology, 55*, 685–694.

Gilbert, D. T., Pelham, B. W., & Krull, D. S. (1988). On cognitive busyness: When person perceivers meet persons perceived. *Journal of Personality and Social Psychology, 54*, 733–739.

Gilovich, T. (1981). Seeing the past in the present: The effect of associations to familiar events on judgments and decisions. *Journal of Personality and Social Psychology, 40*, 797–808.

Gilovich, T. (1987). Secondhand information and social judgment. *Journal of Experimental Social Psychology, 23*, 59–74.

Glass, D. C. (1977). *Behavior patterns, stress, and coronary disease*. Hillsdale, NJ: Erlbaum.

Glass, D. C., & Singer, J. E. (1972). *Urban stress*. New York: Academic Press.

Glick, P., DeMorest, J. A., & Hotze, C. A. (1988). Self-monitoring and beliefs about partner compatibility in romantic relationships. *Personality and Social Psychology Bulletin, 14*, 485–494.

Glick, P., Zion, C., & Nelson, C. (1988). What mediates sex discrimination in hiring decisions? *Journal of Personality and Social Psychology, 55*, 178–186.

Goethals, G., & Klos, D. S. (Eds.). (1970). *Experiencing youth: First-person accounts*. Boston: Little, Brown.

Goethals, G. R., & Darley, J. M. (1987). Social comparison theory: Self-evaluation and group life. In B. Mullen, &

G. R. Goethals (Eds.)., *Theories of group behavior* (pp. 21–48). New York: Springer-Verlag.

Goethals, G. R., Cooper, J., & Naficy, A. (1979). Role of foreseen, foreseeable, and unforeseeable behavioral consequences in the arousal of cognitive dissonance. *Journal of Personality and Social Psychology, 37,* 1179–1185.

Goffman, E. (1952). On cooling the mark out: Some aspects of adaptation to failure. *Psychiatry, 15,* 451–463.

Goffman, E. (1959). *The presentation of self in everyday life.* Garden City, NY: Doubleday.

Goldberg, P. (1968). Are women prejudiced against women? *TransAction, 5,* 28–30.

Golden, J. S., & Johnston, G. D. (1970). Problems of distortion in doctor-patient communications. *Psychiatry in Medicine, 1,* 127–149.

Goldstein, J. H., Davis, R. W., & Herman, D. (1975). Escalation of aggression: Experimental studies. *Journal of Personality and Social Psychology, 31,* 162–170.

Goodman, M. E. (1952). *Race awareness in young children.* Reading, MA; Addison-Wesley.

Goranson, R. E., & Berkowitz, L. (1966). Reciprocity and responsibility reactions to prior help. *Journal of Personality and Social Psychology, 3,* 227–232.

Gordon, S. L. (1981). The sociology of sentiments and emotions. In M. Rosenberg & R. H. Turner (Eds.), *Social psychology: Sociological perspectives* (pp. 562–592). New York: Basic Books.

Gorn, G. J., & Goldberg, M. E. (1980). Children's responses to repetitive TV commercials. *Journal of Consumer Research, 6,* 421–425.

Gottman, J. M. (1979). *Marital interaction: Experimental investigations.* New York: Academic Press.

Gottman, J. M., & Krokoff, L. J. (1989). Marital interaction and satisfaction: A longitudinal view. *Journal of Consulting and Clinical Psychology, 57,* 47–52.

Gouldner, A. W. (1960). The norm of reciprocity: A preliminary statement. *American Sociological Review, 25,* 161–179.

Granberg, D. (1984). Attributing attitudes to members of groups. In J. R. Eiser (Ed.), *Attitudinal judgment.* New York: Springer-Verlag.

Granberg, D. (1987). Candidate preference, membership group, and estimates of voting behavior. *Social Cognition, 5,* 323–335.

Graziano, W. G., Moore, J. S., & Collins, J. E., II. (1988). Social cognition as segmentation of the stream of behavior. *Developmental Psychology, 24,* 61–72.

Green, S. K., Buchanan, D. R., & Heuer, S. K. (1984). Winners, losers, and choosers: A field investigation of dating initiation. *Personality and Social Psychology Bulletin, 10,* 502–511.

Greenberg, B. S., & Mazingo, S. L. (1976). Racial issues in mass media institutions. In P. A. Katz (Ed.), *Towards the elimination of racism* (pp. 309–340). Elmsford, NY: Pergamon Press.

Greenberg, J., & Cohen, R. L. (Eds.). (1982). *Equity and justice in social behavior.* New York: Academic Press.

Greenberg, M. S., & Frisch, D. M. (1972). Effects of intentionality on willingness to reciprocate a favor. *Journal of Experimental Social Psychology, 8,* 99–111.

Greenwald, A. G. (1968). Cognitive learning, cognitive response to persuasion, and attitude change. In A. G. Greenwald, T. C. Brock, & T. M. Ostrom (Eds.), *Psychological foundations of attitudes* (pp. 147–170). New York: Academic Press.

Greenwell, J., & Dengerink, H. A. (1973). The role of perceived versus actual attack in human physical aggression. *Journal of Personality and Social Psychology, 26,* 66–71.

Greer, S. (1974). Psychological aspects: Delay in the treatment of breast cancer. *Proceedings of the Royal Society of Medicine, 64,* 470–473.

Greer, D. L. (1983). Spectator booing and the home advantage: A study of social influence in the basketball arena. *Social Psychology Quarterly, 46,* 252–261.

Gregory, W. L., Cialdini, R. B., & Carpenter, K. M. (1982). Self-relevant scenarios as mediators of likelihood estimates and compliance: Does imagining make it so? *Journal of Personality and Social Psychology, 43,* 89–99.

Gross, A. E., & Latané, J. G. (1974). Receiving help, reciprocation, and interpersonal attraction. *Journal of Applied Social Psychology, 4*(3), 210–223.

Gross, A. E., Wallston, B. S., & Piliavin, I. M. (1979). Reactance, attribution, equity, and the help recipient. *Journal of Applied Social Psychology, 9*(4), 297–313.

Gruder, C. L., Romer, D., & Korth, B. (1978). Dependency and fault as determinants of helping. *Journal of Experimental Social Psychology, 14,* 227–235.

Grush, J. E. (1980). Impact of candidate expenditures, regionality, and prior outcomes on the 1976 Democratic presidential primaries. *Journal of Personality and Social Psychology, 38,* 337–347.

Grush, J. E., McKeogh, K. L., & Ahlering, R. G. (1978). Extrapolating laboratory exposure research to actual political elections. *Journal of Personality and Social Psychology, 36,* 257–270.

Guerin, B. (1986). Mere presence effects in humans: A review. *Journal of Experimental Social Psychology, 22,* 38–77.

Guidubaldi, J., Perry, J. D., & Natasi, B. K. (1987). Growing up in a divorced family: Initial and long-term perspectives on children's adjustment. In S. Oskamp (Ed.), *Family processes and problems: Social psychological aspects* (pp. 202–237). Beverly Hills, CA: Sage Publications.

Gurin, P. (1985). Women's gender consciousness. *Public Opinion Quarterly, 49,* 142–163.

Gurin, G., Veroff, J., & Feld, S. (1960). *Americans view their mental health: A nationwide survey.* New York: Basic Books.

Guttentag, M., & Secord, P. F. (1982). *Too many women: The sex ratio question.* Beverly Hills, CA: Sage Publications.

Hacker, H. M. (1981). Blabbermouths and clams: Sex differences in self-disclosure in same-sex and cross-sex friendship dyads. *Psychology of Women Quarterly, 5*(3), 385–401.

Hall, E. T. (1959). *The silent language.* Garden City, NY: Doubleday.

Hall, E. T. (1966). *The hidden dimension.* New York: Doubleday.

Hall, J. A. (1978). Gender effects in decoding nonverbal cues. *Psychological Bulletin, 85*(4), 845–857.

Hall, J. A. (1984). *Nonverbal sex differences: Communication accuracy and expressive style.* Baltimore: Johns Hopkins University Press.

Hall, K. R. L. (1960). Social vigilance behavior of the chacuma baboon (*Papio ursinus*). *Behavior 16*(3), 261–294.

Halpern, D. F. (1989). The disappearance of cognitive gender differences: What you see depends on where you look. *American Psychologist, 44*(8), 1156–1158.

Hamill, R., Wilson, T. D., & Nisbett, R. E. (1980). Insensitivity to sample bias: Generalizing from atypical cases. *Journal of Personality and Social Psychology, 39*, 578–589.

Hamilton, D. L., & Gifford, R. K. (1976). Illusory correlation in interpersonal perception: A cognitive basis of stereotypic judgments. *Journal of Experimental Social Psychology, 12*, 392–407.

Hamilton, D. L., & Trolier, T. K. (1986). Stereotypes and stereotyping: An overview of the cognitive approach. In J. F. Dovidio & S. L. Gaertner (Eds.), *Prejudice, discrimination, and racism* (pp. 127–164). New York: Academic Press.

Hamilton, D. L., & Zanna, M. P. (1972). Differential weighting of favorable and unfavorable attributions in impressions of personality. *Journal of Experimental Research in Personality, 6*, 204–212.

Hamilton, M. C. (1988). Using masculine generics: Does generic *he* increase male bias in the user's imagery? *Sex Roles, 19*, 785–799.

Hamilton, V. L. (1978). Obedience and responsibility: A jury simulation. *Journal of Personality and Social Psychology, 36*, 126–146.

Hansen, G. L. (1985). Perceived threats and marital jealousy. *Social Psychology Quarterly, 48*(3), 262–268.

Hansson, R. O., & Slade, K. M. (1977). Altruism toward a deviant in city and small town. *Journal of Applied Social Psychology, 7*, 272–279.

Hare-Mustin, R. T., & Marecek, J. (1988). The meaning of difference: Gender theory, postmodernism, and psychology. *American Psychologist, 43*, 455–464.

Harkins, S. G. (1987). Social loafing and social facilitation. *Journal of Experimental Social Psychology, 23*, 1–18.

Harkins, S. G., & Petty, R. (1981). The effects of source magnification of cognitive effort on attitudes: An information-processing view. *Journal of Personality and Social Psychology, 40*, 401–413.

Harkins, S. G., & Petty, R. (1987). Information utility and the multiple source effect. *Journal of Personality and Social Psychology, 52*, 260–268.

Harkins, S. G., & Szymanski, K. (1988). Social loafing and self-evaluation with an objective standard. *Journal of Experimental Social Psychology, 24*, 354–365.

Harkins, S. G., & Szymanski, K. (1989). Social loafing and group evaluation. *Journal of Personality and Social Psychology, 56*, 934–941.

Harkness, A. R., DeBono, K. G., & Borgida, E. (1985). Personal involvement and strategies for making contingency judgments: A stake in the dating game makes a difference. *Journal of Personality and Social Psychology, 49*, 22–32.

Harris, P. R. (1980). *Promoting health—preventing disease: Objectives for the nation.* Washington, D.C.: U.S. Government Printing Office.

Hartmann, D. P. (1969). Influence of symbolically modeled instrumental aggression and pain cues on aggressive behavior. *Journal of Personality and Social Psychology, 11*, 280–288.

Hastie, R. (1984). Causes and effects of causal attribution. *Journal of Personality and Social Psychology, 46*, 44–56.

Hastie, R., & Kumar, P. A. (1979). Person memory: Personality traits as organizing principles in memory for behavior. *Journal of Personality and Social Psychology, 37*, 25–38.

Hastie, R., Park, B., & Weber, R. (1984). Social memory. In R. S. Wyer & T. K. Srull (Eds.), *Handbook of social cognition* (Vol. 1, pp. 151–212). Hillsdale, NJ: Erlbaum.

Hatfield, E., & Sprecher, S. (1986). *Mirror, mirror . . . The importance of looks in everyday life.* Albany: State University of New York Press.

Hatkoff, S., & Lasswell, T. E. (1979). Male-female similarities and differences in conceptualizing love. In M. Cook & G. Wilson (Eds.), *Love and attraction.* Oxford: Pergamon.

Hauenstein, M. S., Schiller, M. R., & Hurley, R. S. (1987). Motivational techniques of dieticians counseling individuals with Type II diabetes. *Journal of the American Dietetic Association, 87*, 37–42.

Haynes, S. G., Feinleib, M., & Kannel, W. B. (1980). The relationship of psychosocial factors to coronary heart disease in the Framingham Study, III: Eight-year incidence of coronary heart disease. *American Journal of Epidemiology, 111*, 37–58.

Hazan, C., & Shaver, P. (1987). Romantic love conceptualized as an attachment process. *Journal of Personality and Social Psychology, 52*, 511–524.

Hecker, M. H. L., Chesney, M. A., Black, G. W., & Frautschi, N. (1988). Coronary-prone behaviors in the Western collaborative group study. *Psychosomatic Medicine, 50*, 153–164.

Heckhausen, H., & Strang, H. (1988). Efficiency under record performance demands: Exertion control—An individual difference variable? *Journal of Personality and Social Psychology, 55,* 489–498.

Heider, F. (1958). *The psychology of interpersonal relations.* New York: Wiley.

Hendrick, C., & Hendrick, S. (1989). Research on love: Does it measure up? *Journal of Personality and Social Psychology, 56,* 784–794.

Hendrick, C., Hendrick, S., Foote, F. H., & Slapion-Foote, M. J. (1984). Do men and women love differently? *Journal of Social and Personal Relationships, 1,* 177–195.

Hennigan, K. M., Heath, L., Wharton, J. D., Del Rosario, M. L., Cook, T. D., & Calder, B. J. (1982). Impact of the introduction of television on crime in the United States: Empirical findings and theoretical implications. *Journal of Personality and Social Psychology, 42,* 461–477.

Hepworth, J. T., & West, S. G. (1988). Lynchings and the economy: A time-series reanalysis of Hovland and Sears (1940). *Journal of Personality and Social Psychology, 55,* 239–247.

Hessing, D. J., Elffers, H., & Weigel, R. H. (1988). Exploring the limits of self-reports and reasoned action: An investigation of the psychology of tax evasion behavior. *Journal of Personality and Social Psychology, 54,* 405–413.

Hewstone, M., & Jaspars, J. (1982). Intergroup relations and attribution processes. In H. Tajfel (Ed.), *Social identity and intergroup relations* (pp. 99–133). Cambridge: Cambridge University Press.

Higbee, K. L. (1969). Fifteen years of fear arousal: Research on threat appeals, 1953–1968. *Psychological Bulletin, 72,* 426–444.

Higgins, E. T., & Bargh, J. A. (1987). Social cognition and social perception. *Annual Review of Psychology, 38,* 369–425.

Higgins, E. T., King, G. A., & Mavin, G. H. (1982). Individual construct accessibility and subjective impressions and recall. *Journal of Personality and Social Psychology, 43,* 35–47.

Higgins, E. T., Rhodewalt, F., & Zanna, M. P. (1979). Dissonance motivation: Its nature, persistence, and reinstatement. *Journal of Experimental Social Psychology, 15,* 16–34.

Higgins, E. T., Rholes, W. S., & Jones, C. R. (1977). Category accessibility and impression formation. *Journal of Experimental Social Psychology, 13,* 141–154.

Hill, C. T., Rubin, Z., & Peplau, L. A. (1976). Breakups before marriage: The end of 103 affairs. *Journal of Social Issues, 32*(1), 147–168.

Hill, T., Smith, N. D., & Hoffman, H. (1988). Short note: Self-image bias and the perception of other persons' skills. *European Journal of Social Psychology, 18,* 293–298.

Hirt, E., & Kimble, C. E. (1981, May). *The home-field advantage in sports: Differences and correlates.* Paper presented at the annual meeting of the Midwestern Psychological Association, Detroit.

Hochbaum, G. (1958). *Public participation in medical screening programs* (DHEW Publication No. 572, Public Health Service). Washington, D.C.: U.S. Government Printing Office.

Hochschild, J. L., & Herk, M. (1989). "Yes but . . .": Principles and caveats in American racial attitudes. In J. Chapman (Ed.), *NOMOS: Majorities and minorities: Political and philosophical perspectives.* New York: New York University Press.

Hodges, B. H. (1974). Effect of valence on relative weighting in impression formation. *Journal of Personality and Social Psychology, 30,* 378–381.

Hoffman, C., Mischel, W., & Baer, J. S. (1984). Language and person cognition: Effects of communicative set on trait attribution. *Journal of Personality and Social Psychology, 46,* 1029–1043.

Hoffman, M. L. (1981). Is altruism part of human nature? *Journal of Personality and Social Psychology, 40*(1), 121–137.

Hogg, M. A., & Abrams, D. (1988). *Social identifications: A social psychology of intergroup relations and group processes.* New York: Routledge.

Hogg, M. A., & Turner, J. C. (1987). Social identity and conformity: A theory of referent information influence. In W. Doise & S. Moscovici (Eds.), *Current issues in European social psychology* (Vol. 2, pp. 139–182). New York: Cambridge University Press.

Holahan, C. J., & Wilcox, B. L. (1978). Residential satisfaction and friendship formation in high- and low-rise student housing: An interactional analysis. *Journal of Educational Psychology, 70,* 237–241.

Holland, D., & Skinner, D. (1987). Prestige and intimacy: The cultural models behind Americans' talk about gender types. In D. Holland & N. Quinn (Eds.), *Cultural models in language and thought* (pp. 78–111). New York: Cambridge University Press.

Hollander, E. P. (1985). Leadership and power. In G. Lindzey & E. Aronson (Eds.), *Handbook of social psychology,* 3rd ed. (Vol. 2, pp. 485–538). New York: Random House.

Holmes, T. H., & Rahe, R. H. (1967). The social readjustment rating scale. *Journal of Psychosomatic Research, 11,* 213–218.

Holtgraves, T., & Srull, T. K. (1989). The effects of positive self-descriptions on impressions: General principles and individual differences. *Personality and Social Psychology Bulletin, 15,* 452–462.

Holtz, R., & Miller, N. (1985). Assumed similarity and opinion certainty. *Journal of Personality and Social Psychology, 48,* 890–898.

Holtzworth-Munroe, A., & Jacobson, N. S. (1985). Causal attributions of married couples: When do they search for causes? What do they conclude when they do? *Journal of Personality and Social Psychology, 48,* 1398–1412.

Homans, G. C. (1965). Group factors in worker productivity. In H. Proshansky & L. Seidenberg (Eds.), *Basic stud-*

ies in social psychology. New York: Holt, Rinehart and Winston.

Hook, J. G., & Cook, T. D. (1979). Equity theory and the cognitive ability of children. *Psychological Bulletin, 86,* 429–445.

Hornstein, H. A., Fisch, E., & Holmes, M. (1968). Influence of a model's feeling about his behavior and his relevance as a comparison other than observers' helping behavior. *Journal of Personality and Social Psychology, 10,* 222–226.

House, J. S., Landis, K. R., & Umberson, D. (1988). Social relationships and health. *Science, 241,* 540–545.

Houston, B. K., & Kelly, K. E. (1989). Hostility in employed women: Relations to work and marital experiences, social support, stress, and anger expression. *Personality and Social Psychology Bulletin, 15,* 175–182.

Hovland, C. I. (1959). Reconciling conflicting results derived from experimental and survey studies of attitude change. *American Psychologist, 14,* 8–17.

Hovland, C. I., & Janis, I. L. (1959). Summary and implications for further research. In C. I. Hovland & I. L. Janis (Eds.), *Personality and persuasibility.* New Haven, CT: Yale University Press.

Hovland, C. I., Campbell, E., & Brock, T. C. (1957). The effects of "commitment" on opinion change following communication. In Hovland, et al., *Order of presentation in persuasion.* New Haven, CT: Yale University Press.

Hovland, C. I., Harvey, O. J., & Sherif, M. (1957). Assimilation and contrast effects in reactions to communication and attitude change. *Journal of Abnormal and Social Psychology, 55,* 244–252.

Hovland, C. I., Janis, I. L., & Kelley, H. H. (1953). *Communication and persuasion.* New Haven, CT: Yale University Press.

Hovland, C. I., Lumsdaine, A. A., & Sheffield, F. D. (1949). *Experiments on mass communication.* Princeton, NJ: Princeton University Press.

Hovland, C. I., & Pritzker, H. A. (1957). Extent of opinion change as a function of amount of change advocated. *Journal of Abnormal and Social Psychology, 54,* 257–261.

Hovland, C. I., & Sears, R. R. (1940). Minor studies of aggression: Correlation of lynchings with economic indices. *Journal of Psychology, 9,* 301–310.

Hovland, C. I., & Weiss, W. (1952). The influence of source credibility on communication effectiveness. *Public Opinion Quarterly, 15,* 635–650.

Howard, J. A. (1984). Societal influences on attribution: Blaming some victims more than others. *Journal of Personality and Social Psychology, 47,* 494–505.

Howard, J., & Rothbart, M. (1980). Social categorization and memory for in-group and out-group behavior. *Journal of Personality and Social Psychology, 38,* 301–310.

Huesmann, L. R. (1982). Television violence and aggressive behavior. In D. Pearl, L. Bouthilet, & J. Lazar (Eds.), *Television and behavior: Ten years of scientific progress and implications for the eighties:* Vol. II: *Technical reviews.* Rockville, MD: National Institute of Mental Health.

Huesmann, L. R. (1988). An information processing model for the development of aggression. *Aggressive Behavior, 14,* 13–24.

Huesmann, L. R., Eron, L., Lefkowitz, M. M., & Walder, L. O. (1984). The stability of aggression over time and generation. *Developmental Psychology, 20,* 1120–1134.

Huesmann, L. R., Eron, L. D., & Yarmel, P. W. (1987). Intellectual functioning and aggression. *Journal of Personality and Social Psychology, 52,* 232–240.

Hull, J. G., & Bond, C. F., Jr. (1986). Social and behavioral consequences of alcohol consumption and expectancy: A meta-analysis. *Psychological Bulletin, 99,* 347–360.

Hunt, M. M. (1959). *The natural history of love.* New York: Knopf.

Hur, K. K., & Robinson, J. P. (1978). The social impact of "Roots." *Journalism Quarterly, 55,* 19–24.

Huston, T. L. (1983). Power. In H. H. Kelley et al., *Close relationships* (pp. 169–219). New York: Freeman.

Huston, T. L., Ruggiero, M., Conner, R., & Geis, G. (1981). Bystander intervention into crime: A study based on naturally-occurring episodes. *Social Psychology Quarterly, 44*(1), 14–23.

Hyde, J. S., & Linn, M. C. (1986). *The psychology of gender: Advances through meta-analysis.* Baltimore: Johns Hopkins University Press.

Hyde, J. S. (1986). Gender differences in aggression. In J. S. Hyde & M. C. Linn (Eds.), *The psychology of gender: Advances through meta-analysis* (pp. 51–66). Baltimore: Johns Hopkins University Press.

Hyde, J. S., & Linn, M. C. (1988). Gender differences in verbal ability: A meta-analysis. *Psychological Bulletin, 104,* 53–69.

Hyman, J. (1959). *Political socialization.* Glencoe, IL: Free Press.

Inkeles, A. (1983). *The third century.* Stanford, CA: Hoover Institution Press.

Institute for Propaganda Analysis. (1939). *The fine art of propaganda: A study of Father Coughlin's speeches.* New York: Harcourt Brace.

Insko, C. A., Smith, R. H., Alicke, M. D., Wade, J., & Taylor, S. (1985). Conformity and group size: The concern with being right and the concern with being liked. *Personality and Social Psychology Bulletin, 11*(1), 41–50.

Isen, A. M. (1970). Success, failure, attention, and reaction to others: The warm glow of success. *Journal of Personality and Social Psychology, 15,* 294–301.

Isen, A. M., & Levin, P. F. (1972). Effects of feeling good on helping: Cookies and kindness. *Journal of Personality and Social Psychology, 21,* 384–388.

Isen, A. M., & Simmonds, S. F. (1978). The effect of feeling good on a helping task that is incompatible with good mood. *Social Psychology Quarterly, 41,* 346–349.

Isen, A. M., Clark, M., & Schwartz, M. F. (1976). Duration of the effect of good mood on helping: Footprints on the sands of time. *Journal of Personality and Social Psychology, 34,* 385–393.

Isenberg, D. J. (1986). Group polarization: A critical review and meta-analysis. *Journal of Personality and Social Psychology, 50*(6), 1141–1151.

Iyengar, S., & Kinder, D. R. (1987). *News that matters: Television and American opinion.* Chicago, IL: University of Chicago Press.

Jackman, M. R. (1978). General and applied tolerance: Does education increase commitment to racial integration? *American Journal of Political Science, 22,* 302–324.

Jackman, M. R., & Crane, M. (1986). "Some of my best friends are black . . .": Interracial friendship and whites' racial attitudes. *Public Opinion Quarterly, 50,* 459–486.

Jackman, M. R., & Muha, M. J. (1984). Education and intergroup attitudes: Moral enlightenment, superficial democratic commitment, or ideological refinement? *American Sociological Review, 49,* 751–769.

Jackson, J. M., & Williams, K. D. (1985). Social loafing on difficult tasks: Working collectively can improve performance. *Journal of Personality and Social Psychology, 49*(4), 937–942.

Jackson, J. M. (1987). Social impact theory: A social forces model of influence. In B. Mullen & G. R. Goethals (Eds.), *Theories of group behavior* (pp. 111–124). New York: Springer-Verlag.

Jamieson, D. W., & Zanna, M. P. (1989). Need for structure in attitude formation and expression. In A. R. Pratkanis, S. J. Breckler, & A. G. Greenwald (Eds.), *Attitude structure and function* (pp. 383–406). Hillsdale, NJ: Erlbaum.

Janis, I. L. (1967). Effects of fear arousal on attitude change: Recent developments in theory and experimental research. In L. Berkowitz (Ed.), *Advances in Experimental Social Psychology* (Vol. 3, pp. 166–224). New York: Academic Press.

Janis, I. L. (1982). *Groupthink: Psychological studies of policy decisions and fiascoes,* 2nd ed. Boston: Houghton Mifflin.

Janis, I. L. (1983). Improving adherence to medical recommendations: Prescriptive hypotheses derived from recent research in social psychology. In A. Baum, S. E. Taylor, & J. Singer (Eds.), *Handbook of psychology and health* (Vol. 4, pp. 113–148). Hillsdale, NJ: Erlbaum.

Janis, I. L. (1986). Problems of interpersonal crisis management in the nuclear age. *Journal of Social Issues, 42,* 201–220.

Janis, I. L., & Feshbach, S. (1953). Effects of fear-arousing communications. *Journal of Abnormal and Social Psychology, 48,* 78–92.

Janis, I. L., Kaye, D., & Krischner, P. (1965). Facilitating effects of "eating-while-reading" on responsiveness to persuasive communications. *Journal of Personality and Social Psychology, 1,* 181–185.

Janis, I. L., & Mann, L. (1977). *Decision making.* New York: Free Press.

Janoff-Bulman, R. (1979). Characterological versus behavioral self-blame: Inquiries into depression and rape. *Journal of Personality and Social Psychology, 37,* 1798–1809.

Jellison, J. M., & Green, J. (1981). A self-presentation approach to the fundamental attribution error: The norm of internality. *Journal of Personality and Social Psychology, 40,* 643–649.

Jemmott, J. B. III, Ashby, K. L., & Lindenfeld, K. (1989). Romantic commitment and the perceived availability of opposite sex persons: On loving the one you're with. *Journal of Applied Social Psychology, 19,* 1198–1211.

Jemmott, J. B. III, Croyle, R. T., & Ditto, P. H. (1988). Commonsense epidemiology: Self-based judgments from laypersons and physicians. *Health Psychology, 7,* 55–73.

Jemmott, J. B. III, & Locke, S. E. (1984). Psychosocial factors, immunologic mediation, and human susceptibility to infectious diseases: How much do we know? *Psychological Bulletin, 95,* 78–108.

Jenkins, C. D., Zyzanski, S. J., & Roseman, R. H. (1979). *Jenkins Activity Survey.* Cleveland, OH: Psychological Corp.

Jennings, J., Geis, F. L., & Brown, V. (1980). Influence of television commercials on women's self-confidence and independent judgment. *Journal of Personality and Social Psychology, 38*(2), 203–210.

Jennings, M. K., & Markus, G. B. (1984). Partisan orientations over the long haul: Results from the three-wave political socialization panel study. *American Political Science Review, 78,* 1000–1018.

Jennings, M. K., & Niemi, R. G. (1974). *The political character of adolescence.* Princeton, NJ: Princeton University Press.

Jervis, R. (1976). *Perception and misperception in international politics.* Princeton: NJ: Princeton University Press.

Jessor, T. (1988). Personal interest, group conflict, and symbolic group affect: Explanations for whites' opposition to racial equality. Unpublished doctoral dissertation, Department of Psychology, University of California, Los Angeles.

Johnson, J. T., & Drobny, J. (1985). Proximity biases in the attribution of civil liability. *Journal of Personality and Social Psychology, 48,* 283–296.

Johnson, R. D., & Downing, L. L. (1979). Deindividuation and valence of cues: Effects of prosocial and antisocial behavior. *Journal of Personality and Social Psychology, 37,* 1532–1538.

Johnson, D. J., & Rusbult, C. E. (1989). Resisting temptation: Devaluation of alternative partners as a means of maintaining commitment in close relationships. *Journal of Personality and Social Psychology, 57,* 967–980.

Johnson, T. E., & Rule, B. G. (1986). Mitigating circumstance information, censure, and aggression. *Journal of Personality and Social Psychology, 50,* 537–542.

Jones, E. E. (1979). The rocky road from acts to dispositions. *American Psychologist, 34,* 107–117.

Jones, E. E., & Harris, V. A. (1967). The attribution of attitudes. *Journal of Experimental Social Psychology, 3,* 1–24.

Jones, E. E., & McGillis, D. (1976). Correspondent inferences and the attribution cube: A comparative reappraisal. In J. H. Harvey, W. J. Ickes, & R. F. Kidd (Eds.), *New directions in attribution research* (Vol. 1, pp. 389–420). Hillsdale, NJ: Erlbaum.

Jones, E. E., & Nisbett, R. E. (1972). The actor and the observer: Divergent perceptions of the causes of behavior. In E. E. Jones et al. (Eds.), *Attribution: Perceiving the causes of behavior* (pp. 79–94). Morristown, NJ: General Learning Process.

Jones, E. E., & Pittman, T. (1982). Toward a general theory of strategic self-presentation. In J. Suls (Ed.), *Psychological perspectives on the self* (Vol. 1, pp. 231–262). Hillsdale, NJ: Erlbaum.

Jones, E. E., Davis, K. E., & Gergen, K. J. (1961). Role-playing variations and their informational value for person perception. *Journal of Abnormal and Social Psychology, 63,* 302–310.

Jones, E. E., Wood, G. C., & Quattrone, G. A. (1981). Perceived variability of personal characteristics in in-groups and out-groups: The role of knowledge and evaluation. *Personality and Social Psychology Bulletin, 7,* 523–528.

Jones, W. H. (1982). Loneliness and social behavior. In L. A. Peplau & D. Perlman (Eds.), *Loneliness: A sourcebook of current theory, research and therapy* (pp. 238–254). New York: Wiley-Interscience.

Jones, W. H. Briggs, S. R., & Smith, T. G. (1986). Shyness: Conceptualization and measurement. *Journal of Personality and Social Psychology, 51*(3), 629–639.

Jones, W. H., Carpenter, B. N., & Quitana, D. (1985). Personality and interpersonal predictors of loneliness in two cultures. *Journal of Personality and Social Psychology, 48*(6), 1503–1511.

Jordan, W. D. (1968). *White over black: American attitudes toward the Negro, 1550–1812.* Chapel Hill: University of North Carolina Press.

Jose, P. E., & McCarthy, W. J. (1988). Perceived agentic and communal behavior in mixed-sex interactions. *Personality and Social Psychology Bulletin, 14,* 57–67.

Judd, C. M., & Johnson, J. T. (1981). Attitudes, polarization, and diagnosticity: Exploring the effect of affect. *Journal of Personality and Social Psychology, 41,* 26–36.

Judd, C. M., & Park, B. (1988). Out-group homogeneity: Judgments of variability at the individual and group levels. *Journal of Personality and Social Psychology, 54,* 778–788.

Jussin, L. (1989). Teacher expectations: Self-fulfilling prophecies, perceptual biases, and accuracy. *Journal of Personality and Social Psychology, 57,* 469–480.

Jussin, L., & Osgood, D. W. (1989). Influence and similarity among friends: An integrative model applied to incarcerated adolescents. *Social Psychology Quarterly, 52,* 98–112.

Kahneman, D., & Miller, D. T. (1986). Norm theory: Comparing reality to its alternatives. *Psychological Review, 93,* 136–153.

Kahneman, D., & Tversky, A. (1982). The simulation heuristic. In D. Kahneman, P. Slovic, & A. Tversky (Eds.), *Judgment under uncertainty: Heuristics and biases* (pp. 201–209). New York: Cambridge University Press.

Kalick, S. M., & Hamilton, T. E. (1988). Closer look at a matching simulation: Reply to Aron. *Journal of Personality and Social Psychology, 54,* 447–451.

Kallgren, C. A., & Wood, W. (1986). Access to attitude-relevant information in memory as a determinant of attitude-behavior consistency. *Journal of Experimental Social Psychology, 22,* 328–338.

Kandel, D. (1978). Similarity in real-life adolescent friendship pairs. *Journal of Personality and Social Psychology, 36,* 306–312.

Kanin, E. J., Davidson, K. R., & Scheck, S. R. (1970). A research note on male-female differentials in the experience of heterosexual love. *Journal of Sex Research, 6,* 64–72.

Kanner, A. D., Coyne, J. C., Schaeffer, C., & Lazarus, R. S. (1981). Comparison of two modes of stress measurement: Daily hassles and uplifts versus major life events. *Journal of Behavioral Medicine, 4,* 1–39.

Kaplan, K. J., Firestone, I. J., Degnore, R., & Morre, M. (1974). Gradients of attraction as a function of disclosure probe intimacy and setting formality: On distinguishing attitude oscillation from attitude change—Study one. *Journal of Personality and Social Psychology, 30,* 638–646.

Karabenick, S. A., & Knapp, J. R. (1988). Effects of computer privacy on help-seeking. *Journal of Applied Social Psychology, 18*(6), 461–472.

Karlin, R. A., Epstein, Y. M., & Aiello, J. R. (1978). Strategies for the investigation of crowding. In A. Esser & B. Greenbie (Eds.), *Design for community and privacy.* New York: Plenum.

Kassin, S. M. (1985). Eyewitness identification: Retrospective self-awareness and the accuracy-confidence correlation. *Journal of Personality and Social Psychology, 49,* 878–893.

Kassin, S. M., & Lepper, M. R. (1984). Oversufficient and insufficient justification effects: Cognitive and behavioral development. *Advances in Motivation and Achievement, 3,* 73–106.

Katz, D., & Braly, K. W. (1933). Racial stereotypes of 100 college students. *Journal of Abnormal and Social Psychology, 28,* 280–290.

Katz, I., & Hass, R. G. (1988). Racial ambivalence and American value conflict: Correlational and prime studies of dual cognitive structures. *Journal of Personality and Social Psychology, 55,* 893–905.

Katz, I., Wackenhut, J., & Hass, R. G. (1986). Racial ambivalence, value duality, and behavior. In J. F. Dovidio & S. L. Gaertner (Eds.), *Prejudice, discrimination, and racism* (pp. 35–60). New York: Academic Press.

Katz, P. A., & Taylor, D. A. (Eds.). (1988). *Eliminating racism: Profiles in controversy.* New York: Plenum.

Kaufert, J. M., Rabkin, S. W., Syrotuik, J., Boyko, E., & Shane, F. (1986). Health beliefs as predictors of success of alternate modalities of smoking cessation: Results of a controlled trial. *Journal of Behavioral Medicine, 9,* 475–489.

Kaufman, M. R. (1970). Practicing good manners and compassion. *Medical Insight, 2,* 56–61.

Keating, C. F., Mazur, A., Segall, M. H., Cysneiros, P. G., DiVale, W. T., Kilbride, J. E., Komin, S., Leahy, P., Thurman, B., & Wirsing, R. (1981). Culture and the perception of social dominance from facial expression. *Journal of Personality and Social Psychology, 40,* 601–614.

Kelley, H. H. (1950). The warm-cold variable in first impressions of persons. *Journal of Personality, 18,* 431–439.

Kelley, H. H. (1967). Attribution theory in social psychology. In D. Levine (Ed.), *Nebraska Symposium on Motivation* (pp. 192–238). Lincoln: University of Nebraska Press.

Kelley, H. H. (1972). Attribution in social interaction. In E. E. Jones et al. (Eds.), *Attribution: Perceiving the causes of behavior* (pp. 1–26). Morristown, NJ: General Learning Press.

Kelley, H. H. (1979). *Personal relationships: Their structures and processes.* Hillsdale, NJ: Erlbaum.

Kelley, H. H. (1983). Love and commitment. In H. H. Kelley et al., *Close relationships* (pp. 265–314). New York: Freeman.

Kelley, H. H., Berscheid, E., Christensen, A., Harvey, J. H., Huston, T. L., Levinger, G., McClintock, E., Peplau, L. A., & Peterson, D. R. (1983). *Close relationships.* New York, Freeman.

Kelley, H. H., & Thibaut, J. W. (1978). *Interpersonal relations: A theory of interdependence.* New York: Wiley-Interscience.

Kelley, H. H., & Volkart, E. H. (1952). The resistance to change of group-anchored attitudes. *American Sociological Review, 17,* 453–465.

Kelley, H. H., & Woodruff, L. (1956). Members' reactions to apparent group approval of a counternorm communication. *Journal of Abnormal and Social Psychology, 52,* 67–74.

Kelley, S., Jr., & Mirer, T. W. (1974). The simple act of voting. *American Political Science Review, 68,* 572–591.

Kelly, J. R., & McGrath, J. E. (1985). Effect of time limits and task types on task performance and interaction of four-person groups. *Journal of Personality and Social Psychology, 49,* 395–407.

Kelman, H. C., & Cohen, S. P. (1986). Resolution of international conflict: An interactional approach. In S. Worchel and W. G. Austin (Eds.), *Psychology of intergroup relations* (pp. 323–342). Chicago: Nelson-Hall Publishers.

Kelman, H. C., & Hamilton, V. L. (1989). *Crimes of obedience: Toward a social psychology of authority and responsibility.* New Haven, CT: Yale University Press.

Kelman, H. C., & Hovland, C. I. (1953). "Reinstatement" of the communicator in delayed measurement of opinion change. *Journal of Abnormal and Social Psychology, 48,* 327–335.

Kendall, P. C., Williams, L., Pechacek, T. F., Graham, L. E., Shisslak, C., & Herzoff, N. (1979). Cognitive-behavioral and patient education interventions in cardiac catheterization procedures: The Palo Alto medical psychology project. *Journal of Consulting and Clinical Psychology, 47,* 49–58.

Kenrick, D. T., & Gutierres, S. E. (1980). Contrast effects and judgments of physical attractiveness: When beauty becomes a social problem. *Journal of Personality and Social Psychology, 38,* 131–140.

Kenrick, D. T., & Johnson, G. A. (1979). Interpersonal attraction in aversive environments: A problem for the classical conditioning paradigm? *Journal of Personality and Social Psychology, 37,* 572–579.

Kephart, W. (1967). Some correlates of romantic love. *Journal of Marriage and the Family, 29,* 470–479.

Kernis, M. H. (1984). Need for uniqueness, self-schemas, and thought as moderators of the false-consensus effect. *Journal of Experimental Social Psychology, 20,* 350–362.

Kernis, M. H., & Wheeler, L. (1981). Beautiful friends and ugly strangers: Radiation and contrast effects in perception of same-sex pairs. *Personality and Social Psychology Bulletin, 7,* 617–620.

Kessler, R. C., & McLeod, J. D. (1985). Social support and mental health in community samples. In S. Cohen & S. L. Syme (Eds.), *Social support and health* (pp. 219–240). Orlando, FL: Academic Press.

Kidder, L. H., Fagan, M. A., & Cohn, E. S. (1981). Giving and receiving: Social justice in close relationships. In M. J. Lerner & S. C. Lerner (Eds.), *The justice motive in social behavior: Adapting to times of scarcity and change* (pp. 235–259). New York: Plenum.

Kilbourne, B. K. (1989). A cross-cultural investigation of the foot-in-the-door compliance induction procedure. *Journal of Cross-Cultural Psychology, 20,* 3–38.

Kim, M. P., & Rosenberg, S. (1980). Comparison of two structural models of implicit personality theory. *Journal of Personality and Social Psychology, 38,* 375–389.

Kimball, M. M. (1989). A new perspective on women's math achievement. *Psychological Bulletin, 105,* 198–214.

Kinder, D. R., & Kiewiet, D. R. (1979). Economic discontent and political behavior: The role of personal grievances and collective economic judgments in congressional voting. *American Journal of Political Science, 23,* 495–527.

Kinder, D. R., & Sears, D. O. (1981). Prejudice and politics: Symbolic racism versus racial threats to the good life. *Journal of Personality and Social Psychology, 40,* 414–431.

Kinder, D. R., & Sears, D. O. (1985). Public opinion and political action. In G. Lindzey & E. Aronson (Eds.), *Handbook of social psychology*, 3rd ed. (Vol. 2, pp. 659–741). Reading, MA: Addison-Wesley.

King, C. E., & Christensen, A. (1983). The relationship events scale: A Guttman scale of progress in courtship. *Journal of Marriage and the Family, 45*, 671–678.

Kingdon, J. W. (1967). Politicians' beliefs about voters. *The American Political Science Review, 61*, 137–145.

Kipnis, D. (1984). The use of power in organizations and in interpersonal settings. In S. Oskamp (Ed.), *Applied social psychology annual 5* (pp. 179–210). Beverly Hills, CA: Sage Publications.

Kirkland, S. L., Greenberg, J., & Pyszczynski, T. (1987). Further evidence of the deleterious effects of overhead derogatory ethnic labels: Derogation beyond the target. *Personality and Social Psychology Bulletin, 13*, 216–227.

Kirscht, J. P., & Dillehay, R. C. (1967). *Dimensions of authoritarianism*. Lexington: University of Kentucky Press.

Kirscht, J. P., & Rosenstock, I. M. (1979). Patients' problems in following recommendations of health experts. In G. C. Stone, F. Cohen, & E. Adler (Eds.), *Health psychology—A handbook* (pp. 189–216). San Francisco: Jossey-Bass.

Kivilan, D. R., Coppel, D. B., Fromme, K., Williams, E., & Marlatt, G. A. (1989). Secondary prevention of alcohol-related problems in young adults at risk. In K. D. Craig & S. M. Weiss (Eds.), *Prevention and early intervention: Biobehavioral perspectives*. New York: Springer.

Klapper, J. T. (1960). *The effects of mass communications*. Glencoe, IL: Free Press.

Klayman, J., & Ha, Y.-W. (1987). Confirmation, disconfirmation, and information in hypothesis testing. *Psychological Review, 94*, 211–228.

Klein, E. (1984). *Gender politics: From consciousness to mass politics*. Cambridge, MA: Harvard University Press.

Klein, K., & Harris, B. (1979). Disruptive effects of disconfirmed expectancies about crowding. *Journal of Personality and Social Psychology, 37*, 769–777.

Klein, S. B., & Loftus, J. (1988). The nature of self-referent encoding: The contributions of elaborative and organizational processes. *Journal of Personality and Social Psychology, 55*, 5–11.

Klinnert, M. D. (1981, April). *Infants' use of others' facial expressions for regulating their own behavior*. Paper presented at the annual meeting of the Society for Research in Child Development, Boston.

Kluegel, J. R., & Smith, E. R. (1983). Affirmative action attitudes: Effects of self-interest, racial affect, and stratification beliefs on whites' views. *Social Forces, 61*, 797–824.

Kluegel, J. R., & Smith, E. R. (1986). *Beliefs about inequality*. Hawthorne, NY: Aldine.

Knox, R. E., & Inkster, J. A. (1968). Postdecision dissonance at post time. *Journal of Personality and Social Psychology, 8*, 319–323.

Knutson, J. N. (1973). *The human basis of the polity: A psychological study of political man*. Hawthorne, NY: Aldine.

Kogan, N., & Wallach, M. A. (1967). Risk taking as a function of the situation, the person, and the group. In G. Mandler (Ed.), *New directions in psychology* (Vol. 3). New York: Holt, Rinehart and Winston.

Kohlberg, L. (1966). A cognitive-developmental analysis of children's sex-role concepts and attitudes. In E. E. Maccoby (Ed.), *The development of sex differences*. Stanford, CA: Stanford University Press.

Koltun, A., & Stone, G. A. (1986). Past and current trends in patient noncompliance research: Focus on diseases, regimens-programs, and provider-disciplines. *Journal of Compliance in Health Care, 1*, 21–32.

Komarovsky, M. (1967). *Blue-collar marriage*. New York: Vintage.

Komorita, S. S., & Lapworth, C. W. (1982). Cooperative choice among individuals versus groups in an *N*-person dilemma situation. *Journal of Personality and Social Psychology, 42*, 487–496.

Konecni, V. J., & Doob, A. N. (1972). Catharsis through displacement of aggression. *Journal of Personality and Social Psychology, 23*, 379–387.

Konecni, V. J., & Ebbesen, E. B. (1976). Disinhibition versus the cathartic effect: Artifact and substance. *Journal of Personality and Social Psychology, 34*, 352–365.

Konecni, V. J., Libuser, L., Morton, H., & Ebbesen, E. B. (1975). Effects of a violation of personal space on escape and helping responses. *Journal of Experimental Social Psychology, 11*, 288–299.

Korte, C. (1971). Effects of individual responsibility and group communication on help-giving in an emergency. *Human Relations, 24*, 149–159.

Korte, C. (1980). Urban-nonurban differences in social behavior and social psychological models of urban impact. *Journal of Social Issues, 36*(3), 29–51.

Korte, C., & Grant, R. (1980). Traffic noise, environmental awareness, and pedestrian behavior. *Environment and Behavior, 12*, 996–1003.

Koss, M. P., Gidycz, C. A., & Wisniewski, N. (1987). The scope of rape: Incidence and prevalence of sexual aggression and victimization in a national sample of higher education students. *Journal of Consulting and Clinical Psychology, 55*, 162–170.

Kovel, J. (1970). *White racism: A psychohistory*. New York: Pantheon.

Krafka, C., & Penrod, S. (1985). Reinstatement of context in a field experiment on eyewitness identification. *Journal of Personality and Social Psychology, 49*, 58–69.

Kramer, G. H. (1971). Short-term fluctuations in U.S. voting behavior, 1896–1964. *American Political Science Review, 65*, 131–143.

Krantz, D. S., & Deckel, A. W. (1983). Coping with coronary heart disease and stroke. In T. G. Burish & L. A. Bradley

(Eds.), *Coping with chronic disease: Research and applications* (pp. 85–107). New York: Academic Press.

Krauss, R. M., Apple, W., Morency, N., Wenzel, C., & Winton, W. (1981). Verbal, vocal, and visible factors in judgments of another's affect. *Journal of Personality and Social Psychology, 40,* 312–320.

Krauss, R. M., Geller, V., & Olson, C. (1976, September). *Modalities and cues in the detection of deception.* Paper presented at the annual meeting of the American Psychological Association.

Kraut, R. E. (1978). Verbal and nonverbal cues in the perception of lying. *Journal of Personality and Social Psychology, 36,* 380–391.

Kraut, R. E., & Poe, D. (1980). Behavioral roots of person perception: The deception judgments of customs inspectors and laymen. *Journal of Personality and Social Psychology, 39,* 784–798.

Kravitz, D. A., & Martin, B. (1986). Ringlemann rediscovered: The original article. *Journal of Personality and Social Psychology, 50*(5), 936–941.

Krebs, D. L., & Miller, D. T. (1985). Altruism and aggression. In G. Lindzey & E. Aronson (Eds.), *Handbook of social psychology,* 3rd ed. (Vol. 2, pp. 1–71). New York: Random House.

Krech, D., & Crutchfield, R. A. (1948). *Theory and problems of social psychology.* New York: McGraw-Hill.

Krosnick, J. A. (1989). Attitude importance and attitude accessibility. *Personality and Social Psychology Bulletin, 15,* 297–308.

Kruglanski, A. W., & Mayseless, O. (1988). Contextual effects in hypothesis testing: The role of competing alternatives and epistemic motivations. *Social Cognition, 6,* 1–20.

Kuhlman, D. M., & Wimberley, D. L. (1976). Expectations of choice behavior held by cooperators, competitors, and individualists across four classes of experimental game. *Journal of Personality and Social Psychology, 34,* 69–81.

Kuiper, N. A., & Rogers, T. B. (1979). Encoding of personal information: Self-other differences. *Journal of Personality and Social Psychology, 37,* 499–514.

Kulik, J. A., & Mahler, H. I. M. (1989). Stress and affiliation in a hospital setting: Preoperative roommate preferences. *Personality and Social Psychology Bulletin, 15,* 183–193.

Kunda, Z. (1987). Motivated inference: Self-serving generation and evaluation of causal theories. *Journal of Personality and Social Psychology, 53,* 636–647.

Kutner, B., Wilkins, C., Yarrow, P. R. (1952). Verbal attitudes and overt behavior involving racial prejudice. *Journal of Abnormal and Social Psychology, 47,* 649–652.

Laerum, E., Johnsen, N., Smith, P., & Larsen, S. (1987). Can myocardial infarction induce positive changes in family relationships? *Family Practice, 4,* 302–305.

Laing, R. D., & Stevenson, R. (1976). Public opinion trends in the last days of the Nixon administration. *Journalism Quarterly, 53,* 294–302.

Lambert, W. E., & Klineberg, O. (1967). *Children's views of foreign peoples.* New York: Appleton-Century-Crofts.

Landy, D., & Aronson, E. (1969). The influence of the character of the criminal and his victim on the decisions of simulated jurors. *Journal of Experimental Social Psychology, 5,* 141–152.

Landman, J. (1988). Regret and elation following action and inaction: Affective responses to positive versus negative outcomes. *Personality and Social Psychology Bulletin, 13,* 524–536.

Lane, R. E. (1959). *Political life: Why people get involved in politics.* Glencoe, NY: Free Press.

Langer, E. J. (1975). The illusion of control. *Journal of Personality and Social Psychology, 32,* 311–328.

Langer, E. J., Blank, A., & Chanowitz, B. (1978). The mindlessness of ostensibly thoughtful action. *Journal of Personality and Social Psychology, 36,* 635–642.

Langer, E. J., & Rodin, J. (1976). The effects of choice and enhanced personal responsibility for the aged: A field experiment in an institutional setting. *Journal of Personality and Social Psychology, 34,* 191–198.

Langlois, J. H., & Roggman, L. A. (1990). Attractive faces are only average. *Psychological Science, 1*(2), 115–121.

La Piere, R. T. (1934). Attitudes vs. actions. *Social Forces, 13,* 230–237.

Larson, D. (1986). Crisis Prevention and the Austrian State Treaty. *International Organization,* (Winter), 27–60.

Larson, R., Csikszentmihalyi, M., & Graef, R. (1982). Time alone in daily experience: Loneliness or renewal? In L. A. Peplau & D. Perlman (Eds.), *Loneliness: A sourcebook of current theory, research and therapy* (pp. 40–53). New York: Wiley-Interscience.

Lassiter, G. D. (1986). Effect of superfluous deterrence on the perception of others. *Journal of Experimental Social Psychology, 22,* 163–175.

Lasswell, H. D. (1930). *Psychopathology and politics.* New York: Viking Press.

Lasswell, H. D. (1948). *Power and personality.* New York: Norton.

Lasswell, M., & Lobsenz, N. M. (1980). *Styles of loving.* New York: Ballantine.

Latané, B. (1981). The psychology of social impact. *American Psychologist, 36,* 343–356.

Latané, B., & Darley, J. M. (1970). *The unresponsive bystander: Why doesn't he help?* New York: Appleton-Century-Crofts.

Latané, B., & Wolf, S. (1981). The social impact of majorities and minorities. *Psychological Review, 88,* 438–453.

Latané, B., Williams, K., & Harkins, S. (1979). Many hands make light the work: The causes and consequences of social loafing. *Journal of Personality and Social Psychology, 37,* 822–832.

Lau, R. R. (1982). Negativity in political perception. *Political Behavior, 4,* 353–378.

Lau, R. R. (1985). Two explanations for negativity effects in political behavior. *American Journal of Political Science, 29,* 119–138.

Lau, R. R., & Russell, D. (1980). Attributions in the sports pages. *Journal of Personality and Social Psychology, 39,* 29–38.

Lau, R. R., Bernard, T. M., & Hartman, K. A. (1989). Further explorations of common-sense representations of common illness. *Health Psychology, 8,* 195–219.

Lau, R. R., Kane, R., Berry, S., Ware, J., & Roy, D. (1980). Channeling health: A review of televised health campaigns. *Health Education Quarterly, 7,* 56–89.

Lazarsfeld, P. F., Berelson, B., & Gaudet, H. (1948). *The people's choice,* 2nd ed. New York: Columbia University Press.

Lazarus, A. A. (1971). *Behavior therapy and beyond.* New York: McGraw-Hill.

Lazarus, R. S. (1966). *Psychological stress and the coping process.* New York: McGraw-Hill.

Lazarus, R. S. (1984). On the primacy of cognition. *American Psychologist, 39,* 124–129.

Lazarus, R. S., DeLongis, A., Folkman, S., & Gruen, R. (1985). Stress and adaptational outcomes: The problem of confounded measures. *American Psychologist, 40,* 770–779.

Lazarus, R. S., & Folkman, S. (1984). *Stress, appraisal, and coping.* New York: Springer-Verlag.

Lazarus, R. S., & Launier, R. (1978). Stress-related transactions between person and environment. In L. A. Pervin & M. Lewis (Eds.), *Internal and external determinants of behavior* (pp. 287–327). New York: Plenum.

Le Bon, G. (1896). *The crowd: A study of the popular mind.* London: Ernest Benn.

Leary, M. R., Rogers, P. A., Canfield, R. W., & Coe, C. (1986). Boredom in interpersonal encounters: Antecedents and social implications. *Journal of Personality and Social Psychology, 51*(5), 968–975.

Leary, M. R., & Shepperd, J. A. (1986). Behavioral self-handicaps versus self-reported handicaps: A conceptual note. *Journal of Personality and Social Psychology, 51,* 1265–1268.

Leavitt, H. J. (1951). Some effects of certain communication patterns on group performance. *Journal of Abnormal and Social Psychology, 46,* 38–50.

Lee, J. A. (1973). *The colors of love.* New York: Bantam.

Lee, J. A. (1977). A typology of styles of loving. *Personality and Social Psychology Bulletin, 3,* 173–182.

Leigh, H., & Reiser, M. F. (1986). Comparison of theoretically oriented and patient-oriented behavioral science courses. *Journal of Medical Education, 61,* 169–174.

Leippe, M. R., & Elkin, R. A. (1987). When motives clash: Issue involvement and response involvement as determinants of persuasion. *Journal of Personality and Social Psychology, 52,* 269–278.

Leites, N. (1951). *The operational code of the politburo.* New York: McGraw-Hill.

Lemyre, L., & Smith, P. M. (1985). Intergroup discrimination and self-esteem in the minimal group paradigm. *Journal of Personality and Social Psychology, 49,* 660–670.

Leonard, K. E. (1989). The impact of explicit aggressive and implicit nonaggressive cues on aggression in intoxicated and sober males. *Personality and Social Psychology Bulletin, 15,* 390–400.

Lepper, M., Greene, D., & Nisbett, R. (1973). Undermining children's interest with extrinsic rewards: A test of the "overjustification hypothesis." *Journal of Personality and Social Psychology, 28,* 129–137.

Lerner, M. J. (1965). The effect of responsibility and choice on a partner's attractiveness following failure. *Journal of Personality, 33,* 178–187.

Lerner, M. J. (1970). The desire for justice and reactions to victims. In J. McCauley & L. Berkowitz (Eds.), *Altruism and helping behavior.* New York: Academic Press.

Lerner, M. J. (1980). *The belief in a just world: A fundamental delusion.* New York: Plenum.

Leventhal, H. (1970). Findings and theory in the study of fear communications. In L. Berkowitz (Ed.), *Advances in experimental social psychology* (Vol. 5, pp. 120–186). New York: Academic Press.

Leventhal, H., & Cleary, P. D. (1980). The smoking problem: A review of the research and theory in behavioral risk modification. *Psychological Bulletin, 88,* 370–405.

Leventhal, H., & Nerenz, D. R. (1982). A model for stress research and some implications for the control of stress disorders. In D. Meichenbaum & M. Jaremko (Eds.), *Stress prevention and management: A cognitive behavioral approach.* New York: Plenum.

Leventhal, H., Nerenz, D., & Strauss, A. (1980). Self-regulation and the mechanisms for symptom appraisal. In D. Mechanic (Ed.), *Psychosocial epidemiology.* New York: Watson.

Le Vine, R. A., & Campbell, D. T. (1972). *Ethnocentrism: Theories of conflict, ethnic attitudes, and group behavior.* New York: Wiley.

Levinger, G., & Snoek, J. G. (1972). *Attraction in relationship: A new look at interpersonal attraction.* Morristown, NJ: General Learning Press.

Levinson, R. M. (1975). Sex discrimination and employment practices: An experiment with unconventional job inquiries. *Social Problems, 22,* 533–543.

Lewin, K., Lippitt, R., & White, R. K. (1939). Patterns of aggressive behavior in experimentally created social climates. *Journal of Social Psychology, 10,* 271–299.

Lewis-Beck, M. S. (1985). Pocketbook voting in U.S. national election studies: Fact or artifact? *American Journal of Political Science, 29,* 348–356.

Leyens, J. P., Camino, L., Parke, R. D., & Berkowitz, L. (1975). Effects of movie violence on aggression in a field setting as a function of group dominance and cohesion. *Journal of Personality and Social Psychology, 32,* 346–360.

Lichtenstein, M., & Srull, T. K. (1987). Processing objectives as a determinant of the relationship between recall and judgment. *Journal of Experimental Social Psychology, 23,* 93–118.

Liebrand, W. B. G., & van Run, G. J. (1985). The effects of social motives on behavior in social dilemmas in two cultures. *Journal of Experimental Social Psychology, 21,* 86–102.

Life magazine. (1988, Spring). What we believe, pp. 69–70.

Linder, D. E., Cooper, J., & Jones, E. E. (1967). Decision freedom as a determinant of the role of incentive magnitude in attitude change. *Journal of Personality and Social Psychology, 6,* 245–254.

Lindman, R., Jarvinen, P., & Vidjeskog, J. (1987). Verbal interactions of aggressively and non-aggressively predisposed males in a drinking situation. *Aggressive Behavior, 13,* 187–196.

Linville, P. W. (1982). The complexity-extremity effect and age-based stereotyping. *Journal of Personality and Social Psychology, 42,* 193–211.

Linville, P. W., & Jones, E. E. (1980). Polarized appraisals of outgroup members. *Journal of Personality and Social Psychology, 38,* 689–703.

Linville, P. W., Fisher, G. W., & Salovey, P. (1989). Perceived distributions of the characteristics of ingroup and outgroup members: Empirical evidence and a computer simulation. *Journal of Personality and Social Psychology, 57,* 165–188.

Linville, P. W., Salovey, P., & Fisher, G. W. (1986). Stereotyping and perceived distributions of social characteristics: An application to ingroup-outgroup perception. In J. F. Dovidio & S. L. Gaertner (Eds.), *Prejudice, discrimination, and racism* (pp. 165–208). New York: Academic Press.

Linz, D., Donnerstein, E., & Penrod, S. (1984). The effects of multiple exposures to filmed violence against women. *Journal of Communication, 34,* 130–147.

Linz, D. G., Donnerstein, E., & Penrod, S. (1988). Effects of long-term exposure to violent and sexually degrading depictions of women. *Journal of Personality and Social Psychology, 55,* 758–768.

Lisak, D., & Roth, S. (1988). Motivational factors in non-incarcerated sexually aggressive men. *Journal of Personality and Social Psychology, 55,* 795–802.

Little, K. B. (1968). Cultural variations in social schemata. *Journal of Personality and Social Psychology, 10,* 1–7.

Locksley, A., Borgida, E., Brekke, N., & Hepburn, C. (1980). Sex stereotypes and social judgment. *Journal of Personality and Social Psychology, 39*(5), 821–831.

Longley, J., & Pruitt, D. G. (1980). Groupthink: A critique of Janis's theory. In L. Wheeler (Ed.), *Review of personal and social psychology* (Vol. 1). Beverly Hills, CA: Sage Publications.

Lord, C. G. (1980). Schemas and images as memory aids: Two modes of processing social information. *Journal of Personality and Social Psychology, 38,* 257–269.

Lord, C. G., Lepper, M. R., & Mackie, D. (1984). Attitude prototypes as determinants of attitude-behavior consistency. *Journal of Personality and Social Psychology, 46,* 1254–1266.

Lord, C. G., Lepper, M. R., & Preston, E. (1984). Considering the opposite: A corrective strategy for social judgment. *Journal of Personality and Social Psychology, 47,* 1231–1243.

Lord, C. G., & Saenz, D. S. (1985). Memory deficits and memory surfeits: Differential cognitive consequences of tokenism for tokens and observers. *Journal of Personality and Social Psychology, 49,* 918–926.

Lorge, I. (1936). Prestige, suggestion, and attitudes. *Journal of Social Psychology, 7,* 386–402.

Lovibond, S. H., Birrell, P. C., & Langeluddecke, P. (1986). Changing coronary heart disease risk-factor status: The effects of three behavioral programs. *Journal of Behavioral Medicine, 9,* 415–437.

Ludwig, D., Franco, J. N., & Malloy, T. E. (1986). Effects of reciprocity and self-monitoring on self-disclosure with a new acquaintance. *Journal of Personality and Social Psychology, 50,* 1077–1082.

Lurigio, A. J., & Carroll, J. S. (1985). Probation officers' schemata of offenders: Content, development, and impact on treatment decisions. *Journal of Personality and Social Psychology, 48,* 1112–1126.

Lydon, J. E., Jamieson, D. W., & Zanna, M. P. (1988). Interpersonal similarity and the social and intellectual dimensions of first impressions. *Social Cognition, 6,* 269–286.

Lynch, J. G., Jr., & Cohen, J. L. (1978). The use of subjective expected utility theory as an aid to understanding variables that influence helping behavior. *Journal of Personality and Social Psychology, 36,* 1138–1151.

Maass, A., & Clark, R. D. (1984). Hidden impact of minorities: Fifteen years of minority influence research. *Psychological Bulletin, 95,* 428–450.

Maass, A., Clark, R. K., & Haberkorn, G. (1982). The effects of differential ascribed category membership and norms on minority influence. *European Journal of Social Psychology, 12,* 89–104.

Maccoby, E. E., & Jacklin, C. N. (1974). *The psychology of sex differences.* Stanford, CA: Stanford University Press.

MacDonald, W. S., & Oden, C. W. (1973). Effects of extreme crowding on the performance of five married couples

during twelve weeks of intensive training. *Proceedings of 81st Annual Convention of the American Psychological Association, 8*, 209–210.

MacKay, D. G., & Fulkerson, D. G. (1979). On the comprehension and production of pronouns. *Journal of Verbal Learning and Verbal Behavior, 18*, 661–673.

Mackie, D. M. (1986). Social identification effects in group polarization. *Journal of Personality and Social Psychology, 50*(4), 720–728.

Mackie, D. M. (1987). Systematic and nonsystematic processing of majority and minority persuasive communications. *Journal of Personality and Social Psychology, 53*, 41–52.

Mackinnon, C. A. (1986). Pornography: Not a moral issue. *Women's Studies International Forum, 9*, 63–78.

MacKuen, M. B. (1981). Social communication and the mass policy agenda. In M. B. MacKuen & S. L. Coombs (Eds.), *More than news: Media power in public affairs* (pp. 19–144). Beverly Hills, CA: Sage Publications.

Madsen, M. C. (1971). Developmental and cross-cultural differences in the cooperative and competitive behavior of young children. *Journal of Cross-Cultural Psychology, 2*, 365–371.

Maddux, J. E., Roberts, M. C., Sleddin, E. A., & Wright, L. (1986). Developmental issues in child health psychology. *American Psychologist, 41*, 25–34.

Major, B., Cozzarelli, C., Testa, M., & McFarlin, D. B. (1988). Self-verification versus expectancy confirmation in social interaction: The impact of self-focus. *Personality and Social Psychology Bulletin, 14*, 346–359.

Malamuth, N. M., & Briere, J. (1986). Sexual violence in the media: Indirect effects on aggression against women. *Journal of Social Issues, 42*, 75–92.

Malamuth, N. M., & Ceniti, J. (1986). Repeated exposure to violent and nonviolent pornography: Likelihood of raping ratings and laboratory aggression against women. *Aggressive Behavior, 12*, 129–137.

Malamuth, N. M., & Check, J. V. P. (1981). The effects of mass media exposure on acceptance of violence against women: A field experiment. *Journal of Research in Personality, 15*, 436–446.

Malamuth, N. M., Check, J. V. P., & Briere, J. (1986). Sexual arousal in response to aggression: Ideological, aggressive, and sexual correlates. *Journal of Personality and Social Psychology, 50*, 330–340.

Malatesta, C. Z., & Haviland, J. M. (1982). Learning display rules: The socialization of emotion expression in infancy. *Child Development, 53*, 991–1003.

Mann, L. (1977). The effect of stimulus queues on queue-joining behavior. *Journal of Personality and Social Psychology, 35*, 437–442.

Mann, T. E., & Wolfinger, R. E. (1980). Candidates and parties in congressional elections. *The American Political Science Review, 74*, 617–632.

Mansbridge, J. J. (1985). Myth and reality: The ERA and the gender gap in the 1980 election. *Public Opinion Quarterly, 49*, 164–178.

Manstead, A. S. R., Proffitt, C., & Smart, J. L. (1983). Predicting and understanding mothers' infant-feeding intentions and behavior: Testing the theory of reasoned action. *Journal of Personality and Social Psychology, 44*, 657–671.

Marks, G. (1984). Thinking one's abilities are unique and one's opinions are common. *Personality and Social Psychology Bulletin, 10*, 203–208.

Marks, G., & Miller, N. (1987). Ten years of research on the false-consensus effect: An empirical and theoretical review. *Psychological Bulletin, 102*, 72–90.

Markstrom-Adams, C. (1989). Androgyny and its relation to adolescent psychosocial well-being: A review of the literature. *Sex Roles, 21*, 325–340.

Markus, H. (1977). Self-schemata and processing information about the self. *Journal of Personality and Social Psychology, 35*, 63–78.

Markus, G. B. (1979). The political environment and the dynamics of public attitudes: A panel study. *American Journal of Political Science, 23*, 338–359.

Markus, H., & Nurius, P. (1986). Possible selves. *American Psychologist, 41*, 954–969.

Markus, H., & Ruvolo, A. (1989). Possible selves: Personalized representations of goals. In L. A. Pervin (Ed.), *Goal concepts in personality and social psychology* (pp. 211–242). Hillsdale, NJ: Erlbaum.

Markus, H., & Smith, J. (1981). The influence of self-schemata on the perception of others. In N. Cantor & J. Kihlstrom (Eds.), *Personality, cognition, and social interaction* (pp. 233–262). Hillsdale, NJ: Erlbaum.

Markus, H., & Zajonc, R. B. (1986). The cognitive perspective in social psychology. In G. Lindzey & E. Aronson (Eds.), *Handbook of social psychology*, 3rd ed. (Vol. 1, pp. 137–230). New York: Random House.

Markus, H., Smith, J., & Moreland, R. L. (1985). Role of the self-concept in the perception of others. *Journal of Personality and Social Psychology, 49*, 1494–1512.

Marlatt, G. A. (1987). Alcohol, the magic elixir: Stress, expectancy, and the transformation of emotional states. In E. Gottheil, K. A. Druly, S. Pashko, & S. P. Weinstein (Eds.), *Stress and addiction* (pp. 302–322). New York: Brunner/Mazel.

Marlatt, G. A., & George, W. H. (1988). Relapse prevention and the maintenance of optimal health. In S. Shumaker, E. Schron, & J. L. Ockene (Eds.), *The adoption and maintenance of behaviors for optimal health*. New York: Springer.

Marlatt, G. A., & Gordon, J. R. (1985). *Relapse prevention: Maintenance strategies in addictive behavior change*. New York: Guilford.

Martin, C. L. (1987). A ratio measure of sex stereotyping. *Journal of Personality and Social Psychology, 52*, 489–499.

Martyna, W. (1980). The psychology of the generic masculine. In S. McConnell-Ginet, R. Borker, & N. Furman (Eds.), *Women and language in literature and society* (pp. 69–78). New York: Praeger.

Maruyama, G., Fraser, S. C., & Miller, N. (1982). Personal responsibility and altruism in children. *Journal of Personality and Social Psychology, 42*(4), 658–664.

Maslach, C., Santee, R. T., & Wade, C. (1987). Individuation, gender role, and dissent: Personality mediators of situational forces. *Journal of Personality and Social Psychology, 53,* 1088–1093.

Maslach, C., Stapp, J., & Santee, R. T. (1985). Individuation: Conceptual analysis and assessment. *Journal of Personality and Social Psychology, 49,* 729–738.

Matarazzo, J. D. (1980). Behavioral health and behavioral medicine: Frontiers for a new health psychology. *American Psychologist, 35,* 807–817.

Matarazzo, J. D. (1983). Behavioral health: A 1990 challenge for the health sciences professions. In J. D. Matarazzo, N. E. Miller, S. M. Weiss, J. A. Herd, & S. M. Weiss (Eds.), *Behavioral health: A handbook of health enhancement and disease prevention* (pp. 3–40). New York: Wiley.

Mathes, E. W., Adams, H. E., & Davies, R. M. (1985). Jealousy: Loss of relationship rewards, loss of self-esteem, depression, anxiety and anger. *Journal of Personality and Social Psychology, 48,* 1552–1561.

Mathews, K. E., & Canon, L. K. (1975). Environmental noise level as a determinant of helping behavior. *Journal of Personality and Social Psychology, 32*(4), 571–577.

Matlin, M., & Stang, D. (1978). *The Pollyanna principle: Selectivity in language, memory, and thought.* Cambridge, MA: Schenkman.

Matthews, K. A. (1988). Coronary heart disease and Type A behavior: Update on and alternative to the Booth-Kewley and Friedman (1987) quantitative review. *Psychological Bulletin, 104,* 373–380.

May, J. L., & Hamilton, P. A. (1980). Effects of musically evoked affect on women's interpersonal attraction toward and perceptual judgments of physical attractiveness of men. *Motivation and Emotion, 4,* 217–228.

Mazlish, B. (1972). *In search of Nixon: A psychohistorical inquiry.* New York: Basic Books.

McArthur, L. A. (1972). The how and what of why: Some determinants and consequences of causal attribution. *Journal of Personality and Social Psychology, 22,* 171–193.

McArthur, L. Z. (1981). What grabs you? The role of attention in impression formation and causal attribution. In E. T. Higgins, C. P. Herman, & M. P. Zanna (Eds.), *Social cognition: The Ontario symposium* (Vol. 1, pp. 201–246). Hillsdale, NJ: Erlbaum.

McArthur, L. Z., & Baron, R. (1983). Toward an ecological theory of social perception. *Psychological Review, 90,* 215–238.

McArthur, L. Z., & Friedman, S. A. (1980). Illusory correlation in impression formation: Variations in the shared distinctiveness effect as a function of the distinctive person's age, race and sex. *Journal of Personality and Social Psychology, 39,* 615–624.

McArthur, L. Z., & Post, D. L. (1977). Figural emphasis and person perception. *Journal of Experimental and Social Psychology, 13,* 520–535.

McArthur, L. Z., & Resko, B. G. (1975). The portrayal of men and women in American TV commercials. *Journal of Social Psychology, 97,* 209–220.

McCain, G., Cox, V. C., & Paulus, P. B. (1980). *The effect of prison crowding on inmate behavior.* Washington, DC: National Institute of Justice.

McCarthy, D., & Saegert, S. (1978). Residential density, social overload, and social withdrawal. *Human Ecology, 6,* 253–272.

McClelland, D. C. (1976). *The achieving society.* New York: Irvington.

McClintock, C. G., & Liebrand, W. B. G. (1988). Role of interdependence structure, individual value orientation, and another's strategy in social decision making: A transformational analysis. *Journal of Personality and Social Psychology, 55,* 396–409.

McConahay, J. B. (1982). Self-interest versus racial attitudes as correlates of anti-busing attitudes in Louisville: Is it the buses or the blacks? *Journal of Politics, 44,* 692–720.

McConahay, J. B. (1986). Modern racism, ambivalence, and the modern racism scale. In J. F. Dovidio & S. L. Gaertner (Eds.), *Prejudice, discrimination, and racism* (pp. 91–126). New York: Academic Press.

McConahay, J. B., Hardee, B. B., & Batts, V. (1981). Has racism declined in America? It depends upon who is asking and what is asked. *Journal of Conflict Resolution, 25,* 563–579.

McConahay, J. B., & Hough, J. C., Jr. (1976). Symbolic racism. *Journal of Social Issues, 32,* 23–45.

McCormick, N. B. (1979). Come-ons and put-offs: Unmarried students' strategies for having and avoiding sexual intercourse. *Psychology of Women Quarterly, 4,* 194–211.

McCormick, N. B., & Jesser, C. J. (1983). The courtship game: Power in the sexual encounter. In E. R. Allgeier & N. B. McCormick (Eds.), *Changing boundaries: Gender roles and sexual behavior* (pp. 64–86). Palo Alto, CA: Mayfield.

McFarlane, A. H., Norman, G. R., Streiner, D. L., Roy, R., & Scott, D. J. (1980). A longitudinal study of the influence of the psychosocial environment on health status: A preliminary report. *Journal of Health and Social Behavior, 21,* 124–133.

McGrath, J. E. (1984). *Groups: Interaction and performance.* Englewood Cliffs, NJ: Prentice-Hall.

McGuire, W. J. (1964). Inducing resistance to persuasion: Some contemporary approaches. In L. Berkowitz (Ed.), *Advances in experimental social psychology* (Vol. 1, pp. 192–229). New York: Academic Press.

McGuire, W. J. (1969). The nature of attitudes and attitude change. In G. Lindzey & E. Aronson (Eds.), *The handbook of social psychology,* 2nd ed. (Vol. 3, pp. 136–314). Reading, MA: Addison-Wesley.

McGuire, W. J. (1985). Attitudes and attitude change. In G. Lindzey & E. Aronson (Eds.), *Handbook of Social Psychology,* 3rd ed. (Vol. 2, pp. 223–346). New York: Random House.

McGuire, W. J., & Padawer-Singer, A. (1976). Trait salience in the spontaneous self-concept. *Journal of Personality and Social Psychology, 33*(6), 743–754.

McGuire, W. J., & Papageorgis, D. (1961). The relative efficacy of various types of prior belief defense in producing immunity against persuasion. *Journal of Abnormal and Social Psychology, 62,* 327–337.

McMillan, J. R., Clifton, A. K., McGrath, D., & Gale, W. S. (1977). Women's language: Uncertainty or interpersonal sensitivity and emotionality? *Sex Roles, 3*(6), 545–559.

Mednick, S. A., Brennan, P., & Kandel, E. (1988). Predisposition to violence. *Aggressive Behavior, 14,* 25–33.

Meehl, P. E. (1954). *Clinical versus statistical prediction: A theoretical analysis and review of the literature.* Minneapolis: University of Minnesota Press.

Mehlman, R. C., & Snyder, C. R. (1985). Excuse theory: A test of the self-protective role of attributions. *Journal of Personality and Social Psychology, 49,* 994–1001.

Mehrabian, A. (1972). *Nonverbal communication.* Chicago: Aldine-Atherton.

Meichenbaum, D. H., & Jaremko, M. E. (Eds.). (1983). *Stress reduction and prevention.* New York: Plenum.

Merei, F. (1949). Group leadership and institutionalization. *Human Relations, 2,* 23–29.

Messick, D., & Brewer, M. B. (1983). Solving social dilemmas: A review. In L. Wheeler & P. Shaver (Eds.), *Review of personality and social psychology* (Vol. 4, pp. 11–44). Beverly Hills: Sage Publications.

Meyer, A. J., Nash, J. D., McAlister, A. L., Maccoby, N., & Farquhar, J. W. (1980). Skills in training in cardiovascular health education campaign. *Journal of Consulting and Clinical Psychology, 48,* 129–142.

Meyer, D., Leventhal, H., & Gutmann, M. (1985). Common-sense models of illness: The example of hypertension. *Health Psychology, 4,* 115–135.

Meyer, J. P., & Koelbl, S. L. M. (1982). Students' test performances: Dimensionality of causal attributions. *Personality and Social Psychology Bulletin, 8,* 31–36.

Meyer, J. P., & Mulherin, A. (1980). From attribution to helping: An analysis of the mediating effects of affect and expectancy. *Journal of Personality and Social Psychology, 39*(2), 201–210.

Meyerowitz, B. E. (1980). Psychosocial correlates of breast cancer and its treatments. *Psychological Bulletin, 87,* 108–131.

Michaels, J. W., Bloommel, J. M., Brocato, R. M., Linkous, R. A., & Rowe, J. S. (1982). Social facilitation and inhibition in a natural setting. *Replications in Social Psychology, 2,* 21–24.

Michelson, W. (1970). *Man and his urban environment: A sociological approach.* Reading, MA: Addison-Wesley.

Michelson, W. (1977). *Environmental choice, human behavior, and residential satisfaction.* New York: Oxford University Press.

Midlarsky, E., Bryan, J. H., & Brickman, P. (1973). Aversive approval: Interactive effects of modeling and reinforcement on altruistic behavior. *Child Development, 44,* 321–328.

Milavsky, J. R., Kessler, R., Stipp, H., & Rubens, W. S. (1982). Television and aggression: Results of a panel study. In D. Pearl, L. Bouthilet, & J. Lazar (Eds.), *Television and behavior: Ten years of scientific progress and implications for the Eighties. Vol. II: Technical reviews.* Rockville, MD: National Institute of Mental Health.

Milgram, S. (1963). Behavioral study of obedience. *Journal of Abnormal and Social Psychology, 67,* 371–378.

Milgram, S. (1965). Some conditions of obedience and disobedience to authority. *Human Relations, 18,* 57–75.

Milgram, S. (1970). The experience of living in cities. *Science, 167,* 1461–1468.

Milgram, S. (1974). *Obedience to authority: An experimental view.* New York: Harper & Row.

Milgram, S., Bickman, L., & Berkowitz, L. (1969). Note on the drawing power of crowds of different size. *Journal of Personality and Social Psychology, 13,* 79–82.

Milgram, S., & Shotland, R. L. (1973). *Television and antisocial behavior: Field experiments.* New York: Academic Press.

Millar, M. G., & Tesser, A. (1986). Thought-induced attitude change: The effects of schema structure and commitment. *Journal of Personality and Social Psychology, 51,* 259–269.

Millar, M. G., & Tesser, A. (1989). The effects of affective-cognitive consistency and thought on the attitude-behavior relation. *Journal of Experimental Social Psychology, 25,* 189–202.

Miller, A. G. (1976). Constraint and target effects in the attribution of attitudes. *Journal of Experimental Social Psychology, 12,* 325–339.

Miller, A. G. (1986). *The obedience experiments: A case study of controversy in social science.* New York: Praeger.

Miller, A. G., Jones, E. E., & Hinkle, S. (1981). A robust attribution error in the personality domain. *Journal of Experimental Social Psychology, 17,* 587–600.

Miller, D. T., & Ross, M. (1975). Self-serving biases in the attribution of causality: Fact or fiction? *Psychological Bulletin, 82,* 213–225.

Miller, D. T., & Turnbull, W. (1986). Expectancies and interpersonal processes. *Annual Review of Psychology, 37,* 233–256.

Miller, J. G. (1984). Culture and the development of everyday social explanation. *Journal of Personality and Social Psychology, 46,* 961–978.

Miller, L. C., & Kenny, D. A. (1986). Reciprocity of self-disclosure at the individual and dyadic levels: A social relations analysis. *Journal of Personality and Social Psychology, 50,* 713–719.

Miller, L. W., & Sigelman, L. (1978). Is the audience the message? A note on LBJ's Vietnam statements. *Public Opinion Quarterly, 42,* 71–80.

Miller, N., & Brewer, M. B. (Eds.). (1984). *Groups in contact: The psychology of desegregation.* Orlando, FL: Academic Press.

Miller, N., & Brewer, M. B. (1986). Categorization effects on ingroup and outgroup perception. In J. F. Dovidio & S. L. Gaertner (Eds.), *Prejudice, discrimination, and racism* (pp. 209–230). Orlando, FL: Academic Press.

Miller, P. A., & Eisenberg, N. (1988). The relation of empathy to aggressive and externalizing/antisocial behavior. *Psychological Bulletin, 103,* 324–344.

Miller, S. M. (1979). Controllability and human stress: Method, evidence, and theory. *Behaviour Research and Therapy, 17,* 287–304.

Miller, S. M., & Mangan, C. E. (1983). Interacting effects of information and coping style in adapting to gynecologic stress: Should the doctor tell all? *Journal of Personality and Social Psychology, 45,* 223–236.

Mills, R. S. L., & Grusec, J. E. (1989). Cognitive, affective, and behavioral consequences of praising altruism. *Merrill-Palmer Quarterly, 35*(3), 299–326.

Mischel, W. (1979). On the interface of cognition and personality: Beyond the person-situation debate. *American Psychologist, 34,* 740–754.

Mita, T. H., Dermer, M., & Knight, J. (1977). Reversed facial images and the mere-exposure hypothesis. *Journal of Personality and Social Psychology, 35,* 597–601.

Mitchell, R. E. (1971). Some social implications of high-density housing. *American Sociological Review, 36,* 18–29.

Mogielnicki, R. P., Neslin, S., Dulac, J., Balestra, D., Gillie, E., & Corson, J. (1986). Tailored media can enhance the success of smoking cessation clinics. *Journal of Behavioral Medicine, 9,* 141–161.

Molm, L. D. (1985). Relative effects of individual dependencies: Further tests of the relation between power imbalance and power use. *Social Forces, 63*(3), 810–837.

Molm, L. D. (1988). The structure and use of power: A comparison of reward and punishment power. *Social Psychology Quarterly, 51,* 108–122.

Monson, T. C., & Snyder, M. (1977). Actors, observers, and the attribution process: Toward a reconceptualization. *Journal of Experimental Social Psychology, 13,* 89–111.

Moreland, R. L., & Zajonc, R. B. (1982). Exposure effects in person perception: Familiarity, similarity and attraction. *Journal of Experimental Social Psychology, 18,* 395–415.

Morgan, C. J., & Leik, R. K. (1979). Simulation theory development: The bystander intervention case. In R. B. Smith & B. Anderson (Eds.), *Social science methods. Vol. 3: Theory construction.* New York: Halstead Press.

Moriarty, T. (1975). Crime, commitment, and the responsive bystander. Two field experiments. *Journal of Personality and Social Psychology, 31,* 370–376.

Morris, W. N., & Miller, R. S. (1975). The effects of consensus-breaking and consensus-preempting partners on reduction in conformity. *Journal of Experimental Social Psychology, 11,* 215–223.

Morse, S., & Gergen, K. J. (1970). Social comparison, self-consistency, and the concept of self. *Journal of Personality and Social Psychology, 16,* 148–156.

Morton, T. L. (1978). Intimacy and reciprocity of exchange: A comparison of spouses and strangers. *Journal of Personality and Social Psychology, 36,* 72–81.

Moscovici, S. (1985). Social influence and conformity. In G. Lindzey & E. Aronson (Eds.), *Handbook of social psychology,* 3rd ed. (Vol. 2, pp. 347–412). New York: Random House.

Moscovici, S., Lage, E., & Naffrechoux, M. (1969). Influence of a consistent minority on the responses of a majority in a color perception task. *Sociometry, 32,* 365–379.

Moscovici, S., Mugny, G., & Van Avermaet, E. (Eds.) (1985). *Perspectives on minority influence.* New York: Cambridge University Press.

Moss, M. K., & Page, R. A. (1972). Reinforcement and helping behavior. *Journal of Applied Social Psychology, 2,* 360–371.

Mueller, J. E. (1973). *War, presidents, and public opinion.* New York: Wiley.

Mullen, B. (1985). Strength and immediacy of sources: A meta-analytic evaluation of the forgotten elements of social impact theory. *Journal of Personality and Social Psychology, 48,* 1458–1466.

Mullen, B. (1986). Atrocity as a function of lynch mob composition. *Personality and Social Psychology Bulletin, 12,* 187–198.

Mullen, B., Atkins, J. L., Champion, D. S., Edwards, C., Hardy, D., Story, J. E., & Vanderklok, M. (1985). The false consensus effect: A meta-analysis of 115 hypothesis tests. *Journal of Experimental Social Psychology, 21,* 262–283.

Mullen, B., & Hu, L. (1988). Social projection as a function of cognitive mechanisms: Two meta-analytic integrations. *British Journal of Social Psychology, 27,* 333–356.

Mullen, B., & Riordan, C. A. (1988). Self-serving attributions for performance in naturalistic settings: A meta-analytic review. *Journal of Applied Social Psychology, 18,* 3–22.

Mullen, B., Salas, E., & Driskell, J. E. (1989). Salience, motivation, and artifact as contributions to the relationship between participation rate and leadership. *Journal of Experimental Social Psychology, 25,* 545–559.

Murphy, T. J., Pagano, R. R., & Marlatt, G. A. (1986). Lifestyle modification with heavy alcohol drinkers: Effects of aerobic exercise and meditation. *Addictive Behaviors, 11,* 175–186.

Myers, A. M., & Gonda, G. (1982). Utility of the masculinity-femininity construct: Comparison of traditional and androgyny approaches. *Journal of Personality and Social Psychology, 43*(3), 514–523.

Myers, D. G., & Lamm, H. (1976). The group polarization phenomenon. *Psychological Bulletin, 83,* 602–627.

Myers, J. K., Lindenthal, J. J., & Pepper, M. P. (1972). Life events and mental status: A longitudinal study. *Journal of Health and Social Behavior, 13,* 398–406.

Myerscough, R., & Taylor, S. (1985). The effects of marijuana on human physical aggression. *Journal of Personality and Social Psychology, 49,* 1541–1546.

Myrdal, G. (1944). *An American dilemma.* New York: Harper and Row.

National Institute of Mental Health. (1982). Television and behavior: Ten years of scientific progress and implications for the eighties. Vol. I: *Summary report.* Rockville, MD: National Institute of Mental Health.

Nemeth, C. J. (1986). Differential contributions of majority and minority influence. *Psychological Review, 93,* 23–32.

Nemeth, C., & Chiles, C. (1988). Modelling courage: The role of dissent in fostering independence. *European Journal of Social Psychology, 18,* 275–280.

Nemeth, C., & Kwan, J. (1987). Minority influence, divergent thinking, and detection of correct solutions. *Journal of Applied Social Psychology, 17,* 788–799.

Nerenz, D. R., & Leventhal, H. (1983). Self-regulation theory in chronic illness. In T. G. Burish & L. A. Bradley (Eds.), *Coping with chronic disease: Research and applications* (pp. 13–35). New York: Academic Press.

Neuman, W. R. (1976). Patterns of recall among television news viewers. *Public Opinion Quarterly,* 115–123.

Newcomb, T. M. (1943). *Personality and social change.* New York: Dryden Press.

Newcomb, T. M. (1961). *The acquaintance process.* New York: Holt.

Newcomb, T. M. (1968). Interpersonal balance. In R. P. Abelson et al. (Eds.), *Theories of cognitive consistency: A sourcebook.* Chicago: Rand McNally.

Newcomb, T. M., Koenig, K. E., Flacks, R., & Warwick, D. P. (1967). *Persistence and change: Bennington College and its students after 25 years.* New York: Wiley.

Newtson, D. (1976). Foundations of attribution: The perception of ongoing behavior. In J. H. Harvey, W. J. Ickes, & R. F. Kidd (Eds.), *New directions in attribution research* (Vol. 1, pp. 223–248). Hillsdale, NJ: Erlbaum.

Newtson, D., Engquist, G., & Bois, J. (1977). The objective basis of behavior units. *Journal of Personality and Social Psychology, 35,* 847–862.

Newtson, D., Hairfield, J., Bloomingdale, J., & Cutino, S. (1987). The structure of action and interaction. *Social Cognition, 5,* 191–237.

Nickerson, S., Mayo, C., & Smith, A. (1986). Racism in the courtroom. In J. F. Dovidio & S. L. Gaertner (Eds.), *Prejudice, discrimination, and racism* (pp. 255–278). Orlando, FL: Academic Press.

Nie, N. H., Verba, S., & Petrocik, J. R. (1979). *The changing American voter,* enlarged ed. Cambridge, MA: Harvard University Press.

Niemi, R. G. (1974). *How family members perceive each other.* New Haven, CT: Yale University Press.

Nieva, V., & Gutek, B. (1981). *Women and work: A psychological perspective.* New York: Praeger.

Nisbett, R. E., Caputo, C., Legant, P., & Maracek, J. (1973). Behavior as seen by the actor and as seen by the observer. *Journal of Personality and Social Psychology, 27,* 154–164.

Nisbett, R. E., Fong, G. T., Lehman, D. R., & Chang, P. W. (1987). Teaching reasoning. *Science, 238,* 625–631.

Nisbett, R. E., Krantz, D. H., Jepson, C., & Fong, G. T. (1982). Improving inductive inference. In D. Kahneman, P. Slovic, & A. Tversky (Eds.), *Judgment under uncertainty: Heuristics and biases* (pp. 445–462). New York: Cambridge University Press.

Nisbett, R. E., & Kunda, Z. (1985). Perception of social distribution. *Journal of Personality and Social Psychology, 48,* 297–311.

Nisbett, R. E., & Ross, L. (1980). *Human inference: Strategies and shortcomings of social judgment.* Englewood Cliffs, NJ: Prentice-Hall.

Nisbett, R. E., & Schachter, S. (1966). Cognitive manipulation of pain. *Journal of Experimental Social Psychology, 2,* 227–236.

Nisbett, R. E., & Wilson, T. D. (1977). Telling more than we can know: Verbal reports on mental processes. *Psychological Review, 84,* 231–259.

Norman, R. (1975). Affective-cognitive consistency, attitudes, conformity, and behavior. *Journal of Personality and Social Psychology, 32,* 83–91.

Novak, D. W., & Lerner, M. J. (1968). Rejection as a consequence of perceived similarity. *Journal of Personality and Social Psychology, 9,* 147–152.

Ohbuchi, K., Kameda, M., & Agarie, N. (1989). Apology as aggression control: Its role in mediating appraisal of and response to harm. *Journal of Personality and Social Psychology, 56,* 219–227.

O'Kelly, C. (1980). Sex-role imagery in modern art: An empirical examination. *Sex Roles, 6*(1), 99–112.

Oliner, S. P., & Oliner, P. M. (1988). *The altruistic personality: Rescuers of Jews in Nazi Europe.* New York: Free Press.

Olson, J. M. (1988). Misattribution, preparatory information, and speech anxiety. *Journal of Personality and Social Psychology, 54,* 758–767.

Olson, J. M., & Ross, M. (1988). False feedback about placebo effectiveness: Consequences for the misattribution of speech anxiety. *Journal of Experimental Social Psychology, 24,* 275–291.

Olzak, S., & Nagel, J. (1986). *Competitive ethnic relations.* New York: Academic Press.

Orbell, J. M., van de Kragt, A. J. C., & Dawes, R. M. (1988). Explaining discussion-induced cooperation. *Journal of Personality and Social Psychology, 54,* 811–819.

Orlofsky, J. L., & O'Heron, C. A. (1987). Stereotypic and nonstereotypic sex role trait and behavior orientations: Implications for personal adjustment. *Journal of Personality and Social Psychology, 52,* 1034–1042.

Orvis, B. R., Kelley, H. H., & Butler, D. (1976). Attributional conflict in young couples. In J. H. Harvey, W. Ickes, & R. F. Kidd (Eds.), *New directions in attribution research.* (Vol. 1, pp. 353–386). Hillsdale, NJ: Erlbaum.

Osborn, A. F. (1957). *Applied imagination.* New York: Scribners.

Osgood, C. E. (1962). *An alternative to war or surrender.* Urbana, IL: University of Illinois Press.

Osgood, C. E., Suci, G. J., & Tannenbaum, P. H. (1957). *The measurement of meaning.* Urbana: University of Illinois Press.

Pagel, M. D., & Davidson, A. R. (1984). A comparison of three social-psychological models of attitude and behavioral plan: Prediction of contraceptive behavior. *Journal of Personality and Social Psychology, 47,* 517–533.

Pallak, M. S., Sogin, S. R., & Van Zante, A. (1974). Bad decisions: Effect of volition, locus of causality, and negative consequences on attitude change. *Journal of Personality and Social Psychology, 30,* 217–227.

Pancer, S. M., McMullen, L. M., Kabatoff, R. A., Johnson, K. G., & Pond, C. A. (1979). Conflict and avoidance in helping situations. *Journal of Personality and Social Psychology, 37,* 1406–1411.

Park, B. (1986). A method for studying the development of impressions of real people. *Journal of Personality and Social Psychology, 51,* 907–917.

Park, B., & Fink, C. (1989). A social relations analysis of agreement in liking judgments. *Journal of Personality and Social Psychology, 56,* 506–518.

Park, B., & Hahn, S. (1988). Sex-role identity and the perception of others. *Social Cognition, 6,* 61–87.

Park, B., & Rothbart, M. (1982). Perception of out-group homogeneity and levels of social categorization: Memory for the subordinate attributes of in-group and out-group members. *Journal of Personality and Social Psychology, 42,* 1051–1068.

Parke, R. D., Berkowitz, L., Leyens, J. P., West, S. G., & Sebastian, R. J. (1977). Some effects of violent and nonviolent movies on the behavior of juvenile delinquents. In L. Berkowitz (Ed.), *Advances in experimental social psychology* (Vol. 10, pp. 1136–1173). New York: Academic Press.

Parkinson, B. (1985). Emotional effects of false autonomic feedback. *Psychological Bulletin, 98,* 471–494.

Parlee, M. B. (1979, October). The friendship bond. *Psychology Today,* pp. 43–54, 113.

Parrott, W. G., Sabini, J., & Silver, M. (1988). The roles of self-esteem and social interaction in embarrassment. *Personality and Social Psychology Bulletin, 14,* 191–202.

Patterson, M. L., & Sechrest, L. B. (1970). Interpersonal distance and impression formation. *Journal of Personality, 38,* 161–166.

Patterson, T. E. (1980). *The mass media election: How Americans choose their president.* New York: Praeger.

Patterson, T. E., & McClure, R. D. (1976). *The unseeing eye.* New York: Putnam.

Pavelchak, M. A. (1989). Piecemeal and category-based evaluation: An idiographic analysis. *Journal of Personality and Social Psychology, 56,* 354–363.

Pearlin, L. I., & Schooler, C. (1978). The structure of coping. *Journal of Health and Social Behavior, 19,* 2–21.

Pederson, L. L. (1982). Compliance with physician advice to quit smoking: A review of the literature. *Preventive Medicine, 11,* 71–84.

Pennebaker, J. W. (1983). Accuracy of symptom perception. In A. Baum, S. E. Taylor, & J. Singer (Eds.), *Handbook of psychology and health* (Vol. 4, pp. 189–217). Hillsdale, NJ: Erlbaum.

Pennebaker, J. W., & Beall, S. (1986). Confronting a traumatic event: Toward an understanding of inhibition and disease. *Journal of Abnormal Psychology, 95,* 274–281.

Pennebaker, J. W., & Lightner, J. M. (1980). Competition of internal and external information in an exercise setting. *Journal of Personality and Social Psychology, 39,* 165–174.

Pennebaker, J. W., Kiecolt-Glaser, J., & Glaser, R. (1988). Disclosure of traumas and immune function: Health implications for psychotherapy. *Journal of Consulting and Clinical Psychology, 56,* 239–245.

Penrod, S., Loftus, E., & Winkler, J. (1982). The reliability of eyewitness testimony: A psychological perspective. In N. L. Kerr & R. M. Bray (Eds.), *The psychology of the courtroom* (pp. 119–168). New York: Academic Press.

Peplau, L. A. (1984). Power in dating relationships. In J. Freeman (Ed.), *Women: A feminist perspective,* 3rd ed. Palo Alto, CA: Mayfield.

Peplau, L. A., & Perlman, D. (1982). *Loneliness: A sourcebook of current theory, research and therapy.* New York: Wiley-Interscience.

Perlman, D., & Oskamp, S. (1971). The effects of picture content and exposure frequency on evaluations of Negroes and whites. *Journal of Experimental Social Psychology, 7,* 503–514.

Perry, D. G., Perry, L. C., & Weiss, R. J. (1989). Sex differences in the consequences that children anticipate for aggression. *Developmental Psychology, 25,* 312–319.

Pessin, J. (1933). The comparative effects of social and mechanical stimulation on memorizing. *American Journal of Psychology, 45,* 263–270.

Peterson, C., & Seligman, M. E. P. (1984). Causal explanations as a risk factor for depression: Theory and evidence. *Psychological Review, 91,* 347–374.

Peterson, C., Seligman, M. E. P., & Vaillant, G. E. (1988). Pessimistic explanatory style is a risk factor for physical illness: A thirty-five-year longitudinal study. *Journal of Personality and Social Psychology, 55,* 23–27.

Peterson, D. R. (1983). Conflict. In H. H. Kelley et al., *Close relationships* (pp. 360–396). New York: Freeman.

Pettigrew, T. F. (1985). New black-white patterns: How best to conceptualize them? In R. H. Turner & J. F. Short, Jr. (Eds.), *Annual Review of Sociology, 11,* 329–346.

Pettigrew, T. F. (1988). Integration and pluralism. In P. A. Katz & D. A. Taylor (Eds.), *Eliminating racism: Profiles in controversy* (pp. 19–30). New York: Plenum.

Petty, R. E., & Brock, T. C. (1981). Thought disruption and persuasion: Assessing the validity of attitude change experiments. In R. E. Petty, T. M. Ostrom, & T. C. Brock (Eds.), *Cognitive responses in persuasion.* Hillsdale, NJ: Erlbaum.

Petty, R. E., & Cacioppo, J. T. (1977). Forewarning, cognitive responding, and resistance to persuasion. *Journal of Personality and Social Psychology, 35,* 645–656.

Petty, R. E., & Cacioppo, J. T. (1979). Issue involvement can increase or decrease persuasion by enhancing message-relevant cognitive responses. *Journal of Personality and Social Psychology, 37,* 1915–1926.

Petty, R. E., & Cacioppo, J. T. (1984). The effects of involvement on responses to argument quantity and quality: Central and peripheral routes to persuasion. *Journal of Personality and Social Psychology, 46,* 69–81.

Petty, R. E., & Cacioppo, J. T. (1986). *Communication and persuasion: Central and peripheral routes to attitude change.* New York: Springer-Verlag.

Petty, R. E., Cacioppo, J. T., & Goldman, R. (1981). Personal involvement as a determinant of argument-based persuasion. *Journal of Personality and Social Psychology, 41,* 847–855.

Petty, R. E., Cacioppo, J. T., & Schumann, D. (1983). Central and peripheral routes to advertising effectiveness: The moderating role of involvement. *Journal of Consumer Research, 10,* 135–146.

Petty, R. T., Ostrom, T. M., & Brock, T. C. (Eds.). *Cognitive responses in persuasion.* Hillsdale, NJ: Erlbaum.

Petty, R. E., Rennier, G. A., & Cacioppo, J. T. (1987). Assertion versus interrogation format in opinion surveys: Questions enhance thoughtful responding. *Public Opinion Quarterly, 51,* 481–494.

Phares, E. J., Wilson, K. G., & Klyver, N. W. (1971). Internal-external control and attribution of blame under neutral and distractive conditions. *Journal of Personality and Social Psychology, 18,* 285–288.

Piliavin, I. M., Piliavin, J. A., & Rodin, J. (1975). Costs, diffusion, and the stigmatized victim. *Journal of Personality and Social Psychology, 32*(3), 429–438.

Piliavin, I. M., Rodin, J., & Piliavin, J. A. (1969). Good Samaritanism: An underground phenomenon? *Journal of Personality and Social Psychology, 13*(4), 289–299.

Piliavin, J. A., Dovidio, J. F., Gaertner, S. L., & Clark, R. D. (1981). *Emergency intervention.* New York: Academic Press.

Piliavin, J. A., Evans, D. E., & Callero, P. (1984). Learning to "give to unnamed strangers": The process of commitment to regular blood donation. In E. Staub, D. Bar-Tal, J. Karylowski, & J. Reykowski (Eds.), *The development and maintenance of prosocial behavior: International perspectives.* New York: Plenum.

Pilisuk, M., Boylan, R., & Acredolo, C. (1987). Social support, life stress, and subsequent medical care utilization. *Health Psychology, 6,* 273–288.

Pines, A., & Aronson, E. (1983). Antecedents, correlates, and consequences of sexual jealousy. *Journal of Personality, 51*(1), 108–136.

Plous, S. (1989). Thinking the unthinkable: The effects of anchoring on likelihood estimates of nuclear war. *Journal of Applied Social Psychology, 19,* 67–91.

Pratkanis, A. R., Greenwald, A. G., Leippe, M. R., & Baumgardner, M. H. (1988). In search of reliable persuasion effects. III: The sleeper effect is dead. Long live the sleeper effect. *Journal of Personality and Social Psychology, 54,* 203–218.

Prentice-Dunn, S., & Rogers, R. W. (1983). Deindividuation in aggression. In R. G. Geen & E. I. Donnerstein (Eds.), *Aggression: Theoretical and empirical reviews.* Vol. 2: *Issues in research.* New York: Academic Press.

Pyszczynski, T. A., & Greenberg, J. (1981). Role of disconfirmed expectancies in the instigation of attributional processing. *Journal of Personality and Social Psychology, 40,* 31–38.

Rahe, R. H., Mahan, J. L., & Arthur, R. J. (1970). Prediction of near-future health change from subjects' preceding life changes. *Journal of Psychomatic Research, 14,* 401–406.

Ramist, L., & Arbeiter, S. (1986). *Profiles, college-bound seniors, 1985.* New York: College Entrance Examination Board.

Rands, M., & Levinger, G. (1979). Implicit theories of relationship: An intergenerational study. *Journal of Personality and Social Psychology, 37,* 649–661.

Raven, B. H. (1988, August). *French and Raven 30 years later: Power, interaction and interpersonal influence.* Paper presented at the International Congress of Psychology, Sydney, Australia.

Raven, B. H. (1988). Social power and compliance in health care. In S. Maes, C. D. Spielberger, P. B. Defares, & I. G. Sarason (Eds.), *Topics in health psychology* (pp. 229–244). New York: Wiley.

Raven, B. H., & Rubin, J. Z. (1983). *Social psychology,* 2nd ed. New York: Wiley.

Reed, G. M. (1989). Stress, coping, and psychological adaptation in a sample of gay and bisexual men with AIDS.

Unpublished doctoral dissertation, University of California, Los Angeles.

Reeder, G. D., Fletcher, G. J. O., & Furman, K. (1989). The role of observers' expectations in attitude attribution. *Journal of Experimental Social Psychology, 25,* 168–188.

Reeder, G. D., McCormick, C. B., & Esselman, E. D. (1987). Self-referent processing and recall of prose. *Journal of Educational Psychology, 79,* 243–248.

Regan, D. T. (1968). *The effects of a favor and liking on compliance.* Unpublished doctoral dissertation, Stanford University.

Regan, D. T., & Fazio, R. (1977). On the consistency between attitudes and behavior: Look to the method of attitude formation. *Journal of Experimental Social Psychology, 13,* 28–45.

Regan, D. T., & Totten, J. (1975). Empathy and attribution: Turning observers into actors. *Journal of Personality and Social Psychology, 32,* 850–856.

Reich, W. P., Parrella, D. P., & Filstead, W. J. (1988). Unconfounding the hassles scale: External source versus internal responses to stress. *Journal of Behavioral Medicine, 11,* 239–250.

Reinisch, J. M., & Sanders, S. A. (1986). A test of sex differences in aggressive response to hypothetical conflict situations. *Journal of Personality and Social Psychology, 50,* 1045–1049.

Ridgeway, C. L. (1983). *The dynamics of small groups.* New York: St. Martin's Press.

Reis, H. T., & Jackson, L. A. (1981). Sex differences in reward allocation: Subjects, partners and tasks. *Journal of Personality and Social Psychology, 40,* 465–478.

Reis, H. T., Senchak, M., & Solomon, B. (1985). Sex differences in the intimacy of social interaction: Further examination of potential explanations. *Journal of Personality and Social Psychology, 48,* 1204–1217.

Reis, H. T., & Shaver, P. (1988). Intimacy as an interpersonal process. In S. W. Duck (Ed.), *Handbook of personal relationships* (pp. 367–389). New York: Wiley.

Renshon, S. A. (1974). *Psychological needs and political behavior: A theory of personality and political efficacy.* New York: Free Press.

Rhine, R. J., & Severance, L. J. (1970). Ego-involvement, discrepancy, source credibility, and attitude change. *Journal of Personality and Social Psychology, 16,* 175–190.

Rhodewalt, F., & Marcroft, M. (1988). Type A behavior and diabetic control: Implications of psychological reactance for health outcomes. *Journal of Applied Social Psychology, 18,* 139–159.

Rhodewalt, F., & Strube, M. J. (1985). A self-attribution-reactance model of recovery from injury in Type A individuals. *Journal of Applied Social Psychology, 15,* 330–344.

Ritter, C. (1988). Resources, behavior intentions, and drug use: A ten-year national panel analysis. *Social Psychology Quarterly, 51,* 250–264.

Rix, S. E. (Ed.) (1988). *The American woman 1988–89: A status report.* New York: Norton.

Robinson, C. C., & Morris, J. T. (1986). The gender-stereotyped nature of Christmas toys received by 36-, 48-, and 60-month-old children. *Sex Roles, 15*(1/2), 21–32.

Robinson, J., & McArthur, L. Z. (1982). Impact of salient vocal qualities on causal attribution for a speaker's behavior. *Journal of Personality and Social Psychology, 43,* 236–247.

Robinson, J. P. (1971). The audience for national TV news programs. *Public Opinion Quarterly, 35,* 403–405.

Robinson, J. P., Yerby, J., Fieweger, M., & Somerick, N. (1977). Sex-role differences in time use. *Sex Roles, 3,* 443–458.

Rodin, J., & Janis, I. L. (1979). The social power of health-care practitioners as agents of change. *Journal of Social Issues, 35,* 60–81.

Rodin, J., & Langer, E. J. (1977). Long-term effects of a control-relevant intervention with the institutionalized aged. *Journal of Personality and Social Psychology, 35,* 897–902.

Rodin, J., & Salovey, P. (1989). Health psychology. *Annual Review of Psychology, 10,* 533–579.

Rogers, R. W. (1984). Changing health-related attitudes and behavior: The role of preventive health psychology. In J. H. Harvey, J. E. Maddux, R. P. McGlynn, & C. D. Stoltenberg (Eds.), *Social perception in clinical and counseling psychology* (Vol. 2, pp. 91–112). Lubbock: Texas Tech University Press.

Rogers, R. W., & Mewborn, C. R. (1976). Fear appeals and attitude change: Effects of a threat's noxiousness, probability of occurrence, and the efficacy of coping responses. *Journal of Personality and Social Psychology, 34,* 54–61.

Rogers, T. B., Kuiper, N. A., & Kirker, W. S. (1977). Self-reference and the encoding of personal information. *Journal of Personality and Social Psychology, 35,* 677–688.

Rogow, A. A. (1963). *James Forrestal: A study of personality, politics, and policy.* New York: Macmillan.

Rokeach, M., & Mezei, L. (1968). Race and shared belief as factors in social choice. *Science, 151,* 167–172.

Romer, D., Gruder, C. L., & Lizzadro, T. (1986). A person-situation approach to altruistic behavior. *Journal of Personality and Social Psychology, 51,* 1001–1012.

Rose, S., & Frieze, I. H. (1989). Young singles' scripts for a first date. *Gender & Society, 3,* 258–268.

Rosen, B., & Jerdee, T. H. (1978). Perceived sex differences in managerially relevant characteristics. *Sex Roles, 4,* 837–843.

Rosenbaum, M. E. (1986). The repulsion hypothesis: On the nondevelopment of relationships. *Journal of Personality and Social Psychology, 51,* 1156–1166.

Rosenbaum, R. M. (1972). *A dimensional analysis of the perceived causes of success and failure.* Unpublished doctoral dissertation, University of California, Los Angeles.

Rosenberg, M. J. (1960). An analysis of affective-cognitive

consistency. In C. I. Hovland & M. J. Rosenberg (Eds.), *Attitude organization and change.* New Haven, CT: Yale University Press.

Rosenberg, S., Nelson, C., & Vivekananthan, P. S. (1968). A multidimensional approach to the structure of personality impressions. *Journal of Personality and Social Psychology, 9,* 283–294.

Rosenfeld, L. B. (1979). Self-disclosure avoidance: Why I am afraid to tell you who I am. *Communication Monographs, 46,* 63–74.

Rosenfeld, P., Giacalone, R. A., & Tedeschi, J. T. (1984). Cognitive dissonance and impression management explanations for effort justification. *Personality and Social Psychology Bulletin, 10,* 394–401.

Rosenkrantz, P., Vogel, S., Bee, H., Broverman, I., & Broverman, D. M. (1968). Sex-role stereotypes and self-concepts in college students. *Journal of Consulting and Clinical Psychology, 32,* 287–295.

Rosenman, R. (1978). The interview method of assessment of the coronary-prone behavior pattern. In T. Dembroski, S. Weiss, J. Shields, S. Haynes, & M. Feinleib (Eds.), *Coronary-prone behavior* (pp. 55–70). New York: Springer-Verlag.

Rosenstock, I. M. (1966). Why people use health services. *Milbank Memorial Fund Quarterly, 44,* 94ff.

Rosenthal, R. (1986). Media violence, antisocial behavior, and the social consequences of small effects. *Journal of Social Issues, 42,* 141–154.

Roskies, E. (1980). Considerations in developing a treatment program for the coronary-prone (Type A) behavior pattern. In P. O. Davidson & S. M. Davidson (Eds.), *Behavior medicine: Changing health lifestyles* (pp. 38–69). New York: Brunner/Mazel.

Ross, A. S. (1971). Effect of increased responsibility on bystander intervention: The presence of children. *Journal of Personality and Social Psychology, 19,* 306–310.

Ross, L. (1977). The intuitive psychologist and his shortcomings: Distortions in the attribution process. In L. Berkowitz (Ed.), *Advances in experimental social psychology* (Vol. 10, pp. 174–221). New York: Academic Press.

Ross, L., Amabile, T. M., & Steinmetz, J. L. (1977). Social roles, social control, and biases in social-perception processes. *Journal of Personality and Social Psychology, 35,* 485–494.

Ross, L., Greene, D., & House, P. (1977). The "false consensus effect": An egocentric bias in social perception and attribution processes. *Journal of Experimental Social Psychology, 13,* 279–301.

Ross, M. (1975). Salience of reward and intrinsic motivation. *Journal of Personality and Social Psychology, 32,* 245–254.

Ross, M., & Sicoly, F. (1979). Egocentric biases in availability and attribution. *Journal of Personality and Social Psychology, 37,* 322–336.

Rothbart, M. (1976). Achieving racial equality: An analysis of resistance to social reform. In P. A. Katz (Ed.), *Towards*

the elimination of racism (pp. 341–375). Elmsford, NY: Pergamon.

Rothbart, M., Fulero, S., Jensen, C., Howard, J., & Birrell, B. (1978). From individual to group impressions: Availability heuristics in stereotype formation. *Journal of Experimental Social Psychology, 14,* 237–255.

Rothbart, M., & Lewis, S. (1988). Inferring category attributes from exemplar attributes: Geometric shapes and social categories. *Journal of Personality and Social Psychology, 55,* 861–872.

Rotter, J. B. (1966). Generalized expectancies for internal versus external control of reinforcement. *Psychological Monographs, 80* (1, Whole No. 609).

Rotter, J. B. (1971). External control and internal control. *Psychology Today, 5,* 37–42.

Rowland, W. D. (1983). *The politics of TV violence: Policy uses of communications research.* Beverly Hills, CA: Sage Publications.

Ruback, R. B. (1987). Deserted (and nondeserted) aisles: Territorial intrusion can produce persistence, not flight. *Social Psychology Quarterly, 50*(3), 270–276.

Ruback, R. B., & Innes, C. A. (1988). The relevance and irrelevance of psychological research: The example of prison crowding. *American Psychologist, 43*(9), 683–693.

Ruback, R. B., Pape, K. D., & Doriot, P. (1989). Waiting for a phone: Intrusion on callers leads to territorial defense. *Social Psychology Quarterly, 52*(3), 232–241.

Rubinstein, C. M., & Shaver, P. (1982). The experience of loneliness. In L. A. Peplau & D. Perlman (Eds.), *Loneliness: A sourcebook of current theory, research and therapy* (pp. 206–223). New York: Wiley-Interscience.

Rubin, B. (1967). *Political television.* Belmont, CA: Wadsworth.

Rubin, L. (1976). *Worlds of pain.* New York: Basic Books.

Rubin, Z. (1970). Measurement of romantic love. *Journal of Personality and Social Psychology, 16,* 265–273.

Rubin, Z. (1973). *Liking and loving: An invitation to social psychology.* New York: Holt, Rinehart and Winston.

Rubin, Z. (1975). Disclosing oneself to a stranger: Reciprocity and its limits. *Journal of Experimental Social Psychology, 11,* 233–260.

Rubin, Z., Hill, C. T., Peplau, L. A., & Dunkel-Schetter, C. (1980). Self-disclosure in dating couples: Sex roles and the ethic of openness. *Journal of Marriage and the Family, 42,* 305–317.

Rubin, Z., Peplau, L. A., & Hill, C. T. (1981). Loving and leaving: Sex differences in romantic attachments. *Sex Roles, 7*(9), 821–835.

Ruble, D. N., & Stangor, C. (1986). Stalking the elusive schema: Insights from developmental and social-psychological analyses of gender schemas. *Social Cognition, 4,* 227–261.

Runciman, W. G. (1966). *Relative deprivation and social justice.* Berkeley: University of California Press.

Rusbult, C. E. (1980). Commitment and satisfaction in romantic associations: A test of the investment model. *Journal of Experimental Social Psychology, 16,* 172–186.

Rusbult, C. E. (1983). A longitudinal test of the investment model: The development (and deterioration) of satisfaction and commitment in heterosexual involvements. *Journal of Personality and Social Psychology, 45,* 101–117.

Rusbult, C. E. (1987). Responses to dissatisfaction in close relationships: The exit-voice-loyalty-neglect model. In D. Perlman & S. Duck (Eds.), *Intimate relationships: Development, dynamics and deterioration* (pp. 209–237). Beverly Hills, CA: Sage Publications.

Rusbult, C. E., Zembrodt, I. M., & Gunn, L. K. (1982). Exit, voice, loyalty, and neglect: Responses to dissatisfaction in romantic involvements. *Journal of Personality and Social Psychology, 43,* 1230–1242.

Rusbult, C. E., Farrell, D., Rogers, G., & Mainous, A. G. (1988). Impact of exchange variables on exit, voice, loyalty, and neglect: An integrative model of responses to declining job satisfaction. *Academy of Management Journal, 31,* 599–627.

Rush, M. C., & Russell, J. E. A. (1988). Leader prototypes and prototype-contingent consensus in leader behavior descriptions. *Journal of Experimental Social Psychology, 24,* 88–104.

Rushton, J. P., & Campbell, A. C. (1977). Modeling, vicarious reinforcement and extraversion on blood donating in adults: Immediate and long-term effects. *European Journal of Social Psychology, 7,* 297–306.

Rushton, J. P., & Teachman, G. (1978). The effects of positive reinforcement, attributions, and punishment on model-induced altruism in children. *Personality and Psychology Bulletin, 4,* 322–325.

Rushton, J. P., Fulker, D. W., Neale, M. C., Nias, D. K. B., & Eysenck, H. J. (1986). Altruism and aggression: The heritability of individual differences. *Journal of Personality and Social Psychology, 50,* 1192–1198.

Russell, J. A., & Bullock, M. (1985). Multidimensional scaling of emotional facial expressions: Similarity from preschoolers to adults. *Journal of Personality and Social Psychology, 48,* 1290–1298.

Ruvolo, A., & Markus, H. (1988, August). *Possible selves and motivation.* Paper presented to the American Psychological Association annual meetings, Washington, DC.

Ryan, W. (1971). *Blaming the victim.* New York: Vintage.

Saegert, S., Swap, W., & Zajonc, R. B. (1973). Exposure, context, and interpersonal attraction. *Journal of Personality and Social Psychology, 25,* 234–252.

Safer, M. A., Tharps, Q. J., Jackson, T. C., & Leventhal, H. (1979). Determinants of three stages of delay in seeking care at a medical care clinic. *Medical Care, 17,* 11–29.

Sagar, H., & Schofield, J. W. (1980). Racial and behavioral cues in black and white children's perceptions of ambiguously aggressive acts. *Journal of Personality and Social Psychology, 39,* 590–598.

Salancik, G. R., & Conway, M. (1975). Attitude inferences from salient and relevant cognitive content about behavior. *Journal of Personality and Social Psychology, 32,* 829–840.

Sampson, E. E. (1977). Psychology and the American ideal. *Journal of Personality and Social Psychology, 35,* 767–782.

Sande, G. N., Ellard, J. H., & Ross, M. (1986). Effect of arbitrarily assigned status labels on self-perceptions and social perceptions: The mere position effect. *Journal of Personality and Social Psychology, 50,* 684–689.

Sande, G. N., Goethals, G. R., & Radloff, C. E. (1988). Perceiving one's own traits and others': The multifaceted self. *Journal of Personality and Social Psychology, 54,* 13–20.

Sapiro, V. (1983). *The political integration of women.* Urbana: University of Illinois Press.

Sarason, I. G., Johnson, J. H., & Siegel, J. M. (1978). Assessing the impact of life changes: Development of the Life Experience Survey. *Journal of Consulting and Clinical Psychology, 46,* 932–946.

Sarnoff, I., & Zimbardo, P. G. (1961). Anxiety, fear and social affiliation. *Journal of Abnormal and Social Psychology, 62,* 356–363.

Satow, K. L. (1975). Social approval and helping. *Journal of Experimental Social Psychology, 11,* 501–509.

Scanzoni, L. D., & Scanzoni, J. (1981). *Men, women and change,* 2nd ed. New York: McGraw-Hill.

Scarpaci, J. L. (1988). Help-seeking behavior, use, and satisfaction among frequent primary care users in Santiago de Chile. *Journal of Health and Social Behavior, 29,* 199–213.

Schachter, S. (1951). Deviation, rejection, and communication. *Journal of Abnormal and Social Psychology, 46,* 190–207.

Schachter, S. (1959). *The psychology of affiliation.* Stanford, CA: Stanford University Press.

Schachter, S. (1964). The interaction of cognitive and physiological determinants of emotional state. In L. Berkowitz (Ed.), *Advances in experimental social psychology* (pp. 49–80). New York: Academic Press.

Schachter, S., & Singer, J. E. (1962). Cognitive, social and physiological determinants of emotional state. *Psychological Review, 69,* 379–399.

Schain, W. S. (1976). Psychological issues in counseling mastectomy patients. *Counseling Psychologist, 6,* 45–49.

Schaller, M., & Cialdini, R. B. (1988). The economics of empathic helping: Support for a mood management motive. *Journal of Experimental Social Psychology, 24,* 163–181.

Schaufeli, W. B. (1988). Perceiving the causes of employment: An evaluation of the causal dimensions in a real-life situation. *Journal of Personality and Social Psychology, 54,* 347–356.

Scheier, M. F., & Carver, C. S. (1980). Private and public self-attention, resistance to change, and dissonance reduction. *Journal of Personality and Social Psychology, 39,* 390–405.

Scher, S. J., & Cooper, J. (1989). Motivational basis of dissonance: The singular role of behavioral consequences. *Journal of Personality and Social Psychology, 56,* 899–906.

Schifter, D. E., & Ajzen, I. (1985). Intention, perceived control, and weight loss: An application of the theory of planned behavior. *Journal of Personality and Social Psychology, 49,* 843–851.

Schlegel, R. P., Crawford, C. A., & Sanborn, M. D. (1977). Correspondence and mediational properties of the Fishbein model: An application to adolescent alcohol use. *Journal of Experimental Social Psychology, 13,* 421–430.

Schlenker, B. R. (1980). *Impression management: The self-concept, social identity, and interpersonal relations.* Monterey, CA: Brooks/Cole.

Schlenker, B. R. (1986). Self-identification: Toward an integration of the private and public self. In R. Baumeister (Ed.), *Public self and private self* (pp. 21–62). New York: Springer-Verlag.

Schmidt, G., & Weiner, B. (1988). An attribution-affect-action theory of behavior: Replications of judgments of help-giving. *Personality and Social Psychology Bulletin, 14,* 610–621.

Schmitt, D. R., & Marwell, G. (1972). Withdrawal and reward reallocation as responses to inequity. *Journal of Experimental Social Psychology, 8,* 207–221.

Schoen, R., & Wooldredge, J. (1989). Marriage choices in North Carolina and Virginia, 1969–71 and 1979–81. *Journal of Marriage and the Family, 51,* 465–481.

Schoenrade, P. A., Batson, C. D., Brandt, J. R., & Loud, R. E. (1986). Attachment, accountability, and motivation to benefit another not in distress. *Journal of Personality and Social Psychology, 51*(3), 557–563.

Schneider, D. J. (1973). Implicit personality theory: A review. *Psychological Bulletin, 79,* 294–309.

Schofield, J. (1978). School desegregation and intergroup relations. In D. Bar-Tal & L. Saxe (Eds.), *Social psychology of education: Theory and research.* New York: Wiley.

Schopler, J., & Stockdale, J. E. (1977). An interference analysis of crowding. *Journal of Environmental Psychology and Nonverbal Behavior, 1,* 81–88.

Schuman, H., & Johnson, M. P. (1976). Attitudes and behavior. *Annual Review of Sociology, 2,* 161–207.

Schuman, H., Steeh, C., & Bobo, L. (1985). *Racial attitudes in America: Trends and interpretation.* Cambridge, MA: Harvard University Press.

Schwartz, B., & Barsky, S. (1977). The home advantage. *Social Forces, 55,* 641–661.

Schwartz, J. C., & Shaver, P. (1987). Emotions and emotion knowledge in interpersonal relations. In W. Jones & D. Perlman (Eds.), *Perspectives in interpersonal behavior and relationships* (Vol. 1). Greenwich, CT: JAI Press.

Schwartz, S. H. (1977). Normative influences on altruism. In L. Berkowitz (Ed.), *Advances in experimental social psychology* (Vol. 10, pp. 197–241). New York: Academic Press.

Schwartz, S. H. (1978). Temporal instability as a moderator

of the attitude-behavior relationship. *Journal of Personality and Social Psychology, 36,* 715–724.

Schwartz, S. H., & Gottlieb, A. (1980). Bystander anonymity and reactions to emergencies. *Journal of Personality and Social Psychology, 39,* 418–430.

Schwarz, N., & Clore, G. L. (1983). Mood, misattribution, and judgments of well-being: Informative and directive functions of affective states. *Journal of Personality and Social Psychology, 45,* 513–523.

Schwarz, N., Strack, F., Hilton, D., & Naderer, G. (in press). Base-rates, representativeness, and the logic of conversation. *Social Cognition.*

Scott, J. E., & Cuvelier, S. J. (1987). Violence in *Playboy* magazine: A longitudinal analysis. *Archives of Sexual Behavior, 16,* 279–288.

Sears, D. O. (1982). *Positivity bias in evaluation of public figures.* Paper presented at the annual meetings of the American Political Science Association, Denver, CO.

Sears, D. O. (1983). The person-positivity bias. *Journal of Personality and Social Psychology, 44,* 233–250.

Sears, D. O. (1986). College sophomores in the laboratory: Influences of a narrow database on social psychology's view of human nature. *Journal of Personality and Social Psychology, 51,* 515–530.

Sears, D. O. (1988). Symbolic racism. In P. Katz & D. Taylor (Eds.), *Eliminating racism: Profiles in controversy* (pp. 53–84). New York: Plenum.

Sears, D. O. (1989). Whither political socialization research? The question of persistence. In O. Ichilov (Ed.), *Political socialization, citizenship education, and democracy* (pp. 69–97). New York: Teachers College Press.

Sears, D. O., & Allen, H. M., Jr. (1984). The trajectory of local desegregation controversies and whites' opposition to busing. In N. Miller & M. Brewer (Eds.), *Groups in contact: The psychology of desegregation* (pp. 123–151). New York: Academic Press.

Sears, D. O., & Chaffee, S. H. (1979). Uses and effects of the 1976 debates: An overview of empirical studies. In S. Kraus (Ed.), *The great debates, 1976: Ford vs. Carter* (pp. 223–261). Bloomington: Indiana University Press.

Sears, D. O., & Citrin, J. (1985). *Tax revolt: Something for nothing in California,* enlarged ed. Cambridge, MA: Harvard University Press.

Sears, D. O., Citrin, J., & Kosterman, R. (1987). Jesse Jackson and the Southern white electorate in 1984. In L. W. Moreland, R. P. Steed, & T. A. Baker (Eds.), *Blacks in Southern politics* (pp. 209–225). New York: Praeger.

Sears, D. O., & Huddy, L. (1989). Linguistic conflict as symbolic politics: The role of symbolic meaning. Unpublished manuscript, Department of Psychology, University of California, Los Angeles.

Sears, D. O., & Kinder, D. R. (1985). Whites' opposition to busing: On conceptualizing and operationalizing group conflict. *Journal of Personality and Social Psychology, 48,* 1141–1147.

Sears, D. O., & McConahay, J. B. (1973). *The politics of violence: The new urban blacks and the Watts riot.* Boston: Houghton Mifflin. Reprinted by University Press of America, 1981.

Sears, D. O., & Whitney, R. E. (1973). Political persuasion. In I. deS. Pool, W. Schramm, F. W. Frey, N. Maccoby, & E. B. Parker (Eds.), *Handbook of communication* (pp. 253–289). Chicago: Rand McNally.

Sears, R. R., Maccoby, E., & Levin, H. (1957). *Patterns of child rearing.* Evanston, IL: Row, Peterson.

Sears, R. R., Whiting, J. W. M., Nowlis, V., & Sears, P. S. (1953). Some child-rearing antecedents of aggression and dependency in young children. *Genetic Psychological Monographs, 47,* 135–236.

Segal, M. W. (1974). Alphabet and attraction: An unobtrusive measure of the effect of propinquity in a field setting. *Journal of Personality and Social Psychology, 30,* 654–657.

Seligman, C., Bush, M., & Kirsch, K. (1975). Relationship between compliance in the foot-in-the-door paradigm and size of first request. *Journal of Personality and Social Psychology, 33,* 517–520.

Selye, H. (1956). *The stress of life.* New York: McGraw-Hill.

Selye, H. (1976). *Stress in health and disease.* Woburn, MA: Butterworth.

Shakin, M., Shakin, D., & Sternglanz, S. H. (1985). Infant clothing: Sex labeling for strangers. *Sex Roles, 12,* 955–964.

Shapiro, P. N., & Penrod, S. (1986). Meta-analysis of facial identification studies. *Psychological Bulletin, 100,* 139–156.

Shaver, P. (1986, August 26). *Being lonely, falling in love: Perspectives from attachment theory.* Invited address presented at the annual meeting of the American Psychological Association, Washington, D.C.

Shaver, P., & Freedman, J. L. (1976, August). Happiness. *Psychology Today.*

Shaver, P., & Klinnert, M. D. (1982). Schachter's theories of affiliation and emotion: Implications of developmental research. In L. Wheeler (Ed.), *Review of personality and social psychology* (Vol. 3). Beverly Hills, CA: Sage Publications.

Shaver, P., & Rubenstein, C. (1980). Childhood attachment experience and adult loneliness. In L. Wheeler (Ed.), *Review of personality and social psychology* (Vol. 1, pp. 42–73). Beverly Hills, CA: Sage Publications.

Shaver, P., Hazan, C., & Bradshaw, D. (1988). Love as attachment: The integration of three behavioral systems. In R. J. Sternberg & M. Barnes (Eds.), *Anatomy of love* (pp. 69–99). New Haven, CT: Yale University Press.

Shaw, M. E. (1981). *Group dynamics: The psychology of small group behavior,* 3rd ed. New York: McGraw-Hill.

Sheatsley, P. B., & Feldman, J. J. (1965). A national survey of public reactions and behavior. In B. S. Greenberg & E. B. Parker (Eds.), *The Kennedy assassination and the American public* (pp. 149–177). Stanford, CA: Stanford University Press.

Shelton, J. L., & Levy, R. L. (1981). *Behavioral assignments and treatment compliance: A handbook of clinical strategies.* Champaign, IL: Research Press.

Shepperd, J. A., & Arkin, R. M. (1989). Determinants of self-handicapping: Task importance and the effects of preexisting handicaps on self-generated handicaps. *Personality and Social Psychology Bulletin, 15,* 101–112.

Shepperd, J. A., & Wright, R. A. (1989). Individual contributions to a collective effort: An incentive analysis. *Personality and Social Psychology Bulletin, 15,* 141–149.

Shepperd, J. A., & Strathman, A. J. (1989). Attractiveness and height: The role of stature in dating preference, frequency of dating, and perceptions of attractiveness. *Personality and Social Psychology Bulletin, 15,* 617–627.

Sherif, M. (1935). An experimental study of stereotypes. *Journal of Abnormal and Social Psychology, 29,* 371–375.

Sherif, M., & Cantril, H. (1947). *The psychology of ego-involvements.* New York: Wiley.

Sherif, M., Harvey, O. J., White, B. J., Hood, W. R., & Sherif, C. W. (1961). *Intergroup conflict and cooperation: The robber's cave experiment.* Norman: University of Oklahoma Press.

Sherman, S. J., Judd, C. M., & Park, B. (1989). Social cognition. *Annual Review of Psychology, 40,* 281–336.

Sherman, S. J., Presson, C. C., Chassin, L., Besenberg, M., Corty, E., & Olshavsky, R. W. (1982). Smoking intentions in adolescents: Direct experience and predictability. *Personality and Social Psychology Bulletin, 8,* 376–383.

Sherman, S. J., Presson, C. C., Chassin, L., Corty, E., & Olshavsky, R. (1983). The false consensus effect in estimates of smoking prevalence: Underlying mechanisms. *Personality and Social Psychology Bulletin, 9,* 197–208.

Sherrod, D. R. (1974). Crowding, perceived control and behavioral aftereffects. *Journal of Applied Social Psychology, 4,* 171–186.

Sherrod, D. R., & Downs, R. (1974). Environmental determinants of altruism: The effects of stimulus overload and perceived control on helping. *Journal of Experimental Social Psychology, 10,* 468–479.

Sherrod, D. R., Hage, J. N., Halpern, P. L., & Moore, B. S. (1977). Effects of personal causation and perceived control on responses to an aversive environment: The more control, the better. *Journal of Experimental Social Psychology, 13,* 14–27.

Shinar, E. H. (1975). Sexual stereotypes of occupations. *Journal of Vocational Behavior, 7,* 99–110.

Shotland, R. L., & Huston, T. L. (1979). Emergencies: What are they and do they influence bystanders to intervene? *Journal of Personality and Social Psychology, 37*(10), 1822–1834.

Shotland, R. L., & Straw, M. K. (1976). Bystander response to an assault: When a man attacks a woman. *Journal of Personality and Social Psychology, 34,* 990–999.

Siebenaler, J. B., & Caldwell, D. K. (1956). Cooperation among adult dolphins. *Journal of Mammology, 37*, 126–128.

Siegel, D., Grady, D., Browner, W. S., & Hulley, S. B. (1988). Risk factors modification after myocardial infarction. *Annals of Internal Medicine, 109*, 213–218.

Siegel, J. M. (1986). The multidimensional anger inventory. *Journal of Personality and Social Psychology, 51*, 191–200.

Sigall, H., & Ostrove, N. (1975). Beautiful but dangerous: Effects of offender attractiveness and nature of the crime on juridic judgment. *Journal of Personality and Social Psychology, 31*, 410–414.

Silver, R. L., Boon, C., & Stones, M. (1983). Searching for meaning in misfortune: Making sense of incest. *Journal of Social Issues, 39*, 81–102.

Simmel, G. (1903). *Sociology of Georg Simmel.* New York: Macmillan, 1950 (translation of German edition).

Simon, H. A. (1985). Human nature in politics: The dialogue of psychology with political science. *American political science review, 79*, 293–304.

Simonton, D. K. (1981). Presidential greatness and performance: Can we predict leadership in the White House? *Journal of Personality, 49*, 306–323.

Simonton, D. K. (1985). The vice-presidential succession effect: Individual or situational basis? *Political Behavior, 7*, 79–99.

Simonton, D. K. (1986). Presidential greatness: The historical consensus and its psychological significance. *Political Psychology, 7*, 259–284.

Simpson, J. A., Campbell, B., & Berscheid, E. (1986). The association between romantic love and marriage: Kephart (1967) twice revisited. *Personality and Social Psychology Bulletin, 12*, 363–372.

Sistrunk, F., & McDavid, J. W. (1971). Sex variable in conformity behavior. *Journal of Personality and Social Psychology, 17*, 200–207.

Sivacek, J., & Crano, W. D. (1982). Vested interest as a moderator of attitude-behavior consistency. *Journal of Personality and Social Psychology, 43*, 210–221.

Skinner, P. H., & Shelton, R. L. (1985). *Speech, language, and hearing: Normal processes and disorders*, 2nd ed. New York: Wiley.

Skolnick, P. (1977). Helping as a function of time of day, location, and sex of victim. *Journal of Social Psychology, 102*, 61–62.

Skov, R. B., & Sherman, S. J. (1986). Information-gathering processes: Diagnosticity, hypothesis-confirmatory strategies, and perceived hypothesis confirmation. *Journal of Experimental Social Psychology, 22*, 93–121.

Skrypnek, B. J., & Snyder, M. (1982). On the self-perpetuating nature of stereotypes about women and men. *Journal of Experimental Social Psychology, 18*, 277–291.

Slavin, R. (1983). When does cooperative learning increase student achievement? *Psychological Bulletin, 94*, 429–443.

Slivken, K. E., & Buss, A. H. (1984). Misattribution and speech anxiety. *Journal of Personality and Social Psychology, 47*, 396–402.

Slusher, M. P., & Anderson, C. A. (1987). When reality monitoring fails: The role of imagination in stereotype maintenance. *Journal of Personality and Social Psychology, 52*, 653–662.

Slochower, J., Wein, L., White, J., Firstenberg, S., & Di-Guilio, J. (1980). Severe physical handicaps and helping behavior. *Journal of Social Psychology, 112*, 313–314.

Smeaton, G., & Byrne, D. (1987). The effects of R-rated violence and erotica, individual differences, and victim characteristics on acquaintance rape proclivity. *Journal of Research on Personality, 21*, 171–184.

Smith, E. R., & Lerner, M. (1986). Development of automatism of social judgments. *Journal of Personality and Social Psychology, 50*, 246–259.

Smith, M. D., & Hand, C. (1987). The pornographic/aggression linkage: results from a field study. *Deviant Behavior, 8*, 389–399.

Smith, S. S., & Richardson, D. (1983). Amelioration of deception and harm in psychological research: The important role of debriefing. *Journal of Personality and Social Psychology, 44*, 1075–1082.

Smith, T. W. (1984). The polls: Gender and attitudes toward violence. *Public Opinion Quarterly, 48*, 384–396.

Sniderman, P. M. (1975). *Personality and democratic politics.* Berkeley: University of California Press.

Sniderman, P. M., & Brody, R. A. (1977). Coping: The ethic of self-reliance. *American Journal of Political Science, 21*, 501–522.

Snodgrass, S. E. (1985). Women's intuition: The effect of subordinate role on interpersonal sensitivity. *Journal of Personality and Social Psychology, 49*, 146–155.

Snyder, C. R., & Fromkin, H. L. (1980). *Uniqueness: The human pursuit of difference.* New York: Plenum.

Snyder, C. R., & Higgins, R. L. (1988). Excuses: Their effective role in the negotiation of reality. *Psychological Bulletin, 104*, 23–35.

Snyder, C. R., Lassegard, M. A., & Ford, C. E. (1986). Distancing after group success and failure: Basking in reflected glory and cutting off reflected failure. *Journal of Personality and Social Psychology, 51*(2), 382–388.

Snyder, M. (1987). *Public appearances/private realities: The psychology of self-monitoring.* New York: Freeman.

Snyder, M., Berscheid, E., & Glick, R. P. (1985). Focusing on the exterior and the interior: Two investigations of the initiation of personal relationships. *Journal of Personality and Social Psychology, 48*(6), 1427–1439.

Snyder, M., & Gangestad, S. (1981). Hypothesis-testing processes. In J. H. Harvey, W. Ickes, & R. F. Kidd (Eds.), *New directions in attribution research* (Vol. 3, pp. 171–198). Hillsdale, NJ: Erlbaum.

Snyder, M., & Gangestad, S. (1986). On the nature of

self-monitoring: Matters of assessment, matters of validity. *Journal of Personality and Social Psychology, 51,* 125–139.

Snyder, M., & Swann, W. B., Jr. (1976). When actions reflect attitudes: The politics of impression management. *Journal of Personality and Social Psychology, 34,* 1034–1042.

Snyder, M., & Swann, W. B., Jr. (1978). Hypothesis-testing processes in social interaction. *Journal of Personality and Social Psychology, 36,* 1202–1212.

Snyder, M., Tanke, E. D., & Berscheid, E. (1977). Social perception and interpersonal behavior: On the self-fulfilling nature of social stereotypes. *Journal of Personality and Social Psychology, 35,* 656–666.

Sogin, S. R., & Pallak, M. S. (1976). Bad decisions, responsibility, and attitude change: Effects of volition, foreseeability, and locus of causality of negative consequences. *Journal of Personality and Social Psychology, 33,* 300–306.

Solano, C. H., Batten, P. G., & Parish, E. A. (1982). Loneliness and patterns of self-disclosure. *Journal of Personality and Social Psychology, 43,* 524–531.

Sommer, R. (1969). *Personal space: The behavioral basis of design.* Englewood Cliffs, NJ: Prentice-Hall.

Sommer, R., & Olsen, H. (1980). The soft classroom. *Environment and Behavior, 12*(1), 3–16.

South, S. J. (1988). Sex ratios, economic power, and women's roles: A theoretical extension and empirical test. *Journal of Marriage and the Family, 50*(1), 19–31.

Spears, R., van der Pligt, J., & Eiser, J. R. (1985). Illusory correlation in the perception of group attitudes. *Journal of Personality and Social Psychology, 48,* 863–875.

Spence, J. T. (1985). Gender identity and its implications for the concepts of masculinity and femininity. In T. B. Sonderegger (Ed.), *Nebraska Symposium on Motivation: Psychology and gender* (pp. 59–95). Lincoln: University of Nebraska Press.

Spence, J. T., & Helmreich, R. L. (1978). *Masculinity and femininity: The psychological dimensions, correlates, and antecedents.* Austin: University of Texas Press.

Spence, J. T., & Helmreich, R. L. (1980). Masculine instrumentality and feminine expressiveness: Their relationships with sex role attitudes and behaviors. *Psychology of Women Quarterly, 5*(2), 147–163.

Sprafkin, J. N., Liebert, R. M., & Poulos, R. W. (1975). Effects of prosocial televised example on children's helping. *Journal of Experimental Child Psychology, 20,* 119–126.

Sprecher, S. (1986). The relationship between inequity and emotions in close relationships. *Social Psychology Quarterly, 49,* 309–321.

Sprecher, S. (1988). Investment model, equity, and social support determinants of relationship commitment. *Social Psychology Quarterly, 51,* 318–328.

Srole, L. (1972). Urbanization and mental health: Some reformulations. *American Scientist, 60,* 576–583.

Srull, T. K., Lichtenstein, M., & Rothbart, M. (1985). Associative storage and retrieval processes in person memory. *Journal of Experimental Psychology: Learning, Memory, and Cognition, 11,* 316–345.

Srull, T. K., & Wyer, R. S., Jr. (1979). The role of category accessibility in the interpretation of information about persons: Some determinants and implications. *Journal of Personality and Social Psychology, 37,* 1660–1672.

Stagner, R. (1967). *Psychological aspects of international conflict.* Belmont, CA: Brooks/Cole Publishing Co.

Stasser, G., & Titus, W. (1985). Pooling of unshared information in group decision making: Biased information sampling during discussion. *Journal of Personality and Social Psychology, 48,* 1467–1478.

Steblay, N. M. (1987). Helping behavior in rural and urban environments: A meta-analysis. *Psychological Bulletin, 102,* 346–356.

Steele, C. M., & Southwick, L. (1985). Alcohol and social behavior. I: The psychology of drunken excess. *Journal of Personality and Social Psychology, 48,* 18–34.

Steele, D. V., Gotmann, M., Leventhal, H., & Easterling, D. (1983). Symptoms and attributions as determinants of health behavior. Unpublished manuscript, University of Wisconsin, Madison.

Stein, A. H., & Friedrich, L. K. (1972). Television content and young children's behavior. In J. P. Murray, E. A. Rubinstein, & G. A. Comstock (Eds.), *Television and social behavior: Vol. 2. Television and social learning.* Washington, D.C.: U.S. Government Printing Office.

Stein, D. D., Hardyck, J. A., & Smith, M. B. (1965). Race and belief: An open and shut case. *Journal of Personality and Social Psychology, 1,* 281–289.

Steiner, I. D. (1972). *Group process and productivity.* New York: Academic Press.

Stephan, F. F., & Mishler, E. G. (1952). The distribution of participation in small groups: An exponential approximation. *American Sociological Review, 17,* 598–608.

Stephan, W. G. (1985). Intergroup relations. In G. Lindzey & E. Aronson (Eds.), *Handbook of social psychology,* 3rd ed. (Vol. 2, pp. 599–658). New York: Random House.

Stephan, W. G., & Rosenfield, D. (1978). Effects of desegregation on racial attitudes. *Journal of Personality and Social Psychology, 36,* 795–804.

Stern, M., & Karraker, K. H. (1989). Sex stereotyping of infants: A review of gender labeling studies. *Sex Roles, 20,* 501–522.

Sternberg, R. J. (1986). A triangular theory of love. *Psychological Review, 93,* 119–135.

Sternberg, R. J., Conway, B. E., Ketron, J. L., & Bernstein, M. (1981). People's conceptions of intelligence. *Journal of Personality and Social Psychology, 41,* 37–55.

Stokols, D. (1976). The experience of crowding in primary and secondary environments. *Environment and Behavior, 8,* 49–86.

Stokols, D., & Altman, I. (Eds.). (1987). *Handbook of environmental psychology.* New York: Wiley.

Storms, M. D. (1973). Videotape and the attribution process: Reversing actors' and observers' points of view. *Journal of Personality and Social Psychology, 27,* 165–175.

Stouffer, S. A., Suchman, E. A., DeVinney, L. C., Star, S. A., & Williams, R. M., Jr. (1949). *The American soldier: Adjustment during army life.* New York: Wiley.

Straus, M. A., & Gelles, R. J. (1986). Societal change and change in family violence from 1975 to 1985 as revealed by two national surveys. *Journal of Marriage and the Family, 48,* 465–479.

Straus, M. A., Gelles, R. J., & Steinmetz, S. K. (1981). *Behind closed doors: Violence in the American family.* Garden City, NY: Doubleday/Anchor.

Strayer, F. F., Wareing, S., & Rushton, J. P. (1979). Social constraints on naturally occurring preschool altruism. *Ethology and Sociobiology, 1,* 3–11.

Suedfeld, P. (1982). Aloneness as a healing experience. In L. A. Peplau & D. Perlman (Eds.), *Loneliness: A sourcebook of current theory, research and therapy* (pp. 54–69). New York: Wiley-Interscience.

Suedfeld, P., & Rank, D. (1976). Revolutionary leaders: Long-term success as a function of changes in conceptual complexity. *Journal of Personality and Social Psychology, 34,* 169–178.

Suedfeld, P., & Tetlock, P. E. (1977). Integrative complexity of communications in international crises. *Journal of Conflict Resolution, 21,* 169–184.

Sullivan, J. L., Piereson, J., & Marcus, G. E. (1982). *Political tolerance and American democracy.* Chicago: University of Chicago Press.

Suls, J., & Fletcher, B. (1985). The relative efficacy of avoidant and nonavoidant coping strategies: A Meta-analysis. *Health Psychology, 4,* 249–288.

Suls, J., & Mullen, B. (1981). Life change in psychological distress: The role of perceived control and desirability. *Journal of Applied Social Psychology, 11,* 379–389.

Sundstrom, E., & Sundstrom, M. G. (1977). Personal space invasions: What happens when the invader asks permission? *Environmental Psychology and Nonverbal Behavior, 2,* 76–82.

Surgeon General's Scientific Advisory Committee. (1972). *Television and growing up: The impact of televised violence: Report to the Surgeon General.* U.S. Public Health Service, Dept. of Health, Education, and Welfare Publication N. HSM 72-9090. Rockville, MD: National Institute of Mental Health.

Sutaria, S. D. (1985). *Specific learning disabilities: Nature and needs.* Springfield, IL: Charles C Thomas.

Swann, W. B., Jr. (1984). Quest for accuracy in person perception: A matter of pragmatics. *Psychological Review, 91,* 457–477.

Swann, W. B., Jr., & Ely, R. J. (1984). A battle of wills: Self-verification versus behavioral confirmation. *Journal of Personality and Social Psychology, 46,* 1287–1302.

Swann, W. B., Jr., Giulano, T., & Wegner, D. M. (1982). Where leading questions can lead: The power of conjecture in social interaction. *Journal of Personality and Social Psychology, 42,* 1025–1035.

Swann, W. B., Jr., & Stephenson, B. (1981). Curiosity and control: On the determinants of the search for social knowledge. *Journal of Personality and Social Psychology, 40,* 635–642.

Sweeney, P. D., Anderson, K., & Bailey, S. (1986). Attributional style in depression: A meta-analytic review. *Journal of Personality and Social Psychology, 50,* 974–991.

Swensen, C. H. (1972). The behavior of love. In H. A. Otto (Ed.), *Love today* (pp. 86–101). New York: Dell.

Swim, J., Borgida, E., Maruyama, G., & Myers, D. G. (1989). Joan McKay versus John McKay: Do gender stereotypes bias evaluations? *Psychological Bulletin, 105,* 409–429.

Symons, D. (1979). *The evolution of human sexuality.* New York: Oxford University Press.

Tajfel, H. (Ed.). (1982). *Social identity and intergroup relations.* Cambridge, MA: Cambridge University Press.

Tajfel, H., Billig, M. G., Bundy, R. P., & Flament, C. (1971). Social categorization and intergroup behavior. *European Journal of Social Psychology, 1,* 149–178.

Tajfel, H., & Turner, J. C. (1986). The social identity theory of intergroup behavior. In S. Worchel & W. G. Austin (Eds.), *Psychology of Intergroup Relations* (pp. 7–24). Chicago: Nelson-Hall.

Tanford, S., & Penrod, S. (1984). Social influence model: A formal integration of research on majority and minority influence processes. *Psychological Bulletin, 95,* 189–225.

Tarde, G. (1903). *The laws of imitation.* New York: Holt, Rinehart and Winston.

Taylor, D. A., & Katz, P. A. (1988). Conclusion. In P. A. Katz & D. A. Taylor (Eds.), *Eliminating racism: Profiles in controversy* (pp. 359–369). New York: Plenum.

Taylor, D. G., Sheatsley, P. B., & Greeley, A. M. (1978). Attitudes toward racial integration. *Scientific American, 238,* 42–49.

Taylor, D. W., Berry, P. C., & Block, C. H. (1958). Does group participation when using brainstorming facilitate or inhibit creative thinking? *Administrative Science Quarterly, 2,* 23–47.

Taylor, J., & Riess, M. (1989). "Self-serving" attributions to valenced causal factors: A field experiment. *Personality and Social Psychology Bulletin, 15,* 337–348.

Taylor, S., Vardaris, R., Rawitch, A., Gammon, C., Ranston, J., & Lubetkin, A. (1976). The effects of alcohol and delta-9-tetrahydrocannabinol on human physical aggression. *Aggressive Behavior, 2,* 153–161.

Taylor, S. E. (1975). On inferring one's attitudes from one's behavior: Some delimiting conditions. *Journal of Personality and Social Psychology, 31*, 126–131.

Taylor, S. E. (1979). Hospital patient behavior: Reactance, helplessness, or control? *Journal of Social Issues, 35*, 156–184.

Taylor, S. E. (1981a). The interface of cognitive and social psychology. In J. H. Harvey (Ed.), *Cognition, social behavior, and the environment* (pp. 189–212). Hillsdale, NJ: Erlbaum.

Taylor, S. E. (1981b). A categorization approach to stereotyping. In D. L. Hamilton (Ed.), *Cognitive processes in stereotyping and intergroup behavior* (pp. 83–114). Hillsdale, NJ: Erlbaum.

Taylor, S. E. (1981c). The impact of health institutions on recipients of services. In A. Johnson, O. Grusky, & B. Raven (Eds.), *Contemporary health services: A social science perspective* (pp. 103–137). Boston: Auburn House.

Taylor, S. E. (1983). Adjustment to threatening events: A theory of cognitive adaptation. *American Psychologist, 38*, 1161–1173.

Taylor, S. E., & Aspinwall, L. G. (in press). *Psychological aspects of chronic illness.* In G. R. VandenBos and P. T. Costa Jr. (Eds.), Washington, DC: American Psychological Association.

Taylor, S. E., & Brown, J. D. (1988). Illusion and well-being: A social psychological perspective on mental health. *Psychological Bulletin, 103*, 193–210.

Taylor, S. E., & Clark, L. F. (1986). Does information improve adjustment to noxious events? In M. J. Saks & L. Saxe (Eds.), *Advances in applied social psychology* (Vol. 3, pp. 1–28). Hillsdale, NJ: Erlbaum.

Taylor, S. E., & Crocker, J. (1981). Schematic bases of social information processing. In E. T. Higgins, C. P. Herman, & M. P. Zanna (Eds.), *Social cognition: The Ontario symposium* (Vol. 1, pp. 89–134). Hillsdale, NJ: Erlbaum.

Taylor, S. E., Crocker, J., Fiske, S. T., Sprinzen, M., & Winkler, J. D. (1979). The generalizability of salience effects. *Journal of Personality and Social Psychology, 37*, 357–368.

Taylor, S. E., & Fiske, S. T. (1975). Point of view and perceptions of causality. *Journal of Personality and Social Psychology, 32*, 439–445.

Taylor, S. E., & Fiske, S. T. (1978). Salience, attention, and attribution: Top of the head phenomena. In L. Berkowitz (Ed.), *Advances in experimental social psychology* (Vol. 11, pp. 249–288). New York: Academic Press.

Taylor, S. E., Fiske, S. T., Close, M., Anderson, C., & Ruderman, A. (1977). *Solo status as a psychological variable: The power of being distinctive.* Unpublished manuscript, Harvard University, Cambridge, MA.

Taylor, S. E., & Koivumaki, J. H. (1976). The perception of self and others: Acquaintanceship, affect, and actor-observer differences. *Journal of Personality and Social Psychology, 33*, 403–408.

Taylor, S. E., Lichtman, R. R., & Wood, J. V. (1984). Attributions, beliefs about control, and adjustment to breast cancer. *Journal of Personality and Social Psychology, 46*, 489–502.

Taylor, S. E., & Lobel, M. (1989). Social comparison activity under threat: Downward evaluation and upward contacts. *Psychological Review, 96*, 569–575.

Taylor, S. E., & Thompson, S. C. (1982). Stalking the elusive "vividness" effect. *Psychological Review, 89*, 155–181.

Taylor, S. P., & Gammon, C. B. (1975). Effects of type and dose of alcohol on human physical aggression. *Journal of Personality and Social Psychology, 32*, 169–175.

Taylor, S. P., Gammon, C. B., & Capasso, D. R. (1976). Aggression as a function of the interaction of alcohol and threat. *Journal of Personality and Social Psychology, 34*, 938–941.

Taylor, S. P., Schmutte, G. T., Leonard, K. E., & Cranston, J. W. (1979). The effects of alcohol and extreme provocation on the use of a highly noxious electrical shock. *Motivation and Emotion, 3*, 73–81.

Taylor, S. P., & Sears, J. D. (1988). The effects of alcohol and persuasive social pressure on human physical aggression. *Aggressive Behavior, 14*, 237–243.

Taynor, J., & Deaux, K. (1973). When women are more deserving than men: Equity, attribution and perceived sex difference. *Journal of Personality and Social Psychology, 28*, 360–367.

Taynor, J., & Deaux, K. (1975). Equity and perceived sex differences: Role of behavior as defined by the task, the mode and the action. *Journal of Personality and Social Psychology, 32*, 381–390.

Tedin, K. L. (1974). The influence of parents on the political attitudes of adolescents. *American Political Science Review, 68*, 1579–1592.

Tenenbaum, G., & Furst, D. M. (1986). Consistency of attributional responses by individuals and groups differing in gender, perceived ability and expectations for success. *British Journal of Social Psychology, 25*, 315–321.

Tesser, A. (1978). Self-generated attitude change. In L. Berkowitz (Ed.), *Advances in experimental social psychology* (Vol. 11). New York: Academic Press.

Tesser, A. (1988). Toward a self-evaluation maintenance model of social behavior. In L. Berkowitz (Ed.), *Advances in experimental social psychology*, (Vol. 21, pp. 181–227). New York: Academic Press.

Tesser, A., & Collins, J. E. (1988). Emotion in social reflection and comparison situations: Intuitive, systematic, and exploratory approaches. *Journal of Personality and Social Psychology, 55*, 695–709.

Tesser, A., & Conlee, M. C. (1975). Some effects of time and thought on attitude polarization. *Journal of Personality and Social Psychology, 31*, 262–270.

Tesser, A., & Paulhus, D. (1983). The definition of self: Private and public self-evaluation maintenance strategies.

Journal of Personality and Social Psychology, 44, 672–682.

Tessler, R. C., & Schwartz, S. H. (1972). Help-seeking, self-esteem, and achievement motivation: An attributional analysis. *Journal of Personality and Social Psychology, 27,* 318–326.

Tetlock, P. E. (1983). Policymakers' images of international conflict. *Journal of Social Issues, 39,* 67–86.

Tetlock, P. E. (1984). Cognitive style and political belief systems in the British House of Commons. *Journal of Personality and Social Psychology, 46,* 365–375.

Tetlock, P. E. (1985). Accountability: A social check on the fundamental attribution error. *Social Psychology Quarterly, 48,* 227–236.

Tetlock. P. E., Bernzweig, J., & Gallant, J. L. (1985). Supreme court decision making: Cognitive style as a predictor of ideological consistency of voting. *Journal of Personality and Social Psychology, 48,* 1227–1239.

Tetlock, P. E., & Boettger, R. (1989). Accountability: A social magnifier of the dilution effect. *Journal of Personality and Social Psychology, 57,* 388–398.

Tetlock, P. E., Hannum, K. A., & Micheletti, P. M. (1984). Stability and change in the complexity of senatorial debate: Testing the cognitive versus rhetorical style hypotheses. *Journal of Personality and Social Psychology, 46,* 979–990.

Tetlock, P. E., Skitka, L., & Boettger, R. (1989). Social and cognitive strategies for coping with accountability, conformity, complexity and bolstering. *Journal of Personality and Social Psychology, 57,* 632–640.

Thibaut, J. W., & Kelley, H. H. (1959). *The social psychology of groups.* New York: Wiley.

Thompson, S. C. (1981). Will it hurt less if I can control it? A complex answer to a simple question. *Psychological Bulletin, 90,* 89–101.

Thompson, S. C., & Kelley, H. H. (1981). Judgments of responsibility for activities in close relationships. *Journal of Personality and Social Psychology, 41,* 469–477.

Thompson, W. C., Cowan, C. L., & Rosenhan, D. L. (1980). Focus of attention mediates the impact of negative affect on altruism. *Journal of Personality and Social Psychology, 38,* 291–300.

Thompson, L., & Walker, A. J. (1989). Gender in families: Women and men in marriage, work, and parenthood. *Journal of Marriage and the Family, 51,* 845–871.

Thoresen, C. E., & Mahoney, M. J. (1974). *Behavioral self-control.* New York: Holt.

Tilker, H. A. (1970). Socially responsible behavior as a function of observer responsibility and victim feedback. *Journal of Personality and Social Psychology, 14,* 95–100.

Tillman, W. S., & Carver, C. S. (1980). Actors' and observers' attributions for success and failure: A comparative test of predictions from Kelley's cube, self-serving bias,

and positivity bias formulations. *Journal of Experimental Social Psychology, 16,* 18–32.

Toi, M., & Batson, C. D. (1982). More evidence that empathy is a source of altruistic motivation. *Journal of Personality and Social Psychology, 43,* 281–292.

Toris, C., & DePaulo, B. M. (1984). Effects of actual deception and suspiciousness of deception on interpersonal perceptions. *Journal of Personality and Social Psychology, 47,* 1063–1073.

Tourangeau, R., & Rasinski, K. A. (1988). Cognitive processes underlying context effects in attitude measurement. *Psychological Bulletin, 103,* 299–314.

Trimble, J. E. (1988). Stereotypical images, American Indians, and prejudice. In P. A. Katz & D. A. Taylor (Eds.), *Eliminating racism: Profiles in controversy* (pp. 181–202). New York: Plenum.

Triplett, N. (1989). The dynamogenic factors in pacemaking and competition. *American Journal of Psychology, 9,* 507–533.

Trivers, R. L. (1971). The evolution of reciprocal altruism. *Quarterly Review of Biology, 46,* 35–57.

Trope, Y. (1986a). Self-enhancement and self-assessment in achievement tasks. *Journal of Personality and Social Psychology, 37,* 1505–1518.

Trope, Y. (1986b). Identification and inferential processes in dispositional attribution. *Psychological Review, 93,* 239–257.

Trope, Y., & Mackie, D. M. (1987). Sensitivity to alternatives in social hypothesis-testing. *Journal of Experimental Social Psychology, 23,* 445–459.

Trzebinski, J., McGlynn, R. P., Gray, G., & Tubbs, D. (1985). The role of categories of an actor's goals in organizing inferences about a person. *Journal of Personality and Social Psychology, 48,* 1387–1397.

Trzebinski, J., & Richards, K. (1986). The role of goal categories in person impression. *Journal of Experimental Social Psychology, 22,* 216–227.

Tucker, L., Hornstein, H. A., Holloway, S., & Sole, K. (1977). The effects of temptation and information about a stranger on helping. *Personality and Social Psychology Bulletin, 3*(3), 416–421.

Tucker, M. B. (1986). Sex ratio imbalance among Los Angeles Afro-Americans. *ISSR Working Papers in the Social Sciences, 24*(4). Los Angeles: Institute for Social Science Research, University of California.

Turk, D. C., & Kerns, R. D. (1985). *Health, illness, and families: A life-span perspective.* New York: Wiley.

Turk, D. C., & Meichenbaum, D. (1989). Adherence to self-care regimens: The patient's perspective. In R. H. Rozensky, J. J. Sweet, & S. M. Tovian (Eds.), *Handbook of clinical psychology in medical settings.* New York: Plenum.

Turk, D. C., Rudy, T. E., & Salovey, P. (1986). Implicit models of illness. *Journal of Behavioral Medicine, 9,* 453–474.

Turner, J. C. (1985). Social categorization and the self-concept: A social cognitive theory of group behavior. In J. E. Lawler (Ed.), *Advances in group processes* (Vol. 2, pp. 77–122). Greenwich, CT: JAI Press.

Turner, J. C., Hogg, M. A., Oakes, P. J., Reicher, S. D., & Wetherell, M. S. (1987). *Rediscovering the social group: A self-categorization theory.* New York: Blackwell.

Turner, R. H. (1962). Role-taking: Process versus conformity. In A. H. Rose (Ed.), *Human behavior and social processes: An interactionist approach.* Boston: Houghton Mifflin.

Tversky, A., & Kahneman, D. (1973). Availability: A heuristic for judging frequency and probability. *Cognitive Psychology, 5,* 207–232.

Tversky, A., & Kahneman, D. (1974). Judgment under uncertainty: Heuristics and biases. *Science, 185,* 1124–1131.

Tybout, A. M., & Scott, C. A. (1983). Availability of well-defined internal knowledge and the attitude formation process: Information aggregation versus self-perception. *Journal of Personality and Social Psychology, 44,* 474–491.

Tyler, T. R., & Devintz, V. (1981). Self-serving bias in the attribution of responsibility: Cognitive versus motivational explanations. *Journal of Experimental Social Psychology, 17,* 408–416.

Tyler, T. R., & Sears, D. O. (1977). Coming to like obnoxious people when we must live with them. *Journal of Personality and Social Psychology, 35,* 200–211.

Ugwuegbu, D. C. E. (1979). Racial and evidential factors in juror attribution of legal responsibility. *Journal of Experimental Social Psychology, 15,* 133–146.

Uzark, K. C., Becker, M. H., Dielman, T. W., & Rocchini, A. P. (1987). Psychosocial predictors of compliance with a weight control intervention for obese children and adolescents. *Journal of Compliance in Health Care, 2,* 167–178.

Valins, S. (1966). Cognitive effects of false heart-rate feedback. *Journal of Personality and Social Psychology, 4,* 400–408.

Vallacher, R. R., & Wegner, D. M. (1987). What do people think they're doing? Action identification and human behavior. *Psychological Review, 94,* 3–15.

Vallacher, R. R., Wegner, D. M., & Frederick, J. (1987). The presentation of self through action identification. *Social Cognition, 5,* 301–322.

Vallacher, R. R., Wegner, D. M., & Somoza, M. P. (1989). That's easy for you to say: Action identification and speech fluency. *Journal of Personality and Social Psychology, 56,* 199–208.

Valois, P., Desharnis, R., & Godin, G. (1988). A comparison of the Fishbein and Ajzen and the Triandis attitudinal models for the prediction of exercise intention and behavior. *Journal of Behavioral Medicine, 11,* 459–472.

Van Heck, G. L., & Dijkstra, P. (1985). The scope and generality of self-other asymmetry in person perception. *European Journal of Social Psychology, 15,* 125–145.

Vanneman, R. D., & Pettigrew, T. F. (1972). Race and relative deprivation in the urban United States. *Race, 13,* 461–486.

Vinsel, A., Brown, B. B., Altman, I., & Foss, C. (1980). Privacy regulation, territorial displays, and effective individual functioning. *Journal of Personality and Social Psychology, 39*(6), 1104–1115.

Von Baeyer, C. L., Sherk, D. L., & Zanna, M. P. (1981). Impression management in the job interview: When the female applicant meets the male (chauvinist) interviewer. *Personality and Social Psychology Bulletin, 7*(1), 45–52.

Wagner, H. L., MacDonald, C. J., & Manstead, A. S. R. (1986). Communication of individual emotions by spontaneous facial expressions. *Journal of Personality and Social Psychology, 50,* 737–743.

Walker, I., & Mann, L. (1987). Unemployment, relative deprivation, and social protest. *Personality and Social Psychology Bulletin, 13,* 275–283.

Wall, J. A., Jr. (1977). Operantly conditioning a negotiator's concession making. *Journal of Experimental Social Psychology, 13,* 431–440.

Wallbott, H. H., & Scherer, K. R. (1986). Cues and channels in emotion recognition. *Journal of Personality and Social Psychology, 51,* 690–699.

Waller, W. (1938). *The family: A dynamic interpretation.* New York: Dryden Press.

Wallerstein, J. S., & Kelly, J. B. (1975). The effects of parental divorce: Experiences of the preschool child. *Journal of the American Academy of Child Psychiatry, 14,* 600–616.

Walster, E., Aronson, E., & Abrahams, D. (1966). On increasing the persuasiveness of a low-prestige communicator. *Journal of Experimental Social Psychology, 2,* 325–343.

Walster, E., & Walster, G. W. (1963). Effects of expecting to be liked on choice of associates. *Journal of Abnormal and Social Psychology, 67,* 402–404.

Walster, E., & Walster, G. W., & Berscheid, E. (1978). *Equity: Theory and research.* Boston: Allyn & Bacon.

Walster, E., & Walster, G. W., & Traupmann, J. (1978). Equity and premarital sex. *Journal of Personality and Social Psychology, 36,* 82–92.

Walster, E., Aronson, E., Abrahams, D., & Rottman, L. (1966). Importance of physical attractiveness in dating behavior. *Journal of Personality and Social Psychology, 4,* 508–516.

Waltz, M. (1986). Marital context and post-infarction quality of life: Is it social support or something more? *Social Science and Medicine, 22,* 791–805.

Ware, J. E., Jr., Davies-Avery, A., & Steward, A. L. (1978). The measurement and meaning of patient satisfaction: A review of the literature. *The Health and Medical Care Services Review, 1,* 1–15.

Warner, M. G., & Fineman, H. (1988, September 26). Bush's media wizard: A down-and-dirty street fighter reshapes the veep. *Newsweek,* 19–20.

Watkins, M. (1978, January 9). Why N.B.A. teams succeed at home. *The New York Times*, p. C-23.

Watson, D. (1982). The actor and the observer: How are their perceptions of causality different? *Psychological Bulletin, 92*, 682–700.

Watson, R. I., Jr. (1973). Investigation into deindividuation using a cross-cultural survey technique. *Journal of Personality and Social Psychology, 25*, 342–345.

Wattenberg, M. P. (1984). *The decline of American political parties, 1952–1980*. Cambridge, MA: Harvard University Press.

Watts, W. A., & Holt, L. E. (1979). Persistence of opinion change induced under conditions of forewarning and distraction. *Journal of Personality and Social Psychology, 37*, 778–789.

Weary, G., Jordan, J. S., & Hill, M. G. (1985). The attributional norm of internality and depressive sensitivity to social information. *Journal of Personality and Social Psychology, 49*, 1283–1293.

Webb, B., Worchel, S., Riechers, L., & Wayne, W. (1986). The influence of categorization on perceptions of crowding. *Personality and Social Psychology Bulletin, 12*(4), 539–546.

Weber, S. J., & Cook, T. D. (1972). Subject effects in laboratory research: An examination of subject roles, demand characteristics, and valid inferences. *Psychological Bulletin, 77*, 273–295.

Weber, R., & Crocker, J. (1983). Cognitive process in the revision of stereotypic beliefs. *Journal of Personality and Social Psychology, 45*, 961–977.

Wegner, D. M., Vallacher, R. R., Kiersted, G. W., & Dizadji, D. (1986). Action identification in the emergence of social behavior. *Social Cognition, 4*, 18–38.

Weigel, R. H., Loomis, J. W., & Soja, M. J. (1980). Race relations on prime time television. *Journal of Personality and Social Psychology, 39*, 884–893.

Weigel, R. H., Vernon, D. T. A., & Tognacci, L. N. (1974). Specificity of the attitude of a determinant of attitude-behavior congruence. *Journal of Personality and Social Psychology, 30*, 724–728.

Weiner, B. (1979). A theory of motivation for some classroom experiences. *Journal of Educational Psychology, 71*, 3–25.

Weiner, B. (1980). A cognitive (attribution)-emotion-action model of motivated behavior: An analysis of judgments of help-giving. *Journal of Personality and Social Psychology, 39*, 186–200.

Weiner, B. (1982). The emotional consequences of causal attributions. In M. S. Clark & S. T. Fiske (Eds.), *Affect and cognition: The 17th annual Carnegie Symposium on Cognition* (pp. 185–210). Hillsdale, NJ: Erlbaum.

Weiner, B. (1986). *An attributional theory of motivation and emotion*. New York: Springer-Verlag.

Weiner, B. (1988). An attributional analysis of changing reactions to persons with AIDS. In R. A. Berk (Ed.), *The social impact of AIDS in the U.S.* (pp. 163–232). Cambridge, MA: Abt Books.

Weiner, B., Amirkhan, J., Folkes, V. S., & Verette, J. A. (1987). An attributional analysis of excuse giving: Studies of a naive theory of emotion. *Journal of Personality and Social Psychology, 52*, 316–324.

Weiner, B., Russell, D., & Lerman, D. (1979). The cognition-emotion process in achievement-related contexts. *Journal of Personality and Social Psychology, 37*, 1211–1220.

Weiss, R. S. (1973). *Loneliness: The experience of emotional and social isolation*. Cambridge, MA: MIT Press.

Weiss, R. S. (1974). The provisions of social relationships. In Z. Rubin (Ed.), *Doing unto others*. Englewood Cliffs, NJ: Prentice-Hall.

Weiss, W., & Fine, B. J. (1956). The effect of induced aggressiveness on opinion change. *Journal of Abnormal and Social Psychology, 52*, 109–114.

Weldon, E., & Gargano, G. M. (1988). *Personality and Social Psychology Bulletin, 14*, 159–171.

Wells, G. L., & Gavanski, I. (1989). Mental simulation of causality. *Journal of Personality and Social Psychology, 56*, 161–169.

Wells, G. L., & Murray, D. M. (1984). Eyewitness confidence. In G. Wells & E. Loftus (Eds.), *Eyewitness testimony: Psychological perspectives* (pp. 155–170). New York: Cambridge University Press.

Wells, G. L., Taylor, B. R., & Turtle, J. W. (1987). The undoing of scenarios. *Journal of Personality and Social Psychology, 53*, 421–430.

Wells, W. D. (1973). *Television and aggression: Replication of an experimental field study*. Unpublished manuscript, Graduate School of Business, University of Chicago.

Werner, C. M., Brown, B. B., & Damron, G. (1981). Territorial marking in a game arcade. *Journal of Personality and Social Psychology, 41*(6), 1094–1104.

Werner, E. E. (1979). *Cross-cultural child development*. Monterey, CA: Brooks/Cole.

Westen, D. (1988). Transference and information processing. *Clinical Psychology Review, 8*, 161–179.

Wetzel, C. G., & Walton, M. D. (1985). Developing biased social judgments: The false-consensus effect. *Journal of Personality and Social Psychology, 49*, 1352–1359.

White, G. L. (1976). *The social psychology of romantic jealousy*. Doctoral dissertation, University of California, Los Angeles, University of Microfilms No. 77-7700.

White, G. L. (1981). Jealousy and partner's perceived motive for attraction to a rival. *Social Psychology Quarterly, 44*, 24–30.

White, L. A. (1979). Erotica and aggression: The influence of sexual arousal, positive affect, and negative affect on aggression behavior. *Journal of Personality and Social Psychology, 37*, 591–601.

White, R. K. (1970). *Nobody wanted war: Misperception in Vietnam and other wars*. Garden City, NY: Doubleday.

Whitley, B. E. (1983). Sex role orientation and self-esteem: A critical meta-analytic review. *Journal of Personality and Social Psychology, 44,* 765–778.

Whitley, B. E. (1988). Masculinity, femininity, and self-esteem: A multitrait-multimethod analysis. *Sex Roles, 18,* 419–431.

Whyte, W. H., Jr. (1956). *The organization man.* New York: Simon & Schuster.

Wichman, H. (1970). Effects of isolation and communication on cooperation in a two-person game. *Journal of Personality and Social Psychology, 16,* 114–120.

Wicker, A. W. (1969). Attitudes versus action: The relationship of verbal and overt behavior responses to attitude objects. *Journal of Social Issues, 25,* 41–78.

Wicker, A. W. (1971). An examination of the "other variables" explanation of attitude-behavior inconsistency. *Journal of Personality and Social Psychology, 19,* 18–30.

Wicklund, R. A., Cooper, J., & Linder, D. E. (1967). Effects of expected effort on attitude change prior to exposure. *Journal of Experimental Social Psychology, 3,* 416–428.

Wicklund, R. A., & Frey, D. (1980). Self-awareness theory: When the self makes a difference. In D. M. Wegner & R. R. Vallacher (Eds.), *The self in social psychology* (pp. 31–54). New York: Oxford University Press.

Wiebe, D. J., & McCallum, D. M. (1986). Health practices and hardiness as mediators in the stress-illness relationship. *Health Psychology, 5,* 425–438.

Wiesenthal, D. L., Endler, N. S., Coward, T. R., & Edwards, J. (1976). Reversibility of relative competence as a determinant of conformity across different perceptual tasks. *Representative Research in Social Psychology, 7,* 319–342.

Wilder, D. A. (1977). Perception of groups, size of opposition, and social influence. *Journal of Experimental Social Psychology, 13,* 253–258.

Wilder, D. A. (1986). Social categorization: Implications for creation and reduction of intergroup bias. In L. Berkowitz (Ed.), *Advances in experimental social psychology* (Vol. 19, pp. 291–355). New York: Academic Press.

Williamson, G. M., & Clark, M. S. (1989). Providing help and desired relationship type as determinants of changes in moods and self-evaluations. *Journal of Personality and Social Psychology, 56*(5), 722–734.

Williamson, J. B. (1974). The stigma of public dependency: A comparison of alternative forms of public aid to the poor. *Social Problems, 22,* 213–238.

Wills, T. A. (1981). Downward comparison principles in social psychology. *Psychological Bulletin, 90,* 245–271.

Wills, T. A. (1984). Supportive functions of interpersonal relationships. In S. Cohen & L. Syme (Eds.), *Social support and health* (pp. 61–82). New York: Academic Press.

Wilson, E. O. (1971). *The insect societies.* Cambridge, MA: Harvard University Press.

Wilson, E. O. (1975). *Sociobiology, the new synthesis.* Cambridge, MA: Harvard University Press.

Wilson, L., & Rogers, R. W. (1975). The fire this time: Effects of race of target, insult, and potential retaliation on black aggression. *Journal of Personality and Social Psychology, 32,* 857–864.

Wilson, T. D., & Lassiter, G. D. (1982). Increasing intrinsic interest with superfluous extrinsic constraints. *Journal of Personality and Social Psychology, 42,* 811–819.

Winkler, J., & Taylor, S. E. (1979). Preference, expectations, and attributional bias: Two field studies. *Journal of Applied Social Psychology, 2,* 183–197.

Winter, D. G. (1987a). Enhancement of an enemy's power motivation as a dynamic of conflict escalation. *Journal of Personality and Social Psychology, 52,* 41–46.

Winter, D. G. (1987b). Leader appeal, leader performance, and the motive profiles of leaders and followers: A study of American Presidents and elections. *Journal of Personality and Social Psychology, 52,* 196–202.

Winter, D. G. (1988). The power motive in women—and men. *Journal of Personality and Social Psychology, 54,* 510–519.

Winter, D. G., & Stewart, A. (1977). Content analysis technique for assessing political leaders. In M. G. Hermann (Ed.), *A Psychological Examination of Political Leaders* (pp. 27–61). New York: Free Press.

Winter, L., & Uleman, J. S. (1984). When are social judgments made? Evidence for the spontaneousness of trait inferences. *Journal of Personality and Social Psychology, 47,* 237–252.

Winter, L., Uleman, J. S., & Cunniff, C. (1985). How automatic are social judgments? *Journal of Personality and Social Psychology, 49,* 904–917.

Wolf, S. (1987). Majority and minority influence: A social impact analysis. In M. P. Zanna, J. M. Olson, & C. P. Herman (Eds.), *Social influence: The Ontario Symposium,* (Vol. 3, pp. 207–235). Hillsdale, NJ: Erlbaum.

Woll, S. (1986). So many to choose from: Decision strategies in videodating. *Journal of Social and Personal Relationships, 3*(1), 43–52.

Wollin, D. D., & Montagne, M. (1981). College classroom environment. *Environment and Behavior, 13*(6), 707–716.

Wong, P. T. P., & Weiner, B. (1981). When people ask "why" questions, and the heuristics of attributional search. *Journal of Personality and Social Psychology, 40,* 650–663.

Wood, J. V. (1989). Theory and research concerning social comparisons of personal attributes. *Psychological Bulletin, 106,* 231–248.

Wood, W. (1982). Retrieval of attitude-relevant information from memory: Effects on susceptibility to persuasion and on intrinsic motivation. *Journal of Personality and Social Psychology, 42,* 798–810.

Wood, W., & Eagly, W. H. (1981). Stages in the analysis of persuasive messages: The role of causal attributions and message comprehension. *Journal of Personality and Social Psychology, 40,* 246–259.

Wood, W., & Kallgren, C. A. (1988). Communicator attributes and persuasion: Recipients' access to attitude-relevant information in memory. *Personality and Social Psychology Bulletin, 14,* 172–182.

Wood, W., Kallgren, C., & Priesler, R. (1985). Access to attitude relevant information in memory as a determinant of persuasion. *Journal of Experimental Social Psychology, 21,* 73–85.

Woodworth, R. D. (1938). *Experimental psychology.* New York: Holt.

Worchel, S. (1984). The darker side of helping: The social dynamics of helping and cooperation. In E. Staub et al. (Eds.), *Developing and maintenance of prosocial behavior: International perspectives on positive morality.* New York: Plenum.

Worchel, S., & Austin, W. G. (1986). *Psychology of intergroup relations,* 2nd. ed. Chicago: Nelson-Hall.

Worchel, S., & Teddie, C. (1976). The experience of crowding: A two-factor theory. *Journal of Personality and Social Psychology, 34,* 30–40.

Worchel, S., & Yohai, S. (1979). The role of attribution in the experience of crowding. *Journal of Experimental Social Psychology, 15,* 91–104.

Word, C. O., Zanna, M. P., & Cooper, J. (1974). The nonverbal mediation of self-fulfilling prophecies in interracial interaction. *Journal of Experimental Social Psychology, 10,* 109–120.

Wortman, C. B. (1975). Some determinants of perceived control. *Journal of Personality and Social Psychology, 31,* 282–294.

Wortman, C. B., & Dunkel-Schetter, C. (1979). Interpersonal relationships and cancer: A theoretical analysis. *Journal of Social Issues, 35,* 120–155.

Wu, C., & Shaffer, D. (1987). Susceptibility to persuasive appeals as a function of source credibility and prior experience with the attitude object. *Journal of Personality and Social Psychology, 52,* 677–688.

Wurf, E., & Markus, H. (1983, August). *Cognitive consequences of the negative self.* Paper presented to the annual meetings of the American Psychological Association, Anaheim, CA.

Wurtele, S. K., & Maddux, J. E. (1987). Relative contributions of protection motivation theory components in predicting exercise intentions and behavior. *Health Psychology, 6,* 453–466.

Wyer, R. S., Jr. (1974). Changes in meaning and halo effects in personality impression formation. *Journal of Personality and Social Psychology, 29,* 829–835.

Wyer, R. S., Jr., & Srull, T. K. (1980). The processing of social stimulus information: A conceptual integration. In R. Hastie et al. (Eds.), *Personal memory: The cognitive basis of social perception* (pp. 227–300). Hillsdale, NJ: Erlbaum.

Wyer, R. S., Jr., & Srull, T. K. (1981). Category accessibility: Some theoretical and empirical issues concerning the processing of social stimulus information. In E. T. Higgins, C. P. Herman, & M. P. Zanna (Eds.), *Social cognition: The Ontario symposium* (Vol. 1, pp. 161–198). Hillsdale, NJ: Erlbaum.

Wyer, R. S., Jr., & Srull, T. K. (1986). Human cognition in its social context. *Psychological Review, 93,* 322–359.

Wyer, R. S., Jr., Srull, T. K., & Gordon, S. (1984). The effects of predicting a person's behavior on subsequent trait judgments. *Journal of Experimental Social Psychology, 20,* 29–46.

Wyer, R. S., Jr., Srull, T. K., Gordon, S., & Hartwick, J. (1982). Effects of processing objectives on the recall of prose material. *Journal of Personality and Social Psychology, 43,* 674–688.

Yee, D. K., & Eccles, J. S. (1988). Parent perceptions and attributions for children's math achievement. *Sex Roles, 19,* 317–333.

Yuki, G. A. (1981). *Leadership in organizations.* Englewood Cliffs, NJ: Prentice-Hall.

Zajonc, R. B. (1965). Social facilitation. *Science, 149,* 269–274.

Zajonc, R. B. (1968). Attitudinal effects of mere exposure. *Journal of Personality and Social Psychology* (Monograph Suppl., Pt. 2), 1–29.

Zajonc, R. B. (1980). Feeling and thinking: Preferences need no inferences. *American Psychologist, 35,* 151–175.

Zajonc, R. B., & Markus, H. (1984). Affect and cognition: The hard interface. In C. E. Izard, J. Kagan, & R. B. Zajonc (Eds.), *Emotions, cognition, and behavior* (pp. 73–102). Cambridge: Cambridge University Press.

Zajonc, R. B., Pietromonaco, P., & Bargh, J. (1982). Independence and interaction of affect and cognition. In M. S. Clark & S. T. Fiske (Eds.), *Affect and cognition: The 17th annual Carnegie symposium on cognition* (pp. 211–228). Hillsdale, NJ: Erlbaum.

Zanna, M. P., & Cooper, J. (1974). Dissonance and the pill: An attribution approach to studying the arousal properties of dissonance. *Journal of Personality and Social Psychology, 29,* 703–709.

Zanna, M. P., & Fazio, R. H. (1982). The attitude-behavior relation: Moving toward a third generation of research. In M. P. Zanna, E. T. Higgins, & C. P. Herman, *Consistency in Social Behavior: The Ontario Symposium* (Vol. 2, pp. 283–301). Hillsdale, NJ: Erlbaum.

Zanna, M. P., & Hamilton, D. L. (1977). Further evidence for meaning change in impression formation. *Journal of Experimental Social Psychology, 13,* 224–238.

Zeichner, A., & Pihl, R. O. (1979). Effects of alcohol and behavior contingencies on human aggression. *Journal of Abnormal Psychology, 88,* 153–160.

Zillmann, D. (1988). Cognition-excitation interdependencies in aggressive behavior. *Aggressive Behavior, 14,* 51–64.

Zillmann, D., & Bryant, J. (1974). Effect of residual excitation on the emotional response to provocation and delayed aggressive behavior. *Journal of Personality and Social Psychology, 30,* 782–791.

Zillmann, D., & Bryant, J. (1982). Pornography, sexual callousness, and the trivialization of rape. *Journal of Communication, 32,* 10–21.

Zimbardo, P. G. (1960). Involvement and communication discrepancy as determinants of opinion conformity. *Journal of Abnormal and Social Psychology, 60,* 86–94.

Zimbardo, P. G. (1970). The human choice: Individuation, reason and order versus deindividuation, impulse and chaos. In N. J. Arnold & D. Levine (Eds.), *Nebraska symposium on motivation, 1969.* Lincoln: University of Nebraska Press.

Zimbardo, P. G., Weisenberg, M., Firestone, I., & Levy, B. (1965). Communicator effectiveness in producing public conformity and private attitude change. *Journal of Personality, 33,* 233–256.

Zimmerman, D. H., & West, C. (1975). Sex roles, interruptions and silences in conversation. In B. Thorne & N. Henley (Eds.), *Language and sex: Difference and dominance* (pp. 105–129). Rowley, MA: Newbury House.

Zlutnick, S., & Altman, I. (1972). Crowding and human behavior. In J. F. Wohlwill & D. H. Carson (Eds.), *Environment and the social sciences: Perspectives and applications.* Washington, D.C.: American Psychological Association.

Zuckerman, M., Amidon, M. D., Bishop, S. E., & Pomerantz, S. D. (1982). Face and tone of voice in the communication of deception. *Journal of Personality and Social Psychology, 43,* 347–357.

Zuckerman, M., DePaulo, B. M., & Rosenthal, R. (1981). Verbal and nonverbal communication of deception. In L. Berkowitz (Ed.), *Advances in experimental social psychology* (Vol. 14, pp. 2–60). New York: Academic Press.

Zuckerman, M., Larrance, D. T., Spiegel, N. H., & Klorman, R. (1981). Controlling nonverbal displays: Facial expressions and tone of voice. *Journal of Experimental Social Psychology, 17,* 506–524.

CHAPTER 1 1 Marilyn K. Yee/NYT Pictures; 2 Shirley Zeiberg; 4 Eugene Gordon; 7 (top, left to right) Historical American Psychology Archives/University of Akron, Ohio, The Washington Post, The Washington Post (bottom) WHO Photo; 8 UPI/Bettmann Newsphotos; 11 Marily K. Yee, NYT Pictures; 14 Laimute Druskis; 24 James Carroll; 26 U.S. Census Bureau.

CHAPTER 2 36 Rick Kopstein/Monkmeyer; 38 Hugh Rogers/Monkmeyer; 43 Laimute Druskis; 46 Rhoda Sidney; 50 Rick Kopstein/Monkmeyer; 52 Michael Kagan/Monkmeyer; 60 From P. Ekman and W. V. Freisen.

CHAPTER 3 73 J. Isaac/The United Nations; 75 Hays/Monkmeyer Press Photo Genic; 78 J. Isaac/The United Nations; 80 AP/Wide World Photos.

CHAPTER 4 102 Eugene Gordon; 109 Arlene Collins/Monkmeyer; 113 (left) Ken Karp/Sirovich Senior Center (right) Laimute Druskis; 128 Eugene Gordon.

CHAPTER 5 136 Paul Conklin/Monkmeyer; 140 AP/Wide World Photos; 146 AP/Wide World Photos; 150 Paul Conklin/Monkmeyer; 161 Charles Gatewood; 166 UPI/Bettmann Newsphotos.

CHAPTER 6 171 UPI/Bettmann Newsphotos; 173 UPI/Bettmann Newsphotos; 175 Buckingham-Wile Co., NY; 178 Donald Getsug/Photo Researchers; 194 Laimute Druskis; 198 Russ Kinne/Photo Researchers; 200 Marc P. Anderson.

CHAPTER 7 206 Larry Kolvoord/Photo Researchers; 208 (top to bottom, left to right) AP/Wide World Photos, Barbara Rios, Photo Researchers, Irene Springer, Laimute Druskis; 210 Shirley Zeiberg; 211 Laimute Druskis; 215 Larry Kolvoord/Photo Researchers; 219 (top) Will McIntyre/Photo Researchers (bottom) George E. Jones III/Photo Researchers; 227 Barbara Rios/Photo Researchers; 230 Teri Stratford.

CHAPTER 8 237 and 238 Charles Gatewood; 242 UPI Bettmann/Newsphotos; 244 Courtesy Western Electric; 248 National Archives; 251 Barbara Rios/Photo Researchers; 252 Ken Karp; 257 and 258 UPI/Bettmann Newsphotos; 259 NYU Film Library.

CHAPTER 9 263 Laimute Druskis; 265 Hanna Schreiber/Photo Researchers; 272 Donald C. Johnson, Click/Chicago; 275 Bill Anderson/Monkmeyer Press; 278 Laimute Druskis; 281 AFL/CIO News; 283 Rick Smolan/Stock, Boston; 287 Handelsman/The New Yorker Magazine, Inc.; 288 Laimute Druskis; 293 (left) Ed Lettau/Photo Researchers (right) Bill Bachman/Photo Researchers.

CHAPTER 10 299 Larry Fleming; 302 Tom McHugh/Photo Researchers; 306 Skjold Photographs; 307 UPI/Bettmann Newsphotos; 309 Meerkamper/Monkmeyer Press; 312 Gus Boyd/Photo Researchers; 313 Lynn McLaren/Photo Researchers; 318 UPI Bettmann Newsphotos; 319 Larry Fleming; 327 AP/World Wide Photos.

CHAPTER 11 333 Strickler/Monkmeyer Press; 334 UPI/Bettmann Newsphotos; 338 Neil Goldstein; 345 Ken Karp; 346 DeSazo-Rapho/Photo Researchers; 351 Suzanne Szasy/Photo Researchers; 352 Photofest; 353 Photofest; 355 Photofest; 356 Strickler/Monkmeyer Press; 360 Photofest.

CHAPTER 12 365 FPG/Hampton, VA; 366 Charles Cocaine/Photo Researchers and Jan Lucas/Photo Researchers; 367 Rhoda Sidney; 371 American Red Cross; 372 George Malave, Stock, Boston; 373 FPG/Hampton, VA; 376 Mimi Forsyth/Monkmeyer; 384 Calogero Cascio/Photo Researchers; 385 Irene Bayer/Monkmeyer.

CHAPTER 13 395 Alan Carey/The Image Works; 397 Ebony/Johnson Publishing Co; 399 UPI/Bettmann Newsphotos; 400 Charles Gatewood; 406 Alan Carey/The Image Works; 412 UPI/Bettmann Newsphotos; 419 AP/World Wide Photos and Donna Gernigan/Monkmeyer Press; 421 U.S. Army Photo and Marc Armstrong; 424 Elizabeth Crews/The Image Works.

CHAPTER 14 428 U.S. Air Force Photo; 429 Ewing Galloway; 432 Howard Dratch/The Image Works, Irene Springer, and Laimute Druskis; 435 The Supreme Court Historical Society; 438 U.S. Air Force Photo; 441 UPI/Bettmann Newsphotos; 447 Ken Karp; 452 UPI/Bettmann Newsphotos; 456 (left) Ken Karp (right) Teri Stratford.

CHAPTER 15 461 Mark Antman/The Image Works; 463 (top, left) Ken Karp (right) J. Latta (bottom) Michael Kagan/Monkmeyer Press; 467 News and Information Service, University of Texas at Austin; 469 Mark Antman/The Image Works; 473 Ken Karp; 480 H. Armstrong Roberts; 481 Laimute Druskis.

CHAPTER 16 486 and 488 American Cancer Society; 491 American Cancer Society; 495 The Christian Science Monitor; 503 Larry Fleming; 507 Laimute Druskis; 512 P. Davidson/The Image Works.

CHAPTER 17 516 AP/World Wide Photos; 521 (top) UPI/Bettmann Newsphotos (bottom) United Nations Photo by M. Tzovarus; 525 AP/Wide World Photos; 527 Bill Fitz-Patrick/The White House; 529 AP/Wide World Photos; 535 AP/Wide World Photos; 536 AP/Wide World Photos; 537 AP/Wide World Photos; 540 AP/Wide World Photos; 542 AP/Wide World Photos.